Chambers
Student
Guide

Careers in the Law

2015

Introduction

Published by Chambers and Partners Publishing
(a division of Orbach & Chambers Ltd)
39-41 Parker Street, London, WC2B 5PQ
Tel: (020) 7606 8844 Fax: (020) 7831 5662
email: info@ChambersandPartners.co.uk
www.ChambersandPartners.com

Our thanks to the many students, trainees,
pupils, solicitors, barristers and graduate recruitment personnel who
assisted us in our research. Also to the researchers of Chambers UK 2014
from which all firm rankings are drawn.
Copyright © 2014 Michael Chambers and
Orbach & Chambers Ltd

ISBN: 978-0-85514-318-3

Publisher: Michael Chambers
Editor: Antony Cooke
Deputy Editors: Sam Morris, Sara Veale
Writers: Alice Saville, Anna Winter, Ben McCarthy, Duncan Scott,
Eleanor Veryard, Emily Rainbow, Georgia Stephens, Jack Watkins,
James Pulford, Natalia Rossetti, Paul Rance, Phil Roe
A-Z Co-ordinator: Tom Hewitt
Production: Jasper John, David Nobakht, Pete Polanyk
Business Development Director: Brad D. Sirott
Business Development Team: Bianca Maio, Catriona Howie,
Liz Brennan, Neil Murphy, Richard Ramsay
Proofreaders: Sally McGonigal, John Bradley, Nicholas Widdows

So you want to be a lawyer...

Welcome to the 2015 edition of the *Chambers Student Guide* to careers in the law. We've written this book to give you the information, tools and confidence to help you make a sound career decision.

This guide is the only publication to offer these four key ingredients:

- The True Picture: an insight into the training schemes at 111 law firms, based on in-depth interviews with thousands of trainees. The trainees were selected by us, not by their law firms, and they spoke to us freely and frankly under the protection of anonymity.
- Chambers Reports: a look at life inside 34 barristers' chambers. These reports were written after visits to each of the sets and interviews with pupils, barristers and clerks.
- Law school reviews: compiled after feedback from students who have completed courses at each of the schools, plus interviews with course directors.
- Additional online advice and information in key areas, including details of the recruitment process at all our featured firms, with tips from recruiters and trainees and in-depth interviews with managing partners and training partners detailing their firms' strategies for the future.

Chambers and Partners publishes guides to the legal professions around the world. You will benefit enormously from using our *Chambers UK* guide to refine your search for a law firm or chambers to train with. The best performing firms and sets in over 77 areas of practice are identified by way of league tables in *Chambers UK*, and you can get all this information online, for free, by visiting www.chambersandpartners.com.

All the guides we publish have one thing in common: they are independent. In a market flooded with publications for law students we take great pride in this fact. No one's money influences what we say about them.

This book could be the most useful thing you read this year, so get stuck in, and we wish you great success for your future career.

The *Student Guide* team
October 2014

Contents

This guide, if used properly, can greatly ease the process of pursuing a career in the law

Use this book in conjunction with chambersandpart-ners.com to find your perfect traineeship or pupillage

*"A superb reference guide for those
entering the legal profession"*
DWF LLP

Our Editorial Team

Antony Cooke
Editor. Graduated from Durham University in Russian & French. Taught English at St. Petersburg State University. Previously worked at Michelin as a European project manager, and at PricewaterhouseCoopers as an audit associate in Investment Management. Fluent in Russian and French.

Sam Morris
Deputy Editor. Graduated from the University of Leiden, The Netherlands with a First in Political Science in 2008 and from the London School of Economics with an MSc in Comparative Politics in 2009. Has worked for the Dutch Ministry of Foreign Affairs. Speaks Dutch and German.

Sara Veale
Deputy Editor. Graduated Magna Cum Laude from the University of North Carolina at Charlotte with degrees in English and Dance, and completed an MA in English at University College London. She currently freelances as a literary and dance critic.

Phil Roe
Deputy Editor of Chambers Associate. Joined Chambers & Partners in 2007 from a global executive search firm, where he advised Private Equity clients. Has written extensively for both Chambers Associate and the Chambers Student Guide. Graduated with an MA in English from Oxford University, and is a theatre critic for London-based newspapers in his free time.

Alice Saville
Graduated from Oxford University with a First in English, then completed an MA in Medieval and Renaissance Studies at UCL. She also writes theatre criticism and features for several arts publications.

Anna Winter
Graduated with a BA in English Literature from Balliol College, Oxford. Took journalism qualifications following internships at The Observer and The New Statesman magazine.

Ben McCarthy
Graduated from the University of Reading with a First in History, and also presented a paper at the International Children of War Conference in 2011. Currently writes for a film review site in his spare time.

Eleanor Veryard
Graduated in 2011 with a BA in History before completing an MA in Early Modern History from the University of Sheffield. Previously at University worked as Head of Research and then Editor-in-Chief for a monthly student magazine.

Emily Rainbow
Graduated with a BA (Hons) in English and Spanish from The Queen's College, Oxford in 2013. Spent a year teaching English in Costa Rica and Argentina.

François Le Grand
Graduated from Royal Holloway with a BA in Human Geography. Studied International Relations in Brazil for two years before becoming a full-time translator working in English, Spanish, French and Portuguese.

Georgia Stephens
Graduated in 2012 with a BA Hons in Politics and International Relations at the University of Sussex. Worked at the university as a News Editor for its weekly newspaper and previously worked as Editor-in-Chief of a high school magazine. Currently editing a book about the Kruger National Park in South Africa in her spare time and has sold images and videos from her recent trip to New Zealand to the news agency Barcroft.

Jack Watkins
Graduated with a BA Honours degree in History from the University of Sheffield in 2010.

Natalia Rossetti
Graduated with a First in English & Theatre Studies from Warwick in 2010, then went on to complete an MA in Text & Performance at the Royal Academy of Dramatic Art and an MPhil in Multi-Disciplinary Gender Studies at Cambridge University. In her spare time she collaborates as Associate Producer with a London-based Theatre company. Bilingual Italian/English and fluent in French.

Paul Rance
Graduated from Exeter University with a First in English Literature, and also spent a year abroad at the University of Toronto to read Canadian literature. He completed his MA in English at UCL in 2010.

Becoming a Lawyer

Law Fairs

Law fair strategies:

Depending on which approach you take, you'll get very different things out of your law fair experience. What sort of law fair attendee are you?

1. The magpie: You're passive and blend into the crowd. The most you'll get out of the day is a few pens, plastic bags and chocolate bars.

2. The weight-lifter: You pick up all the literature you can. You'll have sore arms and a mountain of material to plough through at a later date... if you ever get round to it.

3. The explorer: You have a rough idea where you want to work and which areas you'd like to specialise in. This is your chance to scout around, have a chat, and hone in on those firms that really take your fancy.

4. The interrogator: You've done your research, and have pin-pointed which firms you're interested in. Now's your chance to get the inside scoop on the things that matter to you. What pro bono work can trainees do? Are there any diversity initiatives at the firm? If you're lucky, you might even make some contacts you can mention on the dreaded application form.

Calendar of events 2014

Law Fairs

October 2014

15	City University
20	University of Nottingham; SOAS
21	King's College, London
22	University of York; King's College, London
23	Queen's University, Belfast; University of Cambridge; King's College, London
27	Queen Mary
29	Lancaster University; University of Salford
30	University of Leeds

November 2014

4	Cardiff University; University of Liverpool; London School of Economics; Northumbria University
5	University of Sussex and University of Brighton; University of Leicester; University of Reading; University of Bristol
6	University of Hull; London School of Economics; University of Bristol
8	University of Oxford
10	UCL; Newcastle University
11	UCL; University of Warwick
12	University of Birmingham; University of East Anglia
13	University of Essex
18	University of Manchester
19	University of Sheffield & Sheffield Hallam University; University of Exeter
20	University of Central Lancashire
25	University of Durham
26	University of Durham; Lancaster University

Vacation Scheme Deadlines

October 2014

31	Herbert Smith Freehills (winter) Jones Day (winter) Norton Rose Fulbright (winter)

November 2014

1	Boodle Hatfield (application form available on website from November 1) (summer)
2	Stephenson Harwood (winter)
15	Cleary Gottlieb Steen & Hamilton (winter)

December 2014

19	Jones Day (spring)

"Make sure anything you put in your application can be substantiated. It's awful to catch people out."
Trainee

January 2015

6	Freshfields Bruckhaus Deringer
12	Skadden (Easter and summer)
15	Mischon de Reya (Easter and summer) Nabarro (summer) Olswang (spring and summer)
16	Herbert Smith Freehills (spring and summer) Jones Day (summer) Kirkland & Ellis (summer)
28	Cleary Gottlieb Steen & Hamilton (spring and summer) Davis Polk & Wardwell (summer)
29	PwC Legal (summer)
30	Sullivan & Cromwell (summer)
31	Addleshaw Goddard (Easter and summer) Bird & Bird (summer) Bond Dickinson (Easter and summer) Clyde & Co (Easter and summer) CMS (spring and summer) Covington & Burling (summer) Dechert (summer) Edwards Wildman Palmer (summer) Farrer & Co (Easter and summer) Gateley (summer) Hill Dickinson (Easter and summer) Ince & Co (Easter) Irwin Mitchell (summer) Kennedys (summer) King & Wood Mallesons (Easter and summer) Macfarlanes (Easter and summer) Mills & Reeve (summer) Morgan Lewis (summer) Muckle (summer) Norton Rose Fulbright (summer) O'Melveny & Myers (summer) RPC (summer) SGH Martineau (summer) Squire Patton Boggs (summer) Stephenson Harwood (spring and summer) Stevens & Bolton (summer) Taylor Wessing (summer) Travers Smith (summer) Vinson & Elkins (summer) Watson, Farley & Williams White & Case (spring and summer) Withers (Easter and summer)

Vacation Scheme Deadlines

February 2015

13	Capsticks (summer)
14	Holman Fenwick Willan (spring and summer)
28	Ashfords (summer) Michelmores (summer) Ward Hadaway (summer) Wedlake Bell (summer)

March 2015

8	Arnold & Porter (summer)
17	Browne Jacobson (summer)
31	Lester Aldridge (summer)

April 2015

30	Foot Anstey (summer)

"If you really want to get into this business and think you're suited to it, don't stop at the first knockback – we've taken on some fantastic people who didn't get in the first time around."

City partner

Training Contract Deadlines

January 2015

15	Nabarro
16	Herbert Smith Freehills; Jones Day
31	Bristows (Feb interviews); PwC Legal (for vac scheme)

March 2015

| 31 | Dentons (non-law); Curtis Mallet-Prevost (for 2015); Hogan Lovells (non-law); Simmons & Simmons (non-law) |

May 2015

| 31 | B P Collins; Kingsley Napley (for 2016) |

June 2015

| 1 | Foot Anstey |
| 30 | Brabners; Lester Aldridge; O'Melveny & Myers; Veale Wasbrough Vizards; Wilsons; Winckworth Sherwood |

July 2015

1	Michelmores
12	Freeth Cartwright
15	Gide Loyrette Nouel; Mishcon de Reya
17	McDermott Will & Emery
20	Hill Dickinson
31	Addleshaw Goddard; Ashfords; Ashurst; Baker & McKenzie; Berwin Leighton Paisner; Bingham McCutchen; Bircham Dyson Bell; Bird & Bird; Bond Dickinson; Boodle Hatfield; BPE Solicitors; Bristows (Aug interviews); Browne Jacobson; Burges Salmon; Charles Russell; Cleary Gottlieb; Clyde & Co; CMS; Covington & Burling, Cripps; Davis Polk; Dechert; Dentons (law); DLA Piper; DWF; Edwards Wildman Palmer; Farrer & Co; Gateley; Gordons; Government Legal Service; Harbottle & Lewis; Higgs & Sons; Hogan Lovells (law); Holman Fenwick Willan; Ince & Co; Irwin Mitchell; K&L Gates; Kennedys; Kings & Wood Mallesons; Kirkland & Ellis International; Latham & Watkins; Macfarlanes; Mayer Brown; Mills & Reeve; Memery Crystal; Morgan Lewis; Muckle; Norton Rose Fulbright; Olswang; Orrick; Osborne Clark; Paul Hastings; Reed Smith; RPC; SGH Martineau; Sheridans; Shoosmiths; Sidley Austin; Simmons & Simmons (law); Skadden; Speechly Bircham; Squire Patton Boggs; Stephenson Harwood; Stevens & Bolton; Sullivan & Cromwell; Taylor Wessing; Thomas Cooper; TLT; Travers Smith; Trethowans; Vinson & Elkins; Walker Morris; Ward Hadaway; Watson Farley & Williams; Wedlake Bell; Weil Gotshal & Manges; White & Case; Withers; Wragge & Co

August 2015

1	Trowers & Hamlins
3	Arnold & Porter
11	Capsticks
31	Hewitsons; Maclay Murray & Spens

*"Before you hit send on an application, ask yourself
whether the things you really like about the firm are
clear on your application. We like to see enthusiasm
and evidence that you distinguish us from other firms."*
                                                    HR representative

What kind of lawyer do you want to be?

Let's start with one of the most basic questions – do you want to be a barrister or a solicitor?

Barrister

"Have you ever heard a barrister say, 'I wish I had been a solicitor instead'? No!" star QC Dinah Rose exclaimed when we interviewed her in December 2012. At first glance the role of a barrister certainly looks a lot cooler than that of a solicitor. You know the deal – it's all about striding into courtrooms, robes flowing, tense moments waiting for missing witnesses and razor-sharp cross-examinations. Glamorous? It's downright sexy! The truth, of course, is that there's a great deal more to it than looking good in a wig…

Essentially barristers do three things:

- Appear in court to represent others
- Give specialised legal advice in person or in writing
- Draft court documents

The proportion of time spent on each depends on the type of law the barrister practises. Criminal barristers are in court most of the time, often with only an hour or two's notice of the details of their cases. By contrast, commercial barristers spend most of their time in chambers, writing tricky opinions and advising in conference on complicated legal points.

Barristers must display the skill and clarity to make complex or arcane legal arguments accessible to lay clients, juries and the judiciary. Their style of argument must be clear and persuasive, both in court and on paper. It has been some time since barristers have had exclusive rights of audience in the courts, though. Solicitors can train to become accredited advocates in even the higher courts.

This encroachment hasn't been an utter disaster for the Bar, although solicitor advocates are handling a lot more of the most straightforward cases. When it comes to more complicated and lengthy matters, barristers are usually still briefed to do the advocacy, not least because this is often the most cost-effective way of managing a case. As a point of interest, solicitor advocates do not wear the wig and gown, and are referred to as 'my friend' rather than 'my learned friend'.

Solicitors value barristers' detailed knowledge of the litigation process and their ability to assess and advise on the merits and demerits of a case. A solicitor will pay good money for 'counsel's opinion'. Certainly, in the area of commercial law a barrister must understand the client's perspective and use their legal knowledge to develop solutions that make business or common sense as well as legal sense. If you think a career as a barrister will allow you to rise above the rigours and scraping of modern-day capitalism, think again.

Of the UK's 15,500 or so barristers, approximately 80% are self-employed. This is why you hear the expression 'the independent Bar'. The remainder are employed by companies, public bodies or law firms, and they make up 'the employed Bar'. To prevent independence from turning into isolation, barristers, like badgers, work in groups called 'sets', sharing premises and professional managers, etc. Barristers do not work for their sets, just at their premises, and as 'tenants' they contribute to the upkeep of their chambers. A percentage of their earnings also goes to pay their clerks and administrators. Unlike employed barristers and solicitors, those at the independent Bar get no sickness pay, holiday pay, maternity leave or monthly salary. What they do get is a good accountant.

To enter practice, law grads need to complete the Bar Professional Training Course (BPTC) before starting a much sought-after year of 'pupillage'. Non-law grads need to first complete the Graduate Diploma in Law (GDL) before taking the BPTC. After the pupillage year, hopefully, the set you're with will then take you on as a tenant, though you may have to look elsewhere. Once tenancy is established, you're home free (well, except for the gruelling schedule, high pressure, concerns over how much you'll earn, dedicated wig maintenance…).

The competition to become a barrister is truly fierce. The main difficulty is that there are many more aspiring barristers than can possibly achieve a career at the Bar. If you want to know more, take a look at the final section of this book, where we provide details on the recruitment process, practice areas, terminology and the difficulties that aspiring barristers may encounter. The **Chambers Reports** give invaluable insight into the lives of pupils and junior barristers at some of the best sets.

The Bar's professional body is the Bar Council, and it is regulated by the Bar Standards Board.

Solicitor

According to the Law Society, there are 127,676 solicitors in England and Wales (as of July 31 2013), with practising certificates issued annually by the Solicitors Regulation Authority (SRA). Over 87,800 of them are in 'private practice' in solicitors' firms, and of those 44,000 are employed in London. Many thousands work in-house for companies, charities or public authorities.

After an undergraduate degree, law school beckons. Law grads need to take the Legal Practice Course (LPC). Non-law grads must first complete the Graduate Diploma in Law (GDL) before being eligible for the LPC.

Next comes the practical training. The most common way of qualifying is by undertaking a two-year training contract with a firm of solicitors, law centre, in-house legal team or public body. Much of the rest of this book deals with the nature of training contracts at different firms and how to procure one. The SRA's website gives all the fine detail you could wish for as to the requirements for training.

Upon satisfactory completion of their training contract and the mandatory Professional Skills Course (PSC), a person can be admitted to the roll of those eligible to practise as a solicitor and apply for a practising certificate. They are then fully qualified.

Where people often trip up is not being fully aware of when they should apply for a training contract. Most big employers recruit two years in advance. If you are studying law and you want to work in a commercial firm, the crucial time for research and applications is early on during your penultimate year at uni.

If you are a non-law student intending to proceed straight to a GDL 'conversion course' before going to a commercial firm, you'll have to juggle exams and career considerations in your final year. Smaller firms and high-street practices often recruit closer to the start date, and often after a trial period of working as a paralegal.

Larger commercial firms more often than not cover the cost of their future trainees' law school fees and other basic expenses. However, for students hoping to practise in smaller firms financial assistance is far from likely, and this can make law school a costly and uncertain endeavour.

Needless to say, your choice of firm will shape the path of your career. A firm's clients, its work and its reputation will determine not only the experience you gain but probably also your future marketability as a lawyer. At Chambers and Partners, we've made it our business to know who does what, how well they do it and what it might be like working at a particular firm.

Our parent publication *Chambers UK* will also be an incredibly useful resource for you. Its league tables show which firms command greatest respect from clients and other professionals in different areas of practice right across the country. You can search the entire thing for free and use it to help create a shortlist of firms to apply to.

In the **True Picture** section of this guide we've profiled the leading legal employers in England and Wales. Our goal is to help you understand what kind of firm might suit you and the kind of work you can expect to undertake when you get there. It is the product of many hundreds of interviews with trainees, and we think you'll really benefit from making it your regular bedtime reading or favourite bookmark on your smartphone.

We've also interviewed recruiters, training partners and managing partners to give you the lowdown on firms' business models, plans for the future and recruitment strategies. You should also read through the **Solicitors' Practice Areas** section of this guide to gain an understanding of what's involved in different fields of practice.

Different types of law firm

There are nearly 11,000 private practice firms in England and Wales. All offer a very different experience. The following will help you drill down.

London: magic circle

The membership of this club traditionally extends to Allen & Overy, Clifford Chance, Freshfields Bruckhaus Deringer, Linklaters, and Slaughter and May. To those for whom bigger is better (bigger deals, bigger money, bigger staff numbers), this is the place to be. Corporate and finance work dominates these firms, as do international big-bucks business clients. By organising their training on a massive scale, these firms can offer seemingly unlimited office facilities, great perks, overseas postings and excellent formal training sessions.

Although these five giants top many lists, not least for revenue and partner profits, consider carefully whether they'd top yours. Training in a magic circle firm is CV gold but not suited to everyone. One factor to consider is the requirement to work really long hours to keep profits fat and international clients happy. A great camaraderie develops among trainees, but be prepared to not see your other friends too often…

London: large commercial

The top ten City of London firms (including the magic circle) offer roughly 800 traineeships between them each year, representing approximately 16% of all new training contracts registered with the SRA. In terms of day-to-day trainee experiences, there's not such a huge difference between the magic circle and the so-called 'silver circle' firms such as Ashurst, Herbert Smith Freehills and a few others.

Training contracts at these chasing-pack firms are strongly flavoured with corporate and finance deals and, again, international work. The salaries match those paid by the magic circle, which is only fair given that many of the lawyers work equally hard.

Many of these firms have recently enlarged further thanks to mergers with large US, Canadian and Australian firms: Norton Rose Fulbright (formerly Norton Rose) and Hogan Lovells (formerly Lovells) are just two examples.

London: American firms

Since the 1970s, there has been a steady stream of US firms crossing the Atlantic to take their place in the UK market. Currently around 40 of them offer training contracts to would-be UK solicitors, with new schemes popping up all the time. We'd suggest staying eagle-eyed if you've a thing for stars and stripes.

At the risk of over-generalising, these firms are characterised by international work (usually corporate or finance-led), small offices, more intimate training programmes and very long hours. On the other hand they usually give trainees a good amount of responsibility. Famously, many of them pay phenomenally high salaries. Lawyers at the hotshot US firms frequently work opposite magic circle lawyers on deals; indeed many of them were previously magic circle and top-ten firm partners or associates. We've also noticed that since these firms' training contract numbers are often small, many don't look much further than Oxbridge and London for their trainees: they can afford to be selective.

As we've already mentioned, UK and US firms are increasingly merging with each other, and with Aussie and Canadian firms, further blurring the definition of which are 'American' and which are not. Some firms are quite happy to be labelled as American; others prefer to be described as 'international'. Look at their websites to get an idea of which term to use.

London: mid-sized commercial

Just like their bigger cousins, these firms are mostly dedicated to business law and business clients. Generally, they don't require trainees to spend quite so many hours in the office; however, some of the most successful mid-sizers – eg Macfarlanes and Travers Smith – give the big boys a run for their money in terms of profitability.

Generally, the size of deals and cases in these firms means trainees can do much more than just administrative tasks. The atmosphere is a bit more intimate than at the giants of the City, with the greater likelihood of working for partners directly and, arguably, more scope to stand out within the trainee group. You shouldn't expect such an international emphasis to all the work.

London: smaller commercial

For those who don't mind taking home a slightly more modest pay cheque in exchange for better hours, these firms are a great choice. After all, money isn't everything.

There are dozens of small commercial firms dotted around London: Wedlake Bell and Boodle Hatfield are just two examples. Usually these firms will be 'full-service', although some may have developed on the back of one or two particularly strong practice areas or via a reputation in certain industries. Real estate is commonly a big deal at these firms. Along with commercial work, a good number offer private client services to wealthier people. At firms like these you usually get great exposure to partners and there's less risk of losing contact with the outside world.

Niche firms

London is awash with firms specialising in areas as diverse as aviation, media, insurance, shipping, family, intellectual property, sport… you name it, there's a firm for it. Niche firms have also sprouted in areas of the country with high demand for a particular service. How about marine law in Plymouth? If you are absolutely certain that you want to specialise in a particular field – especially if you have already worked in a relevant industry – a niche firm is an excellent choice. You need to be able to back up your passion with hard evidence of your commitment, however. Many of these firms also cover other practice areas, but if any try to woo you by talking at length about their other areas of work, ask some searching questions.

Regional firms

Many of you will agree that there is more to life than the Big Smoke. There are some very fine regional firms acting for top-notch clients on cases and deals the City firms would snap up in a heartbeat. There is also international work going on outside the capital.

The race for training contracts in the biggest of these firms is just as competitive as in the City. Some regional firms are even more discerning than their London counterparts in that applicants may have to demonstrate a long-term commitment to living in the area. Understandable, as they hardly want to shell out for training only to see their qualifiers flit off to the capital.

Smaller regional firms tend to focus on the needs of regional clients and would therefore suit anyone who wants to become an integral part of their local business community. Salaries are lower outside London, in some cases significantly so, but so is the cost of living. There's a perception that working outside London means a chummier atmosphere and more time for the gym/pub/family, but do bear in mind that the biggest and most ambitious regional players will expect hours that aren't so dissimilar to firms with an EC postcode.

National and multi-site firms

Multi-site firms are necessarily massive operations, some of them with office networks spanning the length and breadth of the country and overseas. To give you just two examples, Eversheds has nine branches in England and Wales, plus many overseas; DLA Piper has six in England and many more overseas. These firms attract students who want to do bigger-ticket work outside London – a sometimes unwelcome consequence of which is doing London levels of work for a lower salary.

Some of the multi-site firms allow trainees to stay in one office, whereas others expect them to move around. Make sure you know the firm's policy or you could end up having a long-distance relationship with friends, family and your significant other while you move to a new town for a few months or are saddled with a punishing commute. The work on offer is mostly commercial, although some private client experience may be available.

General practice/small firms

If you're put off by the corporate jargon, City-slicking lifestyle and big-business attitude of some of the firms in this guide, then the small firm might be just what you're after. If you want to grow up fast as a lawyer and see how the law actually affects individuals and the community in which you practise, then a high-street firm may be the best option for you. We provide a lot more information on this type of outfit on our website.

Larger firms may take up to half a dozen or so trainees a year; the smallest will recruit on an occasional basis. It is in this part of the profession where salaries are the lowest. The SRA's minimum required salary for trainees was scrapped from 1 August 2014. Employers now only have to adhere to the national minimum wage, which was bumped up to £6.50 in October 2014.

Many high-street firms depend on legal aid funding, and anyone thinking of entering this sector should be aware of the dramatic cuts being made to public funding of legal services. We discuss this in considerable detail on our website.

What is a training contract?

Basically, a training contract is the step between your academic life and your life as a qualified solicitor.

Most training contracts are taken on a full-time basis and last two years. Part-time options are much rarer. The part-time-study training contract lasts between three and four years, allowing you to learn while you earn, balancing the LPC and/or GDL with part-time training at a firm. The part-time training contract is an option for those who have already completed their LPC. It involves working a minimum of two-and-a-half days per week for up to four years.

Training contracts must comply with SRA guidelines. The most important of these are:

- It's a *training* contract, not an *employment* contract. This means it is nearly impossible for you to be sacked. For a training contract to be terminated there must be mutual agreement between the firm and trainee, a cancellation clause (like failing the GDL or LPC), or a formal application to the SRA when issues cannot be resolved internally. Instances of trainees being fired are extremely rare.
- Trainees must gain practical experience in at least three areas of English law and develop skills in both contentious and non-contentious areas. Some firms send trainees on litigation courses that fulfil the contentious requirement without them having to do a full contentious seat. Firms can also arrange secondments for trainees to gain contentious experience.
- Trainees must complete the Professional Skills Course. The firm has to allow trainees paid study-leave to attend these courses and has to pay the course fees.

The norm is to spend time in four departments over the two years (six months in each). Each stint is called a seat. At some firms you'll find yourself doing six four-month seats or some other more bespoke arrangement. At very small firms it's likely that your training won't be as structured. Sometimes trainees repeat a seat, especially during six-seat schemes. Typically, repeat seats are in either the firm's largest department or the department in which you hope to qualify.

Besides the SRA's contentious/non-contentious requirement, some firms may require that you do a seat in one or more particular departments over the course of your training. For the other seats, firms usually ask you to identify your preferred departments and try to best accommodate your wishes. However, seat allocation isn't always a simple task, and you might not get what you want. It usually depends on the needs of departments and trainee seniority.

You will be allocated a supervisor in each seat who will be responsible for giving you assignments and (hopefully) helping out with any questions you have. Supervisors are typically mid-level to senior associates/assistants or partners. Usually you will share an office with your supervisor or sit near them in an open-plan setting. You may also have the opportunity to spend a seat (or part of one) seconded to one of your firm's clients or one of its overseas offices. Appraisals are important, and most firms will arrange a formal meeting between trainee and supervisor/HR at the end of each seat and probably also midway through.

What the experience entails:
- Long hours are almost a given; however, they are more likely when you work at a large, international or corporate/finance-focused firm. They are less likely at litigation-led firms and smaller domestic advisory or boutique firms.
- There is a hierarchical structure to law firms, and while this is felt more strongly at some firms than others, trainees should be prepared to start at the bottom. Salaries usually follow the hierarchy too, rising with seniority rather than being based on performance.
- Trainee groups tend to be close-knit and most firms provide some sort of budget for trainee socialising. Larger firms with larger intakes of trainees tend to have more active social scenes.
- You're not guaranteed a job at the end of it. If you've done well, the firm will retain you on qualification, finding you a job in a department that you've come to love… or in a department that needs new junior lawyers. The firm that trained you is not obligated to keep you. Our research shows that about 81.1% of qualifying trainees stayed at their firms in 2014; the rest either elected to look elsewhere or were forced to. You should regard your training contract as a two-year job interview.

One training partner put it perfectly when he said: *"Trainees should view the training contract as an opportunity to be a sponge and soak up all the right ways to be the lawyer they want to be. A degree of open-mindedness about your career is imperative."*

Trends affecting the recruitment market

In a competitive recruitment market where the standards keep getting higher and higher it pays to know your stuff. Here are the main issues you should be aware of.

The economy: the only way is up?

In the three months between April and June 2014 UK economic output finally returned to the level at which it had stood in the first three months of 2008. Socially speaking this crisis isn't over: on a per capita basis people are still poorer than back in 2007/08, taking into account rising prices and a population increase of 2m.

But businesses are optimistic: both the services and manufacturing sectors have been growing, and overall the UK economy expanded by 1.7% in 2013. The IMF has predicted growth of 3.2% in 2014 and 2.7% in 2015 – the highest rate of any developed major economy. So the news on the business front is good. But recruiters will still want you to be able to understand the journey the UK economy has been on in the past few years and how trends in different sectors are affecting their firm. Law firms are becoming increasingly innovative: firms are aware that their future success depends on prudent and efficient handling of finances, and gaining work by offering better quality services than competitors at home and abroad.

The value of UK M&A transactions was up 108% in the first half of 2014 compared to the same period in 2013 (although the number of transactions remained flat); both the value and volume of non-residential property transactions rose in 2013 (to £86bn and 59,000 respectively), the highest numbers since 2008. Lawyers working in areas like finance, corporate and real estate now find they are fully engaged again. Areas like litigation, employment and regulation also remain busy. Most big commercial firms have seen their revenues increase during 2013 and 2014.

Trainee recruitment

The up-tick in the economy has not led firms to go on a massive trainee hiring bonanza. Recruitment numbers at most of the biggest commercial firms are down compared to where they stood five or six years ago. For example, the six elite City firms known as the 'silver circle' told us they were looking to recruit 305 trainees when we asked in 2008, but want just 237 when we asked this year. The same story is true outside the capital: the five big national firms (Addleshaw, DLA Piper, Eversheds, Pinsent Masons and Squire) were in the market for 325 trainees in the 2008/09 recruitment cycle, but are looking for just 255 in 2014/15. These numbers reflect an overall market trend: while the number of training contracts offered in 2012/13 was up on the previous year (to 5,302), this number is still 16% lower than the 6,303 training contracts registered in 2006/07. The trend for cuts has been felt up and down the market, from the high street to the City.

It's unlikely that demand for junior lawyers will return to pre-crash levels any day soon. With tighter budgets, clients are demanding greater value for money. They are no longer willing to pay for a junior lawyer to sit in a room photocopying if a temp can do the same for peanuts. The recession led many firms to tighten their belts and they've learnt to do more with less. New technology is also hitting demand for trainees. Many functions can be performed by legal software, and globalisation means that firms can easily outsource low-level tasks to countries like India and South Africa. City firms are finding that even more complex legal and administrative work can be performed by staff based outside London.

We don't want to come across as the harbingers of doom: there are still literally thousands of training contracts up for grabs each year. The world will always need lawyers, and good graduates will always have a chance of making it in the profession. English law is increasingly popular overseas for doing business deals and resolving disputes (especially in the BRIC countries and the Middle East). For a structured career path that almost guarantees a solid lifetime income, the law is right up there. But we certainly wouldn't want to encourage anyone to try to become a lawyer just because they think it's an easy way of getting a cushy job. It isn't.

Our point is: if you have a passion for the law and the right skills, then there's no need for doom and gloom. At the same time, the days when students could waltz into a top job by being bright, young and perky are over – forever. Yes, there are thousands of training contracts on offer, but there are also thousands of candidates. Applicants are expected to have exactly the right professional skills firms are looking for, need to know the firms they are applying to inside out, and must have a stash of solid life experiences as evidence of their professed skill set.

Law firm mergers

You may have heard talk of consolidation in the market. What this means is that there are fewer law firms about. Some have gone into administration: many high-street outfits have ceased operations in the past few years, and some major law firms too – Halliwells, Dewey & LeBoeuf, Cobbetts, Davenport Lyons – have gone the way of the dodo. These big casualties were all victims of financial mismanagement exposed by worsening market conditions. There are still firms out there in financial difficulty, with costs rising and profits plummeting. In 2013 the SRA went so far as to announce that it was closely monitoring the finances of 30 top-200 firms at risk of failure.

For the moment, however, law firm mergers are a much bigger trend than failures. In the past few years such mergers have gone from being unusual events to frequent occurrences. Nearly a quarter of firms profiled in the 2009 *Student Guide* have since undergone a major merge, and many others are considering the option. Mergers happen for all manner of reasons. Some are genuine attempts to strategically expand a firm's areas of practice or gain a national presence; the Charles Russell Speechlys tie-up is an example of the former, while the merger which created Bond Dickinson is one of the latter. International and transatlantic mergers are common too: they aim to make firms which were previously merely international truly global. Quite a few Brits have paired up with US or even Australian outfits: Norton Rose recently merged with Texas' Fulbright and Ashurst with Australia's Blake Dawson. Meanwhile, SJ Berwin became the first ever UK firm to join arms with an Asia-Pacific firm, King & Wood Mallesons, in 2013. Elsewhere in the market CMS, Orrick, Mayer Brown and Eversheds are all firms which have made noises suggesting they're in the market for a US or other overseas tie-up. A merger can boost internal client referrals and offer economies of scale by sharing overheads. Quite a few mergers have been tie-ups between a stronger firm and one which was in some financial difficulty. Recent examples of this include Slater & Gordon's takeover of Pannone, CMS's of Dundas & Wilson, and Wragge & Co's merger with Lawrence Graham.

Trainees' contracts are honoured when firms merge. And, for the moment, many merged entities appear to be continuing to recruit similar numbers to their legacy halves. Even in the case of firm failures, rival outfits where large numbers of out-of-work lawyers have been taken on have subsequently increased their trainee intakes or even instituted entirely new schemes. For more on this topic go online and read our feature on **Law firm mergers: a developing trend**.

Legal education and training

The big legal training news of 2014 was an announcement made with little fanfare by the SRA on 1 July: from that day on it became possible to qualify as a solicitor without doing a training contract. How? Paralegals who have completed the LPC can become qualified solicitors after a 'period of recognised training'. To make this happen an employer recognised as an 'authorised training provider' is required simply to notify the SRA that a recognised period of training has begun. The SRA can intervene if it is 'not satisfied that a trainee is receiving adequate training' to 'impose any condition necessary'.

As these regulations are brand new it's unclear how they will operate in practice. But we put out some feelers to see what our sources thought. *"I can honestly say I don't think I would want to be called a solicitor if I had never completed a training contract,"* said one trainee who had previously worked as a paralegal. Another, with the same background, told us: *"It's dangerous to let this happen – we must maintain respect for the profession by operating by the highest of standards."* Mark Stobbs, director of legal policy at the Law Society, made the same point more diplomatically in the *Law Society Gazette*: *"We support flexible routes to qualification. But we question whether many paralegals will be able to satisfy the new requirements. It is important the SRA consults properly on any significant changes to ensure that standards are maintained."*

Some firms are finding other creative ways of offering alternative routes into the profession or a leg-up to those seeking more work experience. These include legal apprenticeships (launched by Kennedys, Shoosmiths and Addleshaw Goddard among others) and Plexus Law's graduate pathways programme.

The Law Society doesn't mince its words about the risks involved starting out on the path to becoming a lawyer: 'Qualifying as a solicitor is not easy,' intones its website. 'Many trainee solicitors finish their training with debts. Others are not able to finish their training because they cannot get a suitable job. There is no guarantee of getting a job either as a trainee or as a solicitor.' We couldn't agree more. Be warned that the biggest LPC providers like BPP and the University of Law are profit-making businesses and have a vested interest in more graduates studying with them. So: you should consider your options very carefully before parting with any hard-earned debt to pay for law school. Most trainees we interviewed for this guide secured their training contracts before starting law school, and this is the course we advise you to follow. Starting law school without a training contract lined up will always be a calculated gamble.

As an added incentive most commercial firms will pay all or part of your LPC fees as well as a living allowance; smaller non-commercial firms do not usually do this. See our **Table of salaries and benefits** on page 482 for full details.

We should also point out that your future is in your hands: whether you land a traineeship or NQ job depends on how hard you work at getting the right experience, learn what firms are looking for, and target the right employers. For more advice on this topic read our feature **How suitable are you and what do recruiters want?** on page 28.

Public spending cuts

Unless you've been living in a cave for the past four years, you will have read about the sweeping public spending cuts being brought in by the coalition government. The cuts have been affecting law firms in various ways. First, firms which rely heavily on public funding – sectors like healthcare, housing, local government, transport, education, infrastructure, charities – have found themselves in a spot of bother. A good example is Bevan Brittan, which has seen revenues fall by a fifth in the past five years, and cut its trainee intake in half. Firms like this are branching out to do more private sector work.

Meanwhile, the public funding of litigation through legal aid is being severely cut, with the Ministry of Justice aiming to trim the legal aid budget by a quarter. Combined with other funding changes, this is squeezing lawyer fees in areas like crime, housing, family, employment and personal injury. While larger commercial firms which practise in these areas are not affected (their clients pay privately), the cuts are affecting recruitment at smaller firms: Fisher Meredith, a London firm with a strong legal aid practice long covered by the *Student Guide*, does not feature in our pages this year because recruiters told us the firm is unsure if and when it will be hiring trainees again. Barristers and solicitors have taken to the streets to demonstrate against the legal aid cuts, but the changes are going ahead regardless. For more on this topic, take a look at the **Solicitors' Practice Areas**, and go online to read our feature on **Legal aid cuts and reforms**.

The Legal Services Act

The Legal Services Act 2007 has now fully come into force. In a nutshell, the Act aims to liberalise and regulate the market for legal services. First, it makes it possible for non-solicitors to become partners in law firms, forming so-called multidisciplinary partnerships or MDPs. Second, under Alternative Business Structures (ABS) lawyers are now able to team up with other professionals to offer a range of services to clients. The idea is still relatively new, but in the near future a commercial firm could handle a business' accounts and its contract disputes, while a high-street firm might advise an individual on securing a mortgage as well as all the conveyancing. ABSs will also allow firms to seek external investment. National firm Irwin Mitchell is one of the most innovative players here, having gained five ABS licences in late 2012. Other firms have since followed suit: Gateley, PwC Legal and Slater & Gordon have all recently gained ABS status. Head over to our website to read more about **Alternative Business Structures**.

Ultimately, the Legal Services Act aims to make legal services as easily accessible as your local supermarket – quite literally. In the not-so-distant future it may be possible to write your will at a bank or buy divorce services alongside your groceries. 'Tesco law' – regarded only a few years ago as comical and dangerous by some – is now here. Co-op Legal Services was the very first business to win an ABS licence in the UK. It employs 500 staff and offers services including fixed-fee family advice. It recruited ten trainees in 2013, but has shelved more ambitious plans announced in 2012 to recruit 100 trainees annually by 2017. Recruiters have been spotted at law fairs, however, so this is one to keep your eye on.

Some observers thought that liberalisation of the market would lead to an influx of private equity cash into the profession. But, for the moment, neither firms nor investors are keen on this idea, partly because of the financial requirements it would place on firms and partners.

Pay and prospects

Despite the profession being under pressure, lawyer salaries at commercial firms remain generous. Previously, the SRA set a minimum salary for trainees which was well above minimum wage, but as of 1 August 2014 this has been scrapped, and firms will only be obliged to pay the national minimum wage (currently £6.50 per hour). Advocates of this change say it will allow small firms to employ more trainees, while detractors have suggested it will mean trainees can be exploited as low-paid lackeys.

The good news is that none of this will affect the top of the market. Salaries at the biggest firms both in and outside London are as robust as ever, and at some they are even on the up. Several firms – from the magic circle to regional outfits like Bond Dickinson, Lester Aldridge and Ashfords – have recently announced increases in trainee pay. According to figures provided by the SRA in summer 2014, average trainee salary in the City is £35,825; the lowest is in Halifax, averaging £16,447; the national average stands at £26,984. For more information check out our **Table of salaries and benefits** on page 482.

If you do manage to win a training contract you should be well placed for the future. The number of trainees who stay with the firm they trained with varies from employer to employer, but on average the firms we surveyed in 2014 retained 81.1% of their trainees upon qualification. There was a noticeable dip in retention in 2009 and 2010, but over the past four years the figure has hovered around the 80% mark. Go to our website for further retention analysis and retention stats for every firm we've covered in the *True Picture* since 2000.

Some other career options

Solicitors and barristers may think they're the be-all and end-all of the legal profession, but there are numerous other respectable career paths out there. Here are a few.

Working in-house for a company

According to a report by the Solicitors Regulation Authority 25,600 solicitors work in-house for a company, for example in the financial services, manufacturing, retail, construction, media, transport and telecommunications sectors. The numbers have doubled since 2000 partly due to companies bringing legal work in-house in an attempt to cut outsourcing costs.

As an in-house lawyer, your day-to-day role depends on the work the business in question conducts, but the experience is nonetheless likely to be broad. One day you might be handling an employment issue, the next drafting a commercial contract or advising on a potential M&A transaction. Indeed, in-house lawyers are fully embedded within the company they work for and have to know the ins and outs of the business down to a tee.

The number of training contracts offered in-house is much smaller than that of private practice, and unfortunately there's no centralised system that gathers all commercial in-house opportunities. As such, it can take a good deal of effort to track one down. The reality is that around 500 companies have permission to offer training contracts, but most recruit on an ad-hoc basis, taking newbies as and when they're needed. Your best bet is to target the organisations and sectors in which you have the most knowledge and/or experience and check their online recruitment info regularly.

The number of individuals who begin in-house training contracts represent around 3% of the total number of training contracts offered each year. Examples of companies that take in-house trainees include BT, Standard Life and PwC.

Unless an organisation publicises its vacancies, it's likely the company recruits trainees from a pool of candidates who already work there in some other capacity – as a paralegal, for example. Even then aspiring trainees are advised to exercise discretion when trying to obtain a contract. A softly-softly approach more in line with the tortoise than the hare usually works best.

We spoke to one junior solicitor who completed their training in-house with a major international company. *"I began working there as a legal secretary and was encouraged to go to law school when they discovered I had a law degree."* The company paid for our interviewee's LPC and even tasked them with finding out how the organisation could become an accredited training contract provider. These days, this source works as a content in-house lawyer. *"I get such a mixed bag of work – I can start the day doing contracts and end on regulatory work."* Flexibility and good time management are important aspects of the job – *"all day people will turn up at your desk and ask for five minutes of your time"* – as is the ability to take a generalist approach: *"We are the GPs of the legal world as we are not the master of anything but cover a wide area."*

In-house lawyers don't lose touch with private practice; in fact, a big part of the job involves selecting and instructing law firms to provide specialist advice. This dynamic often keeps them knee-deep in invites to parties, lunches and sporting events as different law firms curry favour.

Good remuneration is one of the biggest perceived pluses of an in-house training contract. In terms of pay, the salary at the junior end of the scale is more pleasing (in comparison with private practice), though it's important to keep in mind compensation becomes less so (again, as a comparison) as lawyers progress and gain seniority with a company. The decent work/life balance is also something to consider. Indeed, it's true to some extent that the hours are better than those at commercial firms – it's not exactly a nine-to-five schedule, but in-house lawyers generally find they have more control over their working lives than their private practice counterparts.

If the in-house route seems like the one for you, take a look at the Commerce and Industry Group, which makes promoting in-house legal careers a priority and *"has a mentoring system for trainees and hosts networking dinners."* It's also worth keeping an eye on the legal press and *The Times* on Thursdays to see who's recruiting, as well as making your interests known in the relevant circles. Finding out which companies offer training is *"all about networking and making contacts,"* according to our sources. The Law Society's in-house division is a good place to look for advice and keep up to date on the latest issues. Aspiring in-house barristers should get in touch with the Bar Council.

Law Centres

Law Centres are not-for-profit legal practices with local management committees and a remit to 'help people to stay in their homes, keep their families together and get into employment or education'. Advice and representation are provided without charge to the public, with funding coming from local authorities, the Legal Aid Agency and some major charities like the Big Lottery Fund. Cuts to Legal Aid and funding from local authorities have affected services across the country. A spokesperson from the Law Centres Network told us: *"The majority of Law Centres have so far managed to survive the cuts to their legal aid income, through restructuring and robust fundraising. In almost every case legal aid and other cuts have led to a reduction in the level of service they can provide to their local communities as staff have had to be laid off."* Nine law centres were forced to close as a result of the legal aid cuts although others are managing to flourish. *"Reductions in Law Centre services and closures in particular will leave many very vulnerable people without access to justice."* Law Centres' horizons tend to be broader than those of Citizens Advice Bureaux, and they tend to take on cases with a wider social impact, including community care, all types of discrimination, education, employment, housing, immigration, asylum and public law matters. Legal problems handled may vary from one Centre to another, but all who work in the sector are considered social welfare law specialists.

The network of Law Centres in the UK now numbers over 50 and most employ several lawyers. If you're attracted to the idea of colleagues with shared ideals and a social conscience, it's worth investigating a career in the sector. Routes to a Law Centre position are as varied as the work each handles: newly qualified solicitors with relevant experience in private practice are taken on, as are those who have worked as paralegals for non-profit agencies and gained supervisor-level status. As a newly qualified solicitor your salary at a Law Centre will roughly match private practice on the high street or local authority salary scales – that's £24,000 to £30,000 (or more in London). However, Law Centres tend to lose their competitive edge when seeking to appoint more experienced lawyers. Let's just say such organisations tend to attract those who feel there is more to being enriched than being rich. Law Centres regularly take on volunteers and are an excellent way of both giving back to the community and gaining valuable experience. Law Centres operate along different lines from private practices: there's less hierarchy and more of an equal say for staff at all levels – some even operate as collectives with all staff drawing the same salary. Terms and conditions at work emulate those in local government: pensions, holiday provisions and other such benefits are decent, and flexible or part-time working options are readily available. Law Centres are keen on the equality and diversity fronts, and many actively seek out trainees from their local community. It is an exciting environment, and many lawyers go on to take up influential roles outside of the movement.

A client with a consumer dispute is less likely to receive assistance than someone who is affected by, say, a local authority's decision on rent arrears. Law Centres identify trends and then use individual cases as a springboard for changing the big picture, perhaps by way of a test case that makes it to the highest courts and the broadsheets. Law Centres are also eager to involve the communities they operate within, providing legal training and education. As a Law Centre employee you might even find yourself at a local comprehensive imparting your legal know-how to teenagers. Recent reforms to the provision of legal aid have required Law Centres to become more target-oriented, but there is still a strong campaigning angle to the sector. Candidates for positions at Law Centres are only considered if they respond to an advertisement. Look out for these in *The Guardian* (on Wednesdays), in local newspapers, on individual Law Centres' websites and the Law Centres Network website. Applicants can enhance their prospects by demonstrating their interest in social justice – for example, earning some stripes through committees or community group participation or taking advantage of relevant law school schemes. Work placements at a local authority also offer a taste of the fields Law Centres plough.

Government Legal Service

The GLS ostensibly has only one client – the Queen. In practice, however, 'clients' include policymakers and managers within various government departments, while lawyers act as full-time litigators and solicitors who draft new legislation and advise ministers how best to legally put policy into practice. Despite ongoing government budget cuts, the GLS is still currently recruiting. Before you apply, it's important to consider whether you'll be happy working at the interface of law and politics and dealing with matters that directly impact UK society. If this sounds appealing, read our True Picture and Chambers Report features on the GLS.

Local government

There are around 4,300 solicitors as well as a host of paralegals, legal executives and barristers employed in the local government sector. Local government lawyers advise elected council members and senior officers on a wide variety of topics including commercial/contracts, conveyancing/property, employment issues, information management, administrative law and governance.

Additional work depends on the type of local authority involved and can include litigation/prosecution, social care, children, consumer protection, environmental, highways and planning, education and housing matters, to name but a few. Lawyers tend to maintain broad practices in the smaller authorities, while those in larger ones usually specialise in a single area like housing, planning, highways, education or social services. Duties include keeping councils on the straight and narrow, making sure they don't spend their money unlawfully and advising councillors on the legal implications of their actions. The typical salary for a local authority solicitor is between £29,700 and £39,900, though some senior solicitors can earn more than £40,000.

Local government services are funded by central government and the taxpayer so large funding cuts are having a big impact on legal departments. Some are stripping back services to basics while others are bringing outsourced work back in-house. Several boroughs have started to share services between councils while others are considering converting to Alternative Business Structure to offer more flexibility in services and resources. Luckily this is *"likely to expand the opportunities and work available for both trainees and qualified solicitors,"* Joanna Swift, head of legal and democratic service, Chiltern and South Bucks District Councils tells us. What's clear is that local government lawyers are increasingly required to be adaptable to changes both in departmental structure and the services they are expected to deal with.

Local government trainees usually follow the same seat system as those in private practice but have rights of audience in courts and tribunals that outstrip those of their peers. Trainees shadow solicitors and gradually build up their own caseload. Most authorities offer summer placements to give aspiring solicitors a sneak preview of what it's really like, and some are even paid. Contact the head of legal services at a local authority to ask for further information – the more experience you can get the better. Most applicants are graduates, but there is a chance for non-graduates to pursue a career in this direction by starting their training as a legal executive. Many lawyers switch between public and private practices and beginning your career in one won't bar you from continuing in the other. In fact North West Leicestershire District Council partners up with private firms in order to offer wider development opportunities and training to its junior solicitors and trainees.

Be prepared to wade through the bureaucratic bog and at times be driven to distraction by the slow machinations of local government. Still, the benefits of a government training contract – variety in your day-to-day work, flexible hours and a sense of serving the community – generally outweigh the downsides. *"It is the variety and complexity of local government work that continues to make the job interesting and challenging,"* Joanna Swift tells

us, *"as well as knowing that what you do does make a difference to the local community."* A major plus is the ease with which many climb the career ladder – there's the option to hop from authority to authority, plus the general perception that the glass ceiling is less prevalent in local government than it is in City law firms. In fact, 50% of local authority chief executives have trained as solicitors. Training in local government can also open doors to careers in private practice, the Crown Prosecution Service and the GLS.

There are currently around 130 trainees with registered training contracts in local authorities, and while government cuts and job freezes are affecting recruitment, we have it on good authority that a solid number of councils are expected to continue recruiting trainees in upcoming years. That said, one Essex council solicitor we spoke with told us in Essex and Southend people are expected to work as a paralegal for two years before applying for training contracts *"as the competition is so fierce these days."*

Because each of the 400-plus authorities in England and Wales acts as a separate employer, there's no central list of vacancies or single recruitment office. As such, finding out about training contract opportunities is somewhat of a challenge in itself, as is determining which councils offer sponsorship for the GDL and/or LPC. A good starting point for research is www.lgjobs.com. Most authorities advertise vacancies on their own website and in the *Law Gazette* and *The Lawyer*, so those are worth a look too. Other helpful resources include: www.localgovernmentlawyer.co.uk, which offers useful job-search functions; www.slgov.org.uk, which provides a career brochure outlining career profiles and advice; and www.jobsgopublic.com. You can also try the law and public service job ads in *The Times*, *The Guardian* and *The Independent*, or even approach local authorities directly.

Crown Prosecution Service

The Crown Prosecution Service is the government department responsible for bringing prosecutions against people who have been charged with a criminal offence in England and Wales. The CPS handles all stages of the process, from advising the police on the possibility of prosecution, right through to the delivery of advocacy in the courtroom.

The CPS employs over 2,700 lawyers to handle more than 1.2m cases in the magistrates' and Crown Courts. Over 640,000 prosecutions alone were brought between 2013 and 2014. Its prosecutors review and prosecute criminal cases following investigation by the police, and also advise the police on matters of criminal law and evidence in order to combat the problem of failed prosecutions. Specifically, lawyers advise the police on appropriate charges for certain crimes, and generally split their time between preparing cases in the office and prosecuting in the Magistrates' Court. A special band of lawyers entitled Crown Advocates prosecute Crown Court cases including murder, rape and robbery.

The CPS put its training programme on hold in 2011 because of government cutbacks, but in spring 2012 relaunched graduate recruitment with its Legal Trainee Scheme. In 2014 the Service offered 20 traineeships and pupillages. This is double the number offered in 2013, but competition for jobs remains fierce. The deadline for applications was 31 May 2014 for pupillages/traineeships starting in November 2014. Successful candidates were put through a rigorous application process involving case studies, online testing, a presentation and interview. It is not yet known what the timetable for recruitment in 2015 will be – unlike commercial law firms the CPS only decides a short while in advance how many graduates it's going to recruit and what the application process will look like. Recruitment has shown an upward trend over the past few years, however, and we would expect the Service to recruit trainees and pupils again next year. Head over to the careers section of the CPS website to find out more.

The armed forces

Unsurprisingly, the army always needs lawyers, and in good army no-nonsense fashion, it knows how to sell the position: 'No billing, no timesheets, no rat race – a job to be proud of', declares the website. In fact the more you consider it it's less of a job and more a vocation. Fully qualified barristers and solicitors with a good understanding of army activities and preferably some work experience under their belt can join the Army Legal Services (ALS) and expect to see all sorts of work, from court-martial to international cases. You should be physically fit and aged between 24 and 32 and don't need previous military experience. Legal Officers can expect to get involved in the three main areas of the ALS's work – prosecution, general advisory and operational law. Major Hannah Giles at the ALS told us: *"You'll need leadership skills, integrity, courage, a practical mind, determination and the ability to work under pressure. You might be briefing a room of 700 soldiers about to be deployed on Operations, or you could just as easily be advising a senior general who needs clear and concise legal advice quickly."*

Recruitment goes as follows: once or twice a year up to nine suitable candidates are called for interview before attending the Army Officer Selection Board at Westbury in Wiltshire for a three-day selection process. Successful applicants are then offered a Short Service Commission in ALS, which lasts four years, including an 18-month initial probational period. Six months of training will lead on to your first legal appointment, usually at home or in Germany or Cyprus. Major Giles suggested that

those who've made an application to the ALS might like to think about attending one of the familiarisation visits held at the the Adjutant General's Corps HQ at Worthy Down: *"Come and see what Army life is really like. You get to spend time in the Officers' mess, enjoy the food and even test yourself on the obstacle course."* Lawyers and other professionally qualified officers are commissioned as Captains, with a starting salary of £38,847. Army officers are entitled to 30 days' paid leave a year, plus bank holidays, while the other benefits include *"opportunities for sport, travel and adventurous training which come as part of Army life."* Further international opportunities occasionally arise in Afghanistan, Kenya, Australia and Canada. NATO and the UN are also worth bearing in mind as future job prospects.

The Royal Air Force also employs barristers and solicitors to deal with criminal cases and prosecutions, both at home and abroad. The Air Force's legal department is small, but the work is juicy – areas of law covered include Air Force law, the law of armed conflict, new legislation plus the host of civil issues that affect RAF personnel. A linear career path can see you rise to the position of Squadron Leader after four years and Wing Commander after a further six. Throughout your career there'll be opportunities to explore new areas such as international humanitarian law. Previous legal officers have found themselves providing advice to people in Iraq, the Falklands, Kosovo and Germany. The starting salary is £37,915 after training, and recruitment is done according to needs rather than annually. Applicants must be aged between 21 and 35. Visit the RAF website to learn more.

The Navy doesn't have such a clear recruitment path and expects its lawyers to serve as officers before taking up a legal role. We've been told that qualified lawyers should sign up as a Logistics Officer in the first instance. From there officers are streamed depending on their skills, so there's a good chance you'll be considered for legal work if there are vacancies. The Navy careers website has a live chat where you can talk through options with an advisor.

The police

Only Sherlock Holmes can operate for and outside of the law and get away with it. All other members of the police force are as accountable as everyone else and therefore need good legal representation when their own conduct is called into question. This is where police lawyers step in. They also provide guidance on policing at events and public order and advise officers on legal problems or clarify particular points of law. As well as the aforementioned civil actions, they might find themselves working in corporate governance; employment law and discrimination; personal injury; and neighbourhood safety matters (for example, issuing ASBOs or Sexual Offences Protection Orders). There are also a small number of 'duty lawyer' roles in police stations across the country. 'Duty lawyers' work independently of the police and provide detainees with free legal advice on their rights.

We were told by Alpa Patel, head of professional support at the Metropolitan Police, that the Met's in-house legal department plans to *"undertake recruitment campaigns for qualified lawyers according to needs of the service and the levels of work coming in."* In other words: because of cuts to public spending in recent years, the Met no longer has an annual recruitment drive. Unfortunately, it's a similar story across the rest of the country for qualified lawyers seeking a career with the police. Vacancies are few and far between. It's worth bearing in mind that there are occasionally opportunities in areas like forensics, operational policing and criminal justice units, and you don't necessarily have to be a qualified solicitor to get in there. Check online with your local police force for information about any vacancies.

Legal executive

Becoming a qualified lawyer doesn't mean you have to start your career with a training contract. You can still become an advocate, partner in a law firm or even a judge through the CILEx route. The Chartered Institute of Legal Executives (CILEx) has helped over 95,000 members secure a successful career in law in the last 25 years alone. There are currently over 20,000 Chartered Legal Executive lawyers and trainees across England and Wales, all of whom are independently regulated.

Taking the Chartered Legal Executive route means aspiring lawyers can earn as they learn and gain valuable practical experience in one fell swoop. Once their CILEx studies and qualifying employment are complete, they can call themselves qualified lawyers straight away without having to undertake an LPC or wait for an elusive training contract. CILEx members are employed across the full spectrum of legal services, from private practice to government departments, and within the in-house legal teams of major companies. Around 60% of students are funded by their employer.

For those with no prior legal training, the CILEx Level 3 Professional Diploma in Law and Practice is the first stage of the academic training. The second stage of the CILEx route is the Level 6 Professional Higher Diploma in Law and Practice, which is assessed at honours degree level. For those with a qualifying law degree obtained within the last seven years, CILEx offers the Graduate Fast-Track Diploma. The qualification can help you become a Chartered Legal Executive lawyer instead of becoming a solicitor or barrister through the LPC or BPTC. CILEx has seen a significant rise in fast-track students.

While being a Chartered Legal Executive can be a rewarding career in its own right, don't forget CILEx can provide a useful route to qualifying as a solicitor. Most people can seek exemptions from much of the GDL (having already covered its core subjects) and, more crucially, they're also usually exempt from the two-year training contract, provided they are already a qualified Chartered Legal Executive before completing their LPC.

Paralegal

Traditionally, a stint paralegaling could fill space after law school or before commencing a training contract, offering a broad taste of the legal experience. With fewer and fewer training contracts on offer, however, a job as a paralegal can act as a feasible longer-term option.

Legal employers tend to view any time spent paralegaling favourably as it demonstrates a commitment to the profession and enables candidates to gain industry insight and experience. *"A major factor in getting my training contract was that I could talk about my responsibilities as a paralegal: attending court, going to client meetings, drafting documents,"* said a source. What's more, the job remains a valuable position in its own right. It's a good idea to take into account factors such as a firm's size and number of trainees when making applications – a smaller trainee intake often means you'll get to see much better quality work. And it's not just wannabe solicitors who should consider a stint paralegaling, either: some recruitment agencies now specialise in putting pre-qualification barristers in paralegal positions.

The term 'paralegal' is quite generic and the job duties that paralegals encounter can vary drastically: some are given their own files to run, while others end up with dull document management tasks for months on end. *"I was given better work because I had previous business management experience,"* one source said, *"but on average it's rare that you get exposure to true legal work as a paralegal."* At the end of the day *"experiences depend entirely on the firm."*

In July 2014, the updated RSA training regulations state that paralegals who have completed the LPC can now qualify as solicitors without undergoing a formal training contract. This change caused controversy in the legal world and some of our sources expressed concerns, stating that *"it's dangerous to let this happen – we must maintain respect for the profession by operating by the highest of standards."* Another commented: *"I can honestly say I don't think I would want to be called a solicitor if I had never completed a training contract."*

Legal secretary

"Being a legal secretary is a good way to get your foot in the door," explained one of our lawyer contacts. This particular source would know – it's exactly how they started their career. For anyone unsure of whether they want the full-bore pressure of working as a solicitor, this

route could be perfect. *"A major pro is that you're working in law without the more intense responsibility of being a lawyer."* It's also a smart way to spend a few years if you're struggling to get your finances back on track and can't yet contemplate law school.

According to the Institute of Legal Secretaries and PAs (ILSPA), taking a legal secretarial role is suitable for anyone with an interest in law or a background in administrative work. That said, it's important to know that the market is pretty full right now – many firms are reducing their support staff to reduce costs, and there's a lot of competition for jobs.

People can take on legal secretarial positions at any stage of life, be it instead of university, after a degree or as a complete career change. Whenever you take this step, you'll need to be certain that you have the right qualities and temperament: you need to work well under pressure and have a lot of patience, as well as be detail-oriented, organised and articulate. You must also quickly get to know your boss and become their surrogate brain.

Her Majesty's Courts & Tribunals Service

HM Courts & Tribunals Service is an agency of the Ministry of Justice. It is responsible for the administration of the criminal, civil and family courts and tribunals in England and Wales, and non-devolved tribunals in Scotland and Northern Ireland. Its aim is to 'provide for a fair, efficient and effective justice system delivered by an independent judiciary.'

The agency employs around 18,000 staff. Most HM Courts & Tribunals Service jobs are administrative in nature. However, it recruits judicial assistants (JAs), who are assigned to one of the Court of Appeal's senior judges for a period of up to 12 months. Applicants need at least a 2:1 degree and must be lawyers who have completed or are about to complete pupillage or a training contract.

HM Courts & Tribunals Service also employs legal advisers who are qualified solicitors or barristers and play a crucial role advising magistrates and district judges. Their responsibilities include managing the court room, advising the Bench on law, practice and procedure, and drafting of Justices' reasons and the use of delegated judicial powers for the purpose of effective case management. Research and the verbal and written delivery of findings are thus a big part of the role, and a commonality among all legal advisers is the ability to think on their feet and deal confidently with people.

There are no current plans to recruit legal advisers. However, when positions are available, for both judicial assistants and legal advisers, they are advertised in the national press and legal periodicals, as well as on GOV.UK and the civil service jobs portal.

The Law Commission

Constant reform is needed to ensure that the law is fit for purpose in the modern age. However, the government is not always best placed to see where reforms could be made. The Law Commission, an advisory non-departmental public body sponsored by the Ministry of Justice, was set up by Parliament in 1965 to review the laws of England and Wales and propose reform where necessary.

The Commission is engaged in about 20 projects at any one time. Recent topics have included: how the outdated law that governs firearms may be modernised and simplified; how to ensure that there are more wills and that fewer wills are invalid; how the law can protect the rights of people who lack the capacity to consent to necessary medical care. For the first time, the Commission is also looking specifically at Welsh law.

It's not just a case of repealing laws that are clearly archaic; it's equally important not to accidentally remove the legal basis for someone's rights. Researchers for the Commission analyse many different areas of law, identifying defects in the current system and examining foreign law models to see how they deal with similar problems. They also help draft consultation papers, instructions to Parliamentary Counsel and final reports.

The Commission takes on 10 to 12 researchers annually on year-long contracts. These researchers are normally law graduates and postgraduates who *"tend to leave in order to qualify as lawyers – it's a good jumping-off point for a legal career."* The Commission also recruits qualified lawyers throughout the year.

Candidates should have a First or a high 2:1, along with a keen interest in current affairs and the workings of the law. The job suits those with an analytical mind and a hatred of waffle. They must also love research, because there's a lot of it – be it devising questionnaires and analysing the responses, studying statistics or examining court files.

To find out just which proposed reforms have been implemented and rejected, read the Law Commission annual report.

Keep up to speed with the Law Commission's recruitment needs on their website. December is usually the month when they start looking for people.

The Legal Aid Agency (formerly the Legal Services Commission)

The Legal Aid Agency (LAA) was formed in April 2013 to replace the Legal Services Commission (LSC), which in turn replaced the Legal Aid Board in 2000. The LAA was created as part of the reforms to legal aid funding introduced by the Legal Aid, Sentencing and Punishment of Offenders Act (LASPO) – which became law in May 2012 – and is an executive body of the Ministry of Justice, giving ministers closer control over the government's legal aid budget. The LAA now shares headquarters with the Ministry of Justice in Westminster and has a further 11 offices across England and Wales. These branches manage the distribution of public funds for both civil legal services and criminal defence services. The agency aims to make savings by sharing administrative resources with the Ministry of Justice. The LAA has implemented a number of reforms to criminal and civil legal aid that aim to deliver savings to the legal aid fund and make the legal aid scheme more sustainable for the future. The LAA will oversee a new competitive tendering process for duty provider contracts and has introduced a new online system for law firms making applications, submitting bills and applying for payments.

The work of the LAA is essentially divided into Civil Legal Aid and Criminal Legal Aid. In Civil Legal Aid, the LAA works with legal aid solicitors, Law Centres, local authority services and other organisations. Caseworkers assess the merits of individual applications for legal funding, and a means test is required of civil legal aid applicants. In addition, the LAA is responsible for a national advice line for England and Wales which provides a specialist advice service to people who qualify for legal aid under the revised scheme, in debt, education, discrimination, family, housing, and welfare benefit appeals. In Criminal Legal Aid the LAA manages the supply of legal advice to those under police investigation or facing criminal charges using local solicitors accredited by the service. It does so by the operation of a Duty Solicitor Scheme, which covers criminal legal aid procurement areas throughout England and Wales. It also performs an audit role in relation to authorised providers of criminal legal advice. The Public Defender Service (PDS) also comes under the LAA's aegis, though it provides independent advice to clients separate to the agency. Its five offices, set up in 2001, advise members of the public 24/7. They are located in Cheltenham, Darlington, Pontypridd, Swansea and London. An advocacy unit was established in 2013.

For more information on the Legal Aid Agency, visit www.gov.uk/government/organisations/legal-aid-agency

Students interested in working for the Civil Service should go to the Civil Service Jobs Website: www.civilservicejobs.service.gov.uk/csr/index.cgi

Patent attorney

Over 2,000 patent attorneys are registered in the UK, usually in private practice firms, large companies and government departments. Their job is to obtain, protect and enforce intellectual property rights for their owners. It typically takes four or five years to become a UK Chartered Patent Attorney and/or a European Patent Attorney. All candidates must have a scientific or technical background (usually a related degree) and the aptitude for learning the relevant law. Attention to detail, good drafting skills and a very logical, analytical mind are crucial.

Candidates who wish to become a patent attorney typically find a post with a patent attorney firm or in-house, then sit both foundation and advanced examinations, which are run by the Chartered Institute of Patent Attorneys. Once qualified, there's the opportunity to obtain a further qualification that entitles the successful candidate to conduct litigation in the High Court, although all patent attorneys have the right to conduct litigation and appear as advocate in the specialist Patents County Court. In order to become a European Patent Attorney, candidates must complete another set of examinations. The website for the Chartered Institute of Patent Attorneys (CIPA), www.cipa.org.uk, has a useful careers section and job vacancy listings.

Trade mark attorney

A trade mark is a form of intellectual property used to distinguish a manufacturer or trader's particular brand from its competitors. It can be anything from a logo or picture to a colour – in 2012 Cadbury successfully trade marked the distinctive purple hue that's made its packaging famous. Trade mark attorneys provide advice on the suitability of words or logos as trade marks, on the action needed to safeguard a protected trade mark, and on how to deal with infringements by another parties. *"It's quite a pedantic job,"* commented one insider, *"and requires you to pay a lot of attention as you're constantly dealing and playing with words."*

There are about 855 fully qualified trade mark attorneys in the UK, all registered with the Institute of Trade Mark Attorneys (ITMA). Most work for large companies or at firms of patent and trade mark attorneys. In 2013, 51 individuals qualified as trade mark attorneys. To become a trade mark attorney you must complete two training courses and a period in practice. A degree isn't a prerequisite to qualification, although it can offer exemption from some coursework and is sometimes viewed as desirable by some employers. There's no central admissions procedure, so students need to approach firms or in-house trade mark departments directly. Check out www. itma.org.uk for more information.

Compliance officer or analyst

Banks and other financial services companies occasionally recruit law and non-law grads into their compliance units, which take on the vital role of advising senior management on how to comply with the laws, regulations and rules that govern the sector. Due to the proliferation of financial regulation, the importance of compliance departments has grown enormously so that in larger banks they're often equivalent in size to in-house legal teams

The role of compliance officer or analyst requires astute advice, clear guidance, reliable professional judgement and the ability to work in a team. Attention to detail and a determination to see the consistent application of compliance policies and practices are essential.

A minimum 2:1 degree is standard for successful applicants, and salaries are typically comparable with other graduate trainees in the City. With some compliance teams numbering more than 100 staff, there's plenty of scope for career development. Several banks run a two-year compliance analyst training scheme, over the course of which a trainee will gain a broad base of business knowledge and technical experience.

Barristers' clerk

Barristers' clerks should not be confused with any other type of clerk, as their role is very different. They help provide all the admin services a barristers' chambers needs by: liaising and organising meetings with solicitors (and the CPS); negotiating and collecting fees; allocating cases and planning their duration; administering databases, timetables, finances and diaries; and marketing their set's members. The most brilliant barristers aren't always the best at selling themselves, and so a good team of clerks can be a godsend in this respect.

The traditional image of a barristers' clerk is that of a Cockney barrow boy – think Philip Greene – with a wide tie-knot, wheeling around a trolley of legal briefs just like his father did before him. As with most professions, clerking these days is now more mixed, with plenty of women and people from other backgrounds, though there are still many burly, earthy types. Certain forward-thinking sets have retitled their clerks as 'practice managers', but it's essentially the same job under a different name.

Clerks are usually school leavers, and the minimum academic requirement is four GCSEs at C or above. Some clerks also have A levels and degrees, but it's personality coupled with legal, business or court administration experience that matter most.

Policy and regulatory work

So you did a law degree because you eventually wanted to end up writing the law of the land yourself? Unfortunately, the harsh truth is that the winter of discontent is well and truly upon us when it comes to recruitment into the (quasi-)public sector and the policy/regulatory world. That's not to say that all organisations have frozen recruiting altogether (though many have), but the onus is on you to dig a little deeper.

If you're prepared to be dynamic, the policy route provides a fascinating and rewarding career path. But how to make that first step? Knowing people who can champion your cause and offer you work experience here and there doesn't hurt. We suggest you start networking early. Internships with think tanks, charities, NGOs and international organisations are a must. Otherwise, it's a question of researching which government departments and regulators might interest you and contacting them directly to ask about recruitment.

For ideas, try typing 'policy' into the Guardian Jobs website search engine every so often, as well as checking regularly on the websites of organisations such as the Judicial Appointments Commission and Queen's Council Appointments. The Law Society, Solicitors Regulatory Authority, Bar Council and Bar Standards Board websites are all worth looking at for vacancies, as are various industry ombudsmen (check out www.ombudsmanassociation.org). The Financial Conduct Authority also runs a graduate training scheme: see www.fcacareers.org.uk for details.

How suitable are you and what do recruiters want?

So you've got a degree? No biggie. So will everyone else. Now is the time to make sure your CV and experiences square with what recruiters demand and build your self-confidence to improve your prospects.

Did we mention that competition for training contracts and pupillages is fierce? To win yourself one you will need not just an excellent academic record, but a stash of experiences to prove you have the ability to dive into the professional world with greater confidence than your rivals. Applying directly out of university with one or two interesting extracurricular experiences under your belt works for some. However, our research has shown that an increasing number of those entering the profession made an effort to gain substantive life experience before starting to make applications. It's no bad thing if you've already taken several steps up the career ladder by the time you start a traineeship or pupillage.

How impressive is your degree?

Having a law degree is no reason to assume entitlement. From the top sets at the Bar to the little-known solicitors' firms on the high street, non-law graduates are just as able to secure training positions as their LLB peers. In the few cases where employers prefer law grads they will specify this, so unless you hear differently, conversion route applicants may proceed with confidence. Many recruiters tell us just how highly they regard staff with language skills and scientific or technical degrees, particularly where their clients' businesses will benefit, and humanities degrees require many of the research, analytical or communication skills needed by lawyers.

Many solicitors' firms and barristers' chambers subscribe to the idea of a pecking order of universities; at some the bias is undeniably evident. If you worry that your university isn't one of the best regarded, then you should make sure you get the best degree result possible and work on enriching your CV in other ways.

As obvious as it may sound, working for good results throughout your degree is crucial. Be aware that you may already be applying for training contracts and vacation schemes in your second year, so if most of your first-year marks are thirds or 2:2s, you'll not get far.

Most firms and sets in this guide require recruits to have at least a 2:1. If you get a First that will definitely impress (at least on paper); if you wind up with a 2:2, you're go-

ing to have a tough time. Many recruiters will tell you that they take exceptional circumstances into account, but these circumstances do truly need to be exceptional – e.g. the star student who suffered a serious accident as finals loomed. In addition, you will need something pretty awesome to overcome that 2:2 – a year or more in a great job, a further degree or impressive voluntary work might cut it. Of course, none of these is a guaranteed fix. *"If you have average or less than average grades, you're really going to struggle,"* one recruiter told us. *"I sometimes feel that no one warns students about that early enough."* A Desmond is not likely to get you far a professional career, so work your socks off at university.

Extra-curricular activities

Addicted to Buzzfeed or obsessed with online cat pictures? Get over it. To succeed in your aim of becoming a lawyer, you will need to devote a large chunk of your free time at university and thereafter to undertaking worthwhile, constructive pursuits. Take advantage of the practically unlimited opportunities on offer. Every university has societies, meeting groups and sports clubs. Better still, set up your own event, society, club or business or social venture. Being able to show you are entrepreneurial and can achieve concrete results working on projects is increasingly important to recruiters. But you cannot undertake these pursuits just as CV fodder. Do something you are genuinely interested in; recruiters are always telling us they want to see that individuals have a passion for the things they have done.

Some kind of legal experience, whether it's organising events for your university law society or shadowing your aunt's neighbour's lawyer friend, is crucial since you need to convince prospective employers that you're serious about the profession. *"If you haven't been in a firm before, you'll have a hard time convincing us,"* says a managing partner. *"It's far better to see that candidates have experienced what lawyers do and still want to do it."* You can acquire experience later on through open days and vacation schemes, but it's never too early to start, not least because vac schemes and open days are now devilishly hard to get onto. Non-legal extracurriculars can be just as useful to show that you play well with others. It also gives you something to write about when an application form says: 'Discuss a time when you worked with a group to achieve a common goal'.

Many universities run law-specific career seminars in association with solicitors' firms or barristers' chambers. Be savvy, go along and find out as much as you can by talking to trainee solicitors and recruiters. Networking is a key tactic you should be employing. Our website has further advice on **The niceties and no-nos of networking.**

Researching firms

When you apply, research should be your watchword. Demonstrating your understanding of what a firm is about and what the work will entail, and being able to explain honestly and realistically why you want to do it, are among the most important things to get across when you make an application. Adopting a scattergun approach works for some, but simply sending the same covering letter to 50 firms will get you nowhere. Recruiters can tell very easily which applicants have a genuine interest in their firm and which have put in minimal effort. On our website, you can find a feature on **How to research firms properly.**

Commercial awareness

If you want to become a commercial lawyer you'll need this thing they call commercial awareness. Try and gain a sense of what's going on in the business world. The key issue to be aware of is how the current economic climate is affecting the way businesses and other organisations operate. Big topics of the day include: the implications of the crisis in Ukraine and sanctions against Russia; the efforts to boost the British economy; the impact that Scottish independence would have on business; and the greater emphasis placed on regulation in the financial services sector. Why not follow the news on a specific industry which you're interested in? Energy, technology and the media are particularly vibrant sectors at the moment.

Read the *Financial Times*, *The Economist* (it has great podcasts too) or any newspaper's business section. BBC Radio 4's *Today* programme also puts out a good daily business podcast. *The Student Guide's* Facebook page often links to stories that will broaden your knowledge of the business world and private client law.

It's also important to understand the role of a lawyer as a service provider. Lawyers must be able to relate to their clients and know something about their businesses. If the firms you apply to have certain specialisms or target certain industry sectors, then find out about those sectors.

Students looking to go into criminal law should be aware of recent legislation and current issues. Future family

lawyers should be able to discuss the major cases that have hit the headlines. Anyone interested in administrative and public law issues will have a full-time job keeping up to date with all the various developments in that field; Radio 4's *Law in Action* podcasts should be a real help. Hopeful crime, family and human rights lawyers should also be aware of the ways in which legal aid cuts are hitting these practices.

Travel

International travel in a gap year can broaden your horizons and teach you new organisational and problem-solving skills. Overseas experience is usually only valued by employers if you've spent time working, perhaps undertaking a project for a charity or in business. If you don't want to travel, don't worry: you can stand out in other ways. Above all, be original (as much as it's possible) in the experiences you pursue.

Mature candidates

Many employers now welcome mature applicants, and some – often smaller niche or regional outfits – actively seek out those with previous career experience. With age comes wisdom and probably an impressive set of transferable skills and industry knowledge. We've chatted with successful barristers and solicitors who've done everything from secretarial work, professional football, radio DJing, forensic science, physiotherapy and music production to accountancy, consultancy, piloting, policing and soldiering.

But when is old too old? If you're still in your 20s, that's fine. If you're in your 30s, ask what it is you can offer a law firm that will make your application stand out. And if you're older still? Never say never. Over the years we have run into a number of 40-something trainees, all of whom were glad to have made the career change. These much older trainees tended to have one thing in common: they brought advantageous industry experience to their firm. Figures collected by the Law Society show that 12.5% of solicitors admitted to the Roll in 2012/13 were aged 35 to 54, and 0.9% were aged 55 or over. But just as a rough guideline, the average age was 29.7 years.

Diversity

Women and ethnic minorities are increasingly present at the young end of the profession. In the year ending 31 July 2013, 59.1% of those admitted to the Roll were female and 23.7% were from ethnic minority backgrounds. In the course of our research this year 110 firms provided us with lists identifying their trainees. In most, the girls outnumber the boys – something we would expect to see given that more women have gone into the profession than men for well over a decade. The names on most of these lists also reflect a healthy spread of ethnic backgrounds. It is worth mentioning, however, that female and ethnic minority trainees still have too few senior role models, and there are always a small number of legal sector sex or race discrimination claims going through the employment tribunals. You can find more information about diversity, social mobility and diversity affinity groups on our website, as well as diversity statistics for firms in the *True Picture*.

Coming from overseas

If you're a non-Brit and you want to become a lawyer in the UK, your best bet is study here and then follow the standard route to qualification. Some people do join the profession after completing studies overseas, but the recognition of foreign degrees and qualifications is a complex and sketchy business. A specific programme called the Qualified Lawyer Transfer Scheme exists for those who are already practising lawyers overseas and are moving to the UK. We devote more attention to **Qualifying from overseas** on our website.

Regional connections

Regional firms and sets are sometimes more comfortable recruiting candidates with a local connection, be this through family or education. Quite simply, they want to know that whoever they take on will be committed to a long-term career with them. The picture across the UK is a variable one: some firms clearly state their preferences for local lads and lasses; others tell us that most of their applicants do have links with the region but that they are happy to consider anyone.

And finally...

What with studying hard, following the business and professional news, helping out at the CAB, captaining your rugby team, debating, acting as student law society president and attending careers events, you'll hardly have time for a pint. Your years at university are supposed to be fun, but don't waste valuable time that could be spent CV building.

How to make successful applications

We can't emphasise this more strongly: bulk applications rarely end well. Here are some tips on how to proceed.

Law firms are not homogeneous; each of them offers something unique. The applications you send off should be just as unique. Whenever we ask trainees for their words of wisdom on this subject, we often get an answer like this: *"It's so important to know the ins and outs of the firm you're applying to. If you're submitting an application that could easily be for just about any firm out there, then you'll get found out very quickly."* Recruiters think along the same lines: *"What I've found with many unsuccessful candidates is that they err towards rehearsed answers. Not knowing your subject really well can be your downfall."*

None of this means that you should be putting all your eggs in one basket and merely targeting one or two firms. Given that the market's so competitive today, it makes sense to identify several firms that suit you best – no matter how many that may be – and then take it from there. But you stand a much better chance of success if you've tailored each and every application to the firm in question. In addition, some informal contact or networking with the firms you apply to can help you on your way.

Do your research

If you do manage to secure a training contract at a firm, bear in mind that you're likely to be there for a minimum of two years. In other words: it's a big decision to make. As such, it's essential for you to find out which firms best match your personality and interests. Some can have pretty gruelling working hours attached to them, for example; others allow you to get home for the 6pm showing of The Netflix. Of equal importance is pinpointing the areas of law you're interested in and coupling that with the firms specialised in those areas. If you have an interest in a certain industry sector – healthcare, education, retail – it's worth taking that into account and looking at firms with the appropriate focus. As for useful resources, here are a few for you to cherish:

- *The Student Guide*. The **True Picture**, the **Chambers Reports**, the **Solicitors' Practice Areas**, **Practice Areas at the Bar** and our **Application & Selection** and **Salaries & Benefits** tables are all designed to help you work out which employer and area of law is right for you. We provide a **'How to get a training contract at...'** article for each firm in the True Picture that details its application and selection process.
- Our parent publication *Chambers UK*. It identifies and ranks all the best firms in over 70 areas of practice and can be read online for free at www.chambersandpartners.com.
- The legal press. *The Lawyer, Legal Week* and the *Law Gazette*, as well as legal gossip websites, can all be of value. Things to look out for include information on firms' business strategies as well as case and deal highlights.
- Law firms' websites. Study them vigorously! On top of laying out the key facts, they'll give a valuable insight into what that firm essentially stands for and how it sees itself. A firm's recruitment pages will also list its minimum requirements. Check your qualifications and abilities match up. **The Applications and selections table [on page 479]** should help with this, as should the **law firm profiles** at the back of this book.
- Industry journals and the local press. Find out more about the sectors a firm works in or its involvement in the local community. Read the national and international business press too, to build up your commercial awareness.

Get organised

- Law firm recruitment is a veritable deadline fest. Be aware of them, put them in your diary. The deadline calendars in this book will help you.
- Application forms take far, far longer to complete than you'd expect, especially when they're done well.
- Some barristers' chambers use the Pupillage Gateway; some don't. Make sure you know which is which. Check their websites. The **Bar** section of this guide discusses the Pupillage Gateway in more detail.
- Increasingly firms are digitising the application process and only accepting full applications from those who perform well enough in online tests – often verbal and numerical reasoning. You can find examples of these types of tests online or ask your careers service.

Tighten up your CV

- Chronological gaps can easily tarnish your CV, no matter how much work experience you've gained. If you've taken time off, put it down and be prepared to explain why.
- Content is more crucial than style. Don't waste time with photos or unusual fonts. Saying that, bullet points can make things more eye-catching.
- Don't just say what you did at uni – mention sports teams, work experience and volunteering, and be prepared to talk about the skills an activity gave you, or how it tested you.
- Mistakes can be damning. Recruiters are constantly telling us about basic spelling and grammar errors they encounter. Such mistakes provide an easy and legitimate reason to put your application straight in the bin. Check spelling thoroughly, and get a friend to read over your CV and applications.
- A CV should not be a brochure – keep the page count to one or two, and only move onto a third if you've won Nobel Prizes. Recruiters have to read countless numbers of them, so avoid flowery language and non-pertinent information. Part of a lawyer's skill set is effective communication. A third page signals a waffler and a weak communicator.
- Every point needs some evidence behind it. Putting down that you're fascinated by a particular area of law isn't enough; you're going to have to prove your passion with examples. Speak to lawyers whenever you can – it all helps to show that you understand the reality of practice. *"Nothing replaces face-to-face interaction, however you can achieve it,"* a graduate recruitment partner suggests.
- You can use any kind of work to prove you have commercial awareness. Even if you worked in a pub, you can still talk about being aware of costs, budgeting and marketing.

Nail that application form

- Answer questions directly – no cutting and pasting or repetition.
- Don't use glossy terms or jargon. Be clear and be concise.
- If a word limit is indicated, stick to it. It usually indicates how much detail you should go into. If you fall short, don't worry: it's better to be clear and concise than just to waffle on for no reason.
- Keep copies of everything you send out. Before an interview or assessment day you will need to remind yourself of what you wrote. Recruiters will most likely use your application as a basis for their questioning.

Don't undersell yourself

- Prizes, professional qualifications, impressive A levels, vac schemes – these things are obvious essentials on any CV.
- Experiences should demonstrate as many of the following as you can muster: teamwork, problem-solving skills, judgement, decision-making, leadership, dedication, the ability to thrive outside your comfort zone, a commercial outlook, and commitment to becoming a lawyer.
- Explain what you learned from your experiences rather than just listing them.
- If you can demonstrate that you're a real grafter who paid their way through uni, then do so.
- It won't always be appropriate to list all your part-time employment, so you might need to group some jobs into a more general category. Unless the list is extensive, indicate the key aspects of your role in each position.
- If you studied a musical instrument to a high level then say so – it shows you can commit to something and work diligently to achieve it. The same goes for other pastimes or pursuits.
- Sports are good application fodder. Again, the commitment factor will come through, and if it's a team sport you play it will confirm you're a team player
- Were you ever selected – or, better still, elected – to a position of responsibility? To be chosen by your peers as a student representative, for example, suggests that people admire you and have confidence in your abilities.
- If you are still at university, or have very recently graduated, mentioning things from your later school days is still permissible. If it has been some time since you left uni, however, then you need to find some more recent examples.

There's no room for error

You may think you're the ideal candidate, but any mistakes on your applications, no matter how minuscule, will almost certainly cost you. Recruiters want people who are likely to be a roaring success and not make mistakes. A final word goes to this recruitment partner: *"We're not looking for people who will do the job of a trainee and NQ, but won't be able to go any further than that. In a nutshell, we're looking for the partners of the future."*

How to succeed at interviews and assessment days

Interviews and assessment days are to be celebrated, not dreaded. You'll send out dozens of application forms and get blanked by many firms. So when you do get an interview, give it your all.

Interviews

Well done on bagging an interview. That may have been hard work, but it's no guarantee that you've got the job. Now it's time to ratchet things up another notch. Turn on the charm, stand up straight, dress smartly and be thorough with your homework.

Before any interview:

Read and think about your application form. Interviewers will pick up on what you wrote and question you on it. A lot of the time, they'll discuss your application form as an icebreaker. It's your chance to speak about things that interest you and to build up rapport. Chat, be expansive, maybe even flash the pearly whites. If you fibbed on your application form, this is when you'll be found out, so don't lie.

Research the firm. A stock question is 'Why this firm?' Recruiters tell us this is where many people trip up. Make sure you've got something good, innovative and non-generic to say. Read the **True Picture** reports and find out about the firm's strengths, its history and what is being said about it in the legal press. Ideally you will find a topic or two that can be developed into a reason why you and the firm are a perfect match.

Research the people who are interviewing you, if possible. Know your enemy. Practice areas, precedent-setting cases they've won, previous firms they've worked at, their favourite sport – all of this is gold, and firm websites often contain such details. Don't quote it all back at them though… that's creepy.

Have a finger on the pulse of legal news and current affairs. *The Lawyer, Legal Week, Solicitors Journal* and *Law Gazette* are all very good, as is Thursday's law supplement in *The Times*. And have you signed up to the *Student Guide*'s Facebook page? Be ready to see the connections between law and the real world of politics, society and business.

Practise answers, but not too much. It's not hard to guess what sort of questions you're going to get; something

along the lines of 'Why do you want to be a lawyer?' is a bona fide cert. It is wise to rehearse a little to collect your thoughts, but you've got to be ready to deviate from the script. Speaking off the cuff makes you sound more interesting and often a classic question will be slightly altered, so you need to be ready to adapt. Almost no firm will directly ask questions about black-letter law, although some do favour enquiries about lawyerly ethics or client confidentiality designed to be appropriate for graduates of all fields.

Think about what skills you can offer. Increasingly, interviewers are asking competency-based questions. Common examples include 'Give an example of a time you successfully achieved a set goal'; 'Tell me about how you've dealt with a difficult person in a team'; and 'What do you think constitutes excellent client or customer service?'. Before an interview think about how the skills you've acquired in your work and life experiences can benefit the law firm you're interviewing with.

Expect the unexpected. Some firms are known for asking quirky questions: 'If you were a biscuit what type would you be?' or 'If I put your iPod on shuffle what track would be likely to come up?' are just two examples. Ideally, your answer should say something about your personality or at least show that you're quick-witted. Interviewers may also challenge your views or hit you with an unexpected question. If you encounter this, the best strategy is usually to stand your ground and explain the reasoning behind what you've said.

The default setting when going into an interview is to want to be liked, but remember that the interview is a crucial opportunity for you to figure out whether you like the firm back. You should have a couple of questions prepared to ask the firm. There are so many things you might ask, so do pick something that isn't already covered in the firm's own literature. You could find out what your interviewers like about the firm or ask them about when they trained. You could ask them what the firm is doing in reaction to a major development in the legal or business world. Be confident: *"If you've made it to the interview stage, on paper you're a good candidate,"* a training principal tells us. *"The thing that tends to elevate people is confidence."*

The usual interview tips apply:

- Arrive early. Have a contact number ready in case some cruel act of divine vengeance makes you late.
- Dress appropriately.
- Be polite to everyone, including receptionists and support staff.
- Shake hands firmly (but avoid the 'bone crusher' handshake) and make eye contact. Smile non-menacingly.
- Speak to everyone on the panel, ensuring you make eye contact with all present.
- Don't fidget or sit awkwardly. Don't allow your body to tense.
- Do mock interviews beforehand and get feedback from whoever tests you. Even family members and friends can be surprisingly good at this if you explain what sort of questions you want them to ask. They may identify an annoying verbal tic. Do what you can to eradicate any rogue erms and umms.
- Listen carefully to questions so you can establish what it is the interviewer seeks. Don't just shoehorn in prepackaged answers. *"Recruiters really don't like it if people are too polished and give standard answers,"* a trainee told us.
- Finally, be yourself. The interview process is *"about showing your personality, showing yourself as you are normally,"* one graduate recruiter told us. *"There's nothing worse than seeing someone trying to be what they think we want them to be."*

Assessment days

Even though you might have an LPC distinction, a First, 5 A*s at A level, 29 GCSEs and a gold star from Mrs Haslem's nursery class, many firms will want to see you in action and test you out with their own assessments. In their arsenal, firms have written and negotiation exercises, personality profiling, research tasks, group tasks, in-tray exercises and presentations. Often, an assessment day will also include an interview. Different firms prefer different methods. In the **How to get a training contract at...** features alongside each **True Picture** online, we detail the hoops you'll need to leap through at each firm.

"I felt the assessments were pitched at testing social confidence and whether you are a friendly person," recalled one trainee at a City firm. Most group tasks and exercises are serious in tone: examples include mock client meetings, an email inbox full of correspondence to deal with, or a feedback session with a partner and an associate. Advertising pitches to faux clients and pretend minitransactions are also common, but be warned that firms frequently change the make-up of their assessment days.

A (decreasing) number use more unusual methods: over the years we've heard of scenarios where groups of candidates were asked to build Lego towers, determine the allocations of eggs to different parts of a country, and debate who should be allowed to leave a hypothetical cave first.

Remember: however out of the ordinary an assessment, it is still aimed at testing business skills, and your attitude should at all times remain professional and aimed at showcasing your competencies. Recruiters are especially keen to see whether you can work in a team. Be careful not to dominate group tasks too much or fade into the background.

Don't relax too much if there's a social event as these are often just as important when it comes to making a good impression. Some firms have lunches where you sit round with three or four partners and a handful of other applicants and make small talk. Who will your prospective supervisor want to hire? The girl who kept her eyes on the plate for the entire meal and whispered unintelligible answers to every question? The chap who drank too much and spent most of the meal calling him 'buddy'? Or the nice young man who made some pertinent observations on the Eurozone crisis and showed an interest in his kite-surfing hobby?

Similarly, a drink with the firm's trainees is an opportunity to strike up a rapport with them, not to start making comments about how your vac scheme at Ashurst was soooo much better.

Either as part of the assessment day or application process, you may be asked to complete one or more psychometric tests. Some look at verbal or numerical skills, while others test your judgement when confronted by certain scenarios. You can find examples of these types of tests online, or by asking your careers service.

Verbal and numerical reasoning tests usually consist of multiple-choice questions with right and wrong answers. Accuracy, intellectual rigour, efficiency and mental agility are imperative. Personality and situational judgement tests aim to find out whether you are a leader or a follower, a planner or impulsive, etc. In theory, these have no correct answers, but before you expose your soul to recruiters, it's worth thinking about why they have set this test and what they are looking for: profiling yourself as an emotionally fragile control freak isn't going to help you.

And finally...

The sad fact is that for many people it could take a while to succeed. Don't let rejection bring you down: ask recruiters why you didn't make the cut and learn from it.

Managing job offers

After all the hard work involved in securing a training contract offer, you'll need to know what to do when you actually land one.

The Solicitors Regulation Authority publishes a 'voluntary code to good practice in the recruitment of trainee solicitors', which you can find at http://www.sra.org.uk/trainees/period-recognised-training/voluntary-code-recruitment.page

Read through these guidelines if at any stage you are in doubt as to what you should do. They address the conduct expected of both recruiters and students. Law firms are not obliged to follow these guidelines, though most will.

On offers, the guidelines say:

- If you're still an undergrad, a training contract offer should not be made before 1 September in your final undergraduate year. If you've impressed a firm during a vacation scheme or period of work experience, it must wait until this date before making you an offer.
- At an interview, you will be told if there is a further stage to the selection process. You should also be told within two weeks of reaching the end of the process whether or not you have been successful.
- Offers should be made in writing. If you receive an offer by phone you don't need to say yes or no: you can ask the firm to send a formal offer in writing for you to consider.

On deadlines, the guidelines say:

- No deadline for accepting an offer should be earlier than four weeks from the date of that offer. If you need more time to mull over an offer, firms are supposed to consider your request 'sympathetically', provided you have a good reason. No definition of 'good reason' is given in the guidelines.
- If a firm is going to pay your law school fees it should set out the terms and conditions of the arrangement in the training contract offer letter. A firm's willingness to provide financial assistance should not affect the time limit for accepting the contract.

- If you feel you need more time, you will have to enter into diplomatic discussions with the law firm, telling them how much longer you need, and the date by which your decision will be made. Ask for written confirmation of any extension to the deadline so both parties are clear what has been decided.

You may want to hang on to an offer from one firm while you pursue applications with others. This is okay, but the SRA guidelines suggest the following (again, these rules are not binding):

- You should not hold more than two (as yet unaccepted or declined) offers at any one time.
- Students are supposed to respond promptly to a firm that's made an offer, either by accepting or rejecting it. The word 'promptly' is not defined in the code.
- Because offers can and will be made with time limits for acceptance, do guard against allowing a deadline to elapse. The stupidity tax you may otherwise pay doesn't bear thinking about.
- Once you have accepted your preferred offer in writing, you must then confirm to everyone else that you are withdrawing your application. This is only fair to busy recruiters and other applicants who may suffer if you clog up a shortlist.

The guidelines are silent on the issue of what happens if a student changes their mind after accepting an offer. It's a rare firm that will be particularly sympathetic to a post-acceptance withdrawal but, on occasions, these things do happen. We can give no general advice on this subject, as each individual case will have its own merits. What we can say is that the smooth running of the whole trainee recruitment market relies on most parties playing by the above 'rules'.

So what if a law firm puts pressure on you to accept an offer earlier than the guidelines say they should? Again, there is no simple answer as the SRA's code of conduct is voluntary. If this situation arises you will have to enter into delicate negotiations with the law firm. You could also discuss the problem with your university or college careers adviser and ask if they can recommend a course of action.

Pro bono and volunteering

Deriving from the Latin pro bono publico, meaning 'for the public good', the idea of providing free legal advice has been ingrained in the legal profession for centuries.

The past decade has seen the rise of structured pro bono programmes at law firms, sets of chambers, law schools and universities. Bringing these all together, ProBonoUK. net was started in 2003 and is the most comprehensive resource on pro bono activities in the UK. 2014's National Pro Bono week runs from 3rd to 7th November.

Why participate?

The legal aid bill is being cut thick and fast. On top of £350m already removed from the scheme's £2.2bn annual budget, Justice Secretary Chris Grayling announced a further £220m cut to criminal legal aid. The government estimated that around 600,000 people will lose access to legal advice as a result, and former Labour legal aid minister Lord Bach estimated that the cuts will remove 86% of funding which law centres receive to provide advice and 'legal help'. Birmingham Law Centre was forced to close in summer 2013 (although Coventry Law Centre later stepped in to help set up a new one), and it's feared that other centres will experience similar problems. Check out our online feature on **Legal aid cuts and reforms** to find out more.

As a result of paid jobs going, involvement in some form of pro bono or volunteering work is becoming increasingly important, not just because there are people out there who need your help, but because pro bono experience can really help boost your CV. Being able to demonstrative proactive involvement in a cause and achieving real results for those in need will help get your application to the front of the queue. Practising lawyers can – and perhaps ought to – continue to help their communities by providing free legal advice via organisations like LawWorks.

Law schools make a particular effort to introduce students to pro bono. As Jessica Austen, joint director of pro bono at BPP, told us: *"Being involved in pro bono can make a huge difference to a student's engagement with the courses they are undertaking. They can see the law they are studying come to life in a practical sense and the impact their participation can have on the community around them. This is particularly true now, given access to justice is so much more challenging following the legal aid cuts."*

Many firms now have formal pro bono relationships with organisations such as community legal advice centres. Arguably the increased scope and visibility of pro bono work is in part due to the greater importance placed on pro bono activities by the influx of US law firms into the UK market. Certainly more home-grown law firms now recognise the business case for doing this kind of work, not least because of the PR benefits.

Real life

In light of the threats posed to law centres across the country, more universities, like Liverpool John Moores, have been opening their own legal advice centres (LJM's is supported by LawWorks). Many law schools now offer extensive pro bono programmes. Cardiff Law School has the Innocence Project, for example, which deals with long-term prisoners who maintain their innocence and have exhausted the initial appeals process. Kaplan Law School has developed a close relationship with Amicus and sponsors students to attend training sessions that allow them to assist with defence counsel representations for those facing execution in the US. At the other end of the pro bono spectrum, BPP works in conjunction with the charity Own It to provide free IP advice to the creative industries. And as if you needed a greater incentive than a warm glow in the pit of your belly, there are various national prizes on offer for students who excel in this field, including the Law Society's annual Junior Lawyers Division Pro Bono Award. At university level, student pro bono opportunities traditionally used to be more limited, as it was seen as too risky for inexperienced undergrads to provide real-life legal advice. But this is changing now as undergraduates are receiving more support. For example, Kent Law School's law clinic recently got one undergrad very closely involved with the case of a man from Afghanistan who won asylum in the UK because he was an atheist. You can go to www.studentprobono.net for a comprehensive list of opportunities at each institution.

If you hope to go to the Bar or become a solicitor specialising in any contentious area of law then you should seriously consider becoming a ratified member of The Free Representation Unit (FRU), a charity founded in 1972 to provide legal advice, case preparation and advocacy for people who aren't able to claim legal aid.

Vacation schemes

Not only are vac schemes CV gold, many firms treat them as an integral part of the training contract application process. So if you want to bag a training contract get yourself on a vac scheme. Here's how...

Still at uni and unsure if you really want to be a lawyer? If so, then giving up a week or two of your hard-earned holiday during Christmas, Easter or the summer to sample law firm life is a small price to pay. As one training partner told us, vacation schemes are a great opportunity to test the waters, *"a chance to gain an insight into life as a lawyer, get feedback on your work and grow from the experience."* And as a trainee recalled of their vac scheme at a City firm: *"It gives you a very good picture of what life as a trainee will be like."*

But be under no illusions: you will also be on trial, because in this ever-more competitive market most firms (and some more than others) treat the vac scheme almost as a pre-screening exercise when it comes to handing out training contracts. The prime example of a firm that relies heavily on vac schemes is City firm Nabarro, which now takes almost all of its trainees from people it sees on its three-week placement. Another is US giant Skadden, which informs us: *"We do accept applications from those who haven't done vacation schemes with us, but we really only look at those if something has gone wrong with our placement and it hasn't thrown up enough quality candidates."*

This stance is not (yet) the prevailing recruiting model, and many firms who offer vacation schemes have no hard and fast rules about how many they will aim to recruit from them: some firms have just as many trainees who haven't done one as those who have. But the message is clear: whichever vac scheme you end up doing you'll be assessed, no matter how informally, and you should plan and act accordingly.

How do you get on one?

Our table of vac schemes will tell you exactly what places are available with the firms covered by this guide and when to apply. Timing your application is important: certain schemes are targeted at penultimate-year law grads or final-year non-law grads, which can leave other students frustrated. Suffice to say, law undergrads need to start thinking about their application campaign during the summer after their first year at university.

The application deadlines for the majority of vac schemes come in January and February, but some firms run schemes in the Christmas and Easter holidays and the deadlines for applying to those can be as early as October. Don't miss out! You'll generally find full details of exactly how to make your application on firms' recruitment websites.

What do firms look for when recruiting for the vac scheme? *"Same as the training contract really,"* one tells us: *"Strong academics and an interest in our practice areas."* For smaller firms with a more concentrated or specialist array of practice areas, take note of this training principal's advice: *"Given the limited spaces that we have, we want to feel that candidates have chosen us for a particular reason. Some applicants have a 'shotgun' approach. That doesn't work for us: we don't have the number of spaces to just say 'oh, we'll just take a punt on those five'. We really want people who really want us."* As competition for training contracts gets more intense, it's no surprise that competition for vac scheme places is equally so. Obvious conclusion: you'll need to put as much effort into vac scheme applications as you do into training contract applications. For some tips on how to do this refer to our feature on **How to make successful applications.** On our website we also provide detailed advice on the application procedures for each of the firms covered in the **True Picture**.

The strongest applicants always manage to secure a clutch of offers, but don't despair if you can't secure a place – it doesn't necessarily mean you'll never get a training contract. Try and build your CV up in other ways – say with voluntary work or other legal or commercial experience – and then have another stab at vac scheme applications. Even if you navigate the vac scheme obstacle course perfectly, don't get complacent. You'll still need to prepare well for a training contract interview.

What will I get to do?

At some firms, vac schemes are structured down to the minute with talks about the firm and its training contract, followed by tasks and social engagements. At others, vac schemers may be tied to a trainee or qualified solicitor and what they do will depend on that individual. Elsewhere, panhandling for work and knocking on doors to find assignments will be the name of the game, which can be a blessing or a curse, depending on how you look at it, as this trainee told us: *"It's good because it forces you to engage with people throughout the firm, who you might not have otherwise met, but if you're not used to knocking on doors it can be very difficult."*

The best vac schemes get students involved in ongoing cases and deals and puts them in the heat of the action – or at least lets them feel that way. *"You are expected to contribute to real work,"* recalled one ex-vac schemer. *"I remember doing some very serious assignments – although looking back I probably thought they were more serious than they actually were."* For detailed information on each firm's vacation scheme, go to our website.

What should I look out for?

When on a vac scheme, become an anthropologist. Observe your environment and its inhabitants; figure out the social structures, the hierarchies, the shared values that bond people (if indeed there are any). Watch how the trainees fit in with all of this. Eavesdrop. You've got to be on your guard, though, because people will be conscious you're there, and some of our sources did end up concluding: *"It can be an artificial exercise – you see what they want you to see."* Your aim is to peer beyond the mask at the living, breathing, sweating entity behind it.

Try also to get a feel for how different departments work by reading as much as you can. A starting point would be our **Solicitors' Practice Areas**. It'll help you figure out what sort of work might suit you best and will enable you to ask intelligent questions of your supervisors. Intelligent questions pave the road to success, so lay as many down as possible without becoming annoying.

How will I be assessed?

"The vacation scheme is a great way of meeting prospective trainees and giving them a real taster of what life is like here," one recruiter explains. But don't forget that also *"it's a good way to see them in action."*

Vac schemers are often given research to do as a way of evaluating their abilities; expect to be given some specifics to look into before reporting back to solicitors with your findings. You might be asked to shadow someone, helping them out with their workload. This is an excellent opportunity for you to find more out about the firm while proving yourself at the same time. You might even get to go to client meetings or visit court. Regardless of the task, attention to detail cannot be underestimated, as minor errors may not go unnoticed and could well come back to haunt you. One recruiter told us: *"Sometimes, vac schemers are instructed to copy someone into an email, and they fail to do that; it's a criticism we've raised in the past."*

Last, but certainly not least, are the mini-assessment tasks and projects designed to test your ability to present, argue and work as a team. *"Don't be over-assertive, but don't fade into the background either. Remember to ask other people what their opinions are – you have to look like a team player."* Some projects may require vac schemers to balance their more competitive instincts with their ability to function within a team, as this recruitment contact told us: *"We divide the vac schemers into two groups, and they are given a negotiation exercise which they will later have to act out during the final assessment, so there's that element of competition between the groups."* Other assessments we heard about involved advertising pitches to faux potential clients, mock mini-transactions and business advice scenarios.

How should I act?

"Those who are successful have the drive, imagination and confidence to see the scheme for the learning opportunity it really is rather than just an assessment centre in which they are competing with other students," one training partner at a larger outfit advises. *"Students become part of the firm when they arrive; many make friendships. And the firm will always make room for excellent candidates it sees on the scheme, whatever the numbers."*

While you're busy watching everyone else, don't forget that they're watching you, watching them, watching you. This recruitment lark is a delicate dance, so attune yourself to the characters around you and follow their lead. More than anything else, people will be trying to see if you 'share the firm's core values'.

Ultimately, 'professionalism' should be your watchword. This is a job interview, even when you're eating lunch in the canteen. Don't be late for work. Switch off your mobile phone when in the office. Don't bitch or send stupid emails. Thinking about browsing Facebook in a slack moment? Why take the risk?

Okay, so don't be an idiot. That much is obvious. But how can you impress? As one recruiter says, it's all about *"marketing yourself well."* Does that sound a little intimidating? It's really not. After all, you marketed yourself well on paper when you sent your application form in; now you are just doing it in person. Asking well-timed questions and showing an interest is an easy way of doing this. Just remember, *"seeking out work and raising your profile without pestering people is a fine line to walk."* It may be a fine line, but it's one worth treading, and being proactive is key, as this partner suggests: *"If you get given a piece of work, think about what happens next. Think about that next stage in the transaction, and if you don't know what it is then go find out. You've got to show initiative – that's how you grow and develop and get handed other pieces of work going forward."*

Coming for a quick drink? Bankers, lawyers, doctors and even priests all know how effective alcohol can be when it comes to greasing the wheels. But the trick is to drink the right amount or none at all. Even when firms take vac schemers out to snazzy clubs, recruiters' mental notepads will still be out. So gauge the situation: is the firm boozy or abstemious?

At the end of the day, a law firm is just like any other office workplace in that you'll find all sorts of characters. You'll also find variety within any group of vac schemers. *"You get the quiet ones, the loud ones, the ones who say inappropriate things, the ones who're always smiling."* Obviously, you're being assessed on how good a lawyer you're likely to be, but don't underestimate how far having a normal, attractive personality will get you.

"A small intake means trainees are very much exposed in their role, for better or for worse. Think about whether your personality and working style are suited to that when choosing a firm."
                                    City graduate recruitment source

Vacation Schemes

Firm Name	Vacancies	Season	Duration	Remuneration	Deadline
Addleshaw Goddard	65	Easter and summer	1-2 weeks	not known	31 January 2015
Allen & Overy	not known	Winter and summer	1-3 weeks	not known	not known
Arnold & Porter	8	Summer	2 weeks	not known	8 March 2015
Ashfords	24	Summer	1 week	Unpaid	28 February 2015
Ashurst	60	Easter (final-year non-law and grads) & summer (penult-year law)	2-3 weeks	£250 p.w.	not known
Baker & McKenzie	not known	Easter and summer	not known	not known	not known
Bates Wells & Braithwaite	12	Easter and summer	2 weeks	£300 total	March 2015
Bird & Bird	30	Summer	3 weeks	£275 p.w.	31 January 2015
Bond Dickinson	40-50	Easter and summer	not known	not known	31 January 2015
Boodle Hatfield	6	Summer	2 weeks	not known	not known
BP Collins	15-20	Easter and summer	1-2 weeks	not known	31 March 2015
Bristows	No vac scheme – two day workshops	Winter, spring and summer	2 days	not known	22 November 2014 (winter); 31 January 2015 (spring and summer)
Browne Jacobson	not known	Summer	not known	not known	17 March 2015
Burges Salmon	36	Summer	2 weeks	£250 p.w.	not known
Capsticks	24	Summer	2 weeks	not known	13 February 2015
Cleary Gottlieb Steen & Hamilton	35 (5 in winter, 10 in spring and 20 in summer)	Winter, Easter and summer	2 weeks	£500 p.w	15 November 2014 (winter); 28 January 2015 (spring and summer)
Clyde & Co	not known	Easter and summer	2 weeks	not known	31 January 2015
CMS Cameron McKenna	80	Easter and summer	2 weeks	£250 p.w.	31 January 2015
Covington & Burling	24	Summer	1 week	£300 p.w.	31 January 2015
Davis Polk & Wardwell	not known	Summer	2 weeks	£500 p.w.	28 January 2015
Dechert	20	Summer + spring open days	2 weeks	not known	31 January 2015
Dentons	8	Summer + open days	1 week	not known	not known
DLA Piper	130	Summer (law students only) + open days (other applicants)	2 weeks	not known	not known
DWF	140	Summer (law students only) + Winter open days (other applicants)	2 weeks	not known	not known
Edwards Wildman Palmer	8	Summer + open days	2 weeks	£300 total	31 January 2015
Eversheds	not known	Summer	2 weeks	£225-250 p.w.	not known
Farrer & Co	30	Summer	2 weeks	£275 p.w.	31 January 2015
Foot Anstey	20	Summer	1 week	Unpaid	30 April 2015
Freshfields Bruckhaus Deringer	not known	Summer	not known	not known	6 January 2015
Gateley	not known	Summer (aimed at penult-year undergrads)	2 weeks	not known	31 January 2015
Government Legal Service	10-15	Summer	1 week	£200 p.w.	not known
Herbert Smith Freehills	not known	Summer	not known	£350 p.w.	31 October 2015 (winter); 16 January 2015 (spring and summer)
Hewitsons	not known	Summer	not known	not known	not known

Vacation Schemes

Firm Name	Vacancies	Season	Duration	Remuneration	Deadline
Hill Dickinson	60	Easter and summer	4 days-1 week	not known	31 January 2015
Holman Fenwick Willan	Up to 30	Easter and summer	1-2 weeks	£300 p.w.	14 February 2015
Ince & Co	not known	Easter	2 weeks	£250 p.w.	31 January 2015
Irwin Mitchell	not known	Easter and summer	not known	not known	31 January 2015
Jones Day	70	Summer	2 weeks	£400 p.w.	31 October 2014 (winter); 19 December 2014 (spring); 16 January 2015 (summer)
K&L Gates	12	Summer	2 weeks	£300 p.w.	31 January 2015
Kennedys	12	Summer	2 weeks	£275 p.w.	31 January 2015
King & Wood Mallesons	50	Summer and Easter	1-2 weeks	£270 p.w.	31 January 2015
Kirkland & Ellis	16-18	Summer	2 weeks	£350 p.w.	16 January 2015
Latham & Watkins	40	Easter and summer	not known	£350 p.w.	31 December 2014 (Easter); 31 January 2015 (summer)
Lester Aldridge	8	Summer	2 weeks	not known	31 March 2015
Linklaters	40	Summer	not known	not known	not known
Macfarlanes	55	Summer	2 weeks	£300 p.w.	31 January 2015
Maclay Murray & Spens	6-7	Spring (finalists) and summer (penult-year undergrads)	2-3 weeks	not known	January 2015
Mayer Brown	45	Easter and summer	3 weeks	not known	31 January 2015
Memery Crystal	No vac scheme – open days offered	Summer	N/A	N/A	N/A
Michelmores	16	Summer	1 week	Unpaid	28 February 2015
Mills & Reeve	not known	Summer	2 weeks	£270 p.w.	31 January 2015
Mishcon de Reya	30	Summer	2 weeks	not known	15 January 2015
Morgan Lewis	not known	Summer	1 week	not known	31 January 2015
Muckle	not known	Easter and summer	not known	not known	31 January 2015
Nabarro	55	Summer	3 weeks	£225-£275 p.w.	15 January 2015
Norton Rose Fulbright	45	Summer and winter	1-2 weeks	£300 p.w.	31 October 2014 (winter); 31 January 2015 (summer)
Olswang	20	Summer	not known	£275 p.w.	15 January 2015
O'Melveny & Myers	not known	Winter (finalists and grads) and summer (penult-year undergrads) + open days	not known	not known	31 January 2015
Orrick	open days	Easter and summer	1 day	not known	not known
Osborne Clarke	not known	Summer	2 weeks	not known	not known
Pinsent Masons	100	Summer	2 weeks	£250 p.w.	31 January 2015
PwC Legal	22	Summer	3 weeks	Paid	29 January 2015
Reed Smith	24	Summer	2 weeks	£300 p.w.	31 January 2015
RPC	24	Summer	2 weeks	£275 p.w.	31 January 2015
SGH Martineau	24	Summer	2 days	not known	31 January 2015

Vacation Schemes

Firm Name	Vacancies	Season	Duration	Remuneration	Deadline
Shoosmiths	not known	Summer	1 week	not known	not known
Simmons & Simmons	not known	Easter and summer	1-3 weeks	not known	not known
Skadden	c.40	Easter and summer	2 weeks	£300 p.w.	12 January 2015
Slaughter and May	72-80	Summer (penultimate year law students), September (penultimate year non-law students), Easter (penultimate year law and non-law) + open days	1-3 weeks	not known	not known
Squire Patton Boggs	40-50	Easter and summer (penult-year law & non-law)	2 weeks	£225-240 p.w.	31 January 2015
Stephenson Harwood	40	Easter and summer (penult-year students) + open days	1–2 weeks	£260 p.w.	2 November 2014 (winter); 31 January 2015 (spring and summer)
Stevens & Bolton	8	Summer	1 week	not known	31 January 2015
Sullivan & Cromwell	not known	Winter, Easter and summer	2 weeks	£500 p.w.	30 January 2015
Taylor Wessing	40	Summer	2 weeks	£250 p.w.	30 January 2015
TLT	not known	Summer (penult-year law and final-year non-law)	1 week	£230 p.w.	not known
Travers Smith	60 – (15 in winter and 45 in summer)	Winter and summer	2 weeks	£275 p.w.	31 January 2015
Trowers & Hamlins	24	Summer	2 weeks	not known	not known
Veale Wasbrough Vizards	16	Summer	1 week	Unpaid	not known
Vinson & Elkins	c.20	Summer	1 week	£250 p.w.	31 January 2015
Ward Hadaway	10-12	Summer	1 week	not known	28 February 2015
Watson, Farley & Williams	not known	Easter and summer	2 weeks	not known	31 January 2015
Wedlake Bell	8	Summer	3 weeks	not known	End of February 2015
White & Case	75 (15 in Easter and 60 in summer)	Easter and summer	2 weeks	£350 p.w.	31 January 2015
Wilsons	5	Summer	1 week	not known	31st March
Winckworth Sherwood	8	Summer	3 weeks	£150 p.w.	not known
Withers	18	Easter and summer	2 weeks	not known	31 January 2015
Wragge Lawrence Graham & Co	40 (summer)	Easter and summer	2 weeks	not known	not known

Gender and the law

Female solicitors are more represented in lower paid areas including employment, family and welfare benefits, while male solicitors dominate better paid areas including business, commercial and criminal law

In 2014, Linklaters became the first magic circle firm to set gender diversity targets, aiming for a 30% female executive committee within four years

34.7% of practising barristers are female

86% of female lawyers believe that firms adopting more flexible working practices is critical for more women to reach senior roles

One of 11 Supreme Court Justices is female

61.5% of new trainees in 2013 were women

Female solicitors' salaries were 30% lower than males' in 2013; the UK-wide gender pay gap is 10%

Fewer than one in 10 senior lawyers at the UK's biggest law firms are women

Law School

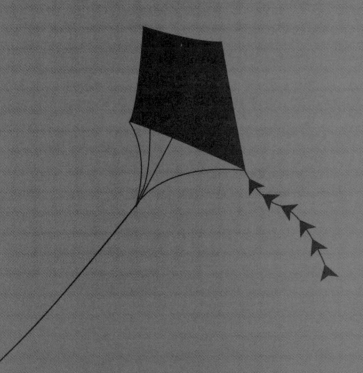

Solicitors' Timetable

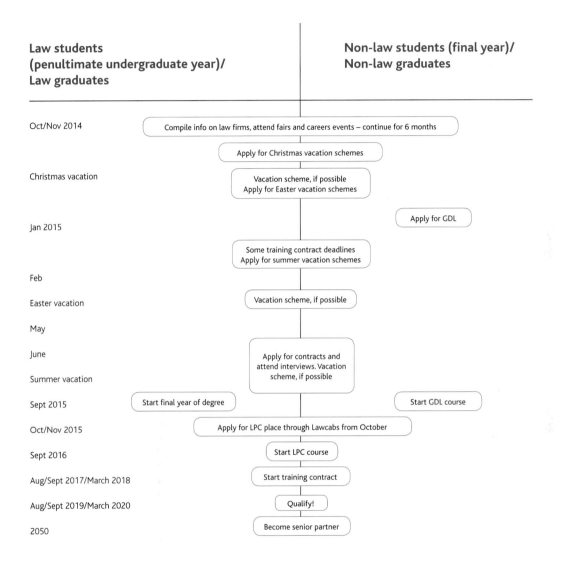

**Law students
(penultimate undergraduate year)/
Law graduates**

**Non-law students (final year)/
Non-law graduates**

Oct/Nov 2014	Compile info on law firms, attend fairs and careers events – continue for 6 months
	Apply for Christmas vacation schemes
Christmas vacation	Vacation scheme, if possible Apply for Easter vacation schemes
Jan 2015	Apply for GDL
	Some training contract deadlines Apply for summer vacation schemes
Feb	
Easter vacation	Vacation scheme, if possible
May	
June	Apply for contracts and attend interviews. Vacation scheme, if possible
Summer vacation	
Sept 2015	Start final year of degree	Start GDL course
Oct/Nov 2015	Apply for LPC place through Lawcabs from October
Sept 2016	Start LPC course
Aug/Sept 2017/March 2018	Start training contract
Aug/Sept 2019/March 2020	Qualify!
2050	Become senior partner

Notes

1   It is important to check application closing dates for each firm as these will vary.
2   Some firms will only accept applications for vacation schemes from penultimate-year students, whether
    law or non-law. See 'firm profiles' for further information.
3   Some firms require very early applications from non-law graduates.
    See A-Z pages for further information.
4   The timetable refers primarily to those firms that recruit two years in advance. Smaller firms often recruit
    just one year in advance or for immediate vacancies.
5   This timetable assumes students will progress straight through from university to law school and a train-
    ing contract. This is not necessarily the most appropriate or achievable course of action for all students.

Barristers' Timetable

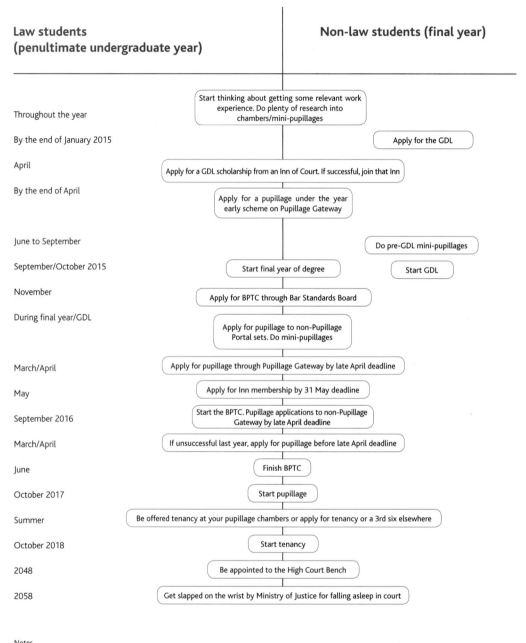

**Law students
(penultimate undergraduate year)**

Non-law students (final year)

Throughout the year	Start thinking about getting some relevant work experience. Do plenty of research into chambers/mini-pupillages
By the end of January 2015	Apply for the GDL
April	Apply for a GDL scholarship from an Inn of Court. If successful, join that Inn
By the end of April	Apply for a pupillage under the year early scheme on Pupillage Gateway
June to September	Do pre-GDL mini-pupillages
September/October 2015	Start final year of degree — Start GDL
November	Apply for BPTC through Bar Standards Board
During final year/GDL	Apply for pupillage to non-Pupillage Portal sets. Do mini-pupillages
March/April	Apply for pupillage through Pupillage Gateway by late April deadline
May	Apply for Inn membership by 31 May deadline
September 2016	Start the BPTC. Pupillage applications to non-Pupillage Gateway by late April deadline
March/April	If unsuccessful last year, apply for pupillage before late April deadline
June	Finish BPTC
October 2017	Start pupillage
Summer	Be offered tenancy at your pupillage chambers or apply for tenancy or a 3rd six elsewhere
October 2018	Start tenancy
2048	Be appointed to the High Court Bench
2058	Get slapped on the wrist by Ministry of Justice for falling asleep in court

Notes

This timetable assumes students will progress straight through from university to law school and a pupillage.
This is not necessarily the most appropriate or achievable course of action for students.

The Graduate Diploma in Law (GDL)

Whether you chose to spend your undergrad years exploring the ritual ceremonies of Amazonians, immersing yourself in Chaucer and Langland, or grappling with some insoluble questions existentielles, you can still come to the law via a one-year conversion course known as the Graduate Diploma in Law (GDL).

NB: The course is also referred to as the CPE (Common Professional Exam) or PgDL (Postgraduate Diploma in Law).

Because skills like textual analysis, research, logical argument, and written and oral presentation can be acquired in a whole range of disciplines, from English lit to zoology, legal employers tend not to make a distinction between applicants with an LLB and those who take the GDL route.

The GDL is essentially a crash law degree designed to bring you up to the required standard in the seven core legal subjects that are typically taught in the first two years of an LLB. So that's two years of study crammed into one – not exactly a walk in the park. Taken full-time it lasts a minimum of 36 weeks and can demand up to 45 hours of lectures, tutorials and personal study each week. It's possible to take the course part-time over two years, and you'll find course providers offer a surprisingly wide range of flexible study options, from distance learning to weekends or evening-only classes.

The standard requirement for admission is a degree from a university in the UK or Republic of Ireland. It is possible for non-graduates to get onto a course if they've shown the requisite drive and determination, and have exceptional ability in some other field. Such candidates – and those with a degree from an overseas university – must obtain a Certificate of Academic Standing from the Bar Standards Board or Solicitors Regulation Authority before enrolling on the GDL.

Assessments tend to be written exams taken at the end of the academic year. These make up the bulk of your final grade, so make sure you are adequately prepared. Most GDL providers offer their students the opportunity to take mock exams throughout the year, and while these are generally optional, it's probably a good idea to get as many as you can under your belt. If nothing else, they give you an indication of your progress and the chance to receive feedback from tutors. Other assessments and essays completed during the year can count for up to 30% of your final grade, so don't underestimate their importance. Coursework does allow for a degree of flexibility, meaning students can write about areas that aren't necessarily explored in depth on the course, such as immigration or copyright law. Depending on the institution, there is more or less emphasis on academic essays, written problem questions or practical preparation for classroom debates.

Because the institutions that offer the GDL vary in perceived quality, approach and composition of their student bodies, it's well worth doing your research before you apply. City University and Nottingham are renowned for offering more academic courses, thought to be ideally suited to students headed to the Bar. In London, BPP and the University of Law, meanwhile, are packed with plenty of City types and place special emphasis on helping you gain practical legal skills.

Be aware that an increasing number of City firms are appointing a particular law school as their preferred provider. If you have your heart set on doing your training contract with a certain law firm, do your research and find out whether they have a preferred provider before you apply to the schools.

There's a huge amount to take in, so you need to be disciplined. Try to work out a study timetable early on, and stick to it. Don't count on being able to catch up, as time will fly by. You're there to learn a set curriculum, not to think outside the box. That said, it's important that you gain an overall understanding of how the law works, so avoid studying each subject in isolation. Perhaps the best use of your creativity is to come up with amusing ways of remembering case names. Above all else, attend classes! Especially if you've already secured a training contract before starting the GDL, as some law schools will report on attendance (if asked by your future employer).

The following are the areas of law students have to wrap their heads around during the GDL:

Contract

As a practising civil lawyer, you'll apply your knowledge of contract law on a daily basis as it underpins nearly every single legal relationship. Students start by studying the rules that determine when an agreement becomes legally binding and enforceable, and which formalities are required to create a contract. You'll then move on to study what terms are permissible and find out what happens when you omit to read the small print. You'll hear about the doctrine of misrepresentation, mistake and duress, and you'll find out what your remedy is when an art dealer has neglected to tell you the Jackson Pollock you've just bought is actually the product of his son's finger painting. Armed with your knowledge of the Sale of Goods Act, you may be tempted to bring any number of small claims against the high-street retailers whose products fall apart the minute you get them home.

Tort

Broadly defined, the law of tort is concerned with remedying wrongs committed by one individual against another, via the civil rather than the criminal courts. Beyond this very sensible definition hides one of the most intellectually challenging and stimulating courses on the GDL. The law of negligence is the big subject in tort, and you'll devote the best part of the year to getting your head around it and applying it to specific situations such as clinical negligence. The course also covers wrongs ranging from defamation to private nuisance. This is the field that fuels the so-called compensation culture and gives 'ambulance-chasing' lawyers a bad name. While studying tort you'll hear about the fate of victims of gruesome work or road traffic accidents, and catastrophic events such as the Hillsborough disaster. But you'll also come across downright comical stories, including snails in bottles of ginger beer or a case of compensation for scratchy underwear.

Public law

Public law, as it's generically referred to, is a course that includes the study of constitutional law, human rights and administrative law (the order may vary depending on where you study). If you have no interest in politics (shame on you), you may find the whole subject a little obscure, but with over ten years since the passing of the Human Rights Act, and with several constitutional reforms in the works, now is arguably the best of times to study this fascinating subject. The course normally kicks off with an analysis of the UK's constitutional arrangements. This part is largely academic and covers the doctrines of Parliamentary sovereignty, the Rule of Law, the Royal Prerogative and Responsible Government. Those with politics degrees should be able to hit the ground running. You're also likely to enjoy the constitutional bit of the subject if you're a history or philosophy buff. If you

don't fit the description, why not Google 'Dicey' and see where that takes you.

You'll also be taught about the Human Rights Act, with particular emphasis on the concepts of freedom of speech, the right to privacy, the right to a fair trial and the nitty-gritty of exactly how much force the police can use when they throw you in the back of their van. After the academic bit is over, a large chunk of the rest of the course is devoted to judicial review, the process by which individuals with sufficient standing can challenge the decisions of public authorities. Those who don't enjoy the theoretical feel of constitutional law should appreciate the more practical nature of judicial review.

Crime

Whether it's through reading crime novels, watching *Law and Order* or simply perusing newspaper headlines, you're in contact with criminal activity on a daily basis, and you could be forgiven for thinking the law begins and ends at crime. Studying criminal law will allow you to discover the reality behind the storylines. The syllabus takes you through assault, battery, sexual offences, criminal damage, theft, fraud and homicide. Also covered are the liability of accomplices, attempted offences and the defences available to those accused of committing criminal acts.

Whether your interest is in policy or the gruesome things that people do to one another, the crime course should provide plenty to engage and surprise. Overall, the subject follows a logical pattern and doesn't hide many difficult philosophical concepts. You will find out early on that you always need to identify the actus reus (the guilty act) and the mens rea (the guilty mind) in order to establish an offence. Follow this structure religiously and you can't go wrong. By the end of the course you'll also be in a better position to explain why killing someone is not necessarily unlawful, or why you could be guilty of theft without actually making off with somebody else's property.

Equity and trusts

This course provides an introduction to the fundamental principles of equity, an intriguing area of law that calls upon the idea of conscience to remedy injustices brought about by the application of black letter law. Also on the agenda is the concept of trust, which is the legal arrangement whereby one person holds property for the benefit of another.

One preconception about the subject is that it is the preserve of those who have their heart set on Chancery work at the Bar or wish to practise in the private wealth sector. While this is partially true, equity and trusts form a particularly dynamic area of law, and you'll not only

The GDL Providers

Aberystwyth University (ft)

Aston University (ft/pt)

Birmingham City University (ft/pt)

Bournemouth University (ft/pt)

BPP Law School, Birmingham (ft/pt)

BPP Law School, Bristol (ft/pt)

BPP Law School, Cambridge (ft/pt)

BPP Law School, Leeds (ft/pt)

BPP Law School, Liverpool (ft/pt)

BPP Law School, London (ft/pt)

BPP Law School, Manchester (ft/pt)

University of Bradford (ft/pt)

University of Brighton (ft/pt)

Brunel University (ft/pt)

Cardiff University (ft/pt)

University of Central Lancashire (ft/pt)

City University Law School (ft)

De Montfort University (ft/pt)

University of East Anglia (ft)

University of Huddersfield (ft/pt)

Kaplan Law School (ft)

Keele University (ft)

University of Law, Birmingham (ft/pt)

University of Law, Bristol (ft/pt)

University of Law, Chester (ft/pt)

University of Law, Guildford (ft/pt)

University of Law, London (ft/pt)

University of Law, Manchester (ft/pt)

University of Law, York (ft/pt)

Leeds Metropolitan University (ft/pt)

University of Lincoln (ft)

Liverpool John Moores University (ft/pt)

London Metropolitan University (ft/pt)

London South Bank University (ft/pt)

Manchester Metropolitan University (ft/pt)

Northumbria University (ft)

Nottingham Trent University (ft)

Oxford Brookes University (ft/pt)

University of Plymouth (ft)

University of Sheffield (ft)

University of South Wales (ft/pt)

Staffordshire University (ft/pt)

Swansea University (ft)

University of Sussex (ft)

University of the West of England (ft/pt)

University of Westminster (ft/pt)

learn about the creation of gifts and trusts in the family context, you'll also see that the concept has many uses in the commercial and financial worlds, particularly where tax evasion or the tracing of misappropriated funds are concerned. The topic is mostly precedent-based, meaning that you'll have to memorise a huge number of cases. On the bright side, these can be amusing and memorable. You'll hear about adulterous husbands trying to set up secret trusts for their mistresses and illegitimate children, or wealthy eccentrics attempting to set up a pension for a beloved pet. Be aware that the concept of equity pervades the GDL course, so what you've learned here will also be relevant to your land law and contract modules. Past students report that there's a mathematical side to this module, and that the complex nature of some of the concepts promotes a different way of thinking.

Land law

This module will teach you everything you need to know about the ownership of land, starting with the startling realisation that all of it ultimately belongs to Her Majesty the Queen. Many students may find the subject off-putting to begin with because it uses archaic, mind-numbing jargon and calls on concepts such as overreaching, flying freeholds or overriding interests, which defy any sense of logic. Give it some time and everything will start to fall into place. You'll find the topic has practical implications for your everyday life, including tips on how to handle a dispute with your landlord or how to arrange your first mortgage. The course will also take you through the basics of conveyancing and how to acquire interests in land such as easements or covenants, before going through the detail of how those interests operate.

The subject is formalistic and particularly statute-heavy. In addition to remembering loads of cases, you will be required to memorise countless statutory provisions on the creation and registration of interests in land. Don't wait to familiarise yourself with the most important sections of the Law of Property Act: start creating flowcharts and checklists early on and you will laugh your way through the exam. As with most topics on the GDL, you will need to gain a good overall understanding of land law to be able to deal with specific matters, so don't bet on revising selected subjects for the exam. There can be important overlap between them, particularly with equity and trusts.

EU

Whether the *Daily Mail* likes it or not, EU law now affects our lives in many ways. This course should help dispel a few misconceptions about the British membership of the European Union – it touches on far more than the way in which EU bureaucrats regulate the shape and size of bananas. You'll learn that the European Court of Justice (ECJ) is effectively the highest court of appeal for all the member states, and that EU law plays a cen-

Law School

tral role in the creation of new rights against discrimination on grounds of age, disability, race, religion or sexual orientation, for example. Students become familiar with the institutional framework, foundations and underlying principles of the European Union before going on to explore certain areas of substantive EU law. Big subjects include the free movement of goods and workers, competition law and the freedom of establishment, as well as the incorporation of the European Convention on Human Rights into our national law. For Euro-philes, this course will provide a fascinating mix of politics, history, economics and comparative jurisprudence, but its case law contains some of the longest and most tongue-twisting names you're likely to see.

How to apply

In addition to the seven core subjects, certain GDL providers, particularly those with a City slant, also offer optional classes designed to ease your passage into the corporate world. These may include additional lectures or seminars on company law, intellectual property and international law. Most also organise mooting competitions and pro bono work. These should give you an early opportunity to try your counselling and advocacy skills and find out if a legal career is really for you, particularly if you're headed for the Bar. A number of providers have degree-awarding powers allowing you to upgrade your qualification to an LLB, either upon successful comple-

tion of your GDL and LPC or after a summer course following the GDL. Unlike the GDL, the LLB gives you an internationally recognised accreditation.

All GDL applications are made online through the Central Applications Board. Remember, there's an application fee and it's worth getting your application in as early as possible if you have your heart set on a particular institution, particularly as Lawcabs needs your referee to respond to them before your application is passed on to the schools you're interested in. Many law schools now offer January as well as September starts for their GDL programmes, and so the application timetable has been reformed to accommodate this. Replacing the old process involving first and second round offers, law schools will now recruit GDL students on a rolling basis.

The application forms for courses beginning in 2015 are now available, and commencing early November these applications will be sent to law schools who may then make offers to students. The later you apply the more flexible you may have to be about where you study. Applications for part-time courses should be made directly to the providers. If you intend to do an LPC or BPTC at a popular institution you might stand a better chance if you choose it for your GDL, as many providers guarantee places to their GDL graduates. Our website has a table detailing all the GDL providers, their stated fees and loads of other useful information.

The Legal Practice Course (LPC)

Before starting your glorious career as a solicitor, you'll need to jump through the unavoidable hoop that is the LPC. Just don't let all of those flexible and alluring study options distract from the underlying truth that the LPC is intense, costly, and not a guaranteed pass to a training contract.

The nuts and bolts of the LPC

It's important to remember that the LPC is not an academic course – it's vocational. Treat it like the first year of your professional life. The LPC requires good time management, organisation and preparation, and even though some providers have open-book exams, it's far from advisable to be sitting at your desk with an exam paper in front of you searching furiously through the textbooks at your side. Keep on top of things as the course progresses, and perhaps even think about sharing the revision workload with classmates.

Many students complain that the *"learn, apply, regurgitate, pass"* approach of the LPC isn't as stimulating as an undergraduate degree. However, the course isn't designed to be stimulating; it's meant to get you ready to start a training contract. With classes on semicolons and spelling, it can feel like you're back at school, but you'll pick up plenty of tricks and tips along the way, including:

- How to conduct an interview (usually a strong handshake accompanied by the offer of a beverage);
- How to sign off a letter – not 'lots of love' or 'peace', as a rule;
- How to minimise tax exposure – it's about avoidance, not evasion;
- How many directors it takes to make a board meeting – this isn't a bad joke;
- When litigation documents must be served on the other side – you will curse the day bank holidays were invented;
- Whether you or your landlord is responsible when the roof leaks; and
- Why it's never a good idea to dabble with clients' money.

Also, let's not forget that virtually all the law schools that run the LPC have a raft of interesting extracurricular opportunities on offer – a nice side dish to complement the main course. For example, pro bono work is easy enough to come by and can range from getting involved in the school's legal clinic to undertaking projects with external organisations.

The numbers game

There's been a lot of chit-chat over the years about whether the current legal education system needs a massive overhaul, not least with the release of the Legal Education Training Review (LETR) report in June 2013, which was intended to be *"a big shake-up of the legal profession"* but ended up being somewhat of a damp squib instead. The course leaders we spoke to certainly felt the LPC still had an important part to play in training the next generation of lawyers. *"I do think the LPC is underrated in PR terms,"* said one. *"It's a highly relevant course and highly regarded within firms, so I don't see an immediate need to totally change it."* However, they did acknowledge that the current education system has one key failing: *"The problem isn't the course itself – it works very well. What doesn't work well is matching the number of LPC grads with the number of available jobs."*

According to The Law Society the number of new training contracts registered between July 2011 and July 2012 totalled a dismal 4,869. This is a 10.5% drop on the previous year when the number of training contracts had actually risen to 5,441. The latter rise can be attributed to the cohort of trainees who started with firms in 2011 having had their start dates deferred from 2010. The number of training contracts is going through a classic peaks and troughs experience as the market right-sizes itself while the country continues to dust itself off from the recession. In fairness, the latest statistics make for slightly better reading compared to that underwhelming total the year before, with 5,302 new training contracts registered between July 2012 and July 2013.

In any case, here is the cold truth: the number of available contracts isn't huge and there are far too many aspiring lawyers for everyone to get one. The good news – if you can call it that – is that the number of LPC enrollments isn't exactly astronomical. According to The Law Society, in 2013-14 5,198 students enrolled on the LPC. Still, the decline in LPC numbers remains smaller than the decline in the number of training contracts – and don't forget that there are hordes of individuals out there who graduated the LPC in previous years and still don't have a training contract.

As you would expect in a competitive market, some LPC providers are doing better than others. The National College of Legal Training (NCLT) and Oxford Brookes both ceased their LPC provision in 2013 because of dwindling application numbers, with the universities of Plymouth and Aberystwyth following suit in 2014. The likes of BPP and the University of Law (ULaw) continue to post strong enrolment results, though, and the latter's relocation of its York branch to Leeds in September 2014 has meant a further increase in the number of students it can accommodate.

So you don't need to be the next Einstein to figure out that not everyone who completes the LPC will get a training contract – as the SRA gently points out: *"If you are planning to apply for a training contract, you need to know that the number of employers able to offer training contracts may be dictated by economic factors and can be significantly lower than the number of LPC graduates."* The SRA claims that it has no power to cap the number of places that institutions are validated for, so effectively institutions can continue to invite people to the party, even though the dance floor is already full.

Course providers have told us that increasingly *"firms [especially smaller outfits] are very keen to take on LPC graduates as paralegals and not offer training contracts,"* as trainees are more expensive and smaller firms are not willing to take the risk. *"For a small firm, taking on a trainee is an onerous burden and a risk because if it's the wrong decision, then you're saddled with an ineffective person for a long period of time."* Crucially, a recent change to the SRA rules has meant that paralegals who've done the LPC can now qualify as solicitors without having to complete a training contract. It'll be fascinating to see the impact this has on firms and their willingness to take on LPC graduates as paralegals.

Law schools are very proactive when it comes to delivering careers advice to their LPC students, but it is really up to the individual to take a long, hard objective look at their prospects of securing a training contract after the course.

An apt question

The Bar Standards Board has introduced a compulsory aptitude test for the BPTC (the vocational course all prospective barristers must pass before being called to the Bar). The aim of the test (called the BCAT) is to assess applicants' chances of securing a pupillage before spending one year and many thousands of pounds on a qualification they may never use.

While many feel that aptitude testing is the way forward for the LPC, the LETR rejected the proposal and earlier attempts to do so by Kaplan Law School were thwarted by the SRA. Most providers aren't exactly enthralled by the idea anyway: *"An aptitude test for what? The market is so broad, and there's quite a bit of difference between someone who wants to be a back-room tax lawyer and someone who wants to be a corporate high-flyer. If you introduce an aptitude test then you can be sure as hell that people will be hot-housed for it. Where would the diversity be?"*

Size matters

Another trend over the last few years has been law school expansion. The two big course providers – BPP and ULaw, who collectively dominate the market – have opened up new centres up and down the country in recent times, and both now boast full university status. More schools outside the major city centres are to be welcomed, as they allow students the less-expensive option of studying from home and they generally cost less than their City counterparts.

However, having BPP or ULaw open up in your city can be detrimental, as Anglia Ruskin found out when BPP set up camp in Cambridge: the former was forced to scrap its part-time course due to lack of student interest. Will we see much more expansion from the two legal education powerhouses? A source at ULaw told us in 2012 that *"we now have a centre in every region, so I'm comfortable in saying that we wouldn't want to expand any further."*

However, when the news came through in March 2013 that Oxford Brookes was ceasing its LPC provision, ULaw stepped into the void and agreed to deliver its course on the university's campus for 2013/14. Both providers are keeping their ears to the ground in relation to international expansion, too. ULaw has already tapped into the Singapore market, while BPP is also looking at potential overseas opportunities through the US education company Apollo, which it became a part of in 2009.

Money on my mind

Wherever you choose to do it, the LPC is an expensive affair. Unless you've been hooked up by a generous commercial law firm that's sponsoring you, it's time to dig deep. While some providers have frozen their fees, most have inevitably risen and will continue to do so year by year. After the University of Glamorgan was incorporated into the new University of South Wales in April 2013 its full-time fees were increased from £7,150 to £9,000.

£9,000 is par for the course at most providers but at the top end you could be shelling out a whopping £14,000. And that's before you factor in living expenses. For a comprehensive comparison of course fees look at the LPC Providers Table online. For advice on how to fund your trip to law school, see our feature on **How to fund law school**.

Law schools are a business: they sell the LPC to prospective solicitors for around £10k and welcome in as many people as they can without compromising on quality. A 2:2 degree will pretty much guarantee you a place on a course, but finding a firm that will want to train you afterwards is an entirely different proposition. When faced with a 2:2 candidate, firms usually expect a pretty good reason for the grade (ie valid extenuating circumstances), some outstanding features on your CV or, if you're a more 'mature' candidate, a strong first career under your belt, which show that your degree results are historic and not a true reflection of your abilities.

Some law schools, like Kaplan and Nottingham, take an *"ethical approach"* by asking for a 2:1 in most cases, while others are less prescriptive, earning them some fierce criticism from former students: *"They are taking the piss with how many people they are taking on who are not good enough to get training contracts. It's not fair."* One such provider does assure us that students with a 2:2 receive *"specialist advice – we always say that they must be alive to the fact that they need to demonstrate something over and above. It's not impossible, but they must also be prepared to struggle more to get a vac scheme, and seriously consider paralegal work."*

Make the right choice

When and how: Timetables can vary wildly between providers, and while some course providers have taken advantage of the fact they're allowed to condense teaching into three or even two days, either mornings or afternoons, others still require attendance four days a week alongside a sizeable chunk of self-study. Term dates and even the length of the whole course can vary substantially. Students can opt to spend anywhere between seven months and five years studying for the qualification. Think realistically about what timetable structure will fit most easily into your life. Also think about whether or not you will need a job during the course because, while all providers are reluctant to acknowledge that students will be able to fit in a part-time job, they are increasingly aware that this may be unavoidable, so the majority offer the choice of studying part-time.

Meanwhile, the use of online learning is becoming even more pervasive. BPP, for example, has rolled out an entirely distance learning-based LPC; a 'blended' approach that makes physical attendance entirely unnecessary (well, almost: the SRA dictates there must be a mini-

mum of ten hours face-to-face interaction). Students at Birmingham City University can access work from virtual law firm 'BCU Solicitors', while ULaw has replaced the passive lecture format with i-tutorials. Some students thrive on electronic learning methods, and part-time students in particular appreciate being able to fit the work around their already busy lives. However, working from home does require a degree of dedication and self-discipline, so think carefully about what mode of teaching will suit you best before you sign up. Can you actually focus in pyjamas with *Game of Thrones* on in the background?

Assessments: The vast majority of providers examine their students using open-book exams and written assessments. A notable minority, including BPP, have stuck with the closed-book approach. Although it's easy to feel drawn to the open-book approach, the timeframes are such that you have very little time to trawl through books in the exams.

Facilities: For every provider at which students must search plaintively for a quiet study corner, there is another where they can spread out in blessed peace in their own 'office'. Take the LPC at a university and you'll belong to a proper law faculty surrounded by chilled-out undergrads and deep-thinking postgrads; elsewhere, leather sofas and acres of plate glass might make you think you've strayed into the offices of a City firm. Given the importance of IT to the LPC, you should consider whether the institution offers endless vistas of the latest flat screens or a few dusty computers in a basement.

Atmosphere and direction: A large institution may appeal to students keen to chug anonymously through the system. Conversely, the intimacy of fewer students and easily accessible tutors may tip the scales in favour of a smaller provider. Some places are known to attract corporate types destined to be City high-flyers; others cultivate the talents of those headed for regional practice. Still, others purport to attract a broad a mix of students, so the commercially minded can mingle with future high-street practitioners.

Money and location: Fees vary and so do the providers' policies on the inclusion of the cost of textbooks and Law Society membership, etc. Even if you have sponsorship, living expenses still need to be taken into account. The cost of living in London can be an especially nasty shock – according to the National Union of Students, the average yearly living costs for students in the capital is a whopping £13,388. Plenty of students find that tight finances restrict their choice of provider. Although it might seem reprehensible to some, living with the parents will obviously save you a packet. If you're desperate to strike out on your own (or you haven't lived with The Olds for some time), then it's worth considering what you like or don't like about your university or GDL provider and whether you want to prolong your undergraduate experience or escape it. When weighing up providers in large cities, find out whether the campus is in the city centre or out on a ring road.

Extra qualifications: A current trend among providers is the offer of a top-up LLM, with students using their LPC credits to count towards a Masters in legal practice. Students at ULaw can top up their LPC with an LLM in either Professional Legal Practice or International Legal Practice, while BPP now offers all its students a new MA programme ('LPC with business'). A handful of providers also have degree-awarding powers, which means you can turn your GDL and LPC into an LLB.

Social mix and social life: Hip, student-infested cities such as Nottingham and Bristol are always a lot of fun, but the bright lights of the capital may be irresistible. Experience tells us that compared to those in other cities, many students in London tend to slink off the moment classes end rather than socialise into the evening.

Making applications

The Central Applications Board administers all applications for full-time LPCs. The application timetable has been overhauled in response to the fact that several course providers have introduced January and February start dates. LPC admissions will now be processed on a rolling basis with the application form available from early October. Beginning early November applications are sent to law schools week by week and the course providers may make offers to students immediately.

Obviously the later the application the less secure a place, but it should be remembered that almost every school will have more validated places than enrolled students on its both full-time and part-time courses. Some of the most popular institutions must be placed first on the Law-Cabs application form – see our LPC Providers Table online – but students can apply for up to three. Check also whether your university, GDL provider or future law firm has any agreement or relationship with a provider. Applications for part-time courses should be made directly to the individual provider.

LPC Provider Reports

See our website for a comprehensive table detailing all the providers – compare their fees, student numbers, available subjects and other helpful info. Read the reports below for extra background plus feedback from past students and course leaders...

Anglia Ruskin University

Number of places: 60 FTE
Fees (2014/15): £8,755

The course

ARU used to run the LPC out of both its Cambridge and Chelmsford campuses, but, for now at least, the latter has been suspended – the reason being that *"the two programmes ran in very different ways and we believe our Cambridge form of delivery is the more effective going forward,"* according to course leader Louise McKeon. Students here therefore attend just two sessions a week every Tuesday and Thursday, enabling them *"to balance the course with any other commitments they might have."* Class sizes are relatively small, especially in the workshops, where there are around 16 to 20 students in each, and all sessions are complemented by *"a very extensive digital library containing all the essential course materials."* A distinguishing feature of Anglia Ruskin's LPC is the use of mock assessments for every area of the course, with McKeon telling us *"the feedback we've received shows they're incredibly useful for helping to prepare students for the heavy diet of exams."* Stage One entails all the core modules, while Stage Two sees students pick three electives from a list of five – the options are *"partly based on input from our partners in the profession,"* adds McKeon.

The location and facilities

Back in 2011 Anglia Ruskin invested a whopping £35m to revamp its Cambridge campus, and LPC students are now fully reaping the benefits of *"state-of-the-art"* facilities including various lecture rooms, a library and a mock courtroom. The campus is in a decent spot too: it's within walking distance of the train station and the prestigious University of Cambridge, as well as all the nearby shops, bars and restaurants situated in the heart of the city. A word of warning on the crowds though, as masses of tourists clutter the streets of Cambridge all year round (and it gets particularly hectic in the summer).

Careers services and prospects

Although the law school doesn't have formal ties with any firms, it has developed *"a close relationship with most of the well-known firms that have a presence in Cambridge,"* McKeon says. ARU regularly welcomes practitioners from the region who come in to give career-oriented talks, and students receive frequent bulletins updating them on law-related job opportunities – *"not just locally but nationally too."* As for the positions Anglia Ruskin's LPC graduates end up in, McKeon reveals that *"many go to mid-sized firms with some national coverage, while others will go to much smaller local firms. We've even had a considerable number go into local government."*

The *Chambers Student* verdict

With only two sessions a week to attend, ARU will suit students who wish to pursue other commitments alongside their LPC studies – just as long as you don't mind the throng of tourists in Cambridge's city centre.

Birmingham City University

Number of places: 60 FT, 40 PT
Fees (2014/15): £9,000

The course

The LPC at Birmingham City University incorporates a mix of large and small group sessions, the latter having a *"target number of no more than 16 students at a time,"* admissions tutor Martin Burnett tells us. And with the current set-up allowing for plenty of interaction with tutors, it's no surprise that *"there are no plans to change that structure."* Both full and part-time options are on offer here: full-timers can expect to be on campus on Monday, Tuesday and Wednesday – the last two days of the week are freed up to allow other commitments – while those on the part-time option typically attend classes on Tuesday and Thursday evenings. Alongside face-to-face teaching, there's a robust online offering in the form of the school's 'Virtual Solicitors' Office' – *"a virtual space you can log into to help prepare for the sessions ahead. It provides a funkier and more accessible way of approaching the modules."*

The location and facilities

A big development on the horizon is the law school's relocation to The Curzon Building in September 2015, as part of the university's move to a brand-new campus in the city centre. *"The facilities will be newer, better and more dedicated,"* says Burnett, who adds that *"the physical closeness to the city centre is going to be a major benefit for us."* Facilities in the building will include two libraries, numerous study areas and work rooms, and a raft of student services. While the hustle and bustle of Birmingham's city centre won't be to everyone's tastes, we should note that it's currently undergoing a redevelopment of its own after a 20-year 'Big City Plan' was launched in 2010. Students can get stuck into local pro bono projects served up by the likes of CABs, the local council and various legal advice charities, and Burnett says: *"We even have many LPC graduates who stay in contact with us and eventually help to generate pro bono work."* In addition there's a mentoring scheme run in conjunction with prominent law societies and firms in the region, in which students get paired up with a lawyer or another professional, depending on their career desires. Burnett hints that the school's upcoming move to the new digs will see its pro bono and mentoring programs expanded, presumably to make use of the central location.

Careers services and prospects

The school's dedicated careers service *"mainly builds on contacts with local practices,"* Burnett explains. For example, several guest presenters come in and give career-oriented talks during the course, and students receive membership to the Birmingham Law Society as part of the overall fee, which *"gives them access to all the networking events and other opportunities that we encourage them to go to. It tends to be an effective way for gaining employment."*

The *Chambers Student* verdict

Affordable fees, small class sizes and an interesting online component make this LPC an attractive Midlands option – and the move to a snazzy new building in 2015 might just seal the deal.

Bournemouth University

Number of places: 85 FTE

Fees (2014/15): £11,000

The course

Bournemouth University is a well-established name among LPC providers, having first delivered the course back in 1994. Offering both full-time and part-time options, the LPC at BU entails a healthy blend of teaching modes: *"Students have told us they still want face-to-face interaction with tutors,"* explains senior lecturer Julie Pick, *"so as a result we have a mix of large and small group sessions."* The bigger classes take place in a *"funky lecture theatre"* (as Pick describes it), while the smaller offerings typically hold around a dozen students in each. On top of all that there's an extensive collection of online resources. Pick adds: *"We have our own intranet, on which all PowerPoint slides are placed along with materials for the small group sessions. Then, providing we have permission from the tutor, we also allow some of the large group sessions to be recorded and uploaded."* Full-timers attend four sessions a week, with Wednesday usually being a class-free day (barring formal assessments), whereas those who've opted for the part-time option are taught two or three days each week over two years. The electives, of which there are seven to choose from, incorporate both high-street and commercial-oriented areas of work.

The location and facilities

The university is spread across two sites – Talbot Campus and Lansdowne Campus. The latter is arguably the more appealing when it comes to location: it's right near the seafront and Pokesdown train station, as well as the array of shops and eateries situated in the town centre. Fortunately for LPC students, it's also home to the Department of Law, which resides in the *"still relatively new"* business centre there. However, bear in mind that Talbot Campus is where many of BU's key buildings are – like the students' union, main library and all the sports facilities – and it's too far a walk from Lansdowne Campus for even the most zealous of wayfarers.

Careers services and prospects

Pick tells us that the university has strong ties with the likes of the Junior Lawyers Division and Bournemouth & District Law Society, plus a bunch of local firms (including one of Bournemouth's top dogs Lester Aldridge). She also says many of the tutors *"know the profession incredibly well"* thanks to their active roles in the local legal community, *"and can drum up work opportunities for students."* These links are complemented by plenty of careers events put on at the university, such as guest lectures led by solicitors, magistrates, expert witnesses and government reps. We'll end by pointing out that, while there's nothing stopping BU's LPC graduates from pursuing the bright lights of London – *"or even further afield than that"* – a good chunk tend to nab jobs in or around the region.

The *Chambers Student* verdict

Bournemouth University's LPC is well worth a punt for favourable levels of tutor interaction and the possibility of embarking on a career in the South. Just remember to pack your boogie board.

BPP Law School

Number of places: 3,307 – see below for breakdown by city

Fees (2014/15): see below for breakdown by city

The course

Now boasting full university status, BPP is one of the top dogs around for the LPC. *"Our ethos has very much remained the same,"* says the course's joint director Jo-Anne Pugh. *"It's still a case of professionals teaching professionals, as well as maintaining our close links with many of the best-known law firms out there."* Taking a closer look at the course itself, it's clear BPP keeps the profession in mind at all times. A prime example of this is a recently introduced programme that enables students to study for a unique MA ('LPC with Business'). *"The commercial acumen that students get from that part of the course has proved very appealing to firms,"* Pugh adds. Students who take up this option carry out two extra business modules and a 'business intelligence project' on top of their LPC studies.

There's a raft of additional module choices as part of the package, all of which help to tailor the course to students' career desires and boost their chances of securing a job afterwards. The 'Preparing for Practice' module *"focuses on presentation and negotiation skills, as well as many of the other skills that employees are on the lookout for,"* while the 'Law Firm as a Business' module gives students an idea of what it's like to be a trainee solicitor. There's also a module for those looking to join high street firms, and you can study a fourth elective entirely online (though it isn't formally assessed).

The list of study options is just as exhaustive. For some of the firms that BPP is partnered with – such as Slaughter and May, Freshfields and Hogan Lovells – there's a 'fast-track' option that sees the course condensed into seven months, though this is currently only available in Birmingham and London (Holborn). In return for the shortened course, students have to take on two more hours of face-to-face teaching and three additional hours of self-study per week. Current trainees who'd done the fast-track LPC at BPP felt it was a *"very intense experience,"* but appreciated getting it all wrapped up quicker.

Even on the more conventional full-time or part-time routes, there are quite a few variations on offer. Full-timers can choose between two, three or four days a week, as well as morning or afternoon classes. Meanwhile, those seeking part-time can select between two evenings, one day, every other Saturday, or a full weekend every three or four weeks. All these options aren't necessarily available in every centre – the full weekend option for part-timers is exclusive to Holborn, for example – so we advise checking BPP's website to see if the centre and study option you have in mind match up.

Even on the more conventional full-time or part-time routes, there are quite a few variations on offer. Full-timers can choose between two, three or four days a week, as well as morning or afternoon classes. Meanwhile, those seeking part-time can select between two evenings, one day, every other Saturday, or a full weekend every three or four weeks. All these options aren't necessarily available in every centre – the full weekend option for part-timers is exclusive to Holborn, for example – so we advise checking BPP's website to see if the centre and study option you have in mind match up.

The location and facilities

Birmingham
Number of places: 150 FTE
Fees (2014/15): £11,303 FT; £11,295 PT

Given the busy city centre location, it might be a tad annoying if you're having to commute by car each day – though BPP does lend a hand by offering a discount for one of the nearby car parks. The Birmingham site is only around four years old and has over a dozen classrooms, numerous study zones, a library, a student lounge, a breakout area and a computer-based assessment centre.

Bristol
Number of places: 80 FTE
Fees (2014/15): £11,303 FT; £11,295 PT

Bristol has a reputation for being one of the nicest – and booziest – cities in the country. *The Sunday Times* says it's the best city to live in in Britain – you might question the publication's bold statement, but one way to test it is to join BPP's Bristol centre. It's situated in Queen Square, a largish open garden that sits among Georgian town houses in the heart of the city. *"The branch is in a really good and convenient location,"* echoed a graduate. Bristol Temple Meads station and the main shopping district (Broadmead) are both around a ten-minute walk away, as are performance venues like the O2 Academy and the Hippodrome. Alumni praised the *"nice and shiny"* premises. Noteworthy facilities include ten classrooms kitted out with audio-visual equipment, a computer-based assessment lab and a student lounge.

Cambridge

Number of places: 80 FTE
Fees (2014/15): £11,303 FT; £11,295 PT

The Cambridge branch was only established in 2011. Its central location means POIs like the Grafton, Lion Yard and Grand Arcade shopping centres are all within reasonable walking distance, as is the sprawling University of Cambridge. When it comes to the location's inconveniences, we'll make the same point as we did for Anglia Ruskin (another Cambridge-based provider): swarms of tourists visit the city all year round, so if crowded streets get your goat then consider yourself warned. What's more, the train station is roughly a 20-minute walk away, so to get there swiftly you might have to buy into the city's love of cycling. The site itself contains air-conditioned classrooms and a library, among other facilities.

Leeds

Number of places: 374 FTE
Fees (2014/15): £10,583 full-time; £10,575 part-time

The centre is around a five-minute wander away from the train station and the recently opened shopping centre Trinity, while venues like the O2 Academy and the Grand Theatre are slightly further away. On-site features include a few mock courtrooms, a library with several study areas and a 155-seat lecture theatre. The careers service, CV-boosting Pro Bono Centre, and the hi-tech teaching tools come strongly recommended.

Liverpool

Number of places: 80 FTE
Fees (2014/15): £10,583 full-time; £10,575 part-time

BPP's Liverpool branch is in the city's legal district, close to the crown and youth courts plus a host of well-known law firms, like Slater & Gordon, Hill Dickinson and Brabners. Also in its vicinity are three train stations, and this is a decent location for bars, restaurants and shopping. As one of the smaller BPP centres, it has just a handful of classrooms and less seating in its library and breakout area than some of the bigger ones (such as Holborn and Leeds), though the range of facilities is still on a par with the rest of the BPP family.

London (Holborn)

Number of places: 1,850 FTE
Fees (2014/15): £14,393 full-time; £14,385 part-time

BPP actually has two centres in London, but the one at Waterloo is no longer running the LPC – for now, at least. As for Holborn, it's home to BPP's most populated branch and is where a sizeable chunk of the institution's partner firms ship their future trainees off to. A few of the graduates we spoke to described the Holborn site as *"lovely and modern,"* and said it has *"fantastic"* facilities, including *"more than enough computers to accommodate everyone."* Also included on the branch's list of features are 35 classrooms, a few mock courtrooms, a common room and a large lecture theatre. It's close to the Inns of Court and Law Society, Holborn and Chancery Lane tube stations, and the buzzing throngs of Covent Garden, Soho and Leicester Square.

Manchester

Number of places: 411 FTE
Fees (2014/15): £10,583 full-time; £10,575 part-time

Manchester is BPP's biggest northern branch. Being based in the city's academic heartland (near Oxford Road station) means there's a huge amount on the doorstep to distract a student in this excellent city. It's also a short hop away to Spinningfields, where many of the city's top firms reside. As for the branch itself, it has a 108-seat lecture theatre, ten classrooms, a library to house 200 and the usual pro bono centre.

Careers services and prospects

BPP prides itself on the close ties it has with many of the UK legal market's major players. It has an exclusive partnership with over 30 firms, from magic circle megafirm Allen & Overy to national powerhouse DWF – and everything in between. *"Over the years, we've built up our expertise of knowing exactly what these firms are looking for,"* Pugh says. *"We know how they're recruiting and what their thought processes are, and we're able to replicate that."*

BPP has a wide range of careers services, including advice and assistance regarding applications, CVs, cover letters, assessment centres and interviews – the latter two involves mock sessions. Crucially, these can be utilised as soon as incoming students have accepted their place on the LPC, so you can easily plan ahead if you're still in search of a training contract. Students can also get involved in an array of pro bono projects to add some sparkle to their CVs, from the legal advice clinic and Streetlaw programme to the Human Rights Unit.

Of course, despite the reputation BPP has within the profession, that doesn't mean its students are invariably going to secure their dream jobs straight away. With that in mind, there's a careers guarantee on offer: *"If you haven't managed to get a job in the legal sector within six months of completing our LPC, we're happy to let you study for another qualification at no extra cost."*

Graduates say...

"In some ways, whether or not you've already secured a training contract dictates the type of experience that

you have here. You might be a little more confident and relaxed if you've got one, for instance."

The *Chambers Student* verdict

It may be on the pricier end (even with the interest-free payment plans, scholarships and loans up for grabs), but when you consider the comprehensive package that BPP provides, it's not a bad deal at all.

Bristol Institute of Legal Practice at UWE

Number of places: 60-65 FT, 35 PT
Fees (2014/15): £10,300 FT, £5,150 PT per year

The course

Students keen to connect with South West firms flock to UWE's Bristol-based campus. Our trainee solicitor sources had nary a bad word to say about the course, which offers all the charms of surf, sea and student life, combined with the substantial benefits of dedicated teaching staff. One reported that *"you could always knock on tutors' doors to ask questions, and I had no problem getting extra assistance or feedback."*

Full-time students choose to take their tutorials on two consecutive days, Monday to Thursday, getting around 11 hours of contact time a week. Part-timers either study once a month on Friday and Saturday, or join the full-timers one day a week. Unusually among LPC students, they benefit from the same amount of contact time as full-timers over their two-year course, though taking time off during regular working hours may not suit those with 9-5 jobs.

The standard course is taught in four two-and-a-half-hour workshops, and one lecture a week. The workshops split students into groups of three or four to simulate an office environment, with the tutor acting as a facilitator to set up tasks. Lectures take place on a separate day, with slides and recordings available online for students who want to view them remotely. There's a pretty exhaustive list of electives covering everything from big-bucks finance and corporate law to public childcare, housing, personal injury and private client.

The location and facilities

The course is based on UWE's Frenchay campus, four miles outside Bristol. Principal Dagmar Steffens tells us that *"because we are a university, not a commercial outfit, we can offer a wider community of undergraduate and postgraduate students, societies, sports facilities, and student bars. There's a lot of continued opportunity for student life."* For anyone who feels past doing Jägerbombs with 18-year-olds, there are also the practical advantages of a 24-hour law library, and plenty of parking for commuting in.

Careers services and prospects

The school is the preferred provider for nearby outlets Burges Salmon, TLT and Harrison Clark Rickerbys. The admittedly biased Steffens tells us *"you'd be hard pressed to find a local firm that doesn't have at least one of our alumni working there."* Certainly, as the main provider in the region it seems right that it should populate South West firms. As one junior told us, *"I didn't want to go to London, because I didn't want to end up in a London firm."*

Although precise information isn't available, Steffens estimates that about 20% of students start the course with a training contract, and around 40% have secured one by its end, at a roughly even mix of high street and commercial firms.

Graduates say...

"I loved the flexibility – I wanted to commute to save money, so the fact I could condense the course into two days a week was great."

"Overall it was a really positive experience. The facilities were great, and the lecturers were on great form."

The *Chambers Student* verdict

This sunny campus uni is a great place to prolong the *"student lifestyle"* for another year, and to plan for a legal future in the South West.

Bristol Institute of Legal Practice at UWE Bristol

Bristol Institute of Legal Practice, University of the West of
England, Coldharbour Lane,
Bristol BS16 1QY
Email: fbl.sat@uwe.ac.uk
Website: www.uwe.ac.uk/bilp

Contact
For further information about
all of our courses, please
contact us via email on
fbl.sat@uwe.ac.uk or visit our
website www.uwe.ac.uk/bilp.

Institute profile
The Bristol Institute of Legal Practice (BILP) at UWE Bristol is a leading provider of professional legal education with an established track record of excellence. We offer flexible
study, a choice of timetabling options, superb facilities and are large enough to provide a
range and depth of quality provision. Our courses are designed and taught by experienced
solicitors/barristers teaching within their own subject areas. The emphasis is on practical
learning within a supportive environment and on providing students with the skills and
knowledge to ensure they are 'practice ready'.

Graduate Diploma in Law (GDL) full and part time
Our GDL enables non-law graduates to progress with confidence to the LPC/BPTC and is
supported by a dedicated team of tutors who understand the demands of the GDL. Teaching
is not shared with undergraduates. The curriculum is divided into two teaching blocks with
assessments after each block.

Legal Practice Course (LPC) full and part time
We are one of very few providers nationally to have consistently achieved the highest possible grading of 'excellent' from our regulator. Students are offered a broad based Stage 1
designed to prepare them for the full variety of practice followed by a selection of 13 elective subjects.

Bar Professional Training Course (BPTC) full and part time
Our BPTC equips students to excel at the Bar and beyond. We provide outstanding opportunities in advocacy, research, conference and mediation skills, which will help in securing
pupillage. We also have exceptional links with the local Bar.

University of the
West of England

Cardiff Law School

Number of places: 220 FT, 20 PT
Fees (2014/15): £10,800 FT, £11,050 total PT

The course

Most of Cardiff's LPCers have degree-based or family ties to the area, but others come especially for the Russell Group prestige and stately location of the university's law school. Students here get more contact time than at other LPC providers – 12-14 hours of contact time a week, all of which takes place between 9am and 5pm on Mondays, Tuesdays and Wednesdays. Teaching is split between four non-compulsory lectures, which students can view online if they prefer, and four two-hour tutorials in groups of around 16. These tutorials often involve working in smaller groups on unseen problems and then coming together to discuss the results.

The ten or so electives students can choose from include all the usual suspects, from IP and commercial litigation to family and employment.

The location and facilities

A recent revamp to the law school has seen the old legal practice library replaced with a new computer-filled postgraduate study centre, and the addition of electronic whiteboards and recording facilities to classrooms. The school occupies two buildings in Cardiff's leafy civic centre, which features grand neoclassical buildings and formal gardens laid out along the River Taff. Those in search of more modern diversions will be pleased to know it's a short walk from the city's bustling centre.

Careers services and prospects

Around half of students trickle in from Cardiff's undergraduate course. Although the university's LPC is probably the highest-profile course in Wales (not to mention considerably larger than rival Aberystwyth), there aren't actually that many Cymraeg training contracts to go round. Course leader Byron Jones was reluctant to divulge how many graduates end up with training contracts at Welsh firms and suggested that many regional firms are more likely to recruit through the paralegal route.

The law school's careers service offers one-to-one advice sessions and a programme of regular talks and visits from law firms. Cardiff's aspiring lawyers also have the chance to boost their practical skills through the law school's work placement scheme, which sources a fortnight of legal work experience – either at law firms or other legal employers such as the Welsh National Government – for at least two-thirds of students.

Graduates say...

"The tutors are helpful and make the course very interesting. There are lots of opportunities for e-learning alongside plenty of face-to-face lectures and seminars."

The *Chambers Student* verdict

Cardiff's LPC course offers lower fees and more work experience than rival providers, but students have to wade, not paddle, into applications to score a local training contract.

City Law School, London

Number of places: 86 FT
Fees (2014/15): £12,500

The course

This pint-sized provider is sheltered under the City University umbrella and is lodged in the heart of legal London. With around 80 students to nine teachers, it offers a high staff-to-pupil ratio. Its fees are slightly lower than BPP and University of Law, a reflection of its less established reputation on the London law school scene. The plus side is, as director David Amos explains, the law school's small size means *"students get an individualised timetable and their own pigeon-hole. We treat them as individuals, which is really good preparation for practice."*

Students can choose to attend classes during the morning or afternoons, with Wednesdays left free. Stage one of the LPC entails between 15 and 18 hours of contact time a week, which drops down to 13.5 hours in stage two. Teaching is split between tutorials and skills sessions. Tutorials take place in groups of 16 students, who are divided into subteams of four for regular group work in an interactive approach that, as Amos tells us, *"is designed to get them used to working alongside other people and swapping ideas. The tutor is more of a facilitator."* Skills sessions take place in groups of eight and zoom in on students' drafting and writing skills.

The location and facilities

A short walk from Chancery Lane tube station, the law school is surrounded by a host of City of London law firms and barristers sets, and is a stone's throw from the Royal Courts of Justice. And although throwing applications through their windows as you pass – let alone stones at our country's primary seat of law – might not bag you a training contract, the atmosphere could be inspiring preparation for life as a fully fledged legal eagle.

City's lecture hall looks out onto the 17th-century Gray's Inn Gardens, which hosts picnicking LPCers at lunchtime. A two-minute walk away, the newly refurbished tutorial facilities have equipment that allows students'

Cardiff Law School

Centre for Professional Legal Studies, Cardiff University, Museum Avenue,
Cardiff CF10 3AX
Website: www.law.cardiff.ac.uk/cpls

University profile
Cardiff Law School is one of the most successful law schools in the UK and enjoys an international reputation for its teaching and research, being ranked 7th in the UK for research. Cardiff offers opportunities for students to pursue postgraduate study by research leading to the degrees of MPhil and PhD and a broadly based Masters (LLM) programme which is offered in full and part-time mode. Cardiff also has a Pro Bono Scheme which gives students an opportunity to experience the law in action, work alongside volunteer legal professionals and develop transferable skills to add to their CVs.

The Law School is the leading provider of legal professional training in Wales and is validated to offer the GDL, LPC and BPTC. Students are taught by experienced solicitors and barristers who are specifically recruited for this purpose. The Law School prides itself on its friendly and supportive teaching environment and its strong links with the legal profession. Placements with solicitors' firms or sets of chambers are available to students pursuing the vocational courses.

Graduate Diploma in Law (full-time or part-time)
The GDL is a one-year (full-time) or two-year (part-time) course for non-law graduates to convert to law. This intensive course covers all of the essential topics of a qualifying law degree. Completion of the GDL allows you to progress to the professional stage of training – the LPC for solicitors and the BPTC for barristers.

Legal Practice Course (full-time or part-time)
Cardiff has delivered its LPC since 1993 and is highly regarded by both students and employers. Cardiff offers the LPC both full-time (3 days a week) and part-time (1 day a week). Through both courses the Law School provides an excellent learning experience which includes a high degree of hands-on teaching. Placements with solicitors' firms are available to some students without training contracts or recent legal work experience.

Bar Professional Training Course
Cardiff delivers a top quality, highly regarded BPTC. There is a relatively small student cohort and the course provides a truly supportive learning environment with high levels of individual tutor feedback on all skills performances. The learning mostly takes place in small groups. There is a focus on the development of advocacy skills, with two hour classes in groups of six or fewer almost every week across all three terms. Students are offered two weeks of placements, giving them the opportunity to marshall with both a Circuit Judge and a District Judge in addition to undertaking a mini-pupillage.

LLM in Legal Practice
Cardiff offers a one year LLM in Legal Practice which can be taken part-time or by distance learning. The LLM is open to students who have successfully completed the LPC, BPTC or BVC, whether at Cardiff or another recognised institution. Assessment takes the form of a practice-based dissertation.

Facilities
The Law School has dedicated accommodation for the vocational courses which houses a postgraduate study space, a suite of classrooms with interactive teaching and audio visual equipment and extensive computer facilities. In addition, the main law library contains one of the largest collections of primary and secondary materials within the UK. The Law School is housed in its own building at the heart of the campus, itself located in one of the finest civic centres in Britain.

classroom performances to be recorded and visualisers to display students' work on screens. Students can get involved in over 20 different pro bono opportunities, including a popular scheme based in South Africa and two tutor-run advice clinics.

Careers services and prospects

The school has a training contract advisory service run by a former partner from a City law firm and assisted by a partner from a regional firm. Students go in for one-to-one sessions to polish their CVs and cover letters even before they start the course, and also have access to mock interviews and help from their assigned personal tutors. They've got access to further career advice and resources courtesy of City University's career service.

Graduates say...

"For me, it was exactly what I wanted: a small course with small classes. I got good feedback and individual attention from the tutors."

The *Chambers Student* verdict

City Law School might not have the reputation of London LPC powerhouses like Kaplan, BPP or University of Law, but for students looking for a more personal experience, it could well be a little gem.

De Montfort University

Number of places: 80 FT, 80 PT
Fees (2014/15): £8,500

The course

Programme leader Oliver Bennett picks out two particularly alluring aspects of De Montfort's LPC: *"Firstly, it's important to highlight that we're extremely competitively priced in comparison with other providers,"* he says. *"Secondly, because of our size we can provide an incredibly high level of one-on-one attention to all of our students."* Indeed, all face-to-face teaching is done in small groups, with each one consisting of around 16 to 18 students. Full-timers attend just two sessions a week every Monday and Tuesday, and there are also live lectures taking place on Wednesdays throughout Stage One – though these are optional and can also be accessed online. For part-time students, classes are mainly taught at the weekends so they can fit the course around full-time employment (or other outside commitments). Stage Two sees those on the course choose three electives to study from a blend of private client and commercial-oriented options. One of the latter offerings is sports and media law, which Bennett says *"is one of our USPs and we have a leading expert in the field who teaches it."*

The location and facilities

DMU's law school is housed in a £35m building that's energy-efficient and, perhaps most crucially of all, entirely purpose-built. *"It's important that our LPC students have their own space,"* explains Bennett, *"so the building contains a password-protected dedicated LPC library, they have their own common room and all of their teaching rooms are designed for postgraduate students."* On a wider note, the university's campus is currently undergoing a £136m redevelopment and work for that is expected to be completed in 2016, so future joiners will be able to benefit from the ongoing transformation. There are several pro bono opportunities on offer. These include a law clinic where *"students can give real-life legal advice to other students and employees of the university,"* as well as the 'Streetlaw' initiative, which sees students present legal topics to members of the local community.

Careers services and prospects

DMU provides various avenues for students to obtain both work placements and permanent positions. For example, the university co-ordinates with a bunch of organisations in the not-for-profit and public sectors to secure placements for students, including the likes of international child abduction charity Reunite, and Leicester's local council. Beyond those, DMU has ties with a number of high-profile firms including national giant Irwin Mitchell, as well as prominent bodies like the Citizens' Advice Bureau. It's also worth mentioning that those on the LPC are guaranteed a spot on a mentoring scheme with local solicitors – an opportunity that results in some gaining a training contract with their respective mentors' firm.

The *Chambers Student* verdict

With relatively cheap fees, smallish class sizes and strong links to the profession, the LPC at DMU is a good alternative to the pricier LPC providers out there.

University of Hertfordshire

Number of places: 80 FT
Fees (2014/15): £10,500

The course

The University of Hertfordshire's LPC is only offered on a full-time basis, and it combines distance and on-campus learning. Students attend one session every Wednesday in groups of around 16 to 20, while the remainder of the week is freed up for them to prepare for sessions from home using 'StudyNet', the law school's intranet system. Senior lecturer and mooting director Neal Geach describes the classes as *"pretty intensive,"* and with good reason: students are taught from 9am until 5pm during stage one, and between 9am and 7pm throughout stage two; the electives stage. *"A benefit of this is there's flexibility to manage the rest of your life simultaneously,"* he points out.

Students have 11 electives to select from, among them personal injury, IP and mediation. Speaking of mediation, it's worth noting that students can also undertake a post-graduate diploma in commercial and workplace mediation at the university before or after completing the LPC.

The location and facilities

It was only in 2011 that Hertfordshire's law school relocated to a brand-new multimillion-pound building on the university's Havilland campus, so we weren't surprised to hear that everything remains in tip-top condition. The *"absolute crown jewel,"* according to Geach, is the mock courtroom: *"It's fantastic for providing a realistic environment to nurture students' courtroom skills,"* he says. There's also the school's mediation centre – a place for budding mediators in the region to learn their trade.

There certainly isn't the same buzz around here that you find in major cities (or even other towns), so bear that in mind if vibrant nightlife is on your checklist.

Careers services and prospects

The school's careers service has recently been revamped and now hosts drop-in advice centres and CV clinics, and lists vacancies via StudyNet to help students secure a post-LPC job. The school has solid links with some of the big local firms – Taylor Walton, for one – and St Albans Crown Court, where a number of students head each year to shadow judges. Most students stay local after completing the LPC, although London-based opportunities arise through some tutors' affiliations with bodies such as the West London Law Society.

The *Chambers Student* verdict

This package suits those who want a considerable emphasis on distance learning and a chance to hone their mediation skills – while enjoying swanky facilities.

University of Huddersfield

Number of places: 80 FT, 35 PT
Fees (2014/15): £9,000

The course

While the focus of this feature is on Huddersfield's standalone LPC, principal lecturer Emma Seagreaves points out that *"our major course in terms of professional practice is the exempting degree,"* which *"has really taken off and is the primary way our students pursue legal careers."* This option sees students study the LLB and LPC in tandem over three or four years.

But back to the LPC. Both full-timers and part-timers are taught together for certain sections. Part-timers normally attend sessions one day a week – Monday in the first year and Tuesday in the second year – while full-timers are on campus for both those days. *"We recognise that even on the full-time course, people still need to work,"* says Seagreaves, *"so we decided to make it flexible enough to allow time for outside commitments as well as self study."* The university also offers *"block elective teaching at different times of the year,"* meaning that *"students don't have to do all their electives simultaneously."*

We heard there *"isn't much in the way of standard lectures,"* and even in the large classes *"it remains very student-centred and transactional."* Huddersfield deliberately keeps its class sizes small to allow for maximum student-teacher interaction – large group sessions normally contain between 30 and 40 students each, while small group sessions hold between 12 and 20.

The location and facilities

The law school is based in one of the university's flagship buildings and is kitted out with a mock courtroom, dedicated teaching rooms and various IT facilities. More exciting developments are on the horizon: according to Seagreaves, the school has plans to move to a brand-new building at some point in 2016.

Although not a city outright, Huddersfield is one of the biggest towns in the UK and has a swarm of well-known shopping outlets and restaurants in its bustling centre, which is not far from the university. One shopping centre is home to the school's legal advice clinic, which was launched in late 2013 and allows students to get involved in advising members of the public.

Careers services and prospects

One of the university's more prominent careers services for LPC students is its Partners in Law scheme. The firms involved – which include big-hitters like Pinsent Masons, DLA Piper and Eversheds, as well as some smaller local firms – help generate networking and mentoring opportunities for students. The law school also arranges occasional careers events throughout the course, like CV and interview workshops run by legal recruitment consultants.

The *Chambers Student* verdict

If you're aiming to balance the LPC with a job or aren't a fan of conventional big-group lectures, Huddersfield's offering might be worth a look.

Kaplan Law School

Number of places: 300 FT
Fees (2014/15): £13,645

The course

The former Kaplan students we spoke to were keen to point out that the school *"is significantly smaller than its main London competitors"* – namely BPP and the University of Law – and felt it *"offers a more personal experience"* as a result. In the small group sessions, for example, there are no more than 21 students in each, and head of operations Juliette Chase adds that the course *"is still very much driven by face-to-face contact."* Indeed, while other providers have placed less emphasis on delivering the content in person, the LPC at Kaplan sees students attend sessions Monday to Thursday, with Fridays kept free for independent study or outside commitments. That's not to say there isn't an online element though: Chase tells us *"all the lectures used to be mandatory, but now only around a third of them are. The rest of them can be viewed online by students in their own time."* In an exciting new development, Kaplan will now be offering an LLM option as part of the LPC. *"Students who don't opt out of it have two choices: they can either take the simple dissertation route or one which is more centred on employability,"* explains Chase, *"meaning they look at aspects like commercial awareness and the profession in further detail."*

The location and facilities

Chase reveals that in September 2014 the law school upped sticks to a new building complete with a lecture theatre, library, computer labs and various study rooms. *"The facilities are all student-friendly and the emphasis is on maximising the space we have,"* she says. The school itself is based around the South Bank and is a few minutes' walk away from London Bridge station, as well as Southwark Cathedral and Borough Market. According to Chase, Kaplan's main pro bono offering is its legal advice centre, run in conjunction with Anthony Gold Solicitors: *"It's on every week and students who want to get involved in it can offer advice to members of the local community, usually on employment or housing issues."*

Careers services and prospects

Kaplan is renowned for its high employability rates, with 91% of its 2013 LPC graduates having secured a training contract (note: that figure includes those who started the course with one). The school has formal ties with around a dozen firms – among them Mayer Brown, Shearman & Sterling and Farrer & Co – and part of the deal involves teaching these firms' future trainees the LPC. *"We have a wide range of client firms, but what they all have in common is that they're not part of the magic circle,"* says Chase. *"We're much more about the mid to large-sized firms that have anything from a handful to 20 or 25 trainees."* Alongside these affiliations, Kaplan runs a number of careers events and services throughout the course: *"Students can make as many appointments as they like with our careers team, and no application needs to be sent off without being thoroughly checked by us first."* What's more, when training contract hopefuls manage to nab an interview or a spot at an assessment centre, the careers crew will carry out mock interviews with them beforehand. The one-on-one careers assistance is complemented by employer-led workshops and presentations, while each week there's a 'breakfast club' which students can attend to stay in the loop about current trends in the legal market.

Graduates say...

"If you're going into the LPC without a training contract then they make sure you get the attention you need."

The *Chambers Student* verdict

Kaplan's impressive employability statistics understandably make it a standout option, and the course will especially suit those who prefer to be taught on campus as part of a smallish cohort.

Kaplan Law School

179-191 Borough High Street, Southwark, London, SE1 1HR
Tel: (020) 7367 6455
Email: admissions@kaplanlawschool.org.uk
Website: www.kaplanlawschool.org.uk

Contact
Apply to GDL & LPC Central
Applications Board
www.lawcabs.ac.uk

College profile

Kaplan Law School offers highly regarded professional postgraduate courses with excellent pass rates and a truly hands-on and proactive careers service.

Face-to-face tuition is key; Kaplan's teaching model is based around small groups to help student learning, as well as give tutors more contact time with each student. Our tutors are all qualified lawyers with a proven track record in practice and legal education.

At Kaplan we do not offer places to fill bums on seats. Our strict admissions criteria ensures that all students on the course have a realistic chance of gaining a training contract. Our 2013 employability rates reflect this; of our intending solicitors, 91% gained a training contract whilst consulting with our careers service.

Our careers service is run by a former graduate recruiter, so we know exactly what law firms are looking for. Students can make weekly appointments and never need to send off an application until it has been checked. When students get through to the next stage of the application process, they will be given mock interviews bespoke to the firm they are interviewing at.

GDL: Graduate Diploma in Law (full time)

Designed for any non-law graduate who intends to become a solicitor or barrister in the UK, with most teaching weeks taking place over three days giving students flexibility to work or make applications. Kaplan's GDL places the academic subjects into a work related context so that students are more prepared for practice.

LLM LPC: LLM Legal Practice Course (full time)

From September 2014 Kaplan will be offering an LLM LPC. Students study core modules and then choose elective subjects to specialise in. Awarded by Nottingham Trent University, the LLM LPC offers students the chance to develop a higher level of knowledge whilst gaining invaluable practical and commercial insight.

Those sponsored by one of our client firms also participate in our Bridge to Practice course, an umbrella programme designed to get students ready for their training contract.

Careers & open events

Kaplan runs a full programme of careers events throughout the year, designed to help you make the decision of whether to pursue law, give you the opportunity to meet people from the profession and in some cases bolster your CV. Alternatively students can visit for a guided tour and the opportunity to sit with our careers service to see how they will work with you. Students can bring with them an application they are working on.

Scholarships

Kaplan offers a scholarship programme across all courses including one free place for the GDL and LPC.

University of Central Lancashire (UCLan)

Number of places: 80 FT, 40 PT
Fees (2014/15): £8,200

The course

Students on UCLan's full-time LPC can expect to be on campus for the first three days of the week, with occasional assessments on Thursdays and Fridays, while part-timers usually attend an all-day session every Wednesday. Acting dean Jane Anthony tells us one of the course's main strengths is *"the high level of interaction, not only between staff and students but also among the students themselves."* Indeed, the group sessions that make up the course all have an interactive spin, and each of the smaller ones tends to accommodate between 15 and 20 students – *"there's no hiding at the back of the class."* Each module is supported by online resources, such as interactive quizzes for students to complete prior to the session.

According to Anthony, UCLan's LPC will incorporate an LLM component from September 2015. *"Students here no longer have the tough choice of whether they should do a Master's or the LPC."*

The location and facilities

Students spend the majority of their learning time in the university's Harris Building, where the law school is based. Facilities include a dedicated moot courtroom, LPC resource rooms, and 'skills development' rooms containing recording and playback equipment. There's also a law section in the library for students.

UCLan's Preston campus is centrally located, only a short stroll away from the train station and the city's two main shopping centres. Bear in mind that Preston itself isn't going to win any prizes for nightlife, especially when compared to the likes of Manchester and Liverpool, though these are both about an hour's train or car journey away.

The school's biggest pro bono offering is its *"very popular"* law clinic. *"Students who get involved in it really reap the benefits,"* Anthony tells us. *"From a CV point of view, it shows they've done something over and above the course itself."*

Careers services and prospects

Alongside the university's central careers service, some of the law school's staff *"take on the responsibility of helping students by looking at CVs, practising interviews and providing general guidance."* An *"extensive programme of visiting speakers"* sees judges, trainees and former UCLan students come in to share their experiences in the profession, and there's also an annual careers fair packed with legal and public sector entities. The law school advertises vacancies on behalf of several firms and bodies in the region – including Vincents, Duncan Gibbins and Lancashire County Council – and screens students' initial applications to them.

The *Chambers Student* verdict

Provided you're not on the hunt for party central, the LPC at UCLan is a solid contender, with its interactive set-up and robust careers services.

The University of Law

Number of places: 4,752 FT; 2,000 PT
Fees 2014/15: see below for breakdown
Awards: 20 awards of £5,000 each, subject to 2:1 degree and online skills assessment

The course

At over 100 years old, University of Law (formerly known as the College of Law) is the UK's oldest legal training provider. The institute is keen to swat off young upstarts BPP and Kaplan to become the country's biggest provider, too. *"We have trained more solicitors in current practice than anyone else, so there's a huge amount of name recognition out there,"* head of students at UoL Chester Stuart Bladen notes. Indeed, UoL has centres scattered across major cities – including two in London – and has struck up firm-specific course deals with Linklaters, Clifford Chance and Ashurst to school their incoming trainees.

The pressures of maintaining this national network and lucrative law firm contracts mean UoL is a slicker and more commercial outfit than LPC courses offered by traditional universities. In 2012 the institute launched a so-called international LPC, which has wooed big firms like Dechert and CMS with its emphasis on global law. UoL's pioneering and fast-growing online LPC is another exercise in innovation. Students study online over a period of 22 months, attending campus only for induction, certain training sessions and exams.

Full-time students can choose from ten-month or accelerated seven-month courses. The former offers ten hours of contact time over two or four days a week – slightly lower than smaller providers. These are supplemented with i-tutorials, online tests and independent study. The seven-month accelerated version, which starts in January, involves 12 hours of contact time a week and is available in all centres except Bristol and Chester. A part-time study option isn't available at all centres; those that do offer it vary in length and scope. Students can choose to study during the day, evening or at weekends, over either 18 or 22 months.

As you'd expect, teaching standards and student experiences vary from centre to centre, though the basic structure and course materials are the same across all. Several alumni complained *"there were too many internet modules to watch on your own in lieu of face-to-face sessions where you could ask questions as you went along – that made it less personal than is ideal."* Still, the general consensus was that *"the course is very well structured and offers useful materials, and the quality of the seminar and group discussions is good."*

A couple of sources suggested that rival provider BPP's business credentials mean it's more of an *"organised, well-oiled machine."* They also mentioned that the University of Law's lengthy two-and-a-half hour workshops *"sometimes feel laboured, whereas at BPP the sessions are more focused and efficient."*

Some students seek out UoL especially for its famed open book exams. *"I'm not suggesting the exams are easy, but I liked being able to find what I needed quickly once I had a grasp on the question. I think that's a more realistic idea of how being a real lawyer works – you can just go back to the statute books when needed."*

The location and facilities

Birmingham
Fees (2014/15): £11,515 FT
The small Birmingham branch comprises several *"well-equipped"* teaching rooms in the city's central Jewellery Quarter. Grads told us *"the lecturers were really good at helping with exam preparation and were always on hand to offer advice."* The course here stands out for its French exchange programme, whereby students with conversational French skills can do work experience in Birmingham's twin city Lyon.

Bristol
Fees (2014/15): £11,515 FT
UoL Bristol is located in Temple Quarter, the city's financial and legal district. *"The building's only been open for a few years, so the facilities all still feel very new."* Our sources agreed the course here is *"very well run."* As one recalled: *"The tutors were lovely and enthusiastic, and were very familiar with the course. It's small enough that it feels personal and friendly."*

Chester
Fees (2014/15) £10,965 FT
Chester's branch is just outside the city's historical centre, which boasts Tudor houses and several medieval city walls. We picked up on a bit of rivalry between this centre and its larger sister one in Manchester, with former students declaring the facilities in Chester *"way better. The library is really good, and there are always spaces to sit, even when it's busy."* They were also keen on the school's campus, set across 14 acres of parkland. *"It's*

a very peaceful location with beautiful scenery – you're surrounded by green fields and right by the River Dee."*

Guildford
Fees (2014/15): £11,815 FT
Like Chester, Guildford is a good option for countryside lovers. Here UoL occupies a manor house set in 23 acres of parkland. The *"really nice and very rural"* campus is a 20-minute walk from Guildford rail station and has plenty of parking for drivers. In keeping with its outdoorsy surroundings, there are several sports societies, including polo, rowing and golf. If the attractions of chi-chi Guildford don't suffice, London is just 35 minutes away by train.

Leeds
Fees (2014/15): £10,965 FT
This branch recently upped sticks from York, perhaps to capitalise on the growing numbers of law firms in what's now Britain's second-biggest legal market. According to UoL, the branch hopes to *"replicate the corporate setting of a professional law firm"* with its glass-clad, seven-storey building, which includes a student cafe and top-floor balconies overlooking the Leeds skyline. It's five minutes from the train station, and a hop, skip and jump away from the many nightclubs that have cropped up to satisfy the city's bloated student population (one of the biggest in the country).

London Bloomsbury
Fees (2014/15): £14,765 FT
There's a casual rivalry between the UoL's centre in Bloomsbury – its largest – and the City-focused Moorgate alternative. One grad of the Bloomsbury course called the campus *"a lot more lively and less corporate-focused than Moorgate. There's a wider variety of people here, and fewer students have City training contracts lined up already."* The potential downside of that is that *"more money is pumped into Moorgate."* One source complained that *"the facilities are not great, given the level of fees people pay. The building is kind of run-down and dingy, and doesn't have any water coolers."* Still, students are just a short walk from the big-city charms of Tottenham Court Road and Oxford Street, and can pile onto the lawns of Bedford Square for lunchtime picnics.

London Moorgate
Fees (2014/15): £14,765 FT
For one source, *"it was a bit of a shock to the system moving from Bloomsbury to Moorgate after my GDL – everything's much slicker, and it's set up very much like a law firm, so everything is shiny."* As the name suggests, these facilities are a short walk from Moorgate Tube station, smack in the middle of the Square Mile. The likes of Ashurst and Linklaters send their future trainees on tailored LPCs at this branch, and we're told "the tutors are

generally pretty clued-up on law firm life." Class sizes are large here – with 20 or more per class – and a few sources grumbled about the "lack of space in the library, especially during the exam period."

Manchester

Fees (2014/15): £10,965 FT

UoL's Manchester premises may be brand new, but they're *"still quite basic facility-wise – it takes up a few floors of a tower block, and when the trams go past it rattles. Likewise, you can feel it shake when people in the gym upstairs drop their weights."* Accordingly, Manchester emerged as the underdog in our research. *"A lot of staff are part-time so I found it hard to pin anyone down,"* one source recalled. *"A lot of us felt there wasn't enough support and that we were rushed through the course."* That said, others added that *"the materials were good enough that you could learn from home, and the teachers seemed to know what they were talking about. You're very much treated like a young professional."*

Careers services and prospects

UoL has not been shy about boasting the stat that 98% of its 2013 students found employment within nine months of graduation. However, it doesn't divulge whether these jobs were top-flight training contracts or stacking the shelves at Tesco, so we don't suggest setting too much store by that figure.

The sheer size of UoL means the level of individual attention students receive during their job hunt varies from centre to centre. Still, there are some notable careers services on offer, including the ten-stage programme StEP, which incorporates online employability exercises, links and workshops. Each centre also has its own dedicated professional advisor on hand, as well as an employability service that arranges one-to-one advice sessions, talks, visits from law firms and mock interviews. UoL's is long-established enough that's it's built up relationships with firms across the country, making for well-attended law fairs, mentoring schemes and a job database of its own.

The school also has ties with local pro bono organisations and offers a range of pro bono opportunities across its offices – these typically include law clinics, work for local charities and practice-specific schemes in areas like employment or criminal law.

Graduates say...

"It's a well-run course that sets you up well for going into a corporate firm."

"I thought the course was pretty boring, and a lot of it was structured in a very formulaic way. But then again, the answers they're looking for are very formulaic, so

perhaps that's to be expected."

"There's a real divide between those who come in with City training contracts and those who don't have anything lined up. It's difficult for teachers to manage the varying needs of students."

The *Chambers Student* verdict

Bigger isn't always better, but plumping for this vast outfit virtually guarantees access to a bevy of online resources and work experience opportunities.

Leeds Beckett University (formerly Leeds Metropolitan)

Number of places: 105 FT, 45 PT
Fees (2014/15): £7,500

The course

The emphasis here is very much on fostering a close-knit experience. As such there are no lectures, but rather *"interactive three-hour workshops with activities done in pairs and small groups,"* explains course leader Yvonne Marsh. These typically hold no more than 16 students in each, and when it comes to some of the core modules, the class sizes are essentially split in half. Full-time students can expect to be on campus on Monday, Wednesday and Thursday, while those pursuing the part-time route attend two evening classes a week – these are usually on Tuesdays and Thursdays in Stage One, while the sessions during Stage Two depend on the electives chosen. Speaking of electives, there are two new ones on the roster: commercial dispute resolution and mental health law, both of which were introduced *"in response to demand."* The group sessions are supported by extensive online resources, including podcasts, quizzes and preparatory materials. In an effort to enhance students' employment prospects, there's now a four-day introductory course for both full and part-timers, involving a series of talks on topics like CVs, applications, social media and networking. This culminates in a mini assessment centre taking place on the final day, with local solicitors coming in to provide feedback. *"In particular, they really value the feedback they get from the pros,"* Marsh adds.

The location and facilities

The law school currently resides in Cloth Hall Court, situated in the midst of the city's legal neighbourhood. *"We have our own dedicated floor with a resources room and recording suite,"* says Marsh, *"and it's a short walk away from the train station and Trinity"* (a brand-new shopping centre that opened in March 2013). However, Marsh goes on to reveal that the school will be upping sticks next year to occupy part of a university building closer to Leeds Met's main campus, so future starters will have a different habitat from those on the course right now.

Careers services and prospects

The school has its own set of services to assist LPC students with their career aspirations. Strong links with the Leeds Law Society have paved the way for students to undertake voluntary legal positions, while a professional mentor scheme sees students paired up with local practitioners who offer regular support. Marsh says: *"Many solicitors studied at Leeds Met and are still loyal to us; as well as the mentor scheme, they keep us updated on vacancies for training contracts or paralegal positions."* What's more, a few nationally recognised firms with a local presence – namely Eversheds, DWF and Pinsent Masons – have close ties with the school and actively participate in career-oriented sessions and other aspects of the course.

The *Chambers Student* verdict

This will suit folks after a small-scale experience with plenty of focus on employability. Probably best to support a different football team though – Leeds United ain't what it used to be...

Liverpool John Moores University

Number of places: 32 FT, 44 PT
Fees (2014/15): £8,585FT, £4,300PT

The course

If all you need is law, studying in the Beatles' hometown could be just the ticket. JMU's LPC places a big emphasis on the academic side of legal practice. According to principal Fiona Fargher, *"we offer a higher percentage of face-to-face contact than many other institutions, with a real focus on providing a university environment."* That said, class sizes here are larger than at rival providers, with up to 20 students per class.

Full-timers' contact time adds up to between 12 and 15 hours Monday to Wednesday, while part-time students have six hours across either one day or two evenings a week. One graduate complained that *"a lot of the lecturers just gave us handouts to do. I hoped it would be more involved for the amount of money."* However, Fargher insists *"all of our lectures are interactive and can involve role-playing court appearances, interviewing and drafting documents."* Outside of class students are expected to do 40 hours of prep a week with the aid of online course materials.

Law students have the chance to boost their LPC to an LLM by doing an extra dissertation, although it's worth noting the extra letters after your name will likely impress law firms less than your granny.

The location and facilities

JMU recently splashed out a cool £38m on its new Redmonds Building, complete with a mock courtroom, amped-up IT facilities and Starbucks. It's located in the centre of town, a short walk from Liverpool Central rail station and all its nearby restaurants and bars. According to university estimates, £6,000 to £8,000 a year should be enough for students to cover their living expenses – this might see students living on Pot Noodles, but there's no denying it's an attractive figure when compared to the sky-high costs of London.

Careers services and prospects

The LPC at JMU is primarily a local course for local folk: three-quarters of students on the course are returning undergraduates, and the remainder tend to be people already living and working in Liverpool. The electives offered (among them family, personal injury and criminal litigation) are skewed towards high street rather than corporate practice – another suggestion this is not the place to go for a career in the City.

"The majority of our students end up in the North West," Fargher confirms, adding that most graduates *"are likely to work as paralegals before getting a training contract."* She estimates around 30% of grads end up with a training contract during the course or shortly after leaving. Students keen to boost their chances can sign up to the law school's solicitor mentoring scheme.

The *Chambers Student* verdict

It's not the most all-singing, all-dancing of options, but those staying local should find this a handy place to train.

London Metropolitan University

Number of places: 192 FTE
Fees (2014/15): £8,900

The course

London Metropolitan's LPC consists of three-hour sessions that hold a maximum of 16 students in each. *"We teach most of the course face-to-face because we believe that's the most effective mode of delivery for our students to learn,"* explains course director Sarah Campling. The classes are interactive and thus enable plenty of active student participation; the first hour is normally teacher-led, with the rest of the session led by students. When it comes to the timetable, full-timers tend to be on campus on Tuesdays and Thursdays, while part-timers have the flexibility of choosing between one day or two evenings a week, allowing ample time for their outside commitments. Campling tells us the course *"focuses mainly on litigation rather than business law,"* and this is reflected in the electives – though there are a few commercial-oriented options on the menu too. The face-to-face sessions are accompanied by a wealth of online resources, including tests, legal databases and revision materials. On top of the LPC, there's a 'barrister to solicitor' conversion course on offer at LMU – ideal for those who have already done the BPTC but wish to pursue the solicitor route instead – as well as a top-up LLM option.

The location and facilities

The law school is based near the unmistakable Gherkin and Aldgate station (think nights out on Brick Lane for hit-and-miss curries). The building that's home to the school has all the facilities you'd expect, such as a mock courtroom, coffee shop, various teaching rooms and a dedicated resource centre for LPC students. LMU's pro bono offering isn't the most comprehensive, especially when pitted against other providers, but Campling points out that *"we do have support in place to help students find pro bono work,"* which takes the form of a dedicated pro bono supervisor.

Careers services and prospects

The school's big focus at the moment is on the recently revamped mentoring scheme: *"It's like a mentoring family tree in a way,"* Campling says. *"The idea is that LPC students mentor the undergraduate law students, then in turn we have professional mentors to mentor the LPC students."* Beyond that, there are normally a fair few work placements up for grabs at firms, court and not-for-profit organisations, then every March there's a week devoted to careers events as the school *"provides services like CV advice, networking workshops and mock interviews."*

The *Chambers Student* verdict

This LPC stands out for its interactive spin and emphasis on face-to-face teaching, though bear in mind the fact that it's tailored slightly more towards aspiring litigators.

Manchester Metropolitan University

Number of places: 168 FT, 72 PT
Fees (2014/15): £9,500
Awards: three scholarships of £4,000 each; 10% discount for MMU graduates

The course

Manchester Metropolitan University runs Manchester's longest-established LPC. MMU doesn't have the national clout of BPP or University of Law, both of which have Mancunian outposts, nor does it enjoy the same reputation for getting its students training contracts. Still, its fees are a good £1,000 less than these providers (though not, as MMU's website boasts, a full 20% less).

Most MMU students come from the North West with the intention of landing training roles with high street firms or other smallish outfits. The condensed schedule of the LPC means even full-time students have time to keep up part-time jobs through the course. Full-timers get between 12 and 15 hours of contact time a week, spread over two days, while part-timers have six to seven hours, consolidated on one day a week.

Teaching takes place in workshops of 16 to 20 students and is supplemented with online resources like questionnaires, podcasts and drafting exercises. Part-time students can spread their modules over 16 or 24 months. There are a dozen or so electives on offer, among them commercial property, employment, family, media and criminal litigation.

The location and facilities

MMU's law school is right in Manchester's city centre, next to 'student alley' and has a host of cheap eateries and bars. LPC students have access to an LPC resource room stocked with practitioner texts and computing facilities, two other study rooms, and a 24-hour law library.

The law school offers a range of pro bono work through organisations like the Manchester Mediation Service, Trafford Law Centre, Manchester CAB, Shelter, Personal Support Unit and Innospace. PSU trains students to support litigants in person, while Innospace is a more commercial option, offering a helping hand to small businesses and start-ups.

Careers services and prospects

According to MMU, 90% of LPC students find legal-related employment after graduating – a claim we suggest taking with more than a mere grain of salt. For starters, that category is suspiciously vague and could cover anything from a top training contract down to a stint pushing the tea trolley at a high street firm. What's more, there's no time period on that statistic, suggesting it takes some several years after graduating to land a job in the sector.

In any case, MMU helps its LPC students find jobs for up to three years after they graduate. Students have access to personal tutors, mock interviews, practitioner mentoring sessions, one-to-one advice appointments, and various talks. The law school lacks the networking prowess of BPP and University of Law, both of which have struck up deals to provide tailored LPCs to incoming trainees at some of Manchester's largest legal players, but MMU does have ties with small firms in the area and offers a pro bono programme in which students assist local solicitors on judicial review cases.

The *Chambers Student* verdict

This course is an economical option in a vibrant legal hub. Be sure to approach employment-related stats with a degree of caution, though.

Northumbria University Law School

Number of places: 150 FT, 100 PT
Fees (2014/15): not disclosed for 2014; estimated at £9,400

Awards: 15% discount for a 1:1 at undergraduate, 10% discount for a 2:1, additional 10% discount for Northumbria graduates

The course

Aspiring north eastern solicitors have their pick of the more established Newcastle University or its cooler young sister Northumbria. As one graduate of both institutions put it, *"you could make assumptions about the quality of the course based on the fact that Newcastle's a red brick and Northumbria's newer, but I actually found Northumbria better in certain respects. It's less of a traditional read-your-textbooks kind of place, and more about practical exercises and group work."*

LPC students are taught in a mixture of lectures, small group sessions and workshops that take place in classes of around 16. Full-time students can opt to come in either two or four days a week, while part-timers study one weekday. They can choose between general or commercial practice course routes, and incorporating electives that range from commercial – IP or corporate finance, for example – to more niche options like mental health law. There's a particularly popular student law office option, which sees students work on live pro bono cases. *"The fact that I was handling live clients in my final year definitely gave me the edge at interviews, as it demonstrated I could handle the pressures of real work,"* said one grad.

The location and facilities

Northumbria's lecture theatres are modelled on Harvard's, and in true American style the law school even has a Starbucks. The university's not too far from the regenerated docklands area, which plays host to plenty of riverside drinking and dining opportunities, plus the vast, modern Baltic Gallery.

Northumbria's alumni were particularly keen on the law school's *"forward-thinking"* approach, which sees students outfitted with iPads as study aids. There's also a mock courtroom with DVD recording facilities.

Careers services and prospects

One trainee who'd successfully made the leap from Northumbria LPC student to local trainee told us *"quite a lot of trainees from my course went on to work in big firms in the region – it has a good reputation in the North East."* The student law office links up with Ben Hoare Bell solicitors to run a legal advice scheme for members of the public, and the university also has a relationship with Ward Hadaway, which offers two honour roll students bursaries of £1,000 and four weeks of work experience.

Students can sign up for work experience or mentoring sessions with nearby firms or organisations with legal teams, and they also have access to practice interviews, careers advice sessions and the annual law fair.

Graduates say...

"I was surprised by the quality of the resources and the IT system. The law and business school is all very new."

"The way the LPC is taught is hands-on – we got lots of opportunities to try drafting and advocacy."

"The student law office is why I decided to go there – there's a chance to work with qualified lawyers giving real advice."

The *Chambers Student* verdict

Come for the modern facilities; stay for the ties with staples of the Newcastle legal scene.

Nottingham Law School

Number of places: 650 FT, 100 PT
Fees (2014/15): £11,400

The course

New to Nottingham Law School's LPC this time around is the incorporation of an LLM award, which principal lecturer Jason Ellis believes *"brings a lot of extra value to the course."* Students can opt out of the LLM element altogether, but if they choose to pursue it then they're required to submit a 5,000-word project or 7,500-word dissertation during Stage Two. This is preceded by 'professional legal practice' in Stage One, a module comprising various workshops and a series of lectures from experts within the profession.

All the core modules are taught in Stage One, while Stage Two sees those on the course pick three electives to study from a list of ten.

Although delivery methods differ according to the module, Ellis tells us the course is generally underpinned by *"four pillars that collectively highlight our blended approach to learning: lectures, vodcasts, small group sessions/work-*

Nottingham Law School

Nottingham Law School, Burton Street, Nottingham NG1 4BU
Tel: (0)115 848 4460
Email: nls.enquiries@ntu.ac.uk
Website: www.ntu.ac.uk/nls

Contact
Nottingham Law School
Burton Street
Nottingham Trent University
Nottingham NG1 4BU
Tel: (0)115 848 4460
Email: nls.enquiries@ntu.ac.uk
Website: www.ntu.ac.uk/nls

Law School

School profile

One of the largest and most diverse law schools in the UK, we are committed to retaining strong links to practice. We seek to ensure that all our clients, from students to experienced practitioners, receive the best practical legal education and training. You will be taught by a unique mix of qualified lawyers with a proven track record in practice and legal education.

Nottingham Law School has an excellent reputation for graduate employability. Our focus on practical skills, award-winning pro bono scheme and dedicated careers and recruitment service has helped to keep our training contract and pupillage rates consistently high. We also have a number of competitive scholarships for our postgraduate and professional courses.

Graduate Diploma in Law (full time or distance learning)

This conversion course is designed for any non-law graduate who intends to become a solicitor or barrister in the UK. The intensive course effectively covers the seven core subjects of an undergraduate law degree in one go. It is the stepping stone to the LPC or the BPTC and to a legal career thereafter. It is possible for the Law School to award a Graduate LLB degree to students who have achieved the LPC or BPTC after completing the GDL with us.

Legal Practice Course (full or part time)

At Nottingham Law School (NLS) we are confident that our LPC will provide you with the best training currently available. Our careers expertise and experienced and supportive teaching staff will help you get your career off to a flying start.

Our LPC has recently been enhanced so that the successful completion of all its elements will result in the award of a Masters degree: LLM Legal Practice Course. As well as providing you with an internationally recognised qualification, you will leave NLS with enhanced insight into the legal profession and better equipped to succeed.

Students who do not wish to study for the full masters award can still study for the award of a postgraduate diploma, that is, the "traditional" LPC award. However, all students will benefit from the enhanced the LPC.

Bar Professional Training Course (full time)

Nottingham Law School designed its BPTC to develop to a high standard a range of core practical skills, and to equip students to succeed in the fast-changing environment of practice at the Bar. Particular emphasis is placed on the skill of advocacy. The BPTC is taught entirely by qualified practitioners, and utilises the same integrated and interactive teaching methods as all of the school's other professional courses. Essentially, students learn by doing. Students are encouraged to realise, through practice and feedback, their full potential.

Masters in Law (LLM)

Our taught masters in Law programme offers a wide range of subject pathways taught by tutors whose research is nationally and internationally recognised.

Subject areas include: Corporate and Insolvency, Health Law and Ethics, Human Rights and Justice, Intellectual Property, International Trade and Commercial, Sports, and Oil, Gas and Mining Law.

LLM Legal Practice (distance learning)

This new LLM award is for those with professional legal qualifications, for example the BPTC or LPC (or their precursors). Credit points are awarded for these professional qualifications and students can then 'top-up' these points with a dissertation or publishable article to gain this LLM.

shops and then, surrounding all of that, independent learning and study." Full-timers usually attend sessions on Monday to Thursday with Fridays kept free, plus they have the flexibility of choosing to be taught either in the mornings or afternoons during Stage One. Meanwhile, those on the part-time option attend a large group session on Friday then smaller group sessions at the weekend. Techies might also be interested to know that every LPC student gets a nifty tablet as part of the package. Result!

The location and facilities

The law school received a facelift back in 2011 and now "offers everything you'd expect any good law school to offer," such as mock courtrooms, moot rooms and numerous teaching rooms. What's more, the university itself is in the midst of a mammoth redevelopment project across all three of its campuses, so future joiners can expect brand-new facilities all-round. The school is in a decent spot too: it's situated on NTU's City campus, which is a short drive away from the railway station as well as the city's two main shopping centres. The only annoyance is that Clifton campus isn't within walking distance, so if you need to head there for whatever reason (like for the sports facilities) then a bus/car/bike ride will be needed. Pro bono is a pretty big deal here. A bespoke pro bono centre houses a work area and interview rooms, and students can get involved in an array of opportunities, from the on-campus advice clinic to projects provided by external bodies like Nottingham Citizens Advice Bureau, Nottingham Law Centre and Streetlaw. There's also a chance to tackle Employment Tribunal cases in conjunction with the Free Representation Unit – the offshoot in Nottingham is actually the only one outside of London.

Careers services and prospects

A former student deemed the school's dedicated careers service "one of the best things about the entire place," while another told us: "The support in terms of helping me get a training contract was good." The careers crew consists of a number of legal gurus who specialise in certain areas, and they assist students with the likes of CVs, interviews and initial applications. On top of that, there's a mentoring scheme – run in connection with law firms such as Eversheds, Browne Jacobson and Shoosmiths – which sees trainees provide those on the LPC with some words of wisdom and a personal perspective on life in the profession.

The *Chambers Student* verdict

Nottingham's LPC fuses a multimedia approach with a considerable focus on employability: two thumbs up.

University of Sheffield

Number of places: 180 FT, 35 PT
Fees (2014/15): £10,350

The course

The University of Sheffield is one of only two Russell Group universities to run the LPC (Cardiff is the other). Students here can expect a practical focus. "It wasn't simply a case of coaching us for the exams," recalled one former student. "They offered a really comprehensive experience, covering commercial areas as well as legal issues." As the end of their first stage nears, students can choose to study parts of their core modules from either a commercial or general perspective. "We don't ask them to explicitly state whether they want to go into general or commercial practice, though," senior lecturer Clare Firth clarifies, "on the basis that most of them don't know for certain in the beginning."

The course is primarily delivered via workshops comprising up to 18 students, so don't come here expecting many large group lectures. In fact, "we only formally get the whole cohort together a few times during the course," Firth says. These workshops all take the form of case study-based learning, and are supported by screencasts and a wide variety of interactive tasks, including multiple-choice quizzes and drag and drop exercises. Full-timers here attend sessions four days a week, usually from Monday to Thursday, while those on the part-time route tend to be on campus every Friday. Students studying full-time can choose to be taught in the mornings or afternoons (during stage one, at least).

The location and facilities

The law school building has recently undergone some improvements, including refurbished computer rooms and a bigger cafe – "it's no longer just a coffee cart!" jokes Firth. There are also seminar rooms, student common rooms and a moot courtroom, and while the building doesn't house a library, the one on the main campus is only a short walk away. The university is situated right on the leafy edge of the city centre. Most pro bono opportunities take place here through the Innocence Project and the FreeLaw clinic. The latter sees students provide advice to locals on areas like employment, housing and contractual disputes – under the supervision of a solicitor, of course (who is usually part of the law school staff).

Careers services and prospects

The law school has dedicated careers advisers who assist with CVs, cover letters, applications and interviews (this includes arranging mock interviews with local solicitors). "We work with virtually all the firms in the local area and have alumni in most of them," Firth says. According to the university's latest statistics, over 80% of its students start the LPC without a training contract, but around 70% will have secured one within two and a half years of completing the course.

The *Chambers Student* verdict

The practical nature and small group set-up give this LPC a distinctive flavour. And let's not forget the Arctic Monkeys are Sheffielders – they're still cool, right?

University of South Wales

Number of places: 90 FT, 40 PT
Fees (2014/15): £9,000

The course

The University of South Wales – the result of the April 2013 merger between the University of Glamorgan and the University of Wales, Newport – incorporates lectures and workshops into its LPC. *"We have one-hour 'briefing sessions', which are akin to typical lectures, and three-hour 'practice sessions' that essentially put theory into practice,"* deputy director Tricia Morrissey says. *"The practice sessions are designed in consultation with local practitioners and aim to simulate real-life professional environments."* These typically hold around 15 students in each, as opposed to the larger-scale lectures. Full-timers attend sessions Monday to Thursday, with Fridays kept free *"for independent study or work experience."* Meanwhile, part-timers are on campus one day a week – Tuesdays in the first year, then Wednesdays in the second.

The university also runs a four-year MLaw course. This fuses the undergraduate law degree with the LPC, meaning students gain a masters-level degree alongside the qualification required to become a trainee solicitor.

The location and facilities

USW has five sites in total, with the law school situated on the relatively petite Treforest campus. The school was recently renovated and houses all the facilities you'd expect, including a mock courtroom, study areas and dedicated resource rooms for LPC students. One of the other campuses, Glyntaff, is within walking distance, while the remaining three are spread across Cardiff and Newport. Although decent transport links ensure both of these cities can be reached in around half an hour by car or train, they're not exactly right on your doorstep – in other words, you'll be left disappointed if you're after a city centre location.

In November 2013 the university launched its legal and financial advice clinic, which *"gives LPC and undergraduate students the chance to put their knowledge into practice by assisting qualified solicitors in advising clients,"* says Morrissey. *"We're currently looking at inte-* *grating the LPC into the clinic so the students' involvement can become part of their learning."*

Careers services and prospects

One of the main ways students here can boost their legal experience is by completing one of the work placements offered as part of the LPC. The firms involved range from small outfits like Cardiff-headquartered Hugh James all the way up to international juggernauts like Eversheds, and students have a fair amount of flexibility when it comes to how many days they're on placement for. *"We introduce it during stage two, when the programme is less demanding and more flexible,"* Morrissey tells us. *"The scheme has been very well received by students. In 2012/13 all who applied successfully secured a place."*

Graduates say...

"They have quite a good contact network within Cardiff for law students. A handful of students from USW have come to the firm I'm at for work experience."

The *Chambers Student* verdict

South Wales' LPC is a good shout for those who want to be taught via a mix of lectures and workshops, in a location close to – though not smack dab in the middle of – the action.

Staffordshire University

Number of places: 150 FTE
Fees (2014/15): £10,250

The course

'Flexibility' is the catchword surrounding Staffordshire University's LPC; there are more study options available here than you can shake a stick at. If you're after the full-time offering, for example, you can opt for sessions four days a week, narrow it down to two, or spread it across one day and two evening classes. Meanwhile, part-timers used to be able to choose between one day, two evenings or a combo of day and evening classes per week, but the option for two evenings has now been scrapped because *"students working alongside their studies were finding it quite difficult to cope,"* explains LPC award manager Catherine Edwards. On top of all this, the full and part-time routes both offer a 'blended learning' option, which sees roughly 90% of the course delivered online with the remainder saved for face-to-face teaching. If you don't pick that, however, then expect to be taught via a mix of lectures and workshops, the latter usually containing no more than 20 students in each. The flexibility of Staffordshire's LPC extends to the LLM path: students can study for it alongside the LPC, or pursue the top-up LLM route when they complete the LPC.

The electives are designed with the profession heavily in mind. In fact, the vast majority of them have direct input from firms and legal bodies: *"One of our specialist electives is public child law,"* Edwards tells us, *"and that's developed in collaboration with Staffordshire County Council. Then for others we'll have firm reps come in and lead some sessions, as lawyers from Knights do for private client."*

The location and facilities

The law school can be found on the university's Stoke-on-Trent campus, which is a stone's throw away from the railway station as well as the Potteries shopping centre. The school itself has a mock courtroom with video equipment, group study rooms and a law library. What's more, all the workshops are taught in 'Practice Offices' – spaces kitted out with computers, printers and e-resources – and students can also use them for private study. On the pro bono front, Staffordshire's legal advice clinic is one of the main ways for students to get involved. Edwards hints that *"the university is looking to develop the level of advice the clinic can provide,"* so watch this space.

Careers services and prospects

Careers lectures and workshops are put on by a dedicated careers tutor and law school alumni, who *"can talk about their own experiences in the legal world. It shows we don't just wave goodbye to our students once they leave,"* Edwards says. The careers tutor is also on hand to *"give specialist advice,"* and stages mock interviews and drop-in sessions, among other careers-related services. There's a mentoring scheme too, enabling students to be paired up with practitioners in the local area. *"They alert us to vacancies at their respective firms,"* Edwards tells us, *"and ultimately help add to our bank of knowledge surrounding the local legal market."*

The *Chambers Student* verdict

Busy bees with work commitments will no doubt be attracted to Staffordshire's extensive menu of study options for the LPC.

Swansea University

Number of places: 100 FTE
Fees (2014/15): £10,000

The course

A hallmark of Swansea University's LPC is its guarantee of ample class contact time, explains associate professor Michael Draper, *"for the simple reason that student feedback shows there's still a strong desire for it."* As such, those on the full-time course go along to three sessions a week, each one lasting around four or five hours, with part-timers attending two a week – one in the day and another in the evening – over two years. These are all taught

through a combo of large and small group sessions; the smaller ones have a somewhat practical spin, focusing on real-life case studies and transactional tasks, while the bigger offerings *"are backed up by electronic materials on our Blackboard site,"* Draper tells us.

The course is essentially split into two. Stage One takes place over the initial 24 weeks and covers the core practice areas, and is then followed by Stage Two, which has students picking three electives to study out of the following six: advanced commercial law; business leases; employment law & practice; advanced criminal practice; family & child care law and practice; and personal injury and clinical negligence. Draper picks out the business leases elective as a bit of a USP: *"Seeing as it focuses on leases in particular, it's a very different option to the standard commercial property module that most other LPCs offer,"* he says.

The location and facilities

'In a park, by the beach, near the city' – that's how the university summarises its location on its website. And who could deny the appeal of that? Nestled among parkland and stunning botanical gardens, the campus looks out onto Swansea Bay and is on the fringe of the Gower Peninsula. It's fair to say the scenery's rather different from that of inner-city law schools – plus the lively city centre is only a 10-minute drive away. What's more, when we spoke to Draper the law school was is in the midst of receiving a welcome dose of TLC: *"All our teaching rooms are being redeveloped this year,"* he reveals, *"so for the 2014/15 intake everything will be brand new."* There are also plenty of extracurricular opportunities available to give students' CVs that extra gloss. The Pro Bono Clinic enables those on the LPC to impart their legal wisdom to other students at the university, and Draper adds that it's *"currently being revamped to reflect our close ties with the Citizens Advice Bureau."* Interestingly, the law department itself has started taking on students for work experience, an initiative that will expand over the coming months and lead to paid internships being offered in the summer.

Careers services and prospects

While law students can make use of the university's main careers service, Draper tells us that *"many actually turn to us, the tutors, for careers guidance."* Thanks to a lot of the staff boasting affiliations with the local legal market and holding esteemed positions outside the university – Draper himself is a member of the Wales Committee Law Society – it proves an effective way for some to secure a relevant job to walk into after the LPC. On top of this, students are granted the unique opportunity of picking the brains of firm reps on a few Fridays during Stage Two of the course.

The *Chambers Student* verdict

If you can handle the occasional bouts of torrential Welsh rain, then the LPC at Swansea University is a great shout with its idyllic setting, extracurricular offerings and eclectic mix of teaching modes.

University of West London

Number of places: 60 FTE
Fees (2014/15): £9,470

The course

Those on UWL's full-time LPC can expect to attend full-day sessions every Tuesday and Thursday, plus half-day sessions on Wednesdays, while the part-time offering is normally taught on Tuesdays in the first year and then on Thursdays in the second year, with an additional class on Wednesday evenings. Sessions *"usually comprise two-hour workshops with a brief introductory lecture at the start followed by student-led work for the remainder,"* senior lecturer Khalid Butt tells us. Class sizes are relatively small, with no more than 20 students in each. Among the many online resources available are preparatory materials accessible through the school's Blackboard site.

A key feature of the university's LPC is an integrated careers module: *"During the electives stage, there's a weekly programme run by the careers service that offers interviewing and CV-writing advice, and tips about networking,"* explains Butt. He adds that *"the feedback element of our course is very strong – we make sure we give students feedback rather than waiting for them to come to us."* Indeed, the university runs a one-on-one appraisal scheme throughout the course.

The location and facilities

As part of UWL's ongoing multimillion-pound redevelopment, the Ealing law school has been given a full makeover in recent years. One of the newest features is an in-house mock courtroom, *"where we run our moot and advocacy sessions,"* Butt says. This complements the university's other mock courtroom, which was introduced in 2013, and is based on the main campus and used for open days, judicial training and national mooting events. There's also the main library, which includes a dedicated room for LPC students. Topping the school's pro bono offering is its Community Advice Programme, an advice clinic run in conjunction with the Ealing Equality Council. *"It used to be separate but is now housed within the school,"* Butt says, *"so that's given students much greater access to it."*

Careers services and prospects

To boost students' employment prospects the law school runs work placement schemes with a handful of local firms. The school's close relationship with the Middlesex Law Society also offers students the chance to pick the brains of solicitors and trainees based in the area.

Something else to add a bit of gloss to students' CVs is a recently introduced law school magazine, *"to which students can contribute researched articles of specific interests. It's a great outlet for them to put their thoughts into writing,"* says Butt.

The *Chambers Student* verdict

The integrated careers module makes this provider a decent option on the employability front. Plus, there's no denying Ealing's a pretty swish neighbourhood.

University of Westminster

Number of places: 120 FT, 64 PT
Fees (2014/15): £11,500 FT, £5,750 PT

The course

Westminster Law School is handily placed just off Oxford Street, and offers its students more than just fashion bargains thanks to significantly lower fees than other London providers. The catch? Less than stellar rates of students with prestigious training contracts and less flexibility than neighbouring schools.

Teaching for full-timers takes place three set days a week, on Mondays, Tuesdays and Thursdays from 10:30am to 4:30pm. Part-timers are allocated two evenings a week out of Tuesday, Wednesday and Thursday, from 5.45pm to 9pm. Tutorials last for two and a half hours, and take place in groups of around 15, and there are also hour-long lectures which are a mixture of online and in person. There are tutorial handout and online tests available through the school's intranet.

Students can pick from a decent spread of private client and commercial electives. There's also pro bono work on offer, including land registry and immigration work from the school's dedicated centre, which offers seven or so opportunities a term. Students doing the school's popular clinical elective escape the stress of exams and get to learn on the job – they're assessed by writing a report and then doing a viva on the pro bono work they've done.

The location and facilities

The LPC is part of a law school that's based away from the rest of the university. The building has recently been refurbished to add a new lecture theatre, and also offers a library, a dedicated LPC study room, and an on-site cafe.

Careers services and prospects

The school's relatively limited careers service has a dedicated careers adviser on hand who helps with applications and arranges CV and psychometric test workshop sessions, as well as organising an annual careers fair. The school also offers a mentoring scheme, which pairs up current students with former Westminster LPC students who are in practice. Course administrator Miles MacLeod reports that *"we had a couple of success stories this year where students got their CVs looked at by their mentor's firms and ended up with training contracts, although obviously there are no guarantees."*

Around 40% of the cohort are students taking the course externally through the University of London. Students who hail from London often have 2.2s. Graduates most commonly end up at high-street firms in and around London, or work as paralegals.

Graduates say...

One graduate of the law school's GDL course reported that *"Westminster wasn't necessarily a centre of excellence but they did their best. By and large the quality of the other students wasn't hugely high, but I had good relationships with the tutors."*

The *Chambers Student* verdict

The Oxford Street location's great for shopaholics, but you'll have to do some serious shopping around to bag a training contract that's off the high street.

University of Wolverhampton

Number of places: 60 FT, 30 PT
Fees (2014/15): £9,250

The course

Wolverhampton's LPC is largely defined by its small intake, course leader Chris Busst tells us: *"Students have always loved having so much access to the tutors, so we've always tried to maintain that."* Every subject entails a one-hour lecture followed by a couple of small group workshops that consist of only 12 to 15 students each. Full-timers attend these classes during the first three days of the week, while part-timers are on campus twice a week. There are also extra skills assessments that run on Fridays for full-time students and Saturdays for those on the part-time option. The extensive collection of online resources available includes pre-recorded lectures, multiple-choice quizzes, handbooks, legal databases and other materials – all of which are uploaded to 'Wolf', the uni-

versity's intranet. The week leading up to Christmas sees students team up to form individual 'firms' and follow instructions set for them via the portal. It's worth noting that an LLM top-up is available at a reduced sum of £720.

The location and facilities

The law school's on-campus location means that *"all the university's services are right on our doorstep,"* Busst points out. The school has its own set of dedicated facilities to boot, including a specialist resources room in the library and a courtroom that plays host to the Bar and Mooting Society. Wolverhampton isn't exactly the most glamorous of cities, though the powers that be are doing their bit to change its image: the local Mander shopping centre is currently undergoing a £30m transformation, and there are plans for revamp of the train station too.

One of the school's most notable extracurricular offerings is its legal advice clinic, based in the Mander shopping centre. Busst highlights a couple of other initiatives for obtaining legal experience, such as the McKenzie Friend scheme run by the National Centre for Domestic Violence: *"They recently extended it to allow students to get involved."*

Careers services and prospects

The school has expanded its careers services considerably over the past year or so. The long-standing mentoring scheme run in connection with local firms has been extended through a partnership with top-20 UK powerhouse DWF – members of its Birmingham office now offer Wolvo's law students guidance on topics like how to obtain a training contract and, more generally, life in the profession. A number of other professionals come in throughout the year to give career-related presentations too, and November 2013 saw the university host its first ever law careers fair, which saw the likes of Mills & Reeve, Irwin Mitchell, Eversheds and DWF attend.

The *Chambers Student* verdict

If you like the sound of petite class sizes and an active careers service, this is an option worthy of consideration. The course is predominantly inhabited by Wulfrunians and those from surrounding areas, but Busst says: *"We also encourage applications from students who aren't local."*

Ethnicity and the law

Christian Frederick Cole was the first black African to be called to the Bar in 1883

Over a hundred Indian men were called to the Bar in the 1880s, including Mahatma Gandhi in 1888

13% of barristers pro-moted to QC in 2014 were from ethnic minority backgrounds

27.5 % of trainees registered in 2013 with known ethnicity were drawn from BME groups

13.1% of solicitors come from a minority ethnic group. 8.2% of these are of Chinese and Asian origin; black lawyers tend to be proportionally under represented.

*Figures from the Law Society and Bar Council.

The Bar Professional Training Course (BPTC)

The BPTC is the necessary link between either an LLB or GDL and pupillage for would-be barristers. Nine law schools are authorised by the Bar Standards Board (BSB) to teach the course at locations in London, Bristol, Cardiff, Nottingham, Manchester, Leeds and Newcastle. The full-time course lasts a year; the part-time option is spread over two. Those with the gift of the gab, step up please.

A career at the Bar? You may need your health checked

Unfortunately it's not just LPC students who are finding it increasingly difficult to find employment at the end of a time-consuming and costly course: those chasing a career at the Bar are also facing the prospect of being well trained and highly qualified, but with little more than a £15k-sized hole in their pockets to show for it.

The current disparity between the legions of BPTC graduates and the relatively miserly amount of available pupillages means the BSB has deemed it necessary to put out a 'health warning' to prospective barristers: *"We need to give a signal to those who aren't up to it that they're wasting their money* [or risk] *gaining an army of enemies,"* says Lady Deech, Chair of the BSB (whose stint will finish at the end of 2014). Strong words, but a quick glance at the recent employment statistics of those called to the Bar would give even the next Dinah Rose something to ponder.

The BSB states in its health warning that applicants should 'consider some of the facts and figures concerning a career at the Bar before you commit yourself'. It outlines that approximately 1,700 students take the Bar course each year but typically only around 480 are offered pupillages.

According to the BSB, in 2010/11 there were 1,407 students who enrolled on the BPTC (after 3,099 applied), but only 446 first-six pupillages were up for grabs that year. (The Bar Council was unable to provide us with any more recent statistics.) It's important to also bear in mind that the BPTC has a lifespan of five years, so this figure includes graduates from previous years who were unsuccessful in their first, second, third or even fourth attempt. Over 3,000 individuals may be applying for pupillage in any given year, while chambers regularly receive over 100 applications for a single position.

The odds are clearly stacked against aspiring barristers, and most students will have to strike the right balance between *"realism and optimism; they know it's tough, but then again you always think that you will be the one to get a pupillage."*

The quest for a pupillage can look almost as daunting as Frodo's ring-destroying adventure when you consider the qualifications of those who do make the cut; the academic records of new tenants are quite simply terrifying. Some 35% hold First-class degrees (less than 5% of new tenants graduated with 2:2s) and a similar percentage attended Oxbridge. Another third will have attended a Russell Group university. Throw into the mix a bountiful array of MAs, PhDs, academic prizes, scholarships and languages and you can see that the competition is fierce.

As Lady Deech says: *"If you're tone deaf, don't go to music school; if you have two left feet don't go to ballet school"* – with reference to BPTC students who lack the required command of the English language. The point is, winning arguments over the dinner table and fancying yourself as Atticus Finch or Mark Darcy just isn't going to cut it. You really need to make a cold, hard assessment of whether you can cut it in the profession.

In 2009 and 2010, the BSB piloted an aptitude test for the BPTC as a more proactive way of protecting wide-eyed students, while also looking to ensure the future strength and quality of the Bar. Now all prospective students have to undertake the BCAT and they must achieve a minimum required standard in logic and reasoning questions in order to take up their place on the BPTC. Oh, and they must also shell out a £150 fee to take the test.

The move to give the go-ahead for this test has been a controversial one, with the Law Society flagging up various concerns about the viability of the BCAT, especially since the Legal Education and Training Review rejected proposals for an aptitude test for LPC students on 'diversity grounds'. A homogenisation of the Bar has been predicted by some, but Legal Services Board chief executive Chris Kenny told the *Solicitors Journal* that the validity of these concerns is *"impossible to verify in absolute terms at this stage."* The BSB is therefore undertaking a five-year data gathering and evaluation period, after which a decision will be made about the ongoing use of the BCAT.

BPTC providers (apart from Kaplan, which already ran an aptitude test) were on the whole *"unconvinced that aptitude tests tell you much more than a paper application."* Sources at Nottingham Law School, which runs the exact same course as Kaplan but without a prerequisite aptitude test, said that *"the profile of the students at both institutions is remarkably similar,"* and that exam results demonstrate an equal level of *"those who are competent and those who aren't."* One welcome outcome is that the test is likely to protect certain misguided students from the burden of a heavy debt unnecessarily incurred, but we'll have to wait a few more years before the true worth of an aptitude test is fully known.

2:2 boohoo

A second contention in enlisting quality candidates onto the BPTC arises from course providers. The BSB's minimum requirement for admission onto the courses is a 2:2 at degree level, and a pass on the GDL (where taken). Several providers have chosen to up the ante. Kaplan, for example, now requires all applicants to possess a 2:1, and even those subsequently shortlisted will have to attend an assessment day, where they undertake a written advocacy exercise, an oral advocacy exercise and an interview. As sources there say: *"We need students who can fire on all cylinders."*

In fact, most providers will be looking for students with at least a 2:1, and according to recent statistics over 60% of BPTC students across all providers had this qualification or higher. One course leader told us: *"In line with BSB requirements we never outrightly say no to someone with a 2:2, but increasingly we have looked to recruit people with at least a 2:1 and mini-pupillage or practical experience. They have to have a fighting chance."*

Success at the Bar is based on more than impeccable academics and most providers are on the lookout for an applicant's commitment to practice, either through public speaking, such as mooting or debating, or relevant work experience. This is no different for the sets offering pupillage, so if a life at the Bar is the one for you, do everything you can to stand out from the crowd.

The mismatch between BPTC graduates and the number of pupillages is tempered to a certain extent by those individuals who have decided that the Bar is simply not for them, and by the significant number of international students (estimated at between 20 and 25% of all BPTC

students) who return home rather than seeking pupillage in England and Wales.

The international contingent may be set to fall as many course providers, prompted by the BSB, are getting tougher on their entry requirements as concerns English language ability. Currently the BSB requires all students whose first language is not English or Welsh to demonstrate that they have a minimum 7.5 IELTS standard, or equivalent. Over the past few years we've heard rumbling criticisms that some students' English just isn't up to scratch, which causes difficulties in the classroom for other students practising key skills that rely on rhetorical ability. It seems that law schools are finally reacting, taking steps to ensure applicants possess the required standard of English.

Mad skillz

The BPTC has been designed to ensure that wannabe barristers acquire the skills, knowledge, attitudes and competencies needed for practice. Cue: developing students' advocacy, drafting, opinion writing, conferencing, case analysis and legal research skills. As for knowledge, students are schooled in civil litigation and remedies, criminal litigation and sentencing, evidence, and professional ethics.

These core areas, especially ethics, are essential because *"barristers are individuals, and they get thrown to the wolves more often. When you're a solicitor you have the protection of the firm around you – barristers have to be equipped with all the knowledge they can get."* In the final term, students select two option subjects in areas they're targeting for practice.

Almost wherever you study the emphasis is very much on face-to-face teaching – usually to groups of about 12, but for all-important skills there's often six students or fewer. Still, many use computers in lectures to make learning more stimulating, while writing skills classes often involve the use of whiteboards.

Oral skills classes make increasing use of video-recording equipment in role-plays so students can improve by assessing their own performance as well as that of their peers. The skills acquired are then examined using a variety of assessments in the second and third terms.

Written skills are tested through a mix of unseen tests and 'homework', and the BSB recently permitted students at BPP to type their written skills assessment for the first time. Professional actors are commonly drafted in to take part in oral assessments.

One area where the BPTC differs most from its predecessor (the Bar Vocational Course) is its focus on alternative dispute resolution (ADR). A new 'resolution of disputes out of court' module replaced the old negotiation skills course, heralding a broader approach to avoiding litigation.

Though skills assessments will continue to be set and marked by the individual providers, the future of testing knowledge has changed. The BSB now sets standardised and centralised exams for civil litigation, criminal litigation and ethics to ensure confidence in the parity between course providers. The exams consist of a blend of multiple choice questions and short answer questions. The latter are still marked locally by the providers, while the former are centrally marked by a computer. The BSB then samples and moderates the written exam papers.

This was all introduced for the first time in 2012 and the response from both providers and students hasn't been hugely positive. Providers' responses ranged from moderate annoyance to full-on fury: *"I'm upset about it, to the point where I want to run to the BSB with a pitchfork in hand."* Students were also unimpressed, and hundreds signed a petition to the BSB expressing their dissatisfaction. As one provider subsequently put it: *"As long as I can remember exams were set locally; if you did the course at Nottingham, then Nottingham set the exams and marked them. The assessments were aimed at what students could be expected to know based on the teaching at that institution. It's just inevitable when exams are centralised that the questions are going to be one step removed from the providers – the exams may cover things that students haven't come across before."*

While some students haven't done as well under the new system, others have actually thrived, and providers told us that *"in the end our students ended up doing more or less how they expected they would. Our pass rates are not dissimilar to what they were last year."* The problem, then, seems to be with the stress of having to revise a vaster body of material than ever before...

All systems go

Course directors tell us that the BPTC is *"a very demanding, intensive and rigorous course."* The timetable is described as *"undulating"* – *"intense in parts and boring in others"* – and often the course is *"front-loaded."* But don't use the quieter times to relax. This is your chance to improve your pupillage prospects, as one student advised: *"Organise dining with the Inns, mooting, debating, pro bono, mini-pupillages, marshalling and the like to give your CV a fighting chance of reaching interview stage."*

It's essential to look carefully at the extracurricular opportunities offered at each provider and throw yourself into everything you can. Most providers will deliberately keep days free of classes to allow students this opportunity.

How to apply through BPTC online

An application for the BPTC costs £40, and the process is all done online. There is no cap on the number of providers you may apply to, although during the first phase of the process only your top-three choices will look at your application. While many providers will say that it's not vital that you put their institution as a top choice, many popular providers fill their places with first and second-choice applicants alone. Prioritise your favourites if you want to avoid disappointment.

How to pick a provider

The fight for pupillage is a truly testing one, so choose your course provider carefully. Read through prospectuses and websites, attend open days, try to speak to current or former students. Read our **BPTC Provider Reports** and consider the following criteria:

Cost: London is clearly going to be pricier than Northumbria, but even in the capital there's variation. If you're an international student, look at the differential in price. Part-timers should note whether fees increase in the second year.

Location: Regional providers may be the best option for those looking for pupillage on the regional circuits, not least because of their stronger links and networking opportunities with the local Bar. London students benefit from proximity to the Inns of Court and easier access to London sets for pupillage interviews. However, compulsory dining and advocacy training courses in the Inns enable regional students to maintain their links with the capital's beating legal heart.

Size: Smaller providers pride themselves on offering a more intimate and collegial environment, and student feedback indicates that this does make a positive difference to the experience. You can also expect a noticeably different feel at the providers that are within universities to those that aren't.

Facilities: Students can tap into a far wider range of support services, sports and social activities by taking the BPTC at a university. Library and IT resources vary from one provider to the next, as does the level of technology used in teaching. Some providers make technology a key feature of the course.

Option subjects: Available option subjects vary. For example, although judicial review and immigration are popular, they're not offered everywhere. Check out our **Table of BPTC Providers** online to see what's on offer at each one. This table also compares fees and offers provider-specific application tips.

Pro Bono: Opportunities range from minimal to superb across the nine providers. Again our **Table of BPTC Providers** has the details.

Law School

BPTC Provider Reports

Which of the law schools teaching the BPTC will be right for you? All quotes come from course directors or other official sources at the providers.

BPP Law School

Number of places: 360 FT, 144 PT (see 'location and facilities' for full breakdown)
Fees (2014/15): £14,740 in Leeds and Manchester, £17,925 in London

The course

BPP is one of the leading BPTC providers, and it continues to add to its impressive offering. In 2013 the legal education giant introduced new software to help students speed up their opinion writing and drafting assessments, and recently added electives in international trade; public international criminal law; and asylum, detention, deportation and extradition (note: these are currently only available in London). It's also launched a BPTC offering in its Manchester centre. According to co-director Anna Banfield, *"we're looking more outside the core requirements of the course to help students prepare for practice, and we're also striving to establish links with more barristers' chambers."*

Along with the new Manchester course, BPP offers the BPTC in London (Holborn) and Leeds; Banfield assures us *"the course is identical across all three centres."* Full-timers attend sessions four days a week, with Monday or Friday usually freed up; meanwhile part-timers pop along to classes one weekend a month over the course of two years.

Most sessions are taught in small groups, partly because *"we have to comply with the BSB rulebook"* and partly because *"a lot of what we teach is skills-based, and it doesn't make sense for that to be done in large groups,"* Banfield tells us. Advocacy sessions consist of just four students each. The entire cohort is occasionally brought together for lectures, but most of these can be viewed online, a decision made in response to student feedback, Banfield says: *"They prefer to watch those in their own time to make sure they digest the info properly."* Our sources confirmed this, with one telling us: *"I appreciated not having to go to every lecture. Other providers make you do a certain number of hours each week, but I don't think that necessarily benefits your final grade."*

Feedback is pretty frequent: oral feedback is given during each small group session, and students are critiqued on each of their oral skills performances. They also receive formal written feedback on at least two bits of work.

Students who complete the BPTC at BPP are able to study additional credits in order to graduate with an LLM in professional legal practice or a law with business MA.

The location and facilities

London (Holborn)
Number of places: 264 FT, 96 PT

The majority of BPTC students head to Holborn. The branch has more than 300 computers, as well as a 94-seat student common room, mock courtrooms and a library with silent study areas. The campus is handy for budding barristers as it's a pebble's throw away from the Inns of Court and a flock of barristers' chambers. Of course, nobody wants to spend all their downtime roaming around the stamping grounds of folks in the profession, so we should add that the vibrant Covent Garden, Soho and Leicester Square are all within walking distance too.

Leeds
Number of places: 48 FT, 48 PT

Leeds may be a smaller branch than Holborn, but it's in just as convenient a spot. The train station and Trinity – a brand spanking new shopping centre – are both in close proximity, and if you're into your gigs and theatrical spectacles then know the O2 Academy and Grand Theatre aren't too far away, either. The centre itself contains much the same as the others, including mock courtrooms, a library and lecture theatre.

Manchester
Number of places: 48 FT

Still relatively new to the BPTC scene, BPP's Manchester offshoot only offers the full-time option for now and thus has the smallest cohort of the three centres. Oxford Road and Piccadilly train stations are two and ten minutes away respectively, and also nearby are the Arndale shopping centre, the Palace Theatre, the Opera House, and the many bars and eateries that comprise Spinningfields. More importantly, there are a good number of barristers' chambers close to campus, which has a 108-seat lecture theatre, ten classrooms, a library with 200 students and, like the others, a pro bono centre.

Careers services and prospects

BPP offers an array of services to aid students in their quest for a pupillage. A careers team is on hand to offer general guidance on CVs, cover letters and applications, and there's also a BPTC careers officer who arranges mock interviews and talks from legal pros. The provider organises mock trial and mooting events across the year – with practitioners and members of the judiciary coming in to judge them – as well as pupillage-related lectures and court visits.

BPP students have to commit at least five hours to pro bono. The pro bono centre collaborates with bodies like FRU, Liberty, Streetlaw and the Royal Courts of Justice, and it's possible for students to bring in their own matters too, subject to approval.

Following in the footsteps of its LPC, the BPTC at BPP now comes with a career guarantee. This means those who haven't secured pupillage within six months of completing the BPTC are able to study another qualification at BPP free of charge. This includes the LPC. *"There's always a worry that really bright students won't want to take a risk by pursuing the Bar,"* Banfield says, *"so it's crucial for the profession that we look at ways to help students succeed."*

Graduates say...

"They do a good job of introducing you to the basics of civil and common law, and the advocacy sessions are quite useful too. Some of the other modules seem a little less helpful, though."

The *Chambers Student* verdict

If you can afford the fees, BPP is well worth considering, not least for its wealth of electives and career services.

Bristol Institute of Legal Practice at UWE

Number of places: 84 FT, 48 PT
Fees (2014/15): £12,965 FT, £6,483 PT (year one)
Awards: 15% discount for UWE graduates

The course

BILP's full-time BPTC involves 16 hours of contact time spread over three to four days a week, with Fridays kept free for pro bono or private study. Part-time students, meanwhile, have a four-day induction period followed by 11 study weekends a year. Teaching groups are small, with about six to ten students in each. Electives include clinical negligence, criminal, employment, competition, commercial, family, international trade, and refugee and asylum law.

Students here have the opportunity to qualify as commercial mediators at no extra cost. They can also qualify as family mediators at a discounted rate. It's worth bearing in mind the law school doesn't offer one-to-one advocacy training like pricier providers such as City.

The location and facilities

BILP's BPTC is run on the university's Frenchay campus, four miles outside Bristol. Barristers in training have access to a 24-hour law library, a canteen for cheap nosh and the university's vast fitness and sports centre, complete with an indoor climbing wall.

BILP's Community Legal Advice and Representation Service (CLARS) – which sees students team up with practitioners on the Western Circuit to assist during hearings at Bristol's civil courts – is the centrepiece of its pro bono offering. Back on campus the law school puts on regular practice trials involving professional actors in its mock courtrooms, which are fitted with recorded equipment. (Of course, the subject matter is likely to be more 'alas, you got nicked' than 'alas, poor Yorick.')

Careers services and prospects

BILP's links with the Western Circuit extend to advocacy master classes and practice pupillage interviews with local practitioners. Local chambers sponsor three advocacy competitions and a mooting competition through the year. These links certainly come in handy when pupillage applications roll round, though it's worth remembering there are only a handful of pupil places a year to fight for in Bristol's smallish legal scene.

The *Chambers Student* verdict

With its rural location and close ties to local sets, this school is a good bet for those interested in forging a career in the Western Circuit.

Cardiff Law School

Number of places: 84 FT
Fees (2014/15): £13,000

The course

Most students on this course are drawn in by the opportunity to study at the only Russell Group university to run a BPTC. It doesn't hurt that Cardiff guarantees its aspiring barristers a two-week placement scheme and offers more contact time than rival providers, either. Students here attend 14 hours' worth of sessions a week, which take place between 9am and 5pm, Monday to Thursday. These mix knowledge and writing skills seminars, which take place in groups of 12, with advocacy classes in smaller groups of six.

The two-week placement includes a mini-pupillage at a local barristers set and a stint marshalling with a district or circuit level judge. Optional extras include a day-long expert witness handling seminar, a day of arbitration training and a Welsh advocacy course for fluent students.

location and facilities

BPTC students attend class in two buildings on the university campus, which is just outside Cardiff city centre, near Cathays Park. The park plays host to civic buildings like Cardiff Crown Court and the National Museum, as well as rolling lawns and formal gardens. When students aren't lolling on the grass, they benefit from teaching rooms equipped with electronic whiteboards and recording facilities; they also have access to the substantial university library opposite the law school. The university recently replaced its dedicated legal practice library with a computer-laden study space for postgraduate law students.

Pro bono opportunities include work for Welsh rugby clubs, the NHS continuing healthcare scheme and children's charity Cerebra. Students also have the chance to train with Cardiff's Personal Support Unit, which sees them advise litigants.

Careers services and prospects

Cardiff's careers services group runs a mixture of large group sessions on CV writing and pupillage applications, and one-to-one sessions for advice and mock interviews.

Course leader Jetsun Lebasci tells us only a handful of students here secure pupillages by the end of their BPTC year, although more may go on to do so later. The course's high proportion of international students is likely a contributing factor, as is the fact that Cardiff lacks the established reputation of rival operators.

The *Chambers Student* verdict

This course is worth crossing the border for if you want to undertake the BPTC at a well-known university. There's no need to speak Welsh to study in Cymru's capital, either.

City Law School, London

Number of places: 360 FT, 30-36 PT
Fees (2014/15): £17,500

The course

City's BPTC used to be known as the Inns of Court Law School, a prestigious operator that trained four British prime ministers – Tony Blair, Margaret Thatcher, Clement Atlee and Herbert Asquith – as well as Mahatma Gandhi and just about every 20th-century British barrister. The school might have lost its monopoly on training barristers back in 1997, but its prestige value remains. In exchange for the heftiest fees of any provider, it offers a location in the heart of legal London and an array of legal superstars popping back in to lecture, including retired High Court judge Dame Linda Dobbs and controversial Lord Chancellor Chris Grayling – history doesn't relate if he needed an armed escort.

Another bonus of the school is that your class lecturer may have literally written the book on the course areas – tutors are experienced practitioners and academics who've written many of the BPTC course manuals. Teaching is structured so that topics are introduced by lectures, then followed up by seminars in groups of 12. There are also two one-on-one advocacy classes, as well as student advocacy performances, lecture videos and course notes available on the school's intranet. Full-time students attend classes on three days a week. They get 12 hours of contact time, scheduled between 10.30am and 6pm to miss rush hour fare prices. Part-timers come in on two set evenings a week from 6-9pm.

There are electives in social security, advanced crime, commercial law, company, domestic violence, employment, family, fraud and economic crime, employment, landlord and tenant, and professional negligence.

The location and facilities

City's barristers-in-waiting are ensconced right in the midst of some of the lawyerly lairs they'll hope to join. The school's lecture hall overlooks Gray's Inn Gardens, and you pass numerous other barristers' sets on the two-minute walk to the newly refurbished tutorial facilities.

Law School

The course's highly active student society gets a budget to organise regular moots and has sent teams to compete as far afield as the European Court of Human Rights in Strasbourg. There's also similarly international pro bono work, including a scheme where three students work on human rights issues over the summer in South Africa, and a death row appeal programme in conjunction with Amnesty.

Careers services and prospects

City Law School is cagey about the proportion of its students that gain pupillages, pointing to the large and established quotient of overseas students. Still, although shelling out for the hefty course fees certainly won't guarantee anyone a pupillage, the school's established reputation means it won't hold back talented aspiring barristers either.

Help is at hand both from City University Law School's careers service and from a dedicated pupillage advice service staffed by teachers on the course, which offers one-to-one advice and mock interviews.

Graduates say...

"The cost places expectations unrealistically high, so I can understand that some people feel frustrated by the number of hours. But overall it's a good course, and I thought the staff were mostly very motivated and committed to it."

The *Chambers Student* verdict

If prestige is what you're after, City's course has it by the yacht-load. It's pricey but in fact a few hundred pounds less than its chief rivals, BPP and University of Law.

University of Law

Number of places: 240 FT, 48 PT
Fees (2014/15): See below for breakdown
Awards: £1,500 alumni discount; 10 awards of £5,000 each for students with a 2:1, subject to online skills assessment

The course

The University of Law's BPTC hasn't got the starriest of reputations or alumni compared to longer established providers like City University. Still, the course has the might of a national legal education juggernaut behind it and looks set on upping its game. Following Kaplan's recent closure of its widely praised BPTC course – which at 55% boasted the highest pupillage rates of any provider – UoL managed to land Kaplan's former BPTC head Lynda Gibbs to redesign its own course, making for an exciting range of employability-boosting changes. The institution now offers enhanced learning materials, advocacy com-

petitions sponsored by London chambers, a mentoring scheme in conjunction with the school's alumni, and extracurricular advocacy and conference classes.

Still, it's unlikely UoL's laser focus on the financial bottom line will see it emulate Kaplan's rigorous admissions procedure, wherein only students with a 2:1 or above were admitted. Bar Standards Board reports show a high proportion of UoL students don't meet that threshold, particularly at the Birmingham branch.

Full-time BPTC students get up to 17.5 hours of training a week, including up to three and half hours of one-to-one sessions. Part-timers study 14 weekends a year over two years – each weekend involves up to 14 hours of contact time. Classes are generally delivered in small groups of no more than 12 and last for a marathon three and a half hours each. There are also advocacy sessions conducted in groups of between two and six. Electives range from criminal litigation and judicial review to family, personal injury, and immigration practice and asylum.

UoL boasts that its BPTC offers three times as much advocacy training as the Bar Standards Board minimum requirement. Students can put these polished advocacy skills on trial at practitioner events, where they perform in front of real judges and barristers in real courtrooms. In 2013, 225 barristers attended such events, so they're a good place to see and be seen. UoL also runs regular mooting competitions and pro bono opportunities through organisations like Liberty Letters and the National Coalition Against Domestic Violence.

The location and facilities

Birmingham
Fees: £13,450
The small Birmingham branch has *"well-equipped"* facilities in the heart of the city's Jewellery Quarter. The area houses hundreds of workshops that make and shops that sell British-worked gems, plus museums, bars and restaurants. Among the centre's features are course-specific workshop rooms – complete with courtroom furniture – plus a student common room and a handful of quiet study areas.

London
Fees: £17,700
The most prestigious BPTC provider in London is City Law School. UoL shares joint second place in reputation with BPP, though it's worth noting that both of these institutions charge several hundred pounds more in fees for their BPTC course. Grads of the Bloomsbury branch, the largest in the UoL system, spoke of a *"lively atmosphere"* thanks to the institution's large size and wide mix of peo-

The University of Law

Braboeuf Manor, Portsmouth Road, St Catherines, Guildford GU3 1HA
Freephone 0800 289997 International (+44) (0)1483 216000
Email: admissions@law.ac.uk
Website: www.law.ac.uk
Twitter: @UniversityofLaw

University profile

At The University of Law you'll get the best possible start to your legal career. We've been around for over 100 years and have trained more lawyers than anyone else. We offer first-class careers advice and support and have an outstanding employability record. With eight centres across the country, we're the first choice for aspiring solicitors or barristers looking for effective legal training. Our innovative courses are designed and taught by lawyers, with a clear focus on building the practical skills, commercial awareness and independent thinking you need to succeed in legal practice.

Graduate Diploma in Law – full-time/part-time/i-GDL (supported online learning programme)

The University of Law GDL is designed to build knowledge and skills that more than match a law degree – with a clear focus on preparing you for life in practice. Academic training is built around real-life examples and case studies and you'll be given research assignments that directly reflect the way you'll work as a lawyer. In addition, its unique Preparing for Practice module equips you with the professional skills you'll need as a modern lawyer.

The University of Law GDL is the first choice of many leading law firms and over 30 send their trainees exclusively to us.

LLM Legal Practice Course – full-time/part-time/i-LLM LPC (supported online learning programme)

When you study your LPC at The University of Law, you can qualify with a Masters. Our LLM in Legal Practice LPC, as well as being your LPC, is also an internationally-recognised Masters qualification with the scope to specialise in international or national legal practice. The cost of the LLM LPC is the same as for a traditional LPC and if you want to qualify with a Masters, you'll need to complete a Professional Practice Dissertation.

Graduating with The University of Law LLM LPC, means you will be better prepared and more employable for modern legal services than graduates from any other law school. Your LLM will be recognised globally as the leading qualification in legal services.

The University of Law LPC is the first choice of many leading law firms and over 30 send their trainees exclusively to us.

Bar Professional Training Course – full-time/part-time

The University of Law BPTC has been designed to resemble practice as closely as possible. Study follows a logical, realistic process from initial instruction to final appeal and learning is based around the seven core skills and three knowledge areas stipulated by the Bar Standards Board. Most of your learning will be in small groups and you'll have plenty of opportunities to put your learning into action through: practitioner evenings, mock trials, court visits, mooting, negotiating and advocacy competitions, and pro bono. A new selection process is being introduced for 2015 courses, involving interviews and assessment.

LLM Masters Degree – full-time/i-LLM (a supported online learning programme)

Our LLM in International Legal Practice is a truly professional qualification and reflects cutting-edge approaches to legal practice. We offer a wide choice of flexible, specialist modules to suit your area of interest and enhance your expertise.

Events

We run events of all types, including open days, law fairs, insight days and online webinars. Take a look at what's available on our website: law.ac.uk/events79

Contact
Freephone: 0800 289997
International:
+44 (0)1483 216000
Email: admissions@law.ac.uk
Website: www.law.ac.uk

GDL & LLM LPC full-time
Apply to: Central Applications Board
www.lawcabs.ac.uk

GDL & LLM LPC part-time
Apply to: The University of Law
www.law.ac.uk/postgraduate

BPTC full & part-time
Apply to Bar Standards Board (BSB)
www.barprofessionaltraining.org.uk

LLM Masters Degrees
Apply to: The University of Law
www.law.ac.uk/postgraduate

Law School

The University of Law
incorporating The College of Law

ple. The centre has an on-site courtroom and a four-floor legal library, plus a hefty pro bono programme. UoL recently updated its IT systems, though sources mentioned the facilities as a whole are slightly on the shabby side.

Careers services and prospects

UoL's employability service is open to all students. It's notably comprehensive, with its own job database and online careers materials. Staff also provide students one-to-one advice. Take note: the broad range of students the service advises does mean those on the BPTC might not receive the same tailored service offered by smaller providers.

UoL doesn't release statistics on how many of its graduates land pupillages.

The *Chambers Student* verdict

A little help from the legal education whizzes at Kaplan could be just thing to help this provider's employability rates justify its hefty fees.

Manchester Metropolitan University

Number of places: 108 FT, 48 PT
Fees (2014/15): £13,250

The course

Thanks to its strong links to the Northern Circuit, this course is a solid choice for someone looking to do the rounds of barristers' sets in Manchester and beyond. *"Virtually the whole teaching team is made of barristers with a significant number of years of experience each,"* course director Joanne Lewthwaite tells us. *"We recently worked out that we have 187 years call between the 12 of us."*

The brigade holds course sessions four days a week for full-timers. In the past the part-time option has been cancelled due to lack of interest, but when it does run it involves a full day of teaching one Monday a fortnight, supplemented by pre-recorded lectures and podcasts. Lectures take place in groups of 12, which are then split into groups of six for the advocacy training. This sees barristers who are still in full-time practice help students prepare for getting on their feet. They also have the chance to get extra experience acting as witnesses in the Northern Circuit's pupil training programme.

There are six electives on offer: advanced crime, family, personal injury, advanced civil, employment and business.

The location and facilities

Manchester Met's law school is in the city centre, close to the train station and plenty of cultural activities. The school has mock courtroom facilities, resource rooms and new DVD recording equipment for advocacy and conference classes. Students have access to the university's broader facilities, including its substantial law library and student union.

Manchester Met has ties with the Personal Support Unit at Manchester Civil Justice Centre and the Manchester Mediation Service. Mediation monkeys can take their interest further still by gaining a professional mediation qualification at no extra cost. There's also an imaginative scheme that hooks aspiring barristers up with trainee police officers for some realistic advocacy practice.

Careers services and prospects

Students have access to both the law school and the university careers services. There are personal tutors to help with pupillage applications.

Most students who secure a pupillage end up at sets around the North West, although a few go to London each year. Manchester Met wouldn't reveal what proportion of their alumni end up with pupillages, but you can bet competition's stiff for the relatively small number of North West spots. According to Lewthwaite, many grads who stay local continue to be involved in the school years on.

The *Chambers Student* verdict

This small operator is a good bet for students keen on advocacy-focused training and hoping to break into the North West legal circuit.

Northumbria University Law School

Number of places: 100 FT, 24 PT
Fees (2014/15): £12,500

Awards: 15% discount for a 1:1, 10% discount for a 2:1; additional 10% discount for Northumbria graduates

The course

Northumbria's Bar course has the distinct honour of being England and Wales's cheapest. Students here work in small groups on case studies under the supervision of current or former barristers from the region. senior practitioners and judges also deliver regular talks. Full-time students study from Monday to Thursday, with Fridays off for private study or pro bono. Meanwhile, part-timers attend one day a week: Monday, Tuesday or Thursday.

Manchester Metropolitan University

Manchester Law School, Manchester Metropolitan University, Sandra Burslem Building,
Lower Ormond Street, Manchester M15 6BH
Tel: (0161) 247 3046 Email: law@mmu.ac.uk
Facebook: /manchesterlawschool Twitter: @mmu_law

College profile

Manchester Law School is one of the largest legal education providers in the UK, with a long history of providing top class training at the centre of the UK's second largest legal hub. As part of Manchester Metropolitan University, Manchester Law School benefits from exceptional facilities, with the additional advantage of being adjoined to our £75m Business School and Student Hub.

Students gain huge benefits from regular contact with the legal profession due to strong, long-lasting links and the advantage of many staff still being in practice. Outstanding Pro Bono programmes, careers support, mentoring schemes and work experience opportunities make Manchester Law School a popular choice for postgraduate and professional study.

Each year over 1500 students study on a range of undergraduate, postgraduate and professional programmes, including the LLB (Hons), Legal Practice Course (LPC), Bar Professional Training Course (BPTC), Graduate Diploma in Law (GDL) and LLM.

We offer the following postgraduate courses, on a full and part-time basis:

GDL

If you are a non-law graduate looking for a legal career, our GDL is the perfect start. Our new 'Legal Skills and Practice' module will equip you with all the skills you need to train as a solicitor or barrister. We offer high levels of face-to-face teaching, innovative teaching methods and exceptional extra-curricular opportunities.

LPC

Our LPC is the perfect training for aspiring solicitors. You will receive all the vocational training you need for your future career, delivered by our innovative teaching team. You will also benefit from our excellent links to the local legal profession and the opportunity to gain work experience in your chosen elective subjects.

BPTC

We have a long and successful history of training barristers and our BPTC is rigorous, interactive and practical. We have outstanding, lasting links to the local Bar, giving you a great start to your career as well as significantly more advocacy training than the BSB advises. You will also receive the opportunity to obtain an independent professional qualification in mediation at no additional cost.

LLM

Our legal masters programme has been tremendously popular since its inception in 2010 and has two exciting routes. The taught LLM is for those with an LLB/GDL or a degree in social sciences. It allows you to research an area of the law that interests you and provides an excellent addition to your CV. The "top-up" LLM route is for those who already have an LPC/BPTC. It is a streamlined, fast-track way of getting a masters – you only complete one taught module and a research project.

Scholarships are available for the GDL, LPC and BPTC, visit law.mmu.ac.uk/scholarships for details.

For further information on our programmes visit www.law.mmu.ac.uk

Contact

GDL
law@mmu.ac.uk

LPC
lpc@mmu.ac.uk

BPTC
bptc@mmu.ac.uk

LLM
law@mmu.ac.uk

To apply

GDL & LPC full-time
Central Applications Board
www.lawcabs.ac.uk

BPTC
BPTC online
For details, please see
www.law.mmu.ac.uk/bptc

Part-time GDL
Directly to Manchester Law School
www.law.mmu.ac.uk/gdl

Part-time LPC
Directly to Manchester Law School
www.law.mmu.ac.uk/lpc

LLM
Directly to Manchester Law School
www.law.mmu.ac.uk/llm

Manchester Metropolitan University

Another distinction of Northumbria's BPTC is that it gives barristers in training the chance to have a go at handling live work – this can be done through the Student Law Office either as an elective or in their spare time, and involves contentious as well as advisory work for members of the public. Recent students have assisted with GP inquests and attended small claims court.

Other electives range from family and criminal to employment, housing and personal injury.

The location and facilities

Northumbria's law school is based right in the bustling centre of Newcastle, not the rolling countryside its name suggests. As such, students have easy access to the city's high street shopping and many wining and dining outlets. The law school building features curved glass encased in stylish steel bars. Inside, however, the conditions are anything but prison-like. One former student told us: *"I was pleasantly surprised by the quality of the resources and the IT. The facilities are all pretty new."* For barristers-to-be, there are mock courtroom facilities, complete with recording capabilities.

Careers services and prospects

A recent report by the Bar Standards Board found a decent pupillage conversion rate at Northumbria: about eight out of 30 home students gain pupillage, while some 28 of 30 overseas students find pupillage equivalent roles on their return, aided by the fact that the course is recognised by the Bar Council of India.

Where other institutions rely on telephone interviews, Northumbria goes further by flying to meet overseas applicants, although the aforementioned report notes concerns about the standards of English of some overseas students. UK students need a 2:2 or above and a demonstrable commitment to the profession, although recently introduced fee discounts for students with higher classes of degrees suggests the law school is keen to raise academic standards.

The *Chambers Student* verdict

Northumbria's low fees belie the quality of the facilities and experience on offer.

Nottingham Law School

Number of places: 120 FT
Fees (2014/15): £13,800
Awards: Four £3,000 scholarships, plus a progression discount for former Nottingham University students

The course

This course has a reputation for getting a sizeable proportion of its students pupillages – a sizeable proportion by super-competitive BPTC standards, that is. With about four times as many applications as places, getting a place on it doesn't come easily. Principal Ian Fox tells us recruiters look for not only stellar academics but *"a genuine commitment to the profession. We ask for three weeks of legal work experience – these could be mini pupillages, law firm vacation schemes or marshalling with a judge – plus evidence of contested advocacy over and above what's required on the GDL or LLB."*

Applicants who make the cut join a smallish programme taught from Monday to Thursday, with Fridays left free for prep. There are 10 to 12 hours of contact time a week, which is slightly lower than other providers – students are expected to cover much of the factual side of the course during independent study. They attend advocacy and oral skill classes in groups of six, and seminars in groups of 12. These are largely focused on skills like opinion writing and drafting statements of case. There are also one or two lectures a week.

The location and facilities

The low cost of living is Nottingham is often a draw for students here, as is the city's accessibility. As the law school's website proudly boasts, 89% of England and Wales' population resides within two hours' drive of Nottingham, so the location often proves handy for commuters or those attending pupillage interviews out of town.

The law school is based in Nottingham Trent's City campus, in the historic heart of Britain's most haunted city. Although Nottingham has buildings that date back to the 1100s, the law school is up-to-date, with newly built mock courtrooms, a nearby law library, and ample intranet and tech facilities. The school recently started offering i-Pads to all students.

In other developments, the school has just opened a new legal advice centre with specially built facilities. Students can train here to become Free Representation Unit (FRU) representatives, or take part in programmes like The Innocence Project or ones that work to rehabilitate prisoners. Further CV-boosting opportunities are available in the form of mooting competitions sponsored by nearby barristers' sets.

Careers services and prospects

The careers service offers assistance with pupillage applications and interview preparation, and there's a mentoring scheme that offers places to all applicants. The school has close relationships with local sets and often arranges for judges and barristers to participate in open days or visit the campus to deliver talks.

Fox estimates around 30% of students will have scored a pupillage by the January after graduation – a reasonably healthy proportion for a profession with a notoriously fraught path to entry.

The *Chambers Student* verdict

Nottingham gave rise to the legend of Robin Hood, but you won't need to raid the sheriff's coffers to get a place on this top-flight course.

Law School

How to fund law school

It's now completely plausible that you'll be saddled with upwards of £30,000 of debt by the time you complete your undergraduate degree. Given that a GDL, LPC or BPTC course is by no means cheap either, how can you ease the increasingly intimidating financial burden of law school?

Secure sponsorship before starting your training contract

If you're interested in commercial law or want to work at one of the larger firms in the UK, there's a chance you might be able to find a firm that will sponsor you through law school. These firms tend to recruit two years in advance of the start of the training contract, so you'll need to get your act together well ahead of time. Not only will such firms cover the cost of course fees (LPC and usually GDL too), they may well give you a few thousand pounds towards the cost of living. Details of what solicitors' firms are offering their future trainees are given in our Salaries and Benefits table, P.482.

The lucky minority of BPTC students will already have a pupillage lined up. At the more affluent sets, the size of the pupillage award is now comparable with City trainee/ NQ salaries. Usually a decent chunk of the pupillage award can be drawn down to cover BPTC expenses. At the more modest sets there may be no money available for the BPTC at all. Further information about funding is given in the Bar section of this guide.

The Inns of Court

If you're training to be a barrister you can apply for a range of GDL and BPTC scholarships from the Inns of Court. Around a quarter of BPTC students get some funding, and there's just under £5m up for grabs. Check out our Inns of Court table for more information.

Law school scholarships

Individual law schools have scholarship programmes. See our LPC Providers Reports and BPTC Provider Reports for details. But be wary: the SRA has recently issued a warning about phony providers and scam emails offering to pay for part of your LPC.

Where to study

Studying in London could set you back as much as double what it would elsewhere, say in Sheffield, Cardiff or Nottingham, and the quality of training isn't necessarily going to be any better. Our online tables on the GDL Providers, LPC Providers and BPTC Providers will allow you to compare the prices of all the relevant law school courses.

Career Development Loans

First of all, if the loan isn't from Barclays or the Co-op then it isn't really a Career Development Loan (CDL), it's just a bank claiming there will be no repayments to make while you study. Though that may be the case, it doesn't mean there is no interest accruing – it could just be piling up, ready to swamp you once your studies finish. A true CDL allows you to borrow up to £10,000, with the interest paid by the Skills Funding Agency while you study.

Because the CDL interest rate may be higher than another loan, some people recommend taking a CDL and, when the interest-free honeymoon is over, paying it off using another unsecured personal loan with a lower interest rate. Unfortunately, the GDL is no longer covered by the scheme, just the LPC and BPTC.

Bank loans

There's a good chance that you've already emptied the last pennies out of your student overdraft, but never fear – you may still be eligible for more debt. Despite the credit crunch, there's still money to be had, so check the interest rates of various banks.

Since 2010 most banks have withdrawn the special packages for customers entering the legal profession. However, check out graduate accounts, because they sometimes offer slightly better overdraft terms. Both Lloyds and TSB provide loans of up to £10,000, and repayment is made over a maximum period of five years. Whatever you do, don't make any decisions lightly; loans involve a big commitment that only continues to grow once the debt starts to accrue.

Get a job!

Law firms are increasingly interested in applicants' commercial awareness and ability to cope in a professional office environment, so what used to be an undesirable option can now be deployed in an interview as proof of your suitability for a career in law. Course providers tell us that part-time enrolments are on the rise as students increasingly look to ease the financial burden of law school by working jobs alongside their studies. While this option does stall your legal career by another year or so, it does help you avoid the heavy debts accrued by the average law student. Even students on full-time courses will look to boost their cash flow with evening shifts or weekend work. Be sure to set yourself a manageable schedule, though. You don't want to end up flunking your course for the sake of saving a few extra quid.

Benefits, benefactors, begging

So bunking up with ma and pa during your course isn't a dream come true, yet sometimes needs must. Forget ideas of declaring bankruptcy to evade student debt; consider other creative ways to ease the burden.

- A student card will get you low-cost travel, discount haircuts, cinema tickets and even drinks in some places. If nothing else, it'll make you feel young.
- Websites such as www.studentdiscountbook.co.uk and www.studentbeans.com have discounts and deals for meals, entertainment and more.
- Law books are pricey, so don't get overzealous before term starts. College libraries will have the core texts and you're sure to find former students hawking books. Check out notice boards and online for second-hand tomes.
- A number of law schools, chambers and solicitors firms run competitions. Do a Google search to find them. Winning may bring kudos as well as cash.
- Market research focus groups will pay decent money for an hour or two of your time.

Some scholarships

- Many law schools offer funding. For instance, national provider the University of Law offers various scholarships to those studying full-time LPC or BPTC courses. It also offers 35 Gold Awards worth £3,000 for students about to start a GDL who have a First or a distinction at Masters level.
- Universities also offer a miscellany of scholarships: Oxford, for example, has many for students wanting to take its BCL or MJur courses.
- The Law Society Diversity Access Scheme supports talented people who face obstacles to qualification.
- The Inderpal Rahal Memorial Trust supports women from an immigrant or refugee background. Contact irmt@gclaw.co.uk for more details.
- The Kalisher Scholarship works with each of the BPTC providers to ensure that every year at least two talented but financially disadvantaged students gain a free place on the course. In addition, it offers a variety of awards and bursaries, including a £5,000 essay prize.
- The Leonard Sainer Foundation provides interest-free loans of £10,000 each to help fund either the LPC of BPTC.
- The Student Disability Assistance Fund can award up to £500 for people studying on a full-time or nearly full-time basis.
- Universities and publicly funded colleges have discretionary college access funds available to especially hard-up students. The major LPC/BPTC providers usually have a number of scholarships to assist select students with fees, etc.
- The HM Hubbard Law Scholarship is for trainees and solicitors who want to study the law and legal procedures in France, Spain or Canada. Recent scholarships have ranged between £14,000 and £27,000.
- The Human Rights Lawyers Association will provide around five awards from a maximum annual bursary fund of £5,000 to those who wish to undertake unpaid/poorly paid human rights work, either during their training or soon after.
- The Foreign and Commonwealth Office's Chevening Scholarships are available for overseas students wishing to study in the UK. In 2012 the scholarship fund totalled £22m.
- Postgrad Solutions offers a small number of £500 bursaries for LLM students.

Average trainee salary: £26,976

In central London: £34,875

In outer London: £24,303

In South West: £22,351

In South East: £21,464

In Yorkshire: £20,526

In the Midlands: £19,721

In the North West: £19,773

In Eastern England: £19,587

In the North East: £19,011

In Wales: £18,299

Figures provided by the SRA,
summer 2014

Solicitors' practice areas

Banking & Finance

In a nutshell

Banking and finance lawyers may work in any one of the specialist areas described below, but all deal with the borrowing of money or the management of financial liabilities. Their task is to negotiate and document the contractual relationship between lenders and borrowers and ensure that their clients' best legal and commercial interests are reflected in the terms of loan agreements. It is a hugely technical, ever-evolving and jargon-heavy area of law.

Straightforward bank lending: a bank lends money to a borrower on documented repayment terms. **Acquisition finance:** a loan made to a corporate borrower or private equity sponsor for the purpose of acquiring another company. This includes **leveraged finance**, where the borrower uses a very large amount of borrowed money to meet the cost of a significant acquisition without committing a lot of its own capital (this is called a leveraged buyout or LBO). **Real estate finance:** a loan made to enable a borrower to acquire a property or finance the development of land and commonly secured by way of a mortgage on the acquired property/land. **Project finance:** the financing of long-term infrastructure (eg roads) and public services projects (eg hospitals), where the amounts borrowed to complete the project are paid back with the cash flow generated by the project. **Asset finance:** this enables the purchase and operation of large assets such as ships, aircraft and machinery. The lender normally takes security over the assets in question. **Islamic finance:** Muslim borrowers, lenders and investors must abide by Shari'a law, which prohibits the collection and payment of interest on a loan. Islamic finance specialists ensure that finance deals are structured in a Shari'a-compliant manner. **Financial services regulation:** lawyers in this field ensure that their bank clients operate in compliance with the relevant financial legislation.

What lawyers do

- Meet with clients to establish their specific requirements and the commercial context of a deal.
- Carry out due diligence – an investigation exercise to verify the accuracy of information passed from the borrower to the lender or from the company raising finance to all parties investing in the deal. This can involve on-site meetings with the company's management, so lawyers can verify the company's credit profile.

- Negotiate with the opposite party to agree the terms of the deal and record them accurately in the facility documentation. Lenders' lawyers usually produce initial documents (often a standard form) and borrowers' lawyers try to negotiate more favourable terms for their clients. Lawyers on both sides must know when to compromise and when to hold out.
- Assist with the structuring of complicated or groundbreaking financing models and ensure innovative solutions comply with all relevant laws.
- Gather all parties to complete the transaction, ensuring all agreed terms are reflected in the loan and that all documents have been properly signed and witnessed. Just as in corporate deals, many decisions need to be made at properly convened board meetings and recorded in written resolutions.
- Finalise all post-completion registrations and procedures.

The realities of the job

- City firms act for investment banks on highly complex and often cross-border financings, whereas the work of regional firms generally involves acting for commercial banks on more mainstream domestic finance deals. If you want to be a hotshot in international finance, then it's the City for you.
- Lawyers need to appreciate the needs and growth ambitions of their clients in order to deliver pertinent advice and warn of the legal risks involved in the transactions. Deals may involve the movement of money across borders and through different currencies and financial products. International deals have an additional layer of difficulty: political changes in transitional economies can render a previously sound investment risky.
- Banking clients are ultra-demanding and the hours can be long. On the plus side, your clients will be smart and dynamic. It is possible to build up long-term relationships with investment bank clients, even as a junior.
- Working on deals can be exciting. The team and the other side are all working to a common goal, often under significant time and other pressures. Deal closings bring adrenaline highs and a sense of satisfaction.
- You need to become absorbed in the finance world. Start reading the *FT* or the City pages in your daily newspaper for a taster.

Current issues

- The UK economy recently returned to its pre-recession level and the IMF has forecast it will be the fastest growing economy among developed nations in 2015.
- The IMF's World Economic Outlook reported that financial markets continued to improve during 2014 and the expectation is that this trend will last throughout 2015. However, the report highlighted that this was predominantly driven by advanced economies while emerging markets were seeing increased financial volatility.
- Higher levels of regulation will continue to affect the market and commentators suggest that banks will increasingly be dealing with regulators and ensuring they comply with standards.
- The Banking Reform Act came into effect in December 2014 with the aim of improving and protecting the banking sector in the wake of the 2008 financial collapse. Measures include protecting taxpayers by separating money belonging to individuals and small businesses from that used in wholesale trading and imposing criminal sanctions when reckless misconduct causes banks to fail.
- The Financial Conduct Authority continues to strongly enforce regulations. This includes launching a new approach to dealing with serious failings of standards in companies. 'Enhanced Supervision' is intended only for exceptional circumstances and focuses on the fundamental causes of deficiency by targeting managerial policy and demanding commitments from a firm's board to resolve any issues.
- The ramifications of the Libor interest rate-fixing scandal continue to be felt. Major UK firms are advising institutions under investigation by the FCA.
- In the wake of the Libor scandal, allegations emerged that some foreign exchange traders rigged foreign exchange market rates. After an initial enquiry was established by the FCA, the Serious Fraud Office launched a full criminal investigation into the matter.
- Global regulators recently postponed the implementation of Basel III, a group of measures designed to strengthen regulation and minimise risk in the banking sector. Initially the measures were intended to come into force between 2013 and 2019 but will now be gradually introduced from 2015. Expect law firms to provide advice and guidance to the banking sector on how to stick to the new rules.
- The Small Business, Enterprise and Employment Bill (expected to be introduced in May 2015) has been driven by a desire to create a more transparent financial market. The Bill proposes to improve financial access for small businesses and streamline contact between creditors and insolvency practitioners.

Read our True Pictures on...

Addleshaw Goddard	Lester Aldridge
Allen & Overy	Linklaters
Ashfords	Macfarlanes
Ashurst	Maclay Murray & Spens
Baker & McKenzie	Mayer Brown
Berwin Leighton Paisner	Memery Crystal
Bird & Bird	Michelmores
Bond Dickinson	Mills & Reeve
Brabners Chaffe Street	Muckle
Browne Jacobson	Nabarro
Burges Salmon	Norton Rose Fulbright
Charles Russell	Olswang
Cleary Gottlieb	Osborne Clarke
Clifford Chance	Paul Hastings
Clyde & Co	Pinsent Masons
CMS	Reed Smith
Cripps	SGH Martineau
Dechert	Shearman & Sterling
Dentons	Shoosmiths
DLA Piper	Sidley Austin
DWF	Simmons & Simmons
Eversheds	Skadden
Farrer & Co	Slaughter and May
Foot Anstey	Squire Patton Boggs
Freeths	Stephenson Harwood
Freshfields	Stevens & Bolton
Gateley	Taylor Wessing
Gordons	TLT
Herbert Smith Freehills	Travers Smith
Hill Dickinson	Trethowans
Hogan Lovells	Trowers & Hamlins
Ince & Co	Veale Wasbrough Vizards
Irwin Mitchell	Ward Hadaway
Jones Day	Watson, Farley & Williams
K&L Gates	Wedlake Bell
King & Wood Mallesons	Weil, Gotshal & Manges
Kirkland & Ellis	White & Case
Latham & Watkins	Wragge Lawrence Graham

Capital Markets

In a nutshell

The world's capital markets are trading floors (either real or virtual) on which cash-hungry businesses obtain funding by selling a share of their business (equity) or receiving a loan (debt) from lenders. Capital markets lawyers advise companies ('issuers') and investment banks ('underwriters') on these complex transactions. Here are some of the terms you'll encounter.

Equity capital markets: where a private company raises capital by making its shares available to the public by listing itself on a stock exchange and executing an initial public offering (IPO), as a result of which it becomes a public company (or plc). The London Stock Exchange (LSE) and New York Stock Exchange (NYSE) are the most prestigious exchanges, but companies may list in many other exchanges worldwide. Once listed, a company's shares can be bought and sold by investors at a price determined by the market. **Debt capital markets:** where borrowers raise capital by selling tradable bonds to investors, who expect the full amount lent to be paid back to them with interest. **Structured finance:** this area can get gloriously complicated, but its aims are simple – to increase liquidity and limit or trade on risk, which in turn offers up extra funding for borrowers. **Derivatives:** financial instruments used by banks and businesses to hedge risks to which they are exposed due to factors outside of their control. The value of a derivative at any given time is derived from the value of an underlying asset, security, index or interest rate.

What lawyers do

- Carry out due diligence on issuers and draft prospectuses which provide information about the company and its finances, as well as past financial statements. A prospectus must comply with the requirements of the EU's prospectus and transparency directives.
- Negotiate approval of a listing on the stock exchange. This involves the submission of documentation, certifications and letters that prove the client satisfies the listing requirements. As soon as a company undergoes an IPO, it will be subject to all the rules and requirements of a public company, so the necessary organisational structure must be in place before then.
- Work with underwriters and issuers to draw up the structure of a security and help the parties negotiate the terms of the structure. The underwriter's lawyers draft most documents related to a bond issue. An issuer's lawyers will comment on them and negotiate changes.

- With derivatives, lawyers communicate back and forth with the client discussing legal issues and risks related to various possible structures for the product, as well as suggesting ways to resolve or mitigate those problems and issues.
- Issuer's and underwriter's counsel work together with a team of bankers, accountants, insurers and an issuer's management to get securities issued.

The realities of the job

- Capital markets lawyers are mostly based in the City. The biggest firms have specialist departments focused on capital markets or one of its subgroups, while midsize firms may lump capital markets work in with corporate.
- Clients can be very demanding and lawyers work very long hours. On the plus side, large law firms usually have strong and close relationships with investment bank clients and financial institutions, meaning that trainees and NQs can get frequent client contact.
- Lawyers have to gauge the needs and personality of the company they're working with and require an aptitude for responding to and resolving issues as they arise.
- Capital markets lawyers feel all the highs and lows of market forces – if you're trying to get a deal done market conditions often matter more than the willingness of the parties involved. Even if a deal has been organised, unpredictable market conditions can mean it falls through.

Current Issues

- The effects of the 2008/09 recession and the ongoing European sovereign debt crisis continue to be felt by the markets.
- However, in terms of IPOs and capital raised globally, the first quarter of 2014 was the best since 2011. According to Ernst & Young, London more than held its own, with 24 IPOs (main market and AIM) raising cumulative funds of £3.9bn. It kept it up in Q2, too, with a whopping 37 IPOs raising £7bn. As of 30 June 2014, the London market had seen the strongest first half of the year since 2007, almost matching the level of activity for the whole of 2013.

Practice Areas

- While the bond market has fared well in recent years, some of the biggest investment funds are wrestling with the prospect of the US Federal Reserve pushing up interest rates by 2015, and also bringing its $1tr a year bond buying programme to a halt before summer 2014. This could increase inflation and commodity prices and hinder the recovery of markets across the globe.
- At the end of this year's first quarter, online takeaway service provider Just Eat became the first company to join the LSE's High Growth Segment (HGS), raising £360m. "*The float is one of the largest technology listings to have taken place on the London market for some time,*" said Ernst & Young.
- An area of particular interest to magic circle firms is high-yield financing and the European bond market, traditionally the stomping grounds of US law firms. High-yield products provide an increasingly popular alternative financing strategy for businesses struggling because of a lack of traditional bank lending. The growing popularity of high-yield financing has also contributed to the continuing success of US firms in the UK.

Read our True Pictures on...

Addleshaw Godard	Linklaters
Allen & Overy	Mayer Brown
Ashurst	Memery Crystal
Baker & McKenzie	Nabarro
Berwin Leighton Paisner	Norton Rose Fulbright
Bird & Bird	Olswang
Burges Salmon	Osborne Clarke
Charles Russell	Pinsent Masons
Cleary Gottlieb	Shearman & Sterling
Clifford Chance	Sidley Austin
Covington & Burling	Simmons & Simmons
Davis Polk & Wardwell	Skadden
Dechert	Slaughter and May
Dentons	Squire Patton Boggs
DLA Piper	Stephenson Harwood
Eversheds	Taylor Wessing
Freshfields	Travers Smith
Herbert Smith Freehills	Trowers & Hamlins
Hogan Lovells	Watson, Farley & Williams
Jones Day	Weil, Gotshal & Manges
K&L Gates	White & Case
King & Wood Mallesons	Wragge Lawrence Graham
Latham & Watkins	

Practice Areas

Competition/Antitrust

In a nutshell

It is the job of the UK and EU regulatory authorities to ensure that markets function effectively on the basis of fair and open competition. The rules in the UK and EU are substantially similar, but the UK bodies concentrate on those rules that have their greatest effect domestically, while EU authorities deal with matters affecting multiple member states. The UK regulators were the Office of Fair Trading (OFT) and the Competition Commission (CC). In light of the Enterprise and Regulatory Reform Act 2013, their functions were combined under a single body: the Competition and Markets Authority (CMA). Responsibility for the consumer credit industry was passed over to the Financial Conduct Authority (FCA). The European Commission is the regulator for matters which affect other EU countries. Additionally, there are industry-specific regulatory bodies, such as Ofcom for the media and telecoms industry.

Competition authorities have extensive investigative powers – including the ability to carry out dawn raids – and can impose hefty fines. The OFT became more proactive and litigation-minded in the years before it was subsumed into the CMA, and the European Commission continues to dole out big fines.

What lawyers do

- Negotiate clearance for acquisitions, mergers and joint ventures.
- Advise on the structure of commercial or co-operation agreements to ensure they can withstand a competition challenge.
- Deal with investigations into the way a client conducts business.
- Bring or defend claims in the Competition Appeal Tribunal (CAT).
- Advise on cross-border trade or anti-dumping measures (preventing companies exporting products at a lower price than normally charged in the home market).
- Regulators investigate companies, bring prosecutions and advise on the application of new laws and regulations.

The realities of the job

- You won't get much independence; even junior lawyers work under the close supervision of experienced partners. In the early days the job involves a great deal of research into particular markets and how the authorities have approached different types of agreements in the past.
- You need to be interested in economics and politics.
- The work demands serious academic brainpower twinned with commercial acumen.
- As a popular area of practice it's hard to break into. Work experience with a regulator or at the Commission in Brussels will enhance your prospects.
- Advocacy is a relatively small part of the job, though you could end up appearing in the High Court or the CAT.
- In international law firms you will travel abroad and may even work in an overseas office for a while, perhaps in Brussels. Fluency in another language can be useful. There is also a trend for lawyers to switch between private practice and working for the regulators.

Current issues

- Competition law continues to increase its profile as greater regulatory activity is undertaken by the UK, EU and USA. In 2012 the European Commission slapped a EUR1.5bn fine on a group of electronics companies, including Philips and LG, for agreeing to fix the price of cathode-ray tubes. The OFT ordered airlines and other travel companies to abolish hidden debit card fees.
- The OFT was criticised for offering immunity to competition whistle-blowers and has begun conducting more 'own initiative' investigations.
- The Department for Business, Innovation and Skills also plans to introduce a new regime for class actions to enhance access to justice for consumers who have suffered because of anti-competitive behaviour. The planned changes will see the introduction of 'opt-out' collective actions, which means a legal action can be brought on behalf of all affected individuals for example by a consumer body.
- Competition lawyers are increasingly drawing on the experience of colleagues, such as financial regulation, tax, litigation and white-collar crime specialists.
- As the technology sector continues to grow it's coming under increasing scrutiny from regulators. Google is facing off against Microsoft and TripAdvisor over claims it had been giving itself an unfair competitive advantage by filtering search results.
- Online service providers are increasingly on the CMA's radar, especially for misleading pricing infringements, and the EU has passed a new Common European Sales Law to facilitate cross-border online transactions.

- The government has given the newly established CMA a "*strategic steer*," and recommended it assesses particular sectors in order to stimulate competition and boost the British economy. These include: 'knowledge intensive' sectors (eg engineering); financial services; and infrastructure sectors (eg energy).
- Lengthy investigations were often the bugbear of big companies who longed for a swifter process: some were scrutinised by the OFT for one year, and then by the CC for an additional two years. The establishment of the CMA marked the government's attempt to cut duplication between the two bodies and quicken the administration of competition law. However, the CMA's arrival has also produced some concerns. Questions over the body's internal governance and how transparent it will be have been raised, while doubts linger over whether the CMA can maintain the levels of consumer protection once delivered by the OFT and CC.
- The globalisation of competition law enforcement is on the up. The recent Libor and auto parts investigations have demonstrated the sheer scale and international co-operation involved in such operations. The Libor investigation involved regulators in at least ten countries spanning three continents, while global efforts to investigate the automotive industry have increased significantly over the past few years: the USA has fined over 20 car parts producers more than $2bn, while the European Commission has recently fined suppliers almost EUR1bn for fixing the price of ball bearings.
- Dechert partner Miriam Gonzalez told us that sanctions are becoming the weapon of choice: "*Regulators are creating a new army of people without weapons, and that can have a tremendous effect in some countries.*" Advisory work tied to such sanctions is therefore likely to keep competition/antitrust lawyers busy in the months ahead. Go online to read the full interview.
- After a public consultation, the government its announced intentions to introduce a new 'opt-out' system which will change the way in which competition/antitrust class actions are brought: an 'opt-out' arrangement means that a legal action can be brought on behalf of all affected individuals (for example, by a consumer body). In contrast, the current 'opt-in' arrangement requires those who are bringing the action to source potential claimants to willingly participate in the proceedings. The legislative provisions needed to implement this change were introduced in January 2014 via the Consumer Rights Bill. The House of Lords is currently scrutinising this Bill, and a decision as to whether to adopt these changes or not is expected later in 2014.

Read our True Pictures on...

Addleshaw Goddard	Linklaters
Allen & Overy	Macfarlanes
Ashurst	Maclay Murray & Spens
Baker & McKenzie	Mayer Brown
Berwin Leighton Paisner	Nabarro
Bond Dickinson	Norton Rose Fulbright
Browne Jacobson	Osborne Clarke
Burges Salmon	Peters & Peters
Cleary Gottlieb	Pinsent Masons
Clifford Chance	Reed Smith
Clyde & Co	Shearman & Sterling
CMS	Shoosmiths
DLA Piper	Sidley Austin
DWF	Simmons & Simmons
Eversheds	Slater & Gordon
Freshfields	Slaughter and May
Herbert Smith Freehills	Squire Patton Boggs
Hogan Lovells	Stevens & Bolton
K&L Gates	TLT
King & Wood Mallesons	Travers Smith
Kingsley Napley	Wragge Lawrence Graham
Latham & Watkins	

Construction

In a nutshell

Construction law can broadly be divided into non-contentious and contentious practice. The first involves lawyers helping clients at the procurement stage, pulling together all the contractual relationships prior to building work; the second sees them resolving disputes when things go wrong. In the past the relatively high monetary stakes involved and the industry trend for recovering building costs through the courts made construction a litigation-happy practice. Since the 1990s most new contracts have contained mandatory procedures to be adopted in case of dispute. Adjudication of disputes has become the industry norm and these tend to follow a swift 28-day timetable. Others are resolved through mediation or arbitration; however, some disputes are so complex that the parties do still choose to slug it out in court.

What lawyers do

Procurement

- Negotiate and draft contracts for programmes of building works. Any such programme involves a multitude of parties including landowners, main contractors, subcontractors, engineers and architects.
- Work in conjunction with property lawyers if the client has invested in land as well as undertaking a building project. Together, the lawyers seek and obtain all the necessary planning consents as well as local authority certifications.
- Where the developer does not own the land, liaise with the landowner's solicitors over matters such as stage payments, architects' certificates and other measures of performance.
- Make site visits during development.

Construction disputes

- Assess the client's position and gather all related paperwork and evidence.
- Extract the important detail from huge volumes of technical documentation.
- Follow the resolution methods set out in the contracts between the parties.
- Where a settlement is impossible, issue, prepare for and attend proceedings with the client, usually instructing a barrister to advocate.

The realities of the job

- Drafting requires attention to detail and careful thought.
- It's essential to keep up to date with industry standards and know contract law and tort inside out.

- People skills are fundamental. Contractors and subcontractors are generally earthy and direct; structural engineers live in a world of complicated technical reports; corporate types and in-house lawyers require smoother handling. You'll deal with them all.
- The construction world is often perceived as a male-dominated environment, but while some clients might see a visit to a lap-dancing club as par for the business entertainment course, there are many successful female construction lawyers, architects and engineers who avoid such activities.
- Most lawyers prefer either contentious or non-contentious work, and some firms like their construction lawyers to handle both, so pick your firm carefully.
- A background in construction or engineering is a major bonus because you'll already have industry contacts and will be able to combine legal know-how with practical advice.

Current issues

- The construction industry still hasn't completely recovered from the recession – it's still around 10% shy of its pre-crash best. The industry experienced another slowdown between March and May this year, with output falling by 0.8% compared to the previous three months.
- However, it's expected that the residential market will usher in new growth, thanks to government schemes like Help to Buy and Funding for Lending. Indeed, housebuilding has increased at its fastest rate for nearly a decade, and has even resulted in shortages of bricks and bricklayers. However, prices for such materials have soared as a result.
- Mortgage lenders like RBS have had to clamp down on large mortgages for fears of a bubble growing in the London property market. Figures from Nationwide show that UK house prices hit a new peak in May – breaking the previous record set before the financial crisis.
- Thanks to a new infrastructure programme announced by Downing Street, there will be a whopping 150,000 new construction jobs available over the coming years. A whopping £36bn in funding will be spent on new projects like the Mersey Gateway Bridge, the Sheffield Don Valley flood relief scheme and Heathrow's Terminal 2 upgrade.
- However, as building activity picks up there is a burgeoning risk of a rise in deaths and serious injuries on construction sites. According to an ex-Labour adviser, the construction industry is sitting on "*a ticking timebomb*," as more and more inexperienced workers

are being recruited since the budget of the Health and Safety Executive was cut by 35% in 2011.

- Construction industry disputes are getting longer. According to building consultancy EC Harris they are now taking on average 12.9 months to be settled, compared to 8.7 months the previous year. This has been attributed to both economic conditions and the growing complexity of projects. Often disputes arise over payment; building work is now under greater scrutiny as companies search for any excuse not to pay. Recently, a subcontractor was forced to pay £800,000 in damages for delaying the construction of the Shard by 42 days.

Read our True Pictures on...

Addleshaw Goddard	Lewis Silkin
Allen & Overy	Macfarlanes
Ashfords	Maclay Murray & Spens
Ashurst	Mayer Brown
Baker & McKenzie	Michelmores
Berwin Leighton Paisner	Mills & Reeve
Bond Dickinson	Muckle
Brabners Chaffe Street	Nabarro
Browne Jacobson	Norton Rose Fulbright
Burges Salmon	Olswang
Charles Russell	Osborne Clark
Clifford Chance	Pinsent Masons
Clyde & Co	Reed Smith
CMS	RPC
Cripps	SGH Martineau
Dentons	Simmons & Simmons
DLA Piper	Slaughter and May
DWF	Speechly Bircham
Eversheds	Squire Patton Boggs
Foot Anstey	Stephenson Harwood
Freeths	Stevens & Bolton
Freshfields	Taylor Wessing
Gateley	TLT
Gordons	Trowers & Hamlins
Herbert Smith Freehills	Veale Wasbrough Vizards
Hill Dickinson	Vinson & Elkins
Hogan Lovells	Ward Hadaway
Jones Day	Wedlake Bell
K&L Gates	White & Case
Kennedys	Wragge Lawrence Graham
King & Wood Mallesons	

Corporate/M&A

In a nutshell

Corporate lawyers provide advice to companies on significant transactions affecting their activities, including internal operations, the buying and selling of businesses and business assets, and the arrangement of the finance to carry out these activities.

Mergers and acquisitions (M&A) involve one company acquiring another by way of a takeover (acquisition), or two companies fusing to form a single larger entity (merger). The main reasons for a company to execute an M&A transaction are to grow its business (by acquiring or merging with a competitor) or add a new line of business to its existing activities. During a recession, mergers are also a means of strengthening two or more existing companies facing financial trouble. M&A can either be public (when it involves companies listed on a stock exchange) or private (when it concerns companies privately owned by individuals). **Corporate restructuring** involves changes to the structure of a company and the disposal of certain assets, either because the company wants to concentrate on more profitable parts of its business, or because it is facing financial difficulties and needs to free up liquidity.

What lawyers do

- Negotiate and draft agreements – this will be done in conjunction with the client, the business that is being bought or sold, other advisers (eg accountants) and any financiers.
- Carry out due diligence – this is an investigation to verify the accuracy of information passed from the seller to the buyer. It establishes: the financial strength of the company; the outright ownership of all assets; whether there are outstanding debts or other claims against the company; and any environmental or other liabilities that could reduce the value of the business in the future.
- Arrange financing – this could come from banks or other types of investors; they will wish to have some kind of security for their investment (eg participation in the shareholding, taking out a mortgage over property or other collateral).
- Gather all parties for the completion of the transaction, ensuring all assets have been properly covered by written documents that are properly signed and witnessed. Company law requires that decisions are made at properly convened board meetings and recorded in written resolutions.
- Finalise all post-completion registrations and procedures.

The realities of the job

- The type of clients your firm acts for will determine your experiences. Publicly listed companies and the investment banks that underwrite deals can be extremely demanding and have a different attitude to risk than, say, rich entrepreneurs, owner-managed businesses (OMBs) and small to medium-sized enterprises (SMEs). To deal with such clients, a robust and confident manner is required and stamina is a must.
- Corporate transactions can be large and complicated, with many different aspects of the company affected in the process. Lawyers need to be conversant in a variety of legal disciplines and know when to refer matters to a specialist in, say, merger control (competition), employment, property or tax.
- Corporate deals involve mountains of paperwork, so you need to be well organised and have good drafting skills. Above all, corporate is a very practical area of law, so commercial acumen and a good understanding of your clients' objectives is a must.
- Corporate work is cyclical and therefore the hours lawyers work can vary depending on the general state of the market and the particular needs of the clients, whose expectations have risen even further since the widespread use of instant modes of communication. It's fair to say there can be some very late nights.
- The most junior members of a deal team normally get stuck with the most boring or unrewarding tasks. The banes of the corporate trainee's life are data room management (putting together and caretaking all the factual information on which a deal relies) and bibling (the creation of files containing copies of all the agreed documents and deal information). More challenging tasks quickly become available to driven junior lawyers.
- You need to become absorbed in the corporate world. If you can't develop an interest in the business media then choose another area of practice pronto.
- A sound grounding in corporate finance makes an excellent springboard for working in-house in major companies. Some lawyers move to banks to work as corporate finance execs or analysts. Company secretarial positions suit lawyers with a taste for internal management and compliance issues.

Practice Areas

Current Issues

- The UK is traditionally Europe's biggest market for M&A deals, but since the start of the economic downturn it has been a story of gradual decline. In the first quarter of 2014, M&A activity targeting the UK stood at £11bn, the lowest quarterly value since Q3 in 2009. However the value of UK M&A is now at its highest since 2008, with a 108% increase in deal value in the first half of 2014.

- The value of total global deals dropped to $978.8bn in the first half of 2013, down from $1.07 trillion in the first half of 2012, marking the weakest performance since the first half of 2009. M&A deals in Europe accounted for just 22.6% of the global total, a 16-year low. In 2014, however, global deal values reached $1.75 trillion, the highest mid-year levels since 2007.

- The level of activity has remained low in the UK, with the trend of fewer, but bigger deals making the headlines in 2014. Companies are opting for quality over quantity, however the US's deal volume is starting to pick up, which indicates that the UK is about to follow suit.

- Consumer products was the most active sector by value in the first half of 2014 with 162 deals, followed by media and entertainment (111) and oil and gas (66).

- The upward trend seen during the first half of 2014 is predicted to continue, with the upcoming year considered the ideal period for transformative deals, according to Ernst & Young.

- Cash-rich investors have their pick of the best assets and often acquire businesses at a significant discount due to lower company valuations. There has been growing interest from emerging markets investors and sovereign wealth funds, particularly from the Middle East, in acquiring assets in the UK and elsewhere. Although the USA is still the largest overseas bidder for UK companies, emerging market bidders like China and India are catching up fast.

Read our True Pictures on...

Arnold & Porter	Lester Aldridge
Addleshaw Godard	Lewis Silkin
Allen & Overy	Linklaters
Ashfords	Macfarlanes
Ashurst	Maclay Murray & Spens
B P Collins	Mayer Brown
Baker & McKenzie	Memery Crystal
Berwin Leighton Paisner	Michelmores
Bird & Bird	Mills & Reeve
Bond Dickinson	Mishcon de Reya
BPE Solicitors	Muckle
Brabners Chaffe Street	Nabarro
Browne Jacobson	Norton Rose Fulbright
Burges Salmon	Olswang
Charles Russell	Osborne Clarke
Cleary Gottlieb	Paul Hastings
Clifford Chance	Pinsent Masons
Clyde & Co	Reed Smith
CMS	RPC
Covington & Burling	SGH Martineau
Cripps	Shearman & Sterling
Dechert	Shoosmiths
Dentons	Sidley Austin
DLA Piper	Simmons & Simmons
DWF	Skadden
Eversheds	Slaughter and May
Farrer & Co	Speechly Bircham
Foot Anstey	Squire Patton Boggs
Freeths	Stephenson Harwood
Freshfields	Stevens & Bolton
Gateley	Taylor Wessing
Gordons	TLT
Harbottle & Lewis	Travers Smith
Herbert Smith Freehills	Trethowans
Higgs & Sons	Trowers & Hamlins
Hill Dickinson	Veale Wasbrough Vizards
Hogan Lovells	Ward Hadaway
Irwin Mitchell	Watson, Farley & Williams
Jones Day	Weil, Gotshal & Manges
K&L Gates	White & Case
King & Wood Mallesons	Wragge Lawrence Graham
Latham & Watkins	

Crime

In a nutshell

Criminal solicitors represent defendants in cases brought before the UK's criminal courts. Lesser offences are commonly dealt with exclusively by solicitors in the magistrates' courts; more serious charges go to the Crown Courts, which are essentially still the domain of barristers. Everyday crime is the staple for most solicitors – theft, assault, drugs and driving offences. Fraud is the preserve of a more limited number of firms, and the cases require a different approach from, say, crimes of violence. Criminal practice is busy, often frantic, with a hectic schedule of visits to police stations, prisons and magistrates' courts meaning plenty of face-to-face client contact and advocacy. The area is also known for having the lowest pay in the profession.

What lawyers do

- Attend police stations to interview and advise people in police custody.
- Visit prisons to see clients on remand.
- Prepare the client's defence using medical and social workers' reports.
- Liaise with witnesses, probation officers, the CPS and others.
- Attend conferences with counsel (ie barristers).
- Represent defendants at trial or brief barristers to do so.
- Represent clients at sentencing hearings, explaining any mitigating facts.
- Fraud solicitors need a head for business as they deal with a considerable volume of paperwork and financial analysis.

The realities of the job

- Hours are long and can disrupt your personal life. Lawyers who are accredited to work as duty solicitors will be on a rota and can be called to a police station at any time of the day or night.
- Confidence is essential. Without it you're doomed.
- In general crime you'll have a large caseload with a fast turnaround, meaning plenty of advocacy.
- The work is driven by the procedural rules and timetable of the court. Even so, in 2012 nearly 32,000 magistrates' and Crown Court trials did not proceed on the appointed day.
- Your efforts can mean the difference between a person's liberty or incarceration. You have to be detail-conscious and constantly vigilant.

- You'll encounter horrible situations and difficult or distressed people. Murderers, rapists, drug dealers, conmen, paedophiles – if you have the ability to look beyond the labels and see these people as clients deserving of your best efforts then you've picked the right job.
- It can be disheartening to see clients repeat the same poor choices, returning to court again and again.
- Public funding of criminal defence means there's a good helping of bureaucracy. It also means you'll earn very little, certainly in your first few years of practice.
- Trainees in fraud find the early years provide minimal advocacy and masses of trawling through warehouses full of documents. Caseloads are smaller but cases can run for years.

Current issues

- The world of criminal legal aid has entered a long dark winter of despair. The Legal Aid, Sentencing and Punishment of Offenders Act 2012 came into force on 1 April 2013. It aims to cut £220m annually from the £1.1bn criminal legal aid budget by 2018/19, and remove entire areas – such as employment and immigration – from the scheme.
- Since 2013 there have been mass walkouts by barristers and solicitors in protest at the cuts, which will lead to 500,000 fewer instances of legal help to individuals and 45,000 fewer instances of legal representation. In June 2014, barristers and solicitors protested outside the Old Bailey and MoJ with a giant effigy of Justice Secretary Chris Grayling.
- Cuts in criminal legal aid fees of 17.5% on average for solicitors and 6% for barristers were confirmed by Grayling in February 2014.
- In July 2014 the president of the Law Society sent a letter to criminal law practitioners across the country warning that hundreds of solicitors firms will close if the government doesn't postpone and reconsider cuts to fees and changes to duty contracts for solicitors covering police stations and magistrates' courts. There are currently about 1,600 duty contracts but this will be reduced to 525 under the new scheme overseen by a quango, the Legal Aid Agency. Firms may form consortia to bid for contracts.
- Many firms that have previously excelled in crime are moving out of the area entirely or no longer accept publicly funded clients. Firms affected by the cuts (or those looking to pre-empt financial difficulties) are either abandoning legal aid altogether, merging, or shifting their focus from the high-street criminal cases to fraud and more serious financial crimes.

- The traditionally close relationship between barristers and solicitors could be threatened by the rise of public access work, which allows barristers to bypass solicitors to gain clients, with fixed fees agreed in advance.
- The number of legal aid firms has steadily declined in the past decade since the Legal Services Commission introduced a compulsory quality mark in 2000. In 2011, there were around 1,700 criminal legal aid firms, compared to 2,900 in 2000. The government's 'Transforming Legal Aid' proposals aim to cut that number to just 400, as well as require firms to bid on contracts to represent defendants, which will squeeze fee income. It's predicted that many smaller practices will be forced to merge as a consequence.
- The most controversial element of the Transforming Legal Aid proposals – depriving defendants of their right to choose their own solicitor – was quickly dropped after loud disapproval from the legal sector.

Read our True Pictures on...

Foot Anstey	Kingsley Napley*
Higgs & Sons	Peters & Peters*
Irwin Mitchell	Slater & Gordon*

*These firms have a strong focus on crime

- Since the Jimmy Savile saga and the start of Operation Yewtree, there has been a huge rise in the number of historic sex abuse allegations being brought. The heat of the Savile case and the surrounding furore means that many cases are being brought on the strength of one allegation alone.
- Check out www.clsa.co.uk for other news and discussion on major developments in criminal practice.

The criminal courts of England and Wales

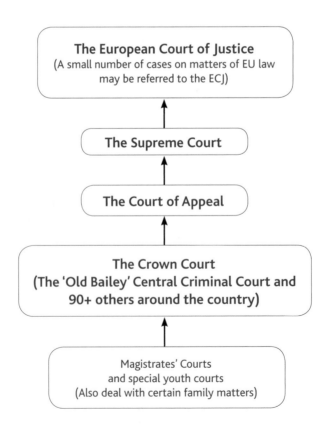

The European Court of Justice
(A small number of cases on matters of EU law may be referred to the ECJ)

The Supreme Court

The Court of Appeal

The Crown Court
(The 'Old Bailey' Central Criminal Court and 90+ others around the country)

Magistrates' Courts
and special youth courts
(Also deal with certain family matters)

Employment

In a nutshell

Employment lawyers guide their clients through workplace-related legislation and are intimately involved in the relationship between employers and employees. The divide between employers' and employees' lawyers is often clear-cut so bear this in mind when you pick your firm. Most will work either largely for employers or largely for employees; a few will straddle both sides of the fence. Usually the job includes both advisory work and litigation.

Disputes are almost always resolved at an Employment Tribunal, or before reaching one, and appeals are heard at the Employment Appeal Tribunal (EAT). The grievances leading to litigation fall into the following broad categories: redundancy, unlawful dismissal, breach of contract, harassment and discrimination. This last type of claim can be brought on the grounds of race, religious or philosophical belief, gender, sexual orientation, disability and age.

What lawyers do

Employees' solicitors...

- Advise clients on whether they have suffered unlawful or unfair treatment and establish the amount to be claimed. This will either be capped or, in the case of discrimination, can include additional elements to cover loss of earnings, injury to feelings and aggravated damages.
- Gather evidence and witnesses to support the claim.
- Try to negotiate a payment from the employer or take the matter to tribunal. If there is a breach-of-contract element to the claim, it might be heard in a court rather than a tribunal.
- If the matter does reach tribunal, the solicitor may conduct the advocacy.

Employers' solicitors...

- Defend or settle the sorts of claims described above.
- Negotiate employment contracts or exit packages for senior staff.
- Negotiate with unions to avoid or resolve industrial disputes.
- Formulate HR policies and provide training on how to avoid workplace problems.

Realities of the job

- You quickly develop an understanding of human foibles. By their very nature employment cases are filled with drama.

- Clients may assume your role is to provide emotional support as well as legal advice, so you need to take care to define your role appropriately.
- Solicitors who want to do their own advocacy thrive here, although barristers are commonly used for high-stakes or complicated hearings and trials.
- The work is driven by the procedural rules and timetable of the tribunals and courts.
- The law is extensive and changes frequently. You'll read more than your fair share of EU directives.

Current issues

- The appetite for redundancy exercises has not tailed off completely, and although it's not as strong as it was in 2008, many clients are still looking to make cost savings by restructuring, outsourcing or simply cutting staff.
- There has been a rise in TUPE work as staff are transferred or outsourced by companies looking to cut costs. In cases where staff have been dismissed or made redundant, or have had changes made to their contracts, there has been more scope for proceedings.
- Employers are increasingly concerned about staff leaving to set up a competing business, leading to a rise in attempted enforcement of restrictive covenants and confidentiality agreements.
- Some law firms have a team of HR specialists or a dedicated hotline to deal with low-cost, day-to-day employment queries.
- Many organisations have consolidated their employment legal spend by putting out to tender just one contract and are now looking for a sole legal provider to handle all their needs. This has naturally increased the level of competition between employment practices.
- Many companies are still leveraging the effects of the recession to make changes at board and senior management level. This has led to an increase in demand for advice on high-value contract termination work from both employees and respondents.
- The coalition government introduced radical reforms to the tribunal process. More decisions can now be made by legal officers rather than employment judges or a full tribunal. Plus, from April 2012 the amount of time an employee needs to have worked at a company before being able to bring an unfair dismissal charge has been increased from one to two years. Employers naturally see these proposals as a good thing; trade unions are angry.
- As of April 2013 legal aid has been cut from all employment cases, except those related to discrimination. This is leading to more people representing themselves.

- The Enterprise and Regulatory Reform Act 2013 brought about a number of changes to employment law. Whistle-blowing was one affected area: protection was reduced for whistle-blowers, who now have to show that it's in the public interest to complain about an employer's unlawful act. Also, employers are allowed to have a 'protected conversation' with an employee encouraging them to leave with a pay-off (settlement agreement).
- The government's new owner-employee contracts will offer employees shares in return for waiving employment rights including unfair dismissal, training rights and the right to ask for flexible working hours. It remains to be seen what the take-up rate for these new contracts will be, but observers say they will probably be unpopular with employers and employees alike.
- From 30 June 2014, the Children and Families Act gave all employees (provided that they have worked at least 26 weeks for the same employer) the legal right to request flexible working hours – this right had previously been reserved for just parents and carers. Employees submit a statutory application, and employers are legally obliged to provide a valid reason for refusing such requests. Employers can revert to the ACAS Code of Practice, in order to wise-up on how to approach flexible working requests, but confused employers are just as likely to turn to employment lawyers for some advice. This change to the law has also led to predictions of increasing discrimination and other tribunal claims: the government itself has estimated that the new law could give rise to up to 150 extra tribunal cases a year – with employers shelling out an average of £5,900 for each one.
- In January 2014, the Capital Requirements Directive (CRD) IV imposed a cap on bonuses within the financial sector, to tackle what has been deemed excessive risk-taking that has produced a global 'big bonus' culture. Banks that break the rules run the risk of receiving hefty fines, so lawyers have been helping their clients draft policies which: a) ensure that employees affected by the cap are renumerated within the remits of the CRD IV, and b) are compensated in a way that rewards strong performance and keeps British banks competitive.
- The Enterprise and Regulatory Reform Act 2013 set out to alter the procedures and penalties which tribunals have traditionally adopted. Throughout 2014, further amedments were implemented: discrimination questionnaires were scrapped; financial penalties were imposed on employers in breach of employment rights; claimants were asked to register details of their claim with ACAS before formally submitting it; and (from October 2014) tribunals were given the power to order equal pay audits if employers were found to have breached equal pay.
- The Department for Business, Innovation & Skills (BIS) has also been busy devising new changes to TUPE (pronounced 'tu-pee') transfers. On 31 January

Read our True Pictures on...

Addleshaw Goddard	Latham & Watkins
Allen & Overy	Leigh Day
Ashfords	Lester Aldridge
Ashurst	Lewis Silkin
B P Collins	Linklaters
Baker & McKenzie	Macfarlanes
Bates Wells Braithwaite	Maclay Murray & Spens
Berwin Leighton Paisner	Mayer Brown
Bird & Bird	McDermott Will & Emery
Bond Dickinson	Memery Crystal
BPE Solicitors	Michelmores
Brabners Chaffe Street	Mills & Reeve
Browne Jacobson	Mishcon de Reya
Burges Salmon	Muckle
Capsticks Solicitors	Nabarro
Charles Russell	Norton Rose Fulbright
Clifford Chance	Olswang
Clyde & Co	Osborne Clarke
CMS	Pinsent Masons
Cripps	Reed Smith
Dechert	RPC
Dentons	SGH Martineau
DLA Piper	Shoosmiths
DWF	Simmons & Simmons
Eversheds	Slater & Gordon
Farrer & Co	Slaughter and May
Foot Anstey	Speechly Bircham
Freeths	Squire Patton Boggs
Freshfields	Stephenson Harwood
Gateley	Stevens & Bolton
Gordons	Taylor Wessing
Harbottle & Lewis	TLT
Herbert Smith Freehills	Travers Smith
Higgs & Sons	Trethowans
Hill Dickinson	Trowers & Hamlins
Hogan Lovells	Veale Wasbrough Vizards
Irwin Mitchell	Ward Hadaway
Jones Day	Watson, Farley & Williams
K&L Gates	Wedlake Bell
Kennedys	Wilsons
King & Wood Mallesons	Withers
Kingsley Napley	Wragge Lawrence Graham

2014, these changes were implemented, and new rules concerning (among many others) redundancy consultations; service provision changes; and the meaning of an 'economic, technical or organisational' (ETO) reason for dismissal were established.

Practice Areas

Environment

In a nutshell

Environment lawyers advise corporate clients on damage limitation and pre-emptive measures, and they defend them from prosecution. In other words, the majority of private practitioners work for, rather than stick it to, big business. Opportunities do exist at organisations like Greenpeace and Friends of the Earth, but these jobs are highly sought after. Another non-commercial option is to work for a local authority, a government department such as the Department for Environment, Food and Rural Affairs (Defra) or a regulatory body like the Environment Agency. However, be aware that hiring freezes and cutbacks have been hitting the public sector hard.

Environment law overlaps with other disciplines such as property, criminal law, corporate or EU law. Environmental issues can be deal breakers, especially in the modern era of corporate social responsibility. However, the small size of most law firms' environment teams means there are relatively few pure environmental specialists around.

What lawyers do

Lawyers in private practice
- Advise on the potential environmental consequences of corporate, property and projects transactions.
- Advise on compliance and regulatory issues to help clients operate within regulatory boundaries and avoid investigation or prosecution.
- Defend clients when they get into trouble over water or air pollution, waste disposal, emission levels or health and safety. Such cases can involve criminal or civil actions, judicial reviews and even statutory appeals. They may also be subject to damaging media coverage.

Lawyers with local authorities
- Handle a massive variety of work covering regulatory and planning issues plus waste management and air pollution prosecutions.
- Advise the authority on its own potential liability.

Lawyers working for Defra
- Are responsible for litigation, drafting of subordinate legislation, advisory work and contract drafting on any of Defra's varied mandates.
- Work in a team of 50 lawyers, including Government Legal Service trainees. Defra aims to promote sustainable development without compromising the quality of life of future generations.

Lawyers working for the Environment Agency
- Prosecute environmental crimes – this involves gathering evidence, preparing cases and briefing barristers.
- Co-operate with government lawyers on the drafting and implementation of legislation.
- Work in Bristol and eight regional bases and are responsible for protecting and enhancing the environment. They also regulate corporate activities that have the capacity to pollute.

The realities of the job
- In this competitive and demanding field, all-round skills are best complemented by experience in a specific area. The way in which environmental law spans disciplines requires commercial nous and a good understanding of corporate structures.
- Excellent academics are essential to help wade through, extrapolate from and present research and complex legislation; so too are sound judgement, pragmatism and the ability to come up with inventive solutions.
- A basic grasp of science helps.
- If you want to change environmental laws or crusade for a better planet, then stick to the public or non-profit sectors. The sometimes uncomfortable realities of private practice won't be for you.
- Client contact is key and relationships can endure over many years. Environmental risks are difficult to quantify and clients will rely on your gut instincts and powers of lateral thinking.
- With visits to waste dumps or drying reservoirs and a workload that can span health and safety matters, corporate transactions and regulatory advice all in one day, this is neither a desk-bound nor a quiet discipline.
- Research constantly advances, and legislation is always changing in this field, so you'll spend a lot of time keeping up to date.
- A taste for European law is essential as more and more EU directives prescribe the boundaries of environmental law in the UK.

Current issues
- Despite significant and high-profile budget cuts the Environment Agency has continued to strongly enforce regulations. Commentators observed heightened activity in the monitoring of waste and chemicals, with the EA increasingly pursuing and closing down illegal waste sites. The introduction of REACH (Registration, Evaluation, Authorisation and Restriction of Chemicals) in 2007 continues to drive companies to law firms for advice on complying with the regulations.

- The fracking debate has dominated UK news after large deposits of shale gas were found across Britain. Supporters highlight the importance of the UK becoming self-reliant in its energy supply while anti-fracking campaigners have protested against the detrimental environmental impact. Volatility in areas which traditionally supply European energy, such as the Middle East and Ukraine, will ensure the debate continues.

- Nuclear energy is still a hot topic. The planned development of a nuclear plant at Hinkley Point, Somerset, has caused fierce and widespread debate. With several emerging plans to develop further sites, it's set to remain a sensitive issue. Law firms are helping companies negotiate the minefield of regulations and prepare applications for nuclear development opportunities.

- Renewable energy is at the heart of the Electricity Market Reform which plans to invest £110bn in renewable energy and electricity infrastructure in the UK. The reform aims to make it easier for low-carbon electricity generation to compete with the fossil fuel market and enable the UK to reduce its carbon emissions by 2030. Legal commentators believe this reform will create a fundamental change in the renewable energy market.

- Investment in wind and solar projects has continued to grow in the UK, with other renewable energy projects, such as wave and tidal, benefiting from increased investment. In 2013 the Department for Energy and Climate Change reported that investment in renewable energy stood at £8bn, continuing the trend of investment which has taken place since 2010.

- While UK investment may have increased, globally there was a reduction in renewable investment in 2013 due to uncertainty over policies. Revisions to European Market Infrastructure Regulations (EMIR) came into force across 2013 and 2014, requiring companies to increase their reporting measures and risk management standards. MiFID 2 (Markets in Financial Instruments Derivative) should come into effect in 2016, altering how stocks, bonds and derivatives are traded and reported in the hope of creating a more transparent market. Consequently law firms have seen a drop in work as environmental investors wait to see how these changes will affect the market.

Read our True Pictures on...

Addleshaw Goddard	K&L Gates
Allen & Overy	King & Wood Mallesons
Ashurst	Leigh Day
B P Collins	Linklaters
Baker & McKenzie	Macfarlanes
Berwin Leighton Paisner	Maclay Murray & Spens
Bond Dickinson	Mayer Brown
Brabners Chaffe Street	Mills & Reeve
Browne Jacobson	Nabarro
Burges Salmon	Norton Rose Fulbright
Clifford Chance	Osborne Clarke
Clyde & Co	Pinsent Masons
CMS	Shoosmiths
Dentons	Simmons & Simmons
DLA Piper	Slaughter and May
DWF	Squire Patton Boggs
Eversheds	Stephenson Harwood
Freshfields	Stevens & Bolton
Herbert Smith Freehills	TLT
Hogan Lovells	Travers Smith
Irwin Mitchell	Wragge Lawrence Graham
Jones Day	

- Despite a slowing down in the environment market there are still plenty of opportunities for environment lawyers, particularly among City firms where there is increasing demand for them. Law firms are also building and consolidating environmental practices rather than simply relying on sourcing in lawyers from elsewhere as and when required.

- Keep on top of changes in environmental law courtesy of websites like the UK Environmental Law Association. Most environmental lawyers are members of UKELA, and students are welcome to attend events across the country. The charity ELF provides a referral service for members of the public, organises lectures in London and produces regular newsletters for members.

Family

In a nutshell

Lawyers are involved with almost every aspect of family life, from the legal mechanics and complications of marriage and civil partnerships to divorce, disputes between cohabitants, inheritance disputes between family members, prenuptial and cohabitation agreements, and all matters relating to children. Whether working in a general high-street practice with a large caseload of legally aided work, or for a specialist practice dealing with big-money divorces and complex child or international matters, family solicitors are in court a good deal and fully occupied back in the office.

There is effectively a division between child law and matrimonial law, with many practitioners devoting themselves exclusively to one or the other; others plant a foot in each. Unfortunately, family law is one that has and will be seriously affected by legal aid cuts.

What lawyers do

Matrimonial lawyers

- Interview and advise clients on prenuptial agreements, cohabitation arrangements, divorce and the financial implications of divorce. This can involve issues like inheritance and wills, conveyancing, welfare benefits, company law, tax and trusts, pensions and even judicial review.
- Prepare the client's case for divorce and settlement hearings, including organising witnesses and providing summaries of assets/finances, which will require dealing with accountants and financial and pensions advisers.
- Attend conferences with barristers.
- Represent clients in hearings or brief barristers to do so.
- Negotiate settlements and associated financial terms.

Child law lawyers

- In private cases – interview and advise clients on the implications of divorce with regard to child contact and residence. In some instances this will result in court action. Deal with disputes between parents or other family members over the residence of, and contact with, children.
- In public cases – represent local authorities, parents, children's guardians or children themselves on matters such as children's care proceedings or abuse in care claims. Social workers, probation officers, psychologists and medical professionals will also be involved in cases.

The realities of the job

- When it comes to relationships and families, no two sets of circumstances will ever be the same. Advocacy is plentiful.
- You will encounter a real mix of clients, some at a joyful moment in their lives, others facing deeply traumatic times. A good family law practitioner combines the empathetic, sensitive qualities of a counsellor with the clarity of thought and commercial acumen of a lawyer. You need to remain detached to achieve the result your clients need.
- Tough negotiating skills and a strong nerve are vital as your work has immediate and practical consequences. The prospect of telling a client that they've lost a custody battle does much to sharpen the mind.
- A pragmatic and real-world outlook is useful, however you'll also need to spend time keeping abreast of legal developments.
- On publicly funded matters you'll face your share of bureaucracy, and it certainly won't make you rich.

Current issues

- London is arguably the divorce capital of the world and is becoming known for 'divorce tourism'. Today one in six cases handled passing through the English courts involve a foreign national or have an international dimension. For example, in 2011 Russian oligarch Boris Berezovsky paid out a settlement of £220m to his former wife – Britain's biggest ever divorce settlement. London is also the most generous jurisdiction for women – so it's probably no surprise that Berezovsky's ex-wife understatedly labelled the verdict "*superb.*"
- There has been an increase in the popularity of prenuptial agreements following the *Radmacher v Granatino* divorce. In 2014, the Law Commission recommended that prenups should be legally binding in divorce settlements, but only after the needs of the separating couple and children have been taken into account.
- The Supreme Court's landmark 2013 ruling in *Prest v Petrodel Resources* established that a divorced spouse can lay claim to an ex-partner's assets even if they are tied up in company assets.
- Same-sex marriage became legal in the UK in 2014. This development brought with it the significant benefits that come with marriage, like the provision for a transferable nil-rate tax band.

- Family law no longer qualifies for legal aid, thanks to cutbacks that came into force in April 2013. More and more people are now representing themselves in court. In response, the Bar Council has issued a guide to representing yourself, including the advice that it's best not to copy the lawyers on TV, because *"judges hate it."*

- According to the Children and Family Court Advisory Service, the total number of applications to have children put into care has reached a record high. This has been dubbed 'the Baby P effect'.

- Social workers are under increased scrutiny, and the family courts have been opened up to the press. Many lawyers say that this has made it much harder to do their jobs and has more to do with justice being seen to be done rather than anything else. The family courts have been heavily criticised for the length of time it takes to reach decisions in child law cases. In response, the government has implemented a six-month limit for the completion of child care cases. Critics say this will have an impact on the quality of decisions and on children's welfare.

- The government has also pledged to pour money into publicly-funded family mediation in the hope of diverting cases away from the courts. In 2013, for example, the government pledged an additional £10m – taking the total spent up to £25m.

Read our True Pictures on...

Ashfords	Irwin Mitchell
B P Collins	Kingsley Napley
Bircham Dyson Bell	Lester Aldridge
Boodle Hatfield	Michlemores
Brabner Chaffe Street	Mills & Reeve
Burges Salmon	Mishcon de Reya
Charles Russell	SGH Martineau
Collyer Bristow	Slater & Gordon
Cripps	Speechly Bircham
DWF	Stevens & Bolton
Farrer & Co	TLT
Foot Anstey	Trethowans
Gateley	Ward Hadaway
Higgs & Sons	Withers

Practice Areas

Human Rights & Immigration

In a nutshell

Human rights lawyers protest injustice and fight for principles at the point of intersection between the state's powers and the rights of individuals. Cases usually relate in some way to the UK's ratification of the European Convention on Human Rights (ECHR) through the Human Rights Act and crop up in criminal and civil contexts, often through the medium of judicial review, a key tool in questioning the decisions of public bodies. Civil contexts include claims regarding the right to education or community care under the Mental Health Act, cases of discrimination at work and even family issues. Criminal contexts could relate to complaints against the police, prisoners' issues, public order convictions following demonstrations or perhaps extradition on terror charges. Immigration lawyers deal with both business and personal immigration matters – the former has been embraced by the government in its quest to manage economic migration. In this more lucrative area, lawyers assist highly skilled migrants to obtain residency or leave to remain in the UK and help non-nationals to secure visas for travel abroad. They also work with companies that need to bring in employees from overseas. Personal immigration lawyers represent individuals who have fled persecution in their country of origin. They also take on cases for people whose right to stay in the UK is under threat or indeed entirely absent.

What lawyers do

Business immigration lawyers

- Advise and assist businesses or their employees in relation to work permits and visas. They need to be up to speed on all current schemes, such as those for highly skilled migrants and investors.
- Prepare for, attend and advocate at tribunals or court hearings; or where necessary instructing a barrister to do so.

Personal immigration lawyers

- Advise clients on their status and rights within the UK. Secure evidence of a client's identity, medical reports and witness statements, and prepare cases for court hearings or appeals. Represent clients or instruct a barrister to do so.
- Undertake an immense amount of unremunerated form filling and legal aid paperwork.

The realities of the job

- The competition for training contracts is huge. Voluntary work at a law centre or specialist voluntary organisation, or other relevant experience, is essential.
- A commitment to and belief in the values you're fighting for is essential in this relatively low-paid area. Work in the voluntary sector or taking on important cases pro bono can provide the greatest satisfaction.
- Because much of the work is publicly funded, firms do not usually offer attractive trainee salaries or sponsorship through law school.
- Sensitivity and empathy are absolutely essential because you'll often be dealing with highly emotional people, those with mental health issues or those who simply don't appreciate the full extent of their legal predicament.
- Strong analytical skills are required to pick out the legal issues you can change from the socio-economic ones beyond your control.
- In the battle against red tape and institutional indifference, organisational skills and a vast store of patience are valuable assets.
- Opportunities for advocacy are abundant, which means that knowledge of court and tribunal procedures is a fundamental requirement. Often cases must pass through every possible stage of appeal before referral to judicial review or the ECJ.
- If working within a commercial firm, the clients will be businesses and public sector organisations. As such there will be less of a campaigning element to the work and you will not necessarily feel you are 'on the side of the angels'.

Current issues

- Issues of asylum (including detention and deportation) and people seeking permission to stay in the UK on human rights grounds never cease to arouse strong opinions. The government is cracking down on all forms of immigration, but despite this – or perhaps because of it – the number of asylum appeals has been decreasing over the past few years.
- The advent of the Freedom of Information Act and increased transparency in the public sector in line with Article 6 of the ECHR mean law firms have seen a greater willingness from the public to challenge the decisions of authorities.

Practice Areas

- Many human rights and civil liberties cases have related to issues arising out of Guantanamo Bay, Iraq, terrorism, stop-and-search powers and national security. These cases have taken the form of judicial reviews and public inquiries. The much-publicised Binyam Mohamed judicial review, and the Baha Mousa and Al-Sweady inquiries are examples of such investigations.
- Other recent big social justice cases have related to equality rights, privacy rights and asylum seeker rights.
- The Points Based System (PBS) of immigration means every employer now needs to obtain an immigration licence under the PBS before being able to issue a Certificate of Sponsorship for each employee it wishes to employ. Some argue that the scheme is now so technical that employers are constantly at risk of unlawful employment. Critics believe that restricting highly skilled migrants from working in the UK is farcical. In May 2014, the Government released two new statutory Codes of Practice, one on a civil penalty scheme for employers and the other on avoiding unlawful discrimination while preventing illegal working.
- Non-EU immigration has been affected by new policies since the coalition government came to power; for example the annual capping on non-EU skilled workers at 21,700 in 2011, which was frozen until April 2014. For further details check out migrationobservatory.ox.ac.uk
- The past decade has seen an enormous growth in human rights litigation, in UK and European courts – like the General Court (formerly the Court of First Instance), European Court of Justice, European Court of Human Rights – as well as international tribunals. This case-driven development of human rights law is based on fundamental rights standards common to legal systems throughout Europe.

Read our True Pictures on...

Baker & McKenzie	Leigh Day
Bates Wells Braithwaite	Lewis Silkin
Bird and Bird	Mishcon de Reya
Clyde & Co	Morgan Lewis
DWF	Speechly Bircham
Irwin Mitchell	Squire Patton Boggs
Kingsley Napley	

- The 2014 Immigration Act purports to be "*an Act to make provision about immigration law; to make provision about marriage and civil partnership involving certain foreign nationals; to make provision about the acquisition of citizenship by persons unable to acquire it because their fathers and mothers were not married to each other and provision about the removal of citizenship from persons whose conduct is seriously prejudicial to the United Kingdom's vital interests.*"
- The death of Jimmy Mubenga has shed light on deportation and the extent to which force can be used in immigration removals. The 2010 incident, when the husband and father of three suffered cardio-respiratory collapse on a flight to Angola after being restrained by three G4S guards, was making headlines again in March 2014 when a manslaughter charge was bought against the perpetrators.
- Trenton Oldfield, activist and disruptor of the 2012 Oxford and Cambridge boat race, faced deportation to his native Australia after serving two months of a six-month sentence. Towards the end of 2013, his appeal was accepted and he was allowed to remain in the UK.

Insurance

In a nutshell

Insurance is the practice of hedging against physical and financial risk. This practice and its fallout require a lot of legal work. Insurance and reinsurance (even insurers are vulnerable to financial risk and they transfer part of their risk on to reinsurers) are practised by a significant number of specialist law firms and general commercial outfits across the UK. Insurance can be split into many sub-specialisms (see below). Firms may offer all or some of these services. Personal injury and clinical negligence (including public liability, employers' liability, accident-at-work claims etc) are also insurance-related practice areas – you can read more about them (page 129). Maritime insurance was the first type of insurance to exist. You can read more about shipping law (page 141).

It's possible to insure pretty much anything against almost any eventuality. Put differently, insurance is taken out to cover risks: human error, accidents, natural disasters etc. The most common types of insurance which lawyers deal with are: insurance against the destruction of tangible assets (eg property), insurance against the loss of intangible assets (eg revenue streams) and insurance against mistakes made by professionals (professional indemnity – the insurance-related bit of professional negligence). So, insurance lawyers work on cases related to property damage, product liability, fraud, insolvency, directors' liabilities (D&O), aviation, business interruption, mortgage losses, political events, technology, energy, environment, construction, finance... the list goes on. Disputes arise between the insured policyholder and the insurer; between the insured plus the insurer and another party; or between the insurer and the reinsurer.

Other lawyers specialise in the transactional aspects of the insurance industry, advising on tax, regulations, restructurings, drafting insurance policies, and M&A activity between insurance companies.

What lawyers do

Professional indemnity
- Represent professionals accused of malpractice and their insurers. Professions most often affected include engineers, architects, surveyors, accountants, brokers, financial advisers and solicitors as well as GPs, dentists, surgeons etc.
- Investigate a claim, assess its authenticity and look into the coverage of a given insurance policy to determine an insurer's degree of liability.
- Take advice from experts on professional conduct.
- Draft letters in response to claims.
- Prepare documents for court or out-of-court settlements.

- Attend pre-trial hearings, case management conferences and trials if a case goes to court.
- Attend joint-settlement meetings, arbitrations or mediations in out-of-court cases.

Commercial insurance disputes
- Work on claims related to things as varied as properties damaged by flood or fires, oil rigs destroyed by hurricanes, or gold mines nationalised by socialist governments.
- Work on disputes between insurers and the insured over insurance payouts and what insurance coverage consists of, or act for the insurer and the insured together in litigation with a third party.
- Assess coverage and the insurer's liability.
- Interview witnesses to find out how events occurred.
- Value the claim and build up the case for what the client feels is an adequate settlement.
- Attend court or mediations/arbitrations in order to come to a settlement.

Transactions
- Broadly similar to the work of a general transactional lawyer. There are extra rules and regulations governing insurance transactions which lawyers need to take into account.

The realities of the job
- While several legal practice areas fall under the insurance umbrella, the insurance industry itself is a distinct, single block within the City and the UK as a whole. There are a few big well-known insurance companies out there, but over 400 are registered with the famous insurance market Lloyd's of London.
- London is the global centre for insurance and reinsurance. It has been ever since Lloyd's of London was founded almost 330 years ago. The industry is extremely well established and has its own rules, traditions and obscure terminology. Businesses based overseas will often be insured with a London firm, and the biggest disputes often have an international angle to them.
- The insurance industry has a reputation for being a bit dull. However, the legal side kicks in when calamities occur, making it quite eventful – as any 'wet' shipping lawyer will tell you. Often, insurance lawyers are involved in investigating exactly what happened following a catastrophe, as this is the essence of a claim – how do you think they dealt with the insurance aspects of the missing MH370 plane?

Practice Areas

- It is a complex and technical area – reading policy wording is not easy! Stints in insurance seats are challenging for trainees, even those who have taken an insurance law elective on the LPC.
- Insurance lawyers are known for their precise and fastidious working style. Good organisational skills are crucial, because lawyers in high-volume firms are often dealing with a host of claims at various stages.
- Lawyers have to pay special attention to potentially fraudulent claims or parts of claims.
- Insurance cases range from huge international disputes to small local squabbles. Trainees might run a small case themselves, but only work on a component of a large high-value dispute. Lower value work is usually done by small or mid-size regional and national firms, while the largest disputes are the preserve of City firms.
- Many firms regularly act for both insurance companies and insured policyholders. There is a trend towards firms specialising in either policyholder or insurer work.
- The insurance industry is regulated by the newly-established Financial Conduct Authority.

Current issues

- There is an increasing emphasis on using fixed-fee and capped-fee arrangements to save costs and create stability when it comes to spending.
- There have been many catastrophic events and natural disasters in the past few years. From the Arab Spring and the Fukushima earthquake to the aftermath of the Deepwater Horizon oil spill, the UK riots and 2013 European floods, all had massive insurance implications. In the long term such disasters will affect the reinsurance market too, causing reinsurance premiums to rise. The insurance market is called 'soft' when premiums are low and 'hard' when premiums are high because of a recent catastrophe or disaster (for example, the market 'hardened' after 9/11).
- The EU's Solvency II directive – aimed at harmonising EU insurance regulations to enhance consumer protection – is due to come into force on 1 January 2016. It is already having a major impact on the insurance industry as companies seek legal advice on compliance.
- Much to the surprise of many observers, the insurance markets have held up well during the recession. Insurance firms are – for the most part – doing well. The recession has led to a slight increase in speculative and fraudulent claims by individuals and businesses looking to make a bob or two, but again not to the degree expected.

Read our True Pictures on...

Addleshaw Goddard	Holman Fenwick Willan
Allen & Overy	Ince & Co*
Ashurst	K&L Gates
Berwin Leighton Paisner	Kennedys*
Bond Dickinson	Linklaters
Browne Jacobson	Maclay Murray & Spens
Clifford Chance	Mayer Brown
Clyde & Co*	Mills & Reeve
CMS	Norton Rose Fulbright
Covington & Burling	Pinsent Masons
DLA Piper	Reed Smith
DWF	RPC*
Edwards Wildman Palmer*	Sidley Austin
Eversheds	Simmons & Simmons
Freshfields	Slater & Gordon
Herbert Smith Freehills	Slaughter and May
Hill Dickinson	Wragge Lawrence Graham
Hogan Lovells	

*These firms have a strong focus on insurance

- The recession has caused an upsurge in the number of professional negligence claims against mortgage brokers and other financial advisers over their advice on investments and financial products.
- The Legal Aid, Sentencing and Punishment of Offenders Act 2012 banned the use of referral fees for lucrative personal injury claims (often whiplash-related) from April 2013. Some insurance firms have set up alternative business structures to get around the ban.
- The Insurance Contracts Bill is currently before parliament and believed to be the most significant change to insurance law for at least 100 years. Essentially, it aims to increase transparency in the rules that govern contracts and reduce the overall number of legal disputes.
- Telematics is a growing area in auto insurance. A device in a car can track the driver's behaviour and send that info to the insurance company, who will charge premiums accordingly based on that driver's risk of accident. In August 2014, BMW announced that it will produce the world's first factory-fitted telematics.
- The scandal of mis-sold payment protection insurance is ongoing and claims continue to be dealt with. Add-on insurance is the next scandal-prone area. In 2013, a large insurer was fined for amassing £97m from policies that customers bought without being told that they were optional extras and separate from the core cover.
- New risks to insure against are arising all the time. Lately, protecting companies from cyber attacks has gathered steam.

Intellectual Property

In a nutshell

Lawyers, patent attorneys and trade mark attorneys work to protect their clients' intellectual property assets. Technical solutions to technical problems are deemed to be inventions, usually protectable via **patents** that provide their proprietor with the exclusive right to stop others working in the claimed area for a period of usually up to 20 years. Preparing a patent specification is a highly specialised task requiring particular scientific/technical expertise and knowledge combined with experience and knowledge of complex application procedures.

Trade marks used to sell goods or services are protectable by way of a registration procedure and provide a potentially perpetual monopoly right. The aesthetic shape and way a product is designed is also protectable via **registered design protection** for a limited period of time. **Unregistered** rights also exist for a time for various designs of products. Then there is **copyright** which lasts during the lifetime of the creator and for a period after their death, and which arises automatically on the creation of music, artwork, works of literature or reference, databases and web pages, for example.

A single product such as a mobile phone will be protected by several different forms of IP in countries all around the world. For would-be competitors wanting to make or sell something similar, a first costly hurdle is simply finding out what these rights are and who owns them. Worst-case scenario, getting it wrong or overlooking an IP right might result in being on the wrong end of a court injunction or costly damages (fearsomely so in the USA), and ignorance is no defence! The work of an IP lawyer is not only specialist in itself, but increasingly it requires close collaboration with other specialists in areas such as IT, media, competition, telecommunications, life sciences and employment.

What lawyers do

- Search domestic, European and international registers of patents, trade marks and registered designs to establish ownership of existing rights or the potential to register new rights.
- Take all steps to protect clients' interests by securing patents, trade marks and registered designs; appeal unfavourable decisions; attack decisions that benefit others but harm the lawyer's own client.
- Write letters to require that third parties desist from carrying out infringing activities or risk litigation for damages and an injunction.

- Issue court proceedings and prepare cases for trial by taking witness statements, examining scientific or technical reports and commissioning experiments and tests. Junior lawyers may find themselves conducting consumer surveys and going on covert shopping expeditions.
- Instruct and consult with barristers. Solicitor advocates can appear in the Patents County Court; the advantages of having a specialist IP barrister for higher court hearings are obvious.
- Draft commercial agreements between owners of IP rights and those who want to use the protected invention, design or artistic work. The most common documents will either transfer ownership or grant a licence for use.
- Work as part of a multidisciplinary team on corporate transactions, verifying ownership of IP rights and drafting documents enabling their transfer.

The realities of the job

- Lawyers must be able to handle everyone from company directors to mad inventors. Clients come from manufacturing, the hi-tech sector, engineering, pharmaceuticals, agrochemicals, universities and scientific institutions, media organisations and the arts.
- A degree in a relevant subject is common among patent lawyers. Brand and trade mark lawyers need a curiosity for all things creative and must keep up with consumer trends. Both need a good sense for commercial strategy.
- Attention to detail, precision and accuracy are all important. You must be meticulous, particularly when drafting, as correct wording is imperative.
- In trade mark and design filings and prosecution, everything has a time limit. You will live by deadlines.
- In patent filing, procurement and strategy, you'll need to work seamlessly with a patent attorney. There are hardly any solicitors who are also patent attorneys (and vice versa).
- The volume of information and paperwork involved can be huge on patent matters, though on the plus side you could get the opportunity to visit research labs or factories to learn about production processes etc.
- The stakes can be high. Commercial research and development in the pharmaceutical sector is motivated by profit, not philanthropy. The investment involved will have been colossal, and even a day's loss of sales can be eye-watering. Success or failure in litigation can dramatically affect a company's share price.

Practice Areas

- Manufacturing, pharmaceutical and research companies usually employ patent specialists and there tend to be in-house legal teams at all the larger companies. In the media, major publishers and television companies employ in-house IP lawyers.

Current issues

- UK copyright law has for some time failed to reflect the way that people use digital material and modern technology, and many questions have continued to occupy this ambiguous territory. Whether people infringe copyrights by linking to copyrighted material on websites, buying and selling second-hand digital content like MP3 files or imitating the layout of a photograph is still up for debate. The 2011 Hargreaves Report was commissioned to address problems like these, and the final drafts of the new Exceptions to Copyright regulations were presented to Parliament in March 2014. At the same time, the government also produced eight 'plain English' guides that explain the recent updates.
- The financial crisis led to a growing awareness of intellectual property as a valuable asset. Businesses have become more aggressive in protecting their rights and litigation is on the rise. The English courts' reputation for being patent-unfriendly has been challenged by recent judgments.
- International efforts are being made to harmonise aspects of patent procurement. In January 2014, the Global PPH (Patent Prosecution Highway) pilot programme was launched, allowing applicants to speed up patent examinations where claims have already been allowed by a first participating office.
- After many years of discussion and planning, the EU has finally got closer to establishing a Unified Patent Court, after a treaty was signed in February 2013. The court will hear cases involving European patents which are valid in the participating states, meaning that the need to organise separate litigation in each country will become obsolete. The court will be based mainly in Paris, but will also have subdivisions in London and Munich. Law firms are keeping busy advising businesses on the introduction of both the UPC, which will be operational at the end of 2015, and the attendant EU patent.
- In the US, claims over tech patents make up almost half of patent lawsuits. The high-profile Apple v Samsung case – in which Samsung was found to have infringed patents which covered, for instance, the capacity to zoom into a picture by double-tapping the screen – has spurred on a ream of tech companies to patent a whole range of screen gestures. This pick-up in patenting has, perhaps inevitably, led to an increase in litigation too, although a peak could soon be reached – a decision by the US Supreme Court in June 2014 will limit patent protection for 'computer implemented' inventions.

Read our True Pictures on...

Arnold & Porter	K&L Gates
Ashfords	King & Wood Mallesons
Addleshaw Goddard	Latham & Watkins
Allen & Overy	Lewis Silkin
Ashurst	Linklaters
Baker & McKenzie	Macfarlanes
Berwin Leighton Paisner	Maclay Murray & Spens
Bird & Bird*	Mayer Brown
Bond Dickinson	Michelmores
Brabners Chaffe Street	Mills & Reeve
Bristows*	Mishcon de Reya
Browne Jacobson	Muckle
Burges Salmon	Nabarro
Charles Rusell	Olswang
Covington Burling*	Pinsent Masons
Cripps	Reed Smith
Dechert	RPC
Dentons	SGH Martineau
DWF	Shoosmiths
Edwards Wildman Palmer	Simmons & Simmons
Eversheds	Slaughter and May
Farrer & Co	Speechly Bircham
Foot Anstey	Squire Patton Boggs
Freshfields	Stevens & Bolton
Gateley	Taylor Wessing*
Harbottle & Lewis	TLT
Herbert Smith Freehills	Ward Hadaway
Hill Dickinson	Wedlake Bell
Hogan Lovells	Wragge Lawrence Graham

*These firms have a strong focus on IP

- In the trade mark arena many clients are seeking strategic advice on how to tackle the growing problem of counterfeit goods. L'Oréal's case concerning eBay's liability in relation to counterfeit goods sold on its auction site was referred to the ECJ by the French courts. Its decision was heralded as a triumph for luxury brand owners utilising selective distribution channels. The trend for digitalisation is bringing online IP issues to prominence; in its eagerly awaited ruling on Interflora v Marks & Spencer, the ECJ agreed with the High Court that M&S's use of the Google AdWords search term 'Interflora' infringes the flower business's trade mark.

Litigation & Dispute Resolution

In a nutshell

Litigation solicitors assist clients in resolving civil disputes. Disputes can concern anything from unpaid bills or unfulfilled contract terms to problems between landlords and tenants, infringement of IP rights, construction-related claims, the liabilities of insurers, shipping cases, defective products, media and entertainment industry wrangles... the list is endless. And that's just in the commercial sphere. The most common types of litigation involving private individuals are discussed at length in our personal injury overview.

If disputes are not settled by negotiation, they will be concluded either by court litigation or an alternative form of dispute resolution – thus litigation is a type of dispute resolution. The most common other methods are arbitration and mediation. The former is often stipulated as the preferred method in commercial contracts, while the latter is generally achieved through structured negotiations between the parties, overseen by an independent mediator. These methods can still be problematic: mediation is not necessarily adequate for complex matters, and some argue that opponents can use it as a means of 'bleeding' money from each other or as covert interrogation.

Confusingly, there are two divisions of the High Court dealing with major cases – the Chancery Division and the Queen's Bench Division (QBD) – and each hears different types of cases. For instance, the QBD hears various contract law and personal injury/general negligence cases, whereas the Chancery Division handles matters relating to trusts, probate, insolvency, business and land law.

What lawyers do

- Advise clients on whether they have a valid claim, or whether to settle or fight a claim made against them.
- Gather evidence and witnesses to support the client's position; develop case strategies.
- Issue court proceedings or embark on a process of alternative dispute resolution if correspondence with the defendant does not produce a satisfactory result.
- Represent clients at pre-trial hearings and case management conferences.
- Attend conferences with counsel (i.e. barristers) and brief them to conduct advocacy in hearings, trials and arbitrations.
- Attend trials, arbitrations and mediations with clients; provide assistance to barristers.

The realities of the job

- Work is driven by procedural rules and the timetable of the courts. Good litigators understand how best to manoeuvre within the system while also developing winning case strategies.
- The phenomenal amount of paperwork generated means that young litigators spend much of their time sifting through documents, scheduling and copying them in order to provide the court and all other parties with an agreed bundle of evidence.
- Litigators need to express themselves succinctly and precisely.
- Unless the claim value is small, the solicitor's job is more about case preparation than court performance. Solicitor-advocates are gaining ground, and once properly qualified they can appear in the higher courts. Nonetheless, barristers still dominate court advocacy and the performance of some solicitor-advocates has been criticised by the judiciary.
- Trainee workloads largely depend on the type of firm and the type of clients represented. Big City firms won't give trainees free rein on huge international banking disputes – they might not even go to court during their training contract – but they will be able to offer a small contribution to headline-making cases. Firms handling much smaller claims will often expect trainees to deal with all aspects of a case, from drafting correspondence and interim court applications to meetings with clients and settlement negotiations.
- There are a number of litigation-led law firms that handle cases of all sizes, and these present the best opportunities for a litigation-heavy training contract. The competition for litigation jobs at NQ level is fierce, so concentrate on litigation-led firms if you are certain of your leanings.
- The Solicitors Regulation Authority (SRA) requires all trainee solicitors to gain some contentious experience. People tend to learn early on whether they are suited to this kind of work. Increasingly in big City firms, SRA requirements can be fulfilled by a litigation crash course. It's also worth bearing in mind that more specialised areas, like real estate litigation and employment, can satisfy this contentious requirement.
- Despite a few firms starting up in-house advocacy units, the courts remain dominated by barristers, who are felt to have the edge when it comes to the skills and expertise needed to advocate. If you are determined to become both a solicitor and an advocate, certain areas of practice have more scope for advocacy – for example, family, crime, employment and lower-value civil litigation.

Current issues

- London has long been a popular forum for international litigation and arbitration, and the sheer volume of cases it receives (from places as disparate as Russia and South America) does not appear to be slowing. Research in 2012 showed that London was still the most preferred and widely used seat of arbitration.

- In October 2013, *The FT* wrote that there's 'no end in sight to the London courtroom oligarch litigation boom.' Disputes between Russian oligarchs have certainly been playing into the hands of the Capital's lawyers of late: the dispute between Boris Berezovsky and Roman Abramovich, for example, generated £100m in legal costs and one barrister took home somewhere between £3m and £10m for representing Mr Abramovich.

- Huge technology patent disputes – like the one between Apple and Samsung – have also been lining the pockets of London's lawyers over the past few years, and the outlook shows that this is one area that won't be flagging any time soon. Indeed, Norton Rose's most recent peek into the latest litigation trends showed that in the UK, telco/smartphone dipsutes continue to dominate the court's time: they took up a third of it in 2013, and, at the point of publication NR's findings stated that over 40% of allocated court time in 2014 had already been taken up by such spats.

- The Jackson Reforms came into effect in April 2013. They represented the most significant changes to the English courts in more than a decade, and tackled the costs involved in English civil litigation. Among various changes, claimants were no longer able to recover success fees from the losing party, reducing the burden on defendants. One year on from the introduction of these reforms, opinion is still divided on what impact they will eventually have on the flow of cases making their way through the courts. A key reform (which required parties to provide costs budgets for each phase of litigation) has been extended to affect a wider pool of claims, so lawyers are increasingly under pressure to get their budgets exactly right. Other impacts include an increased use (and obligation to consider) ADR methods like mediation.

- Post-Jackson, it has become harder to fund commercial litigation. Step up, third party litigation funders (TPFs). This type of funding means that organisations that are not directly involved in the case – like a bank or a private equity company – can choose to bankroll litigation for a share of the winnings. Such funders are members of the Association of Litigation Funders of England & Wales, and are required to maintain access to £2m worth of capital. Ever since Jackson's reforms were introduced, the number of TPFs has increased, along with demand for them. Solicitors therefore need to get up to speed with the latest alternatives to funding, as clients expect to be advised on what options (like TPF) are open to them. TPFs tend to be picky about which claims they are willing to stump up cash for though: usually high-value, where the expected damages in a case far outweigh the legal costs. This is

Read our True Pictures on...

Addleshaw Goddard	Jones Day
Allen & Overy	K&L Gates
Ashfords	Latham & Watkins
Ashurst	Linklaters
Baker & McKenzie	Macfarlanes
Berwin Leighton Paisner	Maclay Murray & Spens
Bird & Bird	Mayer Brown
Bond Dickinson	Michelmores
BPE Solicitors	Mills & Reeve
Brabners Chaffe Street	Mishcon de Reya
Bristows	Muckle
Burges Salmon	Nabarro
Charles Russell	Norton Rose Fulbright
Cleary Gottlieb	Olswang
Clifford Chance	Peters & Peters
Clyde & Co	Pinsent Masons
Covington & Burling	Reed Smith
Cripps	RPC
Dechert	SGH Martineau
Dentons	Shoosmiths
DWF	Sidley Austin
Edwards Wildman Palmer	Simmons & Simmons
Eversheds	Skadden
Farrer & Co	Slaughter and May
Foot Anstey	Squire Patton Boggs
Freshfields	Stephenson Harwood
Gateley	Stevens & Bolton
Gordons	Taylor Wessing
Herbert Smith Freehills	TLT
Higgs & Sons	Travers Smith
Hill Dickinson	Trethowans
Hogan Lovells	Veale Wasbourgh Vizards
Holman Fenwick Willan	Ward Hadaway
Ince & Co	White & Case
Irwin Mitchell	Wragge Lawrence Graham

bad news for small-to-medium enterprises, which will find funding their humbler claims much more difficult.

- Disputes are becoming increasingly global: a spike in regulatory probes and corporate crime investigations has seen certain cases play out in multiple jurisdictions. Take the Libor scandal for instance: several big-name financial institutions – like Barclays, Deutshe Bank and RBS – found themselves at the heart of the investigation, which spanned three continents and drew in regulators from at least ten countries.

Pensions

In a nutshell

Pensions law revolves around long-term management of large sums of money. Pensions lawyers advise on the creation, structure and funding of pension schemes, their management and resolving any associated disputes. Often created under the form of a trust, pensions are highly regulated and governed by a vast amount of complex and ever-changing legislation. Solicitors typically advise employers, trustees of pension funds and pension providers. There are several different types of pension scheme that individuals may buy into; broadly these can be divided into 'occupational pensions' and 'personal' or 'individual' pensions. All employers are required to offer their employees membership of a pension scheme – roll-out of this system began in October 2012 with the biggest employers. An overwhelming majority of individuals who contribute to this form of retirement saving will be members of an employer-sponsored occupational pension scheme.

Most pensions are subject to specialist tax regimes, which makes them very attractive as long-term investments. Members are entitled to tax relief on contributions and a tax free allowance applies to pension income. Solicitors structure pension funds to take maximum advantage of the tax regime and advise on compliance with the law and regulations in this area.

Pensions teams also work very closely with a firm's employment and corporate departments. Mergers and acquisitions of businesses may involve the movement of employees from one company to another, alongside the assets etc. of the target company. This change of ownership will have implications on who has responsibility for funding the pension schemes raise and questions over which employees (old or new) can become members of a scheme and whether the target company's pension scheme will even continue to exist or if it will be merged into or amended to mirror that of the bidding company.

Pension funds need to be well-funded, managed and invested for the money to grow and support the fund's members in their retirement. The difficult economic climate recently has had an impact on pension schemes, with low return on investments contributing to funding deficits in pension funds. Pensioners are living longer than had been predicted or planned for, and some companies are struggling to find the resources to keep paying members' pensions for longer periods of retirement alongside funding the scheme for current employees. Such issues affect the public sector just as much as private enterprise – see Royal Mail, for example, which in 2009 had a £10.3 billion deficit in its pension fund. Pensions lawyers help companies with restructuring and re-funding their pension schemes where there is such a shortfall and advise on the particular issues arising where companies collapse. Public sector occupational pensions are also subject to the will of the government, and lawyers have to be able to anticipate and negotiate amendments to schemes.

Most pension schemes are set up in the form of a trust and therefore strict rules apply to those in charge of administering the money. Trustees often seek legal advice on the discharge of their duties and litigation frequently occurs where they or other parties have failed to administer the funds diligently. One of the best examples of financial mismanagement is the Equitable Life scandal, which lost its members millions of pounds.

What lawyers do

- Draft documentation relating to the creation, amendment, closure or freezing (closing funds to new members) of pension funds.
- Advise employers on their obligations towards members and pension funds.
- Advise on who can become a member of a pension fund and when to pay out of a fund.
- Advise on restructuring or securing pension funds which are underfunded or in financial difficulties, including on issues associated with the Pension Protection Fund.
- Advise on regulatory and legislative compliance with tax regimes.
- Handle disputes and litigation related to pension schemes.
- Advise trustees of pension funds on their duties.
- Advise companies, pensions providers and trustees on their interactions with the Pensions Regulator, which regulates UK work-based pension schemes.
- Assist the corporate teams on M&A deals by undertaking due diligence on potential liabilities.
- Negotiating amendments to pension plans with clients.

The realities of the job

- If you're working to corporate deal timetables then the hours can be long.
- Pensions law is technical, highly regulated and often closely intertwined with tax law, which means a lot of time spent reading and interpreting complex statute books. A keen eye and ability to understand very technical information is essential.
- Pensions lawyers need to think long-term and anticipate what policy decisions and legislative proposals the government may make in the area.

Practice Areas

- Contentious negotiations with employee/trade union representatives often arise over proposed amendments to employees' pension plans (especially in the public sector).
- Clients call every day for advice on small issues such as when to pay funds out of a pension scheme.
- Pensions lawyers need to be personable and able to explain complex law in layman's terms.

Current issues

- In 2013, proposals were announced to radically reform the state pension system. The huge number of different state pensions and tax credits are to be consolidated for women, the self-employed and low earners, into a single minimum rate (£144 per week), paid for by higher-income earners. Experts think this will encourage more people to save and boost the introduction of auto-enrolment for company pensions schemes.
- The new flat rate pension means that couples qualify for the full payment as individuals, rather than receiving the less generous 'couples rate'.
- The compulsory retirement age of 65 has been abolished and the age at which an individual can access a state pension will be raised to 67 by 2028.
- Automatic enrolment of employees on to a company pension scheme began in 2012. This means that every employer automatically enrols workers into a workplace pension scheme if they are between 22 and state pension age and earning more than £10,000 a year.
- As the UK population is living longer, defined benefit (or final salary) pensions are becoming unsustainable for employers to fund. By 2028, It is expected that the UK will have 626,900 people over the age of 100, with 21,000 ages 110 or above. This is more than 53 times greater than the current number of centenarians.
- In March 2014, chancellor George Osborne unleashed 'the pensions revolution' in the Budget. People are no longer required to buy an annuity, which is a financial product that converts a retiree's pension pot into a guaranteed retirement income. Now, pensioners over 55 can access their pension savings and spend them any way they want. While Osborne insists that new pensioners can be trusted to organise their own finances, others, like pensions minister Steve Webb, worry that they will instead blow it on Lamborghini sports cars.

Read our True Pictures on...

Addleshaw Goddard	Macfarlanes
Allen & Overy	Mayer Brown
Ashurst	Mills & Reeve
Baker & McKenzie	Nabarro
Berwin Leighton Paisner	Norton Rose Fulbright
Bond Dickinson	Osborne Clarke
Burges Salmon	Pinsent Masons
Clifford Chance	Reed Smith
CMS	Shoosmiths
Dentons	Simmons & Simmons
DLA Piper	Slaughter and May
DWF	Speechly Bircham
Eversheds	Squire Patton Boggs
Freshfields	Stephenson Harwood
Gateley	Taylor Wessing
Herbert Smith Freehills	TLT
Hill Dickinson	Travers Smith
Hogan Lovells	Ward Hadaway
Jones Day	Wragge Lawrence Graham
Linklaters	

- Osborne also promised free, impartial guidance for pensions savers in the Budget. However, it was unclear who will provide this help, and critics wondered whether the pensions industry would surreptitiously push products onto customers, under the 'free guidance' guise. Since then, the government has decided that guidance will be provided through independent organisations like the Pensions Advisory Service or Money Advice Service.
- Pension liberation scams are becoming increasingly prevalent. Scammers claim that it's possible to unlock pensions early, but don't explain the risk of losing 70% through tax losses. Some also suggest moving pensions into bogus investments. The Pensions Regulator has revealed that almost half a billion pounds has been lost by victims of pension scams.

Personal Injury & Clinical Negligence

In a nutshell

Personal injury and clinical negligence lawyers resolve claims brought by people who have been injured, either as a result of an accident or through flawed medical treatment. The claimant lawyer usually acts for one individual, but sometimes a claim may be brought by a group of people – this is a class action or multiparty claim. The defendant lawyer represents the party alleged to be responsible for the illness or injury. In most PI cases the claim against the defendant will be taken over by the defendant's insurance company, which will then be the solicitor's client. Local authorities are common defendants in relation to slips and trips, while employers usually end up on the hook for accidents in the workplace. In a majority of clinical negligence cases, the defendant will be the NHS, although private medical practitioners and healthcare organisations are also sued.

What lawyers do

Claimant solicitors
- Determine the veracity of their client's claim and establish what they have suffered, including income lost and expenses incurred.
- Examine medical records and piece together all the facts. Commission further medical reports.
- Issue court proceedings if the defendant doesn't make an acceptable offer of compensation.

Defendant solicitors
- Try and avoid liability for their client or resolve a claim for as little as possible.
- Put all aspects of the case to the test. Perhaps the victim of a road traffic accident (RTA) wasn't wearing a seatbelt. Perhaps the claimant has been malingering.

Both
- Manage the progress of the case over a period of months, even years, following an established set of procedural rules.
- Attempt to settle the claim before trial or, if a case goes to trial, brief a barrister and shepherd the client through the proceedings.

The realities of the job

- The work is driven by the procedural rules and timetable of the court.
- There is a mountain of paperwork, including witness statements and bundles of evidence.

- Claimant lawyers have close contact with large numbers of clients, who may be significantly injured or vulnerable. Therefore, great interpersonal skills are a must.
- Defendant lawyers need to build long-term relationships with insurance companies. Clin neg defendant lawyers need to be able to communicate well with medical professionals and health sector managers.
- PI lawyers have large caseloads, especially when dealing with lower-value claims.
- There is some scope for advocacy, although barristers are used for high-stakes or complicated hearings and trials. Solicitors appear at preliminary hearings and case management conferences.

Current issues

- April 2013 saw the introduction of the majority of the reforms to civil litigation costs recommended by the Jackson Report. PI and clin neg are the two areas which are most affected. For example, legal aid has largely been withdrawn for clinical negligence, and successful claimants will no longer be allowed to recover success fees from the losing party. Instead, they will have to pay lawyers' fees from damages received, making controlling costs even more important. This will obviously have a profound effect on 'no win, no fee' arrangements. Successful parties in personal injury claims can also no longer claim back after-the-event insurance premiums from the losing party, meaning that claimants have to either fund the premium from their own pocket or risk having to pay out damages if their claim is unsuccessful. Firms may now turn away low-value claims for being too risky.
- The strongest signal so far of the courts' tough line on following new cost rules is the Mitchell case (aka 'plebgate'), where claimant lawyers were heavily penalised for failing to file their costs budget on time.
- The reforms have also placed a ban on referral fees, impacting the relationship between lawyers and claims management companies. The fees were seen to be fuelling a growing compensation culture and so far the ban appears to be having the desired effect: the Claims Management Regulation Unit (CMRU) posted figures which show that the number of companies handling personal injury claims fell from 2,435 in March 2012 to 1,700 in June 2013.

Practice Areas

- At the same time, personal injury lawyers are being required to increase their use of the RTA Portal, which processes low-value personal injury claims. RTA claims are a significant source of work for PI lawyers, and the Motor Accident Solicitors Society estimates that 2,000 solicitors work in the sector, dealing with 500,000 cases each year. But the Portal is also facing a squeeze on costs.
- The expectation is that personal injury fee income will decrease significantly over the next couple of years. In this climate, larger PI firms may look to diversify their practice and branch out into clinical negligence, as this area is more profitable and not covered by fixed costs rules. Practitioners in specialist clinical negligence firms argue this trend poses dangers for quality and cost. To find more experienced practitioners, look for members of panels like the Clinical Negligence Law Society, or firms with the SQM (specialist quality standard).
- Mergers may be the only option for some, continuing the trend for consolidation in the legal market.
- The opening up of the legal market to alternative business structures may have a significant impact upon this practice area, as individual clients on the claimant side could be an ideal target group for the kind of service which might be offered by high-street brands (eg The Co-op entering the legal market.
- Concerns have been raised over the quality of defence available to clinicians. The NHS Litigation Authority has reduced the number of firms on its panel, and increasingly demands that those that remain adhere to very strict rules when responding to claims.

Read our True Pictures on...

Browne Jacobson*	Leigh Day*
Baker & McKenzie	Mayer Brown
Bates Wells Braithwaite	Michelmores
Burges Salmon	Mills & Reeve
Capsticks Solicitors*	Nabarro
Charles Russell	Pinsent Masons
Clyde & Co	RPC
DWF*	Shoosmiths*
Eversheds	Slater & Gordon
Foot Anstey	Stevens & Bolton
Freeths*	Taylor Wessing
Herbert Smith Freehills	TLT
Higgs & Sons	Trethowans
Hill Dickinson	Veale Wasbrough Vizards
Irwin Mitchell*	Ward Hadaway
Kennedys	Wragge Lawrence Graham
Kingsley Napley	

*These firms have a strong focus on PI and clin neg

Private Client & Charities

In a nutshell

You have money. You need to know how best to control it, preserve it and pass it on: enter the private client lawyer. Solicitors advise individuals, families and trusts on wealth management. Some offer additional matrimonial and small-scale commercial assistance; others focus exclusively on highly specialised tax and trusts issues or wills and probate.

Charities lawyers advise on all aspects of non-profit organisations' activities, including the defence of legacies bequeathed to a charity in a will. These specialists need exactly the same skills and knowledge as private client lawyers but must also have the same kind of commercial knowledge as corporate lawyers.

What lawyers do

Private client lawyers
- Draft wills in consultation with clients and expedite their implementation after death. Probate involves the appointment of an executor and the settling of an estate. Organising a house clearance or even a funeral is not beyond the scope of a lawyer's duties.
- Advise clients on the most tax-efficient and appropriate structure for holding money and assets. Lawyers must ensure their clients understand the foreign law implications of trusts held in offshore jurisdictions.
- Advise overseas clients interested in investing in the UK and banks whose overseas clients have UK interests.
- Assist clients with the very specific licensing, sales arrangements and tax planning issues related to ownership of heritage chattels (individual items or collections of cultural value or significance).
- Bring or defend litigation in relation to disputed legacies.

Charities lawyers
- Advise charities on registration, reorganisation, regulatory compliance and the implications of new legislation.
- Offer specialist trusts and investment advice.
- Advise on quasi-corporate and mainstream commercial matters, negotiate and draft contracts for sponsorship and the development of trading subsidiaries, manage property issues and handle IP concerns.

- Charities law still conjures up images of sleepy local fund-raising efforts or, alternatively, working on a trendy project for wealthy benefactors. The wide middle ground can incorporate working with a local authority, a local library and schools to establish an after-school homework programme, or rewriting the constitution of a 300-year-old church school to admit female pupils. Widespread international trust in English charity law means that you could also establish a study programme in Britain for a US university or negotiate the formation of a zebra conservation charity in Tanzania.

The realities of the job

- An interest in other people's affairs is going to help. A capacity for empathy coupled with impartiality and absolute discretion are the hallmarks of a good private client lawyer. You'll need to be able to relate to and earn the trust of your many varied clients.
- Despite not being as chaotic as other fields, the technical demands of private client work can be exacting and an academic streak goes a long way.
- A great deal of private client work is tax-based, particularly involving income and estate tax. Specialists in this area also need their corporate tax knowledge to be up to scratch as it's not unusual for the families they work for to have multimillion-dollar businesses to their names.
- The stereotype of the typical 'country gent' client is far from accurate: lottery wins, personal injury payouts, property portfolios, massive City salaries and successful businesses all feed the demand for legal advice.
- If you are wavering between private clients and commercial clients, charities law might offer a good balance.

Current issues

- Private client practices have become increasingly busy in recent years and competition between them remains high.
- The UK's ageing population is creating a growing amount of wills and probate work for private client practices. With more people preparing their own wills there has been a rise in clients seeking legal advice rather than products. This has created further work in contentious trusts and probate; incorrectly prepared wills are being increasingly challenged, generating yet more business for law firms.

- Overseas clients are increasingly investing their assets into the UK, often into property, and law firms are continuing to deal with large numbers of foreign clients, many of whom come from the Middle East.
- The introduction of alternative business structures has allowed some firms with a substantial private client base to expand their products and offer private client advice typically outside areas covered by law firms.
- Charities are coming under growing pressure from government initiatives. The Lobbying Act restricts charities' campaigning abilities during an election period. Although intended to create transparency in lobbying, critics argue the Act restricts charities from holding the government to account on issues they represent. Charities will have to be careful to ensure any campaigning during elections cannot be viewed as an attempt to influence votes so expect to see law firms increasingly advising on campaigns as the general election draws near.
- Tightening regulations have seen an increase in charities seeking legal advice in an effort to avoid falling foul of the regulators. Changes proposed by the Charity Commission would require charities to declare how much is spent on campaigns and whether a financial review has been carried out. If accepted the proposed changes would come into force into 2015 and represent a wider push to ensure transparency and accountability in the charity sector.
- With economic uncertainty still in the air charities are under pressure to deliver services with increasingly limited funding. Top charity practices have advised on a number of charity restructuring or mergers.
- Charities are also being forced to look at alternative funding solutions such as social impact bonds. An SIB is an investment based on achieving a broad outcome, such as improved quality of life for pensioners, rather than specific actions, such as increasing the number of elderly people attending day centres. Investors provide initial funding for the project and are repaid by the government dependent on whether outcomes have been achieved, rather than project costs.

Read our True Pictures on...

Addleshaw Goddard	Leigh Day
Ashfords	Lester Aldridge
B P Collins	Macfarlanes*
Baker & McKenzie	Maclay Murray & Spens
Bates Wells Braithwaite	Michelmores
Berwin Leighton Paisner	Mills & Reeve
Bircham Dyson Bell*	Mischon de Reya*
Bond Dickinson	Muckle
Boodle Hatfield*	Pinsent Masons
Brabners Chaffe Street	SGH Martineau
Browne Jacobson	Shoosmiths
Burges Salmon	Speechly Bircham*
Charles Russell*	Stevens & Bolton
Collyer Bristow*	Taylor Wessing
Cripps*	TLT
DWF	Trethowans
Farrer & Co*	Trowers & Hamlins
Freeths	Veale Wasbrough Vizards*
Gateley	Ward Hadaway
Gordons	Wilsons*
Hewitsons	Winckworth Sherwood
Higgs & Sons	Withers*
Hill Dickinson	Wragge Lawrence Graham
Irwin Mitchell	

*These firms have a strong focus on private client and charities

Private Equity & Investment Management

In a nutshell

Private equity and investment firms operate funds that pool the investments of anybody prepared to part with their money for a sustained period of time. Private equity firms use investors' cash (equity) in combination with money raised from banks (debt) to buy companies or other assets with the goal of selling them on at a profit. When the targeted company's assets are used as leverage and a significant amount of bank debt is employed, the transaction is known as a leveraged buyout (LBO).

Venture capital is a subset of private equity that sees investors put money into start-up companies or small businesses in the hope they will be sold to a private equity firm or taken public. Although this typically entails high risk for the investor, it has the potential for above-average returns. This high risk is typically offset by investing smaller amounts over a shorter timespan. **Investment management** is the professional management of various securities (shares, bonds etc.) and assets in order to meet specified investment goals. Investment management lawyers advise on the structuring, formation, taxation and regulation of all types of investment funds. A **hedge fund** is a private, actively managed investment fund. It aims to provide returns to investors by investing in a diverse range of markets and financial products, regardless of whether markets are rising or falling. Using the derivatives market helps hedge funds achieve this. A **mutual fund** is a collective investment vehicle that pools money from many investors to purchase securities. The term is most commonly applied to collective investments that are regulated and sold to the general public. A **real estate investment fund/trust** is a publicly traded investment vehicle that uses investors' money to invest in properties and mortgages. Both hedge funds and mutual funds generally operate as **open funds**. This means that investors may periodically make additions to, or withdrawals from, their stakes in the fund. An investor will generally purchase shares in the fund directly from the fund itself rather than from the existing shareholders. This contrasts with a **closed fund**, which typically issues all the shares it will issue at the outset, with such shares usually being tradable between investors thereafter.

What lawyers do

- Advise private equity firms on how to structure new funds.
- Help private equity firms negotiate the terms on which investors contribute their money.
- Act for private funds when they buy and sell investments.
- Assist clients throughout the fund-raising process. This includes the preparation of offer materials and partnership agreements, advising on and documenting management and compensation arrangements, and closing fund formation transactions.
- Conduct diligence and negotiate contracts.
- Draft the numerous organisational documents necessary to form an investment fund. The private placement memorandum is key – it's a prospectus detailing the terms of the investment, minimum investor requirements, risk factors, who the investment manager is, and the strategy to be employed by the fund. If the fund is a limited partnership, it will need a limited partnership agreement, and if it's a limited liability company, it will need an operating agreement, as well as an investor subscription agreement.
- Inform and advise clients on the constantly changing regulatory and compliance issues arising under UK and international securities and tax law.
- Provide day-to-day advice with respect to issues such as performance and advertising and brokerage and portfolio trading practices.

Realities of the job

- Small teams mean that trainees can get high levels of responsibility and client exposure rather than being stuck doing more mundane tasks. You can expect to be involved in drafting key documents and reviewing transfer agreements and to play a part in large-scale negotiations that could involve hundreds of parties at the same time.
- Structuring funds requires an intimate familiarity with the relevant securities and investment company rules. Understanding and being able to apply knowledge of key financial legislation is a vital skill.
- Setting up funds also requires a significant amount of tax and general finance industry knowledge. Funds lawyers often work in close collaboration with their tax and finance colleagues.
- Good people skills and a tough attitude are a must. Private equity lawyers work closely with clients to offer advice on a wide range of areas and need to be able to explain the constantly evolving private fund markets to them as well as understanding the time-sensitive nature of fund organisation. Fortunately, clients are entrepreneurial and tend to have a good understanding of the world of business, meaning they can pick up on issues quickly.

Practice Areas

Current issues

- Recent years have been tough for UK private equity, as investors are reluctant to pay high fees – driven in part by very high management salaries – in an economic climate where returns are low. But buyout groups are making a comeback and looking at some pretty huge deals.
- Private equity funds prefer to invest in real estate and companies with steady income streams but cheap stock prices. Any industry facing the need to increase efficiency, but with guaranteed demand for its products and services, is potentially a good investment.
- Economic conditions mean firms are finding it hard to find safe places to invest their money. Increasingly popular choices include consumer products and retail, technology companies – especially software providers – and the energy sector. In Summer 2014, Cath Kidston made headlines by selling a large chunk of shares to an Asian private equity house. Much coverage was also afforded to the takeover of Boots by US giant Walgreens in a £5bn deal spanning three years.
- The coalition government's spending cuts have led a move towards privatisation. Private equity firms and other commercial organisations are bidding against public sector providers for public service contracts. So far the healthcare and social housing sectors have been the main targets for private equity buyouts, but firms are also moving in on educational institutions.
- Law firms are also finding that private equity firms are taking advantage of the new rules on alternative business structures to invest in public-facing areas of law like conveyancing, wills and personal injury.
- The EU and the Financial Conduct Authority (FCA) are looking to extend the same rules which already govern banks and investment firms to private equity firms. The EU's Alternative Investment Fund Managers Directive (AIFMD) puts hedge funds and private equity funds under the supervision of an EU regulatory body, with tougher rules on risk management and new limits on pay and bonuses.

Read our True Pictures on...

Addleshaw Godard	Linklaters
Allen & Overy	Macfarlanes
Ashurst	Mills & Reeve
Baker & McKenzie	Nabarro
Berwin Leighton Paisner	Norton Rose Fulbright
Bird & Bird	Olswang
Burges Salmon	Orrick
Cleary Gottlieb	Osborne Clarke
Clifford Chance	Pinsent Masons
CMS	Reed Smith
Covington & Burling	Sidley Austin
Dechert	Simmons & Simmons
DLA Piper	Skadden
Eversheds	Slaughter and May
Freshfields	Speechly Bircham
Herbert Smith Freehills	Squire Patton Boggs
Hogan Lovells	Stephenson Harwood
Jones Day	Taylor Wessing
K&L Gates	Travers Smith
King & Wood Mallesons	Weil, Gotshal & Manges
Kirkland & Ellis	White & Case
Latham & Watkins	

Practice Areas

Projects & Energy

In a nutshell

Projects

Projects lawyers work hand in hand with finance and corporate lawyers to enable complex construction, redevelopment and infrastructure projects to come to fruition. A few City firms and the largest US practices dominate the biggest international projects, but there's work countrywide. Many projects relate to the energy sector (see below), while road, rail and telecoms infrastructure projects are also big business. UK lawyers also work on overseas natural resources and mining projects, while domestically waste and utilities projects provide work for many regional firms. The Private Finance Initiative (PFI) – an aspect of Public Private Partnerships (PPP) – has also been an important source of work. PFI introduced private funding and management into areas that were previously public sector domains.

Some law firms consistently represent project companies, usually through a 'special purpose vehicle' (SPV) established to build, own and operate the end result of the project. Often the project company is a joint venture between various 'sponsor' companies. An SPV could also be partially owned by a government body or banks. Other firms consistently represent organisations which commission projects. Then there are the firms that act purely on the finance side for banks, guarantors, export credit agencies, governments and international funding agencies.

Energy

If a firm has an energy practice, most of its work will be based around oil and gas. This breaks down into upstream and downstream work. Upstream refers to the locating and exploiting of oil and gas fields (think 'drill, baby, drill' and you get the picture). Downstream refers to everything related to transport, processing and distribution – pipelines, refineries, petrol stations, etc. Many firms that do energy work trumpet their renewable energy and climate change expertise, but at any firm this will be a very small practice area. Power and utilities, and environment/regulatory are two other areas which are often considered to fall under the energy/projects umbrella.

What lawyers do

Projects

- The work of an energy or projects lawyer mirrors that of a corporate lawyer – drafting, due diligence, getting parties to sign agreements – with several added layers of complexity.

- There are several components to any project: financing, development and (often) subsequent litigation. Lawyers usually specialise in one of these areas, although they do overlap.

- The field also encompasses specialists in areas like construction, real estate, planning, telecoms, healthcare and the public sector.

- The financing of a project is riskier for lenders than other transactions are, as there is no collateral to act as security for the loan. For this reason risk is often spread across several stakeholders including the SPV, shareholders, the contractor, supplier, etc. The agreements which govern the relationship between the parties are the primary domain of lawyers acting for the project company.

- Lawyers who act for lenders check over all project documentation, paying attention to the risks the lender is exposed to.

- Site visits and meetings on location are common.

Energy

- Internationally, energy lawyers work on the contracts and licences agreed between international energy companies, governments and local companies. The upstream component of energy work often involves governments as they have the exclusive rights to certain natural resources.

- Domestically, lawyers often interact with the Department for Energy and Climate Change (DECC). Energy is a highly regulated sector, and there are many government programmes and stimuli to encourage certain types of energy projects. EU regulations also frequently come into play.

- Some energy lawyers work on energy infrastructure projects, but usually an energy lawyer is someone who works on contracts and agreements over (oil and gas) resources already being tapped. For example, they might produce so-called Production Sharing Agreements, which detail what proportions of profits go to different parties.

- Because energy companies have very deep pockets, many energy financings happen without the need for a loan (this is called 'off-balance-sheet financing').

- Disputes in the energy sector are often resolved through arbitration, particularly when they have an international element to them (which is often).

The realities of the job

Projects require lawyers who enjoy the challenge of creating a complex scheme and figuring out all its possibilities and pitfalls. Projects can run for years, involving multidisciplinary legal work spanning finance, regulatory permissions, construction, employment law and much more.

The value of transactions can vary from a few million pounds for projects to build domestic waste plants to deals worth billions to exploit massive oil fields. You have to get your head around these big numbers and understand what they actually mean: often the sum of money involved is the (potential) value of a joint venture or natural resource deposit. One of the things projects lawyers like about their job is that the product of their deal-making is tangible: they can usually watch a mine, bridge or oil refinery being built before their eyes.

The world's energy resources have helpfully positioned themselves in some of the world's most politically unstable or dubious countries (Venezuela, Russia, Saudi Arabia, Iraq, Iran, Nigeria, etc). This adds an extra layer of interest and intrigue to many transactions. For example, the due diligence on building a diamond mine in West Africa might involve consideration of how many AK-47s and armoured personnel carriers the mine will need to operate.

Current issues

- The debate over fracking continues to rage after substantial deposits of shale gas were discovered across the UK. Concerns over the environmental impact led to widespread anti-fracking campaigns. However, supporters assert that the process could supply a substantial amount of the UK's future energy. With Europe reliant on energy sourced from volatile areas such as Ukraine and the Middle East, the recent turmoil in both regions will push the debate further into the spotlight.
- The Electricity Market Reform (EMR) is intended to invest £110bn in upgrading the UK's electricity infrastructure, and provide renewable and reliable energy supplies. The UK's carbon emissions need to be reduced by the 2030s and the reform seeks to ensure that low-carbon generation of electricity is able to compete with traditional fossil fuels.
- Contracts for Difference (CfD) is one such incentive implemented by the EMR. The government-owned Low Carbon Contracts Company will provide 'eligible generators' with a CfD, with the intention of reducing exposure to volatile price shifts in the electricity market.

Read our True Pictures on...

Ashurst	Ince & Co
Addleshaw Goddard	Latham & Watkins
Allen & Overy	Linklaters
Baker & McKenzie	Maclay Murray & Spens
Berwin Leighton Paisner	Mayer Brown
Bond Dickinson	Memery Crystal
Burges Salmon	Mills & Reeve
Clifford Chance	Nabarro
Clyde & Co	Norton Rose Fulbright
CMS*	Pinsent Masons
Dentons*	Shearman & Sterling
DLA Piper	Simmons & Simmons
DWF	Skadden
Eversheds	Slaughter and May
Freeths	TLT
Freshfields	Vinson & Elkins*
Gateley	Watson, Farley & Williams
Herbert Smith Freehills*	White & Case*
Hogan Lovells	Wragge Lawrence Graham

*These firms have a strong focus on projects & energy

- Investment for renewable energy projects and infrastructure has continued to grow, particularly for wind and solar projects. The Department for Energy and Climate Change reports that investment in renewable energy in the UK was £8bn in 2013, continuing the upward trend witnessed since 2010.
- Investment in Africa continues to grow, with law firms witnessing a surge in financing arrangements for large-scale energy projects across the region. Currently there is great demand for investment on the continent; in July 2014 the USA and Nigeria signed a memorandum of understanding to increase US support for energy development in the West African nation and encourage investment in sub-Saharan Africa.
- Overseas investment into UK infrastructure was at its highest level in 25 years during 2014. Over 1,800 projects in a variety of areas were financed by foreign investment.
- Chancellor George Osborne has said he wants to increase investment in Northern cities to better balance the North/South economic divide. Recently Leeds, Liverpool, Manchester, Newcastle and Sheffield recently issued proposals to improve infrastructure in the North after years of underinvestment outside of London.

Practice Areas

Property/Real Estate

In a nutshell

Property lawyers, like their corporate law colleagues, are essentially transactional lawyers; the only real difference is that real estate deals require an extra layer of specialist legal and procedural knowledge and there aren't quite so many pesky regulatory authorities. The work centres on buildings and land of all types, and even the most oblique legal concepts have a bricks-and-mortar or human basis to them. It is common for lawyers to develop a specialism within this field, such as residential conveyancing, mortgage lending and property finance, social housing or the leisure and hotels sector. Most firms have a property department, and the larger the department the more likely the lawyers are to specialise. Note: 'property' and 'real estate' are entirely interchangeable terms.

What lawyers do

- Negotiate sales, purchases and leases of land and buildings and advise on the structure of deals.
- Record the terms of an agreement in legal documents.
- Gather and analyse factual information about properties from the owners, surveyors, local authorities and the Land Registry.
- Prepare reports for buyers and anyone lending money.
- Manage the transfer of money and the handover of properties to new owners or occupiers.
- Take the appropriate steps to register new owners and protect the interests of lenders or investors.
- Advise clients on their responsibilities in leasehold relationships and on how to take action if problems arise.
- Help developers get all the necessary permissions to build, alter or change the permitted use of properties.
- Manage property portfolio investments and advise real estate funds.

The realities of the job

- Property lawyers have to multi-task. A single deal could involve many hundreds of properties, and your caseload could contain scores of files, all at different stages in the process. You'll have to keep organised.
- Good drafting skills require attention to detail and careful thought. Plus you need to keep up to date with industry trends and standards.
- Some clients get antsy; you have to be able to explain legal problems in layman's terms.
- Despite some site visits, this is mainly a desk job with a lot of time spent on the phone to other solicitors, estate agents, civil servants and consultants.
- Your days will be busy, but generally the hours are more sociable and predictable.

Current issues

- Arguably the most cyclical legal area around, property practice will always and has always followed the market. In a downturn, there's less demand for properties and new developments, values plummet and conventional bank lending becomes increasingly hard to find. Still, the UK property market is getting a boost from alternative sources of investment and government stimuli – as the economy recovers, the real estate sector is bound to perk up too.
- Demand for housing remains strong; house prices increased by an average of £18,000 from July 2013 to July 2014 – a jump of 10.6%. However, the pace of growth has slowed due to stricter mortgage rules, and there was a 20% drop in mortgage approvals between January and May.
- The government is in the process of clearing the way for more residential developments by removing red tape. From June 2014, planning applications in England for schemes of fewer than 10 homes no longer need to be accompanied by a 'design and access statement'. What's more, in many areas of the country planning permission is no longer required to use office buildings for residential purposes. However, many local authorities are hoping to undo these changes.
- Of the big cities outside of London, Manchester and Birmingham are the most appealing investment opportunities. Interest in Edinburgh and Glasgow has been dampened by the prospect of Scottish independence owing to uncertainty over currency, tax and regulation. Similarly, the prospect of a UK exit from the EU could have a profound effect on the economy and investors' willingness to come here.
- The residential property market has been boosted by recent government stimuli, which support buyers of new-build homes. Among these is the Help to Buy scheme, though a number of economists and think tanks have called on the scheme to be made less generous to cool Britain's bubbling housing market. Lloyds has already reduced the amount that it will lend to first-time buyers.
- Apart from big government infrastructure projects like Crossrail and the Hinkley Point nuclear power station, the public sector real estate market has slowed. Social housing has been hit particularly hard.
- Social change is creating interest in alternative investment opportunities. For example, the ageing population makes retirement living and the healthcare sector a good bet. Student accommodation is also likely to attract investors, thanks in part to increased university acceptances for EU and international students increasing competition.

- Labour's campaign to tackle "the cost of living crisis" could see caps on rent increases in the private sector, and no more letting fees for estate agents. However, the Residential Landlord Association has warned that rent controls would undermine investment in new homes to rent.
- Generally, property litigation is a booming area, even though matters are not necessarily going all the way to court due to cost implications.

Read our True Pictures on...

Addleshaw Goddard	Lester Aldridge
Allen & Overy	Linklaters
Ashfords	Macfarlanes
Ashurst	Maclay Murray & Spens
B P Collins	Mayer Brown
Berwin Leighton Paisner	Memery Crystal
Bircham Dyson Bell	Michelmores
Bird & Bird	Mills & Reeve
Bond Dickinson	Mischon de Reya
Boodle Hatfield	Muckle
BPE Solicitors	Nabarro
Brabners Chaffe Street	Norton Rose Fulbright
Browne Jacobson	Olswang
Burges Salmon	Paul Hastings
Charles Russell	Pinsent Masons
Clifford Chance	Reed Smith
Clyde & Co	SGH Martineau
Cripps	Shoosmiths
Dentons	Sidley Austin
DWF	Simmons & Simmons
Eversheds	Speechly Bircham
Farrer & Co	Squire Patton Boggs
Foot Anstey	Stephenson Harwood
Freeths	Stevens & Bolton
Freshfields	Taylor Wessing
Gateley	TLT
Gordons	Travers Smith
Herbert Smith Freehills	Trethowans
Higgs & Sons	Veale Wasbrough Vizards
Hill Dickinson	Ward Hadaway
Hogan Lovells	Wedlake Bell
Irwin Mitchell	Wilsons
Jones Day	Winckworth Sherwood
K&L Gates	Wragge Lawrence Graham
King & Wood Mallesons	

*These firms have a strong focus on projects & energy

Practice Areas

Restructuring & Insolvency

In a nutshell

Insolvency law governs the position of businesses and individuals who are in financial difficulties and unable to repay their debts as they become due. Such a situation may lead to insolvency proceedings, in which legal action is taken against the insolvent entity and assets may be liquidated to pay off outstanding debts. Before a company or individual gets involved in insolvency proceedings, they will probably be involved in a restructuring or an out-of-court arrangement with creditors to work out alternative repayment schedules. The work of lawyers in the field can therefore be non-contentious (restructuring) or contentious (insolvency litigation), and their role will vary depending on whether they act for debtors or their creditors. What follows are some of the terms you'll come across.

Debtor: an individual or company that owes money. **Creditor:** a person or institution that extends credit to another entity on condition that it is paid back at a later date. **Bankruptcy:** term used in the USA to describe insolvency procedures that apply to companies, but not in the UK, where the term applies to individuals only. **Restructuring:** a significant modification made to the debt, operations or structure of a company with its creditors' consent. After a restructuring, debt repayments become more manageable, making insolvency proceedings less likely. **Insolvency proceedings:** generic term that covers a variety of statutory proceedings aimed at rescuing or winding up an insolvent company.

Insolvency proceedings include the following actions. **Company voluntary arrangement (CVA):** If it is clear that a business could survive if debt repayments were reduced, it can enter a CVA agreement with its creditors. Under this legally binding agreement, a struggling company is allowed to repay some, or all, of its historic debts out of future profits, over an agreed period of time. **Administration:** When in administration, a company is protected from creditors enforcing their debts while an administrator takes over the management of its affairs. If the company is fundamentally sound, the administrator will implement a recovery plan aimed at streamlining the business and maximising profits. If it is apparent that the company has no future then it can be sold or liquidation can commence.

Receivership: Unlike administration, this is initiated by the company's creditors, not the company itself. A receiver is appointed by the court and must look to recover as much money as possible in order to settle the claims made by creditors. Under receivership, the interests of the creditors clearly take precedence over the survival of the company. **Liquidation:** Procedure by which the assets of a company are placed under the control of a liquidator. In most cases, a company in liquidation ceases to trade, and the liquidator will sell the company's assets and distribute the proceeds to creditors. There are two forms: voluntary liquidation brought about by the company itself or compulsory liquidation brought about by court order. **Distressed M&A:** The sale of all or a portion of an insolvent business is an efficient way to preserve going-concern value and avoid the potential for substantial loss of value through a piecemeal liquidation. **Pre-pack sale:** Refers to a deal made with an interested buyer to sell the insolvent company's business and assets, negotiated before an administrator is appointed and completed immediately on appointment. Such schemes are becoming increasingly popular and more frequently used in the current economic climate.

What lawyers do

Debtors' lawyers

- In a restructuring, advise the insolvent company on the reorganisation of its balance sheet (such as closing down unprofitable businesses or refinancing its debt) and assist in negotiations with creditors.
- Assist in insolvency filings, and once proceedings have commenced, work closely with the insolvency officeholders (that is, those appointed as administrators, receivers or liquidators) and accountants to achieve the goals set for the insolvent company.
- Provide advice to directors of insolvent companies, explaining their duties to creditors.
- Advise on the sale of assets or mergers and acquisitions of troubled companies.
- Assist clients in insolvency litigation and appeals. Provide preventative advice to debtor clients on liability management and ways to avoid insolvency proceedings.

Creditors' lawyers

- Assist in negotiations with debtors and insolvency officeholders.
- Represent clients in insolvency litigation and appeals.
- Assist in the tracing and valuation of debtors' assets.
- Provide training to their clients on how to deal with insolvent companies.

The realities of the job

- Large City firms deal almost exclusively with large-scale corporate restructurings and insolvencies, and the representation of creditor groups in these matters. Smaller regional firms mostly assist on smaller corporate and personal insolvency cases.

Practice Areas

- Lawyers need to be conversant in a variety of legal disciplines or know when to refer matters to specialists in employment, banking, property, litigation, corporate, etc.
- When financial difficulties arise in companies, the rapid deployment of a legal team is necessary to provide immediate assistance. This area of law is extremely fast-paced, and lawyers are often asked to deliver solutions overnight.
- Insolvency and restructuring involves mountains of paperwork, so lawyers need to be organised and able to prioritise their workload, particularly when dealing with multiple assignments. With so much at stake, attention to detail is paramount when drafting asset sale agreements or documents to be filed at court.

Current issues

- Law firms have recently seen a drop in the number of insolvency instructions as corporate insolvency dropped by 25% between 2012 and 2013. There's also a general shift towards restructuring, prompted by the reluctance of companies to declare insolvency and instead attempt reform before bankruptcy looms. However, despite a recovering economy, commentators predict that any subsequent rise in interest rates could cause an increase in the number of insolvencies.
- A recent report by KPMG suggests Asian companies will continue to use English courts for their restructuring after the number of Asian companies in debt rose by 130% between 2012 and 2013. The English system has proved popular with foreign companies as it is more flexible than other insolvency regimes; France and Spain are currently attempting to amend their practices along English lines in the hopes of attracting more business.
- Schemes of arrangement have become increasingly popular both in the UK and abroad. The scheme, entailing an agreement between a company and its creditors to restructure an insolvent company by reducing debts, is viewed as more affordable than other restructuring tools.
- Pre-pack sales have come under fire in the Graham Review into pre-pack administrations (June 2014). The review called for several changes to the process, including strengthening the Statement of Insolvency Practice 16. The process, during which Insolvency Practitioners (IPs) communicate to all creditors any actions they intend to take and any details of assets, transactions and consultation, will be revised to better clarify expectations of both sides.
- One aim of the Small Business, Enterprise and Employment Bill (expected to come into force in May 2015) is to simplify communications between creditors and IPs. The Bill also hopes to make it easier for shadow directors to be held to account in cases of insolvency. Fast-track Individual Voluntary Arrangements (IVAs), an arrangement where creditors receive additional money to that usually recouped in bankruptcy,

Read our True Pictures on...

Addleshaw Goddard	Linklaters
Allen & Overy	Maclay Murray & Spens
Ashfords	Mayer Brown
Ashurst	Michelmores
Baker & McKenzie	Mills & Reeve
Berwin Leighton Paisner	Muckle
Bingham McCutchen	Nabarro
Bond Dickinson	Norton Rose Fulbright
Brabners Chaffe Street	Olswang
Browne Jacobson	Osborne Clarke
Burges Salmon	Paul Hastings
Charles Russell	Pinsent Masons
Clifford Chance	SGH Martineau
Clyde & Co	Shearman & Sterling
CMS	Shoosmiths
Dentons	Sidley Austin
DLA Piper	Simmons & Simmons
DWF	Skadden
Eversheds	Slaughter and May
Freeths	Speechly Bircham
Freshfields	Squire Patton Boggs
Gateley	Stevens & Bolton
Herbert Smith Freehills	Taylor Wessing
Hill Dickinson	TLT
Hogan Lovells	Travers Smith
Irwin Mitchell	Veale Wasbrough Vizards
Jones Day	Ward Hadaway
King & Wood Mallesons	Weil, Gotshal & Manges
Kirkland & Ellis	White & Case
Latham & Watkins	Wragge Lawrence Graham
Lester Aldridge	

would cease to exist after being declared an 'abuse'.
- Waste, energy, shipping and infrastructure have all been areas which have seen large numbers of restructurings in the past year. Other trends have seen negligence claims lodged against directors of insolvent companies and an increasing number of consumer fraud scams in personal insolvency, the latter no doubt prompted by the current economic client. As the market continues to develop lawyers should be prepared to deal with restructuring and insolvency in a wide range of areas.
- The number of personal insolvencies in England and Wales in 2013 fell 7.9% from 2012, their lowest level in eight years, prompted by low interest rates. Bankruptcy made up the smallest part of insolvencies due to the increasing number of Debt Relief Orders, a cheaper option aimed at those on low income with smaller debts. IVAs also continued to be a popular recourse.

Shipping

In a nutshell

Shipping lawyers deal with the carriage of goods or people by sea, plus any and every matter related to the financing, construction, use, insurance and decommissioning of the ships that carry them (or are arrested, sunk or salvaged while carrying them). Despite being the preserve of specialist firms, or relatively self-contained practice groups within larger firms, the discipline offers varied challenges. The major division is between 'wet' work relating to accidents or misadventure at sea, and 'dry' work involving the land-based, commercial and contractual side. In extension, disputes or litigation relating to contracts mean there is also a contentious side to dry work. While some lawyers in the area may be generalists, it is more common to specialise.

What lawyers do

Wet lawyers

- Act swiftly and decisively at a moment's notice to protect a client's interests and minimise any loss.
- Travel the world to assess the condition of ships, interview crew or witnesses and prepare cases.
- Take witness statements and advise clients on the merits of and strategy for cases.
- Handle court and arbitration appearances, conferences with barristers and client meetings.

Dry lawyers

- Negotiate and draft contracts for ship finance and shipbuilding, crew employment, sale and purchase agreements, affreightment contracts, and the registration and re-flagging of ships.
- May specialise in niche areas such as yachts or fishing, an area in which regulatory issues feature prominently.
- Handle similar tasks to wet lawyers in relation to contractual disputes but are less likely to jet off around the world at the drop of a hat.

The realities of the job

- Wet work offers the excitement of international assignments and clients, so lawyers need to react coolly to sudden emergencies and travel to far-flung places to offer practical and pragmatic analysis and advice.
- Despite the perils and pleasures of dealing with clients and instructions on the other side of the world, the hours are likely to be steady beyond those international-rescue moments.
- Non-contentious work touches on the intricacies of international trade, so it's as important to keep up with sector knowledge as legal developments.

- Dealing with a mixed clientele from all points on the social compass, you'll need to be just as comfortable extracting a comprehensible statement from a Norwegian merchant seaman as conducting negotiations with major financiers.
- Contentious cases are driven by the procedural rules and timetable of the court or arbitration forum to which the matter has been referred. A solid grasp of procedure is as important as a strong foundation in tort and contract law.
- Some shipping lawyers do come from a naval background or are ex-mariners, but you won't be becalmed if the closest comparable experience you've had is steering Tommy Tugboat in the bath as long as you can show a credible interest in the discipline.
- Though not an all-boys club, parts of the shipping world are still male dominated. Women lawyers and clients are more commonly found on the dry side.
- In the UK, shipping law is centred around London and a few other port cities. Major international centres include Piraeus in Greece, Hong Kong and Singapore. Some trainees even get to work in these locations.

Current issues

- The shipping market was quite severely blown off course in the recession. Some suggested that the top end of the market plummeted between 90% and 100% in a matter of weeks.
- The global shipping market remains volatile. Some areas are slowly recovering, but tanker and dry bulk rates are still dire.
- Decreased demand for raw materials has hit the industry hard. Because shipments and ships are big, slow and expensive, the shipping market is not very versatile. The recent fall in oil prices, however, has enabled shipping companies to operate more profitably.
- The tonnage on order at shipyards has increased over the past year, but shipping finance is still in the doldrums. New deals are being done though. For example, Singapore's Neptune Orient Lines recently secured $1.1bn worth of financing for the building of 12 new container ships. As this example indicates, the Asian market is doing better than most, with the Chinese government providing financial backing and Chinese commercial banks doing a lot of lending. 2012 figures show freight turnover in China increased 12.4% year-on-year.
- The amount of contentious work arising directly from the economic crisis has tailed off as contracts have been renegotiated and remaining businesses have stabilised their positions in the market.

- Piracy remains a significant concern, although the number of incidents of Somali piracy off the coast of East Africa has fallen dramatically. Firms have subsequently reported an increase in the amount of piracy work emanating from West Africa instead. In practice, shipping law tends to focus on the ships themselves rather than the pirates, and as yet, no pirates have been brought to trial in the UK (although this could happen in future).

- The liquefied natural gas (LNG) market has witnessed a reassuring amount of activity. Seen as a cleaner alternative to oil, demand for LNG has increased, as has the work to extract it from large shale deposits in China and the US. This trend has been welcome news for shipyards, which have been bidding to build LNG tankers to transport this resource across the globe. Competition between shipyards in China, Japan and South Korea has increased, and China's Hudong-Zhonghau Shipbuilding has come out on top: it won a $1bn contract to build four LNG carriers for ExxonMobil and Japan's Mitsui OSK line, as well one from a consortium encompassing the US' ConocoPhillips, Australia's Origin Energy and China's Sinopec. Shipping lawyers at firms like Ince & Co, Stephenson Harwood and Reed Smith have indicated that this is a growth area for them, and that work has involved facilitating vessel operations, as well as advising on floating LNG project work.

- Firms which have a presence in Greece's busy port city of Piraeus may find themselves at an advantage, as shipbroking heavyweight Clarksons has reported that Greek shipowners now sit at the top of the global shipping economy: together they control a gross tonnage of 164 million tons, more than Japan, which controls 159.4 million tons. Greece has also reportedly spent over $6.8bn on vessel acquisitions throughout the first quarter of 2014.

Read our True Pictures on...

Ashfords	Lester Aldridge
Clyde & Co*	Norton Rose Fulbright
Eversheds	Pinsent Masons
Gateley	Reed Smith*
Hill Dickinson*	Stephenson Harwood*
Holman Fenwick Willan*	Thomas Cooper*
Ince & Co*	TLT

*These firms have a particularly strong focus on shipping

- Academics in China and the UK have presented a series of talks in 2014, which focus on how China's laws, combined with its position in global trade, will influence the future of the shipping industry. Speakers posited that China's maritime law (which has historically been influenced by English maritime law) has been evolving into a new framework which will go on to have an impact on areas such as international trade law, pollution liabilities, ship arrest and the carriage of goods by sea.

- Firms have reported that many charterers are close to bankruptcy: one of the most high-profile is South Korea's STX Group, which encountered a severe debt crisis in 2013 and entered into rehabilitation proceedings (South Korea's equivalent of Chapter 11), after it failed to reimburse a variety of owners with hire payments.

- There has been a global increase in shipbuilding work: during the first quarter of 2014, shipping companies placed 792 new orders, and injected over $25 billion worth of capital into the newbuild market. While this may sound good in the short-term, firms like Holman Fenwick Willan have highlighted that the world's fleet is already oversupplied, and are predicting another burst of shipbuilding disputes over the next three years.

Sports, Media & Entertainment

In a nutshell

Advertising and marketing lawyers offer advice to ensure a client's products or advertisements are compliant with industry standards, plus general advice on anything from contracts between clients, media and suppliers, to employment law, corporate transactions and litigation. Entertainment lawyers assist clients in the film, broadcasting, music, theatre and publishing industries with commercial legal advice or litigation. Strictly speaking, sports lawyers work in an industry sector rather than a specific legal discipline, and firms draw on the expertise of individuals from several practice groups. Reputation management lawyers advise clients on how best to protect their own 'brand', be this through a defamation suit or an objection to invasion of privacy.

What lawyers do

Advertising and marketing
- Ensure advertising campaigns comply with legislation or regulatory codes set out by the Advertising Standards Agency or Ofcom.
- Advise on comparative advertising, unauthorised references to living persons and potential trade mark infringements.
- Defend clients against allegations that their work has infringed regulations or the rights of third parties. Bring complaints against competitors' advertising.

TV and film
- Advise production companies on every stage of the creation of programmes and films.
- Assist on the banking and lending transactions which ensure financing for a film, as well as tax exemption rules for UK films.
- Help engage performers; negotiate a multitude of ancillary contracts; negotiate distribution and worldwide rights.

Music
- Advise major recording companies, independent labels and talent (record producers, songwriters and artists).
- Advise on contracts, such as those between labels and bands, or between labels and third parties.
- Offer contentious and non-contentious copyright and trade mark advice relating to music, image rights and merchandising.
- Offer criminal advice when things get old-school rock 'n' roll.
- Assist with immigration issues.

Theatre and publishing
- Advise theatre and opera companies, producers, agents and actors on contracts, funding and sponsorship/merchandising.
- Advise publishing companies and newspapers on contractual, licensing, copyright and libel matters.
- Assist with immigration issues.

Sports
- Assist with contract negotiations, be they between clubs and sportspeople, agents and players, sporting institutions and sponsors, broadcasters and sports governing bodies.
- Handle varied employment and immigration issues.
- Advise on corporate or commercial matters like takeovers, public offerings, debt restructuring and bankruptcy, or the securing and structuring of credit.
- Enforce IP rights in the lucrative merchandise market and negotiate on matters affecting a sportsperson's image rights.
- Work on regulatory compliance issues within a sport or matters relating to the friction between sports regulations and EU/national law.
- Offer reputation management and criminal advice.

Reputation management (incl. defamation and libel)
- Claimants' lawyers advise individuals – commonly celebrities, politicians or high-profile businessmen – on the nature of any potential libel action or breach of privacy claim, usually against broadcasters or publishers, before it either settles or goes to court.
- Defendants' lawyers advise broadcasters or other publishers on libel claims brought against them. With the burden of proof on the defendant, the lawyers must prove that what was published caused no loss to the claimant or was not libellous.
- Help clients stay out of hot water by giving pre-publication advice to authors, editors or production companies.

The realities of the job
- Advertising lawyers must have a good knowledge of advertising regulations, defamation and IP law.
- Many advertising disputes will be settled via regulatory bodies but some, particularly IP infringements, end in litigation.
- Entertainment lawyers need to be completely immersed in their chosen media and have a good grasp of copyright and contract law.

Practice Areas

- Reputation management lawyers need a comprehensive understanding of libel and privacy laws and an ability to think laterally. Individual claimants will be stressed and upset, so people skills, patience and resourcefulness are much needed.
- Solicitors prepare cases, but barristers almost always get the glory.

Current issues

- Web-based interactive, 'smart' advertising is throwing up all kinds of data protection and privacy issues. The attempt to regulate online content in the wake of the Digital Economy Act and the Audiovisual Media Services (AVMS) Directive is increasing demand for legal services.
- There is an intensified public interest in sensitive areas such as gambling, alcohol and products targeting children. Various changes have been made to advertising codes by the Committee of Advertising Practice (CAP), which is the ASA's sister organisation.
- Regulatory changes permitting product placement in TV shows haven't been as lucrative as advertisers hoped, bringing in only 2% of the expected revenue.
- Overseas investment in UK film and television continues and has been boosted by government tax credits. The UK film production sector generated a total spend of £1.075bn in 2013, a 14% increase on 2012's £945m.
- Online television has grown a great deal and broadcasters are attempting to generate new revenue streams to offset a commensurate decline in advertising revenues.
- Efforts to tackle online piracy are gaining teeth. In the USA, pirate sites are being barred from hosting adverts by big companies like Google and Yahoo – the Internet Advertising Bureau (IAB) in the UK is working on a similar scheme.
- The rise of smartphones and tablets has created an explosion in demand for related services like apps, feeding a deluge of opportunities for new players in the market. It's also becoming clear which digital and audio-visual services consumers are and are not willing to pay for. Media outlets are developing ways to negotiate the digital economy, deciding whether to offer free content online or put up pay-walls. This is directly affecting print media too, with online competition forcing *Time Out* to switch to free print distribution.
- The music industry continues to face challenges: illegal downloading and piracy are the biggest concerns. Sales of physical products are declining rapidly, so deals that combine physical sales with merchandising and live appearances are increasingly common.
- The 2010s have been hailed as a 'golden decade' of sporting events for the UK. Following on from the Olympics was the 2013 Ashes and this year's Commonwealth Games. These precede the 2015 Rugby World Cup, the 2017 Athletics World Championships and the 2019 Cricket World Cup.

Read our True Pictures on...

Addleshaw Goddard	Hogan Lovells
Baker & McKenzie	K&L Kates
Bates Wells Braithwaite	Lewis Silkin*
Berwin Leighton Paisner	Macfarlanes
Bird & Bird	Mishcon de Reya
Bond Dickinson	Olswang
Brabners Chaffe Street	Osborne Clarke
Bristows	Peters & Peters
Charles Russell	Pinsent Masons
CMS	Reed Smith
Collyer Bristow*	RPC
Dentons	Sheridans*
DLA Piper	Slaughter and May
Eversheds	Squire Patton Boggs
Farrer & Co	Taylor Wessing
Gateley	Travers Smith
Harbottle & Lewis*	Withers
Herbert Smith Freehills	

*These firms have a strong focus on media law

- Football clubs' finances have continued to hit the headlines. Aldershot Town and Coventry City both went into administration in 2013 following Rangers' fall from grace in 2012. The Financial Fair Play regulations that were implemented to stop clubs spending beyond their means are also in force.
- Premiership Football is an increasingly lucrative affair. Enhanced TV deals are providing clubs with improved revenue streams and the Premiership's broadcasting rights for 2013 to 2016 are worth a whopping £5.5bn.
- The 2013 Defamation Act means that claimants can only sue for defamation if they have suffered serious harm to their reputation, and if they are companies they must demonstrate financial loss. It will also limit (but not halt) 'libel tourism' by making it much harder for individuals who live outside the country to be sued in the London courts. The changes could mean a decrease in the number of cases coming before the courts, but lawyers will continue to be needed for their advice on what does and does not constitute a viable defamation case.
- After Sally Bercow's notorious tweet 'Why is Lord McAlpine trending? *innocent face*' was ruled libellous, there's a new focus on what can and can't be said on social media. Defamation lawyers are involved in getting libellous statements taken off the internet fast.
- The aftershocks of the Leveson Inquiry are still being felt, with phone-hacking claims against News International continuing. Cross-party talks on implementing the Leveson Report broke down in March 2013, and it's unclear how any reforms will be carried forward.

Tax

In a nutshell

Tax lawyers ensure that clients structure their business deals or day-to-day operations such that they take advantage of legal breaks and loopholes in tax legislation. Although it's predominantly an advisory practice area, on occasion matters can veer into litigation territory. Tax law is most often used in private client and corporate matters.

What lawyers do

- Handle tax planning for clients, making sure they understand the tax ramifications of the purchase; handle ownership and disposal of assets, including advising on structuring corporate portfolios in the most tax-efficient way.
- Offer transactional advice when working with corporate lawyers on M&A deals, joint ventures and property portfolio acquisitions.
- Deal with investigations or litigation resulting from prosecution by Her Majesty's Revenue & Customs (HMRC). Litigation is always conducted against or brought by the government.
- Work alongside private client lawyers on matters of private wealth.

The realities of the job

- This is an intellectually rigorous, rather cloistered area of law and is ideally suited to the more academic.
- Corporate tax lawyers are very well paid, treated with reverence by their colleagues and find intellectual stimulation in their work.
- Lawyers must not only have the ability to translate and implement complex tax legislation, but must also be able to advise on how to structure deals in a legitimate and tax-efficient way to avoid conflict with HMRC.
- If you don't already wear specs, expect to after a couple of years of poring over all that black letter law. The UK has more pages of tax legislation than almost any other country, and there are changes every year.
- In time extra qualifications, such as the Chartered Tax Adviser exams, will be useful.
- Read our True Picture on the Government Legal Service to find out about working at HMRC.

Current issues

- After a number of well-known companies and individuals hit the headlines in the UK for tax avoidance (which, unlike tax evasion, is legal), law firms have witnessed an increase in the number of clients paying close attention to their taxes in a bid to avoid publicly scrutiny and exposure in the press. As tax becomes more political, and will even more so in the run up to the 2015 General Election, tax lawyers will increasingly be in demand.
- In 2013 HMRC recouped £2.7bn after challenging tax avoidance schemes. Overall the tax authority collected £23.9bn in the 2013-2014 tax year, an increase of £2bn on the previous term. HMRC expects to raise £100bn in taxes by March 2015 by continuing to hone in on tax evaders.
- The Finance Bill 2014 included provisions which allows HMRC to compel the payment of contested tax in advance of disputes going to court. Clamping down on tax avoidance is a big issue for the authority; further measures include making public the kind of scheme it views as tax avoidance. Those currently involved in such schemes will have to pay the required tax to HMRC within 90 days of being notified.
- The fight to close loopholes in stamp duty land tax was won by HMRC after the High Court quashed appeals against an initial ruling. The loophole allowed schemes to transfer property ownership to an offshore company. When the property was then sold, the buyer would purchase the company as a whole to reduce stamp duty.
- The introduction of the Patent Box into the UK in 2013 offered tax relief on company profits gleamed from UK held patents. Intended to attract research and development to the UK, the Treasury estimates the scheme costs £1bn a year. Further tax relief incentives include video game relief, introduced in 2012, to encourage development in the UK.
- Inversion, whereby companies acquire a foreign company to which they intend to transfer their tax base, has become increasingly popular with American companies, who are targeting British and Irish firms. The process, which is legal under certain conditions, allows companies to transfer tax bases to countries with decreased corporate tax. It's become increasingly popular for companies in the US, which has one of the highest corporate tax rates at 35%. The trend of acquiring British and Irish companies is expected to continue until the US corporate tax rate is lowered.

Practice Areas

- Over the last year law firms have reported seeing an increase of Initial Public Offerings (IPOs) and real estate tax related work. The latter has been prompted by Real Estate Investment Trusts (REITs) who are granted special tax considerations in the UK and promise high returns for investors.
- Personal tax allowances in the UK will continue to increase until 2015 alongside a reduction in starting rates for income tax savings. Individuals will also be encouraged to invest in social enterprises by the introduction of a tax relief on social investment tax.

Read our True Pictures on...

Addleshaw Goddard	Linklaters
Allen & Overy	Macfarlanes
Ashurst	Maclay Murray & Spens
Baker & McKenzie	Mayer Brown
Berwin Leighton Paisner	Mills & Reeve
Bond Dickinson	Nabarro
Brabners Chaffe Street	Norton Rose Fulbright
Burges Salmon	Olswang
Clifford Chance	Osborne Clarke
CMS	Peters & Peters
Dechert	Pinsent Masons
Dentons	RPC
DLA Piper	Shoosmiths
DWF	Sidley Austin
Eversheds	Simmons & Simmons
Foot Anstey	Skadden
Freshfields	Slaughter and May
Gateley	Squire Patton Boggs
Herbert Smith Freehills	Stephenson Harwood
Hogan Lovells	Stevens & Bolton
Irwin Mitchell	Travers Smith
Jones Day	Weil, Gotshal & Manges
King & Wood Mallesons	Withers
Kirkland & Ellis	Wragge Lawrence Graham
Latham & Watkins	

Practice Areas

Technology, Telecoms & Outsourcing

In a nutshell

Technology lawyers distinguish themselves from general commercial advisers because of their specific industry know-how. They combine a keen understanding of the latest advances in various technologies with a thorough knowledge of the ever-changing law that regulates, protects and licenses them. As forms of media and new technologies converge, clients have come to rely on technology lawyers' innovation and imagination in offering rigorous legal solutions to maximise and protect income and ideas. The majority of the top 50 firms possess dedicated groups of lawyers. There are also specialists within smaller commercial firms and a number of niche firms.

What lawyers do

- Advise on commercial transactions and draft the requisite documents. There is a heavy emphasis on risk management.
- Assist in the resolution of disputes, commonly by arbitration or other settlement procedures as this is a court-averse sector. Many disputes relate to faulty or unsatisfactory software or hardware.
- Help clients police their IT and web-based reputation and assets. Cybersquatting, ownership of database information and the Data Protection Act are common topics.
- Give clients mainstream commercial, corporate and financial advice.
- Specialised outsourcing lawyers represent customers and suppliers in the negotiation and drafting of agreements for the provision of IT or other services by a third party.

The realities of the job

- You need to be familiar with the latest regulations and their potential impact on your client's business. Does a website need a disclaimer? What measures should your client take to protect data about individuals gathered online?
- You need a good grasp of the jargon of your chosen industry, firstly to write contracts but also so you can understand your clients' instructions. Read trade journals like Media Lawyer and Wired or magazines such as Computer Weekly or New Scientist.
- In this frontier world, gut instinct matters. One in-house lawyer made what looked like a risky move from BT to little-known internet auction site, eBay. Six years later he moved to head up Skype's legal team.

- The ability to think laterally and creatively is a must, especially when the application of a client's technology or content throws up entirely new issues.
- High-end private sector outsourcing involves complex, high-value and increasingly multi-jurisdictional work. Mostly, it is the larger law firms that handle such deals. In the public sector, deals involve UK government departments, local authorities and the suppliers of services to those entities.

Current issues

- In the UK, the technology sector has recovered well post-recession.
- As tech companies battle for the smartphone and tablet market, there has been an upsurge in patent disputes, most notably between Apple and Samsung. Their court war reached breaking point in August 2014, when both agreed to drop all litigation between them outside of the US.
- Digital convergence throws up many legal problems as the business opportunities created by new technologies move beyond the capacity of existing legal or regulatory structures. For example, the virtual currency Bitcoin is difficult to track as it can be traded anonymously; 3D printing brings IP implications; and copyrighted material can be downloaded onto handheld devices.
- The public are becoming much more aware – or sceptical, rather – of how information is collected and dispersed in the digital sphere, in the wake of the controversy surrounding Edward Snowden's revelations about US spying capabilities. In 2014, Google, Microsoft, Facebook and Yahoo! went to court to protest the gag order preventing them from disclosing the information they are compelled to hand over to the US government.
- Many firms and their clients now believe that technology, media and telecoms are no longer three distinct markets and structure their departments accordingly.
- A trend for mergers and joint ventures in the telecoms sphere continues. Think of T-Mobile and Orange's UK operations merging to create 'EE' and Telefónica O2, Vodafone and EE entering a joint venture agreement to provide billing services to consumers.
- The EU 'Cookie Law' now requires websites to obtain consent from visitors to store cookie information on their device. The law was designed to make people aware of their right to privacy – whether it does is another matter.

- The most interesting telecoms work is taking place overseas, particularly in Africa and Asia. India's Bharti Airtel's $9bn takeover of Zain (South African telecoms) is the ultimate example of this. There is plenty of room for manoeuvre in the emerging markets, unlike Western Europe.
- Mobile messaging applications like WhatsApp are slowly overtaking traditional SMS text messaging. Analysts also anticipate the replacement of traditional phone calls with calls made over the internet – like on Skype.
- IT outsourcing began in the late 1980s, followed by business process outsourcings (BPOs) that involve handing responsibility to third-party service providers for functions like human resources, finance and accounting. Today, the lines between technology outsourcing and BPOs are blurred. Smart outsourcing – the concept of outsourcing parts of a company, one part at a time, often using different suppliers – is in vogue at present, as is multisourcing (using many different suppliers on shorter term contracts).
- With the proliferation of cloud computing in business, data protection has become an area of huge expansion for many law firms. For example, if a New York-based official in a multinational company accesses HR data for staff based in London, they may well be in breach of the Data Protection Act because UK and EU laws are that much stricter than US ones.
- The government has announced plans to roll out a UK-wide super-fast broadband network by 2015. Initially, £830m was earmarked for the project, though in 2014 Culture Secretary Maria Miller announced that a further £250m will be invested. Defra Rural Affairs Minister Dan Rogerman said that "*nothing will have a more spectacular effect on the rural economy than the roll-out of super-fast broadband.*"
- Social networking websites have admitted to conducting experiments on their users without permission, sparking complaints on ethical grounds. In 2014, Facebook admitted to having conducted an experiment on nearly 700,000 users, where the company manipulated news feeds to control the emotions the users were exposed to. Labour MP Jim Sheridan has called for an investigation into the matter.

Read our True Pictures on...

Addleshaw Goddard	Latham & Watkins
Allen & Overy	Linklaters
Ashfords	Macfarlanes
Ashurst	Maclay Murray & Spens
Baker & McKenzie	Mayer Brown
Berwin Leighton Paisner	Michelmores
Bird & Bird	Mills & Reeve
Bond Dickinson	Muckle
Brabners Chaffe Street	Nabarro
Bristows	Norton Rose Fulbright
Browne Jacobson	Olswang
Burges Salmon	Osborne Clarke
Charles Russell	Pinsent Masons
Clifford Chance	Reed Smith
Clyde & Co	RPC
CMS	Shoosmiths
Dentons	Simmons & Simmons
DLA Piper	Slaughter and May
DWF	Squire Patton Boggs
Eversheds	Stephenson Harwood
Freshfields	Stevens & Bolton
Gateley	Taylor Wessing
Harbottle & Lewis	TLT
Herbert Smith Freehills	Travers Smith
Hogan Lovells	Ward Hadaway
Irwin Mitchell	Wedlake Bell
Jones Day	White & Case
K&L Gates	Wragge Lawrence Graham
King & Wood Mallesons	

The True Picture

The True Picture reports on 111 firms
in England and Wales, ranging from
the international giants to small
regional practices. Most handle
commercial law, although many
also offer private client experience.

The True Picture

Think all law firms are the same? They're not. Even superficially similar firms can be worlds apart in how they operate internally. Fortunately, one tool exists to sort the Christmas crackers from the old knackers, the breakthrough indie bands from the One Direction fans... the True Picture.

Between them, the 111 firms covered in the True Picture have thousands of training contract vacancies to fill. With luck, one of them could be yours. Even if none of these 111 firms wants you, reading the reports will teach you a great deal about the nature of legal training and the experience of working within a law firm.

How we do our research

Every year we spend many months compiling the True Picture reports on law firms in England and Wales, ranging from the international giants to small regional practices. Our purpose is to get to the heart of what you need to know about a prospective employer – what it can offer you in terms of work and working environment. You'll want to know how many hours a day you'll be chained to your desk, the tasks that will keep you occupied and who you'll be working with. Importantly, you'll want to know about a firm's culture and whether colleagues will turn into party animals or party poopers come Friday night.

Most of our chosen firms handle commercial law, although many also offer private client experience. There are a few general practice firms offering publicly funded advice to their local communities. To take part in the True Picture a firm must provide a complete list of its trainees. After checking the list is complete, we randomly select a sample of individuals for telephone interviews. Our sources are guaranteed anonymity to give them the confidence to speak frankly. The True Picture is not shown to the law firms prior to publication; they see it for the first time when this book is published.

If you'll allow us to blow our own trumpet for a minute, we're the only publication that conducts our research in this way. By chatting to trainees rather than sending them formulaic questionnaires, we can follow up on leads, delve deeper into what makes firms tick and what challenges they face. We think that leads to better, more detailed information for our readers.

Trainees tell us why they chose their firm and why others might want to. We put on our serious faces and talk about seat allocation, the character and work of different departments, the level of supervision and what happens to people on qualification. And we flirt shamelessly to get the gossip on firm politics, office oddities and after-hours fun. We look for the things trainees agree upon, and if they don't agree we present both sides of the argument.

We also speak to senior sources at every firm – managing partners, training partners, recruiters. You'll notice their comments scattered throughout the True Picture features and published in more detail online. We conduct these management interviews to get their insights on what their firm's strategy is for the coming years. We know that by the time you, our readers, hopefully begin your training contracts in 2017 and beyond, market conditions might be very different, so we've tried to make this a forward-looking guide. Additionally, the True Picture feature isn't supposed to simply be a review of a training contract, but rather a broader picture of a firm as a whole. After all, it's not much use knowing that 'trainees at Firm X are happy/sad and work reasonable/terrible hours' but don't have a clue about the commercial environment in which Firm X operates. Again, we're the only publication to go into this much detail.

What kind of firm do I choose?

Your choice of firm will be based on location, size and the practice areas available... then it's a matter of chemistry. Some firms are stuffier, some are more industrious and some are very brand-aware, involving trainees heavily in marketing activities. Some work in modern open-plan offices; others occupy buildings long past their sell-by date. Some focus on international business; others are at the heart of their local business communities. Some concentrate on contentious work; others transactional. The combinations of these variables are endless.

What we found out this year

The redundancies and falling profits of 2009 and 2010 are now fading into the mists of time, corporate activity has recovered somewhat and more firms are starting to talk about growth. This should not imply that the profession is out of the woods yet. The economy is still on shaky ground, government cuts are biting, the Eurozone crisis is lurching to goodness knows what conclusion – the effects on law firms have been and will continue to be profound. Read more about all this in our feature on **Trends affecting the recruitment market** on page 19.

A word on law firm mergers or closures. Mergers are an increasingly regular occurrence in the profession. This is partly due to the recession – strength in numbers, and all that. However, it is also a result of globalisation. The firms with large international networks seem to feel that unless they have offices absolutely everywhere, they will be left out of an emerging global elite. When firms merge, trainees' contracts are honoured, though of course it does mean that new recruits find themselves in a different firm to the one they signed up to. Closures are rarer, but as we've seen with the cases of Halliwells in 2010, Dewey & LeBoeuf in 2012 and Cobbetts in 2013, they do happen and trainees can find themselves out on their ear.

Since the recession many firms are announcing their qualification job offers extremely late, making it difficult for those who needed to look elsewhere for employment. Pre-recession, usually just over 80% of qualifiers stayed with the law firms that trained them. After a dodgy couple of years, total retention at our True Picture firms recovered in 2011, and has remained fairly strong since then. It stood at 78.5% in 2013, slightly lower than the two previous years. At the same time, many firms have been cutting their trainee intakes and it is to be hoped that firms have managed to 'right-size' themselves. If you intend to use retention rates as a determining factor in your choice of firm, do be wary of the statistics being bandied around. Law firms make their own rules on how to calculate retention rates – you may not be getting a full picture from them. We collect our own statistics and include them in each law firm feature. We have collated statistics since 2000 and publish them on our website.

What we hear every year

- Some seats are more popular than others and there are no guarantees of getting a specific seat. Employment and intellectual property are perennial favourites.

- Levels of responsibility vary between departments. In property you might have your own small files. In corporate you will generally work in a very junior capacity as part of a team.

- The experience in litigation depends entirely on the type of cases your firm handles; usually a trainee's responsibility is inversely proportionate to the value and complexity of a case.

- In times of plenty, corporate and finance seats mean long hours, commonly climaxing in all-nighters. The size and complexity of a deal will determine your role, but corporate and finance usually require the most teamwork.

- Most firms offer four six-month seats; some offer six four-month seats and others operate their own unique systems. Trainees switch departments and supervisors for each seat. Some share a room and work with a partner or senior assistant; others sit in an open-plan office, either with the rest of the team or with other trainees. Occasionally trainees have their own room.

- All firms conduct appraisals: a minimum of one at the conclusion of each seat, and usually halfway through as well.

- Client secondments help you learn to understand clients' needs. They can be the highlight of a training contract.

- The Solicitors Regulation Authority requires all trainees to gain experience of both contentious and non-contentious work. Additionally most firms have certain seats they require or prefer trainees to try. Some firms are very prescriptive, others flexible. Remember, a training contract is a time to explore legal practice to see what you're best at and most enjoy. You may surprise yourself.

And finally...

Use the True Picture to help you decide which firms to target. No matter how easy or hard securing a training contract is for you, you'll want to end up with the right one.

Jargonbuster

We're not massive fans of lawyer jargon, but some of the phrases do actually mean something. If you want to brush up on your legalese for an interview, here's a handy guide to sounding like a pro.

- **ABS** – Alternative Business Structures: newly permitted arrangements for law firms, which allow non-lawyers to have a financial stake in the business.
- **Agency work** – making a court appearance for another firm that can't get to court.
- **AIM** – a 'junior' stock market run by the London Stock Exchange, which allows smaller companies to float stock within a more flexible system.
- **Antitrust** – the US term for competition law.
- **Adjudication** – the legal process by which an arbiter or judge reviews evidence to come to a decision.
- **Arbitration** – a type of dispute resolution where the parties agree to abide by the decision of one or more arbitrators.
- **Associate** – a term used to denote solicitors not at partner level but more senior than an assistant solicitor.
- **Bench** – the judge or judges in a courtroom.
- **Best friends relationship** – a situation where two firms have no organisational or financial ties, but use each other as the first port of call when referring work.
- **Bibling** – putting together sets of all the relevant documents for a transaction.
- **Billing target/chargeable hours target** – the number of hours lawyers are required to record working for a client; time is usually recorded in six-minute chunks; trainees do not usually have billing targets.
- **Boutique** – a small firm which works only on one area of law.
- **Brief** – the instructing documents given to a barrister when they are instructed by a solicitor.
- **Bundling** – compiling bundles of documents for a court case.
- **The City** – the commercial and financial centre of London; also known as the Square Mile.
- **CMC** – case management conference.
- **Coco** – company-commercial department/work.
- **Conditional fee arrangements** – also called 'no win no fee'; an arrangement whereby a solicitor acting in a claim agrees only to be paid a fee if he wins the case; such payment is usually made by the losing party.
- **Contentious matters** – legal disputes between parties.
- **Conveyancing** – the transfer of the ownership of property from one person to another.
- **Counsel** – a barrister.
- **CSR** – Corporate Social Responsibility: the practice of companies taking responsibility for the impact of their activities on society; in reality 'CSR committees' at firms will run projects where lawyers paint schools, plant trees and clean playgrounds.

- **Damages** – a sum of money which one person or organisation has to pay to another for not performing a certain duty.
- **Data room duty** – used to involve supervising visitors to rooms full of important documents, helping them find things and making sure they don't steal them. With electronic data rooms the job becomes more of a desktop exercise.
- **Disclosure** – making relevant documentation available to the other parties in a dispute.
- **Dispute resolution** – litigation, mediation, arbitration, etc.
- **Document management** – dealing with the more administrative side of deal documentation.
- **Due diligence** – the thorough investigation of a target company in a deal.
- **Equity partner** – a partner who receives a contractually agreed share of the firm's annual profits. A part owner of the firm. The other type of partner is a salaried partner.
- **Fee earner** – a lawyer or a paralegal who bills time to a firm's clients. The term doesn't include lawyers who act in a more supportive role.
- **FTSE 100 (pronounced 'footsie')** – an index of the 100 most valuable companies listed on the London Stock Exchange; the value of these companies used to give an indication of the health of the UK's business world.
- **Grunt work** – administrative (and boring) yet essential tasks including photocopying, bundling, bibling, paginating, scheduling documents, data room duties and proof-reading or checking that documents are intact.
- **High net worth individuals** – rich people; commonly used when referring to private client.
- **Highly leveraged** – the practice of having a ratio of few partners to lots of solicitors; leverage is also a term used in finance – the two are not connected.
- **Infant approval** – court authorisation for a settlement involving a minor.
- **In-house lawyer** – a solicitor or barrister who is employed by a company or public body rather than a law firm or barristers' chambers.
- **Injunction** – a court order requiring a party to do, or to refrain from doing, certain acts.
- **IPO** – the Initial Public Offering of shares in a company to the public on a stock market; also known as flotation.

- **Judicial review** – the legal process by which the actions of the government or public bodies can be challenged.
- **Junior Lawyers' Division** – a sub-group within the Law Society set up in 2008 to represent student members of the Law Society, trainees and lawyers up to five years' PQE.
- **Law Society** – the official representative body of solicitors in England and Wales.
- **Legal Aid** – a government-funded system which pays for legal representation in criminal and some civil cases for individuals who would otherwise be unable to afford it.
- **Legal Disciplinary Partnership (LDP)** – a business structure whereby a law firm can take on non-lawyers as equity holders. Up to 25% of a partnership can be non-lawyers.
- **Legal Services Act** – the 2007 Act of Parliament encourages the development of one-stop shops that deliver packages of legal services at the convenience of consumers and provides an alternative path for consumer complaints.
- **Limited Liability Partnership (LLP)** – a way of structuring a professional partnership such that no partner is liable to any of the firm's creditors above and beyond a certain sum.
- **Litigation** – a method of settling disputes through legal proceedings in court.
- **Lockstep** – the practice of increasing solicitor's salaries based purely on seniority.
- **M&A** – mergers and acquisitions; the buying, selling and combining of companies; often the main focus of firms' corporate teams.
- **Magic circle** – the name given to five of the leading London-based law firms; it is generally held to consist of Allen & Overy, Clifford Chance, Freshfields Bruckhaus Deringer, Linklaters and Slaughter and May.
- **Managing partner** – the main boss of a law firm, who leads the partnership and/or management committee in running the business and devising its strategy.
- **Master** (in the High Court) – a judge in the High Court ranking lower than a High Court judge, chiefly responsible for case management. They are called 'Master' regardless of whether they are male or female.
- **Mediation** – A type of dispute resolution where a dispute is resolved with the help of a neutral third party.
- **Moot** – a mock trial used to train or test advocacy skills.
- **Nearshoring** – the outsourcing of work to another organisation, usually in a part of the UK where overheads and salary costs are lower.
- **Niche practice area** – a practice that is specialised and not in a mainstream area.
- **Notary public** – a qualified lawyer appointed by the Archbishop of Canterbury, who is authorised to authenticate and certify estates, deeds, powers-of-attorney and other documents, especially for use abroad; the majorities of notaries are also solicitors.

- **NQ** – a newly qualified solicitor.
- **(Offshore) outsourcing** – hiring in an external organisation (overseas) to perform a part of a company's activities.
- **Overseas seat** – same concept as a seat (see further down the list), except that it's undertaken in an international office.
- **Panel** – a group of law firms or lawyers chosen for regular consultation by a certain business.
- **Paralegal** – a non-lawyer, often with some legal training, who assists qualified lawyers on legal matters.
- **PFI** – Publicly Financed Initiative; a way of creating 'public-private partnerships' (PPPs) by funding public infrastructure projects with private capital.
- **PLUS** – a stock exchange in London founded in 2005, which lists small and mid-sized companies especially from the retail industry.
- **Power of Attorney** – the legal authority to act on someone else's behalf.
- **PQE** – post-qualification experience.
- **Pro bono** – from the Latin 'pro bono publico', meaning 'for the public good'; legal work done without payment as a public service.
- **Public procurement law** – regulates the purchasing by public sector bodies of contracts for products, works or services.
- **Profits per equity partner (PEP)** – the annual profits of a law firm divided by the total number of equity partners in the firm; this statistic is often used to indicate the financial health of a firm, but it can easily be manipulated by altering the number of equity partners.
- **PSC** – Professional Skills Course; a compulsory course taken during the training contract.
- **Restructuring exercise** (in the context of a law firm) – the reorganisation of a business, usually to make it more efficient or more attractive to clients; often a euphemistic way of talking about staff/lawyer redundancies.
- **Reverse commute** – living in a city, working on its outskirts (or even further away) and commuting that distance every day.
- **Rights of audience** – the right of a lawyer (either a solicitor or barrister) to appear and conduct proceedings in court.
- **Rotation** (when referring to seats) – when a trainee moves from one seat onto the next.
- **Salaried Partner** – a partner who receives a salary but has no contractual claim on the firm's profits; the other type of partner is an equity partner.
- **Seat** – time spent by a trainee working in a department, usually four or six months.
- **Secondment** – the practice of 'lending' trainees and qualified solicitors to a firm's client to work in their in-house legal department for a certain period.
- **Silo-ing** – encouraging people to work in a specific field rather than being generalists; teams working very independently of others within a firm.

- **Silver circle** – a group of elite English law firms, generally considered to fall just outside the magic circle. This tends to include Herbert Smith Freehills, Ashurst, Berwin Leighton Paisner, King & Wood Mallesons, Macfarlanes and Travers Smith.
- **SRA** – Solicitors Regulation Authority; the body that regulates the professional conduct of solicitors in England and Wales.
- **Superinjunction** – the informal term for an injunction whose existence and details may not be publicly disclosed.
- **Swiss Verein** – a business structure consisting of a number of independent offices, each of which is independently liable for its own obligations.
- **Tesco Law** – a nickname for the effect of the Legal Services Act.
- **TMT** – technology, media and telecommunications; an increasingly common area of practice.
- **Tort** – a breach of duty owed to someone else (a 'civil wrong') which leads to injury to a person or their property.

- **Training contract** – a two-year period of working in legal practice in which someone who has completed their LPC is trained by an accredited organisation to become a qualified solicitor.
- **Training partner** – the partner who oversees the training scheme.
- **Trainee partner** – a trainee who acts like a partner.
- **Tribunal** – specialist judicial bodies that decide disputes in a particular area of law.
- **Vacation scheme** – a placement with a law firm designed to familiarise a prospective trainee with a firm and vice versa; sometimes called 'vac schemes' or 'summer placements', they are usually held during the summer or at Easter and can last anywhere between one and four weeks. The vast majority of firms offer this.
- **Verification** – the aspect of a deal in which lawyers ensure stated information is accurate.

The True Picture

Firms by size in the UK

		London	Overseas	Yorkshire & NE	East	S & Thames Valley	South West	Wales	Midlands	Trainees	True picture
1	Government Legal Service	•								35	279
2	Pinsent Masons	•	•	•					•	150	382
3	Eversheds	•	•	•	•			•	•	105	256
4	Clyde & Co	•	•			•				80	221
5	DLA Piper	•	•	•					•	154	248
6	Simmons & Simmons	•	•				•			83	408
7	DWF	•		•			•		•	96	251
8	Allen & Overy	•	•							190	162
9	Bond Dickinson	•		•		•	•			43	190
10	Linklaters	•	•							224	333
11	Herbert Smith Freehills	•	•							150	284
12	CMS	•	•				•			160	227
13	Clifford Chance	•	•							c.200	224
14	Freshfields Bruckhaus Deringer	•	•							187	268
15	Addleshaw Goddard	•	•	•						61	159
16	Irwin Mitchell	•		•			•		•	79	301
17	Wragge Lawrence Graham & Co	•	•						•	63	473
18	Hogan Lovells	•	•							125	292
19	Norton Rose Fulbright	•	•							110	366
20	Slaughter and May	•	•							156	414
22	Berwin Leighton Paisner	•	•				•			85	180
22	Shoosmiths	•			•				•	39	401
23	Hill Dickinson	•	•	•						58	289
24	Gateley	•		•					•	30	271
25	Mills & Reeve	•		•	•				•	33	351
26	Squire Patton Boggs	•	•	•					•	37	420
27	Nabarro	•	•	•						51	363
28	Kennedys	•	•	•	•	•	•		•	36	310
29	Osborne Clarke	•				•	•			37	375
30	Dentons	•	•			•				34	245
31	Ashurst	•	•							85	171
32	Stephenson Harwood	•	•							32	423
33	Reed Smith	•	•							50	385
34	Charles Russell	•	•			•	•			33	215
35	Taylor Wessing	•	•		•					44	428
36	TLT	•								32	433
37	White & Case	•	•							63	462
38	Burges Salmon	•					•			51	210
39	Trowers & Hamlins	•	•						•	38	442
40	Baker & McKenzie	•	•							70	174
41	Browne Jacobson	•					•			18	207
42	King & Wood Mallesons	•	•							72	313
43	Macfarlanes	•								51	336

Firms by size in the UK

	Firm	London	Overseas	Yorkshire & NE	East	S & Thames Valley	South West	Wales	Midlands	Trainees	True picture
44	Brabners									12	201
45	Mishcon de Reya	•	•							24	354
46	Freeths	•		•		•			•	26	265
47	Travers Smith	•	•							46	437
48	RPC	•								40	389
49	Holman Fenwick Willan	•	•							29	295
50	Bird & Bird	•	•							36	187
51	Farrer & Co	•	•							20	259
52	Mayer Brown	•	•							30	342
53	Olswang	•	•			•				25	369
54	Capsticks	•		•		•			•	16	213
55	PwC Legal	•	•							20	N/A
56	Ward Hadaway			•						19	450
57	Maclay Murray & Spens	•								8	339
58	Foot Anstey						•			12	262
59	Ashfords	•					•			19	167
60	Lewis Silkin	•				•		•		12	331
61	Speechly Bircham	•								22	417
62	Latham & Watkins	•	•							41	324
63	Jones Day	•	•							31	304
64	Watson, Farley & Williams	•	•							27	453
65	Withers	•	•							25	469
66	Ince & Co	•	•							25	298
67	Veale Wasbrough Vizards	•					•			17	445
68	Michelmores	•					•			13	349
69	Leigh Day	•								18	327
70	SGH Martineau	•							•	16	393
71	Shearman & Sterling	•	•							16	396
72	K&L Gates	•								15	307
73	Winckworth Sherwood	•				•				12	467
74	Wedlake Bell	•								12	457
75	Bristows	•								19	204
76	Bircham Dyson Bell	•								14	185
77	Kingsley Napley	•								10	317
78	Dechert	•	•							24	241
79	Stevens & Bolton					•				8	426
80	Weil, Gotshal & Manges	•	•							23	459
81	Kirkland & Ellis	•	•							16	321
82	Fladgate	•								8	N/A
83	Sidley Austin	•	•							22	405
84	Gordons			•						9	277
85	Lester Aldridge	•				•	•			18	329
86	Cripps	•				•				16	235

Firms by size in the UK

		London	Overseas	Yorkshire & NE	East	S & Thames Valley	South West	Wales	Midlands	Trainees	True picture
87	Sullivan & Cromwell	•	•							4	N/A
88	Higgs & Sons								•	11	287
89	Skadden	•	•							16	411
90	Bates Wells Braithwaite	•			•					9	177
91	Harbottle & Lewis	•								11	282
92	Boodle Hatfield	•				•				10	193
93	Hewitsons				•				•	11	N/A
94	Muckle			•						6	360
95	BPE Solicitors	•								5	198
96	Cleary Gottlieb	•	•							25	218
97	Edwards Wildman Palmer	•	•							12	254
98	Wilsons	•		•			•			6	465
99	Covington & Burling	•	•							14	233
100	Trethowans					•	•			5	440
101	Collyer Bristow	•								8	230
102	Sheridans	•								3	399
103	Orrick	•	•							9	372
104	Memery Crystal	•								8	347
105	Paul Hastings	•	•							8	378
106	Bingham McCutchen	•	•							4	183
107	B P Collins					•				7	196
108	Morgan, Lewis & Bockius	•	•							10	357
109	Davis Polk & Wardwell	•	•							5	240
110	Arnold & Porter	•	•							2	165
111	McDermott Will & Emery	•	•							4	345
112	Thomas Cooper	•	•							6	431
113	Vinson & Elkins	•	•							8	448
114	Peters & Peters	•								5	380
115	O'Melveny & Myers	•	•							7	N/A
115	Gide Loyrette Nouel	•	•							8	274
117	Curtis Mallet-Prevost	•	•							2	238

Addleshaw Goddard LLP

The facts

Location: London, Leeds, Manchester
Number of UK partners/solicitors: 177/430
Total number of trainees: 61
Seats: 4x6 months
Alternative seats: overseas seats, client secondments
Extras: pro bono – Hillside Legal (Leeds), Legal Advice Centre Stockwell (London); language classes

On chambersstudent.co.uk...

How to get into Addleshaw Goddard
Diversity at AG
Interview with the new training
   principal Aster Crawshaw
Berezovsky v Abramovich

Up there with the big dogs in London, an undisputed leader in Yorkshire, and rapidly expanding overseas, Addleshaw Goddard is a growing force with an impressive portfolio of clients.

Three is a magic number

With offices in London, Leeds and Manchester, and a team of over 600 lawyers, Addleshaw Goddard is a leading firm in the North and an established force in the capital. Having gradually acquired overseas offices in Oman, Qatar, Hong Kong, Dubai and Singapore it's a smooth global operator too. The firm's main practice areas are corporate, commercial, finance and projects, litigation, private capital and real estate. Trainees across all three offices were attracted to the firm's *"solid status as a strong corporate player,"* to the *"international flavour"* of its work and to its reputation as a firm where trainees are *"not just transient help, but very involved in matters and building relationships with clients."* Sources who had undertaken a vac scheme (about 80% of the current cohort) unanimously identified Addleshaws' *"warm and welcoming atmosphere"* as a pivotal factor in their decision to accept a traineeship. Vac schemes and training contracts are available in all three offices; at the time of our research, out of 66 trainees 17 were in Manchester, 17 in Leeds and 32 in London.

Recently Addleshaws has undergone a series of management reshuffles. John Joyce has taken over as managing partner (his predecessor Paul Devitt bowed out of the job a year early), and new international regional heads have been installed for the Gulf and Asia offices. There were also over 20 lateral hires in the 2013/14 financial year. A trainee commented: *"The firm hasn't quite had the growth it hoped for in recent years and is definitely undergoing a period of transition: major new hires have been handled swiftly and are clearly a big statement about the firm's determination to put together the best team for the job."*

There's clearly a drive to attract new high-profile clients too: in July 2014 Addleshaws won a spot on BP's UK legal panel, a big achievement and perhaps a sign that recent strategic reshuffling efforts are paying off.

Playing FTSE

The seat allocation system works homogeneously across the three UK offices: trainees are not able to choose their first seat, which the firm allocates *"having considered CVs, backgrounds and interests."* At every subsequent rotation trainees list four seat options in order of preference. Most sources were happy with the system, although as can be expected from a firm this size a few trainees were left disappointed not to be able to do the seats they wanted. Sources did note that HR is working to address this.

Despite reports of it having long hours in all three offices, corporate is a popular seat, attracting trainees with the thrills of *"exciting high-profile deals."* Northerners described corporate as *"offering a steep learning curve"* – while they started with *"basic trainee tasks"* like due diligence, taking board minutes, drafting stock transfer forms and preparing other ancillary documents, interviewees reported eventually *"being left to take an active*

> **Seat options:** corporate; banking; real estate; litigation; commercial; asset finance; employment; infrastructure projects energy; pensions; BSR (restructuring); funds; construction and planning; tax; financial regulation

The True Picture

Chambers UK rankings

Aviation	Information Technology
Banking & Finance	Insurance
Banking Litigation	Intellectual Property
Capital Markets	Litigation
Charities	Local Government
Competition/European Law	Outsourcing
Construction	Partnership
Consumer Finance	Pensions
Corporate Crime & Investigations	Planning
	Private Client
Corporate/M&A	Private Equity
Defamation/Reputation Management	Product Liability
	Professional Negligence
Education	Projects
Employee Share Schemes & Incentives	Public Procurement
	Real Estate
Employment	Real Estate Finance
Energy & Natural Resources	Real Estate Litigation
	Restructuring/Insolvency
Fraud	Retail
Health & Safety	Social Housing
Healthcare	Tax
Hotels & Leisure	Transport

role within smaller deals." Several London sources described their work as that of *"a project manager, bringing together information from across the firm – corporate is something of a hub in that respect."* Londoners reported working on *"IPOs, corporate support, and divestments for banks,"* while a Leeds source told us about *"doing private equity work which was fast-paced and made me feel like I was in the eye of the storm."* Client contact is common, and we heard from trainees who had *"attended companies' AGMs and met directors and key company figures in the build-up to transactions."* AG ranks as one of the country's top ten corporate advisers to FTSE 100 companies. Recently it advised Sainsbury's on the launch of its new mobile phone network, advised Britvic on the production and distribution of its Fruit Shoot drink in India, and acted for William Hill and GVC as they acquired online gambling group Sportingbet for a casual £485m.

London trainees enjoyed the *"strategic nature"* of the approach to work in litigation. Despite some reports of trainees not getting much independence *"because the cases are very high in value so a trainee's work always needs to be checked,"* there are opportunities to *"attend court, watch barristers in action, and go along to interviews with witnesses."* Litigation is notoriously bundle-heavy, but sources who *"went in with an awareness that it comes with the territory"* ultimately found that *"generally there's less admin than in some other seats."* As we've reported in past editions, it's worth bearing in mind that although there are no advocacy opportunities in London, on rare occasions the opportunity does arise in the northern offices. One interviewee in the capital had however got to work on a Court of Appeal case – an experience they described as *"the absolute highlight of the training contract so far."* Our interviewees reported doing a high volume of international work in this seat, either because of international clients or cross-border issues. A recent highlight was a $1bn international fraud case in which the claimants were the largest property development company in the Middle East, Dar Al Arkan, and a Bahraini investment bank, Bank Alkhair. Both were AG's clients. Word is that it could be the largest claim in the Commercial Court in 2014/15. Oooh. Get you.

In real estate, trainees get their own files to handle from the off, along with all the thrills that come with that responsibility. One trainee was *"managing conditions precedent and compiling CP lists, which requires a lot of co-ordination!"* Another recalled *"a lot of lease reviews, getting to know some pretty niche bits of property law, and plenty of form filling for the Land Registry,"* adding that *"by the end of the seat you'll be able to recite those forms in your sleep!"* Sources also reported plenty of client exposure: a Leeds source commented that *"real estate is fantastic for it – from day one you're phoning and e-mailing clients on your own"* although *"supervision is always there when you need it."* One source in the Big Smoke was disappointed that *"there was not a lot of residential work, which you'll want to do if you like law that relates to day-to-day life. But there's just no need for a firm as big as AG to take on that kind of work."* There's plenty of excitement to be had however; the London team for example has recently been busy with international work, advising a large Malaysian investment fund on the acquisition of a trophy London property. Other London clients include Sainsbury's, Primark and Hobbs on the retail side, as well as the Royal College of Music, which AG advised on its big new student accommodation scheme.

'Shaw me the money

There are different strands of banking which trainees can experience but most of our interviewees had undertaken a seat in the core banking seat, the imaginatively named 'banking 1'. Described by London trainees as *"mainstream"* or *"conventional"* finance, it is a transactional seat involving both lending and acquisitions. The firm operates within the mid-market and clients include Barclays, HSBC and the Co-op Bank, as well as a number of FTSE blue-chips. Like in corporate and litigation there are *"lots of standard trainee tasks to do: compiling CP checklists, dealing with post-completion filings, corporate support, and the drafting of ancillary documents."* Responsibility levels left sources more than satisfied: one commented that *"you have the opportunity to work on small files of your own,"* while another *"partook of client meetings and really learnt the graft of being a banking lawyer."* On the Leeds menu it's client exposure with all the trimmings: one source worked on a *"brilliant fun"* 24-hour completion during which they got to go for a fancy pub lunch with clients. 'Banking 2' is basically real estate finance, although this is a less frequented seat.

There are plenty of client secondments on offer, and trainees from all the offices can head off to spend time with some of AG's most prominent clients, including British Airways, Sainsbury's and Diageo. Some sources expressed concern at the *"sheer number"* of secondments, observing that *"partners use trainees as currency to keep clients happy. So there is some pressure to go on them. We also take on secondees from clients, who are occasionally given priority in seat allocation."* However, trainees who had undertaken a client secondment were satisfied with the exposure to different work and reported huge day-to-day variation in tasks compared to what's on offer back home with the firm.

Besides client secondments, AG now also offers overseas seats: trainees can spent time in Dubai, Hong Kong and Oman. Sending people abroad like this is a new thing for AG, and we weren't surprised to hear that there have been some teething troubles. Overseas seat allocation has caused a bit of a stir – mainly among the Leeds and Manchester bunch – after the third overseas seat in a row was offered to a London trainee. *"The issue was raised and is being addressed by HR,"* one interviewee assured us, while a recruitment source was adamant that *"the overseas seats are open to all trainees."* We were assured that the Northern offices will get a better look in from now on. Throughout the training contract there are regular meetups with HR to discuss seats and qualification hopes, and trainees believed these are *"a good forum"* to raise any issues they encounter.

One issue that would probably not need raising is supervision. Trainees across the firm felt supervisors performed well on this front. There's no formal mentoring system for trainees at the moment (although first-years do have a second-year 'buddy'), but sources were under the impression that HR is considering introducing one. There are mid-seat and end-of-seat appraisals for all – *"the end-of-seat review does have a written element to it, but the meetings themselves are pretty informal."*

Laying foundations

As we've reported in the past, every autumn AG organises a CSR trip to Romania for its incoming trainee group, along with four or five partners. Before getting stuck into bundles and CP lists, rookies get their hands dirty building houses for the charity Habitat for Humanity. Our sources this year were yet again singing the praises of this *"incredible experience and brilliant initiative"* which is *"totally un-work-related and a great chance to meet the intake across all three offices."* Another source added: *"It means that when I have to e-mail or call trainees in another office I know who they are, which makes things much easier!"* The firm keeps up its efforts for Habitat throughout the year, with recent fund-raisers for the Philippines typhoon rescue effort raising almost £20k.

Working hours at Addleshaw Goddard really depend on what seat you're in, but trainees across all three offices reported the very occasional all-nighter scattered among the average ten-hour day. *"There isn't a face-time culture here,"* a Leeds source said. *"When you've finished your work you're actively encouraged to leave."* As well as working hard, playing hard is also definitely part of the firm's ethos, with each office organising its own regular events as well as a few firm-wide bashes on special occasions. The Leeds office loves its monthly 5pm Friday drinks. A trainee noted: *"You can use that time to catch up with people from previous seats you've worked in. It's useful to stay in touch particularly if you're thinking about qualifying into that department."*

The location and amenities of the London office were described by one source as a *"major pull for prospective trainees."* The office is centrally located in Moorgate and interviewees appreciated that *"the canteen is subsidised – it's not super-cheap but it's cheaper than going out somewhere so trainees usually try and meet there and eat together."* The Manchester office is located just off Oxford Street near Manchester Central and *"has great views from the higher floors,"* while Leeds boasts *"a big glass atrium at the centre, plus it's right on the river, which is lovely."*

AG recruits heavily from Russell Group universities in London and around Leeds and Manchester, as well as Warwick, Newcastle and Oxbridge. However, an HR source told us that the firm's recruitment ethos is *"non-restrictive and grounded in valuing social mobility and transferable skills acquired in all areas of work, including retail and hospitality."* The firm's A-level requirement of BBB is a little lower than some firms, broadening the potential scope of recruitment.

And finally...

The qualification process at AG is *"relaxed and informal"* and retention rates are about average for a commercial firm, with 29 out of 34 trainees being kept on in 2014.

Allen & Overy LLP

The facts

Location: London

Number of UK partners/solicitors: c.181/668

Total number of trainees: 176

Seats: 3 or 6 months long

Alternative seats: overseas seats, client secondments

Extras: pro bono – Toynbee Hall Free Legal Advice Centre, Battersea Legal Advice Centre, Fair Trials International, Amicus and many others; language classes

On chambersstudent.co.uk...

How to get into Allen & Overy
A potted history of the firm

Growing income and global footprint mean it's cheers all round at Lavanda, A&O's very own bar and terrace.

Seat-ing comfortably

"I was attracted to A&O by its banking and geographical strengths," one fairly representative trainee told us, although while banking is a big part of Allen & Overy's business, it is by no means the be-all and end-all. The global finance world's bounce-back in the years since the Great Recession helped A&O report record results in July 2014 – profits were up 7% in 2013/14 to £532m, with turnover 2% higher at a neat £1.23bn. *"A&O has a big presence in China – with offices in Beijing, Shanghai and Hong Kong,"* another trainee pointed out, trying to explain the glowing financials. Geographic expansion has indeed continued apace, helping to drive growth. Last year we reported new offices in Hanoi and Ho Chi Minh City; this year Myanmar is the latest pin on A&O's map of the world, bringing the total up to 44. At the same time, A&O has undergone a massive streamlining operation in the past few years. In a headline-grabbing move, it shifted its European and US support staff to Belfast in 2011. Improved efficiency and cost-savings are paying dividends. The Support Services Centre now employs some 350 staff.

Such is the importance of Spitalfields-headquartered A&O's international network of offices – and cross-border nature of much of its work – that many trainees spend the last six months of their training contract abroad. *"Most go all around the globe – Dubai, Washington, Shanghai, Moscow, Paris..."* The list seems almost endless. Many of those who stay at home for their last seat will go on client secondment, although some will miss out either through choice or because their desired destinations were too popular. *"I was delighted to get my secondment – international opportunities were one of the*

reasons I joined the firm. I understand that a few people were pretty annoyed that they didn't get theirs, or got a client secondment they didn't put down." Nevertheless, opportunity knocks even louder for the most globally minded, because there are usually *"a dozen or so NQ jobs across the international network"* each year.

Generally, though, interviewees spoke very positively about seat allocation. *"The best thing about the training contract is the ability to work in any department I wanted to work in. Seat selection is very good. I got all my first-choice seats."* A couple of months before the end of their accelerated, A&O-tailored LPC, future trainees attend a fairly comprehensive open day, a bit like a careers fair, in which the various departments set up a stall each and showcase what they have to offer. *"You also get a brochure from HR which describes the various groups and subgroups. You then submit a form noting down groups you're interested in and HR will then allocate people's first seats."* Three or four months into your training contract, you'll sit down to discuss your next two six-month seats, one being your 'priority seat' and one your 'request seat'. Sources praised this process as people usually get what they want. Furthermore, you can specify a subgroup and even a particular trainer (as supervisors are called here) – maybe you've heard good things about them, or met them at the information day and felt you 'clicked'. *"They're very good at getting you where you want to go,"* reiterated one junior. *"By and large everyone gets what they want,"* confirmed another.

A&O has two intakes each year, one in September and one in March. While there are lots of seat options on offer, as you'd expect in a magic circle firm, each trainee must do

Chambers UK rankings

Administrative & Public Law	Insurance
Asset Finance	Intellectual Property
Banking & Finance	International Arbitration
Banking Litigation	Investment Funds
Capital Markets	Life Sciences
Commodities	Litigation
Competition/European Law	Outsourcing
	Partnership
Construction	Pensions
Corporate Crime & Investigations	Pensions Litigation
Corporate/M&A	Private Equity
Data Protection	Projects
Employee Share Schemes & Incentives	Public International Law
	Real Estate
Employment	Real Estate Finance
Energy & Natural Resources	Real Estate Litigation
	Restructuring/Insolvency
Environment	Social Housing
Financial Services	Tax
Fraud	Telecommunications
Information Technology	Transport

seats within two of the three core practice groups: banking, corporate and international capital markets (ICM). From 2014, they can do two banking seats rather than one. Other options include litigation, real estate and tax. There are some three-month seats, although they're rare: *"You can do three months in litigation, then three months somewhere else like banking* [litigation]*, pensions, environment – niche areas – but they do change a lot."* Trainers tend to be senior associates and, less often, partners.

Banking on success

The giant banking group is subdivided internally into different 'B' teams, each with its own number. We won't list them all here, but B2, for example, is structured and asset finance (like aircraft and ship financing), which is now separate from B3, which is leveraged finance and general lending. B4 is restructuring. You get the idea. A trainee might ask to do a banking seat and will be put into one of the Bs – or they might request a specific subgroup in advance. Banking clients include lenders like Barclays, HSBC and Goldman Sachs, borrowers like Marks & Spencer and advertising conglomerate WPP, and financial sponsors including CVC, Charterhouse, Cinven and HgCapital.

On a typical deal, said one interviewee, *"I got to go to lots of internal meetings, and all-party meetings to discuss the terms of the financing. Towards the end of the deal I co-ordinated board minutes, and went to the client's office for the day to review documents with another*

firm." Another trainee told us: *"I spend quite a lot of time liaising with counsel and local parties, and circulating documents. You spread yourself over two or three deals. It's nice to deal with other jurisdictions."* Occasional travel abroad is one perk we heard about in a banking seat. Trainees described banking as *"very, very busy"* – a good thing for getting more responsibility *"out of necessity, because trainers are so swamped! Mine gave me a lot of drafting, got me involved in internal discussions, let me loose on clients."* Another did *"extensive drafting of documents I'd never seen before, for my trainer to review."*

Corporate subteams are similarly divided into numbers. C6 in particular is one to watch right now, as half of what it does, private equity, is an area *"the firm is investing in heavily"* (the other half of C6 is oil and gas work). For example, it recently brought in a heavy hitter from Ashurst, Stephen Lloyd, to co-head the group, as well as other lateral partners. General M&A is the bread and butter for corporate lawyers, and sources spoke of the usual peaks and troughs in this type of work. *"I had a fair amount of client contact and was taking calls myself towards the end of it. The amount of work goes up and down. When there's a lot going on people expect you to pull your socks up and be there. When it's quiet you can leave."* Another experienced *"high-level work"* in this seat – *"I was thrown into the fire on a big transaction. I worked on four or five different things. There was a lot of drafting work and client contact, drafting memos based on research, legal documents – generally I felt I was contributing."*

Among many notable work highlights, lawyers in the Paris office (located next to the Arc de Triomphe) advised French multinational Vivendi on the €17bn sale of its phone unit SFR to European cable group Altice. In another highlight, A&O advised on the complex £3.4bn loan and bond refinancing for broadcast transmission provider Arqiva, a transaction which involved partners in departments including banking, corporate, ICM and tax. Lawyers in London, Germany, Romania and the US recently advised Romanian state-owned electricity company Electrica on its dual listing and IPO on the Bucharest and London stock exchanges.

With over 450 lawyers worldwide, A&O's ICM practice is huge too, and trainees for the most part enjoyed their time here. Clients like Bank of America Merrill Lynch, Deutsche Bank, Credit Suisse and Citibank benefit from brainy legal advice involving concepts like derivatives, securitisation, structured finance and intercreditor issues – if, like our chancellor George Osborne, the question 'what is seven times eight?' makes you break out into a cold, silent sweat, then probably best to avoid this one if you can. Thankfully, said one trainee, *"my trainer was great and has kept in touch throughout my training contract."*

TOILing away

Quite a few avoid doing a formal litigation seat, racking up their 40 hours SRA-required contentious experience in pro bono matters instead. Employment is a popular team – *"very competitive but they fitted us all in. It's a smaller team, so you get more exposure to each other's working styles. The hours are probably better than in the transactional teams because there's less business-critical work where you have to find a deal and it must be done tonight. By contrast, employment follows tribunal dates so it's easier to plan ahead. You get work requests from all of litigation in a general e-mail, and you can chip in ad hoc on anything if you're not busy. But generally you only do work for your subteam."* Other litigation sub-teams include arbitration (where *"people can have wildly different experiences"*), finance/regulation, commercial litigation and intellectual property. *"You're better valued as a trainee in transactional groups,"* some found. *"Litigation is hierarchical – trainees do bundles and legal research. You can't really have trainees running round and sending emails. There is a lot of copy checking, bundling – not stuff you can give to a secretary, but not the most exciting legal work."* Litigation is a strategic priority for A&O, so expect to see further growth here in the coming years. In one recent case, the firm acted for private equity firm CVC in a dispute over monies owed following the onward sale of a beer company to Molson Coors.

When it comes to appraisals, trainees get a *"very helpful"* mid-seat informal review – *"it's good to hear where you stand before the formal end-of-seat review."* A 'buddy' in your first six months *"mostly answers silly questions like how to turn on the computer."* Trainees update their 'record of experience' as they go along, ticking off the types of work each department does as they do it. They're graded between one and five at the end of each seat, one being the best and five the worst. *"It's good to show progress, but some trainers never give more than a three, while some always give one,"* we heard, although *"there is a meeting between partners to iron out inconsistencies. There's trainee gossip about more lenient departments, but the system works."* In reviews, trainers *"give input, and advice about what to focus on in the next seat."*

And what of those notorious magic circle hours? *"When I started I thought 'how will I ever do such long hours?' But the days go so fast a lot of the time. You work on quite interesting stuff, so you're happy to see it through to the end. Plus, the rest of the team is there with you."* There were rumours of sleeping pods, whose existence was confirmed by more than one source: *"Yes, I've seen them! There are four, like tiny hotel rooms, with a single bed and en suite bathroom."* People can take time off in lieu (known as TOIL) if certain mega-hours and *"business targets"* have been met, but more commonly *"lots of departments operate a discretionary system."* Most interviewees regularly worked well into the evening every weekday, sometimes past midnight, but equally felt able to leave much earlier (5.30pm or 6pm) during quieter times. *"A&O is good at distributing work evenly, so the week after a really hard shift I was given less work. Some trainees can get quite stressed, but everyone's part of a team and the firm does look for resilient characters."*

Is it all work and no play? *"Before I started I thought people would be driven, high-achieving, but they're also normal and sociable."* A&O's very own café/restaurant-by-day, bar-by-night, Lavanda (whose name may or may not be a pun on the lavender plants on its terrace), is ever-popular. As the office has *"one foot in the City, and one in Shoreditch,"* there are tons of hipster pubs, bars and restaurants nearby, including The Gun, and The Water Poet. This year's trainee ball was in the *"jungle room"* of the Barbican Centre (a hidden gem, we can assure you), while various sports and arty things (like a choir and theatre) are available for those so inclined. The basement gym is a *"social hub,"* as is the *"mini sports hall"* which hosts things like football, badminton and classes like spinning and *"boxercise."* However, *"the tennis club seems to have more social functions than actual games!"* A&O has long-established pro bono links with Toynbee Hall and Battersea Legal Advice Centre, among other places. And in 2009 the firm launched its 'Smart Start Experience' for underprivileged Year 12 students to sample a week in A&O's office.

And finally...
82 of the 99 qualifiers in 2014 stayed on.

Arnold & Porter (UK) LLP

The facts

Location: Londonw

Number of UK partners/solicitors: 18/25

Total number of trainees: 2 (every two years)

Seats: 4x6 months

Alternative seats: occasional secondments and overseas possible

Extras: TrustLaw Connect, FRU, Waterloo Advice Centre

On chambersstudent.co.uk...

How to get into Arnold & Porter

5 minutes with training partner Richard Dickinson

A&P London's foray into white-collar crime

Once every two years, two bright-eyed candidates are selected to train at Arnold & Porter, an American outfit in the City whose work has a distinct pharma bent.

Life will find a way

The UK arm of Washington, DC-headquartered Arnold & Porter is strongly associated with its work in areas like life sciences, IP and competition. But the office is broadening its scope: the corporate practice has grown in recent years, while the white-collar crime group was kept busy by the furore surrounding the *News Of The World* phone hacking and bribery cases. Renovation work in the office has also triggered talk of further expansion, and one interviewee observed: *"They've taken out leases for extra floors, so maybe they're thinking of hiring more people. We don't know yet..."*

Interviewees targeted A&P because they were looking for a specialised firm geared towards their areas of particular interest. Of the two trainees and two NQs with the firm at the time of our calls, three had science degrees (in microbiology, biochemistry and chemistry), while the fourth had studied law. Previous careers in the pharma industry are common too. We recommend you check out the firm's website to get an idea of what degrees and backgrounds A&P's London lawyers commonly have, although the firm stresses that a science background is not a prerequisite.

For a small firm with only two trainees there are a surprising number of seat options, six in fact: life sciences, intellectual property, corporate, competition, international arbitration and white-collar crime. A stint in life sciences or corporate is pretty much inevitable. A new partner hire in financial services could mean opportunities in this area for trainees soon. Business needs and informal chats determine where A&P's trainee pair end up going at each rotation. The two quickly come to understand what all the departments do, making it easy for them to work out where they might want to spend time. In addition, *"if the team you're officially sat with is a bit quiet you can ask for work from different areas – it helps to be proactive."* Further flexibility is added by occasional client secondments – trainees will likely spend between two and six months away from the office during one of their seats.

Building blocks

Life sciences is the office's biggest department and undoubtedly the jewel in A&P's crown. The firm is top-ranked in *Chambers UK* for regulatory, product liability and general life sciences work – a feat unmatched by any other firm. Clients include recent potential merger partners Pfizer and AstraZeneca, as well as that other behemoth of the pharma industry, GSK. On the product liability side, London lawyers recently defended German pharma company Grünenthal against damages claims tied to the historical testing and marketing of thalidomide in the UK – product liability work doesn't get any bigger or more serious than that. Regulatory advice, meanwhile, may touch on equally serious issues like clinical testing, generic substitution laws and the borderline between medicines and devices. Trainees are given administrative tasks like bundling, but also undertake research, draft

Seat options: corporate (inc telecoms and employment); IP; competition; white-collar crime; international arbitration; life sciences; financial services

Chambers UK rankings

Competition/	Life Sciences
European Law	Product Liability
Intellectual Property	Retail

memos and respond to enquiries. *"I felt heavily involved in all the cases,"* one trainee confirmed. *"The seat is a great introduction to the world of pharmaceuticals."*

A quarter of A&P's London lawyers work in the IP department, which does a mix of patent litigation, soft/commercial IP and trade mark portfolio management. Work ranges from assisting pharma giants with asthma inhaler patents, to advising media clients like Disney, ITV and MTV. The firm recently acted for the first of these in a dispute over the IP rights to the name 'The Avengers'. Sources reported that some of the work has a European focus. For example, lawyers acted for GSK in a dispute about the delivery of a new form of diabetes medication, in which the opposing parties were Swiss company Ypsomed (which makes the disposable pen and injection needle) and Germany's Vetter (which makes the syringe cartridges). Trainees told us they had taken part in client meetings, drafted provisions for contracts, attended cases at the Patent Court, and done copyright and trade mark research.

The corporate group is home to just seven lawyers. Although it's *"not the main strength of the London office,"* lawyers have been working to build up the firm's mid-market M&A reputation. Partner Anna Buscall was hired from Allen & Overy in 2012, and the latest *Chambers UK* research suggests the firm's efforts are paying off. The group focuses on life sciences and retail work (for which the firm is *Chambers*-ranked) and a lot of the work streams in from the US. For example, lawyers recently represented UK designer outlet manager McArthurGlen on a €435m joint venture with Simon Property, the largest mall owner in the US. When the department's busy, trainees are given administrative tasks to help get deals done, and at the height of closings may stay at work until the wee hours. During quieter times, trainees pick up company secretarial work – *"setting up new company registers, dealing with changes of directors etc."* There's some capital markets work too – almost exclusively sovereign debt offerings for non-European governments like Israel, Brazil, Tunisia and Honduras.

A&P is recognised by *Chambers USA* as one of the ten best firms in America for competition work (or 'antitrust' as the Yanks call it). The London competition practice is well regarded too, winning a *Chambers UK* ranking and working on *"high-value deals worth billions of dollars."* The six-lawyer team works closely with the ten-strong Brussels office (which is exclusively competition-focused). Ad hoc secondments to the city of Tintin and Euro-federalism are available to trainees, especially *"if there's a filing going on with the European Commission."* There's a focus on training in this seat with a lot of multi-jurisdictional research as well as the chance to *"listen and learn"* on conference calls with clients.

Faking it

There are hardly any American lawyers knocking around A&P's London office, which means the firm has the feel more of a small City outfit than a strapping American. Firm-wide e-mails, annual meetings with *"the head honchos from the States,"* and regular video conferences help keep links with the US alive. After qualification, NQs are flown to the DC HQ in order to hobnob with the latest cohort of junior associates joining the firm stateside. It's an occasion where *"the ethos of the firm"* is really rammed home. *"It was very cheesy,"* reported one source, *"with lots of rousing speeches!"*

While tub-thumping is not the done thing in A&P's London office, one imported American tradition is the weekly drinks social: *"In DC everyone goes up to the roof terrace on a Thursday evening to socialise so we do the same."* The event is held in the impressive-sounding Garden Room, though before you imagine a cornucopia of dense foliage and exotic orchids we can confirm the room in fact contains one rather fake-looking conifer. Even though the flora may not be so impressive, the views are: A&P is based on the 30th floor of the City's Tower 42 (formerly the NatWest building).

Besides the weekly Garden Room bash there are end-of-deal drinks and client events to be enjoyed as well, but interviewees warned that *"you can't join A&P expecting a lot of trainee socialising."* That isn't a surprise given there are only ever two trainees around at any one time. Iit makes up for this in work/life balance, however: the hours are reportedly not as intense as at most other US or City firms. While there are still times when trainees might be *"slammed"* and have to burn the midnight oil (especially in corporate), on average lawyers can merrily trot out of the office by about 7.30pm.

And finally...
Since 2006 all eight trainees who've qualified at the firm have been kept on, most joining the life sciences and IP departments.

Ashfords LLP

The facts

Location: Exeter, Bristol, London, Plymouth, Taunton, Tiverton

Number of UK partners/solicitors: 74/102

Total number of trainees: 19

Seats: 4x6 months

Alternative seats: secondments

On chambersstudent.co.uk...

How to get into Ashfords
Interview with training principal
    Charles Pallot
Doing business in the South West

Already a front-runner in the South West, Exeter-based Ashfords is jockeying for position in London.

Country capital

Ashfords' West Country roots stretch back several centuries, and today the firm maintains a steady focus on the region, operating five local offices that service a host of regional clients between them, including Devon & Exeter NHS Trusts, Taunton-based Viridor Waste, and Exeter City Council. Some notable national and international players make the books too, including HSBC and National Australia Bank. Beyond the regions there's a London base, which has grown considerably stronger since its 2012 merger with Rochman Landau. In the past few years this office has welcomed a handful of lateral hires, upped sticks to swanky new digs near Holborn Circus and become the focus – along with the Bristol and Exeter branches – of the firm's plan to offer professional, non-legal services such as project management and regulatory advice.

That said, the Exeter HQ remains at the forefront of Ashfords' operation, not least in size: with a staff of 300, it vastly outnumbers Taunton, the next biggest office and home to just over 50 employees. At the time of our calls, there were 11 trainees in Exeter, five in Bristol, and two each in London and Taunton, while the Tiverton and Plymouth offices nabbed one apiece. It's common for them to undertake seats in more than one office. *"We encourage people to consider moving across our locations, if they can, because it gives them an opportunity to get to know the firm as a whole,"* training principal Charles Pallot explains.

Ashfords' main strengths lie in its three key practice areas: commercial, private client, and property and infrastructure. All have earned high *Chambers UK* rankings

in the South West. The firm also dabbles in some fairly niche areas, among them shipping, agriculture and rural affairs, and equestrian sport. The latter practice, top-ranked nationwide, is headed by a former National Hunt jockey and advises everyone from top-class trainers to the British Horseracing Authority. In 2013/14 the firm posted an 8% increase in turnover, clocking in at a cool £31.8m.

A double-dip apprenticeship

Trainees get to state their top three choices each time rotation rolls around. One pick has to be from the property and infrastructure division, one from commercial, and one is a free choice from any of the three main divisions. Luckily, within each division there is *"an ample number of seats to choose from."* Quite a few of our interviewees had done a repeat seat, telling us the option *"makes you feel like you're specialising, which is satisfying."* We should add that while repeat seats do happen, they're contingent on business need. *"People who haven't done a certain seat before will get priority."* Additionally there are client secondments available with companies like Lloyds Bank and South West Water.

The corporate/commercial team is a big player in the West Country, advising local heavyweights like Devon-

> **Seat options:** commercial property; planning; projects; construction; property litigation; commercial; corporate; IT/IP; banking/tax; employment; restructuring and insolvency; personal injury; business risk and regulation; marine; commercial litigation; trusts and estates

Chambers UK rankings

Agriculture & Rural Affairs	Local Government
Banking & Finance	Planning
Construction	Private Client
Corporate/M&A	Real Estate
Employment	Real Estate Litigation
Family/Matrimonial	Restructuring/Insolvency
Information Technology	Shipping
Intellectual Property	Social Housing
Litigation	Sports Law

based engineering company Centrax and Plymouth's The Una Group. Much of the work involves M&A and fund matters. Links via London mean the team has access to a batch of international clients too, among them NYSE-listed Schlumberger and Canadian-based Enghouse Systems. City lawyers recently oversaw Haydon Mechanical & Electrical's buyout of a Mears Group subsidiary and advised Sprue Aegis, a supplier of home safety products, on its successful defence of a £34.8m takeover bid by major shareholder BRK. According to trainees, the *"fast-paced"* department sees them *"dip in and out of work, helping out whenever the partners need assistance."* Most of the work requires *"a lot of senior contact,"* so trainees tend to fill their time with ancillary tasks. *"I did a lot of drafting for documents that weren't fundamental to the agreements we were working on,"* one testified, adding: *"I was given free rein with them, so I got some great exposure."* Likewise, seniors generally handle the face-to-face client contact, though we heard from plenty of interviewees who'd e-mailed and phoned clients themselves. Like most corporate practices, *"when it's really busy you can expect to work very long hours – sometimes past midnight."*

The commercial property team is home to the largest development practice in the South West and has worked on some hefty matters of late – for example, helping the Homes and Communities Agency obtain a £24m loan to fund the construction of a relief road to ease traffic in Berkshire. Quite a bit of work involves renewable energies, and the team counts wind farm developer Airgen Renewables among its key clients. Those who'd spent time in the department showered the seat with praise. *"You're given heaps of responsibility and told to give it a go,"* said one. *"You get to run a lot of work for the smaller matters, and if your supervisor is confident in you, you might even get to do things like explain something directly to clients."* Fortunately, we were told, *"you never feel out of your depth; if you're struggling you can easily get help."*

Over in commercial litigation clients range from small start-ups to high net worth individuals to sizeable multinationals. The team, one of the largest in the region, recently advised Italian bank Comune di Forli on a €50m

SWAP dispute with Dexia Bank and acted for the Indian Farmers Fertiliser Co-operative on a $7.5m charter party dispute. It's not all contractual disputes though: our sources had worked on a good amount of clinical negligence work, which we hear *"allows trainees to get a lot of frontline client contact"* thanks to tasks like taking witness statements. *"Once you're given the chance to speak to a client one-on-one, you realise it's not as scary as it seems."* On the whole, interviewees gave the seat a confident thumbs-up, praising the variety of work and *"high levels of respect and trust shown to trainees."*

Ashfords' construction group handles both contentious and non-contentious matters for an array of clients, from contractors and utility companies to waste management businesses and local authorities like the London Borough of Enfield and Cornwall County Council. Lawyers recently advised Gleeson Regeneration on a handful of issues concerning a multimillion-pound housing regeneration project in Manchester, and have lately dedicated an increasing amount of time to energy-related projects spanning the waste energy, biomass and solar spheres. Trainees here reported tough hours, with one describing *"regular 11 to 12-hour days, plus some weekends. They tried to give me interesting work to do, but ultimately the team was so busy that I ended up doing mostly administrative work like bundling and filing."* Grunt work aside, sources also told of more *"satisfying"* experiences such as attending trials and managing low-value files on their own.

Like construction, the employment department also flits between contentious and non-contentious work, mixing tribunals with advice for local authorities. The firm recently made headlines helping whistle-blowing cardiologist Raj Mattu win an unfair dismissal case – the longest-running and most expensive whistle-blowing matter in NHS history. The victory landed group head Stephen Moore a spot on *The Times*' 'Lawyer of the Week' list. Trainees spoke positively about a seat here, reporting *"a lot of drafting"* of documents like employment contracts, staff handbooks, grounds for resistance and witness statements. *"Your first draft is always considerably amended, but it's nice to know you're not just stuck doing the bundling,"* said one. Interviewees also praised the high amount of client contact and said *"the team is great at sending you along to hearings and letting you get experience that way."*

Saturday night breather

Last year we heard some grumbles about Ashfords' approach to training, but this year's interviewees had positive things to say all around. *"I feel really supported,"* one shared, telling us: *"I spent the first week doing very thorough training, and I've had regular sessions ever since. People appreciate that as a trainee you're starting afresh every six months, so they're always understanding if you need help."* All offices but Tiverton are open plan, and usually trainees sit in close vicinity to their supervisor and other partners, a set-up that *"facilitates discussion – you can bounce ideas off your colleagues rather than sitting and stewing over it."* This proximity also proves useful for picking up training tips. *"One of the best ways to learn is by overhearing what the partners are doing and how they act."*

Our sources extended their praise to the work/life balance the firm affords, agreeing that *"it's definitely not the kind of place where you feel like you need to stay in your seat until the partner goes home."* While we did hear from some trainees who'd worked weekends, we're told this is a relatively rare occurrence. *"I've only worked three Saturdays in my whole time here,"* shared a second-year. Still, as our interviewees pointed out, reasonable hours don't come without some kind of compromise – in this case low wages. *"All South West firms pay less than London of course, but our salary could be better,"* they admitted. Trainees in the regions start on £20,000, although they do progress to £34,000 upon qualification.

Interviewees agreed that *"friendliness and a relaxed atmosphere"* prevail firm-wide but noted that the day-to-day environment varies between offices. Like Bristol, London is *"small enough that everybody knows everybody,"* though the latter has *"more of a modern vibe."* The Tiverton branch, on the other hand, is housed in a 300-year-old building and *"feels like a high street practice is some ways,"* which our sources hastened to add *"is no bad thing."* Meanwhile, Taunton exudes a *"family atmosphere – it's really friendly, and somebody's always bringing in cake."* And then there's Exeter, *"which definitely feels like the headquarters"* thanks to corporate amenities like sleek meeting rooms, a canteen, a free gym

and a bread delivery service. *"It's really big and as such can be seen as more impersonal – you know the people on your floor, but it's impossible to know everyone."* Still, insiders had lots of praise for the premises, mentioning its *"lovely facilities"* and *"really good transport links."* They went on to assert that the firm as a whole *"feels very connected. They're really keen to make sure we operate under one brand, so work feeds through different offices and they hold firm-wide parties where they pay for everyone's travel and accommodation."*

One such event is the firm's summer do, which in 2014 was *Pirates of the Caribbean*-themed. Other annual goings on include departmental Christmas parties and the nomination of a charity for the year. The latter lends itself to a series of fund-raising events, among them fun runs, cyclathons and even sponsored climbs of Mount Kilimanjaro. Trainees are encouraged to get involved in networking groups like the Junior Lawyers Division, which provide access to various professional events, and things are buzzing on the informal side too, although both Exeter and Taunton are located in business parks slightly out of town, so piling into the local pub after work is not as convenient here. Still, *"while things are harder to organise, that doesn't mean it doesn't happen,"* Exeter sources stressed.

The qualification process has become more transparent in recent years. These days the firm releases a list of available jobs, and second-years apply and interview for their desired position. All of our interviewees were eager to stay on and seemed confident, despite last year's lower than usual retention rate of ten out of 17. At the time we went to press Ashfords had confirmed it was giving NQ jobs to six of 14 qualifiers, although that number could go up as 11 jobs were up for grabs.

And finally...

Ashfords attracts a mix of fresh-faced graduates and enthusiastic career-changers – some of the current partners worked as surveyors, engineers or accountants before joining as trainees and rising up the ranks.

make *your* presence felt

Ashurst offers its clients and trainees a clear alternative to other elite law firms by cutting through complexity. With 28 offices spanning the world, we offer the scale to attract global mandates.

We operate at the cutting edge of the financial, corporate, infrastructure, disputes and resources markets with advice that is commercially acute as well as technically accurate.

For our clients this means getting to the heart of issues with speed and clarity. For trainees, our strong culture of collegiality means you will be encouraged to apply your intellect and make your presence felt right from the outset.

To find out more about our training contract and vacation scheme opportunities or find a recruitment event relevant to you, please take a look at our website.

www.ashurst.com/trainees
www.facebook.com/AshurstTrainees
www.youtube/AshurstTrainees

leading international law firm

Ashurst

The facts

Location: London

Number of UK partners/solicitors: 122/228

Partners who trained at firm: 34%

Total number of trainees: 85

Seats: 4x6 months

Alternative seats: overseas seats, secondments

Extras: pro bono – IPSEA, RCJ CAB, Reprieve Toynbee Hall Legal Advice Centre; language classes

On chambersstudent.co.uk...

How to get into Ashurst

What is the 'silver circle'?

Ashurst's founders

Overseas seats

Ashurst was born and bred in the City but has spent the last few years moulding itself into an international marvel.

A slice of the wedding Blake

There's been no shortage of Aussie-Brit relationships in recent years – Peter Andre and Katie Price's inimitable class inspired it all, no doubt, and then later came Shane Warne and Elizabeth Hurley's whirlwind on/off romance (which now looks to be firmly off). Hopefully City slicker Ashurst's recent union with Blake Dawson, one of Australia's 'Big Six', will have more of a fairytale ending than those two former couples. In 2012 Ashurst welcomed Blakes to the family by integrating its Asian operations under the banner Ashurst Australia, and the pair went on to tie the financial knot fully in November 2013. *"Basically we lived together first before we got married,"* jokes graduate recruitment partner Helen Burton, who goes on to reveal that the months since the tie-up have proved a relatively easy-going honeymoon period: *"The energy the merger generated has reignited everybody within the firm, and it's helped propel us forward with a really credible global footprint."* Indeed, with over 1,700 lawyers spread across 28 offices in 16 countries, the power couple is certainly a force to be reckoned with.

In London Ashurst has a 350-lawyer team and is a member of the silver circle. (In case you're unfamiliar with that term, it refers to the set of firms that are one step below the illustrious magic circle but post significantly greater profits than the rest of the UK's legal market.) Many of the trainees we spoke to had made a conscious decision not to apply to the magic circle firms, justifying this with the belief that Ashurst handles work of similar quality but couples it with more of a *"supportive, jovial environment."* We've more on the latter part of this claim later, but for now let's focus on the work. There's no doubting the standard is high: the firm notches up over 40 rankings in *Chambers UK*, many of which – including capital markets, banking, investment funds and high-end M&A – slot into the its hard-hitting corporate and finance practices. Lawyers excel in other areas to be sure, but these practices are Ashurst's pillars, and the ones that nab the biggest deals – for example, Hypothekenbank Frankfurt's £4bn sale of its UK commercial real estate portfolio. With that in mind, it's little wonder trainees are required to complete a finance seat at some point. A stint with the banking or securities and derivatives group satisfies this.

We heard HR has taken strides to make seat allocation an increasingly transparent process in the past year. Rather than simply e-mailing in their preferences, as has been the case in years past, trainees these days kick off their training contract with a meeting with HR in which they discuss what they want to focus on during their two years. *"They offer good advice on whether your choices match up to qualification chances, which is helpful – there's a huge drive to help us succeed from the beginning."* The majority of our sources had secured their first or second choices almost every time.

Seat options: banking; competition; corporate; disputes; employment; energy resources and infrastructure; intellectual property; media and telecoms; real estate; regulatory; restructuring and insolvency; securities and derivatives; tax; technology

The True Picture

Chambers UK rankings

Banking & Finance	International Arbitration
Banking Litigation	Investment Funds
Capital Markets	Life Sciences
Competition/European Law	Litigation
	Local Government
Construction	Outsourcing
Corporate Crime & Investigations	Pensions
	Planning
Corporate/M&A	Private Equity
Employee Share Schemes & Incentives	Product Liability
	Projects
Employment	Real Estate
Energy & Natural Resources	Real Estate Finance
Financial Services	Real Estate Litigation
Fraud	Restructuring/Insolvency
Information Technology	Tax
Insurance	Telecommunications
Intellectual Property	Transport

Supermarket sweep

Ashurst's corporate department is home to a hatful of subgroups, including equity capital markets, private equity and general corporate. Trainees can dedicate their time exclusively to one or opt to take on work from a few. The firm has handled some hefty deals of late in this arena: lawyers recently advised supermarket big'un Morrisons on its £300m agreement with online grocer Ocado, which resulted in the chain adding an online delivery function on its website, and acted for betting giant William Hill on its £485m acquisition of fellow gambling guru Sportingbet. If you remain unconvinced about the magnitude of the team's work, consider these other big-name clients: Lloyds, RBS and Merlin Entertainments, the second-most visited theme park operator on the planet after Disney. We hear all the standard trainee tasks are on offer in a corporate seat – due diligence, fact verification and legal research – and that *"client contact is plentiful – you're often helping advise them on day-to-day activities."*

The firm's finance faction has a host of domestic and international financial institutions on the books, including Santander, Barclays, HSBC and Wells Fargo. One of the team's latest undertakings saw lawyers advise a group of banks – among them Bank of Ireland and RBS – on the £375m refinancing of chain café Pret A Manger. Much like corporate, the finance department is split into various subsets, including securities and derivatives, structured finance, banking and real estate finance. The first is *"a very technical area,"* so trainees in this seat are primarily tasked with minor undertakings like proof-reading and document management. Our sources took a positive view of this, telling us such tasks are *"great for helping you*

find your feet and getting to grips with basic concepts." Meanwhile those who'd sat with the banking team encountered a reasonable level of responsibility working on the *"huge headline deals"* the team handles – for example, Barclays' 2014 collaboration with BlueBay Asset Management. According to our insiders, such matters typically see the group *"broken down into small teams that usually include a partner, senior associate, associate and trainee. Trainees are responsible for knowing all the ins and outs of a given deal so they can assist accordingly."*

The energy resources and infrastructure (ERI) group – one of the most sought-after destinations for trainees, we might add – excels on the power as well as the oil and gas side, regularly advising investors, funders and corporations on projects like pipelines and nuclear plants. Lawyers recently oversaw the development of the first privately financed wind project in Kenya, and assisted with the financing of the biggest concentrated solar power project in Africa. Closer to home, the team has spent the last decade advising on the UK's Crossrail project, one of the largest rail projects in the world at the moment. *"As a junior member of the team you're encouraged to work in as many areas as you can,"* our interviewees said, mentioning involvement across the oil and gas, project finance and waste disposal sectors. They reported passing their days drafting and proof-reading ancillary documents, liaising with clients and opposing counsel, and reviewing contract clauses. *"The documents are huge – as in hundreds of pages long – so there's a lot to look over."*

Walking in the Westfield of gold

Ashurst's real estate department is filled to the brim with big-ticket matters for household names like Tesco, Samsung and Mitsui. Westfield is one of the largest clients on the books; the team recently advised the Aussie shopping centre group on its £1bn regeneration of Croydon, which entails redeveloping and combining the town's two main shopping centres, the Whitgift Centre and Centrale. Sources who'd spent time in the department reported juggling between *"five and 20-plus files at once – it's rather different from a finance seat, where you only manage a handful at a time."* It's not uncommon for trainees to take a crack at the first drafts of licences and agreements, and they're also assigned post-completion tasks like preparing SDLT returns and land registry applications.

The dispute resolution crew's work spans the energy, financial services and automotive sectors, among others. As a result the client base is noticeably varied: alongside financial hotshots like RBS are telecoms giant Telefónica, coach operator National Express and cigarette manufacturer Imperial Tobacco. The team recently defended Goldman Sachs against a multimillion-pound claim by French energy giant GDF regarding an alleged breach of warranty in a Teesside power station. Trainees praised the *"interesting mix"* of tasks on offer in a seat here, which range from carrying out research, interviewing clients and drafting early-stage documents to more basic undertakings like bundling and doc review. *"The high-value nature of the work means you don't quite get as much responsibility as you do in other teams,"* one interviewee remarked, *"but it's still great to see how these disputes play out – plus you get plenty of exposure to the court system."*

Overseas secondments are a pretty big deal at Ashurst. *"The firm recognises law is becoming increasingly global, so they see them as really beneficial."* Stints are available in six offices: Dubai, Hong Kong, Madrid, New York, Singapore and Tokyo. We hear in light of the Blakes merger there's talk of a seat opening up in Australia in due course too. If an overseas seat doesn't appeal, don't fret; there are several client secondments up for grabs too, including spots at several major financial and household-name clients.

Sleepy-eyed pod

Our sources were frank about the fairly gruelling schedule a firm with flagship practices in corporate and finance can incur. *"There's no denying the hours here can be brutal,"* one insider admitted, and indeed we heard a couple of horror stories involving after-hours activity: one source told of finishing at 4am *"three or four days in a row,"* while another recounted the time they went to take a much-needed late-night power nap in one of the firm's sleeping pods *"only to find they were all occupied. That tells you a lot."* As terrifying as these anecdotes sound, however, it's important to recognise they aren't the norm. *"A lot of the work is cyclical by nature, so things get busy then go back to being more stable."* It also helps that Ashurst compensates for arduous shifts with days off in lieu, free food after 7pm and taxi rides home after 10pm. On the whole, interviewees agreed: *"Working on headline-grabbing matters like the ones we handle make the tough hours worth it,"* with one adding bluntly *"if you arrive at a City firm expecting to go home at 5pm every day, there's something wrong with you."*

As you can probably tell, new recruits are unlikely to find a training contract at Ashurst a cushy ride. Any assump-

tions that it might be are likely to be down to the firm's nickname, 'Lashurst', which arose a few years ago as an ode to its work hard/play hard philosophy. Our sources were keen to set the record straight, though: *"It's easy to misconstrue Lashurst as meaning we don't take our work very seriously,"* one grumbled, *"not to mention that it wrongly implies we have a 'laddish' culture here. However, it really just points to the fact we're encouraged to let our hair down every now and then."* Indeed, there are plenty of opportunities for lawyers to let off some steam when they're not beavering away in the office. Trainees are put in charge of organising a yearly ball (the latest one was a nautical affair, complete with sea shanties and sailor hats), and they can also kick back at departmental gatherings, sports clubs, drinks trolleys, charity events and partner-hosted shindigs. For all its revelry, however, *"Ashurst isn't a place where you're forced to go out all the time if you're not that sort of person,"* insiders noted.

There's an age-old perception that Ashurst caters almost exclusively to the Oxbridge crowd, but while that was largely the case back in the day, trainees from recent intakes have been significantly more varied in their backgrounds. *"Most of us do come from prestigious universities, but it's far from being all Oxbridge graduates,"* one confirmed. *"What unites us is a sense of confidence and conviction; there isn't anyone who makes you wonder how they got a training contract here."*

Stars and stripes and all things nice

With Ashurst and Blake Dawson now settled in as newlyweds, all eyes will be on this firm's next endeavour. As insiders noted, *"Ashurst has been looking to make more of a name for itself in the US market for a while now,"* so it's likely management will turn its attention Stateside, where the firm's presence is confined to a 50-person New York branch and ten-person DC outpost. Indeed, while the firm's talks with three American firms between 1998 and 2003 all fell through in the end, the idea came up again in 2013, with partners partaking in fresh discussions regarding the possibility of a US merger. We'll have to wait and see whether Ashurst pursues an American sweetheart, but one thing is certain: *"Our future is looking bright as we continue moving closer to becoming a part of the global elite."*

And finally...

Ashurst's top-quality work and majestic international presence make it a great alternative to the magic circle. In 2014 the firm kept on 43 out of 49 qualifiers.

Baker & McKenzie

The facts

Location: London

Number of UK partners/solicitors: 84/202

Partners who trained at firm: 35%

Total number of trainees: 70

Seats: 4x6 months

Alternative seats: overseas seats, secondments

Extras: pro bono – Bethnal Green Legal Advice Centre, A4ID, TrustLaw UNHCR, Amicus, and others; language classes

On chambersstudent.co.uk...

How to get into Baker Mac
Understanding Swiss Vereins
Why Myanmar?

You have to search far and wide to find part of the planet this megafirm hasn't planted its flag.

My how you've grown

If you believe that size matters, you'll certainly be impressed by Baker & McKenzie. The Chicago-founded firm, one of the two largest in the world, just added bases in Myanmar and Brisbane in 2014, upping its headcount to a walloping 4,100 lawyers spread across 76 offices in 47 countries. If that hasn't got you hot under the collar, consider its global revenue: in 2013/14, turnover clocked in at a cool $2.42bn, making B&M the world's second highest-grossing firm, with only fellow bigshot DLA Piper standing in the way of the gold medal. *"We're more than just a huge international outfit,"* declared one insider: *"We're basically a brand."*

Given the juggernaut is only 65 years old, it's clearly been living life in the fast lane. Behind B&M's massive growth is the Swiss Verein structure it adopted in 2004, which allows each international office to remain independent and benefit from limited liability. Whereas conventional mergers can be lengthy, complex and expensive, Vereins allow firms to expand fast – B&M, for example, was able to launch nine new offices between 2011 and 2014 alone.

Something to note about B&M: it's a US firm by birth only. In fact, just 20% of the firm's lawyers are based in the US; London is now Bakers' biggest bastion. For all its magnitude, however, the firm is far from the largest you'll find in the capital, taking a sound 35 to 40 trainees a year. *"It's a good size – there are a lot of resources, but you never feel lost in the crowd."* B&M London originally built up its name with its corporate and finance practices, but today the office operates as an all-rounder, earning more than 50 *Chambers UK* rankings. Top marks are awarded for areas as varied as construction, employment, IT, IP and private client.

All four corners of the globe

Trainees at B&M submit three seat choices before each seat rotation and are guaranteed a top choice at least once. Corporate is the only compulsory seat, though in recent years dispute resolution has proved *"very popular – it's a big department with a lot of work going on."*

The corporate department boasts some A-list clients like Carlsberg, Siemens and Sony, and in 2013 completed deals worth a collective value of $15bn. On the M&A side the firm handles cross-border deals for big multinationals like Unilever and Macquarie Group. One recent whopper saw B&M advise Korea Electric Power Corporation on its $30bn nuclear power plant development in UAE. Indeed, many of the biggest instructions have an energy slant, with the firm looking after a swathe of mining and oil and gas companies. *"It's one of the only industry-specific departments."* Other recent representations include advising Yamal Development on its $2.94bn acquisition of a 60% stake in Arctic Russia, and assisting Alliance Oil during its $840m joint venture with Repsol. *"I had a surprising amount of responsibility during my time with the team,"* remarked a trainee. *"I drafted some intricate documents like bespoke agreements, which really tested my intellectual ability."*

The corporate department is also home to a *"newish and quite niche"* restructuring and insolvency team that spe-

Seat options: corporate; banking; structured capital markets; dispute resolution; EU competition and trade; employment; IP; IT/communications; pensions; real estate; tax; wealth management

Chambers UK rankings

Administrative & Public Law	Immigration
Banking & Finance	Information Technology
Banking Litigation	Intellectual Property
Capital Markets	International Arbitration
Commercial Contracts	Investment Funds
Competition/European Law	Litigation
Construction	Media & Entertainment
Corporate/M&A	Outsourcing
Data Protection	Pensions
Employee Share Schemes & Incentives	Pensions Litigation
Employment	Private Client
Energy & Natural Resources	Private Equity
Environment	Product Liability
Financial Services	Professional Discipline
Franchising	Public International Law
Fraud	Public Procurement
Hotels & Leisure	Real Estate
	Sports Law
	Tax
	Telecommunications

cialises in cross-border business transformations. As one source summed up: *"We co-ordinate frequently with our overseas offices to help multinationals reorganise their group structure."* Trainees here are typically charged with a *"project management role, which means you're the one liaising with these offices."* Reviewing bibles, spreadsheets and checklists, and drafting company documents, board minutes and resolutions is also commonplace.

B&M's banking group excels in the acquisition finance, securitisation, bank lending, financial regulatory and project finance spheres. *"We have some experts who know their area really well."* The team recently advised telecoms company MTN Nigeria when it was raising $3bn in debt facilities, and also counts private equity group EQT and Standard Chartered among its recent clients. According to trainees, *"you're given whatever work you prove you can handle here."* As one told us: *"I was drafting not just board minutes but security documents, which are generally reserved for qualified solicitors. It was gratifying to know I was in the thick of it, doing jobs that keep the deals moving."* Sources also praised the responsibilities to be found on the *"incredibly friendly"* structured capital markets team. *"My main job was co-ordinating the due diligence procedure on a big project, but I also got to draft various amendments and carry out some important research,"* testified one. *"It's a good seat in that no one looks over your shoulder every two minutes. You can shout out if you're drowning of course, but overall they let you get on with it."*

The Skylon's the limit

Business is booming in B&M's dispute resolution group, where lawyers service the likes of Shell, McClaren and the BBC Trust, the regulatory body that oversees the activities of the Beeb. The firm's been the latter's sole independent legal adviser since it became operational in January 2007, so it was B&M lawyers tasked with handling the fallout of the Jimmy Savile revelations, as well as the wave of complaints that came in after BBC journalists posed as LSE students during *Panorama's* 'North Korea Undercover' programme. *"I spent most of my time with the department involved in one large trial,"* recalled an interviewee. *"I had to do all the bundling, which took a long, long time and wasn't too enjoyable, but everyone was appreciative. Later on I helped with witness prep and attended the trial to see it all come together, which made it all worthwhile."* Like their counterparts in dispute resolution, trainees in employment looked upon their responsibilities with a glass-half-full attitude. *"Contentious seats do involve a lot of bundling, which isn't very glamorous, but I didn't mind it too much as I also got to attend witness statement interviews and take a stab at writing up those, which is really an associate task."* Clients here include big'uns like Google, British Airways and Lloyd's of London. Overseas seats are big news at B&M and consistently prove a lure for applicants. Said one trainee: *"They really deliver on this front – there are so many places you can go!"* The most frequented destinations are Hong Kong, Moscow and Brussels, but trainees can also head to San Francisco, Johannesburg, Sydney, Singapore and Chicago, among others. Stints to faraway shores last three or six months and it's common to do one as a fourth seat. Those interested are asked to submit a CV listing the matters they've worked on and put forward a business case – *"basically, explaining why you're a good fit and how you going would benefit the firm."* Trainees can also spend six months working in-house for a high-calibre client.

"I get the impression that most people come to the firm because of the international experience and cross-border work it offers. You'll find international outlooks common here – a lot of trainees have travelled extensively or were born in different countries. You don't have to speak five languages to work here, but something like that would likely be of interest to the firm." Our sources went on to describe their colleagues as *"a nice mix of people,"* telling us: *"There's a good spread of universities among us, and a lot have had other careers beforehand. It's not all 22-year-olds fresh out of university."* As a result, they felt, *"you don't find hardcore yuppie wannabes here; people are pretty chilled out and intelligent."*

A chilled-out personality certainly comes in handy at the Christmas party, where first-years are tasked with putting on a show for the rest of the firm. *"Last year's theme was Broadway musicals, so we made a hilarious video of really senior partners, including the MP, doing skits to*

Broadway songs. Everyone loved it. That's a pretty good illustration of how easy-going and friendly everybody is." Another big event on the social calendar is the trainee summer party – most recently hosted at swanky South Bank eatery Skylon – and there are also monthly Friday night drinks held in the office canteen. Outside of these formally arranged activities, *"you can always find trainees in the pub together on a Friday."*

Trainees loved the *"great central location"* of B&M's London home – just off Fleet Street and in the shadow of St Paul's Cathedral. *"It's really conveniently placed within the City, and certainly makes the court run easier,"* laughed one source, pointing out the proximity of the Old Bailey. Another chirped: *"There's a variety of good pubs and lunch spots off Fleet Street, too. Head to Carter Lane – you can get some great falafel there!"* If you don't fancy going out, you'll be pleased to hear that the office canteen received rave reviews, which is lucky, as one interviewee was apoplectic that the firm *"got rid of all the good biscuits recently! I don't like the new batch!"*

While the hours were considered *"far from hellish,"* there's no denying that training at Baker Mac will require some hard graft. *"Usually the average working hours are 9.30am to 7pm, which is completely reasonable,"* a trainee said. *"But you have to accept that there'll be times you're here until 2am as well."* Another source remarked: *"You can't avoid the occasional all-nighter, but work/life balance is valued, too. Even when my hours have been long, I've never felt they were unnecessarily long. I've never had to stay just for the sake of it."*

"I know 95% of the people"

Trainees appreciated that B&M London is *"not some faceless place where you don't know the guy four doors down."* As one said: *"I can name everyone on my current team, and they all know who I am. Even in corporate, our biggest department, I know 95% of the people."* Trainees share offices with their supervisors, *"which is an invaluable experience – you can pick up their mannerisms on the phone and get a glimpse into what makes them successful."* There's no need to fret about cramping their style, either – *"I've never had a partner kick me out of the room when they were having a discussion. They're not possessive over their office space."*

Our interviewees also had good things to say about the firm's *"strong culture of feedback."* Elaborated one: *"I'd say the environment is a nurturing one. People are conscious of your development and often suggest ways you can improve or gain more experience. I never feel like I am burdening someone by asking them a question."* Added another: *"It's clear they want us to be comfortable. My supervisor even told me he was as invested in me as he is in his clients. This is our training contract, and they encourage us to speak up if things aren't going right."*

IP partner and management committee member Paul Rawlinson was appointed to succeed Gary Senior as B&M's London MP in July 2013, and our sources were unanimously positive about the impact he's had in the months since. *"We're all excited to have him on board. He's got a great vision and the ability to drive us forward."* So what can we expect from B&M in the coming years? *"Even though we have extensive global coverage, we're always looking for new places to go,"* sources concurred, telling us there's a *"big push"* to increase the firm's presence in Africa. The firm opened a Johannesburg office in 2012, and interviewees confirmed that *"it's steadily increasing its numbers."* Following B&M's merger with a Dubai-based firm in 2013, it's likely the Middle East will be another area of focus in coming years, but don't expect the firm to pass on viable opportunities that present themselves elsewhere. *"Expanding globally is what we do best. Wherever there's the business, B&M will ensure it's there."*

And finally...

B&M's retention rates have topped 75% for each of the last five years. In 2014 this trend continued, with 34 of 40 qualifiers staying on.

Bates Wells Braithwaite

The facts

Location: London
Number of UK partners/solicitors: 30/47
Partners who trained at the firm: 27%
Total number of trainees: 9
Seats: 2x6 + 3x4 months
Alternative seats: occasional secondments
Extras: pro bono – South West London Law Centre

On chambersstudent.co.uk...

How to get a Bates Wells Braithwaite training contract
Social finance and social impact bonds: what's it all about?

BWB bridges the public and private sector, balancing commercial and social goals.

Crowning glory

NSPCC, Barnardo's, Samaritans – some of the biggest names in the charity world and all clients of Bates Wells Braithwaite. This Londoner derives some 60% of its client base from the third sector and is the firm of choice for the Royal Foundation, representing the many charitable endeavours of Will, Kate and Harry. Meanwhile, over on the immigration side, its ability to do battle with the Home Office is well documented. Both BWB's charity and immigration practices pick up top *Chambers* rankings, but don't be fooled into thinking it's a one-trick pony. In fact, the firm's got a bustling commercial side, one that's been shining ever more brightly in recent years. *"Our corporate and commercial department has existed for a while, but its profile has changed rapidly since 2010, when Mark Tasker joined as head,"* sources said. Indeed, the group has played a big role in the EU Commission's proposal for a Common European Sales Law, and now commercial work is one of the firm's biggest earners alongside its not-for-profit practice.

Balancing these public and private sector ambitions has proved a challenge as the firm grows on the latter front. *"Last year you could feel the tension between our commercial development and charity focus,"* revealed a trainee, *"but management has really taken a step back and figured out the direction – over the next few years we'll be focusing on the intersection between the two by looking further and further into social enterprise and finance work."* The firm's trainees praised it for being *"so responsive to the market,"* telling us eagerly how *"we've just converted to an ABS and brought in an accountancy team that specialises in measuring social impact and turning that into figures for funders. We're leading the charge in that respect."*

Like the firm at large, BWB's seat system is far from standard. Incoming trainees select from four 'flight paths' which determine the combination of seats they'll encounter during their training contract. Each path is made up of five seats – two six-month ones followed by three four-month ones – and includes rotations in both charity and dispute resolution. It all sounds fairly rigid, but trainees told us there's a degree of flexibility involved, with some swapping the order in which they completed seats to realign them with qualification interests. *"It's quite an easy process, and HR is fairly relaxed about it."*

Bond, Impact Bond

Charity is BWB's biggest department, *"and its motor."* For the record, lawyers here have amassed over 3,000 charity clients, which span *"all manner of social enterprise, from the tiniest theatre in Ealing to international organisations."* Interests represented include everything from governance and public procurement to campaigning and compliance, and trainees are given the freedom to pair up with relevant partners or fee earners to explore certain ones. The *"meaty and interesting"* matters our sources had encountered include charities in high-risk situations – like those operating in Syria, for instance – and innovative instruments like social impact bonds (SIBs). The team has been busy advising the Cabinet Office on the development of these bonds, providing guidance notes and model contracts to simplify and boost the SIB market. Typical trainee tasks on such matters include

Seat options: charity; dispute resolution; employment; corporate/commercial (coco); immigration; property

Chambers UK rankings

Administrative & Public Law	Healthcare
Charities	Immigration
Data Protection	Local Government
Defamation/Reputation Management	Media & Entertainment
Education	Partnership
Employment	Professional Discipline
	Real Estate
	Real Estate Litigation

carrying out research and drafting articles of association, charity applications and letters of advice.

The immigration department works with both individuals and businesses – *"you might be representing maids working here illegally, or equally companies transferring staff from the US or the EU."* Indeed, high-profile matters of late include advising global software company Mastek on an inward TUPE, an issue which eventually led to the Home Office amending its Sponsor Guidance principles, and helping a high-profile TV personality secure domestic worker visas for their staff. When it comes to challenging the Home Office, BWB has a superb track record: over the past year, not one appeal against a Home Office decision has been lost. Trainees here are often given their own files to run. *"You meet the client and then draft letters of advice or lead on relevant applications. Some can become very complex – for example, if an immigrant has been living in the country for a prolonged time and the Home Office wants to see detailed evidence of that."*

Dispute resolution is split into a number of subgroups which cover commercial disputes, fraud cases, defamation and media matters, property disputes, trade mark infringements and judicial reviews. On the media side, bright lights like the Royal Shakespeare Company, English National Opera and British Film Institute dot the client list. Lawyers here recently advised the Young Vic on various production matters for a handful of upcoming shows, while their colleagues in defamation successfully represented sports journalists David Walsh and Alan English during their attempt to recover damages paid to infamous fibber Lance Armstrong. A trainee's role in litigation largely revolves around *"supporting your supervisor and anyone else who needs your help with research. You're also the one drafting the simpler documents within court procedure, like application notices and claim forms."*

Coco is BWB's fastest-growing department in monetary terms – since 2010, turnover emerging from the corporate side has increased by over 300%, with commercial contracts work up by more than 50% during the past two years. Lawyers here have their eyes trained on small to mid-market transactions, like the £20m sale of technology company iter8 to AIM-quoted Quindell Portfolio, and also undertake contracts work for charity clients too – for example, advising Technology Trust on various commission and reseller agreements. Sources with experience here reported exposure to the *"standard 'terms of' contracts all the way through to big M&A transactions and AIM listing work."* Said one: *"On a couple of occasions I drafted agreements based on precedent, implemented all the instructions and amended the agreement following the client's review."*

Armadillo blues

According to our interviewees, BWB *"attracts lawyers interested in using their knowledge for social benefit."* They went on to tell us that this *"shared sense of purpose"* goes a long way in solidifying the working culture: *"People are very easy to get along with – knowing we're all doing worthwhile work helps with that."* It also helps that lawyers here tend to stick around for awhile. *"Many of the senior partners trained at the firm. In some ways it feels like one big family."* While we're on the topic of shared traits, it's worth noting that trainees tend to be a bit older at BWB than at many other firms. *"No one in our intake has come straight from uni and the LPC; we've all had jobs beforehand, whether it's in charity and campaign work, or politics or media. Everybody's in their late-twenties to early-thirties."* Indeed, while fresh-faced undergrads are very welcome, work experience in a relevant area, combined with a demonstrable interest in the third sector, can stand applicants in good stead. The firm runs cross-departmental sector groups like public procurement, social finance, arts and competition.

Trainees are encouraged to join at least one of these groups according to their preference, and the groups organise monthly know-how meetings open to lawyers across the firm.On the social side, *"things have snowballed"* – trainees told of watching the theatre world's finest perform at the Globe, struggling to remain sober at gin tastings and getting into the spirit of things at Christmas pantomimes. The firm's summer party is a highlight on the calendar and was most recently held at the London Zoo. *"We got to choose an animal to meet up close, but there was a setback – the armadillo we wanted wasn't available, so we got an owl instead. It was a massive owl, though."* Decent working hours mean availability for such outings isn't too hard to come by – a *"normal and good day"* typically finishes by 6.30pm. *"If you're still in the office by 6.30, people start to ask if you're okay."*

Last year's trainees characterised the way qualification was handled as *"disastrous,"* but the 2014 crop of qualifiers were much more satisfied with the firm's approach. *"They've put a lot of effort into addressing previous issues and have definitely learned from their mistakes. It's been very hands-on this time around."* The group received job offers by the end of April, and in the end three of four qualifiers stayed on with BWB.

"It's important to do vac schemes at as many places as you can. Many firms look similar on paper but feel totally different in person depending on your personality. Getting a taste of the kind of people you'll be working with makes all the difference."

Trainee

Berwin Leighton Paisner LLP

The facts

Location: London
Number of UK partners/solicitors: 159/315
Partners who trained at firm: 12%
Total number of trainees: 85
Seats: 4x6 months
Alternative seats: overseas seats, secondments
Extras: pro bono – Sonali Gardens Legal Advice Clinic

On chambersstudent.co.uk...
How to get into BLP
The London real estate market

From bricks and mortar to stocks and shares, this sterling top-20 firm offers a wealth of matters to explore.

Down with BLP (yeah you know me)

Berwin Leighton Paisner is one of the big law firm success stories of the noughties. Created via a merger in 2001, it thrived through the recession, despite its reliance on the particularly hard-hit property industry, and even managed to achieve coveted silver circle status. It hasn't been all smooth sailing post-recession, though: the past couple of years have seen a wobble in profits and a spate of high-profile partner departures – including head of real estate finance Laurence Rogers and head of finance Matthew Kellet – and in 2013 the firm slashed salaries and cut 58 legal roles. Still, BLP's lawyers are convinced a rosy future lies ahead. *"We've had a rough patch, but this is still an exciting place to work,"* said trainees, nodding to *"innovative"* strategies like the firm's freelance service 'Lawyers On Demand' and forthcoming legal service delivery team in Manchester. *"You can feel the firm becoming more international too,"* they added, mentioning its growth in the Far East. BLP added a Beijing office in mid-2013, bringing its overseas office count to eight, and is picking up more and more work from mainland China. *"We've moved from a more easy-going firm to one that's stepping it up and refusing to rest on its laurels."*

BLP's success initially sprung from its expertise in all things real estate, but the firm is currently turning its attention to its expanding corporate finance offering, bringing in laterals like ex-A&O partner Simon Baum. According to our interviewees, this push has caused a slight divide to emerge in the firm's working culture: *"They're trying to lessen the gap between us and the magic circle, and things have become noticeably more high-octane on the corporate finance front, whereas real estate remains quite protective of its slower-paced culture and working*

hours." Indeed, sources in the latter practice reported *"a predictable 9am to 7.30pm day,"* while those in the former said *"it's increasingly the norm to stick around until 9 or 10pm, and there are times when you have to stay late into the night."*

When it comes to seat allocation, *"the party line is that you should do both a corporate and a real estate seat, though it's not a hard and fast rule."* New recruits list up to five seat choices each rotation, then discuss them with HR. *"It's a two-way process; you have to fight your corner sometimes."* This is particularly true on the overseas seats front: *"There are only a few, so it's not as easy to get them; this isn't a firm with guaranteed international opportunities."* At the moment, seats are available in Moscow (corporate), Brussels (competition), Abu Dhabi (contentious construction) and Singapore (finance). There are also a handful of client secondments on at any given time, including a major financial institution and a national retailer.

Trainees had positive views on BLP's custom of sending new joiners off to the University of Law in Moorgate for

Seat options: core real estate; planning & environment; construction & engineering (non-contentious); investment management; corporate finance; restructuring & insolvency; commercial; EU, competition & trade; employment, pensions & incentives; banking; structured debt; projects; asset finance; real estate finance; real estate disputes; insurance; commercial dispute resolution; contentious construction; IP; tax; private client

Chambers UK rankings

Asset Finance	International Arbitration
Banking & Finance	Investment Funds
Banking Litigation	Licensing
Capital Markets	Litigation
Charities	Local Government
Commercial Contracts	Media & Entertainment
Competition/European Law	Outsourcing
Construction	Parliamentary & Public Affairs
Corporate Crime & Investigations	Pensions
Corporate/M&A	Planning
Defamation/Reputation Management	Private Client
Employment	Private Equity
Energy & Natural Resources	Projects
Environment	Public Procurement
Financial Services	Real Estate
Fraud	Real Estate Finance
Healthcare	Real Estate Litigation
Hotels & Leisure	Restructuring/Insolvency
Information Technology	Retail
Insurance	Social Housing
Intellectual Property	Sports Law
	Tax
	Telecommunications
	Transport

their LPC: *"A big plus of that is that you have a ready-made group of friends when you arrive."* Once they start their training contract, rookies benefit from *"very well-organised training – it's something the firm does well."* Tutelage comes in the form of regular department sessions and in-house PSCs, some of which involve external modules like an advocacy course. *"It's kind of front-loaded at the start of your seat, but it's pitched at the right level and helps you prepare for all sorts of things that come up."*

Such great heights

Most of our sources had done at least one real estate-oriented seat. The team achieves top *Chambers UK* rankings for its big-ticket and hotels and leisure work, and it also scores on the real estate finance front. Recent highlights include advising Ballymore on the £105m sale of Victorian gem Old Spitalfields Market, and helping King's Cross Central sell a site to Google for the tech giant's massive new UK headquarters. The hefty practice is split into five divisions. *"In general the work they do overlaps a lot,"* though there is one group devoted solely to work for Tesco, one of the firm's biggest and longest-running clients. The supermarket chain cemented this status by dropping former co-advisers Ashurst, naming BLP its go-to firm for purchase and site development work. Our

sources who'd sat in the core group *"completely loved"* the levels of responsibility they'd encountered: *"I had huge exposure to clients and was running my own files from early on."* Such matters typically include licenses and leases, land registry registrations, and tax returns for a mix of London-based and nationwide clients. Meanwhile, those who'd spent time with the retail team spoke of lease management work for big merchants like John Lewis, Nike and Apple: *"I was conducting property searches, writing up reports on titles and arranging insurance – all sorts of things crop up in this type of work."*

Most of BLP's real estate clients are domestic, but the firm has seen an increase in work for international investors lured in by the UK's rocketing property values. For example, real estate finance lawyers recently assisted Californian healthcare REIT Griffin with its acquisition of 44 senior housing and care facilities in England, Scotland and Jersey. The team also advises financial institutions like Aviva, Barclays and ING on the funding and refinancing pf property developments. Such matters regularly run into the millions or hundreds of millions, and the loan facilities and agreements at hand tend to be complex. *"The seat is pretty overwhelming at first – it's quite technical, and they expect a high level of performance from trainees from the off. Plus, it's common knowledge we've lost some important people recently. The hours can be pretty intense, but a trade-off of that is the high level of client contact."* Trainees reported there's *"lots of scope for drafting"* in the way of security and corporate authorisation documents, and also spoke of running conditions precedent lists, *"which have real estate, finance and tax conditions to be satisfied on a short timescale. It can be challenging co-ordinating all the people involved."*

National Grift

Sources who'd spent time in funds and financial services agreed that *"the responsibility levels drop off here compared to real estate. Trainees mainly review documents, work on company search reports and take minutes at board meetings."* Much of the work has a real estate flavour, and there's more work still for Tesco – lawyers recently advised the grocer on a £490m secured loan for four stores and three sites under development. The team also holds lucrative spots on panels for RBS, Barclays, Santander, HSBC and Credit Suisse.

This side of the practice also incorporates an asset finance team that specialises in aviation, rail, equipment and shipping finance. *"It's a good seat if you want to see things from the start to finish,"* said one trainee, who went on to praise the international dynamic of the practice: *"Sometimes there are tons of jurisdictions involved with the financing of one small aircraft – you're delivering it to Chinese clients one day and then leasing it to a South American operator the next."*

The True Picture

BLP makes a strong showing on the corporate side, scoring high rankings in *Chambers UK* for its mid-market M&A work. The team recently advised gaming software development company PlayTech during its £424m sale of its stake in William Hill Online, and counselled professional services firm Towers Watson on the $250m disposal of its global reinsurance broking business. A note of caution from trainees: *"A lot of our clients are insurers and pension funds with property assets in their portfolio, so it can feel like you're doing real estate deals in a corporate wrapper."* Indeed, the firm is certainly trying to grow this line of work, but it's doing so by way of its real estate forte, so those with their heart set on a more pure corporate offering might want to think twice.

You could cook a meal and wash up afterwards courtesy of litigation clients Tesco (yes, again), Thames Water and National Grid. BLP's team is big in the financial services, real estate construction, sport and energy sectors, and nearly half of its work involves cross-border elements. Lawyers recently acted in the biggest cartel damages action to hit the English courts, advising National Grid on a £350m damages claim after it was overcharged for power substation components by cartelists across six countries. The firm has also been representing the shareholders of Bumi in the wake of a $1.5bn internal investigation at the Indonesian coal producer. In line with the firm's growing finance offering, *"we're very much pushing banking litigation,"* sources said. Indeed, BLP has recently added a spate of (unfortunately confidential) international financial institutions to its client roster, which already features the likes of HSBC. Trainees with litigation experience told of encountering clients and counsel *"from all over the world. The matters are very big here, so the trainee role usually revolves around bundling and doc review, though you can get meatier stuff too – I got to take a stab at drafting witness statements, and I even got to go in front of a master at one point."*

Not so Magnus-ificent

New recruits at BLP usually share an office with a senior associate or partner supervisor. Our sources praised this arrangement, telling us that *"it's nice to have someone nearby who can keep an eye on you and your workload."* Each rotation feature mid and end-of-seat reviews, the format of which depends on individual supervisors. *"Some offer helpful and constructive advice while others might engage in a casual chat without much detailed feedback."* There were a few grumbles about this lack of uniformity, with trainees lamenting the way *"different departments have different measuring systems."* Still, they mentioned additional support on hand from assigned mentors and in general felt *"pretty positive"* about qualification, although we heard that the process was delayed this year. In 2014, the firm retained 31 out of 39 qualifying trainees.

BLP's digs are split between two buildings in London Bridge: *"Adelaide House is nicer to work in – it's a quirky old art deco building, with a really cool décor and front entrance, and it has our canteen; Magnus House next door is kind of dark."* Either way, sources agreed the location is a big plus: *"We're just over the bridge from Borough Market, and our canteen looks right onto the river, which is lovely in summer."*

Our *"very sociable"* sources told us the trainee cohort – big though it is, with 85 trainees – is *"really close; you're very quickly assimilated into the crowd."* Trainees often make for river-front seafood peddlers The Oyster Shed or the Fine Line on Friday nights, and there's a trainee social committee that hosts regular outings – recent dos include a casino night, a summer boat party and a riotous evening of *"curry on Brick Lane, followed by bowling and karaoke."* A number of social events surround the firm's charity efforts, too: *"We've done lots of things for Mind, our 2014 charity of the year, including a dress-down day, quiz and Grand National sweepstake."* There aren't too many firm-wide soirees to attend, but individual departments have their own traditions – for example, the projects team's Friday Beer Club – and client events often prove a *"good source of fun. I got to go to the races at Ascot, complete with a coach and champagne and dinner!"*

And finally...

With 494 lawyers in total, BLP's medium size proved just right for one Goldilocks trainee, who told us that *"we're small enough to have a more personal feel than the magic circle but big enough that there's still a wide selection of seats you can do."*

Bingham McCutchen (London) LLP

The facts

Location: London

Number of UK partners/solicitors: 20/29

Partners who trained at firm: none

Total number of trainees: 4

Seats: 4x6 months

Alternative seats: none

Extras: pro bono - LawWorks

On chambersstudent.co.uk...

How to get a Bingham McCutchen training contract

This finance-focused firm is a good fit for those who get a thrill from having "nowhere to hide." Welcome to the intimate world of Bingham London.

Bing-dong!

Bingham London burst onto the scene back in 1973 to serve the needs of the then Bank of Boston's British base. The office has evolved greatly since then, but its focus on finance remains very much intact. In recent years Bingham's UK lawyers have cemented the firm's reputation in this area with big-ticket representation after big-ticket representation – the firm acted for the bondholders of Iceland's crashed banks as well as the noteholders during the €1.3bn restructuring of the QUINN Group. For their sterling efforts, *Chambers UK* bestows Bingham an elite ranking for its restructuring work in London, and also gives nods to its banking litigation, tax and debt capital markets expertise.

The trainees we spoke with had made a beeline for Bingham as an alternative to the magic circle. What they sought was what they got: a small intake of just two trainees each year, along with the *"high-quality work and independence"* American outfits in London are generally known for. They also confessed to being lured in by the NQ pay packet – at £100k it's one of the biggest in town – and counted the firm's *"reassuringly stable"* strategy as another plus: *"Our plan in London revolves around organic growth; change at Bingham is not an overnight thing."* Indeed, Bingham's known as a wary lateral hirer and in recent years has only made a few additions, to flesh out its anti-trust/competition and funds offerings.

First-seaters are put *"wherever there's business need,"* but after that get to discuss their preferences with a recruitment partner during mid-seat reviews. *"They try to give us a choice, but with so few trainees there are always limitations."* Many end up completing seats in the firm's

core areas of financial restructuring, corporate, finance and litigation, but trainees can also dabble in some of the smaller teams, like tax and competition: *"Even if you don't qualify into one of those, it's good to get an idea of what people there do."*

Keys to the Bingdom

The financial restructuring group (FRG) is Bingham's *"leading and biggest department,"* and consequently *"much of the office revolves around it."* Lawyers here act for a heady mix of bondholders, noteholders and mezzanine lenders on some of the most significant matters of the day, including those emerging from the debt bailouts and banking crisis across Europe. The deals are huge – as in $33bn huge – the amount in bonds that were lost in the Icelandic banking crisis of 2008, which Bingham is unravelling on behalf of its clients. Luckily, new recruits are *"eased into it all naturally – there's time to read into these matters and talk them through with your supervisor."* Typical trainee fare includes *"doing the initial research before restructurings take place in order to find out what type of companies are involved, and then writing notes to provide the client with information."*

Following a restructuring, clients often need a bit more advice – this is where the firm's corporate lawyers step in. The team is particularly known for its distressed M&A

Seat options: financial restructuring group (FRG); corporate; finance; finance litigation; tax; financial regulatory; investment funds; competition

The True Picture

Chambers UK rankings

Banking Litigation	Restructuring/Insolvency
Capital Markets	Tax
Financial Services	

work, but trainees made it clear that there are a good number of standalone deals on the books too. Key clients comprise a mixture of hedge and investment funds seeking advice on their investment strategies, so lawyers regularly counsel on things like the probable outcome of a takeover bid. The trainee role here is pretty drafting-heavy – sources told of taking a crack at ancillary documents like board minutes and resolutions as well as portions of more complex shareholder agreements.

Litigation at Bingham is primarily centred around financial disputes. Some cases are fed in through the restructuring group, while others might emerge from the complete dissolution of companies, like the team's representation of Ernst & Young in a range of pensions disputes arising from the professional services firm's role as liquidators of Sea Containers. Trainees *"don't get to go to court very often,"* but we heard of instances where some requested the exposure and were in turn *"permitted to attend a couple of times."* Sources agreed the pace here is *"slightly less frantic"* than in transactional teams: *"We often get in-depth research tasks that take a week or so to complete."* There's also research and doc review as well as the chance to draft client memorandums and the odd witness statement.

A stint in regulatory sees trainees charged with *"keeping on top of changes in the regulatory space so we can advise clients on how to comply with new regimes."* Sources told us it's not uncommon to spend many an hour writing legal opinions and pouring over EU legislation, directives and regulations. Tax, meanwhile, is widely considered a *"difficult but enjoyable"* seat. *"It's perfect if you love technical-puzzling-over-the-sentence work – most of what we do is look at provisions, break them down and analyse them to work out the answers."*

Bingham's Got Talent

Our interviewees were adamant that Bingham London *"doesn't have an overly American feel – it's just not a major influence."* Posited one: *"I think it's because our*

headquarters are in Boston rather than New York. American firms with flagship NYC offices tend to be more intense and require longer hours." Trainees also pointed to the fact that *"quite a lot of the work originates here, so we're pretty autonomous – more so than other US firms in London, some of which are satellite offices subject to the whims of bosses elsewhere."*

Sources claimed that the firm's approach to hours is another departure from its American peers in the City. *"We get a pretty good deal – everyone looks at the salary and automatically assumes that we work all hours under the sun, but I've actually met associates here who say they work less and get paid more than when they worked at magic circle firms."* Of course, that hardly means trainee schedules are a walk in the park. *"It's very up and down,"* one confirmed. *"There are weeks when I finish at 6.30pm, and then weeks when I'm leaving at 10pm every night."* Broadly speaking, FRG tends to require the longest hours, with corporate a *"close second."* Having the stamina and initiative to handle these longer hours is something the firm looks for when recruiting, we're told: *"They don't hire people who need to be spoon-fed or constantly reassured; you have to be willing to push yourself and go the extra mile here."* Accordingly, confidence and enthusiasm go down a storm during interviews: *"It's all about showing you're proactive. You don't have to be aggressively vocal or anything; there are plenty of opportunities to say what you want and make things happen."* With this in mind, sources suggested *"the training is what you make of it here – if you want to enrol on an external course, for instance, they'll be happy to send you. All you have to do is ask."*

While sources assured us the firm knows how to hold a stellar Christmas party, they went on to declare that *"this isn't the firm for people interested in a social life more than anything else."* Indeed, there are no trainee social committees here, though we did hear there's *"plenty of scope"* for the odd departmental wine-tasting now and then. And it's after-work tipples all-round come August, *"when work tends to quieten down a bit."*

The 2014 qualification round *"happened quickly and early"* – the dream combo for many an anxious trainee. Given the small intake, *"it's all quite informal – there are no interviews; we knew where we wanted to qualify and just signed a qualification contract."* All qualifiers got places.

And finally...

A genuine interest in the world of finance is a must at Bingham – if the thought of reaching for the nearest copy of the FT each morning gives you the willies, you're unlikely to make it beyond the first recruitment round.

Bircham Dyson Bell

The facts

Location: London

Number of UK partners/solicitors: 46/74

Partners who trained at firm: 41%

Total number of trainees: 14

Seats: 4x6 months

Alternative seats: secondments

Extras: pro bono – Migrants Resource Centre

On chambersstudent.co.uk...

How to get into Bircham Dyson Bell

Interview with training principal
  Nick Evans

Planning law

If you've got a bridge that needs erecting or Tube line that needs burrowing, give Bircham Dyson Bell a call – you might find it does a lot more than just infrastructure.

The AA-team

BDB + AA = a 47-partner practice with a combined annual turnover in excess of £33m. Bircham Dyson Bell's biggest story this year came through its merger with the small, four-partner London outfit Ambrose Appelbe. *"It was primarily to strengthen the family and private wealth side of our practice,"* training principal Nick Evans explains. The move has also brought about a £2m bump in top-line figures. *"We're happy to have seen growth not only in revenues, but also in profitability,"* reports Evans – profits per equity partner rose by 4.3% in 2013/14.

The AA merger is part of a wider strategy to incrementally develop all of the firm's key practice areas: government and infrastructure (G&I), real estate, private wealth, litigation, corporate, charities and employment. The G&I department is BDB's headline act, known for getting its hands dirty with some of the nation's leading infrastructure projects – think the massive £33bn HS2 project or the £800m upgrade of Victoria Station for London Underground. Within this department are the firm's nationally recognised parliamentary agency and public law teams, which often play a key role in getting these projects off the ground. One trainee reflected: *"I wanted to train at a mid-sized firm where I would get more responsibility without compromising on the quality of the work."*

Before starting, trainees submit preferences for their first seat via e-mail. In the run-up to each subsequent rotation, rookies *"meet with the training principal and HR to discuss where they would like to move next."* Sources said their views *"are always taken into account, but the decision is also determined by business needs."* There are no compulsory seats but *"given the size of the real estate*

department and the fact that it takes in three trainees at a time, it would be unusual not to spend time there."

G&I is the Knuts(ford)

The real estate department offers up three different seats: residential, commercial and projects. In the first of these, trainees spoke of their involvement in leasehold and conveyancing work in some of London's swankier postcodes (BDB represents property firms like South Kensington Estates). The commercial arm spends a lot of time advising private banks lending to high net worth borrowers looking for prime bits of property. Young guns are often responsible for *"drafting leases and licences,"* while there are also opportunities to *"correspond directly with the client and liaise with solicitors on the other side."* The odd source had even been given smaller transactions to handle on their own.

The projects team often plays the role of *"supporting national infrastructure projects."* For example, it's been helping National Grid secure all the necessary land rights needed for the new Hinkley Point C nuclear power station. This of course means there's a lot of crossover with the G&I team (which offers a distinct seat). BDB is able to advise on the multitude of planning, environmental, compulsory purchase, regulatory, public affairs and parliamentary issues that big UK projects throw up.

Seat options: real estate; litigation; private wealth; government and infrastructure; corporate and commercial; employment; charities

Chambers UK rankings

Administrative & Public Law	Planning
Agriculture & Rural Affairs	Private Client
Charities	Public Procurement
Family/Matrimonial	Real Estate
Local Government	Real Estate Finance
Parliamentary & Public Affairs	Real Estate Litigation
	Transport

Trainees told us the G&I department had seen a large emphasis on planning recently: the team is a dab hand at obtaining development consent orders (DCOs) under the 2008 Planning Act. It recently sought one for the Hinkley Point project mentioned above, and on behalf of the Highways Agency for improvements to the A556 between Knutsford and Bowden. Trainee tasks include *"doing research, making submissions to the Planning Inspectorate, drafting letters and witness statements, attending conferences with counsel and going to public inquiries."* Some of our sources had been heavily involved in HS2 work: *"It made no difference that I was a trainee – I was treated like any other lawyer,"* said one interviewee. *"I attended client meetings and drafted notes and board minutes."* Another concurred: *"You're given a long leash to organise your workload and can take charge of drafting documents. The supervision is good, but you are expected to take on a lot of responsibilities."*

ACID trip

Nick Evans told us BDB is *"looking to grow the business services side of the firm"* – that includes the employment, charity and corporate/commercial teams. The last of these in particular is gaining momentum, says Evans, with lateral partner hires bolstering the ranks. For example, in May 2014 the firm hired corporate/commercial partner Philip Lamb from Lewis Silkin. The firm isn't *Chambers*-ranked for corporate M&A (yet), but has been winning more praise for commercial contracts work. Trainees told us they work on deals with values ranging *"from £70,000 to £80m,"* and reported *"drafting confidentiality agreements, shareholders' agreements, memorandums and articles of association."* The firm frequently acts for organisations in the non-profit, health and education sectors, advising on anything from outsourcing to technology to IP. Clients include ABF The Soldiers' Charity and ACID, which isn't as trippy as it sounds, but is in fact a designers' non-profit and stands for 'Anti Copying In Design'.

The litigation department handles a whole range of commercial, property, regulatory and family disputes, and has been carving out a niche for itself working on judicial reviews. *"As well as dipping in and out of more complex matters, an effort is made to ensure there are smaller claims knocking about for trainees to work,"* a source told us. Interviewees felt they had *"real ownership"* over these cases, as they could *"draft claim forms and witness statements."* One trainee concluded: *"It's a great seat for getting out to court. I even managed to do a bit of advocacy!"*

Ligne claire

The firm underwent a rebrand in 2013 themed around the concept 'Accentuating The Positive' (we kid you not). This produced a pleasingly symmetrical new 'BDB' logo and a website filled with stylish line-drawings of the Houses of Parliament and big Mayfair townhouses. Trainees were decidedly upbeat about the firm's *"progressive"* new image. One said: *"We are still quite a traditional firm but there is a push, not to change who we are, but to make sure we're keeping up to date and offering the best service we can."* Trainees told us that *"it's drilled into us from the start that we should act as a 'trusted adviser' to clients and be able to do lots of different things for them."*

Despite trying to keep up with the Joneses, BDB retains a preference for *"recruiting trainees who are a little bit older than those in your average cohort."* One interviewee observed: *"A lot of us are career changers – the firm values people with experience who are a bit more mature."* This also *"affects the tone"* when it comes to BDB's social scene. *"We're not all out drinking every night,"* remarked one second-year. *"A lot of us have families and have moved on from that a bit."* That said, trainees do like to go for lunch together and will usually sink a few swift ones before heading home on a Friday. We also heard the ski lodge-themed Christmas party is a guaranteed winner, while the annual quiz night *"is much loved and one of everyone's favourite social events of the year."*

As well as being a little older, BDB's trainee intake is also female-heavy. When we conducted our interviews only 20% of the cohort were male. But despite the strong female presence in the lower ranks, this has as yet failed to translate through to the partnership – just 24% of partners are female. Rectifying this stat is important, says Nick Evans: *"We had consultants come in to appraise us five years ago and as a result we established a board-level diversity and inclusion group,"* he told us. *"So it's something we take seriously."* According to Evans the number of female partners has risen sharply recently – it stood at just 13% a few years ago.

And finally...

BDB's retention rates have been a little shaky since the recession, and in 2014 just three of seven qualifiers were kept on.

Bird & Bird

The facts

Location: London
Number of UK partners/solicitors: 81/159
Partners who trained at firm: 9%
Total number of trainees: 36
Seats: 4x6 months
Alternative seats: overseas seats, secondments
Extras: pro bono – LawWorks, South Westminster Legal Advice Centre

On chambersstudent.co.uk...

How to get into Bird & Bird
Fågel och Fågel: the firm's Nordic nests

This was an early bird on the tech scene, but that's just one feather in its multi-sector plumage.

The True Picture

Electric avenue

Flashes of inspiration have played a fundamental role in Bird & Bird's ascent, IP-slanted as this firm is. Indeed, the eureka effect has prompted many an inventor to seek patent advice from the Londoner's trusty team over the years, though light bulb moments aren't just the preserve of the firm's clients; after taking over the practice from his father in 1884, WB Montford Bird had his own 'Aha!' experience and went on to form one the world's first electric light bulb companies (the resulting enterprise remains a client to this day). As technology has advanced and bright ideas abounded in the decades since Mr Bird's dabbles in the electric sector, his firm's penchant for IP work has served it well. Towards the turn of the 20th century, it took on its first trade mark case – an application on behalf of the predecessor to Kodak – and shortly thereafter made its patent debut. And when the computer age dawned, Bird & Bird (commonly nicknamed 'Twobirds') soared straight to the head of the flock, carving out niches in the IT, electronics and telecoms sectors.

"We're definitely not a pinstripe and shoulder-pads type of firm," one insider said, emphasising that *"we operate at the cutting edge of the technology and media world. It might seem strange to describe a law firm as trendy, but there you are."* Certainly, fustiness is definitely not a quality that springs to mind when perusing the client roster, which includes the likes of Microsoft, Adobe, Nokia, Everything Everywhere and Yahoo!. That said, servicing the digital elite is only part of Twobirds' mission. Having established a sector-based business model in 1998, the firm works across a variety of industries, among them aviation, healthcare, food and beverage, and life sciences. *"Our scope is very broad,"* interviewees confirmed, add-

ing that *"it's not like going to one of the big City firms and just doing finance and corporate work for banks; many of our clients are completely different from one another – there's Microsoft and then there's the Ministry of Justice. You can undertake a commercial seat and find yourself doing anything from data protection to sport to energy work."*

This sector diversity is matched by a network of 26 offices, with branches in Europe, Asia and the Middle East. Twobirds increased its wingspan through strategic tie-ups with Australian, Danish and Swiss outfits in 2013, and in early 2014 become the first major law firm to land in Korea after entering an agreement with the Seoul-based Hwang Mok Park.

Go to the mattresses... IP-style

None of the eight seats on offer are compulsory, though it's common for trainees to pass through IP and commercial, both of which *"are very popular – they're the biggest departments and often a major reason why people want to come here."* The sport seat is also highly sought-after. Sources were pleased to report that *"the graduate recruitment team is really attentive and does its utmost to give you at least three out of the four seats you ask for. If you don't get a seat you want in your first year, they'll ensure you get it in your second."* Fledgling trainees submit seat preferences before they begin and before each rota-

---

Seat options: commercial; dispute resolution; IP; corporate; finance; real estate; employment; sport

Chambers UK rankings

Asset Finance	Intellectual Property
Aviation	Life Sciences
Banking & Finance	Litigation
Capital Markets	Media & Entertainment
Corporate/M&A	Outsourcing
Data Protection	Private Equity
Employee Share Schemes & Incentives	Public Procurement
	Real Estate
Employment	Real Estate Finance
Franchising	Sports Law
Fraud	Telecommunications
Healthcare	Travel
Information Technology	

tion attend chats with graduate recruitment about where they'd like to head next. *"It's quite a personal training contract,"* trilled one, and indeed those especially keen on IP will be pleased to hear it's not unheard of to wangle your way into two seats there.

The commercial department takes in work from many of Twobirds' core sectors, including healthcare, energy, media and aviation. *"We handle quite a lot of work in particular for start-ups like new apps or online businesses."* Aerospace and defence giant BAE, the Department of Energy and Climate Change, King's College NHS Foundation Trust and mattress manufacturer Tempur-Sealy are among the *"pretty eclectic"* client list, with lawyers recently handling a sizeable franchise restructuring project for the latter. Typical trainee tasks here include drafting agreements, attending client meetings, co-ordinating signings and proof-reading contracts. *"On low-fee matters you'll get the most responsibility,"* one interviewee said, telling us: *"I got to draft all the policies for one client's website, including the terms and conditions, privacy policy and methods of payment. Then I had to go through every page to check everything was scripted correctly and nothing was misleading."* We also heard from sources who'd contributed to public sector projects, put together sub-contracting agreements for solar farms and assisted banking clients with IT platforms.

When it comes to IP, Twobirds has a high-flying reputation and the lofty *Chambers UK* rankings to match. It's boffinry all around for these solicitors – 75% of the London contingent holds a degree in a scientific or technical subject. As such, the team is well equipped to handle 'hard' IP work like patent litigation. Lawyers recently helped pharmaceutical mammoth Teva protect the patent for its multiple sclerosis drug and represented Microsoft in a patent-related scrum with Motorola. Those more au fait with Byron than biochemistry need not fear, however; there's plenty of 'soft' work on offer too, such as trade mark disputes and brand portfolio reviews. This arm of the practice recently helped the makers of Monster en-

ergy drink achieve a settlement in a trade mark dispute with rival Shark Energy. Trainees in the thick of such cases are typically tasked with *"quite a few admin jobs"* – think taking attendance notes, bundling, photocopying and writing letters – though we did hear from some who'd cut their teeth on *"more exciting"* endeavours like attending court and drafting witness statements.

Tech... no? Tech – yes!

Banking matters are often filtered in through other departments. As one insider explained, *"the commercial department might have a relationship with a communication services provider that wants to raise some finance, for example, so they'd be referred on to us."* To that end, our sources were keen to distinguish between Bird & Bird's banking work and the finance fare at other City outfits: *"You'll do lots of transactions relating to tech firms here, usually acting for the borrower rather than the lender – stuff like consumer credit or general regulatory work for an electronic trading platform. If you want to do highly complex derivatives lending or specialised financial products on behalf of financial institutions, this isn't the place for you."* This caveat aside, trainees agreed the department is a good destination for those seeking *"a lot of experience and responsibility – there are only three or four partners, so they rely on us a lot."* This translates into plenty of drafting – securities documents, shareholder resolutions, board minutes – and a good whack of client contact, *"which is a great opportunity as a trainee."*

By contrast, the dispute resolution team is large enough to take up two floors. Lawyers here handle a mix of general litigation and international arbitration, much of which spans the technology, telecoms, energy and transport spheres. Big-name clients on this front include Nokia, BT and Virgin Atlantic, and at the time of our calls the team was leading the way on one of the financial sector's biggest shareholder disputes, a £4bn claim against RBS for alleged misrepresentation. For trainees *"there's an enormous amount of supporting work to be done like undertaking disclosure exercises and reviewing masses of documents. You also assist with drafting correspondence and the like."*

Insiders had nothing but praise for the sports team, which nets a top *Chambers UK* ranking and handles commercial, brand management, governance, regulatory, disciplinary and dispute resolution matters for a whole line-up of eminent organisations, including the FA, Premier League, Six Nations Rugby and World Anti-Doping Agency. *"You could be working on allegations of doping against a boxer one day and then reviewing contracts for the Rugby World Cup the next,"* chirped one, adding: *"Often I'd see something in the sport pages and think 'that might be on my desk on Monday', and sure enough it would be! I even ended up working on an incident in a game I was watching live. That 'real-time' feeling is great."* Others with experience in the seat had encountered match-fixing cases, sponsorship agreements, broadcasting disputes and doping allegations, telling us cases on the latter front can be *"particularly emotive – someone's career is being decided upon, and there are often a lot of grey areas."* In such matters, trainees typically review case law, put together documents and attend tribunals.

Client secondments are available for those completing sports, commercial, IP or dispute resolution. Among the more *"well entrenched"* of these is a three-month stint with a high-profile sports organisation. *"Stepping into the shoes of an in-house lawyer is an interesting experience,"* remarked one interviewee with secondment experience, explaining that *"you're a lot more autonomous than here at the firm, and you get to see clients' commercial concerns first-hand – something that might not strike you here, where you're looking at things from a purely legal perspective."* Trainees also have the chance to spend time in certain overseas offices, though these seats are offered on a more ad hoc basis. Brussels is a regular feature of the training programme, but some trainees have also recently roosted in Abu Dhabi, Madrid and Paris.

Feathered friends

"We're very well looked after here," our sources agreed when asked to what extent they're taken under the wing of senior solicitors. *"Associates are pretty good at remembering how it feels to be a trainee and the challenges you face, and there's a good level of mentoring. We all get a junior associate mentor, who's very useful to meet up with now and again, and there's also the buddy system, wherein first-years are paired with second-years for extra support."* As one summed up: *"They give you as much responsibility as you can handle, but there's always someone available to help if you need it."*

None of our sources were disgruntled about *"working long hours fairly regularly,"* taking the pragmatic view

that *"you shouldn't go into law if you want to go home at 6pm every day; it's just not going to happen."* That said, they agreed *"Bird & Bird is relatively relaxed on this front – if you finish up early and don't have anything that needs to be done, there's no pressure to stay. It's just that it fluctuates a lot."* According to one, *"the standard trainee schedule is probably 9am until anywhere between 6.30 to 9.30pm,"* while another said: *"I probably leave on average around 8pm most nights."*

Interviewees went on to characterise Twobirds' sector-based structure as *"progressive,"* telling us that concern for the client is key to preserving the firm's forward-looking approach. *"This is a modern, entrepreneurial place – everyone has on their commercial hat as well as their legal one. It's important that lawyers here have an innovative attitude and think along the same lines as clients."* Around the office we hear *"there aren't any stuffy overtones; people are genuinely friendly. There's a hierarchy of course, but everyone gets on with one another, and there's a lot of banter between different levels of solicitors."* The firm is currently split between three separate buildings, each a few minutes away from the others, though there are plans to bring the whole flock together under one roof by 2016. *"I think there's going to be a social hub in the new building, which would be great. We have the Bird Table canteen at the moment, but it's only so-so – you wouldn't rush to get there."* Meanwhile, there's plenty going on outside the office, from department drinks and sponsored trainee outings to CSR projects, an inter-office football tournament and regular Friday pub gatherings.

When it comes to qualification, *"it's out of our hands. There's no formal process or jobs list; we just have a meeting and make our preference known."* Trainees have historically enjoyed a high retention rate, which continued in 2014, when 15 out of 17 new qualifiers stayed on.

And finally...

"Technology is the theme that links much of our work at Bird & Bird, and it's something prospective trainees should be interested in."

Bond Dickinson

The facts

Location: Bristol, Leeds, London, Newcastle, Plymouth, Southampton, Stockton-on-Tees, Scotland

Number of UK partners/solicitors: 151/584

Partners who trained with firm:

Total number of trainees: 43

Seats: 4x6 months

Alternative seats: secondments

On chambersstudent.co.uk...

How to get into Bond Dickinson
The Newcastle legal market

Fresh from a two-way merger, Bond Dickinson is making a bid for national stardom. Keep reading to find out how...

Painting the town yellow

One trainee at this newly national firm told us that *"on the first day of the merger all the walls were painted bright yellow overnight. For some people it was a bit of a shock to the system, but if you ask me, the brighter the better!"* The metaphorical paint might still be drying on the merger that created Bond Dickinson in 2013, but the firm's ambitions are as clear and bright as its sunny new branding. Management's '2020 vision' entails one very ambitious goal: to become a top-20 firm by 2020.

Formed from South West stalwarts Bond Pearce and Newcastle's biggest firm Dickinson Dees, BD boasts a spread of offices across England's top right-hand and bottom left-hand corners. Training contracts are available in Newcastle, Leeds, Bristol, Southampton, Plymouth and Stockton-on-Tees, and the firm revealed they'll probably advertise for training contracts starting in 2016 in London too. At the time of our calls there were 16 trainees in Newcastle, eight in Bristol, seven in Southampton, five in Leeds, four in Plymouth and two in Stockton.

The firm has capitalised on its new national reach by winning legal panel spots with hygiene giants Colgate Palmolive and pensions administrators Suffolk Life. It's also lured a top private client/charities team in Bristol from rivals Osborne Clarke, and made some high-level lateral hires in other offices and practice areas. These hires are part of a bid to extend the merged firm's full-service capacity across seven key sectors: energy, waste and natural resources; retail and fast-moving consumer goods; real estate; financial institutions; chemicals and manufacturing; transport and infrastructure; and private wealth. Expansion in London is also a strategic priority. This office is essentially the glue that bonds the firm's northern and southern halves together: the capital was the only location where both legacy firms had an office.

Combined revenues for the two legacy firms amounted to £98.3m in 2012/13, putting the new entity at roughly 35th place in the UK revenue stakes. So there's a long way to go to get to that top-20 place. And we'll tell you one thing: this firm is not going to get there by just hiring a few new trainees or partners here and there. Keep your eyes open for more ambitious expansion in the future.

Fancy pants

It's time we turned our attention to trainee matters (though we'll have more to say about the merger later on). For training purposes the firm is split into four distinct groups: corporate/commercial, litigation, real estate and private wealth. Trainees are encouraged to complete one seat in each of these areas, although there's plenty of choice within each group. Trainees let HR know their seat preferences, nominating their top three choices for each rotation. Bristol and Newcastle are the two largest offices and offer the most seat options (they're Bond Pearce and Dickinson Dees' former HQs respectively). Trainees in the smaller offices – Leeds, Plymouth, Southampton – find that *"there's a bit more flexibility"* when it comes to the requirement to do a seat in each of the

Seat options: oil and gas; real estate; planning; casualty risk; professional risk; corporate; employment; property litigation; finance; commercial litigation; banking and insolvency; commercial; private capital; IP/IT; public services; regulatory; insurance

Chambers UK rankings

Agriculture & Rural Affairs	Media & Entertainment
Banking & Finance	Pensions
Charities	Pensions Litigation
Commercial Contracts	Planning
Construction	Private Client
Corporate/M&A	Product Liability
Data Protection	Professional Negligence
Employment	Public Procurement
Energy & Natural Resources	Real Estate
Environment	Real Estate Litigation
Information Technology	Restructuring/Insolvency
Intellectual Property	Retail
Licensing	Social Housing
Litigation	Tax
Local Government	Transport

groupings mentioned above. There is also the option of completing a seat in another office to broaden one's experience, or even a split seat across two offices. Looking at the other end of the trainee pipeline, interviewees felt the qualification process is *"managed well,"* and of 2014's 21 qualifiers, 18 stayed with the firm.

Under the real estate umbrella trainees can complete seats in planning, residential property, commercial property, real estate finance, agriculture and property litigation. Most of our interviewees had spent time in at least one of these areas and told us a stint here *"offers a fantastic mix of public and private work for individuals, companies and developers."* Clients include Network Rail, Ben Sherman, House of Fraser and Newcastle property businesses Bellway and Grainger. One trainee reported: *"I was given smaller matters to run on my own, including debt recovery files and property portfolios."* Trainees also get involved in bigger matters like *"sales for big social landlords offloading properties to their tenants"* and *"the transfer of property portfolios from one part of a company to another."* Interviewees told us there is *"a lot of client contact and you get taken along to all the meetings."*

The Bristol corporate team advised Piper Private Equity on its £8m investment in designer swimwear company Orlebar Brown (makers of the swimming trunks worn by Daniel Craig in *Skyfall*), as well as helping energy group npower sell off its subsidiary Telecom Plus for £218m. Newcastle is notable for its transport-focused corporate subgroup, which works for several major rail and bus clients. Trainees in the seat reported *"helping draft documents for rolling stock leases, as well as working on some large national and international transport projects."* In Leeds, interviewees believed, *"the firm has a strong grip on the North East and works for quite a few Yorkshire-based and national businesses."* For example,

the team recently advised the University of York on its joint venture with Leeds-based property developer Evans for a new residential college on its Heslington Campus. Typical trainee tasks here include *"preparing the first draft of documents, including some you might not expect to get your hands on as a trainee, like sales agreements."* There's also company secretarial work to do for some of the firm's long-standing clients, as well as proof-reading and drafting of ancillary documents.

The legacy Dickinson Dees private client team in New-castle is well established in the market and consistently top-ranked by *Chambers UK*. A trainee here told us: *"I got quite a lot of client contact and spent time helping with the drafting of wills over the phone. It's a nice change to have a personal chat with someone rather than having to deal with a corporate entity."* Interviewees also reported working on powers of attorney, estate planning and other larger financial matters for high net worth individuals. The clients are a mix of *"entrepreneurs based in Leeds, owners of landed estates in the North East and other businesspeople."* Down south, Bond Pearce never really had much of a presence in this area, so the new team from Osborne Clarke is a welcome addition. Prior to their move, the OC team worked on the sale of the late Lord Wraxall's stately home Tyntesfield to the National Trust.

Postman splat

Newcastle's commercial litigation team recently acted for a subsidiary of bus company Arriva after it was excluded from providing bus services from London Victoria to Luton airport, despite clocking nearly 30 years on the route, and it also defended IBM in proceedings arising from the company's controversial decision to wind up part of its pension plan. The smaller Bristol team acts for a number of leading energy clients, as well as betting agents Coral and the Post Office. One trainee involved in a large piece of litigation told us: *"I helped prepare court bundles, undertook disclosure exercises and organised inter-party correspondence – this was all for one huge case which took up most of my time in the first few months."* South-ampton offers a specific professional risk/insurance litigation seat. The department primarily defends negligent professionals, including surveyors, barristers, trustees and marketing agents. Lawyers act for the insured and their insurers, counting major firms like AIG, QBE and Allianz among its clients.

In Newcastle trainees can do a split seat in banking/finance and insolvency. *"The work runs from one end of the financial spectrum to the other: from deals worth tens of millions of pounds to individuals in debt. It's great to see big transactions going off and get experience on smaller insolvency cases at the same time."* The finance team represents the key big banks operating in the North East, including HSBC, Santander, Lloyds and the Newcastle Building Society. The firm also takes on work from local businesses and organisations, recently helping Tees Valley Unlimited set up a £10m scheme to support local companies with the help of the European Regional Growth Fund. The split seat option is also available down in Bristol. Across the firm, juniors found that on bigger banking deals *"there's plenty of administrative work and little bits of minor research to do – I had to handle a number of minor documents which needed duplicating with just the names changed."* The insolvency side of the seat involves a mixture of contentious and non-contentious work for both businesses and individuals. This includes *"some pro bono for individuals to ensure they don't go bankrupt for very small debts,"* plus work on the turnaround or restructuring of failing businesses.

Poles apart

When we spoke to trainees in May 2014, it had been a year since the Dickies-Bond merger. So how were the two halves of the firm getting on? *"There's a natural geographical divide that means day-to-day we don't come across the northerners much,"* admitted one southern trainee, before quickly adding: *"But there is a genuine effort to integrate us all,"* including cross-office team-building days. New recruits now receive their initial training together over a couple of days in Newcastle before congregating in Bristol for PSC training sessions. Interviewees believed *"the two legacy firms were fairly compatible in terms of culture, so the merger has gone pretty smoothly. There are still residual separate identities, but no factionalism."*

This is good news. To give you a bit of history on this merger: while Bond Pearce (like many Bristol firms) was swimming along nicely with an optimistic outlook and no trouble at t'mill, Dickie Dees was having a bit of an identity crisis – a friendly, open-minded management team was trying to grow the firm, but trainees spoke of 'dinosaur' partners who didn't want to change with the times. Operating in the long-suffering North East business market didn't help either, and the firm was stagnating somewhat: while BP's revenue grew by 11% in the year leading up to the merger, DD's was up just 4% and lower than it had been before the recession hit.

All the same, it was our South West interviewees who were more likely to chafe at some of the changes brought on by the merger, complaining of newly centralised social budgets and teething troubles merging the two legacy firms' IT systems. Still, across the offices our sources found that *"you just have to try to get on with people and be confident about the future."* We detected a somewhat more convivial culture down south, whereas northern sources appeared ambitious and hard-working while also recognising that *"everyone has their own life to get back to away from the office."* Fortunately working hours, which average 9am to 6.30pm, allow for both, leaving time for hobbies, sports or family life.

You can be sporty inside the firm too: across the offices are netball, football and cricket teams, and Southampton counts triathletes and even ultramarathon runners among its numbers. In Leeds the firm arranged a Tour de Yorkshire for cycling solicitors and clients. *"We couldn't have had worse weather,"* recalled one trainee, *"but spirits were high!"* Besides Christmas parties and summer barbecues, there is informal socialising too: Newcastle trainees sometimes congregate at the Pitcher & Piano on the Quayside on Friday evenings; meanwhile Bristol's *"really sociable"* group heads to riverside gastro-tent Yurt Lush. The most recent office Christmas party there was held at Bristol Zoo. *"It was really funny – the real estate team dressed up as penguins."*

They might have their silly side, but in a difficult market for mid-sized firms everyone at Bond Dickinson will have to put their business development thinking caps on to capitalise on the firm's new national network of offices. Trainees are well aware of this. *"It's all about the clients,"* said one. *"Knowing what they want and staying ahead of their business needs is what we do."* The firm's dreams of top-20 stardom are quite an ask and inevitably mean an increased push for efficiency and drive. As one trainee reflected: *"We might have to change some of our attitudes and become a little bit more ruthless. I hope we can retain our laid-back attitude, but there probably will be pressure to work more hours."* It's a story we've heard before and a path many other firms have successfully trodden. Will Bond Dickinson be able to do so too?

And finally...

Trainees advised applicants that *"it's paramount to get on the vac scheme,"* particularly in the Newcastle office, where *"almost all of us have done it."*

Boodle Hatfield LLP

The facts

Location: London, Oxford
Number of UK partners/solicitors: 34/40
Partners who trained at firm: 21%
Total number of trainees: 10
Seats: 4x6 months
Alternative seats: none

On chambersstudent.co.uk...

How to get into Boodle Hatfield
Poussin the envelope: Boodle takes
   on art fraud

If you've a hankering for property or private client work, and baulk at the big City bruisers, then Boodle might be your bag.

High society

This may be the century of Google Glass, contactless debit cards and lab-grown lungs, but let's not forget the past is still very much part of the present. Heritage matters – this is England, after all, home to landed gentry, peers, aristocracy. *Tatler* keeps tabs on these elites, and Boodle Hatfield services them by the yacht-load. The firm, which has been working with the wealthy for nearly 300 years, has all the proud pedigree of a coiffed Crufts champ.

Boodle was founded in 1722 by the estate manager for the Grosvenor family, which owns much of Mayfair and Belgravia. The estate remains a client to this day and is now headed by Gerald Grosvenor, the 6th Duke of Westminster and the UK's wealthiest landlord (not to mention the highest-ranked Briton on the Forbes World's Billionaires list). But there are other family estates of eye-watering wealth on Boodle's books. Take the Bedford Estate, which encompasses most of Bloomsbury, or the Howard de Walden Estate, Marylebone's main landlord. Other major clients – the ones we're allowed to name, anywho – include Marriott International and the Telegraph Media Group.

Historically the firm's resided in – where else? – Mayfair, a decision that's cost management quite a bit in rent over the years. In July 2014, however, lawyers moseyed south of the river to a brand new abode in Bankside, no doubt saving a few pennies in the process. They haven't cut ties with West London, though; at the time of the move the firm launched a new, smaller base in Mayfair. There's also a small branch in Oxford, which mainly deals in private wealth for the more regional clients.

A hotel on Mayfair, please!

Finance aficionados looking to do big business with the big banks might consider looking elsewhere for a training contract. Most of the seats at Boodle span the private client and property spheres, with interviewees citing the firm's stellar reputation in these areas as a big draw. The firm scores *Chambers UK* rankings for both practices, but its focus on private wealth doesn't mean Boodle is some crusty outfit full of braying old chaps in red trousers. *"It's not stuffy or pompous here,"* confirmed our sources, telling us *"there really is an open community feel. It's a supportive place."* Also encouraging is the fact that, in addition to a sizeable number of female associates and trainees, *"there are a lot of younger partners, many of whom are women."* In fact, women make up nearly half of the partnership (and 58% of the equity partnership).

Trainees characterised seat allocation as *"a fairly oblique process,"* noting: *"We're a small firm, so we don't have that corporate culture where there's a set procedure for everything."* Trainees have periodic meetings with HR to discuss their preferences and felt overall that these are taken into account, though one warned that *"if you don't make a big noise about family, you might not get it."* Everyone is required to complete a property seat, *"and actually most people do two property seats."* The scale of the department is such that there are three separate branches – Grosvenor work, other residential estate work and

Seat options: property; private client & tax; litigation; corporate; family

Chambers UK rankings

Agriculture & Rural Affairs	Private Client
Charities	Real Estate
Corporate/M&A	Real Estate Litigation
Family/Matrimonial	

commercial/development work – so spending 12 months there hardly means retreading the same territory.

On the residential property front, lawyers handle *"licence work for the bigger estates, plus sales and purchases for private clients."* One source proudly told of *"helping sell a cottage and sorting out freehold issues"* during their time with the team, while another reported *"lots of agricultural work for a client buying up huge tracts of farmland. I handled the right of way issues that emerged. One transaction alone involved 15 rights of way."* Meanwhile, commercial property lawyers advise on developments for offices, hotels, shopping centres and petrol stations. Trainees with experience in this group recalled *"drafting lease and title reports, and helping put together documents for commercial transactions and financings. You get a lot of direct contact with the other side."* Apparently *"there's some crossover between the residential and commercial elements, which is nice because you get an idea of what's going on with both."*

Those assigned to Grosvenor-specific work can expect to handle basic applications from tenants based in Mayfair and Belgravia, such as for the use of roof terraces or the keeping of pets. *"You also review leases,"* added one trainee, telling us *"that kind of work never gets boring because there are different elements involved every time."* The past few years have seen the team keep busy assisting Grosvenor with the development of a luxurious boutique hotel in Mayfair that will feature a restaurant, spa and, according to our sources, a newly commissioned Antony Gormley sculpture. Posh!

It's not uncommon for trainees in property to find themselves *"running files from day one. It's a very involved seat, and the work is of incredibly high-quality."* For this reason property can be *"quite a scary first seat."* Elaborated one source: *"I was getting bombarded with e-mails from other people's solicitors in my first week and had no idea what I was doing. People are always happy to help you, but I found it a reactive sort of supervision."* That said, interviewees took a positive view generally, acknowledging that *"it's nice to have as much responsibility in property as we do. You feel like a member of the department in your own right."*

Private lives

Boodle's private client lawyers advise on asset protection, long-term wealth devolution and tax advice matters for high net worth individuals located at home and abroad (think landed estates and appallingly wealthy families). The majority of matters have an international element – for example, overseas tax planning or international philanthropy projects. Partners tend to have long-established relationships with their clients, so it's uncommon for trainees to be the ones ringing up Old Rupert for a chat about his assets; rather they keep busy *"drafting wills, deeds and appointments, and working on tax calculations and trust administration. Everything is supervised and checked."* There's also a good bit of research to be handled. The team collaborates regularly with colleagues in Oxford, and trainees have the option to go on secondment in that office, though we heard nobody's taken this offer up in the past few years.

The six-member family team works closely with the private client department to help wealthy individuals to sort out prenups, divorces and custody cases. A recent matter saw Boodle represent a prominent private equity manager in a financial remedy case against his ex-wife. The value at stake was approximately £40m of liquid assets, among them various London properties, a Scottish castle, a Swiss chalet and a yacht in Antibes. There's scope for trainees to get *"heavily involved"* with files here, with one telling us they'd *"attended court hearings alone with clients and counsel."*

Over in litigation lawyers tend to specialise in either property or commercial work, though trainees *"are not necessarily confined to one area."* On the property front are Grosvenor-related residential cases *"which you manage yourself with lots of supervision."* Commercial cases, on the other hand, *"tend to be larger and more complex, so you get small piecemeal tasks like copy-checking and doing the court run."* There's also the chance to get involved with some art world disputes, which the team has cultivated a particular penchant for. Boodle litigators have spent the past few years representing one Mr Lancelot William Thwaytes in a professional negligence claim against Sotheby's regarding a painting he sold through the auction house. Sotheby's maintained the work was a Caravaggio knock-off, but the successful bidder, a Caravaggio scholar, declared it to be an original.

Boodle's Guetta talent

Interviewees agreed that *"trainees are fairly different in terms of personality here,"* although they did highlight some similarities among the current cohort: *"We're all very organised – you have to be to thrive here because it's sink or swim. And people are definitely academic."* Said one trainee: *"Three out of the five in my year are from Oxbridge, but overall I think there's a good balance of universities represented across the firm."*

When it comes to hours, sources were happy to report that *"work/life balance is really good here."* Indeed, schedules are largely civilised – *"past 6.30pm or 7pm, people are thin on the ground."* This leaves plenty of time for socialising, which Boodle lawyers do not shy away from. The annual and much-beloved 'Boodle's Got Talent' contest is one of the biggest events on the calendar. In 2014 the office manager's acoustic rendition of David Guetta's 'Titanium' landed first prize, while the second-year class came in as the runners-up with a no doubt illuminating rap performance. Sadly the first-year group's poetry slam, which mimicked *"the style of a six-month*

appraisal," failed to place. Still, *"by the end everyone was singing and had their arms around each other,"* so it couldn't have been too poor a performance. Those with a flair for athletics rather than theatre will be pleased to know Boodle has a sporty side too – there are football, netball and cricket teams, plus yoga sessions.

We hear the qualification process is *"quite informal. You have a chat with HR in April, and they come round a few week later to tell you if you have a job."* In 2014 the firm retained four out of five second-years.

And finally...

For those who need extra convincing: "*Boodle has an incredible history. To train at a place that's been working with the same families for literally hundreds of years is such a unique experience.*"

B P Collins LLP

The facts

Location: Gerrards Cross
Number of UK partners/solicitors: 15/32
Total number of trainees: 7
Seats: 4x5 + 1x4 months
Alternative seats: none

On chambersstudent.co.uk...

How to get into B P Collins
What goes on in Gerrards Cross

A relaxed home counties location, famous neighbours and a wide range of practice areas – what's not to like about B P Collins?

Postcode lottery winner

Sitting alongside the local library, a pet shop and a bathroom supplies business, B P Collins could easily be mistaken for a high-street outfit by the casual observer. In fact, this is a full-service law firm with expertise ranging from family law to commercial property. It attracts eight regional rankings in *Chambers UK*, testament to the high-profile local business and private clients it attracts. *"I didn't fancy working for a big City firm,"* reflected one trainee, *"but I was looking for somewhere full-service, which did commercial work and acted for private clients too."*

And private clients there are aplenty. Gerrards Cross is no run-of-the-mill home counties town: a 2013 Experian survey named it as the country's third wealthiest postcode. The area has been dubbed 'mini-Hollywood' for its glut of high-profile residents, which includes James Corden, Peter Jones (of *Dragons' Den* fame) and Fern Britton. Despite the town's beautiful rural location in South Bucks it's far from being in the back of beyond: London Marylebone is just 19 minutes away by fast train, so this is the ideal repose for those high net worth individuals who want to pay a premium for a gentle commute.

For B P Collins this means a constant supply of high-value divorces to litigate, wills to write and estates to manage. This is complemented by commercial and corporate work for companies looking to escape London rates – many of the firm's clients are businessmen and company directors, so they can send commercial work the firm's way once B P Collins has untangled the complications in their personal lives. This all leads to quite an interesting mix of work for trainees.

B P Collins' recruitment cycle isn't a rigid affair and there's *"a degree of flexibility regarding start dates."* So to make sure no one gets *"out of sync,"* first seats can vary in length from a single month all the way to a very rare eight. Trainees are able to sit in litigation, corporate/commercial, employment, private client, property and family, and usually undertake four five-month seats followed by a single four-month stint in the department into which they wish to qualify. Before arriving at the firm, each new starter is asked for a seat they *"most want to experience"* and one they *"really want to avoid."* All of our sources had been able to avoid their bogey seat, and the majority had already gained experience in their favoured one. Every trainee usually does a litigation seat, with corporate and private client the next most common destinations.

Matters of life and death

Litigation is (by a hair) the firm's largest department with three partners and five associates. *"I got to know everyone really quickly,"* said one trainee. *"They took me out for lunch on my first day. And the team made a real effort to make me feel involved. I've been taken along to client meetings and to meetings with counsel in London."* The department's work is *"mostly a mix of property and general commercial litigation,"* but trainees were excited to point out that recently *"it has expanded into contentious probate, which is a really interesting area."* Recent work highlights range from defending a client accused of regu-

Seat options: family; litigation; property; private client; corporate & commercial; employment

Chambers UK rankings

Corporate/M&A	Litigation
Employment	Private Client
Environment	Real Estate
Family/Matrimonial	Real Estate Litigation

latory breaches to suing for failure to honour a commercial supply contract. Trainees also reported working on the termination of tenancies, disputes over covenants and trade mark infringements. The department acts for executives and business managers, as well as smaller companies (usually with an annual turnover below £100m) like pharma manufacturer Norgine, Hayes-based TMD Technologies and electronics retailer Misco. The firm does also attract larger clients including the (South Bucks-based) Epilepsy Society and Biffa Waste Management.

Biffa is also a client of the corporate/commercial group, which in addition acts for translation company RWS and top pesto brand Sacla. The team consist of five partners and two associates. It recently advised Jason Gardiner and James Gay, the founders and only shareholders of IT services provider ICCM, on the sale of their company to OpenText. Most deals are in the £5–10m range, but one trainee did proudly tell us they were *"attending a completion meeting at the offices of a City firm in two days' time."* On the commercial side tasks include company secretarial work like drafting agreements, registering offices, filing annual accounts, and revising terms and conditions for websites.

Property work is *"predominantly commercial but with some residential work thrown in."* The three-partner, ten-associate team recently took over from a City firm advising on a £30m creative industries office and music studio development near Kings Cross. Trainees deal with their own residential conveyancing, leasehold and commercial lease files. *"There's lot of drafting – I really like it!"* exclaimed one. There are also larger matters which *"take up the time of a partner and a few associates."* These include large leases, concession agreements and the acquisition of big plots of lands. For example, the team has been advising Beaconsfield-based Chartridge Developments on the acquisition of land in Arkley, Gerrards Cross and Cobham to build new luxury homes.

When we asked about the private client department, we were slightly taken aback to hear interviewees refer to *"the living team and the dead team,"* but further questioning revealed that one side of the department deals exclusively with probate issues (dead) and the other handles work like trust administration, powers of attorney and the drafting of wills (living). A trainee reported: *"I was given some basic files to run myself, and did the admin work on more complex trusts. I also attended trustee meetings and drafted lasting powers of attorney."* The department also offers the opportunity to *"come into contact with the great and good of Gerrards Cross."* Unfortunately the client list is entirely confidential, but we can reveal it consists mostly of managing directors and chief execs rather than any celebs.

The crazy days, city lights

"There's a very good atmosphere in all the departments," interviewees agreed. *"People are always bouncing ideas off one another and trainees are encouraged to express their opinions."* Many senior lawyers at the firm joined from London outfits later in their careers, but sources didn't feel this gave the office a sharp or hard-nosed edge. Quite the opposite, in fact. *"Outsiders tend to adapt to our more relaxed and less frantic approach quite quickly,"* said one trainee. *"It's often why they've made the move here, after all!"* The hours trainees work are pretty un-Citylike too: our interviewees tended to get between 8am and 9am and leave at 5.30 or 6.30pm. *"Litigation tends to have the longest hours, as you have to react immediately if something comes in. But you rarely stay later than 7.30pm."*

B P Collins' location means *"people travel in to work from quite a wide catchment area"* so *"it's not that easy for everyone to head out for drinks after work on a Friday."* However, trainees do take advantage of GX's impressive range of chain restaurants and regularly go for lunch together, *"especially if someone's just joined or is leaving."* Each quarter trainees are given a £25-a-head social budget which is often spent on a jaunt down to London, sometimes to the glitz and bright lights of the West End, but sometimes for something darker: *"Last year we did a Jack the Ripper tour of Whitechapel."* B P Collins is also involved in the local community: the firm has sponsored the switching on of GX's Christmas lights and the local fun-run, which even some partners have been known to participate in.

The True Picture

And finally...

B P Collins only recruits a small number of trainees, but retention rates are usually pretty decent. In 2014 two out of threequalifiers stayed with the firm.

BPE Solicitors LLP

The facts

Location: Cheltenham
Number of UK partners/solicitors: 21/45
Total number of trainees: 5
Seats: 4x6 months
Alternative seats: none

On chambersstudent.co.uk...

How to get into BPE
All about Cheltenham

The idyllic Cotswolds: an unlikely setting for a hard-hitting law firm with an impressive caseload.

Horses for courses

Cheltenham might be best known for its royal races, but this quaint spa town is also home to another type of pedigree. BPE mixes country living with high-profile clients – an option to consider if you're looking to avoid the rat race and take a different course. Of course, the firm's Gloucestershire postcode doesn't mean lawyers can simply hang up their suits. *"While you're not expected to slave away until ten every night, this isn't a place where you can kick off your shoes and coast,"* warned trainees, who assured us there are plenty of times when they find themselves *"incredibly busy."* With big hitters like NatWest, BMW and Holiday Inn on the books, it's no surprise that BPE cracks the whip.

Luckily for them, our interviewees were no strangers to hard work. Most arrived at the firm following stints as paralegals or in other law-related employment – a route managing partner John Workman can empathise with. After training at a London firm, he weaved his way through various industries, from money-printing to pharmaceuticals, before finally finding his feet as head of BPE.

Since Workman took to the reins in 2005, BPE has grown to a team of 21 partners across ten departments. The recession temporarily knocked back trainee figures, but it looks like things have settled into a pretty steady rhythm now, with the firm taking on about four newbies a year. BPE has traditionally excelled on the property front, and that team made a bold bid for the front this year, finishing only one place from the top spot in the regional *Chambers UK* rankings, alongside the firm's corporate department.

Racing ahead

With only 45 or so lawyers among its ranks, BPE is the kind of place where *"everyone knows who you are as a trainee; you're not just a number on the 17th floor."* The fact that there aren't scores of trainees to herd around means the firm can afford to take a flexible approach to seat allocation. There are a few restrictions – everyone has to visit property and litigation, and HR decides where a trainee sits first – but we hear HR does its best to accommodate those with a burning passion for a specific area, and trainees can even repeat a seat if it strikes their fancy.

Many trainees start out in property, BPE's biggest department. Those daunted by the bevy of household names on the client list – among them Superdry, Lloyds and Barclays – need not worry; our interviewees assured us: *"It's a process-driven seat, so you can get your head around things relatively quickly."* Indeed, leasehold acquisitions and contract exchanges pave the way for research, while trainees get plenty of chances to hone their drafting skills through Land Registry applications and stamp duty returns. Sources agreed it's not uncommon to see multiple files through to completion and deal with clients on a regular basis.

Corporate is another big group and handles a range of matters, from joint ventures and flotations to restructurings and private equity buyouts. In one of the bigger deals handled in 2013, the firm advised Lloyds TSB on

> **Seat options:** commercial property; commercial litigation; corporate; commercial; employment

Chambers UK rankings

Construction	Litigation
Corporate/M&A	Real Estate

a refinancing worth £30m. Meanwhile, Mears Group is a long-running client on the M&A side, with lawyers recently overseeing the social housing repairs firm's £22.5m acquisition of ILS. *"It feels more like a normal job than a training seat,"* said one interviewee of their time in corporate. *"You're treated as a member of the team and never micromanaged."*

Can you hack it?

BPE operates under the mantra that training should take place on the job. Elaborated one trainee: *"We're always supervised, but that doesn't mean we're mollycoddled; partners are really good at recognising how much supervision we need at each stage."* Others assured us that *"you're encouraged to ask if you don't understand anything"* and said the open-plan working environment helps a great deal on this front: *"It's not daunting to bother a partner with a question because you can just turn to them and they're sitting right there."*

Training principal Philip Radford sits with the litigation team and proves a handy resource for trainees in all departments. *"He's been involved with training since the year dot,"* said one source, *"and is always happy to discuss any issues."* Sources on his team told of collecting evidence, preparing appeals, attending mediations and even meeting with QCs in court. Cases are often long-running, whereas those on the employment side tend to be short enough for trainees to see through from start to finish. Here typical tasks include bundling, tribunal prep and writing up the particulars of claims. Meanwhile those in construction reported a lot of drafting, telling us *"this type is a whole new ball game – construction contracts are very different to commercial contracts."* The team handles both litigious and non-contentious matters and in 2013 advised on the construction of a stem cell research lab in Guy's and St Thomas' hospital in London.

The commercial department is split between two partners who handle general commercial and IP matters, respectively. The latter faction caters to both national and international clients, and the Estonian government even features on the books. The science and technology team, on the other hand, has a much narrower focus, handling *"all manner of obscure matters"* – research grants and offshore renewable work, for instance – for STEM fund providers and societies. Here you can learn about public

funding in the sciences, but be warned that *"the clients are demanding, and the hours are long."*

The firm also has private client and matrimonial teams, and hopes to offer a seat combining these practices in the future. Watch this space.

The final furlong

BPE has demonstrated a great retention rate in recent years, having offered permanent roles to each of its last five trainees. 2014 was no different, with three out of three new qualifiers kept on. The qualification process is not overly structured; *"it's up to you to take the initiative and press the firm for responses."* That said, insiders took care to point out: *"They'll never leave you out on a ledge. HR is always very conscious of where trainees are headed and will try to gauge whether there'll be opening in their favoured department upon qualification. If there isn't space, they'll help you to find something elsewhere or perhaps give you the option to spend half a year with another team before joining the team you wanted originally."*

Our sources agreed: *"There's no one certain type or image the firm looks for"* when recruiting, although being *"business-driven and hard-working"* is a must. Said one insider: *"A lot of people look at BPE and assume it'll be a cushy training contract, but you shouldn't see it that way. This is a place where you're encouraged to progress and can quickly work above your station if you're good."*

A breakfast club and regular lunches out give trainees a chance to unwind together, and there are seasonal parties like summer barbecues and a Gatsby-themed Christmas bash that see everyone from partners to secretaries involved. There's also a monthly drinks event that keeps lawyers in the loop about the firm's ambitions. Insiders shared that recent discussions have revolved around the firm's efforts to avoid being swallowed up in the trend of mergers and takeovers prevalent in the legal sphere these days, and that it's keen to make a name for itself helping get start-ups off the ground, as evidenced by its new Launch Pad Programme.

It's true you won't rake in a City salary at BPE, but that's partly balanced out by the lower cost of living in ye olde Cheltenham and the reduced chance of finding yourself sorting through documents in the wee hours of the AM. *"For the client exposure and support I've been given, it seems like a fair trade-off,"* testified one source. *"You don't work through the night here; partners encourage you to have a decent work/life balance."* What's more, there's a free golf membership. Turns out *"life in the sticks isn't so bad after all."*

And finally...

Fun fact: BPE's managing partner is Estonia's honorary consul in Cheltenham, so the office technically doubles up as the Estonian consulate.

"One of the best questions to ask at a law fair is 'what parts of your job don't you enjoy?'. That tells you a lot about the working culture."

Trainee

Brabners LLP

The facts

Location: Liverpool, Manchester, Preston
Number of UK partners/solicitors: 68/205
Partners who trained at firm: 30%
Total number of trainees: 12
Seats: 4x6 months
Alternative seats: secondments
Extras: pro bono – Liverpool University Pro Bono Clinic

On chambersstudent.co.uk...
How to get into Brabners
Sports law guru Maurice Watkins

It's got a sports practice to rival any in the land, but this North West powerhouse can offer so much more besides.

United (and it feels so good)

Bringing together Liverpool and Manchester sounds like a recipe for disaster. The rivalry between the two cities is such that a union might be doomed to the Romeo and Juliet treatment. But perhaps our views are clouded by rivalries on the football pitch, because the harmonious merger of Merseyside's Brabners and Manny's Chaffe Street back in 2002 appears to have dispelled any myths that the two cities can't work in tandem. Of course, a rebranding exercise in 2013 did see 'Chaffe Street' dropped from this firm's name, but we're assured this wasn't due to any uncomfortable friction; rather, *"it was about simplifying our message,"* confirms director of training Tony Harvey.

Indeed, this is a firm that has little time for superfluousness. Despite major growth over the past decade, the trainee intake remains on the modest side, with just 13 in residence at the time of our calls: seven in Liverpool and six in Manchester. Note that Brabners' petite Preston outpost occasionally takes on a single trainee, but it's not in a position to recruit every year. Between them, the offices have cultivated an impressive reputation on the social housing, private client and employment fronts. *Chambers UK* awards top-band rankings for these three practices, plus a host of others, including IP, family and charities. There's also a solid corporate offering, and the firm boasts a nationally renowned sports practice too.

Ooh! Aah! Cantona!

Trainees don't have a say in their first seat, but we didn't hear any complaints on this front. For their remaining rotations new recruits get to put forth three preferences each time, and we hear it's possible to split or even repeat a seat. There are no compulsory seats, although a turn in the property department – Brabners' biggest – is generally encouraged. There's also a highly coveted client secondment to Manchester United on offer to a lucky first-year every 18 months.

Bear in mind a stint with the sports team is only on offer in Manchester, so it can be hard for Liverpudlians to find themselves a chair. The team is headed up by former Manchester United director Maurice Watkins, who represented French footballer Eric Cantona after he was charged with assault for kung fu-kicking a fan in 1995. These days Brabs remains a beautiful prospect for the beautiful game, boasting a client roster that includes more than three-quarters of FA Premier League clubs and the Professional Footballers' Association itself. Last year the firm advised Man U on the £27.5m acquisition of Marouane Fellaini and instructed Italian fireworks-enthusiast Mario Balotelli on his move to AC Milan from Manchester City. There's plenty of work beyond the football sphere too – British Cycling, British Swimming, the Rugby Football League and Commonwealth Games England are all on the books too.

The team has both commercial and regulatory arms. The latter handles *"the things that affect matters on the pitch, such as big transfers or UEFA's recent Financial Fair Play regulations."* Meanwhile, the commercial limb advises on sponsorship deals, image rights and advertising matters. With high-profile clients comes high expectations, so

Seat options: commercial; corporate; employment; family; litigation; private client; property; sport (Manchester); social housing and regeneration

Chambers UK rankings

Agriculture & Rural Affairs	Litigation
Banking & Finance	Media & Entertainment
Charities	Private Client
Construction	Real Estate
Corporate/M&A	Real Estate Litigation
Employment	Restructuring/Insolvency
Environment	Retail
Family/Matrimonial	Social Housing
Information Technology	Sports Law
Intellectual Property	

"you're not given too many big responsibilities as a train-ee here," sources admitted. That said, *"bits and pieces of drafting"* are the norm, particularly on the regulatory side.

Choppers and chicken shops

Almost all new joiners complete a property seat, but not just to keep their employer happy. *"It's known as the best department for letting trainees manage themselves under supervision."* Of course the biggest matters are still partner-led, but rookies here can expect a lot of responsibility right from the off. *"I was thrown straight into various transactions,"* reported one Liverpudlian; *"almost immediately I was drafting leases, producing title reports and acting as point of contact for clients. It was a bit of shock!"* The team mainly handles commercial property matters for *"major shopping retailers,"* but the firm is also big in the renewable, student and healthcare sectors, and does a bit of residential development work too. Those who take up a social housing seat generally find themselves dealing with *"a real mix of work,"* from conveyancing and construction matters to grant funding and tenancy disputes. *"It's a great team – they let you take the lead as much as possible, though they're careful not to bombard you with responsibilities you can't handle."*

Brabners' corporate contingent has achieved a high degree of respect in the region for its work on mid-market transactions. The team acts for entrepreneurs right through to AIM-listed companies, with deals generally ringing in at somewhere between £1m and £10m, though they're occasionally known to go *"above and beyond"* this – for example, Bristow Helicopters' £74m sale of a stake in FB Heliservices to Cobham, which the Mancunian side recently oversaw. In a more typical deal, Liverpudlian lawyers recently advised Goodmans Law on its £4m sale to Slater & Gordon. *"I started off drafting board minutes and share certificates,"* a second-year said of their time with the team, *"but as time went on I got more involved in transactions and got to meet with clients, undertake post-completion work and oversee the due diligence process."*

Those interested in client contact should head to the family team, where the work is *"hands-on from the word 'go',"* and trainees are *"constantly following up with clients and going to court."* The department chiefly acts for high net worth individuals with money maladies, handling dodgy divorces, prickly pre-nups and complicated custody cases involving children. There's a big crossover between clientele here and in the private client group – *"for example, we had one lady getting married who wanted to change her will and get a pre-nup drawn up."*

Meanwhile the likes of J D Wetherspoon, Nando's and AXA Insurance have all sought out Brabners' employment expertise in recent years, the former for advice on staffing issues as it launched in the Republic of Ireland. Our sources gave rave reviews of the team and told of drafting settlement agreements and attending tribunal matters. That said, we heard the recent changes to the court fees system mean *"things have been quieter than usual recently – a lot of our contentious work has just disappeared."*

That Friday feeling

"I've found the offices are more integrated now than when I started," said a Liverpool source; *"I recently helped out a partner from Manchester with a Preston-based client – that's a great example of the three branches working in tandem."* That said, *"there's not too much crossover between trainees"* either work-wise or socially. Still, our interviewees were content with the dynamics of their individual offices: Liverpudlians praised their branch's *"efforts to find the right balance and create a supportive atmosphere. Everyone makes themselves approachable here."* Meanwhile, over in Manchester trainees had good things to say about their office's open door policy. *"Of course we all roll our eyes when they call it that, but it really is possible to ask anybody a question here, whether they're in your department or not."* Trainees also waxed lyrical about the perks on offer in their respective locales. *"We have fresh fruit every day, you can leave an hour early on your birthday, and there's 'Friday feeling', which sees a beautician come on the last Friday of the month,"* sung a Liver bird. This last benefit is not on offer to those in Manchester, although as one resident there pointed out: *"If that's the only complaint I have, it's probably not too bad!"* Sources agreed *"the hours are very reasonable – generally you've had a hard one if you're not home by 7pm."* In 2014 two of Brabners' six qualifiers stayed on with the firm.

Both offices put on end-of-the-month drinks, run plenty of sports teams and organise events like trips to the races. A yearly staff conference sees everyone in the firm come together for a day-long programme of events. *"Early on it's all about the boring stuff – how the firm is doing and so forth,"* joked a source, *"but then things liven up with a meal and a party in the evening!"*

The True Picture

"If you're applying to a sector-focused firm, make sure your background reflects an interest in at least one of the key sectors it targets. If you don't have evidence to show you're interested in healthcare or energy or IP or whatever, it will be hard to get hired by firm that centres its work on those areas."

The True Picture

Trainee

Bristows LLP

The facts

Location: London

Number of UK partners/solicitors: 38/83

Partners who trained at firm: 26%

Total number of trainees: 19

Seats: 3 or 6 months

Alternative seats: secondments

Extras: pro bono - Waterloo Legal Advice Centre, A4ID, People United

On chambersstudent.co.uk...
How to get into Bristows
The Unified Patent Court

Those more corporate-minded should find themselves increasingly at home at this London firm, traditionally known for its IP expertise.

A philosophical maze

Think Bristows and it's likely intellectual property springs to mind. However, there's far more to this firm than that. *"We're a full-service firm, and you'd be wrong to think that our corporate or commercial departments are peripheral,"* insiders were keen to stress, pointing out that these practices are *"actually major growth areas for us."* Indeed, says training principal Mark Hawes: *"Competitors like to put us in a box, but growing our transactional side is at the heart of our strategy."* At the time of our interviews the firm had trainees sitting in departments as diverse as real estate, employment and competition.

Still, Bristows does have a well-known – not to mention enviable – reputation in all things IP. The Londoner's *Chambers UK* rankings are dominated by techy practices like patent litigation, life sciences, IT and data protection. Bristows' close connections to all things scientific stretch back to 1837, when founding partner Robert Wilson drafted the patent for the first electrical telegraph. In the intervening 177 years, the firm's had a hand in some landmark developments – for example, the laying of the first transatlantic telephone line and the invention of the jet engine. Today's client list remains as impressive as ever, boasting multinational giants like Diageo, Google, Samsung and McDonald's.

Bristows' identification with innovation is visible in its offices in Unilever House, which feature external meeting rooms named after prominent inventors and scientists. A nice touch, though a potentially confusing one, as one trainee pointed out: *"I spent at least half an hour on my first day searching for a partner named Adam Smith*

before realising that 'he' was a room just down the corridor!"

We hear space within the building, located at 100 Victoria Embankment, is increasingly at a premium, with three lawyers to an office now a common occurrence. *"We definitely seem to be expanding, although there's still enough room to squeeze a few more people in,"* our sources observed.

Have a break, have a...

The training contract includes both three and six-month long seats depending on business needs in that area. A full six months in IP litigation is guaranteed, an arrangement our sources were happy to abide and even characterised as *"one of the best things about Bristows."*

Incoming trainees used to arrive to find their entire two years carefully mapped out in a lovely colour-coded spreadsheet. However, the seats they undertook in the end rarely corresponded to those assigned, so as of 2013 new seats are doled out at the six-month mark. *"A few weeks before rotating, you'll have a chat with HR,"* the newest joiners explained. *"They're very good at taking preferences into account, business needs permitting."* Even

Seat options: IP litigation; regulatory; competition; corporate; commercial disputes; employment; real estate; commercial IP/IT

Chambers UK rankings

Data Protection	Media & Entertainment
Information Technology	Outsourcing
Intellectual Property	Partnership
Life Sciences	Telecommunications
Litigation	

those who'd experienced the old system testified that *"you're never pushed into doing something unwillingly."*

As the largest single department and a mandatory pit-stop for trainees, IP litigation always has a few juniors poking around. The work is visibly divided into contentious patent-related matters and softer ones related to brands and advertising. Trainees often switch supervisors at halfway through their time with the group in order to get a taste of the full range of work on offer and meet as many people as possible. *"It really feels like two different seats in the same department,"* sources agreed.

On the patent side, Bristows has regular dealings with household names. Lawyers are currently handling Thomas Pink's claim that the ever racy Victoria's Secret is infringing on the luxury clothing brand's trade mark with their signature 'Pink' range. Other recent activities include helping the BBC protect its beloved 'Desert Island Discs' brand by forcing the revocation of trade marks for 'Desert Island Movies' and 'Desert Island Films', and acting on behalf of Cadbury and Kraft to block attempts by Nestlé to register the shape of a Kit Kat as a protected trade mark. According to insiders, trainees' experiences in this seat vary greatly depending upon which cases are approaching trial. For one lucky soul, *"one month in and it was all guns blazing! I spent my last ten days at trial."* Still, most can expect to undertake research, help manage the disclosure process and respond to questions from counsel. *"You're made to feel like an important part of the team and involved in all aspects of the work – even witnessing major strategy discussions."*

The other side of the department busies itself with long-term management of trade marks and image rights. Essentially, the aim here is to avoid litigation as far as possible. Our interviewees told of researching industry experts and presenting the findings to clients, as well as drafting pleadings and letters. *"They make an effort to give you a first go at things,"* we heard. *"Sometimes your work is redrafted, but occasionally you get a big flush of pride as something goes out almost unchanged."*

Commercial IP/IT is another IP-related seat. The work here typically falls into the advisory sphere – namely data protection and outsourcing issues. The team recently advised Viacom and its subsidiaries on their online operations. The team also has ties with some other household names that must remain confidential – find out once you

get a contract there. One trainee recalled *"attending a lot of client meetings and helping amend various documents,"* telling us: *"The team makes a big effort to involve you. I learned a lot about privacy policies."*

Out of the office; try again later...

Trainees with experience in commercial litigation characterised the seat as varied, telling us *"you'll take on a mixture of stuff – there are copyright and design rights cases, and then there's the more general commercial stuff."* The team broadly handles financial and technology-related disputes for big'uns like Microsoft, Volvo and Chrysler. The firm's kept busy representing the latter in one of the longest-running international fraud litigations to date: the $400m collapse of Canadian finance and property bigwig Castor Holdings.

Still, it's important to note that Bristows has made its name chasing mid-market matters rather than those on the above scale – think in the tens, rather than hundreds, of millions. On the competition side, lawyers recently defended Google against charges that it's abusing its dominant position in the online mapping and search markets, while the real estate team has has been busy advising garden centre brand Blue Diamond on its lease and redevelopment of farm shop Fermoy's. Trainees sitting in the latter department informed us the group mainly works on commercial property deals and offers *"great exposure – you get to see things through from start to finish, and you're constantly on the phone with letting agents, clients and other solicitors."*

Over in corporate, trainees toil away by undertaking research and completing filings for Companies House. Meanwhile, their counterparts in employment reported *"plenty of drafting"* and told of researching some, shall we say, *"interesting"* topics – for example, the terms of employment for a pole-dancer.

Clients secondments are big news at Bristows – almost every trainee undertakes one at some point. Recent destinations include Capgemini, Google, Sony and WPP. Our sources praised the experience, calling it *"a really useful insight into what our clients want from us."* Said one secondee: *"It's very strange being on the other side – that is, giving instructions and receiving advice. It really makes you think about how to give relevant advice as a lawyer."*

As is the case with any firm, office hours vary with the workload. *"If you're preparing for a trial, the hours can really rollercoaster – be prepared for late nights,"* one source advised. Still, when pushed, that same interviewee admitted that *"the latest I've ever left the office is 11pm"* – not too shabby when compared to other City firms.

Technical talents

In 2013 Bristows received nearly 1,800 applications for just eight training contracts, making it one of the most competitive firms to land a spot with by our reckoning. Our interviewees were reluctant to highlight just which of their many talents had helped them succeed, but they did identify *"sociability"* and *"a strong academic background"* as traits shared by many at the firm. *"Everyone is super-intelligent and very technically qualified."* Indeed, a quick look at the firm's website reveals that around a quarter of the current crop holds a master's degree.

While standard subjects like history, politics and law are represented among Bristows' trainees year on year, there's no denying its science slant – the firm deliberately targets science types with a special science and engineering open day, and at the time of our research, ten of the 19 trainees had science degrees. Still, our sources were adamant that a science background is no particular advantage, with Mark Hawes telling us the firm is keen to increase its appeal to students of other disciplines. *"It's important to us to strike that balance,"* he says, pointing out that *"our IP department is so broad that while it appeals to scientists, it shouldn't put off arts and law students."* In any case, trainees agreed that *"above all, the firm values people who are enthusiastic about their work – we all have a geeky side!"*

According to our interviewees, Bristows *"makes a big effort to create an environment where people can build relationships and stay connected."* As such, hyper-competitive personalities *"really don't go down well. No one here is out to stab anyone else in the back to get ahead; on the contrary, loads of people volunteer to help whenever anyone needs a hand."* One trainee summed up their co-workers as *"bright, helpful and very nice. They do a very good job of finding people in tune with the firm's warm and inviting philosophy."*

Part of that philosophy includes maintaining a relatively flat hierarchy. *"Almost every partner I've worked with has given me one-to-one advice,"* said one trainee, while another reported that Bristows' senior figures *"make an effort to be easy to talk to and work with; they don't come across as scary or superior."* What's more, *"they're great at giving you feedback. You always get a pat on the back when you've done something well."*

Movie makers

On the social calendar each year is a departmental Christmas party, an annual pub quiz, and a spring dinner and dance which sees future trainees invited to partake in a bit of black-tie boogie. For the 2014 spring fling (which was fast approaching at the time of our interviews), we heard trainees were granted an increased budget for entertainment. *"We're hiring a videographer to help us make a video poking a little bit of fun at the partners!"* Monthly drinks in 'The Hub', the office's social area, are also on the cards. The gathering features plenty of beer and wine to help everyone unwind, with most lawyers making a concerted effort to *"drop by and show their faces. At the pub, too, the partners will stop in, buy a round of drinks and then head off."*

Our interviewees were very appreciative that Bristows' qualification process *"doesn't involve the stress of preparing for an interview of any kind."* Rather, trainees express their preferences to HR, and the firm's partners collectively discuss each candidate. In 2014 eight out of nine qualifiers stayed on with the firm.

And finally...

Take note: in 2013 Bristows replaced its vacation scheme with three annual workshops. Check out our website for more on this new approach.

Browne Jacobson LLP

The facts

Location: Nottingham, Birmingham, London, Manchester, Exeter

Number of UK partners/solicitors: 98/184

Partners who trained at firm: 26%

Total number of trainees: 18

Seats: 4x6 months

Alternative seats: occassional secondments

Extras: pro bono – ProHelp, Planning Aid, Environmental Law Foundation

On chambersstudent.co.uk...

How to get into Browne Jacobson
Interview with training principal
   Mark Hughes

This mighty midlander is steadily becoming a national player thanks to its growing commercial offering.

How now, Browne Jacobson

Born and raised in the heart of the Midlands, this firm is now a five-site operation, its branches spanning from Devon up to the North West. As its office openings in Exeter and Manchester in 2012 illustrate, Browne Jacobson is in growth mode, though we'd be remiss not to mention that it has been for some time. *"We've actually quadrupled in size since 1997,"* remarked one of its young guns, pointing out: *"We continued climbing throughout the recession, a time when other firms were struggling to stay afloat."* Indeed, revenue has risen steadily over the years, with BJ achieving a record turnover of £50.2m in 2013/14.

The past year has seen a record number of partner promotions made across Nottingham and Birmingham, bringing the firm's total partnership to 98 at the time of publication. According to training principal Mark Hughes, it's not just the mighty Midlands pushing forward. *"We're increasingly investing in Manchester – which doubled its headcount last year – as well as London and Birmingham."* Of particular focus is the firm's IP offering in London, which recently poached partner Alex Watt from IP boutique Redd.

If the current trainee tribes' comments are anything to go by, there's a real buzz around the firm at the moment. *"It's an exciting time to be here – we're going from strength to strength."* BJ maintains a long-held reputation in the health, insurance and public sectors, and it also has a booming education-related arm that earns a top-band *Chambers UK* ranking, though it's the firm's business side that's drawing the most attention of late. *"These days our commercial offering is as strong as the other parts of our business,"* says Hughes, revealing *"roughly 50% of*

our turnover is now drawn from that." He goes on to say that the firm's diverse output was one of the key reasons it weathered the economic downturn. *"We're one of only a handful of firms to do this combination of work. We offer different services for different clients, but there's plenty of crossover, too – for example, we often handle commercial work for our public sector clients."*

Seats here fall into four broad areas: business and professional risk (BPR); business services (BS); insurance and public risk (IPR); and property. At the time of our calls there were 12 trainees in Nottingham and five in Birmingham. New starters don't get much say in their first seat, *"but we do get an e-mail from HR asking if there's anything we're keen on."* Second-years have priority (as per usual) and receive the seat list first before each rotation. They give their top three choices, then first-years give their three picks from what's left over. Luckily *"there are always more seats than trainees; you're never forced into an area you don't want."*

A few seats – environment, for example – are only on offer in Nottingham, but one insider told us *"the Birmingham office is getting so big there's very little you can't do here*

> **Seat options:** commercial dispute resolution; construction; employment; financial and professional risks; banking; commercial; corporate; government and infrastructure; private client and charities; tax; administrative law; health; personal injury; social care; development and housing; education

Chambers UK rankings

Administrative & Public Law	Information Technology
Banking & Finance	Intellectual Property
Clinical Negligence	Litigation
Construction	Local Government
Corporate/M&A	Personal Injury
Court of Protection	Private Client
Data Protection	Professional Negligence
Education	Projects
Employment	Real Estate
Environment	Real Estate Litigation
Health & Safety	Restructuring/Insolvency
Healthcare	Retail
	Social Housing

these days. I've been pleasantly surprised by how many opportunities there are." In any case, trainees are encouraged to sample life in both Midlands mainstays, and indeed many complete a rotation or two away from their home base. We hear London occasionally offers a seat – there was one available in 2014 – *"in the right circumstances."*

Egg-cellent inventions

Commercial litigation, employment and construction all fall under the BPR banner. British Gas, Wolverhampton City Council and sugar beet trade association NFU Sugar are some of the sweetest names on the commercial litigation team's client list, with lawyers recently representing the latter in a £2m pricing dispute against British Sugar. Alongside commercial cases like shareholder and contract disputes are plenty of insolvency matters, which trainees often have a hand in. Sources with experience here told us they'd split their time between assisting members of the team on the big cases and running small ones, like *"bankruptcy cases winding up,"* on their own – *"with supervision, of course."*

Trainees who'd sat in employment praised the top-ranked team for offering *"a lot of responsibility without the pressure of feeling you're doing it all on your own."* Nottingham tends to delve into more commercial and education-related cases, while Birmingham occupies itself with health sector disputes, and between the two are a good whack of advisory matters, too. *"The firm advertises it as a mixed seat."* Lawyers are frequently instructed on unfair dismissal and discrimination claims, both of which see trainees attend tribunal hearings. Said one trainee of their time with the team: *"My responsibilities were initially limited to supporting the fee earner, but eventually I got to run my own case – and we won, which was pleasing. That entailed meeting the clients, interviewing witnesses, drafting their statements and even doing a bit of advocacy."*

A stint in construction also sees trainees grapple with both litigious and advisory elements. Big retailers like Wilkinson and Alliance Boots are on the books, but insiders told us that *"clients can be anyone in the involved in the process, from the person who wants the building to those constructing it to the end occupant."* The team is big in the public sector, particularly on the education front. *"We handle a lot of academy conversions. As a trainee you usually get to run those by yourself, which is a really interesting experience."*

IP is a popular destination for rookie lawyers. The team handles a whole raft of patent, trade mark, licensing and co-branding cases, acting for both private and public sector clients. One of the tastiest cases the team has been involved with recently was carrying out an IP audit on Pork Farms' new soft-boiled egg product, which can be eaten on the go by adding hot water. According to our interviewees, *"they have no problem putting you in front of clients"* on this team. One told of overseeing a client's visit to the office – *"I took the notes in the meeting and was given research to follow up on"* – while another reported handling client calls in addition to drafting claims and working on schedules. *"It's a good seat for that kind of responsibility."*

Taking care of business

Like IP, corporate is also a sought-after destination in the business services division. Nottingham's contingent, the largest corporate finance team in the region, excels in the healthcare sector, recently acting for CARE Fertility Group on its purchase of a London-based fertility clinic, and also handles a good bit of private equity work. The firm has been taking on an increasing number of matters with an international scope lately – for example, the 2013 sale of Dynamic-Materials to US-based ceramics manufacturer CoorsTek. *"The files are usually quite big, so we do all the little tasks at the beginning and end of deals – stuff like bibling, Companies House registrations and article amendments."* Interviewees also told of managing ancillary documents and negotiating with the other side.

There's some education work to be done within corporate, but the firm has its own standalone practice in the field – one *Chambers UK* deems among the best in the country, in fact. The team boasts more than 1,000 sector organisations on its client roster and has become increasingly active since the coalition sent shockwaves through the sector with reforms like academy conversions and changes to the national curriculum. A lot of instructions involve advising education charities and sponsors on Free School projects, and insiders said academy-related work also takes up a significant chunk of the workload.

Over in the commercial department undertakings span the retail, insurance, financial services and technology sectors, and involve clients as varied as Thornton's, The National Trust and Vodafone. *"We have a growing advertising team that focuses specifically on brands,"* said a Birmingham source; *"my time in the department was mostly spent investigating claims that came in through that and offering advice on whether they had any standing. I also dabbled in some data protection and competition matters."*

Meanwhile, under the IPR umbrella is BJ's healthcare group, which is nationally renowned and sits on the NHS Litigation Authority and Medical Protection Society panels. The re-appointment to the former in 2014 was particularly significant, given that the panel was recently reduced. Clients include both private and public entities, and much of the work involves the takeover of health groups – such as Source Bioscience's £12m acquisition of Vindon Healthcare – though there's plenty of inquiry and inquest work too. Matters of the latter type often make use of BJ's expertise on the mental health front – lawyers recently represented Birmingham & Solihull Mental Health NHS Foundation Trust during an inquest into the death of a man who took his own life following his diagnosis of psychotic depression.

Clinical negligence cases likewise concern sensitive issues, with lawyers representing NHS trusts and other authorities during claims from people who've sustained injuries having fallen getting out of ambulances or had issues with cancer surgery. Because work is primarily defendant-side, *"there's a slight level of removal from the saddest cases,"* one source pointed out. Personal injury work, too, is done on behalf of defendants, which include both public entities like the London Borough of Hackney and private insurance companies. Trainees said there are some *"squeamish"* cases to contend with here – particularly when they fall into the catastrophic injury category – but agreed the work is *"satisfying. We tend to assist on the high-value claims that partners are running, but they also trust us with a lot. I was allowed to go off on my own to meet a brain injury client."*

The property side of the business includes seats in retail, development, and public authority and healthcare. The former counts Morrisons and the Louis Vuitton Moët Hennessy Group among its clients, with one trainee saying: *"There's some document organisation that trainees can't avoid, but I got to do a lot more than that – by the end of my seat I was basically drafting all day."* Meanwhile, the development team handles residential and social housing work for bodies like Waterloo Housing and Bournville Village Trust, while the public authority and healthcare arm works regularly with the education team on issues like academy conversions, and gets involved in hospital leases as well.

Progress report

When Browne Jacobson's trainees talked to us about the firm's culture, *"approachable"* regularly cropped up in their reports. One source in Birmingham recounted the time *"our ex-MP came over and sat down to start a casual conversation with me – a trainee! That's just how it is here."* As a rookie in Nottingham summed up: *"This is the kind of place where the environment is inclusive and there aren't barriers between lawyers of different levels. You can walk up to any equity partner here and ask them a question without feeling unwelcome."* This *"progressive"* approach goes a long way in creating an environment *"in which everybody's opinions are valued,"* trainees said. *"The firm is open to new ideas about taking the business forward, even if they've come from a trainee. I approached a senior colleague with some thoughts on how to build our client base, and now those have been put on the agenda."* We're told management does its part to make sure this info-sharing is a reciprocal process. *"Each year the managing partner goes around each office and talks to everybody about the strategy and current state of the firm,"* said one source, telling us these are known as 'roadshows'. *"The firm does a good job communicating with us which direction they want to go."*

Given BJ's steady expansion in recent years, some of our interviewees questioned whether its identity and core values will stick around in the long run. Most, however, were confident the firm will keep its culture intact as it expands. *"We're steadily moving from being a regional to a national firm, but we remain an integrated network,"* said one, pointing out that *"we work as departments, not just as offices, so there's a lot of interaction and a shared approach to things like team meetings and planning."* While Nottingham and Birmingham *"have always been well linked,"* trainees told us they increasingly collaborate with their colleagues in London and Manchester. *"It's nice to have those connections. Now if I go down to London for the day, I can pop into the office and work from there; I wouldn't be ushered away because I'm not a Southerner."*

The entire trainee cohort tries to get together for events every once in a while, with a Nottingham source telling us *"there's a big effort to make sure Birmingham people aren't sidelined."* At the time of our calls the whole group had just returned from *"an awesome weekend in Birmingham where we hired out a penthouse, went go-karting and relaxed at a spa."* Back at home, trainees enjoy outings like rock-climbing, wine tasting and cocktail dos, in addition to firmwide events like holiday drinks and an annual family day.

And finally...
This is an ambitious and commercially savvy operator. In 2014 seven of nine qualifiers took up NQ jobs at BJ.

The True Picture

Burges Salmon LLP

The facts

Location: Bristol

Number of UK partners/solicitors: 79/213

Partners who trained at firm: 30%

Total number of trainees: 51

Seats: 6x4 months

Alternative seats: secondments

On chambersstudent.co.uk...

How to get into Burges Salmon

A rough guide to Bristol

Don't be fooled by the Bristol postcode; this firm is a headline act and often outshines its city rivals.

Reeling 'em in

A couple years back one of Burges Salmon's more prominent graduate recruitment adverts prompted aspiring trainees to question whether they were sardines or salmon. Its implication that life in Bristol offers a rose-tinted alternative to sweaty commutes on the packed Central Line was part of a broader pitch to persuade City hopefuls to consider the firm on par with the London outfits they might be targeting. While this is a marketing angle the firm has since decided to ditch, its current trainees – weary of deflecting assumptions that Burges Salmon is some small-fry regional outfit – remain keen to emphasise the firm's respectable market standing and the various perks of training there.

"It's frustrating the opinion still pervades that we aren't as well trained as those at City firms," said one. *"It's a real shame – we do excellent work and are given a huge amount of responsibility early on. What's more, the trainee wage is fantastic, and Bristol is a phenomenal city with loads going on."* Indeed, most felt the salary, though obviously lower than at your average London firm, actually sways the balance in their favour once cost of living is factored in. There's also the area's stability to consider – Bristol proved particularly resilient during the economic downturn and even continued to grow between 2008 and 2010, a time when most other cities were shrinking. At the time several London firms like Simmons & Simmons flocked to the scene to snap up fresh candidates from the region's law schools, but Burges Salmon has steadfastly held its own.

In fact, if there was an award for best independent firm outside London, this one would certainly be a contender. Burges Salmon hauls in top *Chambers UK* regional rankings across nearly all of its practices, and it's flagged as a national leader outside London for construction,

corporate/M&A, employment, IP, litigation and real estate work. Where other firms have merged and opened offices across the country, Burges Salmon has stayed a one-site operator, and it looks set to run as such for the foreseeable future. This hasn't stopped the firm from reeling in big-ticket clients, though; its books are swimming with both home-sprung and global companies – from Bristol airport to Eurostar and Starbucks – plus a host of governmental bodies, such as the Department for Transport, the Ministry of Defence, the Home Office and the Met Police. *"The South West is certainly an important region for us, but the vast majority of our work comes from outside the region – either London, the wider UK or overseas,"* says trainee recruitment partner Keith Beattie. The firm has a swanky hub in New Street Square for meeting its many and varied clients, though this space doesn't house anyone permanently; Burges Salmon's 300 lawyers and 50-strong trainee cohort are based in its similarly swish, waterfront premises in One Glass Wharf. Still, trainees can expect to find themselves *"hopping on and off trains to London"* throughout their contract, we're told.

Taking the bait

Trainees undertake six seats here, each lasting four months. Seat options fall into three broad groups: real estate, contentious and transactional. A pick each from the first two categories is compulsory, and most spend

Seat options: real estate; planning; construction and engineering; environment and energy; dispute resolution; real estate litigation; banking; commercial; corporate; employment; pensions and incentives; private client and wealth structuring

Chambers UK rankings

Agriculture & Rural Affairs	Investment Funds
Asset Finance	Litigation
Banking & Finance	Local Government
Capital Markets	Outsourcing
Charities	Partnership
Competition/European Law	Pensions
Construction	Pensions Litigation
Corporate/M&A	Planning
Employment	Private Client
Energy & Natural Resources	Professional Negligence
Environment	Projects
Family/Matrimonial	Public Procurement
Health & Safety	Real Estate
Information Technology	Real Estate Litigation
Intellectual Property	Restructuring/Insolvency
	Tax
	Transport

their sixth seat in the practice they're planning to qualify into. Our interviewees appreciated the broad experience and exposure to different lawyers this system offers – in fact, it was one of the most commonly cited reasons for choosing the firm in the first place. They also had good things to say about HR's role in the allocation process: *"They try to give your first choice wherever possible."*

Real estate is one of the firm's biggest departments and in 2014 won a coveted place on the Crown Estate's legal panel for its rural portfolio and Windsor estate, which covers forests and agricultural land along with residential and commercial properties. The group is also big in the energy sector and recently advised Low Carbon on negotiations for a series of UK solar projects. These are just two highlights of a very busy year – lawyers closed nearly £1bn worth of deals in December 2013 alone. *"There's so much going on that they really let trainees go for it,"* said interviewees who'd sat in the general real estate seat. *"You're in charge of matters from inception to completion. It's daunting to deal with clients on your own, but by the end of the seat you have so much confidence in your own abilities."* Those who opted for planning, meanwhile, reported attending planning inspectorate tribunals to get planning permission for energy projects such as offshore wind farms. *"It's brilliant to experience a more niche department like this – there's still a lot of high-end work."*

Many fulfil their contentious requirement with a stint in commercial disputes, which covers areas as varied as arbitration, IP, insurance, agriculture and sport. It's considered one of the more demanding seats in terms of hours, but *"it's more rewarding as a result of that,"* our sources agreed. Most had spent their time here drafting witness statements and instructions to counsel, handling disclosure, putting together bundles for hearings and attending trials. Construction also counts as a contentious seat and is a popular trainee pitstop. *"It's a small team, so you get to work directly with partners."* The group frequently collaborates with the real estate and environmental teams on large matters – for example, asset manager Bluefield's acquisition of a £21m solar farm in Swindon, a deal which involved all three teams, plus reps from corporate and banking.

What a catch!

Over on the transactional side, there's the commercial team, which handles competition, IT, IP and projects matters for a mix of private and public sector clients, among them Bristol University, the Ministry of Justice, HMRC and Coca-Cola HBC. Much of the work falls into the energy, transport, renewables and defence sectors – on the latter front, the firm recently advised joint venture DiSCS on its bid to act as a service provider for a £6bn Ministry of Defence project. We hear it's a *"fun team with great socials,"* but insiders assured us the work is far from light. There's plenty of drafting for trainees to get on with in the way of pitches, tenders, and contract clauses and summaries, plus research and, if you're lucky, negotiations with clients. One trainee spoke of attending one client's office *"every single day on my own for a few weeks – it was like an unofficial mini-secondment."*

Spending some time with the corporate team *"gives you a good oversight of the whole structure of a deal and a proper taste of cross-departmental work,"* interviewees agreed. Indeed, the team regularly works in tandem with lawyers from Burges Salmon's banking, insurance and tax arms, operating across five key sectors: energy, food and drink, leisure, financial services and transport. A major client in the latter sphere is FirstGroup, which lawyers recently assisted with the £79m sale of two of the company's London bus operations. Other highlights of late include advising The Competition Commission in connection with BAA's £1.5bn disposal of Stansted airport, and assisting tech company Cobham with its £85m acquisition of Axell Wireless. Trainees told us drafting, research and completion exercises comprise a decent chunk of their role. *"We're responsible for checking all the documents that come in electronically,"* said one. *"There can be some long nights leading up to closure, but it's worth it when you see the press coverage and realise how you were part of making that happen."*

Interviewees who'd opted for a spell in banking had worked on insolvency matters and amendments to loan agreements. *"The partners like to get us roped into big projects so we get an understanding of what's going on in the department – I got exposed to some very complicated pieces of work."* The team primarily handles mid-market work and counts the likes of HSBC and JPMorgan Chase among its esteemed clientele. Deals here often have a cross-border component – for example, Beechbrook Capital's funding for the acquisition of a consultancy with subsidiaries in France, Luxembourg and the States.

Pensions has proved a popular destination among the current cohort. *"You'd expect it to be dull, but nearly everyone who spends time there loves it – the team is known as one of the best in the UK."* Meanwhile areas like employment, tax and wealth structuring are all slightly less subscribed, though we did hear positive reviews from trainees who'd sat with these teams.

The firm regularly offers client secondments: *"There always seems to be at least one person on a placement at any one time."* Recent ones have been undertaken in the energy and environmental sectors. Reflected one trainee with in-house experience: *"You get much closer to the business by spending time with their legal team. You learn how to approach matters as a lawyer while remaining commercial in your outlook."*

Give a man a fish...

With *"substantial amounts of responsibility"* on offer for trainees, how does Burges Salmon ensure they're up to the task? For starters, trainees sit directly alongside their supervisor, usually a senior associate, *"which makes it easy to learn by example."* They're also assigned a trainee buddy from the year above and a dedicated partner principal, though sources revealed that in practice this is *"someone you'd only really go to if you'd exhausted all other routes."* Finally, there's plenty of structured training: *"Every time you move seats you have at least ten training sessions. On top of that are optional talks and seminars, and each department has its own training day."* New starters might be disappointed to learn that 'October Fest' is one such day rather than the piss-up the name implies.

Still, there's no shortage of opportunities to grab a beer with fellow lawyers. Trainees can join a social club that organises tickets to sports events and other outings, and on the last Friday of the month the firm puts on free drinks and food, a gathering well loved firmwide. *"They make a big effort to encourage people to socialise. Trainees go out at least once a week together, and we all go away for a weekend together each year."* Indeed, only one of the 46-strong cohort missed out the latest annual trip, which took place in Wales. The group is comprised of a mix of fresh grads and more seasoned workers, newcomers to Bristol and others with ties to the area alike. *"We're all hard workers but remain pretty modest about it – that's what I'd say trainees here have in common."*

According to interviewees, Burges Salmon takes its charity efforts as seriously as it does its socialising. It has a nominated charity of the year and carries out periodic fundraising initiatives on behalf of that cause. Over 2013 the firm managed to raise more than £100,000 for that's year's charity, the Grand Appeal. Meanwhile, everyone is permitted a day off a year to volunteer with an organisation of their choice, and the firm also offers legal assistance to various charities.

At the time of our calls, the firm's second-years had just received news of its retention results for 2014 – of 22 qualifiers, 20 netted an NQ role. The process is fairly simple: *"You meet with a member of HR and give your first and second choice of department, then you wait to hear,"* explained one insider. *"I get the impression that if you're flexible, your chances of a job are pretty good. The firm's growing, so management is keen to take people on."* As another interviewee reflected: *"It was great how many supervisors came out to congratulate people who'd landed roles. You don't expect that of an organisation with 600 people in it, but it's so easy to get to know people here on a personal level."*

And finally...
The work/life balance is not to be scoffed at here, where departures around 8pm constitute *"a fairly late night,"* according to trainees.

Capsticks Solicitors LLP

The facts

Location: London, Birmingham, Leeds, Southampton

Number of UK partners/solicitors: 51/161

Partners who trained at firm: 20%

Total number of trainees: 15

Seats: 6x4 months

Alternative seats: none

Extras: pro bono – Wimbledon pro bono law centre, Wimbledon Guild

On chambersstudent.co.uk...

How to get into Capsticks

The Health and Social Care Act

This specialist firm has a handle on one of the leading healthcare practices in the country.

Old Mews

Much like the Wombles, Capsticks has long called Wimbledon its home. Whereas its furry neighbours have spent the past 30 years singing the praises of recycling, however, Capsticks has used that time to build up its health and social care expertise (an equally commendable endeavour in our opinion). Today the firm is a leading light in both sectors, earning top-band nationwide *Chambers UK* rankings for its clinical negligence, professional discipline and healthcare practices, plus top marks for its social housing work in the South following the 2013 acquisition of a 25-strong social housing team from Coffin Mew.

Most of Capsticks' output is done on behalf of the NHS, looking after national entities like the Department of Health, the NHS Litigation Authority and NHS England. Lawyers also advise regional trusts. Lawyers have lent their expertise to inquests into the Hillsborough disaster, the 7/7 bombings and the Jimmy Savile scandal. Insiders rightly pointed out that while the firm's scope lends itself to an array of interesting cases, it would be foolhardy to sign on hoping to work outside the health and social care spheres. *"It's all healthcare clients here,"* confirmed one, adding: *"The upside to that is that you get a really deep insight into the industry."*

Until 2008 Capsticks was a one-site operator, but openings over the previous six years it expanded to Birmingham, Leeds and Southampton. *"There's no sense that the enthusiasm for growth is waning, either,"* chimed in a trainee. *"The firm has an ambitious growth plan and is determined to continue expanding in its key areas. It's an exciting time to be involved here."* At the time of our interviews there were 12 trainees in London, plus one each in Southampton and Leeds, and as of September 2014 there's a Birmingham trainee too. It's worth noting that in 2013/14 all 14 of the firm's trainees were women. The firm indicated that this was a bit of a fluke – two male trainees started in September 2014.

Tearjerkers and tummy ticklers

Trainees work their way through six four-month seats drawn from the firm's five departments: clinical law, real estate, employment, dispute resolution and commercial. Generally they complete a seat in every department and then return to the area they'd like to qualify into for their final four months. *"Towards the end of each seat we meet with someone from HR and give our preferences,"* one source explained. *"Second-years get priority, but you know you'll get your top picks at some point."*

Clinical law is the firm's largest department and contains both negligence and advisory branches. The former tends to attract greater interest thanks to the *"gripping and often pretty squeamish"* cases it handles. *"Sometimes you'll get a bit of shock when you flick through a medical record and come across some unpleasant pictures."* There are some *"quite upsetting"* cases – for example, matters involving disabled or brain-damaged children. *"With those you have to try to stand back and be impartial, which can be difficult."* Balancing these out are *"lighter"* files wherein people have fallen off chairs or out with their

> **Seat options:** clinical law; real estate; employment; dispute resolution; commercial

The True Picture

Chambers UK rankings

Administrative & Public Law	Healthcare
Clinical Negligence	Professional Discipline
Employment	Social Housing

therapist. Quite a bit of responsibility is doled out to trainees for both types of cases. *"It's a really busy department, so they rely on us to contact experts and claimant solicitors."* As one testified, *"half my time was spent handling my own matters, some of which were six-figure cases. I got to draft the defences and make settlement offers, and even attended a hearing in central London."*

Capsticks' dispute resolution group has commercial, property and regulatory teams. *"We basically deal with health regulators seeking to remove doctors, dentists or pharmacists who've breached their duties,"* summed up a trainee of the latter team. *"The work is really interesting. I've done a bit of bundling, but I've also taken witness statements and prepared court documents."* Meanwhile the commercial contingent oversees contractual disputes, fraud cases and procurement challenges *"wherein companies providing services to the NHS are unhappy with the way things have been carried out."* This group delves into a bit of IP work too. Finally there's the property subset, which has seen *"a big influx of work recently"* owing to the newly added social housing group in Southampton as well as the abolition of Primary Care Trusts (PCTs) following the 2012 launch of the Health and Social Care Act. *"I've been helping my supervisor with some cases involving squatters living in old medical centres,"* reported one interviewee, while another told of advising a trust on their options when a number of patients refused to leave their hospital beds.

The firm's real estate lawyers advise both public and private sector healthcare clients, recently overseeing Community Health Partnerships' takeover of 294 health estates worth a whopping £1.5bn following the dissolution of PCTs. *"The department is smaller than some, so occasionally you're given low-value matters to handle yourself."* Over in commercial it's all about *"getting to grips with NHS structure and how it operates."* Shared one trainee: *"I worked on mergers, acquisitions, procurement contacts and competition matters, and I helped advise trusts on how to implement savings."*

Dr. Feelgood

The firm runs department-specific training throughout the year to help bring newbies up to scratch with the ins and outs of the sectors it dabbles in. Trainees are expected to rock up to as many sessions as possible, which those based in the regions can access via video conference. Additionally everybody's assigned an associate supervisor for each seat who handles reviews. *"Most work comes through your supervisor,"* we're told, though we hear the open-plan office *"makes it easy to pick up tasks from anyone in the department."*

Atmosphere can vary between departments, but Capsticks is *"a sociable and accessible place."* Sources credited the open-plan set-up with preventing *"a head-down approach where everyone's cordoned off in their own little space; generally there's a bit of banter in the office. You'll get into a lift and actually talk to the people because you've already seen them around."* They also told us sitting among their superiors goes a long way in lessening the barriers between ranks. *"All of the partners here are very nice – I feel like I can interrupt them with questions about anything,"* said a London resident. Meanwhile in Leeds *"the seniors are all very approachable. It's so nice to have people you respect willing to stop to have a cup of tea."*

Trainees in London can often be found propping up a bar on a Friday night or even taking weekend trips together. Regional trainees occasionally join in on get-togethers if they're in town and told us they're *"looking forward to the future when there are more trainees out here and therefore some more organised activities."* The firm likes to keep things low-key for the most part, but we hear festivities can get a little rambunctious around Christmas, when Londoners participate in the firm's time-old tradition of donning *"dubious"* seasonal garb and parading around the firm, selling cakes for charity. *"It's a quite embarrassing right of passage,"* one told us.

The firm recently established a junior lawyers' committee to provide a forum for planning social activities as well as *"a platform for people to express any grievances they might have. The head of HR came to our last meeting – they're willing to take on board our feedback."* In 2014 Capsticks retained four of its six qualifiers.

And finally...

"A lot of people who get the training contracts here have some kind of connection to medical law or the healthcare sector. If you can't demonstrate knowledge of the current issues, you'll struggle."

Charles Russell LLP

The facts

Location: London, Cheltenham, Guildford

Number of UK partners/solicitors: 93/221

Partners who trained at firm: 19%

Total number of trainees: 33

Seats: 4x6 months

Alternative seats: Geneva, secondments

Extras: pro bono – Surrey Law Centre; Bethnal Green Law Centre; RCJ CAB; LawWorks

On chambersstudent.co.uk...

How to get into Charles Russell Speechlys

More on the CR-Speechly merger

Interview with senior partner Christopher Page

Charles Russell will be adding Speechlys to its name and £57m to its revenue once it merges with fellow private client big'un Speechly Bircham in late 2014.

Wedding Speech

Charles Russell has achieved the rather unusual feat of operating under the same name since its establishment in 1891. Things will change on this front after the Londoner's merger with Speechly Bircham in November 2014, but only just: the new firm will be known as Charles Russell Speechlys. Of course, there are far bigger changes in store from a foundational point of view – the merger will be quite the shake-up for Charles Russell, more than doubling its lawyer head count (bringing it up to 500) and boosting revenue enough that the newly beefed-up shop will sit comfortably in the UK's top 30 firms. Speechlys' current managing partner James Carter is set to head up the newly merged entity from November onwards.

For Charles Russell, the union will, among other things, help it economise on its expensive London premises; meanwhile Speechlys will benefit from the new-found ability to offer lower rates for certain types of work through Charles Russell's well-established offices in Guildford and Cheltenham. This merger is a meeting of minds as well as pockets. Both firms are best known for servicing well-heeled private clients – each has a long track record of *Chambers UK* rankings in this area – though they're keen to consolidate their other practice areas. There are plans to reorganise into four primary divisions: business services; litigation and dispute resolution; private client; and real estate and construction. Both firms will increase their respective international presence as well. Both Charles Russell and Speechlys have an office in Geneva, but the latter's European presence also comprises bases in Zürich, Luxembourg and Paris;

meanwhile Charles Russell brings some Middle Eastern coverage to the table, recently launching a construction and real estate-focused office in Doha to complement its existing outpost in Bahrain. According to our sources, further international expansion will be a priority post-merger.

Because of their wealthy clientele – which, for these firms, includes landed gentry and celebrities alike – private client shops often attract a reputation for being traditional in their dealings. In previous years trainees at Charles Russell have told of *"a certain charm"* echoed by the firm's wood-panelled meeting rooms and ever so polite partners; Speechlys, on the other hand, has long favoured some slightly more modern touches – including open-plan offices and an elaborate recycling scheme – and has made no bones about its desire to grow on the corporate finance and IP sides. With the latter's MP at the helm of the new firm, we wouldn't be surprised if these ways of working prevail under the new Charles Russell banner.

Guildford youth

At the time of our calls, Charles Russell had 25 trainees in London, eight in Guildford and four in Cheltenham.

> **Seat options:** family; private client; real estate; property litigation; employment; insolvency; litigation; construction and engineering; banking; corporate/commercial; IP

The True Picture

Chambers UK rankings

Agriculture & Rural Affairs	Intellectual Property
Banking & Finance	Litigation
Capital Markets	Media & Entertainment
Charities	Planning
Construction	Private Client
Corporate/M&A	Professional Discipline
Defamation/Reputation	Professional Negligence
Management	Real Estate
Employment	Real Estate Litigation
Family/Matrimonial	Restructuring/Insolvency
Fraud	Retail
Healthcare	Sports Law
Information Technology	Telecommunications

Seat allocation sees trainees list three preferences at the start of each seat. Post-merger options haven't yet been confirmed but in London will most likely include a few new areas like IP and technology, plus a newly widened range of secondments and overseas seats. There's a smaller choice of seats in the regional offices, with secondments and the Geneva seat reserved for Londoners.

Charles Russell is one of five firms in London that earns top rankings in *Chambers UK* for private client work, and post-merger the firm will dominate the market in size as well as reputation. A seat with the team is a popular choice. Interviewees reported working with landed estates, super-rich foreign clients and even royalty. *"I got to visit an estate owner at their beautiful house in West London to take instructions, but with overseas clients it's mostly by telephone or Skype."* Work here ranges far and wide: on the advisory side there's tax and trust structuring, probate and estate administration, Court of Protection and immigration advice; meanwhile the contentious trusts side of the practice handles trust, probate, charity litigation, and Court of Protection and property ownership disputes. *"It's the most traditional department in the firm, with a clear hierarchy, though that works well – there's very much a teacher/pupil structure, which is good for learning. You're always invited to meetings to talk through clients' needs, and once you understand the nature of the department, there's a lot of responsibility."* Trainees with experience here had completed first drafts of wills and trusts and assisted with powers of attorney. The latter task *"is the kind you oversee yourself, dealing with the clients from the off. Having to take accurate instructions and translate them into a final document really hones your skills. By the end of my seat I was contributing to meetings."*

The firm also runs a private client seat in Geneva, where lawyers help expats manage their finances, investments and tax responsibilities. It's not uncommon for trainees here to get involved in calculation-heavy Liechtenstein disclosures, part of a taxpayer compliance programme under which people who haven't paid tax to HMRC on offshore assets can escape criminal proceedings. *"It's very rare that you meet such clients – they tend to stay as far removed from the process as they can."* Among the spoils of residing abroad is *"a very posh flat in a massive old terrace of houses, ten minutes' walk from Lake Geneva. There's a good social life in the office, plus lots of cultural festivals in the summer."*

Coco-nuts

At the time of our calls Charles Russell's corporate/commercial department was split into three subgroups – corporate M&A, banking and capital markets, and commercial contracts – with trainees able to do a split seat between two of these areas. The commercial group works with an impressive range of clients, including Nike, ITV, Wagamama, Tesco and Sotheby's. The team recently assisted the Barbados government with endeavours to grant licences for offshore oil and gas exploration, and defended Paddy Power against objections to *"cheeky"* publicity stunts like the high-street bookie's 2014 'money back if he walks' campaign aired during the Oscar Pistorius trial. Over in corporate, lawyers have kept busy advising Travelzest on its administration following its failure to take naturist holidays mainstream, a matter which involved the sale of two (clothes on, thankfully) Canadian subsidiaries. *"It's pretty low responsibility at first – you're mostly doing research and helping out on secretarial stuff,"* said a source with experience on the M&A side. *"But eventually there's a chance to draft ancillary documents. Partners keep a close supervisory role, but there's enough responsibility to keep things interesting."* Elsewhere, a trainee who'd focused on finance described their role in a mezzanine financing of a property development: *"There were lots of parties involved, which made it complicated. I gathered conditions precedent, did the fact checking, drafted the first draft of our opinion and attended the completion. It was a good level of experience."*

Litigation is one of the firm's biggest departments, with disputes spanning the sport, IP, property, pharmaceutical, fraud and commercial spheres. High-profile representations of late include acting for Baker Tilly as liquidators in a $9.2bn fraud case against Awal Bank, and defending The FA against an appeal made in light of its decision to relegate the Doncaster Rovers Belles from the top tier of the Women's Super League. Debt recovery cases are typical trainee fare – *"essentially you issue proceedings against old clients who haven't paid, which gives you really valuable experience going back and forth with them"* – and though advocacy isn't terribly common among new recruits, one did report *"going to court on a case for a cost-conscious client. It was just me and the barrister, which was a great experience."* Others told of taking notes, attending meetings with counsel and taking a crack at first drafts of letters to clients, claims and cost schedules *"where possible."*

Good-time Charlies

Sources tell us a major priority post-merger is *"getting everyone in London under one roof as quickly as possible,"* most likely in one of the legacy firm's existing offices. Charles Russell's City branch, *"right in the thick of things, near St Paul's,"* is no doubt a tempting choice. The modern edifice has marble floors and *"glass everywhere,"* plus a subsidised canteen dubbed Charlie's. *"It's a nice place to get chatting to people around the firm."* Still, the lower rents in Speechlys' New Street Square premises make it a more likely destination for the economically minded new firm. Over in Guildford, interviewees were excitedly awaiting a move, telling us *"the current office is quite tired, but the new one is very modern and spacious."* The roomier the better, seeing as this branch might well play host to outsourced support staff post-merger. Cheltenham, on the other hand, remains still a bastion of tradition for now. *"It's old and designed like a rabbit warren, with a big wooden Georgian staircase straight out of a Jane Austen novel."*

Among our interviewees, the consensus was that *"we're a traditional firm, and that's by no account a bad thing. It's a testament to the standard of quality we've perpetuated over the years and simply means we have a reputation to uphold."* It helps that *"there are lots of Russells still running around,"* including recently retired senior partner Patrick Russell, who *"still pops in now and again. It's nice to have that family atmosphere."* Trainees told of certain steadfastly old-school elements of life at the firm – *"hard-copy memos are returned formally, for instance"* – and even mentioned a few downright old-fashioned customs like the way *"certain people rely on Dictaphones rather than more computer-savvy methods of note-taking."* The Cheltenham office, as its rich interiors suggest, *"particularly likes to cater to our heritage. We have wood-panelled meeting rooms, and partners prefer you to use a fountain pen when you meet a client."*

As you might expect, *"Charles Russell attracts a certain type of person – there's a fairly strong South East, Oxbridge contingent here."* Still, sources were keen to say: *"People shouldn't be put off by that; we're not all twin-set and pearls Oxford grads."* In any case, this distinctive demographic is likely to be diluted after the merger. The firm doesn't run many trainee-specific socials, *"but we do meet up for lunch whenever we can, and people often pile into the pub next door after work, especially when the weather's nice."* As far as firm-wide events go, there's a sports dinner held each year in a fancy London restaurant, though couch potatoes need not fear – *"it only has a very loose reference to sports."* There's also a summer boat party and a well-received Christmas carol concert. *"Last year we listened to a couple of partners and associates who'd formed a string quartet, then we all choked back mince pies and mulled wine."*

With merger plans simmering away, it's little surprise qualification proved a tricky process in 2014. Our interviewees – who were in the middle of applying at the time of our calls – revealed that several commercial and litigation roles were retracted after appearing on the jobs list. *"It all feels slightly chaotic and up in the air. We haven't got much information."* In the end the firm managed to keep on 12 of its 19 qualifiers.

And finally...

Applicants interested in Charles Russell should keep their ears open and eyes peeled for news on the coming merger and how it will affect future trainees. The firm's growing international ambitions suggest foreign language skills in particular will be at a premium in years to come.

The True Picture

Cleary Gottlieb Steen & Hamilton LLP

The facts

Location: London

Number of UK partners/solicitors: 14/50 (+ 23 non-UK-qualified)

Total number of trainees: 25

Seats: 4x6 months

Alternative seats: overseas seats; secondments

Extras: pro bono – LawWorks

On chambersstudent.co.uk...

How to get into Cleary

Internationalists

Interview with graduate recruitment
   partner Richard Sultman

If you're a right clever clogs with an eye for international work, this could be the firm for you. Just *"don't apply if you have sharp elbows."*

Clear vision

A small assemblage of lawyers founded Cleary Gottlieb in New York and Washington, DC in 1946, and paddled the Atlantic a mere three years later to set up shop in Paris. Upon its arrival to the Old World, this Yankee firm suited up and got to work mopping up the gargantuan mess that was post-war Europe, its efforts spurred on by George Ball – one of the founding partners – and his close relationship with the chief architect of the European Community. Lawyers had a hand in advising on the Marshall Plan (aka the European Recovery Program) as well as an economic strategy for the war-weary continent, a move that paved the way for the foundation of the European Coal and Steel Community, the first treaty organisation of the EU.

Today Cleary remains one of the most reputable firms in the world for sovereign finance work, having scooped numerous industry awards over the years, including a handful for its role as international counsel during Greece's €206bn debt restructuring in 2011. London – part of an eight-office European network – busies itself with finance, capital markets and M&A work in particular, all of which comes highly recommended by *Chambers UK*. Lawyers also handle tax, antitrust, regulatory, IP, litigation and arbitration matters.

It's not just Europe that's welcomed Cleary: the firm has six more outposts across Asia, Latin America and, thanks to its 2012 debut in Abu Dhabi, the Middle East.

Musical chairs

As part of its *"hallmark generalist culture,"* Cleary operates under a non-departmental structure. For trainees this translates into being formally assigned to seats, but still given the freedom to flit between practice areas in search of work. Trainees do have a supervisor who assigns them work too. According to graduate recruitment partner Richard Sultman, the reasoning behind this fluid approach is that *"it makes lawyers more adaptable to market situations, and gives people the opportunity to gain transferable skills and develop as a whole."* While we hear darting back and forth between unrelated files *"is not for the faint-hearted,"* our interviewees praised the system for allowing them to tailor their interests and see matters *"all the way through, even if your seat is over."* They also told us that specialisation isn't impossible; there are a few areas – including litigation, competition, tax and employment – where lawyers *"tend to work almost exclusively within their practice."*

Trainees communicate their seat preferences to HR before they join the firm, and then before each seat change. *"People almost always get their first or second choice,"* sources said, adding that preference is given to second-years. *"It's a positive experience – HR does a fantastic*

Seat options: capital markets; finance; M&A; emerging markets M&A; funds; disputes; competition; tax; financial regulation; IP; employment

Chambers UK rankings

Banking & Finance	Corporate/M&A
Banking Litigation	Litigation
Capital Markets	Private Equity
Competition/European Law	

job of listening to us and making recommendations." Finance, M&A and capital markets – the house specialities – were the most common seats across our sample of interviewees.

International seats are incredibly popular at Cleary; the current options are New York, Washington DC, Abu Dhabi, Hong Kong, Beijing, Moscow, Paris and Brussels. Language skills are a factor in who goes where: *"English is generally fine, but it's likely they'll prioritise people who speak the local language."* Those who don't fancy taking the overseas plunge still have plenty of chances to interact with their cross-border colleagues. In fact, our interviewees told of working on *"almost exclusively international"* matters back at home, with some even reporting they'd *"never been involved in a deal that was purely based in the UK."*

When the music stops

"The firm makes no pretensions that it expects a lot from its trainees," agreed our sources, telling us *"you're treated like a lawyer from day one."* This is especially visible in the capital markets seat, where *"there's not much handholding,"* and headline-worthy, high-profile transactions are the norm. *"It's scary at first,"* admitted one trainee, *"but you get better quickly because of the experience."* The team specialises in emerging markets, particularly those in eastern Europe, sourcing a good deal of work through the Moscow office. In 2013 Cleary continued its streak as the principal international legal adviser to Russia by counselling on its $7bn senior unsecured bond offering – one of the largest local currency Eurobonds, and the largest ever for the rouble. Lawyers also recently advised the underwriters in a $1bn senior unsecured bond offering by Nigeria.

For trainees, capital markets work often takes the form of IPO filings, which typically involve research, annotation, prospectus drafting, reviewing capital markets opinions and, in many cases, liaising directly with clients. *"Every deal I did involved a different industry, from supermarkets and fruit wholesalers to terminal operators and pharmaceutical companies,"* testified one, while another told of working on a bond issuance for *"a company with operations in Bulgaria, Greece, Romania and Ukraine. A lot of the deals we work on involve multiple jurisdictions."*

While an M&A seat often saddles trainees with *"lengthy amounts of due diligence,"* we hear it's a good department for *"volunteering yourself to take the plunge – they make no secret that you can take on as much responsibility as you feel you need."* One trainee excitedly reported: *"I encountered the highest level work I've had so far here. I was left to conference call with clients on my own, and the senior lawyers were even happy for me to correspond with clients without copying them in."* Trainees can expect a lot of private equity work, much of which draws on the expertise of other offices in Cleary's network – for example, the firm's recent representation of Bank of America Merrill Lynch in a $1bn acquisition by Julius Baer, which covered more than 20 jurisdictions and involved lawyers in New York, Paris, Rome, Milan and Hong Kong. Other clients in recent years include investment giants like TPG and Renaissance Capital, as well as global behemoths Coca-Cola and American Express.

Like their M&A counterparts, trainees in finance described high levels of client contact. Typical tasks here include assisting issuers in ongoing disclosures, keeping up to date with regulatory developments, coordinating documents for clients and listing agents, and producing first drafts of ancillary documents. Speaking of the department's high expectations, one source said: *"You'll be given work that you're in complete control over; if it's not done right, someone will catch it, but you'll likely piss that someone off."* In one major deal of late, the firm acted as counsel for Greece during its recent loan agreements with the European Financial Stability Facility, a matter which involved debt facilities in excess of 150bn.

The competition team has also got its hands on some newsworthy matters lately, including Google's $12.5bn acquisition of Motorola Mobility. We're told that the technical nature of the work and the fact that *"decisions tend to be made with input from a lot of people"* mean that trainees here see *"slightly less"* responsibility in this seat than in others. Still, there are plenty of *"interesting"* tasks on hand, from preparing documents and responding to requests for information to reading annual reports and undertaking legal research. *"We work closely with Brussels when matters involve European elements, which is an informative experience."*

Divide and conquer

Before they step over the threshold of City Place House in Moorgate, trainees must complete the LPC at the nearby University of Law, a requirement they saw no problem with. *"On day one, you join among friends."* The friendliness doesn't stop there; our sources enthusiastically described a *"nice"* and *"relaxed"* atmosphere across the firm in which *"there is a readiness to help people out, to make time, to chat about work and to share what you're doing with other people."* An emphasis on teamwork means sharp elbows don't go over well. *"Self sufficiency is expected, but you won't do well if you're the kind of person who hoards work and doesn't play well with others."*

When it comes to hierarchy, we're told it's *"pretty flat,"* a dynamic that sees trainees' views *"respected and considered. There's no monopoly on smarts here; you don't feel like you have to keep schtum just because you're not a partner."* Perhaps this willingness to listen to those on the lower end of the totem pole comes from the *"high value"* the firm places on academics. According to our insiders, *"the calibre of intellectual engagement is very high here, and they look for driven, successful people."* Cleary doesn't limit its recruitment to a specific pool of institutions, but partner Andrew Shutter does admit that *"inevitably, many of the best CVs come from Oxford and Cambridge"* and other top universities like Durham and London. That said, he's quick to point out that *"we like to diversify in terms of where people come from,"* and indeed our sample of interviewees was hardly limited to Oxbridge grads.

While the London office is *"nothing to write home about,"* insiders agreed the *"dated"* digs are *"very comfortable"* and *"do the job."* There are *"spacious"* work areas dotted around the firm's three floors (which strangely are the ground, third and fifth levels), plus a subsidised cafeteria that serves *"great hot food."* Those with their eyes on something a little more glitzy will no doubt be pleased with the rumours that management is considering upping sticks to a more spacious locale in 2015. The firm's London digs are certainly bulking up: in 2014 all 11 qualifiers were kept on.

For the time being, the Cleary bunch looks set to continue frequenting their pub of choice, Davy's, a nearby watering hole favoured *"largely for geographical reasons."* Weekly five-a-side football games and periodic wine and cheese evenings provide additional forums for cross-generational socialising, while the 24-strong trainee group makes an effort to assemble as a whole *"maybe once or twice a month."* Of course, it's not uncommon for busy schedules to keep the social stuff at bay. *"When it gets busy, you can be in the office all night,"* our sources confessed, *"and sometimes you're called into work on evenings or weekends at very little notice."* Fortunately, such disruptions only happen rarely. Said one source with more than a tad of relief: *"When I joined, I thought the hours would mean I'd have to kiss my boyfriend goodbye, but it hasn't been like that at all."*

And finally...
Past years have seen male trainees vastly outnumber their female counterparts at Cleary, but we're happy to report there's no skew in this year's evenly split cohort.

Clifford Chance LLP

The facts

Location: London

Number of UK partners/solicitors: 161/526

Total number of trainees: 200

Seats: 4x6 months

Alternative seats: overseas seats, secondments

Extras: Mary Ward and other legal advice centres; language classes

On chambersstudent.co.uk...

How to get into Clifford Chance

A history of the firm

More on seats and secondments

There's no denying that Clifford Chance works its trainees hard, but those who can stand the heat are given excellent opportunities for international travel and can work on some of the world's top deals.

All that glitters is gold

Management at magic circler Clifford Chance must be feeling pretty smug right now. Revenue in 2013/14 reached the highest levels ever, up 7% on the previous year to £1.359bn, and new offices in Saudi Arabia and Indonesia have lifted the office count to 36 in 26 countries. There's no doubt this firm is one of the world's global legal heavyweights: it picks up tons of rankings in *Chambers Global* and our other guides, with over a dozen tier-one rankings at a global-wide level, for practices including banking and finance, capital markets, corporate/M&A, projects and insolvency.

As this list suggests, it's transactional work that rules the roost at CC, and within that it's traditionally the finance practice that shines the brightest: areas like banking and finance, capital markets and asset finance do just a smidge better in *Chambers UK* than the corporate and litigation practices. We don't want to belabour that point too much, though; the litigation and corporate teams are still among the very best in the global and UK market. But everything's relative when your best is so very, very good.

London trainees can bask in the fact that they work in the firm's global nerve centre – the UK produces 35% of total revenue. Many massive deals are run from London, and trainees cooed to us about working on ground-breaking transactions that are *"part of economic history."* For example, Clifford Chance advised HSBC on its role in the Treasury's inaugural offering of an Islamic sukuk bond, valued at £200m. Lawyers also acted for 13 banks (including Goldman Sachs, Commerzbank, ING, Sumi-

tomo Mitsui and the Royal Bank of Canada) on a £1.4bn post-IPO facility for Royal Mail, cementing that institution's transformation from government-backed entity to corporate colossus.

Given the firm's transactional prowess, it's unsurprising trainees are expected to visit the core areas of finance, capital markets and corporate. Now, imagine you're trying to navigate this expectation surrounded by 200 fellow trainees who are also vying for their top preferences. This will give you an impression of the juggling act that is seat allocation at CC. Still, our interviewees were all happy with the seats they'd undertaken, saying the firm is prepared to turn a blind eye if the odd trainee wants to sidestep a compulsory seat. Some years seats in the smaller practices are heavily oversubscribed, but trainees this year found *"there's not so much competition for things like employment."* That said, most of our interviewees had concentrated their training contracts on finance and corporate seats, so expect similar if you get a place at CC.

Seat options: project finance; asset finance; insolvency finance; general banking and finance; derivatives and regulatory; real estate finance; capital markets; M&A; private equity; financial institutions; private funds; antitrust; technology, media and telecommunications; litigation and dispute resolution; real estate; real estate planning and environment; real estate litigation; construction; tax pensions; employment; employee benefits

Chambers UK rankings

Administrative & Public Law	Insurance
Asset Finance	International Arbitration
Banking & Finance	Investment Funds
Banking Litigation	Litigation
Capital Markets	Outsourcing
Commodities	Parliamentary & Public Affairs
Competition/European Law	Partnership
Construction	Pensions
Corporate Crime & Investigations	Planning
Corporate/M&A	Private Equity
Data Protection	Projects
Employee Share Schemes & Incentives	Public International Law
Employment	Real Estate
Energy & Natural Resources	Real Estate Finance
Environment	Real Estate Litigation
Financial Services	Restructuring/Insolvency
Fraud	Retail
Hotels & Leisure	Social Housing
Information Technology	Tax
	Telecommunications
	Transport

The levers of global capitalism

Under the heading of 'finance' trainees can pick from quite a number of seat options: general banking; asset finance; project finance; derivatives and regulatory; real estate finance; and insolvency. In the general banking group, you could end up working on *"huge leveraged finance deals worth billions."* A lot of the work has cross-border features too. For example, along with colleagues in New York, Luxembourg, Amsterdam, Frankfurt and Warsaw, London lawyers recently advised a group of six major global banks on a €1.97bn loan to private equity firm BC Partners to support its acquisition of German publishing house Springer. A trainee's role often revolves around project management; this invariably involves co-ordinating lawyers across different jurisdictions. *"The qualified lawyers are incredibly busy, so it falls on me to make sure everything gets done,"* said one interviewee. Trainees also get to oversee the signing and closing processes, and often serve as a go-between for client and team – *"clients often prefer to call a trainee because they can ask basic questions without looking stupid."*

An alternative option within the practice group is asset finance. A lot of the work revolves around aircraft transactions, although one source joked that the closest you're likely to get to a jet plane is a slip of paper outlining its value. Rookies are soon trusted to run small deals by themselves, drafting documents, meeting clients and taking care of closings. In the derivatives seat, *"It was exciting but challenging to work on cutting-edge transactions which had never been done before in the market,"* said one source. *"Even partners had a job trying to get their heads around them at times."* The financial regulation seat is more research-based, and working in the aftermath of the financial crisis means trainees have to keep abreast of rapidly developing EU and UK policy. *"It can be quite a political seat at times."* There's a lot of client contact: one interviewee had to pinch themselves when the general counsel of a bank asked for their business card following a presentation they'd given.

Trainees told us that in capital markets they'd taken a stab at drafting a whole range of documents and had been given plenty of chances to escape the office when driving across town to meet clients. Current trainees had been tasked with running company board meetings, and guiding clients and lawyers around a room in which they'd set out hundreds of documents for signing. *"Because of the type and size of the deals we do, it's usually a large part of the company or borrower's business that's at stake."* Structured debt work is *"very technical,"* and sources who'd sat with the team had particularly enjoyed conducting the complex research these transactions necessitate. CC has made sure to tap into the emerging markets base. The group recently worked on a $400m Eurobond issued by the Rwandan government.

Like finance, the massive corporate group has a glut of subgroups: M&A; private equity; private funds; financial institutions; technology, media and telecommunications; and antitrust. Deals here regularly reach into the billions, and the team is pretty much on a par with finance in terms of the clients it attracts – top ones include HSBC and Shell. Trainees in the M&A seat need only switch on *BBC Breakfast* to find out that a deal they've worked on has successfully closed overnight.

Visit chambersstudent.co.uk, where we have a lot more to say about Clifford Chance and its corporate and disputes work, its overseas seats, and the lifestyle and culture at this *"huge, hardcore, corporate firm."*

What is a 'good' university in the eyes of a recruiter?

Should I do a Master's degree?

How do I get work experience?

How diverse are my chosen firms?

Which law firms give away the best freebies at job fairs?

The True Picture

We answer all these questions and more on
Chambersstudent.co.uk

Follow us on Twitter and Facebook for commercial
awareness updates.

Clyde & Co LLP

The facts

Locations: London, Guildford, Oxford, Manchester
Number of UK partners/solicitors: 164/939
Total number of trainees: 80
Seats: 4x6 months
Alternative seats: overseas seats, secondments
Extras: pro bono; language classes

On chambersstudent.co.uk...

How to get into Clyde & Co
Barlow (C)Lyde & Gilbert
A guide to Guildford
Clyde worldwide

From Sydney to London, Clyde & Co has a formidable international reach to complement its broadening skill set.

The big Clyde world

Clyde & Co has long been a part of the international scene after establishing its first overseas outpost in Hong Kong nearly 30 years ago. That said, it's only over the past few years that this London-headquartered firm has propelled itself towards global stardom. After merging with fellow insurance guru Barlow Lyde & Gilbert (BLG) in November 2011, Clydes went on to open offices in Tripoli, Sydney, Perth, Madrid, Atlanta and Beijing, and, since the start of 2014, three further areas – Cape Town, Johannesburg and Orange County – bringing its office tally to 36 (and counting). Trainees told us they'd be surprised if such expansion efforts tailed off any time soon, and praised the firm for its *"well-thought-out strategy of moving into the markets where our clients want us to be."* This MO has certainly paid off from a financial perspective: Clydes' revenue rose by 17% in 2012/13, and by a further 8.5% in 2013/14. It now stands at more than £365m.

Clydes' UK presence spans bases in London, Oxford, Manchester and Guildford. Together, these rake in around 60% of the firm's total earnings. At the time of our calls, seven of the firm's 80 trainees were stationed in Manchester, with the rest based in London. Those who are pursuing a training contract at the headquarters should know that *"the way departments are set up means you're very likely to have to make do with a seat in Guildford,"* although as one source pointed out, *"there isn't enough space for everyone to go, so if Guildford isn't your thing, you might find yourself lucky."* In any case, trainees with experience there have consistently told of favourable working hours and high-quality work over the years. And, as one added, *"there are far worse places in the world than Guildford!"*

Clydes is best known for its litigation, shipping and insurance practices, although *Chambers UK* recognises that the firm's breadth of expertise, awarding rankings to practices as varied as insurance (contentious and non-contentious), real estate, personal injury, shipping finance and mid-market M&A. And we'd be remiss not to mention Clydes' impressive headway on the transactional front in recent years. The firm's corporate and transactional practices experienced a 17% hike in revenue in 2013/14, and insiders revealed that *"the focus going forward is on strengthening that aspect of our work."*

Stirring up trouble

In addition to expressing three-seat preferences before each rotation, trainees can submit a written summary of their current seat experience during the seat allocation process. *"It's not compulsory, so not everyone does it, but it is useful, especially if you want a particular seat."* said one. As one trainee pointed out, Clydes *"should be one of the first names on your list"* if you're after a firm with a top-notch insurance offering. Strong on both contentious and non-contentious sides, the department acts on behalf of virtually every major insurer in the country, including Aviva, Zurich, AXA, AIG and Direct Line, to name but a few. The team also handles matters for companies with

Seat options: professional and commercial disputes (PCD); employment; general corporate; corporate insurance; projects and construction; casualty and healthcare; marine, construction and energy insurance; catastrophic injury; international trade/arbitration; aviation litigation; property; banking and ship finance

Chambers UK rankings

Asset Finance	International Arbitration
Aviation	Litigation
Banking Litigation	Pensions
Clinical Negligence	Personal Injury
Commodities	Planning
Construction	Police Law
Corporate/M&A	Product Liability
Data Protection	Professional Discipline
Employment	Professional Negligence
Energy & Natural	Projects
Resources	Public International Law
Environment	Real Estate
Fraud	Real Estate Finance
Health & Safety	Real Estate Litigation
Healthcare	Retail
Information Technology	Shipping
Insurance	Transport

operations far beyond UK shores – in 2013, for example, lawyers represented Ironshore Insurance in a dispute surrounding hurricane damage to some offshore oil wells in the Gulf of Mexico. On the non-contentious side, lawyers have been busy assisting Enstar with the Bermuda-born group's $692m purchase of global insurance specialist Torus Insurance Holdings.

The department houses a number of subgroups, including general insurance, insurance/reinsurance, political risk and marine, construction and energy – all of which take on trainees. *"You'll find yourself receiving work from both your designated team and the other teams in the department. It all depends on where the demand is, really."* Marine, construction and energy is among the biggest of the subgroups and provides trainees with a healthy spread of tasks: *"There's in-depth research, bundling and filing, plus a fair amount of drafting too for things like witness statements, claim forms, settlement agreements and correspondence with courts."* The team is big on the industry networking scene, so *"expect to attend a lot of client functions."*

There's no shortage of contentious seats at Clydes. The most coveted of these is PCD, which trainees noted is a legacy BLG department and *"could almost be a standalone firm in its own right,"* such is its size. Much of the work here revolves around professional negligence claims, an area in which the firm has made a real name for itself. At the time of writing, the team was defending magic-circle member Clifford Chance in a high-profile case concerning a financial derivatives transaction brought against it by a German public body. There are pockets of other types of work available in the team too, including property and commercial litigation. It's not uncommon to get court exposure during the seat: one inter-

viewee was tasked with taking notes at a hearing at the Royal Courts of Justice within their first couple of weeks, while another got to observe a mediation not long after starting. But back at the office, it's all about case-specific research, drafting letters to clients and the opposing side, and handling bundling and doc review.

Casualty and healthcare – another popular contentious seat – covers personal injury and clinical negligence work. *"The exposure is great – claims vary wildly in size, and fee earners can have between 30 and 40 cases going on at any one time."* Typical trainee tasks in this seat include detailing settlement and cost estimates for insurer clients, carrying out witness interviews, *"often without any supervision,"* and attending hearings with counsel.

Meanwhile, the employment group has a stellar client base featuring big-name entities such as UPS, Santander, the *Financial Times* and Estée Lauder. Lawyers regularly advise the latter on its employment law requirements in the UK, recently assisting with disciplinary proceedings against nine members of staff following inappropriate comments posted on Facebook (we're guessing they forgot about the privacy settings). In this case, trainees prepared witness statements and compiled case summaries for clients as well taking on non-contentious duties like advisory work for trade unions.

That sinking feeling

Shipping law remains at the heart of Clydes' overall practice, and its crew of nautical eggheads advises on some of the most significant shipping incidents around. Take, for example, the 2013 sinking of the MOL Comfort – the firm's lawyers have been investigating the loss of roughly $350m worth of cargo aboard the ship; the biggest container vessel to have ever been lost at sea. International trade/arbitration is one of several shipping seats up for grabs. Sources who'd taken up that option enjoyed the unique nature of the work: *"The clients we work for are huge multinational companies working across a range of jurisdictions – it's really interesting trying to enforce arbitration awards in jurisdictions that aren't so accepting of those awards."* Elsewhere, the ship finance seat involves *"the buying and selling of ships,"* with work split between *"commercial vessels – things like oil tankers and cargo carriers – and super yacht-related matters."* Trainees here normally handle the bureaucratic elements that accompanies such matters; a big part of which is dealing with ship registries and local counsel. *"There's a fair amount of tedious paperwork to be completed, and when a completion goes down you have to head to the registry office to hand over all of the forms."*

On the transactional front, recent successes include the firm's appointment by the Guinean government to advise on the ongoing $20bn Simandou South iron-ore mining project, as well as its part in Nigerian contractor Sea

Trucks' five-year, $575m Norwegian bond issue. Transactional seat options are divided into 'cores', among them corporate insurance (Core 3), general corporate (Core 4), and a *"mishmash"* seat encompassing energy, construction and projects, real estate, and banking/finance work (Core 5). It's important to note that in wide-ranging seats like Core 5, trainees can opt to focus on a single stream of work such as construction or real estate. Our sources praised their responsibility levels across all these cores. Those with experience in corporate insurance told of drafting confidentiality and settlement agreements for *"major"* transactions, while insiders in construction reported *"drafting a fair few contracts and getting heavily involved in arbitrations. There even matters where I had direct exposure to clients and did most of the work without any oversight."*

Sherlock homes

If you skim through Clydes' latest graduate recruitment brochure, you'll likely notice a recurring word: 'an altogether better choice', 'an altogether ambitious firm', 'an altogether hands-on experience' – the list goes on. With that catchword in mind, we wondered whether there is a strong sense of unity at the firm, particularly in light of the 2011 merger with BLG. Our sources certainly thought so, telling us that Clydes has slowly but surely made the transition into becoming a more cohesive unit since tying the knot. *"There's been an obvious effort from the senior figures to make people feel like they're part of a united work force. Even with two separate buildings here in London, it now feels like a truly integrated firm."*

The firm's headquarters are in fact split between two sites: St Botolph Building and Beaufort House, both of which are just a stone's throw away from Aldgate station. The former has a striking bright blue exterior, and inside *"it looks a bit like an Ikea showroom, with white walls, glass windows and lots of fancy lifts."* Fans of *Sherlock* will be pleased to know that Benedict Cumberbatch recently graced the building with his presence (during filming, we should add, not as a client). By contrast, Beaufort House (a legacy of BLG) has a *"slightly dated"* look, although it does boast spacious interiors and a *"homely"* feel. Meanwhile, we hear that Manchester is *"not a bad place to be,"* what with its *"impressive reception and lovely views."*

Sources agreed that Clydes' hunger for growth, both in the UK and internationally, has had a real bearing on the working environment. *"Every so often we get the news that we're opening a new office somewhere, or have done something no other firm has done yet – that creates a real buzz. It feels like everyone is constantly trying to better themselves and it's exciting to be at a place like that."* The approachability of senior lawyers has long been a hallmark of the firm's working environment, both in London and Manchester. *"You can talk to the vast majority of people here without worrying about stepping on any toes or pissing anyone off,"* said a source in the capital, while a Mancunian added: *"Our office is open-plan, so we sit right among the senior folks. That helps keep things open and even."* Interviewees in both offices characterised day-to-day proceedings as *"down to earth"* and *"devoid of any stuffy traditions."*

This feel-good vibe is complemented by a reasonably busy social calendar. In London there's a Christmas bash, regular events organised by the trainee social committee and drinks held every other Thursday in St Botolph's top-floor bar. Meanwhile, lawyers in Manchester benefit from firm-wide events every other month. *"The last one was a Brit pop night at a local karaoke bar. People came dressed up as Oasis and the Spice Girls – partners included!"* If sports are more your thing, the firm has a raft of teams to join, including the netball and football sides. The latter competes in the London Legal League, although *"we didn't do as well this time compared to the previous year,"* one trainee lamented. Here's hoping for a more successful campaign next season.

And finally...

For those seeking a wide-ranging training contract with a strong international flavour, Clydes is one to watch out for. In 2014 the firm retained 42 of its 43 qualifiers.

CMS

The facts

Locations: London, Bristol, Scotland

Number of UK partners/solicitors: 204/472

Partners who trained at firm: 14%

Total number of trainees: 160

Seats: 4x6 months

Alternative seats: overseas seats, secondments

Extras: pro bono – LawWorks, Trustlaw, Islington Law Centre, Advocated for International Development; language classes

On chambersstudent.co.uk...

How to get into CMS

CMS in Bristol and Scotland

More on the D&W merger

If you're hankering after a firm with a huge international network and a guaranteed secondment, look no further.

Is this the real life?

CMS is a global network of ten independent member firms. Together, these employ 3,000 legal professionals in 58 offices across the world. The UK incarnation of CMS oversees outposts in London, Bristol and Scotland, as well as a further ten international locations. *"It's certainly not your traditional law firm,"* one current trainee chuckled.

In fact, even most of our trainee interviewees were struggling to understand how the firm operates. One even described it as *"a sexually confused teenager,"* going on to admit: *"I had to look up exactly what the CMS network is even though I've been here for two years. I'm never quite sure how everything interlinks..."* Another source helpfully broke things down for us: *"In simple terms, we're structured as a network of firms that make up one big firm, and there is a degree of integration between all of the offices."* A concerted effort has been made to strengthen the branding in recent years, *"tidying things up"* to help avoid any confusion. A second-year trainee commented: *"We try to refer to ourselves just as 'CMS' now rather than 'CMS Cameron McKenna' like we used to. And that applies throughout the network, so no matter which office a client works with the firm has the same name."* For our part, we think the firm still has a bit of tidying up to do – even its own website refers to the firm as 'CMS United Kingdom' and 'CMS Cameron McKenna'. But perhaps a major rebrand is temporarily on hold. There have been rumours in the past few years that the firm is considering a merger with a big US firm, so watch this space.

Speaking of mergers: the big news of 2014 was a tie-up with major Scottish firm Dundas & Wilson, which took place in May. This added a Glasgow office to the network and strengthened the firm's financial services and energy offerings in Edinburgh and Aberdeen. In 2013/14 CMS also opened in Istanbul and Oman to bolster its European and Middle East presence. Looking at the international network trainees commented that *"CMS's unique selling point is its presence in Eastern Europe."* Very true. The network has 15 offices across the region in unusual locations like Sarajevo and Tirana, as well as more regular spots like Warsaw and Moscow.

Trainees told us that further international integration is important to the firm. In February 2014, Penelope Warne was appointed as senior partner. Formerly based jointly in London and Scotland, Warne had previously taken charge of the opening of offices in Aberdeen, Edinburgh, Brazil, Mexico and Dubai, so she seemed to be the ideal person to continue the integration push. *"CMS really wants to put a stamp on its image, refine it, and make sure people understand it is a global firm,"* said one forthright trainee. New overseas seats in Mexico, Dubai and Beijing

Seat options: infrastructure and project finance; corporate and leveraged finance; corporate recovery; banking litigation; technology and commercial litigation; EU competition; financial services; insurance; employment; pensions; corporate; tax; energy; disputes and construction; projects; real estate; planning; real estate disputes

Chambers UK rankings

Banking & Finance	Intellectual Property
Banking Litigation	International Arbitration
Capital Markets	Life Sciences
Commercial Contracts	Litigation
Competition/European Law	Media & Entertainment
Construction	Outsourcing
Corporate/M&A	Pensions
Data Protection	Planning
Employee Share Schemes & Incentives	Product Liability
Employment	Professional Negligence
Energy & Natural Resources	Projects
Environment	Public Procurement
Financial Services	Real Estate
Hotels & Leisure	Real Estate Finance
Information Technology	Restructuring/Insolvency
Insurance	Retail
	Tax
	Telecommunications

are certainly bringing the network closer together from a trainee perspective. *"You regularly find yourself working with the other offices,"* one interviewee explained. *"In fact about 70% of the matters I've worked on have involved at least two CMS offices."* As you might suspect, language skills are warmly welcomed.

Is this just fantasy?

Trainees list four preferred seats before each rotation. A stint in either corporate or banking is compulsory, although an overseas seat can satisfy this requirement too. Four trainees are taken on in Bristol each year, where the seats on offer are banking litigation, insurance litigation, real estate and commercial/technology. *"Everyone will usually spend their second seat out on secondment,"* we were told. Trainees can go abroad, to a client or spend time in another UK office. *"The secondments really appealed to me,"* said one interviewee, *"and as everyone goes away, there's no need to feel that you're at a disadvantage for missing out on another seat within the firm."* Client secondments can be done at Amazon, Erste Bank and the Wellcome Trust, while overseas seat options include Vienna, Prague, Rio de Janeiro, Sofia and Bucharest. Wherever the trainees were sent they waxed lyrical about the *"phenomenal"* experience. "They just throw you in at the deep end and you're not treated like a trainee at all," said one source. *"CMS makes the process as seamless as possible, especially as you're given an amazing flat to live in that you could never afford in real life."*

CMS's corporate team can bust a move or two at the high end of the market – it was one of several firms to work on the £5.6bn Royal Mail initial public offering (IPO) – but

it also shines in the upper mid-market. CMS regularly completes deals in the £50m to £250m range, and has a noteworthy focus on the energy, technology, consumer and retail sectors. For example, it recently acted for Computer Software Holdings as it was sold to the Advanced Computer Software Group for £110m. *"One of the good things about the corporate seat is that you're not pigeon-holed into one particular area,"* a first-year told us. *"There's an unofficial policy that you can hunt down whatever work you want. Over the course of my six months there I did private M&A and private equity work, as well as a public takeover."* There is the odd bit of bundling or proofreading for trainees, but sources said they were also taken along to client meetings and had *"drafted board minutes, articles of association and non-disclosure agreements."* A source even mentioned that one trainee has even been flown overseas to *"single-handedly"* negotiate a confidentiality agreement.

The banking practice has a number of well-known clients including Lloyds, RBS and Barclays. It works for both borrowers and lenders, and has an international and pan-European presence. For example, lawyers recently acted for a consortium including Cheung Kong Infrastructure (the largest listed company in Hong Kong) on the EUR940m acquisition of Dutch energy company AVR Afvalverwerking. The practice is split into four sub-teams: corporate recovery, leveraged finance, infrastructure and project finance, and banking litigation. Trainees are specifically assigned to do a seat with one of these. A Bristol source told us of doing some smaller-cap litigation work: *"There's quite a high volume of files, so I found myself in charge of 15 or so lower-value matters. My work included drafting witness statements and other court documents, and I was also sent to London to attend a strike-out hearing."*

The infrastructure and project finance seat allows trainees to get involved in a fair number of real estate transactions such as the refinancing of a hotel in London. *"We acted for the borrower who was a high net worth individual,"* a source informed us. *"I was often involved in the meetings, which were, rather unusually, held around the client's dining table. I also worked on conditions precedent, and got to help negotiate the loan agreement and write advice emails to the client."* Some of the projects work has an international flavour – think wind-farm projects in Jordan or waste plants on the Gulf – but there's plenty of UK-based work too. For example, a team of nearly 20 lawyers from different departments is currently advising the National Grid on a £2bn-plus carbon capture project.

Caught in a landslide

Energy is a major focus for CMS, and a seat in the department is a popular destination among trainees. *"It's a powerhouse for the firm – where it's all happening,"* enthused one source – the team wins a top-tier ranking for this practice in *Chambers UK*. The department has four sub-groups: oil and gas; power and utilities; renewables and alternative energy; and energy disputes. Clients across these areas include BP, British Gas, Conoco Phillips and Norwegian oil giant Statoil, who CMS advised when it sold off $3bn worth of interests in UK oilfields. CMS has also been a key player when it comes to advising the offshore wind sector on the next wave of mega-projects in UK waters. These include the first floating offshore wind farm, Hywind, and the £32bn Forewind project – the biggest offshore wind development in the world. The magnitude of these projects mean they throw up all manner of legal concerns, from tax issues to disputes. Luckily CMS is on hand to help out. *"I was mainly involved in disclosure and drafting various parts of procedural documents,"* said one trainee. *"I really enjoyed my time in this seat because energy is something I'm really interested in."*

The employment team has been boosted by the arrival of two new legacy Dundas & Wilson partners. It advises on both contentious and non-contentious matters, and does corporate support work for clients like BT, Royal Mail and General Electric. *"The team leader is amazing and took me along to meetings with him,"* one trainee enthused. *"When I wasn't doing that I drafted employment contracts, severance agreements and various litigation documents like witness statements."*

If you look at CMS's website you'll see that below the firm's name is the subtitle 'Law.Tax'. "It is a little confusing, as people sometimes think we're accountants," admitted one trainee, but the tag is supposed to draw attention to the firm's tax capability across Europe and the world. In London, the tax team is home to 17 fee-earners, but has reportedly been booming in the last few years, with turnover growing by a third since 2011. It works on matters related to all the firm's key sectors: energy, infrastructure, technology and retail – for clients like Lloyds, Aviva Investors and Sainsbury's, and it was also active in the Royal Mail IPO. "That led to a pretty chaotic period,"

recalled one trainee. *"I did a lot of research into tax law and undertook other discreet tasks – tax is a very technical area."* The small size of the team means *"you are expected to work with everyone, and that is something that gets looked at in your appraisals."*

No escape from reality

Sources told us that CMS is *"really interested in your development as a lawyer,"* and that *"everyone is willing to share knowledge."* A first-year told us: *"I feel very much at ease here – I don't feel I have to walk on eggshells if I go into a partner's room, and I don't wake up in the morning fearing that I'll get a bollocking that day."* This attitude is also prevalent in Bristol. *"There isn't anybody here who I consider to be difficult or unreasonable,"* said one source. While the Bristol cohort had nothing but good things to say about their London counterparts (and vice versa), it's worth noting that there's little interaction between the two trainee groups. *"We're encouraged to get on the train and attend socials in London, but that never really happens,"* said one Bristolian. *"But both groups do get together for our induction, and once a year for the trainee ball, so there is some effort to integrate the two offices more closely."*

The Dundas & Wilson merger obviously has the potential to throw a spanner in the works of the firm's culture and operations. While D&W was primarily a Scottish beast, it also had a significant London office that, at our last count, was home to 25 trainees. Some trainees were wary of *"two competing cultures trying to merge together,"* but sources said that so far *"it all seems to be coming together quite nicely."* However, when it comes to qualification, 12 D&W trainees were thrown into the CMS pool for 2014, with only a few additional jobs made available. *"That was pretty stressful,"* admitted one source, who recognised that the retention rate would be *"quite poor"* as a result. *"Good people have missed out on jobs,"* said one source, *"but all the people I know who didn't find a place here have landed on their feet elsewhere."*

And finally...
The recent merger with Dundas & Wilson and potential future tie-ups make this an *"exciting"* time to be at CMS. In keeping with the firm's ambitious outlook, the London office is moving to new digs at Cannon Place in 2015.

Collyer Bristow LLP

The facts

Location: London
Number of UK partners/solicitors: 30/27
Partners who trained at the firm: 19%
Total number of trainees: 8
Seats: 4x6 months
Alternative seats: occasional secondments
Extras: pro bono – law centres, Zacchaeus 2000 Trust

On chambersstudent.co.uk...

How to get into Collyer Bristow
More about the commercial
    practices
The Collyer Bristow art gallery

Not a fan of the City's concrete jungle? Take a stroll down the leafy streets of Bloomsbury to Collyer Bristow, where a *"small-firm feel"* and *"challenging, interesting work"* is on offer.

The True Picture

Aah, Bristow!

Don't expect this little London-based firm to remain quite so little for much longer. Partnership director Phillip Palmer told us in mid-2014: *"We are committed to growing the firm's capabilities and, in particular, our leading and high-potential practices. Over the last year we have added partner capacity including to some of our key practices – financial disputes, IP, real estate, tax and estate planning."* Collyer Bristow might be renowned for its work with individuals (its defamation/reputation management, family and private client teams all pick up *Chambers UK* rankings), but Palmer says the firm's focus probably gets a bit skewed: *"We focus equally on corporate and commercial clients and revenue is evenly split between individuals and commercial organisations."*

Therefore, practices such as financial disputes have developed over the past few years. *"Collyer Bristow saw a gap in that market and has moved into it successfully,"* trainees agreed. CB has a strong international practice which is a key strategic focus: around 30% of revenue comes from non-UK clients. *"As such we expect our trainees to have an international outlook,"* explains Palmer. *"Our trainees will get the opportunity to spend time working on cross-border matters and for overseas clients."* The firm already boasts an office in Geneva, and has Italian, Russian, Spanish and US desks to help service those who are based outside of Blighty.

Trainees can make their preferred seats known before each changeover, but allocation is always dependent on business needs and the whims of second-year trainees. Nothing is compulsory, but *"people do tend to do two*

seats in dispute resolution as it's the biggest department, generates the most revenue, and takes the most trainees at any time."

Coat of many Collyers

Within DR the work covers defamation/reputation management, IP, employment, financial services and real estate litigation. While rookies will be nominally allocated to one of these, *"you are never entirely restricted as the work tends to be pooled."*

Many big names seek out the defamation/reputation management group's expertise – it represented the 51 core participants in the Leveson Inquiry, and over 80 other victims of phone-hacking. In addition to traditional defamation and privacy claims, it handles disputes involving online publications, harassment and cyber-stalking. *"It's quite an emotive environment to work in,"* reflected a trainee. *"Often, with high-profile clients, tasks have to be done immediately, but also with sensitivity."* Push the emotions to one side though and there's plenty of good work to be found.

"There is the occasional bit of bundling," commented a first-year trainee, *"but as soon you prove you're capable they're happy to give you greater responsibility. I've had an awful lot of contact with clients to keep them updat-*

Seats options: dispute resolution; family; tax and estate planning; property; corporate and commercial

Chambers UK rankings

Defamation/Reputation Management	Family/Matrimonial
	Private Client

ed about what's going on." Another source said: "I was given the opportunity to do the first drafts of cease and desist letters. They were always checked, but it was high-quality work." The rise of social media and its implications for the Defamation Act (take note: careful who you slag off in your tweets) also keeps trainees busy. "The laws are ever-changing," one remarked. "So you have to keep on top of them and help out with any crossover work it throws up for our media and IT teams."

With financial services "going from strength to strength" over the last few years, all those who pass through DR tend to do at least some work in that area. CB represents a lot of claimants in the Libor manipulation scandal, but delves into the "whole world of banking disputes." Trainees found that their personal workloads varied. A first-year told of "a lot of research and bundling," but added "that always meant you were taken along to the meeting and were an active part of the case." Another source mentioned: "I was heavily involved in one matter, where I was compiling documents, attending conferences with counsel and clients, and assisting with witness statements."

Although the real estate team's work is broad, the focus is on litigation, with a lot of landlord and tenant cases. While partners may take a "softly, softly" approach with trainees as they learn the ropes, responsibility can ramp up quickly. "I never felt I was handed work on the basis that someone else didn't want to do it," reflected a first-year trainee. "I spent a lot of time liaising with clients in the good old-fashioned way – over the phone – and could help draft letters." A second-year worked on a construction case that saw them "assist the partner in creating a defence for clients with negligence claims against them." Despite the long-ish leash, "if you don't understand something, there's no question that you can't ask someone for an explanation."

The employment group represents both employers and employees in key sectors such as education, hospitality, transport and the arts. "It's known as being one of the best teams for utilising trainees," a source informed. "I went to client meetings, reviewed settlement agreements and contacted the other side with regard to them." Another rookie told us: "I attended tribunal hearings and took control of the doc management leading up to those. There's also the odd bit of non-contentious work as well, so that I could help draft employment contracts."

Trainees in the corporate/commercial department will find that their workload is largely dependent on the part-ner they sit with. "It's never too uneven, but you will get more of their specific area," explained a first-year. On the corporate side, there's a number of M&A deals involving SMEs (small to medium-sized enterprises), including the recent merger between film and education charities, Filmclub UK and First Light. Trainees working on such deals could be tasked with "drafting board minutes, share transfer agreements and other ancillary documents." On the commercial arm, trainees were immersed in "film-option agreements, website terms and conditions, and commercial contracts for large international companies."

Bristow Inferno

Would a firm that has a 250-year history be bogged down by traditional stuffiness? Not at Collyer Bristow, which is "free of those horrible formalities – you can talk to whoever you need to," said a first-year. "No one is so precious that you can't approach them. You never feel like you have to tiptoe around the place." Not that this means your eyes aren't firmly on the ball: "Nobody is flippant or takes things lightly – we do some serious work."

This is not a mega-firm, and that helps breed a "close-knit and cooperative" environment, especially within the trainee intakes, which are at most five strong per year. "We all get on well, and there isn't that competitive nature you might find at other firms," reflected a second-year. It turns out that bitching and backstabbing would have been redundant this year anyway as all five of CB's 2014 qualifiers were retained.

To have such a chummy cohort does not mean that Collyer Bristow is chock full of identikit trainees. "There's not a common thread between us," said one. Flick through their profiles and you can see that there are numerous universities represented, with a good mix of law and non-law graduates, and many embarking on this as a second career. "You couldn't sum the trainees up in one characteristic," our source explained. "It's full of individuals who work together successfully."

They might be very different, but they were uniformly chirpy about the quaint charm of their Bedford Row home. "Compared to the glass and steel monstrosities you often get, it's wonderful," one said of the Georgian townhouse. Being just on the outskirts of the City also helps brighten the mood: "I imagined everything in London would be giant, grey, depressing buildings," reflected a trainee. "It's so nice to be on a tree-lined street with Gray's Inn fields next door."

Collyer Bristow offers a nice blend of the past and present though, with its own bespoke modern art gallery showcasing emerging talent for nearly two decades now. What did the trainees make of the works on show? "Interesting," was the diplomatic response. However, "it's *something we're quite proud of, and it's always a good conversation point. It shows we're not just purely a legal business and are interested in things beyond the law."* A first-year concluded: *"It's nice that they are happy to let*

trainees talk to clients about it and give us responsibility in a social context. Although I must admit I normally have to wing it on the art front."

And finally...

Collyer Bristow likes a knees-up. In addition to the big Christmas and summer shindigs, there are monthly events organised by the social committee. And if that doesn't tickle your fancy, then trainees tend to prop up Old Nick's bar on a Friday night.

Covington & Burling LLP

The facts

Location: London
Number of UK partners/solicitors: 19/40
Total number of trainees: 14
Seats: 4x6 months
Alternative seats: secondments, overseas seats
Extras: pro bono – LawWorks, TrustLaw, A4ID

On chambersstudent.co.uk...

How to get into Covington
The new Brussels secondment

Covington offers a training contract with a tech and life sciences edge to it, in an academic, intellectual atmosphere.

Doing drugs

Covington's London office opened in 1988 and represented the Washington DC firm's first foray into the world outside the US. Since then the firm has expanded its international presence with offices in Beijing, Brussels, Seoul and, most recently, Shanghai. Trainees gain plenty of exposure to international work, and in September 2013 the first overseas seat was introduced: a stint in Brussels working on food and drug regulatory matters.

In its home town, Covington has a full-service practice but is best known for its lobbying and government practice. On this side of the pond the firm stands out for its life sciences (ie pharmaceuticals) and IP/IT work. This work acts as a lure for many trainees. As one told us: *"I wanted to work for a small to medium-sized London firm that did corporate work but wasn't entirely finance-focused. Technology, IP and life sciences were all areas I was interested in."*

Trainees are required to spend six months each in the firm's two core departments: dispute resolution and corporate. Trainees tend to do these two first, *"leaving the remaining two as free choices."* The other seat options are life sciences transactional, life sciences IP, employment, arbitration, and technology and media. Client secondments to leading pharma companies are also regularly in the offing. We touched on a few issues with seat allocation last year, but these appear to have been resolved. Incoming trainees are now asking to *"list all the optional seats on offer in order of preference"* before they start. Sources felt that *"overall HR tries hard to take our choices into account."*

Revenge of the Nerds

The life sciences department (in either its transactional or IP guise) is visited by all trainees, whether at the firm or on a client secondment. When asked to describe the transactional seat. one trainee simply said: *"I loved it!"* Another, more expansive, source told us: *"The work relates to all the commercial aspects of the pharmaceutical industry, from licensing arrangements to research and development collaborations."* For example, the firm recently advised AstraZeneca on an exclusive agreement with Moderna Therapeutics to develop and market a new RNA-based drug designed to treat cancer, and heart and kidney diseases. Trainees often start the seat with *"a fair amount of research and proofreading"* – it pays to start easy, as matters can be *"incredibly complex and are invariably multi-jurisdictional."* Another source commented that as their knowledge increased during the seat, they *"became more confident and began doing more drafting."*

Corporate is the London office's largest department. It mixes M&A with venture capital, private equity and capital markets IPO work, making it *"perfect for those who aren't sure what kind of corporate work they're most interested in."* Trainees generally assume a support role, drafting board minutes, assisting with due diligence, bibling and doing company searches. The department is *Chambers*-ranked for its AIM work and has recently

Seat options: corporate; dispute resolution; employment & incentives; life sciences regulatory; life sciences transactional; tax & incentives; technology & media

Chambers UK rankings

Capital Markets	Investment Funds
Corporate Crime &	Life Sciences
Investigations	Parliamentary & Public
Corporate/M&A	Affairs
Data Protection	Private Equity
Insurance	Product Liability
International Arbitration	

advised several pharmaceutical, technology and energy companies on capital markets transactions. *"I helped advise an American client on an AIM flotation,"* reported one trainee, *"and I really saw the cross-border nature of the work come to life – there was a lot of back and forth between our US and UK teams."* While there's a noticeable pharma and technology slant to the work here, other clients have called on the firm's services too, including luxury brand Armani – one trainee told us they were thrilled to find themselves *"proofreading documents signed by Giorgio Armani himself!"*

The dispute resolution team, so the firm tells us, has two notable strengths: insurance and energy. Covington is top-ranked by *Chambers UK* for its policyholder work (so it doesn't act for the insurers themselves). Trainees tend to be tasked with *"examining policies, sourcing experts to back up arguments and undertaking background research."* One told us: *"It was nice to be left to my own devices. I'd often be given a big box of files to summarise and then be asked to report back later."* The firm recently acted for American brokerage firm Howden in commercial court proceedings brought by its London insurers. Other litigation clients include Ryanair, Harley Davidson and Bacardi.

Clients of the tech and media team include big names like Facebook, Microsoft and Wikimedia (the parent company of Wikipedia). The team offers regulatory advice to tech and media companies, and also deals with trade sanctions work, an area that's been quite active recently. *"It throws up lots of thorny issues with no clear answers,"* one interviewee revealed. Most recently, we hear, *"events in Ukraine and Russia have been a preoccupation for the group."* The more regular work of the department includes trying to make sense of *"woolly regulations from Brussels,"* which counts as *"a test of common sense and commercial awareness as well as legal knowledge."* As this implies, *"there's a lot of looking at black letter law, and a ton of research – much more than in the other*

seats." Day-to-day tasks include drafting advisory memos and documents like terms and conditions for websites. Like the trade work, tech and media is topical too: *"The Snowden revelations coloured a lot of the work – new regulations were coming in from the US and the EU. Tech and media are constantly changing areas, and that makes the work we do here quite exciting. Oh, and as you may have guessed, this is quite a nerdy department."*

Listen to Sam the Eagle

Covington trainees were not afraid to admit the firm has a culture of *"comfortable intellectualism"* and is *"quite academic."* When quizzed on how this manifests itself, they explained *"people are very smart and feel comfortable knowing that everyone else here is too."* We also heard that *"good writing and presentational skills are seen as very important – typos are not tolerated! But luckily you improve quickly as you get a lot of feedback."* The atmosphere is not strictly professorial, though: *"There's a certain ease of conversation between people, regardless of rank; there's no strong sense of hierarchy."*

Trainees praised what they called *"the Covington way,"* telling us: *"We're made to feel there is a strong focus on investing in the personal development of each individual trainee."* Interviewees said *"your work is often praised when you do well, which carries a lot of weight."* While there are no formal training sessions for those starting new seats, litigation, life sciences and corporate all have ongoing training programmes, often bringing in outside speakers like doctors and accountants to give talks.

Trainees were also positive about the firm's approach to hours. *"It would be wrong to say the hours are never bad, but we are actively encouraged to go home at 6pm when it's not busy,"* commented one interviewee. *"You are sometimes expected to knuckle down and put in the hours, but if you're working late, it's always for a purpose, a tight deadline. Then I'll stay until 8.30pm or sometimes midnight. A really late night would mean staying until 1 or 2am."*

As well as not eschewing the hard work typical of American lawyers, Covingtonites are also happy to unfurl the Stars and Stripes every Fourth of July for a barbecue on the office terrace with hotdogs, burgers and music. More regular shenanigans include a monthly drinks trolley, and *"on Fridays trainees and NQs will all head out for a drink – usually to Dalys Wine Bar."*

And finally...
Covington has always had a pretty good retention record, and 2014 was no different, with five of seven qualifiers kept on.

Cripps LLP

The facts

Locations: Tunbridge Wells, Kings Hill, London
Number of UK partners/solicitors: 47/42
Partners who trained at firm: 16%
Total number of trainees: 16
Seats: 6x4 months
Alternative seats: none

On chambersstudent.co.uk...

How to get into Cripps
A glance at Tunbridge Wells
Five minutes with managing
   partner Gavin Tyler

A vibrant rebrand, relaxed atmosphere and country idyll are on offer at this leading Kent-based firm.

The orange revolution

Cripps' striking new orange logo may be a bit much for Tunbridge Wells, but it fits a new, bolder version of Cripps Harries Hall, which is fresh from its merger with corporate specialists Vertex Law. *"We weathered the recession well, but wanted to grow,"* managing partner Gavin Tyler explained, *"When the opportunity to merge with Vertex arose, it allowed us to balance our significant real estate offering with a larger corporate and commercial department."* The choice to merge with Vertex was also helped along by Vertex being managed by a lot of former Cripps solicitors.

Cripps rules the *Chambers UK* rankings in Kent, taking gold in a string of practices, from agriculture to IP to real estate, with the latter earning the firm national recognition. Recent client wins include Prudential and worldwide real estate investors Kennedy Wilson. They join veterans Eurotunnel, Shell UK and the Home Office. The current crop of trainees was drawn by *"top-quality work without having to work in the City."* One trainee explained, *"I didn't want someone standing over me with a whip at 11pm. A life outside work is important, and Cripps wears that ethos on its sleeve."* Another told us *"I wanted responsibility and progress – Cripps have allowed me to get my teeth into different practice areas."*

The firm offers six, four-month seats, *"which meant I didn't feel pigeon-holed into just one type of law,"* one source said. Seats are chosen in advance after receiving an overview of the departments from past trainees. Although competition can be fierce for family and employment, there is the option of *"chatting among ourselves and rearranging"* if people aren't happy.

Clockwork Orange

Real estate is the largest department, and has the greatest variety of seats for trainees: residential investment, residential conveyancing, plot sales, portfolio property, development, and property dispute resolution. The Home Office, Environment Agency and UK-wide developers British Land are among the firm's national clientele, alongside international clients such as real estate investors Liberty Property and M&G Real Estate.

"Cripps entrusts you with responsibility and expects you to take the initiative; in the residential conveyancing seat you're running your own files." Expect to get *"heavily involved"* in transactions, exchanges, drafting covenants and leaseholds, transferring contracts, and liaising with clients including big agricultural estates and ultra-high-net-worth individuals. Working with the latter often entails purchasing second homes or properties in London. In the past the team has assisted with the sale of a £5.7m Knightsbridge property and a £13.5m London townhouse. Closer to home the team also assists clients buying locally. *"I was involved every step of the way,"* commented one trainee, while another elaborated: *"taking an active role in conversing with clients is highly gratifying."*

Portfolio property *"eases trainees in"* through drafting leases, deeds of easement and licences to alter and occupy, and fielding client enquiries. Research entails specific

Seat options: advisory group; residential conveyancing; family; residential investment desk; development; plot sales; portfolio property; corporate; commercial; commercial disputes; employment; specialist disputes; property disputes

Chambers UK rankings

Agriculture & Rural Affairs	Intellectual Property
Banking & Finance	Litigation
Charities	Partnership
Construction	Planning
Corporate/M&A	Private Client
Employment	Professional Negligence
Family/Matrimonial	Real Estate Litigation
Information Technology	Social Housing

legal points or the more bizarre: *"I had to research the meaning of a lake for one transaction."* Clients include real estate investors Hermes, who own Milton Keynes shopping centre thecentre:mk. By the end of their seat, trainees have the opportunity to run their own files. *"Being handed the reins for a significant client was exhilarating."*

"As the first port of call for enquiries from overseas clients you spend a lot of time replying to emails about developments, sales and exchanges," reported a source in residential investment. *"Prioritisation is crucial,"* in this seat, a source wistfully recalled. *"One morning I had 110 enquiries."* Trainees can get bogged down in transactional processes and we heard that the seat was more admin heavy than others on offer. However, interviewees were keen to emphasise that this contact was a *"fantastic opportunity to establish working relationships."*

When things come tumbling down Cripps' property dispute team steps in. The team is a national leader outside London, and clients such as Shell UK and the Crown Prosecution Service speak for the department's appeal. It recently represented Crossrail in a dispute over compulsory purchase compensation claims. The team also assists private clients, and there are plenty of neighbour and boundary disputes. Trainees advise clients on niche points of law, consult with barristers and attend court. One trainee was even involved with ejecting squatters from a commercial property.

The whole spectrum (but mainly orange)

Cripps' dispute department acts for both private and corporate clients, including food distributor Brake Bros and Nikwax waterproof products. Trainees can expect to work on will and estate disputes, and clinical and professional negligence cases. *"There's a whole spectrum of litigation available – one day I could be dealing with will validity and the next with drink-driving offences."* Client meetings and drafting trial documents are punctuated by attending conferences and court hearings.

Court outings were also a feature of the family department, which deals heavily with divorce, separation and custody suits for high net worth individuals. *"You can be entrusted with a large amount of responsibility to liaise with counsel and clients"* trainees told us. Although you're not chained to the photocopier, trainees will inevitably have to prepare bundles. Other typical tasks are drafting questionnaires and divorce petitions, and reviewing financial statements.

Administration of estates and trusts and execution of wills and probate dominates the private client department. But there's also tax advice, which proved to be a *"daunting area"* for some of our trainees as *"it's complex, but prior research gives you confidence. Explaining issues in simpler terms to clients is a great challenge."*

Specialising in mid-range sales and acquisitions, the corporate and commercial department has been significantly bolstered by the merger. Recently, they advised Kent vineyard Chapel Down in the sale of shares to raise £4.35m for expanding operations. The seat entails drafting board minutes and management agreements, establishing new companies and changing registered offices. Over on the commercial side, trainees commented that *"the diversity of drafting is brilliant training."* Our interviewees in this department had been involved in drafting contracts and confidentiality agreements, software developments and IP rights. *"My supervisor ensured I really understood a business before drafting for them,"* one reported. *"It's such an invaluable skill."*

Oranjeboom

Overall, the hours are *"never horrendous - you usually finish at 6.30pm, but sometimes you'll stay until 8pm."* *"There's no pressure to stay late for the sake of it,"* we're told, but if it's necessary *"your effort is acknowledged."* Regular feedback and appraisals from supervisors ensure trainees are kept abreast of their progress and supervisors *"channel a lot of time and effort into reviewing work with you."*

"At Cripps, people are encouraging and value your contribution to the team," one trainee acknowledged. Another told us, *"if you need anything they're almost universally helpful. Starting somewhere new can be nerve-racking, but at the welcome drinks everyone wants to get to know you."*

Social life at the firm caters to the sporty – there are netball, football and cricket teams – and the more sedentary, through the regular drinking sessions at Sankeys. The summer ball was upon us as we conducted interviews, organised by second-years around the theme of 'Secret Garden Party'.

In the wake of the merger with Vertex, integration between the two firms has been *"seamless,"* we were told. Trainees described both firms as culturally similar, reporting that the atmosphere was *"relaxed but not informal,"* and the merger with Vertex has encouraged this. *"We weren't overly traditional,"* one trainee explained, *"but Vertex have infused us with a more modern feel and we're now even more communicative and approachable."*

The re-branding aims to emphasise this with its *"vibrant"* colours and *"cleaner"* name. Most trainees felt it was *"fresh and bold,"* with one declaring, *"it's suc-*ceeded in helping us stand out from the crowd."* *"We're a different kind of law firm,"* managing partner Gavin Tyler explained. *"When a client approaches us we look at the whole picture to understand what that client wants to achieve and then we adapt ourselves to give them the best we can."*

"Cripps is looking really exciting," trainees told us, *"the rebrand is kicking in, the head count is increasing, and we're moving into new offices in 2016. There's a real sense the firm is growing."*

And finally...
The firm hopes to increase its trainee intake next year, and adopt a staggered entry system to maximise the opportunity for trainees to qualify in their desired department.

Curtis, Mallet-Prevost, Colt & Mosle LLP

The facts

Location: London
Number of UK partners/solicitors: 1/4 (+ 9 US partners)
Total number of trainees: 2
Seats: none
Alternative seats: New York

On chambersstudent.co.uk...

How to get into Curtis
Interview with deputy managing
   partner Winta Jarvis

A compact New York native with international expertise, Curtis offers a pretty distinctive training contract.

Globetrotters

It isn't just the sprawling Goliaths of the legal landscape that can exert a truly global grip. New York-based Curtis might be a bantam weight compared to some of the behemoths out there, but in the international ring it packs a formidably powerful legal left hook. Founded by a couple of cousins from Connecticut way back in 1830, Curtis was one of the first US law firms to expand abroad, and has since developed into a thoroughly cosmopolitan enterprise. Nowadays, it has a total of 16 offices, including some in mysterious and exotic locations like Istanbul, Almaty and Ashgabat, as well as South America and China.

The London office, established in the 1970s, concentrates on international arbitration, investment management and corporate work for a range of multinationals, state-owned companies, financial institutions and governments. As the portal to the firm's burgeoning African practice, the City branch is a key component of the Curtis network. Oil, gas and energy issues constitute much of the African work – clients include the governments of Algeria and Uganda, and the Ghana National Petroleum Corporation. Of late, the firm has been advising the last of these on the development of Ghana's Jubilee oil field. A lot of work emerges from the Middle East too, so if you're not turned on by the prospect of multi-jurisdictional matters, then this probably isn't the firm for you. Our interviewees were all drawn to the firm's international outlook as well as its small size. In terms of head count, the London office is pretty dinky – at the time of our calls, there were three trainees among 15 qualified lawyers.

Curtis's training contract doesn't involve a conventional seat system. Rather than sit with different supervisors for separate seats, trainees have their own office from the beginning. *"The trainee supervisor is very good at giving out work and divvying it up between available trainees,"* so newcomers aren't left to flounder. Once trainees have acclimatised and *"got their feet on the ground"* by getting to know folk around the office, it's up to them to *"approach partners to get involved with assignments"* according to where their interests lie. A trainee commented: *"You define how your training develops. The firm really allows you to specialise in what you want."* Interviewees explained that *"you're treated as an associate. You have to be a self-starter to go out and speak to partners. But that system is typical in the US, where they don't have a rotational training system."* Sources noted with satisfaction that *"when you walk around, all doors are open – you're encouraged to build a personal rapport with partners and associates."* And while trainees might get to tailor their training, that doesn't mean the SRA requirements are thrown out of the window – the standard requirement to gain both contentious and non-contentious experience still applies. And if the firm can't cover the contentious requirement they'll be sent on a course.

An energetic business

On the international arbitration front, Curtis has recently advised the government of Uganda on a $500m tax-related dispute brought in London by oil company Heritage Oil. Trainees have the opportunity to really immerse themselves in this type of case. *"I spent the best part of a year working on one big arbitration, but I took on other matters in parallel,"* explained one interviewee. *"The teams that handle arbitrations are very small, so as a trainee you're very much involved. I went to client meet-*

ings and did the legal research. I also got to do the first draft of a witness statement, which seemed really daunting at first! But once you get your head around the fact that there'll be about 20 edited drafts before the final version, you let go of the fear and just do the best you can."

An interviewee recalled that *"when I was on an arbitration there were some very busy times and then slower patches, so in the downtime I did corporate work."* We were told that a lot of this *"comes through the Middle East and New York, and you might also have to work alongside lawyers in the other European offices such as Frankfurt, Paris and Milan."* A source noted: *"I worked on a matter for a big corporate client in New York, which had an office in London. We had to figure out all the laws that applied to the UK arm and if their implementation would affect the larger parent company."* The work is *"mainly commercial stuff, rather than M&A."* That's not to say that acquisitions are off limits – one interviewee had *"assisted the Paris office with a large M&A transaction."* Our sources had also handled *"companies house work, drafted shareholder agreements and negotiated contracts between franchisees and franchisers"* as well as *"taking on a bit of finance, such as the restructuring of a bank."* Meanwhile, the funds team advises financial institutions, high net worth individuals and families from around the world on their investment activities. For a trainee, this area involves *"a lot of due diligence and fund formation work."*

Welcome to Wall Street

As they approach qualification, trainees jet over to New York and spend around ten weeks in the firm's HQ as part of the 'summer associate programme' (the US equivalent of a vac scheme). Fortunately, they aren't required to pass the New York Bar Exam or jostle for position with their American colleagues. An insider told us: *"You won't be expected to advise on New York or federal law – you're fully entrenched, but still doing your own work from London."* The Big Apple *"mother ship"* has an open-door policy, but *"more of a distinct hierarchy that arises from*

its age. In London, the atmosphere is more congenial because the office is still fairly new and very small."* In addition to this stint across the pond, enthusiastic sources confirmed that there are *"opportunities to go abroad, especially to Dubai or Oman."* This is on an ad-hoc basis, depending on overseas demand.

Do trainees work Wall Street hours? Well, you certainly shouldn't expect to knock off at 5pm. *"Obviously, working in the corporate department of a New York law firm means that you have to be flexible. If there's a deadline to meet, you're expected to stay until the work is done,"* said one source. The average hours are 9.30am to 7.30pm, although one trainee commented: *"Finishing at 4am once was a particular low point!"*

Trainees were pleased to report that *"everyone is so approachable here – it's a small office so everybody has to get on!"* Curtis' cultural cohesion *"stems from the recruitment process – the firm looks for the right fit. If you don't fit, you don't get in."* So what qualities might constitute the *"Curtis fit"* besides the usual academic achievements? Trainees agreed that *"you have to be proactive. You're in your own office where no-one supervises you, so you need to go out and get work. Plus, they want someone who isn't put off by the fact that we don't just work on traditional, text-book English legal issues, someone who won't be fazed when confronted with an issue relating to, for example, Kazakh Law."* Despite the firm's international scope, trainees pointed out that language ability isn't compulsory.

Given the office's compact size, there isn't a bulging social calendar in place. *"It's left up to the employees to organise things themselves, but celebrations like birthdays or someone qualifying quickly turn into an office-wide affair that the firm will sponsor."* Interviewees also emphasised that *"the partners are young and they treat you as an adult rather than just telling you that things have to be done a certain way. You don't feel like a small cog in a big machine, but like an associate who's capable of making a real contribution to a matter."*

The True Picture

And finally...

Sources weren't scared about their prospects of landing a job with the firm. *"There's never been an instance when someone hasn't been retained."* Lo and behold, all three qualified in 2014.

Davis Polk & Wardwell LLP

The facts

Training contract begins: Aug 2014
Location: London
Number of UK partners/solicitors: 10/40
Total number of trainees (from Sept 2014): 5
Seats: 4x6 months (including time in New York)
Starting salary: £50k (TC); £100k (NQ)

"Our first trainees have just started. We have our second intake lined up for August 2015 and expect to take between four and six trainees per year in the future."

A new training contract is in town, and with its chart-topping TC and NQ salaries, it's clear that this eminent Wall Street firm is serious about growing its new English law practice. We visited the office to get the inside scoop...

Please note: Davis Polk's first trainees only started in August 2014, so we are unable to provide a True Picture for this firm. The full article online is based on on-the-record conversations with representatives of the firm in November 2013 and September 2014.

Big Apple bigwig Davis Polk set up shop in London more than four decades ago, but it was only in 2012 that the firm debuted its English law practice, a move designed to *"join the dots"* between its existing corporate offerings in New York, Hong Kong and London, according to training principal Will Pearce. *"We can now handle domestic and international capital markets transactions, and are equipped to do M&A transactions pretty much anywhere in the world,"* he says, underscoring DP's single biggest aim: *"To remain one of the world's premier corporate finance-focused law firms."*

Indeed, corporate finance is the name of game at DP's City branch. *"We cover capital markets, M&A, credit and restructuring transactions, with corporate tax and financial services regulatory lawyers on top of that,"* Pearce sums up, telling us the firm's *"strong relationships"* with investment banks and listed companies – among them Citigroup, Goldman Sachs and Credit Suisse – *"drive the nature of the practice here."* Bear in mind there are no plans in place to start a litigation practice any time soon, so we suggest looking elsewhere if you're keen to get in the courtroom.

The firm scores *Chambers UK* rankings for its capital markets work on both the debt and equity fronts, with lawyers handling some hefty deals of late, including a smattering of cash tender offers and notes offerings for RBS – together worth a whopping $17.6bn. Pearce is optimistic that involvement in such matters will carry on unabated in coming months, and adds *"We've had a great 12 months working on a number of M&A deals including ARM, Aetna, Morgan Stanley and Tesco, and on IPOs by ISS and OneSavings Bank."*

A spate of lateral partner hires in recent months – all from the likes of Freshfields, Ashurst and Herbert Smith Freehills – has helped build up a 20-strong core for the English practice, but management is hoping for *"organic growth"* from here on. Enter DP London's shiny new training contract, which has seen five trainees join ranks in August 2014. *"Our first trainees have just started. We have our second intake lined up for August 2015 and expect to take between four and six trainees per year in the future,"* reveals Pearce.

Chambers UK rankings

Capital Markets

To read the full review on what awaits trainees at DP's London office, visit chambersstudent.co.uk

Dechert LLP

The facts

Location: London

Number of UK partners/solicitors: 41/72

Total number of trainees: 24

Seats: 6x4 months

Alternative seats: overseas seats, secondments

Extras: pro bono – A4ID, Islington Legal Advice Centre, Advocates for International Development, Community Matters, LawWorks, Citizens Advice Bureau, The Prince's Trust, Raising Her Voice.

On chambersstudent.co.uk...

How to get into Dechert

A lawyer with cojones: Miriam Gonzalez interview

Interview with grad recruitment partner Andrew Hearn

US outfit Dechert has ballooned into a sizeable international player in recent years, but its brand recognition is still playing catch-up in London.

Taking a (brief) breather

Dechert's roots date back to 1875, but a burst of 21st-century expansion has given the American firm a significant makeover. Since the millennium, it's added a whopping 17 new offices (ten international and seven stateside) to its network in a bid to enrich its scope and pulling power. While Dechert's CEO designated 2013 as a year of consolidation for the firm, co-head of graduate recruitment Andrew Hearn tells us *"we're always looking to do more and more."* Indeed, rumours abound over a potential office opening in Singapore and, in 2012, China's Ministry of Justice granted a license for Dechert to launch a Shanghai base, so it's safe to say that a bigger presence in Asia is in the works.

Over in Europe, Dechert's London branch is its star performer. *"We're the gateway that connects the East with the US,"* says Hearn, who explains *"we handle Anglo-American work on one hand, but we're also the hub for matters from places like Russia, Kazakhstan, Georgia and, more generally, Asia."* London has not escaped the firm's expansion plans: a ream of lateral hires in 2011 and 2012 from the likes of DLA Piper and the late Dewey & LeBoeuf has swelled the office's revenue by a not-too-shabby 44%, with much of the growth taking place on litigation and financial services. The 2012 addition of Dewey's 25-strong capital markets team had a particularly profound effect, causing a shift towards *"decidedly more emerging market-oriented work,"* according to insiders. *Chambers UK* acknowledges the office's capital markets capabilities on the debt and securities side, and

awards rankings for its corporate, funds and real estate practices, among others.

Our interviewees told us they had Dechert in their sights for several reasons, including its sizeable amount of international work, mid-size trainee intake and its six-seat system. Trainees can choose from *"a range of corporate and finance seats, plus more niche areas like employment and IP,"* although it's important to note *"this is not a huge office, so you won't be able to go where you want every single time."* Still, sources praised graduate recruitment manager Stephen Trowbridge for making seat allocation a transparent process, telling us *"you can always talk to him about where you're thinking of going."* The firm recently added Dubai to its list of overseas seats, complementing existing options in Brussels, Dublin and Moscow. Meanwhile, there are a handful of client secondments on offer each year with some big names in finance among others.

AA: Acronyms anonymous

Over two-thirds of Dechert's corporate deals have an international and/or emerging markets component. A cor-

Seat options: corporate and securities; complex commercial litigation; international arbitration; white-collar; government trade sanctions; IP; tax; real estate; employment; finance; financial services and investment management

Chambers UK rankings

Banking & Finance	Intellectual Property
Capital Markets	Investment Funds
Corporate Crime &	Litigation
Investigations	Partnership
Corporate/M&A	Real Estate
Employment	Tax
Financial Services	

porate seat sees trainees work for the whole department, dipping in and out of the M&A, private equity and capital markets subgroups. *"No two deals are the same,"* said interviewees, who told of drafting agreements, reviewing contracts and putting together due diligence reports during their stint with the department. The capital markets team is known for its work with sovereign nations and banks in the Gulf region – *"we have some of our biggest rainmakers there."* Meanwhile, private equity lawyers have made their own waves of late, recently signing global asset management firm The Carlyle Group as a client and assisting on packaging giant Crown Holdings' $1.6bn purchase of a Spanish food can manufacturer.

Navigating the *"niche, intangible"* world of financial services can induce a migraine in the finest of minds, so trainees kindly summed up the team's remit, telling us *"basically, we launch a variety of funds and deal with regulatory matters arising from these."* Clients include established investment management firms like Legg Mason as well as banking kingpins Barclays and Wells Fargo. While it's not uncommon to encounter *"quite a bit of bibling"* in the beginning, trainees here progress onto more involved tasks such as writing the first draft of an agreement, going to client meetings and sitting on partner calls. *"It's important that we gain an understanding of certain investment structures and how certain tax provisions are worked to see why clients choose certain options."* However, be warned there are *"a whole lot"* of pesky acronyms to come to terms with, although fortunately there are plenty of research tasks in place to help trainees memorise these.

Things are a bit more straightforward in the finance and real estate group, which focuses on originating, acquiring and disposing of large commercial real estate loans. As a smaller team, *"you get more responsibility as a trainee. By the end of the seat I was running my own matters under supervision,"* said one interviewee. The team recently advised LA-headquartered CBRE on its role as facility and security agent for a €2.3bn loan used to secure a German real estate portfolio.

Hot under the collar

The litigation department is one of Dechert's biggest, with separate seats available in complex commercial disputes, white-collar and international arbitration, and then a smaller opportunity in government trade and sanctions. While trainees are assigned to one team, however, *"we often get pulled onto other teams if they need extra manpower for things like doc review,"* sources said. Commercial and arbitration are the most common areas. The disputes are large and multi-jurisdictional: lawyers are currently representing Bob Diamond, former group chief executive of Barclays, in proceedings regarding traders' alleged manipulation of Libor interest rates, and recently acted for Deutsche on a handful of cross-border enforcement matters. For trainees, involvement in such cases is not always glamorous, particularly during the discovery stage. *"We had a bank trying to establish a claim, and my job was to sift through 15,000 emails they'd sent over,"* one reported. On the other hand, it's not uncommon for those joining the team as a case goes to trial to help draft witness statements, go to court and organise exhibits.

The white collar team, poached in 2011 from DLA Piper, has seen an influx of work recently now that many of the prosecutions of the Bribery Act of 2010 are coming to fruition. The top-ranked practice handles a heady array of issues, from insider dealing and money laundering matters to fraud and corruption cases. Our sources praised the fast-paced seat for many reasons, not least that it offers the unique chance to work with forensic accountants who trace money flows between various companies. *"The hours are long but rewarding."* Trainees who'd wangled a government trade and sanctions seat were equally excited to report on the topical work that team has advised on of late, including the latest sanctions and asset-freezes imposed on Russians after the annexation of Crimea. A word of warning though: as *"thrilling"* as the subject matter is, the day-to-day work for trainees does involve its fair share of low-level tasks like doc review.

Insiders tell us the IP department is small enough that *"you get maximum exposure – everything comes to you!"* The work spans both the contentious and non-contentious spheres, and on the client books are basmati rice brand Tilda, holiday dream-maker Thomas Cook and online fashion juggernaut ASOS. The team spends a good chunk of its time managing trademark portfolios, an undertaking that sees trainees draft oppositions to trademarks that have infringed those of the firm's clients, and take on plenty of research. One interviewee said: *"I've drafted a number of articles on IP issues, including data protection law – a hot topic right now."* Research also crops up frequently in the tax department, where *"academic and technical"* work reigns supreme.

Sources praised Dechert's *"very structured"* approach to feedback. Supervisors schedule informal mid-seat appraisals to give trainees a heads-up on their progress and how to improve, while end-of-seat reviews act as a formal assessment of a trainee's oral, written and time-management skills: *"You're assigned a panel partner when you first join who sits in on all of your reviews to get a rounded view of your development."*

Stuck in the middle

"Mid-Atlantic" was a term our interviewees threw around to describe Dechert's identity in London. *"We're not drenched in American culture by any means, but we do have the very entrepreneurial drive of our US roots,"* said one trainee, explaining *"the firm looks for clients in places other firms don't and, even as trainees, we're encouraged to be proactive and seek opportunities out."* Another visible Americanism is the incorporation of pro bono work – all fee earners in the City branch are required to complete 25 hours of it a year. One associate, Victoria Fitzpatrick, set a sterling example by journeying to Washington, DC to assist on the case that challenged the constitutionality of the controversial Defense of Marriage Act (DOMA). Trainees, while exempt from formal requirements, are encouraged to take part on the pro bono front, with many attending clinics at the Islington Legal Advice Centre and the Prince's Trust. However, one thing that hasn't spilled over from across the pond, however, is the demanding hours frequented by many US outfits, although sources did note there are clusters of lawyers at Dechert who tend to follow the *"typically American pattern of starting late and finishing late."*

For all their talk about US versus UK influences, of course, trainees were keen to emphasise that *"in the end we are an international firm with an international outlook."* Indeed, Dechert's rapid expansion has seen it lean evermore towards an identity defined by its global scope and transcontinental presence rather than its Yankee roots. With this growth comes the hope that retention rates will improve in London, where they've historically been rather poor. Our sources were optimistic about their chances at the time of our calls, and appreciated the firm's efforts to make the qualification process *"clear and structured – we know which departments have roles and what it entails to get them."* Ultimately seven of ten qualifiers stayed on with the firm in 2014.

A few trainees drew our attention to the NQ salary, which is £68,000, telling us *"on qualification the firm runs the risk of losing people to the American firms – Kirkland & Ellis or Bingham McCutchen, for example – that pay a lot more money."* That said, it's worth bearing in mind that Dechert's NQs still take home more than their magic circle counterparts, and their salary is not a million miles away from that of Jones Day, another US firm.

The social agenda is pretty low-key at Dechert, but the Christmas party is one highlight not to be missed. In past years, the swanky event has included treats like magicians and nail-painting booths, and in 2013 the pampering continued as lawyers kicked back and relaxed with massages. *"It sounds kind of weird, but it was nice!"* A Robbie Williams tribute act and Posh and Becks lookalikes rounded off the event, although these went down a bit like Marmite: *"People either loved or hated the cheesy 1990s angle."* The small trainee cohort is a close bunch, having had the chance to bond during their LPC at what's now the University of Law. The group recently hosted a networking event called Dechert Uncorked, with the aim of promoting the firm's profile in the business community. *"I went to an event recently and encountered people who didn't know how to pronounce Dechert! It's important that our profile matches the quality of work we're putting out."* Thanks to the success of Dechert Uncorked, trainees now receive a budget for similar events. *"They're all for us trying new ideas."*

Fresh ideas aren't limited to a business context: *"There's always the opportunity to start a sports team or organise a tournament."* Our sources weren't shy on the field either; many had found the time to participate in the football, cricket, netball or sailing teams. The latter competed in Britannia's 2014 Legal Cup, although it unfortunately lost out to Allen & Overy's nautical prowess. *"That so many of us get involved is a testament to the hours here. If they were that bad, no one would have time to go and play netball."*

And finally...

Given Dechert's enviable docket of work, our interviewees were confident that this firm's name will resonate more vibrantly in the years to come.

The True Picture

Dentons. The new Global Elite
law firm created by Salans,
FMC and SNR Denton.*

Join Dentons and you will launch your career in
a fast-paced, dynamic global firm. Join Dentons
and you will have access to the calibre of training,
support and practical experience that leads to
success. Join Dentons and you will be given all
the responsibility you can handle, right from the
start. Interested?

Learn more and apply at
dentons.com/uk-graduates

DENTONS ▷ Know the way

* Acritas Global Elite Law Firm Brand Index 2013.

© 2014 Dentons. Dentons is a global legal
practice providing services worldwide
through its member firms and affiliates.
Please see dentons.com for Legal Notices.

Dentons

The facts

Location: London, Milton Keynes
Number of UK partners/solicitors: 124/231
Total number of trainees: 34
Seats: 4x6 months
Alternative seats: overseas seats, secondments
Extras: pro bono – CAB, PopLaw Clinic

On chambersstudent.co.uk...

How to get into Dentons
More about seats
The Milton Keynes office
Dentons around the world

The True Picture

A succession of mega-mergers over the past few years has elevated this firm to spectacular heights – and it doesn't look like it's coming down any time soon.

Going for gold

Like a pubescent boy destined for a career as a high jumper, Dentons has been growing – and growing quickly. It all kicked off in 2010, when City mid-sizer Denton Wilde Sapte joined forces with American superstar Sonnenschein Nath & Rosenthal to form SNR Denton. With 1,400 lawyers plying their trade across 16 offices worldwide, this combined firm was among the 30 biggest ones on the planet by head count.

The next major development came in November 2012. Hopping aboard the expansion express train once more, the firm announced a three-way merger with Fraser Milner Casgrain and Salans. The former was one of Canada's most prominent firms, the latter a Parisian with a hefty international footprint. The newly forged legal giant was christened Dentons and launched in March 2013, shooting straight up the law firm charts. In fact, with roughly 2,600 lawyers in its ranks, it's one of today's top ten largest firms, with a mighty workforce spread across a whopping 79 offices, including locales as far afield as Doha, Beirut and Johannesburg (not to mention the equally exuberant Milton Keynes, which we'll get to shortly). It's worth noting that the firm is structured as a Swiss Verein, meaning its regions keep their profit pools separate from one another.

So, what do trainees in London – Dentons' biggest office – make of all this change? According to one, *"everyone is much happier under the Dentons brand than under SNR Denton. It looks better, sounds punchier and, as far as London is concerned, more effectively highlights our roots as a specialist in emerging markets and banking*

work, as well as our growth in newer areas like TMT." Certainly, banking has long been one of the firm's cornerstones in the UK and is a requisite pit-stop for trainees. Other historic strengths include energy and real estate, though the firm scores *Chambers UK* rankings across a whole host of practices, from construction to data protection to telecoms.

Dentons' UK presence is rounded off by – you guessed it – a Milton Keynes branch, which like the firm as a whole *"is very much in expansion mode right now."* The small trainee cohort there can choose between seats in construction, corporate, dispute resolution, employment, property litigation and real estate. Visit our website for the full scoop on this office.

Learning the ABCs

The 2013 merger gave Dentons a stonking number of extra practice and sector groups. These now slot into five broad divisions: Middle East; EIPF (energy, infrastructure and project finance) and real estate; corporate; litigation; and banking. Trainees don't have a say in which seat they start off in, but they do get to express three preferences before each subsequent rotation. We've

Seat options: banking and finance; competition; construction; corporate; dispute resolution, employment and pensions; energy; property litigation; real estate; technology, media and telecoms; transport and infrastructure

Chambers UK rankings

Administrative & Public Law	Litigation
Asset Finance	Local Government
Banking & Finance	Outsourcing
Banking Litigation	Pensions
Capital Markets	Planning
Commercial Contracts	Professional Negligence
Commodities	Projects
Construction	Public Procurement
Corporate/M&A	Real Estate
Data Protection	Real Estate Finance
Employment	Real Estate Litigation
Energy & Natural Resources	Restructuring/Insolvency
Environment	Retail
Hotels & Leisure	Sports Law
Information Technology	Tax
Intellectual Property	Telecommunications
	Transport

heard complaints in the past about the way assignment is handled, but this year's cohort voiced few objections, so it looks like any wrinkles in the system have largely been smoothed out.

With over 100 lawyers UK-wide, the firm's banking practice is one of the biggest in the country and draws in business from a multitude of major financial institutions across the funds, Islamic finance and acquisition finance spheres, among them Standard Chartered Bank and Investec. Trainees here get to choose between three subgroups. Group A covers general banking and real estate finance matters, while group B does asset finance, project finance and trade finance. Meanwhile group C handles derivatives, capital markets, regulatory and structured finance matters. All three are similar in size and can hold an even share of trainees at once.

According to our sources, each subgroup dishes out a reasonable level of responsibility off the bat, *"and tasks get gradually more advanced throughout the course of the seat."* Case in point: *"I started off with menial tasks like proofreading and post-completion stuff, but it wasn't long before I was trusted to speak to clients directly."* We hear the working hours in banking are *"more erratic than in most other departments,"* but insiders agreed: *"It's worth it for the thrill of helping close huge deals."*

Real estate is another colossal department packed with top-notch clients, including the likes of Sainsbury's, John Lewis and the London Borough of Hammersmith & Fulham. *"A lot of property work is done in Milton Keynes,"* a source shared, *"so that clients can have Dentons' quality work without the City rates."* A sizeable chunk of the team's work revolves around the rail industry, especially

following the firm's appointment to Network Rail's legal panel in April 2013. Dentons was one of only five firms to make the cut and has since been advising the rail company on recently proposed regulatory changes. On the trainee side *"there are numerous files to run on your own,"* and more than one interviewee told of acting as *"the first port of call for clients."*

Dispute resolution is one of a handful of contentious seats on offer. The department makes full use of Dentons' repertoire of banking clients, recently representing big shots Deutsche Bank and Société Générale, and advising DEPFA on the German-Irish bank's multimillion-pound dispute with UBS and German water supply company KWL. Trainees described their role as *"varied,"* telling us: *"There's a lot of involvement in the court process"* in the way of drafting court applications, carrying out disclosures and preparing bundles.

Given the firm's global outlook, it's hardly surprising that an international aroma pervades many of its departments. We heard from some sources who'd collaborated with the firm's US and European branches, although *"as a trainee, you can expect most of the international work to relate to the Middle East and Africa,"* such is Dentons' *"knack for sniffing out work in emerging markets."* Many of our interviewees had actually applied to the firm with these regions in mind.

There are normally a few overseas seats on offer, with Dubai, Abu Dhabi and Muscat all featuring as recent destinations. *"If you're not interested in the Middle East, then you might find the options disappointing."* That said, things might be changing, with trainees telling us: *"The firm is keen to provide more because there's a real appetite for it."* Graduate recruitment partner Sarah Dyke confirms: *"It's something we're constantly assessing,"* but emphasises that business needs must come first. *"It's important that we send trainees to offices that can provide appropriate work for them to do."* There are also a handful of client secondments available.

Check out our website for more on Dentons' other seats, including energy, competition, and transport and infrastructure.

If you can't stand the heat...

Over a year on from its latest merger, Dentons' hallways continue to buzz with glee. *"It's an exciting backdrop to work against,"* trainees agreed, telling us: *"People are pulling together and putting in the hard graft."* Of course, gargantuan growth doesn't come without its own set of trade-offs. *"With all this expansion taking place, you could say there's a bit more of a corporate vibe here now than there was pre-merger,"* said one source. *"It feels like business has really picked up, and there is heaps of ambition on show."* As another pointed out, one only need look to the firm's graduate recruitment campaign over the past few years for evidence of a top-down shift: *"When I applied, the slogan in our ad was 'Wherever we are in the world, we're down to earth'; then a year later it became 'Can you take the heat?'"*

Mention of this shift prompted us to ask our interviewees whether the firm is on the hunt for a different breed of trainee these days. *"It seems to me that they want to appeal to the sort of people who would previously only look at the magic circle, because they feel they can now match those firms with the quality of work,"* commented one, while another chimed in to say: *"I think we're attracting more driven candidates than before. When we visit law fairs, we get students who are overtly interested in the recent mergers and where the firm is heading."* Despite all this talk of ambition, however, our sources were keen to emphasise that *"we haven't become corporate monsters overnight or anything. In fact, in many ways we've maintained the close-knit environment Denton Wilde Sapte was known for."*

Trainee-partner relations were cited as one such example. *"The partners are very aware of how we're getting on, and it's rare to come across any Demon Headmaster types."* Dealings are even chummier in the trainee ranks, with the cohort regularly heading for Friday drinks at the nearby Jamies Wine Bar or the Corney & Barrow (conveniently situated under the office). The firm also does its bit, mind you. A raft of social events are put on throughout the year, from quiz nights and drinks evenings to sponsored walks. And if you consider yourself to be of the athletic sort, there are over 20 sports teams to get involved in too. One recent do on most trainees' lips was the 2013 summer party – *"the first since the tripartite merger became official. They put up a marquee by the Tower of London, the firm's band played a few tunes, and one of the trainees even did a rap. It went something like, 'I got 99 problems, but this pitch ain't one.'"* Move aside, Jay-Z; there's a new hip-hop maestro on the block.

Keep calm and keep us on

Dentons' qualification process has received some much-needed TLC over the past couple of years. We used to hear frequent grumbles about a needlessly complex system that saw second-years forced to submit a written application, go through two interviews, carry out a drafting exercise and complete a Watson-Glaser aptitude test. Thankfully, the process has since been streamlined – the drafting exercise and Watson-Glaser test have been dropped. What's more, the list of available NQ jobs is now released in May to ensure hopefuls are informed of the outcome a lot earlier than in the past. *"They've been good at explaining everything to us,"* insiders shared. *"It's given us all confidence that we're going to get a fair crack of the whip."*

Retention rates have proved another source of contention in previous years. Just under three-quarters of qualifiers were kept on in 2013, and the same was true in 2012. That might sound like a decent return, but when pitted against the average for London firms – around 79% in 2013 – it's nothing to write home about. The second-years we chatted to this year were upbeat about their chances nonetheless. *"It feels like business has been booming,"* thought one, *"so I hope the retention figure reflects that."* In the end, 25 of 32 qualifiers stayed on in 2014.

So what does the future hold for this ever-growing legal titan? If its merger talks with America's McKenna Long & Aldridge in late 2013 are anything to go by, a bigger presence in the US seems to be on the cards. These eventually fell through, but in April 2014 the firm was at it again, entering discussions with DC native Patton Boggs and Cleveland-founded Squire Sanders over a potential tie-up. Sarah Dyke remains tight-lipped on any specifics, but after our conversation with her we were left with the clear impression that the firm may consider making up for the remaining gaps in its global footprint. In other words: watch this space.

And finally...

It'll be intriguing to see if this firm undergoes further changes over the coming year. Of course, with an already immense network of offices and bucketfuls of ambition, now seems as good a time as any to join the Dentons family.

DLA Piper LLP

The facts

Locations: Birmingham, Leeds, Liverpool, London, Manchester, Sheffield, Edinburgh

Number of UK partners/solicitors: 264/771

Total number of trainees: 154

Seats: 4x6 months

Alternative seats: overseas seats, secondments

Extras: pro bono – A4ID, Hillside Legal Advice Clinic, i-Probono, LawWorks, Prince's Trust, ProHelp, National Pro Bono Centre, TrustLaw

On chambersstudent.co.uk...

How to get into DLA Piper
The world's biggest law firms

The number of lawyers under DLA Piper's roof may be a world record, but its trainees don't feel lost in the crowd.

Big Friendly Giant

With nearly 80 offices – including six across England's biggest legal markets – and a staggering 4,200 lawyers worldwide, this young firm dwarfs all of its longer-established City rivals. You might think that smashing the record for world's largest firm – before the age of ten, no less – would prompt management to stop and take a breath, but a push to grow further is central to DLA's strategy. In 2013 the firm launched a new office in Seoul and entered an alliance with an outfit in Indonesia, although the past few years have seen it take some more painful strategic decisions too. The firm's consolidation of its Singapore and Hong Kong offices prompted a spate of partner exits in July 2014, bringing the number of partner defections from the DLA's Asia Pacific region since May 2013 to a discouraging 19. In the UK, the firm began 2013 by entering consultations for one of the biggest rounds of lay-offs since 2008, which ultimately resulted in it closing its office in Glasgow and divesting its defendant insurance arm. Then it ended 2013 by cutting 69 support staff.

Our sources attributed all this chopping and changing to the way that *"there's no sense of complacency at DLA. They drill it into us that our aim is to become the leading global law firm and, despite our size, the firm feels it's still got a long way to go."* According to training principal Duncan Mosley, *"we've filled in the major holes in our geographical spread at this point, so now we're concentrating on exploiting what we've got to the full. We have to integrate our network fully with the US to be a truly global firm."* Indeed, while the firm's global presence touches on locations as far-flung as Tbilisi, Bangkok and Caracas, it maintains a concentrated presence in the US and UK – more than half of its lawyers reside between the two, with around 860 across the latter. Former Linklaters managing partner Tony Angel was hired in 2011 to increase integration between the firm's UK and US offices, but he's stepping down from the role of global co-chair in 2015. For now though, the firm's UK and US factions remain financially independent of each other, and our trainee sources reported little contact with their US counterparts.

That said, there has been an increasing amount of interaction between lawyers on UK shores. *"They're pushing a 'one UK' policy, which promotes the sharing of workloads between offices."* As a trainee in Sheffield pointed out, this push has more to do with keeping costs down than promoting collaboration, but: *"Regional rates are often cheaper, so we've seen a lot of London work filtering in through here lately, although the firm isn't neglecting its local ties."*

Tale of two cities

DLA Piper's London office, split between two City buildings, is easily its biggest in the UK and takes a whopping 30 trainees a year. At the same time, with annual intakes of around ten trainees each, the full-service branches in Birmingham, Manchester, Leeds, Liverpool and Shef-

Seat options: corporate; employment; finance and projects; IP and technology; litigation and regulatory; real estate; restructuring; tax (see online for breakdown by office)

Chambers UK rankings

Asset Finance	Investment Funds
Aviation	Licensing
Banking & Finance	Litigation
Banking Litigation	Local Government
Capital Markets	Media & Entertainment
Commodities	Outsourcing
Competition/European Law	Parliamentary & Public Affairs
Construction	Pensions
Consumer Finance	Planning
Corporate Crime & Investigations	Private Equity
Corporate/M&A	Product Liability
Data Protection	Professional Negligence
Employment	Projects
Energy & Natural Resources	Public International Law
Environment	Public Procurement
Fraud	Real Estate
Health & Safety	Real Estate Finance
Healthcare	Real Estate Litigation
Hotels & Leisure	Restructuring/Insolvency
Information Technology	Retail
Insurance	Sports Law
Intellectual Property	Tax
International Arbitration	Telecommunications
	Transport

field are still among the biggest firms in their respective cities. *"I get to live in the North, but still make use of my language skills thanks to the international work we do,"* said a Liverpudlian. There's a wide range of seats on offer at each office, and before each rotation trainees submit three or four seat preferences. There's the option to spend six months in another office if it offers a seat you're particularly interested in, and there are also around ten corporate secondments on offer to household-name clients. *"I was worried the decision as to who gets to go would be London-centric as many of them are based there, but it's not,"* said a source up North. *"Trainees all around the country can go to these."* Given the firm's international network, it comes as little surprise there are numerous overseas seats up for grabs too. More on these later.

The nearly 80-strong trainee cohort kicks off the training contract by gathering for a week of training at a hotel; the 2013 programme took place in Crewe. *"You do your PSCs during the day and get to socialise in evening at dinner – one evening there was a festival theme, complete with an ice cream truck and a band. It really got us all excited about working together."* A few days of *"intense training"* also take place at the beginning of each seat rotation. *"Trainees from the whole practice group will come together in one office or join up via video-link."*

When it comes qualification time, trainees can apply to any office and any department. *"You fill in forms detailing the experience you've received, and then you interviews for the role. We get a lot of guidance about what we should be doing at each stage."* Every year, a few regional qualifiers end up moving to London. Trainee sources told us that *"most offices will ask about your commitment to working in a certain region when you apply for a training contract"* However, a recruitment source told us candidates are in fact no longer asked about this in trainee interviews, as the firm is keen to have a mobile workforce. In 2014, DLA retained 70 of its 89 qualifying trainees.

Capital gold

DLA's corporate practice scores top *Chambers UK* rankings in Sheffield, Birmingham, Leeds, Manchester and London, reflecting the impressive range of national and international work on offer. Trainees in the latter branch had encountered M&A, private equity and capital markets matters, and told us *"the deals are really high in value, so sometimes it's hard to know exactly what's going on – you end up doing a lot of verification work."* Lawyers here recently represented Discovery Communications on its $1.7bn acquisition of a Scandinavian broadcasting business, and advised Etihad Airways on its $600m partnership with Indian airline Jet, as well as its acquisition of a stake in Serbian airline Jat (the latter is conveniently renaming itself Air Serbia to avoid confusion). Out in the regions, sources told us *"the bread and butter work is M&A,"* but we did hear from some who'd had a broader experience than that. *"I actually worked on a few capital markets matters with international companies alongside work for regional clients,"* said a trainee in Birmingham. *"I got to draft almost every document on one sale, apart from the main purchase agreement, and went to lots of client meetings."*

Chambers UK ranks DLA as top dog for litigation in Liverpool, Sheffield, Birmingham and Manchester, and the London team also gets a nod. The team there is split into litigation, arbitration and corporate crime factions, and has had a hand in some very high-profile proceedings of late, including representing Andy Coulson during criminal allegations of phone hacking as well as several parliamentary and judicial inquiries. Over in arbitration, there's the chance to attend the London Court of International Arbitration or even the International Courts of Justice in The Hague. *"It's usually big-ticket cases in these courts, so as a trainee you have input into a lot of small tasks like compiling exhibits."* Meanwhile, we heard from trainees in the regions who'd encountered shipping, coal mining, IT, fraud and insurance disputes between them. *"There are also a lot of high-volume small claims like debt cases, which you can see progress from start to finish in the same seat."* On bigger matters *"you don't have too much freedom,"* but interviewees assured us *"everyone tries to get trainees involved in meaty tasks like disclo-*

The True Picture

sure or drafting wherever possible." We heard from a few who'd liaised with counsel overseas and attended client dinners, and even one who told of *"travelling down to London for an international arbitration, which was fantastic experience."*

DLA's real estate arm counts a number of household names as clients, including British Airways, EAT, easyJet and JD Sports. Trainees here are asked to step to the plate early on. *"I was handed over 30 files on my first day,"* said one. *"It's a big ask, but taking them and running with it makes you feel like an NQ."* Those based in London and Leeds found themselves assisting with portfolio management, refinancings and restructurings for national financial institutions like RBS and NatWest. *"It's great to be part of a deal involving hundreds of properties nationwide, even if your role is mainly administrative. On one portfolio I was in charge of managing all the deeds."* Meanwhile, trainees outside the capital reported *"a lot of small tenant and landlord matters"* for local clients. *"You liaise daily with the clients, and you do a lot of crossover work with corporate and finance too."* Indeed, the three teams recently joined forces in Liverpool to oversee the several sales for Dutch property investor Wereldhave, including that of the Dolphin and Towngate Shopping Centres in Poole.

Trainees on the projects side had encountered *"some really interesting infrastructure, public procurement and energy work"* in London. Over in Manchester, the team frequently works for local education authorities and hospital trusts, and we're told renewables work *"is really taking off in Leeds – we've had wind farm deal after wind farm deal."* The Manchester, Liverpool, Leeds and London groups recently teamed up to advise on the £600m Mersey Gateway Project, which will result in a new 1km-long bridge over the River Mersey. *"There's a lot of proofreading and research day to day, but once you show you're capable of doing more, they let you."* Indeed, sources reported drafting contracts and meeting clients on their own.

Oh Dla Dla!

Roughly a quarter to a third of trainees go abroad at some point during their time with the firm, choosing from seats in Dubai, Abu Dhabi, Singapore, Moscow, Madrid,

Bangkok, Sydney and Hong Kong. *"You used to be able to apply based on destination, but now they've decided to attach certain practice areas to certain places"* – eg Sydney, Dubai and Moscow all offer corporate seats. Singapore is particularly social as *"there are about 50 trainees out there from various firms at any one time."* A source with experience there praised the experience, telling us *"I got to travel around most of Asia – we'd literally go on a trip every other weekend."* We also heard good things about the responsibility on offer overseas – *"I got to make calls about what advice to give clients"* – and the experience of grappling with new jurisdictions: *"It's really valuable to learn about the way the international network operates, particularly from a client's point of view."*

We didn't hear many complaints from trainees at DLA, but one recurring grumble we did hear came from regional trainees and regarded hours: *"It's fair to say our hours are tougher than at other local firms – sometimes it feels like we're working London hours, but only getting paid a regional salary."* At the same time, *"you feel valued for the work and hours you put it, so it's not all bad."* According to our interviewees, trainees are encouraged to *"take the wheel from the get-go – the onus is on you to throw yourself into the team and to find out as much as you can about something before you start asking questions. That can be daunting, but it does pay off when you realise how much input you've actually had in a certain deal or case."* Despite heavy workloads, *"people here make an effort to enjoy themselves – you can have more fun here than you might expect of such a big firm."*

Indeed, trainees described the social scene as *"one of the best things about life at DLA. It's almost too much fun."* We don't know about that, but we can tell you there trainees across the firm regularly enjoy drinks with their fellow officemates – *"that can get quite messy"* – and the trainee cohort at large. *"We meet up for training sessions regularly, and we always argue over which office is the best."* We're inclined to vote Birmingham, which is home to an *"amazing"* chef who whips up tiffin and cakes for an 11am tea, although Sheffield's breakfast fry-ups deserve an honourable mention. Another cross-office get-together is the Burns Night gathering hosted in Edinburgh, complete with a ceilidh, bagpipes, haggis and Champagne.

And finally...
DLA may be big in size, but big egos need not apply. *"People here are down to earth and easy to get on – hoity-toity does not go down well."*

DWF LLP

The facts

Locations: Birmingham, Bristol, Coventry, Leeds, Liverpool, London, Manchester, Milton Keynes, Newcastle, Preston, Teesside, Scotland, Northern Ireland

Number of UK partners/solicitors: 270/643

Total number of trainees: 96

Seats: 6x4 months

Alternative seats: occasional secondments

Extras: language classes

On chambersstudent.co.uk...

How to get into DWF

DWF's stratospheric growth

An astounding period of growth has transformed this dynamic Northerner into a national marvel.

Hunger Games

We all have goals we strive to accomplish in life, whether it's realising a lifelong dream of winning an Oscar (it'll happen one day, Leo) or aiming for something smaller like getting that promotion. For DWF, becoming a top 20 UK law firm based on revenue was the aspiration topping its bucket list in 2013. Having secured top 30 status by the start of that year – thanks largely to its combination with five (yes, five) firms between January 2012 and February 2013 – the home-grown Mancunian set itself a 2015 deadline for levelling up. However, in a fortunate and remarkable twist the firm managed to nab the number 19 spot by the end of 2013, achieving its feat two years ahead of schedule. *"It is a fantastic result and means that in terms of our size and reach we're now a major national player,"* says graduate recruitment partner James Szerdy. *"In 2013/14 we've been concentrating on integrating all of our people, systems and processes."*

The firm's expansion drive kicked into gear long before 2013 though. Once just a compact regional outfit with four offices up north, DWF has undergone a lot of pivotal changes since Andrew Leaitherland took charge in 2006 at the tender age of 36. A year into his appointment as managing partner, DWF merged with Ricksons, another neighbour in the North, upping its workforce to 800-strong and its turnover to more than £50m. A truckload of lateral hires followed over the next few years, and then came the impressive string of mergers in 2012/13, which culminated in the acquisitions of professional indemnity maven Fishburns and a big chunk of collapsed Manchester firm Cobbetts. These days, DWF has around £200m in revenue and 2,500-plus staff working wonders across 12 offices in England, Scotland and Ireland.

It all sounds rather exciting, doesn't it? Of course, we've seen firms step on the gas like this before, racing towards the upper echelons of the legal world only to crash and burn along the way. Fortunately, DWF's management isn't oblivious to the concerns some might have about being the next Halliwells. *"The challenges faced by rapidly growing firms have been well documented,"* says James Szerdy, *"and we're aware there are suggestions we're expanding too quickly."* It's been pretty smooth sailing so far though: the £17m DWF spent on its expansion efforts in 2012/13 was a small price to pay for the 84% hike in turnover it achieved in the process, and debt levels remain relatively low for the moment.

Insurance work has long been at the core of DWF's practice, and it accounts for roughly half of the firm's overall takings. The personal injury defence team is the jewel in the crown, as illustrated by its top-tier nationwide ranking in *Chambers UK*. *"Given how big our insurance offering is, it's likely you'll do a seat there at some point,"* an insider shared. Commercial services comprise the other half of turnover, and the DWF has been making some impressive headway on that front. Recent months have

Seat options: casualty; catastrophic personal injury; insurance; occupational health; professional indemnity; commercial insurance; claims; healthcare; asset finance; banking; commercial; corporate; corporate tax; pensions; private client; construction, infrastructure and projects; planning; real estate; business restructuring; commercial litigation; employment; family; finance litigation; insured litigation; real estate litigation; regulatory (see online for breakdown by office)

The True Picture

Chambers UK rankings

Administrative & Public Law	Intellectual Property
Banking & Finance	Licensing
Banking Litigation	Litigation
Charities	Local Government
Civil Liberties & Human Rights	Parliamentary & Public Affairs
Competition/European Law	Partnership
Construction	Pensions
Consumer Finance	Personal Injury
Corporate/M&A	Planning
Education	Police Law
Employment	Private Client
Energy & Natural Resources	Product Liability
Environment	Professional Negligence
Family/Matrimonial	Projects
Health & Safety	Real Estate
Information Technology	Real Estate Litigation
Insurance	Restructuring/Insolvency
	Retail
	Social Housing
	Transport

seen some big client additions, among them M&S and Metro Bank, as well as the hiring of Pinsent Masons' former financial institutions head, Stephen Miles, who was brought on board in April 2014 to lead the commercial services division.

Set the CAT among the Pigeons

This year's trainees spoke glowingly about DWF's six-seat system: *"You get a great breadth of experience by working across so many teams, which really helps with the decision of where you want to qualify."* Seat options differ depending on the office, with the biggest selection in Liverpool and Manchester, but *"you're not confined to the office you're based in. They publish the list of options nationally, and if you want to do a seat offered in another office, it's easy enough."*

The firm's insurance expertise encompasses just about every area of the practice there is, from catastrophic injuries to fraudulent claims, and many of the industry's biggest hotshots are on its books, including Aviva, QBE, Zurich and Allianz. In most cases lawyers act on behalf of defendants, who are usually insurers or brokers. Occupational health is one of several seats up for grabs in the department. *"I dealt with a lot of death and disease claims concerning people in the workplace,"* said one source with experience in the seat, telling us *"it was really fascinating."* Interviewees told us that on high-value claims, *"you're usually just assisting other fee earners with one-off tasks, like drafting statements or conducting research,"* while cases with a lower value *"grant you*

more free rein. You'll be drafting things like court documents, instructions to counsel and witness statements."

Another insurance seat is catastrophic personal injury (CAT PI), which involves injury defence work for insurers. The group is one of the largest of its kind in the UK and in late 2013 it welcomed a 47-strong team, including 11 partners, from insurance specialist Greenwoods – a development that prompted DWF to launch a small operation in Milton Keynes. The subject matter handled in CAT PI is pretty heavy – think amputations and spinal injuries.

Blazin' squad

Insiders were adamant that DWF's real estate practice *"is thriving right now,"* and a look at the figures shows they're right on the money, thanks largely to the Cobbetts takeover, the department raked in £13.5m during the first half of 2013/14 – a whopping 92% increase on the same period the previous year. Consequently, real estate work now accounts for around 15% of the firm's total earnings. *"The team is very busy, so it's a bit crazy when you start,"* remarked one source, adding *"that means you get plenty of responsibility."* Trainees typically find themselves liaising with clients and preparing lease reports, and we're told *"you get to run a few of your own files from start to finish."* The clientele spans a range of sectors, including hotel and leisure (Premier Inn), education (Liverpool John Moores University) and retail (adidas), and lawyers also collaborate with their banking colleagues on property finance matters for big-name banks like RBS and Barclays.

A stint in commercial litigation comes with a mouth-watering assortment of work, from negligence claims to contentious probate matters. This variety can be chalked up to the array of sectors the firm covers, among them food and drink, sports, retail and the public sector. In 2013, lawyers handled some particularly high-profile cases, including the Liverpool team's representation of fitness club Langstone Leisure in one of the biggest professional negligence battles of the year. Trainees' involvement in such cases is likely to err towards the lower-level end of the scale, but litigation trainees across the firm had plenty of praise for the levels of responsibility they'd encountered, gleefully reporting heaps of court experience. *"I got to attend the Royal Courts of Justice as well as a few mediation meetings – both were great for my development,"* said a Leeds source.

DWF's banking lawyers act for most of the major banks, including Santander, Nationwide and Barclays, and excels in property finance and social housing matters in particular. The Newcastle team recently advised Lloyds Bank on a £25m financing for luxury property developer Story Homes, while colleagues over in Manchester helped Warrington Borough Council secure funding for the redevelopment of a former RAF airbase. One trainee in Liverpool said: *"Our team focuses mostly on public finance. I ran a lot of my own files and got some good exposure to clients. There was a fair bit of business development too – I attended a ton of networking events."*

Meanwhile, those in employment told of encountering unfair dismissal and whistle-blowing claims, as well as matters involving directors and executives. *"Cases are quickly turned over pretty quickly, so you get to see a lot from start to finish."* The group nabbed some impressive clients in recent years, including Newsquest and Iceland Foods.

Walkie Scorchie

Trainees in years past have called DWF a *"fun-loving"* and *"down-to-earth"* place, with one 2012 source insisting that *"the staff comes before the work here."* Given the firm's astronomical transformation over the past two years, we were keen to find out whether these characteristics still hold true today.

According to the current crop of trainees, they most certainly do. *"There have been so many changes since we began as trainees, especially after the mergers last year, but it's all settled down nicely, and things are going as well as ever,"* said one, confirming that the arrival of new colleagues has done little to upset the status quo. *"Like us, both firms had very people-oriented cultures, so their lawyers have proved a good fit."* A jam-packed social calendar has gone a long way in helping everybody get acquainted. In addition to dedicated integration socials, there have been summer and Christmas bashes, quiz nights, sports tournaments, charity balls and countless networking events dotted across the past year. Each office is treated to a monthly drinks event known as Friday Fridge, and we hear that trainees regularly meet up for lunch and after-work boozing too. *"DWF invests a lot of time in making sure we're happy. Overall, we're not as austere as some firms, particularly large ones, appear to be."*

Our interviewees praised the prominent role that managing partner Andrew Leaitherland plays in ensuring they don't just feel like another cog in the DWF machine. The man at the helm is heavily involved in the recruitment process, and hosts a biannual trainee dinner that doubles as a forum for questions and concerns. *"We get first-hand information about where the firm is heading, and we get to put forth our own ideas of how things could be improved. It's great to have that face-to-face interaction with the executive board – they're not just names you see at the bottom of an email."* Sources also had good things to say about their day-to-day exchanges with senior figures, with one telling us *"my volume of stupid questions is endless, but people are always happy to listen to them. It's clear they value everyone here, regardless of their seniority."*

DWF isn't exactly famed for its presence in London, but the firm's taking steps to change this. In early 2014, management announced plans to move into the iconic Walkie Talkie building on Fenchurch Street. You may have come across this 37-storey skyscraper before: it made the news for all the wrong reasons in September 2013 by inadvertently frying a bike and bits of a Jaguar, giving new meaning to the phrase Hot Property. *"London is becoming a major area of growth for us,"* trainees told us, and it looks like the office's population is set to expand. *"We've always taken a cautious, measured stance towards our growth strategy in London,"* says James Szerdy, *"but we have recently brought in some significant lateral hires and will continue with that strategy."* The past years have seen the London cohort welcome a wave of partners from Stephenson Harwood, TLT, Wragge & Co and Lawrence Graham (note: these last two firms have since merged), and Szerdy's comments suggest that more hires will follow. That said, he makes a point to stress that *"a key factor to the London growth is the strategy around the expanding teams working with our regional offices,"* so don't expect DWF to suddenly become a London-centred firm.

Consolidation looks to be the next step in DWF's master plan. *"It's all about cementing our position in the top 20 at the moment,"* insiders confirmed. It would take something pretty drastic for DWF to break into that illustrious top ten any time soon, but there's no question that the mantra onwards and upwards is already on management's mind. *"We're always trying to better ourselves and maximise business opportunities where possible,"* one interviewee summed up. *"This is a very exciting firm to be a part of, especially as a trainee."*

And finally...

Last year DWF's retention rate *"suffered a slight blip by its own immaculate standards"* – an unfortunate consequence of the 2013 takeovers, which doubled the contingent of second-year trainees. Luckily, things are back on track: the firm kept on 39 out of 48 qualifiers in 2014.

The True Picture

Edwards Wildman Palmer UK LLP

The facts

Location: London

Number of UK partners/solicitors: 26/37

UK partners who trained at firm: 15%

Total number of trainees: 12

Seats: 4x6 months

Alternative seats: secondments

Extras: pro bono – Fair Trials International, LawWorks, RCJ CAB, Own-It; language classes

On chambersstudent.co.uk...
How to get into Edwards Wildman

A series of mergers carried this ambitious US firm across the Atlantic, where it has a *"relaxed and chatty"* London office.

Merger of red, white and blues

The London branch of this 600-lawyer firm has little in common, at least culturally, with its American parent. Back in 2008, US shop Edwards Angell Palmer & Dodge merged with UK insurance outfit Kendall Freeman, then went on to strengthen this transatlantic partnership further by adding Chicago native Wildman, Harrold, Allen & Dixon into the mix in 2011. Because of Kendall Freeman's long-standing roots in the UK, we're told the London office *"maintains a distinctly British feel,"* despite being part of a predominantly US firm. *"We don't get crazy American salaries, either,"* added a trainee. *"But equally they don't expect every hour of the day from us."* In addition to London and the dozen US offices, Edwards Wildman has bases in Tokyo, Hong Kong and, as of 2013, Istanbul.

While trainees acknowledged that *"all the changes in the past few years mean the firm today isn't the same one we applied to years ago,"* they were keen to point out *"it's certainly going in the right direction."* Revenue in London hit a hefty £23.4m in 2013/14, and the firm has onboarded some notable clients in recent years, including Warner Brothers, Guardian Media and renowned muggle JK Rowling. Kendall Freeman's historic insurance offering still forms an important part of the practice, while commercial litigation, IP and corporate comprise the other cornerstones. All of these are ranked by *Chambers UK*.

Take a seat

While none of Edwards Wildman's seats are compulsory, most trainees pass through litigation and business law at some point. New recruits meet with HR before each rotation to discuss their preferences, but seats are allocated predominantly on business need. *"They don't see any point in sending trainees to departments where there isn't enough work; you learn more in the busy ones,"* said one source, telling us: *"Most people end up happy with the way it's done."*

Sources took an equally positive view of the firm's training programme, which entails a week-long induction followed by *"drip-fed"* training. *"At least once a week partners hold lunch sessions on subjects like instructing counsel or writing witness statements. Everybody finds them really useful."*

The insurance practice counts Centre Re, Munich Re and Swiss Re among its more well-known clients. The contentious team recently represented all three in a £500m asbestos dispute over T&N Asbestos Trust's liability policy, while the advisory side assisted Fairfax Financial Holdings on the regulatory aspects of its recent acquisition of American Safety Re. *"It's a very technical seat, but you get a lot of support, and it's easy to ask ques-*

Seat options: insurance and reinsurance; commercial litigation; restructuring and insolvency; business law; employment; competition; IP

Chambers UK rankings

Corporate/M&A	Litigation
Insurance	Public International Law
Intellectual Property	

tions," insiders told us, adding that trainees *"can get involved in everything from complex litigation and arbitration to minor policy review work and small disputes."* Day-to-day tasks include putting together cost assessments and researching technical points, and several sources had attended High Court hearings. *"I was able to draft parts of a closing submission and meet with clients day in, day out."*

Over in commercial litigation lawyers tackle asset recovery, anti-corruption cases, international arbitrations *"and everything in between."* This variety is apparent from the team's client roster: Tata Steel, Bambino Holdings, money broker Tullet Prebon and the government of Nigeria have all sought the firm's advice in recent years. In 2014 the team defended Amazon after cosmetics company Lush accused the superstore of trade mark infringement. Much of the trainee work here centres around research, *"often on subjects that are niche and difficult to explore. I had to look into the Bribery Act's impact on the insurance industry, which meant going to the British Library to look in the national archives."* This academic approach might seem snooze-worthy to some, but our insiders took a bright-eyed view: *"All the research is relevant, and you can see how it's used."* When they're not hitting the books, trainees are generally grappling with documents. *"When you're acting for a foreign government, the stakes are high, so I think we're all happy to get on with it."*

Amazonian Wildmans

Business law covers private equity, banking, M&A and corporate matters for a mix of small start-ups and bigger names like Citibank, Morgan Stanley and telecoms service provider GTS. Lawyers recently advised the last of these on its €546m sale to Deutsche Telekom. Such transactions typically see trainees *"sitting in on the call, rather than leading it"* and getting stuck into *"standard trainee fare like due diligence, data rooms and board minutes. You also get to draft things like loan note instruments."* During start-up matters, on the other hand, *"you're kind of left to fend for yourself, which is great. I got to run investment rounds on my own, draft shareholder resolutions and research how to get rid of company*

directors. It's a great seat for learning how companies and certain business procedures work."*

Those interested in life on the other side will be pleased to know the firm runs client secondments with some of its high-profile clients, including Amazon, Warner Brothers and Citibank. Nearly every trainee does one. *"That was a major draw for me, and I wasn't disappointed,"* said one interviewee of their experience in-house. *"I got an astronomical amount of responsibility and was engaging with clients from day one. Without a supervisor, you're forced out of your comfort zone, but the payoff is tons of hands-on experience and an up-close view of how legal advice comes across to clients.* The firm doesn't offer overseas seats, but trainees did mention *"much of the work we do has international elements – for example disputes involving an Iraqi oil field or Caribbean jurisdictions."* We even heard of a few travelling abroad for certain cases, though we're told *"this is rare; it usually makes more sense for an associate to go."*

Where the Wild things are

The firm's London base is *"pretty much on top of Liverpool Street station,"* and its subsidised cafe, football tables, and cake and ice cream trolleys all prove big hits with trainees year after year. The interiors go down well, too: *"There are huge picture collages from people's holidays. It's a bright and friendly place to work."* Indeed, *"it's not an enormous office, so you can get to know everyone,"* sources told us, adding: *"That's easy anyway – people are always joking around and chatting over coffee. The firm is driven and ambitious, but that doesn't mean things aren't relaxed at the office. We're not one of those firms preoccupied with trying to take over the world at the expense of everything else."*

Trainees were generally pleased with their work/life balance, telling us: *"There's no such thing as face time here; when there's a slow period you're encouraged to go home."* Of course, *"hours do fluctuate – the corporate department can become particularly rammed at times."* There's plenty to get on with when the work's done. On the social front, we heard about everything from annual quizzes to summer picnics to mechanical bull-riding – the last took place at the 2013 Wild West-themed winter social. The more formal Christmas do that year was held in the office. *"It was a really good night – they converted one of the floors into a Winter Wonderland, with a vodka ice sculpture."*

And finally...

Last year the firm suffered a disappointing retention round, with only three of eight qualifiers gaining places. In 2014 four of seven NQs took up jobs with Edwards Wildman.

Eversheds LLP

The facts

Location: Birmingham, Cambridge, Cardiff, Leeds, London, Manchester, Newcastle, Nottingham, Ipswich, Scotland

Number of UK partners/solicitors: 288/1068

Total number of trainees: 105

Seats: 4x6 months

Alternative seats: overseas seats

On chambersstudent.co.uk...

How to get into Eversheds
Interview with training principal
Ian Gascoigne

Across the eight of its offices offering training contracts, Eversheds provides great opportunities to do high-quality national and international work.

Extrasheds

Some firms have a lot of UK offices; some firms do very wide-ranging work; some have a big network of international offices; some work on really big cases and deals. And Eversheds? It does all of these things. Is it trying to be all things to all people? Yeah, just a bit. Work ranges from education and energy to private equity and arbitration, and trainees come in all shapes and sizes too, from City slickers and transnational globetrotters to true-born Yorkshiremen and lasses from the Valleys.

"When I first applied what I noticed was the firm's aggressive expansion plan," said one trainee. *"It was nowhere in the early 2000s – and now we're everywhere."* 'Sheds has 53 offices around the world, from Milan and Madrid to Shanghai and Singapore. Judging by comments from trainees, its eggs are in a lot of baskets: *"Africa is quite a big focus at the moment,"* said one, while another believed the firm *"is trying to crack emerging markets like the BRICs,"* and a third said: *"We're thinking about merging with an American firm."*

For a while now Eversheds has been running its strategy plan in three-year cycles: *"The first aimed to make us full-service in the UK, the second international, and now we're going global!"* said one trainee. The current 2012-15 cycle is part of a '2020 vision' to be 'the global law firm that sets the standards'. This all sounds a bit highfalutin', but it seems the firm's ambitions really do match up to this statement. When we spoke to training principal Ian Gascoigne he made it clear that the firm's ambition to be 'global' involves establishing an increasing number of international outposts. Autumn 2013 saw the launch of the Eversheds Africa Law Institute, which provides link-ups with law firms in an impressive 33 countries. Ian Gascoigne also revealed that the firm *"is looking at the US"* and is investigating how it can best serve clients here and in other locations where it does not yet have a presence.

At present the overwhelming majority of the LLP is still UK-centred: 90% of the £376m it raked in during 2012/13 came from the UK, with 5% coming from continental Europe and 5% from the rest of the world. There are a growing number of overseas seat options, though – Paris, Hong Kong, Shanghai, Singapore and Doha all make the current list. While winning an overseas placement is competitive, *"no preference is given to trainees from London or any particular office; quite a lot of regional trainees end up going abroad."* Interviewees also agreed that *"if you want international work in the regions – especially somewhere like Manchester or Cardiff – Eversheds is definitely your best option."*

The firm recruits trainees in London, Birmingham, Leeds, Manchester, Cardiff, Cambridge, Nottingham and Newcastle. The first five of these are the biggest recruiters and offer the most seat options. Moving between

Seat options: banking; commercial; commercial disputes; competition; construction litigation; corporate; employment; environmental real estate; financial services; financial services, disputes and investigations; health and safety regulatory; insurance litigation; pensions; planning; real estate; real estate litigation; restructuring; shipping; tax (see online for breakdown by office)

Chambers UK rankings

Administrative & Public Law	Investment Funds
Banking & Finance	Licensing
Banking Litigation	Litigation
Capital Markets	Local Government
Commercial Contracts	Outsourcing
Competition/European Law	Parliamentary & Public Affairs
Construction	Pensions
Consumer Finance	Pensions Litigation
Corporate Crime & Investigations	Planning
Corporate/M&A	Product Liability
Data Protection	Professional Discipline
Education	Professional Negligence
Employee Share Schemes & Incentives	Projects
Employment	Public International Law
Energy & Natural Resources	Public Procurement
Environment	Real Estate
Financial Services	Real Estate Finance
Health & Safety	Real Estate Litigation
Healthcare	Restructuring/Insolvency
Information Technology	Retail
Insurance	Shipping
Intellectual Property	Social Housing
International Arbitration	Tax
	Telecommunications
	Transport

locations isn't required, but *"there's nothing to stop you applying for seats in other offices,"* especially if it's a seat not available where you're based. We spoke to several trainees who'd moved for this reason. Seat allocation itself was viewed as a well-run process. *"Generally it's done fairly, but of course it's difficult to come up with something everyone is happy with."* Pretty high praise for a firm this size.

Qualifiers who want a job are required to put in an application and undergo an interview. As one second-year pointed out: *"I think it's a fair system as the firm is trying to encourage the idea that trainees can apply to different offices and to departments they haven't sat in."* In 2014 51 out of 58 stayed with the firm on qualification.

Everything everywhere

Eversheds' corporate team is a market leader in Manchester, Birmingham and Leeds, while in London the firm is a top-of-the-mid-market player, with clients like John Lewis, Cisco Systems, Kier and BAE Systems. The Manchester team recently advised Manchester Airport on an £800m joint venture to develop a commercial/logistics airport hub. Besides M&A, trainees get involved in IPOs, restructurings, private

equity transactions and disposals. *"My tasks ranged from drafting ancillary documents like stock transfer forms and disclosure letters to organising the schedule for the share purchase agreement,"* said one interviewee. While trainees aren't spared administrative tasks like proofreading, scanning documents and bibling, they did report liaising with clients and attending completions.

Eversheds doesn't shy away from doing smaller deals and 'nuts and bolts' work for clients, which is good news for trainees. But nuts and bolts work doesn't have to be small-scale: *"I worked with one client who we serve in nearly all our offices,"* reported one source. *"We co-ordinate what's going on for them in all manner of jurisdictions."* The firm has around 30 core clients it acts for firm-wide, including Swiss security firm Tyco and the International Air Transport Association, with which the firm recently signed a multimillion-pound fixed-fee contract to provide legal advice in 158 countries. Some offices have a distinctive flavour to their corporate work. For example, Cambridge often acts for educational institutions, recently advising on the merger of Glamorgan and Newport universities.

Speaking of *materion Cymreig*, Eversheds is the biggest national law firm with a presence in Wales, and *Chambers UK* awards it an impressive sweep of top-tier rankings in the principality. The Cardiff corporate department is big on renewable energy, as is the commercial group. Clients include Centrica, EDF, Germany's RWE and Norway's Statkraft. *"We do a lot with renewable energy incentives,"* said one trainee. *"We deal with energy suppliers, and handle power purchase agreements and grid connection contracts."* Besides energy work the firm-wide commercial department is active on consumer contracts, procurement, contractual management, transport, franchising and IP/IT. The last of these is particularly big in Nottingham, which offers distinct intellectual property and IT projects seats.

Fast Food Rockers

Real estate is a central pillar of the firm, and most of our interviewees had done a seat here. The practice wins top-tier *Chambers UK* rankings in Manchester, Leeds, Cardiff and Birmingham. *"Our clients are big national and international businesses,"* a Birmingham trainee told us, *"and the projects we deal with are not just Birmingham-based."* For example, lawyers are advising on the £400m redevelopment of Westgate shopping centre in Oxford and helping Taylor Wimpey get a £210m housebuilding scheme off the ground in Northamptonshire. The firm also recently won a spot on the legal panel of Yum! (the company behind Pizza Hut and KFC) to provide employment and real estate advice. Property management and occupier work gives trainees the chance to run their own small files, like leases, licences, renewals and other dealings between landlords and tenants. *"That involves a*

The True Picture

lot of ongoing monitoring of procedural transactions," a trainee told us.

A commercial disputes seat is available in every office that takes trainees. Interviewees outside the capital harangued us about the calibre of their work: *"Just because we're in Leeds doesn't mean we don't have the calibre of clients you'd associate with City firms,"* blasted one. For example, a Leeds-headed team recently acted for GDF SUEZ in a multimillion-pound breach of warranty claim over the purchase of Teesside Power Station. Other clients include GE, British Gas and Lloyds Bank. Trainees said the work in litigation is *"heavily administrative."* One told us: *"80% of the time I was bundling or doing document management; 10% of the time I was researching law and liaising with counsel, and the other 10% I spent on juicy work like drafting witness statements."*

A seat in financial services disputes and investigations (FSDI) can be completed in every office except Newcastle. Work ranges from FCA investigations, fraud and financial crime to banking litigation and consumer finance disputes. Lawyers recently advised Xcap Securities during an FCA enforcement investigation which resulted in a £120,900 fine for not adequately protecting client money and assets. *"I drafted reports for the FCA and did research on procedural rules. Once it came to litigation there was a huge amount of indexing and bundling to do, too."*

The competition seat (available in London and Leeds) is popular with trainees and offers *"long hours, hard work and interesting assignments."* There's plenty of *"research into black-letter law"* and investigations into *"large organisations which may or may not have done something naughty."* Activities are heavily geared towards Brussels and the EU, with work on merger control and contested takeovers sitting alongside cartel cases. We mentioned long hours above; one trainee told us: *"Mine were pretty horrendous – I was regularly staying until 11pm or midnight."*

Competition is not the only team with long hours. *"For two weeks on one deal I was getting in at 9am and leaving at 10pm,"* a corporate trainee told us. We also heard from trainees who said real estate was *"steadily busy the whole time until 7pm or 8pm."* Although we did come across some pockets of regional resistance to long hours, *"the idea that the regions don't work a lot is far from the truth."* However, trainees all agreed that *"if it's not busy then you don't have to stay late and can leave at 5.30 or 6pm."* Some trainees linked this *"focus on work/life balance"* to the firm not paying top dollar to trainees or NQs. It was a gripe among some that *"salaries have remained static in recent years."*

Seek and ye shall find

Eversheds makes a big thing of its ability to share assignments between offices and have London work done in the regions at a cheaper rate. It calls this approach 'Networked Law'. *"I really noticed it in my disputes seat,"* one trainee told us. *"A lot of our arbitration work is handled in Paris, but that work was flowing into London as well. Every other day I was liaising with a colleague in Paris."*

This is all part of management's proactive approach to keeping the business shipshape, and 'Sheds hasn't been afraid to make redundancies to keep profits buoyant either (even as recently as 2013). A proactive approach is expected from rookies too: *"It's a trainee's duty to seek supervision and feedback,"* one interviewee told us. *"You have to be assertive and ask for it."*

Eversheds' offices are sociable places to work, perhaps because of their sizeable trainee cohorts: London has 30, followed by Birmingham with 20. Manchester, Leeds and Cardiff have a dozen trainees each, and Nottingham, Newcastle and Cambridge half a dozen each. Limiting ourselves to the larger branches, here's what we heard about office social life: the Birmingham base is in an *"excellent location"* on Colmore Row, and *"some teams have drinks trolleys on Fridays;"* in 2013 Cardiff held an all-staff Christmas party at the Radisson Blu hotel across the road from the office; in Leeds, teams enjoy sports days and *"outings to go gorge-walking,"* and a bar is set up in the canteen one Friday every month, though the prevalence of commuters does mean there's *"not a culture of everyone going down the pub on a Friday."* Manchester, by contrast, is known for its loyalty to the Briton's Protection pub as well as its noteworthy away-days – *"recently one team went to the Lake District and another did the Crystal Maze."* While Londoners bemoaned *"the lack of a budget for trainee social events"* (no office has one), they can enjoy a subsidised drink in the firm's own ground-floor bar, where *"a double with a mixer is £3, and a bottle of wine is a tenner."* Finally, Nottingham has *"the Roundhouse pub about 15 feet from the front door"* and is the only office to have a dress-down Friday – *"I'm not sure how they swung that one by national management!"*

And finally...

"Although every firm cares about the bottom line, I feel that people here are acutely concerned about client relationships. Everyone works very hard and gives 100% – it can be pretty intense."

Farrer & Co LLP

The facts

Location: London
Number of UK partners/solicitors: 74/160
Partners who trained at firm: 60%
Total number of trainees: 20
Seats: 6x4 months
Alternative seats: secondments
Extras: pro bono – Mary Ward Legal Centre; language classes

On chambersstudent.co.uk...

How to get into Farrer & Co
Charles Dickens' lawyer

It's not just moustache-twirling trustees who seek advice from Farrer; this firm represents publishers, entrepreneurs and some of the country's best-known charities.

A tale of two firms

Farrer is somewhat of a dichotomous firm. The private client outfit is steeped in history thanks to client relationships that stretch back hundreds of years, but at the same time its strides in the media sphere and extensive work for entrepreneurs see it plunging headfirst into the 21st century. Age-old clientele like Queen Victoria and Charles Dickens have been replaced by Bauer Media and the publisher of *heat*, and it seems the lawyers themselves are changing too. According to this year's trainees, Farrer is trying to move away from the stiff Oxbridge stereotype that plagues its ranks by seeking out candidates from more walks of life. *"These days they want people who've done something other than just uni and law school – something that adds more dimension to what they can offer."* Indeed, when you're talking to the richest individuals in the country, it certainly helps to have some real-world experience to keep you tethered.

Of course, it's difficult to get too far away from associations with Oxbridge when Oxford University itself is one of the key clients on the books. Farrer's website, littered as it is with artsy photos of ballerinas and violinists, furthers the suggestion that the firm is a refined one, nodding to its ties with institutions as genteel as the British Library and the V&A. Still, despite nabbing top *Chambers UK* rankings for its work advising private clients and elite educational institutions, this firm is no Old Boys' tax avoidance club. Private client matters vary from big institutional mergers to more altruistic ventures like setting up a trust for a worthy cause. On that note we should mention Farrer's charities practice, which one of the best in the country. Meanwhile the agriculture and employ-

ment teams both earn top-band kudos, and the firm's also recognised for its corporate, family and media practices, among others.

As trainees pointed out, this balance between private and commercial work has kept Farrer in good stead over the years, especially recent ones. *"During the recession, a lot of corporate firms experienced huge profit fluctuations, but we chugged along quite steadily."* It seems this firm knows what it's good at, and that's unlikely to change much in the coming years.

Ghosts of clients past

Trainees rotate through six seats – one each from the private client, property, litigation and commercial arenas, plus a 'wildcard' option that offers a bit more freedom. Ideally they spend their sixth seat in the department they plan to qualify into. Our sources were happy with this system, telling us: *"Second-years take priority, but trainee managers are really responsive and bend over backwards to give everyone what they want."* Everybody's guaranteed their top two choices at some point during their training contract.

Seat options: corporate; employment, IP and commercial; banking and financial services; commercial property; estates and private property; family; disputes; private client onshore; private client international; tax; media; charity and community

Chambers UK rankings

Agriculture & Rural Affairs	Fraud
Charities	Intellectual Property
Corporate/M&A	Litigation
Data Protection	Media & Entertainment
Defamation/Reputation	Partnership
Management	Private Client
Education	Real Estate
Employment	Real Estate Finance
Family/Matrimonial	Sports Law

The private client department is divided into several sub-teams, like onshore, offshore and tax. That said, *"none of the teams work in isolation; most of the work crosses over between at least two."* Trainees sitting in the group are on the receiving end of a big variety of tasks, from sorting out parking disputes and advising on inheritance tax to drafting wills and assisting with huge international trust structures. *"I attended meetings with counsel and collected witness statements in addition to a whole lot of research,"* reported one, telling us: *"The seat was much more varied than I expected; it's not just pure advisory work."* The firm has extensive experience offering planning advice to landed estates and historic houses in the UK, and it also represents super-wealthy foreigners on succession and asset protection matters. According to our insiders, such work isn't usually driven by tight deadlines, but handling 20 or so small jobs at once – as is often the case – can be quite a balancing act. There are also clients to worry about, as trainees are regularly given their own files to manage and expected to deal with any concerns that crop up. One source characterised their time in the department as *"tough work,"* but added: *"I look back on it fondly – I really grew in confidence over the course of my time with the team."*

Separate commercial, residential, and estates and private property subteams comprise Farrer's property department. Certain families have been on the estates books for generations, so it's little surprise many of the matters that group handles involve 'old money'. We hear tasks here can be reminiscent of university study at times, with trainees asked to rifle through dusty cabinets in search of 18th-century deeds that will piece together the story behind a certain property. The commercial team, meanwhile, has kept the firm's royal connections alive by advising the Duchy of Cornwall on the development of an urban community in Dorset, though it's important to note matters increasingly involve corporate banks and Middle Eastern investors these days. The group also represents charities, educational institutions and sports clubs. Such work lends itself to *"lots of hands-on tasks"* like registering estates and granting renewing or licences.

The disputes team includes the contentious trusts group, and it's not uncommon for cases to have international el-ements. Reported one trainee: *"I worked on huge trust structures that stretched from the Cayman Islands to Georgia – the work touches on all kinds of weird and wonderful places."* At home, disputes range from landlord/tenant disagreements to those between parents and schools. One interviewee had tried their hand at advocacy in the Royal Courts of Justice, while another had worked primarily on some arbitrations, reminding us *"not everything has to go through the courts."* If you're really keen to see the inside of a courtroom, head to the family seat, where *"trainees get tons of court experience"* representing clients in divorces, prenups and cohabitation disputes. Such cases, particularly those concerning children, can take a real toll on the parties involved, so a soft touch is imperative. *"Some days can be difficult – vulnerable clients often need emotional support, not just legal advice."* That hardly makes this a soft area though; as one source pointed out, *"we take a lot of cases to the Supreme Court – the team really makes the law."*

Hard times

Farrer has a long history of representing national newspapers, but the infamous News International phone hacking scandal saw Rupert Murdoch's News Group, once a major client, crossed off the books. The press biz at large is experiencing hard times, and the firm's media team has adjusted accordingly, swinging from 95% defendant work to 75% claimant in just three years. Trainees told us a seat on the disputes side, while *"great fun,"* can at times can feel like a stint in PR. *"We do a lot of reputation management these days, which requires a less legal and more practical approach."* Indeed, when they're not defending publishers like Bauer Media (owner of mags like *Grazia* and *FHM*) against defamation and libel complaints, lawyers are busy acting for celebs who don't want salacious allegations paraded across the tabloids or compromising pics circulating the web. The seat is fast-paced and the deadlines tight, especially on Fridays, when the weekend papers go to print. It's juicy work, though one downside of that is the trying task of keeping schtum when a silver screen starlet breezes by the offices seeking a super-injunction. *"What's the point in hearing great goss if you can't tell anyone about it?!"* The team also works with well-known libraries, museums and galleries as they move towards online archiving and contend with the various privacy issues this entails.

Like we said, the firm's charities team really is at the top of its game, and our interviewees had great things to say about their time sitting with the team. *"It's one of those areas where you're constantly doing new things. At the same time, you get to work with clients who've been on the books for hundreds of years, since their inception. It's fascinating getting out the old deed boxes and digging through documents from the 1500s."* Lawyers advise on a good number of charity mergers and restructurings in particular, leading the way on the merger between Age

Concern and Help the Aged in 2009, and more recently advising the Save the Children Fund on its amalgamation with Merlin, an NGO specialising in emergency medical relief. Other high-profile clients of late include Age UK, BAFTA and the Bill & Melinda Gates Foundation.

The corporate team mainly tackles mid-market M&A deals and is often instructed by entrepreneurs and family businesses, with the private client group proving a handy feed for the latter. According to our sources, the team's scope is becoming increasingly international as it takes on more and more transactions involving offshore trust companies. In 2014 the $80m sale of a stake in a US/UK-based hedge fund was the largest deal on the books. The banking and financial services group also deals with funds – *"everything from hairy hedge fund stuff to registered charity funds,"* in fact. The work here is technical, so *"it can be hard for trainees to get to grips with the law,"* but on the plus side *"you get to work directly with the partners."*

New recruits are unlikely to go on secondment, though there are a number available after qualification. Recent destinations include the Natural History Museum, WWF and the British Olympic Association.

Not so bleak house

Farrer's office dominates a corner of Lincoln's Inn Fields and hasn't really changed much since it was purchased in 1790. Interviewees appreciated the *"beautiful heritage"* and *"lovely high-ceilinged rooms"* of the building. The employment and property teams are stationed down the road, close to the Royal Courts of Justice. Trainees sit opposite their supervisors in pods – *"the perfect combination of privacy and openness. It's really easy to approach people with questions, and you can learn so much by just listening to them work."*

Our sources told us with conviction: *"You can't beat the work/life balance here."* They reported finishing between 6 and 7pm most nights, and found that while their salaries aren't quite on a par with the magic circle, *"it's a small price to pay for having a life."* Many were surprised by the welcoming nature of the working environment. *"On the vac scheme I became convinced they were hiding something – how could everyone be so nice?"* recalled one trainee. *"But it's just a really lovely place. I've never found it difficult to work with anyone,"* they continued, putting this down to the fact that many of the partners

trained at the firm and still remember what it's like to be a trainee. *"There's a real culture of nurturing."* Another recounted the story of an associate who left for a different firm but only managed one month there before returning to *"no ill feelings"* at Farrer. *"She's not the first person who's come back here, either."*

An undeniable perk of training at a private client-led firm is the copious wining and dining that takes place to maintain long-standing client relationships. One interviewee reported attending an exclusive private viewing at the National Gallery in the name of business development, telling us: *"It's nice to be given the responsibility of acting as the face of the firm."* The firm holds its own parties and drinks events throughout the year, and most trainees can be found sharing a pint with partners at Ye Olde White Horse on a Friday evening. The cohort also goes away together for a few days in the summer, a tradition that stretches back to when partners were young recruits, and participates in charitable events like the London Legal Walk. That said, the most popular event of the year is the 'annual revue' trainees present each Christmas, a punerific sketch that sends up those in charge. In 2013 they enacted a murder mystery game set at the partners' annual conference. *"It's slightly terrifying, but it's a good chance to bond, and a good way of making sure nobody at the firm takes themselves too seriously."*

The firm recently introduced Farrer Connected, a young professionals network designed to help junior lawyers build up networking contacts. The organisation holds events like pub quizzes and seminars. Trainees can also volunteer at legal advice centres and take on pro bono projects to up their professional cred. According to our sources, such work is *"very much led from the bottom up – if you have an idea, you can run with it."*

Over the past five years Farrer has kept all but one of its trainees; in 2014 the firm kept on nine of its ten qualifiers. We hear the firm is *"relaxed and open"* when it comes to qualification. *"They try to avoid formality and make it as mutual a process as they can. We're kept in the loop."* Balancing trainees' desires with business needs isn't always easy, but our sources found the training principal *"a useful source of wisdom"* and told us the firm puts a good deal of effort into gauging their thoughts on potential options. *"For all the stress of qualifying,"* one mused, *"this is a very special place to work – that's why we're all so eager to stay!"*

The True Picture

And finally...

"The client base here is unparalleled – beyond the big names we've got tons of amazing clients that we can't even mention because they're confidential."

Foot Anstey LLP

The facts

Location: Bristol, Exeter, Plymouth, Taunton, Truro

Number of UK partners/solicitors: 44/133

Partners who trained at firm: 5%

Total number of trainees: 12

Seats: 4x6 months

Alternative seats: occasional secondments

On chambersstudent.co.uk...

How to get into Foot Anstey

Islamic finance

Interview with acting training
  principal Peter Singfield

"Work/life balance is where the firm excels," but high-quality work comes first at this expanding West Country wonder.

Bigger Foot

Foot Anstey has called the South West home for over a century, but it's only really put its foot down over the last decade or so. Following a host of mergers and lateral hires in recent years, this firm has taken a deep breath of fresh coastal air and woken up to its status as one of the largest firms in the region, with 170-plus lawyers and five offices scattered around the area: Bristol, Exeter, Plymouth, Taunton and Truro. Over the last five years, Foot Anstey has punted £9m into bringing in more lawyers to up this headcount. *"We're confident we can grow profitably with the right people and the right work,"* says acting training principal Peter Singfield. Bristol stands out as the office with the most gains so far: it opened with three employees in 2011 and now has around 100. They include partners who arrived from Debevoise & Plimpton and Pinsent Masons in summer 2014. The firm also recently nabbed a partner from Addleshaw Goddard to head up the procurement practice in Exeter.

This approach is paying off – literally. Since 2009 the firm has increased its overall turnover by 35%, jumping from from £24.2m to £27m in 2013/14. In 2013 Foot Anstey adopted a three-year plan to up the quality of its clientele and as such the firm's been focused on strengthening its existing corporate, commercial, real estate, employment and dispute resolution capabilities – all of which score regional *Chambers UK* rankings – as well as upping its ante on the media and Islamic finance fronts. While we're talking strengths, we should mention Foot Anstey's highly regarded clinical negligence and personal injury practices too. *"It's no secret we aspire to become the region's premier law firm,"* said one of our trainee sources.

"I think we stand a good chance of meeting that target." In any case, it's off on the right foot.

Getting your feet wet

Each seat rotation, trainees list their top three preferences, and second-years get priority. There's no formal sit-down with HR, but trainees can chat to the training principal if they want to discuss a particular interest. *"If you're proactive during the process, you'll be rewarded,"* suggested one. At the time of our calls, six trainees were based in Exeter, three in Plymouth and two each in Bristol and Taunton. It's common to move between offices (including Truro) during the training contract. *"That's something to keep in mind if you want to apply – there's quite a considerable distance between our offices in Truro and Bristol, for instance, but it's possible you'll be asked to move between them at six weeks' notice."* According to Singfield, this is because *"we think trainees get the most out of their seats if they do them where the practices are most established."* As such, those completing a stint in IP disputes typically head to the Exeter office, while the Islamic finance seat takes place in Bristol.

Foot Anstey's commercial real estate group covers planning, construction, property litigation and real estate finance matters, including Islamic finance transactions for clients like Dimah Capital and Qatar Islamic Bank. The

Seat options: corporate; commercial; employment; dispute resolution; construction; property litigation; commercial property; clinical negligence and mental capacity

Chambers UK rankings

Agriculture & Rural Affairs	Education
Banking & Finance	Employment
Banking Litigation	Intellectual Property
Charities	Licensing
Clinical Negligence	Litigation
Construction	Pensions
Corporate/M&A	Personal Injury
Court of Protection	Private Client
Crime	Real Estate
Defamation/Reputation	Real Estate Litigation
Management	Tax

Plymouth team recently advised investment company Akkeron on the development of a new £50m leisure development at Higher Home Park Plymouth, while lawyers in Exeter acted for Park Bay in its £4m land sale to Bovis Homes. It's common for trainees here to draft commercial contracts and leases; some are able to take on a few residential files themselves. *"Having my own files meant I could have a direct relationship with clients and build on my pre-existing skills,"* one trainee recalled. *"A lot of trust is placed on you in that instance, but you're always supervised."* The Plymouth team is big in the renewable energy sector, while Exeter specialises in agricultural matters. *"I found working with registered land really interesting,"* a trainee who'd spent time with the latter team enthused. *"You're usually acting for a farmer who's had the same land for generations and never registered it, so what we end up doing is submitting an application based on old plans and maps."*

The firm is home to the largest claimant-focused clinical negligence team in the South West. Lawyers in Exeter specialise in personal injury and abuse claims, while those in Truro take on a lot of group action and Court of Protection work, and the Taunton group mainly handles birthing injury claims. Understandably, a seat here *"can be tough: sometimes you're dealing with stillbirth cases, and you know the only reason clients have come to you is because the worst has happened."* Still, we heard the firm is generous with its emotional support, particularly in Taunton, where there are *"extended tea breaks"* to recuperate. On the whole, our sources gave the seat a thumbs-up for experience. *"You get a lot of varied work – I was assisting on a few large and medium cases, and running a few small ones on my own."* Day to day trainees write letters of instruction to experts, taking witness statements, review reports and apply for medical records. *"You also get a lot of contact with clients, barristers and experts."*

Working boots

Foot Anstey's employment team earns a premier regional *Chambers UK* ranking and counts Odeon, Screwfix and the Eden Project among its key clients of late. The group was recently appointed the role of Halfords' legal adviser, covering 460 stores and 10,000 employees, and it's also worked for rival retailer Robert Dyas. In addition to commercial and tactical advice for employers, the firm provides HR law coverage like employment tribunal assistance and advocacy. *"As a trainee you can dip in and out of different types of matters as you like, and it's pretty hands-on – you might be drafting witness statements for tribunal claims one day, then contracts of employment or termination the next."*

The corporate group works for regional business owners right up to big businesses like property advisory firm 90 North Real Estate Partners. While Exeter brings in a lot of healthcare clients, Bristol and Plymouth tend to attract more media-related clientele – for example, UBM and Teachers Media International. The corporate group operates as a single team across the region, so *"trainees get work from every office – it can be difficult to balance all of it sometimes, but it's good to have that kind of responsibility and learn to manage your time effectively."* Generally *"there isn't a huge deal of face-to-face client contact, but you do get to draft small documents and deal with ancillary work."*

Trainees flagged the firm's commercial practice as *"one of its fastest-growing teams. The workload has increased a lot in the past few years."* As Singfield confirms: *"We're increasing our focus on the commercial side and aiming to keep pulling in larger commercial clients because we endeavour to cross-sell our services and generate repeat business."* Trainees here enjoyed the variety of clients on offer: *"It can be a social enterprise one day, an IT company the next and a charity after that."* Indeed, University of Bristol Students' Union, Warner Music, mobile gambling company Betfuze and Chinese takeaway chain Hotcha are all among its recent clients, along with Bristol City Football Club, which lawyers are advising on its £45m stadium redevelopment. Our interviewees reported a lot of drafting here, as well as reviewing contracts and terms of business, working on IP agreements and conference-calling clients. Some even do a *"virtual secondment"* in this seat, wherein a trainee works in-house for a client for a few hours per week.

Finding your feet

The Bristol and Truro offices might be separated by 165 miles of countryside, but our sources insisted the firm's offices feel united. *"Work constantly flows in from all over the place,"* one asserted, telling us: *"I work mainly

The True Picture

in Exeter, but the majority of my work comes in from Bristol, so I go there once a week." Both Bristol and Exeter are conveniently located in their respective city centres, while the Plymouth and Truro bases have more of an aquatic theme, taking in the *"beautiful views"* of the adjacent Sutton Harbour and Truro River. By comparison, Taunton sits next to the busy M5, though we heard it's *"probably the friendliest office out of all of them, so we can't complain too much."*

All of the offices are open plan, with trainees, partners, fee earners and support staff mingling. *"It's nice to see people working together – nobody has their head down or keeps things to themselves. And from a trainee's point of view, it's a dream – you can learn by observation, and if you need help people are right there."*

Sources last year complained the formal training was lacking, but this year's trainees were all smiles: *"There's a focus on retaining us, so the training is pretty good in turn – they aim to give us the tools to do the job."* These tools come by way of a two-week induction in the Plymouth office, plus additional training sessions over trainees' first six months. Everybody also receives a formal end-of-seat review, but supervisors *"are flexible about having more if you want – for one of my seats, I had a review every month."*

Footloose

Culturally, Foot Anstey *"has a friendly regional feel despite being a firm that attracts multinational clients."* We're told that *"if you walk into an office and don't know anyone, people will come and introduce themselves,"* and that *"there's always friendly chatter going on in the background."* One trainee even claimed to have *"some of my best friends here."*

This warm and welcoming mood makes for a sociable atmosphere. At the time of our calls, interviewees were looking forward to the inaugural firm-wide summer party at St Mellion International Resort. Charity fund-raising events also provide opportunities for interoffice mingling – past efforts include a 12k obstacle course and camp-out in Plymouth. The extent to which trainees gather for impromptu outings depends on office location: *"Being centrally located makes it easy,"* said a Bristol source, noting *"it's a little more difficult in Taunton, where people have to drive to find a local pub."* In comparison, Exeter trainees can typically be found five minutes down the road at The Cosy Club or Rendezvous Wine Bar on a given Friday evening.

According to our sources, the firm's 'lifestyle hour' policy – wherein everybody gets a free hour each week to use as they see fit – goes down a treat. *"You can use it to come in at 10am one morning, or meet a friend for a long lunch; it's also very popular on Friday afternoons."* The firm offers 'family hours' too *"for things like going to see your child's special assembly."* As one summed up: *"Work/life balance is where the firm excels. My hours have always been really good, and I'm still doing high-quality work."* A few Bristol sources pointed out their salaries aren't as high as some other firms in the area, like Burges Salmon, but concluded: *"The quality of life is worth it here."*

Interested applicants should know a commitment to remain in the South West is a must at Foot Anstey, as is a good dose of commercial awareness. *"We want people who have enough of an understanding of business to be able to get off the fence and give recommendations,"* stresses Peter Singfield. *"We also want people who understand this is a service industry – people who have fantastic people skills and the ability to present information in an understandable way."*

And finally...

Foot Anstey has traditionally boasted high retention rates, and 2014 was no different – six of seven qualifiers stayed on.

Freeths LLP

The facts

Location: Nottingham, Leicester, Derby, Birmingham, Manchester, London, Stoke-on-Trent, Milton Keynes, Sheffield, Oxford, Leeds

Number of UK partners/solicitors: 118/149

Partners who trained at firm: 21%

Total number of trainees: 26

Seats: 4x6 months

Alternative seats: none

On chambersstudent.co.uk...

How to get into Freeths
All about recent mergers
Freeths' legal assistant foundation
   programme

This thriving firm won't be freezing its freething any time soon.

Freeth up

The firm formerly known as Freeth Cartwright is no longer just a small Midlands outfit; this Nottingham-founded firm has embarked on an impressive bout of expansion right through the recession, merging with regional firms in Milton Keynes (in 2011), Stoke (2012) and Oxford (2013), and launching branches in London, Birmingham, Sheffield and, most recently, Leeds, upping its total office-count to 11. The newly national firm has smartened up its branding too, streamlining the bewildering array of different names across its regional bases so nearly the whole firm now goes by Freeths, except for Oxford which remains 'Henmans Freeth'. This fricative-heavy moniker might not exactly glide off the tongue, but as current trainees at the firm pointed out, *"everyone just called us Freeth before anyway, so it isn't a big change."* Accompanying the rebrand is a slick new black and gold colour scheme –*"a reflection of how we're becoming more sleek and sophisticated as a firm"*– and a slew of activities designed to get the spread of offices working together as one. For example, the lawyers from all around the network recently participated in 'Tour de Freeths', a three-day cycling relay that covered nearly 500 miles and raised a cool £20K for Cancer Research.

Freeths earns its highest *Chambers UK* rankings in the property sphere: it's placed in the top regional band for construction, real estate, real estate litigation, planning and social housing. Other strengths include corporate, banking and employment, plus some practices *"that not a lot of big firms do,"* such clinical negligence, personal injury and private client. *"I chose the firm because of its broad range of departments,"* said one interviewee, explaining: *"There's room to adapt and make a decision about where you want to go."* Other sources told us they were drawn to the firm by *"its reputation for treating staff*

well. Some places are a little more factory-like in their approach to trainees, whereas we're treated as individuals."

At the time of our calls, there were 21 trainees in total spread across the Oxford, Milton Keynes, Leicester, Manchester, Nottingham, Birmingham and Derby branches. There will also be a trainee in Sheffield from 2015 and one in Leeds from 2016. New joiners across the firm *"get an awful lot of training,"* starting out with a two-week PSC whizz-through at the University of Law Birmingham. *"It's a solid nine-to-five in a hotel. Spending all that time together helped us really get to know each other."* Trainees also convene periodically for sessions in Nottingham – these are administered by external lecturers, with topics ranging from legal writing and client relationships to how to get the best out of performance reviews.

Before each seat, trainees *"make a list of options we do and don't want to do – they pay a lot of attention to the seats you don't want."* Second-years' choices are prioritised, and trainees in smaller offices like Milton Keynes have the option of completing seats in nearby branches of the firm if they're particularly keen.

Brain Freeths

Real estate is broadly considered *"the engine room of the firm,"* and has construction, real estate, real estate litigation, planning and social housing subgroups. The

Seat options: employment; family; real estate; real estate litigation; dispute resolution; commercial; corporate; drinks, hospitality and leisure; clinical negligence; personal injury; private client; construction

Chambers UK rankings

Agriculture & Rural Affairs	Licensing
Banking & Finance	Litigation
Charities	Local Government
Clinical Negligence	Personal Injury
Construction	Planning
Corporate/M&A	Private Client
Employment	Professional Negligence
Energy & Natural	Real Estate
Resources	Real Estate Litigation
Family/Matrimonial	Restructuring/Insolvency
Intellectual Property	Social Housing

core real estate team works on multimillion-pound refinancings and transactions for the likes of construction giant LaFarge Tarmac and Yorkshire-founded Ideal Care Homes, which designs, constructs and runs its own retirement homes. Lawyers recently helped Porthcwlis secure £1bn worth of investment to build up to 11,000 new homes across Wales, and assisted Loughborough University with negotiations on a lease in London's Queen Elizabeth Olympic Park. According to a Nottingham source, *"the clients are big enough that they supervise you closely. Still, I was encouraged to sit in on client meetings to get a feel for each transaction, and got to take on landlord and tenant work like rent review situations and stamp duty and tax returns."* Meanwhile, a trainee with experience in real estate litigation reported *"doing the main bulk of drafting on defences, witness statements and claims. I worked quite closely with a partner, who talked me through all my work – that gave me a lot of confidence."* Among the team's varied workload are rent review disputes, dilapidations, contentious lease renewals and trespassing cases.

There's a specialist drinks, hospitality and leisure (DHL) team based in Milton Keynes that handles sales, leases and property portfolios for industry clients like Wells & Youngs, Heineken and Novus Leisure, owner of the Tiger Tiger chain. Sources with experience here told of handling their own pub leases and licences to alter, as well as researching stamp duty and franchising issues. *"I assisted in a lot of due diligence and post-completion work, and I also got to draft a few documents on small projects."*

The litigation department counts gaming group Gala Coral, professional services giant Deloitte and industrial supplier Flogas among its key clients. The Sheffield team specialises in international arbitration and competition matters, while Milton Keynes litigators obtain a good bit of crossover work from DHL clients. Over in Nottingham, however, the scope is much wider, with insurance, construction, private client and insolvency disputes just some of the cases on hand. *"All the litigators in the office*

sit together, so as a trainee you come across a wide variety of work. One day you might be working on boundary disputes, another day winding up wills." A source here reported *"working closely with barristers on a judicial review, drafting witness statements and putting together trial bundles,"* while an interviewee in Milton Keynes spoke of *"analysing over 1,200 pages of financials on a breach of trading case – that was a big meaty task to get into."* For one source *"going to the High Court in London was definitely a highlight of my seat – I got to spend time in chambers with counsel, and the adrenalin was brilliant. I also got to go down to the court here in Leicester for small matters like orders of sale or applications for possession."*

Freeths' commercial team works on a mixture of public sector, finance, IP and corporate matters. Nottingham sources reported taking a stab at drafting documents like debentures, distributorship agreements, public sector contracts and finance facilities, while one in Leicester commercial team said: *"I've spent most of my time helping out the licensing team and got to assist with several regulatory licensing issues for a large supermarket chain. I've also helped out with some regulatory matters, like coroner's inquests, for local authorities."*

Freeths spirits

All of Freeths' offices are open plan, and they've recently become a bit shinier thanks to a fresh lick of black and gold paint. Trainees in smaller offices described a *"family feel"* to their respective digs, with Leicester sources telling us: *"The entire office often goes out for drinks together, which is really fun."* Meanwhile in Nottingham *"things tend to be organised by department,"* though *"a lot of people rally on Friday night – there's almost always someone asking if anyone's up for the pub. We used to always go to the Roundhouse, but now we've moved on to The Crafty Crow."* Most offices have their own social committee to organise periodic outings and there are also quarterly cross-office trainee socials, most recently a barge ride in Birmingham and a trip to the races in Worcester. Additionally there are various charity events sprinkled across the social calendar. Lawyers in Notts recently organised 'FC Live', an *X Factor*-style fundraiser featuring 11 acts, a live band and *"celebrity"* judges like local newsreaders. *"Trainees, partners and everyone in between came along, and the winner got to record their song at a proper studio!"*

Our sources found *"there's a sense of unity at the firm – the whole trainee group gets to see a lot of each other through the various different training events and socials."* At the same time *"we're quite open about the fact that each office has its own feel and its own client base. Management tries to get us to mingle so we don't come across as a faceless corporate entity, but they understand that each office does things in its own way."* On the whole interviewees across the firm spoke of *"a laid-back, inclusive atmosphere in which trainees are made to feel part of the wider firm."* Many credited the open-plan office layout with *"fostering a good dialogue. The attitude is that two minds are better than one."* Said one: *"I've visited firms where it felt like senior management was inaccessible, but here they care about us and devote a lot of resources to looking after us."* Indeed, interviewees were full of praise for the training on offer and called the mid and end-of-seat review process *"constructive – fee earners are interested in your personal progression and give you action points to work on so you can improve."*

When it comes to hours, *"people recognise you're an individual with a life and therefore are flexible about your needs,"* we heard. Many interviewees reported heading home around 6.30pm most nights, though of course *"it varies – there are occasional weeks where you have to stay late, but luckily no one tends to stay past midnight very frequently."* As such, there's plenty of time to enjoy the array of firm-sponsored hobbies on offer, among them football, rugby, rowing and choral singing.

Trainees told us *"there's no fixed mould"* on the recruiting front. *"Basically they want people who are affable, down to earth and have something interesting about them that makes them stand out from a crowd. Commercial awareness is important too – show you can build a rapport with people and understand how to interact with clients."* Increasingly, new recruits come to the firm by way of a nine-month legal assistant foundation programme, which hires graduates as support staff. Go to our website to read more about this.

Our interviewees shared positive feelings about Freeths' future, telling us: *"All our mergers show we're an ambitious, growing firm. This is a good place to come, particularly if you want to work outside of London – there are plenty of career development opportunities here."* Most were confident about their qualification chances, noting that the majority of opportunities come up in core departments like real estate and commercial. It's common for trainees to return to the area they want to qualify into for a second seat. In 2014 the firm retained seven of its eight qualifiers.

And finally...
Our sources advised applicants to get up close and personal with the firm. *"Engage with the representatives at law fairs and contact people afterwards so they remember you."*

Freshfields Bruckhaus Deringer LLP

The facts

Location: London

Number of UK partners/solicitors: 148/499

Total number of trainees: 164

Seats: 3 or 6 months long

Alternative seats: client secondments, overseas seats

Extras: language classes

On chambersstudent.co.uk...

How to get into Freshfields

Halo (Freshfields' LGBT network) and The Stephen Lawrence Scholarship

CSR at Freshfields

A push on various diversity fronts is yet another big plus at this distinguished Fleet Street-gone-global institution.

The True Picture

Flexible friends

Interested in magic circle firms but have no clue how to differentiate them? Fleet Street-based Freshfields' trainees were unanimous about the distinguishing characteristic of their training contract: its flexibility. *"I was sceptical that it would be as flexible as they made out,"* one admitted, looking back, *"but it has been incredibly flexible."* Not only is there the option of three-month seats here, it's *"a bit of a luxury to apply for seats as you go through the training contract rather than at the start."*

If you find you don't like a particular seat, you can move on after three months and try to direct your future seats as your interests develop. *"People generally go where they want to go, but not necessarily in the order they want,"* trainees explained. *"Therefore, you can't rank seats."* You might try the dark arts, though, and *"express cryptically, strongly or less strongly, where you want to go."* Unsurprisingly, with over 2,600 lawyers in 27 offices worldwide, Freshfields offers awesome work, often with an international angle, as well as client and 'network' (overseas) secondments, which are usually popular among trainees finishing up their training contracts.

Glittering clients

Founded centuries ago, in 1743, Freshfields advises its first-ever client, the Bank of England, to this day. It's historically a corporate superstar (specifically for private and public M&A) and today's *"three behemoth departments of corporate, finance and dispute resolution"* each contain numerous sub-teams for trainees to spend time in. Then there are smaller *"specialised departments"* including: antitrust, competition and trade (ACT); employment, pensions and benefits; intellectual property and information technology (IP/IT); real estate; and tax.

When applying for seats, you need to set out the reasons why you want to work in a particular area (and office or client, in the case of secondments). How does the type of work fit into your *"qualification plan?"* You must *"justify where you want to go."*

Trainees spoke of Freshfields' *"glittering client list and great work."* Let's have a peek at some recent work highlights to see what they mean. The initial public offering (IPO) market has taken off again in 2014 after years of caution following the Great Recession (though it remains volatile), and Freshfields has been in the thick of the action, advising on the flotations of well-known companies like Poundland, property website Zoopla and SSP Group (owner of sandwich favourite Upper Crust, and Millie's Cookies). In late 2013, Freshfields lawyers advised the government on the flotation of the Royal Mail.

Headline deals for the large corporate/M&A practice – which *Chambers UK* ranks in its highest tier – include engineering and tech company Invensys's £3.4bn takeover by France's Schneider Electric; acting for BT on its acquisition of ESPN's UK and Ireland television channels business; advising the London Stock Exchange on taking a majority stake in clearing house LCH.Clearnet; and helping China's Bright Food Group (makers of the delicious White Rabbit sweets, among other treats) when it bought a stake in Israel's biggest food company, Tnuva. Freshfields topped Thomson Reuters' M&A charts for the first half of 2014 both by volume and value, closing 41 transactions worth a whopping $71.1bn – almost 50%

Seat options: antitrust, competition and trade; corporate; dispute resolution; employment, pensions and benefits; finance; real estate; tax

Chambers UK rankings

Administrative & Public Law	Information Technology
Asset Finance	Insurance
Banking & Finance	Intellectual Property
Banking Litigation	International Arbitration
Capital Markets	Investment Funds
Competition/European Law	Litigation
Construction	Outsourcing
Corporate Crime & Investigations	Pensions
Corporate/M&A	Private Equity
Employee Share Schemes & Incentives	Product Liability
Employment	Projects
Energy & Natural Resources	Public International Law
Environment	Public Procurement
Financial Services	Real Estate
Fraud	Real Estate Finance
Hotels & Leisure	Restructuring/Insolvency
	Retail
	Tax
	Telecommunications
	Transport

more than nearest magic circle rival Slaughter and May, who advised on 21 deals worth $36.2bn.

Heady heights

Most interviewees had spent time in corporate, which is divided into four main teams. 'Corporate A' is financial regulation; 'B' is private equity-related; 'C' is energy; and 'D' does more general corporate advisory work. *"I was thrown in at the deep end,"* one trainee reported of their corporate seat, consistent with the feedback from others. *"In corporate, you work on ten to 15 matters, so you need less time to get struck in. I drafted less important documents and researched precedents. An associate asked me to call up the other side's lawyers and negotiate. There was lots of pubic and private M&A work. My supervisor was good."*

Another recalled of their stint in corporate: *"It was intense. People who love corporate talk about peaks and troughs – for me it was one very high plateau. The informal structures are a lot more supportive than the formal. Supervisors are mixed – some are nice, some too busy. People here thrive on adrenaline. I attended client meetings and conference calls at all sorts of strange times of the day."* Working across different time zones only adds to the unpredictable nature of the hours. *"You don't realise what working 75 to 80 hours in a week is like until you've experienced it yourself,"* a trainee reported. *"It's just something you go through."*

The hours can be equally demanding in Freshfields' superb finance practice, where seats include restructuring and insolvency (R&I); structured finance and debt capital markets; and banking. In the latter, *"they like trainees who are willing to take on as much as possible, especially grunt work. But I also got a lot of client contact from day one. Anything you can do to make processes easier will help you stand out. My hours were worst in this seat – 100 hour weeks, 20 straight days without a day off. I took a taxi home one night, showered, then came back to work – no sleep. Though when it's quiet you can leave early."* Another said: *"I learnt a lot, but finance is not what I want to do."* This is where a major benefit of the three-month seat system kicks in: you can cut your losses and move on.

Some interviewees who thrived in finance and corporate seats found their dispute resolution seats a little *"slow-paced"* by comparison, while others relished the different working environment. *"In litigation, deadlines are so much further ahead, so it's easier, even for trainees, to manage your time,"* one reflected. *"Hours can be as long, although you can see them coming, unlike in corporate."* Contentious seats include: environmental, planning and regulatory (EPR); financial institutions disputes; commercial disputes; engineering, procurement and construction (EPC); intellectual property; and the European Union (competition law) disputes group. This trainee's feedback was fairly typical: *"I did a lot of drafting expert reports, and had conferences with experts and counsel. I did a lot on the technical side of litigation and also the project management side. A junior associate was very good at giving me the same kind of work she was doing, then giving detailed feedback."*

You can only stay three months in the smaller, popular dispute resolution sub-teams, and some would have preferred to stay on. *"As soon as you get settled, you're off,"* one lamented. Working on a long-running case or cases, *"it's hard to be useful in a couple of months. Responsibility is low because you're not in a position to make decisions."* With so many trainees in a firm of Freshfields' ginormous size, experiences varied, and others found they had more responsibility, *"doing a lot of research, working on presentations, going to client pitches."* While some DR teams are more *"hierarchical"* than transactional teams, for some trainees they were *"friendlier than corporate – I found they care more about your development."* Others felt the opposite. *"The training can be a bit hit and miss,"* more than one had found. High-profile litigation includes fallout from the Russian oligarch wars between Chelsea FC owner Roman Abramovich and the late Boris Berezovsky, which recently settled on the eve of another mega court battle. Freshfields litigators also won an $8bn case for Deutsche Bank in its fiendishly complex dispute with Norwegian investment fund Sebastian Holdings, and is defending engineering giant ABB in a groundbreaking cartel case brought by the National Grid.

Stay Fresh

While interviewees praised the flexible training contract and the opportunity to try lots of things out in shorter, three-month seats, they did caution that you might not get every single seat you want – *"you can't choose all eight seats. The seat allocation process is not always transparent. You submit your choices to trainee development and they let you know where you're going."* In such a huge training programme, this is only to be expected, and such gripes were minor in the grand scheme of things.

So, how do trainees cope with the long hours and challenging work? Most revel in it. And colleagues are generally friendly: *"I preferred Freshfields' people,"* one said when contrasting the vacation scheme here with another big firm's. *"More genuine, less stuck up, very nice."* Secretarial and other admin support is greater here than at smaller firms, although inevitably *"sometimes someone can get stuck on a massive task for ages, like due diligence, reviewing hundreds of documents. But these jobs have to be done. Everyone has a shared PA. They help during the day. There's also a centralised documents team that helps with things like pdfs and photocopying."*

Lifestyle-wise, one source commented: *"I plan my weekends carefully and don't sleep in on Saturdays until two in the afternoon (tempting as it is). I see friends, work out. I see other trainees at weekends a lot too, which helps. You go through it together."* More formally, *"trainee development sends you an email if you work more than 60 hours in a week, asking 'are you okay?'"* Free dinner in the *"really nice"* canteen afer 7pm and free cabs home after 9.30pm also help to soften the blow of late nights. For the hardest core, there are rumours of sleeping pods – bedrooms with bathrooms – in the office.

Many Freshfields trainees look forward to doing a client or overseas secondment, typically in their final six months. Most offices in Freshfields' network participate, and the most popular are (surprise, surprise) the more exotic locations like New York, Tokyo, Singapore and Hong Kong. Client secondments include the Bank of England, Sony, Tesco and the Stock Exchange, and pro bono secondments are at Oxfam and Tower Hamlets Law Centre. You don't just apply to an office, like Berlin, but to a practice area as well, like competition or regulatory: *"You apply for the type of work as well as the office."* Landing your preferred secondment can be competitive and depends on experience gained in your previous seats, so it's wise to start thinking early and strategically about where you might like to go. Freshfields usually provides and pays for a serviced flat *"within walking distance of the office"* to those who get to go on secondment. In more expensive cities like Tokyo the firm raises your salary to reflect the higher cost of living.

Reviews take place every three months with a partner (a 'trainee intake partner', or TIP), who has feedback from everyone you've worked with. Sometimes trainees have buddies too – *"a more junior associate, though not senior enough to action anything."* Responsibility *"depends on how well you prove yourself in the early weeks. Make a mark. But if you're on a huge case there may be relatively menial work to do – you're a small cog in a big machine."*

Rainbows of fun

What of the social scene? *"Different departments have a different social profile – something you should be aware of when starting your training contract."* Transactional teams *"tend to have more social events and are more organised, putting more emphasis on socialising – because the ebb and flow of deals lends itself more to social activities, like lunch celebrating a closing. And also because the personalities tend to be more sociable by nature. In dispute resolution the social side is sometimes lacking, as it doesn't have the same work cycle, and the personalities are different, more bookish."* Bigger departments, like banking, invite trainees on their annual ski trip and help with the cost. But *"litigation doesn't take trainees on its ski trip."*

Pub-wise, regular trainee haunts are happily within milliseconds of the Fleet Street HQ: the Hack & Hop and, merely a few doors further down Whitefriars Street, The Harrow, a rather smart 18th-century affair. Also popular is the nearby Witness Box, as people are still *"very insistent"* on calling it, even though it's been a Jamies Wine Bar for some time now. There are sports teams aplenty for those who are interested, including sailing off the Isle of Wight and in Devon. Diversity-wise, trainees were *"pleasantly surprised about how keen partners are to engage women, especially those with kids."* There's also been a big push recently to improve LGBT visibility through the Halo group – read our online bonus features for more. Trainees get involved in various charity fundraising events, including the London to Paris Bike Ride, and there's a regular workshop at a school in Haggerston. Freshfields also recently launched the Stephen Lawrence Scholarship, which aims to help black and ethnic minority students from less-than-privileged backgrounds get a foothold in the law.

Another nice thing Freshfields does is with the *Big Issue*. Over to a trainee to explain: *"A Big Issue vendor comes into the office once a week. As part of trainee induction, two trainees go with a vendor to help them pick up the magazines, then help sell them on the streets. It was the most memorable day of my induction. We have our own job stresses – this helped put a perspective on things."* Well quite.

Gateley

The facts

Location: Birmingham, Nottingham, Leicester, London, Manchester, Leeds, Scotland

Number of UK partners/solicitors: 152/249

Total number of trainees: 28

Seats: 4x6 months

Alternative seats: none

On chambersstudent.co.uk...

How to get into Gateley

Getting Gateley out there

There's a strong emphasis on training and responsibility at this national firm.

Up and down and all around

Take a look at Gateley's website and you're treated to a game of 'Guess the Landmark'. The Gherkin, Edinburgh Castle and Dubai's famous sail-shaped hotel Burj Al Arab are all visible in an illustrated cityscape hugging the homepage – a nod to this firm's slightly unusual spread of offices, which span from Edinburgh down to London, taking in Glasgow, Leeds, Manchester, Nottingham, Leicester and Birmingham in between. The last of those is the headquarters, and Gateley also has a small outpost in Dubai (hence the Tower of the Arabs mention).

The top-50 firm performs well in the *Chambers UK* mid-market tables, picking up rankings in areas as diverse as real estate, pensions, IP and family. Gateley's individual offices top the board in certain areas: the Birmingham tax group is one of the city's best, while Leicester is highly regarded on the corporate and employment fronts; meanwhile Nottingham is top of the market in restructuring and insolvency. Corporate and real estate are the firm's biggest practices, so it's little surprise that in most offices trainees are required to complete seats in both, along with a contentious stint. Remaining seat options vary by office – shipping, for example, is only available in London, and smaller offices on the whole tend to have fewer options.

At the time of our calls, Manchester had 11 trainees, Birmingham ten, London five, Nottingham three and Leicester two. Several of the Manchester trainees had transferred from training contracts offered, but not commenced, with Halliwells after Gateley bought a slice of the defunct firm in 2010 and fully integrated its office in 2012 – a move that brought the firm 200 new staff (some of whom went to London) and an extra £8m in profits. Trainees can also do ad hoc client secondments, and there's also the chance to undertake a three-month corporate seat in Dubai.

Jewels in the Gateley crown

Gateley's corporate practices in Manchester and Birmingham score high *Chambers UK* rankings, but it's the Leicester and Nottingham teams that get top marks. Together Gateley's corporate lawyers advised on deals amounting more than £1.2bn in 2013. The Leicester team recently advised luxury jeweller Aurum on its £165m sale to US private equity firm Apollo Global Management, while the Notts group has taken up work for global software business Descartes Systems and auto parts manufacturer Belton Massey in recent years. Other notable clients of late elsewhere include Halsall Toys, tapas eatery La Tasca and homeware provider Lifetime Brands. Trainees here typically undertake due diligence and draft ancillary documents for private equity transactions and M&A deals. Big matters often see new recruits *"grinding through admin work,"* although *"there's enough variety to stop things from getting stale – partners are keen to expose you to all parts of the transaction if they can. You're often taken to client meetings, which is good for getting to understand the business world."* A few interviewees across the East Midlands reported taking on their own small files on the side, for example reclassifying a com-

---

Seat options: commercial; corporate recovery; construction; pensions; tax; corporate; employment; private client; real estate; residential development; commercial dispute resolution; banking; shipping

Chambers UK rankings

Banking & Finance	Pensions
Banking Litigation	Planning
Construction	Private Client
Corporate/M&A	Real Estate
Employment	Real Estate Litigation
Energy & Natural Resources	Restructuring/Insolvency
	Shipping
Family/Matrimonial	Social Housing
Information Technology	Sports Law
Intellectual Property	Tax
Litigation	Transport

pany's shares, *"which can be scary, but you learn a whole lot as it's up to you to get it right."*

Banking falls under the firm's corporate umbrella – in London trainees split a seat between the two. The group is big in the private equity, acquisition finance and real estate financing spheres in particular. Across the firm trainees reported *"backstage tasks – we're usually the ones drafting ancillaries like company check-lists and loan notes. I like to think of it as client care rather than admin,"* said one. The Birmingham team recently assisted Lloyds Bank with its £39m financing of West Midlands golf resort The Belfry, and also counts HSBC, RBS, Santander and Allied Irish Bank among its recent clientele. *"You meet a lot of great clients during a seat here,"* said a Brum source. *"There's exposure to some really big deals. As a trainee you're responsible for pulling all the documents together with minimal supervision."* HSBC and Lloyds are also customers of the Manchester and Nottingham branches – lawyers in the latter office recently advised HSBC on its provision of development and investment facilities to Hazleton Homes.

Corporate seats generally require the longest trainee hours, we're told. Our Birmingham sources reported a few midnight finishes during deal completions, while those in London had stayed as late as 2am during busy periods. Fortunately when completion isn't approaching, trainees tend to clock off at a more reasonable 7pm, as is the case in most other departments. Sources were keen to note *"this isn't a place where you're chained to your desk"* and added *"there's no pressure to stay late just for the sake of it."*

Let's all do the Gateley Poznań!

Gateley's commerce, media and technology department advises on commercial contracts, regulatory matters and IP litigation across a range of sectors, including IT, sport, social media and hospitality. The Manchester group has strong links with Manchester City FC, where trainees can go on secondment, and recently assisted the club with

various image rights agreements. Entertainment-related issues, meanwhile, dominate the London office, where clients include Pulse Films, Trinity Productions and Peppa Pig creators The Elf Factory. *"It's a much broader seat than corporate – you need to be a jack of all trades and are often dealing with things that are new to both you and the partners. You never really repeat the same task."* We hear six months in CMT *"will improve your drafting by a mile and is a great grounding in contract law."* Research is a common trainee task – our sources had looked into everything from chemical regulations to statutory rights. On the IT side trainee fare often involves drafting software licences, data protection and privacy policies, while IP cases generally undertake bundling, and occasionally attend mediations and trials.

Commercial dispute resolution (CDR) and corporate recovery are the most common contentious seats, but trainees can also fulfil the requirement by spending six months in construction, property, employment or shipping. Sources praised the high levels of responsibility on offer in CDR, where trainees are charged with managing debt files on their own. *"I also know people who've represented the firm at negotiations by themselves. There's a lot up for grabs here."* Similar praise was lavished on corporate recovery, which predominantly covers insolvency matters. *"They're keen for us to understand how court applications and processes work, so you're given a lot of forms to file and documents to churn through, and you get brought along to court to see how all that pans out. There's a good level of client contact too – you spend a lot of time attending meetings and taking minutes."* The Birmingham and Nottingham groups often work together, recently teaming up to assist business advisers BDO with the administration of rail maintenance firm Railcare.

"Real estate covers such a broad range of transactions it can be hard to get a detailed grasp of any one aspect of work," one source informed us, *"but the client contact is great – going to meetings all the time really improves your communication skills."* When they're not schmoozing with clients, trainees can typically be found drafting lease agreements, assisting with lease negotiations and searching Land Registry documents for corporate clients like NatWest and financial services adviser Mattioli Woods – the Nottingham group recently helped the latter transfer some of its portfolio to a real estate investment trust. Over in Manchester lawyers have been busy refinancing various properties for the development of £150m residential and leisure complex Cains Brewery Village. *"I ended up doing a lot of project managing because of how many properties were involved,"* said one trainee who'd worked on the matter. *"It was a lot of pressure, but an exciting time all the same."*

Birmingham also handles residential development matters for clients like Taylor Wimpey, the Berkeley Group and Redrow Homes – lawyers recently advised Redrow on a £204m grant as part of the Help to Buy scheme. Trainees here keep busy drafting contracts and deeds of easement, compiling legal reports, and undertaking due diligence. *"It's a fast-moving department, so you get stuck in and learn very quickly about the commercial realities at hand. You might be handling up to 40 files at a time, and no one's going to chase you up on them; it's up to you, which is thrilling."*

On the whole our interviewees were pleased with the supervision they'd received. *"The partners strike a good balance between getting involved in your schedule and being hands off,"* a Nottingham trainee told us. Elsewhere interviewees praised the way supervisors *"actively seek out a variety of work for you and give you a good first-knock at things before reviewing them."* They also deemed their mid-seat appraisals useful, telling us: *"They address any problems you're having and make sure you're being exposed to the right training. The emphasis is on developing your skills; they don't see simply hitting targets as a way to create better lawyers."*

Trainees kick off their training contract by gathering in Birmingham for a two-week induction. This covers certain PSCs, plus broader topics like how to handle difficult clients. Various department-specific sessions follow in their first year covering everything from insurance subjects to presentation skills. Trainees can also attend lunchtime training sessions outside their specific department – invitations are sent out nearly every week and are not, as one trainee feared, an email error. The firm broadcasts these sessions across all the offices.

Deal or no deal?

While the bulk of trainees' cross-office interaction takes place through training, certain departments offer *"loads of opportunities to work with people elsewhere and make those beneficial connections."* Our Manchester sources told us their property group works closely with those in Leeds, Birmingham and London. *"I'm regularly on the phone with them for property stuff, and I've also spoken with London's corporate team,"* said a Mancunian. Likewise the corporate recovery teams in Birmingham and Manchester often collaborate, particularly on insolvency matters. *Grapevine*, Gateley's weekly magazine, and regular emails alert employees when partners visit other offices so lawyers can make the most of the occasion.

Birmingham is the largest office, but *"you still feel you know everyone – people are encouraged to work together and ask questions. I find everyone's very friendly and approachable."* Nottingham sources told us their office is also tight-knit, while over in Leicester *"everyone's willing to point you in the right direction."* In Manchester, we hear Halliwells' outgoing, sociable nature still lingers on: *"It's definitely a work hard/play hard place. On the whole I'd describe it as pretty jolly and relaxed. Everyone is happy to muck in here; you don't find much of a pronounced hierarchy."* The relocation of several Halliwells lawyers to London a few years back has likewise livened up that office, according to insiders there: *"It feels increasingly youthful and dynamic."*

Every year Gateley hosts a firm-wide induction party at the Birmingham office for its new trainee intake. 2013's do saw new joiners participate in a *Deal or No Deal*-themed quiz. *"Associates would ask you a question about yourself – nothing embarrassing – and you had to answer. It was great fun and a relaxed way to meet everyone. We even had actual Deal or No Deal boxes!"* Other highlights on the social calendar include the annual Midlands rounders tournament and barbecue – the most recent of which saw the Birmingham corporate team take home the coveted first place – and individual office Christmas parties. *"Birmingham turns one floor of the office into a Christmas grotto for a day so everyone can bring their kids. One of the partners has played Santa for years, and they always rope in a few trainees as elves."*

Our sources were heavily involved in their respective offices' social committees and told us about past outings like visiting the Shard, attending comedy festivals, going bowling and karaoke. Leicester and Nottingham each host regular departmental drinks, and trainees there told us: *"We attend a lot of young professional events with other young lawyers in the area."* Manchester and Birmingham groups are also *"very involved"* with their local junior law societies.

In 2014 Gateley retained just eight of its 17 qualifiers. Trainees can apply to any office and for multiple positions if they wish. The firm holds interviews for every position, even if there's only one applicant. Some competitive seats require an additional exercise – like a drafting task – but insiders told us the firm's made an effort this year to ensure the process is as fast and transparent as possible.

The True Picture

And finally...

Half of the current trainee cohort joined the firm after undertaking a vacation scheme. *"It's a good way to suss out the type of people who work here."*

Gide Loyrette Nouel LLP

The facts

Location: London

Number of UK partners/solicitors: 9/13 (+ 6 non-UK-qualified)

Total number of trainees: 8

Seats: 4x6 months

Alternative seats: overseas seats

Extras: pro bono; language classes

On chambersstudent.co.uk...
How to get into Gide
Gide around the world

There's a groaning buffet of international opportunities on offer at Gide – just the ticket if your taste for continental stretches further than your breakfast preferences.

Parisian chic

Gide is France's biggest international law firm. Its Paris headquarters command a formidable reputation and are complemented by 17 overseas offices that offer a handy summary of France's historical reach, taking in Vietnam, Eastern Europe, Russia, North Africa and China among them. Gide remains the only French firm to have planted a flag in London, though its 30-strong City operation maintains a definite international slant: trainees benefit from a range of jet-setting opportunities – with two overseas seats the standard undertaking – and characterised themselves as *"very internationally minded,"* telling us that *"even people who haven't worked or lived abroad have a lot of knowledge of other countries."* We heard that most came to Gide on the basis of its strong brand in francophone countries.

The firm represents some glorious stalwarts of French culture, including Pernod Ricard, owner of a multicultural cocktail cabinet of brands including Absolut Vodka, Beefeater Gin and Malibu. Admittedly, the firm's London office has yet to earn any *Chambers UK* rankings, but this is perhaps a reflection of the firm's global rather than UK-centric reach. As one trainee explained, *"because we're the London presence of a huge French firm, it doesn't make sense to compete strategically with the London and American firms here."* Training partner Margaret Boswell has this to say: *"Much of our work comes through the Paris connection and international network, which I see as a huge benefit of working here. But it's not true that our only role is to service the rest of the firm."* It's important to note that the London office occupies a *"financial niche"* rather than operating a full service, *"which means*

you need to be certain you're interested in finance before you come to the firm."

Our interviewees were conscious of the firm's modest reputation in London. One put it bluntly: *"At the moment, saying you work at Gide only means something to French people."* A recent rebrand has seen the firm drop the cumbersome 'Loyrette Nouel' from its logo in the hopes of revitalising its image both at home and in Paris. *"The name used to be quite a mouthful, but now it's not so old school and looks much better,"* sources concurred.

La vie en rose

Trainees were tickled pink with the *"excellent level of responsibility"* on offer at Gide. Said one: *"I didn't want to be a cog in a big machine or repeat what I'd done as a paralegal. I knew trainees here did much higher level work than that."* What's more, *"because it's a small office, everyone knows your name and comes to you with questions."* Of course, the firm's small size is accompanied by an equally small scope, so those looking for a generalist training might be better off elsewhere. *"We're pretty much entirely focused on finance and disputes. If you want to be a corporate lawyer here, forget about it."*

Seat options: banking and finance; projects and infrastructure; structured finance and derivatives; capital markets/securitisation; financial regulation/tax; litigation/arbitration

Because of its narrow focus, the firm encourages trainees to complete two seats abroad in an effort to broaden their training. Our interviewees saw this policy as a *"massive bonus"* and appreciated *"the fantastic experiences these international opportunities can give you."* Overseas options include Paris (international arbitration), Hong Kong (banking, corporate and employment) and Moscow (banking and finance).

First seats are allocated by the firm, after which trainees can put in requests, although the small size of each practice group means that business need is a necessary factor in their final placement. Five of the six seat options fall within the finance sphere – with stints in banking, structured finance and capital markets among them – but there is a joint litigation and international arbitration seat to satisfy SRA requirements.

Unsurprisingly, Gide's client base largely consists of banks and other financial institutions, including hardhitters like Goldman Sachs, JPMorgan and Société Générale. On the structured finance side lawyers handle securitisation, asset-backed finance and covered bond transactions, many of which cover multiple jurisdictions. The team recently advised BNP Paribas on a €650m securitisation transaction involving subsidiaries located across ten different countries. *"I had the chance to draft part of an agreement and organise the closing for a deal,"* reported one source, while another told of *"negotiating and getting to grips with some corporate documents."*

Over in banking and finance, *"fast and furious"* commercial deals complement debt work for international development banks, while lawyers in projects and infrastructure often find themselves working for French institutions. *"A lot of projects work originates through our global infrastructure in Africa, Asia and Eastern Europe – they deal with the project side, and we handle the finance elements as they fall under English law."*

Trainees warned that those after a very structured training contract will find *"this is not the firm to go for."* Indeed, Gide's approach – which reflects the less sheltered path to lawyerhood favoured by firms in France – sees trainees responsible for managing their own training. They are given a yearly budget of £750, *"which you can spend on whatever courses you feel you need."* Language classes – particularly French lessons – are a common choice, and many opt for conferences and training schemes at professional bodies like Kaplan on top of that. *"We treat trainees like adults and ex-*

pect them to take responsibility for their own careers," affirms learning and development consultant Paula McMullan.

Entente Cordiale

While some of our interviewees were blissfully oblivious to any visible effects of Gide's Parisian heritage on day-to-day dealings at the firm, others felt that having *"quite a few French people in the office"* has some evident repercussions. *"People like to play on the French/English divide here,"* said one trainee, *"but it's something everyone takes very lightly and with a smile. My French colleagues are culturally different, but I see that as a positive point. We often laugh about how things that might seem rude to an English person are normal to a French one – for example, lift etiquette."*

With just nine trainees, the cohort is already small, but factor in the firm's fondness for overseas seats and it's clear that big group socialising isn't the way at Gide. *"There are often only two or three other trainees around in London, so we don't all go out as a gang."* That said, there is some company to be found next door at Italian firm Chiomenti, with which the firm works closely as part of a 'best friends' agreement. *"We have training lunches twice a month there, and we also get together with them after work."*

Each trainee shares an office with their supervisor, and most benefit from a *"pretty good view"* of the glittery skyscrapers dotting the Square Mile. Insiders agreed that the Paris headquarters, housed in a Haussmann-designed building, vastly outshine the City branch in the style stakes. *"It looks like it could be an embassy – there are winding corridors, views of the Seine and a massive wooden staircase straight out of some kind of country manor."* Those who'd spent time in Paris found a warm welcome awaiting them alongside these fancy interiors. *"They're very, very hospitable to London trainees,"* testified one, telling of *"frequent"* lunches and drinks with the stagiaires (entry-level French lawyers).

Languages aren't a prerequisite at Gide, but there are a good number of French speakers at the firm, and our interviewees were adamant that *"being bilingual would put you in a pretty good position at interview."* We also hear that *"a genuine interest in finance"* helps too. On the personality front, *"you need to be relaxed and natural, as well as professional of course. People don't take themselves too seriously here."* Finally, *"it's imperative to be open-minded."* Indeed, we're told *"some people come here and have difficulties with the culture clash, so if you're stuck in your ways it's best to stick to a national firm."*

And finally...
Gide retained one of its two qualifying trainees in September 2013, and three of four in 2014.

"Bear in mind firms have different goals. Some are very ambitious and looking to grow, grow, grow, while others are more established and don't expect to change much in coming years. Consider the type you think you'll feel most comfortable at and stick to those when you make applications."

Trainee

Gordons LLP

The facts

Location: Leeds, Bradford
Number of UK partners/solicitors: 35/56
Partners who trained at firm: 17%
Total number of trainees: 9
Seats: 4x6 months
Alternative seats: none

On chambersstudent.co.uk...

How to get into Gordons
The Yorkshire legal market
Where to bury Richard III?

Gordons marries Northern charm with big-city grit. Big Six, budge up...

Shaken, not stirred

Change is in the air at Gordons, which has been thirsting after national recognition for some time now. In recent years the *"straightforward, plain-talking"* Yorkshire shop has onboarded big-dog clients like Morrisons and Santander, welcomed a raft of new hires (including a four-strong pensions team from Eversheds), set up an apprenticeship scheme for school leavers – the first of its kind – and undergone a cosmetic revamp to its Leeds HQ, with insiders telling us *"the finished product will emerge soon."* For all its efforts, however, the firm's revenue fell flat in 2013/14 – the first time in over decade. *"Our big clients protected us from the immediate effects of the recession, so we're feeling the delayed repercussions now,"* training partner and head of commercial property Barbara Rollin explains. *"That combined with the investments we've made means we can't report growth as we have in years past. Still, we're already ahead of target for the first quarter and have plans to keep rejigging our practice in order to keep up with our competition."*

Property and personal law are the two biggest departments at Gordons, and the firm earns nods from *Chambers UK* for both practices. Its banking and finance, construction, corporate and real estate practices are also among those recognised. First-years' seats are allocated according to business needs, so they don't get a say in seat allocation, though *"they're pretty accommodating"* when it comes to placing second-years. That said, *"often trainees who are unhappy will end up swapping around, which can displace everyone – you basically don't know what seat you're doing until you're literally sat there doing it."* According to the firm, this is something HR is working on. A stint with the personal injury team is no longer compulsory like in years past, although most trainees still end up there at some point. In any case, new recruits can expect to spend at least one seat in the Bradford office.

More of what matters

Several sources voiced complaints about the personal injury seat, telling us: *"It's not commercial in nature, and there aren't NQ jobs in the department, so it feels a bit like a wasted seat."* That said, we heard only positive things about about the levels of responsibility they'd encountered. *"You're often there for your first seat, and you really hit the ground running. Your role is to be a claims handler for things like road accident claims – I was passed 80 files and told to run them. There's supervision, but it's pretty sink or swim."* This sees trainees tasked with speaking with clients, taking witness statements, liaising with insurers and, for some, attending hearings. Morrisons is one of the team's biggest clients and brings in *"all sorts of work, like lorry drivers getting into small accidents, or someone suing the company."*

The commercial litigation team's 2013 headline-grabbing representation of the descendants of Richard III in a challenge to the decision to re-inter the late king in Leicester rather than York remains legendary within the firm; other notable ongoings of late include acting for Morrisons during the supermarket chain's opposition to a judicial review challenge regarding planning permission, and securing a retainer to act for Santander UK on its mortgage fraud and professional negligence recoveries work. Ac-

Seat options: commercial property; commercial litigation; personal injury; property litigation; employment; corporate; banking and finance; private client

The True Picture

Chambers UK rankings

Banking & Finance	Litigation
Construction	Pensions
Corporate/M&A	Private Client
Employment	Real Estate
Intellectual Property	Restructuring/Insolvency

cording to our sources, *"commercial litigation is the seat where you do the most 'trainee' work, like bundling and writing letters. It does get better as you go along and prove yourself, though – I've attended client meetings, and I know trainees who went to several hearings and even did some advocacy of their own."*

Interviewees praised the firm's banking and insolvency arm for its *"collaborative, supportive nature"* and *"great supervision."* Santander is also a big client here, along with big hitters like KPMG, Deloitte and Bank of Ireland. Trainees generally work on the insolvency side of the practice and agreed *"it's a good mixture of corporate and litigation,"* though several complained about the lack of client contact, with one commenting: *"I didn't get to go to a single client meeting in the whole six months."*

Meanwhile, a stint in private client drew praise for offering *"brilliant client exposure,"* so trainees keen to put a face to their work's name should put in a bid for this department, which sources described as *"a great group with a great reputation."* Said one: *"You get to work with little old ladies and high net worth individuals at the same time, visiting care homes and estates – if that's your cup of tea it's great."* Lawyers here handle wills and trusts, tax planning and probate matters, plus estate administration, *"often for clients who aren't able to act for themselves. It's a good seat if you like to see things through from beginning to end."*

Fix up, look sharp

Our interviewees had only good things to say about Gordons' *"modern and quite centrally located"* Leeds HQ, which is situated right on the River Aire. *"Sometimes we get together and go running along the canal at lunchtime."* We heard the Bradford digs *"could probably do with a facelift,"* though sources were quick to justify this by informing us the office is housed in a *"charm-*

ing" Grade II-listed building. Both branches have recently acquired *"thinking areas"* complete with sofas, white boards and complimentary sweets, and participate in various cross-office activities with one another – for example, 'Tour of Gordons', which involves *"exercise bikes scattered across the offices and everyone having a go at out-distancing each other. We also hosted a 'Gordons' Got Talent' event last year. A few partners did songs and dances, but I'm afraid not much talent was actually showcased!"*

We detected a slight tension between the firm's long-standing *"approachable, people-oriented"* image and its eagerness to catch up with Leeds's so-called 'Big Six', with several sources citing concerns over what they perceived to be an *"increasingly corporate image."* Here's what Barbara Rollin has to say on the subject: *"It's certainly a challenge as we get bigger to retain the image we've grown to embody, but we do a lot to promote our core values. A few partners have even organised to give talks about our brand so that people can live and breathe it."* Closing the gap between Gordons and its Big Six competitors would likely see the firm boost trainee and NQ salaries, but our sources weren't especially concerned with this, telling us: *"One good thing about not being in that club is not working such intense hours."* Indeed, sources spoke positively about their work/life balance, reporting an average working day of 8.30am to 7pm. *"The firm makes it clear future trainees should approach Gordons for the experience it offers, not the money."*

Last year's qualifying round, which saw five out of seven trainees stay on with the firm, was a pleasing change from the low numbers of 2012. Unfortunately, the numbers dipped back down in 2014, with only one out of four new qualifiers retained. *"It's aggravating – halfway through the process, it emerged that the firm had been advertising externally without letting anyone know. Still, overall it was the trainees' choice not to stay, which says something."* Rollin admits things could have been handled differently: *"From now on trainees will be made aware that going forward we'll be advertising NQ roles externally alongside our interviews from internal candidates – the reason is to make sure we get the absolute best people."* This approach prompted our sources to take the view that *"Gordons is a great firm to have on your CV, but it's just wise to bear in mind there isn't a total commitment to keeping trainees on."*

And finally...

Gordons doesn't run a vac scheme, but candidates in the past have managed to swing some work experience before applying, so it's worth picking up the phone and putting yourself forward if the firm appeals.

Government Legal Service (GLS)

The facts

Location: London
Number of solicitors: 1,634
Total number of trainees: 35
Seats: 4x6 months
Alternative seats: none

On chambersstudent.co.uk...

How to get into the GLS
Ofwhat? Government departments
  explained

If you want to work on high-profile, politically charged matters that are always in the headlines, the Government Legal Service is the place for you.

The corridors of power

Imagine working on matters that change the political, legislative and social make-up of the entire country. Your clients include the Home Office, the Ministry of Justice, the Attorney General's Office and the Ministry of Defence, and your work relates to crucial legislation like the European Convention on Human Rights and the Freedom of Information Act. You could be handling judicial review claims relating to the conduct of the British Army in Iraq and Afghanistan, or in court rallying against multinationals doing everything they can to avoid paying their taxes. This is life at the GLS. Look around you and the GLS's influence on law and policy is discernible across pretty much every aspect of society, whether it's how we tackle climate change or how much booze mini-breakers are allowed to bring back from the continent. *"I often wake up to hear my team's work being talked about on the radio,"* said one of our interviewees.

"The work here is seriously high-profile and cutting-edge," one trainee told us when we asked why they'd applied. Another added: *"I thought public law looked much more interesting than corporate law, and I didn't want to be stuck in one department after qualification like you are at a firm."* GLS trainees come from all walks of life, and it's fair to say there are far fewer fresh-faced grads here than at your typical law firm – many of our interviewees had worked previously in other industries. In 2014 the GLS revised its policy of only accepting applicants with a 2:1 or above – if you've got a 2:2 you'll get a look in now too. Insiders praised the fairness of the competency-based application process, with one source saying: *"I found it very straightforward. You don't have to write thousands of words in response to a series of crazy and arcane questions."* Instead questions are structured around clearly defined skills and competencies, and assessments have a firm practical base.

TSol asylum

The majority of incoming trainees slot into the Treasury Solicitor's Department, or TSol, a rather misleadingly named organisation that works on much more than just public finance and Her Majesty's money. Nearly all ministerial departments use TSol's lawyers: the Cabinet Office; the Department for Culture, Media and Sport (DCMS); the Ministry of Justice (MoJ); the Department for Education (DfE); the Department for Transport (DfT); the Ministry of Defence (MoD); the Department for Environment, Food and Rural Affairs (Defra); the Department for Energy and Climate Change (DECC); Department for Work and Pensions (DWP); the Department of Health; the Department for Communities and Local Government (DCLG); the Treasury; and the Home Office. *"This opens up some incredible opportunities – there's a huge variety of work,"* trainees agreed. Some of the departments mentioned above used to take in their own GLS trainees, but their legal departments have recently been merged with TSol as a result of government belt-tightening. A duo of departments do still take in their own trainees from each GLS crop: Her Majesty's Revenue and Customs (HMRC) and the Department for Business, Innovation and Skills (BIS).

A TSol training contract typically consists of two litigation seats and two advisory seats. The latter can touch on anything from education to employment and prisons to property. The first year is usually spent in TSol's Kemble Street HQ just off Kingsway, and then trainees are farmed out to two government departments for their second-year

The True Picture

advisory seats. (Not all trainees do the litigation and advisory seats in this order.) When it comes to the allocation process, we heard that *"you're given the first seat, but after that they're very good at handing out the seats you want. Ultimately, though, it sort of depends on which departments need trainees."*

On Her Majesty's Civil Service

The litigation seats see TSol trainees getting stuck into anything from land registry disputes to inquests concerning Her Majesty's Prison Service. *"The prison work largely involves personal injury and mistreatment claims made by prisoners and prison employees against the MoJ. It's very, very interesting and you work with a lot of highly sensitive information."* Sources who'd spent a seat doing this work spoke of taking witness statements, drafting defences, instructing counsel, going to court, and meeting prison officers in the clink. They did note that it can be emotionally gruelling work at times.

Immigration was another seat popular with our TSol sources. *"We defend the Home Office when an immigrant makes a judicial appeal against its decision to deport them,"* explained one source. *"Some of the cases are very high profile and end up in the Supreme Court – often it's the kind of story tabloids love to get hold of."* There are tons of these cases coming through all the time, so trainees have a lot to be getting on with. *"You either instruct counsel or draft the defence yourself, depending on how complicated it is,"* one insider said. *"I found that my view really mattered – civil servants were asking for my opinion all the time."*

In one of TSol's advisory seats you could be working with the DfT on a judicial review for a mega-important infrastructure project like HS2, or helping the Treasury with a major government initiative like Help to Buy. You might even find yourself answering ad hoc queries from the Royal Parks – managers of Regent's Park, Hyde Park and Kensington Gardens – during a stint at DCMS. *"The advisory seats involve classic governmental work – what everyone imagines when you tell them you're in a government department. You might be working closely with a minister, preparing answers for parliamentary questions or helping a bill get passed through Parliament,"* a source told us. DWP's Pensions Act is one piece of legislation we heard TSol trainees had recently been working on.

An insider who'd sat in the Department of Education reported: *"I spent a lot of time working with policy officials, giving them advice on specific issues relating to the bill they were trying to pass. That meant writing speech notes for ministers, drafting parts of the bill and attending debates in Parliament. I loved all the interaction that came with that – there's always an incredible buzz around Parliament."* Another source said of their time in the Attorney General's Office: *"I was working*

with the criminal team, dealing with sentences that could be considered unduly lenient. It's often high-profile work that's passed on to the Court of Appeal. I had the chance to work with the Attorney General himself and with the Solicitor General, the two most senior lawyers in government. It's just incredible – you don't get this kind of opportunity in private practice."

Maxin', relaxin', it ain't too taxin'

After TSol, HMRC has the largest trainee population in the GLS. The department has been particularly busy recently: UK tax inspectors collected an additional £23.9 bn in taxes during 2013/14 – nearly £1bn more than the target set by the Chancellor. *"I wasn't sure that tax law would be my kind of thing,"* admitted one interviewee. *"I didn't do much number crunching at school or uni, but I'm chuffed to be here now."* As with TSol, trainees tend to do two litigation seats followed by two advisory seats, switching between Whitehall and the gloriously neoclassical Bush House, situated on the Aldwych. Bush House was formerly the home of the BBC World Service and, allegedly, the place that gave George Orwell the idea for Room 101. Luckily, we're told the place is pleasingly free of ravenous rats. Instead, trainees here get stuck into dealing with VAT duties, personal tax, business tax, and criminal and information law.

A seat in the business and property tax litigation team involves *"working on a lot of stuff related to what you're taught on the LPC – it's largely property law and civil litigation, so I was referring back to my old course books all the time!"* Another source reported: *"There's a huge amount of big-ticket group litigation we're involved in, like taking huge companies to task for unpaid corporation tax. We're up against accountancy firms and magic circle law firms on a daily basis."* One trainee was more than happy with their experience: *"I absolutely love going to court. In my first seat I was attending hearings all the time, and I got to do advocacy."* The sheer size of these cases, and the fact that some of them are in litigation for years and years, means that trainees are also tasked with a good portion of support work.

Alongside the hit-squad tasked with chasing dodgy tax-avoiding businesses, HMRC has a team dedicated to pursuing individual tax issues. As one trainee told us, it's not all about tracking down the likes of Jimmy Carr and Gary Barlow and making them cough up: *"Tax avoidance cases do take up a lot of your time, but every day offers something different. At the minute I'm fielding enquiries about National Insurance contributions, sorting out bundles for a non-domicile case, drafting responses to a litigant and speaking with a senior lawyer about a case on a public law issue."*

Over on the advisory side at HMRC, *"a seat in criminal and information law is fast-paced and practical. You're dealing with real-life stuff – when the police have a warrant to search a property, they might call us first to make sure what they're doing is legit."* In the VAT advisory seat *"there are head-scratching arguments and a lot of kinks to straighten out because the law is always changing. A lot of it is rooted in EU directives, and you get stuck into researching VAT law in other countries too."* Speaking of their time at HMRC more generally, trainees agreed *"it's important to remember that while this is tax law, it isn't accountancy – you aren't expected to do arithmetic every day; we aren't all mathletes!"*

Plain living and high thinking

No matter where they were stationed, our interviewees agreed that the quality of training and support offered by the GLS is excellent. *"There are tons of opportunities to attend specific training sessions,"* one source said. *"You're very much encouraged to go to all of the training in your home department, but it's also very easy for a TSol trainee to pop over to a session at HMRC if it looks useful."* Juniors also meet with their supervisor twice in the course of each seat for an appraisal, and *"you can ask for feedback at any time – they're happy to give it out."*

Much is always made of the cushty civil service lifestyle – but what's the reality? The sources we spoke to tended to work 9am to 5.30pm pretty much every day. *"The culture is different to City law firms,"* one source explained.

"You're encouraged to be fast and efficient. There are no prizes for macho posturing or showing your worth by hanging around in the office for days on end." Another source added: *"I've found there's a real respect for the fact that part of the reason we joined is because we don't want to work all night."* The occasional 9 or 10pm finish does happen, but it isn't the norm.

Hours aren't the only difference between the GLS and your standard London law firm – the salary is well below the big bucks paid out in the City, and the offices aren't all polished steel and water features. *"Government expenses are a bit of a sore spot right now, so things are done on a low budget,"* said one interviewee. *"Don't expect a roof garden with panoramic views of London, a full suite of gym equipment or a fancy staff restaurant."* The offices themselves are largely open-plan, and some operate a policy of hot-desking – thought to be *"a bit of fad"* by some trainees – meaning staff can sit wherever they like when they arrive in the morning.

Year after year the GLS's retention rate puts its private practice peers to shame. In 2014 it once again retained 100% of its trainees. *"It's a job for life,"* our sources agreed, without exception. *"You're given real responsibility, the hours are excellent, the people are great, and the work is bigger and better than pretty much anything out there. What's not to love?"*

The True Picture

And finally...

"One of the most exciting things about a job here is the long-term opportunities. People move around a lot, so you could end up anywhere, be it in MI5 or at the European Commission in Brussels."

Harbottle & Lewis LLP

The facts

Location: London
Number of UK partners/solicitors: 33/42
Partners who trained at firm: 10%
Total number of trainees: 11
Seats: 4x6 months
Alternative seats: secondments

On chambersstudent.co.uk...

How to get into Harbottle
Interview with training partner
 Sandi Simons
More on media and entertainment

Much like Kylie Minogue, this firm is small in stature but a big name in the entertainment world.

Glitz and glam

Ben Sherman, Chelsea FC, David and Victoria Beckham, Microsoft, DreamWorks, the Royal Household – Harbottle & Lewis's client register reads like a who's who of today's glitterati and creative industry giants. Indeed, some of the biggest names in the advertising, digital media, fashion, film, gaming, music, publishing, sport, television and theatre spheres seek commercial advice from the legal eagle, whose media and entertainment practice is among the best in the country.

Don't be lured into thinking this is some niche little boutique, though. Current trainees were keen to point out that Harbottle is a full-service outfit and in fact often acts as a one-stop shop for its celeb clientele. The reputation management group recently secured a public apology for cricketer Kevin Pietersen after a Specsavers advert implied he'd tampered with his bat during the Ashes, and also scored libel damages for long-haired lothario Russell Brand after *The Sun on Sunday* said he'd cheated on Jemima Khan. Meanwhile the property team has kept busy negotiating a lease for Mrs Beckham's flagship shop on London's Dover Street.

Despite these flashy connections, however, interviewees warned against pursuing a career at Harbottle in the hopes of hanging onto the coattails of the rich and famous. *"You don't come here because you want to meet the Beckhams or because you think it'll be like working at heat magazine,"* said one. *"No one here is in it for the glitz and glamour of spotting celebs; we all have a very keen interest in and understanding of the commercial realities of the industries we work in."* Noted.

Hacks, paps, divers and duchesses

Trainees inform the firm of their seat preferences before starting their training contract. *"The training partner does her best to allocate what you want,"* sources agreed, though they did acknowledge *"that isn't always possible."* New starters have all four rotations mapped out for them in their induction week, but *"it's not totally inflexible from that point; if you have a big problem you might be able to switch them around."* The media seat is understandably *"very popular,"* as is the standing secondment to Virgin Atlantic. No seats are compulsory, though everybody does a turn in either litigation or employment to fulfil SRA requirements.

The media rotation, which takes two trainees at a time, offers work in a variety of areas: theatre, film, television, music, sport and IP. Harbottle built its reputation on the theatre industry, and its work here shines to this day: the firm earns top-band *Chambers UK* rankings for its many West End credits, among them advisory roles on The National Theatre's worldwide production of *War Horse* and the theatre arm of Warner Bros.' adaptation of *Charlie and the Chocolate Factory*. Lawyers also lent their nous to the producers of the deliciously devilish *The Book of Mormon* during its transfer from Broadway to the West End. Meanwhile on the film and TV side, Harbottle has ties with all the big studios, from Universal Pictures to

Seat options: corporate; litigation; property; technology, media and entertainment; family, tax and private client; employment

Chambers UK rankings

Charities	Information Technology
Corporate/M&A	Intellectual Property
Defamation/Reputation	Media & Entertainment
Management	Private Equity
Employment	Real Estate
Family/Matrimonial	Sports Law

DreamWorks to Carnival, recently advising the latter on its financing and production of series five of *Downton Abbey*: *"It's exciting and interesting stuff."*

Meanwhile, solicitors on the sports side of things delve into issues like sponsorship, broadcasting and image rights. The firm recently assisted video game developer EA SPORTS with a contract with Lionel Messi that will see the Argentine footballer become the global face of the FIFA franchise. Lawyers also advised Olympian Tom Daley on the establishment of his own image rights company. *"I gained a lot of hands-on experience drafting various types of agreements,"* reported one trainee, adding: *"It's a client-facing seat – I sat in on a number of meetings, which I really appreciated. On top of that I had a chance to write an article for an online sports website."*

Many of the firm's media clients hit up the corporate team for assistance on transactions like sales and acquisitions, the majority of which are worth less than £100m. The firm also advises start-up companies seeking venture capital. *"I got to step into an associate's shoes after he left mid-transaction, which meant I was drafting and negotiating with the other side. My experience was pretty intense, but it's indicative that if you show you're willing and able, the firm will happily to put you into a more senior role."* Of course, trainees have got to put in the appropriate groundwork first, namely in the form of due diligence and document management. Even so, sources took a 'glass half full' view of this, acknowledging that *"going through the nuts and bolts of transactions is a good grounding for the remainder of the seat."*

When they're not undertaking commercial cases like contract disputes, Harbottle's litigators can be found tackling issues of privacy and defamation. The firm's lately been wrapped up in *"a lot of phone-hacking litigation,"* having advised more than 80 victims of the News International scandal, and has also kept busy with its work for the Royal Family, recently assisting the Duchess of Cambridge with the fallout after French tabloid *Closer* published topless pictures of her. Salacious as such scandals are,

however, most of our interviewees had spent their time on the commercial side. There's no escaping some low-level disclosure and research tasks, but new recruits are given their own debt collection files to run. *"Having that responsibility actually exceeded my expectations,"* said one. *"If I qualify now, I know I could do the job of an associate."*

Geniuses in a (Har)bottle

As we mentioned, a desire to wine and dine celebs won't get you far with this firm. *"That's not what we do. You have to actually know about the industries we service and what they want from their lawyers."* Historically a good number of trainees have sampled life in creative industries like publishing or theatre before coming to Harbottle, though this isn't requisite. Still, *"it's important to show you're enthusiastic and passionate about our work – take a look at your background and try to show the firm what you can bring to the table."* More crucial is some legal work experience, though bear in mind this will have to be done elsewhere as Harbottle doesn't run a vac scheme.

Our sources characterised ideal recruits as people who are *"approachable, have a good sense of humour and aren't arrogant."* We have a collaborative environment, and the firm prides itself on maintaining a mutual sense of respect across all levels of seniority, right down to the support staff."* One of the ways Harbottle encourages this cross-rank co-operation is through free lunches for all employees. *"Everyone sits together in the canteen, which makes it easy to talk to people you don't come across in your everyday work,"* said one insider. *"It's a small thing, but it makes a big difference – you really feel like part of the firm."*

While trainees admitted that *"there's a natural competitiveness between us seeing as a lot of people want to qualify into media,"* we were assured *"this doesn't manifest itself negatively."* Indeed, trainees find plenty of time to enjoy one another's company during jaunts to the nearby Duke of York and end-of-seat nights out. *"We've had some fun ones like bowling. There's also a treasure hunt in the summer, and we have a legendary Christmas party. Last year it was masquerade-themed."* Back at the office, located on Hanover Square, the firm hosts quiz nights in the James Bond-themed kitchen. The proximity to Oxford Street and all its shops can be *"tough on the bank balance,"* but sources agreed: *"It's a great central location. You can pop out to do anything you need to at lunch – when you're not having it here, that is."*

And finally...
Don't forget there's much more to this firm than just its media practice. In 2014 the firm retained three of its five NQs.

Herbert Smith Freehills

The facts

Location: London

Number of UK partners/solicitors: 160/540

Partners who trained at firm: 61%

Total number of trainees: 150

Seats: 4x6 months

Alternative seat: overseas seats, secondments

Extras: pro bono – Whitechapel Legal Advice Centre, Fair Deal Sierra Leone; language classes

On chambersstudent.co.uk...

How to get into HSF

The rush to Seoul: an in-depth analysis

Privatisation and the law

With 24 offices around the world, this City stalwart could take you to Tokyo, Moscow or Abu Dhabi on trainee secondment.

A match made in heaven

"Much like any successful marriage, you have to keep working at a merger," HSF's graduate recruitment partner Matthew White tells us. The first two years of any marriage are crucial, so it's a good sign that disillusionment hasn't set in just yet between Herbert Smith and Aussie 'Big Sixer' Freehills. Indeed, two years on and things are looking pretty peachy for the recently wed pair: a global revenue of £800m coupled with recent openings in Frankfurt, New York and Seoul suggest the combined firm is en route to take the world by storm. *"We've already achieved our goal of becoming one of the largest firms in the Asia-Pacific region, and now we're focused on consolidating our presence there and becoming the leading firm in the region,"* White confirms.

For trainees, the change hasn't gone unnoticed on the ground. *"There are always quite a few Aussies knocking about on secondment, and they bring a bit more casualness to the place,"* one said. *"They're enthusiastic, and it makes it an exciting place to work."* Another was slightly less effusive, pointing out the *"horrendous new logo"* born out of the merger, which became the butt of a joke in the press for its likeness to a certain part of a cat.

Traditionally, Herbies has always been a corporate and disputes powerhouse, and it continues to amass strings of top rankings in *Chambers UK* across its core practices. When it comes to trainee departmental postings, HSF has a penchant for codifying the seats to near incomprehensibility – a stint in corporate LC6S might be followed by a period in litigation LL4, but what does this mean in real terms? Firstly, seats are structured around five divisions: corporate; dispute resolution; finance, real estate and

projects; employment, pensions and incentives; and competition, regulation and trade. All trainees sit in at least one corporate and one litigation seat, but these are split into specialist areas such as IP, tax, energy and M&A. Secondments also prove a popular choice, with about 90% opting to spend one of their seats with a client or in one of HSF's international offices.

The winning formula

The corporate department distributes its trainees among four specific subgroups, all with M&A at their core. Across the department lawyers specialise in areas such as TMT, energy, manufacturing and consumer products, and in 2013 helped BSkyB buy rival O2's customer accounts, making it second only to BT in the UK broadband market. Other recent highlights include representing Lloyds on its £550m sale of Scottish Widows to Aberdeen Asset Management. The *"really, really busy"* group suits those up for a challenge – one source described the level of responsibility as *"through the roof"* and got a kick from taking control of smaller matters on their own. For another, the most exciting work had perversely come when *"assisting supervisors with the more boring elements of*

Seat options: corporate; disputes; IP disputes; competition, regulation and trade; employment, pensions and incentives; tax disputes; corporate tax; real estate; property construction; planning; property disputes; corporate real estate; finance; international arbitration; in-house advocacy unit

Chambers UK rankings

Administrative & Public Law	Investment Funds
Banking & Finance	Life Sciences
Banking Litigation	Litigation
Capital Markets	Local Government
Competition/European Law	Outsourcing
Construction	Partnership
Corporate Crime & Investigations	Pensions
Corporate/M&A	Pensions Litigation
Data Protection	Planning
Employee Share Schemes & Incentives	Private Client
Employment	Private Equity
Energy & Natural Resources	Product Liability
Environment	Professional Discipline
Financial Services	Professional Negligence
Fraud	Projects
Health & Safety	Public International Law
Hotels & Leisure	Public Procurement
Information Technology	Real Estate
Insurance	Real Estate Finance
Intellectual Property	Real Estate Litigation
International Arbitration	Restructuring/Insolvency
	Retail
	Tax
	Telecommunications
	Transport

interesting deals," like drafting board minutes, managing due diligence on companies, and helping draft articles.

The compulsory disputes seat can be spent in any one of nine sector-focused teams, which cover *"the full spectrum,"* from fraud to media to financial services. It's one of the most hardcore disputes teams in the country (and the world, says *Chambers Global*), with 54 partners and 281 other lawyers, and many of the trainees we spoke to originally applied to the firm to get a bite of some of the meatiest cases around. HSF recently defended Bernie Ecclestone against allegations of fraud and bribery surrounding the sale of F1 shares. For trainees, there's a fair bit of billing clients and preparing bundles, but they stressed that the department is *"very good at encouraging trainees to go to court,"* even for cases they're not working on themselves.

Trainees told us they can get a *"lot of exposure to human rights work"* in the department. LGBT and torture issues tend to prove *"particularly interesting"* and come about as a result of having a *"very active pro bono department."* Apparently a previous trainee even had the chance to go to Jamaica and advocate in a trial over there. In general, pro bono *"isn't considered less important than other work"* and is a *"good opportunity to take on more responsibility."* Quite a few trainees trot down to the Wh-

itechapel legal advice clinic once a week, taking on a mix of housing, employment and contract dispute cases. *"It takes up quite a bit of time but is rewarding if you can get results for the clients,"* one told us. Others had helped teach GCSE languages, mentored promising but underprivileged kids, and helped out with workshops hosted at the firm's offices.

First-class postings

The finance department is comparatively small when pitched against the mammoth corporate and disputes groups, though Matthew White adds that the finance group is working *"absolutely flat out"* thanks to improvements in the economy at large and the resurgence of lending activity across various sectors. The department recently advised the government of Nepal on the development of a number of hydroelectric power projects, drawing on the firm's expertise in the energy sector. It's split into four distinct seat options: general and acquisition finance; energy, natural resources and infrastructure finance; restructuring, insolvency and real estate finance; and debt capital markets, securitisation and structured finance. According to our sources, *"everyone does a bit of general banking finance"* too. Sources suggested that being a smaller department there's *"much more responsibility in this seat."* One had liaised with local counsel in Ghana on energy projects, while another said they'd *"met with clients all the time"* and attended *"lots of signings and the parties after deals closed."*

In real estate there's the chance to *"run low-value matters yourself,"* corresponding with clients, taking care of small licences and handling property management. On big-ticket deals, such as the development of a 200,000 sq ft office and retail complex above a West End Crossrail station, trainees help by conducting doc review and proofreading contracts. Those who'd sat with the real estate disputes team had worked with clients such as Standard Life, which owns a string of shopping centres across the UK, and Farnborough Airport after it became embroiled in a row with local residents over the effect of noise pollution on house prices. Other cases tend to revolve around commercial landlord/tenant disputes, and trainees had frequently been to court.

The employment group offers opportunities in pensions or incentives, as well as core employment cases. The teams do a fair bit of transaction support but also win work off their own backs. Since *"a lot of the work involves small matters that can be turned around within a week,"* it's a good place to see things through from start to finish. Like employment, the competition, regulation and trade seat also mixes contentious and non-contentious matters. Though the department only takes on a handful of trainees at a time, don't be fooled into thinking matters will be comparatively small fry. The group recently

The True Picture

advised Royal Mail on the competition and regulatory aspects of its controversial IPO.

Sources who'd opted for a client secondment had ended up at huge organisations across the energy, telecommunications and banking industries. One of the few gripes sources had about the Herbies training contract was that *"there isn't an awful lot of client contact,"* so secondments are a good way to *"make contacts and get exposure to some pretty senior business leaders."* If you'd rather go abroad, then you can draw on HSF's network of offices around the globe. Of course, you're expected to *"pull your weight"* wherever you go, though when London trainees move out to places like Singapore together, there can be a bit of a *"back to uni feel"* about the experience, with *"weekend travel balancing out all the hard work."* Perhaps out of necessity, word has it the firm hands out a pack on respecting local laws and how not to get arrested.

Herbies goes bananas

"I think that HSF has carried a slight chip on its shoulder because it's not seen as a magic circle firm," one trainee admitted. *"Our disputes team is globally recognised, and our finance and corporate groups are City-strong, but luckily for us the firm hasn't lost the humility associated with not being one of those exclusive five."* Trainees described their peers as *"down to earth, sociable and not overly competitive,"* and found partners *"involved and easy to talk to."* That said, there were some muffled suggestions that certain departments – litigation especially – can be quite hierarchical at times.

Such gripes were quickly forgotten, though: *"Team socials take place every six weeks or so, and they are great levellers,"* sources told us. *"Departments really take time to get to know their trainees."* New joiners *"take the social side seriously,"* organising trips away together and going for drinks in Exchange Square or nearby

Shoreditch on Friday evenings. The firm plays its part by organising a trainee ball every two years, most recently held at Kensington Rooftop Gardens, and there is *"a whole programme of other events put on throughout the year."*

With around 150 in the ranks, it's not a huge surprise that trainees are *"quite a mixed bunch. People come from all over the world – it's quite unusual in a top firm to not just see a line of white faces."* One trainee said it looks as though HSF is currently trying to recruit heavily in India, putting this down to the fact that there are no international firms there: *"It makes sense to have a strong base of lawyers to help Indian clients from London."* The firm currently funds flights and accommodation for Indian students who win a place on the London vac scheme – a nod perhaps to its longer-term intentions.

What trainees do have in common is the ability to withstand some pretty gruelling hours at times. Though there are no official targets, you might get *"slammed for a couple of weeks"* when approaching a trial or exchange. *"They're appreciative when you work hard,"* though *"it's very much a team effort; you never find yourself slogging away on your own."* If you do stay late, the firm forks out for dinner in the canteen or a takeaway. *"It's always better to go for the takeaway option,"* one trainee advised. *"You get more money that way, and if you're staying until 2am you're going to need some serious snacks."*

Towards the end of their second year, trainees are issued with a list of vacancies for NQ jobs, kick-starting the qualification process. Only some departments interview, but *"everyone has a fair shot, whether they've sat with the team or not."* As with everywhere really, it's not considered a particularly nice process, but sources suggested the firm *"does everything it can to make it as pleasant as possible."* In 2014, 79 of 89 trainees accepted NQ positions.

And finally...

While some feel the firm carries a *"slight chip on its shoulder because it's not seen as a magic circle firm,"* there are also big pluses about joining HSF: *"Partners take their role of nurturing us very seriously,"* reflected one source, *"and the trainees are also very close – we're not at each other's throats fighting over work to boost our status."*

Higgs & Sons

The facts

Location: Brierley Hill

Number of UK partners/solicitors: 31/52

Total number of trainees: 11

Seats: 4x4 + 1x8 months

Alternative seats: none

Extras: pro bono – Birmingham Employment Advice Clinic, Birmingham CAB

On chambersstudent.co.uk...

How to get into Higgs

Interview with managing partner
  Paul Hunt

Black Country native Higgs is a hearty regional firm with a *"family feel."*

Country corkers

Higgs & Sons has been around since 1875, when it was forged in the iron-clad heart of the industrial Black Country. And like the Black Country, Higgs has evolved over the years. It still plucks many of its clients from the local manufacturing and engineering industries, but today this single-office outfit offers a full service and is one of the area's most prominent firms, earning top regional *Chambers UK* rankings for its clinical negligence, corporate, employment, family, litigation, personal injury, private client and real estate practices. As one trainee chuckled, *"if you apply to Higgs expecting a poky high-street firm, you're going to be surprised."*

For all its development, however, Higgs very much remains at one with its roots. For starters, the firm still houses a resident Higgs – David, great-grandson of the founder and today a legal consultant. What's more, it has no plans to abandon the community that built up its business. *"Our Black Country identity is strong, and we like being a big fish in this pond,"* says managing partner Paul Hunt, adding: *"We don't really need to go anywhere else, either; we have a growing reputation as a leading regional firm and already serve clients nationwide."* There has been one recent change, albeit a relatively minor one: in 2014 the small Kingswinford office, which primarily handled private client and residential property work, upped sticks and moved into Higgs' headquarters in Brierley Hill. *"We want to offer all of our complementary private client and business skills under one roof,"* explains Hunt about the move.

Try before you buy

The seat system at Higgs is unique: new recruits sample four areas for four months each, then return to whichever one they deem their favourite for an eight-month mega-seat. *"The theory is that this creates a seamless transition into an NQ role,"* explained one trainee. *"By the time you qualify, you'll have already spent a year in that department so you'll be able to hit the ground running."* Trainees choose their first four seats before they commence their training contract, though we hear there's room for adjustment as you go along. *"People often ask to move around over the course of their training contracts – HR is very accommodating."*

Higgs has an excellent reputation for its private client work and is home to the only ranked – and top-ranked at that – practice in the whole of the Black Country. Our sources had positive things to say about the department, the firm's biggest, telling us a stint there offers *"substantial amounts of client contact – the partners are really good at getting you into client meetings very early on."* The team works for both high net worth individuals and your average Joe, and its remit includes wealth preservation, Court of Protection matters, and a good whack of estates and trusts administration, including work with charities. Our interviewees told of drafting wills and letters, meeting with accountants, carrying out research, and even running files for small estates. *"It's interesting to work with individuals rather than companies – many aren't businesspeople, so you find yourself spending more time walking them through things,"* remarked one. Given this focus on client interaction, excellent people skills are a must for trainees here. *"The firm specifically*

Seat options: personal injury; family; private client; private criminal; regulatory and motoring; corporate/commercial; dispute resolution; commercial property; residential property; employment

Chambers UK rankings

Clinical Negligence	Litigation
Corporate/M&A	Personal Injury
Employment	Private Client
Family/Matrimonial	Real Estate

looks for presentable people who can easily hold their own in conversation when recruiting. They need to know that when they put you in front of a client you'll be able to handle it."

Like private client, the personal injury and clinical negligence seat is a popular trainee stop. The former contingent deals with road traffic collisions and also handles liability cases following events like accidents at work and asbestos complications. Meanwhile clinical negligence lawyers tackle everything from delayed cancer diagnosis to birth injuries. Typical trainee fare here includes liaising with insurers, taking witness statements, assessing medical records and preparing financial schedules. There's even a chance for advocacy. *"I got to attend an approval hearing solo and speak before the judge,"* reported one source.

Over in the corporate department, a decent chunk of the clientele includes local engineering, manufacturing, technology and franchising businesses. The team gets involved further afield, too, with lawyers recently representing American-led machine tool builder Hardinge in its $34m acquisition of Forkardt from Illinois Tool Works. Interviewees reported work across the M&A, insolvency, tax and banking spheres, telling us their primary job is *"to help the fee earners keep on top of all the documents that come in."* This requires, in addition to due diligence and bundling, *"quite a lot"* of drafting of documents like contracts and Companies House forms. We hear the seat has been *"quite busy lately"* and *"is definitely one of the harder ones in terms of hours."*

The dispute resolution department is on the up, having increased its fee income by 30% between 2012 and 2013. The practice handles a mixed bag of work – from construction disputes to financial mis-selling cases to professional negligence claims – and recently represented Butcher Woods during its recovery of £60m of missing assets and money from property developer Arck LLP.

Trainees found the seat here *"extremely unpredictable"* but ultimately rewarding. *"The team brings in a lot of small claims work that trainees can get involved in – I took full control of a few and even went to court on my own twice,"* reported one.

Shin-diggs

The firm's swanky headquarters reside in Brierley Hill's Waterfront Business Park and boast a huge glass-roofed atrium, where employees regularly gather for lunches and get their downward-facing dog on during weekly yoga sessions. Once a month management hosts a business forum in the space which sees staff discuss firm developments over drinks and nibbles. *"They make a big effort to keep us up to date."*

Such efforts go a long way in fostering a *"one-team ethos,"* interviewees agreed. *"I never hesitate to knock on a senior partner's door here,"* said one, adding: *"In fact I socialise as much with partners as I do with other trainees."* The firm's smallish size certainly helps on this front. *"There's a big feeling of community – you can get to know everyone. At the same time, we're big enough to compete with the city firms in Birmingham, so we're not short on opportunities in that respect."* On that note, our sources pointed out that while their salaries might fall short of their Brummie counterparts', *"it's a lot cheaper to live here, and we're paid quite a lot more than other Wolverhampton firms."*

Another plus? *"It's never mental hours-wise. The office usually shuts at 8pm, so you've got no choice but to go home. And if you're here at 6pm on a Friday, they'll probably tell you to go home anyway."* As such, it's little surprise our interviewees held an overwhelmingly positive view of their work/life balance. *"It's awesome to know you don't have to write off the next ten years as one with no social life!"* While the firm's location doesn't lend itself easily to impromptu drinks after work, trainees have plenty of opportunities to socialise during various sports and networking events run by local organisations like the Birmingham Trainee Solicitors' Society and the Wolverhampton Junior Lawyers Division. The cohort also organises its own informal get-togethers, and there are good times to be had at Higgs' annual winter and summer parties, which usually include future trainees.

And finally...
Higgs prides itself on internal recruitment – more than half of its current partners trained with the firm, including the managing partner. In 2014 all four qualifiers stayed on with the firm.

Hill Dickinson LLP

The facts

Location: London, Liverpool, Manchester, Sheffield

Number of UK partners/solicitors: 186/230

Total number of trainees: 34

Seats: 4x6 months

Alternative seats: Singapore seat, secondments

Extras: pro bono – Liverpool and Manchester University Legal Advice Clinics, LawWorks St Hilda's Legal Advice Clinic

On chambersstudent.co.uk...

How to get into Hill Dickinson

The firm's history

A look into historic abuse cases

Once lawyers to the 1912 Titanic mess, Hill Dickinson is no sinking ship. Originally a Liverpudlian maritime firm, it has since built up a reputation in insurance and healthcare, and added ports around the country.

From the Mersey to the Med

Looking at Hill Dickinson's flat revenue over the past two years, which has hovered around the £112m mark, you might assume the Liverpool-headed firm has been chugging along steadily. Sadly this isn't the case – the firm's been angling for growth since 2010, when it took over the collapsed Halliwells' Sheffield and Liverpool bases, but a restructuring launched in April 2013 saw it cut 83 jobs and sell its Chester office to Knights Solicitors, costing it another four partners and 20 staff. A further blow was dealt in July 2014, when HD held redundancy talks over 39 roles in its counter fraud group. *"As with all growth,"* head of the trainee committee Alastair Gillespie explains of the cuts, *"it was necessary to carry out a bit of internal restructuring to make us slimmer and fitter for the years ahead."*

Despite these setbacks, HD has no plans to stop pushing forward on the growth front. The marine department is one of the main driving forces behind this. In 2013 the firm supplemented its shipping-focused bases in Singapore and Greece with new offices in Hong Kong and Monaco. *"It was particularly important for our yacht team to have a presence in Monaco, and we also wanted to reach out to our clients who do a lot of work in Hong Kong,"* Gillespie tells us. *"Both offices deal with marine matters, but we're hoping to make them more rounded over the years to come."* If London's anything to go by, this shouldn't be too hard: the capital branch, traditionally strong in shipping law, has grown outwards in a number of directions, including energy and reputation management. The City base recently announced the launch of a new sport, media and entertainment team, along with

the addition of seven lawyers to its aviation group, and in 2013 relocated to shiny new premises in Broadgate Tower.

It's important trainees think carefully about which office they apply to since seat offerings vary substantially between them (see our full table online). Liverpool and Manchester offer the most options, and it's common to move between the two – so much so that *"it doesn't really matter which you belong to officially."* Sheffield only has a handful of seats to its name, so trainees there are also likely to spend one or more seats in another branch, most likely Manchester. London seats, meanwhile, largely centre around shipping work, with trainees in the capital required to undertake at least one seat in marine law. A shipping seat is available in Singapore – typically taken up by Londoners – and Gillespie predicts places in Monaco and Hong Kong will be available *"in the not too distant future."*

At the time of our calls there were 17 trainees stationed in Liverpool, nine in London, six in Manchester and three in Sheffield, plus two abroad.

Seat options: banking; commercial and IP; construction; corporate; employment; fraud; healthcare; insurance; health litigation; professional risks; property; shipping cargo and logistics; commercial and IP; commercial litigation; commodities; corporate commercial; marine regulatory; yachts; aviation (see online for breakdown by office)

Chambers UK rankings

Banking & Finance	Intellectual Property
Banking Litigation	Litigation
Clinical Negligence	Police Law
Commodities	Private Client
Construction	Professional Discipline
Corporate/M&A	Professional Negligence
Court of Protection	Real Estate
Crime	Real Estate Litigation
Education	Restructuring/Insolvency
Employment	Shipping
Health & Safety	Social Housing
Healthcare	Transport
Insurance	Travel

Have you had an accident at work that wasn't your fault?

A few years back Hill Dickinson realigned its practices into four 'business units' which function firm-wide. Insurance forms one, health another, marine, trade and energy the third, and business services – a combo of property, construction, employment, commercial litigation, banking, pensions and company commercial – completes the set.

All offices offer at least one seat within insurance. The department forms one of the largest insurance practices in the country – poaching 30 lawyers from DLA Piper in 2013 can't have hurt. The group nabs a nod from *Chambers UK* for its contentious claims work and is divided into sub-teams that cover an array of areas, among them catastrophic injury, professional indemnity, motor claims, regulatory and fraud. Big names like Aviva, Tesco, M&S, Royal Caribbean and the NHS Litigation Authority have all sought out advice in recent years.

The casualty claims team works across the retail, travel and leisure, manufacturing, logistics, and utilities sectors, acting exclusively defendant-side. Trainees with experience here told us it's their job to look into *"meaty"* compensation claims arising from issues as varied as slips and trips, harassment and false imprisonment. Alongside incoming claims are historic allegations – one interviewee told of researching apprenticeships in the 70s to shed light on an asbestos claim and investigating the origins of a company now caught up in a hearing loss dispute. This research, coupled with drafting court forms and bundling duties, makes for *"a good litigious grounding – you get to see pretty much every stage of a claim, from pre-action to trial,"* said a Sheffield source.

Those who'd encountered the abuse and social care side of the practice told of working on *"particularly sensitive and often unsettling"* matters like child abuse claims and GP investigations. Like the casualty claims team,

work here is exclusively defendant-side, with lawyers representing insurers, local authorities, private clients and charities. The firm recently acted for Royal & Sun Alliance in a multimillion-pound liability case brought by 170 former pupils of a Catholic residential care home alleging that three decades of physical and sexual abuse took place at the institute. The firm's argument that the defendants should not be held vicariously liable for abuse sustained before they took over management was taken all the way to the Supreme Court. *"You have to be mindful that this is a sensitive area – that can be a challenge."*

The professional risks, fraud and regulatory teams could respectively see trainees defend vets or fellow solicitors from liability claims, don a detective's coat to stake out those who dare defraud an insurance company, and work to protect the reputation of footballers. Defamation might not seem like a typical strand of regulatory work, but those on the team told us its scope spans *"a ton of interesting areas, like media, sport, and health and safety."* Said a Liverpudlian: *"There's a lot of research and drafting – I worked on letters to the other side, instructions to counsel and letters of advice. You also get the chance to be involved with mock trials, which are good fun. I helped organise one for a health and safety client, and everybody had a good laugh trying to keep a straight face."*

Healthcare is a big success story for HD, and the firm's reputation on this front was cited by several sources as a reason for applying in the first place. The group, which is nationally ranked by *Chambers UK*, represents more than a hundred NHS and private sector clients, including Care Quality Commission, NHS England and NHS Litigation Authority. Among its specialisms on the litigation front are offender healthcare, child protection, coroners' inquests and corporate manslaughter matters. *"You name it, we do it."* The team has played a role in a number of historic public inquiries, including the landmark Redfern Inquiry into organ retention at Alder Hey Children's Hospital in 1999, and more recently the Francis Public Inquiry into Mid Staffordshire NHS Foundation Trust after a death sparked concerns over poor care and high mortality rates. Sources here told of meeting clients to discuss clinical negligence matters, preparing bundles for inquests into nursing home care plans and looking into hospital records for General Medical Council proceedings.

That sinking feeling

When the Titanic sunk in 1912, Hill Dickinson rushed on board to represent its woeful insurers, and when the Lusitania fell foul of German torpedoes just three years later, the firm was again quick to the scene. A century later and HD continues to advise on maritime tragedies – its shipping department is one of a few firms called upon to deal with the wreck removal issues posed by the sinking of the 'Costa Concordia', and lawyers also recently advised

The True Picture

the owners of the cruise ship 'Marco Polo' on passenger liabilities after it ran aground in Norway. Alongside maritime arbitrations and salvage and collision matters is a fair bit of personal injury work – for example, someone falling ill on a cruise ship or a diver having an underwater accident. These types of at-sea accidents fall under the remit of the marine personal injury and regulatory team, while the transaction yachts group deals primarily with sales and purchases of multimillion-pound super-yachts. Here trainees can try their hand at drafting and reviewing contracts for high net worth sea aficionados.

Though the firm is well known for its insurance, healthcare and shipping expertise, the business services side of the practice is substantive in its own right, earning a smattering of regional *Chambers UK* rankings in areas like banking and finance, real estate, and employment. The Liverpool corporate team is a heavyweight in the area and stands alone at the top of the city's rankings table. Big clients here include British infrastructure company Stobart Group and Everton Football Club, while on the other side of the Peak District there's Sheffield Wednesday topping the client roster. The Liverpool and Sheffield teams recently joined forces with the Singapore office to advise a Singapore-based tech company on its acquisition of manufacturer S3 ID. Trainees in both offices told of drafting board minutes and shareholder resolutions, and completing Companies House forms, while a source in Manchester reported taking part in client meetings and handling verification notes: *"It's very detailed stuff – we had to go line by line and verify each sentence of a huge offer for takeover document with an external source."*

One direction

Over the years HD has been vocal about plugging its 'one firm' vision, a hint that its four bases perhaps aren't as unified as management would like them to be. Indeed, our trainee sources characterised the London branch as a bit of an enigma to those based up North: *"There's definitely a divide – it feels a bit like a firm in its own right. I think we can all agree it would be nice if there was more overlap."* According to Alastair Gillespie, this is something the firm's clocked and is working on: *"Bringing the offices together poses a logistical challenge, but we can't grow our business unless they're working together. We encourage everybody to get out and about and work from other offices when they can. Part of the reason we realigned our groups was so there wouldn't be geographical barriers between them."*

At the moment it's safe to say the Liverpool and Manchester residents are pretty chummy, thanks in large part to trainees' frequent toing and froing between the two. The Sheffield cohort gets an occasional look in on the social front, though the London lot tends not to cross the dreaded Watford gap. Still, trainees stressed this is purely *"a practicality issue"* and said when they do all get together they have a good laugh. Doing the LPC-plus, a nine-day training course in Liverpool before the start of the training contract helps, as it *"gives you the chance to get to know everyone before starting."* Firm-wide PSCs offer a chance to build on those foundational friendships, though most training is office-specific. We're pretty jealous of the Liverpudlians who shipped off to Salford Keys recently for *"a day of training followed by sailing."*

Each office has its own quirks, but on the whole the vibe across them is *"supportive and fairly down to earth."* In Liverpool and Manchester there's a lot of camaraderie among the troops, most of whom have some kind of connection to their respective city. The latter is smaller, leading one source who'd spent time in both to conclude *"people know each other better there."* That said, *"Liverpool definitely has the better building – it's much newer and bigger, with air-con and fabulous views."* Those in Sheffield had good things to say of the social dynamics in their office, telling us *"everybody's really approachable,"* while Londoners revealed a predilection for *"midweek mingles"* and praised their new digs in Broadgate Tower. *"It's on the edge of the City, right by Shoreditch – the best of both worlds."* Trainees firm-wide agreed there's no set type among them: *"They're as interested in people who came straight from uni as they are people with families and previous careers."*

We described last year's low retention rate, a consequence of HD's restructuring, as *"a bit of a blip."* In 2014 the figures edged up, with 15 of 19 qualifiers taking up a place with the firm.

And finally...

Managing partner Dave Wareing turns 60 this year and has pledged to run eight half-marathons in the name of fund-raising. Don't worry if you're a fitness-phobe, though; legal advice clinics and Prince's Trust events are another way to *"get involved with the wider community."*

Hogan Lovells

The facts

Location: London

Number of UK partners/solicitors: 151/372

UK partners who trained at the firm: 35.5%

Total number of trainees: 125

Seats: 4x6 months

Alternative seats: overseas seats, secondments

Extras: language classes; pro bono - RCJ CAB, A4ID, numerous charities

On chambersstudent.co.uk...

How to get into Hogan Lovells

Interview with training partner Andrew Hearn

Interview with EU law expert Miriam Gonzalez

It's been five years since the mega-merger between City firm Lovells and DC hotshot Hogan & Hartson, and trainees say HogLov has reached that anticipated *"happy point."*

Mind the gap

Happy, happy, happy – that's the vibe we're getting from Hogan Lovells this year. After a couple of years of posting static or slipping results, the firm's global turnover has risen by a promising 5.2%. On top of that a new CEO, Steve Immelt, took the reins in July 2014, replacing former co-CEOs Warren Gorrell (of American-led Hogan & Hartson) and David Harris (of City staple Lovells), and signalling the consolidation of the two firms' integration following their merger in 2010.

HogLov has made good on its ambitions in the emerging markets sphere, opening up a São Paulo branch in early 2014, joining forces with Mexican firm BSTL in August 2014, and merging with South African firm Routledge Modise. According to insiders, the latter move will *"affect the London office more than others – we're closely connected to the work originating from Africa."* Closer to home, the firm launched a new low-cost centre in Birmingham in 2014 to deal with all the dreaded doc review and due diligence that emerges from its City base. Trainees welcomed the news, confident the operation will *"make our lives easier and our work even more interesting."* Now the firm's presence stands at 45 offices spread over 24 countries, and while management still has its eye on expansion, our sources suggested any growth in the future will *"likely be done organically."* Next stop Australia?

In London we hear that *"closing that gap between us and the magic circle"* is high on the agenda, a goal the firm plans to achieve by beefing up its corporate and finance capabilities. *"Lovells was historically famous for its litiga-* *tion practice, but post-merger our corporate department has become huge. Now we're aiming to compete and get bigger and better deals."* In February 2014 HogLov took a step towards this by nabbing former Allen & Overy corporate partner Don McGown, a man known for both his electrifying stage presence (he famously managed charity productions of *Oklahoma!* and *Carmen* via A&O's music programme) and his prowess in the M&A field.

Best laid plans?

HogLov's five main practices are corporate, litigation, finance, IP and government regulatory, all of which score highly in *Chambers UK*. Sources were keen to emphasise that *"we primarily do corporate, finance and litigation work, so if you come here looking to do lots of niche seats, you'll probably end up disappointed."* Indeed,

Seat options: corporate, commercial, regulatory and environment; private equity, infrastructure and energy; corporate finance; real estate; pensions; financial institutions; tax; competition, public and EU law, antitrust, competition and economic regulations; IP, technology, telecommunications and media; financial services disputes; commercial litigation, product liability and insurance; corporate litigation, investigations, contentious insolvency and fraud; international arbitration, projects, engineering and construction; employment; business restructuring and insolvency; capital markets; banking; infrastructure, energy, resources and projects (banking); infrastructure, energy, resources and projects

Chambers UK rankings

Administrative & Public Law	International Arbitration
Asset Finance	Investment Funds
Banking & Finance	Life Sciences
Banking Litigation	Litigation
Capital Markets	Media & Entertainment
Commercial Contracts	Outsourcing
Commodities	Parliamentary & Public Affairs
Competition/European Law	Pensions
Construction	Pensions Litigation
Consumer Finance	Planning
Corporate/M&A	Private Equity
Data Protection	Product Liability
Employee Share Schemes & Incentives	Professional Negligence
Employment	Projects
Energy & Natural Resources	Public International Law
Environment	Public Procurement
Financial Services	Real Estate
Fraud	Real Estate Finance
Hotels & Leisure	Real Estate Litigation
Information Technology	Restructuring/Insolvency
Insurance	Retail
Intellectual Property	Tax
	Transport

trainees are required to complete both a corporate and a finance seat, and while offerings like competition, public law and employment are available, they're notoriously hard to land. Those who'd triumphed made it clear that stating an interest from the get-go is an absolute must. Said one: *"I wrote it on my application form, mentioned it in interviews and as soon as I started met the partners and senior associates in that department."*

Fortunately, as insiders went on to point out, the options available within the corporate, finance and litigation arms are plentiful. *"It's not like everybody's doing the same standard corporate work; there are tons of seats to choose from: real estate, financial institutions, private equity..."*

Seat allocation goes as follows: new joiners express a preference for their first seat before they join and once they're at the firm go on to attend a series of introductory lectures on other available groups. They then note six preferences including secondment, from which a fixed seat plan is formulated. Our interviewees either raved or ranted about this system depending on whether they'd been allocated the seats they wanted. On the cons side was the argument that this approach *"takes away some of your power to determine your career progression,"* though the pros contingent countered this with the opinion that *"it's nice to know what's coming up so you can plan accordingly."*

Around half of the trainees end up going on either an international or client secondment at some point during their training contract. There are between eight and ten overseas seats available each rotation, though with 30-ish trainees in each intake, competition for these can be tough. New York and Hong Kong in particular tend to be oversubscribed, and for a stint in Paris, for example, an A level in French would work in your favour. As for client secondments, there are usually 20 or so available each rotation; recent destinations include John Lewis and ExxonMobil.

D-Unit!

Chambers UK top-ranks the firm's litigation practice within the 'elite' band, placing it alongside Freshfields and Herbert Smith Freehills as one of the best in the City. The likes of Barclays, ExxonMobil and Vodafone dot the client roster, and cases here are often high-value and high-stakes. Take BTA Bank's £6bn – plus claim against its former chairman, Mukhtar Ablyazov, for instance, which has spurred more than 100 hearings in the UK and is the largest set of fraud proceedings currently before the English courts. Seats within the department often straddle different areas – 'D3', for example, encompasses corporate litigations, fraud and insolvency disputes. Trainees are encouraged to sample the various strands available and work with many people.

Sources with experience on the pensions litigation side told of attending trials for global cases, and we also heard from those who'd dabbled in fast-paced and disclosure-heavy commercial cases. International arbitration is particularly popular with trainees – sources here enthusiastically described gearing up for hearings at the London Court of International Arbitration (LCIA) and participating in oil and energy-related matters. Real estate litigation, meanwhile, drew praise for the fact that *"you can actually respond to client queries here because the cases are small enough that trainees don't have to be kept one step removed."*

Over in the corporate department, M&A is a strong suit. Those who'd taken up a seat in insurance M&A enjoyed working closely with industry experts on multi-jurisdictional matters such as Enstar's $262.6m acquisition of Atrium, which involved lawyers as far afield as Singapore, the USA, Canada and Brazil. Such deals see trainees undertake general research tasks, draft sections of contracts and attend negotiation meetings. Those with experience in the retail banking group – *"the regulatory side of corporate"* – found themselves dishing out advice on new payment technologies and consumer credit regulation. *"It's quite technical, but they teach you really well here – by the end of the seat, I was drafting advice notes and helping deliver training sessions to clients!"* According to our sources, the advice-driven group *"lends itself to more consistent hours than transactional-focused ones."*

The True Picture

Tax, share schemes and pensions seats also fall under the corporate umbrella.

Tough competition

HogLov earns numerous finance-related rankings from *Chambers UK*, including nods for its banking, capital markets and asset finance work. The latter team is *"relatively small in comparison to the rest of the practice"* and handles a good whack of work in the aviation and shipping realms. Clients include *"all the top banks"* – among them BNP Paribas, Barclays and UBS – and financings are often *"innovative and complex,"* like the firm's recent oversight of aircraft lessor ALAFCO's first US EXIM-backed bond financing of two Boeing planes for Garuda, Indonesia's national airline. Trainees' role during such matters is to liaise with foreign counsel, oversee document signings and *"make sure everything's ready for completion."* In project finance, meanwhile, deals typically involve a consortium of banks or institutional investors, and work spans both the lender and borrower side. Trainee work on this end is largely administrative, though there is the chance to take a crack at first drafts of fee letters and legal opinions.

In the *"coveted"* IP department, trainees can choose from the patent, brands or TMT sub-teams. The former handles a good number of disputes within the mobile phone market – it currently acts for five of the top ten smartphone manufacturers, with HTC recently soliciting HogLov's assistance in a dispute with Nokia. Over in brands, it's all about trade mark work for household names like ASOS and Mars. Trainees here spend much of their time *"reviewing trade mark watch notices and reporting back to the client – there's quite a lot of contact, mainly by email."*

Spots in the competition and public law groups are highly competitive. The latter team spends its time assisting corporate clients looking to challenge government decisions, and advising on public bodies on procurement matters. *"We're in contact quite regularly with the Brussels office as much of the work is European."*

That's soooo post-merger

"I got my training contract just before the merger was announced, and now that I'm sitting in this post-merger world, it seems no different to the firm I first applied to," said one trainee, summing up the general attitude of our interviewees regarding the firm's transition from Lovells

to HogLov. *"We've got the best of both worlds – the friendly environment Lovells was known for is still very much intact, but now it's strengthened by a global network of lawyers and clients across various jurisdictions."* Lest you think there's any divide between legacy Hogan & Hartson lawyers and those from Lovells, consider this trainee's account: *"It took me at least five months to realise which partners came from which firm – they've really integrated in that respect."* Fortunately, the Yankee side did not bring over a *"stereotypically American"* approach to hours. *"There's no culture of constant 2am finishes here. And if you do have to work long hours, it's always met with gratitude from partners and associates."*

Trainees are assigned contact partners upon starting their training contract *"so we can bounce ideas off them and talk about our career trajectory."* The firm's ears are open to input from its junior lawyers as well: management recently made amendments to the secondment application form off the back of trainee feedback, and at the time of our calls trainees were involved in a survey about the training contract. *"We've had focus groups and filled out confidential questionnaires – we can address anything we like."* Interviewees also pointed to the establishment of a new board role for equity partners under the age of 45, which they said *"shows the firm is thinking about the next generation and its views."*

With 125 trainees, when all is said and done it can be understandably difficult to wrangle everybody together for impromptu socialising. Luckily there's a very conveniently placed wine bar in the basement of HogLov's Chancery Lane digs, so nobody has to go too far to unwind after a hard day's work. Interviewees told us intakes tend to band together – *"just like you would in a university year group"* – with some hitting the town on a weekly basis. As far as firm events go, the summer party is by far *"the big affair"* of the year. The past few have been held at the HAC Artillery Garden and featured a fun fair, among other delights.

The firm releases NQ job lists in April and October, and trainees are welcome to apply for a seat they haven't sat in. In keeping with HogLov's efforts to beef up its corporate and finance offerings, there have been fewer litigation jobs on offer in recent years, and the same goes for niche areas like public law. We're told the firm makes the qualification process *"as transparent as possible – they talk us through it and advise us on how to prepare for interviews."* In 2014, 52 out of 67 qualifiers stayed on with the firm.

And finally...

Hogan Lovells has been on fine form of late, and it looks like that trend is set to continue. Come here if you're game to mine its core practice areas, not because you're hell-bent on becoming a competition lawyer.

Holman Fenwick Willan LLP

The facts

Location: London

Number of UK partners/solicitors: 76/171

Total number of trainees: 29

Seats: 4x6 months

Alternative seats: overseas seats, secondments

Extras: Morden Legal Advice Centre, LawWorks; language classes

On chambersstudent.co.uk...

How to get into HFW

Piracy: an international problem

Life as an expat in Hong Kong and Singapore

These undisputed leaders in the shipping sector offer *"adventurous and proactive"* trainees a contentious-heavy experience and the opportunity to go far.

Confessions of a shipaholic

Holman Fenwick Willan is a fine example of why it pays to go international. In shipping this is more of a bog-standard requirement, but still, the firm has properly embraced it of late: by permanently relocating a senior partner to Asia, *"we're demonstrating great commitment to the Asia-Pacific region,"* says training principal Toby Stephens. Across offices in London, Paris, Brussels, Piraeus, Dubai, Shanghai, Hong Kong, Singapore, Melbourne, Sydney, Perth and São Paulo, the firm's goal is to *"have a truly global management,"* Stephens tells us. *"We always make sure that all our international offices feel empowered. They're not just satellites."*

Shipping has been the firm's mainsail since Frank Holman, a mariner's son, and shipping and insurance mogul John Holman set up a legal practice in London in 1873. Over the last few years, HFW has adopted a slightly different tack to its competitors: when the economy hit the poop deck many were forced to diversify, but Holman instead focused on its areas of expertise. As Stephens puts it, *"we managed to stick very close to our roots and have concentrated on what we're good at. Other areas are definitely considered complementary to the main area in which we operate."*

No surprises, then, that the shipping team has been top ranked in *Chambers UK* since the dawn of time. The group's expertise evolved over the years and spread into areas like commodities, aviation and logistics, which today also earn first prize in *Chambers UK*. A huge chunk of the firm's business therefore consists of shipping, from

wet to dry, via shipping litigation and ship finance. Big clients include RSA, Barclays, Rolls-Royce and Eni.

Plenty of fish

Seat options include: energy and resources (split into commodities; construction; EU/competition, fraud and insolvency; and corporate); shipping (litigation and finance); insurance and reinsurance; aerospace; and international (the overseas seat). Before joining the firm, recruits indicate a preference for their first seat. *"Usually this is a bit of a stab in the dark,"* our sources commented, with one laughing it off: *"I had absolutely no idea what to put down!"* Sources agreed that the firm does its best to play fairly and accommodate trainees' preferences as much as possible, gauging willingness to travel and qualification hopes. We advise thinking carefully about which contentious seats you do, because options are more limited abroad. *"The rule is that we have to do at least one transactional seat, and the other three will be litigious. Usually in other firms it's the other way around, but we're a heavily litigious firm."*

All trainees are expected go abroad for at least one seat, *"and of course we all want to, or we wouldn't have applied to work here!"* Decisions on when and where to

Seat options: shipping litigation; ship finance; commodities; offshore/ general commercial; construction; fraud and insolvency; energy; EU/competition and regulatory; corporate; insurance; aerospace

Chambers UK rankings

Asset Finance	Insurance
Aviation	Litigation
Commercial Contracts	Shipping
Commodities	Transport
Construction	Travel

send trainees on secondment depend on the overseas offices' requirements. As one interviewee put it, *"they do whatever makes commercial sense, so you don't always get your first choice, but it's the way it should be."* At the time of our calls, out of 31 trainees 24 were in London, two were in Hong Kong, and the rest were scattered between six overseas offices. A willingness to travel is a must at Holman Fenwick Willan; Toby Stephens describes ideal candidates as *"proactive and adventurous."* Several sources had chosen to qualify abroad and were staying on as NQs in Asia and elsewhere in Europe.

International seats vary in focus. Options can include non-contentious versions of energy, shipping, EU/competition and insurance as well as contentious options including shipping, insurance and commodities. Whatever you end up doing, trainees promised *"exciting work"* such as *"advising the Thai government on EU arbitrations to do with trade negotiations, which was cool!"* Other topics we heard about included the import of rainbow trout and the cigarette trade. One source raved that *"it was so interesting, I didn't expect to be doing any of this, and my own international background certainly came in handy – the firm values it a lot."* In the overseas offices the international seat involved *"advising my foreign colleagues here on UK law and how it works, as well as liaising with clients since I'm the one who speaks English best."*

Probates of the Caribbean

"I could talk for ten hours about everything I've done in six months," gushed a trainee about the shipping seat, which all sources named their favourite, *"for obvious reasons! It's so alive as a subject and a really hot topic. It's a very commercial field where people are constantly trading."* Across the 'wet' and 'dry' disciplines, *"the tasks vary massively."* In the shipping litigation and admiralty departments the emphasis is on wet work, particularly in the overseas offices, including *"high-profile"* vessel collisions, groundings and salvage. Trainees find themselves on the front line: *"Clients ring up for quick advice – for example about trying to arrest their opponent's assets."* SMIT, a leading salvage firm, is a huge client, as are BP and COSCO Bulk Carrier, and HFW also works for P&I clubs and shipowners. In the Piraeus office, *"you have very good clients who throw everything your way: finance work, charter party work, or if things go bad at sea they'd instruct you to proceed with salvage,"* said one overseas

trainee. Another reported that *"a Supreme Court case is coming, so we're doing a lot of prep work for that, assembling witness statement exhibits."*

Dry shipping work for one source included *"charter party disputes and two arbitrations, for which they flew me home for from my secondment!"* Another reported: *"They let me have a crack at drafting witness statements for the High Court, and sometimes clients even came to me first to find out what was going on."* In the overseas offices *"you always get more responsibility because they're all smaller than London, so trainees are naturally given more of their own work,"* sources agreed. *"When I was in Shanghai,"* a trainee explained, *"there was a High Court matter and I had to liaise with partners in the London office entirely on my own."*

The newly created energy and resources seat (*"part of the firm's effort to show we're cradle to grave when it comes to commodities"*) sees trainees join an internationally operated team, which recently brought an Australasian group on board. It handles matters relating to oil and gas at all stages of production, energy trading and offshore work, energy dispute resolution and energy insurance, as well as EU/competition law. Sources in commodities felt they were working in an expanding department, acting for *"some big clients – mostly commodities houses."* As a trainee involved in high-level shipbuilding or energy arbitrations, *"you do a lot of bundling, but I also got to go to attend a very heated dispute."* In EU/competition interviewees found the work *"really rewarding."* One gave an example: *"I was working on sanctions, and I had a couple of small advisory cases by myself. It all gets checked of course."* The firm's major clients still include global energy beast Eni, Australia's largest independent oil and gas company Woodside, and UK leader EnQuest. A recent case involves acting for Hellas Gold in a dispute over the terms of acquisition of a gold mine.

The recently opened aerospace department offers trainees a predominantly contentious seat option, where work includes large PI claims following accidents, convention claims, and research into contractual and insurance matters. *"In this seat you have to be able to synthesise facts quickly,"* one observed, while another remarked: *"I had lots of responsibility, and was able to run one small file by myself and bigger ones almost singlehandedly!"* One source got at least one of their five-a-day working on *"the transportation of a large batch of asparagus,"* while another *"investigated the rules of remoteness"* and *"went to court once with a barrister. In the end the judge threw the case away, which was great for our client."* Finally, one interviewee *"worked on a few high-profile helicopter crashes you would have heard of in the media recently,"* such as the 2013 Vauxhall helicopter crash.

You've got bail

The atmosphere in the London office is *"generally friendly if a bit old-fashioned,"* sources told us. In the past we've reported that the firm could be more nurturing towards trainees. Our sources didn't deny this, confirming that there isn't really a formal mentoring system in place, but they ultimately agreed that *"you're never abandoned. If it's not your official mentor, there will always be your direct supervisor in that particular seat who is ready to listen and help out."* And is there any truth in the legends of the terrifying partners? The consensus was that while *"generally, all the partners are lovely and approachable, there are those three or four you know to avoid,"* with one source stoically confessing: *"I had to work for one in particular who was a total ball-buster. But it didn't take away anything from the seat."* Our interviewees were realistic about their lot: *"It's all based on business needs – no one forces you to stay late, but if there's something to finish you'll want to get it done."* Our research continues to show that HFW is suited to resilient types who are ready to accept every challenge a partner might throw at them.

It isn't all work, though. The firm hosts regular parties at Christmas and in the summer, with events like the office-wide boat party on the river. Every department has its own social scene too, and shipping is rumoured to be particularly keen for a pARRRty (sorry). Sources agreed that overall the social side of things probably isn't as structured at HFW as it is in other firms, but this is part of the firm's overall policy of hiring and growing proactive, independent individuals who can easily be left to their own devices. As put by Toby Stephens, *"the kinds of people we hire aren't those who need their social life organised by the firm."* Fair enough.

So what kind of person do they hire? While the firm does value second languages, these are by no means required. They are, however, looking for candidates with an interest in international business, a degree of commercial awareness, and the desire to know more. At the time of our interviews, not all trainees had come straight out of uni; several had prior legal work experience, and a few had come from different careers altogether. The firm hires from across the country, from London to St Andrews, with the current trainee list encompassing 21 different institutions.

And finally...

HFW is seeking to *"feed its fast-growing network with clever young people,"* with the encouraging (provisional) retention rate of 16 out of 18 trainees in 2014 to prove it.

The True Picture

Ince & Co

The facts

Location: London

Number of UK partners/solicitors: 50/91

Partners who trained at firm: c.70%

Total number of trainees: 25

Seats: 4x6 months

Alternative seats: occasional overseas seats

On chambersstudent.co.uk...

How to get into Ince & Co
The 'Costa Concordia' disaster
Ince's international presence

Shipping, insurance and energy are the three pillars of this Londoner, where trainees benefit from the flexibility of a non-departmental structure.

I-aye, captain!

WhatsApp, Instagram, Google Maps, the magical add-on that predicts what you'll look like in 20 years – these are just a few of the apps that have found their way onto the average person's iPhone in recent years. Ince & Co's international emergency hotline app might not fit into quite the same bracket of popularity, but for adventurers stranded at sea or mariners fending off pesky pirates it could prove a lifesaver – a quick dial of the 24/7 emergency number will beckon a squadron of Incies to the rescue. This is but one example underlining Ince's know-how in the nautical field. The firm has handled the legal wreckage of some of the biggest shipping disasters around, including the ill-fated 'Costa Concordia' sinking in January 2012, and *Chambers UK* deems it one of the best in the country for its shipping work, which encompasses both 'wet' and 'dry' matters. Ince also earns solid rankings in the shipping finance and commodities spheres, among others. For the record, shipping makes up around a half of Ince's overall business, while the rest of its undertakings are split between energy (20%), insurance (20%) and international trade and aviation (10%) work. This pie chart has generally produced steady financial results, though in early 2014 the firm was forced to axe ten fee earners off the back of a below-par financial performance across its key sectors.

While the vast majority of the work at Ince is contentious, our trainee interviewees told us the firm's aim going forward is to boost its non-contentious offering. *"I don't think we'll end up strengthening our non-contentious side to the same extent as other shipping firms like Holman Fenwick Willan have,"* mused one, *"but over the next two years we should be much busier in that respect."* An earmark of Ince's training contract is that virtually all the work has an international dimension. *"It's not just that many of our clients are international; a lot of the work itself is based abroad too, so we collaborate with our other bases regularly."* The firm has a pretty extensive network of offices: aside from the London crew stationed in St Katharine Docks, Ince has lawyers on deck in Paris, Hamburg, Le Havre, Monaco, Piraeus, Beijing, Shanghai, Singapore, Hong Kong and Dubai.

All hands on deck

It's crucial to note that Ince is structured a little differently from most other City firms: lawyers here aren't rigidly assigned to departments, so there are no boundaries when it comes to trainee seats. As one source summed up: *"You move physically in the sense that you sit with a different partner every six months, but your workload moves with you too."* Our interviewees appreciated the benefits of this way of doing things. *"There's the chance to get involved in the more substantive tasks of a particular matter since you don't have to start anew every six months,"* said one. *"I'm basically managing all my own matters at this point. Another plus is that you get work from a variety of partners."* At the same time, trainees agreed *"it's by no means a perfect system."* One recurrent criticism was that *"it can sometimes be unclear how much work everyone has on, so some end up taking on far more than others."* Additionally, there's the challenge of *"juggling several different types of matters simultaneously."* The firm does have some measures in place to deal with these issues – for example, there's a traffic light system through which trainees can declare their availability every week, although we're told *"that's not something widely used in the junior ranks."* Ultimately the onus is on trainees to

Seat options: aviation; energy and offshore; insurance and reinsurance; international trade; shipping

The True Picture

Chambers UK rankings

Asset Finance	Insurance
Aviation	Litigation
Commodities	Professional Negligence
Energy & Natural Resources	Shipping

make sure they're on top of everything, a dynamic which requires a certain level of confidence: *"Put simply, if you wouldn't be comfortable telling someone you've already got enough on your plate, you'd struggle here."*

There are a few ways for trainees to go about obtaining work. First up is *"the walkabout, where you go and knock on doors to introduce yourself,"* though trainees told us most of their work in the end comes from *"replying to e-mails advertising available matters. They're usually first come, first served, so you have to move quickly if you're interested."* We also heard that *"impressing a partner on a previous matter is a possible way to generate future work opportunities."*

When the ship hits the fan

When the firm's shipping supremos aren't swooping in to sort out live maritime mishaps, they're busy mopping up the post-incident clutter. In July 2013, for example, Incies secured a $167m judgment on behalf of the owners and insurers of bulk carrier 'Ocean Victory', which ran aground and eventually snapped into pieces after it tried to leave Japan's Port of Kashima during hazardous weather. Similarly, the Ince crew has been acting for the parties behind 'Astipalaia' following the tanker's collision with a container ship in Singapore back in 2008, recently winning them a claim for $6m worth of lost earnings.

Nearly all of our interviewees had soaked their feet in the shipping department, with some even dabbling in both the wet and dry sides of the practice. Wet shipping is typically viewed as the more glamorous of the two. *"A lot of it is assisting with the early stages of emergency responses,"* shared one source, *"so you have to gather as much information from as possible to ensure the team is sufficiently briefed when they arrive on the scene. It's fascinating to witness how the firm is set up to respond."* When they're not contributing to these urgent missions, trainees can often be found prepping expert witnesses for hearings – *"you go through each statement line by line to make sure they have their story straight"* – before attending the hearing itself to *"carry out small deeds like passing bundles to witnesses."* Rest assured dry shipping has its fair share of thrills and spills too. One interviewee reported working almost exclusively on charter party disputes over issues like unsafe cargo. There's even cause for international travel occasionally, given that many of Ince's shipping clients reside outside the UK. Trainees'

dockets tend to be filled with minor tasks here – namely assembling bundles and reviewing documents – but as cases progress there, so do chances to draft pleadings, witness statements and letters to opposing parties.

Insurance work might not sound as exhilarating as answering distress calls from pirate-infested vessels, but dig a little deeper and you'll find Ince's insurance practice spans a number of juicy industries, among them international trade, aviation, energy, technology and, of course, shipping. It's worth noting that roughly half of the firm's overall undertakings contain an insurance element of some kind, so there's no getting away from the practice's importance within the Ince set-up. The firm recently helped a fleet of international maritime insurers investigate a casualty on the vessel 'DC Merwestone', and advised on the liability and quantum of potential claims arising from the incident. Lawyers have also kept busy acting for various underwriters of the 'Galatea', a yacht that caught fire in late 2011 and generated a spate of insurance-related court proceedings. Trainees undertaking insurance work typically encounter both contentious and non-contentious matters, each of which serve up a decent spread of tasks. Those on the contentious side reported some detective-style research into certain documents *"with the aim of finding evidence of insurance fraud."* Meanwhile a source on the latter front told of drafting terms for business reviews and service agreements, plus analysing *"some pretty interesting insurance arrangements."*

Energy rounds off the trio of sectors central to Ince. The majority of clients in this sphere are contractors, many of which operate in the oil and gas and offshore wind markets. The firm recently advised on a contract package for the post-lay inspection and burial of several sub-sea cables at London Array, the world's biggest offshore wind farm, and acted for Golar on a charter agreement between the Bermuda-headquartered company and the Jordanian Ministry of Energy and Mineral Resources intended to pave the way for the construction of a floating storage and regasification unit. Energy matters come in both big and small packages, and a trainee's role varies accordingly. Recalled one: *"I had a large case that mainly just entailed doc review – a very important task in this area of law, but also a very boring one! That said, I was also put on some smaller-scale disputes, and on those I got to write detailed advices to clients and assist them with technical points of law."*

Those hoping to nab an overseas seat will be happy to know there are usually a couple or so on offer each year. Destinations tend to differ; in recent years stints have been available in the Paris, Monaco, Hamburg, Piraeus and Shanghai offices.

The True Picture

Growth from withInce

Many law firms rely on lateral hires to boost their head-count, but not Ince; nearly three-quarters of its partners trained at the firm, a high statistic in today's legal market. Our sources felt this organic growth has gone a long way in creating a *"homely environment – the partners who've been here for a long time remember what it was like when they were trainees, so they're very understanding of our situation. If you're working late, they'll always check in to make sure you're okay."*

Operating in old-school sectors like shipping has given Ince a somewhat conservative image, but trainees told us *"the firm is striving to ensure onlookers we belong in the modern era."* One way of doing this is *"making sure we recruit a good mix of trainees and not just those from Oxbridge."* Indeed, our interviewees over the years have represented a range of universities between them – including former polytechnics University of Westminster and University of Central Lancashire – supporting assertions that *"the firm doesn't take a narrow view of who belongs here."* Interviewees also told us the firm's day-to-day atmosphere bears little whiff of conservatism. *"Take the dress code – most people are only fully suited and booted when they're going to court or a client meeting. Culturally it's very fluid too; there isn't a rigid hierarchy."*

According to current trainees, *"the majority of us haven't come straight out of uni; it's common for people who apply here to have some work experience beforehand."* In previous years we've spoken to trainees who've dabbled in roles as varied as government researchers, paralegals and hedge fund traders, but our sources were keen to emphasise *"you shouldn't be put off if you're looking to come here directly after finishing your studies; plenty of people do that."* According to one second-year, a common attribute among Incies is that healthy helping of confidence we alluded to earlier: *"It's a very pleasant environment here, but coping with the non-departmental system is demanding, and it takes someone with a lot of self-belief to be comfortable with that."*

The *"sociable nature"* of the sectors the firm services lends itself to a fairly robust social scene. Client events are plentiful and include seminars and marketing dos alongside purely social gatherings like the annual shipping party. *"You can even get involved in them even as a first-year."* There are also quarterly drinks held at various nearby venues, departmental shindigs and a budget for trainees to go paint the town red every now and then. One of the most anticipated events on the social calendar is the May ball, the latest of which went down in memory thanks to a speech by a member of the HR team. *"Every year we have a mystery speaker, and people place bets on who it's going to be. The guy this year was brilliant – he could easily be a professional stand-up! At one point he started drawing lipstick on his eyebrows."* Make of that what you will.

And finally...

Ince's retention rates have been generally good over the years, barring a slight blip in 2013 when only ten of 15 second-years gained an NQ position at the firm. It was similar in 2014, with 11 out of 16 qualifiers kept on.

Irwin Mitchell

The facts

Location: Birmingham, Bristol, Cambridge, Leeds, London, Manchester, Newcastle, Sheffield, Southampton, Scotland

Number of UK partners/solicitors: 201/402

Total number of trainees: 79

Seats: 3x4 + 1x12 months or 4x6 months

Alternative seats: none

On chambersstudent.co.uk...

How to get into Irwin Mitchell
The firm's conversion to an ABS
Other seats at Irwin Mitchell

An ever-growing set of business services complements a long-standing reputation in all matters personal at this national firm.

Injury lawyers for you

On the occasions when somebody causes somebody else injuries far more severe than anything a plaster and a lollipop can fix, it's usually time for a lawyer to step in. As the famous saying goes, where there's blame, there's a claim – and when it comes to personal injury claims, Irwin Mitchell's got a stronghold among a sea of wobbly ladders. Over the course of its 102-year history, this top 25 UK firm has become a top dog in the personal injury and medical negligence world, accumulating a raft of first-class *Chambers UK* rankings in both spheres. It also excels in other people-oriented areas like court of protection and family law.

That said, you shouldn't assume that money-spinning corporations aren't welcome here. On the contrary, IM's work for business clients has become a real growth area of late: restructuring and insolvency, commercial litigation, and IP are just some of the teams that have recently been bolstered by a string of lateral hires. *"The aim is for our business side to match the heights of our personal legal services,"* trainees confirmed, and although that feat has yet to be achieved, the signs are certainly promising.

It's not terribly common for a firm to dedicate such attention to two contrasting areas of law, but then again Irwin Mitchell isn't exactly the conventional sort. Its transformation into an Alternative Business Structure (ABS) in August 2012 was big news in the legal press at the time, and it remains the largest firm to date to convert. *"It's exciting to be part of an innovative force that's always looking to be one step ahead of the competition,"* said our sources, nodding to the fact that this isn't a firm content with resting on its laurels. Case in point: after obtaining a £60m joint loan from HSBC, Lloyds and RBS to fuel its plans for future expansion, IM went on to open its tenth national office, in Cambridge in June 2014. The firm now

has fingers in most of the UK's major legal markets and has reaped the resulting financial rewards, with turnover standing at over £200m in 2013/14. In other developments, managing partner John Pickering departed in April 2014 after a 37-year stint at the firm; former head of personal legal services Andrew Tucker has since taken up the position.

In keeping with its propensity for bucking trends, IM's training contract is unlike most others in structure. Before they join ranks, incoming trainees pick one of two 'streams': personal legal services (PLS) or business legal services (BLS). We're told there's very little scope for completing seats outside one's designated stream, so new recruits are encouraged to think long and hard about which is best suited to their career goals. *"Neither stream is too restrictive,"* trainees were keen to clarify; *"there's still a decent level of variety in each."* Still, it's important to note that seat options decrease with office size – in fact, Newcastle, Bristol, Cambridge and Southampton (the smallest offices) only offer the PLS stream. At the time of our calls, there were 17 trainees in the Sheffield HQ, 16 in London, 13 in Birmingham, ten apiece in Leeds and Manchester, four in Bristol and two in Newcastle.

BLS streamers complete the standard four six-month seats, but those in PLS undergo three four-month seats

Seat options: court of protection; medical law and patient rights (clinical negligence); workplace injury/illness; international travel litigation; commercial litigation; employment; serious injury; insolvency; construction; real estate; regulatory and criminal investigations; family; product liability; contentious probate; public law; banking and finance; corporate

Chambers UK rankings

Administrative & Public Law	Family/Matrimonial
Aviation	Fraud
Banking & Finance	Information Technology
Charities	Litigation
Civil Liberties & Human Rights	Personal Injury
Clinical Negligence	Police Law
Corporate/M&A	Product Liability
Court of Protection	Professional Discipline
Crime	Professional Negligence
Employment	Real Estate
Environment	Restructuring/Insolvency
	Tax
	Travel

before moving on to a year-long 'qualification seat'. Most interviewees on this end were fans of this system, telling us it helps ease the transition from trainee to NQ. *"You're basically doing NQ-level work and have your own caseload by the time the training contract is up,"* elaborated one, *"so you're already ahead of the game when you qualify."*

It's a personal matter

Clinical negligence, or medical law and patient rights, is a most popular PLS destination, and rightly so – Irwin Mitchell's prowess in this arena is virtually peerless. The firm boasts lawyers at the top of their trade across a ton of specialist areas, such as brain and spinal injuries, amputation cases and sexual assault allegations in the medical profession. All work primarily on the claimant side. Interestingly, this area of law has seen a sizeable uptick in activity lately – in 2013 alone the number of medical negligence claims brought against the NHS rose by 22%. IM's Birmingham team recently secured a £5.5m settlement for a 12-year-old girl suffering from severe physical and cognitive problems in a claim alleging that a doctor's oversight during her mother's pregnancy resulted in these health problems. Taking on initial enquiries is a big part of the trainee role here – *"you basically jot down all the info related to a potential client and make a judgement call as to whether they should proceed with their claim."* There's also the chance to try your hand at drafting – typically for items like court documents, letters of claim and instructions to experts – and client contact comes in bucketloads, with insiders reporting regular meetings with counsel and experts brought on board to offer advice.

IM's court of protection team is one of the biggest in the country. The practice *"essentially involves looking after the rights of those who don't have capacity – like someone who's been in a car accident and suffered a severe brain injury. As soon as they're admitted, we're appointed to manage the money they receive from the settlement."*

The seat is *"considerably more admin-heavy"* than others, and trainees are tasked with reviewing paperwork, liaising with potential investors and drafting applications to the Court of Protection. There's plenty of client interaction too, *"which gives you a good grounding for dealing with matters of a sensitive nature."*

The serious injury practice, as you might have guessed, is all about severe incidents that occur on the road or in the workplace. Specifically, the firm concentrates on brain, spinal, amputee and disease cases, with settlement amounts ranging from five and six-figure sums to millions of pounds. Our interviewees described a broad spread of tasks, from liaising with road traffic accident investigators to *"considering liability and quantum"* for incoming claims. *"We always represent the injured party,"* explained one, *"so a big part of our role is looking for evidence to determine whether or not the other side was at fault."* Drafting is par for the course here, encompassing court applications, witness statements, schedules of loss and letters to experts.

Family is a different proposition from the other PLS seats mentioned here. Much of the department's workload is centred on divorce cases, but there are *"less run-of-the-mill"* matters too, such as international child abduction cases and custody disputes – *"you might have a mother who wants to take her child to live in another country, but it's being contested by her partner."* On the divorce side of the practice, trainees reported preparing forms for divorce petitions, analysing financial documents, helping arrange settlements and drafting the paperwork that accompanies court proceedings. Speaking of which, there's ample court action in this seat, though *"you only really occupy the role of note-taker when you go to hearings."*

Business needs

Much like the firm's BLS offering as a whole, corporate is *"an ambitious and growing part of Irwin Mitchell that increasingly picks up impressive work on a national level."* Each of IM's offices has its own set of corporate specialisms: lawyers in Sheffield focus on M&A, private equity, corporate restructuring and capital markets work, for example, while the crew in London primarily handles private capital and equity deals. The former team recently advised Sheffield City Trust on least interest purchases made in connection with a £140m deal underwritten by Sheffield City Council, a transaction that saw it work closely alongside the real estate and commercial departments. A good whack of IM's corporate clients belong to the manufacturing, digital and IT, and financial sectors – like leading mechanical seal manufacturer AESSEAL and financial services giant IFG. Trainees here regularly draft board minutes and Companies House forms, and *"we're given a lot of research to do. The work can be tricky to do on your own, but it's nice not having someone breathing over your shoulder all the time."*

According to one interviewee, commercial litigation *"doesn't yet have the same calibre of clients"* as other teams, though the smattering of household names on the books – River Island, Toni & Guy, Cardiff City FC – seems to suggest otherwise. Insurance matters are the biggest source of business for the department, with lawyers recently representing Arc Legal Assistance and Arag in a landmark case concerning the use of panel solicitors in the legal expense industry. Trainees agreed one of the best parts about sitting with the team is the chance to interact with clients and counsel. *"We get to travel regularly to attend conferences, mediations and trials."* Back at their desks trainees conduct research, draft correspondence to opposing parties, write instructions to counsel and prepare bundles.

The real estate department has grown substantially since the hiring of four ex-SJ Berwin partners back in 2010. IM's Sheffield and London offices are particularly strong in the field – the former regularly advises River Island on the retailer's acquisition of new stores and re-sites, while lawyers in the capital recently assisted Wells Fargo with its part in a £4bn property loan book from a subsidiary of Commerzbank. Other big-name clients across the department include Thorntons, ITV and British Land. Post-completion tasks are a common trainee assignment, namely Land Registry and SDLT forms that need to be filled out. *"They can take quite a while to do in the beginning, but it's not long before you start churning them out rapidly."* Lower-value deals grant trainees more of a lead role – *"on those you're negotiating with the other side, trying to sort out lease terms."*

AB... who?

IM's conversion to an ABS certainly made waves in the press in 2012, but trainees told us that life at the firm *"has remained the status quo"* since the change. *"We haven't felt any of the tremors at ground level. It's mainly just reasserted our approach as a forward-thinking business."*

According to our interviewees, the offices with both PLS and BLS streams can *"definitely feel the divide – it's almost like a tale of two firms, though not in a West Side Story kind of way; it's more that we sit on different floors and hardly interact."* Several sources on the BLS side told us the growth from their end has contributed to *"an extra air of excitement. The vibe has become a bit more corporate, though that doesn't mean anyone is aggressive or that working hours have become more demanding."* In fact, working hours are *"consistently reasonable"* across both streams, though we did come across a few trainees who'd had some run-ins with late-night shifts. *"There was a period when I was working 12-hour days pretty regularly,"* reported one, *"but that's unusual. Most days I leave around 6pm."* An apparent compromise for this healthy work/life balance is a salary our interviewees deemed *"fairly rubbish."* In 2013 the firm bumped starting pay up to £25,000 in the regions; London first-year salary was further increased in 2014 to £36,000.

Aside from a yearly charity quiz held via video conference, firm-wide shindigs are few and far between thanks to IM's vast geographical spread. Fortunately each branch has a sprightly social scene of its own. Most hold office-wide gatherings over the summer and Christmas periods, plus the odd celebration to mark the end of the financial year, and athletic types can join one of the many sports teams each office has to offer. There are also occasional drinks dos, networking events and impromptu nights out dotted across the social calendar.

And finally...
Provided you're sure which career path you want to head down, Irwin Mitchell's excellent calibre of work makes it an attractive option all round. In 2014 the firm kept on 36 of its 45 second-years.

Jones Day

The facts

Location: London

Number of UK partners/solicitors: 65/90 (+10 non-UK-qualified)

UK partners who trained at firm: 40%

Total number of trainees: 31

Seats: none

Alternative seats: Dubai

Extras: pro bono – Waterloo Legal Advice Service, LawWorks, FRU, Amicus, Reprieve

On chambersstudent.co.uk...

How to get into Jones Day

Interview with graduate recruitment partner David Smith

More on non-rotational training

Confident and outgoing individuals will thrive on Jones Day's non-rotational training contract.

That'll be the (Jones) Day

Given this American giant's 41-strong arsenal of offices, you'd be forgiven for assuming London's just another notch on the tally chart. You'd still be wrong, though. Jones Day's City branch is in fact its largest post outside the US and has experienced some not insignificant developments in the past few years. For starters there have been some fairly high-profile lateral hires of late, including banking and finance whiz Brian Conway, who joined from fellow Yank Latham & Watkins in late 2014. At the time of our calls the Tudor Street office was undergoing a complete refurbishment, in part to increase capacity and accommodate such hires.

"We're also seeing a greater percentage of our work become multi-jurisdictional," says recruitment partner David Smith, explaining that *"the firm is focused on increasing the presence of London as a hub for its international work."* Indeed, the office will be the subject of continued investment as its lawyers contend with cross-border matters like the $215m financing of Kenya-based Kwale Mineral Sands Project and Eurasian Resources' £3bn takeover of London-headquartered natural resource company ENRC. As the latter deal illustrates, Jones Day has real clout on the corporate/M&A front, gaining impressive *Chambers UK* rankings for both its mid-market and high-end work. The firm also wields a formidable reputation in the civil fraud, litigation and restructuring arenas, among others.

The story of a US firm flexing some muscle in the City is hardly an anomaly in this guide, but there is one thing that distinguishes JD from its peers: in lieu of a tradi-

tional seat system the firm offers a non-rotational training contract, with trainees expected to procure their own work from day one. *"We have to manage things ourselves, which suits people who are confident and want to get as far as they can,"* remarked a current trainee. *"You definitely aren't treated as a glorified photocopier here."*

These halls were made for walking

Trainees told us there are two primary ways to source assignments. *"Everybody's expected to walk the halls and knock on people's doors. Even if partners don't have any work for you at that moment, they'll remember that you expressed an interest and make an effort to come back to you. You'll also find when partners and fee earners are feeling democratic, they'll send out emails saying soliciting assistance – in that case, the fastest finger first usually gets it."*

Our sources found many different reasons to praise this system, with some citing it as a primary reason for signing on with JD. *"I think it's brilliant because it helps you build up confidence for dealing with people outside the firm. If you're able to go and talk to a senior partner, then you can do it with a client,"* said one, while another told us: *"You have control over what you work on and are able to step away from things you don't like in a way that's not possible with a conventional training contract."* Others still mentioned: *"If nothing else it's a great way to get to know everyone in the office."*

At the same time, *"it's not a perfect system,"* interviewees acknowledged. As one explained: *"You end up working*

Chambers UK rankings

Banking & Finance	Litigation
Banking Litigation	Private Equity
Commodities	Real Estate
Construction	Real Estate Finance
Corporate/M&A	Restructuring/Insolvency
Employment	Tax
Environment	Telecommunications
Fraud	

for a few different people at the same time, none of whom keep track of your overall workload. They're in their own world with clients pressuring them to get results, and so it's easy for trainees to take on too much work and become overwhelmed. You have to be assertive enough to say no to people, though tactful enough that you can do this without stepping on anyone's toes."

Most trainees gain experience of at least a few of Jones Day's primary practices – corporate, real estate, banking and finance, litigation and regulatory – and there's also the chance to dive into IP, energy, competition and projects matters. *"On a given day you could be working on matters across several different departments,"* voiced one excited (if slightly frazzled-sounding) trainee. *"I've learned so much – my commercial knowledge in particular has improved drastically."* The non-rotational system means it's hard to fit overseas seats neatly into the training contract, but the odd trainee does fly out to Dubai for a six-month stint, spending their time there doing corporate and litigation work.

Knights of the round table

Almost all our interviewees had dipped a toe into the corporate practice. The team consistently posts one of the highest deal counts in the City, with funds and listed companies comprising the majority of the client base. Lawyers recently advised Russian retail bank Sovbcombank on its acquisition of GE Money Bank, Cabot Credit Management on its buyout by J.C. Flowers, and Veolia Environnement on the auction of its offshore marine services division. Trainees reported encountering a wide spectrum of case values, telling us: *"The work you do changes in relation to that – on the bigger deals you can expect due diligence, but when there's a bit less at stake we draft the main transactional documents, liaise with counsel and generally manage the deal. They know how to get trainees involved."*

The experience is similar in litigation. *"On big cases you spend a lot of time doing doc review, but there are also pivotal tasks they trust to us,"* said one trainee. *"I've drafted letters of complaint, researched case strategy and handled clients – one of them just asked me to lunch, actually!"* The team is big on the fraud front and

also handles a good number of high-value cross-border disputes, recently defending Texas Keystone against Excalibur's Ventures' $1.6bn claim regarding a stake in Iraqi oil blocks – one of the longest-running commercial trials in recent years. *"That matter actually demonstrates the benefits of our training system,"* says recruitment partner David Smith, explaining: *"A trainee started on the case the day she joined and got to see [the 57-day trial] through to the end; she didn't have to move on and leave it behind after six months."* Litigators also act for the likes of Procter & Gamble, RBS, Goldman Sachs and Master-Card, with lawyers defending four of MasterCard's subsidiaries against claims totalling £1.5bn. *"Sometimes you feel under pressure with such big amounts at stake, but luckily there's always someone there you can ask for help. Partners expect you to ask questions."*

JD's real estate practice, which has both finance and litigation branches, advises some of the largest real estate investment trusts in the country – including British Land – as well as private companies, funds and financial institutions. Trainees agreed *"you can find a bit more responsibility here than in the other departments – they seem happy to give you a long leash."* One told of running *"several small leases and rent reviews where I was the first port of call for clients,"* while another described their role on a developer's acquisition as *"pretty intensive. I handled all the research, reviewed the results and helped prepare the certificate titles on my own."*

Sourcing your own work as a newbie might appear daunting, but interviewees were quick to assure us *"most of the partners and senior associates trained here, so they'll be expecting you to come and introduce yourself."* It helps that there's a *"relatively flat"* hierarchy. *"[Partner-in-charge] John Phillips knows who I am and has no qualms in speaking to me,"* said one trainee, telling us: *"That's something that permeates across the whole office."* Sources went on to say: *"Everyone has their name on their door but not their position, which means you don't have to think twice before popping in to ask someone a question, no matter how stupid it is."*

Of course, there's no getting around the reality that this set-up doesn't lend itself to all personalities. *"You have to be a confident, decisive person to cope here,"* trainees agreed. *"If the idea of a helping hand is more up your street, this might not be the best place for you. That's not to say people here are brash or arrogant; we just all have a lot of self-motivation and are comfortable in our own skin."* Indeed *"everyone is astute and sharp but also friendly. Nobody's a peacock – you won't find people who are here for show or looking to boast about their bank balance."*

With 16 stateside offices, Jones Day has far more offices in the US than any other country it operates in. Still, sources agreed *"London isn't smothered by the American side of the firm. Pretty much everyone here is UK-qualified, and apart from the fact that the answer phone messages are recorded in an American accent, there isn't a huge influence. We're very self-sufficient."* In fact, *"we identify as a global firm more than anything,"* they continued, explaining: *"You're as likely to work with someone in Asia as you are with an American here."* Many credited the 'New Lawyer Academy' – a training programme which sees all new starters flown out to DC prior to the start of the training contract – with driving this point home. *"You get to meet all the other juniors from across the network, which really gives you a sense of our size and global scope."*

Harrow-ing Friday nights

At the time of our calls the firm's swanky renovation was nearing completion. *"It's a complete refurb – they're stripping everything out and adding in fancy, top-end furniture, a gym and an internal auditorium. They're also revamping the communal areas with coffee lounges. I think the firm is going for the 'let's make life as pleasant as possible if we have to work long hours' approach."* If our trainees' reports are anything to go by, hours can indeed be long. *"A comfortable day for me would be getting in at 8am and leaving by 7.30pm,"* said one, a timetable many agreed was standard. Later than that, though, and things start to vary. *"I've never stayed past midnight,"* claimed one interviewee, while another told of *"coming in on a Wednesday and going home on Friday. I think*

most people expect that kind of thing from time to time." Fortunately on the latter occasion *"the whole team was also there; it's not like the partners just waltzed out at 6pm and left us to it."*

Rather unusually, trainees used to get their own office here, but now the firm has them share with a fellow trainee or other junior lawyer. *"It's going really well actually,"* beamed one young gun. *"My roommate has done a lot of different work from me, so we're both able to lean across the table and mine the other when we don't know something. Luckily we haven't worked out how much we irritate each other yet!"*

Our sources spoke enthusiastically of the social life at JD, praising the frequency of events and *"sincere friendships across the ranks."* In addition to drinks on the last Friday of the month, JD hosts quarterly shindigs, heaps of sports teams, and plenty of departmental events. *"Since we're not assigned to a particular group, you can turn up to whichever ones you want. Corporate and real estate always have a huge barny over whose are the best, but I personally think employment gives as good as it gets."* If informal gatherings are more up your alley, you'll find a large number of JD lawyers propping up the bar of The Harrow on Friday nights. *"Objectively it's quite a dire place, but the staff are great. It's not so bad that I won't have a pint."* Sold!

And finally...

"The general ethos regarding qualification is that if you're good enough you will be kept on. As a result, there isn't head-to-head competition between trainees." The firm retained nine of its 11 qualifiers in 2014.

K&L Gates

The facts

Location: London

Number of UK partners/solicitors: 54/69 (+2 non-UK-qualified)

UK partners who trained at firm: 5%

Total number of trainees: 15

Seats: 4x6 months

Alternative seats: secondments

Extras: pro bono – Battersea Legal Advice Centre, Bliss

On chambersstudent.co.uk...

How to get through the K&L Gates

K&L Gates' financial transparency

Interview with London administrative partner Tony Griffiths

With its *"relaxed"* outlook and *"civilised"* hours, K&L Gates' City branch is not your typical American firm.

Unlikely neighbours and royal eyebrows

K&L Gates is Yankee-born and internationally bred. Thanks to a 2013 merger with Aussie unit Middletons, it's now one of the biggest firms in the world by headcount, with over 2,000 lawyers across 48 offices (26 of which are Stateside). The City branch has a somewhat convoluted history: its humble roots go way back to 1858 via mid-sized *"everyfirm"* Nicholson Graham & Jones, which merged with Pittsburgh hard hitter Kirkpatrick & Lockhart in 2005, and then again with Seattle bigwig Preston Gates & Ellis two years later.

These days K&L's London lawyers handle their wheeling and dealing at the swanky One New Change, an edifice famous for causing the Prince of Wales to raise a scornful eyebrow at its über-modern design (keep in mind this is the same guy who once professed to prefer the rubble left by the Luftwaffe to certain postwar architectural efforts). Of course, lawyers hankering for a fix of tradition need not look far: the *"futuristic"* building – which is drizzled with melting chocolate-like curves and swathed in coffee-coloured glass – is but a schoolgirl's stone's throw from the venerable St Paul's Cathedral.

The London office has been chugging along at a dazzling pace in recent years: in 2014 it posted a 23% increase in revenue, pushing its figures up to a solid £40.5m. Principal practice areas include corporate, real estate, finance, construction, IP and dispute resolution. As *"one of the major European offices,"* a fair few Eurocentric deals flow through London – for example wireless enterprise Brightstar's recent acquisition of 20:20 Mobile, which involved 13 jurisdictions across Western Europe and Scandinavia.

LitiGates

Around ten seat options are on offer, including some less-than-standard ones like white-collar crime and insurance litigation. A stint in commercial litigation, white-collar crime, employment or insurance satisfies the contentious requirement. According to our sources, corporate, litigation and real estate – *"our principal departments"* – are the most visited areas.

Trainees don't get to choose their first seat; rather, HR assigns them *"based on your background and the interests that came across in your CV and interview."* Still, *"they do a good job – I would have picked my first seat anyway,"* testified one source. From there on, trainees meet with the firm's director of lawyer development and diversity, Tina Two, before each rotation to discuss their preferences. *"I try to really get to know the trainees so I can play to their strengths and weaknesses,"* says Two, explaining that *"often what people want at the beginning changes as they develop – we want to reflect that."* Our sources were content with this approach, telling us: *"We get quite a lot of influence on where we go."*

Seat options: corporate; finance; competition; IP; planning; employment; litigation; white-collar crime; real estate; insurance litigation

Chambers UK rankings

Capital Markets	Licensing
Construction	Litigation
Corporate/M&A	Projects
Environment	Real Estate
Insurance	Real Estate Finance
Investment Funds	

Insiders described corporate as a *"fantastic seat"* due to its *"importance within the firm."* The department specialises in inbound M&A for US corporate clients, recently overseeing special metal producer ATI's $605m sale of its tungsten materials arm to Pittsburgh-based tool supplier Kennametal. Our interviewees told of splitting their time between M&A and capital markets matters, working *"equally between the two."* Both areas are highly ranked by *Chambers UK*, so there's a lot to learn. There's a lot of collaboration with other departments – for example tax and finance – and typical trainee tasks include drafting ancillary documents, preparing board minutes and handling due diligence across matters both small and large. *"No day is ever the same. More often than not you're involved in the smaller transactions as a trainee, which lend themselves to some exciting things like having the first go at drafting."*

When it comes to litigation, K&L is big in the financial disputes, insurance claims and civil fraud spheres, acting for clients as diverse as Puma, WWE, Capita and the London Underground. Trainees sitting with the white-collar crime team reported involvement with financial crime cases and investigations such as corruption probes – *"really exciting stuff."* In addition to administrative tasks like bundling, which can become *"intense"* during trial preparations, there's also a fair bit of communication with clients and the other side. *"I got to attend interviews to help carry out an internal investigation, which was really cool,"* said one source, speculating that *"I think they allow you as much responsibility as you want as long as you're doing well."* Said another: *"You get to see how an investigation starts, develops and concludes. I'm not sure how many trainees at other firms get to see the complete picture like that."*

Chambers UK awards rankings to K&L's real estate practice for its involvement in high-value matters like Capita Asset Services' ongoing loan and real estate workout management programme, which is valued at more than £1bn. The group's principal clientele are real estate investment trusts that manage retail businesses and commercial properties, though we're told a seat in this department sees trainees contend with *"lots of different clients, from large investors and high net worth individuals to local councils."* Work tends to err towards commercial, with trainees assigned a certain number of properties and tasked with handling all the matters related to them –

for example, rent review memos, lease assignments and portfolio sales. *"You're heavily supervised at first, but as soon as you've got a month or so under your belt, you find yourself managing your own files."*

Considering K&L's enormous global network and the fact that *"the vast majority"* of its undertakings involve international elements, it's always been a bit surprising that the training contract doesn't offer overseas seats for trainees. *"It's rumoured that this comes down to London being too busy an office to spare a trainee,"* insiders speculated. In any case, London administrative partner Tony Griffiths tells us that *"international seats are something the firm has looked at from time to time, and the growing feeling is that they would be a good thing. It's just a matter of making sure all the pieces are in place now to make it happen."* For now, options to get out of the office include occasional client secondments and the odd work-related travel opportunity. Suggested one source: *"If you desperately want to go abroad as a trainee, you might be better off at another firm."*

The Gates beyond the States

Trainees agreed that despite K&L Gates' Pittsburgh headquarters, *"it doesn't seem to have an overly American ethos."* Elaborated one: *"We've definitely retained our English roots here. It's hard to pin down exactly how this manifests itself, but basically we seem to be less target-orientated and more collaborative than other American firms in London."* Indeed, collaboration is something the firm does well: much of the work involves more than one office, a strategy facilitated by K&L's 'one firm' approach, which sees a single governance system and profit pool applied across the network to discourage competition between individual offices. The firm also uses the same designer for each office, meaning lawyers feel at home no matter where they find themselves working. *"I've been to the New York branch, and it's identical,"* confirmed one insider, revealing that white marble is one of the signature touches of the K&L Gates brand.

Another way in which the firm departs from typical American associations is its lack of *"silly US salaries,"* a feature our sources accepted unchallenged as it generally means *"we aren't expected to do the same silly hours as trainees at other US firms."* Indeed, *"don't kill yourself"* seems to be the mantra at work here: *"We of course do high-quality work, but people talk about the importance of having a work/life balance here and actually mean it,"* one trainee told us. *"On the whole, people are quite laid-back and have lives outside of work."*

Sources assured us there's *"no pressure"* to join in on work-sponsored socialising; still, those keen to get in some more times with friends at the firm have plenty of options, most of which are informal in nature. We hear K&L's *"not a heavy-drinking firm,"* but when a tipple is in order lawyers tend to hit their building's roof-top bar at One New Change or one of the nearby watering holes – Ping Pong and Ye Olde Watling are particularly favoured. When it comes to organised events like the office-wide Christmas party, trainees are invited before they've even joined the firm. We heard one festive soul showed up to the 2013 do dressed as a reindeer, but we reckon a tux or gown should suffice.

And finally...
In 2014 three out of seven qualifiers stayed on with the firm.

Kennedys

The facts

Location: London, Manchester, Birmingham, Cambridge, Chelmsford, Maidstone, Sheffield, Taunton, Belfast

Number of UK partners/solicitors: 116/253

Total number of trainees: 36

Seats: 4x6 months

Alternative seats: Hong Kong, secondments

On chambersstudent.co.uk...

How to get into Kennedys
The firm's regional offices
Interview with partner Andrew Coates

Kennedys' contentious-heavy training contract serves up an appetising dish for litigation lovers.

Whoa, Neddy!

Kennedys – named after partner Charles Kennedy – was founded in London at the tail-end of the 19th century and chugged along merrily for nearly a century as a single-site firm. Following the opening of a Belfast office in 1996, however, things started to change – and fast. Since 2000 Kennedys has ushered 17 more offices into the fold, now boasting branches in locations as far-flung as Auckland, Dubai and Hong Kong. Its most recent expansion efforts saw it merge with aviation specialist Gates and Partners in 2013, a move which added 70 employees and a Brussels base. But Kennedys hasn't exactly stopped to gorge on chocolates or sample the local bière, as its latest financial results demonstrate: in 2013/14 revenue grew by 10% to £128.5m, three-quarters of which was generated by UK activity.

If professional practice partner Andrew Coates' words are anything to go by, the Gates merger is emblematic of the firm's approach to growth going forward. *"We've continued to grow organically, but as an ambitious firm we need to be doing more than that,"* he says, telling us *"we're always on the lookout for suitable acquisitions or lateral hires."* Of course, *"we do try to keep the feel of the place as we grow,"* he adds, assuring us the firm won't be expanding at the expense of its character – *"we think quality of life is important."*

Other sources at the firm were keen to stress that *"anyone applying to Kennedys should know we're primarily an insurance firm."* Explained a current trainee: *"Knowing that gives a lot of context to the work we do – we deal with a lot of claims in areas like construction and personal injury."* The vast majority of the firm's work

is contentious, and it earns top *Chambers UK* rankings for its work in the aviation, professional negligence, and health and safety arenas. *"Energy and marine sectors are next on our list,"* Coates adds.

At the time of our calls, 25 of Kennedys' 36 trainees were nestled away in its London office, which has the major players of the insurance industry on its doorstep, literally: Lloyd's of London is just across the road. *"It's really cool to be surrounded by all of our clients."* Meanwhile, there were three apiece in Manchester and Birmingham, two apiece in Sheffield and Chelmsford, and a lone trainee beavering away in Taunton. Seats span four main departments – insurance, liability, company/commercial and workplace (which deals with employment and health and safety matters) – but the regional offices don't offer all the options London does. Chelmsford, for example, only runs liability seats, while options in Cambridge (which only occasionally takes trainees) largely revolve around clinical negligence work. Accordingly, some trainees don't have much choice when it comes to seat allocation. *"You're usually just put into seats one after the other – I've never submitted anything formally, although if you have a preference they'll usually try to accommodate it,"* said a source in Manchester. That said, the sources we spoke to in Birmingham and Sheffield mentioned

Seat options: professional indemnity; construction insurance; insurance/reinsurance; product liability; aviation; clinical negligence; personal injury; employment; health and safety; insolvency; commercial litigation; professional indemnity; costs

Chambers UK rankings

Aviation	Partnership
Clinical Negligence	Personal Injury
Construction	Product Liability
Employment	Professional Negligence
Health & Safety	Real Estate
Insurance	Transport
Litigation	Travel

discussing their preferences with HR during mid-seat appraisals, telling us *"if you don't get your first choice, you'll get it next rotation."*

From 2011 Kennedys began sending the odd trainee to Hong Kong, and when there's a business need it also runs secondments with some of its insurer clients.

Brit insurance ACE

Kennedys' jumbo insurance department is home to over 200 lawyers and scores high *Chambers UK* rankings for its contentious claims work. The team, which rakes in the majority of the firm's revenue, specialises in property, construction, professional indemnity and financial claims, and has more than 50 of the world's leading insurers under its wing, including ACE, Zurich and AIG. Much of the work is kept tightly under wraps, but we can say a good whack of it stretches into the billions. Alongside the confidential matters are plenty of newsworthy ones – lawyers recently scored RSA £10m in compensation following an attack on the Sony warehouse during the 2011 London riots. Trainees visiting the department have their pick of four different seats, among them construction, professional indemnity and general insurance. The latter covers *"lots of broad areas, from property damage to insurance for kidnapping,"* while a spot in insurance and reinsurance is more centred around technical points of research. *"I was buried in textbooks most of the time,"* said one source, explaining: *"It's an intellectual area and something you can really immerse yourself in. At the same time, it's so technical partners usually need to look over what you're doing."*

Construction, meanwhile, is primarily a contentious seat, with cases ranging into the millions – for example, the firm's defence of subcontractor Essex Services against a £5.2m claim for water damage brought by the developer of Greenwich Millennium Village. Such matters are generally *"large and slow-moving,"* meaning trainees tend to chip at the icebergs while the more heavyweight lawyers steam through. *"Sometimes you get cases that are decades old,"* said one interviewee, adding: *"My first few weeks were taken up going through one huge file. The seat is very document-heavy, and as the cheapest person in the room you're the one who has to go through it all."* As another pointed out, there's a plus side to this: *"Even-*

tually they trust you to become the source of knowledge for a particular area, and then you turn into the go-to person. I felt like a valued member of the team in that respect."* Client contact here is *"very much encouraged,"* and many trainees are able to get in some drafting experience too, taking a first crack at contractual documents, notices of adjudication and witness statements.

Professional indemnity is another major stop-off on the insurance front. The team is one of the largest in the firm, hosting around 75 lawyers in London alone. Lawyers primarily represent professionals accused of dropping the ball – for example, property consultants alleged to have overvalued a property – and work across the finance, education, construction and media sectors, to name a few. The firm is tight-lipped about the specifics of the claims it handles, but we can say they often run into the millions and involve some of the biggest names in insurance, like AIG, XL and Allianz. As such, trainees take a *"smallish"* role in proceedings. *"Most matters are so big that you don't experience the whole litigation process from start to finish; instead, you have to hope your seat coincides with enough of the important stages to get a general overview."* Sources went on to report that much of their time with the team revolved around attending mediations and hearings, putting together trial bundles, and conducting research. The latter is *"a big feature, but that's not a bad thing,"* reflected one source. *"It's very hands-on, and you actually get to see your findings being used in the cases."* Alongside the mega cases are occasional chances to grab a bit more responsibility: *"If you show you're interested early on, people are very willing to give you as much as you can handle. I ran three or four small files with supervision."*

Oh my God! You killed Kenny!

Kennedys' liability practice is split into clinical negligence and personal injury teams. The former's biggest client is the NHS Litigation Authority Panel, which sees Kennedys act on behalf of over 60 NHS trusts. The team also represents individual clinicians like GPs and dentists via its links with the Medical Protection Society. *"The work can be distressing,"* trainees said, telling us: *"We see a lot of high-value claims involving babies with brain damage – nearly every case has a tragedy involved."* Fortunately, *"the partners tell you at the start it's fine if you don't want to deal with certain issues."* Sources went on to describe the seat as *"very hands-on."* Said one: *"I had a big caseload, including some of my own files to run. That gave me a lot of experience corresponding with experts, drafting witness statements and writing letters of instruction. You need good organisational skills to keep on top of everything here."*

The majority of trainees we spoke to had undergone a stint in personal injury, a department that's highly ranked by *Chambers UK* and specialises in employers' liability, public liability, motor claims and coverage issues. *"Most of our work involves road traffic accidents,"* clarified one trainee, *"though there are also a lot of catastrophic injury claims too."* In the past, the group has taken instructions from insurance gurus like Chubb and Acromas. Trainees praised the tasks they'd encountered here, with one saying: *"I was given a few of my own files to run myself, which meant I got to organise deadlines, ring up clients and take statements. Even though the files weren't worth a great deal, it was a brilliant experience."* New recruits also help out with heftier matters by gathering evidence and conducting site visits, and some even get to try their hand at advocacy: *"I went to a court hearing, where I was just handed a file and asked to stand for someone."* With this level of responsibility on offer, it's easy to sink below the surface, sources agreed. *"About three weeks in I felt totally overwhelmed!"* one admitted. *"Fortunately, I raised it with my supervisor, who sorted it. It's important to let people know when you've got a lot on."*

Last year's interviewees raised some grumbles regarding supervision, but this year's sample indicated an improvement on this front. *"I think the main thing to bear in mind is that supervisors vary across the board. Some will come and speak to you all the time; others you'll need to stick your hand up. They're busy people, but they'll help you out if you need it."* When it comes to formal training, the feedback was all-around positive. *"I've definitely felt supported,"* testified one Londoner, telling us trainees firm-wide are carted down to the capital at the start of their training contract. *"It's a few weeks to get to know the different departments and get a big chunk of the PSC out of the way. It's also a great way to get to know all the regional trainees."*

Drinks and dragon boats

All of Kennedys' offices are open-plan, with trainees situated in pods alongside partners and solicitors. Interviewees praised this layout for allowing them to watch partners in action, and for encouraging collaboration. *"Everyone mucks in together, and there are no closed doors – literally. I can happily walk up to anyone and ask a question."* Moreover, *"it's really easy to get to know people quickly. You get a lot of hellos from lots of people as you walk down the corridor."*

London-based trainees are treated to some of the firm's best views, thanks to the wrap-around balcony at 25 Fenchurch Avenue. *"You can see pretty much all of the*

famous skyscrapers – the Gherkin, the Cheesegrater, the Walkie Talkie."* Inside are plenty of perks too, including well-loved cafe The Writz, where trainees can tuck into sandwiches as well as breakfasts of fruit and toast. Sources in regional branches admitted their pads are *"not as swanky as London,"* but we're told most offices share similar decor and are centrally located in their respective locales. Naturally, salaries in the regions are lower than in the capital – up to £9,000 lower in some cases – though our interviewees broadly agreed with the trainee who said *"I don't have a problem with it – it's all down to the cost of living."*

There may be a lengthy 250 miles between Manchester and Maidstone, but trainees across the firm agreed that Kennedys *"feels really connected,"* telling us firmwide charity fund-raising efforts *"go a long way"* in making this the case. At the time of our calls 33 lawyers had recently returned from scaling Mount Toubkal in Morocco, bagging over £40,000 for War Child in the process. Another major event took place in July 2014, when two teams of Kennedys employees competed in a 26-mile dragon boat marathon. The firm also unites its lawyers by bringing all the regional offices down to London every other year for a Christmas bash. *"Last year's was really good,"* enthused one trainee. *"Everything was paid for – drinks, hotels, you name it!"*

Abiding by its motto, which promises to deliver legal advice 'in black and white', Kennedys maintains a straightforward style, sources thought. *"What you see is what you get here. It's very transparent, and there isn't much of a hierarchy; we're always told about things going on up high."* Indeed, across the firm partners hold frequent departmental meetings to discuss Kennedys' financial performance and general business plan. *"The 'black and white' strapline wasn't dreamt up by some PR person; it was coined by one of the partners over 20 years ago,"* says Andrew Coates. *"We really do live by it!"*

Sources were keen to emphasise the *"refreshing lack of competition"* among trainees. Explained one: *"We have great retention rates, so it's not dog-eat-dog. In fact, at times we even rescue each other. Once a trainee had some files that had to be into the court that day, but right outside the courthouse a double-decker bus drove through a puddle, and the files were completely destroyed! Luckily another trainee rushed down with fresh ones!"* In 2014, 13 of 18 new qualifiers stayed on.

And finally...

"Don't apply thinking we're the same as DLA Piper or Eversheds just because we're a full-service national firm. Show that you understand we do a lot of litigation and insurance work, and demonstrate your interest in that."

King & Wood Mallesons LLP

The facts

Location: London

Number of UK partner/solicitors: 88/189

Partners who trained at firm: 22%

Total numbers of trainees: 72

Seats: 4x6 months

Alternative seats: overseas seats, secondments

Extras: pro bono – Toynbee Hall Debt Clinic, International Lawyers for Africa; language classes

On chambersstudent.co.uk...

How to get into KWM
Private equity made public

Analysts suggest that the 21st century will be an 'Asian Century'. It certainly looks that way for the formidable City force that is KWM.

Frankie goes to... Hong Kong

China is fast becoming the world's dominant economic power, a fact that's now had a direct impact on the fortunes of one major UK law firm. On 1st November 2013 King & Wood Mallesons became the first Asia-Pacific firm to merge with a City outfit, shacking up with private equity pro SJ Berwin to form a $1bn firm. KWM was already the result of a 2012 tie-up between top Australian shop Mallesons and Hong Kong-headquartered King & Wood (which, rather oddly, never had any partners called either King or Wood – the name was chosen because it sounded reliable to Western ears). All of this left the UK firm with the rather clunky name King & Wood Mallesons SJ Berwin, or KWMSJB for short, but as of 2014 the firm shortened this to the simpler title of King & Wood Mallesons.

Before KWM came on the scene, there'd been rumblings of an SJB tie-up with a heavy-hitting American firm, but nothing came of them – the Chinese swooped first. So what were London's reasons for going East rather than West? *"It was a completely unique proposition. The growth potential in the Asian market is incredible,"* says UK graduate recruitment partner Nicola Bridge. *"We wanted to connect the world to Asia and connect Asia to the world."* This grandiose vision explains the thinking behind the firm's (somewhat ungrammatical) new slogan, 'The Power of Together'.

So what's it like on the inside now that SJB has joined forces with KWM? *"It would have been awful if we'd applied to work at one firm and ended up at another as a result of the combination, but that hasn't been the case at all,"* trainees agreed. *"The firm hasn't lost the feel of SJB."* So what was it that sold our insiders on SJB in the first place? *"I wanted to work for an ambitious and forward-thinking firm with an international reach and a great client list,"* said one source, *"and when I saw the roof terrace and the views of London, I couldn't say no."*

Chambers UK ranks KWM for both its mid-market and high-end corporate/M&A work, while the private equity, investment funds, litigation, banking and finance, and competition practices (among others) are also roundly respected. But it's corporate and private equity work for which the firm is most noted: it recently advised music moguls Universal on the £487m sale of the Parlophone label to Warner Music, and acted for US private equity giant Warburg Pincus as the leader of a consortium providing up to $600m worth of funding to Delonex, a new Africa-focused oil and gas explorer.

Two corporate and one contentious seat are compulsory. But then again, as one trainee queried, *"why would you come here if you weren't really interested in corporate law?"* Beyond this requirement, trainees are free to choose where they go. *"The allocation process is han-*

Seat options: corporate; energy and infrastructure; finance; funds and indirect real estate; financial markets; international funds; reconstruction and insolvency; commercial litigation; employment; EU, competition and regulatory; IP; planning and environment; property litigation; commerce and technology; construction; EU, competition and regulatory; real estate; tax

The True Picture

Chambers UK rankings

Banking & Finance	Investment Funds
Banking Litigation	Litigation
Competition/European	Parliamentary & Public
Law	Affairs
Construction	Partnership
Corporate/M&A	Planning
Employment	Private Equity
Environment	Real Estate
Financial Services	Real Estate Finance
Fraud	Real Estate Litigation
Hotels & Leisure	Restructuring/Insolvency
Information Technology	Retail
Intellectual Property	Tax

dled very well and people tend to get their first choice for most seats," insiders agreed. We hear seats in commercial and employment are the most competitive to get, by virtue of the smaller size of those departments.

We three (corporate) kings

The corporate practice is split into three core teams: team A deals predominantly with public M&A and real estate finance; team B is concerned with private equity transactions; and the third, the incongruously entitled international funds, works on fund formation. *"These are big teams – the real lifeblood of the business,"* one source told us. In team A, *"you get the chance to work on some really huge transactions – so big that you often don't see the whole picture."* Recent clients include Westfield, Ladbrokes and Lion Capital. One recent real estate transaction saw lawyers advise British Land on the £470m purchase of Paddington Central, a mixed-use estate close to Paddington station. The size of the deals means trainees usually take charge of managing documents, but we also heard there are opportunities to draft ancillaries, and on smaller matters you might get to draft a whole suite of documents.

Trainees in team B work on the purchase and sale of portfolios of companies for private equity houses. *"Quite a bit of the work involves household names and high-street brands, but there's more niche work going on too."* The firm recently advised Duke Street on its £185m sale of Oasis Healthcare to the owners of Pret A Manger and Virgin Active. *"We also do a lot of work in emerging markets like Russia and Africa, so trainees get stuck into some really interesting international work,"* one source said. As in team A, there's a lot of document management and drafting of ancillary documents like board minutes, but we also heard *"once you've proved yourself they give you the good stuff, like drafting sale and purchase agreements."* One source reported: *"I managed to meet most*

of the clients we had during the course of my seat, which was a great experience."

The international funds group works mostly on fund formation – for instance, *"negotiating limited partnership agreements"* – for private equity houses, hedge funds and occasionally the investors themselves. *"We go through the process of negotiating with all the new investors that come on board to form a fund,"* one trainee told us. *"New deals are closing all the time – the work goes at a phenomenal rate."* Recent partner departures have had an adverse effect on the firm's standing in the private equity and investment funds market, but trainees nonetheless hyped up the *"impressive academic credentials"* of the partners on this team. It seems they impart their knowledge on trainees too: *"The funds market is really diversifying,"* observed one well-informed young gun. *"For instance, there are more and more funds investing in infrastructure debt."* Funds is a specialist area, and this is recognised by the firm, which lays on *"really in-depth training sessions"* once a week. The rest of the learning curve is provided through involvement in negotiations and the answering of ad hoc queries from fund managers and investors.

A seat in litigation means working on *"a really broad range of matters – you could be staffed on a banking dispute, an arbitration, a fraud case or a general commercial matter. It's a real smorgasbord."* Morgan Stanley, Hilton, Universal and the Crown Estate are all clients, and the firm recently successfully defended BSkyB in a trade mark battle with a Hong Kong telecoms group over the name of its internet TV service, Now TV. Several of our sources spoke of going to court during their time in the seat, and trainees also draft witness statements, do research and – inevitably – get stuck into bits of bundling. *"The team is home to some brilliant personalities, and they're great to work with. That really lightens the load when there's a lot of pressure on,"* one insider told us.

Lingua franca

The popular EU, competition and regulatory seat gives trainees the chance to get involved in everything from anti-cartel work and international merger control to regulatory matters. Major clients include the BBC, Dixons and Diageo, among others. It's not unusual for trainees to be despatched to the European Commission in Brussels, and one insider called the seat *"a genuine intellectual challenge. The work is very engaging."* Typical tasks for trainees here include drafting witness statements and consent orders, attending conferences with counsel, and doing black-letter law research. Interviewees cooed appreciatively about the department *"winning some incredible work"* – this includes advising RBS on the competition aspects of the European Commission's Libor fraud investigation.

Speaking of transnational issues, we should also mention the overseas seats the firm offers. The current options are Paris, Madrid, Frankfurt and Dubai. *"There are some fantastic opportunities out there, particularly if you speak foreign languages,"* insiders agreed. The KWM combination is set to open up new opportunities too. Graduate recruitment partner Nicola Bridge told us: *"We want to get people moving between the offices as much as possible at all levels. For trainees, there'll hopefully be a posting to Australia before too long."* The firm also seconds trainees to big-name multinationals.

When we asked about working hours, our sources shrugged off the suggestion that KWM is any more punishing than its rivals. *"The bottom line is that if you're working at a City law firm, there will be long hours and late nights,"* said one. *"We've got a bit of a reputation for bad hours, but I don't think I'm putting in any more time than my friends at other City firms."* We were pleasantly surprised to hear that an average day looks something like 9am to 7.30pm and that weekend work is relatively rare. That said, there can be late nights back to back in some of the transactional teams when a deal is closing, so don't forget your energy tablets.

The perks of not being a wallflower

"In the past we've had a bit of a reputation for being aggressive but that's more to do with our approach to winning work rather than our attitude towards each other in the office," one trainee was quick to tell us. *"For such a young firm* [SJB was founded in 1982] *we've done a great job of expanding rapidly and muscling in on others' turf, but that doesn't mean people are forceful or difficult to work with in the office – there are a lot of laughs here."* Another insider said: *"When the work needs to get done we're very focused and driven, but there are times when*

it feels relaxed too – it's a healthy balance. I'd say your typical trainee here is confident, sociable and resilient. It's not the kind of place that attracts wallflowers."

Our sources spewed superlatives when we asked about the newly formed KWM's growing international activities. *"I've already worked with Chinese investors and Australian clients,"* one source said. *"There's only going to be more of that to come – increased chances to work on global mega-deals and some amazing opportunities to travel too!"* Another interviewee added: *"I really came to appreciate just how international the firm is when they flew our team out to Europe and I randomly bumped into a Spanish associate I'd been working closely with for months!"* So what should we expect from the firm in the future? *"We want to grow and develop across Asia – that's the priority,"* says Nicola Bridge. At the same time, our trainee sources believed, a US merger could still happen too. *"Management considered it seriously before joining up with King & Wood Mallesons, even entering merger talks with US firm Proskauer, and I don't think they've dropped the idea of an American alliance just yet."*

Homing back in on KWM's London office on Queen Street Place (by Southwark Bridge), pretty much all of our sources singled out the firm's roof terrace as one of the major perks of the workplace. *"There was a great party on the terrace when they announced the KWM combination, and there are often drinks and networking events up there too."* Another nice bonus is Stanley's, the in-house restaurant named for the firm's founder Stanley Berwin, where trainees can enjoy a complimentary meal every day. (Is there such a thing as a free lunch?) And watering holes such as The Banker, The Anchor and The Oyster Shed are favourites among trainees looking for a drink after work on a Friday.

The True Picture

And finally...

The qualification process has been a bit of a sore spot for trainees here over the past couple of years. *"If they published a list of jobs it would all be a lot clearer,"* our sources implored. In 2014 the firm kept on 28 of 39 qualifiers.

Kingsley Napley

Cool.
Calm.
Collective.

When trouble is brewing and your reputation is at stake, getting the right legal advice is crucial. At Kingsley Napley we recognise the need for sensitivity, trust and discretion, and have been advising high profile clients for over 75 years.

Looking after our clients is a serious business. We ensure our lawyers have the right tools and environment to focus on their clients, remain calm in their crisis and give the best advice possible. The firm's core values of teamwork, respect, integrity and fairness is how we do things around here. We do all this because we want our lawyers to be the best and many of them already are.

FOR MORE INFORMATION VISIT US AT
KINGSLEYNAPLEY.CO.UK
OR CALL US ON
+44 (0) 20 7814 1200

Kingsley Napley LLP

The facts

Location: London
Number of UK partners/solicitors: 46/70
Partners who trained at firm: 6.5%
Total number of trainees: 10
Seats: 4x6 months
Alternative seats: none
Extras: pro bono – CAB

On chambersstudent.co.uk...

How to get into Kingsley Napley
Senior partner Jane Keir on women
    in law

This firm's criminal cases frequently make headlines, and it also possesses a formidable reputation in the clinical negligence, regulatory and immigration spheres.

In Dire Straits?

If you're a high-profile personality in a legal pickle, Kingsley Napley should be on your radar. The Londoner, founded in 1937 by Sidney Kingsley and Sir David Napley, has built up a stellar reputation for handling cases for the famous and infamous alike. On Napley's roster were General Pinochet, murderer Jeremy Bamber and notorious rogue trader Nick Leeson, plus various disgraced politicians. Beyond defending the dastardly, he had a keen interest in miscarriages of justice, taking up the cause of government whistle-blower Sarah Tisdall and working on the notorious Newcastle one-armed bandit case that inspired *Get Carter* (not to mention a song by Mark Knopfler). Nowadays, KN's criminal caseload remains as headline-grabbing as ever. Solicitors are busy acting for Rebekah and Charlie Brooks as they stand trial for phone hacking and perverting the course of justice. They're also representing Rolf Harris over allegations of historic sexual abuse emerging from the Operation Yewtree investigation, acting for Conservative MP Andrew Mitchell in the wake of 'Plebgate', and recently defended footballers Steve Cook and André Santos over respective charges of indecent assault and dangerous driving.

But KN does much more than helping celebs and Establishment folk out of serious spots of bother. This year's trainees put it best when they said *"lots of people come here because of the crime group's reputation, but it's not like all the other departments are poor cousins."* Indeed, the firm has made waves with its professional discipline, clinical negligence and immigration practices – all of which earn top *Chambers UK* rankings – and many of our sources pursued the firm with these top-notch groups

in mind. The petite intake proved another prominent reason for joining up. Said one interviewee: *"I knew I wouldn't flourish as one of many, but here there are only five trainees per year. That plus the high quality of the work made me think I'd get a really good training."*

Before they begin at the firm new recruits submit their top four seat choices to HR, one of which has to be a non-contentious option. Most of our sources noted with satisfaction that they'd got *"pretty much everything I asked for. The firm works very hard to give us what we want."* Seat patterns are confirmed in advance of their training contract, a tactic interviewees appreciated as *"it means you don't have to spend the last few months of every seat feeling anxious about where you'll be plonked next."* What's more, added one, *"you can start building relationships with people you know you'll be working with in future and keep an eye on what's going on in their departments."*

Court in the limelight

Given the crime department's repute, it's understandable why it's one of the most popular pit stops for trainees. The seat takes on two trainees at a time and *"really is a mixed bag,"* according to interviewees. *"We do everything from*

Seat options: crime; clinical negligence and personal injury; regulation and professional discipline; private client; dispute resolution; immigration; corporate and commercial; family; real estate; employment

The True Picture

Chambers UK rankings

Administrative & Public Law	Family/Matrimonial
	Financial Services
Clinical Negligence	Fraud
Corporate Crime & Investigations	Immigration
	Professional Discipline
Crime	Real Estate
Employment	

administrative stuff to solicitor-level tasks like analysing documents. We're asked to be jacks of all trades." At the time of our calls the department was aflutter with the fervour surrounding the Brooks case. "It's incredibly exciting to open up a newspaper and read about the trial – you feel like you're genuinely part of the most important case of this decade." While trainee contributions to such high-profile matters "aren't always the most exciting" (think taking notes at court and bundling), it seems some found themselves "thrust into the heart" of this particular one. We heard reports of one trainee "directly assisting counsel for Charlie Brooks over a discrete piece of evidence" and another "sitting in Rebekah Brooks' house with the best QCs and lawyers in the country, briefing her." Such in-depth involvement is the norm for small general crime cases, which trainees often handle with minimal supervision. One source told of representing a client in court following their failure to provide a breath sample when pulled over by the cops and later attending a week-long trial for a sexual offence case. "You get to attend a lot of client meetings on your own and are responsible for the outcome."

The clinical negligence team works exclusively on the claimant side, handling complex, high-value compensation cases for conditions like spinal injuries. "It's been interesting to see how the department has adjusted to civil litigation reforms following the Jackson report," mused a trainee. "There's now a big emphasis on operating cost-efficiently, with the fee earner doing work appropriate to their level." Here interviewees had got the chance to review medical records, draft letters of instruction to experts, take witness statements, research case law and attend inquests. "You're supervised a lot, but there is a big element of interacting with clients, which is nice."

Hearing aids

Over in the regulatory and professional discipline team, major clients include the Health and Care Professions Council (HCPC), the Solicitors' Regulation Authority (SRA), the General Dental Council (GDC) and the Chief Police Officers' Staff Association (CPOSA). "They don't really teach this area of law on the LPC, so I had no idea what it was before I started," recalled one interviewee. "Basically the department prepares cases for hearings when allegations have been made against registered pro-

fessionals – for example, paramedics or social workers – and their fitness to practise is called into question." Lawyers take on cases mainly from the prosecution side, but a bit of defence sometimes creeps in. "From day one I was given my own cases," reported a source, telling us "these were supervised of course, but it was immediately challenging. I interviewed a witness within a few days of starting, and quickly found myself attending hearings and drafting statements. Slightly later in the seat I got to conduct vulnerable witness interviews."

A stint in private client also allows trainees to shoulder "real amounts of responsibility. The team is small, so they really need you; you're not just a bag carrier." Said one interviewee: "I was able to handle small probates myself with limited supervision and regularly went to client meetings." Other trainee fare includes drafting wills and applications for powers of attorney, and "tackling complicated tax planning for high net worth individuals who have a lot of assets." Trainees are also given exposure to the department's deputyship team, which handles work "for people who lack capacity – for instance, if a child with a brain injury receives a multimillion-pound settlement, their guardians will seek advice from us about the management of that fund." Such clients often get referred internally by the clinical negligence department.

Strikers and sopranos

Trainees unanimously praised the working environment at KN, telling us "everyone here is very approachable and helpful. It sounds so cheesy, but we're really lucky to be here!" Hours are "very civilised on the whole," which also pleased interviewees, many of whom reported regularly leaving the office around 6pm. Of course, late nights are by no means off the table, particularly when a big case is on the books. "I had some 2am finishes in crime," reported one trainee, "but they happened during the Brooks case, so I was always up for it – I knew how lucky I was to be involved with something like that." On the social front "there's loads going on," including sports teams, baking competitions, a firm choir and trainee-only socials. "We get a budget every month and usually end up doing something like ping-pong or urban golf. Luckily everyone is pretty outgoing; nobody's too corporate or bland." Easter is all about the egg hunt, summer ushers in a bash open to family and friends, and Christmas is marked by "about six celebrations." And in between holidays "you can always find someone to go for a drink with on a Friday."

Kingsley Napley has a history of recruiting its fair share of graduates with work experience "either in a law firm or in another profession." In recent years the cohort has featured ex-journalists, ex-drummers from Blur, estate agents and salespeople, plus a couple of paralegals, but the firm would like to stress that it's also interested in taking on new graduates. When it comes to qualification,

The True Picture

a job list is released, and then there's a formal process of applications and interviews. In 2012 and 2013 KN's retention rate was a resounding 100%, but this year there were only four jobs on offer, so second-years entered the process knowing not everyone would stay on. *"It's disappointing, but we know it's nothing remotely personal,"* said one stoically. In the end, the firm kept on four out of five qualifiers in 2014.

And finally...

Women comprise nearly half the partnership at KN, with both the senior and managing partner roles occupied by women. *"It's nice to have so many successful role models to look up to across the firm,"* noted one female trainee.

Kirkland & Ellis International LLP

The facts

Location: London

Number of UK partners/solicitors: 41/62 (plus 22 US-qualified lawyers)

Total number of trainees: 16

Seats: 4x6 months

Alternative seats: overseas seats

Extras: pro bono – LawWorks, A4ID, Impetus PEF

On chambersstudent.co.uk...

How to get into Kirkland & Ellis

More info on dispute resolution

A beginner's guide to private equity

Life in the restructuring group

It takes a tough mind and a whole lot of resilience to stay in the fast lane at this firm, which flaunts a type A personality.

Crystal clear

The London base of this prestigious American powerhouse sprang into action in 1994, when two partners crossed the pond to try their hand at bolstering a European practice. Today, the firm has around 140 lawyers toiling away in the City's iconic Gherkin building, working primarily on corporate and finance matters. *Chambers UK* consistently places Kirkland's investment funds practices in the top-ranked realm, and the firm's banking and finance faction scores equally highly.

2013 saw a few significant lawyer departures from Kirkland's corporate and restructuring teams, but things are looking up as the European M&A market improves. Trainees pointed to a clear strategy: *"Management wants to build a stronger finance practice, especially on the capital markets and high-yield bonds side. We're a firm that's very good at what it wants to be good at; it's safe to say we're not looking to start a real estate department any time soon."* The firm added that this growth isn't lopsided and is channelling investment into all core areas.

Our interviewees had precise reasons for joining Kirkland's ranks. Many were attracted to the big-ticket corporate/finance lilt, specifically the prevalence of private equity work, while others confessed it was the Yankee paycheque that drew them in. (Trainees here start on £41,000, NQs on £97,560.) For everybody, the prospect of working in a smallish office proved particularly appealing. *"You get the opportunity to be an individual here, to carve out your career and take on a lot of responsibility."*

The firm usually takes on between seven and eight trainees a year, meaning the cohort's small enough that seat allocation is a relatively informal process. *"During mid-seat reviews, HR will ask you what you're thinking of doing and then go away and work their magic."* Stints in corporate and either restructuring or litigation are required, and trainees also have the option to spend a seat in the Hong Kong or New York office. The former tends to be more popular and generally has more business need, *"so they take trainees at least once a year, sometimes twice."*

Entering the complex world of finance can be daunting, so for their first six months trainees attend introductory sessions (three a week) on all practice areas. *"It's nice to gain that insight into why certain things are done the way they are during deals."* Helpful as they found this training, however, sources acknowledged *"the nature of this kind of work is such that listening to lectures only goes so far; eventually you just need to put things into practice and learn by doing."*

Sweet dreams are made of this

Private equity is a key focus of the corporate group, the office's largest. The firm counts most of the major players of the PE world on its books, including Sun Capital and Bain Capital. Lawyers recently helped the latter acquire a 90% stake in German clutch maker FTE automotive. There's *"a fair bit of due diligence"* to be done from the trainee end, although responsibilities grow as deals close.

Seat options: corporate; debt finance; international litigation and arbitration; funds; restructuring; regulatory, IP, antitrust and competition; tax

Chambers UK rankings

Banking & Finance	Private Equity
Capital Markets	Restructuring/Insolvency
International Arbitration	Tax
Investment Funds	

"You have to track so much information! The best thing you can do is excel at execution and make sure things go smoothly at the signing stage."

In 2013 Kirkland's market-leading investment funds group saw its best year for fund-raising since the global financial crisis. There's a good mixture of funds to get to grips with in this seat: recent work has seen the team advise Blue Water Energy on an $861m first-time energy fund, AMP Capital on a €400m infrastructure debt fund, and Vitruvian Partners on a £1bn private equity fund. *"You get the sense that you're working on the best deals in the most profitable areas,"* remarked trainees, who told us: *"The work is very complex and technical – a lot of it's linked to European directives or the constant fluctuations of EU or US tax statutes. You have to be ready to be thrown into the deep end here. As a trainee you have to pitch in on the phone calls and high-level discussions going on."*

Funds also crop up as clients in the firm's debt finance group, which handles leveraged buyouts, debt portfolio purchases and restructurings, much of them international – for example CVC Capital Partners' €875m high-yield bond offering for the acquisition of German energy provider ista International GmbH. *"We don't operate in just one jurisdiction; you'll spend a lot of your time as a trainee on calls to places like Peru or Mexico, co-ordinating with local counsel."* Sources were in agreement that a seat here is *"fast-paced and very demanding. We're often put in charge of the conditions precedent checklist, and while at other firms you might be allocated point A or B on that list, here you'll be responsible for the whole thing. Those lists cover a lot! Luckily you learn quickly as you go along."*

Tough and ready

Kirkland's junior associates stateside were quick to flag their type A personalities to our sister publication, *Chambers Associate*, but what do trainees in London make of that classification? One summed it up best when they said: *"That applies more to the firm as a whole than individual people. Our working culture is driven and com-*petitive, which comes down to our clients, who want to get things done and fast."* Of course, while they insisted Kirkland lawyers aren't ruthless or aggressive, they did paint a picture of people who *"are confident and work extremely hard. You have to be tough-minded and resilient to work the hours we do."*

And those hours can be tough. Though the run-around in the lead up to a closing *"is probably not that dissimilar to other City law firms,"* sources suggested Kirkland's small stature means gruelling patches come more frequently. Explained one: *"With a larger intake, lawyers might be able to take a break after finishing a big deal, but here there aren't the numbers to allow that. You'll come off a deal and go straight onto another one – that's the rough that comes with the smooth."*

Fortunately there's plenty of smooth, according to our sources, who had endless praise for Kirkland's entrepreneurial culture, wherein *"we're encouraged to say, 'This is what I want to do' or 'Can I do something this way?'"* They also appreciated the way *"you don't get put into a box here – just because you're at a certain stage doesn't mean you have to do X, Y and Z; rather they just give us as much responsibility as we can handle."* Our interviewees saw these aspects as American influences, though they were quick to point out the firm's Yankee roots don't have an overbearing influence on operations. *"London doesn't rely on the US offices for work; we're the head of the European practice."* They did mention a few transatlantic traditions on the social side, however, including Halloween parties and Thanksgiving get-togethers on top of the usual Christmas and summer fare. Trainees admitted they're *"not quite as social as firms with a larger intake,"* but assured us *"at the end of the working week we're all on the same wavelength and want to let our hair down."* On any given Friday you can find a cluster of tired-but-still-exhilarated Kirkland trainees toasting another week at one of the many bars surrounding their Square Mile digs.

Connections throughout the Kirkland network are forged via video conferences with Stateside colleagues – *"there's a lot of knowledge-sharing"* – as well as the annual attorney retreat, which sees Londoners unite with their Munich counterparts. The retreat is held in a country manor and is sprinkled with interdepartmental meetings, plus a spate of team-building exercises. Last year's featured, bizarrely enough, zombie ambushes. *"We had to focus on a certain task while being attacked by zombies!"* For the record, no one was seriously harmed – a company was hired especially to play the dreaded undead.

And finally...

The *"simple and remarkably stress-free"* qualification process amounts to a chat with HR and the partners in one's targeted department. In 2014 all five of the firm's qualifiers took up NQ posts there.

"The best candidates I've come across are those who have an interest in the law but also know what's going on in the broader business world."

City training principal

Latham & Watkins

The facts

Location: London

Number of UK partners/solicitors: 51/112 (+58 non-UK-qualified)

Total number of trainees: 41

Seats: 4x6 months

Alternative seats: overseas seats

Extras: pro bono; language classes

On chambersstudent.co.uk...

How to get into Latham & Watkins
The flat hierarchy at US firms
Latham around the world

Megafirm Latham has remained true to its Californian roots, but don't think that means trainees here get an easy ride.

Let's get together and feel all right

LA-born Latham has always boasted a one-firm, one-heart mantra, even as it's expanded into a 31-office behemoth with a global turnover topping $2bn. *"London feels no less powerful or important than New York,"* said trainees in the City, who went on to reveal that nearly all their undertakings involve co-ordination with other branches on the Latham family tree. Work here is based around the core practices of corporate, finance and litigation, and the size and stature of matters are such that the firm naturally draws comparisons to the magic circle, though a training contract here comes with some considerable distinctions. For starters, international travel is virtually guaranteed: the majority of trainees spend one of their four seats abroad, and associate academies offer the chance to visit America at least three times upon qualification. And then there's the famed Yankee paycheck, which translates into one of the highest trainee salaries in the City. Unsurprisingly, fat wallets come with an expectation to work some pretty gruelling hours at times, but overall our interviewees were content with the way Latham *"has preserved the non-conservative and relaxed attitude it was founded on."*

The likes of Barclays, Goldman Sachs and RBS all make the client roster, and the firm scores top *Chambers UK* rankings for its banking, capital markets and restructuring practices. Its energy, IT and restructuring arms also receive nods. Strong litigation and tax departments prop up the corporate and finance contingents, and in 2013 all four practices came together to work on Liberty Global's acquisition of Virgin Media, valued at a whopping $23bn. The firm's onboarded some significant laterals in recent months to keep up with its high-value workload: between

January 2013 and January 2014 it welcomed five new partners, including former head of private equity at Clifford Chance, David Walker.

Trainees are expected to complete seats in corporate, finance and litigation, although the latter can be substituted with a two-week course at the College of Law. Our sources suggested getting your qualification choice out of the way early on *"so you can spend your last seat abroad without having to worry so much about making an impression in the UK."* At the same time, most years at least one trainee opts to qualify abroad.

Searching for an answer

A stint with the banking and finance team sees trainees work on hefty financing transactions for investment big'uns like Deutsche and Morgan Stanley. The team has historically been strong on the lender front, but it now does a fair amount for borrowers too, among them VTB Capital and Douglas Holdings. Highlights for the group in recent years include leading the refinancing of Thomas Cook and representing JP Morgan during Nokia's acquisition of Siemens. On big deals like these, a trainee's role generally revolves around transaction management – running through conditions precedent checklists, for example – though most of our interviewees had also

Seat options: corporate; finance; litigation; property; tax; banking; restructuring; project finance; technology transactions; private equity; capital markets; competition; employment

Chambers UK rankings

Banking & Finance	Intellectual Property
Banking Litigation	International Arbitration
Capital Markets	Investment Funds
Competition/European Law	Litigation
Corporate/M&A	Outsourcing
Employment	Private Equity
Energy & Natural Resources	Projects
Information Technology	Public International Law
	Restructuring/Insolvency
	Tax

tried their hand at drafting ancillary documents and legal opinions at some point. One even reported dealing with clients and local counsel, and running *"substantial work-streams all by myself! I felt more like a junior associate than a trainee."*

The project finance team has closed some particularly high-profile matters recently, including the development of a $7bn greenfield phosphate site in Saudi Arabia and Turkey's first infrastructure bond. Among the sectors lawyers work across are transportation, telecoms and lique-fied natural gas (LNG). Those with experience here told us that trainees are unlikely to see deals through from start to finish – *"projects can take years to orchestrate"* – but nevertheless praised the experience gained by participating in *"super high-value deals. I got to negotiate the term sheet for a contract on a huge LNG deal, which taught me a lot."*

Trainees sitting in corporate are encouraged to seek work from multiple subgroups in the department, among them M&A, private equity and investment funds. In 2013 lawyers here topped their main triumph from the previous year – representing Watson Pharmaceuticals in its €4.25bn acquisition of Actavis, 2012's largest leveraged buyout – by helping the new Actavis-Watson megacorp take hold of Irish pharmaceutical company Warner Chilcott for a cool $8.5bn. Other clients on the department's books include insurance giant Aviva, car manufacturer Nissan and internet star Yahoo!. You might expect such big names to remain out of reach for trainees, but our sources reported talking to clients on a regular basis. They also told of co-ordinating with local counsel, handling verification, and drafting disclosure letters and agreements. *"They encourage us to take on whatever responsibilities are available so we can learn as much as possible. It's a great seat for developing your drafting skills in particular,"* said one, while another told us: *"I even got to take the lead on a few small deals."*

Trainees in smaller departments like employment and tax tend to spend most of their time on corporate support work. Those with experience in the former told us *"the team is small enough that you get to work with everyone*

and have a lot of scope to get involved with things like drafting."* The department works primarily on the employer side, working with companies as varied as Amazon, Manchester United and Royal Caribbean. *"I found the team less manic than corporate, which meant I had more time to think things through,"* said one interviewee. *"That was helpful – cases often come down to subtle points of law, so everything needs to be thoroughly researched."* Tax is another research-heavy seat revolving around intricate, complex points. *"You can spend three days looking for an answer and not even find it. That can be challenging, but the team is really friendly and supportive, so that helps."*

What's the alternative?

In 2013 the growing litigation department welcomed Simon Bushell, former co-chair of corporate fraud at Herbert Smith Freehills, into the fold. Latham's litigators frequently work alongside corporate and banking lawyers, representing corporations, private equity houses and financial institutions in arbitrations, fraud proceedings and financial disputes. The department has recently taken on a spate of restructurings sparked by the credit crunch, devoting a fair share of time to issues like layoffs and unpaid debts arising from those, and lawyers have also kept busy with arbitrations – an increasingly popular alternative to litigation as clients become more and more alert to the monetary and reputational costs associated with going to court. Several of our interviewees had spent time with the arbitration team and told us matters there tend to be *"more bitty"* than in transactional seats. Nevertheless, *"the academic concepts involved can be difficult to grasp. It's a really interesting area."* They told of pitching in on judicial reviews and ICSID arbitrations by conducting research, writing memos on various topics and compiling info for disclosure exercises. *"They actually use the arguments we write for statements and responses, which is gratifying."*

A stint in technologies transactions comprises IP, IT and commercial work. As you might expect, the seat is *"massively varied,"* with trainees drafting commercial contracts, conducting IP filings and researching data protection issues, in addition to carrying out due diligence as corporate support. Said one source: *"It's a very small team, so you end up taking on work above your level as a trainee. That holds true for many of the smaller seats, actually. Here I was expected to go to meetings with clients and ask them questions myself."* Another told of acting as the sole London representative during conference calls with Chicago and New York. *"They trusted me to offer a UK law perspective on US deals, which was an amazing learning experience."*

To prepare trainees for such responsibilities, the firm has them spend their first three weeks in training sessions and PSCs. *"They show you everything from research re-*

sources to how to use your phone. It's a great way to get to know the cohort, and they usually let you leave around 4pm, so there's plenty of time to grab drinks after work." Additionally, trainees receive formal practice area overviews at the start of each seat, though our sources found their on-the-job learning the most helpful form of training. *"I learned much more quickly once I started doing things for myself, and I think most people here work best that way,"* said one, adding: *"We share an office with our supervisor, and that helps a lot – you can ask them any questions you have about the work."*

California dreamin'

"It's normal to work really long hours here," one trainee said frankly, a point our other interviewees agreed was fair. *"I get the impression that we're expected to be on call more than trainees at English firms – there's slightly more encroachment into your personal life here."* Indeed, hours can be *"very intense"* as deal closures loom, particularly on the banking side of things, and as one source pointed out sadly, *"there's no such thing as a lunch hour at Latham."* Still, trainees stressed that *"there genuinely is no facetime here,"* which they agreed makes the quiet times, infrequent though they are, *"lots more enjoyable. You're never going to be sitting there with nothing to do; if the work is done, you can leave."*

Indeed, *"we're left to manage our own workloads,"* our sources said, telling us it's not uncommon for a trainee to pop out for a haircut during the day or head downstairs for a spot of table tennis with colleagues. *"They respect that you need downtime during the day and treat you like an adult."* This is perhaps a reflection of the way the firm's junior associates in America, who join as fully qualified lawyers, are treated. Like their Yankee colleagues, Latham trainees are held to billable targets, although we heard that *"no one really gives a crap about them to be honest – not until you actually qualify, that is."* Trainees have a *"loose target"* of 1,200 billable hours a year, and for NQs that's upped to 1,900. The latter expectation is matched with a *"very handsome"* salary of no less than £98,000. *"I think we're all happy to accept the hours we do considering how well we're paid."*

Trainees were in agreement that there's a *"laidback"* vibe about the office, which many chalked up to Latham's California roots. *"The firm as a whole embraces a re-*laxed approach – we don't wear ties, people dress down on Fridays, and it's totally normal to see trainees having a joke about with the partners."* They also credited the firm's American side with promoting a *"go-getter"* culture in which *"trainees are encouraged to push for developments like creating a secondment where there isn't an existing one – they won't say no on technicalities if you come up with a good idea."*

From our calls, we could tell the current trainee cohort has bonded well, though some found the social side of the firm lacking: *"They could do more to organise things that aren't just for the sake of business development."* That said, management does fork out for four trainee socials a year – a recent one involved a curry followed by drinks at Mahiki – plus monthly breakfasts, lunches and drinks. *"Generally there's a lot of free food available here,"* one trainee happily reported.

It's no secret that US firms tend to take pro bono a lot more seriously than their UK counterparts, and Latham is no exception. It's not mandatory for trainees to get involved, but pro bono is *"highly encouraged and well supported – all hours count towards billable targets, and they make it clear it's a great area for us to practise our skills."* One source had this to say of the pluses: *"As a junior lawyer pro bono matters let you can take control in a way you wouldn't otherwise be able to – you get to draft documents, talk to the client and generally oversee a case, all the while knowing you're doing something worthwhile."* Those who prove particularly committed can have the title 'Guardians of Justice' stuck on their door – what more incentive could you want?

When it comes to qualification, we hear there's competition for Latham's smaller departments, *"but there are generally more NQ places than trainees across the firm, so people aren't too worried about being kept on."* The process, like the firm at large, is pretty relaxed: *"There are no formal interviews or anything; it all comes down to informal conversations you have with partners, who will tell you what they think of you qualifying in a particular area."* Trainees then submit two options. *"It's never just a stab in the dark; everybody has an idea of which team will take them."* In 2014, 16 of 18 trainees accepted NQ roles at the firm.

And finally...

Interviewees agreed there's no set Latham type. *"People here range from the super geeky to really cool. If you're a nice person who works hard, you should fit in just fine."*

Leigh Day

The facts

Location: London
Number of UK partners/solicitors: 30/104
Total number of trainees: 18
Seats: 2x12 months
Alternative seats: secondments

On chambersstudent.co.uk...

How to get into Leigh Day
More on PI, clin neg and abuse claims

Human rights struggles, battling negligent healthcare providers, suing faulty product manufacturers, helping Jimmy Savile victims... this is a firm on a mission.

Leigh'll help you

This firm is very different from all the others in this guide. Leigh Day's work is serious, serious stuff, so forgive us for putting the *Student Guide*'s cringe-making levity [*surely 'much-cherished'? Ed.*] temporarily on hold. Human rights abuses on an industrial scale abroad and horrific cases of clinical negligence, product liability and (increasingly) child abuse cases at home are just part of what this campaigning 130-lawyer outfit does for a living. As you flick through firms' glossy graduate recruitment brochures and meet people at careers fairs, you'll hear many talk the talk about 'making a difference', but Leigh Day actually walks the walk when it comes to helping people, day in, day out. *"I was particularly impressed by the nature of the cases Leigh Day takes on,"* remembered one trainee about why they bust a gut to get hired here. *"Leigh Day fitted with my philosophy,"* explained another.

Leigh Day's Clerkenwell-based lawyers are often in the news. As well as case victories, news items frequently quote partners about some hot topic of the day, like abuse team head Alison Millar speaking to the BBC in July about the Westminster child abuse scandal. Here's a snapshot of some other recent assignments. At the High Court, Leigh Day succeeded in winning a full judicial review for Afghan interpreters seeking help from their former employer, the UK government, to relocate themselves and their families safely outside of Afghanistan. The firm is representing an Ethiopian farmer taking the UK to court over a *"brutal"* resettlement policy funded by British aid, and a Libyan politician, Abdul-Hakim Belhaj, over his MI6 rendition which led to him being tortured. (Leigh Day is working with legal charity Reprieve.)

A few years back, Leigh Day represented over 100 victims of abuse in the Stafford Hospital care scandal, and it's currently working with patients at the latest headline-grabbing NHS basket case, Morecambe Bay. Another team helps people residing at Her Majesty's pleasure. Some prisoners' human rights cases are guaranteed to make *Daily Mail* readers' blood boil. Take the case of client 'Mrs C', who received a bumper payout from taxpayers because the prison service didn't move her to an open prison after a year (as required) to complete the remainder of her two-and-a-half year sentence (it lacked the adequate wheelchair facilities she needed). Elsewhere, solicitors won a settlement for the family of a man who died after his GP failed to refer him to hospital, despite his cardiac symptoms; they're also acting for victims of Jimmy Savile; and investigated whether a local authority could have done more to prevent the suicide of a 16-year-old abuse victim in its care.

Day of reckoning

Unusually, trainees do two year-long seats. The options are: clinical negligence (the biggest department); international and group claims (IGC); human rights; employment (part of human rights); product liability (part of IGC); and personal injury. Two six-month secondments are also available each year: one to Shadow Attorney General Emily Thornberry at the Houses of Parliament (who gets it is decided by an essay competition, judged

Seat options: international group claims; clinical negligence; human rights; personal injury

Chambers UK rankings

Administrative & Public Law	Education
Civil Liberties & Human Rights	Employment
	Environment
Clinical Negligence	Personal Injury
Court of Protection	Product Liability

by a partner), and one to a trade union. The first seat is allocated to you, and you express your preference for the second. The downside of year-long seats is that you don't get to try out many different types of law in the two years, and some would like to see shorter seats. *"The difficulty is, in human rights and IGC especially, because the cases are so big and take so long, you can't get to grips with cases after only six months,"* a trainee reported. There has been some discussion about potentially shorter seats, and *"the new HR manager is keen to get everyone's opinions. I wonder whether they might change it in future. Six months would be fine in clin neg and PI, but in international six months would be difficult because they are huge cases: you need longer."*

Clinical negligence *"represents a good proportion of the firm's income. It covers a wide variety of injury claims, especially brain injury, birth injury (to babies and mothers) and late diagnosis of cancer claims, but also lower-value claims. Though thanks to new regulations to send lower-value claims to County Courts, we now rarely do cases worth under £50,000 – but if it is and there's a big injustice, the firm may take it on."* The varied cases are *"interesting and rewarding"* to work on, sources found. *"My supervising partner has a lot of oversight. I give my drafted instructions and get feedback. I feel I have an active role in running cases, yet I'm not dropped in the deep end."* Tasks are *"legal and medical. I learn about complicated medical stuff, on the phone and by letter with medical experts. Also by liaising with the Legal Aid Agency – less glamorous, but it gives me an insight into funding."*

One trainee confessed: *"I became a bit of a hypochondriac in clin neg! It's strange because it impacts you more than international human rights – it could be you or a family member."* Birth injury claims, a big focus, arise from any number of poor care factors, including handling and diagnosis. One particularly distressing example is brain damage caused when a nurse's syringe needle inadvertently penetrates the fetal brain during amniocentesis (a procedure which tests for abnormalities in the fetus). This *"used to be more common, before ultrasound,"* but sadly cases still occur from time to time. Money-wise, clin neg cases are *"all no win, no fee. Some people have legal expenses insurance. Legal Aid has gone now, although there is still provision for birth injury cases like cerebral palsy."*

Striving for justice

International and group claims (IGC), led by co-founder Martyn Day, *"is split in two – one holds governments to account for abuses abroad, and the other holds multinationals to account, mainly extractive industries like oil and gas. This department can involve a lot of travel"* – for example, to Nigeria to investigate oil spill pollution. Supervision is *"very hands-on. Feedback is daily."* Product liability sits within IGC. Here, *"you spend your entire time doing one or two products"* for lots of clients who have the same problem, which *"can get a bit tedious"* compared to clin neg, where you might work on *"30 different cases with 30 different injuries."* Faulty medical products include dodgy hip replacements, specifically metal-on-metal versions which leak poisonous toxins into the blood supply, and *"vaginal mesh – quite a new one."* This is used to treat women with stress urinary incontinence (SUI), which occurs during coughing or sneezing. Sub-standard mesh can cause inflammation, perforate organs, and/or cause bleeding and more incontinence, among other injuries. Various products the team sees include *"cosmetics, pharmaceuticals products, knee replacements, fridges that blow up, laptops..."*

The personal injury department has a group dedicated to cyclists – such a boom area that it opened a Manchester office in April 2014 to cover cycling up north. In one case, Leigh Day is representing the families of two cyclists from Aberdeen Asset Management who were run over by a lorry in Cornwall at the start of their charity cycle ride from Land's End to John O'Groats. The driver later pleaded guilty to causing two deaths by dangerous driving and is going to prison.

Hours are reasonable: *"It's 9.30am to 5.30pm officially. I've been pleasantly surprised by the number of times I've left then. My supervisor caught me working late once and told me to go home."* The social life revolves around two pubs near Clerkenwell's ancient St John's Gate: Bear on the Square and the White Bear. In 2014 four of six qualifiers will be staying with the firm to sample their wares for a little longer.

And finally...

Many join Leigh Day hoping to do human rights. What does it look for in candidates? *"Increasingly, people who have an interest in other areas of the firm, mainly clinical negligence,"* reckoned one trainee.

Lester Aldridge LLP

The facts

Location: Bournemouth, Southampton, London
Number of UK partners/solicitors: 42/47
Partners who trained at firm: 20%
Total number of trainees: 18
Seats: 4x6 months
Alternative seats: none

On chambersstudent.co.uk...

How to get into Lester Aldridge
Interview with training principal
   Susan Cowan
A beginner's guide to Bournemouth

A staple of the South Coast legal scene, Lester Aldridge is a good option for trainees willing to *"roll up their sleeves."*

LA Times

Lester Aldridge may be only 89 lawyers strong, but the South Coast firm still manages to make a splash in the region, earning nods from *Chambers UK* for a host of local practices, from planning and litigation to private client and real estate. LA is particularly hot on the latter, wielding one of the largest real estate teams in Southampton, and the firm also nabs national rankings for its specialist work in the healthcare, shipping and consumer finance spheres. *"If you're looking to stay local, we've got a great reputation,"* said its current trainees, many of whom had ties to the area through family or university. *"And the size is just right – this is the kind of place where you can get to know people and become part of the fabric of the firm. There aren't a thousand of us kicking around."*

Bournemouth is LA's head office and houses the majority of trainees, with seven based there at the time of our calls; meanwhile the firm's smaller Southampton and London branches played host to three trainees apiece. New recruits should know that while completing seats in multiple offices isn't a formal requirement, business needs mean that trainees do generally end up flitting between at least two. *"Nobody will force you to experience all three offices, but they sort of expect you to move around,"* said interviewees, who agreed *"a sense of willingness will stand you in good stead."* They went on to tell us that taking up a seat in Bournemouth is *"particularly useful as that office's size lends itself to more opportunities,"* though noted this is by no means compulsory. Before each rotation trainees receive a list of available seat options, some of which are reserved for second-years; they then rank their preferences along with *"commentary on why you should get a particular seat."* As has been the

case in years past, we heard a few laments about this process. *"It's kind of a mystery how they end up allocating the seats. I've always gotten my first choice, but I know people who never have, and even some who've been landed with their fifth or sixth choice,"* said one source. This confusion was compounded by suggestions that some trainees approach partners directly to get the seats they want, though sources were keen to clarify that such behaviour isn't the result of a sneaky environment where clandestineness gets you far, but rather a reflection of the way *"we're encouraged to express our goals and make the most of our training contract."*

I'm on a boat

Real estate is big business at Lester Aldridge, and trainees are *"extremely likely if not outright guaranteed"* to land a seat here. The department's client base ranges from commercial lenders and investment vehicles to sheltered housing and care home developers, with Santander, Care South and Big Yellow among the biggest names on the roster. It's predominantly receivership and insolvency work in Southampton, while commercial and residential conveyancing matters reign supreme in Bournemouth, where lawyers recently oversaw the region's largest office letting in five years. *"The exposure is completely different from seats where matters are drawn out and approached in a win/lose situation; here both sides are working to-*

Seat options: real estate; insolvency; corporate; care; employment; family; marine; dispute resolution; personal injury; trusts, tax and wills (TTW); banking and finance; international probate; contentious probate

Chambers UK rankings

Charities	Partnership
Consumer Finance	Planning
Corporate/M&A	Private Client
Family/Matrimonial	Real Estate
Healthcare	Real Estate Litigation
Litigation	Shipping

wards the same goal." On the planning side there's *"quite a lot of research and registrations of unregistered properties,"* one interviewee said, while others told of working on behalf of receivers on issues like grants of leases and acquisitions of land. *"It's a great seat for learning quickly – I was completing deals within my first month."*

Trainees who'd sat with the marine team happily reported high levels of responsibility and client exposure. *"I sat in several meetings with clients, which I hadn't done before, and I got my own files to handle. The partners give you enough freedom to work on your own, and they encourage you to be proactive."* Much of the department's work revolves around contractual disputes, often involving insurance companies, though lawyers also advise on vessel sales and purchases, oversee marine mortgages and vessel repossessions, handle charter party disputes, and assist with personal injury claims. *"We have a lot of different types of clients – P&I clubs, insurers, lenders, vessel operators. I helped draft a contract for a very high-profile shipowner."* Jack Sparrow perhaps? A source went on to mention that matters, while *"not of terribly high value,"* tend to vary greatly, *"which keeps things interesting – I got a lot out of my time there."*

According to our interviewees, LA's contentious seats generally offer the best opportunities for hands-on work. Those who'd sat with the corporate/insolvency team proudly told of racking up hours in the courtroom by filing motions, liaising with counsel and sitting in on qualifier hearings. *"I've been to court by myself twice now. There's some bundling that goes along with it all, which can be a bit mind-numbing, but it's a great exercise for really getting to know a file."* The team here acts for both corporate and personal insolvencies, and also represents creditors in debt recovery cases. Over in dispute resolution, the group excels in the marine, defence and financial sectors, and the team counts the major providers of anti-malware software ESET and Wessex Petroleum, as well

as natural hair dye company Herb UK, as clients. A seat here sees trainees get to grips with disclosure, witness statements, claim forms and statements for court costs. *"You're never just standing in front of a photocopier."*

I got 99 problems, but a beach ain't one

Past trainees have gushed about their satisfaction with the work/life balance at LA, and this year's crop was no different, with many citing decent hours as a reason for joining ranks. *"The hours are never terrible, even in London. On a good day you can leave at half past five."* That said, *"the firm is wary of advertising itself as a cushty alternative,"* sources revealed, and indeed as training principal Susan Cowan stresses: *"Applicants shouldn't think it's an easy ride here. If someone suggests that during their interview, we say 'goodbye'."*

Keeping that in mind, sources described the firm's day-to-day atmosphere as *"serious but friendly."* Said one: *"We work very hard, but we also know how to have fun as well."* Indeed, at the time of our calls, trainees had recently returned from a trip to outdoor adventure centre Go Ape, where they *"did just that."* Back at the firm there are monthly happy hours in Bournemouth, where teams take turns setting up an in-house cocktail bar, while Southampton and London lawyers enjoy regular breakfasts and lunches. *"On the whole Bournemouth is probably the most formal office, mostly by way of being the biggest,"* trainees agreed, explaining that *"it's a seven-floor building, so naturally the hierarchy is a little more pronounced."* Meanwhile London *"is a little more relaxed, as is Southampton – it has a real family feel and is somewhat akin to a high-street firm in that sense."*

Last year one trainee observed they *"could be earning more working in Topshop,"* a point many of our interviewees conceded, although they did so laughingly. *"It's not great, which makes it difficult sometimes, but for the regions it's not that bad."* It's worth noting those working in London are given a tax-free weighting bonus each month, *"though the NQ salary there is pretty low, which is concerning."* On the whole, however, sources agreed *"the exposure you get to hands-on work here is a good trade-off, as is the lack of crazy hours – how many trainees can say the latest they've ever stayed was midnight, and that was only once?"*

And finally...
Trainees have historically benefited from high retention rates, and 2014 was no different, when four out of six qualifiers stayed on with the firm.

Lewis Silkin LLP

The facts

Location: London, Oxford, Cardiff

Number of UK partners/solicitors: 61/112

Partners who trained at the firm: 23%

Total number of trainees: 12

Seats: 6x4 months

Alternative seats: occasional secondments

Extras: pro bono – National Pro Bono Centre, Own-It, Mary Ward Legal Advice Centre, PRIME, LeGaL BesT (LGBT network in the legal sector); language classes

On chambersstudent.co.uk...

How to get into Lewis Silkin

In a lather: toiletries trademark tussle

If the thought of big City fare makes your eyes glaze over, take a long look at Lewis Silkin...

A rare breed

Beyond the competitive pack of thundering racehorses that dominate the arena of corporate law, you'll spot a quite different creature – a piebald pony that prefers to graze in the fertile legal land between the City and the West End. Here, away from the sweaty braying of the Square Mile, it excels at an unusual variety of practices, from social housing to sorting out libelled celebs. We're referring, of course, to Lewis Silkin. Like the piebald pony, this firm is characterised by variegation, with clients as diverse as Saatchi & Saatchi and Islington & Shoreditch Housing Association, Credit Suisse and TV chef Heston Blumenthal. A hoofful of golden *Chambers UK* rosettes for media, employment and mid-market corporate work attest to its presence in these areas. Founder Mr Lewis Silkin was minister for town and country planning in Clement Attlee's government, and his firm has an enduring commitment to social housing projects. Clients today include Peabody Trust and Notting Hill Housing Trust.

Despite its formidable clout, the firm promotes a sense of approachability – this is, as the website puts it (contrary to our horse-based metaphor) a 'rather more human law firm'. Plenty of places might make out that they mix the cuddly with the corporate, but what's the reality here? *"The training contract interview I had at Lewis Silkin was the only one where I felt properly comfortable and not intimidated,"* an insider told us – a sentiment echoed by others. Happily, the 'more human' slogan *"isn't just marketing spiel – it lives up to the reputation of being a different type of law firm. I've seen people leave and come back!"* Six consecutive years on the *Sunday Times'* list of the '100 Best Companies to Work For' also lends

credence to the suggestion that this isn't the most soul-crushing of corporate enterprises.

The chosen half dozen trainees taken on each year complete six seats of four months, so there's the chance to sample all five departments (*"you get to see how the firm fits together"*) along with a repeat seat or secondment. While some thought this breadth of experience was *"brilliant,"* others felt that *"changing so regularly means just as you start to settle into a seat, you're wrenched away and thrust into something unfamiliar."* Overall sources reckoned that *"the way they allocate seats isn't that transparent,"* although there's the opportunity to discuss preferences with HR and pick out two priority seats. *"The process can be a bit difficult, but it's just because everyone wants to do the same two seats – MBT (media, brands and technology) and employment,"* summarised one. A few interviewees mentioned that several in their cohort hadn't been able to do a corporate seat *"because of requests from clients to do secondments."*

The Don (Draper?) of advertising law

The media, brands and technology department takes on contentious and non-contentious work such as IP disputes, commercial contracts, defamation and reputation management cases from across the film, TV, music, theatre, publishing, interactive and advertising sectors. The lat-

Seat options: employment, reward and immigration (ERI); media, brands and technology (MBT); real estate; corporate; litigation

The True Picture

Chambers UK rankings

Construction	Media & Entertainment
Corporate/M&A	Partnership
Defamation/Reputation	Real Estate
Management	Real Estate Litigation
Employment	Retail
Immigration	Social Housing
Intellectual Property	Sports Law
Litigation	

ter is an important area of business for Lewis Silkin. Former chairman Roger Alexander was known as 'the Don' of advertising law during his 40-year tenure; in the 1980s the firm became the first to advertise on a billboard. Along with Saatchi & Saatchi, clients include multinational communications companies like Publicis Groupe and modish independent agencies such as Mother London. Recently the firm helped Jaguar Land Rover create that Bond-style telly advert featuring the combined thespian might of Tom Hiddleston, Mark Strong and Ben Kingsley. For this, trainees *"spent time working out the contractual rights of the actors and summarising them to the client."* Another had toiled over a talent agreement *"for a footballer who was going to be a pundit at the World Cup."* On the contentious side, the firm recently acted for cosmetic chain Lush in a hefty trade mark dispute with Amazon. *"There was bundling obviously, but I also drafted witness statements and was able to attend hearings and conferences with QCs,"* recalled a trainee. *"I was in the thick of it. If you put in the hard yards then they'll give you a lot of responsibility."*

About 40% of Lewis Silkin's revenue comes from employment work, which perhaps isn't surprising given the size of the department – comprising 94 employment law specialists, it's the second largest in the UK. Trainees warned that *"getting seen across the department can be hard if you want to qualify into it, so it's best to sit there twice."* The majority of work is on the employer side, although some claimant issues are taken on. Financial services clients make up a big chunk of business, along with clients from the media, advertising, retail and technology sectors such as MTV, Marks & Spencer and Nokia. Fellow firms Freshfields and Linklaters also turn to Lewis Silkin for help with employment matters. *"The work ranges from small tribunal claims for individuals through to big High Court stuff,"* trainees noted. *"I ran a grievance procedure by myself, which meant drafting all the letters and submissions. There was some photocopying and bundling, but I felt like I was doing an awful lot of valuable work."* Another source *"worked on settlement and compromise agreements, and helped to draft employee handbooks."*

Hive of activity

Over in the corporate department, there's a focus on work from the media and technology industries, with plenty of M&A activity among major companies and start-ups. Recently, the firm helped Publicis Groupe acquire a 75.1% stake in media agency Walker Media from M&C Saatchi for £36m. On acquisitions, typical trainee fare includes *"drafting share purchase agreements, shareholder resolutions and board minutes."* Some sources reported tackling an AIM flotation, which allowed for *"very good exposure to clients. I led a meeting to talk through various sections of an admission document that I'd drafted."* Research tasks are also *"a classic part"* of the corporate seat.

The real estate/development department covers commercial and social housing work. A stint in the former group exposes trainees to *"big deals with tech, advertising and retail clients."* The trainee workload might involve *"some research, looking into tax issues and responding to client enquiries as well as drafting simpler leases on small projects – for example if a client is just taking one floor of a building."* Social housing involves *"loads of contact with housing association clients to organise their insurance or licences. I helped one of the councils to organise a lease."* This obviously isn't Candy brothers-esque stuff – the firm works on the affordable housing element of projects like the £1.5bn regeneration of Elephant & Castle. *"It isn't especially glamorous,"* muttered an interviewee. *"Things move quite slowly."* It seems that both halves of the department have a Marmite effect on trainees: *"Some love it, but it's not for everybody."*

Interviewees were fairly chipper about their hours: *"I can get away by 7pm pretty consistently and rarely work at weekends."* Of course, *"at peak times you stay later."* When the day's legal business is done, sources told us that *"there's always somebody to go for a drink with."* The small trainee intake is fairly close-knit (*"they've chosen people who bond quite strongly"*), and there's a budget for social events. Firm-wide, there are annual summer and Christmas bashes, with drinks trolleys regularly doing the rounds. Charity *"is taken seriously"* here, so there are frequent fund-raising events. Some intrepid trainees completed a sponsored cycle ride from London to Amsterdam, while others reassured us that the firm is still keeping bee hives on the roof – the resultant honey is sold in the canteen, raising funds for a good cause. *"Ultimately it's still a business,"* said trainee of the firm's fêted culture. *"But they're very supportive. They want you to succeed and stay with them."* In 2014, three out of six qualifiers were kept on.

And finally...

"There isn't a type – apart from being unpretentious – although a lot of trainees have previous experience in creative industries."

Linklaters

The facts

Location: London

Number of UK partners/solicitors: 179/548

UK partners who trained at the firm: c.60%

Total number of trainees: 224

Seats: 4x6 months

Alternative seats: overseas seats, secondments

Extras: pro bono – Mary Ward Legal Advice Centre and others; language classes

On chambersstudent.co.uk...

How to get into Linklaters

Linklaters in America

"You'll work harder here than you ever thought possible, but that's what we thrive on."

The strongest link

Home to 2,600 lawyers across 20 countries, London-born Linklaters is one of the largest and most successful firms in the world. Corporate, banking and capital markets are the strongest links in this powerhouse's chain: *Chambers UK* deems each practice among the City's best. Of course, Linklaters' work is very wide-reaching both within these groups and beyond them, so we suggest you check out the full *Chambers UK* listings – which awards over 50 rankings, many of them top-tier – for a fuller idea of the firm's considerable might.

"It can be difficult to differentiate Links from its magic circle rivals, but when I first interviewed here I felt it was a more personable, team-oriented environment than other places I looked at," one interviewee said of their decision to join up. *"I think a lot of people come here because they see something of themselves in the way the firm as a whole operates."* Links is a great shout in particular for those who want a hand in matters that visibly impact the economies and sectors involved: the firm is one of the 100 British companies that generate 13% of the nation's GDP, and it handles deals that *"regularly make the front page news."* Take Co-op Bank's £1.5bn recapitalisation, for example.

The chance to dabble in matters that reach beyond the UK shores also proves a big draw for candidates year upon year. *"The international opportunities here are outstanding – they're above and beyond what a lot of other firms can offer."* Indeed, global names aren't sprinkled so much as splattered across the client roster – think Morgan Stanley, HSBC, Glencore – and big-hitting cross-border matters appear in the docket regularly, like European private equity firm Triton's £1bn purchase of French power

giant Alstom's German-based components business. What's more, around two-thirds of trainees spend a full seat abroad, with Hong Kong, Singapore and Tokyo proving popular destinations of late.

As they approach the end of the Linklaters LPC at the University of Law, incoming trainees list four groups they'd be happy to undertake for their first seat. Midway through that seat, they draw up another list, comprising eight seats in total, which forms the basis for their remaining three seats. *"HR has a pretty tough task trying to organise us all – I don't envy them that."* Fortunately, trainees are able to swap seats if the worst comes to the worst, provided there's space. This is a transaction-heavy firm, so you can count on around half of its 225 or so trainees sitting in a corporate, banking or capital markets-focused seat at any one time. Seats outside these realms can be particularly competitive, so sources advised getting your hat in the ring early if you're interested in a smaller group like IP or competition.

Seat options: banking; capital markets (equity and debt markets; derivatives and structured products; structured finance); competition; corporate; employment and incentive; environment and climate change; financial regulation; investment management; litigation and arbitration; pensions; projects; real estate; restructuring and insolvency; tax; technology, media and telecommunications, IP (TMTIP); trusts

The True Picture

Chambers UK rankings

Asset Finance	Intellectual Property
Banking & Finance	International Arbitration
Banking Litigation	Investment Funds
Capital Markets	Life Sciences
Commodities	Litigation
Competition/European Law	Outsourcing
	Pensions
Corporate Crime & Investigations	Pensions Litigation
Corporate/M&A	Planning
Data Protection	Private Equity
Employee Share Schemes & Incentives	Projects
	Public Procurement
Employment	Real Estate
Energy & Natural Resources	Real Estate Finance
	Real Estate Litigation
Environment	Restructuring/Insolvency
Financial Services	Retail
Fraud	Tax
Information Technology	Telecommunications
Insurance	Transport

Pushing the envelope

RBS, BP, Lloyds and Repsol are just a few of the big names on Links' corporate client roster. Lawyers recently advised Vodafone on its €7.7bn purchase of Kabel Deutschland, Germany's largest cable company, and oversaw Schneider Electric's £3.4bn bid for a London-based listed tech company. *"The scale and scope of our deals is really exciting. I worked with a lot of FTSE 100 companies, plus colleagues in Europe, Africa and South America,"* one insider said. Links divvies its corporate practice into sector-based groups like energy, private equity and insurance. Given the size of the matters at hand, *"you can easily spend your whole six months on a single transaction,"* though we did speak to a number of trainees who spent their seat balancing a handful of smallish matters instead. New recruits are often left to look after doc review, due diligence and data room management, though meatier tasks like drafting board minutes and confidentiality agreements are not out of reach.

Links' vast banking group is split between four floors of its Silk Street HQ. *"We've got distinct restructuring and insolvency, and mainstream borrowing/lending factions, but you'll be working with a lot of the same people."* The collapse of Lehman has proved a big money-spinner for the practice – one of the many developments the firm has advised on during the company's long-running insolvency is its distribution plan to return $9bn of assets to customers. Lawyers have also represented the likes of RBS, JP Morgan, Deutsche Bank, Citi, Barclays and Goldman Sachs in recent years. For trainees, proofreading and research are staple tasks, and there's *"a whole lot of transaction management,"* which sees them become well acquainted with checklists. We also heard from insiders who'd drafted deeds and securities documents, and headed up communications with overseas counsel.

On the capital markets side, work falls into three groups: DSP (derivatives and structured products), EDM (equity and debt markets) and SFG (structured finance group). Each houses around ten trainees at any one time. Interviewees across these groups affectionately characterised the work as *"a bit nerdy,"* telling us *"it's very technically challenging and thought-provoking, which suits a certain type of mind."* We're told SFG, which covers utilities and bond work, is *"one of the busiest groups across the whole firm – you get a heck of a lot of client contact here. There's also a lot of drafting of ancillaries to be done."* The team is one of the largest dedicated structured finance practices in the world, and in 2013 its portfolio sales and purchases topped a whopping £10bn in worth.

A key figure in DSP is Chambers-ranked partner Simon Firth, who as one insider gleefully pointed out *"wrote the textbook on derivatives – he knows everything there is to know!"* (As it happens, 'Derivatives: Law and Practice' retails at a cool £925, so perhaps it's one to look out for in your university library.) Work here is *"very bespoke, very challenging and very techy."* The team is big on the derivatives clearing front in particular, and regularly works in tandem with Links' tax, banking and M&A groups, among others. Trainees here reported regular client contact in addition to drafting prospectuses and working on advisory research tasks. *"You're left to do a lot of the small repackagings on your own, which is great. These can become a little repetitive, but they go a long way in building your confidence."* EDM, meanwhile, advises on bond and equity issues, liability management and restructurings. The group has garnered attention recently for its role in Royal Mail's £3.3bn IPO following the government's controversial decision to float the postal service on the London Stock Exchange.

Accept it and move on

It's easy to get distracted by the top-tier work going down in the transactional teams, but Links' solid litigation arm is well worth a mention. *"As a trainee you're a group resource, so you encounter all kinds of cases,"* sources with experience here said, mentioning property, insolvency and regulatory matters. Back in 2012 News International brought the firm on board to advise on the fallout from News of the World's phone-hacking scandal, but that's not where the team's high-profile representations end. Unfortunately, the firm remains tight-lipped on its biggest cases, but we can mention the ongoing advice it's been providing Grant Thornton on its entanglement in a $9.2bn fraud case. *"It's a very paper-heavy seat – litigators love their files and coloured paper in a way most of the transactional lawyers don't,"* one insider revealed, telling us their role largely revolved around research tasks and doc review. Other trainees mentioned drafting witness statements, disclosures and memos during their time with the team.

"I won't lie; the hours can be savage. But that's what life is like at a top City firm." This was a view we heard from several interviewees. When it's busy in corporate and banking, trainees *"can easily be there until midnight for weeks on end,"* and that's to say nothing of the occasional overnighters required. *"When it's quiet, you'll probably head out at 7.30pm, but it's very up and down."* Meanwhile, litigation schedules tend to be more predictable, though the days are still long here – *"often 12 hours or so."* On the bright side, *"there can be great camaraderie here when everybody's in the trenches together,"* trainees chirped, though they did agree that *"the cheer goes away when you're working long hours under high pressure over a long period of time."* Fortunately, sleeping pods, days in lieu and taxis home go some way to alleviate the pain, though it's hard to imagine these were much comfort to the trainee who reported working *"until 3am every night for three weeks in a row. That was brutal – it took a lot longer than my single day off in lieu to recover."*

All the same, our sources were keen to shatter any conceptions of the firm as *"cold or calculated."* Said one: *"I'd characterise the atmosphere as a constructive one – people are easy to approach and care about your career."* Many put this down to the firm's efforts to *"recruit people who are well-rounded. It's not just bookworms who live in the office here; you get all sorts, including people with some truly impressive quivers to their bows – someone I know recently revealed he's a grade-8 violinist, and I know others who speak four or five languages."* Sources also pointed out that *"a good number of trainees here have grown up abroad, which increases the diversity of experience coming to the table."*

Hong Kong calling

Links offers a staggering selection of overseas seats – recent destinations include Hong Kong, Singapore, Tokyo, Abu Dhabi, Dubai, Moscow, Madrid and Paris – and *"almost everyone who wants to go abroad will go."* Typically the focus is on capital markets, banking or corporate work. Sources who'd jetsetted had plenty of praise for the experience, with one saying: *"They put you up in a swish apartment and give you a generous stipend on top of your salary. There's even an allowance for language lessons if needed and books before you go. What's not to love?"* The firm also sends trainees in-house fairly regularly to big banks and financial institutions.

Our interviewees called the training they'd received *"fantastic,"* pointing to both the three-week induction upon arrival and the ongoing practice-specific, partner-led seminars. They also praised the willingness of senior lawyers across the firm to help out junior colleagues in need. *"You never feel ill-equipped to deal with the things they throw at you because there are resources all around you."* Indeed, each trainee shares an office with a 'principal' designated to *"look out for you, get you interesting work and shield you if too many tasks are coming your way."* Appraisals take place midway through and at the end of each seat. According to our sources, the quality of the former *"depends on who your principal is – some skip it because they're just so busy, which can be frustrating."* Luckily the end of seat review is *"generally pretty thorough,"* and sees trainees graded across a range of criteria and given formal feedback from those they've worked alongside on major matters.

Forget about roof gardens, beehives and fatuous notions of urban bliss; Links' Silk Street HQ goes for the gut when it comes to amenities. There's a GP, dentist, physio and manicurist on hand (bundling is not so kind on the hands, don't you know), plus a gym that runs yoga and Zumba classes, a canteen that serves up *"excellent"* grub, a few 24-hour shops, and even an on-site dry cleaner. *"You really feel the benefits when you realise it's your sister's birthday tomorrow, the last post is being collected in 20 minutes, and you're still able to buy a card and get it off to her in time. In that respect, the work/life balance swings back in your favour."* Trainees also had rave reviews of Links' document production and review services, which run 24 hours a day, seven days a week.

Insiders agreed that *"one of the benefits of doing the LPC together is that those bonds last in a professional context."* When they're not busy beavering away in the office, lawyers have plenty of forums to flex those bonds, whether it's playing on the firm's cricket, football, hockey or netball teams, or just commandeering the drinks trolley as it rolls round the office each Friday. There are also two trainee parties a year, summer and Christmas dos for every practice, and regular departmental city-breaks and ski trips too.

Retention is generally high at Links, and trainees appreciated the firm's *"efforts to keep us in the loop qualification-wise."* In 2014 the firm retained 103 of its 115 new qualifiers.

And finally...

In honour of its 175th birthday in 2013, Links commissioned a pomp-tastic history called *Passing the Flame*, available for download on the firm's website.

Macfarlanes LLP

The facts

Location: London

Number of UK partners/solicitors: 81/196

Partners who trained at firm: 59%

Total number of trainees: 51

Seats: 4x6 months

Alternative seats: secondments

Extras: pro bono - LawWorks, Great Ormond Street Hospital, Virgin Unite

On chambersstudent.co.uk...

How to get into Macfarlanes

The firm's private client work

This City thoroughbred has a keen eye for quality, a classy feel and an intimate training environment.

Silver lining

A stalwart of the City for 140 years, Macfarlanes is one of a coterie of six firms known as the silver circle. Corporate work is traditionally the biggest breadwinner here, drawing in 41% of revenue in 2013/14 (a year during which the firm's total turnover grew by a whopping 22% to nearly £140m). But this isn't your typical City slicker: the firm has a busy private client practice which brings in 13% of revenue and serves the needs of wealthy businessmen, oligarchs and sheikhs. *"For those who don't want to devote all their time to corporate law, a training contract here is a great option,"* sources said.

Turning to the *Chambers UK* rankings, you'll see that Macfarlanes' corporate group picks up two rankings: one placing it at the very top of the mid-market, the other showing that it's a force to be reckoned with when it comes to the biggest and best deals out there. Elsewhere, the firm's private client practice is also placed in the top tier. *"You'll see more of the same from us in the future,"* sources said when we asked where the firm is going. *"The only slight change is that our regulatory work is now more of a focus and is going from strength to strength, as are some of the more specialist practices."*

Unsurprisingly, a Macfarlanes traineeship is heavily weighted towards corporate. Spending six months in 'mainstream' M&A is compulsory, as are another six months in one of the 'specialist' corporate seats like banking and finance or investment funds. Trainees can, however, express their preferred choices for the remaining two seats. *"They give you a 'to die for' seat and do their utmost to accommodate you there,"* one source told us, while another confirmed: *"We're all pretty happy with*

how seats are handed out." A word to the wise: seats in the smaller, specialist practices can be hard to come by and getting one is competitive. So if you're interested in employment, pensions or competition, for example, make your desires known early on. Macfarlanes also offers a few client secondments, but sources agreed: *"It's seen as a bonus, and they're certainly not something people single out as their reason for joining the firm."*

One big phone bill

The M&A group recently worked on Verizon's much-publicised purchase of the 45% stake in Verizon Wireless owned by Vodafone. The £84bn price tag made this one of the biggest deals ever, and certainly the biggest US-based corporate transaction since 2001. Hacks in the legal press were quick to point out that working on this deal was a significant coup for Macfarlanes. You might have expected the job to go to one of the magic circle. Typically the work isn't all 11-digit deals – you're just as likely to be staffed on a mid-market matter. Trainees tend to do either private or public work, though for some there's a mix of the two. *"There's a huge amount of responsibility in terms of project management,"* sources agreed, which means a sizeable chunk of due diligence and co-ordinating checklists. On smaller matters juniors

Seat options: M&A; investment funds; banking & finance; employment pensions & benefits; commercial; competition; derivatives and trading; financial services; corporate tax; real estate; private client; tax; dispute resolution

Chambers UK rankings

Agriculture & Rural Affairs	Fraud
Banking & Finance	Information Technology
Capital Markets	Intellectual Property
Charities	Investment Funds
Commercial Contracts	Litigation
Competition/European Law	Media & Entertainment
	Partnership
Construction	Pensions
Corporate/M&A	Private Client
Employee Share Schemes & Incentives	Private Equity
	Real Estate
Employment	Real Estate Finance
Environment	Real Estate Litigation
Financial Services	Tax

try their hand at drafting ancillary documents, and if you're lucky you might get a first stab at a share purchase agreement or similar.

The other transactional teams work for some big-name clients: Lloyds and Citibank are just two of the major international banks that have lined the pockets of the banking and finance group recently. For trainees sitting here, there's no split between borrower and lender work, so they can get stuck into both. *"It's a fantastic seat,"* crowed one trainee, claiming they were doing *"associate-level work."* Well, maybe. When pushed for examples, this source told us they had been *"running checklists and drafting and negotiating ancillary documents."* Sounds like pretty standard trainee fare to us. For some there's corporate support work too, which can include getting stuck into the leveraged finance side of an M&A transaction. Client contact can be in short supply, but we heard that it does come through in dribs and drabs when a matter is coming to a close.

Corporate support work takes up part of trainees' time in tax too. *"The group is split between a lot of small to mid-size private equity work and corporate reorganisations and disposals,"* said one source. Another added: *"It's a completely different seat from M&A, where you're moving rapidly from one thing to the next. In tax you spend a lot of time thinking about issues and doing research. There's much more black-letter law and it's exceptionally interesting – if your brain is wired that way."*

As a trainee in the disputes practice, *"the work really comes in from all angles. If you're sitting with the construction group but you really want to do some trusts work, for example, and you make that known, they'll be sure to deliver it to your desk if they have it."* The clients come from a range of different areas, so you could be dealing with anyone from private clients to the FCA. In 2014 the team secured a judicial review victory for

Russian metal moguls RUSAL in a dispute with the London Metal Exchange (which is not a forum for hard-rock bands) about rules governing metals warehouses. *"You could easily get staffed on a massive case that goes on for months,"* a trainee told us. *"But I mostly worked on smaller claims, which was great as it meant I got more responsibility. This included taking witness statements and drafting letters to clients."* That said, there's a fair share of doc review, research and bundling to be done too.

From Kensington to Qatar

"There's been a shift in the kinds of people the practice works with," trainees said of the private client department. *"I imagine once upon a time it was all pipes and tweed jackets, but for a while now we've been pushing into new money coming from Russia and the Middle East, as well as managing offshore and non-dom wealth."* Trainees work on domestic and offshore trusts, estates, wills, probate and tax arrangements. *"It's astonishing how well the partners know their clients,"* we heard. Even the basic research is reportedly *"amazing and of genuine academic interest,"* so never fear if you get tasked with that. Otherwise, there's plenty of drafting to be done. *"The seat is renowned for the quality of work on offer and offers really good client contact,"* trainees told us. *"And if a partner saw me doing menial work, they'd stop me and tell me to do something more interesting!"*

When we asked about hours, trainees said they vary significantly depending on your seat and supervisor. As a rule of thumb, the transactional seats have the longest hours and are least predictable: *"In banking it can be very tough – there are periods when you're working till two or three or four in the morning."* The same experience was common in M&A. Happily it's a slightly different story on the contentious and regulatory side, where 9am to 7.30pm is pretty standard.

During the first month or so in each seat trainees are given regular, intensive training, usually rolled out over two or three lunchtimes each week. These classes cover the basics and are designed to allow you to 'learn by doing' during the rest of the seat. *"I've found them really useful,"* said one source. *"The seniors and partners running them do a good job of making the material relevant and interesting. The only thing they could improve is the sandwiches they put out!"* Each trainee shares an offices with their supervisor – usually either a partner or a senior associate – which provides *"an invaluable chance to learn from those with the most experience."*

When it comes to the appraisal process, trainees sit down with their supervisor twice in the course of each seat. The mid-seat review *"is very informal, and your supervisor might just tell you that everything's fine before giving you three targets to work towards and sending you on your way."* The end-of-seat review is a little more formal

The True Picture

and trainees discuss their performance with a partner and training principal Seán Lavin based on written feedback supplied by those they've worked with. Additionally, juniors have a checklist their supervisor signs off each month to ensure they're on top of things. *"The feedback is great,"* sources agreed. *"It's particularly helpful in the first couple of seats when you don't really know how or what you're doing."*

Fifty shades of grey

Look out for Macfarlanes' grad recruitment brochure, notable for its tasteful black-and-white (and grey) photographs of the firm's young guns at work. With bowed heads and pressed suits these bright young things evoke a finer, more sophisticated age where valets and butlers tended to the needs of their employers with rigour and care. Is this what life's actually like on the inside? *"The idea that this is an old-school place is laboured a little too much,"* sources agreed. *"It's true that most men wear a tie and women tend to be in suits too, but when it's dress-down Friday some of the men wear chinos and leave the tie at home!"* Other sources suggested that the last vestiges of Macfarlanes' past are discernible in the firm's *"uncompromising commitment to excellence."*

Looking back five years, we used to give Macfarlanes a bit of a drubbing for the lack of diversity in its trainee group. It doesn't deserve any harsh words from us anymore: 49% of trainees are female while 20% are non-white – that's pretty standard for the City. *"We're definitely starting to see the incoming classes get more diverse,"* said one trainee, while another added: *"It's not just middle-class white people who went to Oxbridge."* It's worth highlighting the fact that Macfarlanes recently joined a small circle of firms operating a CV-blind recruitment policy for vacation schemes and training contracts. Note that the 'blind' part of this refers to the interview and testing stage rather than initial selection. While the overwhelming majority of the sources we spoke to for our research had been to either Oxbridge or a Russell

Group uni, it does look like the recruitment pool is getting broader.

Capture the castle

We were sad to hear that Macfarlanes' all-singing, all-dancing drag cabaret (yes, really) is a thing of the past, but the social scene is far from dead and buried. The Castle on Furnival Street is a timeless classic and still a favourite watering hole for lawyers across the firm on a Friday night. More formally the quasi-articled clerk committee, or QUACC, organises trainee events. ('Articled clerk' is what trainees used to be called before the 1980s.) These include Christmas and summer parties, and drinks each time a new intake joins. We'd certainly like to hear what the partners thought of a recent trainee neon fancy-dress roller disco extravaganza.

The most recent firm-wide Christmas party saw everyone get together for a night of Prohibition era-themed, moonshine-fuelled revelry in the West End. A particular highlight for several of our interviewees was seeing Charles Martin, the firm's senior partner, participate in a mock police shoot-out that culminated with him being shot and dragged across the stage by a couple of cops. Others gleefully recalled alcoholic afternoons in the idyllic confines of the White Swan in Twickenham, a pub owned by John Hornby, the firm's former head of graduate recruitment.

When it comes to qualification, Macfarlanes has a straightforward approach that sees September qualifiers apply for jobs in early May, interview two weeks later and hear if they have an offer two weeks after that. All in all there were no complaints about the mechanics of the system. Sources said that *"from about March onwards you start to see trainees and partners ducking out for coffee and lunch together. It certainly pays to show your hand to the right people and make your interests known."* While the numbers took a tumble in 2013, Macfarlanes' retention rate is typically strong and steady. In 2014, 26 of 30 qualifiers were kept on.

And finally...
Intellectual, hard-working, polite and courteous – that's a Macfarlanes trainee. *"But we're not bookish and boring – this is a sociable place to work, and you need to show at interview that you're good at holding a conversation."*

Maclay Murray & Spens LLP

The facts

Location: London, Scotland
Number of UK partners/solicitors: 60/124
Total number of trainees: 8 (in England)
Seats: 3x8 months
Alternative seats: none
Extras: pro bono – RCJ CAB

On chambersstudent.co.uk...

How to get into MMS
Refashioning the high street

Trainees suggested there's a real push at Maclays to be *"seen as a UK-wide firm with offices in Scotland, rather than a Scottish firm with a London add-on."* Those in the City certainly don't seem to be left out on a limb.

To buy or not to buy

The past few years have hardly been a smooth run for Glasgow-headquartered Maclay Murray & Spens. After a proposed merger with Bond Pearce fell through in 2012, redundancies ensued and profits took a dip (13% in 2013). That said, Maclays is not alone. The past two years have seen a number of mergers in the Scottish legal market, with McGrigors sacrificing its name to the Pinsent Masons brand, and Dundas & Wilson suffering the same fate with CMS Cameron McKenna. In the light of prevailing economic conditions, MMS has done well to hold its own. And if it can weather this, we predict the forecast will be bright for the firm.

Despite its recent woes, Maclays remains an attractive choice to London trainees. Sources were drawn to it as a *"medium-sized commercial firm that does interesting work across a range of sectors"* – somewhere they could feel *"like a bigger fish in a smaller pond."* They assured us, however, that the London office *"stands in its own right"* and the teams there *"feel very interlinked"* with the firm's offices in Aberdeen, Edinburgh and Glasgow. Inductions, conferences and social events in Scotland mean there are plenty of chances to get to know the rest of the trainee cohort, and the Scottish slant means London trainees can get involved in some interesting oil and gas deals taking place up north. Other clients come from the financial services, food and drink, gaming, charities, life sciences, healthcare, retail and public sectors, and comprise a glorious variety, from Baxters (think canned soup) to Lloyds Bank to British Polythene Industries (bin bags and cling film).

Trainees rotate through just three seats, spending eight months in each, so they need to choose wisely. New starters are asked to rank their preferences, and, as in BBC's *To Buy or Not to Buy*, the firm strives to honour at least two of those, with the third being *"more of a wildcard."* Everyone does a contentious seat (commercial dispute resolution or employment) and most a corporate seat (or banking or financial services). Sources said the firm *"tries hard to ensure everyone experiences a good spread of practice areas."* You might think a three-seat system would hinder this, but trainees instead praised the way it allowed them to *"really make a contribution"* in each stint.

A close-knit team

Trainees in the corporate department can get involved in mid-market M&A work for food and drink clients like The Restaurant Group (which owns chains Frankie & Benny's and Garfunkel's), and financial institutions brought in by the Scottish offices, such as Aberdeen Asset Management. In 2013 trainees were able to help out on the mysteriously named Project Panther – in layman's terms, Aberdeen's purchase of Scottish Widows for £550m. On big deals like this, trainees told us they're *"left in charge of ancillary tasks like drafting board min-*

Seat options: corporate; banking and finance; financial services; commercial dispute resolution; employment; property

The True Picture

Chambers UK rankings

Financial Services	Social Housing
Public Procurement	

utes or smaller pieces of documentation." On smaller matters they might also draft resolutions and sections of shareholder agreements, submit due diligence reports, and deal with procedural tasks like amending articles. They appreciated being *"given lots of exposure to the deals which were going on,"* and found that being taken to meetings and listening in on calls enabled them *"to understand the bigger picture."*

Of late, the reorganisation of the high street has proved particularly fruitful for the firm. In June 2014 Maclays was for the second time chosen to advise Edinburgh Woollen Mill on the administration of Jane Norman, having previously advised the retailer back in 2011 when it bought the budget chain along with its sister company Peacocks. Around 24 Jane Norman shops have now gone into administration, and Maclays has been called upon to untangle the mess.

Banking clients consist mostly of insurers like Aviva and financial institutions like Santander and RBS. The team recently advised Scottish Equity Partners on its majority stake investment in marketing company Pure360. For trainees, banking tasks regularly revolve around property finance. *"It often falls on trainees to take care of post-completion paperwork, which can drag on for years after the original signings. Chasing documents from solicitors' firms and sending out relevant notices can be quite demanding,"* one told us. That doesn't mean they can't try their hand at drafting, though – security documents, deeds of confirmation and director certificates could all be on the menu.

Pub brawls

Trainees described the commercial dispute resolution seat as particularly varied – you might be working on a dispute between technology companies one month, and a large oil and gas litigation the next. Classic trainee tasks like bundling, copy-checking, and drafting witness statements are interspersed with the chance to *"draft lengthier documents, such as advice to clients"* and to run small files, such as debt matters, on your own. It's common for senior lawyers to take a trainee with them when they give advice at the Citizens Advice Bureau – *"a good learning opportunity for trainees and a chance to get involved with pro bono work."*

Trainees can run small matters themselves in property, but they can also find a role on big deals for clients such as oil and gas company Nexen and cheap-booze provider J D Wetherspoon. Interviewees had gotten to know the ropes by doing *"a fair bit of land registry work and research"* before moving on to *"more sophisticated legal work"* in the second half of the seat, such as lease reporting and drafting transfers.

Keen apprentices

With a small intake that fluctuates between three and five trainees each year, there isn't the *"rigid, structured training programme"* you might find at a big City firm. *"The low recruitment means they focus a lot on your development,"* with a view to retaining *"as many trainees as possible at qualification."* In 2014 the firm kept on 21 out of 25 qualifiers across the firm (note, this figure includes the Scottish offices). Sources stressed that *"everyone is very patient and takes time to teach you,"* and that *"there's no hierarchy, so you can go to partners with even the smallest question."*

Having a compact bunch of recruits also means *"trainees have bonded well"* and do their best to *"help each other out."* Interviewees suggested the social committee has upped its game lately, so it looks like the lull in events we wrote about last year has been rectified somewhat. Now trainees usually go for drinks together at the end of the week, on top of a spring fair, softball evening, business development and fund-raising events, and barbecues hosted by partners. An annual dinner in Scotland sees the office fly up to Edinburgh or Glasgow (they alternate responsibility for the event) and is a *"chance to let your hair down"* and, for *"those who are still standing,"* to have a dance.

The firm puts a lot of effort into integrating the London office; sources told us there's *"no weird divide"* between the offices and said Scottish partners regularly come down to London to check in on the teams. There may be another reason they're keen to visit the city, though: one trainee described the 1 London Wall office as reminiscent of the opening scenes of *The Apprentice*, with *"floor-to-ceiling windows and spectacular views across the capital."*

The London lifestyle doesn't seem too bad, either. Trainees leave the office by 6 or 7pm most days, and weekend work is rare. They'd experienced some pretty late nights when working on big deals but had found it *"worth it for the experience."* There are no billable targets as a trainee, and the general consensus was *"the pay is definitely okay for the hours we work."*

And finally...

Trainees are welcome to apply for jobs in the Scottish office, though most opt to stay in London (perhaps owing to the higher salary there).

"I'm a light-hearted, smiley person, and the interviews I failed were the ones where I tried to act all serious. It can be tempting to come across the way you think a firm wants you to, but really it's best to let your natural personality shine through so it's clear whether or not you're a good match."

Trainee

Mayer Brown International LLP

The facts

Location: London

Number of UK partners/solicitors: 88/139

Total number of trainees: 30

Seats: 4x6 months

Alternative seats: overseas seats, secondments

Extras: pro bono – RCJ CAB, Mediation Advice Clinic, LawWorks, A4ID, Amicus, TrustLaw, PILnet

On chambersstudent.co.uk...

How to get into Mayer Brown

Mayer Brown in Asia

The London branch of this global heavyweight might have struggled financially in the post-recession years, but it still offers top-quality training with a distinctly international flavour.

Golden Brown

Mayer Brown is one of the world's largest firms, with its 20 worldwide locations pulling in combined revenues of $1.14bn in 2013. Although the London office saw revenues fall in both 2011 and 2012, fee income rose again by 12% in 2013, according to the firm's management. It competes admirably well with the City's native elite in areas like corporate, capital markets and litigation, and picks up a host of *Chambers UK* rankings in areas ranging from energy to construction.

Although mighty, Mayer Brown has reduced its trainee intake in recent years – there were just 30 trainees with the firm in September 2014, compared to 54 in September 2011. Recruitment partner Dominic Griffiths assures us this was done with the best intentions. *"It's partly a decision to match the needs of the business but also to ensure that we deliver on our commitment to provide long-term career opportunities with the firm for all our trainees,"* he informs us. The decision to reduce the intake seems a wise one as *"there is a certain amount of disconcertion around the retention rates as they are."* The figure has hovered uneasily around 60% for the past five years and dropped to an unimpressive 12 out of 23 in 2014. Just before NQ jobs were announced, a final-seater told us: *"I think I've got a chance, but I won't be putting all my eggs in one basket – you'd be an idiot not to apply elsewhere."*

Still, even those who were unsure of their futures at MB were upbeat about the experience the firm had given them. *"Lots of other firms will look favourably on my time here,"* a second-year remarked. *"Mayer Brown is held in pretty high esteem."* It's easy to see why. The training con-

tract offers a heady mix of opportunities both at home and abroad, and this was a major lure for current trainees. An overseas or client secondment is mandatory. Trainees can jet off to MB's offices in Hong Kong or New York for six months, but sources believed the extra-office possibilities in Britannia are equally appealing. *"The client secondments are among the best things the firm offers,"* asserted one. *"We have a wide-ranging client list, and it's invaluable to get the opportunity to spend six months in-house."* A range of spots are available at banks and other financial institutions, while the Hong Kong secondment can now be combined with experience in the offices of a financial services client.

Mayer Brown's boys (and girls)

In addition to the mandatory secondment, trainees must undertake one contentious and one non-contentious seat, but other than that the remaining rotations are free of restraints. Rookies give four preferences before each changeover and are allowed to completely change their selections from move to move. While interviewees were *"not entirely sure what goes on behind the scenes,"* they believed *"HR tries to respect our choices as much as possible."* The big corporate and finance practices usu-

Seat options: corporate; banking and finance; real estate; commercial dispute resolution; construction; insurance; employment; pensions; IP/IT; tax; EU and competition

Chambers UK rankings

Banking & Finance	Litigation
Banking Litigation	Outsourcing
Capital Markets	Pensions
Construction	Pensions Litigation
Corporate/M&A	Product Liability
Employment	Professional Negligence
Energy & Natural Resources	Real Estate
Environment	Real Estate Finance
Hotels & Leisure	Real Estate Litigation
Information Technology	Restructuring/Insolvency
Insurance	Tax
Intellectual Property	Telecommunications

ally receive a fair amount of clamour, while insurance is another popular choice.

Mayer Brown's corporate group has a global management structure and focuses primarily on three industries: energy, funds and insurance. This brings a cross-border flavour to many of London's deals. For example, the team recently acted for GAW Capital on the €240m acquisition of the Waterside Building – the global headquarters of Marks & Spencer – on behalf of a Korean consortium. Trainees are exposed to this international side of things too, with one telling us they had recently been *"dealing directly with American clients."* Another told us: *"I received a lot of responsibility, and on my appraisal I was told I had been doing associate-level tasks. For example, I was liaising with clients every day and making sure their requests were adhered to. I built up a relationship with them and felt in control. That was a great insight into what life is like when you qualify."* Corporate trainees aren't bound to one specific area, although they tend to follow their supervising partner's lead. *"I mainly worked on corporate insurance as that was my supervisor's speciality,"* one interviewee said.

Trainees in finance are usually given free rein. *"I've been involved in a wide range of matters,"* one source informed us. *"Nobody specialises until they're about three years PQE, so you can get that invaluable all-round experience."* Although it's common to come across due diligence, proofreading and the like, our interviewees also reported being *"very much thrown in the deep end."* One remarked: *"From day one I was part of a major deal – I liaised with a client and with local counsel. I really enjoyed the work and felt like I was part of something important."* Another interviewee did offer a quick word of warning: *"The transactional seats are pretty unpredictable, and there are long hours to contend with a lot of the time – it goes with the territory. In the last five weeks I haven't left before midnight."*

The dispute resolution group is the firm's largest. It comes highly recommended by *Chambers UK* and includes commercial, construction, employment and insurance subgroups. Its client list boasts big names like UBS, Unilever and HSBC, with the firm recently advising the first of these in a major cross-border dispute relating to credit default swaps. A source told us: *"The UBS case has been a primary focus for the commercial dispute resolution team for a while now. There is other work for trainees to do though, which is actually a godsend as I really enjoyed getting to grips with a range of smaller commercial matters. Those cases had fewer people working on them than the UBS dispute, so I had a good amount of client contact and felt very involved in the overall process."*

Insurance has been the hot ticket for trainees recently, and time spent in this department involves both contentious and non-contentious work. The team has some of the sector's biggest movers and shakers as clients, including AIG and Zurich. One source said that *"the big plus of working on this team is that cases are quick enough that in six months you can follow them all the way through, from the drafting of initial documents to being taken to court."* A second-year added: *"I was given some typical bundling tasks, but most of my work involved drafting applications or witness statements, and reviewing contentious points in contracts. I was even included in strategic discussions about how to proceed with the case."*

Home and away

Whether secondments were undertaken with clients or abroad, trainees gave a massive thumbs up to the experience. Do bear in mind that a trip to New York is essentially a finance seat while Hong Kong is corporate-focused, so spending time abroad will likely make your training contract transaction-heavy. However, for those so inclined: *"You get a lot of responsibility because of the way training is organised abroad,"* one export to the Big Apple told us. *"They don't have trainees in the US, so you're usually treated like a junior associate. On some matters I was just expected to draft documents and deal with clients on my own. It was quite scary but a great way to learn."* An interviewee who'd had experience in Hong Kong added: *"It was a fantastic experience to meet the Asian team and expand my knowledge. I had two weeks of post-secondment blues after I finished."*

Back in Blighty, all trainees are paired up with a different supervisor in every seat. *"If you want, you can specify who you want to sit with,"* a trainee reported. *"It's easy to do some background research and get opinions from other trainees about what each supervisor is like."* Another interviewee commented: *"Some of the supervisors are excellent and take a personal and professional interest in you, making sure you're happy with life at Mayer Brown and with life in general. Others are different; in some seats you don't do much work for your supervisor at all."* Sources agreed that occasionally you will have to roll with the punches as *"every group is different. Real estate, insurance and construction are known for being friendly, while the working culture of corporate and finance is generally a bit colder and more hard-nosed."*

In general though, trainees felt there is an *"open environment"* at MB. *"If you look at the higher-ups you don't really see anyone pulling rank,"* commented a first-year. *"I feel I can walk into any partner's office to discuss a matter or ask questions. The experience hasn't been as daunting as I thought it would be at a firm like this."* A lack of top-down communication had been a bit of a bugbear for trainees in past years, but this now seems to have been rectified. *"One of the main criticisms I read about when I was looking at Mayer Brown was that information wasn't filtering down to trainees,"* considered a second-year. *"But they've taken those concerns on board. We've had meetings with* [London senior partner] *Sean Connelly, who gives presentations on how the firm is doing and its future strategy. That's been a key development."*

The London office was said to have an *"intimate, personal feel"* despite MB's global footprint. This stems from trainees being placed together on the LPC at Kaplan. *"You get to know the entire group before you start,"* a second-year explained. *"We were all fellow travellers before the training contract started. And as we've got a demanding job with quite long hours, that closeness makes a world of difference."* This feeling of camaraderie is evident in the higher ranks as well: *"You can see that the seniors and partners who trained here know each other really well too."*

Stars and stripes for never

Although Mayer Brown was born and raised in Chicago, this isn't a firm that thrusts deep-dish pizza or other stateside mainstays down the throats of its UK employees. *"Outsiders always have the impression that we are* *a very American firm, but on the ground there's nothing about our culture that's particularly American,"* observed a second-year. Perhaps this stems from the London office's origins as Rowe & Maw, a City firm with which Mayer Brown merged in 2002 to expand its London presence. Our interviewees suggested another reason for the un-American feel to the place: internationalism. *"If you look at our client base you'll see that we have a global focus, and that we don't cater solely for UK and US businesses,"* reflected one. A colleague concurred: *"I'm constantly working with four or five of our offices around the globe on different matters. It's great to know we have that presence in other countries – it means you can talk to someone about issues in all kinds of jurisdictions as and when you need to."*

We heard *"there's no stereotypical Mayer Brown trainee. There are a lot of different personalities here, and yet somehow we all seem to gel together."* Luckily the workplace does seem to be free of *"big characters who are difficult to work with."* Trainees said the keys to success here are a propensity for hard work, an outgoing nature, confidence, commercial awareness and *"an international mindset that recognises we are a global firm."*

There's *"not a strong social emphasis"* to life at MB currently, partly as a result of budget cutbacks in the post-recession years. However, there should still be more than enough to keep you occupied. Drinks trolleys make their way around each department on occasion, and trainees *"now and then"* get together for a bevvy at The White Horse or another watering hole near MB's Bishopsgate home. In addition, there is *"a culture of celebrating large deals being completed with drinks and dinners."* A number of events are also held in support of the firm's charity of the year – the Royal Marsden Cancer Charity in 2014. *"We organised Mayer Brown's Got Talent recently,"* one trainee relayed. *"Some of the partners got up and sung – and some were surprisingly good."*

And finally...
The mandatory secondment at Mayer Brown means this firm suits *"outgoing and confident individuals"* who are willing to test themselves.

McDermott Will & Emery UK LLP

The facts

Location: London
Number of UK partners/solicitors: 21/15
Total number of trainees: 4
Seats: 4x6 months
Alternative seats: overseas seats, occasional secondments
Extras: pro bono – LawWorks, Trustlaw

On chambersstudent.co.uk...

How to get into McDermott
Interview with training principal
   Rohan Massey
McDermott goes to Africa

Only a couple of candidates each year get to sample what MWE has to give: a training contract focused on corporate, energy, tax, IP and employment.

Here there and everywhere

This US gem established itself in Chicago as a tax practice in 1934, and since then MWE's rep has fanned out far from the Windy City. It has nine offices in the States and a further nine overseas (all but one of those in Europe), as well as a strategic alliance in China. The London office was opened in 1998 and besides typical City corporate work is notable for some more specialist practices: IP, energy, tax, private client, regulatory and employment. Training principal Rohan Massey tells us: *"In London, we're a small, dynamic and cohesive group, and we are looking to grow in our core areas, which tie in to the global platform of McDermott, allowing us to better use our network."*

Back in 2009, the firm pruned its bolt-on practices and rejigged management to make it the more streamlined outfit it is today. Things have settled down now. Trainees told us *"the message coming out of the States is that London is very important – management has a strong belief in the resilience of the market here, and is keen to invest further."* While sources admitted they weren't always *"privy to the big management machinations,"* they did tell us *"the firm is looking to invest heavily in private client, energy and corporate."* Private client isn't a familiar face in the usual cluster of corporate and finance practices at US firms, but it's an area that's growing at MWE: in recent years two partners from private client pro Withers have been lured over.

Seats are allocated on the basis of a chat trainees have with HR and Rohan Massey. Due to the number of options available, repeat seats *"aren't that common, as HR likes you to get a feel for as many different departments as possible."* Client secondments *"pop up now and again,"*

but *"with only a few trainees here, whether someone can actually go depends on what the office can cope with."* There are overseas seats too, and *"if you have the language skills then you can usually go."* In 2013/14 trainees spent time in both Paris and Düsseldorf.

Sugar and spice

A stint in corporate is a *"common starting point"* for trainees – all of our interviewees had sat in this department first. The team blends sector work in areas like energy and food and beverages, with an eye on emerging markets across the CIS and Africa. For example, MWE recently advised Olam International, a global food processing company, during its acquisition of a 50% interest in USICAM, a company which owns cocoa-handling and processing facilities in Cameroon. There are *"lots of deals which have a US side to them, and the department often gets ancillary work coming in from the States."*

Trainees' typical tasks include drafting board minutes and compiling bibles, but sources were also able to test their mettle on weightier documents like share purchase agreements, confidentiality agreements and side letters. Trainees described MWE's energy department as *"very much a corporate team with an energy focus, as quite a bit of the work surrounds the sale and purchase of energy assets."* The team recently advised South Africa's national oil company, PetroSA, on its acquisition of an interest in Ghana's Jubi-

Seat options: corporate; energy; intellectual property; tax; employment; private client

Chambers UK rankings

Commodities	Employment
Data Protection	Intellectual Property

lee oil field. There are other elements to the work too, and the department handles a mix of transactional, projects and regulatory matters for a heady brew of governments, private equity investors, and independent power and gas producers. Trainees reported a similar experience to corporate in some respects (in that they were drafting SPAs and side letters), but were also able to sink their teeth into the regulatory side of things too – for example, by *"looking into FCA rules and notifying clients when changes to the law occurred."*

The employment seat offers both contentious and non-contentious experience. While sources felt more *"ba-bysat"* here than in the other departments, they also flagged up the fact that this is a prime seat for developing presentation skills: *"Every week a bundle with new case law is produced, so trainees have the opportunity to prepare that and get used to presenting the information."*

The tax team focuses on corporate support. It recently advised Lord Sugar's Amsprop Estates on the tax aspects which emerged from the sale of the IBM building to private Middle Eastern investors for over £100m. Trainees draft stamp duty applications and conduct research on points of tax law. Interviewees loved the pace of this seat: *"Everyone takes a step back and thinks about what it all means from a legal perspective – it's a very different take compared to how corporate lawyers think about deals."*

The IP team slimmed down in size after one of the litigation partners left to join Baker & McKenzie in early 2014. As a result, a trainee told us, *"there's currently a lot more commercial work: software agreements, e-commerce stuff, data protection."* A lean team did mean good levels of responsibility for trainees, who found themselves drafting software licence agreements and providing trade mark analysis – *"things that would normally be done by a two-year PQE lawyer."* It's also worth mentioning MWE's rep in the food and beverages industry. Trainees reported undertaking *"a lot of regulatory work for these clients – there's a strong portfolio of them in the States, so when they operate in the EU we advise them."*

Everything is awesome!

Office culture may be *"pretty British,"* but the US offices and HQ aren't remote twinkling lights on the horizon – they oversee and connect with London in a few ways. First, *"the head of the firm comes over frequently to give talks and tell us what the plans are – Americans have a special way of making everything sound amazing, and the 'State of the Firm' address is very rousing!"* Second, on a logistical level, *"everything goes through Chicago: financial decisions, hiring, targets, time billed etc."* Third, London receives *"a lot of referrals from the States,"* especially when it comes to corporate deals, and sources mentioned they had worked *"closely with the New York and Chicago offices."* It's not all about the US though; trainees noted that *"there has been a concerted movement to strengthen ties between the European offices."* A French partner now resides in the London office, sealing relations with Paris, while *"London and Düsseldorf share a couple of big clients"* on the corporate front. The firm is also continuing to build an African practice, particularly in projects and energy. Check out our online bonus features to find out more.

Speaking of corporate, interviewees told us this department *"invariably has the longest hours,"* but overall trainees were more satisfied on this front than their peers at some other US firms. *"I've had a few all-nighters, but that's very rare, and it's never just you burning the midnight oil – the partners and senior associates do as well. They don't just dump things on your desk and run away!"* People tend to start a bit later than at most firms – *"they're quite strict about not coming in before 9.30am"* – and on average leave by 7.30pm. As a consequence, interviewees felt that working at MWE had not left their social life *"badly damaged."*

The firm itself is a pretty sociable place: *"We'll get a good crew of people down to the pub on a Friday."* Most of this sociability is spontaneously conjured up in MWE's office in Heron Tower (which we note is now officially called the 'Salesforce Tower London' – ugh). This skyscraper – the tallest in the City – was only completed in 2011, and the interior was described by trainees as *"swish"* and *"amazing."* The building is well known for its jaw-dropping 70,000 litre aquarium, but for trainees the focus was on *"the clear lifts whizzing up and down – you have to get used to them!"* For those with no head for heights, you have been warned.

And finally...

At this small firm you *"hold your destiny in your own hands"* when it comes to qualification. An initial discussion kicks off the process at the start of May and trainees find out if they are staying by mid-June. Three out of five qualifiers were kept on in 2014.

Memery Crystal LLP

The facts

Location: London

Number of UK partners/solicitors: 20/30

Partners who trained at firm: 5%

Total number of trainees: 8

Seats: 4x6 months

Alternative seats: none

Extras: pro bono – A4ID

On chambersstudent.co.uk...

How to get into Memery Crystal

AIM explained

Memery Crystal's website

Gulf Keystone

Hats off to this pint-sized City shop for showing that size is no barrier to success.

In recent Memery

The fantastically named Memery Crystal wields considerable clout, despite its small stature. Founded in 1978, the Londoner has taken just three and a bit decades to develop one of the country's best capital markets/AIM practices, with an impressive roster of clients and a top *Chambers UK* ranking to boot. MC is also strong on the real estate, M&A, commercial contracts and litigation fronts, and has made a big effort of late to develop its private client and technology teams, beefing up the latter with the addition of two partners and a solicitor from Davenport Lyons in 2014. *"We've found that a lot of our work has a technology angle to it,"* says HR manager Helen Seaward of this push, *"and this will let us offer our AIM clients the full service."* On the flip side of the equation, the firm waved goodbye to its fledgling family team in 2013 when its one and only partner, Ursula Danagher, jumped ship for Mishcon de Reya. A couple of editions back we relayed one trainee's claim that *"you come to Memery Crystal to do corporate law or dispute resolution; you don't come here to do family."* It seems they were right after all.

Indeed, most trainees undertake seats in corporate and dispute resolution, the firm's two biggest departments. Those who want to skip out on the latter will find that spots in real estate or employment also satisfy the contentious requirement. Seat allocation is a relatively informal affair: trainees discuss their preferences among themselves before having a chat with HR. *"We're small enough that everyone generally gets what they want,"* a trainee told us. *"If two people want to go to the same place, they just have to decide who gets to go there first."*

Second-years are given priority during this process, and trainees don't get to pick their first seat.

AIM high

MC's corporate department covers M&A, venture capital and private equity transactions, but it's the group's capital markets/AIM arm that shines brightest. A quick recap: the Alternative Investment Market is a submarket of the London Stock Exchange that allows small companies to float shares and raise funds flexibly. The MC team works for around 50 companies quoted on the AIM or Main Market, including Gaming Realms, Gulf Keystone and house builder Mar City, which MC advised on its £35m placing with brokers WH Ireland and Shore Capital. *"Our clients tend to be the owner of the company at hand. It's really rewarding to feel like you're helping them."* Much of the department's work involves the natural resources and technology sectors, and dealings often have an international dimension. Indeed, in late 2013 the team advised Australian gold exploration company Nyota Minerals on its disposal of a 75% stake in an Ethiopian operation.

Trainees in corporate usually start off with admin tasks like house forms and due diligence. *"You progress quickly though,"* said a source. *"I soon became responsible for seeing several Main Market listings through to admission and managed some of my own smaller files."* Trainees

Seat options: corporate; dispute resolution; tax; real estate; employment/commercial

Chambers UK rankings

Capital Markets	Energy & Natural Resources
Commercial Contracts	Litigation
Corporate/M&A	Real Estate
Employment	Real Estate Litigation

went on to tell us *"there's always a deadline that you're working towards, so there's never time for this seat to get boring – unless you're doing verification, which feels like hitting your head against a wall for a few days!"* Time can also get tough when deals are reaching completion, at which point it's not uncommon to find yourself staying well into the AM. *"Luckily there are usually two trainees per rotation, so if one is overwhelmed, the other can pick up the slack."*

The dispute resolution department reels in nearly a third of the firm's total revenue. Recent years have seen the firm cash in for Gulf Keystone on a widely reported, $1.65bn case centred around exploration rights to oil-fields in Kurdistan, and represent three members of dance troupe Diversity – the 2009 winners of *Britain's Got Talent* – in a dispute over management and use of group funds. Bundling and filing comprise a big part of the trainee role here, and we also heard from those who'd undertaken detailed research and had the first go at drafting letters between opposing parties.

8x8 = $18.4m?

The tiny tax team often collaborates with colleagues in the corporate, property and employment departments. MC's corporate and tax lawyers recently teamed up to advise the shareholders of Voicenet Solutions following the company's $18.4m acquisition by communications company 8x8. *"Trainees mainly do employee incentive work, like share option schemes and EMI plans,"* which generally involves *"a great deal of research."* With only four people in the department, *"you're in the thick of it right away – eventually clients call you directly."* As one trainee recalled: *"I was responsible for several important deadlines. My time there required a lot of initiative."*

Over in employment the team predominantly advises employers but also tackles employee-side work for senior executives and the like. Both contentious and non-contentious matters are at hand, and trainees encounter both. *"You could be going to a tribunal on one day and drafting sections of an employee handbook another."* Among

the key clients here is cosmetic surgery giant The Harley Medical Group, which the firm recently assisted with a series of claims involving discrimination and disciplinary procedures. *"The partners are happy for you to deal with clients directly, which is really great experience."* Occasionally, trainees here can split their seat with the neighbouring commercial contracts team.

Trainees had lots of praise for the top-end work they'd encountered but were keen to assure us new recruits aren't shoved off the diving board without knowing how to swim: *"They made a big effort to ease us into it – at the beginning we had IT training and introductions to each departments, and then there were regular training sessions after that,"* said one interviewee. *"I've felt supported throughout – everyone's always happy to walk you through the complicated stuff."*

Energy Crystal

Our sources agreed Memery Crystal *"definitely feels like a young firm,"* though as one elaborated, *"not in the sense that it's immature; rather it's more that it's full of energy – lots of our clients are young go-getters looking to list on the AIM market, which helps."* They went on to describe a *"personal and friendly atmosphere,"* which they chalked up to MC's small stature: *"It's easy to get to know everyone when there are only 50 or so lawyers."*

While trainees were nothing but enthusiastic about their colleagues, the same can't be said for their verdict on the office. *"It's really close to Chancery Lane, which is a great location, but it's split over six floors, so some departments can feel a little isolated,"* one source explained. *"There aren't any communal areas, so you easily go weeks without seeing people from other teams."* Fortunately, trainees make a big effort to meet up regularly. *"We often go out for lunch or drinks at the Grand Union."* It's a bit more difficult to get the full house together, but the firm-wide Christmas bash is well attended – last year's saw chief executive Lesley Gregory recite a version of 'The Night Before Christmas' adjusted to include a spate of firm-related puns. *"It trod the line between awful and hilarious,"* confided a trainee. *"There were definitely a few groans among the laughs!"*

Interviewees gave their work/life balance a thumbs-up, though we heard *"there are some dark times when things get hectic. Corporate deadlines wait for no man! Luckily these are never prolonged, and people acknowledge when you've been working hard."*

And finally...

Memery Crystal shouldn't be overlooked if you're after an AIM market pro. In 2014 three of MC's four qualifiers stayed on with the firm.

Michelmores LLP

The facts

Locations: Exeter, London, Bristol, Sidmouth
Number of UK partners/solicitors: 57/80
Total number of trainees: 13
Seats: 4x6 months
Alternative seats: secondments

On chambersstudent.co.uk...

How to get into Michelmores
Interview with HR director Colette
  Stevens
Working in the South West

This growing firm has come up trumps in Devon, and its presence is now extended across wider plains.

Harry Potter and the increase in revenue

Like Harry Potter's Aunt Marge, this Devonshire native is inflating rapidly. The past 14 years have seen Michelmores conjure up an impressive increase in revenue, rising from £5m to £26m and landing a spot in the UK top 100 table. Turnover grew by 15% for both the 2012/13 and 2013/14 financial years, and HR director Colette Stevens says: *"We're anticipating similar growth next year."* That said, *"this will be achieved through lateral hires and work for bigger clients rather than through mergers,"* she explains, referring to the firm's 2012 takeover of Wilsons' Bristol branch. Michelmores has bases in London and Sidmouth alongside this office and the Exeter HQ.

Stevens goes on to mention that international work now accounts for 10% of Michelmores' turnover. *"At the moment, our focus is broad, but we're looking at developing our expertise in Russia, Africa and China in particular. Our London office is pivotal to this strategy, as it takes on the most cross-border matters."* As our trainee sources pointed out, that the firm is even focused on its international prospects is indicative of *"quite a dramatic transformation when you remember that we started out as a high-street firm with local clients."* These days, Michelmores operates a full-service shop, working across three broad areas: business, real estate and private client. The latter division has expanded *"vigorously"* in recent years, thanks largely to the agricultural team that was onboarded in 2012, and it now rakes in 25% of the firm's turnover. The team receives top marks from *Chambers UK* for its work in Exeter and the surrounding area. But Michelmores is no one-trick Exmoor pony; top-band regional rankings also go to its corporate, IP and restructuring practices, among others.

Most trainees set up shop in the Exeter HQ, which houses the broadest selection of practice areas and is by far the largest office, with 120 lawyers. (By comparison, London and Bristol have around 20 each.) However, there's a commercial litigation seat up for grabs in London, and the firm offers a single training contract in Bristol that centres around private client and agricultural litigation work. Trainees submit their seat preferences a month before each rotation, including the first. While we heard *"it's best to be proactive during this process,"* trainees assured us that *"it's fair – if you don't get your first choice, you usually get it next time."* The firm runs occasional secondments to clients such as the Met Office or Plymouth University.

Down on the farm

Michelmores' private client group is one of the biggest outside of London, and counsels landed estates, wealthy individuals and family owned companies on everything from offshore tax planning to structuring farming interests. Naturally, we can't mention any individual cases due to confidentiality, but we can say that many amount to millions of pounds. Typical trainee work includes drafting wills and lasting powers of attorney, and handling trust administration, although we heard they often carry out research, attend court, draft witness statements and collate financial reports too. Heavy client contact is a given, although it's not for the faint-hearted: *"I did some death-bed planning and went to the hospice the day before the client died. That side of the practice can be upsetting, which is why some wouldn't touch this seat with a barge pole."*

Over in commercial litigation – a popular trainee stop – sources reported *"a lot of disclosure, which can be dull, but*

Chambers UK rankings

Agriculture & Rural Affairs	Intellectual Property
Banking & Finance	Litigation
Charities	Planning
Clinical Negligence	Private Client
Construction	Projects
Corporate/M&A	Real Estate
Employment	Real Estate Litigation
Family/Matrimonial	Restructuring/Insolvency
Information Technology	

it does give you a good understanding of what's going on." We also heard from those who'd drafted letters and instructions to counsel, drawn up cost schedules, attended client meetings and even tried some minor advocacy in front of a practice master. In Exeter, the team counts the Met Office, Legal Aid Agency, and Torbay and South Devon Health and Care NHS Trust among its recent clients, successfully defending the latter against a £1m contractual claim brought by a care home owner. Trainees taking up the seat in London have access to cross-border disputes – *"I came across matters involving Malaysia, Israel, New Zealand and the Cayman Islands"*– and have the chance to dabble in peripheral practices such as insolvency and insurance litigation, alongside standard commercial disputes.

Veni, Vidi, Vinci

Among the corporate group's more notable clients are international construction company Vinci, NatWest and Exeter Rugby Group, which lawyers recently advised on a £7.5m bond issue. The team's remit includes private equity, M&A and corporate finance transactions, and it's also been building its expertise on the emerging markets side, carrying out an increasing number of deals in the Middle East, sub-Saharan Africa and South East Asia. While it's unlikely for trainees sitting here to escape low-level tasks like bibling and due diligence, our sources were pleased that they'd been able to tackle meatier fare by way of drafting ancillary documents and shareholder agreements. As is usually the case in corporate, work comes in peaks and troughs, so trainees might find themselves burning the midnight oil. *"I've stayed until 1am,"* one said, *"although working that late is usually a one-off."*

The real estate department specialises in public sector and development work for clients like Barratt Homes and City North Finsbury Park, which it recently advised on the creation of a new £200m residential development. Trainees who'd encountered large-scale development projects told of previewing surveys and leases, drafting leases and *"generally playing a project management role;"* meanwhile those working on smaller transactions like land sales busied themselves with completion statements and client correspondence.

Purple velour suit

Our interviewees agreed that *"even the most senior partners here are approachable and friendly. You never have to be afraid to ask them silly questions."* Luckily, such questions tend to be dispelled anyway through the *"umpteen hours of training"* new recruits are treated to during their first weeks at the firm. *"If you can think of it, we were trained in it."* Trainees also receive mid-seat appraisals from their supervisors and informal feedback along the way. *"I've found my supervisors really helpful. On the few occasions I've felt the work was too much for me, my supervisor talked it through with me instead of just saying 'deal with it'."* It helps that the London and Exeter offices are open-plan: *"You can see very easily to see whether or not it's a good time to bug someone about where to get an envelope."*

According to our sources, *"Michelmores works hard to make sure that this culture is carried out across all the offices."* We heard *"whenever there's a big get together, the other offices are always invited,"* which means lawyers firm-wide were treated to the no-doubt transcendent tunes of Michelmores' in-house rock band, The Disclaimers, when they performed at the summer party at Powderham Castle last year. (Apparently, the guitarist donned a purple velour suit and energetically pogoed across the stage.) *"The firm really pushes the boat out with parties,"* – trainees told of masquerade balls, champagne towers and one Willy Wonka-themed drinks event complete with people dressed up as Oompa Loompas. The Exeter HQ is located outside of town on an business park, so impromptu booze-ups can be hard to organise due to driving obligations. However, the office does come equipped with a gym and a conservatory serving up snacks alongside views of the surrounding hills.

And finally...

In 2014 all six qualifiers stayed on with the firm. If you aspire to follow in their footsteps, don't fall at the first hurdle – it's pronounced *'Mitchell-mores'*.

Mills & Reeve LLP

The facts

Location: Cambridge, Norwich, Manchester, Birmingham, Leeds, London

Number of UK partners/solicitors: 115/273

Partners who trained at the firm: 12%

Total number of trainees: 33

Seats: 6x4 months

Alternative seats: occasional secondments

Extras: pro bono – LawWorks, ProHelp, Cambridge and Birmingham FLAG

On chambersstudent.co.uk...
How to get into Mills & Reeve
The techy revolution in divorce law
Pro bono at Mills & Reeve

Mills & Reeve has amassed an impressive collection of clients over the years, including top dogs from the education and healthcare sectors. For students eager to travel the country, there are plenty of opportunities to hop between offices.

The True Picture

Knowing Mills, Knowing Reeve

Steve Coogan claims to have put Norwich on the map, but Mills & Reeve made the city its home long before Alan Partridge. Alan eventually decided to settle in a hotel just half way down the M11 to London; Mills & Reeve has proved a little more adventurous. Since its Norwich founding in 1880, it has opened offices in Cambridge, Birmingham, Leeds, London and Manchester. It now has the largest private tax team outside of London, plus a sizeable first-class family law team.

For many of the trainees we spoke to, it was the firm's educational and healthcare slant that proved its biggest draw. It wins high rankings in *Chambers UK* for its work in the sectors though continues to operate as a full-service firm. *"I liked the idea that I could work with health sector clients without necessarily being tied to a healthcare firm – we do pretty much everything here,"* one source reflected. To take the Norwich office as an example, it has no fewer than 25 top-tier rankings to its name in the East Anglia tables. If you've never read *Chambers UK* before, know this is exceptional.

Only the Birmingham, Cambridge, Norwich and (most recently) Manchester offices take on permanent trainees, but if you want to experience something not offered there you can always spend a seat in Leeds or London. Interviewees told us the firm *"really encourages us to spend at least one seat in another office,"* and trainees can even

qualify somewhere they didn't train. Trainees hand in a 'wish-list' of seat preferences, and though first-years are somewhat subject to *"the luck of the draw,"* second-years are guaranteed priority. Add to that a six-seat rotation, and *"there's plenty of chance to cover the areas you'd like to."* Only a contentious seat is compulsory (plenty of teams fall under that umbrella), though trainees suggested the firm *"likes you to do a real estate seat too."*

Putting family first

A lot of the trainees we spoke to had started their contract with a spell in family law. This is considered a *"good teething period"* in a sociable department, where interviewees enjoyed *"an awful lot of client contact."* They'd been taken to negotiations, mediations and final hearings, and had attended tribunals in court with just counsel and client. One confessed all this had come at the cost of more administrative tasks, but that wasn't much of a

Seat options: public law and regulatory; commercial disputes; healthcare; employment; insurance; real estate; construction; family and matrimonial; private tax; planning; agriculture; corporate; banking; technology; corporate tax; projects; insurance; pensions; private client; real estate disputes; commercial (See online for breakdown by office)

Chambers UK rankings

Administrative & Public Law	Insurance
Agriculture & Rural Affairs	Intellectual Property
Banking & Finance	Licensing
Charities	Litigation
Clinical Negligence	Pensions
Construction	Planning
Corporate/M&A	Private Client
Court of Protection	Private Equity
Data Protection	Professional Discipline
Education	Professional Negligence
Employment	Projects
Energy & Natural Resources	Public Procurement
Family/Matrimonial	Real Estate
Healthcare	Real Estate Litigation
Information Technology	Restructuring/Insolvency
	Tax

gripe. Cases here range from standard prenups to those carrying allegations of domestic violence, and in the latter kind *"it's important to be able to support the client on a personal level."* It's a particularly tech-savvy team that's managed to capitalise on the UK's growing divorce market in a number of quirky ways – check out our website to find out how.

Most trainees will sit in a real estate team, but that could mean anything from agricultural property to construction or planning. Work often involves the healthcare and education sectors – recent examples include advising Addenbrooke's Hospital in Cambridge on plans to double its size, and acting for Northampton Uni on its proposed £33m campus relocation. For trainees, pro bono files can be a good way to get responsibility without being shunted with the grunt work. Sources had worked with local philanthropic groups, drafting commercial leases and deeds of variation, and helping with post-completion tasks. Hours are longer than in family but never *"disastrously"* so, and interviewees had enjoyed working in such a busy team. Planning is much smaller, but trainees there get the opportunity to attend inquiries with barristers and clients, and see through smaller matters on their own. A trainee who'd sat in construction told us it's *"a useful introduction to contracts without being an exclusively non-contentious seat."*

Commercial is another seat that mixes transactional and contentious work. On the non-contentious side, trainees are expected to draft commercial contracts and distribution agreements, and to *"prevent disputes from arising in the first place."* The team counts the Department of Health and Ministry of Defence among its top clients, and has advised the British Council on a number of projects, including remote video-teaching and a radio programme broadcasting British music around the world.

On the contentious side, trainees had helped draft witness statements and court documents, and had learned to deal with people on the other side who *"aren't always that nice."* The Manchester office advises on sports disputes, representing high-profile clients like the Court of Arbitration for Sport and the Professional Footballers' Association.

Trainees in projects are unlikely to be given their own matters as *"they're all massive,"* but they'd enjoyed visiting sites and going to meetings on their own. In 2013 the team advised insurance giant Aviva on projects totalling an impressive £140m, including the building of 11 new fire stations in Staffordshire. The banking team does a similar kind of public financing work, often with an education slant. Trainees remembered how exciting it was to work on *"things that had never been done before,"* such as the launch of a £350m public bond issuance by the University of Cambridge in 2012, and a similar £300m one by the University of Manchester in 2013.

Corporate's worst-kept secret

In addition to general practice group seats like those already mentioned, trainees can sit with a more sector-specific team like education or healthcare. Trainees had found education *"interesting and fast-paced,"* with *"lots of running in and out of court,"* while those in healthcare described work as *"out of the ordinary"* since it concerns *"real-life decisions."* Healthcare clients include over 100 NHS bodies, along with independent providers such as Bupa. The team offers all the standard commercial advice but also represents institutions in patient matters like mental health sectioning orders, Court of Protection decisions and even assisted suicide litigation. Interviewees had helped prepare for inquest hearings and filed emergency 'best interest' applications – one claimed to have loved it so much they would have done it *"for zero pay."*

The employment group also represents both the education and healthcare groups' clients, along with more general corporate clients. Trainee tasks here vary from giving general redundancy advice to drafting policies for clients. Interviewees had been to High Court cases in London and to lots of tribunals, regularly popping over to the client's premises to help draft witness statements. A stay in corporate proved *"a bit of a shock"* to some, given it's such a busy team, but they'd been pushed to do *"as much drafting as possible,"* which helped them gain experience quickly. Clients range from higher education institutions, charities and medical firms to well-known companies like Weetabix and holiday website Secret Escapes. Work sometimes has a technology focus – in 2013 the team advised on the sale of a bug-free code developer business to Facebook (so your cringey photos from 2007 look safe for now).

With trainees stationed across at least four offices at any one time, training courses provide a good chance to catch up. First-years start the contract with a four-day residential course and then visit Cambridge, Norwich and Birmingham for further PSCs. One told us: *"It's nice to have other trainees put us up while we do the PSC. It's a good way to get to know each other, and they usually take us out."* Another commented that training *"is very much tailored to the individual,"* mentioning one-on-one sessions with a coach designated to help trainees prepare for interviews before the NQ process. All offices are open-plan, meaning trainees can pick up clues from how the solicitors around them act and have quick access to partners if they're stuck. And you needn't worry about keeping your guard up: *"A lot of the partners are very funny,"* so you can always *"have a joke with them."*

To hell and back

Trainees firm-wide told us they'd *"never felt uncomfortable or intimidated,"* and that *"everyone is really supportive and keen to get you involved as much as possible."* That said, each office does have its own particular quirks. Since we last checked in, the Manchester office has expanded thanks to a merger with local firm George Davies in 2013. It's still relatively small, though, meaning *"you get to know everyone."* The office sits right in the middle of Piccadilly Gardens, and trainees admitted it can get quite chatty at times. They assured us it has a *"decent social scene,"* with *"drinks on Friday nights and lots of lunches out."*

The Birmingham office is also in a good location, with the law courts to one side, and shops and bars on the other. A source told us: *"There's a community for young professionals that you can tap into quite easily,"* and trainees tend to show their faces at events put on through that. *"We all get on really well and go out together every week or so."* They can also get involved with various CSR ventures, such as the Birmingham FLAG pro bono project, which provides free legal advice to people in the local community. In 2013 the office benefited from the addition of a nine-strong insurance team from DLA Piper.

Norwich is no longer the firm's biggest office, but trainees were nonetheless surprised at how many people they'd come to know over the contract. It's also home to the paralegal support team that's *"very sociable. Most of them are of a similar age to us, so there's always a group of young people up for a drink after work."* A sports and social committee *"tries to arrange events monthly,"* such as cinema trips and wine-tasting nights, and local junior lawyers' division events always *"pull in a large crowd."* Trainees told us they're encouraged to help with business development and added that *"charity work is a great way to get to know others in the office"* – they were recently filmed cooking 'Hell's Kitchen'-style to raise money.

The Cambridge office (the firm's largest and, according to interviewees, *"the busiest"*) moved to a brand-new building in 2012. It now looks out from six floors of glass windows over the university's botanical garden and is considered *"a very supportive place to be,"* even though *"not everyone knows each other."* Juniors often go out for drinks after work on a Friday, though one did lament the fact that lunchtime meet-ups had recently subsided as *"everyone's really busy at the moment."* Most IP work takes place in Cambridge, so those interested in the area can opt for a seat with the technology and commerce team there. The same goes for projects and banking, though for insurance they must head elsewhere. It's quite common for trainees to swap and change between offices. *"The firm is very helpful with finding you accommodation when you move for a seat."* Mills & Reeve is doing its best to promote a "one-firm feel," and the heads of each team try to spend some time working in each office so everyone can get to know their faces. *"They're also trying to encourage cross-office working,"* another trainee told us. *"Some people even split their job between two offices, spending half the week in one and half in another."*

Trainee salaries don't vary between offices, so what may seem fair in Norfolk doesn't go so far in pricey Cambridge. Across the offices, though, it seems that you can be out by about 7pm if there's no urgent work to finish. *"Different teams have different working patterns, but partners generally appreciate you have a life outside of the office and encourage you to leave if you're finished."*

And finally...

The jobs list is published pretty early at Mills & Reeve, and trainees insisted *"they really do try to accommodate you if you're a good candidate."* In 2014, 16 of 19 trainees stayed with the firm on qualification.

Mishcon de Reya

The facts

Location: London

Number of UK partners/solicitors: 94/177

Total number of trainees: 24

Seats: 4x6 months

Alternative seats: occasional secondments

Extras: pro bono – Queen Mary University's Pink Law Initiative

On chambersstudent.co.uk...

How to get into Mishcon
Interview with training principal
Jonathan Berman

Glitzy clients and a corporate boost are driving this rapidly expanding London firm forwards.

Stars in their eyes

"You know the opening of 'The Big Bang Theory' with the planets whirling around the sun and everything happening increasingly quickly? That's how I'd describe Mishcon," one source proclaimed. Mishcon's expansion over the past five years has certainly been explosive: revenue has doubled from £47.3m in 2008/09 to £97.8m in 2013/14, and the firm has just beaten its financial target for a fourth year running. Celebrity clients and a considerable litigation, private client and real estate offering have long been associated with this once firmly West End firm, which also sports notable art and media law practices. But now Mishcon is also establishing itself as a mid-size corporate player: the department has long had a top lower mid-market ranking in *Chambers UK*, but our latest research shows it has been making significant inroads into the main mid-market too. Demonstrating the corporate department's capability, in 2014 the team advised Qatari investor Al Mirqab Capital on its $1.5bn takeover of Heritage Oil. The firm also added real estate investors Hermes and Prestige Finance to a commercial client list which includes Delancey (redevelopers of the London Olympic Village) and Investec Bank.

Mishcon retains its links to celebs and smaller clients, though: the firm recently acted for social news start-up Premium Interest in a multimillion-pound trade mark dispute with Pinterest, while Alice Temperley and Christian Louboutin followed in the footsteps of Lady Gaga and Gordon Ramsay and received IP advice from the firm. Private client work remains important, and the firm is *Chambers*-ranked for this area as well as for its family and defamation work. Management recently announced the launch of 'Mayfair Private', an independent private client business operated in conjunction with Opus Private. It aims to advise high net worth individuals on personal and business matters not typically handled by law firms.

Current trainees arrived by a variety of routes, legal or non-legal. *"There's no typical Mishcon trainee,"* one interviewee believed. *"We're a diverse bunch."* A large number of our interviewees were recruited via the vac scheme, and from 2015 onwards trainees will only be recruited via this route. *"We've been considering this for a while, and everyone we've spoken to internally feels it's the best option for us. We want to get to know prospective trainees over a couple of weeks first rather than just an assessment day,"* explains training principal Jonathan Berman.

Trainees can do seats within six broad areas: litigation, corporate, real estate, family, private client and employment. For each rotation trainees submit three choices to HR, who then allocate places; most trainees were relatively happy with the results. Like last year, interviewees informed us that forging relationships with key partners can help you get what you want. *"Demonstrating that you're interested works in your favour – it pays to speak*

Seat options: corporate litigation; corporate; employment; family; litigation (banking & finance, IP, fraud, fraud defence); private client (contentious, immigration, tax and wealth planning); real estate; real estate litigation; corporate tax

Chambers UK rankings

Commercial Contracts	Intellectual Property
Corporate/M&A	Licensing
Defamation/Reputation	Litigation
Management	Private Client
Employment	Real Estate
Family/Matrimonial	Real Estate Finance
Fraud	Real Estate Litigation
Immigration	Sports Law

to people," one interviewee believed, while another concluded that *"it can be political."*

Mishcontentious

Within litigation, fraud is the biggest area of work, and trainees who do a seat here often visit court. *"That could be for anything from a mini-trial to a 20-minute application seeking an injunction."* One trainee had even *"helped obtain a bench warrant for someone's arrest."* The flip-side is the admin work – *"you can't get away from it; it's mainly trial bundling."* Trainees also draft witness statements and affidavits, organise expert witnesses, and assist with injunction preparations. Heavyweight clients include Microsoft, American Express and Dell, and the department specialises in cross-border cases and injunctions. Over the past year one notable case saw the firm act for ten defendants in a $500m dispute over funding for property assets in Montenegro. The high-profile nature of the cases means trainees *"understandably never get to take charge of one ourselves, but do get really interesting work."*

IP – for which Mishcon is *Chambers*-ranked alongside magic circle firms and specialists like Harbottle & Lewis and Arnold & Porter – is another contentious seat option. Fewer matters go to trial here, but if you're lucky enough to catch one be prepared to liaise with counsel and clients, and draft application orders and witness statements. Last year the department acted for lingerie chain Victoria's Secret in a trade mark dispute with clothing brand Thomas Pink. Trainees can also do a seat in banking and finance litigation. The cases here are usually big, meaning less responsibility for trainees: interviewees told us of undertaking tasks like budgeting, filing and bundling. There are occasionally smaller cases too, which allow you to *"stretch yourself mentally,"* drafting correspondence to clients and analysing legal positions.

Because of the demands of taking cases to trial, the hours in all the litigation seats are notoriously varied and can sometimes see trainees staying until midnight or the early hours of the morning. *"Staying late actually makes me feel lucky as it means I'm working on some really fascinating matters,"* said one particularly Panglossian trainee, although others didn't feel quite so 'lucky' to be working late. Elsewhere, we're informed, unless it's *"ridiculously busy"* you can head home around 7pm.

Real estate offers both a contentious and a non-contentious seat. The property litigation department acts for both big commercial clients and high net worth individuals. The team recently acted for Gordon Ramsay in a dispute with film director Gary Love over an alleged falsified signature on a leasehold for the York & Albany pub in Camden. While trainees have contact with larger clients, they typically gravitate towards small-fee work, undertaking tasks like compiling witness testaments, preparing for court days and attending hearings. Non-contentious property work *"unavoidably entails a fair amount of admin work"* such as creating schedules and filing Land Registry applications. When the stars are aligned trainees can get exposure to big portfolio deals, transactions and negotiations; they spend time drafting leases and licences, and leading minor transactions. The department recently advised property developers Minerva on the £460m sale of the St Botolph Building in the City, and is helping the Dutch government relocate its London embassy from Kensington to Nine Elms. *"It's great that the clients are so diverse,"* said one trainee. *"They range from huge institutions to small entrepreneurs, and trainees are encouraged to deal with all of them."*

Mishcorporate and Mishtresses

With an increase in the total value of deals from £6.9bn in 2012 to £27bn in 2013, the corporate department is really carving out a place for itself in the market. Loan management company Prestige Finance recently joined the books, as did DHX Media (the company responsible for the Teletubbies). Trainees work closely with the rest of the team on transactions and can spend months assisting on large deals. Expect to record board minutes and resolutions, and create document lists in preparation for deal completions. The department is getting busier and busier, and spending time here *"can be pretty stressful,"* according to our sources.

A seat in corporate tax allows trainees to get stuck into some *"very technical"* issues – *"there's quite a lot you need to know."* Trainees here conduct research into points of tax law and draft support documents for transactions. The department recently advised Investec Bank on the tax aspects of a £52.5m financing arrangement for investment into East London student accommodation. *"It's a surprisingly brilliant seat,"* one trainee enthused. *"You receive your own set of slightly scary legislation books, but there is a lot of training to get you up to speed."*

Mishcon's private client department offers three seat options: contentious, non-contentious, and private tax and wealth preservation. The latter entails drafting wills and lasting powers of attorney, and advising individuals on residency and tax issues. In the spirit of creating generalists, trainees are encouraged to sample tasks from other areas of private client if their own is fairly quiet. Probate and wills disputes throw up a lot of *"challenging but juicy cases."* One interviewee revealed that when dealing with wills *"everything comes out in the open – a mistress or unknown child might pop up wanting money, or step-parents might fall out with their children over inheritance."* Trainees get regular client contact, but the sensitive nature of cases sees supervisors keeping a relatively close eye on them. While doing a private client seat rookies may also get to work with the specialist art law group, which recently advised on the setting up of the 1:54 Contemporary African Art Fair at Somerset House.

Oh I just can't wait to be... a lawyer

Most trainees felt relatively happy with the supervision they had received, reporting that *"even when busy, supervisors will take the time to break things down."* In some seats the supervisor role is a *"nominal position,"* and trainees work with the department as a whole. Trainees undergo a three-week induction programme upon beginning their contract, and different departments provide training sessions. Overall, interviewees reported that most fee earners are very approachable when it comes to raising queries – *"no one's a monster."* The firm also runs the 'Academy', a programme of lectures featuring big wigs like Shami Chakrabarti, Douglas Alexander and Cherie Booth.

Our sources described Mishcon as *"a vibrant place to work,"* telling us *"everyone is friendly and likes to air their opinions."* Another source added: *"It's definitely not pompous; you're encouraged to speak up."* While some departments such as private client are quite formal, others have a more laid-back atmosphere, with jokes and (apparently) even footballs being kicked around. Keepie uppie aside, we were assured that *"people do conduct serious work, but there is a lot of banter."* On the social side of things we heard mixed feedback from trainees. *"It's not the most sociable of places,"* one interviewee reported, while another said *"it's very sociable! There's always more than a few Mishcon employees in the Bountiful Cow on a Friday night."* This pub is just around the corner from Mishcon's Summit House HQ and is a long-time favourite. Some departments are reportedly better than others at getting everyone out, so trainees' comments likely reflect where they were sat at the time of our calls. The firm lays on summer and Christmas parties, and trainees traditionally supply the entertainment at the latter. *"We did a medley of Lion King songs, rewritten to have a training contract theme,"* reported one interviewee. *"It was pretty embarrassing!"*

In recent years the firm has struggled a bit to get into the right groove due to rapid growth. Several trainees reported a *"lack of transparency"* about management decisions, which they attributed to the lingering small-firm mentality. Generally our interviewees had the sense that even though the firm is growing, it still has the feel of *"an inclusive Mishcon family"* about it. One source commented: *"It's important to management that we don't lose that culture despite expansion and lateral hires. And I reckon we'll be able to do it."* Expansion is having one definite and very physical consequence: in 2015 the firm is moving from Red Lion Square just round the corner to the larger and newly refurbished Africa House on Kingsway.

Trainees' biggest bone of contention this year was the NQ process, which was described as *"quite painful"* by our interviewees. Trainees reported the setting up of *"an increasing number of hurdles as the process went on"* – sources said that while they were aware there would be competition for positions and expected to undergo an interview, they ended up undertaking additional application tasks too. *"Some people had to do two or three written assessments or extra technical interviews, and most of these were sprung upon us with little warning,"* sources reported. *"The goal posts were moved several times, and the relay of information was haphazard and inconsistent."* Most interviewees suspected all this was down to competition for some seats – private client, employment and litigation– being greater than anticipated. Training principal Jonathan Berman had this to say about the issue: *"We allocate NQ jobs to particular departments based on our business plans. Most of our trainees decided to apply for just a few of those positions, which led to competition. We were looking to choose whoever was most suited for each role, so candidates went through a series of interviews. We wanted to make the process fair and open. It wasn't perfect, and we encouraged trainees to make their minds known about it. We will work with them to deal with the issues they brought up and resolve them for next year."* Ultimately the firm retained eight of 11 qualifiers.

And finally...
While this firm still offers nifty family, IP and private client experience, corporate is growing and growing, so expect the training contract and NQ jobs on offer to reflect this.

Morgan, Lewis & Bockius LLP

The facts

Location: London

Number of UK partners/solicitors: 23/24 (+6 non-UK-qualified)

Total number of trainees: 10

Seats: 4x6 months

Alternative seats: overseas seats, occasional secondments

Extras: language classes

On chambersstudent.co.uk...

How to get into Morgan Lewis

Interview with managing partner Peter Sharp

US firm Morgan Lewis' London outpost is thriving and functions as *"the English law platform for the entire firm."*

What Dewey do?

The Titanic is sinking, and the iceberg is labelled 'financial integrity'. But Jack and Rose are long gone, and the partners, associates and trainees of Dewey & LeBoeuf are the ones tumbling from the escape hatches – fleeing the largest law firm collapse in history. Morgan Lewis' London office only started taking on trainees at around the same time, in 2012 – and that's no coincidence. Peter Sharp, current London managing partner and former London head of Dewey, crash-landed into Morgan Lewis. *"A lot of people were rushing around in different directions,"* a former Dewey trainee told us, *"and Peter arranged interviews at Morgan Lewis for a few of us."* Seven trainees eventually made the switch to Morgan Lewis, *"and the firm's training programme was kickstarted overnight,"* says Sharp.

Since then the London office has steamed ahead, and trainees were confident that this is partly thanks to the 18-lawyer team from D&L. There have been other lateral hires too: in January 2014 the firm hired private equity partner Tom Cartwright from Taylor Wessing, while corporate partner Stephen Walters arrived from Bird & Bird in April. The office was also boosted when the firm retained its single qualifying trainee in summer 2014. *"London is becoming more than a satellite office,"* said one interviewee. *"It's starting to make a name for itself."* So far our *Chambers UK* research doesn't yet agree with this observation – at present the firm is only ranked for its business immigration work. But further expansion and winning new work can only change this.

London does corporate/M&A, finance, dispute resolution, energy, tax and employment work. Peter Sharp

rightly points out that the last of these *"has always been a trophy practice area for the firm in the US"* – the practice wins a top-tier ranking in *Chambers USA*. ML's stateside origins lie in Philadelphia, which is still the firm's HQ, but from there it has successfully expanded across the US and around the world. It now employs 1,600-odd legal professionals in 25 offices around the world. Culturally, a London trainee told us, *"while it's clear that we've got a US parent, and we have celebrations for the Fourth of July and Thanksgiving, on a day-to-day basis you don't get the sense we have an American culture. It actually feels quite English here."*

ML has just eight trainees, so seat allocation's a doddle, and trainees usually get what they want. *"You have an informal chat with HR about what you want next as part of your mid-seat review,"* a source explained, *"and because the firm's quite small, we trainees tend to discuss where we want to go among ourselves too."* One source warned that, *"while this is a system that works well when there aren't many trainees, if and when the firm expands it will need something a bit more formalised."*

From Russia with love

For those after hands-on experience, the litigation department is a very worthwhile stop. Matters are high in value and often international in nature. For example, the firm recently defended the former owner of Kazakhstan's Al-

Seat options: banking finance; corporate; employment; energy; private investment funds; litigation

Chambers UK rankings

Immigration

The True Picture

liance Bank against a $1.1bn fraud claim. The 11-strong team, headed by Peter Sharp, is particularly strong in the energy, insurance and finance sectors, and often attracts international clients from Eastern Europe, Africa and Central Asia. The department's two resident trainees *"tend to work on matters with one partner and an associate, which means your role is rarely just to do the filing or photocopying."* While trainees did admit to doing their share of bundling and proofreading, they can also nab more substantive work. *"I got to draft things from scratch,"* boasted one trainee. *"I also conducted legal research, and prepared memos with my findings and conclusions to send to the client."*

The six-lawyer employment team was recently strengthened by the arrival of an associate from Fieldfisher. Given the prowess of this department in the US, the London team has a lot to live up to, but thankfully impressive client rosters run in the family: insurance broker Willis, American defence company General Dynamics, Facebook and Amnesty International all recently called on the firm for advice. Trainees do a mix of contentious and non-contentious work, which translates into heaps of experience. One said: *"I do anything and everything: drafting witness statements, putting together cost schedules and proofreading."*

The business and finance department offers experience in M&A, banking, energy, and private investment funds. Although trainees are usually allocated to one of these areas, they *"can sometimes take on work from the others too."* Interviewees said they get stuck into things like drafting board resolutions, updating contracts, preparing bibles and conducting disclosure. *"It's not the most technically demanding work – you don't get to run your own files and usually the partners take the lead – but it's good to learn how all the documents are constructed."* Through its close ties to the Moscow office, the team handles numerous international cases from Russia and the other CIS countries. For example, lawyers advised an affiliate of one of Russia's largest pension funds, Blagosostoyanie, on its €35m acquisition of Aviva's Russian insurance and pension business.

Some trainees take the Russian relationship even further and parachute into Moscow for six months in that office's corporate department. Well, we say corporate department – in reality trainees tend to help out on all kinds of things. *"As well as corporate, I did banking, energy and employment work,"* one reported. Trainees lauded the experience, as you get *"as much, if not more, responsibility than in London."* Expect a steep learning curve. *"For one project I attended negotiations that went on for 12 hours,"* one interviewee told us. Trainees can also go on secondment to an insurer client, and from 2014/15 will be able to do overseas seats in Dubai and Brussels too.

Your cup of tea?

Like quite a few American firms, ML sees pro bono work as quite important. Trainees are required to put in at least 20 hours a year. *"It's a great way to get more experience,"* said one source – pro bono cases are much smaller than the firm's usual fare, so trainees usually get to run them themselves. *"You're left to draft documents from scratch and run cases from start to finish, but someone does usually look in to check up on you from time to time."*

Thanks to the office's small size, so say trainees, *"it's easy to learn everyone's names, and we have a friendly, amiable atmosphere."* One source commented: *"The people here are really easy to have a chat with – for example if you're making yourself a cup of tea in the office kitchen."* Trainees sit with either a partner or an associate, and sources were quick to point out the value of the one-to-one relationship which develops. *"My supervisor has been really good at training me up, and I feel comfortable asking partners questions,"* said a first-year. Sources were a bit less impressed with their work/life balance. *"When deadlines are set, come rain or shine, the work needs to get done,"* said one trainee. *"There was a period where my team and I worked until 11pm every day."* But *"the hours aren't horrendous – a really busy period probably rolls around once every few months."* A more regular working day lasts from 9am to 7pm.

Trainees' hours still allow them to socialise with colleagues outside work. Besides a black-tie Christmas dinner, there are cheese and wine evenings, bowling nights and pancake parties. The Christmas do in particular attracted rave reviews: *"Everyone just lets go – it's really wild! There were dance battles between partners and HR, and lots of jumping up and down!"*

And finally...
Morgan Lewis offers trainees a bumper deal on international work: *"Every day I'm in touch with clients from all over the place – just this week I've contacted Russia, the US and Africa."*

"Try to attend open days if you can – they usually offer a good outline of the application process, so if you make it to an assessment day you already know what to expect and have some tips for succeeding under your belt."

Trainee

Muckle LLP

The facts

Location: Newcastle

Number of UK partners/solicitors: 26/46

Partners who trained at the firm: 15%

Total number of trainees: 6

Seats: 4x6 months

Alternative seats: none

Extras: pro bono – LawWorks

On chambersstudent.co.uk...

How to get into Muckle

The Newcastle legal market

Its independence is the only fierce thing about this sociable firm, a staple of the Newcastle legal scene.

Quite something

Muckle's playful website is a good illustration of how it's a bit different from your average firm. *"We are enthusiastic, committed to looking after you and, we hope, quite good fun to work with – only 'quite' because, after all, we are still lawyers!"* broadcasts the homepage. This bubbly blurb is reinforced by our most recent round of interviewees' insistence that the Geordie outfit is *"less stuffy than other local firms,"* a sentiment they put down to the way *"it's run less like a law firm and more like a business."* Elaborated one: *"Management is really open and keeps us in the loop about what's going on – they're aware what they do impacts the firm as a whole."* Indeed, even vac schemers are treated to this type of transparency, kicking off their visit with a talk from accounts about how the financial side of the firm works.

Muckle is proud of its status as the largest Newcastle-only firm in 'toon', and insiders were emphatic that *"we've got no plans to merge or branch out into other cities like all the other commercial firms here seem to be doing."* According to managing partner Steve McNicol, *"we're absolutely steeped in the local community, which is why we retain control of our own destiny in Newcastle and why we're so good at looking after local businesses – we understand who they are and what they want."*

Of course, *"we don't lack ambition,"* McNicol continues, explaining that *"technology and travel make it possible for us to service clients in Hong Kong, Ireland, the US and the South of England quite comfortably from our office here."* Still, the majority of Muckle's clients are based firmly within the UK. These include neighbourhood banks Clydesdale Bank and Newcastle Building Society, as well as national financial institutions like HSBC and Santander, all of which are drawn to the firm's banking and finance capabilities, top-ranked in *Chambers UK* in Newcastle. Muckle also scores highly for its corporate, construction, litigation, IP, real estate and employment work in the area, and has historically been recognised for its expertise in the charities sector.

Banking on it

During their first year, trainees are allocated seats *"mainly based on business need, but by second year it's made clear they'll try to accommodate you, especially if you've got a burning desire to do a specific seat."* Corporate and real estate are among the most common pit-stops, with most visiting at least one, and many both. Trainees meet with graduate recruitment head Kevin Maloney mid-seat and at the end to chat about *"how we're doing and where we'll go next."*

Despite its relatively small size, Muckle's banking and restructuring team is big news with local clients, making for a *"busy seat. The team works very hard, so you can expect some late nights."* Lawyers recently advised Durham County Cricket Club on some multimillion-pound funding arrangements with two local councils, and have

> **Seat choices:** banking; corporate finance; real estate; construction and engineering; employment; dispute resolution; commercial

Chambers UK rankings

Banking & Finance	Information Technology
Charities	Intellectual Property
Construction	Litigation
Corporate/M&A	Real Estate
Employment	Restructuring/Insolvency

overseen various transactions for a slew of major national banks over the past few years. One insider reported *"registering charges on Companies House and handling pre-completion searches,"* while another told of *"drafting board minutes and ancillary documents for a big refinancing. As the seat moved on I got to draft loan agreements under the supervision of fee earners and found myself doing much of the work for smaller deals myself."*

The construction team is split into contentious and non-contentious subgroups which take on a trainee each. *"We've got a national reputation, so we get clients from all over,"* our sources boasted, adding that Chambers-ranked Rob Langley, head of the contentious division, is *"one of the best construction lawyers out there – he's the go-to guy in the region. Being able to talk through cases with people like him who've got experience and knowledge going back years is extremely valuable."* Because the North East has seen a slow recovery from the recession, Langley's team has seen a recent influx of *"disputes regarding cash flow and finances, plus lots of mediations and adjudications."* This abundance of work lends itself to high levels of responsibility at the trainee level, with one telling us: *"I was given a couple of my own disputes to run under supervision, which involved making my own decisions on tactics and strategy. It was amazing to take a lead role on negotiating rather than just sitting there taking notes."* On the transactional side, we hear there's the chance to *"work with really quite complex contracts."* Said one source: *"I was involved in drafting the building contracts and ancillary documents for a new hotel at a football stadium, which were quite complex."*

Trainees completing a real estate seat get to pick between two groups: property development and corporate real estate. The former sees lawyers handle estate management, land purchases and leases for energy providers and developers like Barratt Homes. *"You get lots of drafting experience pretty early on."* On the corporate side, *"it's a lot of corporate support work."* Reported one new recruit: *"I worked for a charity buying a new property and helped with a really complicated transfer on a portfolio of properties."* On large-scale deals, it's not uncommon to get stuck into *"due diligence and find yourself wading through boxes and boxes of deeds,"* but by the end of the seat, our sources found *"you're allocated your own files and get to make decisions yourself."*

Muckle's corporate group is one of the largest in the North East and harbours specialities in the motor retail, pharmaceutical and energy sectors. Trainees doing a stint in commercial contracts work closely with the corporate team as well as the charities group, which advises local stalwarts like the Hadrian's Wall Trust and bigger names like Greggs. The firm's sports team, which represents The FA, also kicks over some contracts work. *"I got to help with an overseas cricket league's media and advertising rights contracts,"* one source offered.

Beaming ear to ear

Supervision at Muckle isn't limited to one's formally assigned supervisor. *"I'd feel confident talking to anyone across the teams I've worked with,"* said one trainee. *"People are pretty good at keeping us up to speed with how we're doing."* Our interviewees found mid and end-of-seat reviews a helpful way of consolidating this feedback, though the firm's buddy system garnered less praise simply because *"you don't really use it; it's easy enough to just make friends during your seats."*

Regional firms seldom involve the frenetic pace of a London training contract, and Muckle is no exception. *"There's a big focus on work/life balance here; you're not chained to your desk or expected to work ridiculous hours."* Indeed, most recruits reported working a decent 8.30am to 6pm. Sources credited the firm's open-plan office for creating a *"relaxed"* environment, telling us this set-up goes a long way in reducing hierarchy. *"The managing partner does have his own office, but his door's always open."* Other office perks include the *"lovely views of St James' Park"* (non-footie fans, take note that's Newcastle United's grounds, not a peaceful picnic spot) and *"a chill-out area with a kitchen and pool table. There are always a few of us chatting over lunch there."*

One thing our interviewees made clear is that *"Muckle really invests in having a friendly firm."* Take the BEAM team (that's Be Engaged At Muckle), which plays a big role in solidifying ties by organising *"tons of engagement initiatives"* designed to get the whole firm mingling. Our sources spoke of hikes, healthy living weeks, bowling outings, curry nights and parties celebrating landmark birthdays. *"There are 35 this year, which statistically is insane!"* Alongside these firm-driven activities are plenty of impromptu get-togethers. *"We socialise all the time,"* sources said, *"and not just because we're forced to."* Indeed lawyers regularly head to nearby watering hole The Strawberry en masse after work, and recently a particularly mucky bunch of Mucklers took on a filthy obstacle course dubbed Muddy Mayhem.

We get the vibe it takes a positive, bubbly personality to fit into this convivial environment. *"Of course there are lots of different types of people here, but you've got to be someone who can get on with others and easily integrate.*

The True Picture

Talking down to secretaries or thinking you can just do whatever you want regardless of others isn't tolerated." Committing to the area and pitching in with the local community are also expectations of trainees at Muckle – read our web extra on the firm's CSR work in the North East to learn more.

And finally...

The only real frustration we heard from trainees here regarded *"not finding out about qualification a bit sooner – we aren't told anything until June."* In 2014 Muckle retained two of its four qualifying trainees.

Nabarro LLP

The facts

Location: London, Sheffield, Manchester
Number of UK partners/solicitors: 104/270
Partners who trained at firm: 18%
Total number of trainees: 51
Seats: 6x4 months
Alternative seats: Brussels, secondments
Extras: pro bono – LawWorks; language classes

On chambersstudent.co.uk...

How to get into Nabarro
Sheffield, Nabarro and British Coal
Interview with training principal
    James Snape

Nabarro's real estate work is hot property, but applicants shouldn't overlook its other offerings.

Moving on up

Change is in the air at Nabarro. Until recently the mid-sizer's UK presence was limited to its London headquarters and a smaller, though still full-service, Sheffield branch, but in September 2014 the firm added a Mancunian neighbour into the mix. *"Initially it will start with real estate and related work,"* says graduate recruitment partner James Snape, adding: *"We would like to offer a training contract there at some point."* 2014 also saw the launch of a Dubai hub to complement the firm's Brussels and Singapore outposts, and at the time of our calls lawyers in the capital were gearing up to move to deluxe new accommodation at 125 London Wall. The changes don't stop there; according to Snape, *"we're now turning our attention towards growing our revenue and attracting more lateral talent."* Since 2013 the firm has already brought on board a raft of notable laterals from the likes of BLP, Osborne Clarke and Addleshaw Goddard.

Nabarro has long been known for its property work, which consistently wins *Chambers UK* rankings on the real estate litigation and finance fronts. That said, our trainee sources were keen to point out *"you don't necessarily need an interest in property to come here. The firm has a lot of other strengths too."* Indeed, Nabarro has a broad collection of *Chambers UK* rankings comprising areas like private equity, corporate, pensions, IP and planning. The Sheffield branch is particularly big in the natural resources and environment sectors, and recently assisted Britain's largest coal miner, UK Coal, with its restructuring following a catastrophic fire in 2013 at Warwickshire's Daw Mill.

The real deal

At the time of our calls there were 40 trainees based in London and seven in Sheffield. New recruits get stuck into a six-seat system. *"You can get a bit fed up with moving around so much,"* one admitted, *"but on the plus side it does give you exposure to a lot of departments."* Trainees submit four seat preferences per rotation, and sources agreed *"HR is very good at discussing what you want to do and making suggestions."* All trainees have to complete a contentious and property seat, and many try out a spell in corporate. Repeat seats are also an option. Sheffielders can do a stint in London, which has a wider selection of seats on offer, and Londoners can head to Sheff too.

There's an overseas seat in EU/competition available in Brussels, plus a range of client secondments up for grabs with the likes of Mercedes-Benz and Serco. *"I'd absolutely recommend the experience,"* said a trainee who had been in-house. *"You're exposed to a completely different way of working."*

Nabarro's real estate team has more than 140 lawyers and is divided by client into five groups across Sheffield and London. The department generates around 40% of the

> **Seat options:** banking; insolvency; funds and indirect real estate; corporate; EU competition; real estate; planning; commercial litigation; real estate disputes; IP; environment; pensions; employment; infrastructure, construction and energy; tax

Chambers UK rankings

Banking & Finance	Investment Funds
Capital Markets	Litigation
Clinical Negligence	Local Government
Competition/European Law	Pensions
	Pensions Litigation
Construction	Planning
Corporate/M&A	Private Equity
Education	Professional Discipline
Employment	Projects
Energy & Natural Resources	Public Procurement
Environment	Real Estate
Health & Safety	Real Estate Finance
Healthcare	Real Estate Litigation
Information Technology	Restructuring/Insolvency
Intellectual Property	Retail
	Tax

firm's total business, and its client roster is impressive. There's Land Securities, the largest commercial property company in the UK, plus Google – the firm recently advised the tech giant on its acquisition of a site for its new £1bn HQ. Another notable matter of late saw lawyers assist Kuwaiti property company St Martins on its £1.7bn purchase of the More London estate from London Bridge Holdings – one of the UK's largest-ever commercial property deals. *"It's one of those departments that's never quiet,"* a trainee told us. *"I would work 'til 11pm or midnight often."* Many of our interviewees found this seat a bit daunting, particularly the one who described their experience as *"heart attack-inducing. You come in and you're immediately handed like 20 to 40 of your own files and thinking 'how on earth can I possibly manage this?'"* Fortunately these files – typically leases and licenses – *"seem a lot more manageable after you've drafted a bunch."* Alongside this type of work are chances to assist partners with more sizeable matters. *"I worked on an enormous retail portfolio by drafting certain clauses, working on land registry applications and putting together schedules for SPAs."* All in all, *"it's not a great seat for someone who panics quickly, but the supervisors are excellent and sometimes you get involved in high-end responsibilities like negotiating."*

Meanwhile, there's *"a bit less free rein"* in real estate litigation. *"Because the advice we give is so specific, everything has to be checked by someone more senior."* The department does a lot of development work – including vacant possession strategy, rights of light disputes and trespassing issues – for the likes of Saatchi & Saatchi, Hermes and SEGRO. The London team recently advised property developer Hammerson on its multimillion-pound redevelopment of Elliott's Field Retail Park, while the team in Sheffield helped the same client with its redevelopment of Eastgate in Leeds. Trainees praised the

department's extensive supervision, telling us: *"You can easily track your progress – your work goes back and forth between several people and comes back covered in red pen. It's a good feeling when you get to the stage where they tick it and just send it out."* There's *"no escape"* from bundling here, but we also heard from those who'd drafted break notices and advice notes, researched case law updates, put together schedules of dilapidations and attended court. More than one interviewee noted a heaving workload: *"You have to be able to cope with picking up lots of little pieces. Being anal is a plus, as you need to make to-do lists – hundreds of to-do lists."*

ICE, ICE, baby

The construction, projects and energy teams recently merged to form a group dubbed 'ICE', which stands for 'infrastructure, construction and energy'. *"There's a huge variety of work on offer,"* one insider enthused, noting that healthcare, leisure, energy and education are all among the industries covered. *"It's cool to see your work in action – you'll close a matter and suddenly realise that a new school is being built as a result."* A glance over the team's client roster shows DC Leisure, Biffa Waste, Wheelabrator Technologies and Kent County Council among the key clients of late. An increasing amount of work here involves cross-border elements – for example, the team recently advised the shareholders of the Jordan Wind Project Company on the $290m financing of the Middle East's first utility-scale wind farm. The energy sector in particular involves a lot of new legislation, so trainees here can expect heaps of research. *"On some topics you end up knowing as much as the partners do."* They went on to tell us that *"our role also involves making sure everything's ready to go in meetings and the hundreds of documents at hand are all in the right places."*

Over in corporate clients include a mix of entrepreneurial start-ups and large listed companies like utility supplier Telecom Plus, REIT Primary Health Properties and Euromoney Institutional Investor – one of Europe's largest business and financial magazine publishers. The London team recently assisted Sportingbet with its £485m sale of operations in Australia and Spain to William Hill, while lawyers in Sheffield have spent the past few years advising Finance Yorkshire on a series of investments in local businesses. Much of the work sees trainees assume a project management role, briefing associates for meetings and managing documents, though we also heard from those who'd drafted shareholder agreements and risk factors, put together prospectuses, and communicated with clients and banks. *"It's pretty up and down – you'll have a week of staying until 1am, then others where you're out by 5 or 6pm. Luckily there's a good sense of teamwork among those held hostage in the early hours."*

Nabarro's commercial litigation faction specialises in financial services disputes and regulatory work, and counts Nationwide, Mercedes-Benz and the office holders of Lehman Brothers among its recent clientele. In one of its more high-profile matters of late, the London team represented IBM UK Pensions Trust after the company was charged with unfairly changing its UK pension plan to reduce an £890m deficit. There's also a largely Sheffield-based sub-team dedicated to Medical Defence Union work. *"Essentially, this is defending medical professionals against negligence claims,"* one source explained. *"For example, if a doctor failed to diagnose X on Y date, we would construct a chronology of events up until then. It's a bit like being a detective, actually."* Elsewhere interviewees had participated in negotiations, constructed case summaries, drafted witness statements and attended court. That said, *"there's also an awful lot of bundling,"* an insider confirmed. *"At one point I started thinking 'I can't wait to get my own trainee!'"*

Wonder Wall

"We'll all miss Holborn, but our new office is incredible," an excited Londoner said of Nabarro's impending move to Alban Gate near Moorgate. *"It's brand spanking new, with enormous windows overlooking the City and St Paul's."* According to James Snape, it's not just the interiors that will benefit from an update: *"We'll be incorporating cutting-edge technology by skipping a generation of IT and going straight to dictation software and at-desk video conferencing. It'll be the Nabarro of the future."* Trainees in the HQ told us this is all part of a bid to *"make sure we're not just seen as a real estate firm. Everybody knows we're good at real estate litigation and funds and projects, of course, but moving to the City projects a certain image beyond that – it's full of huge firms we want to compete with."*

That said, our sources didn't anticipate the firm adopting a cut-throat approach to work/life balance any time soon. *"They place a big emphasis on having a life outside of work – the ethos is very much 'do it, do it well and don't hang around all night for the sake of it'. We're not just* seen as a pool of resources to be exploited." Indeed, *"I think everyone here feels pretty valued,"* one trainee said, adding that *"it's not stuffy, and it's rare to see a closed door. There are a few dragons here and there, but I think that's true of every firm; generally partners are easy to approach, and a lot even socialise with trainees."*

Sources from both offices described a good relationship between the two branches, which occasionally team up for certain types of work – employment, for example. *"They make a big effort to make us feel connected,"* a Sheffielder said. *"We have departmental meetings via video-link and usually do all of our training down there."* Meanwhile the much-lauded 'Trainees in the North' weekend gets the Londoners swimming upriver. *"I think we're meant to do firm-related activities and training, but in reality the last one ended up being a treasure hunt and a huge night out."* Back at home events often have a networking slant – everybody's encouraged to bring their professional contacts along to the thrice yearly 'Contact Nabarro' dos – though there's plenty going on informally too. *"Pub invitations are always whizzing around on Friday afternoon – and trainees are never allowed to buy the drinks!"* The firm is big on barbecues, we're told, with individual departments often serving up hickory-smoked extravaganzas. At the time of our calls Londoners were eagerly awaiting the next tasty instalment, soon to take place at the London office's summer party at Haberdashers' Hall in Smithfields. Sheffielders have their own take on this event, with several insiders highlighting *"the awesome barn dance last year,"* which we like to think brought a literal meaning to the line 'swing your partner round and round'.

In 2014 the firm retained 21 of its 24 qualifiers. Several sources last year complained that the qualification process lacked transparency, but we hear this has been improved: *"Now, all departments submit whether they have jobs available, and HR can tell you straight away if there's one in the area that you want."* The firm now holds interviews if more than one person applies.

And finally...

The only way into Nabarro is through its vac scheme, which sees candidates spend three weeks in a single department.

Norton Rose Fulbright

The facts

Location: London

Number of UK partners/solicitors: 153/346

Total number of trainees: 110

Seats: 4x6 months

Alternative seats: overseas seats, secondments

Extras: pro bono – Liberty Advice Line, FRU, A4ID, legal advice centres; language classes

On chambersstudent.co.uk...

How to get into Norton Rose Fulbright

Going global: Norton's international network

A series of smart combinations has seen this City banking big-shot balloon into a global behemoth with outposts in Australia, South Africa and the Americas. And there may be more to come...

NRF already?

If law firms were retro arcade game characters – bear with us – Norton Rose Fulbright would surely be Pac-Man. Since 2010 it has gobbled up Australian, South African and Canadian outfits, and in 2013 it swallowed up Texan firm Fulbright & Jaworski. Burp! As if that wasn't enough, 2014 heralded the opening of an outpost in Rio de Janeiro, the firm's 55th office worldwide. So has that sated NRF's appetite, or is there room for more? *"We're particularly interested in establishing an office in Mexico, as well as moving further into Africa,"* reveals trainee recruitment partner Duncan Batchelor.

What do trainees make of all this expansion? *"There's a palpable sense of optimism in the office,"* one said. *"But I think we're still waiting to feel the full force of the Fulbright merger and the opportunities it will open up around the world."* The merger had been live for nearly a year by the time of our calls, so for our part we think NRF needs to hurry up and work out what it's going to do with all its new global goodies. Trainees were pleased to report there haven't been any negative side-effects of all the gobbling up the firm has been doing (heartburn perhaps?). *"Even after all the changes we've been through, the friendly, easygoing vibe we're known for hasn't died, and no one has been lost in the shuffle."*

Know that a training contract at Norton Rose Fulbright has a heavy banking slant. Don't be shocked if six months in disputes means six months of banking litigation. A seat in one of the pedigree banking groups – asset finance, project finance or general banking – is compulsory, as is a stint in corporate and one in disputes groups (fortunate-ly there are lots to choose from in these latter groups). That leaves trainees one free choice. They can opt for one of the niche practices, revisit banking, corporate or disputes, go on a client secondment (mostly banking-based), or take a trip to one of the many overseas offices (more on those below). *"There are some restrictions because of business needs, but people are largely happy with the way seats are dished out."*

Planes, trains and mega big deals

The banking group is recognised by *Chambers UK* for its asset finance, projects, general banking and transport work. If a company wants to buy, build or finance something anywhere in the world, NRF can probably sort them out. Clients include HSBC, Bank of America and Deutsche Bank. Asset finance and project finance are by far the most frequent stops for trainees. *"We're very active in emerging markets like Africa and Russia, and there's a lot of work for lenders in areas like real estate and telecoms,"* observed one.

The asset finance team is recognised by *Chambers UK* for its rail, aviation, shipping and general finance work, and NRF is the only firm to receive top-tier rankings in all four of these categories. The seats on offer are ship-

Seat options: banking and finance; corporate, M&A and securities; dispute resolution and litigation; IP; antitrust and competition; employment and labour; real estate; tax; regulation and investigations

Chambers UK rankings

Asset Finance	Intellectual Property
Aviation	Investment Funds
Banking & Finance	Litigation
Banking Litigation	Outsourcing
Capital Markets	Pensions
Commodities	Planning
Competition/European Law	Professional Negligence
	Projects
Construction	Public Procurement
Corporate/M&A	Real Estate
Employee Share Schemes & Incentives	Real Estate Finance
	Real Estate Litigation
Employment	Restructuring/Insolvency
Energy & Natural Resources	Shipping
Environment	Tax
Financial Services	Telecommunications
Information Technology	Transport
Insurance	

ping and aviation/rail. Clients of the latter team include easyJet, British Airways and Bombardier, the Derby-based manufacturer making the new trains for Crossrail. But a lot of the work stretches far beyond London and Derbyshire: lawyers recently worked with their colleagues in Poland and New York to deliver five Boeing 787 Dreamliners (built in the US) to Polish flagship carrier LOT. *"Our clients are spread all over the world and so are the assets they're buying,"* observed one trainee. There are a lot of ducks to get in a row for these deals to work, and sources commented that *"you need to be seriously organised and capable of staying on top of things – you might end up having to close several different aircraft deals all on the same day."* Trainees spend their time *"managing transactions and keeping notes of which documents have and haven't been signed and agreed."* The experience in this seat can vary from person to person: one source reported that *"there wasn't tons of client contact,"* while another said they'd been managing small deals themselves. There's also the occasional chance to attend deliveries of planes, which are always interesting, champagne-flute clinking events.

The project finance team works on a lot of financings for wind farms and biomass plants, as well as doing oil and gas work. *"Some of the deals that come through are huge!"* said one awestruck interviewee. For example, the firm is advising Dutch bank ING on a $4.1bn project to build a gas and petrochemicals plant in Karakalpakstan, Uzbekistan. *"Trainees are expected to pull their weight on the big deals,"* said one trainee. *"Projects has a bit of bad rep for long hours, but I loved it."* Why? *"I've helped oversee the closings of deals that have been in the press."* We did hear from some sources who'd been stuck doing bibling and due diligence, but they also mentioned com-

pleting discrete drafting exercises and meeting clients. Trainees are a shared resource, so *"you aren't shackled to doing just one kind of work if you're sitting with a partner whose specialism doesn't quite match your interests."*

The banking practice's prowess in areas like energy and natural resources means that many of these matters trickle into the corporate practice too. *"Deal volume has really picked up again,"* said one trainee, thinking back to the dark days of the financial slump. *"And it helps that we're active in emerging markets like Africa and the CIS countries."* NRF is ranked as one of the best firms in the City for high-end M&A by *Chambers UK* – hardly surprising when it picks up deals like Barclays' £1.3bn sale of its Africa operations to its subsidiary Absa. *"Corporate is notoriously busy, and the hours can be long,"* we were told. *"You could be doing 60 hours a week when it's busy – 50 is probably normal."* Another source added: *"I tend to get in at 8.30am and usually head home at about 8pm – but sometimes I leave at 6pm, and sometimes I'm in till 1am."* Insiders here spoke of drafting shareholder agreements and ancillary documents, and breezing through lower-level work like verification and due diligence.

Baby, baby, baby, oooh

The disputes group focuses on areas like transport, trade, energy, insurance and – you guessed it – banking. In addition there's a thriving anti-bribery and corruption team whose work spans the corporate and disputes groups. One recent insurance-related case saw the firm advise several London market insurers including ACE, Brit and Novae on $1bn worth of losses related to the Bernie Madoff Ponzi scheme fraud. Other recent clients include BP, AIG, Munich Re and RBS. *"The work is excellent – I loved being staffed on high-profile, newsworthy matters,"* said one trainee, clearly as impressed with this client list as we are. *"I worked on disputes for supermajors [like Big Oil] and state-owned energy companies,"* another told us. Interviewees spoke of doing court filings and conducting legal research, as well as drafting parts of claims and interviewing witnesses. But these are big, heavily staffed cases trainees are working on – don't they feel rather removed from what's going on? It would seem not: *"I could see where my work was going and how it was contributing, even when I was doing lower-level tasks. I felt like I was actively contributing."*

As mentioned above, trainees described their work as *"incredibly international,"* especially in the transactional departments. If this exposure isn't enough for you and you've got itchy feet, there are plenty of opportunities to complete seats abroad. The firm runs six-month placements to far-flung places like Dubai, Johannesburg, Melbourne, Perth, Sydney, Singapore and Tokyo, as well as locations closer to home like Amsterdam, Milan and Paris. We heard rumours that jaunts to the US and South America may soon be possible too. *"The range of over-*

seas seats is impressive – that was a big draw for me when I was applying," one trainee commented. Paris, Singapore and Australia are particularly competitive destinations, and it's easy to see why. While temporary Sydneysiders can go ride the surf on Bondi Beach, trainees in Melbourne *"get to stay in one of the most exclusive hotels in the city – one person kept bumping into Justin Bieber in the foyer!"* For those not bothered about leaving Blighty, NRF also seconds trainees to clients like Citi, BP and Soc Gen.

NRF offers an extensive suite of formal training opportunities. These includes breakfast meetings, seminars and presentations covering technical issues like changes to banking and tax law, plus soft skills like public speaking and time management. Even after all this, *"there are still times when you don't know how to do something, but there are online resources to help with that, and we have designated 'knowledge lawyers' on each team too."* The firm also provides trainees with both a trainee and a partner mentor. *"I never feel short of people to turn to,"* one commented. *"My partner mentor is brilliant and is really interested in my progress."* Trainees themselves have mid-seat *"quick chat with your supervisor"* reviews and more rigorous end-of-seat appraisals. For the latter, they complete an online self-assessment which is then paired with feedback from those they've worked with. *"Supervisors are also pretty good at giving you feedback on the hoof,"* we heard.

Sing when you're winning

So who gets in here? Naturally a firm that reaches all around the world is never going to have just one 'type', but our sources were able to single out a few key qualities they think NRF values. *"There's a noticeable focus on quality, detail and care here,"* said one source. *"People get impatient if you turn in work with spelling mistakes, for example. So an eye for detail is important."* Another interviewee added: *"They like trainees with international interests and backgrounds."* Indeed, at the time of our calls the trainee group contained quite a few individuals who hailed from foreign climes or had studied abroad, and we were pleased to see a very healthy smattering of non-English names on the list. Legal work experience is common too.

We mentioned the firm's reputation for having a relatively friendly atmosphere earlier, so here's some more of the gushing positive feedback we got from our interviewees this year. *"There's real camaraderie across the firm,"* one source said. *"It doesn't matter whether you're a lawyer, a secretary, a paralegal or one of the repro guys – we all connect really well."* Another added: *"It's genuinely a lovely place to work with a palpable team spirit. And people laugh a lot here."*

We're sure that laughs broke into big gleeful smiles when the firm's choir trounced the bankers at BNP Paribas to win Office Choir of the Year for the second time running as part of the 2014 Music in Offices Awards. *"People here feel a real affinity with the firm, so they're always getting involved in social events."* The firm's More London office even has a music room that offers panoramic views of the Thames and City Hall, and trainees told us they occasionally catch sight of sandy-haired London mayor Boris Johnson on his bike from there.

And finally...

The qualification process was described as *"trainee-friendly."* Hopefuls list three departments they'd like to qualify into in order of preference, and the firm tries to match them up accordingly. In 2014 NRF kept on 41 of its 48 qualifiers.

Olswang

The facts

Location: London, Reading
Number of UK partners/solicitors: 81/146
Partners who trained at firm: 6%
Total number of trainees: 25
Seats: 4x6 months
Alternative seats: overseas seats, secondments
Extras: pro bono – RCJ CAB, various charities; language classes

On chambersstudent.co.uk...

How to get into Olswang
Why Malaysia?
CSR at the firm
A rough guide to Reading

This Londoner's sterling media practice is just one part of its well-rounded offering.

So you're full-service, right?

When Olswang sprang into life in the early 80s, its formative years were defined by a media-centric practice. The firm remains a market leader in this field, earning a top-band national ranking from *Chambers UK*, but graduate recruitment and development specialist Katharine Banbury stresses the current mantra is *"full-service, full-service, full-service."* It might surprise some that a firm with bustling banking, corporate, tax and real estate factions feels the need to shout about its capabilities from the rooftops, but this doesn't spring from nowhere. *"Some applicants haven't caught up with the changes and still pitch their cover letters to the media firm that Olswang used to be in the 90s,"* says Banbury. *"We retain that core strength advising the creative industries, but can also offer exposure to the other sectors, such as technology and telecoms."*

At least she can take comfort in the knowledge the current mob of trainees are well indoctrinated on this point. *"We may have been built on media, but we do the full range of mainstream work,"* our interviewees were keen to point out. Olswang favours a sector-based approach, drawing clients from the banking, leisure, life sciences, media, real estate, retail, technology and telecoms industries. The firm earns over 30 nods from *Chambers UK*, in areas as varied as capital markets, defamation, patent litigation and private equity, and counts Microsoft, ITV and BBC Worldwide among its clients.

Family ties and Russian lies

Trainees at Olswang are given a list of all the available seats before starting, and for the first rotation rank their top three choices. *"You also mark down a priority seat*

that you definitely want at some point during your training contract." As each changeover approaches, trainees get to re-enter preferences and then attend a meeting with HR to discuss them. *"They try to take into account the direction you want to take, but business demand pretty much annihilates personal choice."* Still, *"I don't think anyone feels shafted. There are never any promises of seats that don't come to fruition."* A stint in corporate is required, as is six months in a contentious seat, though our sources mentioned exceptions to both: trainees in years past have completed a three-month external course to get around the contentious requirement, and we also heard that *"in some exceptional cases people have done finance or tax in lieu of a corporate seat."* In any case, MCT (media, communications and technology), IP and real estate consistently prove *"hot tickets."*

There were three recruits based in Reading at the time of our calls. Seats here span the real estate, employment and commercial departments, and trainees can also swing by the capital for up to two rotations. *"If you express the preference, they will try to make it happen."*

The odd trainee may be lucky enough to venture to either the Brussels or Paris office, but these overseas seats are not available at every rotation. Client secondments, however, are more common and, according to our sources, *"more highly valued because they tend to be with exciting big-name companies."* Indeed, trainees in recent years

Seat options: corporate; finance; tax; media, communications and technology; commercial litigation; real estate; real estate litigation; construction; IP; employment

Chambers UK rankings

Administrative & Public Law	Life Sciences
Banking & Finance	Litigation
Capital Markets	Media & Entertainment
Construction	Outsourcing
Corporate/M&A	Private Equity
Data Protection	Real Estate
Defamation/Reputation Management	Real Estate Finance
	Real Estate Litigation
Employment	Restructuring/Insolvency
Hotels & Leisure	Retail
Information Technology	Sports Law
Intellectual Property	Tax
Licensing	Telecommunications

have worked in-house for the likes of MTV, ITV and the BBC.

Olswang's corporate group advises on mid-market transactions for an *"increasingly international"* spectrum of clients. Lawyers recently advised NYC-headquartered Warner Music on its £487m acquisition of Parlophone Label from Universal, and assisted the shareholders of Alexander Mann on the talent acquisition company's £260m sale to a US private equity house. *"Who you sit with plays a big role in the work you end up doing."* Some of our sources had delved into MBOs for private equity houses, others were involved in IPOs for tech start-ups, and others still dealt with retail and leisure acquisitions. Sources agreed *"the work at hand is high-calibre stuff,"* though the degree to which they'd been able to be engaged fluctuated. *"My personal responsibility was next to none,"* sighed one, telling us: *"My six months with the team was largely a paper-pushing exercise."* Meanwhile, another commented: *"I had a huge amount of client contact – the partners were happy for me to have meetings on my own, which I didn't expect. On one deal I liaised with a whole family who'd set up a company."*

Olswang's commercial litigation capabilities span disputes across the banking, pharmaceuticals, construction, manufacturing and energy sectors. The team recently investigated potential breaches of confidence on behalf of ENRC after highly sensitive information was leaked to the media about the natural resources company. There have also been several *"Russian cases"* in the docket of late, including the firm's successful defence of former police officer Pavel Karpov following allegations of torture, murder and fraud made against him during an international publicity campaign waged in the wake of Sergei Magnitsky's death. Such matters require *"a fair amount of printing, making bundles and taking stuff along to court, but equally you can liaise with counsel, research case strategies and draft witness statements."*

The firm's top-ranked defamation/reputation management team also falls under the commercial lit umbrella. Much of the work here revolves around media injunctions in which high net worth individuals try to prevent stories being published or get retractions for ones already in the media landscape – for example, Olswang is currently advising football agent Kia Joorabchian in relation to an article published in the *Daily Mail* concerning the less-than-transparent transfers of Carlos Tevez and Javier Mascherano to West Ham United in 2006.

A stint with the IP team is highly sought after, but with only one or two seats available here, you'll have to accept it might not happen for you. In fact, none of our sources had been privileged with the opportunity. However, with clients like Sky, Vodafone and Stella McCartney, it's no surprise that it's hot property. The group, one of the largest in London, works on both the patent and trade mark sides, and is big in the technology, media, life sciences, luxury brands, sport and leisure industries in particular. A recent case saw lawyers defend ZTE against claims of patent infringement in one of the longest trials heard in the specialist Patents Court in 2014.

The real (estate) deal

Most of our sources had passed through the real estate department, which primarily handles commercial property transactions for big institutional investors. Every one waxed lyrical about their time here. *"I can't speak highly enough about the team,"* said one, telling us *"it's the seat where you manage the most files and get the most responsibility. By the end I had about 40 different matters I was running by myself with minimal supervision. That was daunting, but it was a good chance to prove myself."* Another added: *"The atmosphere is fantastic, all the partners are approachable, the training is great and the hours are decent. I absolutely loved it."*

Olswang's media practice is widely recognised as one of the best in the business. Given its glittering swathe of clients from the TV, film, music, theatre, newspaper, advertising and publishing industries – think MGM, Miramax, Bloomsbury and Warner Bros. – it's easy to see why trainees year after year clamour to sit with the team. *"It's a good seat as you can a do a bit of everything. I was involved with a lot of data protection and privacy matters, website terms and conditions, and general financing agreements."* Others reported working on commercial agreements and celebrity endorsements, plus outsourcing matters for telecoms companies. *"There's quite a broad range of tech and telecoms work. Microsoft is a key client and is always bringing stuff in."* Indeed, the tech giant has called upon Olswang for advice on over 500 matters this past year alone. Trainees with experience on this side of the practice told us *"there's scope to get really involved. Initially you're given a lot of research so you can build up sector knowledge, but once you prove yourself capable* you might find yourself negotiating with clients and drafting extensive sections of contracts."

A few sources had been able to dip their toes into the world of film and TV. Olswang recently assisted ITV with the production and financing of animated television series *Thunderbirds Are Go!*, and advised BT on commercial agreements regarding its upcoming launch of two sports channels. Don't expect six months of relentless excitement, though. *"This type of work is very specialist, so it can actually be quite hard to get too involved as a trainee,"* remarked one of their time with the film team. *"There's a lot of corporate support like due diligence, though I did get to help out with a couple of film production agreements and film financing matters."*

Domestic tiffs and Euro trips

When it came to discussing working culture, our sources praised Olswang for being *"unencumbered by bureaucracy"* and told us *"there's almost a total lack of hierarchy insofar as there has to be a hierarchy – you feel like you can approach almost anyone. We have partners who are absolute gurus on certain subjects, but you can still pop into their office to ask a question."* According to our interviewees, this sense of openness *"breeds a meritocratic environment"* wherein *"nobody automatically discounts your opinions just because you're the most junior person in the room. People here are happy to seek out the person with the most knowledge about something, be that a trainee or a senior partner."* Accordingly, *"the firm makes a big effort to explain things properly and make sure we know what we're doing. Both on-the-job training and feedback are readily available."*

Insiders described close bonds between the ranks, telling us that *"partners generally know what's going on in your life – they're often at the pub with us on a Friday night and hear all the gossip. If you have an off day because you've had a fight with your boyfriend, they're pretty understanding,"* chuckled one, while another recalled: *"I*

once made a stupid mistake on a document and thought they would throw me onto the coals, but I find as long as you're open about these things, people are happy to help out and don't just point the finger."* Of course there are always certain characters who don't jibe, *"but people really stand out here if they're unfriendly or ungrateful."*

Trainees are invited along to the annual fee earners' retreat, which sees lawyers across all offices, including international ones, come together with their fellow practice group members for team bonding and networking. The real estate group recently took a jaunt to Windsor, while the corporate team headed out to Berlin, and litigation went to Madrid. *"No one takes them that seriously,"* laughed one source. *"You'll often find the partners out with you at a grotty nightclub at one in the morning."* The firm also takes strides to make sure its most junior members are kept in the loop – in addition to weekly email updates about firm ongoings there are 'State of the Nation' addresses twice a year. *"One of the best things about Olswang is the way they keep the whole firm – from senior partners down to PAs – abreast of the general strategy and direction. It's especially helpful as a trainee because it gives you an appreciation for what the top-down concerns are."*

Naturally all this talk about strategy prompted us to ask our sources what the future holds in store for Olswang. Both Katharine Banbury and the trainees called international expansion *"a primary focus"* as the firm looks to build on the Paris, Munich and Singapore bases it launched back in 2011, and cement a position in the UK's top 20 by 2016. Asia is a particular area of interest, and we're told Indonesia and Malaysia are currently being weighed up as potential spots for new Olswang outposts.

There's no question that retention rates *"haven't been the greatest the past few years"* – indeed, only 12 of 20 qualifiers stayed on in 2013 – but things looked up in 2014, when 14 of 16 NQs were retained.

And finally...

A word of advice for applicants: *"You have to disassociate Olswang from its media reputation if you want to go far in the application process. Read up and make sure you understand what the firm's focuses are today."*

Orrick Herrington & Sutcliffe (Europe) LLP

The facts

Location: London

Number of UK partners/solicitors: 19/33

Total number of trainees: 9

Seats: 4x6 months

Alternative seats: none

Extras: pro bono with CABI and international health records

On chambersstudent.co.uk...

How to get into Orrick

Interview with training principal
  Simon Cockshutt

San Francisco native Orrick's London presence is small but intent on growing in the London market.

London frown

When Mitch Zuklie took the chairman's reins from Ralph Baxter at Orrick in 2013, he became the California-founded firm's first new head in nearly a quarter of a century. Zuklie's appointment has been marked by a drive to pursue *"global opportunities in the energy and infrastructure, finance and technology sectors,"* as he told our sister publication *Chambers Associate* in 2014. This sector focus has become increasingly apparent across the firm's 25 offices – which span the US, Europe and Asia – though a question mark hovers over London, where trainees flagged an *"unclear strategy"* and spoke of the *"mixed messages"* they've received regarding the firm's intentions. *"We keep hearing that London is a key focus of the firm, but I don't know that they're actually promoting any major growth here."* Does management have a different story? *"We have set no rigid deadlines or specific targets,"* says training principal Simon Cockshutt. Although he continues: *"We would like to expand our corporate and finance offerings, as they are good classic City-type practices."* We should also note the firm's recent lateral hires in the finance sectors, such as a new head of finance arriving from Proskauer Rose, a venture capital partner from Edwards Wildman and a restructuring partner from White & Case.

Headcount in London has remained steadily around the 50 mark for the past few years, although we should note this isn't in line with the former chairman's projected growth to 400 back in 2010. Up until Orrick's recent spate of partner hiring, it suffered several high-profile partner departures, including former London head Martin Bartlam and banking partner Elisabeth Gaunt, plus several failed merger attempts, most recently with New York-based

Pillsbury Winthrop Shaw Pittman in late 2013. These unfulfilled growth forecasts have dented the firm's training programme with deferrals and poor retention rates in recent years – only two of eight qualifiers kept a place in 2013 – but the insiders we spoke with still felt Orrick has something to offer future trainees. They flagged the firm's international scope, which lends itself to a wide range of work, and mentioned that London's small stature means responsibility levels are often high, particularly in corporate and finance seats. Interviewees also praised the high salaries and high-standard clients – a mixture of FTSE 100 companies, leading banks and emerging companies – and told us: *"People here are friendly and good to work alongside."* A must if there ever was one.

A trainee what?

The firm offers seats in four core departments – corporate, finance, real estate and litigation – but there is the possibility of doing IP, competition, employment and tax. A stint in litigation is non-negotiable, and trainees in the past have completed a tax seat, though our sources said this is difficult to get. First seats are allocated before trainees arrive, and from there *"a broad seat plan is mapped out. However, as you go along and state your preferences, this plan morphs – it's pretty flexible."*

Corporate, London's largest department, is broken down into *"classic M&A and capital markets matters"* and

Seat options: corporate; competition; IP; finance; restructuring; real estate; employment; litigation

Chambers UK rankings

Private Equity	Social Housing

"quite niche emerging companies venture capital stuff." Because the former type of work is *"very up and down,"* trainees typically concentrate on the steadier venture capital side of things. Lawyers there regularly advise start-ups and tech companies, recently assisting Mendeley, which owns a desktop and web programme for managing research papers, on a series of venture financings as well as on its sale to Anglo-Dutch publisher Reed Elsevier. *"Quite often you're the one taking a first stab at the term sheet and various other documents, and running the closing process."* For some trainees, this proved a bit too much. As one explained delicately: *"You can work with American lawyers here who aren't that familiar with the trainee role, so sometimes the expectations placed on us are perhaps a little high."* For this reason, sources agreed corporate *"can make for a bad first seat"* and is *"probably a better option further on down the line."*

Thanks to a recent partner hire from White & Case, the finance group now has a restructuring dimension in addition to its energy and projects and structured finance focuses. Most of the group's work comes from foreign offices – Londoners regularly collaborate with colleagues in Italy and New York on structured finance deals, and Moscow for banking matters. Italian and London lawyers recently teamed up to advise China Development Bank on its financing of several solar energy projects in Europe, a deal topping out at more than $100m. Finance only takes one trainee at a time (but this may increase in the future as the new partner hires bring in more work), so again responsibility is high. *"I was given tasks that usually go to senior associates."* Other trainee fare includes managing the conditions precedent process, making amendments to facility agreements and liaising with foreign lawyers. Trainees praised the variety of matters at hand, with one telling us: *"I've worked on insolvency, derivatives and general banking matters all in the same day. I don't know how many places let you do that."*

Over in litigation, there are commercial, employment, competition, real estate and financial services disputes to sample, plus arbitrations. *"It's a bit of a free-for-all, though if you're clued-up, you'll approach the partners you're interested in."* The firm counts Big Four accounting firms among its clientele, and trainees mentioned the strands of litigation attached to these clients *"can come with an awful lot of doc review – I'm talking mind-numbing, 15-hour days flicking through documents."* That said, we heard from sources who'd stretched their wings far beyond this scope, organising exhibits, drafting witness statements and letters to the other side, and attending hearings. *"If something goes to trial, you get taken along; they don't hide you away from the client or*

witnesses. It's nice to feel your comments are just as valid as the other lawyers'."

Many interviewees found real estate *"more controlled and restrictive than corporate or finance."* Said one: *"There's very little responsibility – every single thing is checked, even e-mails."* That said, those who undertook the seat as their first enjoyed the novelty of drafting leases and being *"constantly on the phone."* The department is *"quite top-heavy"* thanks to a slew of partners ferried over from the London arm of the now-defunct Coudert Brothers back in 2005. *"They brought with them some big clients, so most of the time we're keeping things ticking over rather than busying ourselves with attracting new clients."* It's therefore quite a stable, if predictable, seat, though sources did highlight *"you get to see a good spectrum, from commercial lettings to residential long leases for new developments."* Repeat clients in this area are Intu Properties and Notting Hill Housing Trust.

Upstairs, downstairs

We heard mixed reviews of Orrick's working culture. Some felt *"there's a massive divide"* between the firm's two floors, telling us *"people don't mix or talk to each other"* and lamenting that *"the office doesn't feel integrated."* Others, however, dismissed these statements as *"a bit of an exaggeration."* Our sources reached more of a consensus when contemplating integration on a broader scale: *"It feels like management doesn't know what to do with the network outside the US. The main centre is Paris, and that's where the focus is."* Given the recent run of partner departures in London – *"there are lots of empty offices at the moment"* – several insiders noted *"the office feels as if it's stagnating."* We should note that at our time of interviews, the firm hadn't announced the latest partner hires. Still, the more optimistic in the bunch rallied to Orrick's defence and revealed *"there is money being spent – we've had a new restructuring partner join, and qualifying trainees are classed as new hires too."* While we're on the topic, this 'new hire' classification prompted a handful of sources to highlight something they felt was a minus of the Orrick's qualification system: *"Even though you've been working at the firm for two years, they interview you like you're a complete stranger. The qualification decisions have to be signed off by heads of departments in the States, which makes things tough – they don't always understand the needs over here."* That said, *"they've made an effort to make the process more transparent this year – people are being much more open."* After last year's poor retention run, we're happy to report figures are up from last year's 25%, with 2 out of 5 new qualifiers staying on in 2014.

Following the kerfuffle of the 2013 qualification round, the trainee group banded together to establish a forum for discussing improvements they'd like to see made to the training contract. *"It's not like we had a list of demands,"*

The True Picture

said one, *"but there were areas to tackle, like the lack of formal training."* The resultant weekly assembly is known as 'Brainy Thursdays'. *"Trainees get to raise any issues they're having, and then the associates and partners deliver presentations on various topics – we've had lots of interest in it firm-wide."* Trainees have also set about trying to alter the appraisal process so that supervisors get to sit in on appraisals, and bolstering the social scene. *"We make sure monthly drinks actually take place once a month, not once every six months."* So far, though, the revival hasn't proved an overwhelming success: *"They put loads of beer and wine upstairs, but only a fraction of people turn up."* Fortunately, *"there's a healthy culture of popping out for drinks – it's just not very organised."*

And finally...

The next few years will be crucial for Orrick London. This is not the first American firm to have teething problems with its training programme, and it appears that many of the issues – from the lack of training to social budgets to qualification decisions – stem from London's lack of autonomy in the broader network.

Osborne Clarke

The facts

Location: London, Reading, Bristol
Number of UK partners/solicitors: 100/263
Partners who trained at firm: 8%
Total number of trainees: 37
Seats: 4x6 months
Alternative seats: secondments

On chambersstudent.co.uk...

How to get into OC
Sweet Valley High(-tech industries)

It might have been born in the 18th century, but Osborne Clarke is embracing the digital age, with technology and energy among its sector specialisms.

Top cat

Look closely at the Osborne Clarke logo and you'll notice a cat – a pretty slinky-looking predator at that. The feline in question is a fitting symbol for OC, which has been prowling the market and staking out new territory as it ascends the ladder of law firm success. The Bristol native turned London-headquartered firm set up shop in Brussels, Paris, New York and San Francisco in 2013, then opened its doors for business in Amsterdam in 2014. These new hubs join a further nine in Europe, plus another Stateside branch (Palo Alto) and the firm's third UK office, Reading. As OC's network has blossomed, so too has its revenue – in 2013/14, turnover sprang up by more than 25% to reach £142m. It'll always remain a Bristolian beast at heart, but the OC of today is a confident cosmopolitan cat with cash to spare: in summer 2014 all UK staff members received a 2% bonus.

It's not just OC's quadrupedal mascot that sets it apart from the rest of the pack. The firm favours a sector-based approach covering eight main industries: digital business; energy and utilities; real estate and infrastructure; financial services; life sciences and healthcare; retail, transport and automotive; and recruitment. Back in 2001, OC set up its Palo Alto branch to help US tech companies branch into Europe, and while Thames Valley might not hold the same superficial glamour of Silicon Valley, the Reading office plays a similar role in the UK, catering for major players along the tech-heavy M4 corridor. Many of our trainee sources told us they were drawn in by the firm's modish, *"future-focused"* clientele – Google, Netflix, Facebook, to name a few – while its high-flying customers on the IP side piqued the interest of others (here we're talking EE, Virgin Media, Marks & Spencer and Selfridges). Over on the corporate end – which commands premier *Chambers UK* rankings both in and out of London – lawyers recently acted on the AIM flotation of cake purveyors Patisserie Valerie and assisted Carphone Warehouse with its £3.6bn merger with Dixons; meanwhile across the pond the firm's bagged a spot on Apple's $3bn (£1.8bn) acquisition of Dr Dre's headphone and music company, Beats.

With clients like these, a dated website would really let the side down. Never fear, for OC's online offering is blooming with colourful, stylish graphics, plus the suggestion that it's *"the world's least stuffy law firm."* Are there beanbags and retro trainers in abundance here? Well no, but trainees did tell us the open-plan design of all three UK locations means there's *"not much visible hierarchy. The partners sit among everyone else, so there's no problem going up to talk to anyone."* More on the OC culture later.

M4 Corridor of Power

At the time of our calls, there were 15 trainees in Bristol, 14 in London and three in Reading. Across all three, seats in corporate, litigation and real estate (or tax in Bristol) are compulsory. That said, *"there's a level of flexibility,"* we're told. *"Sometimes people do banking instead of corporate, depending on the business need at the time, and*

Seat options: tax; incentives; pensions; employment; competition; corporate; private equity; financial institutions; commercial litigation; property litigation; restructuring and insolvency; banking; real estate; planning; projects; commercial; IP litigation (London only)

The True Picture

Chambers UK rankings

Banking & Finance	Litigation
Banking Litigation	Media & Entertainment
Capital Markets	Outsourcing
Charities	Pensions
Construction	Pensions Litigation
Corporate/M&A	Planning
Data Protection	Private Client
Employee Share Schemes & Incentives	Public Procurement
	Real Estate
Employment	Real Estate Litigation
Environment	Restructuring/Insolvency
Financial Services	Retail
Information Technology	Tax
Intellectual Property	Telecommunications
Investment Funds	Transport

within corporate there's lots of variation – M&A, financial services, public companies." Several client secondments are also available. Overall our sources were happy with the way seat allocation is handled, telling us that *"HR is very willing to listen and take your preferences into account."* Over in London *"we chat openly among ourselves about where we want to go so we can foresee any problems."* Meanwhile those in Reading mentioned that with only two non-compulsory of options to choose from, *"you pretty much know at the outset what's going to happen. It's prescriptive, but at least there are no arguments over who goes where."*

Before plunging into a seat, trainees gather in Bristol or London for a day of introductory training. *"It's useful to get a heads-up about what certain seats might involve and to meet trainees from the other offices."*

OC's corporate department takes in work from all the firm's main sectors. On the tech side it recently advised Carphone Warehouse on its £500m acquisition and reverse takeover of American electronics company Best Buy, while lawyers on the energy end advised Foresight Group on its £44m venture capital funding and acquisition of the Wymeswold Solar project, the largest solar farm in the UK. An interviewee who'd spent much of their seat assisting with private equity work described their time with the team thusly: *"I prepared a lot of ancillary documents for various private equity deals. I also produced due diligence reports, reviewed statutory books and made sure all the documents – about 200 of them! – were organised for signing in the run up to completion. People fly in from abroad for these signing days, so that's very important. Post-completion, I bibled these documents and drafted one stating which parties still had obligations to be fulfilled before a certain date."* M&A work also sees trainees get a grip on ancillaries. *"I drafted a lot of board minutes and shareholder resolutions, plus*

transfers of interest, deeds of variation, and short sales and purchase agreements." Other trainee fare generally includes assisting with filings at Companies House and attending client meetings.

Interviewees spoke enthusiastically of their time in the banking group, which earns top *Chambers UK* rankings in the South West and Thames Valley. *"I was involved in a number of credit facility refinancings of large to medium companies,"* said one, explaining that *"that meant managing the conditions precedent process – ie, keeping track of lots of different documents and making sure they were all in place."* Another told us: *"The banking partners have been very good and really pushed me with complex documents. For instance, I recently drafted a facility agreement, which is the main document in a banking deal. This one was about 30 pages long. They're also happy for me to try a first draft of all the securities documents."*

Out in the open

The firm's real estate group is split between residential and commercial work. The former includes projects for major house builders like Barratt, Linden Homes and Persimmon, while on the commercial end OC looks after property portfolios for investment and pension funds. The firm also works with major retail clients like Marks & Spencer and gets involved with regeneration projects and student accommodation developments such as Campus Living Village's £37m acquisition of three student blocks in Bournemouth. For trainees, tasks include drafting leases, underleases and contracts, and most of our sources reported running small discrete matters independently too, *"like an underlease for a charity. I checked my work with the partner every day, but she gave me the first go at everything."* On big residential projects, trainees *"draft transfer forms and take notes in meetings"* when they're not going on site visits and tackling admin, *"like helping out with stamp duty and making sure returns are paid within the deadline."* According to one cheery interviewee, *"everyone talks about stamp duty as this horrendous task, but it really isn't that bad. During the property seat I also got to colour in plans, which was excellent – I saved it until the end of the day, when I was tired."*

All three UK offices have a commercial litigation department, and trainees in Bristol and London can also sample property and IP litigation to fulfil their contentious requirement. Between its departments, OC deals with all manner of disputes, including international arbitrations. The Bristol team recently acted for several Icelandic financial institutions in a claim against French banking group Société Générale, and represented npower in a multimillion-pound dispute with National Grid regarding metering services. OC also acted for the executor of Jimmy Savile's estate, NatWest, in a dispute over a compensation scheme for the TV presenter's sexual abuse victims. Other hefty litigation clients of late include Dell, HP, Yahoo! and EE.

Typical trainee tasks in litigation include carrying out research, going to court to drop off documents, helping draft opinions and letters to the other side, preparing bundles and managing transcripts. That's not all; a Reading trainee reported *"running a couple of small matters like debt claims myself, acting as the first point of contact,"* while a London source told of getting *"involved in a big case going to the High Court – I went to court every day, met the clients and went to chambers to meet the barristers."* Meanwhile a source who'd spent time in property litigation said much of their time was taken up with *"adjudication, which is a fast-paced dispute resolution system specific to the construction industry. I did a lot of liaising and made sure deadlines were met for documents."*

Across all the offices, interviewees told us they felt *"very well supported"* by supervisors and other solicitors. *"There's a good balance. You're never mollycoddled; you're challenged and have to think for yourself, but equally you know there are people to turn to for help. Working open-plan means it's very easy to ask questions at an appropriate moment."* Trainees also praised this set-up for *"allowing you to observe how others operate, which is a great learning process."* When it comes to responsibility levels, one source summed up the general feeling with the following: *"Obviously it's not all glamorous and great, but if you show you're capable, they'll give you as much as you can handle."* One trainee particularly appreciated being *"named on a team sheet. It's good to know you're not just there to fill in forms and make tea all the time."*

Get unstuffed

It's not uncommon for trainees to find themselves *"bundling for an injunction in the middle of the night"* at some point, though we did hear *"the longest hours tend to be in transactional seats,"* where *"the up and down can keep you here until 2am sometimes."* Fortunately average

schedules ranged between 9am and 7pm for our interviewees. *"If you've finished your work, there's no problem leaving at 5.30pm. And if you do end up staying late, at least senior lawyers make the effort to stay with you; it's not as if a whole load of work is dumped on you alone. Teamwork is part of the ethos here."*

On the subject of firm ethos, we quizzed insiders about the firm's aforementioned self-proclaimed lack of stuffiness. *"They really are as friendly as they say they are!"* exclaimed one, a sentiment echoed by – honestly – all our interviewees. *"I was amazed by how approachable and enthusiastic people were about the work and OC itself,"* said one. *"It first struck me during the vac scheme when a senior partner walked up to me and asked me if I wanted a cup of tea. At first I was taken aback and confused as to whether I should say yes, because I was thinking 'shouldn't I be making him a cup of tea?'"* Of course, that's not to say there's lively chatter and non-hierarchical horseplay all day long. *"It's not a party atmosphere – people work very diligently; it's just that it's easy to get to know people alongside that. The partners here are the kind of people who strike up conversation with you in the lift."*

Trainees firm-wide have a budget for social dos, though Thames Valley folk mentioned *"Bristol and London have bigger social scenes simply because there's more of them."* A Bristolian rattled off some recent trainee events: *"Ice-skating, Laser Quest, cider-tasting, and a cocktail and magic masterclass for vac schemers."* In London, *"we do things every three months like drinks or a meal."* The big firm-wide event of the year *"is a massive fancy dress do – everyone goes all out."* The theme for 2014 was 'What I Want To Be When I Grow Up'. In case you were wondering, *"nobody was dressed as a lawyer."* We don't believe it.

When it comes to retention, our interviewees were pretty confident about their chances of staying on. In the end five out of Bristol's seven qualifiers got jobs, while in Reading one out of one stayed on, as did six out of seven in London.

And finally...
Trainees felt the future of the firm looks bright. *"It's an exciting time – OC is growing and getting more and more cutting-edge work."*

Paul Hastings (Europe) LLP

The facts

Location: London

Number of UK partners/solicitors: 19/31

Total number of trainees: 8

Seats: 4x6 months

Alternative seats: secondments

Extras: pro bono - TrustLaw

On chambersstudent.co.uk...

How to get into Paul Hastings
Commercial mortgage-backed securities

This LA-headquartered big shot is on the rise in London Town. It'll suit those looking for an intense training contract with a real estate/finance bent.

Hard to the core

On its US home turf, Paul Hastings is especially known for the scope and prestige of its work in five core areas: corporate, litigation, employment, real estate and tax. The firm has a network of ten offices across the US, but has had its mind set on the wider world for quite some time now: it first targeted the Asia-Pacific region during the 1970s, and now has ten offices outside the States.

The London branch joined PH's emerging network in the late-1990s, and has slowly but surely gathered steam. *Chambers UK* gives a nod to its real estate finance and capital markets work, and both of these practices have been steadily rising up the rankings in recent years. Revenue is headed north too: it jumped by an impressive 24% in 2013 to $42m. Recent lateral hires have contributed to this bump: the firm recently gained a real estate team from legacy SJ Berwin, a capital markets partner from Weil, a structured finance specialist from Clifford Chance, and a financial regulatory partner from Hogan Lovells.

Given the firm's small size in London, the trainee experience is *"more hardcore than at magic or silver circle firms: there are only seven trainees in the office, so we're a shared resource and it's easy to get pulled in lots of different directions, even if you're assigned to one department. That does mean you get more responsibilities, but it won't suit everyone."* Trainees are expected to gain experience in at least one of the departments which has a real estate component to its work, whether that's capital markets, real estate finance or corporate real estate. Sources also observed that *"litigation is not a massive team, so you're quite lucky if you get to do a seat there."*

Keeping it real

The real estate team which arrived from legacy SJ Berwin brought with it a raft of new clients, including Schroders, Hilton, Allianz Real Estate and Hyatt. As a real estate finance trainee, it's possible to collaborate with PH's capital markets lawyers to get a feel for the world of commercial mortgage-backed securities (CMBS). For example, PH's London lawyers recently represented Capita Asset Services as the servicer of a €1.99bn loan, which was secured with German residential properties. As is expected in transactional areas, trainees should expect peaks and troughs in workload. The sources we spoke to said: *"There's been a lull in CMBS recently,"* (this area was hit hard by the financial crisis) so typical trainee tasks weren't always deal-focused. One source reported: *"We do more standard stuff like proof-reading contracts – but fortunately that means there's not a great deal of bibling to do."* Every cloud, every cloud.

Trainees can also cut their teeth on *"more traditional real estate finance work,"* like the refinancing of London's Heron Tower (now the Salesforce Tower) which involved acting for J.P. Morgan on a £210m repurchase transaction with private investment firm Starwood Capital. This strand of work offers trainees more responsibility, like *"having a first crack at drafting standstill agreements*

Seat options: real estate (property and corporate transactional); corporate M&A and private equity; real estate finance; structured products and funds; corporate restructuring; payment systems and financial services; litigation; and capital markets and securitisations

Chambers UK rankings

Capital Markets	Real Estate Finance

and amending deeds of release and novation agreements." There's also the chance to draft regulatory information notices, which get sent out to the stock market. *"You collate all recent examples of defaults and enforcements on existing loans, interpret what is relevant, condense it down and work out who it needs to be sent to,"* one trainee explained.

The corporate real estate seat is *"like an M&A seat with a real estate flavour."* The work mostly involves private acquisitions, and the team often works with the hotels and hospitality sector: for example, it represented Starwood Capital on the acquisition of 30 hotels from De Vere Venues for over £200m. Responsibility levels were deemed good, with one source stating: *"I dealt with clients directly, and after a while didn't need to ask my supervisor if I could send correspondence out."* Trainees also draft short-form share purchase agreements, as well as disclosure letters, escrow agreements and stock transfer forms. (If all this jargon is starting to make your head spin, check out our online bonus feature which explains things in layman's terms.)

The focus in the general corporate team is very much on cross-border, high-value deals: lawyers here facilitated the European elements of the largest-ever acquisition of a US company by a Chinese buyer, when meat processing company Shuanghui snapped up Smithfield Foods – the US's largest pork producer and processor – for a tidy $7.1bn. What trainees do depends on the stage of the deal: at the start sources were buried deep in due diligence, but were *"grateful to have the opportunity to draft the due diligence report as well."* Towards the end of the deal, trainees are responsible for *"dealing with post-closing duties, like filing Companies House forms, and noting director changes – things you're already familiar with from the LPC."*

In 2013/14 PH's restructuring and insolvency department advised on the restructuring of French water company Saur, Toys R Us, and the government of Belize's private sector international debt. Sources here had worked on a mixture of restructuring and leveraged finance deals, running CP checklists (*"which involves liaising with the client so that they understand what's required of them"*) and drafting *"hefty documents"* like restructuring agreements, security documentation and share charges.

Flat-out buzzy

The weight of the Paul Hastings Tower in LA (yes, the firm has a skyscraper named after it) is *"not that overbearing – you only really notice the American side of the firm when you receive cross-border work which has originated in the US."* Instead, *"you're more aware of PH's international dimensions: we have many Italian lawyers in the office* [there's a dedicated Italian practice]*, and I've had a lot of communication with German lawyers."* One interviewee told us that *"as a trainee you're utilised for various strands of the cross-border work. For example, we proof-read client alerts written in English but produced in foreign jurisdictions."*

For trainees, a good day in the office equates to an 8pm finish, and sources warned of *"unpredictable"* hours: *"You can be expected to stay late at short notice and cancel your plans, so during one of my seats I just didn't make any!"* On the flip side, if things are quiet then *"you are encouraged to take advantage of that, and just get up and go."* We mentioned above that the small size of the office means trainees get called upon to do work for different departments, which, said one trainee, *"is good in some ways, as it broadens your exposure, but it does impact on your hours too."*

Trainees get to let off steam via an array of social events. American-themed shindigs include a Fourth of July picnic and Thanksgiving dinner, while office-wide trips have seen thrill-seeking lawyers let loose at Thorpe Park. There's also a budget which allows trainees to organise three or four socials a year (future joiners are also invited). Recent excursions have included bowling nights, laser tag days, cookery lessons and wine and cheese tastings. When our interviewees first applied to PH *"there were plans to make London one of the largest offices, but that still hasn't happened because of the impact of the economic crisis."* However, the spate of recent laterals and the 24% revenue hike has certainly had a rejuvenating effect: *"There's a renewed buzz, and everyone's flat-out busy."* Sources were also impressed by the attention paid to London by those at the very top, and told us that *"the chairman came over in March to have a meal with us – both he and our office managing partner spoke candidly about London's future, and were also willing to speak to trainees individually away from everyone else."* Of course, it takes some guts to speak head-on with the chairman of a $1bn global operation, and while sources felt that they weren't massive extroverts, they did mention that *"you do have to be fairly outgoing and ambitious in order to thrive at PH."*

And finally...
Paul Hastings kept on both of its 2013 qualifiers and retained all two out of three in 2014.

Peters & Peters Solicitors LLP

The facts

Location: London

Number of UK partners/solicitors: 8/21

Partners who trained at the firm: 75%

Total number of trainees: 5

Seats: 1x9 month, 1x6 month; 1x3 month secondment

Alternative seats: secondments

Extras: RCJ Advice Bureau

On chambersstudent.co.uk...

How to get into Peters & Peters
The civil side of Bernie Ecclestone

This litigation boutique offers a select few trainees the chance to participate in high-end business crime, fraud and civil cases.

Let's be civil about this

You're a Russian oligarch on English shores. You've got a townhouse in Moscow-on-Thames. You've got assets, an art collection and a Harrods store card. But then Mother Russia stirs and demands your return. What are you to do? You'd probably turn to the sage solicitors at Peters & Peters. When it comes to fighting extradition requests from the Russian Federation, this firm is top dog – and it has the *Chambers UK* recognition to prove it. Of late, solicitors successfully defended Russian entrepreneur Georgy Trefilov against extradition; and the department also worked on behalf of Bill Browder, the embattled CEO of Hermitage Capital (formerly the largest foreign investor in Russia), to persuade Interpol to reject the request for a red notice (the international equivalent of a 'Wanted' poster) that Russia tried to place against him.

But extradition is only a tiny proportion of the work which Peters & Peters does. The firm is also renowned for its fraud, business crime and commercial litigation practices. Recently it acted for Charles Saatchi on the well-publicised fraud case against his former assistants, the Grillo sisters, handling both the criminal and civil side of proceedings. But what, you may ask yourself, is the difference between criminal and civil fraud? To save you further head-scratching or misguided Googling here's Peters & Peters' training partner David McCluskey to explain: *"You have to separate the facts from the law that may be applicable to them,"* he says. *"One and the same act can be both a civil and criminal offence. If the claimant in a case chooses to take civil action to recover their alleged losses, that wouldn't preclude criminal investigations. With a civil case, by and large, the claimant is in charge. They have to pay the costs, but they have a great-er degree of control over how things are run than they would in a publicly funded criminal fraud prosecution."*

Two-seater

If you envisage your future self as a corporate ball-buster thrashing out mammoth deals, then this firm probably won't fit your brief. *"I knew I wanted to do contentious law, and that's the experience Peters & Peters provides,"* trainees told us. So, a love of litigation is paramount. Usually two trainees are taken on each year and their training contract is made up of just two seats – generally, a year is spent in business crime, nine months in civil fraud and commercial litigation, and the remaining three months on a secondment *"somewhere where you can gain non-contentious experience to satisfy SRA requirements."* Although the duration of each seat is *"somewhat flexible,"* sources appreciated the opportunity to spend a long period getting immersed in the work of the firm's two departments.

As well as extradition work, the business crime department covers areas such as corporate criminal fraud, money laundering, bribery, corruption, cartels, competition and FCA investigations. Recently lawyers acted for a deputy editor of *The Sun* arrested as part of Operation Elveden, which is looking into inappropriate payments to the police. Peters & Peters has also been instructed by an Egyptian businessman arrested for possession of a gun and ammunition at Heathrow airport. Trainees get

Seats: business crime; civil fraud and commercial litigation

Chambers UK rankings

Corporate Crime & Investigations	Fraud
Crime	Litigation
Financial Services	Tax

involved in *"anything from huge matters brought by well-known clients to quite small criminal cases. You tend to do work for everyone; it's not just fed to you by your supervisor. It's a cliché, but no two days are the same: you might be down at the police station, clerking at a trial or in the office doing research."* Our sources recalled getting to grips with *"large fraud cases and SFO investigations which might involve an international element like working with the US Department of Justice."* Trainees were pleased to report that *"there's an enormous amount of client contact. I've taken attendance notes at a lot of meetings and I've been to court frequently."* Such is the sensitive nature of some of these extradition cases that *"when we're trying to set up meetings, we sometimes have to call in the services of a security firm. It's a bit surreal sometimes, but when a client fears for their safety you have to balance that with what's appropriate in a legal sense."* Other trainee tasks include drafting witness statements and letters of instruction. Thankfully, there's *"not too much mundane filing and photocopying,"* although this is sometimes unavoidable.

Over in the commercial litigation and civil fraud seat, trainees find themselves *"putting bundles together, drafting witness statements or taking instructions from the client."* One source noted: *"I've been doing all kinds of predominately civil fraud litigation for claimants and defendants, both corporations and individuals. I've been involved in a lot of interlocutory work and freezing orders."* Big cases of late include acting for German media group Constantin Medien in a claim brought against pint-sized billionaire Formula One boss Bernie Ecclestone for conspiracy to defraud by the deliberate undervaluation of F1 in order to safeguard his own position as CEO. Another notable recent client is Coca-Cola, which turned to Peters & Peters for advice on a case of employee fraud. Not sure if civil litigation is your thing? Take note that the firm wants applicants who are interested in both its civil and criminal work, so don't think you can get in here just because you're a massive crime wonk.

Meet the oligarchs

"The hours here are very sociable – I can't complain!" exclaimed one trainee, expressing a view which was repeated by others we spoke to. The core hours are 9.30am to 5.30pm, but our interviewees averaged 8.30am to 7pm, though naturally *"on some matters you might need to stay later when required."* When it comes to the working culture at Peters & Peters, sources believed that *"it has elements of a City firm and elements of a small firm – because of our small size everyone knows everybody's name and people are friendly and collaborative. But this is a high-end firm so everything is quite partner-led, although it doesn't feel that hierarchical. It's more relaxed than a big City firm, but saying that it's still a law firm – and the dress code is 'smart'."* The small trainee cohort means that *"there isn't the same opportunity to socialise with your fellow trainees as there is at a larger firm. We all get along, but if we're out of the office at court or meetings then we can go for weeks without seeing one another."* More broadly, sources told us, *"there are lots of things going on socially, like CSR activities, a film club and a ski trip. Plus the firm organises socials with various chambers."*

Of the five trainees with Peters & Peters at the time of our calls, three had previously worked with the firm as paralegals or legal researchers while the other two had entered via the traditional TC route. Given the firm's international expertise *"a lot of trainees speak a second language,"* but this isn't essential. *"The firm is highly specialised so you have to be able to explain clearly why you want to work here,"* insiders told us. *"They won't take people who've just tacked their application onto the end of a stream of applications to City firms."* We also asked head of HR Sue Bachorski what the firm is looking for. *"This is a pure litigation firm, so interpersonal skills are crucial,"* she told us. *"We're looking for a fine balance – not for someone who's too outspoken, but someone who has quiet confidence and good interpersonal skills. Then partners can be confident taking that trainee into a meeting with, for example, a Russian oligarch."*

None of our interviewees seemed particularly worried about their chances of staying on at Peters & Peters. *"The retention rates are very good here,"* asserted one. *"Everyone is presuming there'll be a job for them at the end of their training contract."* And indeed, both qualifiers were kept on in 2014.

And finally...
Peters & Peters' *"rigorous"* application process is quite like that of many barristers' chambers, including as it does an essay paper and a panel interview on a legal problem question. Visit our website to find out more.

Pinsent Masons

The facts

Location: London, Birmingham, Manchester, Leeds, Scotland
Number of UK partners/solicitors: 314/1229
Total number of trainees: 150
Seats: 4x6 months
Alternative seats: overseas seats, secondments
Extras: pro bono – Amicus, A4ID

On chambersstudent...

How to get into Pinsent Masons
The new Middle East training contract
Diversity initiatives

This full-service firm is ramping up its international presence, while its robust network of UK offices remains a hit back home.

2+2 = 5?

The laws of arithmetic seem to have met their match after Pinsent Masons' 2012 merger with Scottish firm McGrigors. *"Two and two made five, really,"* chuckled HR and learning director Jonathan Bond. Come again? *"If you compare the turnover of our firm now to the combined figures of the two legacy firms there's been a marked increase,"* Bond explained. Revenue reached £323m in 2013, which compares very favourably to the £294m which the two firms were worth together in 2011/12. And all those millions don't come from nowhere: PM has over 1,500 lawyers in 21 offices across the UK, Europe, the Middle East and Asia.

Pinsent Masons' long-term goal is *"to become an increasingly international firm,"* says Jonathan Bond. Lately, PM has cut the ribbon on three new European offices in Paris (2012), Munich (2012) and Istanbul (2013). The Asia-Pacific and Gulf regions will be a focus in the coming years though. A new Middle East-focused training contract is a case in point: starting in 2014 the firm is offering four traineeships which allow new recruits to rotate between the offices in Dubai, Doha and London, resulting in an English law qualification and an NQ job in the UAE or Qatar. For more on this new programme, read our online bonus feature.

Back home, Pinsent Masons has strong offices in each of England's four largest cities: London, Birmingham, Manchester and Leeds. All four offer training contracts and receive a strong suit of *Chambers UK* rankings for areas as diverse as capital markets, healthcare, planning, intellectual property, corporate, energy and pensions. But the cherry on Pinsent's cake is its formidable construc-

tion practice, which wins a host of top-tier *Chambers UK* rankings and is recognised as the very best in the UK for supplier-side work.

At the time of our research, 57 trainees were based in London (the head office), 20 were in Birmingham, 18 in Leeds and 15 in Manchester. Large teams like property and corporate can be found in most offices, while teams like competition can only be found in Birmingham and London. But trainees can move between offices if there's a particular seat they have an eye on. It probably helps that there's an awful lot of interoffice collaboration anyway. *"I often have colleagues in Manchester and Leeds calling me and asking if I have capacity to help them,"* a London-based interviewee reported.

Trainees are given a list of all available seats and secondments two months before each rotation, and state their top three preferences to HR. The current overseas seat options are Dubai and the Falkland Islands (a McGrigors legacy), while trainees have also recently spent time with clients BP, RBS, Balfour Beatty and Manchester City FC. *"HR really makes an effort when they sit down with you to talk about what seat you want to do next,"* said a Mancunian source, while a London trainee added: *"I have no*

Seat options: banking; construction advisory and disputes; commercial; corporate; employment; energy & finance; EU competition; financial regulation; insurance; IP; litigation & regulatory; pensions; planning and environment; projects; property; property dispute resolution; tax; restructuring; technology, media and telecoms

The True Picture

Chambers UK rankings

Administrative & Public Law	Litigation
Banking & Finance	Local Government
Banking Litigation	Media & Entertainment
Capital Markets	Outsourcing
Competition/European Law	Parliamentary & Public Affairs
Construction	Partnership
Corporate Crime & Investigations	Pensions
Corporate/M&A	Pensions Litigation
Data Protection	Planning
Education	Private Client
Employee Share Schemes & Incentives	Private Equity
Employment	Product Liability
Energy & Natural Resources	Professional Negligence
Environment	Projects
Fraud	Public Procurement
Health & Safety	Real Estate
Healthcare	Real Estate Finance
Hotels & Leisure	Real Estate Litigation
Information Technology	Restructuring/Insolvency
Insurance	Retail
Intellectual Property	Shipping
Licensing	Social Housing
Life Sciences	Sports Law
	Tax
	Transport

complaints – *I didn't once get a seat that I didn't want or enjoy."*

All new trainees join up for a week of induction and PSC training in one of the offices just after they start – *"it's great because all the trainees get to know each other."* After this, individual departments hold their own training sessions at the start of each seat, *"and this is often followed by supplementary training either in person or via video link."*

Construction zone

As its name suggests, the construction advisory and disputes department chiefly does contentious work. Overall, the firm acts for 18 of the top 20 UK construction contractors, and more than half of the world's top 50, including Carillion, Kier and Balfour Beatty. London trainees told us of working on *"really big construction disputes, which means you won't get your own files,"* while those in Leeds said they often work on *"small, less technical claims, so you can see matters through from start to finish."* Leeds, Manchester and Birmingham do work on heftier matters too. Day-to-day trainee tasks include bundling, as well as drafting letters, claim forms and witness statements. While this seat occasionally gets *"so technical you have*

to consult experts,"* we heard that *"the supervisors are excellent and take the time to explain things properly."*

The projects team works across sectors like transport, waste, education, health, social housing and energy. The last of these is *"at the forefront of people's minds at the moment,"* a trainee told us, *"especially when it comes to renewable energy."* PM recently worked with five Welsh local authorities to develop a new £1.1bn energy-from-waste facility in South Wales. Key clients VINCI, Viridor and Veolia also all have an energy/waste angle to their work, and take note that the ex-McGrigors Aberdeen office is big on oil and gas. *"Because projects work is innovative, you're quite often involved in matters which are the first of their kind,"* reflected one trainee. *"That means the drafting work is much freer than on regular contractual or corporate matters."* PM has played a role in a few impressively large new infrastructure projects, like the London Array wind farm, Sellafield nuclear power station and Crossrail, and it's currently acting for a consortium of major international companies appointed by the Scottish government to build the new £900m Forth Road Bridge. One downside of spending time in this seat is that projects can take years to come to fruition, and because of their size *"can be hard to get to grips with at first."* One trainee said: *"It's a complex and technical area of law, so it can be difficult to get involved with the meaty tasks – I did a lot of admin work: proof-reading, reviewing building contracts, due diligence, putting together warranties..."* But trainees didn't see this as a bad thing. *"I like having my own distinct tasks,"* said one, *"and if something is difficult, then there's always an NQ around who will take you under their wing and answer questions."*

View from the top

Pinsent Masons' 260-lawyer property team has worked on several noteworthy projects recently including the redevelopments of Earls Court and Crystal Palace Park and the £1bn development of the Royal Albert Docks in East London. The team also advised a major US real estate investment trust on its £1.3bn bid for a property company owning 160 UK care homes; other clients include Aviva, the property arm of Legal & General and hotel group Accor. Trainees who had supported fee earners on large matters reported *"taking more of a back-seat role, typically replying to enquiries, reviewing lease reports and performing due diligence."* However, other sources recounted *"running matters with light supervision."* A trainee in Leeds said: *"These are usually property management files – I dealt with tenants directly, tackled lease renewals, amended licences, and assisted with Land Registry applications."* Because there are so many files to deal with, *"you really need good organisational skills to keep on top of things – if not, you will struggle."* Indeed, we heard that this is quite a document-heavy seat: *"The low point for me was having to go through eight boxes of documents searching for one lease!"*

The employment team works for businesses and institutions in the finance, infrastructure, energy and education sectors, and also counts well-known businesses like John Lewis, ASDA, Bupa and William Hill among its clients. On the non-contentious side, trainees help draft schedules for contracts and settlement agreements, while on the contentious side there are witness statements and skeleton arguments to prepare. *"I also ran some straightforward cases like unfair dismissals under minimal supervision,"* a trainee told us. *"I chaired a witness statement call and spent the whole day at the Employment Tribunal with a client."* A trainee who worked on a larger matter told us that *"the partner simply split the workload between us, and we spent a lot of time discussing case strategy."*

During 2013 PM's corporate department worked on 220 deals with a combined value of £11bn – a significant increase on 2012's £8.7bn total. One major matter saw PM advise German chemical company Altana on the UK aspects of its $645m purchase of the clay additives division of Rockwood Specialities. A lot of clients come from the energy, mining, manufacturing, technology and real estate sectors. And for several quarters in a row PM has recently topped the rankings for advising most AIM clients. Sources in corporate appreciated *"getting the view from the top – departments like employment and pensions derive quite a lot of their work from corporate transactions, so it's nice to see where that work originates."* A trainee's role is usually that of project manager: marshalling documents and scheduling. *"The most senior lawyers negotiate and draft the big, chunky documents,"* one source told us, *"while trainees work on the supporting documents like board minutes and disclosure letters."* But this division of work isn't to be scoffed at. *"I was challenged, and could see how my work was feeding into the bigger picture,"* said one trainee. A few late nights are to be expected, *"but only at key points in transactions."*

Overall, sources described their work/life balance as *"reasonable," "manageable,"* and *"better than expected."* A Leeds trainee said: *"Sometimes you do get called in to do things last minute, which is a bit frustrating, but I think that's just the nature of being a lawyer."* A Manchester source told us that *"being in the office from 10am*

to 4pm is compulsory, but beyond that you can be flexible with when you arrive and leave,"* while a Birmingham trainee said: *"I've never worked a super-long day – 12 hours is probably the most I've done in one sitting."* Even Londoners were positive: *"Fridays are sacred – I usually work late four days a week, but when Friday rolls around lots of people will be in the pub by six."*

Put the claws away

London was described as *"having the most 'corporate' atmosphere of all the firm's offices – it's quieter than the others and feels a bit more formal."* But most agreed that *"it's still a friendly place"* and pointed out that *"the office is a lot bigger than our other ones, so maybe that's the reason for its more formal reputation."* In the other offices *"you bump into people a lot more"* and overall trainees dubbed Pinsent Masons *"a really down-to-earth place where everyone gets stuck in together."* One source said: *"No one ever behaves in a bitchy way – if you're busy, you can always e-mail the other trainees asking for help, and they will do what they can regardless of what seat they're in."*

Socially, Pinsent Masons is *"a bit of a party firm."* A Brum-based trainee told us: *"The Christmas party is infamous – people take the fancy dress competition superseriously. This year, each floor was allocated a letter from the firm's name, so people went as Pirates, Insects, Noah's ark, Superheroes... you get the picture!"* One trainee (from the superhero floor) commented: *"I'd never spoken to my head of department before, but there I was, at Christmas, trying on lycra onesies with him."* London tends to be a tad more conventional, favouring black ties over masks and capes at its Christmas bash. But still, last year's do was circus-themed and featured acrobats and trapezes. Over the rest of the year, trainees spend their time attending events like office-wide barbecues, monthly firm drinks, Cluedo-themed mystery nights and garden parties. *"And there's always someone who'll go for a drink with you on a Friday night,"* a Londoner concluded.

The firm puts out a single jobs list for all its UK offices, and second-years can apply to and interview for up to three NQ positions. *"It's a fair and transparent process,"* said one source, and eventually 65 of 83 qualifiers were retained in 2014.

And finally...
If you fancy landing a spot at this *"ambitious firm that just keeps on growing,"* apply for its vac scheme – 70% of trainees joined via this route.

Reed Smith LLP

The facts

Location: London

Number of UK partners/solicitors: 115/207 (+ 6 non-UK-qualified)

UK partners who trained at firm: 45%

Total number of trainees: 50

Seats: 4x6 months

Alternative seats: overseas seats; secondments

Extras: pro bono – Queen Mary Legal Advice Centre, Dellow Centre, Liberty, A4ID; language classes

On chambersstudent.co.uk...

How to get into Reed Smith

Interview with training principal
   Peter Hardy

An Oo-to-Arr of shipping terminology

Reed Smith's London branch is its biggest and offers expertise across the board.

Are you an American or an American't?

Since its humble Pittsburgh beginnings in 1877, this Anglo-American firm has turned gigantic, today spanning three continents and 25 cities. Thanks to office launches in Singapore, Astana and Houston in recent years, Reed Smith now has a hefty 1,800 practitioners on board.

London is the Santa Maria of the fleet, clocking in with more than 350 lawyers. The product of a 2007 merger with London-based Richards Butler, our sources observed that there's *"not much that's American about the office,"* and indeed you'd be mistaken to lump it in with other Yankee-led institutions in the Square Mile. As training principal Peter Hardy astutely points out: *"It's easy to throw around the label 'US firm' due to our history, but we are a truly global firm and our largest office is in London. Our business has transformed in recent years and this label doesn't paint an accurate picture of the type of firm that we now are."* He goes on to note that *"if you were to ask the partners in the London office, most would say they're partners of an established City practice of a global firm."*

The London branch has a long pedigree in the shipping and media/technology sectors, both of which have scored top *Chambers UK* rankings; the other two core disciplines are financial services and energy & natural resources. Of course, we'd be remiss to suggest that the firm's reach ends here; Reed Smith is a mighty all-rounder, achieving UK-wide rankings for its work across the board, from capital markets and data protection to environment and life sciences. Hardy tells us that in recent years the cor-porate, structured finance and disputes teams have *"seen real growth,"* contributing to London's 13% increase in revenue in 2013.

First mates and cabin boys

Seat options for trainees fall into seven categories: corporate, financial industries, commercial disputes, employment, real estate, shipping, and energy and natural resources. *"For your first seat you list your preferences by these industry groups; it's only from the second seat onwards that you get to choose from a proper breakdown of all of the seats and specific supervisors,"* explained one interviewee. There are also several client secondments on offer, plus a handful of international seats, with trainees able to qualify abroad in some circumstances.

When it comes to seat allocation, fourth-seaters get priority, while first-seaters tend to end up with *"what's left over."* Our sources agreed *"you have to be incredibly lucky to get your first choice on your first seat,"* although we did hear from a few who achieved just that. Generally interviewees found it *"a fair process,"* telling us that *"HR will hear you out – if there's a problem, you can always talk to them."*

Reed Smith is one of just three firms with a top *Chambers UK* ranking for shipping. Trainees tell us that *"it's*

> **Seat options:** finance; commercial disputes; shipping; real estate; tax; corporate; media; employment; energy and natural resources

Chambers UK rankings

Asset Finance	Intellectual Property
Banking & Finance	International Arbitration
Banking Litigation	Life Sciences
Capital Markets	Litigation
Commodities	Media & Entertainment
Construction	Pensions
Corporate/M&A	Professional Negligence
Data Protection	Public International Law
Employment	Real Estate
Environment	Real Estate Finance
Fraud	Real Estate Litigation
Information Technology	Shipping
Insurance	

The True Picture

a seat you either love or hate." The majority of our interviewees had taken to the practice like a duckling to water, telling us *"it requires a massive learning curve because there's a whole newfangled list of terms to learn, but it's a really nice department."* However, there were a few in the latter camp. Said one: *"It's an old-school, traditionally academic department, and I actually found it quite intimidating – it's a whole new world of law, and you don't really come in with any prior knowledge."*

Work is divided into wet shipping *("when a ship crashes, and there's damage from a calamity")* and dry shipping (*"the day-to-day movements of vessels around the world, including things like carrying cargo"*). Wet lawyers are often *"master mariners,"* while the dry ones *"tend not to have been to sea,"* and historically their work doesn't overlap. Wet shipping entails *"a lot of investigations work, which involves looking at charts, working out tides, figuring out where the ships are and trying to find out whether a master could be telling the truth about a crash based on where the sun was at the time."* On the dry side, trainees reported advising clients on preventative measures for dangerous areas like the Gulf of Aden, *"where Somali pirates spend most of their days."* Such measures include everything from when to take armed guards on board to when it might be prudent to take an alternative route, and there are also claims to be dealt with following attacks. That said, this dark side of the practice is very much an exception to the rule; trainees made it clear they're much more likely to come across a glitzy superyacht than an ocean-going scallywag, going as far as to call dry shipping *"the glamorous side of the practice,"* what with all the arbitrations and contract disputes going on between wealthy seafarers.

Reed Smith's 2013 office launch in Houston – aka *"the energy capital of the world"* – is evidence of its efforts to beef up its energy and natural resource offerings. Peter Hardy tells us that *"the largest concentration of energy and natural resources lawyers still sits in London, but the offices work very much as a global team."* Once an offshoot of the shipping department, the group has *"grown massively"* in recent years and today advises the likes of Chevron and the European Federation of Energy Traders. The work generally errs on the non-contentious side, with matters like derivatives and emissions trading forming an increasingly large portion of the workload. We're told trainees can expect *"a lot of research, especially pertaining to new EU regulations on things like carbon emissions,"* plus a good deal of paperwork during contentious cases. *"On one construction matter an associate and I dealt with all the disclosure ourselves. It wasn't the most exciting case, but I enjoyed that responsibility."*

Corporate umbrella-ella-ella

Corporate offerings include private equity, competition, media, general corporate, and data protection. Those in general corporate told of *"drafting ancillary documents like share purchase agreements,"* and carrying out due diligence and research for IPOs and public announcements. Meanwhile, those in private equity reported assisting with negotiations, drafting closing documents and interacting with clients and counsel, *"including foreign counsel."* The department handles a good deal of energy-related work and recently represented the government of Kazakhstan in its takeover of Eurasian Natural Resources.

Media is among the firm's most popular seats and even *"one of the reasons that some people come here."* The firm has nabbed a splash of headline-grabbing matters recently, with lawyers scoring a win for pop superstar Rihanna in her claim that Topshop unlawfully distributed t-shirts bearing her image, successfully defending Channel 4 in an age discrimination case brought by the eccentric 'face of racing' John McCririck, and advising the BBC on investigations surrounding the infamous Jimmy Savile scandal. Other top clients include McDonald's, Microsoft, HMV and Samsung. Trainees in this group can expect a busy six months packed with client contact, though rest assured *"you'll only be given what you can handle."* Interviewees reported drafting non-disclosure agreements, reviewing collector licensing agreements and getting their hands on *"a lot of film finance work"* as well as *"numerous client alert and advice memos."*

Data protection is *"more of a niche area"* as it focuses solely on that single area of work. Trainees agreed the *"relatively small team is a very interesting place to be,"* with matters spanning sectors as varied as social media, retail, leisure and life science. One source told us they were *"permitted to make a lot of decisions,"* but let on that *"the majority of the clients are very big US firms, so I didn't have that much contact with them; most of that was done over the phone by the partner."*

On the merry-go-round

The firm's financial industry group (FIG) is divided into real estate finance, banking, commercial restructuring and bankruptcy (CRAB), structured finance, funds, and regulatory seats. Trainees in real estate finance told us much of their work revolves around completing checklists and drafting letters for companies. *"It's a good seat for exposure to clients – you deal with them every day."* Most of these are banks like Barclays, Santander and Lloyds.

Meanwhile, *"banking and finance gives you a good introduction into the commercial areas that make the City go round,"* according to one interviewee, who went on to tell us that lean teams mean *"trainees are trusted with a lot, especially when it gets very busy."* Likewise, structured finance offers *"a great deal of responsibility, so long as you're capable."* One source said: *"I was always on calls with clients and negotiating contracts. There's a real trust between supervisors and trainees on this team."* The group has kept busy of late with *"lots of matters involving Lehman entities that have gone bust,"* recently overseeing the completion of the UK's first Lehman residential mortgage-backed securitisation deal since 2008, a deal that rang in at a whopping £1.1bn.

The current overseas seat options are Piraeus, Abu Dhabi and Dubai, and sources speculated that a rotation in Singapore may soon be in the offing too. Dubai is litigation-focused, while Abu Dhabi is corporate, and Piraeus is a shipping seat. Nabbing one of these coveted spots requires a formal application and interview. The same goes for client secondments, which take place with the likes of Bauer Media and Debenhams. *"The list on offer increases every year."* Placements are popular, and for a good reason – the experience is *"fantastic."* Said one source: *"I learned so much about how the business was run during my secondment. The legal team was tiny, and I got to work on a variety of things, which really built up my confidence."*

Not for 00-scared-of-heights

The firm occupies the top third of the 33-storey Broadgate Tower, which some might recognise from its brief cameo in the latest James Bond instalment, *Skyfall*. We hear the *"phenomenal"* views are swoon-worthy – literally. *"If you're afraid of heights, it's probably not the best place to be!"*

Trainees found that the working environment tends to *"vary between departments"* – the real estate group, for example, *"is quite chilled out and relaxed,"* while the vibe in finance and shipping is *"a little more macho."* On the whole *"it's a noticeably friendly place,"* they agreed, telling us *"there isn't a culture of arrogance or smugness, and the atmosphere is such that nobody is ever ashamed of asking questions."* A trainee's hours likewise vary depending on which department they're sitting with. Clocking out around 8pm is *"usual,"* but the unpredictable nature of certain types of work – namely, shipping and corporate – occasionally lends itself to longer hours than that. Fortunately, *"it's not like you're just sitting there pretending to work. There's no expectation to stay for the sake of staying."* What's more, *"late nights aren't taken for granted; you're always thanked for staying."*

When it comes to who fits in here, trainees told us that ironically *"the main similarity between all of us is probably our differences."* Elaborated one: *"There are a lot of backgrounds, personalities and interests represented among my intake. I think that's a positive thing – it means we have a mix of strengths across the firm."* There is one visible commonality, however: *"Everyone is chilled but hard-working."*

Among the ongoings at this *"quite sociable"* firm are regular curries on nearby Brick Lane, departmental pizza lunches, occasional sports tournaments, and farewell and welcome drinks to mark seat changes. There are also some *"amazing"* holiday dos. *"We've got nearly 600 people in this office, so when there's an event it's pretty big."* Previous extravaganzas include a summer boat party featuring ice sculptures, and a Hollywood-themed Christmas shindig complete with cut-outs of James Bond and Martinis galore.

The True Picture

And finally...
It's not unheard of for qualifiers who aren't retained to be offered temporary paralegal positions or placements with clients. In 2014, 20 of 22 new qualifiers stayed on with the firm.

4.
THE
PRACTICE
MAKES
PERFECT

We only take on the top talent. And then we help make them even better. It's not just the training, it's not just the resources, it's not just the review and support. Take those as read in any leading firm. But where a traditional firm ends is where RPC begins. Ours is a true partnership that puts the emphasis on excellence, development and open access. That's why we're in an open plan office where it's easy to talk to others. That's why you'll find yourself bouncing ideas off the partner you're sitting next to. That's why RPC lawyers find themselves lead associates while their contemporaries are still playing second fiddle. And that's why, in the profession's major independent survey, clients rated RPC lawyers top for quality of legal advice.

Read the full manifesto and find out more at
RPC.CO.UK/MANIFESTO

RPC   THE LAW CAREER FOR PIONEERS

RPC

The facts

Location: London, Bristol

Number of UK partners/solicitors: 69/184

Partners who trained at firm: 25%

Total number of trainees: 40

Seats: 4x6 months

Alternative seats: secondments

On chambersstudent.co.uk...

How to get into RPC

More on merit-based NQ pay

With a flourishing corporate practice to complement its long-standing insurance pedigree, RPC gives trainees plenty to choose from.

#Progressive

As recently as 2005, RPC's partners were eating lunch in their own dining room and 90% of work was insurance-related. Since then, the firm has undergone a complete identity overhaul: it now divides its time equally between its core insurance practice and a blossoming corporate/commercial side. The latter attracts top *Chambers UK* rankings for commercial contracts, lower mid-market corporate M&A and publishing/media work. Ten years ago RPC was seen as quite a traditional firm, but that's all changed now amid trainee-run Twitter feeds (@lifein-alawfirm), swanky open-plan offices and a graduate recruitment campaign based around energetic slogans like 'rip up the rulebook'. In September 2014 RPC will also become the first firm to introduce merit-based pay for NQs – go to our website to read more about this.

"You can look back and see for yourself how much the firm has changed and grown," said one of our interviewees. *"Just three years ago, we were a one-office firm with no plans to expand; now we have four offices."* Indeed, RPC recently opened three offices in quick succession, in Singapore (2011), Hong Kong (2012) and Bristol (2012), the last of which specialises primarily in insurance and took on its first trainees in September 2013. While this investment led to a £2.8m increase in debt, it also helped revenue jump 20% in 2012/13. Further growth is on the agenda and we heard rumblings that a mainland China office might be on the menu at some point in the future. The firm is also currently moving some of its lower-value insurance and real estate work to Bristol.

Trainees are required to do at least one insurance and one commercial seat, and to gain both contentious and non-contentious experience. But, observed one trainee, *"we are a litigation-heavy firm,"* so expect this to be reflected in your training contract. Prior to each rotation, the firm runs 'seat spotlight sessions' for trainees, which involve *"partners and associates in each department giving a presentation about what the seat entails."* We heard that *"some departments only offer one seat, and if five or six people go for it, many are left disappointed,"* but sources also told us *"there has been a drive to make the seat allocation process more transparent through trainee forums and meetings with HR."*

Test of strength

RPC clocks up *Chambers* rankings in a host of insurance-related areas, ranging from product liability to professional negligence work. Recent high-profile instructions include advising clients on property damage loss after international earthquakes and counselling insurers following the 2011 London riots. Seats on offer in insurance are: financial risks; professional risks; property and casualty; general liability and life sciences; and construction insurance.

The large construction department mostly does contentious work but has recently seen an increase in trans-

Seat options: corporate; corporate insurance; commercial disputes; construction and projects; employment, pensions and incentives; real estate; insurance; media, IP, technology, outsourcing, competition; commercial contracts

Chambers UK rankings

Banking Litigation	Intellectual Property
Clinical Negligence	Litigation
Commercial Contracts	Media & Entertainment
Construction	Outsourcing
Corporate/M&A	Partnership
Defamation/Reputation	Product Liability
Management	Professional Discipline
Education	Professional Negligence
Employment	Real Estate
Health & Safety	Real Estate Litigation
Information Technology	Retail
Insurance	Tax

actional activity. Major clients include VolkerWessels, Carillion and multinational pharmaceutical company AstraZeneca, which the department is advising on the opening of its new global HQ in 2016. In this seat, trainees usually work on a mix of big high-value cases and lower-value matters on which they're given the chance to take the lead. One reported: *"On large matters I'm part of a bigger team and do the simpler tasks like bundling and cross-scheduling, but for the smaller claims I manage files myself with fairly light-touch management from the partner."* Trainees are often tasked with sourcing construction experts – one described *"attending meetings with engineers to discuss the tensile strength of concrete."*

A seat in the highly regarded professional risks group allows trainees to work in *"one of the firm's bigger, busier insurance departments."* Essentially, it deals with insurance against mistakes made by professionals in the financial, insurance, construction, legal and technology sectors, and acts on behalf of them and their insurers in professional discipline and negligence cases. While some trainees reported doing the bundling or helping with disclosure on larger cases, others told us they got a lot of experience on lower-value matters: *"I was responsible for between ten and 15 files. The learning curve was steep, but I got some awesome exposure."* Often the group works closely with the financial risks team, which deals with the insurance of savings and investments for banks, hedge funds and other financial institutions. Some trainees do a split seat between the two teams. One source reported that these areas of work can be tough to understand: *"I had no idea what half of the language meant when I first started, and I spent the first few months getting used to the insurance world and how it works."* But never fear: *"Eventually it starts to make sense, and you're able to talk with confidence about issues like coverage and policy positions."*

The general liability and life sciences team does personal injury and clinical negligence work. Trainees in this seat are treated to a wealth of clinical cases, from PIP breast implant litigation to claims brought against dentists, GPs and abortion clinics. Due to the confidential nature of the cases we can't disclose any compelling details, but trainees gave the seat a confident thumbs up. One said: *"It's probably one of the seats where you get the most responsibility because there are lots of smaller cases, and trainees are usually left to run them."* Still, *"as it's a specialised seat, you do get a lot of support and work closely with partners."*

Why trainees go to Iceland

Seats on offer on the corporate/commercial side are: real estate; employment; regulatory; commercial disputes; corporate; corporate insurance; and the snappily named 'media, IP, technology, outsourcing, competition and commercial contracts' (MIPTOCC).

The large commercial disputes department is split into subgroups, including banking, general commercial and tax, so *"there's an opportunity to do a variety of work."* RPC has been involved in some headline-grabbing cases, recently representing CF Partners in its €100m claim against Barclays for misusing confidential information. Other key clients include Sports Direct and the Daily Mail and General Trust group, which owns newspapers like the Daily Mail and Metro. With such substantial cases in the offing, trainees are not given their own files. One explained: *"The bigger the matter, the less responsibility you get."* As a result, a seat here is pretty *"bundle-heavy"* and usually involves *"doing more of the grunt work."* But trainees *"are taken to court hearings and get involved with more exciting bits and bobs as well."* For example, some were involved in an attempt to recover money from the crashed Icelandic banks and even travelled to the country.

Corporate is split into M&A, banking and corporate insurance subgroups. Trainees told us that this *"is an area of the firm that's really growing."* Indeed, since 2008 the total turnover of RPC's corporate practice has grown by £4m. While the corporate team generally handles mid-market deals for clients like HTC – recently advising on its $47m acquisition of Saffron Media – it has in the past acted on some major deals. For example, lawyers advised global hygiene company SCA on its €1.3bn acquisition of Georgia-Pacific's European operations, and has since been involved in sales of parts of that business totalling approximately €100m. The banking team can be *"frantic at times, particularly when deadlines are looming. Often e-mails are pinging around on a minute-by-minute basis."* The hours can also be demanding – one trainee admitted to completing a killer 90-hour week. Fortunately, we were assured that *"it's rare for people to work weekends."* Trainee work in this seat tends towards the project management end of the scale, with sources describing *"managing transaction documents, co-ordinating people across timezones and keeping parties up to date."*

Many of the areas the MIPTOCC department works on are highly rated by *Chambers UK*, with publishing and commercial contracts at the top of the class. Counting an enviable collection of national newspapers among its key clients, the publishing group is perhaps best known for its involvement in the Leveson Inquiry. The firm has since played a major role in establishing the new Independent Press Standards Organisation (IPSO). Meanwhile, work in the non-contentious commercial contracts group gives trainees exposure to big-ticket work. Currently the firm's advising three NHS trusts on a deal that will create the largest provider of pathology services in the UK, valued at over £1bn.

While RPC doesn't provide overseas opportunities, Londoners can try a spell in the Bristol office, and client secondments are also on offer. In the recent past insurance secondment options have included AIG, Markel and Chubb, while trainees can also go to clients like Carillion for more construction experience, or to Sports Direct for commercial work.

Raven-claw or Shuffle-puff?

RPC's London HQ stands alongside St Katherine Docks, and the glass-clad building offers excellent views of the neighbouring Tower of London. The Bristol office is based near Temple Meads station in an area popular with law firms. Insiders told us Bristol tends to do lower-value work than London, so trainees here are likely to get a *"greater degree of exposure to clients."* One explained: *"The chances of a trainee being the lead contact on a matter in London are a lot slimmer than in Bristol, where you might have ten to 12 of your own files."*

Both offices are open-plan, with trainees sitting in pods usually consisting of a partner, two associates and a trainee. Trainees found the layout *"great for training,"* as *"you learn a lot just by overhearing conversations and can get involved in discussions because they happen out on the floor."* Trainees also liked the resulting *"lack of hierarchy"* and *"respect for junior employees."* One said: *"There's a very open culture. You can just walk up to a partner and ask questions, and associates are always happy to help."* Many praised the firm's collaborative feel: *"We work as a team here; we're always helping each other."*

Insiders highlighted RPC's sociable atmosphere. All employees are a member of one of three houses: 'Reynolds', 'Porter' or 'Chamberlain'. *"If you just joined a department, you'd probably only socialise with the people in that department, but the houses are much bigger and link people in different teams together – they're always holding events."* Houses compete regularly for the glory of winning the house cup. Among all the inter-house events, 'RPC's Got Talent' stands out as the most popular, with trainees citing singer-songwriter duos and Bollywood dancers as their favourite acts. *"Once you've done a silly dance routine with a partner, you feel much more comfortable approaching them about work!"*

RPC has an excellent retention record: in the past ten years retention has never dropped below 80%. The trend continued in 2014 with 15 of 16 qualifiers staying with the firm.

And finally...

RPC's sociable atmosphere and variety of practices help it attract a mixed bunch of trainees, including career-changers like an RAF pilot, a Cordon Bleu chef and someone who used to work for the president of Brazil.

The True Picture

"If a firm you're interested in is coming to your uni's law fair, do some research beforehand. Most firms have quite a lot of material online about their training contract, and you'll make the most of their visit by coming prepared with some specific questions."

Trainee

SGH Martineau LLP

The facts

Location: Birmingham, London

Number of UK partners/solicitors: 51/79

Partners who trained at the firm: 19%

Total number of trainees: 16

Seats: 6x4 months

Alternative seats: occasional client secondments

Extras: pro bono – Toynbee Hall legal advice centre

On chambersstudent.co.uk...

How to get into SGH Martineau
A beginner's guide to Birmingham

Following a merger in 2011, this Brummie native now takes on trainees in London too. We bring you the inside scoop from those in the 'neau...

Let's talk about secs

The love child of Brummie-born Martineau and City-based Sprecher Grier Halberstam, today's SGH Martineau is a £27.5m turnover firm that focuses on eight key industry sectors: lending institutions; education; energy; industry and manufacturing; investment funds; leisure and retail; restructuring and insolvency; and private capital. The firm has clearly realised that a strong sector focus pays and, according to managing partner Emma Shipp, a recent strategy review confirms this: *"About 65% of our income currently comes from the sectors we specialise in,"* she told us, *"and we hope to push that up to 85% over the next five years."* With more than 100 teaching institutions on the books, education is one area that has supported the firm's business for years, but that doesn't mean it isn't adapting to the times. For example, banking has carved out a niche practice in Islamic finance, while energy lawyers have been building up a reputation for renewables work. *"We're particularly interested in green energy and have done a lot of work with wind, solar and biomass regeneration,"* Shipp tells us. *"There's been an explosion in solar energy work this year and last, and we're excited to be involved in a number of UK projects for international developers."*

London's Sprecher was traditionally less focused on sectors, but Shipp – who headed the office until the merger – remembers how difficult it was to operate as a generalist firm. SGH was able to bring its strong insolvency team to the mix, though, and in Shipp's words, *"putting that together with Martineau's banking practice has been a really good story."* Historically only the Birmingham office has taken on trainees – about seven to ten a year – but since the merger it has been sending a couple down to

sit in London at each rotation. Those trainees obviously made an impression: in 2014 the London office will for the first time be taking on two permanent trainees of its own. HR assured us they'll be making every effort to integrate these newbies into the Birmingham cohort, but it remains to be seen exactly how this will be done.

Trainees rotate through six four-month seats, and told us it's quite common to repeat seats as *"you run out of things you want to try after a while."* Some found the lack of variety slightly frustrating, though others appreciated the opportunity to bulk up their CV with eight months' experience in one area. Trainees chat to HR about their preferences roughly three weeks before each rotation, though there's no guarantee they'll get their first choice. That said, one suggested that *"it can be good to go somewhere you wouldn't have picked yourself"* as *"you never know what might float your boat."* Trainees have to do one contentious and one property seat, though some (like property disputes) fulfil both of these requirement-sat once. They're also encouraged to do a corporate seat where possible.

Seat options: real estate investment and planning; development; construction; banking and support; property disputes; M&A; banking; corporate finance; employment; energy, projects and commerce; IP and technology; private client; family; commercial disputes; real estate; commercial disputes; restructuring and insolvency; M&A; energy. (see online for breakdown by office)

Chambers UK rankings

Agriculture & Rural Affairs	Intellectual Property
Banking & Finance	Litigation
Charities	Private Client
Construction	Professional Negligence
Corporate/M&A	Real Estate
Education	Real Estate Litigation
Employment	Restructuring/Insolvency
Family/Matrimonial	

Getting the boot

The firm's property team is its largest, and about half of trainees sit here for their first four months. As a result, they tend to *"really support each other"* and can share notes on new tasks like how to fill out stamp duty land tax returns. The team eases new starters in with *"standard things like Land Registry forms,"* though trainees soon take responsibility for smaller matters such as small-scale land leases on their own. *"I pretty much ran a residential conveyancing file by myself and was the client's primary contact,"* one told us. *"I conducted meetings, and while there was always a partner present I certainly didn't just sit back and take notes."* Trainees we spoke to had also been involved in some bigger development projects, such as those for the firm's educational clients – in 2013, the group advised the University of Worcester on the development of a new multimillion-pound campus, for example. Other clients include banks like Lloyds – which the firm has been advising since the 1800s, when it was originally incorporated – and high-street names like Selfridges, Claire's Accessories and 99p Stores. More unusually, it represents the Islamic Bank of Britain on real estate matters. Some of our interviewees said they'd helped register Shari'a-compliant mortgages and found the work particularly interesting as *"it really pushes the boundaries of what you learnt on the LPC."*

If a traditional property seat isn't your bag, then you can satisfy the real estate requirement by sitting with the property disputes team, in banking and support, or in construction. Trainees in the disputes team had been *"heavily involved in drafting witness statements, preparing documents and attending conferences with counsel."* Work here is fast-paced: a claim regarding rights of way, for example will often have to be released within a day and heard the next, though more complex environmental disputes can easily span the whole seat. Construction is split into contentious and transactional matters, and is a good place to hone drafting skills while also getting a taste of the various routes that a claim can take – mediation and adjudication are common alternatives to court when building deadlines make litigation a costly option.

Trainees can spend their corporate seat in M&A, banking or corporate finance. In Birmingham the top two tiers of

Chambers UK corporate rankings are dominated by the big nationals like DLA Piper and Eversheds, but SGH Martineau still gets its hands on some fairly high-profile transactions. In 2013, for example, the firm advised on the £300m sale of British boot brand Doc Martens to a private equity company, and the sale of 13 of the Menzies Group's hotels for £85m. As in real estate, Islamic finance is a growing area here. Along with household names like Santander and Clydesdale, the banking group advises Middle Eastern financial institutions like the Qatari Investment Bank on Shari'a-compliant structures and other commercial deals. For trainees, hours are long and the work *"intense;"* one suggested that joining the department is a real *"baptism of fire."* Matters tend to be document-heavy, and trainees we interviewed had helped draft parts of documents that ran to 400 or 500 pages. They'd also drafted share purchase agreements and disclosure letters on the M&A side, got good contact with mid-sized clients in finance, and done a mix of contentious and non-contentious work for the banking team.

npowering trainees

Trainees who haven't already satisfied the SRA's contentious requirement elsewhere or fancy their chances in court can sit with the disputes group in either commercial disputes or professional negligence. We heard about a trainee who'd represented a client in a preliminary hearing on their own, although there's also a lot of bundling and court prep work to do. A big chunk of the work in commercial disputes comes from energy clients – in 2013 the team represented npower on disputes arising from the insolvency of Comet, which occupied 260 of the energy giant's sites. That said, *"the department is not quite as targeted towards the firm's industry sectors as some others; it depends on what people are arguing about on any given day."* Trainee tasks here usually involve researching the nature of a claim, drafting defence and witness statements, and calling clients to talk through strategy. One source told us *"there's less direct client contact and more getting to grips with procedures and nitty-gritty legal points,"* though on smaller claims trainees do deal with clients one to one.

Several seat options fall under the commercial umbrella, including energy, projects and commerce (EPC); employment; and intellectual property and technology. The EPC team does a lot of work for the electricity sector, specifically for National Grid, and a small SGH office in Brussels specialises in energy work with a European dimension. In addition to this, the firm recruited a renewable energy team for its London office in 2012, which just one year in advised on the development of a £32m solar project at Wymeswold airfield – the site was built in less than eight weeks and is the largest of its kind in the UK. A trainee commented that *"it's such specialist work you really do get thrown in at the deep end."* Employment lawyers work on a mix of contentious and non-contentious matters, representing numerous educational institutions. Trainees here had shadowed barristers in court and been invited to lots of client meetings. Others had chosen to sit with the IP team, which advises companies like CEDC (best known for producing Żubrówka vodka) and filter producer BRITA on brand protection matters.

The firm is particularly proud of its private client practice, and rightly so – it wins top *Chambers UK* rankings in the Midlands for its work with private individuals, and for agriculture and rural affairs. Though most client names are confidential, we can tell you that the private capital group acts for a number of landed estate clients, charities and is even the adviser to the Bishop of Birmingham.

A social utopia

When we asked trainees what they most enjoyed about working at SGH, they were all quick to mention the way *"everyone gets on really well."* One even suggested there's a *"Martineau ethos,"* observing that *"everyone is quite closely connected both in and out of work."* Indeed there are clear indications that the firm tries hard to promote a good working environment. It appoints social secretaries, who send an email round each Friday to let everyone know where they're heading that evening – Utopia, Primitivo and Purnell's always prove popular options. *"Partners are much more approachable at work when you've had an informal drink with them at the pub."* The weekly drinks also help when joining a new seat, as *"when you arrive you normally know a few members of the team already."*

On top of these drinks, trainees attend events hosted by the Birmingham Trainee Solicitors' Society, such as the winter ball, and the firm subsidises them to do so. Rookies are also encouraged to get involved with CSR activities and the numerous fund-raising ventures the firm supports – each year trainees sleep rough for a local homeless charity and spruce up a children's ward at Christmas. Even training seems more like a social event than a chore at SGH – interviewees described PSC days at the University of Law as *"a nice day out to catch up with everyone."* More practice-specific training occurs on the job, and the open-plan office layout means you can always *"toddle over and ask partners questions without the nervousness of knocking on doors."* The lack of walls does mean things can get quite noisy, but trainees seem to find this exciting rather than a hindrance – one described the real estate team as *"big, busy and bustling."* In London space is more at a premium of course; sources described the office here as *"cramped but pleasant."*

As a taster of what might be to come in the City office, a trainee who'd spent time there said *"the hours in London are much more reasonable"* than in Birmingham, where they'd *"regularly been working 12-hour days."* Trainees in the Midlands told us some seats demand much longer hours than others. Corporate, for example, can be pretty tough, but *"it's a very sociable team, so in the less busy times they go out for long lunches or drinks in the evening."*

When it comes to qualification, the facts speak for themselves: in the five years from 2010 to 2014, just 32 of 48 qualifiers have been kept on. This is somewhat below the national average for commercial firms, and it means that when it comes to qualification a small, close-knit trainee group is suddenly forced to compete for places in a previously uncompetitive environment. Trainees can apply for as many posts as they want, though, and for uncontested positions NQ interviews are little more than informal chats. If a job has interest from more than one trainee, applicants might be asked to present a mock tender pitch, with questions on a brief lasting a good hour. The pressure doesn't seem to have divided the trainee group, who told us they were all *"pretty open"* about their choices and *"wished each other the best of luck,"* this year. In 2014 six jobs were handed out to a cohort of eight.

And finally...
Take note of this firm's sector focus and the distinct industries and clients it works for.

Shearman & Sterling LLP

The facts

Location: London

Number of UK partners/solicitors: 25/88 (28 non-UK trained)

Partners who trained at the firm: 0%

Seats: 4x6 months

Total number of trainees: 27

Alternative seats: overseas seats

Extras: pro bono – LawWorks

On chambersstudent.co.uk...
How to get into Shearman & Sterling
Shearman's international footprint

If you have a passion for high-end finance, real ambition and an international outlook, Shearman & Sterling might just be the place for you.

Gassing up

Shearman & Sterling first opened its doors in New York in 1873 when Thomas Shearman and John Sterling took the decision to set up shop together. From its earliest days the firm demonstrated a flair for attracting high-profile banking, finance and corporate work. It advised on the 1897 merger which laid the foundation for Citibank, helped German companies such as Siemans and BASF re-enter the US market after the Second World War, and helped the Fords retain control of their company when it went public in 1956.

Today the firm's international reach extends into all the world's major financial centres across Europe, Asia and the Americas. It maintains its outstanding reputation for banking and finance, corporate and projects work with rankings in *Chambers USA*, *Chambers Global* and *Chambers Europe*. The London office is no different, winning its best *Chambers UK* rankings for projects, capital markets and banking work. Recently the firm assisted Nokia with the €1.7bn buyout of Siemens' 50% stake in the two companies' joint venture, Nokia Siemens Networks. Lawyers have also been involved in the recapitalisation of the Co-op Bank and assisted a number of lenders financing the $380m Khauzak-Shady gas field project in Uzbekistan.

Shearman was one of the first US firms to set sail across the pond, opening a Paris office in 1963. London followed in 1972 and the office has grown to become the largest outside the USA. The firm's *"strong global presence," "range of international work"* and *"reputation for taking on the biggest deals"* had excited the interest of many of the trainees we spoke to. During the course of

their training contract rookies have the opportunity to spread their wings and spend six months outside the UK. Potential destinations include New York, Abu Dhabi, Singapore and Brussels.

Financially, the London office is a big hitter, delivering revenues of $134.8m in 2013/14, an increase of 20% on the previous year, making Shearman the ninth-biggest international firm in London. The early implementation of a three-year growth strategy has helped push the office's contribution up beyond 15% of global revenue.

Banking on it

Since September 2013 incoming trainees' first-seat choices have been at the mercy of HR and the requirements of business need. There has been little upset, however, and most trainees felt *"it didn't really make a whole lot of difference."* In theory, no seat is compulsory but everyone must sit in two of projects, M&A or finance – the firm's core departments. This requirement can also be fulfilled by sitting in a transactional group abroad. Although there are contentious seat options (eg arbitration and antitrust) doing one is not a necessity – trainees can complete a two-week course at the University of Law to satisfy SRA requirements. Trainees cautioned that *"finance is effectively compulsory so applicants should be sure they have a real interest in this area before they apply."* This holds

Seat options: finance; antitrust; asset management; employment; financial institutions advisory; international arbitration; litigation; M&A; project development & finance; real estate; tax; capital markets (New York only)

Chambers UK rankings

Banking & Finance	Energy & Natural Resources
Capital Markets	Financial Services
Competition/European Law	Projects
Corporate/M&A	Tax

true on qualification too: *"If your heart is set on real estate, tax or employment, this may not be the firm for you – the opportunities to qualify into those departments are limited."* In 2014 nine of 13 qualifiers stayed with the firm, and six of those joined either finance, projects or corporate.

Finance is the largest department in the London office and usually plays host to six trainees at any one time. The client list includes many of the heavy-hitters of the banking world: Credit Suisse, Barclays, RBS, Goldman Sachs, and Bank of America Merrill Lynch. The department undertakes both leveraged and structured finance; trainees are usually assigned to one or the other but several of our interviewees had undertaken work straddling both. Transactions are often *"monumental"* with one source engaged in a deal *"involving issues spanning 20 jurisdictions from East Asia to South America."* While trainees do undertake some drafting and research, the size of deals means there are also basic tasks like proofreading, document management, running conditions precedent, and organising signings and closings. Trainees weren't unhappy with this though and enjoyed the exposure it gave them. *"We're regularly in contact with clients,"* one interviewee reported. *"It's pretty cool to find yourself talking to the CFO or CEO of a major company!"*

Innovation and original thought – or *"using your brain,"* as one trainee put it – are highly valued. *"When you come across an approach or an idea that no-one else has thought of, people are really appreciative."* The sheer volume of work means that the hours can be *"very up and down,"* trainees told us. *"When it's busy, you're VERY busy: here till early hours, all-nighters – that kind of busy. But when there's not a deal on you can work 9am to 6pm for weeks at a time."* The saving grace is that *"you tend to know in advance when it'll be busy, so it's possible to plan around the tough periods."*

Most project finance work has an infrastructure or energy focus. For example, the firm is continuing to represent Dow Chemical on its massive joint venture with Saudi Aramco (Saudi Arabia's national oil and gas company) to design, engineer, construct, finance and operate a $20bn chemical plant in Saudi. The team also advised Cennergi (a joint venture between Tata and South Africa's second-largest coal producer) in relation to the Amakhala Emoyeni wind farm project in the Eastern Cape Province. As these examples demonstrate, work tends to be on a vast

scale which means it's *"definitely really interesting."* The downside is that *"because the projects are so complicated and long-running, trainees often only get a small snapshot of the whole."* However, interviewees did love the tangibility of the projects, with one explaining: *"Unlike complex financial structures, when someone explains the outcome of a project to you they can draw diagrams and say 'it will look like this!'"* The work trainees undertook in projects was quite varied. One told us: *"I was mostly engaged in typical trainee tasks such as proofreading,"* before going on to describe *"attending meetings in London, Brussels and Paris, and then doing drafting off the back of that."*

Corporate is the third of the firm's core departments. It was boosted in May 2013 by the arrival of three private equity partners from Weil Gotschal & Manges. According to one trainee the arrivals have given the firm extra oomph when it comes to *"mid-market deals in the $25-250m range."* For example, the three ex-Weil lawyers recently advised Goldman Sachs' private equity arm on its $150m acquisition of a 50% stake in Hastings Insurance. According to *Chambers UK* the team's high-end capability remains very strong too – its most recent headline deal was telecoms firm Liberty Global's $23.3bn acquisition of Virgin Media. Other clients include big beasts like General Electric, Citi, the Qatar Investment Authority and steel giants Tata and ArcelorMittal. Interviewees felt the department had offered them *"great exposure to a range of work"* and *"a great deal of responsibility."* Besides drafting board minutes and doing due diligence, trainees find themselves *"liaising with counsel, first-drafting documents, fielding comments from the other side, and processing amendments."*

Take-away'd out

The firm's advisory practices – tax, real estate, employment, financial services, asset management and competition – *"tend to feed off the core transactional departments,"* although they often have their own standalone clients as well. Asset management, for example, handled European regulatory compliance issues for the corporate team during IntercontinentalExchange's $11bn acquisition of securities exchange operator NYSE Euronext. And the tax department deals with *"the tax implications of loans and the buying and selling of companies."* The advisory groups are all smaller than the core departments, and this means more responsibility for trainees, including *"a lot of research into new legislation and how it might affect transactions."*

International arbitration is something of a cornerstone for Shearman globally and in London *"the practice is expanding rapidly."* In one typical case the department secured a $250m payout from the Romanian government at the International Centre for Settlement of Investment Disputes on behalf of Swedish clients who suffered significant losses when the defendant withdrew financial incentives designed to encourage the establishment of a food and drink facility in rural Romania. Most of the work involves upholding individual and corporate compensation claims against sovereign governments before various international arbitrators. One excited trainee told us: *"If you are seen to be capable of handling the responsibility, then the sky's the limit! I drafted the preliminary arguments against the defence made by the other side."*

Each overseas seat allows trainees to gain a different kind of transactional experience in a more exotic location: New York is capital markets focused, Singapore and Abu Dhabi are more varied, but focusing on projects, and Brussels offers antitrust experience. We heard that *"New York is a real challenge as they don't have any concept of trainees in the US so you're treated as an associate,"* and in Singapore you can end up *"working more hours than in London."* Besides the long hours, *"there's plenty of socialising too as lots of other firms send trainees to the same locations we do. And I never felt out of the London loop because I remained on the all-trainee mailing list."*

We touched on hours above, and should reiterate that trainees said working days *"can be pretty dreadful."* One interviewee had this to say about the projects and finance seats: *"When there's a deal on leaving at 10pm is the norm and staying until 3am or 4am is pretty common. I also worked four weekends in a row."* The hours were also central to the one niggle which trainees had about their Appold Street offices, near Liverpool Street: the recent closure of the on-site restaurant. One source commented: *"Although you can order up to £30 worth of takeaway if you're working late, there's only so many nights a week you can face a cheeseburger or noodles."* Interviewees also observed that *"it can be difficult to find time to leave the office during the day to get lunch. And being able to eat in would really help to foster a sense of community."*

Throw me a life jacket!

When asked about Shearman's stateside roots, trainees were quick to correct us: *"The firm prefers to refer to itself as international."* Interviewees also noted that *"the London office is pretty anglicised – and I think there are probably more Australians and New Zealanders here than Americans!"* The relatively small size of the office means *"it's easy to get to know everyone – although it also means that if there's lots of work everyone tends to get swamped at the same time."* The office's small size breeds collegiality: *"Provided you've had a crack at something yourself and you approach the most appropriate person, people are generally willing to answer questions and give feedback on your work."* The trainees are a close-knit group and assist each other as much as possible. One interviewee gave an example of this: *"We've created a Word document that all trainees can access and whenever you make a mistake or have a problem you note down what it was and how you solved it, so everyone else can learn from what you did."*

Socialising is definitely a big thing at Shearman and *"invariably people go out for drinks at least once a week."* Regular haunts include some of Shoreditch's trendier locales: the Light Bar, Rocket, the Whistling Shop and the Electricity Showrooms. If you're less boozy by nature there are also softball, squash and badminton leagues and charity quizzes. Trainees are allocated a generous budget for up to four trainee-only events each year – these usually involve dinner and drinks as well as funded mentor lunches. Departmental socials tend to be a little more imaginative: the corporate team recently hired out space at Boundary to play table football and pool; projects has done the three-peaks challenge and gone go-karting (not on the same day, we hasten to add); and the corporate team went to the Henley Regatta for a spot of dragon-boat racing. *"There was a bit of splashing about,"* recalled one trainee, *"but it was a lot of fun!"*

And finally...
London is *"not just an outpost"* of this international giant. *"Shearman's departments are organised on a global basis so you're constantly in contact with other offices."*

The True Picture

Sheridans

The facts

Location: London
Number of UK partners/solicitors: 35/22
Partners who trained at the firm: 22%
Total number of trainees: 3
Seats: 4x6 months
Alternative seats: occasional secondments

On chambersstudent.co.uk...

How to get into Sheridans
The amazing life of Bernard Sheridan
Social media and the law

World-famous musicians, eminent film stars and prestigious sports bodies – all are part of the package at this dazzling Soho-based media firm.

One does not simply walk into Wardour

Wardour Street, located in the quirky and vivacious slice of London that is Soho, has a deep and rich history in the creative arts. In the 20th century it emerged as the epicentre of the British film industry by housing numerous high-profile film companies, plus there was the late, great Marquee Club, which during its halcyon days played host to some of the greatest acts to grace the scene, including The Rolling Stones, Led Zeppelin and The Who. For Sheridans, a media boutique deeply entrenched in the goings-on of the creative industries, Wardour Street has proven an ideal fit. The firm moved to the neighbourhood in March 2014, a decision largely driven by growth, according to partner Keith Ashby. *"We've continued to expand over the past few years, and so we needed to find larger premises that would also allow for future expansion. After another strong year across the board, we're looking at recruiting in almost every practice area we have."*

A glance at the history books reveals that this firm started out in 1956 as a petite force led by a man intent on haggling the best record deals for upcoming artists. The Sheridans of today, however, has blossomed into a catch-all practice comprising music, film, TV, theatre, gaming, sport and interactive media work, among many other areas. Beyond the media sphere are practices like corporate, banking, employment and family, all of which have begun to flourish in their own right and today rely minimally on the firm's creative channels as a means of securing work.

Sheridans receives oodles of applications each year – up to a thousand, in fact – but only offers one or two training contracts a year, so candidates have to stand out to stand a chance. Most important is *"having substantial knowledge of the sectors in which we work – whether that be music, film and TV, sport or technology – and a demonstrative interest in one or more of those industries."* Of course, this doesn't mean you need to have been a renowned actor or musical sensation in a previous life to cut the mustard here; it's more about showing you're up to speed on developments in the media world and how such ongoings affect the commercial sphere. *"Don't forget the law underlies everything we do."* On top of that, recruits have to possess the confidence to glad-hand the firm's glitterati clients. *"They need people who are very comfortable in social situations – our clients don't want an impersonal approach."*

That's entertainment

Rookies are required to complete both a corporate and litigation seat, and their other two choices largely boil down to what teams need helping hands at the time. *"You don't have much sway, but there is some flexibility – I was able to get one seat changed to another I really wanted to do,"* said one trainee.

Sheridans works much of its magic in the film and TV industries, advising more star names than you'd find at an Oscars afterparty. Over the past year alone the firm's nabbed work on behalf of Billy Connolly, BBC Films and Kudos – the production company behind award-winning

Seat options: corporate/commercial; TV and film; sport; interactive; dispute resolution; music, theatre and media

Chambers UK rankings

Media & Entertainment	Sports Law

ITV show *Broadchurch* – in addition to its representation of longer-standing clients like Channel 4 and the British Film Institute. Lawyers have also been busy handling aspects of a number of TV projects for Buccaneer, a newly crafted company co-founded by the creator of the ever-entertaining *The Only Way Is Essex*. Much of the work in TV and film is rights-based, so a trainee sitting with the department can expect to negotiate and draft plenty of agreements during this seat – for example, contracts between film producers and screenplay writers. On top of this, our sources reported getting involved in script reads, tackling insurance issues and assisting with *"talent-related"* matters such as endorsement deals. It's worth noting that sport-related work used to be incorporated into the TV and film group, but now Sheridans has a separate team for that.

The interactive team, which focuses on gaming and digital media, is the firm's biggest growth area at the moment. The practice is incredibly broad, encompassing pretty much everything that's part of the online world, with a particular focus on app development. The trainees sitting here are often tasked with preparing terms and conditions for websites, managing content for web platforms, and *"protecting the interests of some of the world's best-known video games."* In the case of the latter, this can involve researching the games themselves *"to determine what is actually classed as a video game infringement."* IP matters like these form a sizeable chunk of the team's work. *"I was given my own trade mark portfolio to look after,"* said one trainee.

The firm's corporate contingent is also growing. *"A good bit of work is filtered in through the interactive team – we've been doing quite a lot of work for tech start-ups lately."* Indeed, mobile app developer Buongiorno and telecoms solutions provider Livvy's are both on the roster, though the team draws in business from media-oriented clients too, including Andrew Lloyd Webber's Really Useful Group and London-based production company Raw TV. Trainees with experience here told of preparing ancillary documents, Companies House filings and board minutes during M&A deals, and also mentioned drafting *"meaty"* documents from scratch, like share purchase agreements.

Sheridans' music crew acts for some of the hottest names around, from psychedelic rock gods Pink Floyd to the BBC's 'Sound of 2014' winner Sam Smith. It's not just about famous musicians though; the group also represents the agencies behind them, like Mumford & Son's label Glassnote Entertainment. One of the department's latest successes has been overseeing British record exec Jason Iley's move to New York following his appointment as president of Roc Nation Records, the label owned by the one and only Jay-Z. Oh, and just to throw one more glamorous name into the mix, interviewees said they'd worked closely with Beatles legend Paul McCartney's company MPL Communications: *"It's kind of like being on secondment, but from your own desk."* New recruits here also spoke of preparing agreements for record and talent representation deals.

Merry Sheridans

Trainees described Sheridan's working environment as *"laid-back,"* telling us *"there's a good flow of banter"* trickling through the corridors. Understandably, record producers and TV hotshots are a bit of a different breed from corporate heads and City bankers, so we weren't too surprised to hear the clients themselves play a part in fostering this reasonably chilled character. *"They're usually much less stuffy – you're not expected to wear a tie when you meet them, for instance. In fact, chances are they'd be slightly alarmed if you did!"*

The current trio of trainees, all of whom started back when the firm still resided in Bloomsbury, had only kind words to say about Sheridans' relocation to Wardour Street. *"It's smack bang in the middle of Soho, so we're right in the midst of the buzz this area of London provides. The iconic address has really embedded us into the media world."* The office's interior also drew praise for its panoramic views and open-plan layout, which sources told us has a positive impact on the working culture. *"People know where they stand in hierarchy of course, but it's also a very open and collaborative place, and that's come through a lot more since we've moved here."*

Now we can't promise you'll be schmoozing with A-list celebs at luxurious venues 24/7, but trainees are still treated to a decent spread of social events throughout the year. There's a monthly gathering held in one of the many lively bars dotted around Soho, plus regular firm-hosted client events – *"some of the peeps at Spotify were recently invited to give a lecture,"* for instance. The two main markings on the social calendar are the summer and Christmas bashes. The latest of the latter, held at a private members club in Mayfair, involved a three-course meal and a spoof awards ceremony. *"It was tongue-in-cheek and went down very well!"*

And finally...
In 2014 the firm's single qualifier stayed on as an NQ.

Shoosmiths

The facts

Location: Basingstoke, Birmingham, London, Manchester, Milton Keynes, Northampton, Nottingham, Reading, Southampton, Scotland

Number of UK partners/solicitors: 139/311

Partners who trained at the firm: 5%

Total number of trainees: 39

Seats: 4x6 months

Alternative seats: secondments

Extras: pro bono - Law Works, CAB, Community ProHelp

On chambersstudent.co.uk...

How to get into Shoosmiths

Interview with chief exec Claire Rowe

Full list of seat options by location

Reading: more than just a train station

From Southampton to Edinburgh, Shoosmiths' national ambitions are unlikely to cool in years ahead. Read on if a well-connected network with a pleasing mix of practices is on your wish list.

You're my number one

The aptly named Shoosmiths emerged from Britain's former shoemaking capital, Northampton, during the heyday of Queen Victoria and is now one of the country's top national firms. Of course, it's only in recent years that Shoosmiths has settled comfortably into this identity. The past decade has seen new offices crop up in Birmingham, Manchester and Edinburgh – bringing the total count to ten and in recent years chief executive Claire Rowe has spearheaded a rebranding exercise, a conversion to an LLP and a sizeable lateral hiring spree.

The firm is now in its final phase of a three-year plan launched in 2012, and things are hotting up as a result. *"We've been aiming for 10% growth* [by revenue] *each year, which we've been pursuing more aggressively than ever in year three,"* sources told us. *"We're actually ahead of ourselves,"* Claire Rowe told us. *"Now it's about being the leading national UK law firm, which is famous for the client experience it gives."* 2012's merger with Archibald Campbell & Harley, and the 50 lateral hires in the last five years, all appear to validate the firm's ambition, especially in corporate, commercial and real estate departments. According to insiders, a big part of the firm's bold plan has involved *"moving away from the volume work we've traditionally been known for and towards larger, more complex matters."* In practice this means moving away from high-volume small claims like personal injury and towards courting national names like Telefónica and RBS. The firm has also been endeavouring to link up its practices in the hope of appealing to these bigger clients.

Shoosmiths threads its four core practices – corporate, real estate, private client and commercial – through most of its bases, and financial recoveries is a fifth that crops up in Manchester, Northampton and Edinburgh. What does commercial mean at Shoosmiths? It encompasses litigation, employment and more specialist practices like IP, competition and regulatory. All in all, Shoosmiths has notched up over 50 *Chambers UK* rankings and is regarded as a national leader outside of London in banking and finance, corporate, employment, IP, and pensions in particular.

At the moment the firm recruits trainees in all office except London and Basingstoke. Trainees generally don't get a chance to pick their first seat unless they're an internal candidate who's graduated from the paralegal ranks, though their subsequent three rotations see them sit down with their office's training principal to discuss their next move. *"They often go out of their way to ensure you get one of your top two choices."* Second-years naturally get priority, but *"they do strive to accommodate us – for example, on occasion the firm will put two trainees into a department which usually takes just one."*

Seat options: corporate; insolvency; tax; finance litigation; banking; real estate; planning; construction; real estate litigation; commercial litigation; employment; IP; regulatory; medical negligence (go online to view seats by location)

The True Picture

Chambers UK rankings

Banking & Finance	Outsourcing
Banking Litigation	Pensions
Clinical Negligence	Personal Injury
Construction	Planning
Corporate/M&A	Private Client
Environment	Product Liability
Health & Safety	Real Estate
Information Technology	Real Estate Litigation
Intellectual Property	Retail
Licensing	Social Housing
Litigation	Tax

It's possible to complete seats in different offices. Moreover, Northampton and Milton Keynes are treated as one office for recruiting, but three seats are typically completed in Milton Keynes and one in Northampton. Moves tend to occur when a trainee has a strong preference for a seat their home office doesn't offer. Client secondments are, however, a common undertaking. *"Some clients have ongoing three-month spots, and other opportunities pop up all of the time, like a company that needs a trainee for a couple of days a week. It really comes down to what the client wants."* Thomas Cook and VW are possible destinations.

Yacht's up?

In 2013 the Birmingham branch moved to *"plush"* new offices in Two Colmore Square. *"We've become one of the larger offices now – we've got all the major practices, plus many practice group leaders. A lot of training sessions and inductions are held here too."* Brummie employment lawyers act for the likes of Debenhams, Birmingham City FC and Peugeot Citroën. More often than not the team represents the employer, though some 10% of its output is dedicated to individuals. Brum trainees, told us a stint with the employment team is *"brilliant – you get to attend tribunal hearings and see the whole process through."* There's a fair bit of drafting involved too: contentious issues come with the chance to draft witness statements and parts of settlement agreements, while employment contracts and company handbooks form the bulk of the drafting on the non-contentious side. Birmingham's *Chambers UK*-ranked restructuring and insolvency practice is worthy of a special mention too. Lawyers here recently assisted business adviser Baker Tilly with the administration of a luxury yacht business.

Nottingham, one of Shoosmiths' smaller offices, offers a *"limited range of seats:"* real estate, real estate litigation, commercial, corporate and employment. Its real estate practice is well known and scores a top regional *Chambers UK* ranking. The team recently represented European REIT Stainton International during its joint venture with an international alternative investment fund, leading to the acquisition of 28 industrial estates throughout England and Scotland. Trainees here reported getting to grips with *"the transactional side of the 1954 Act,"* drafting and negotiating leases. *"Partners are keen to get you involved in any negotiations based around documents you've helped draft. I spent three weeks arguing over the use of the word 'reasonably'!"* The real estate litigation team, meanwhile, services a good deal of retail clients like Alliance Boots and Next, and tasks its trainees with *"assisting on issue proceedings and file audits, and making sure the court timetable doesn't slip."*

The Manchester office turns five years old in 2014 and *"we've moved three times since then just to accommodate growth!"* The branch is now full-service, welcoming two trainees a year, but this may increase to three. It offers many seats spread among the core teams of corporate, commercial, real estate and recovery services. *Chambers UK* offers a top-notch nod to Manchester's financial litigation team, which services *"mostly major high-street banks; we don't act for any borrowers."* Trainees here reported keeping busy *"calling debtors"* and attending bankruptcy hearings. It's not uncommon for new recruits to run their own small files. *"You receive instructions from clients, issue proceedings in court, and instruct agents and barristers. The ultimate goal is to secure payment."* Over in banking, lawyers recently acted for RBS during its £5.7m funding of an acquisition that created the UK's biggest audio production company.

Live a lotto

The lively Reading office, home to nine trainees at the time of our calls, is *"generally a bit louder than the others,"* we hear. The IP seat here is split with the Milton Keynes office. The team is big in the clothing, automotive, and food and drink sectors in particular, nabbing clients like H&M, Volkswagen and McDonald's in recent years. IP matters span the contentious and non-contentious spheres. A stint in commercial is *"a bit more technical"* as Shoosmiths offers quite a specialist service in the outsourcing, supply chain and international trade industries.

Milton Keynes offers trainees the chance to dabble in pensions and private client work alongside its bigger commercial and real estate practices. Private clients include a heady array of business-owners, PLC directors, landowners and members of the aristocracy, and lawyers here also counsel lucky National Lottery winners via the firm's position on the Camelot advisory panel. Trainees who'd sat with the team told of working with both high net worth individuals after tax and trust advice and *"people off the street who just want a will."* The latter type of work *"involves getting as much info as possible about the assets at hand, then writing to the people or organisations involved, like insurance companies and banks."*

There were six trainees in Southampton at the time of our research, compared to the four in Milton Keynes. The office is located in a business park next to the motorway. *"It sounds horrible, but we're next to a big lake and a shopping centre, so it's really not that bad."* Chambers UK top-ranks the corporate practice here, which draws in clients from the insurance, technology and retail sectors. Lawyers recently represented Telefónica UK in its sale of 70-plus O2 stores to 16 different buyers. Trainees said the department is very busy at the moment, with one telling us *"I've already seen two deals completed, and I've only been here a few months."* Our interviewees had encountered *"a bit of everything,"* including M&A, private equity and public company transactions. *"There's tons of drafting – you do board minutes, resolutions, loan notes, share certificates and Companies House forms. They give you a bunch of documents and help if you need it."* It's also possible to dip into marine law and shipping work too, which falls under commercial litigation.

Because I'm happeeeeeeeeee

Our interviewees were keen to emphasise *"there's no 'don't speak to me because I'm a partner' nonsense here. People have a good sense of humour and don't take themselves too seriously; trainees certainly aren't seen as minions."* Indeed, Shoosmiths opts for a *"democratic approach,"* one our sources likened to the way the network is structured. *"Many of our offices are similarly sized, and there's no sense that any one is a satellite office; they make it clear each base plays an important part in the bigger picture, the same way it's clear every lawyer here does."*

There are defined links between certain offices and practice groups. Thanks to their proximity, Manchester works frequently with Edinburgh and Birmingham, while Reading lawyers regularly collaborate with their colleagues in Southampton. Meanwhile the big national practices – commercial, corporate and real estate – send out busyness reports each week in an effort to distribute work efficiently: *"If the Reading team is quiet while Birmingham's crazy busy, then they'll spread things out."* Departmental away days and regular hot-desking also help cement these cross-office links.

All incoming trainees gather for an induction in Birmingham, *"which enhances your support network from the get-go."* First-years go on to complete all their PSCs together in Birmingham, occasions that always include a social element. *"You stay overnight in a hotel and partake in some planned evening activities. Note, I'm not talking about a fancy hotel; it's more likely the Premier Inn."*

We're told the firm is interested in recruiting trainees with a 'can-do' attitude: *"Essentially, a willingness to have a go at everything."* This outgoing spirit is evident in the 'New Friday Initiative', a networking programme spearheaded by a former trainee. At various points over the year each office's trainees invite a group of young professionals out for an informal get-together: *"It's fun and very casual – everyone lets their hair down, and there's usually pizza and money behind the bar."* Letting their hair down is something trainees are familiar with here, with many telling us one reason they targeted the firm in the first place is *"the way it prides itself on promoting a good work/life balance. The firm generally attracts people with outside interests and lives."* Of course, *"this is a law firm, so you have to expect the occasional late night."* Fortunately, *"when you do stay late, you'll find the teams are massively in it together, which helps."*

The 2013 retention round was *"bleak,"* with less than half of the trainee cohort retained. Luckily things have improved in the year since – 14 of 23 new qualifiers stayed on in 2014. *"They really took on board comments from last year about how to improve things. In March they brought all of us together in Birmingham to hand out the timetable and go through the different steps to qualification."* The firm did say that it had positions available for everyone; however, they weren't necessarily in first choice locations or departments. Trainees can apply for any of the jobs advertised firm-wide and told us formal seat reviews are very important when it comes to the qualification decision. *"They're basically your CV for job applications, so supervisors take them seriously and are very thorough."* Given Shoosmiths' national stature, some sources felt that trainee salaries *"are on the low side,"* with one suggesting: *"They should be about 10% higher."* That said, the same interviewees deemed the NQ salary, which is on a par with firms that bill equivalent hours, *"reasonable."*

And finally...

Joining Shoosmiths as a paralegal is an increasingly common entry route to the firm, so bear this in mind when deciding whether to add Shoosmiths to your 'yes' pile.

Sidley Austin LLP

The facts

Location: London

Number of UK partners/solicitors: 31/68 (plus 10 US-qualified)

UK partners who trained at the firm: 8%

Total number of trainees: 22

Seats: 4x6 months

Alternative seats: Brussels, occasional secondments

Extras: pro bono, language classes and CRS

On chambersstudent.co.uk...

How to get into Sidley

Energy expansion

Sidley continues to develop its post-recession identity, which ties its traditional rep for structured finance with know-how in blossoming areas like litigation and funds.

Hail to the chief

Sidley is well known in the States – and not just because it's the place where Barack and Michelle Obama met when the future president came in for a summer placement and Michelle was his associate 'buddy'. Its top-notch, high-quality work – broadly encompassing transactional, litigation and regulatory practices – consistently comes in for praise from *Chambers USA*, which showers the firm with over 30 nationwide rankings. This scope is in part the product of a 2001 merger, which brought together the Midwestern charm of Sidley & Austin with the Wall Street gloss of capital markets maestro Brown & Wood.

It's all worked out rather well, as today Sidley sits up there with the largest global law firms, with 1,800 lawyers beavering away to keep Sidley's name ringing out across the US, Europe and the Asia-Pacific region. While Sidley may have recently closed its Frankfurt base (after deciding that a physical presence in Germany was no longer imperative for clients), the firm certainly hasn't turned its back on Europe, and London remains a strong performer – office revenue grew by 6% in 2013.

"We're hearing our name out there more and more!" trainees observed. Perhaps that's testament to an improving market standing or perhaps it's just a consequence of the new vac scheme making the firm better known among students (the scheme first ran in 2013 – go online to find out more). Besides student interns, lateral hires have also invigorated life in the office: structured finance partner Matthew Cahill joined from Clifford Chance; litigator

Matthew Shankland hopped over from Weil; and Stephen Ross from the Man Group (the world's second largest hedge fund manager) was bagged as the new co-head of investment funds. *"Funds is definitely one to watch,"* trainees told us, adding that we should also expect growth in the litigation and restructuring departments.

Seats are available in the global finance group (GFG), capital markets, funds, corporate, disputes, competition, regulatory, tax, insurance, employment, and restructuring/insolvency. Trainees rank preferences for all seats (even their first one) after receiving a list which reveals where seats are available, and a couple of months before each rotation have a chat with HR. Generally speaking seats are either three or six months long, although at the time of our calls interviewees noted that at the most recent rotation only six-month seats had been available. Trainees predicted that this will be a continuing trend: *"Partners prefer to have trainees for six months; it means they're better able to maximise your utility. And as a trainee a longer stint means that you learn a lot more and can consolidate that experience."* HR was praised for *"trying to accommodate everyone,"* and we heard that

Seat options: corporate and securities (incl. employment, competition Brussels and competition London); tax; capital markets; insurance and financial services; financial services regulatory; global finance group; dispute resolution; corporate reorganisation and bankruptcy; funds group

Chambers UK rankings

Capital Markets	Litigation
Data Protection	Real Estate Finance
Insurance	Restructuring/Insolvency
Investment Funds	Tax

generally *"people have got what they wanted."* The restructuring/insolvency seat has been especially popular recently: four or five trainees applied for the two spots in the department in spring 2014.

GFG: Global Finance Giant

The global finance group – or just 'finance' as we would call it – was singled out by trainees as the firm's main department, although they noted that *"it's not compulsory to do a seat here."* The group is known for its structured finance capabilities, and lawyers recently helped Novatio Capital put through a securitisation programme for solar parks, as well as other renewable facilities, in a matter worth £66m. Lawyers also offer expertise in derivatives, real estate finance, finance litigation and general banking. Trainees sit with their supervisor, who may specialise in a certain area, but at the same time are given *"free rein to work with different people with different specialisations."* Those who'd picked up general banking work were able to draft director's certificates and shareholder resolutions, as well as *"ventures to arrange the security and deed of lease to release security obligations."* Quite. With comments like that getting bandied about, it goes without saying that this is a complex and jargon-heavy area of law – for a basic understanding read our practice area features on banking and finance (p. **101**) and capital markets (p. **103**). As a general GFG rule, *"if it's a large transaction then you won't be heavily involved in drafting and negotiating,"* but on smaller matters trainees are allowed to *"negotiate the main points of the deal and other contested parts of it."* This means you *"learn to think about what matters most to the client, and then justify it so that we succeed on those points."*

The restructuring/insolvency department is *"exceptionally busy,"* and was described by several sources as *"the most intense"* that they'd sat in. Fortunately, *"the work is very interesting,"* and also high-value: the team have just finished representing Blackstone Real Estate and Isobel Assetco in connection to five commercial real estate restructuring matters, the largest of which involved £1bn worth of debt. Another trainee told us: *"I worked on three deals which involved buying distressed debt from a Spanish bank in liquidation: our client was a real estate fund, and the first deal involved buying a shopping centre in Dublin, the second an office block in Prague, and the third a hotel in Barcelona."*

Corporate has *"more junior associates than some other departments"* so responsibility levels here are not quite what they are in finance. Trainees find themselves *"drafting amendments to partnership agreements and board minutes,"* and dealing with *"general what-can-and-can't-we-do requests from companies."* The department does quite a bit of private M&A as well as partnership work for private equity firms and fund managers.

To merge, or not to merge?

Sidley has a strong reputation for finance and derivatives litigation, but trainees who sat with the dispute resolution team insisted that the work there is varied: *"The disputes could be about absolutely anything and could have insurance, insolvency or capital markets elements to them."* A lot of the work has an overseas tinge to it: one recent $1.2bn case saw London lawyers represent a Bermudan reinsurance company, Pulsar Re, during disputes arising from the provisional liquidation of underwriter Lehman Re. *"There's a lot going on all of the time, so it's quite frantic and everyone is incredibly busy,"* said one trainee, while another told us of a *"huge"* disclosure exercise which involved *"three million documents and lasted two and a half months."* While this amount of document drudgery provoked cries of *"horrendous!"* from our interviewees, there is also legal research and court time to enjoy. *"I'm at the Royal Courts of Justice or the Rolls Building almost every day delivering and issuing documents, setting up for trials, organising witness statements, and pulling together videographers and stenographers. I've also been arranging for our American colleagues to come over for the hearing."*

Insurance is *"a very well-established department"* according to trainees and wins *Chambers UK* rankings for both its contentious and non-contentious work. It handles M&A in the insurance sector, as well as contractual issues related to insurance policies. In 2013 it advised Apollo on its acquisition of a stake in insurance holding company Catalina, and acted for Hartford Life on the disposal of its UK life insurance and annuity business. Trainees reported being able to see entire deals end to end and *"get stuck into drafting the ancillary documents, e-mailing back and forth with the client, and putting together the disclosure report."* Sources also told us they had *"sat in on negotiations between two parties, taken notes, dealt with queries and amended parts of the agreement."*

Monster's Ball

The majority of Sidley's London lawyers are UK-qualified, so the firm's American heritage is not immediately apparent. *"There are a few US lawyers who've come over from the States,"* observed one trainee, *"and I feel we have taken their American qualities and merged them with our British ones"* – overall there's more of a 'mid-

The True Picture

Atlantic' bent to the culture. The American influence is most evident in the firm's *"on-call mentality."* A trainee explained: *"You are given a smartphone, and are expected to check it in the evenings – long hours and picking up work outside the office is seen as the norm rather than the exception."* Trainees reported that sometimes they *"get given something super-urgent at 3 or 4pm, and then have to work late."* Sources agreed that *"that is annoying when you've made plans."* Stints in restructuring/insolvency, capital markets and GFG yield the most intense hours (*"there were numerous occasions when I was here until 5am,"* reported one trainee), while advisory seats like competition and regulatory offer a more stable experience.

Events are taken quite seriously at Sidley, and the firm knows how to throw a good party. There are Christmas and summer celebrations, which in the past have come complete with Samba dancers and embarrassing trainee-led renditions of 'What does the Fox Say' – *"the most horrendous song ever!"* The 2013 Halloween party was one of the most extravagant yet: *"The firm spent a huge amount of money on it, and people were able to bring their families too. The theme was* 'Monsters Inc.' *and the firm brought in set designers to transform the meeting rooms into the* Monsters Inc. *bedrooms – there were animals and chocolate fountains too!"*

Trainees described their intake as being pretty close, having already had the chance to squeeze in bonding time during the firm-specific fast-track LPC at BPP. They're quite a sporty bunch too, and get involved in runs, as well as softball and netball teams. Lawyers are not afraid to exercise their vocal chords either: Sidley's choir recently competed in the legal profession's first ever choral competition, 'Legal Harmony': *"The quality wasn't incredible, but we raised over £1,000 for charity!"*

After a stellar 100% qualification rate in 2013, Sidley has again performed well. Jobs were offered to everybody, and seven of nine qualifiers took them up. Second-years throw their hat in the ring by applying with a CV and then undergo interviews, the style of which depends on the department in question: *"Some want to have informal chats with a 'Why do you want to work here?' set-up, while others grill you and ask you a lot more hypothetical 'What would you do in these circumstances?' questions."*

And finally...

Trainees are primarily drawn to Sidley for "*the finance aspects of the work – you have to be if you want to work here.*"

Simmons & Simmons LLP

The facts

Location: London

Number of UK partners/solicitors: 230/800

Partners who trained at firm: 25%

Total number of trainees: 83

Seats: 4x6 months

Alternative seats: overseas seats, secondments

Extras: pro bono – Battersea Legal Advice Centre, LawWorks, A4ID, TrustLaw, International Senior Lawyers Project, Lawyers Volunteering for the Arts

On chamberstudent.co.uk...

How to get into Simmons & Simmons

Interview with recruitment partner Alan Gar

Simmons' art collection

Is this City finance leader trying to shed its *"nice guy image"* in favour of something more hard-nosed?

Don't look a gift course in the mouth

"The indications are that it has been a successful year," says graduate recruitment partner Alan Gar. Revenues rebounded in 2013/14 to £268.6m after a slight dip in the preceding year. Gar attributes the upturn to the firm's openings in Saudi Arabia (2011), Bristol (2012), Singapore and Munich (2013) *"bedding in,"* a number of lateral partner hires, a new alliance with a firm in South Africa, and the increasing emphasis on *"a high-performance culture."* He adds: *"There's certainly been an uptake in work and it's been a busier year for the firm, so we hope to continue to grow further."*

Simmons is known foremost as a financial heavyweight but offers a highly successful full-service practice, picking up *Chambers UK* rankings in everything from employment to pensions. All the firm's output is based around five key sectors: financial services; life sciences; TMT; asset management/investment funds; and energy and infrastructure.

This *"clear sector focus"* drew in a lot of our interviewees. The size of the intake was also cited – *"Some firms take 100 trainees and it feels like you get no attention. Some take five and you feel like there isn't much structure. 35 to 40 trainees is about optimal."* – as was the firm's offer of an MBA course in conjunction with the training contract. Trainees can gain a Certificate in Business during the LPC, then during their first two years with Simmons qualify for a Diploma in Business. Once qualified you will continue to study for a full MBA for a further twelve months. *"No one else was offering that,"* chirped a first-year.

Ranking, banking and overseas tramping

There are 14 seat choices on offer at Simmons, plus the opportunity to undertake an international or client secondment. Before each rotation trainees give their preferences. *"You literally rank them one to 14,"* we were told. *"You have to list everything."* There are four blocks of seats: contentious; corporate/commercial; financial markets (FMD – the 'D' stands for 'department'); and 'other'. Trainees must do at least one seat from within each of the first three blocks, and while secondments are not compulsory they are *"highly encouraged. About 80% of trainees will do one."* Overseas seats can be taken in the Tokyo, Hong Kong, Abu Dhabi, Dubai, Singapore and Paris offices, or you can venture in-house to a range of *"pharmaceutical, energy or financial services companies."*

Most of our sources got their first choices and *"nobody ever gets lower than their fifth unless they're not paying attention to the seats they have to do."* We heard that *"IP is one of the most popular options along with employment,"* while *"financial services is usually sought after because it is such a big sector for the firm. A lot of trainees come here with the intention of doing it."*

Seat options: asset finance; banking; capital markets; corporate; employment; environment; EU; competition and regulatory; financial services; information, communications and technology; IP; litigation; projects; real estate; tax

Chambers UK rankings

Asset Finance	Information Technology
Banking & Finance	Intellectual Property
Banking Litigation	Investment Funds
Capital Markets	Life Sciences
Commodities	Litigation
Competition/European Law	Outsourcing
	Pensions
Construction	Product Liability
Consumer Finance	Professional Negligence
Corporate Crime & Investigations	Projects
	Real Estate
Corporate/M&A	Real Estate Finance
Employment	Restructuring/Insolvency
Energy & Natural Resources	Retail
Environment	Tax
Financial Services	Telecommunications
Fraud	Transport

Financial services, part of the FMD group, contains three subsets: funds, regulatory and derivatives. Across these the firm looks after heavyweight clients like Morgan Stanley, Allianz Global Investors and Lloyds. *"My jobs were mainly proofreading and other administrative-type tasks,"* said one source on funds. *"However I also produced updates of investors' documents, wrote some first drafts and liaised with counsel, translators and clients. For a first seat it was good work actually."*

On the regulatory side we heard *"the work mostly involves sitting in with or calling local counsel to discuss the regulatory requirements for companies in other jurisdictions. Essentially it's creating memos and fact sheets for what they can and can't do."* Another source described it as *"research-y,"* but added: *"I didn't expect to enjoy it so much. I've had excellent supervisors throughout, but my one in this seat was out-of-this-world amazing. I felt I developed the most here."*

The capital markets team is another heavy-hitter within FMD and handles transactions for major banks such as Barclays, Merrill Lynch and HSBC – think high-complexity, multi-jurisdictional IPOs, bonds issuances, swaps, securitisations... one source grumbled: *"It's a very steep learning curve and in reality people don't have time to sit down and explain all the jargon. Overall the seat was very administrative, which was really frustrating."* To counter this, another trainee told us: *"The seat was really good. I was drafting a lot of documents and working directly with the partners on quite a few structured product matters."*

The banking team was strengthened by lateral partner hires from Berwin Leighton Paisner a few years ago that formed a new real estate finance group. *"It's good*

to be in a department that's really thriving and getting stronger every year," offered a trainee. *"I was given a lot of responsibility in a busy department, but there's still the safety net of associates and partners. I was mainly in a project management role – liaising with clients and checking precedents had been satisfied. It was an excellent seat as you can see what your life will be like as your career develops."*

Bundling, bibling and branding

Simmons' corporate/M&A practice works exclusively within the firm's five key business sectors. A recent big deal on the life sciences front saw the team advise Becton Dickinson on the sale of its BD Biosciences Discovery Labware unit to Corning Incorporated for $730m. *"The first thing I will say is that the hours are crazy,"* said one sleep-deprived trainee. *"I was stretched to a whole new level. You're outside of your comfort zone and have to step up to the plate, but when you see a deal you worked on in the* Financial Times *it's all worth it and feels like a massive personal triumph."*

Projects also falls under the corporate/commercial umbrella and here trainees *"mostly worked on infrastructure and energy deals."* One elaborated: *"It's a very, very, very busy department with an awful lot going on so you have hit the ground running. Because the deals are so large (such as advising Mainstream Renewable Power on its $1.4bn joint venture with Actis for delivering wind and solar projects in Chile) a lot of the work is quite secretarial or administrative. I did however handle one or two smaller matters and got a lot of responsibility on those."*

The dispute resolution team has both commercial and financial branches. *"It's a bit of an arbitrary split, though,"* we were told. *"You're essentially a trainee for the whole department and it's really easy to do work in both, but you can express a preference for either."* On the financial side, one whirlwind trainee said: *"I came across a lot of interesting work, including massive fraud and insider-dealing cases. As such there is a significant amount of bundling and bibling. Everyone always grimaces about it, and you will get paper cuts and have to carry hand cream everywhere, but it's important to remember what your role is and how important it is for the bigger picture. By the end I did get to handle a few smaller cases under supervision too."* The commercial branch delves into areas like insurance, professional negligence and white-collar crime. *"As a trainee there's a fair balance between doing the necessary grunt work and the higher-level associate tasks like drafting letters and disclosure obligations."*

IP is one of the most popular seats. The firm draws some *"sexy"* clients from its major industry sectors such as Samsung, Bayer and GlaxoSmithKline. *"It's nice to deal with big-name companies that people have heard of,"*

The True Picture

said one. *"Recently we've been involved in the Apple/Samsung dispute that's been all over the papers."* In case you missed this, the two tech titans have been bickering over alleged patent infringements made by Samsung. *"There's not a huge amount of responsibility, but that goes hand in hand with being a junior in a contentious department,"* reflected a young 'un. *"Often as a trainee you're sent off to pick up infringing products – you look like a lunatic going to buy loads of brands of the same thing! However, you do get a lot of access to client meetings and are given exposure whenever you can."*

No more Mr Nice Guy...

All our sources agreed that Simmons has a *"nice guy image. It has a reputation for being good place to work."* Oddly, though, they said that the firm is trying to shake this representation. *"They don't want 'nice' to be confused with mediocrity,"* explained one trainee. *"Not many people would describe great corporate lawyers as nice."* Another added: *"It can be a friendly place to work, but nice always sounds slightly pejorative. If you have a firm fighting your corner, you want to be the tough one, not the fluffy and cuddly one you can push to one side."*

Simmons' current drive for a *"high-performance culture"* ties with this. *"I think we've realised that we aren't loud enough about the things we are good at – we're a bit modest,"* considered a second-year. *"We've always delivered high performance – and will maintain that – but we need to be a bit more bullish and put it out there in the market to show the firm's ambition instead of trundling on."*

The fear that Simmons has been doing just that – trundling along – was real: *"I worry that we're staying slightly static while other firms are moving on around us,"* pondered a second-year. *"Most of our competitors, like Norton Rose, seem to be merging, and while we have a good presence in Europe and Asia, we still don't have any offices in North America."* Another trainee mused: *"The lack of US offices is a bit ridiculous, despite our alliance with Seward & Kissel."*

Merger talks with Mayer Brown a few years ago never quite got off the ground, but trainees believe *"there is still a drive"* to throw its lot in with a major American player. Graduate recruitment partner Alan Gar had this to say: *"The firm is always interested in new opportunities – we've had an alliance with Seward & Kissel since October 2012. This is a really strong relationship that works well for both firms and we're still committed to focusing our efforts here."*

One trainee concluded: *"The firm generally has a lot of ambition and is really committed to growing internationally. I just think they are cautious about rushing into anything. The culture is quite unique and they don't want to change that."*

...but still quite nice

While to an outside audience Simmons is trying to project a stern and efficient façade, trainees were quick to point out that the internal atmosphere remained inviting. *"They probably won't like me saying this, but it really is a nice place to work,"* asserted one. *"That's a massive selling point in corporate law. Everyone I have come across is approachable and there is a really supportive environment. You do get the occasional oddball partner stuck in the 1970s, but they are few and far between."* Another trainee echoed this: *"It's definitely supportive, which is so important coming into a legal career, as it can take so much out of you, so you need people to fall back on at a professional level. Even when I was on secondment I knew I had a whole department back at base if I needed to ask silly questions. Everyone has so much time for me and that really built my confidence."*

While we were assured there is no such thing as a Simmons 'type', we did hear *"ruthless egoism and a stab-someone-in-the-back-to-get-yourself-ahead attitude is not going to work here. For the couple of trainees who did have that outlook, it really did not go well."* That said, most of the cohort is *"ambitious and wants to impress."* With retention rates somewhat inconsistent in recent years, nobody is resting on their laurels. *"There is of course a bit of competition – this is the legal industry right?"* posed a second-year. *"However, there's a really healthy atmosphere among my intake. You're aware who you might be up against, but it's never vitriolic."* In 2014, 33 out of 39 qualifiers were kept on.

And finally...
In keeping with the firm's friendly atmosphere, Simmons is well known for its commitment to diversity, and its LGBT network in particular picks up a glut of awards.

Skadden, Arps, Slate, Meagher & Flom (UK) LLP

The facts

Location: London

Number of UK partners/solicitors: 30/50

Total number of trainees: 16

Seats: 4x6 months

Alternative seats: overseas seats

Extras: pro bono – LawWorks, TrustLaw, Child Rights Information Network

On chambersstudent.co.uk...

How to get into Skadden

Interview with joint grad recruitment partner Danny Tricot

The failed Pfizer/AstraZeneca merger

Skadden's founders

At one of America's – and the world's – most fearsome firms, who would expect a chummy London office where *"everyone knows everyone by name"?*

Not so dinky

To the uninitiated, everything Skadden is huge and terrifying – the embodiment of ruthless New York BigLaw. But it wasn't always that way: when Joe Flom joined four-month-old Skadden in New York in 1948, it was a *"dinky little firm"* says a former partner, and the going-rate salary was just $3,600 per year. Founded in a three-way partnership of rebuffed Jewish immigrant lawyers, it is perhaps no surprise that this firm's subsequent blinding success was driven by a desire to prove its worth.

The firm's reputation today isn't just based on its size (which is nonetheless considerable, with 1,600 lawyers across 23 offices), but more for the way it churns its way through some of the world's biggest, toughest and costliest cases. *"There's never a run-of-the-mill deal,"* an insider explained. *"There's always something interesting about the work done at Skadden that hasn't been done before."* In 2014 Skadden was named the *Chambers Global* international law firm of the year for its expertise on high-value and high-stakes cases. Work highlights are fittingly headline-grabbing, like advising Pfizer on its proposed multi-billion dollar takeover of AstraZeneca – which would have been one of the global drugs industry's largest ever deals. Skadden also represented Russian oligarch Roman Abramovich in his successful rebuttal of rival Boris Berezovsky's $6bn claim. For more on Skadden's unlikely history, see our bonus features online.

Skadden's class sizes can typically be counted on your fingers, and trainees work in small teams with a partner and around two associates. *"You do have to stand up and be counted,"* a source affirmed, *"because it's not like*

there's any way you can shirk responsibility – there's nowhere to hide."* But most saw this as one of Skadden's major draws: *"I applied because I wanted to do as little photocopying as possible,"* one said, *"and it's certainly lived up to that expectation; trainees are given enormous amounts of responsibility with weighty tasks that you'd expect someone to be doing at a much higher level."* To help them scale this mountainous learning curve, the first few weeks of the training contract are spent on various professional skills courses and internal training sessions. After that, departments hold their own at the beginning of each rotation, and this is supplemented by optional lunchtime training seminars once or twice a week.

Trainees submit three preferences during seat allocation, and need to complete stints in both litigation and corporate at some point. While most were satisfied with the process, a couple expressed concerns over *"a lack of clarity."* One said: *"We know about the process and who decides, but the reasoning behind their decisions isn't always communicated."* Graduate recruitment partner Danny Tricot sheds some light: *"Departments submit how many spaces they have, and the only thing we do as partners is discuss where to keep people busy and engaged. It's never a case of saying, 'I want Joe Smith to come to me next,' and if someone doesn't get their first choice for a particular seat, chances are they'll get it next time around."*

Seat options: corporate; banking; capital markets; litigation and arbitration; funds; tax; investigations

The True Picture

Chambers UK rankings

Banking & Finance	International Arbitration
Capital Markets	Investment Funds
Corporate Crime & Investigations	Litigation
Corporate/M&A	Private Equity
Energy & Natural Resources	Restructuring/Insolvency
	Tax

Olig-arch-enemies

The dispute resolution department in Skadden's London office scores top *Chambers UK* rankings in both litigation and international arbitration. The latter is what this outpost is historically known for, and it's easy to see why: in 2013, the practice handled arbitrations with a combined value in excess of $57bn. Key clients include sovereign states and big banks, and the team has handled its fair share of Russian oil disputes. High net worth individuals also feature in this department's impressive client roster, and the firm is currently embroiled in the latest instalment of headline-hitting oligarch battles, defending Gennadiy Bogolyubov against Viktor Pinchuk in 2014's mega court case (complete with mega fees).

"Skadden is interested in the most difficult cases – they don't just grab any old generic cookie," a trainee enthused. *"We're often tackling new developments, niche questions and unusual circumstances."* With this in mind, it would be a reasonable assumption that trainees take a back-seat role – but that's not the case. *"There's a lot of confidence in your ability,"* an insider confirmed. *"I always thought that one of my main tasks would be bundling, but that's not something that I saw much of. Instead, I was involved in strategy meetings and put on calls with experts alone; I felt like I could run my parts and people would trust my judgement."* Trainees also get stuck into drafting witness statements and keeping tabs on the latest headlines for politically driven cases. *"It's more academic than corporate,"* a source asserted. Working hours range, though there's no face-time requirement. When work picks up, trainees can expect a few late ones: *"The earliest that I left was around five, while the latest I stayed... well, I never left!"*

Over in corporate, the team deals with M&A and capital markets work across domestic and international jurisdictions, especially in high-growth markets like Russia, the Middle East and Central Asia. *"The work was second to none,"* a trainee asserted, *"as some of the deals that corporate gets involved with are the biggest and best."* And that's not an overstatement: back in 2012, Skadden represented AAR in the $56bn sale of its joint venture with BP, TNK-BP, to Rosneft Oil Company. This was the largest M&A transaction in the world in 2012, and the largest globally for more than three years. Other clients include multinational investment management corpora-

tion BlackRock, Nike and Finnish stainless steel manufacturer Outokumpu.

Trainees tackle *"several matters at the same time"* in this department, *"whether it's just doing bits and bobs of research or the entire project."* One said: *"I had to keep track of the articles of associations and memorandums for between 20 and 25 companies."* Trainees talk clients through case developments and draft less-important documents like board resolutions and reports. One said: *"You get a lot of responsibility for certain aspects of the deal, but anything with a commercial risk for the client will be done by the partners."* Sources praised the department's small teams: *"For one matter, it was just the partner and me, so I did all of the drafting and sat in on all the meetings."* Unsurprisingly, trainees get *"a lot of feedback from a high level."* But, like any corporate department, working hours vary: *"You get short, busy periods where you stay past midnight, but then you get a breather for a few weeks when a deal has been signed and you can leave at five."*

A banking seat provides *"a scary amount"* of responsibility. *"I had only been immersed in the corporate world for a couple of months,"* one said, *"but straight away I was left to run a conditions precedent check-list that made up a significant part of the transaction."* The London office acts as a hub for European deals, and the team is currently representing German holding company Joh A Benckiser with the asset financing of its $9.8bn acquisition of Dutch company DE Master Blenders. Trainees get stuck into things like preparing board resolutions and researching market trends. But, due to the department's *"huge volume of work,"* hours can be long at times and trainees can expect to spend a few weekends in the office. *"If the work is there, you're there,"* one said, *"though the opposite is also true, and you occasionally leave at five."*

Meanwhile, *"tax is a technical area, and the learning curve is initially steep."* But, *"it lays good foundations for people who want to qualify into corporate or funds, because almost all transactional structures are driven by tax considerations."* Trainees work across the team, *"so you need to be very organised."* However, major perks include an office of your very own. *"I definitely felt like an NQ,"* one said.

Dog-eat-hot-dog

The stereotype is that US firms are hierarchical, dog-eat-dog sweatshops where lawyers can abandon any hope of seeing daylight over the winter months. But we found a very different story. *"It's actually far from scary,"* a trainee remarked. *"Because it's a small office, everyone knows everyone by name. I'll admit, I thought that it would be an intimidating place before I started, but having been here for a while it's lost that aura and it turns out that behind the curtain these people aren't terrifying monsters –*

you can have a laugh with them." Indeed, the office keeps its sense of humour with typical office japes: *"There are huge chain e-mails of partners and associates chipping in and taking the piss – I remember once someone accidentally sent an e-mail querying somebody's personal hygiene to the whole London office, and chaos ensued!"*

We heard that Skadden *"treats its trainees like adults."* One said: *"You're not constantly monitored and nobody cares if you come in late – you just have to make yourself available and stick around when there's work to be done."* Many agreed that Skadden struggles with an unjust reputation: *"I think that our firm gets more of a bad rep for an awful work/life balance than it should – maybe it's that*

idea of the American firm, or because they pay a lot so there's that impression that they'll want their pound of flesh. I haven't seen that – I work hard, sometimes harder, but overall it's not as bad as people say."

Skadden has an active social life. *"Every Friday without fail, everyone from trainees to partners will go for a pint in one of the bars around Canary Wharf,"* an insider remarked. A tad more formally, we heard that trainees at Skadden had attended Italian ski trips, sampled hot-dog canapés at the 4th of July bash and kicked back with *"fancy"* chicken kievs in Chelsea football club's directors' box.

The True Picture

And finally...

"If you get a training contract here, you're pretty much guaranteed a job at the end of it." And they're not wrong – 100% retention rates are the norm at Skadden. In 2014, seven of seven were retained.

Slaughter and May

The facts

Location: London

Number of UK partners/solicitors: 105/394

Partners who trained at the firm: 82%

Total number of trainees: 156

Seats: 4x6 months (occasional 3-month seats)

Alternative seats: overseas seats, secondments

Extras: pro bono – RCJ Advice Bureau, A41D, LawWorks, TrustLaw; language classes

On chambersstudent.co.uk...

How to get into Slaughter and May

Overseas seats

This 125-year-old City institution expects nothing but the best.

Put your best FTSE forward

Slaughter and May's reputation as one of the most prestigious and profitable firms in the world is hardly unjustified. This magic circle thoroughbred upholds an unfaltering commitment to excellence, and draws in the biggest and the best deals out there. Unlike other magic circle firms, Slaughters hasn't embarked on a rampant, and sometimes perilous, programme of international expansion into every continent, favouring instead a 'best friends' relationship with a network of top corporate firms around the world. As such, it still has access to a bevy of multi-jurisdictional matters without the costs and risks that come with opening offices in volatile markets. That said, Slaughters' global footprint isn't invisible – the firm has offices in Brussels, Hong Kong and Beijing, in addition to its London HQ.

The reputation of the firm's corporate department is second to none, and it works with more FTSE 100 and FTSE 250 clients than any other firm out there. Slaughters was recently called in by Vodafone to help with the sale of its 45% stake in Verizon Wireless to Verizon Communications. The £84bn price tag made this not only the largest US-based corporate transaction since 2001 but one of the biggest deals of all time.

Elsewhere the firm has been instructed by the likes of American Express, British Airways, Diageo, Glaxo SmithKline, Morgan Stanley and Royal Mail. The finance practice is another serious heavy-hitter, and it works with Citibank, Lloyds and RBS, among others. Graphite Capital recently called the firm in to advise on its £35m acquisition of London's Hawksmoor restaurants. Unsurprisingly, Slaughters picks up a slew of stellar rankings in *Chambers UK*, which rates it among the strongest firms

in the City for banking and finance, capital markets, competition, high-end corporate, litigation, pensions, and tax.

If you've seen any of the firm's marketing materials, you'll have noticed its vague and slightly dubious tag line 'Great Minds Think Differently'. We took our insiders to task to see if they could explain what it means. *"Essentially they're looking for strong lateral thinkers. They don't want people who will recite verbatim what they were taught in law school. It's about coming in with new ideas and finding new solutions,"* one source said. Another added: *"It's testament to the range and variety of skills they want us to develop. There's a great emphasis on us being multi-specialists – people who are equally confident working on a share purchase agreement, a joint venture or a corporate restructuring, should one land on your desk at a moment's notice."*

Corporate kings

Considering Slaughters' corporate and finance clout, it should come as no surprise that a seat in both is mandatory. A considerable number of juniors will go on to a second six-month stint in one of these, and most trainees fulfil their contentious requirement by sitting in dispute resolution, though there are alternatives like competition. The firm also offers a small number of three-month seats like tax, pensions and employment, and real estate. And that's to say nothing of the overseas opportunities – a handful of third and fourth-seaters are despatched to

Seat options: corporate; finance; financial regulation; dispute resolution; competition; tax; real estate; IP/IT; pensions and employment

Chambers UK rankings

Administrative & Public Law	Information Technology
Banking & Finance	Insurance
Banking Litigation	Intellectual Property
Capital Markets	International Arbitration
Competition/European Law	Investment Funds
Construction	Life Sciences
Corporate Crime & Investigations	Litigation
Corporate/M&A	Outsourcing
Employee Share Schemes & Incentives	Pensions
Employment	Pensions Litigation
Energy & Natural Resources	Private Equity
Environment	Professional Negligence
Financial Services	Projects
Fraud	Real Estate
	Restructuring/Insolvency
	Retail
	Tax
	Telecommunications

places as far-flung as Hong Kong, New York and Australia to work in either a Slaughters office or one belonging to a 'best friend' firm. *"They gave me all of the seats I requested, so I don't have any complaints at all,"* said one source, and we heard similar things from all of the insiders we spoke to.

Four groups operate under the corporate umbrella, though our insiders were keen to stress that these divisions aren't indicative of any particular specialisms. *"It's purely down to how the groups are staffed. Whichever team you sit with, you'll pick up an incredible range of work,"* we heard. *"You could be working on anything from private equity and capital markets to M&A and IPOs to joint ventures and debt funding. Slaughters doesn't limit itself to any particular sector – it could involve renewable energy or Polish vodka."* Recently the group acted for Bupa on its $355m purchase of Quality HealthCare Medical Services from an Indian healthcare group. Typical tasks for juniors include verification, research, due diligence and drafting ancillaries like board minutes and relationship agreements. *"They don't put you in a straitjacket and tell you to do one kind of work. That can be very, very rewarding but also daunting at times. It's hard to get comfortable, and there's never any chance to rest on your laurels."*

In finance it's a similar story: there are three groups within the department, but whichever of these they find themselves in, juniors are involved in a whole host of matters. *"We work very closely with the corporate practice, and a lot of the work is passed around – that's another facet of us being multi-specialists,"* one source said. Deutsche Bank, Barratt Developments and the Manchester Airport Group are just some of the clients the group works

with – it recently advised the last of these on the £1.2bn financing for its acquisition of Stansted Airport. Project finance, asset finance, debt markets, capital markets and restructuring were all areas our sources had been involved with. *"Pretty much everything I worked on had an international element. There were deals coming out of Africa, Asia, the US and Europe while I was there. People play down the level of international work Slaughters does, but I really felt the force of it in the finance seat,"* one trainee reported. Day-to-day tasks for juniors here include drafting board minutes, resolutions, director's certificates and parts of loan agreements.

Come what may

In dispute resolution *"a huge amount of regulatory investigations work has come through in the wake of the financial crisis, so that side of the practice is booming,"* an insider told us. Elsewhere, sources spoke of working on commercial litigation, tax litigation, IP litigation and arbitrations, among others. Clients include BA, Royal Mail and Alliance Bank. The sheer size of the cases coming through means juniors are often left with some of the more menial tasks. *"The majority of what I did was doc review. It was a case of reading communications for an investigation and collecting evidence. Five hours spent doing that each day isn't the most thrilling thing in the world, but then again the case was on the front page of the FT every day, which was exciting. I always knew more than the hacks."* A second source added: *"All the proofreading and bundling I had to do felt worthwhile when I got to go to court. I also did some really interesting legal analysis."*

Slaughters' competition practice covers merger control and cartel work, as well as litigation, regulatory and state aid matters. *"It used to be a support department, but it stands by itself now and is doing very well,"* one junior said. *"The nature of the work means you're interacting with the Brussels office all the time – it starts to feel like an annex of our office. Some trainees get to do a three-month stint there as part of the seat."* Juniors described their day-to-day chores as *"quite dry"* – there's a lot of data room management and sifting through emails and other communications – but said the legislation itself is *"very cutting edge, very current and very interesting."*

Over in real estate, Slaughters' lawyers work with the likes of Arsenal, the Cabinet Office, Legal & General and ITV. The firm recently advised the Grosvenor estate on the sale of five mansions next to Hyde Park for a combined value of £114m. *"It's a fantastic seat,"* one trainee told us. *"The group is much smaller than corporate, finance or DR, so you get a lot of responsibility. That means you could be taking the first cut at a document or fielding queries from a client directly."* Another source said: *"It was classic real estate. I was helping out on the purchase and sale of some of the big buildings in the City.*

The True Picture

I attended a lot of client meetings and was drafting reports – I felt like more than just an expendable trainee."

Suited and booted

"Getting on one of the overseas seats is a more competitive process here than at other magic circle firms because we have far fewer offices," one trainee told us. Still, around ten trainees in each intake are offered the chance to spend a seat abroad. Recent postings include Amsterdam, Brussels, Hong Kong, New York and Sydney. *"It's not just a six-month jolly, particularly if you're going to one of the best friend firms – you're representing Slaughters, and there's a responsibility that comes with that. Nevertheless, it's a great opportunity, and the firm is very good at taking care of accommodation and making sure you're happy when you're out there."*

"There's a lot of talk about how punishing the hours here are, but the reality has been pleasantly surprising," trainees agreed. Indeed, pretty much every source we spoke to said they never started work before 9.30am and that there are stretches when you're out of the door by 6pm: *"Tie off, books down and you're done."* The bottom line, though, is that you stay until the work is finished. *"There can be weeks – or months – on end when you don't leave until midnight, or later, and 9pm finishes certainly aren't infrequent, even when you're not gunning to get a piece of work done."*

Much has been made of Slaughters' slightly traditional ethos, but our sources were quick to do away with the suggestion that it's all tweed suits and college ties. *"It's not the kind of place where you'd just stroll into a partner's office and start talking about the weather, but that doesn't mean it isn't still an amicable, open environment,"* one insider said. *"It's very academic. You see it in the conversations we have over lunch – they tend to be fairly left-field, involving the rule of law or a point of academic interest. There's not a lot of talk about the football results,"* we heard. *"But the things written about us on certain law blogs are rubbish. It's worth talking to someone who works here or coming in to visit. Then you can make your own decision."*

Ahead of the firm's 125th anniversary in 2014, trainees predicted a low-key affair in keeping with Slaughters' restrained manner. Other social ongoings include a book club, football and netball teams, bake-offs, and regular trainee after-work drinks, and *"there's a black-tie party at the Grosvenor Hotel every Christmas. Apparently it's been the same for the last 20 years, but it's still good fun. Everyone from the London office is invited,"* one source said.

Slaughters historically posts the highest retention rates of the magic circle. In 2014 it kept on 71 of 74 trainees. *"The perception is very much that we'll get kept on if we want to stay,"* our sources agreed. Qualification is reasonably straightforward: HR asks trainees to complete a list of departments they'd go back to (including a first choice, should the department wish them to qualify there) and a list of the departments they're not interested in. *"Then they marry things up with the partners based on their preferences. Of course, if you want to go into a specific department the partners will already know because you'll have done some schmoozing beforehand,"* one source hinted. *"It's a good system – there's no bitchiness or in-fighting. It does take a while for it all to go through, but it doesn't feel like an undue amount of time."*

And finally...

"Trainees share an office with either a partner or an associate. With the former you get the view from the war room; with the latter you're in the trenches. Either way you learn a lot."

Speechly Bircham LLP

The facts

Location: London

Number of partners/solicitors: 70/102

Partners who trained at firm: 8%

Total number of trainees: 22

Seats: 4x6 months

Alternative seats: occasional secondments

Extras: pro bono - Blackfriars Settlement, Kings Legal Clinic

On chambersstudent.co.uk...

How to get into Speechlys

After one broken-off engagement, Speechlys has found a fitting partner in Charles Russell.

Paris magnifique

The date's set: on 1 November the legal world will gather to witness the union of Speechly Bircham and Charles Russell, a merger that will result in the world's largest private client-focused firm, with an annual turnover of £135m. This isn't the first time Speechlys has gone for a high-profile hook-up – in 2013 talks with Withers fell through, perhaps because the fellow Londoner's finances looked less than healthy compared to Speechlys' £37m in the kitty. Speechlys' managing partner James Carter, slated to take up the MP role at the impending entity Charles Russell Speechlys, has this to say on the reasons behind the impending merger: *"The two firms have very complementary practice areas. As well as a very strong private wealth practice, together we will end up with significant practices in a number of commercial areas and increased international reach."* Indeed, Speechlys will gain access to Charles Russell's commercial specialisms in retail and sport, and strengthen its national and international footprint.

Speechlys recently opened in Paris in its bid to expand its capability for offering wealthy expats tax and investment advice. This joins existing outposts in Zürich, Geneva and Luxembourg, all of which were launched within the past few years. *"We've had all these people from the new offices turning up at parties and glamming them up,"* Londoners told us. Charles Russell Speechlys socials look set to be glitzier still, once you factor in CR's Middle East branches in Bahrain and Qatar. Charles Russell will also contribute its offices in Guildford and Cheltenham, giving the newly merged entity the opportunity to offer lower rates for certain services.

Our interviewees told us they chose Speechlys for its *"relaxed and friendly atmosphere"* and *"good reputation in areas outside corporate."* As one added: *"I wanted somewhere mid-size with a broad range of opportunities – Speechlys is big enough to have a lot of practice areas, but small enough that you can get stuck into them."* The firm's practice groups are currently split into three divisions: private client; business services; construction, engineering and real estate. Trainees are likely to gain experience in all three areas, though it's only business services that's compulsory. That said, *"you'll find HR steering you in a certain direction if they don't think you've had a rounded experience."* Once Charles Russell joins the ranks, the combined firm will have a fourth division: litigation and dispute resolution.

Mind your language

Speechlys has spent its 137 years in practice building up its reputation for private client work, and today enjoys *Chambers UK* rankings for its nationwide contentious trusts capabilities as well as its London services. The group collaborates closely with the teams in Zürich and Geneva, and works for a roughly equal mix of onshore and offshore high net worth individuals. *"A lot of it's fairly tax-heavy work – for example, helping clients domi-*

Seat options: real estate; real estate litigation; real estate regeneration; construction; tax, trusts and succession; family and contentious trusts; corporate finance; banking and finance; corporate recovery; IP, technology and data

Chambers UK rankings

Agriculture & Rural Affairs	Intellectual Property
Charities	Investment Funds
Construction	Pensions
Corporate/M&A	Private Client
Data Protection	Projects
Employment	Real Estate
Family/Matrimonial	Real Estate Litigation
Financial Services	Restructuring/Insolvency

ciled abroad understand what their tax position would be if they moved here permanently." According to interviewees with experience here, it's *"a big department, but there's scope work with pretty much everyone. They make the effort to get you involved with lots of different issues."* The firm's super-rich client base can make for some glamorous matters – *"I went around to a fairly big TV celebrity's house to get a will signed"* – and we also heard about more unusual undertakings like *"going to the Westminster archive to look at the adopted children's registry."* More common trainee fare includes grappling with probate matters and drafting wills and lasting powers of attorney. *"You're often invited along to meetings, and sometimes you can even talk through the part of the matter you've handled. It's great to play that kind of active role."* Still, trainees are closely supervised, *"and rightly so – you need years of experience to deal with some of the emotional situations at hand."*

Alongside Speechlys' *Chambers*-ranked agriculture and rural affairs practice is a significant commercial real estate offering. Clients range from big property developers to investment companies to businesses in the leisure and hospitality sectors. Lawyers recently represented Caring Homes on its £300m sale of 44 care homes to American health group Griffin, and advised Derwent on its £8.8m lease of two London office developments to Publicis Groupe, which owns advertising mavericks Saatchi & Saatchi. *"The team works on multimillion-pound deals on a day-to-day basis. Those kinds of transactions see trainees take an administrative role, but you also get small files to handle yourself, like leases and licences for institutional landlords such as pension funds. You also draft a lot of land registry forms. It's all supervised, but you do actually run the file from start to finish, dealing with the clients involved whenever necessary."* Within real estate is a regeneration subgroup that takes on *"development work – essentially it's all about acquiring sites and then making it possible for them to be built on."* As a trainee this might entail negotiating terms of the agreement with a service provider in order to get gas or electricity hooked up to a site.

Speechly's corporate team is top-ranked in *Chambers UK* for its lower mid-market M&A work, and is big in the financial services, natural resources, construction and

healthcare sectors, among others. The team works closely with the private client faction, advising high net worth individuals and family businesses on corporate services, and also shares a number of the firm's real estate clients, including Countryside Properties and Northacre. Other noteworthy clients include the Ecclesiastical Insurance Office (insurers to the Anglican Church) and Sisu Capital, the hedge fund that owns the struggling Coventry City Football Club. Sources here told of drafting board minutes and shareholders' resolutions.

The technology and data team mixes contentious and non-contentious matters, and offers trainees various client secondment opportunities, including a stint in-house with a leading investment bank. The IP part of the team's name proved largely theoretical for our interviewees, who'd ended up doing *"about half and half data and technology work."* Tech lawyers advise on licensing and contract negotiations for pharmaceutical companies, technology start-ups and high-profile media clients, while the *"well-known"* data protection arm has carved out a niche assisting multinationals with privacy issues in the social media, outsourcing and cloud computing spheres. Trainees here reported drafting commercial contracts like non-disclosure agreements, licences and distribution agreements, telling us: *"There's quite a lot of crossover with the corporate team."* For one source, *"the highlight of my seat was helping with the webinars we run every fortnight on various general data protection topics. There are some pretty big clients listening in, so it can be quite daunting to be up there talking for 15 minutes."* Another fondly recalled *"the fantastic experience I got advising a client on a security policy during my second week with the team,"* while a third spoke of the time *"I went on-site with a major client for two weeks to renew some contacts. It was really challenging, but luckily some of the solicitors there were ex-Speechlys, so I felt very well looked after. I felt really glad they trusted me with that – the partners really aren't afraid to rely on trainees."*

Indeed, trainees across the firm reported high levels of responsibility and mentioned the office's open-plan format *"means people are immediately there to offer help."* This set-up lends itself to a bustling work environment, we're told: *"There's a lot of banter flying around, and everyone gets involved in discussions, which makes it quite fun. People here don't just stick on ear defenders and get on with it."* According to our sources, *"work/life balance is a big thing here – the aircon turns off at 7pm, so expectations are judged accordingly."* That said, a training contract at Speechlys is not without its late nights, especially as teams like real estate and restructuring gain traction. Fortunately, *"you get fed and taxied home if you stay late."*

Trainees receive reviews halfway through and at the end of each seat. The first is a *"relatively informal"* meeting with their supervisor to set objectives, while the latter sees them talk through a feedback form with their supervisor and a member of HR. *"It's a really thorough process, and they give you solid feedback."*

Lean mean green machine

Plans are afoot to get the respective Charles Russell and Speechlys bunches under one roof soon after the merger in November. In any case, Speechlys' office in New Street Square is *"modern and sleek,"* and, perhaps more importantly, *"located near lots of bars, which makes for a good social scene after work."* The sleek edifice also contains showers, an underground bike garage and an in-house cafe. *"There's not much variety to the food, but it's all healthy and subsidised."*

Private client firms have a reputation for maintaining a somewhat conservative atmosphere, but sources tell us this only holds partly true at Speechlys. *"The private client department is kind of formal and traditional in the way they approach things – there's some very flowery, polite language going on, but that's dictated by what clients want. We do take on a lot of commercial work, and to that*

end I'd say we're not really reserved or old-school at all." They also mentioned the firm's eco focus as evidence of its modern leanings. *"There's a huge recycling drive – we don't have any landfill waste, and lights aren't left on all night."*

Interviewees told us: *"The firm looks for gregarious, outgoing trainees. This is the kind of place where people all have lunch together and get on really well, so you'd need to fit into that. It's a pretty collaborative, relaxed environment – people make a lot of time for each other."* There's a fair bit of socialising too, with departmental outings, quarterly staff drinks and various events organised by the sports and social committee. Recent excursions include an afternoon shopping at Lille's Christmas market, a jaunt to see *The Book of Mormon* and a World Cup social: *"When England played, they commandeered the TVs upstairs and brought in food and drinks for everyone."* Trainees also spoke of heading en masse on Friday nights to various nearby watering holes in search of a destination for the unofficial *"Speechlys' local boozer competition. We haven't settled on one yet, but I'm determined to make it happen."*

And finally...

Given the impending merger, it's wise to heed the trainee who advised applicants to *"show flexibility and willingness to move with the times – they'll be on the lookout for people who want to try a range of practice areas rather than just private client."*

Squire Patton Boggs

The facts

Locations: London, Leeds, Birmingham, Manchester

Number of UK partners/solicitors: 129/259

Partners who trained at firm: 26%

Total number of trainees: 37

Seats: 6x4 months

Alternative seats: overseas seats, secondments

Extras: pro bono – Paddington Law Centre, Birmingham and Hillside Legal Advice Clinics; language classes

On chambersstudent.co.uk...

How to get into SPB

Who is (or was) Patton Boggs?

Two massive American mergers in under five years have transformed what used to be the UK's Hammonds into a global mega firm...

What's in a name?

"We've had four name changes since I applied here," pointed out several second-years, nearing the end of their training contracts during our calls. They'd applied to Hammonds, a mid-sized UK firm with offices in Leeds, Birmingham, Manchester and London, plus a sprinkling abroad. They'd joined Squire Sanders Hammonds, thanks to the 2011 merger with huge American firm Squire Sanders, headquartered in Cleveland, Ohio. The Hammonds name soon disappeared from the masthead. Then, in May 2014, Squire Sanders agreed to merge with another big US law firm, Washington, DC-based Patton Boggs, known especially for its political lobbying and Middle Eastern practices. Squire Patton Boggs was born. In July, yet another merger, though this time on a much smaller scale, boosted SPB's presence in Tokyo.

All this begs the million-dollar question: is the firm today very different to the one its trainees thought they were joining? *"Yes and no,"* was the verdict. One grasped the nettle with both hands by telling us: *"I worried! I'd applied to Hammonds because it was a smaller, European-focused firm with some international offices. I wanted a more collegiate, less international firm. But my fears haven't materialised."* Others also gave the thumbs-up: *"They have focused on keeping the culture steady. The managing partner has maintained a UK LLP independent spirit."* Squire Sanders had a London office for some time before merging with Hammonds, so it wasn't as if our transatlantic cousins suddenly pitched up out of nowhere, interviewees stressed. On the whole, they hadn't experienced gulp-inducing shifts in culture or the nature of their work, but viewed their firm's vastly expanded international network as *"mutually beneficial"* as it opens up *"more access to work"* – especially for those *"in departments like corporate and banking."* For others on the ground in London and the regions *"there hasn't been a much greater international element than we would have had anyway with Hammonds."*

Second(ment) nature

So, on to future trainees. Two interesting things distinguish Squire Patton Boggs: the fast-track LPC at BPP Law School followed by a three-month client secondment before the training contract begins, and a three-week trainee induction in Leeds when it starts. Pre-TC client secondments – options include concerts and ticketing giant Live Nation – *"give you a bit of a head start. It's good to get into the office environment before starting, and it had been a couple of years since they'd interviewed us. There were lots of opportunities to talk to partners for my particular client, and you get an insight into what clients want."* Next, first-years from all four offices live together in a Leeds hotel for their three induction weeks – a heady mix of *"getting most of the PSC out of the way,"* team-building activities (like making clothes from piles of rubbish for a fashion show), introductions to essentials like IT and research services, social outings (eg a cinema night), and dinners galore. *"It's great to get to know*

Seat options: corporate; environmental, safety and health; financial services; IP and technology; labour and employment; litigation; construction; property litigation; pensions; property; restructuring and insolvency; tax strategy and benefits; planning; asset-based lending; international dispute resolution; regulatory

Chambers UK rankings

Banking & Finance	Litigation
Banking Litigation	Media & Entertainment
Capital Markets	Pensions
Construction	Pensions Litigation
Corporate/M&A	Planning
Data Protection	Private Equity
Employment	Real Estate
Environment	Real Estate Litigation
Health & Safety	Restructuring/Insolvency
Immigration	Sports Law
Information Technology	Tax
Intellectual Property	Telecommunications
Licensing	

people," interviewees reported. *"They can be your gateway in future if you need to pick up the phone to other offices."* Various big hitters like office heads turn up to some events, while others are strictly for trainees only. We can only pray that the 'retro sports day' was restricted to newbies – the spectacle of sweaty partners bouncing around in sacks or racing with eggs on spoons is too mind-boggling for us to imagine.

Trainees loved doing more, shorter seats (the firm runs a six-seat programme) as they *"give you as much exposure as possible."* But sources acknowledged the potential downside that you *"might not get to see things through"* on longer assignments, as you have to up sticks to the next department. There are lots of seat options in each office, and some vary according to when there is or isn't a need in a particular team for a trainee.

Corporate is *"big nationwide and globally"* (though *"not so big in Manchester,"* where *"real estate is the engine, though it all works together a lot, as some is corporate support work"*). The *"bread and butter is M&A, private acquisitions and private equity. The remainder is public company work, and there are some big international clients."* A *"baptism of fire,"* corporate is *"one of the seats where quite a lot is expected of you"* time-wise (*"a few late nights"*), but it also provides *"some of the juiciest, big-value deals."* Another *"worked with the London office on some big cross-border deals. Trainees get involved and run smaller aspects, like the disclosure process. They will give you a certain amount of trust if you show you're capable."* UK transactions are typically mid-market: *"£5m or £6m to several hundred million"* in value. One fairly recent highlight was advising on the UK aspects of US billionaire Shahid Khan's acquisition of Fulham Football Club from Mohamed Al Fayed (a deal which also involved US and Bermuda jurisdictions).

"There's always a bit of grunt work in transactional departments," a source reflected. The financial services team is no different, although people praised responsibility levels here too. *"A partner came into my office and said 'look I'll supervise you, but this is yours'."* Long hours are inevitable as deals head for closure, but so is *"champagne all over the place"* when they do complete. Trainees often find themselves working with colleagues in other offices, as clients include large banks on *"chunky deals,"* and there's *"a lot of cross-referral"* from and to other departments like real estate. For example, lawyers from both teams acted for Lloyds Bank in a large-scale portfolio refinancing by IM Properties (one of the UK's largest privately-owned property companies).

Real estate teams at law firms around the world took a battering during the Great Recession. Here, *"it's picked up outrageously well. Lots of recruiters are on the phone to people interested in real estate roles, and for the first time in six years there's a dearth of candidates for jobs,"* one trainee glowed. The group has been busy for some very large and impressive clients, notably multisite retailers, public bodies (like councils), developers, charities, financiers, even the National Grid. *"This was a seat and a half, I can tell you! I think I forgot I was a trainee in this seat. It was 'here is the file, there you go – over to you'."* There's plenty of work to do on *"huge lease portfolios"* and *"massive refinancing deals,"* among other things. Clients include Cancer Research UK, TfL, Birmingham City Council, and jewellery retailer Signet. *"I ran small files by myself and helped on large transactions as part of the team,"* said one source. Aiding ongoing regeneration in Liverpool, SPB recently advised investors (supported by a government grant) backing the development of the decades-empty iconic Royal Insurance Building into a trendy hotel (not to be confused with the famous Royal Liver Building, which looks pretty similar but is still very much functioning).

The highly regarded pensions team often appeals to trainees not (necessarily) because of the inherent fascinatingness of all things pensions *per se*, but because it provides a good opportunity to experience some black-letter law, and *"mash your brain."* In four months *"you don't have the time to learn all the depth and breath of pensions law, so trainees have more of an assisting role."* Another source said: *"Pensions sounds boring but this couldn't be further than the truth. It has truly lovely people, self-confessed geeks, who are very social."* Lawyers often act for trustees of pension schemes, for example *"drafting deeds of appointment and termination, monitoring a piece of legislation, and updating people if there are any changes."* Clients include the Trustees of the ICI Pension Fund, the Norfolk Pension Fund, and the trustees of two schemes sponsored by Thames Water.

The True Picture

421

Far from boggs standard

In litigation, *"right from the get-go I had high responsibility, running my own files from beginning to end."* A colleague found it was *"the epitome of what you think a lawyer is supposed to be – running into court at the last minute with documents."* Among other things, the department is doing a lot of high-volume PPI (payment protection insurance) claims, acting for the banks. Over in property litigation, people are similarly *"incredibly busy,"* dealing with *"hundreds of properties at any one time,"* often lease renewal claims acting for clients of the real estate team like Cancer Research UK and Signet. Again, *"high-volume work"* means good responsibility in the form of *"lots of client contact by phone, calling into court every day, and filing claims."* Other areas of dispute resolution specialisms include environmental (such as fracking), and health and safety defence work for companies when an employee has been injured at work (or worse). But for one source, the main benefit of their contentious seat was that *"I came out knowing that I didn't want to be a litigious lawyer. You either are or you aren't. I'm not."* Litigation clients include European football governing body UEFA, Chelsea FC, ABN AMRO, and a very large public company, which is being advised on a very big cross-border matter (sorry, we can't be any more specific than that as it's ongoing).

Trainees *"really enjoyed"* their time in labour and employment, describing it as *"an incredible team, really enthusiastic,"* which provides *"good commercial training"* as does work that's very *"contracts-based."* Clients include advertising and PR giant WPP, Investec Bank, US Airways, and hotels group Marriott. In Leeds, SPB has long-standing relationships with (and provides all their employment work for) FTSE 100 companies Tesco, Amec and Smith & Nephew. For these large clients, trainees may get *"decent client contact by phone"* getting stuck into volume-driven work, which can include anything from a *"straightforward misconduct case"* to *"litigation around holiday pay."* Other clients include Greggs, TM Lewin and Rolex. More seat options include IP, which is *"mostly non-contentious;"* regulatory; tax; and restructuring and insolvency, *"a mix of litigious and non-litigious work."* Restructuring can see some huge cases and be *"very document-heavy,"* but also opportunities to meet clients, and take and draft witness statements.

Client secondments are particularly popular among London trainees, though some in all four UK offices do them, usually in their second or third seat. Current options include Tesco and Live Nation. They typically learn what will be coming up during their mid-seat review. Two overseas seats are also available, in Paris and Brussels, the latter being slightly more competitive because it is an English-speaking office. Hong Kong and Madrid used to be options too but aren't any more (Madrid owing to regulatory changes there), and given the firm's recent global expansion it will be interesting to keep an eye on developments to see if any other overseas destinations become offered in the future. We've already heard of a trainee being sent to Riyadh, and one to Sydney, in the past year; you can bet your bottom dollar that similar ad hoc postings will follow, when needed.

The Leeds office is *"about to get refurbished,"* but gossiping trainees didn't know any details apart from believing that the *"traditional layout"* of external offices around a bank of secretaries and paralegals will be preserved. Popular trainee watering holes in Leeds' new Trinity mall are The Alchemist, and The Botanist – *"one of the places we have drinks during induction"* – as well as *"poncy wine bar"* Angelica. *"A lot of support services are based in Leeds too, so it's a very important office,"* one source here was keen to emphasize. Manchester trainees chill out when they can in the city's huge Spinningfields development, which featured in the BBC documentary *Restaurant Wars*, as well as the Ape & Apple and Restaurant Bar & Grill next to the office on John Dalton Street. In Birmingham, Metro is the property team's preferred hangout, while trainees here also visit Utopia, and Asha's (for award-winning Indian cuisine), among other destinations. The *"pretty flashy"* London office, near Liverpool Street Station, has had dollars spent on it recently, we heard, and boasts a top terrace. The Magpie, and Devonshire Terrace, are popular nearby pubs – though we heartily recommend a trip up the road to the American-themed Diner in Shoreditch to make those visiting US colleagues feel at home.

Go online for more info about the Patton Boggs merger, plus tips on the firm's personal approach to hiring from graduate recruitment partner Richard Morton.

And finally...
20 out of 26 NQs stayed with the firm.

Stephenson Harwood LLP

The facts

Location: London

Number of UK partners/solicitors: 92/250

Partners who trained at the firm: 15%

Total number of trainees: 32

Seats: 4x6 months

Alternative seats: overseas seats, secondments

Extras: pro bono – PRIME, Camden Community Advice Centre

On chambersstudent.co.uk...

How to get into Stephenson Harwood
More on international trade and
sanctions

Libor fraud, shipping litigation, aircraft finance. This and more is on offer at this internationally minded City firm.

Seoul searching

While shipping is still one of SH's strong suits (just look at the *Chambers UK* rankings), *"the firm is also strong in a number of other transport sectors, such as aviation and rail,"* says training partner Neil Noble. For example, SH advised Hitachi Rail on its bid to manufacture and maintain the new Crossrail trains; and it counselled Vietjet Air on its £480m purchase of 46 aircraft engines. The firm also attracts high *Chambers UK* rankings for areas as diverse as capital markets, civil fraud and commercial contracts.

International work is very important to Stephenson Harwood. It was one of the first UK firms to venture into Asia – opening a Hong Kong office in 1979 – and expansion in East and Southeast Asia has continued since: the firm now sports outposts in Beijing, Guangzhou, Hong Kong, Shanghai and Singapore. The region is a major market for the firm with 25% of staff based there, while a whopping 60% of fee income is generated from clients based outside the UK. There are also offices in Paris, Dubai and Piraeus. And overseas growth is continuing, with a new office in Seoul now in the pipeline. This move came in the wake of the firm striking up alliances with local outfits in Singapore and Myanmar. A look at the rankings in *Chambers Europe*, *Chambers Asia-Pacific* and *Chambers Global* shows that the overseas offices all perform pretty well in their respective markets, especially in the fields of shipping and aviation.

The current strategy of overseas expansion and practice diversification appears to be working very well. The firm has enjoyed five straight years of revenue growth since 2008, with income reaching £121m in 2013/14, up an impressive 40% from the 2008/09 figure.

Small but MIT

Before arriving, prospective trainees are asked to list three broad departments they would like to sit in first, in order of preference. At later rotations, trainees are able to specify a more narrow sub-group they wish to join. According to interviewees: *"Most people tend to get their first or second choice."* Sources also told us that: *"Commercial litigation is really popular due to its excellent clients – lots of people want to qualify into the department too."* Three trainees are able to sit with the team at any one time and it took in four NQs in 2014. Overall 13 of 17 qualifiers stayed with the firm.

The MIT (marine and international trade) department works on all manner of contractual and insurance-related shipping and trade disputes, as well as non-contentious contractual issues. Recently SH defended RSA Global – a large Dutch marine insurer – against a range of claims related to salvage, pollution and repairs originating from a collision off the Chinese coast. Almost all of the work is international and multi-jurisdictional. For example, the London and Singapore offices recently acted for Dutch geo-surveyors Fugro in a dispute over the cancellation of a construction contract for a £71m survey vessel. Arbitra-

Seat options: commercial litigation; corporate; employment & pensions; finance; marine & international trade; and real estate

Chambers UK rankings

Asset Finance	Insurance
Aviation	Intellectual Property
Banking & Finance	International Arbitration
Banking Litigation	Investment Funds
Capital Markets	Litigation
Construction	Pensions
Corporate Crime & Investigations	Pensions Litigation
Corporate/M&A	Private Equity
Education	Professional Negligence
Employee Share Schemes & Incentives	Projects
Employment	Real Estate
Financial Services	Real Estate Finance
Fraud	Real Estate Litigation
Hotels & Leisure	Shipping
Information Technology	Tax
	Transport

tion of disputes is increasingly popular: *"Rather than going straight to trial, many of our clients now prefer using international arbitration because it's cheaper and more discreet."* On the non-contentious side trainees undertake work *"drafting and updating insurance companies' contracts and terms and conditions."*

A seat in finance is a varied affair, with the department undertaking asset finance involving shipping, aviation and rail transactions, as well as property finance and some corporate finance. Trainees' work tends to mirror their supervisor's sector specialism. While there are administrative tasks like arranging notarial services and organising conditions precedent, one source had *"drafted all ten security documents for one transaction,"* while another said *"there are plenty of chances to meet with clients, especially at closing meetings."* Asset finance lawyers act for lenders including many overseas banks, as well as aircraft leasing companies and *"airlines ordering huge numbers of new planes."* Finance is known for its *"driven, high-pressure"* environment and *"punishing"* hours. While in litigation you might finish at 7 or 8pm, finance is more likely to keep you until 9pm or 9.30pm if there's a deal brewing. One trainee cautioned: *"I knew in advance that the hours would be intense, but they were a lot more challenging to deal with in real life than I'd expected. I didn't anticipate the stamina required."*

Libor litigation and Forex fixing

The commercial litigation team has been involved in some topical financial cases recently, including the Libor and Forex rate-fixing scandals. The firm *"often acts for senior individuals who are under investigation by the FCA or SFO"*– these include Brent Davies, a broker alleged to have conspired with UBS employees to fix Libor, and Chris Ashton, former chief foreign exchange dealer

at Barclays, who is currently under investigation for conspiring in online chat rooms to fix the Forex rate. The department also takes on more commercial matters: it was recently brought in to replace Shearman & Sterling by property tycoon Robert Tchenguiz who is suing the Serious Fraud Office for £300m in damages in relation to dawn raids carried out in reaction to the collapse of the Icelandic banks.

Trainees sitting in litigation have the opportunity *"to get deeply immersed in a few major cases."* One interviewee who'd been working on a *"big defamation case"* told us they had *"drafted witness statements, attended client meetings, sat in on conference calls, and drafted instructions to counsel."* Another trainee was sat with a partner whose practice focused on Africa and was heavily involved in arbitrations involving various African governments. In the course of this they *"proofread transcripts, drafted witness statements, corresponded with counsel and worked on affidavits."* Trainees noted that *"because of the size of the cases you generally get less responsibility in litigation than in other departments."*

The real estate team's assignments are often finance-related. For example, the firm recently represented HSBC and Deutsche Postbank on a £54m development near King's Cross. The department's clients are a varied bunch though: they include the University of Greenwich, which SH assisted with the £40m construction of a 358-bed student accommodation block, and Native Land, which lawyers helped with the £201m acquisition and redevelopment of the former site of Holland Park School. On larger transactions trainees are tasked with *"research, compiling lease summaries, making applications to the Land Registry and carrying out due diligence."* To thrive you have to be adept at multi-tasking, with one trainee informing us that they *"had about 30 matters on the go at one time!"* There is a run-up of *"three to four months"* before you'll be handling this volume of work, and by then *"your supervisor will only give things a cursory glance every now and then, so you really feel like they trust you."*

Schmooze don't snooze!

At every seat rotation trainees have the opportunity to head out to Hong Kong, Dubai or Singapore, apart from the first seat. Each office hosts one or two trainees at a time and offer a corporate/finance-focused experience with plenty of shipping and aviation work thrown in. The work involves *"liaising regularly with local clients – usually airlines or leasing companies."* Those clients include Lion Air and the Industrial and Commercial Bank of China's leasing arm. Trainees who'd been abroad told us they had *"conducted closing calls independently"* and *"worked with SH lawyers all around the world."* One source did note that *"doing aviation finance work, I found that a lot of the aircraft are due to be delivered to places like Paris or Hamburg, so we had to work to European time. That meant deals often closed as late as 4am."* While the Singapore office in particular has *"a bad rep for its long hours,"* trainees did appreciate the *"very nice apartments"* the firm puts them up in and the opportunity to take holiday while in the region and travel to some of Southeast Asia's tourist hotspots. There's also the chance to meet, befriend and socialise with trainees from other firms which send people out to Singapore or Hong Kong.

Back in London, the highlight of SH's social calendar – and *"the only event which brings together the entire firm"* – is the black-tie Christmas dinner, which in 2013 was held at The Brewery in Moorgate. Future trainees are invited too and the evening is *"a great networking opportunity and really makes future joiners feel like part of the firm already."* The trainee group also enjoys *"meeting for casual drinks on Thursdays and Fridays – though whether you can make it depends on your workload."*

Trainees felt that they work in a *"very supportive environment,"* noting that *"supervisors are well chosen."* As one put it: *"No one has jumped down my throat... yet!"* People tend to be of the approachable sort and *"there are*

few who give off a 'steer-clear' vibe," although *"occasionally when people are busy and stressed they might have less time to explain everything like they usually would."* Trainees are encouraged to ask questions and to seek clarification; mistakes are tolerated as an inevitable part of the learning curve, *"so long as you learn from your errors and don't make them again."*

Stephenson Harwood moved into new offices on Finsbury Circus in 2011. That, combined with the firm's growth and drive to expand internationally, has, according to some, affected the atmosphere at the firm. One trainee believed: *"It hasn't eroded our friendly and collegial culture, but it has perhaps made everyone a bit more purposeful and formal."* One of the ways the firm is addressing its newfound larger size is by organising networking events. Trainees and NQs even run one themselves. One interviewee explained: *"We're asked to invite peers from other organisations and SH lays on wine and nibbles."* The idea is to get trainees used to the idea of networking and making connections in the industry. *"Usually it's the partners and senior associates who get to go off to do the schmoozing, wining and dining of potential clients, so it's great to get that opportunity as a trainee too!"*

And finally...
Sign up here if you're looking for a training contract with an interesting mix of litigation, fraud, shipping and finance work at *"a firm with a lot of clout."*

Stevens & Bolton LLP

The facts

Location: Guildford

Number of UK partners/solicitors: 36/72

Partners who trained at the firm: 11%

Total number of trainees: 8

Seats: 6x4 months

Alternative seats: secondments

Extras: pro bono

On chambersstudent.co.uk...

How to get into Stevens & Bolton

A beginner's guide to Guildford

Interview with managing partner
   Ken Woffenden

Cast your gaze out of London towards S&B, where City standards meet Guildford idyll.

City status

Guildford may be but a county town (having failed to gain proper city status on several occasions), but Stevens & Bolton, one of its primary legal eagles, has succeeded in bringing home some City-standard clients over the years. Among S&B's latest recruits are Metro Bank, Fuller's Brewery and Godiva, which now stand alongside long-standing big-hitters like Kia Motors and Papa John's. The firm's genteel Surrey surroundings are undeniably calmer than the hustle and bustle of London, but that's not to say this firm doesn't hold its own against its City counterparts: *Chambers UK* awards S&B top-band regional rankings across a raft of practice areas – including banking, IP and litigation – and deems it a national leader in corporate work outside of London. An equally laudable private client practice complements these commercial offerings.

It's this ability to score big-brand work which tempted many of S&B's current trainees to pursue it. *"The firm sells itself as able to offer City-standard work without the traditional City firm culture, and I've found it's stayed true to its promise,"* said one, telling us: *"I've got some fantastic experience and been made to feel like a valuable member of the team."* Another chimed in to mention S&B's *"genuine dedication to its trainees"* as another *"point that's proved true. Partners make it clear they want to invest in us and give us the best training they can. Throughout my training contract the managing partner has held annual meetings with us to discuss where the firm is going and to listen to what we have to say."*

The firm's six-seat structure also proved a big draw among our interviewees, who praised it for *"allowing you to experience every major practice area"* and *"getting to know lots of different people across the firm."* Allocation is *"quite an informal process,"* we're told: *"Your first seat is assigned, and after that you have a chat with HR before each rotation. If you have certain preferences they take them into account."* All trainees complete seats in corporate & commercial (coco), and dispute resolution or IP are very popular being the contentious seats, and it's possible to repeat a seat.

Variety is key

Those sitting in coco are generally shuffled towards either corporate or banking-oriented roles, though *"in reality you get exposure to most of what comes through the department,"* which includes acquisitions, buyouts, financings and contract issues. On the M&A side a good chunk of deals are cross-border, and big clients of late include tech multinational ENER-G, and South African auto glass repair biz Belron. Some more local businesses, like London-headquartered Fuller's, are also on the books – the team recently advised the brewer on its acquisition of a leading stake in pub and restaurant chain The Stable. Commercial lawyers keep busy working across the IT, healthcare, leisure and retail sectors, recently assisting T.M. Lewin with the shirtmaker's move into Indonesia and South Africa.

Seat options: corporate & commercial (coco); dispute resolution; IP; real estate; personal wealth & families, employment pensions & immigration

Chambers UK rankings

Banking & Finance	Intellectual Property
Construction	Litigation
Corporate/M&A	Partnership
Employment	Private Client
Family/Matrimonial	Real Estate
Franchising	Real Estate Litigation
Immigration	Restructuring/Insolvency
Information Technology	Tax

Sources who'd spent time in coco found the amount of client contact on hand higher than expected, although this is balanced out with long hours: *"The longest at S&B, I'd wager. Of course, they're not as bad as they would be at a London firm; you're never stuck here at 11pm slogging it on your own, and it's always appreciated if you do end up staying late."* When it comes to day-to-day tasks, *"there can be moments when you're doing more admin than is ideal,"* our interviewees admitted, though away from the photocopier there's plenty to get on with in the way of drafting board minutes, reviewing contracts, carrying out research and, for a lucky few, running small files. The latter is *"quite a challenging task, but it's a brilliant experience."*

The firm's contentious arm houses several specialist teams – including IP, insolvency, aviation, construction and property litigation – and services a variety of clients among them, from Kuoni Travel and Cineworld to Standard Life and TGI Fridays. Lawyers working on the IP side have kept busy assisting with trade mark disputes for brands like Accolade Wines and Japan Tobacco. A trainee's experience in the dispute resolution/IP seat *"very much depends on what kind of cases are going on during your seat,"* we heard: *"The team makes every effort to get us involved, but the outstretched nature of litigation is such that you might only scratch the surface of a matter during your four months there."* While some did bundling, others told of getting their hands on meatier tasks like disclosure exercises, drafting letters of action and attending client meetings. *"It's so valuable to watch how the senior partners approach different people and situations."*

S&B's private client faction handles family, charities, personal wealth, and tax and trusts work, with clients ranging from landed estates up to ultra high net worth individuals. There are also commercial names on the books – for example, Monitise, which the firm advised on tax arrangements during its £39m purchase of Grap-

ple Mobile. Unsurprisingly, *"great client contact"* is on offer for trainees sitting with the department. *"One of the most enjoyable things about the seat was meeting people three or four times a week to witness wills or give tax advice,"* one source enthused. *"Sometimes you even get to go off-site to meetings at care homes and the like."* When they're not busy liaising with clients, trainees spend their time carrying out research and drafting wills. *"The hours are very civil – most people leave by 5.30pm or 6pm."*

Opportunities for secondments are becoming increasingly common. *"It's a great chance to experience working independently and learn about a business from the inside-out,"* said one trainee. *"I think they'd like everybody to be able to go eventually."* MP Ken Woffenden adds; *"The firm doesn't have the capacity to undertake a large number of secondments but we are planning to increase the opportunity to do so."*

Ask and you shall receive

"Your first few days as a trainee are daunting anywhere, but it's really easy to talk to everyone here." This report is just one of many we heard testifying to the amicable nature of Steven's & Bolton's working culture. *"No one is pompous or out of reach if you have questions – I feel confident I could go and chat with the managing partner if I wanted to,"* said one trainee, adding: *"It makes a big difference to work in a place where you're on first-name terms with everyone and the senior partners know who you are. It makes you feel valued and means you won't get swallowed up like you might at a larger firm."* S&B's *"relaxed and flexible"* approach to hours was also well received among our interviewees: *"You can expect to leave around 6pm on a regular basis. It's the best of both worlds – you're doing high-quality work but without the crazy schedule."*

Outside of working hours trainees have plenty of opportunities to get to know their colleagues, whether it's through annual events like the Christmas party – where *"everybody from the secretaries to the managing partner mixes"* – or more regular ongoings like charity dos or sporting events. The netball team, which incorporates both men and women, is particularly popular, as is the football team, which competes in the Surrey Law League. At the time of our calls, lawyers were recovering from a charity auction with prizes as exciting as champagne on the London Eye, a tennis game at the Royal Albert Hall and a free week in a holiday. Trainees reported that *"the bidding was fierce!"*

And finally...
S&B trainees have historically enjoyed high retention rates. In 2014 the firm retained four out of its five qualifiers.

Taylor Wessing LLP

The facts

Location: London, Cambridge
Number of UK partners/solicitors: 102/200
Total number of trainees: 44
Seats: 4x6 months
Alternative seats: secondments
Extras: language classes; Lawyers Volunteering for the Arts

On chambersstudent.co.uk...

How to get into Taylor Wessing
Interview with graduate recruitment
 partner Kirstie McGuigan
More on Taylor Wessing's seats

Can you fire off ideas with the rapidity of a flashgun and appreciate a good organic cheese stall after a hard day's work?

The True Picture

Fee-fi-fo-fum

"Cool" – this was our interviewees' word of choice when describing the ins and outs of a training contract at Taylor Wessing. They bestowed the descriptor upon the firm's client base – which includes the likes of Google, Spotify, Tiffany & Co and Louis Vuitton – and its mix of practice areas, which blends standard City fare like corporate and finance with more specialist IP, media and private client expertise. If that doesn't convince you of the firm's coolness, consider this: TW is a place that where *"right-brained thinkers"* are the rule and not the exception; where iPads are dotted around tea stations so 'lightbulb' ideas can be logged and transmitted in a flash; where the latest fixed-fee promo bears a fairytale title ('Tech and the Beanstalk') and promises newbie start-up clients five 'magic beans' of service.

TW centres its focus on what it dubs – in unsurprising fashion – 'the industries of tomorrow': technology, media and communications (TCM); life sciences; private wealth; and energy. In 2011 TW supplemented its Fetter Lane HQ and Cambridge tech hub with an office in the heart of London's Tech City, sealing its rep as a forward-looking firm unafraid to take a chance on many a start-up. It's not a bad approach considering London mayor Boris Johnson's recent statement that the capital's tech economy could *"generate a whopping £12bn of economic activity"* over the next decade. Prioritising the industries it does seems to be working out rather well for TW. Revenue shot up by 6.4% during the 2013/14 financial year, and the firm has been expanding its already hefty international network via a string of alliances across South Korea, Indonesia and Vietnam, plus new bases in

Palo Alto and New York, bringing the total office count to 25. The firm's trainees, all of whom are based in London, envisaged a *"tighter international network"* in years to come and praised the firm for its *"clear identity and direction – this is a firm that's really going somewhere."*

A tweak has been made to the seat allocation process where trainees formally sign off their preferences before each rotation, leading to a fairer and more thoughtful process than in years past. A seat in either corporate or finance is compulsory. Our sources urged candidates to bear in mind that *"seats like trade marks, copyright and media (TCM); employment; private client; and private equity are super-popular and over-subscribed,"* and suggested they look elsewhere if a stint scanning trade marks is their only reason for joining the firm: *"In that case a specialist firm or a larger one where IP isn't so popular might suit you better."*

The firm recently introduced training sessions at the start of the seats in corporate, TCM and construction. The sessions were well received: *"It's nice to get it all out of*

Seat options: construction and engineering; corporate, commercial and projects; corporate finance; corporate technology; disputes and investigations; employment and pensions; financial institutions and markets; finance; information technology, telecoms and competition; patents; private client; private equity; real estate, environment and planning; restructuring and corporate recovery; tax; trade marks, copyright and media

Chambers UK rankings

Agriculture & Rural Affairs	Life Sciences
Banking & Finance	Litigation
Banking Litigation	Media & Entertainment
Capital Markets	Outsourcing
Construction	Pensions
Corporate/M&A	Pensions Litigation
Data Protection	Private Client
Defamation/Reputation	Private Equity
Management	Product Liability
Employee Share Schemes	Professional Discipline
& Incentives	Professional Negligence
Employment	Real Estate
Financial Services	Real Estate Finance
Fraud	Real Estate Litigation
Hotels & Leisure	Restructuring/Insolvency
Information Technology	Tax
Intellectual Property	Telecommunications

the way in the first week of your new seat. They give you pointers on certain subjects and tell you what issues you should be aware of." At the moment there are no plans to roll out the scheme among all departments.

I want it NOW!

TW's corporate practice is broad, to say the least: there's a focus on technology, private capital and real estate matters, but this focus incorporates both private and public finance aspects, and touches upon a range of sectors, including energy, transportation, hotels and healthcare. Corporate, commercial and projects (CCP) is one of a handful of seats trainees can choose from the corporate realm: *"As the name suggests, you get a mix of different matters."* Indeed, some trainees here told of helping facilitate the building of hospitals, while others encountered M&A deals with an energy focus. The team services a good whack of private wealth clients, with one trainee recalling the time *"I had to look up a new corporate real estate law to see how it might affect our client's ownership of certain properties."* In terms of tasks, interviewees reported drafting distribution and exclusivity agreements, and one even *"led the first two points in an M&A negotiation. Fortunately I knew what the parameters were and had been instructed by the partner first. I won one and conceded the other!"* Other corporate seats include private equity, corporate finance and corporate technology. The latter is a hotbed of activity at the moment and is anticipated to grow over the next few years. It handles a lot of investment flowing in from US clients and recently advised London-based Shutl as eBay looked to utilise the start-up's network of couriers to expand its own snappy delivery service, eBay Now.

Real estate is also a growth area, and one of TW's largest practices, contributing over 20% to the firm's overall turnover. The team counts Amazon.co.uk among their clients, as well as global investment manager InfraRed Capital and domestic property company Soho Estates, founded by entrepreneur and so-called 'King of Soho' Paul Raymond. To give you an idea of the scope of transactions handled: lawyers here recently advised iCITY on its bid to develop the press and broadcast centres from the 2012 Olympics, a deal worth more than £1bn, and assisted Canada Life investments with the financing of a 52-property portfolio containing £5bn worth of investments. Alongside these whoppers are small files which trainees can often handle themselves. *"You deal with all the client instructions, so there's a lot of client contact."*

A lot of the firm's real estate work feeds into its finance department, which wins *Chambers UK* rankings for its real estate finance work. Clients include big banks like Santander and RBS, and *"much of the work involves investment and development finance, either for sites in London or big retail sites outside the capital."* The group recently masterminded a heady mix of senior and mezzanine facilities so that client McLaren Property – along with joint venture partner Apache Capital – could finance the £45m acquisition of a property in Paul Street in order to convert it into top-notch student digs. A seat here is *"well known for giving trainees hands-on experience – there's junior associate-level work up for grabs."* Indeed, interviewees here had drafted inter-creditor and subordination agreements, and gotten a hand on key documents like loan agreements for smaller properties *"The attitude is 'if you want it, go for it'."* Alongside real estate finance matters are Islamic and trade finance deals, asset-based lending, investment funds work and restructuring.

Oops! I did it again

TW's TCM team covers a mixture of contentious and non-contentious work, and trainees sitting with the group generally get to sample matters from each of its three strands. *"It's cool to work with names everybody has heard of,"* said one trainee, echoing that word again. Among these are Burberry, Spotify, Toyota and Ferrero. On the media side, TW is big on defamation and libel work, which sources agreed is *"incredibly interesting – you'll have someone call and say: 'Oops, I've posted something online which is not... ideal', and then you'll have a couple hours to respond to the problem. It's fast-paced – the longer something stays up, the worse the fallout is."* Meanwhile trade mark work sees trainees grapple with brand management matters, *"keeping an eye out to make sure no one else is registering similar trade marks to our clients'."* The firm currently manages 30,000 live marks worldwide and recently represented George Lucas' production company Lucasfilm in a long-running copyright dispute over certain props used in the *Star Wars* franchise. *"The variety of matters you encounter is* the best part of the seat – you might be attending a client meeting to discuss a defamation case in the morning, then drafting an IP-related cease and desist letter in the afternoon."

The firm's employment team recently represented easyJet after the airline pilots' trade union, BALPA, brought a multimillion-pound holiday pay claim against the company. Cases like this generate a lot of work for trainees, especially when they settle, *"at which time we have to pull together all of the settlement agreements. This can be complex when there are lots of employees involved."* There's *"a lot you can get stuck into"* besides – our sources had drafted settlement agreement contracts, disciplinary letters and sections of employee handbooks, and told us that *"often you're one of the points of contact during restructurings or redundancies, so you spend a lot of time on the phone with clients' HR teams."*

TW's private client list is strictly confidential, but we can tell you it adds up to a net worth of more than $1bn. Lawyers advise on wealth structures, international tax planning, investments and immigration issues. *"Often it's just you and the partner going for it,"* said trainees, who reported drafting wills and lasting powers of attorney. *"I was surprised by how much contact I had with clients, given the confidentiality involved in most matters – I attended meetings with them several times a week!"*

Sources told us the disputes and investigations practice requires a thick skin. *"It's a high-pressure environment – it's really fast-paced, and if you can't find a document in a box, it can be a really big deal."* Like most seats at TW, trainees are assigned a supervisor but not limited to working that person's speciality. Fraud matters, insurance spats, financial disputes and professional negligence cases are all up for grabs here. *"I was involved closely on a big commercial dispute, drafting estimates of costs as well as a witness statement, and even got to attend the trial,"* enthused one source.

The firm runs client secondments at a range of A-list music and media names. *"You have to earn your reputation first,"* insiders told us, adding that *"the decision also depends on whether or not the client needs a trainee; quite a few don't offer regular positions."* The current crop is pushing for international secondments to become available as well: *"It's disappointing that we don't have them seeing as the training contract is so strong on other fronts."* We're told graduate recruitment is currently working out the practicalities involved, as *"they know it*

could be a deal breaker for certain candidates looking at the firm."

Momma always said...

TW's UK lawyers interact pretty often: those in Cambridge regularly visit the London HQ, and the Tech City branch is staffed with a mixture of lawyers from each one. When it comes to incorporating the international network, we're told the real estate team frequently collaborates with the firm's five German offices, while those in private client often work in tandem with lawyers in Asia and the Middle East. International industry groups also solidify connections: *"They give you an opportunity to broaden your knowledge and not get stuck in your own department. We're encouraged to join at least one, but there are so many people who often end up joining more."*

Our interviewees agreed the firm's strategic pursuit of tomorrow's industries *"definitely influences"* its day-to-day operations back in London, telling us *"the people working in these sectors are not as uptight as typical corporate clients, which means we in turn are less uptight as lawyers. Individuals with an idea that needs backing, for example, generally want to connect with their lawyers in a way that isn't rigidly formal or stuffy."* This carries through to the social environment, which sounds decent by all accounts. *"People have a good sense of humour – it's a fun environment to work in,"* said trainees. *"The disputes team recently went to Paris to celebrate exceeding their target, and they also have a table-tennis set-up they wheel out every now and again; TCM has a weekly tea, where people bring in cakes and other treats; and in private equity they break out the champagne trolley when a deal's complete – even if it's 4am."*

This barrage of social excitement is contained under the roof of TW's 5 New Street Square premises, where trainees are exposed to some amazing artwork: TW sponsors the National Portrait Gallery's Photography Portrait prize, so the halls are lined with an array of *"stunning"* pictures. But it's the cafeteria, Cloud Nine, that's the beating heart of the firm. *"People gather here for lunch regularly, and sometimes they host mini farmer's markets with all these incredible cheese and vegetable stalls!"* Those who prefer outdoor gatherings might be interested to hear about the fundraising activities like the London-to-Paris cycle ride and charitable abseiling. There's also an annual cross-office football tournament. *"Last time we lost to Germany – at the penalty stage, no less!"*

And finally...

Qualification was brought forward this year, so by early June all decisions had been made. In the end 20 of 22 qualifiers took up jobs with TW.

Thomas Cooper LLP

The facts

Location: London
Number of UK partners/solicitors: 15/17
Total number of trainees: 6
Seats: 4x6 months
Alternative seats: overseas seats

On chambersstudent.co.uk...

How to get into Thomas Cooper
P&I clubs
The overseas offices

Intrigued by the prospect of becoming a maritime maestro? Check out this shipping firm, which commands an impressive international presence despite its petite size.

The right plaice for you?

We're not going to beat around the seaweed here: it's best to steer clear of Thomas Cooper if the thought of a maritime-heavy training contract doesn't float your boat. If you do see yourself on board with that idea, however, then joining the ranks of this seafaring firm might well be a savvy move to make. After all, TC's been plying its trade for yonks, having opened its doors way back in 1825. Today, the firm's practice covers just about every nautical eventuality imaginable, from ship fires and hijackings to cargo-related contractual issues. It also works in the shipping and commodities arenas, earning *Chambers UK* rankings for both practices.

Now, the firm does employ a handful of lawyers who specialise in other work – including the likes of oil and gas, international arbitration and insurance – but new recruits shouldn't expect to get much of a look-in on these practices as they're kept busy with not one but two seats in shipping, plus stints in marine and commercial litigation, and finance. It's not uncommon for trainees to do a split seat between the latter two areas to make time for a post abroad at one of TC's overseas branches; Singapore and Piraeus are the two current overseas options. The vast majority of trainees spend some time abroad during their training contract, and it's even possible to qualify into an overseas office.

Most recruits come to TC with at least a splash of interest in maritime matters, but this doesn't mean applicants need the nautical know-how of, say, Captain Birdseye, to stand a chance (although one current trainee does apparently enjoy sailing in their spare time). It doesn't hurt to brush up on your sector knowledge: the insiders we chatted to recommended *"reading the headlines on Lloyd's List"* and *"generally keeping abreast of current affairs. Major developments are often all over the news, without a lot of people even realising it."*

Partner and commander

Thomas Cooper has a broad arsenal of shipping expertise and regularly advises on the legal implications of calamitous incidents like salvages and collisions. In 2013 lawyers handled a slew of ship fires, including one that left a tanker called 'Perla' stranded off the coast of Somalia, sparking several cargo claims.

Trainees in the department can expect to encounter both wet and dry matters. Put simply, *"wet shipping involves things that get wet, while dry shipping mainly deals with paper."* One source gave us a little more detail: *"Dry work primarily involves contractual disputes, often concerning cargo – for example, contamination worries or other questions about the quality of the cargo. Wet shipping, on the other hand, tends to refer to a collision or casualty."* Our interviewees appreciated the chance to soak their feet in both sides of the practice, telling us *"you don't want to specialise too much in what's already a specialist area of law."*

> **Seat options:** shipping, marine and commercial litigation, finance

Chambers UK rankings

Commodities	Shipping

Shipping-related matters come in all shapes and sizes, and a trainee's role varies accordingly. *"You can expect to do mostly minor tasks on the huge issues. On the smaller ones the work is a lot more hands-on – you're drafting letters, e-mails and general advice."* This disparity aside, there's no denying the *"fascinating"* nature of the work. *"It is a bit like a modern-day Patrick O'Brian novel,"* an interviewee enthused. *"One minute you're assisting with a ship stranded in pirate-infested waters, and the next you're handling the fallout from a raging fire aboard a vessel. Does it get any more thrilling than that?"*

Over in the marine and commercial litigation group there's an *"eclectic"* mix of cases on offer, *"from general commercial matters to defence work for P&I clubs. A lot of what we work on contains shipping elements, but there are a good number of cases that don't."* The same goes for finance work: sources reported dabbling in a few shipping finance deals here and there but for the most part had assisted with trade finance matters on behalf of foreign banks. Both teams are generous with the level of responsibility they dish out. *"I had a lot of exposure to the court process in commercial litigation, which really improved my procedural knowledge,"* said one source. Meanwhile, those with finance experience told of *"a lot of drafting,"* mainly in the form of loan agreements and contracts.

An overseas seat is par for the course at TC. *"I can't remember the last time a trainee didn't do one,"* noted one insider, telling us *"it's sort of like a rite of passage. You get so much responsibility."* Indeed, trainees abroad are thrust into the thick of action when they make the trip to one of the firm's bases abroad, all of which are significantly smaller than London. One source who'd been to Piraeus – perhaps the most common destination – recalled *"working with a single partner, which meant there was no backstop to lean against. You can't beat that level of involvement."* Take note: overseas seats are pre-dominantly shipping-based, and the firm *"doesn't send trainees out until they've already done a shipping seat in London."*

A sea of knowledge

According to our sources, Thomas Cooper places *"a great deal of emphasis on education while you're here."* During trainees' first months the firm hosts sessions covering basic principles and concepts like charter parties, bills of lading and P&I insurance – *"everything that's needed to give you a decent grounding in maritime law."* These are also ongoing series of lectures held *"either by partners or external figures like a barrister or general expert. And you can go to lectures at the London Shipping Law Centre for free. It doesn't take long to build up your knowledge."*

At just 36 lawyers strong, the London office is pretty petite compared to other City shipping outfits like Holman Fenwick Willan or Ince & Co – something to keep in mind if you crave the structure and variety of a large work environment. For our sources, TC's small set-up proved just the ticket. *"Everybody knows everybody here. At a mega-firm, there are probably people trainees never, ever speak to, but that isn't the case at all here."* It probably helps that *"everyone is affable and up for a bit of banter."* Said one trainee: *"I think shipping is one of those industries that lends itself well to a boutique nature. It feels very much like a community here; you're by no means a statistic. I think they make a big effort to recruit people who – excuse the corny pun – won't rock the boat."*

Although the firm doesn't host a shipload of formal events, there are plenty of bashes to keep up jolly spirits, including firm-wide summer and Christmas dos (to which the overseas offices are invited) as well as bowling outings, karaoke nights, softball matches and, fittingly, the occasional boat trip. Informal gatherings are also on the menu: cruise by the royal-sounding The Emperor on a Friday night and you're likely to see the TC crew catching up over a bevvy. *"There are also a few other pubs nearby where you'll find some of our partners nattering away."*

And finally...

Each year since 2009 has seen this firm keep on all or close to all of its second-years. It was smooth sailing once again in 2014, as three out of three qualifiers stayed on board with TC.

TLT LLP

The facts

Location: Bristol, London, Manchester, Scotland, Northern Ireland
Number of UK partners/solicitors: 98/200
Total number of trainees: 32
Seats: 4x6 months
Alternative seats: secondments

On chambersstudent.co.uk...

How to get into TLT
TLT's recent growth
The Bristol legal market

With a *"progressive"* mindset and an increasingly national set-up, Bristol-born TLT is now hot on the heels of the UK's top 50 firms.

My, how you've grown!

When we asked trainees about their initial attraction to this firm, many replied with the same answer: its growth and ambition. *"It's a really fast-moving firm that's on the up,"* summed up one, *"so the opportunity to become part of that was too good to turn down."* This is something we've heard for a good few years now, and indeed when you look at the facts, it's fair to say TLT's rapid growth and steep ambition are two fundamental factors in its ascent up the legal ladder in recent years.

TLT has come on in leaps and bounds since its conception following a merger between two Bristol-based firms in 2000. For starters, the £49.6m turnover the firm recorded in 2012/13 was more than thrice the amount achieved back in 2002, and in 2013/14 this figure rose again to £57.9m – a whopping 18% increase from the previous year. It's worth noting that just under two-thirds of TLT's overall income comes from industry sectors like retail, leisure, renewables, housing and financial services. The latter is the firm's biggest money-spinner, raking in roughly 40% of total earnings.

TLT has made significant strides in its geographical coverage too. In 2005 the firm took its first steps into London, and two years later it established an overseas presence in Piraeus following its takeover of shipping supremo Constant & Constant. More recently, TLT opened up shop in both Northern Ireland and Scotland in 2012 – the latter following its acquisition of Scottish firm Anderson Fyfe – and in 2013 it added a Manchester office to the network. The Mancunian crew – which is now around 40-strong thanks to the arrival of 30 ex-Irwin Mitchell employees in late 2013 – has followed in the footsteps of Bristol and London by welcoming a couple of trainees into its ranks.

April 2014 saw David Pester kick off his fifth successive term as managing partner by announcing TLT's latest goal: to hike revenue by 60% and reach a turnover of £80m by 2017. If this feat is achieved, it'll almost certainly propel TLT into the UK top 50.

Banking on success

At the time of our calls there were 16 trainees in the Bristol HQ, five in London and two in Manchester. HR gets in touch with new starters before they arrive to solicit requests for their first seat, though these are not necessarily honoured. For the next three rotations, however, trainees put forth five seat preferences. Our interviewees agreed the allocation system is *"fair"* and *"transparent,"* and we heard few complaints about where people had ended up. London and Manchester offer fewer seats than Bristol, but the smaller trainee intakes there mean *"it's really easy for all of us to sit down and discuss between ourselves which seats we want to do."* No seats are mandatory, though property and banking – *"essentially our biggest practices"* – are two very common destinations.

Seat options: banking litigation; commercial dispute resolution; construction; banking and restructuring; corporate recovery and insolvency; corporate; commercial; employment; commercial property; social housing; planning; family; tax and estate planning; pensions and incentives; professional negligence; commercial/IP

The True Picture

Chambers UK rankings

Banking & Finance	Litigation
Banking Litigation	Partnership
Commercial Contracts	Pensions
Construction	Planning
Corporate/M&A	Private Client
Employment	Professional Negligence
Energy & Natural Resources	Real Estate
	Real Estate Litigation
Family/Matrimonial	Restructuring/Insolvency
Franchising	Retail
Information Technology	Shipping
Intellectual Property	Social Housing
Licensing	

Interviewees said that a seat in professional negligence serves as a *"great introduction"* to life as a TLT trainee. *"There's a really high volume of work available from the off, so it's ideal for helping you get accustomed to managing your own caseload,"* one source explained. Trainees here are typically tasked with *"assessing the merits of a case and advising clients on the prospects of success,"* a process which entails drafting letters, reviewing documents, conducting research and filing court applications. Because many of the group's clients belong to the financial sector – for instance, Bank of Ireland, Barclays and UBS – it regularly works in tandem with the insolvency, corporate recovery, and banking and financial services litigation (BFSL) teams.

The BFSL group, one of the biggest in the country, chalks up a top-tier ranking in *Chambers UK*. This impressive size and standing have helped the team secure a place on the legal panels of national big'uns like RBS, UK Asset Resolution and One Savings Bank; other clients include well-known banks and mortgage lenders across the commercial, investment, corporate and retail spheres. The team is a popular pit-stop for trainees, not least because *"it's one of the seats that gives you the chance to handle a large number of your own cases."* Drafting is part and parcel of a stint here, mainly in the form of witness statements and letters, and trainees get to liaise with clients and counsel too. We're unable to reveal many details about the cases on the firm's docket, but we can tell you a large chunk of them concern recouping fraudulent losses and preventing incidents of a similar nature.

Meanwhile, the banking and finance group is especially strong on the social housing and renewable energy financing fronts, and has a good whack of the UK's major financial institutions on its books, including Barclays, Lloyds TSB and Nationwide. It's not all about the domestic players, though: the team services plenty of foreign entities too – Dutch bank Triodos, for example, which lawyers recently advised on a number of multimillion-pound loans to various housing associations in England

and Wales. Sources who'd completed a banking seat told of drafting ancillary agreements, carrying out due diligence and liaising with foreign counsel *"to make sure the paperwork meets the legal requirements of all jurisdictions involved."* It's unlikely you'll get to manage transactions from start to finish here, but we're told there are opportunities to deal with clients and take the lead on low-value deals.

Green with energy

Property lawyers in Bristol recently advised the Department of Energy and Climate Change on the real estate elements surrounding the government's 'Green Deal' energy policy, and the firm also sits on the legal panel of the London Borough Legal Alliance, which consists of ten local authorities. TLT complements this public sector property work with matters for commercial clients like WHSmith, EDF Energy and Greene King. The practice is split into several specialist teams, among them real estate litigation, social housing and planning – all of which are highly recommended by *Chambers UK* for their work in the South West. Trainees in Bristol are assigned to one of these, while their counterparts in the capital take a more general approach, working between them. *"I was exposed to all sorts of work – commercial property matters, development projects and complex residential matters,"* reported one Londoner. Still, we hear both offices offer a healthy dose of responsibility in the form of reviewing and drafting leases, researching titles, overseeing Land Registry applications, and handling client queries. *"The amount of client contact I got really stuck out to me,"* said one interviewee. *"There were so many opportunities to go to meetings."*

The family team scoops top-band regional *Chambers UK* rankings and falls under TLT's private business umbrella, which also incorporates tax and estate planning work. Divorces and child-related cases like contact disputes and those concerning physical or psychological harm form a large part of the team's workload. *"You have people coming to you whose lives have been turned on their heads, which is a completely different experience from dealing with the massive institutions we handle on the commercial side."* Trainees sitting with the group are often asked to oversee negotiations between parents and their children, on top of drafting witness statements and attending court sessions with counsel.

Baby boomer

At only 14 years old, TLT is very much a young'un as far as law firms go. A major plus to this, according to our sources, is that *"it doesn't have the old-school values of other firms in the area. There's no obvious sense of hierarchy, for example – you never feel intimidated approaching any of the partners, who you'll find are just as likely to make cups of tea as trainees."* The open-plan layout helps immensely with this as *"it requires everyone to be amiable, open and talkative."* Said one interviewee: *"I've been supervised by lawyers of many different levels throughout my training contract, but I wouldn't have necessarily known who was who based on how they interacted with me."*

Last year we heard a few grumbles about a lack of collaboration between the teams in London and Bristol, but according to the current crop of trainees, the firm has taken strides to address this. *"There's been a drive to share expertise and develop a greater one-firm focus,"* sources from both offices said, mentioning that they're *"now interacting quite a lot."* There's not much overlap with the Manchester practice yet, but trainees are kept in the loop about its developments. *"As the team out there grows, I imagine we'll get to work with them on a more regular basis."*

Insiders had few complaints about the firm's digs. The Bristol office resides in a 1970s tower block *"right in the heart of the legal quarter, just along the river."* From the outside it might not look like much – sources compared the building to a car park and, of all things, a cheese grater – but the interiors make up for that, we hear. *"We have a lovely reception area, top-of-the-range facilities and great branding – everything's unmistakably TLT. And because we're in such a tall building, we get fabulous views of the city."* Londoners were equally complimentary about their home ground, praising the *"perfectly convenient location"* by Bank tube station and the *"smart, stylish and contemporary"* interiors.

Social butterflies will be pleased to hear there's no shortage of fun at TLT. *"They recruit people who are just as enthusiastic about being here as they are about law in general. We get up to a lot."* Aside from an annual trainee get-together in Bristol and a firm-wide shindig held every other summer, most mingling is kept to trainees' home office. Rest assured, however, that each contingent enjoys a pretty full social agenda. Bristolians can often be found grabbing after-work drinks at nearby wine bar Toto's or attending events put on by their local Junior Lawyers Division, while the London cohort recently introduced a social committee that organises monthly events like pub quizzes. New trainees across the offices are welcomed with a bowling and pizza outing (an excellent combo in our opinion), and third-seaters are tasked with organising some kind of event every couple of months or so. *"It's usually pretty low-key – something like Laser Quest or pizza-making."*

TLT trainees come from a mix of universities and backgrounds, with fresh graduates and career changers alike making up the current cohort. While TLT *"doesn't go for cookie-cutter personalities,"* there are certain traits trainees tend to possess. *"We've all got quite outgoing personalities and aren't afraid to get stuck into something we've not experienced before,"* insiders agreed. *"Enthusiasm is key."*

The firm's ambitious turnover target for 2017 shows it's not hitting the brakes on its expansion drive any time soon. We hear this thirst for growth feeds heavily into the firm's working culture. *"Everybody's motivated to do their bit and contribute to the firm's fortunes,"* trainees said, telling us *"it's exciting to be part of a confident machine that isn't resting on its laurels. It feels like we're all nurturing our own little baby."* Although TLT still has a little way to go to rival the likes of Burges Salmon and Osborne Clarke – the current top dogs in the Bristol market – there's no doubt the progress it's made in recent years has captured the attention of industry insiders. *"That we're even being compared to those two firms shows we're clearly going places,"* noted one interviewee.

The True Picture

And finally...

TLT's mantra of 'recruit, train and retain' has paid off in recent years, topping the 80% mark every year since 2008. This trend continued in 2014, when ten out of 11 second-years were kept on.

Travers Smith LLP

The facts

Location: London

Number of UK partners/solicitors: 65/195

Partners who trained at the firm: 50%

Total number of trainees: 46

Seats: 4x6 months

Alternative seats: Paris

Extras: pro bono – A4ID, Paddington Law Centre, PEF; language classes

On chambersstudent.co.uk...

How to get into Travers Smith

The basics of private equity

This refined City institution offers tip-top transactional work with a touch of finesse.

Those who wait

"There'll be no fundamental changes." So said David Patient of his impending premiership at Travers Smith when it was announced he'd be taking over for managing partner Andrew Lilley come January 2015. Much has been made of the silver circle firm's resolute independence and modest global footprint over the years, but it's hard to argue with the insider who pointed out that *"it's a model that works incredibly well for us."* Indeed, at £882,000 Travers' PEP is enviably high, and despite being just a mid-size operation the Londoner regularly bags headline work, much of it international – for example, its representation of offshore drilling company Noble in its $9.9bn merger with Noble Switzerland. *"We've been courted by bigger outfits, but what good would rushing through a merger do?"* queried our source. *"We've made our market our own."*

It's important to note that this market is firmly transaction-focused. Travers' corporate group is its largest and has defined the firm since its launch in the early 19th century. *Chambers UK* deems the practice one of the best in the City and also awards top-tier accolades to the firm's private equity and capital markets offerings. Travers is no one-trick pony, though: a slew of practices beyond the corporate sphere – among them finance, employment, dispute resolution, pensions, real estate and tax – consistently pick up rankings too.

The trainees we interviewed told us they were drawn in by the firm's high-calibre work but also cited several other reasons for joining ranks, including a positive impression of their future colleagues – *"everybody I met at law fairs was welcoming, talkative and honest"* – and the belief that a training contract at Travers is *"far more*

personable" than some others in the City. *"You don't get beasted here like you do at magic circle firms."* Sources also highlighted the lack of bureaucracy in the application process as a plus: *"There are no psychometric tests or any of that rubbish; it's straightforward, like the firm as a whole."*

Unsurprisingly, a visit to the corporate department is mandatory, and trainees are also required to undergo a stint in either real estate or finance. Six months in dispute resolution or employment satisfies the contentious requirement, and trainees can also pursue a wildcard option in one of the specialist departments – for example, tax, IP or commercial – if they wish. It all sounds a bit restrictive, but according to our sources these rules aren't hard and fast. We heard of trainees who'd done two specialist seats and others who'd ducked out of a contentious seat altogether by subbing in a two-week litigation course instead. We didn't hear any complaints about the allocation process – *"graduate recruitment is constantly asking us if our preferences have changed"* – though insiders did single out tax and commercial as particularly in-demand options (and therefore somewhat hard to land).

Tuck in

Trainees in the corporate department are parachuted into either the corporate finance or private equity sub-teams,

> **Seat options:** corporate; dispute resolution; employment; finance; real estate; competition; commercial, IP & technology; pensions; funds; tax; financial services and markets

Chambers UK rankings

Banking & Finance	Investment Funds
Banking Litigation	Litigation
Capital Markets	Media & Entertainment
Commercial Contracts	Outsourcing
Corporate/M&A	Pensions
Employee Share Schemes & Incentives	Pensions Litigation
	Private Equity
Employment	Real Estate
Environment	Real Estate Finance
Financial Services	Restructuring/Insolvency
Franchising	Retail
Fraud	Tax
Information Technology	

both of which are housed on Smithfield Street, just over the road from the rest of the firm. It's *"exciting blue-chip work"* for those in the former group, where most matters concern IPOs, funds or mid-market M&A. Lawyers here count over 60 listed companies among their client roster and recently nabbed a role alongside Clifford Chance on the £1.2bn IPO of Pets at Home. Junior members of the team are generally tasked with much of the lower-level work, including verification, research and due diligence, but drafting ancillary documents is also par for the course, and we even heard from a few who'd been trusted to lead conference calls with clients. *"I got to see a deal through from start to finish, which was a real eye-opener,"* one interviewee reported. *"The seat is great for gaining an understanding of how City law firms work and what makes the corporate world tick."*

Meanwhile, those on the private equity side found the work *"very document-heavy"* and told of drafting share certificates and board minutes as well as attending disclosure and completion meetings. The group is the City's largest and primarily handles mid-market matters like the £100m sale of Byron Hamburgers to private equity group Hutton Collins Partners. *"Trainees have to do the bibling – possibly the worst task in the world! – but I also got a lot of exposure to clients during my time with the team, which I wasn't expecting,"* one source said. *"It seems once they trust you, they're more than willing to give you the good stuff."*

The dispute resolution practice's diverse scope means new recruits can find themselves working on anything from banking and property disputes to pensions and tax-related claims. *"No two trainees have the same experience here."* The team – which has a number of big hitters on its client roster, including theme park biz Merlin Entertainments and the Argentine Republic – recently made the papers for its work representing Sebastian Holdings in an $8bn compensation claim against Deutsche Bank. *"Big matters like that see trainees stuck with mostly low-level tasks,"* insiders acknowledged, *"but no one minds*

when the work is that important. That was really driven home when Lord Leveson praised our bundling efforts on a recent case in the Court of Appeals!"* To be fair, it's not all stapling and photocopying; sources also reported some meatier undertakings like meeting with counsel, working on client advice notes and taking witness statements.

Either a borrower or a lender be

Travers' finance practice handles work for both lenders and borrowers, and there's also a compact corporate recovery team. On the borrower side lawyers recently worked on refinancings for Pret A Manger, Ambassador Theatres and Trainline – the latter, valued at £190m, was the largest unitranche financing of 2013. Our sources enjoyed the seat here, telling us: *"There are a lot of tasks trainees can claim as their own,"* such as overseeing the condition precedent and drafting board minutes. *"I was running the due diligence process myself, marking everything up and sending it out. I also got to meet clients and get involved with business development too,"* said one insider.

Those who opt into real estate can get stuck into major commercial transactions across the healthcare, retail and student accommodation sectors, among others. Much of the work is London-based, and the team primarily acts for mid-cap funds, counting Patron Capital, Lothbury Property Trust and Voreda among its recent clients. *"The size of the matters we handle can be daunting, but the seat is great for your development,"* one interviewee told us. *"We aren't just given the grunt work."* Indeed, typical trainee fare includes speaking to clients, drafting ancillary documents and carrying out discrete research tasks, and on top of that there are plenty of lease and licence renewals new recruits are trusted to run themselves. As one source recalled: *"I found myself doing completion calls with qualified solicitors on the other end of the line! That was challenging, though I should note they never give you more than you can handle."*

Tax is one of the firm's most popular specialist seats. The group is split into three teams – funds, private equity and employee incentives – and trainees typically divide their six months between two of these. *"It's an excellent seat for those interested in black letter law,"* one source observed, while another added: *"This is definitely one for the number bods – the work is very technical. I remember one associate telling me that even after five years in the practice there were still rudimentary concepts he was getting to grips with."* Research is the name of the game on the trainee front, where *"you spend most of your time assisting partners on ad hoc queries and drafting notes about your findings."* To that end, *"the learning curve is huge,"* one interviewee pointed out, explaining: *"You're given documents and asked for your opinion, which can be daunting. I really enjoyed it, though. It's slower-paced than other departments, so you have time to focus on producing quality work."*

When it comes to the hours trainees keep, we heard *"they shift a lot more in the transactional seats than in contentious ones – in finance and corporate, for example, you could leave at 5.30pm when it's quiet and at 5.30am when it's incredibly busy."* That said, this isn't the kind of firm that has sleeping pods, quite simply because they wouldn't see much use. Sources assured us that standard days weigh in at something like 9am to 7.30 pm, with all-nighters and weekend visits few and far between. Those who had been roped into staying into the wee hours of the AM took comfort in the knowledge that *"when you're working late it's only because your input is essential. There's never any suggestion that you'd stick around just to be seen."*

Skills to pay the bills

Depending on the department, formal training for trainees kicks in a few months into each seat, with weekly lunchtime classes run by an associate or partner. The format of these sessions varies depending on the department, but the quality of teaching remains steady, according to our interviewees. *"The benefits are immediately obvious – you learn how to put together a document or run a file very quickly."* Every three months trainees benefit from a two-stage review, which involves an informal chat with their supervisor followed by a more formal discussion with the training principal a few weeks later. The latter, we're told, *"is as much a dialogue as a review of your performance and acts as a safety net of sorts – you get another chance to flag up issues and discuss your progress."*

Travers assigns its trainees a mentor when they first arrive, although *"you tend not to see much of each other after your first seat,"* said our sources, who saw this as no bad thing. *"The atmosphere here is such that you can chat to partners and associates easily, so the need for a formal mentor trails off after a bit."* Many credited the firm's room-sharing system – which sees trainees sit alongside a partner and an associate – with fostering this *"close-knit"* vibe. *"I've become as happy taking the mickey out of the partner in my room as I am asking them about their weekend,"* said one, touching on the *"reduced hierarchy"* the set-up encourages. *"It's also a great way of learning – you have immediate access to help if you have a question, and you get to observe how your seniors talk to clients and handle various matters."*

Briefcase in point

When it comes to gender diversity, our sources admitted that *"women are under-represented,"* particularly at partnership level, where they only account for 14% – a figure below par, even for the City. Still, they were keen to assure us *"we aren't by any means an old boys' club; incoming female trainees needn't worry about spending their days struggling to talk about rugby."* Many pointed to the newly established Women's Network – which summons female lawyers across the firm for cocktail evenings and networking events – as evidence of Travers' efforts to address the imbalance, and insisted that any disparities at the trainee level are a consequence of the firm's *"dedication to recruiting the very best candidates, no matter who they are."* According to the firm, women comprise 57% of the incoming trainee class for 2014. *"Obviously when you get to the higher levels, the industry as a whole has its issues, but I have faith in the way they do things here – everybody's on an equal footing."*

Speaking of recruitment, let's talk about who gets in here. Our experience of Travers' trainees over the years has shown them to be modest, bright and well-mannered, typically with an Oxbridge or Russell Group education. Our sources suggested that the *"quiet confidence and self-assurance most of us share"* is rooted in the fabric of the firm itself: *"This isn't a place that shouts about its achievements – we don't have a really glam office, and we're not bothered about becoming a McDonald's law firm with offices on every continent. Of course, that doesn't mean we're not on the ball."* Considering this précis, it's fitting that rather than a bling ring or a ritzy watch, trainees are gifted a trusty briefcase engraved with their initials when they attend the Christmas party in their first year.

In 2013 this do was held at the swanky Millennium Hotel in Mayfair. Other annual shindigs include a trainee dinner hosted by the managing partner and an Easter drinks party to which incoming trainees are invited. Once they're in the door, new recruits have plenty of chances to catch up during jaunts to the nearby The Bishops Finger or long-standing Travers haunt Karaoke Box. *"It's pretty dreadful,"* conceded interviewees of the latter, telling us: *"We should know better, but it's open late and close to the office."* We also heard about ski holidays and trips to the Rugby Sevens. *"The firm is generally quite sporty – there's a lot of football and hockey, and people go on cycling trips too."*

And finally...

Interviewees were happy to report *"there's no sense of competition"* during the run up to qualification. *"We're each running our own race."* In 2014 Travers Smith kept on an impressive 16 of its 17 qualifiers.

Trethowans LLP

The facts

Location: Southampton, Salisbury

Number of UK partners/solicitors: 26/32

Partners who trained at firm: 15%

Total number of trainees: 5

Seats: 4x6 months

Alternative seats: secondments

On chambersstudent.co.uk...

How to get into Trethowans

Trethowans in the community

This Southern stalwart has a respectable personal injury, clinical negligence and commercial offering.

The True Picture

Because you're worth it

In a region that plays host to a number of large national players, including Shoosmiths and Bond Dickinson, Trethowans holds its own admirably. The 50-lawyer shop, divided between offices in Salisbury and Southampton, serves clients well beyond its own turf, among them Lloyds Bank, Chelsea FC and Santander. At the same time, its prowess in the local neighbourhood is not to be underestimated: the firm has one of the best clinical negligence and personal injury practices around – top-ranked by *Chambers UK* in fact – and provides claimant-side representation to a host of Southern residents every year. One trainee summed up the firm's remit best using terms that wouldn't look out of place in a perfume ad: *"National overtones complement our strong regional base."*

Chambers UK awards Trethowans additional top-tier rankings for its agriculture, employment and licensing practices. A handful of its other offerings – including corporate, litigation and private client – also get a mention. The personal injury seat is a popular stop for trainees, as is commercial property. Trainees are encouraged to spend time in both of the firm's offices, but the seat system doesn't stipulate any restrictions beyond that, aside from the standard SRA contentious requirement. New starters get to meet with HR before commencing their training contract, and from there the firm consults with them before every rotation to find out their preferences. *"You can say which ones you want to do and which are definite nos,"* a trainee told us, *"and on the whole our wishes are taken into account."*

This time it's personal

The personal injury department spans both offices and works on both general injury claims – often road traffic accidents or workplace injuries – and clinical negligence. The firm acts mainly for claimants seeking compensation from employers, the NHS, local authorities and/or insurers. The work ranges from *"relatively small RTA claims to cases involving significant spinal and brain injuries."* As this suggests, some of the assignments are rather serious and emotional in nature: *"Injuries during childbirth, fatal misdiagnoses – that kind of thing."* Personal injury claims often run for longer than six months, so trainees rarely see a case all the way through, *"but the supervisors make sure you gain insight into the different stages involved by getting you to work on a number of cases."* Occasionally, second-years even get the opportunity to run a few smaller RTA claims on their own. Interviewees described their more usual workload as *"pretty varied"* including as it does *"drafting instructions to counsel, reviewing medical expert information, and sitting in on meetings with clients and counsel."*

The commercial litigation department deals with matters like landlord-tenant disputes, insolvency cases, and contractual disputes about the supply of products or services. The value of most matters is below £1m – the firm recently defended Toys R Us after it was hauled over the coals

Seat options: agriculture and rural property; commercial litigation; commercial property; employment; family; insurance litigation; personal injury; private client; residential property; corporate

Chambers UK rankings

Agriculture & Rural Affairs	Litigation
Banking & Finance	Personal Injury
Clinical Negligence	Private Client
Corporate/M&A	Real Estate
Employment	Real Estate Litigation
Family/Matrimonial	Restructuring/Insolvency
Licensing	

for not paying for £100,000 worth of toiletry supplies. There are a few seven-figure cases too, for example that of the Monaco-based investment company which wanted its money back after it lent $8.5m to a Ghanaian company to help fund the exploitation of a gold mine. Trainees are fed work from all fee-earners – not just their supervisor – which presents *"a prioritising and time-management challenge."* Typical assignments include completing court forms, bundling, attending hearings and helping to interview clients at meetings.

The firm's commercial property clients include high-street banks like Santander and Lloyds. Trethowans recently assisted the former with the £1.65m refinancing of a care home. Several large pension funds are also clients of the group, most notably Legal & General. Responsibility levels are high, with our sources reporting that *"as soon as you arrive you're handed a bunch of files and told 'these are your matters'."* Trainees handle leases, licences, purchases and sales – *"even a few auction sales which are really interesting."* Interviewees were able to *"contact clients, make decisions about how to progress and essentially run entire matters end to end."*

The employment department acts mainly for employers defending claims brought against them in the Employment Tribunal and the courts. Clients include GPS manufacturer Garmin, clinical trial planner Icon, and timber and plant firm WH Bond. During cases trainees find themselves *"drafting witness statements, attending client meetings, observing hearings and explaining tribunal procedures to clients."* There's non-contentious work too – mostly drafting employment contracts – and one source said they enjoyed *"working with the clients we have on retainer as it's nice to see the same faces regularly."*

I'd do anything

The regular meet-the-team lunches are typical of a firm described as *"a very happy place"* with *"a strong team ethos"* and *"generally relaxed atmosphere."* The Salisbury office is located in a business park on the A30 just outside town. The office is open-plan, although this has the opposite effect to what you might think: *"It's quite quiet really,"* mused one trainee. *"People try not to be overheard or disturb others."* The Southampton office has a very different location and feel: it's a city centre Grade II-listed building. It has a more traditional layout with individual offices. *"People wander around quite a bit to chat to people,"* said one source. *"They always know they can retreat back into their offices when they need to get on with work."* Having said all that, official sources told us the firm plans to move its Southampton office in late 2014; the new location will be more like that of the Salisbury office – we wonder if a slight cultural shift might accompany the move.

Trethowans' trainees are a tight-knit bunch, and often *"go round to each other's houses for dinner."* Those in Southampton find it easier to meet up after work as the office is in the centre of the city, while the business park location of the Salisbury office *"makes it more difficult to nip out for a quick pint."* The firm does make a good effort to lay on social events though. Recent outings include bowling, go-karting and a trip to So'ton's Mayflower Theatre to see *Oliver!* At a firm-wide level there are touch rugby, cricket, football and netball teams to join. There's also a firm-wide Christmas party – most recently held at the fancy Marwell Hotel in rural Hampshire – and a summer party which is usually an outdoor affair: *"There was a barbecue, a hog roast, and games like coconut shying and rounders. It felt a bit like a family outing – lots of people brought their kids and other halves."*

The True Picture

And finally...

Trethowans only takes on a few trainees, but it hasn't been able to offer many of them NQ jobs in recent years. It kept on two of four qualifiers in 2013 and just one of four in 2014.

Trowers & Hamlins LLP

The facts

Location: London, Manchester, Exeter, Birmingham
Number of UK partners/solicitors: 123/166
Partners who trained at firm: c.33%
Total number of trainees: 38
Seats: 4x6 months
Alternative seats: overseas seats
Extras: pro bono – Kaplan Legal Advice Centre

On chambersstudent.co.uk...

How to get into Trowers & Hamlins
The Middle East

This firm is big in the Middle East and mixes public, private and international work.

Sheikh-a-maker

Servicing the needs of London councils and Dubai sheikhs might seem worlds apart, but that's Trowers for you. The firm has long been a pitstop for local authorities and other public sector bodies seeking top-tier procurement and social housing advice, and it also attracts a good deal of attention in the Middle East, where it has four offices and is big on the private client, banking and real estate fronts. That said, the Arab Spring has left the firm, like many, anxiously surveying its presence in the region – the past few years have seen Trowers close its Jeddah office after only one year of practice, withdraw from an alliance with a Riyadh outfit and pull out of Cairo citing concern over Egypt's political instability. Still, the firm remains intent on seeking out opportunities in the Middle East as well as sub-Saharan Africa and South-East Asia, where a Malaysia office was opened in 2012.

Our trainee sources were generally drawn to the firm by a preference for either international or public law work. *"There's a bit of a divide on this front – people interested in the international side of our practice are usually not so interested in social housing."* But as one junior pointed out, there are benefits to embracing both: *"The firm is great at both strands. And public law does have its commercial aspects – you negotiate in the same way, but there's extra interest, thanks to the added layers of consent required."*

Trowers has nine offices total, with four in the UK: London, Manchester, Exeter and Birmingham. The firm has recently reshuffled its UK practices under the following five headings: housing and regeneration, public sector, commercial, property, and projects/construction.

And, said one source, *"there's been a big push to join up the different offices so we operate as more of a national practice."* London offers around 15 training contracts per year, while the growing Manchester and Exeter offices offer two each, and Birmingham will begin taking a single trainee from 2014 onward. The whole incoming class completes PSCs together at Kaplan in London before their first seat – *"it's a good way to get to know your intake in the other offices"* – and after that are occasional practice group training sessions. *"There's an awful lot in housing and regeneration in particular because it's such a niche area."*

Jersey wonders

Trainees' first seats are allocated, with the majority ending up in housing and regeneration. Thereafter they have mid-seat meetings with the firm's graduate recruitment and development manager, during which they rank three preferences for the next rotation. Trainees in Exeter and Birmingham are likely to do a seat in London to round

Seat options: London: housing and regeneration; public sector commercial; banking and finance; international; corporate (including tax and pensions); employment; litigation; commercial real estate; projects and construction. **Exeter:** housing and regeneration; commercial real estate; construction. **Birmingham:** housing and regeneration, projects and construction, employment; commercial. **Manchester:** housing and regeneration; banking; commercial real estate; projects and construction; regional litigation

Chambers UK rankings

Administrative & Public Law	Local Government
Capital Markets	Pensions
Charities	Projects
Construction	Public Procurement
Corporate/M&A	Real Estate
Education	Real Estate Litigation
Employment	Social Housing
Healthcare	Tax

out their training contract, an option that used to be available to Manchester recruits but is no longer thanks to the office's recent expansion into practice areas like banking and construction.

Trowers' housing and regeneration team in London has a decades-strong reputation as the City's best, a title reinforced by top rankings in *Chambers UK* and long-standing relationships with sector staples like the Homes and Communities Agency (HCA). *"There's a stigma that public sector work is not exciting, but actually the firm does its most cutting-edge work here."* Indeed, the firm has tackled the housing crisis head-on by assisting with development deals for hundreds of new flats nationwide. Lawyers recently advised the aforementioned HCA on new subsidy regimes designed to encourage affordable housing, and oversaw the States of Jersey's £250m reformation of its social housing system. *"The level of responsibility I encountered here was incredible,"* said one trainee. *"I was running my own files as a first-seater, which involved liaising with clients, drafting reports and completing SDLT returns. The seat is great for developing organisational and communication skills."* Trainees also found the department *"super-supportive in terms of development – there's a professional support lawyer whose job is to help you get to grips with resources."*

In Manchester the busy commercial real estate team recently handled the sale of a new leisure and cinema complex in Leeds, while colleagues in London have been advising BT on the £900m development and leasing of a production space in the Olympic Park for its broadcasting venture BT Sport, and overseeing a series of leases for retailers in the newly launched London Designer Outlet. The broad-reaching practice lends itself not only to big developers but also high net worth individuals looking to invest in real estate funds. Trainees reported a stint here can be *"hectic but enjoyably so,"* particularly in Manchester's growing team. *"You get a lot of responsibility early on – you have your own files to run and also assist with commercial leases for our really big clients."*

Real estate litigation clients range from housing associations and institutional investors to contractors and wealthy individuals. London lawyers recently represented the relatives of Samantha Cameron in a high-profile, multimillion-pound inheritance dispute, and defended a private landlord against a collective enfranchisement claim resulting in the judgment that sub-let flats used as service apartments count as commercial properties. Meanwhile those in Manchester recently scored a win for Queensway Hospitality during a case regarding dilapidation damages. *"It's a bit difficult to get your own files here, but I can't complain about the levels of responsibility,"* said a Mancunian source, telling us: *"I was calling and e-mailing clients daily and even spoke on their behalf at a few case management hearings. Knowing the team trusted me like that was quite reassuring."* London trainees also reported *"a fair amount of client contact"* during matters like landlord and tenant disputes, liquidations and unpaid invoice claims. *"The construction disputes in particular can get really technical, which can be a challenge."*

Trowers' corporate contingent sources a good number of deals through the real estate department. The London team is big in hotel and leisure sphere, which allows the firm to make full use of its international network – for example, the team worked closely with the Bahrain office during local travel group Kanoo's recent acquisition of Thomas Cook's Lebanon and Egypt businesses. There are also general corporate matters such as Mirfield 1964's £2.9m takeover of celebrity jeweller Theo Fennell, whose lavish creations include a £10,000 silver pot of Sudocrem destined for royal baby George's posterior. Trainees here reported drafting board minutes and corporate resolutions in addition to occasional bouts of research. A finance seat at Trowers also involves work on real estate-related deals and refinancings for property investments. Additionally there's global Islamic finance work to be had – Trowers' team works with financial institutions based in the Middle East, helping them implement complex, multimillion-pound cash-raising structures like Tawarruqs or Murabahahs.

Most juniors complete an overseas seat in the Middle East. Dubai's the most popular destination, though secondments are also available in Bahrain, Oman and Abu Dhabi. A stint in the former offers trainees a *"really diverse workload,"* from litigation and real estate to construction and corporate matters, we're told. *"You can ask around for different types of work so you can get more of what you like."* Lawyers there service local companies as well as overseas businesses looking to set up in Dubai; the British Embassy is also a key client. *"It's a brilliant experience being out there, although the responsibility levels can feel a bit daunting."* Fortunately, *"there's a really nice social vibe in the office, with a good trainee network,"* sources said, telling of trips to waterparks and weekends away to nearby beaches. Meanwhile those who'd been to Oman and Bahrain reported working closely with local partners and businesses. *"The cultural differences weren't as pronounced as I thought – I quickly made local friends."*

Strange delight

In London and Manchester trainees share an office with either their supervisor or another fee earner, while those in the smaller Exeter and Birmingham offices sit open-plan. Both set-ups are *"great for asking questions,"* sources agreed. Trainees receive two *"thorough and constructive"* appraisals per seat, both of which are based on feedback collected from everyone they've worked with. On the whole our interviewees were confident about their chances come qualification, noting that *"the firm makes a real effort to try and retain trainees."* In 2014 13 out of 17 qualifiers stayed on.

In 2012 Trowers relocated its London lawyers to Linklaters' old office in Moorgate. City trainees praised their digs for their *"modern feel and position alongside some of the other big hitters in the corporate world."* Said one trainee, well practised in the art of schadenfreude: *"It's nice to be next to Slaughter and May, not least because you'll find when you're working late, they're always later still. There have been times when I've left at 10pm and laughed to myself about that."* On that note, trainees firm-wide spoke of a healthy work/life balance, with those in the regions telling us they're *"generally gone by 6pm"* and Londoners by *"7pm or so. Of course that fluctuates – sometimes I have weeks where I'm staying until 9 or 10pm consistently, though it's definitely not an all-nighter culture,"* said a source in the capital.

Trowers Manchester is located in the city's stately Albert Square, right by Manchester Town Hall. The 19th century architecture might draw the eye, though inside it's a different story: *"Let's just say the offices have seen better days! There's talk of moving; the decor's looking a bit tired."* By contrast, lawyers in Exeter are housed in a glass-fronted newbuild not far from the city's cathedral – a residence trainees agreed *"is very nice to look at and work in."* The group there is *"quite social"* and regularly goes out for drinks together, while the cohort in Manchester enjoys trainee socials and departmental away days. When they're not hitting up the hipster bars in Shoreditch, London trainees spend their Fridays at the nearby Artillery Arms, *"which is quaint and has a great atmosphere."* They're also known to duck out at lunchtime to foodie haven Whitecross Street Market for artisan cakes and pulled pork burgers, and every few months trainees from all offices meet up for business briefing drinks in the London office.

According to our interviewees, Trowers' slate of work lends itself to *"a real mix of people – you get those who come here wanting to become banking lawyers, and others who are really keen on the public sector."* Within the current trainee cohort are individuals with all manner of work experience, from those who came straight through from university to ex-dancers, chefs and naval officers. *"We represent a lot of different ages and personalities. In general, though, people are down-to-earth, enthusiastic and good at getting on well with others."* Considering the firm's international ties, *"it's important to be someone who's tolerant and accepting of different cultures,"* sources observed. *"We have people who join us from all over, though luckily everyone is up for going out, whether they drink or not."*

And finally...

"There's a decent range of practices to try out here – social housing, public sector work, construction, finance. Trowers is a good place to come to if you want to keep your options open."

Veale Wasbrough Vizards

The facts

Location: Bristol, London

Number of UK partners/solicitors: 50/90

Partners who trained at firm: 23%

Total number of trainees: 17

Seats: 4x6 months

Alternative seats: none

Extras: pro bono

On chambersstudent.co.uk...

How to get into VWV

Trends in the education sector

Dickens and the law

There are plenty of beefy deals to sink your teeth into at this firm, which is still riding high after a London-Bristol merger in 2009.

Raising the steaks

London's Vizards Tweedie and Bristol's Veale Wasbrough merged half a decade ago, and it's been pretty smooth sailing ever since. A new office sprang up in Birmingham at the turn of 2014 to house a recently poached charities team from DWF; this was hot on the heels of the London branch's 2013 incorporation of property and private client boutique George Carter, part of a strategy *"to grow not only the London office but the firm as a whole,"* according to training principal Tabitha Cave. Factor in Bristol's upcoming move to swanky waterfront digs in early 2015, and things are looking pretty good for VWV.

The firm works across five primary industries: education and charities; healthcare; private wealth; family businesses; and the public sector. VWV is particularly big on that first one: it acts for more than 1,000 education and charity clients nationwide – including University College London, London Symphony Orchestra and the France-Hayhurst Charitable Trust – and *Chambers UK* awards nationwide rankings for both practices. Sector work is divided among four departments: litigation and employment; charities, corporate and commercial (CCC); private client; and real estate.

At the time of our calls there were 12 trainees in Bristol and five in London. According to Cave, *"we'll be looking into offering training opportunities in Birmingham as that office grows."* Trainees in Bristol have a little more choice than their City counterparts when it comes to seats, though note that available seats are only finalised right before allocation as the firm prefers to wait and see which departments have space for trainees. Aside from a compulsory contentious stint, *"the firm likes you to do a property seat,"* we're told. There's also the chance to move between offices – requests are considered on an ad hoc basis.

Maturing fast

London's real estate group is its busiest and mixes commercial and residential work, with clients ranging from schools and charities to property development companies and retailers. The addition of George Carter's solicitors has brought with it some interesting private clients too – we heard whispers of a few famous names. Meanwhile down in Bristol, huge corporations like Airbus sit alongside a smattering of government agencies and higher education institutions on the client list. Trainees here are assigned to sector-focused teams, like healthcare, which works with GP practices and pharmacies. The firm sits on the legal panel of the Education Funding Agency and has spent the past few years advising on property and construction matters totalling £50m. Other recent highlights include assisting the Highways Agency with its national property portfolio and advising EDF Energy on the multimillion-pound development of its Hinkley nuclear power station. Across both offices, trainees reported *"great drafting experience"* – mainly through leases – along with *"lots of post-completion tasks like handling land registrations, stamp duty and land tax."*

Seat options: Bristol: corporate; commercial; private client; employment; commercial litigation; commercial property; property litigation; construction; charities **London:** real estate; commercial and corporate; private client; employment; litigation

The True Picture

Chambers UK rankings

Banking & Finance	Litigation
Charities	Partnership
Construction	Personal Injury
Corporate/M&A	Private Client
Education	Real Estate
Employment	Real Estate Litigation
Immigration	Restructuring/Insolvency
Intellectual Property	Tax

Trainees can fulfil their contentious requirement with a stint in property litigation, construction, commercial litigation, employment or contentious probates (part of the private client department). VWV's property litigators recently assisted London Metropolitan University when it sought to obtain possession of a library which had been taken over by protesting students, and oversaw the registration of Esso's entire UK underground fuel pipeline network. Trainees here spoke of attending client meetings, preparing charging orders for court and even trying their hand at advocacy.

Over in the employment department, lawyers have kept busy working on numerous academy conversions in recent years. The team also advises the Crown Prosecution Service on tribunal claims, and acts for local charities like Bristol Zoological Society. One interviewee with experience here spent much of their seat working on a big disciplinary case, advising an individual on settlement agreements and drafting employment contracts, while another recalled doing *"tons of bundling, but luckily that was interspersed with trips to employment tribunals for sex and race discrimination cases."* Others typical trainee fare includes drafting witness statements and letters of action, going to conferences with counsel, and attending Crown Court trials.

Money for old mince

VWV's work with charities is a major draw for students choosing the firm, and it proves a popular seat year upon year. Among the long and varied client list are national outfits like the National Association of Citizens Advice Bureaux as well as independent schools and religious organisations like the Diocese of Gloucester – the firm specialises in advising social care, arts and educational charities in particular. Matters at hand include governance, state aid, joint ventures, property and investment issues. When it comes to school mergers and the building of academies, trainees typically find themselves drafting shareholder agreements and helping out with due diligence. We also heard from those who'd *"looked into subjects not many people know much about, like ecclesiastical law and the church's role in marriage. As you can imagine, there's some very old case law involved in those topics."*

The corporate team worked on more than 100 deals in 2013, totalling £800m. *"The sectors we work in – education, healthcare, family businesses and technology – are really distinct, so the contracts we draft vary a lot depending on which one they involve."* Our trainee sources found it particularly interesting advising family-led businesses: *"You have to consider the family dynamics at play, like members getting along."* The group recently advised Park Garden Centre, a third generation family business, on the sale of its Cheddar and Lechdale businesses, and assisted the Ontario Teachers' Pension Plan on its £220m acquisition of Busy Bees day nurseries. *"On big deals like that you kind of take a backseat role, though partners will still take you to meetings and let you have a go at drafting contractual clauses or share purchase agreements."* Additionally, trainees are expected to help out with the firm's company secretarial service, which sees them help clients file account documents and transfer shares.

The private client team services a mix of old-money families, successful businessmen, private banks, celebs and politicians on tax planning, asset protection and Court of Protection matters. *"Some of our clients have been with the firm for more than a hundred years, so you occasionally find yourself digging through some pretty old deed boxes."* Trainees here also draft wills and assist with estate administration, and sources who'd spent time doing *"extremely fast-paced"* contentious probates work told of working with barristers and attending court for will challenges and Inheritance Act claims.

The commercial team has acted for over 800 independent schools in the UK, including Ellesmere College, which it recently advised on an agreement to establish a new school in Dubai. The group also advises on public sector and energy projects – such as the establishment of a waste-to-energy business for engineering company DPS, which aims to roll out new technologically advanced engineering plants to local authorities, hospitals and supermarkets. Sources told of drafting contracts, carrying out data protection work, investigating possible infringement cases and registering trade marks on such projects. *"Partners are really keen to take you along to client meetings, which is great."*

Meat the Veales

Our interviewees drew attention to the fact that many of VWV's partners trained at the firm, telling us *"this means they understand what we're going through and can relate to us well."* Trainees told us that *"it's easy to talk to partners in confidence"* and applauded the way *"partners speak to the secretaries with the same amount of respect as they do with each other."*

Formal training comes in the way of an induction and team presentations at the start of the training contract, but new recruits also have the chance to learn from their peers: trainees maintain 'rough guides' to each seat during their time there by outlining what one can expect and adding links to suggested reading. Firm-wide trainee knowledge-sharing meetings held by video conference are another opportunity to pass on tips and give incomers an idea of what certain seats entail.

With more than three times as many people in Bristol as London, the latter base *"can sometimes feel like a branch office,"* trainees told us. *"That said, it's definitely expanding, particularly on the real estate front,"* thanks in large part to the 2013 incorporation of George Carter. There's a fair bit of collaboration between the two – interviewees from each reported travelling to the other for real estate team meetings, and we hear other groups are following that lead and holding firm-wide meetings where possible. The entire incoming trainee class used to complete PSCs together in Bristol, but enough gripes about early morning trains over the years have finally convinced the firm to let London trainees take their course in the capital.

Now that the two cohorts don't train together at the start of their training contract, several interviewees felt the firm could do more to integrate the trainee class socially. *"It would be nice to have at least one event a year where the whole year group gets together. They used to pay for London trainees to go to the Junior Lawyers Division ball in Bristol, but they don't any more."* Indeed, when it comes to formal socials, VWV does seem to fall behind firms of similar standing – trainees even have to chip in

for the Christmas do (which, fittingly, usually revolves around a few chips in the pub). If our sources are anything to go by, the young generation does a pretty good job of organising their own entertainment, though – a social committee in Bristol runs book club meetings and sports matches, and in London trainees, assistants and NQs *"always try to make time to eat lunch together."* CSR activities offer another chance to get together – we heard about trainees mentoring in schools and working with human rights charities. *"I wish we had a more coherent pro bono strategy for the offices, though – you have to organise everything off your own back."*

On the plus side, *"the work/life balance is excellent – it's one of the biggest plus points about the firm,"* sources agreed. Those in Bristol told us *"by 6.30pm the office is quiet,"* while others claimed *"the hours are no worse in London. Of course, you can expect some late nights, but you're never staying just for the sake of it."* Trainees were divided on whether this makes up for the fact that salaries have been frozen for the past five years: *"I think the trainee wage is fair considering the flexibility we have,"* sources in both offices said, though one in London pointed out that at £35,000 *"the NQ salary here is below market standard for the type of firm we are. It's something the firm will likely have to address in the next few years."* We didn't hear any complaints about the Bristol NQ wage, which is the same (and more in line with firms in the area).

And finally...

Trainees believed the qualification process had improved on last year, now that it's been pushed forward and there are more jobs on the table. Of ten trainees, eight accepted a place upon qualification in 2014.

Vinson & Elkins RLLP

The facts

Location: London

Number of UK partners/solicitors: 12/19 (+ 2 non-UK-qualified)

UK partners who trained at firm: 8%

Total number of trainees: 8

Seats: 4x6 months

Alternative seats: overseas seats

Extras: pro bono – Toynbee Hall Free Legal Advice Centre, TrustLaw

On chambersstudent.co.uk...

How to get into Vinson & Elkins
A brief history of the firm
Energy law

Grab your cowboy boots and giddy up to this Texan energy firm, which oozes *"Deep South charm."*

The True Picture

"Make me a proposition."

"How would you like to come to Houston?" Vinson asked. Replied Elkins: *"That is the ambition of my life; make me a proposition."* Believe it or not, it was this simple conversation between two Texan lawyers back in 1917 that led to the foundation of V&E, an international hard hitter in the energy world.

The firm today boasts a 15-strong collection of offices worldwide: outposts in London, Riyadh, Hong Kong, Abu Dhabi, Tokyo, Beijing, Moscow and Dubai complement its seven Stateside hubs. Despite its global undertakings, V&E doesn't stray too far from its Texas roots; the vast majority of the firm's activity involves energy work, with matters spanning the oil, gas, electricity and alternative energy sectors. The City branch – one of the first American-led legal ventures in London – may be just 37 lawyers strong, but it remains up there with the big boys, scoring *Chambers UK* rankings for its energy and natural resources capabilities as well as its projects work. At the time of writing this, lawyers were busy representing Iraq's Ministry of Oil in both a $17bn natural gas project and an $18bn pipeline project. Other notable clients of late include Indian energy giant Essar, the State Oil Company of Azerbaijan and Norwegian oil and gas biz Statoil.

While energy work is V&E's calling card, training principal Mark Beeley points out that it's useful to consider the sector as *"definitive of our client base rather than the type of law we do."* Indeed, energy-related matters certainly abound at this firm, but they're spread across an array of practice areas, including litigation, M&A, pro-

jects and tax. Naturally, *"it's pretty much all cross-border work,"* trainees confirmed.

Climbing into the saddle

Seat options for trainees are usually litigation/arbitration, finance, M&A, tax, and ETP (energy, transactions and projects). The firm allocates first seats and *"takes preferences into consideration"* thereafter. *"You usually get what you're interested in."* While seats are formally designated, however, a defining feature of the V&E training contact is that *"you're not really tied to any particular department; you're free to pursue work from different practice groups."* This fluid system was widely praised among trainees. Said one: *"You can take your training contract by the reins and say, 'Thanks for putting me in finance, but actually M&A is my passion, and I'm going to put my foot in that camp.'"*

Another V&E hallmark is the chance to spend six months at one of the firm's offices abroad. According to Beeley, regular secondment opportunities are available in Dubai, Moscow, Hong Kong and Houston, provided there's *"sufficient workflow in each office."* The latter two were the only hits among this year's bunch, who characterised the experience as *"a great opportunity to see interesting transactions we don't always do in London."*

Trainees with experience in the busy finance department described a *"steep learning curve"* involving *"lots"* of

Seat op ons: litigation/arbitration; finance; M&A; tax; and ETP (energy, transactions and projects)

Chambers UK rankings

Construction	International Arbitration
Energy & Natural Resources	Projects

client contact and a *"high level of exposure to hands-on tasks"* like drafting, reviewing documents and consulting with lawyers on the other side. The team's expertise centres around corporate and project finance, with clients ranging from investment banks and funds to developers and sponsors of international projects.

On the M&A front, lawyers act for a number of foreign energy companies, including Chinese bigwig Sinopec and Cairn India. Indeed, much of the work is international, with trainees reporting contact with clients in hubs as far flung as Dubai and Tanzania. Activity appears to come in bursts, so a given trainee's busyness is essentially luck of the draw: one source reported absolute exhaustion thanks to some *"massive"* deals, while another characterised their time with the team as *"quite quiet – I ended up seeking out work from other groups to keep busy."*

The following interviewee's testimony seems to sum up most trainees' experience when it comes to responsibility: *"I've never had endless weeks of just photocopying or filing; you get relevant work that makes you feel like a valued member of the team."* Sources were quick to point out that despite this tall order, *"you're always supervised,"* thanks in large part to firm-appointed mentors and the fact trainees have their supervisors as roommates. *"You never feel out of your depth, because they don't ratchet up the responsibility until they're comfortable that you can handle it,"* explained one. *"It's about building up trust. Often you'll get to a point where you look back and think, 'Bloody hell, I just did that!'"*

Southern hospitality

Our sources were frank about the *"tiring"* schedule a stint at V&E entails. *"Be aware you will work – you can't escape the hours, which are gritty and long at times."* Indeed, we heard from more than one poor soul who'd found themselves stuck in the office *"until the small hours working on bundles."* Still, *"I think that everyone has the preconception that you work all the hours God sends you at an American firm,"* one interviewee noted, *"but the reality is that you only work that hard here when*

you need to. If you have a day where you're done at 6pm, you can leave at 6pm."* Along with this lack of face time are generous starting and NQ salaries (which outstrip those of the magic circle, mind) to ease the blow of a hectic schedule. *"We get an awful lot of money to work this hard."* Yippee ki yay!

Trainees counted V&E's welcoming atmosphere as another plus. *"Everyone's happy to joke around and poke fun at each other, and there isn't a massive hierarchy; you won't find yourself trembling outside a partner's door."* They agreed this stems from the Houston headquarters, where *"the vibe is really warm and welcoming."* Further reminders of the firm's New World roots are visible in the form of *"constant correspondence with the US"* as well as the *"free flow of American partners here – you hear a lot of accents in the hallways."* There are also a few US-inspired social events over the year, including a Thanksgiving dinner and a rootin-tootin' Texas Independence Day celebration complete with lasso, horseshoe and fast-draw competitions. Still, one sphere the Yank influence does not pervade is the dress code, which we were admittedly disappointed to hear *"does not involve cowboy boots and a hat."*

The firm's high-rise digs in Moorgate offer *"one of the best views in London"* and have the dubious honour of housing, according to one source, *"the fourth fastest lifts in Europe."* Monthly 'ViEw' drinks celebrate the impressive vista; meanwhile those keen to get out of the office can mosey on over to the nearby Corney and Barrow, the firm's regular haunt. Karaoke bar K-Box and ping-pong club Bounce are also local favourites.

The firm's trainees characterised the typical V&E recruit as *"someone who's able to fend for themselves, is quite outgoing and has a strong personality."* Elaborated one: *"We're all competitive, but only with ourselves – we're the type of people who are always asking questions and requesting more work."* Mark Beeley reminds applicants to keep in mind the firm's *"unstructured"* approach to seats when applying: *"We need people who can run things on their own and don't need to be spoon-fed."* Indeed, said one trainee: *"I wouldn't choose V&E if you want a place that will cradle you and teach you in a nice little nest. You have to take the bull by the horns here."* Another added: *"We're not mice!"* When asked what animal better represents the ideal V&E trainee, our source answered *"armadillo"* without missing a beat. *"That's Texan, right?"*

And finally...

We heard the complimentary biscuits could be better, but V&E's qualification results, on the other hand, are up there with the best: in 2014, three out of four qualifiers were retained.

Ward Hadaway

The facts

Location: Newcastle, Leeds, Manchester
Number of UK partners/solicitors: 87/108
Total number of trainees: 19
Seats: 4x6 months
Alternative seats: none

On chambersstudent.co.uk...

How to get into Ward Hadaway
The Newcastle legal market

This proud Northerner laid its flat cap in Manchester and Leeds, but don't expect it to succumb to London's bright lights any time soon.

The Quay to success

Much like Newcastle's rapidly regenerating Quayside, Ward Hadaway is going places – and fast. *"We're young, forward-looking and very driven,"* its residents told us, and indeed it's those very qualities that have propelled the Geordie firm – a single-site outfit just a few years back – into a thriving three-office joint with branches in Leeds (opened in 2008) and Manchester (2012). Already these young offices are bursting at the seams. *"We've had to take up extra space for both because they're nearly full up now,"* reveals managing partner Jamie Martin happily.

For a good while Ward Hadaway's comfortably occupied second place in the battle for Newcastle's biggest firm, historically trailing Tyne-Tees top dog Dickinson Dees (today known as Bond Dickinson following a 2013 merger with South West firm Bond Pearce). Now that BD's coverage is more nationally focused, Ward Hadaway has more edge than ever in the region. *"We're the best choice for anyone looking to develop at a large full-service firm with a very strong local identity,"* said current trainees, many of whom were lured in by WH's public sector slant. Indeed, the firm has long-standing ties with NHS trusts and local authorities – some as far afield as London and the South West – which filter in property, healthcare and litigation matters. Still, the majority of the work is commercial. The firm advises various Northern industrial and technology clients in their dealings with big multinationals and overseas investors, and it also works with well-known national corporations like Aldi, Barratt Homes, Barclays and brewmonger Samuel Smith.

At the time of our calls there were 17 trainees in Newcastle, five in Leeds and just two in Manchester. Newcastle newbies get to list two preferences for their first seat before joining, though second-years get priority and traditionally have had the opportunity to stay in the same seat for their third and fourth seat, business needs permitting. The process is similar in Leeds, though it has fewer seat choices than the headquarters. In Manchester, there's no formal rotation as yet; rather trainees divide their time between four teams for the course of their two years.

Reel big fish

Chambers UK ranks Ward Hadaway's litigation team as one of the best in Newcastle and the surrounding area. The large department is omnivorous, taking on *"everything from multinational shareholder disputes to contested wills,"* with plenty of corporate fraud cases, professional negligence claims, insurance disputes and private client work in between. The team recently led the way on one of 2013's biggest professional negligence cases, representing Newcastle Airport in a claim against Eversheds. *"Given all the difficult cases we handle, it's amazing they don't stick us by the photocopier all day,"* said one interviewee, who was *"in awe of the amount of trust we're given as trainees."* Indeed our sources told of briefing witnesses, attending meetings with counsel and travelling to the Royal Courts of Justice for hearings. *"There are quite a few small matters to get on with, so you'll very likely find yourself getting to run some of your own files."*

Seat options: commercial litigation; property; banking; corporate; healthcare; property litigation; employment; private client; IP/IT; insolvency; matrimonial; corporate/commercial

Chambers UK rankings

Agriculture & Rural Affairs	Intellectual Property
Banking & Finance	Licensing
Charities	Litigation
Clinical Negligence	Pensions
Construction	Personal Injury
Corporate/M&A	Planning
Employment	Private Client
Family/Matrimonial	Real Estate
Healthcare	Real Estate Litigation
Information Technology	Restructuring/Insolvency

The firm's healthcare team specialises in clinical negligence work, representing over 60 NHS organisations on matters like inquests, birth injury cases and mental health claims, some of which last years and run to millions of pounds. *"Liaising with all these health authorities really scratches my public sector itch!"* offered one source. Let's hope that itch isn't MRSA, because trainees in this busy seat need all the energy they can get. Our sources recalled their first few weeks with the team as *"a whirlwind – it takes a while to pick up the medical terminology, though the work is really interesting, especially when you get to attend inquests."* They also reported bundling, drafting witness statements and instructions, and attending case management meetings with counsel.

The family practice handles private matters like divorces and finance matters, as well as public sector care cases. Lawyers regularly work with children's guardians during care proceedings, *"which can be challenging – often there's been an injury to the child, and it's quite emotional working out whether it's safe for them to go back to their family. This kind of work takes different skills from commercial work."* On the plus side, sources told us *"trainees get involved with all aspects of cases and aren't left behind in the office while all the fee-earners go out."* Indeed, many reported attending court regularly, adding: *"Advocacy is actively encouraged as soon as you're ready. Standing up against barristers in the County Court is such a good experience."*

Banks of the Tyne

Ward Hadaway's corporate department is split into three teams: banking, M&A and corporate finance. Trainees do a mix of all three. On the M&A front, sources told of filing, drafting board minutes and keeping on top of forms for both domestic and cross-border transactions like Growth Capital Partners' acquisition of multinational healthcare communications outfit Fishawack, and business software supplier Sage's sale of its specialist construction software division. Meanwhile the corporate finance side deals with listings and funding, often for lo-

cal start-ups like Applied Graphene. Lawyers recently oversaw the Teeside manufacturer's £22m AIM flotation.

Over in banking there are plenty of big'uns on the books, among them Barclays, Lloyds Banking and RBS. *"You feel like you're at the sharp end of the international finance scene."* The work here is complex, ranging from acquisition finance and PFI funding arrangements to bonding structures and venture capital funds, but our sources found that *"supervisors take a very structured approach – they make sure you're neither overstretched and therefore panicking, nor sitting around feeling too comfortable."* Most newbies start out working on due diligence before progressing to higher-level tasks like drafting ancillary documents.

WH represents *"a nice mix"* of public and private entities on the property front, including Aldi, Barratt Homes, and several NHS trusts and local authorities. Trainees in this seat found themselves *"dealing with properties from Cornwall to London to Manchester – we have a solid national presence."* The firm recently advised the Borough of Telford & Wrekin on its Building Schools for the Future project, and oversaw more than £20m worth of energy-related developments in 2013. There's been a good bit of work on village green inquiries lately, which one source revealed are *"very contentious, so they almost feel like court cases. I had to travel to Manchester to help take witness statements for one."* Trainees on the whole were happy with the levels of responsibility they'd encountered during their time with the team, telling us: *"Partners are very willing to take you along to meet clients, and they don't just give you little pieces of work; you're closely involved throughout the whole transaction."* In fact most get to take the lead on small files by the end of their seat. There's a separate seat on offer in WH's small property litigation group, which gets involved with *"everything from boundary disputes and trespassing cases right up to massive repossessions."*

According to our sources, supervisors at WH expect trainees *"to require less and less of their help as we progress."* Still, they made it clear seniors are *"always willing to go through and explain work to you. You also get tons of feedback, which is very nice."* Indeed, trainees benefit from mid and end-of-seat sit-downs with the training partner and head of HR, which they found *"incredibly useful – the reassurance is helpful, as is being able to set objectives for your next seat."*

No Tyne like the present

WH's Newcastle headquarters are located by the Gateshead Millennium Bridge in the Quayside district, which has benefited from *"a brilliant resurgence"* in recent years. Staff are split between buildings across the road from one another: Sandgate House and Keel Row House. The former overlooks the River Tyne – *"we have the best views in the country!"* – and contains individual offices, while the latter hosts an open-plan environment much appreciated by trainees. *"It's got a more communal feel, and you can learn so much by listening to partners making calls."* Meanwhile our Leeds sources had plenty of praise for their *"very clean, very bright"* branch, which resides in a new development just down the street from the city's chief railway station. *"We've got all the professional resources you'd expect, but the office is small enough that you really get to know people here,"* said one occupant. WH Manchester is located smack in the middle of town and, like its Leeds counterpart, is expanding steadily, having just taken over another half floor.

The firm makes *"a great effort"* to keep up connections between its three offices, interviewees felt. All trainees gather at the HQ for an induction at the start of their training contract and from there regularly travel between branches for training seminars. There are also periodic departmental sessions held via videolink, and everyone assembles in Newcastle for the firm's annual meeting. *"There's a free bar afterwards – it's a nice chance to mingle with all the trainees across the firm."*

Having got to know their colleagues firm-wide, our sources were confident in their claims that WH attracts *"a diverse range of people – there are a lot of different personalities here, which makes for an environment that's* not too rigid." There are some commonalities among the bunch, though – for starters most come from universities based near the firm's offices. *"The firm looks for a genuine commitment to the area."* And attitude-wise, most trainees are pretty down-to-earth individuals. *"There's no real bluster here; we maintain a sense of calm professionalism."* Of course, that doesn't keep the cohort from kicking back every once in a while. *"I'm reluctant to say we're 'fun', but there's definitely no shirking from going out for drinks together."* Tipples are usually taken at the nearby Pitcher & Piano, which *"has a terrace overlooking the river and is great for relaxing after a long day."* Fortunately the days aren't too long at WH – most sources reported finishing up between 6 and 7pm, leaving plenty of time to get involved with the many sports teams and networking events on offer.

Additional firm-sponsored socialising takes place during the Christmas, spring and summer dos, as well as annual departmental team-building expeditions. Recent destinations include Alnwick Castle – aka Hogwarts in the first two Harry Potter films – and Amsterdam and Dublin. There's also the chance to get involved with the local community through business development events and charity walks. This year's trainees had a blast taking on the Sunshine Fund Trade Up Challenge, which saw them haggle their way from an Ant and Dec-autographed teddy bear right up to a night at a posh Yorkshire hotel.

And finally...
Ward Hadaway usually has pretty decent retention rates but 2014 was something of a blip with only seven of 12 qualifiers kept on.

Watson, Farley & Williams

The facts

Location: London

Number of UK partners/solicitors: 49/97

UK partners who trained at firm: 10%

Total number of trainees: 27

Seats: 6x4 months

Alternative seats: overseas seats

Extras: language classes

On chambersstudent.co.uk...

How to get into WFW

P&I insurance explained

Interview with managing partner
  Chris Lowe

International experience ahoy! Trainees get to do an overseas seat at this specialist firm – and have *"a hell of a lot of fun"* along the way.

They called it the ship of dreams...

Boats, paying for boats, and the stuff that goes in boats: to many that's what Watson, Farley & Williams is all about. But while *Chambers UK* places the firm at the top of the London shipping finance market, there is a lot more going on below deck. The firm has spread its tendrils into related practices like aviation, project and trade finance. WFW is also building in areas more associated with bigger full-service firms, like energy, employment, litigation, capital markets, tax and competition.

When two plucky Norton Rose partners (Messrs Watson and Farley) jumped ship to set out on their own in 1981, the Eighties' commercial frenzy and a thirst for international expansion set their new firm on the right course. It steadily diversified and amassed a network of 12 overseas offices dotted around the world's major ports and financial hubs. The training contract at WFW encourages an international mindset and sends all trainees overseas for one seat.

For the first time ever, 2013 saw the firm's revenue surpass the £100m threshold. The other good news is that it hasn't asked any trainees to defer their start dates this year (although this did come with at least £5,000 compensation in 2013). Current trainees also felt relatively confident about their post-qualification prospects and eventually ten of 14 were retained.

You're gonna need a bigger boat

The two years are split into six seats. *"The seat choices are more limited than they seem if you're looking beyond finance and finance litigation,"* sources felt. Before join-ing, new trainees list three preferences for the first seat. Once through the door *"seat allocation is a much more collaborative process; towards the end of each seat you have a meeting with HR to discuss where you want to go next and why."* Most were happy with their allocations and even those less impressed admitted that *"because a seat abroad, asset finance, litigation and corporate finance are compulsory, most people ultimately end up with a similar training contract, just in a different order."*

Asset finance is WFW's flagship department, so expect *"non-stop high-level work, but also exposure to clients."* This is a world leader in ship finance, so get used to some deals with very big boats, such as acting for Standard Chartered Bank on establishing a $109m loan for four 51,800 DWT MR (get used to vessel nomenclature too) tankers for Leopard Tankers. Ships occupy the large part of the asset finance team, but planes and trains also get a look in. Recent cases include advising Lloyds Bank, Lombard and Barclays on the $300m financing of a portfolio of helicopters for offshore oil and gas operations. *"I found myself doing the kind of work I never thought I'd have the opportunity to do as a trainee,"* said one of many upbeat interviewees. This was down to the generous levels of responsibility: *"I was drafting complete loan agreements to be amended by my supervisor;"* while another was *"running ship delivery files – almost on my own – making sure that all the necessary document lists are up to date, as well as dealing with the oppo-*

> **Seat options:** asset finance; projects, commodities and export finance (PCEF); corporate; litigation; tax; employment; property; competition

WATSON FARLEY
&
WILLIAMS

INQUISITIVE MINDS
MEETING GLOBAL
CHALLENGES EVERY DAY

Chambers UK rankings

Asset Finance	Energy & Natural Resources
Capital Markets	Litigation
Commodities	Shipping
Employment	Tax

site side and directly with the client." The work suits the internationally-minded: *"I was on the phone to lawyers in Panama and shipping agents in Malaysia in the past week, and I went to a ship delivery."*

"Some matters in PCEF go on for years," a trainee told us, *"if not a number of months."* The department is split into construction/projects and finance, with experiences varying between each. In construction, which has *"an energy focus – think wind farms and solar farms,"* trainees typically found themselves *"monitoring data, uploading files, helping to draft client reports and assisting with contract reviews."* Those on the other side were predominantly concerned with finance – *"we usually act for large energy companies or banks"* – a recent client being Deutsche Bank as the lead arranger on the £70m financing of a biomass energy facility in Beckton.

Litigation is a broad practice, but the ubiquitous shipping clients dominate as usual. Our interviewees got involved in some quite interesting and varied work including *"an arbitration over the switchover from analogue to digital TV, time charter issues and swap disputes."* Clients include the government of Pakistan, RBS and Bank of Moscow, and a lot of the disputes involve international trade, natural resources and energy. Typically trainees find themselves *"doing a lot of bundling and photocopying but also undertaking research, participating in contract reviews and sending out emails to the various parties."* One trainee got a particular buzz from *"the weekly court run; it's nice to get out of the office, mingle with bewigged barristers and pretend you know what you're doing."*

The corporate department is *"very big on integrating with the other practices at the firm."* This shows in the firm's headline transactions involving oil tankers, North Sea gas field acquisitions and wind farm takeovers. As is common in a lot of corporate teams, trainees were dealt a *"feast or famine"* style of workload, depending on the stage of the M&A cycle. Interviewees found themselves *"drafting corporate authorities, dealing with company secretarial matters and filings with Companies House."*

"People should make sure they realise that property, employment and tax are niche areas at this firm," warned one trainee. Competition included, these departments are generally *"ancillary to the asset finance, litigation and corporate departments."* In employment *"there were lots*

of immigration issues brought in by existing finance clients,"* for example. Meanwhile those in tax, property and competition dealt with elements of larger finance, corporate or litigation matters. Training is handled department by department, and includes sessions for new joiners at BPP.

Das Boot

The compulsory overseas seat is usually the preserve of much bigger organisations, so our interviewees were naturally rhapsodic about their four-month postings to either Hamburg, Athens, Singapore, Bangkok or Paris. Singapore is *"a hell of a lot of fun,"* apparently. The office is *"very busy"* and trainees were *"handed tasks from loads of different departments."* The fast-paced atmosphere meant *"having to learn to stand on our own two feet,"* and the level of responsibility is closer to *"what a junior associate would expect back in London,"* being *"ultimately responsible for a lot of our own work."* Our interviewees found *"the atmosphere in the Singapore office far more relaxed than in London, and less hierarchical; people at all levels chipped in to do the boring bits."* This gregarious cohort *"puts on a lot more social events than back home."* One trainee had *"played six-a-side football, attended a client horse-racing day and a cricket match – plus an awful lot of pub trips."*

Those who'd ventured to Paris concluded that *"the culture is very different; it's much more face-time oriented. People would never think of leaving the office before 7.30."* One went further: *"I definitely prefer the UK's work-hard, play-hard approach."* But still there is some joie de vivre to be had: *"The teams are much smaller so you form much closer working relationships with people."*

Athens is now the sole office in Greece, having absorbed Piraeus into it. Trainees there are given *"their own transactions,"* which is *"scary to start with, but I came back with loads of confidence,"* said a source. One advantage of going to Greece is that *"many of the people who own the shipping companies we act for are based here, so it's brilliant for client contact."*

Where everybody knows Philippe's name

Back home, the London office is conveniently located behind Liverpool Street station in a building that's *"not especially stylish or glamorous,"* but we do hear *"rumours of it getting updated."* Lawyers sit *"two to an office and these are mostly grouped by department."* Alongside the usual swanky meeting rooms, client suites and canteen, the firm also comes with changing rooms *"equipped with GHD straighteners, which is pretty snazzy."* Less snazzy is that *"the canteen isn't open in the evenings; it would be nice not to have to get so many takeaways,"* grumbled some sources. One turned this into a positive: *"It shows how few people stay in the office late into the night."*

Official business hours at WFW are 9.30-5.30. In reality the day is longer, and trainees found the hours increase significantly in certain seats: *"You're expected to be willing to work long hours in the firm's core departments,"* especially when there's a big transaction closing. One told us of an extreme case where *"I was in the office till 3 in the morning during a particularly manic deal just before Christmas."* Life is *"steadier in tax and employment,"* where *"it would be unusual to have to stay later than 7 or 8pm."* Do partners acknowledge this dedication? *"We're disgruntled by the lack of appreciation,"* felt some interviewees, while others said that *"people will often follow up to say thank you for doing extra work."*

"Shipping is quite a close-knit industry; it feels like a community," mused one recruit. WFW's manageable size, too, presents a *"very unintimidating"* milieu to new trainees, who felt able *"to get to know a wide range of people from across the firm,"* and rarely would they *"go to the kitchen and find people I don't know."* In this environment *"it's easier to make your mark,"* but *"this does mean that all the partners quickly know how good or bad you are."* Our sources depicted a collaborative workplace: *"Everyone is keen that the trainees learn as much as possible"* and *"even when someone has to stay late to answer your questions, they never give you the sense that you're being a pain."*

Each year the firm hosts Christmas and summer parties, fee earners' dinners and welcome drinks for new trainees. There are also *"wine-tasting events and the odd champagne reception."* Year on year, our interviewees go weak-kneed about the firm's French chef Philippe and his exquisite canapés. *"You can always tell when the canapés are about to be brought in as everyone starts edging towards the doors."* This is a sociable firm: *"The trainees go out all the time; I've been told I'm antisocial because I can't make every Thursday and Friday."* All this carousing and still *"there's a disappointing lack of scandal"* – the opportunity to make your mark?

And finally...
With three different finance seats being almost inevitable during a WFW training contract *"aspiring trainees should certainly have an interest in that area of law."*

Wedlake Bell LLP

The facts

Location: London
Number of UK partners/solicitors: 55/67
Partners who trained at the firm: 17%
Total number of trainees: 12
Seats: 4x6 months
Alternative seats: secondments

On chambersstudent.co.uk...

How to get into Wedlake Bell
A chat with training principal
   Hilary Platt
CSR at Wedlake

This thoroughly pleasant London firm provides its trainees with a beguiling mix of private client and commercial work.

Wigs can be deceiving

It'd be easy to assume that Wedlake Bell, a law firm that sits among a flock of barristers' chambers on London's Bedford Row, has an image in keeping with its more traditional, bewigged neighbours. While it's true that WB has a formidable presence in private client and family law (both of which could be viewed as rather traditional practices), a look at the *Chambers UK* rankings reveals that much of its skill set is typical of a modern-day law firm: real estate, corporate/M&A, employment and IP are just a few of the areas it scores highly in. Wedlake Bell's clientele serves as further evidence of its substantial commercial clout, including as it does household names like Tesco, Lacoste and Jaeger.

The firm's merger with small fellow Londoner Cumberland Ellis in April 2012 was big news at the time, and training principal Hilary Platt tells us the tie-up was *"a resounding success. Our office is now almost full and the two firms have integrated very well. We've also made further lateral hires in the past few months."* Although the trainees we spoke to conceded that Wedlake Bell *"is never going to be a gigantic City beast,"* they were more than content with the firm's standing. *"We're not intent on having a ridiculously large workforce, but that's part of our charm,"* said one, before adding that the firm is not stagnant and growth is the order of the day. But it comes at a steady pace: revenue was up by just a few percentage points in 2013/14, according to early reports.

LEGO house

Wedlake Bell's 35-strong property department spends its days handling investment and development work across a swarm of sectors. Healthcare has become a principal source of business lately, with the team currently advising Care UK on the multimillion-pound development of new care homes in Suffolk. Besides lending a hand to virtuosos in the healthcare sector, property lawyers have recently acted for Credit Suisse, Lufthansa and much-adored toy manufacturer LEGO.

While it's not an obligatory pit stop, a stint in property is very likely considering its size. There's a decent selection of property seats to choose from: residential, commercial, property litigation and construction. Commercial property *"is the busiest of these teams."* One interviewee said the stream of work *"comes in waves – there have been some trainees who were absolutely swamped with work, whereas others have had it easier."* Even during these drier spells, trainees are entrusted with their own files to run – *"albeit with oversight from your supervisor"* – and spend time drafting leases and licences, regularly liaising with clients and getting involved in lease negotiations.

Maccy Steve's

As noted last year, the corporate department has *"a ton of ambition"* and benefits from a lot of internal cross-refer-

Seat options: commercial property; residential property; property litigation; commercial litigation; construction; private client; family; business recoveries; IP & commercial; corporate; employment; pensions & employee benefits

The True Picture

Chambers UK rankings

Construction	Real Estate
Employment	Real Estate Finance
Information Technology	Real Estate Litigation
Intellectual Property	

rals – *"from the property and private client teams, for instance."* The group operates in the lower mid-market and typically takes on deals in the £10m to £100m range, a recent example of which was the £36m reorganisation of life sciences company Illumina's UK businesses. Noteworthy clients include British Rowing, IMG and Honest Burgers. For trainees, all the standard corporate tasks are evident, including carrying out disclosure, drafting shareholder agreements and interacting with clients – *"more over the phone as opposed to face to face."*

The employment team brings in some pretty high-profile cases. For example, it regularly acts for Ohio-based IT guru Convergys on the employment aspects of its transactions, such as the $446m sale of one of its divisions to Japanese IT provider NEC. The group also picks up work on behalf of renowned individuals. In last year's edition we mentioned its role in representing McDonald's ex-PR Steve Easterbrook as he parted ways with the fast food giant to become CEO of Wagamama. Since then Mr Easterbrook has actually come back to Maccy D's as global chief brand officer, with WB lawyers acting for him once more on his return. Like corporate, employment has pockets of work drawn in from other practices. *"There's a fair amount of corporate support work,"* one source confirmed. Trainees are tasked with drafting employment contracts, conducting research into relevant topics and providing opinions on the case in question.

WB's private client department is a wide-ranging beast and works on trusts and estates, tax planning, wills and succession planning, and wealth preservation – both for domestic and overseas clients. Unfortunately we can't disclose any specific matters, but we can tell you that the team has previously acted for notable names like the Al-Sabah family (the ruling dynasty of Kuwait), the Earl of Dudley and British art dealer Anthony d'Offay. Our sources were handed some *"fairly administrative tasks"* to begin with in this seat, before moving on to more substantive undertakings like drafting wills, handling offshore trust issues and meeting clients outside the office.

Hey Marnold!

We've long considered Wedlake Bell to be one of the cheeriest firms we cover in the *Student Guide*, and our sources this year said nothing to alter that perception. *"I went on vac schemes at other firms and it seemed like they forgot who I was straight after they'd met me,"* said one interviewee. *"It's not like that here; everyone makes a concerted effort to smile at you and remember your name, and that in turn makes you feel really valued."*

This sense of comradeship is embodied by managing partner Martin Arnold – nicknamed 'Marnold' – who *"everyone thinks is a dude"* apparently (we're guessing that's a compliment). *"He's great at taking the time to talk to all the employees here. If he's leaving the office early in the afternoon, he'll stop by first to see how we're getting on, and he does the same thing when he arrives in the morning."* Trainees also quashed concerns about the Cumberland Ellis merger having any negative bearing on WB's working culture, as they agreed the two firms shared similar characteristics and described the months following the tie-up as a *"seamless transition."*

When it comes to socialising, Wedlake Bell has a decent amount going on. A particular highlight was a weekend getaway to the Lake District in 2013: *"I suppose you could bill it as a team-building trip, but there was never a feeling that we were 'on duty'. Marnold led us on a hike, and there was plenty of eating and drinking involved in between."* At the time of our calls trainees were gearing up for another weekend expedition, this time to the New Forest, so it looks like a country getaway might be becoming a yearly occurrence. On a more regular basis, there are cricket, netball and football teams, a raft of charity events, and impromptu drinks at nearby pubs and bars.

WB doesn't release an NQ jobs list, so it's up to second-years to put forth their preferences of where they want to qualify. *"That system has its pros and cons: although you're not limited to what's listed on a piece of paper, you're also not sure of where the demand is."* However, our interviewees were optimistic about being kept on given the firm's healthy retention rates over the past two years. In 2014, three out of six qualifiers were retained.

And finally...

Wedlake Bell recruits from a mix of universities and doesn't target people from certain backgrounds. Generally speaking, though, *"we do like people with more gregarious personalities, so don't blanch at questions in the interview that aren't centred on law."*

The True Picture

Weil, Gotshal & Manges

The facts

Location: London

Number of UK partners/solicitors: 29/79

UK partners who trained at firm: 4%

Total number of trainees: 23

Seats: 4x6 months

Alternative seats: New York, Paris

Extras: pro bono - LawWorks, A4ID, Battersea Legal Advice Centre

Om chambersstudent.co.uk...
How to get into Weil
Private equity for beginners
Weil and the Wolf of Wall Street

Big Apple-born Weil excels at premier private equity work, though aspiring trainees beware: this is no easy ride.

A taste for the transactional

On the confectionery platter of law firms vying for your attention, Weil is an intensely flavoured, tough American cookie jostling for position against the batches of sturdy City flapjacks and magic circle of plump English scones. The firm's graduate recruitment website indicates it's made of stern corporate stuff, deeming the environment 'challenging, technical and pressurised', but is this an establishment that requires a thick skin and sharp elbows to survive? Trainees thought not. *"I'd dispel the myth that we're a brutal, cut-throat firm,"* said one. *"When I first came in for an interview I thought they were going to tear me to pieces, but actually the people were nice, normal and easygoing. It's definitely a professional place, but it's not scary."* Of course, this doesn't mean training at Weil is a piece of cake. *"This isn't a nine-to-five, chilled-out job; you're challenged all the time."* As one source recalled: *"On my first day I had to call up a senior associate in New York and discuss US securities law. I had no idea what I was doing! It can be tough, and the learning curve is certainly steep."*

Graduate recruitment partner Jonathan Wood has this to say about the firm's proclamation that it's 'not for everyone': *"When we say that, we're really pointing at the fact we're an office which is very focused on transactions (whether that be private equity, restructuring, finance) and dispute resolution – we do have people who specialise in real estate, pensions, employment, IP and other disciplines, but advice in these areas tends to be delivered in a transactional or litigation context. Coming here is not like joining a magic circle firm, where there are very large specialist practices."* His main message for aspiring trainees? This is a training contract for those seeking *"the pace and excitement of a transaction or dispute resolution-type environment,"* but if that *"sounds like the most horrific thing imaginable, then we may not be quite the right fit for you."*

There's no doubt transactional work is Weil's forte, particularly in the private equity sphere. The firm scores premier *Chambers UK* rankings for its work on the buyouts side, and in 2013 its lawyers advised on PE deals totalling $136bn in value, outstripping both Clifford Chance and Freshfields in this feat. *Chambers UK* also ranks Weil's capital markets, corporate/M&A and restructuring practices, among others. All of our sources cited the firm's focus on corporate undertakings as a primary reason for joining up, and many were also drawn to the smallish trainee cohort as well as Weil's established presence in the UK market. The firm may have its roots in New York City, but London hardly plays second fiddle to the Big Apple base; 90% of Weil's City lawyers are UK-qualified, and the vast majority of their workload is home-generated – for example, their representation of Barclays in the restructuring of two healthcare-related securitisation deals, together valued at more than £1.5bn.

In 2013 the City branch faced a handful of high-profile departures – including the defection of capital markets head James Cole and a private equity trio led by partner Mark Soundy – but it's also brought on board a handful

Seat options: corporate; banking & finance; business, finance & restructuring; tax; private funds; employment/pensions; property; IP/IT; real estate; structured finance; litigation

The True Picture

Chambers UK rankings

Banking & Finance	Litigation
Capital Markets	Private Equity
Corporate/M&A	Restructuring/Insolvency
Investment Funds	Tax

of high-flyers in the past year from the likes of Hogan Lovells and Goldman Sachs. Turnover-wise, the firm's steamed ahead regardless, posting a 4.2% increase in revenue in 2014.

Private equity passions

Trainees are assigned their first seat and then go on to have a chat with graduate recruitment before each rotation to discuss where they'd like to go next. Our sources found the reasoning behind HR's decisions *"isn't always clear"* and mentioned that *"if you really want a certain seat, it's on you to go speak to the relevant partner and get your name out there, in addition to talking to HR."* Everybody's required to spend six months with the corporate practice, and a finance seat is also compulsory – a stint in either structured finance or banking finance satisfies the latter requirement.

Given the firm's private equity slant, trainees in the corporate department can expect the majority of work they encounter to be PE-related. Big names on the books include Charterhouse, Providence Equity and Lion Capital – the latter recently enlisted Weil to oversee the sale of its stake in Weetabix to a Chinese food company. Other transactions handled of late include Advent International and Bain Capital's acquisition of RBS's stake in payment processing company WorldPay, and eBay's acquisition of online courier company Shutl. According to our sources, trainees get to grips with *"a lot of document management"* on such deals: *"It's up to us to keep tabs on all the documents in the agenda, keep everybody abreast of all the deadlines and ensure all the regulatory consents and legal opinions get delivered on time."* There's also the chance to review agreements, observe negotiations, draft ancillary documents – for example, board minutes and loan certificates – and attend signing meetings with clients, which involve *"walking them through the documents and making sure nothing gets missed out."* Alongside all this deal-making is plenty of non-transactional work for private equity clients' portfolio companies.

We hear there's a *"considerable"* overlap between the corporate and finance departments, seeing as the latter oversees much of the financing for acquisitions handled by the former. Case in point: lawyers here recently advised PE giant OMERS on the loan financing for its £390m acquisition of Civica, a software system provider. Interviewees told us the firm's finance contingent is *"very ambitious – it's expanding and branching out into*

the bank side of things, rather than acting exclusively for private equity houses."* In 2013 Weil acted for most of the big 'uns in the market, including, Deutsche, Citi and Barclays, advising the latter (along with a group of other banks) on one of the year's largest leveraged financings – Hellman and Friedman's $1.7bn acquisition of Scout24, a German online marketplace retailer.

Our interviewees felt the banking finance seat is *"one of the best for responsibility and exposure to clients,"* telling us *"you're given a lot of independence."* Reported one: *"I talked to lawyers in other jurisdictions regularly and had daily contact with clients. In certain refinancings I was even given the leeway to go ahead and run things on my own."* A typical trainee duty here is running the CP checklist. As one explained: *"Before a bank lends a private equity house a load of money, it has to be sure that certain things are ticked off and conditions are met. For us this means managing, reviewing and updating all the documents, and even drafting some of them, like shareholder resolutions."* Meanwhile, those sitting with the smaller, more technical structured finance team told of grappling with *"complex law"* surrounding derivatives and securitisation matters. *"It's really difficult to get your head around, but a good way to learn the ropes of finance."* Sources here reported tasks like drafting ancillary documents and board minutes, proofreading finance agreements and calling up clients, along with a smattering of research.

At the time of our calls lawyers in the business finance restructuring (BFR) team were busy contending with spin-off work from two whopping insolvencies: Lehman Brothers and MF Global. The team is working alongside KPMG as Special Administrators to the latter, which is one of the largest corporate failures in US history and worth upwards of $2.5bn. A seat here mixes contentious and transactional work, and *"can be quite technical – you have to have the ability to interpret case law and statute."* Our sources told of undertaking research and drafting memos in preparation for trial, and went on to point out that the litigation group works hand-in-hand with the BFR team, so there's a chance to get a hand in the Lehman and MF Global cases in that seat too. Litigators at Weil also handle a good bit of tax litigation, scoring a £1.2bn victory for retailer Littlewoods against HMRC in a case related to overpaid VAT – one of the most significant pieces of tax litigation in recent times. Trainees who'd spent time here had tackled doc review, bibling and bundling in addition to case law research for court hearings.

Meanwhile, over in the private funds team trainees learn *"all about the private equity industry and how it fits together. It's really interesting to look at the challenges funds and investors face during the fund-raising process."*

Weil you were(n't) sleeping...

If you've got your eye on a Weil training contract, bear in mind your nose will be firmly pressed to the grindstone. *"As a trainee you get really good work and learn a lot, but you have to be prepared to work really hard. It takes a lot of commitment and motivation to deal with the long hours."* Just how long are we talking? *"You shouldn't come here expecting anything less than a 12-hour day,"* declared one trainee, expressing an opinion reiterated by several others. Of course, schedules shift depending on a department's ongoings and the type of work it handles. *"Banking lawyers tend to work longer hours than others, and at Weil it's no different. I was working until 1 or 2am every day for three weeks during my seat there,"* testified a source, while another reported the work-stream in corporate *"is more steady – there you don't stay late very often, but you're working consistently until 8 or 9pm."* Fortunately, these timetables are incurred because of actual work: *"Nobody's just sitting around to show their face. If it's quiet and you leave at 6:30pm, nobody's going to ask why."* For those who do have to stay into the AM, a few winks aren't out of the question – the basement contains sleeping pods (*"like little hotel rooms,"* complete with shampoo and conditioner) for such toilsome times. And as trainees pointed out, the toil is handsomely rewarded – Weil's trainee salaries are among the highest in the City, as are its NQ rates.

Our sources acknowledged the firm's small stature and demanding workload *"can be quite daunting"* but agreed *"everyone is willing to help you settle in. You aren't spoon-fed of course – it's not a hand-holding place – but the culture definitely isn't aggressive or hawkish. Supervisors are happy to chat about how you're doing."* Additionally, trainees are assigned a 'responsible partner' to discuss their career progression with.

Interviewees went on to characterise Weil's working environment as *"slightly different across each team – banking is pretty hard-hitting, for example, while you'll find smaller departments are less intense because people are not as stressed."* On the whole, however, *"the atmosphere is positive – we work hard and we have a lot of fun. There's a sense of proper community."* At Christmastime we hear corporate colossus Mike Francies, Weil's managing partner, sends an email around to offer trainees wine from his collection, and in previous years he's also hosted a summer party at his house, complete with a petting zoo. Other regular jamborees include a fancy Christmas party at Lincoln's Inn and annual quiz that involves dressing up and karaoke. *"This year's theme is 'songs from movies' – someone suggested* Pretty Woman*, but I suspect dressing up as a call girl might be a bit controversial,"* tittered one source. Meanwhile the firm's women's committee Women@Weil puts on various dos throughout the year like bowling nights, and trainees also have a budget for their own periodic socials.

When asked if there's a 'Weil type', our interviewees insisted that *"besides high academic achievers, there's no one sort of person who comes here."* They did hit on a few commonalities across the firm, though: *"There aren't any massive egos here; everybody's got a quiet confidence in their own abilities and the strength of their convictions. And we're all very interested in corporate law."* Trainees noted *"the firm is expanding and looking to hire,"* and were confident about their chances of staying on. *"There's no formal application process; you just express your preferences in conversations with partners and HR."* Ultimately, 12 out of 12 new qualifiers stayed on with Weil in 2014.

And finally...

"Actually knowing something about private equity" is imperative at interview for this firm, its trainees stressed. *"You need to be interested in that practice area beyond it just being a job."*

White & Case LLP

The facts

Location: London

Number of UK partners/solicitors: 79/218

UK partners who trained at the firm: 7.5%

Total number of trainees: 63

Seats: 4x6 months

Alternative seats: overseas seats

Extras: pro bono - A4ID, Innocence Network UK, Lawyers Volunteering for the Arts, TrustLaw; language classes

On chambersstudent.co.uk...

How to get into White & Case
Why Kazakhstan?

Have you got the travel bug? If so, hop on board the White & Case express, which guarantees overseas seats and international opportunities aplenty.

Defying gravity

It's rumoured that it took New York lawyers Justin DuPratt White and George Case just $500 ($15,000 in today's money) to get White & Case up and running in 1901. Today that $500 nest egg has begotten a billion-dollar firm, which is one of the world's global heavyweights. W&C picks up over a dozen 'global-wide' rankings in *Chambers Global*, winning the highest plaudits for its finance, projects and arbitration work. At present the firm has offices in 41 locations, spanning the US, Latin America, Europe, Asia, the Middle East and Africa. And it isn't easing its foot off the pedal: 2013 saw the opening of a Madrid office, the establishment of a second base in Kazakhstan, the forming of an association with Indonesian firm MD & Partners, and the firm receiving a licence to practise law in Dubai.

London is one of the sturdiest rocks in the W&C network and *"its own centre of gravity,"* according to trainees. W&C was one of the first US firms to hop across the pond, and today, with over 300 fee earners, London is the second largest office in the W&C web. In 2013 it contributed $207m to the worldwide revenue total of $1.4bn, making this the second largest US firm in London. The firm's core global strengths – notably finance, energy and projects – are also at the centre of operations here, but the office picks up an impressive total of 25 *Chambers UK* rankings. Besides top-tier recognition of the energy and projects practices, W&C also wins recognition for areas including capital markets, litigation, corporate M&A, arbitration, construction, asset finance and restructuring.

One element of White & Case's pitch to prospective trainees is its 'small intake'. Now we rarely call firms out in this way, but we're going to go on record as saying that W&C's intake of 30 trainees a year is not small. Got that? Sure, it isn't mega, but compared to other City firms it's mid-sized; and compared to other US firms it's big (remember that this is the second biggest American in London). One thing the firm does get absolutely right in its graduate recruitment materials is all the talk of a 'guaranteed overseas seat'. Spending six months abroad during your training contract is strongly encouraged. *"If you said you didn't want to go abroad then that would be highly unusual,"* said one trainee. And *"unless there were personal circumstances that prevent you from going,"* you are expected to pack your bags and head for Heathrow. Overseas seats are organised at the beginning of the training contract, so you know when and where you're going in advance, but *"it is possible to change that later on – so there is some flexibility."* The most popular overseas destinations are Tokyo, Singapore and New York, while trainees can also head to Abu Dhabi, Hong Kong, Istanbul, Johannesburg, Moscow, Paris, Prague, Frankfurt, Beijing and Almaty.

Trainees told us their remaining three seats are allocated in *"the fairest way possible,"* with more senior trainees getting priority. First-years (and even those who are yet to join the firm) do get to express a preference though,

Seat options: corporate M&A, private equity, real estate, employment & benefits, construction, litigation/arbitration, IP, project finance, asset finance (EIPAF), bank finance, financial restructuring & insolvency (FRI), capital markets, high yield and structured finance

Chambers UK rankings

Asset Finance	Energy & Natural Resources
Banking & Finance	
Banking Litigation	Financial Services
Capital Markets	Information Technology
Commodities	International Arbitration
Construction	Litigation
Corporate/M&A	Private Equity
Data Protection	Projects
Employee Share Schemes & Incentives	Restructuring/Insolvency
	Transport

which is taken into account. The majority of our interviewees said they'd got their top seat choices and *"if you don't, HR will meet with you to explain why, and try to remedy it in the future."* Seats in smaller departments like employment, intellectual property and real estate can be hard to come by.

The great god Vulcan must be enraged

Capital markets is a common first seat. One trainee reported that *"nine out of 15 of us started there when I joined,"* while a majority of our interviewees had done time here first. Happily the department is known for being *"the nicest and coolest"* in the firm. Trainees can join one of several subteams: high-yield debt, trusts, debt capital markets, equity capital markets and financial regulation.

The high-yield debt team focuses on *"companies below investment grade, which are usually high-risk, so the bonds will pay a high yield in order to attract investors."* Lawyers recently represented Sanitec – a Scandinavian bathware producer – as the issuer of US high-yield bonds worth €250m. Trainees reported working on *"a lot of bonds governed by US law,"* and told us that *"the department is heavily Americanised – there are a lot of loud American lawyers here!"* Trainees *"help prepare the offering memorandum – a book about 400 pages long – as well as conducting due diligence on companies with international branches, collating financial statements and calculating yield rates – it can be quite mathematical!"* The broader capital markets team acts for major banks like Standard Chartered, BNP Paribas, HSBC, Barclays, RBS and Morgan Stanley as well as advising issuers like Coca-Cola Turkey and the company which runs Rome's airports. Lawyers also recently helped the government of Rwanda issue its first $400m Eurobond.

White & Case is a global leader in energy, infrastructure, projects and asset finance, especially involving emerging economies. The deals and projects lawyers work on span the globe and many are stupendously massive. None

more so than the Sadara project: W&C is currently advising Saudi Aramco (Saudi Arabia's state oil company) on this $20bn petrochemical development, having originally advised on the setting up of the joint venture to get the whole thing going. That matter has been running since 2009, so we weren't surprised to hear trainees say that *"projects can take a really long time to complete – sometimes ten to 15 years."* Given this fact, trainees often *"work only on a small short chunk of a deal,"* and their tasks usually consist of *"proof-reading, bibling and collating info for hundreds of pages' worth of construction and finance documents."* Many matters are oil and gas-related, but there is infrastructure work too – the financing of railways and airports, for example. And some of the energy work is a little out of the ordinary: the firm recently advised Landsvirkjun, the Icelandic national power company, on a project which will channel geothermal power from Iceland's volcanoes to supply electricity to the UK.

W&C's corporate practice has particular sector strengths in areas such as healthcare, energy and financial institutions, which help keep the M&A deals coming in thick and fast. While the team services a roster of UK clients, *"none of the deals are solely UK-focused,"* meaning that trainees might need to get to grips with *"stock and purchase rules in Indonesia,"* as well as helping to advise *"companies in Kurdistan active in the oil and gas sector."* The firm lured over *Chambers*-ranked private equity partners Richard Youle and Ian Bagshaw from Linklaters in January 2014, so a few interviewees had been able to work on some private equity matters too (although they suggested the new laterals still needed to bed in a bit).

The road is long

The disputes department is known for its finance, energy, white-collar crime and cartel work. The department does both litigation and arbitration, and as there are *"some people who do mainly litigation, some who focus on arbitration, and some who do a mix,"* trainees tend to get a taste of both. Sources reported that *"some people work predominantly with their supervisors, while others have been able to get different types of work – although it can be difficult to escape your supervisor!"* A lot of cases relate to activities in emerging markets, and when we took a look into the firm's case files we spotted ongoing matters related to Ukraine, Kyrgyzstan, Kazakhstan and Turkey. For example, the team is representing Turkish conglomerate Çukurova in a $2bn shareholder dispute with Russia's Alfa Group over the ownership of Turkcell, Turkey's largest mobile phone company. Trainees told us the department is *"always busy – the busiest in the whole office by some distance."* As a result the hours can be tough, as there's *"always a hearing or a last-minute filing to prepare for, so trainees often need to stay until 2am to get all the bundles ready in time."* Sources linked these long hours to the fact the department has quite a competitive atmosphere. *"If you want to qualify here then you have to do something special,"* said one source, circumspectly.

Disputes isn't the only department known for the tough time demands it places on trainees. *"You have to warn your readers about the hours,"* one trainee implored us. Others agreed: *"At uni you have no idea what it's going to be like physically and mentally to work until 3am and then have to come back to work a few hours later. You have to ask yourself whether that's what you really want."* The attitude towards hours varies by department – some will *"give you days or half days off"* to recover after a tough stretch, while others, like dispute resolution and banking, are home to *"some very enthusiastic people who think that you're lazy if you don't want to come in and work at the weekend."*

Construction is one department which is noted for the fact that *"the hours aren't so bad."* The department is quite small and offers both a contentious and a non-contentious seat. *"There are only a handful of lawyers who do non-contentious construction work,"* but like their colleagues in projects these lawyers work on some major international building schemes, including what will eventually be a $37bn construction project to build four new metro lines and 510 kilometres of long-distance railway in Qatar in preparation for the 2022 World Cup. The department is a good introduction to commercial contracts: *"You encounter a lot of them!"* said one trainee. *"And you get to see how the key clauses are negotiated by attending client meetings."*

United in diversity

We've talked a lot about international work above – a real hallmark of a W&C training contract – and this involves plenty of interaction with overseas offices too, even at trainee level. Just after they joint, first-years get together in Belgium for introductory training alongside their colleagues from the rest of Europe, the Middle East and Africa. *"It's great to have that networking opportunity,"* said one interviewee. *"And when you get back to London that's followed up on with regular cross-office training via video conference."* Trainees described interoffice interaction as *"seamless,"* telling us that *"if you have a question for another office then you just go on a recommendation and send an email or pick up the phone."* One (presumably Europhile) trainee went so far as to compare W&C to the European Union: *"All of the offices/countries operate independently but at the end of the day we're still one firm/entity."* And perhaps this 'European Union' metaphor applies within the London office too: *"All the departments have an incredibly different feel,"* said one trainee, echoing the opinions of others. For example, we hope you picked up on the difference between capital markets (approachable, nice) and litigation (more hard-nosed) above. As one trainee pointed out, *"you'll have a very different experience of the firm depending on your selection of seats."*

To add to this mixed and mingled state of affairs, our interviewees commented that the trainees themselves are quite a diverse bunch. *"A large number of us are not exclusively from the UK,"* said one interviewee. At the time of our calls the trainee cohort contained individuals from Canada, Nigeria, Italy, Germany, Singapore, China and Saudi Arabia, however, almost all have a long-term association with the UK. With this shared international background, most W&C trainees also share a burning desire to *"go abroad and explore new cultures,"* and many also speak a second (or third) language.

And finally...

Qualifiers receive a list of which departments are recruiting trainees (although not how many). There are no interviews, and the *"very efficient"* NQ process is usually wrapped up three months before qualification. In 2014, 26 out of 28 qualifiers were kept on.

Wilsons

The facts

Location: Salisbury, London
Number of UK partners/solicitors: 30/31
Partners who trained at firm: 25%
Total number of trainees: 6
Seats: 4x6 months
Alternative seats: occasional secondments

On chambersstudent.co.uk...

How to get into Wilsons
The London office
Life in Salisbury

A distinguished name in Salisbury's legal circuit, Wilsons is best known for its private client and charities expertise.

www: the Wilsons wide web

Check out Wilsons' rather slick-looking website and you'll notice its legal services are categorised into three types of clients: businesses, individuals and charities. The last two have long been the mainstays of this Salisbury superstar's practice, a point our sister publication *Chambers UK* underpins by awarding top-tier rankings for its private client, charities and agriculture work. We mustn't ignore Wilsons' ever-growing commercial side, though, which earns *Chambers UK* scores in the corporate, real estate and employment spheres.

Something else showcased on Wilsons' website is its green and black colour scheme, which appeared as part of a rebrand in 2012, a year that also saw it shift its operations to Alexandra House (once the home of the Crown Court), appoint a new managing partner and dispose of its Bristol branch – an office only obtained the year before – following a drawn-out disagreement between two partners there. These days things appear to be a bit more settled, with management *"keen to turn its attention to growth,"* according to our sources. *"We're in the process of looking forward, and I think the firm is approaching that in a healthy way,"* speculated one. *"They're aware we've become a little partner-heavy, so there's a focus on nurturing new talent and filling the gaps, which is good news for us trainees."*

New recruits here are required to undertake seats in private client and in one of the property teams: commercial, farms/estates or residential. On the whole the allocation process is pretty informal: *"E-mails are sent around a couple of months before each rotation, and you can request a meeting with HR at any time during a seat."*

Those hoping to sample the firm's small but growing London office, opened in 2009, can head there to do *"a mixed commercial and charities seat."*

A taxing matter

Wilsons' private client offering has a long-standing reputation on the landed estates and farms front, assisting owners with issues like farming agreements and partnerships. Since the Annual Tax on Enveloped Dwellings (ATED) charge was introduced in April 2013, lawyers have kept busy advising clients with residential properties deemed to be high in value on their tax obligations. The team also has a pretty strong international flavour and handles a lot of offshore trusts in particular. Trainees here typically spend their days conducting research, namely on tax legislation and other tax-related issues, which *"can be quite a challenge because of how complex that area of law is."* There's a lot of drafting too, encompassing wills, letters, deeds of appointment and various trust documents.

The firm's trusts and probate practice handles both contentious and non-contentious matters. Legacy recovery cases – *"wherein an individual who's passed away has left a charity a certain amount of money, but the executor either isn't paying up or isn't sending the full amount"* – comprise *"the bread and butter"* of the contentious side.

Seat options: property (residential, commercial and farms/estates); private client; contentious trusts/probate (charities); non-contentious trusts/probate; family; employment; company/commercial; litigation

The True Picture

Chambers UK rankings

Agriculture & Rural Affairs	Employment
Charities	Private Client
Corporate/M&A	Real Estate

"As a trainee, you have to put your investigator hat on and essentially figure out what has happened to the money." Lawyers recently represented the Salvation Army in a case of that ilk, with the dispute revolving around the sale price of a property left by a deceased individual to the charity. Other big-name organisations the team has acted for include Blue Cross, Age UK, and Battersea Dogs & Cats Home. On the non-contentious front, sources reported carrying out routine correspondence with long-running clients, drafting oaths for executors, completing inheritance tax forms, and preparing wills and lasting powers of attorney. *"A lot of the tasks are administrative in nature, but they do help you ease into the job nicely."*

Meanwhile, the real estate department draws in business from rich philanthropists, public schools, well-established landed estates and some of the biggest charities in the country – Help for Heroes, for example, which the firm regularly advises on property-related matters like its recent establishment of a UK network of recovery centres designed to support wounded victims and their families. Trainees who'd spent time in this seat said the team was *"lovely and very welcoming,"* and applauded the broad spread of tasks on offer. *"You get to go through the whole process for a property transaction."* The experience in farm/estates also drew praise. *"I was actually pretty surprised by how much they let me get involved in,"* admitted one source. *"I got to look at new registrations, arrange property charges, deal with land transfers, negotiate contracts and undertake some basic conveyancing work, too."*

Our interviewees agreed working hours at Wilsons are *"very reasonable"* for the most part. Indeed, a 5.30pm finish is *"standard"* across most seats, though those who stay later can take comfort in the fact that *"you'll never be the only one left in the office. The times I've stayed after 7pm I've had partners knocking on my window telling me to go home!"* Said one source: *"I wasn't attracted to the London lifestyle and didn't want to sacrifice my life outside of work, so I applied here on that basis. Thankfully the firm has lived up to its tag of providing a great work/life balance."*

I feel the need... the need for tweed

When we asked our sources to identify some of Wilsons' core characteristics, we weren't exactly expecting mentions of tweed to crop up so frequently in their responses. *"Honestly, I've never seen as much tweed in my entire life as I have during dress-down Fridays,"* chuckled one. *"All the guys wear it, as well as bright cords and mustard-coloured shirts. The particularly daring types come in light pink attire."* While this observation suggests the firm's employees share an impeccable fashion sense (and perhaps a great deal of respect for Sherlock Holmes), it also paints Wilsons as a place without an overly formal atmosphere. *"There's a certain etiquette here in that everything is well presented, but it's far from being stuffy. You can approach any senior figure – everybody's friendly."* This includes managing partner Andrew Roberts, whom trainees praised for *"regularly making sure we're getting on okay"* and *"keeping us updated on upcoming developments."*

Prior to its move to Alexandra House in 2012, Wilsons' workforce was split across four separate buildings. Most of our sources felt the relocation *"has brought everyone closer together in more than just a physical sense,"* though a few did mention that *"some old office cliques"* remain and *"each department retains a somewhat unique identity."* As for the office itself, all were in agreement that it's *"fantastic – the building is lovely and shiny and new, with beautiful white marble floors and lots of seating areas and meeting rooms. The old offices were fine, but this is a vast improvement."* Interestingly, we heard there remain a few empty desks dotted around the premises, though it seems some of these will be filled come September 2014 following this year's qualification round, which saw all five second-years offered NQ positions.

While Salisbury isn't known for the liveliest of social scenes, our sources assured us they make full use of their downtime by attending drinks evening and quiz nights put on by the Salisbury Young Professionals group, as well as firm-sponsored bashes like the summer and Christmas parties. More informally, trainees frequently kick back with after-work drinks and take it upon themselves to arrange lunch outings every Friday. It would surely be a crime for us not to mention The Lawbreakers, a local rock band that includes three of the firm's partners and offers musical stylings on the regular. At the time of our calls, the maestros had recently rocked up to the Wilsons HQ to perform an exclusive acoustic set, which one attendee revealed *"was very good. I'd have to say that anyway, but they actually were!"* We'll take their word for it.

And finally...

"You don't necessarily have to come from Salisbury to get a training contract here, but they certainly want you to make Salisbury your home." Visit our website to learn more about Wiltshire's sole city.

Winckworth Sherwood

The facts

Location: London, Oxford, Manchester
Number of UK partners/solicitors: 48/75
Partners who trained at firm: 17%
Total number of trainees: 12
Seats: 4x6 months
Alternative seats: secondments
Extras: pro bono - London Borough of Southwark

On chambersstudent.co.uk...

How to get into Winckworth Sherwood
The firm's history

This modestly sized London outfit offers trainees experience in some unusual practice areas including social housing, planning, parliamentary agency and ecclesiastical law.

Worth a shot

Take a look at Winckworth Sherwood's website and you'll see a live image of London streamed via a webcam on the roof of the firm's London Bridge HQ. It's fitting that the focal point of the camera is St. Paul's Cathedral – the firm counts eight Church of England dioceses among its clients, as well as the cathedral itself. If the camera panned east, you'd be gazing straight into the heartland of several other key clients: the City's funds and financial institutions and the City of London Corporation; if the camera turned west you might just catch a glimpse of another significant landmark: the Houses of Parliament, where Winckworth drafts and promotes legislation as an official parliamentary agent. Besides these areas, the firm counts private client, housing and litigation among its core practices.

The out-of-the-ordinary work on offer here – variously described by our insiders as *"niche," "quirky"* and *"weird"* – was as much a part of the appeal for trainees as Winckworth's small size and affable training environment. *"I didn't want to work in a corporate snake pit,"* one source said. *"We're just a stone's throw from the City, but in terms of the quality of work given to trainees and our ability to have a life away from the office, we couldn't be further removed."* And the work comes in all shapes and sizes, ranging from small lease renewals for local housing associations to advisory work on the £5.5bn transformation of Liverpool's docklands – the largest planning application in UK history.

The nature of Winckworth's client base means it's pretty much nailed-on that trainees will do a property-oriented seat at some point. This could mean experience in an area like parliamentary agency or ecclesiastical law, or time in a slightly more mainstream department like planning or housing. Incoming trainees are assigned their first seat and after that it's a case of letting your supervisor and the training partner know where you'd like to go next, and they will do their best to accommodate. *"The allocation process has worked pretty well for all of us – you usually get your first choice,"* trainees agreed. We didn't hear any complaints about the NQ process either and in 2014 four out of five qualifiers stayed with the firm.

Safe as houses

Housing is the firm's largest department and it works with 14 of the 15 biggest housing associations in and around London as well as the top six house builders in the UK. Winckworth was recently called in by the Genesis Housing Association to help with its plan to build 700 new homes close to London's Olympic Park. The department is held in high regard by *Chambers UK*, which recognises Winckworth as one of the top three firms for social housing in London. Trainees get stuck into tasks such as drafting leases and licenses, helping to purchase develop-

> **Seat options:** employment; commercial and corporate; private client; matrimonial and family; property and licensing; housing; parliamentary; real estate; planning and environment; housing plot sales; education; ecclesiastical; property litigation; commercial litigation; construction

Chambers UK rankings

Charities	Planning
Education	Real Estate
Local Government	Real Estate Litigation
Parliamentary & Public	Social Housing
Affairs	Transport
Partnership	

ment sites and overseeing Stamp Duty Land Tax returns. *"As well as drafting and amending leases, you're free to phone and email clients directly,"* one trainee reported.

The housing department works closely with planning, though the latter has plenty of its own matters. Winckworth recently helped on plans to build Western Europe's tallest residential tower in the new Nine Elms development in Battersea. Trainees work with local authorities, housing associations and a smattering of private individuals. *"The group is very busy,"* one source said and several others: *"You spend time chasing clients and counsel and when you're not doing that you're working on deeds, doing research or attending meetings."*

A seat in the *"blossoming"* corporate/commercial group is also steeped in housing and property development work, though there are matters relating to areas like digital media, manufacturing and retail too. Typical tasks for trainees include research, proofreading and due diligence as well as drafting board minutes and shareholder agreements. Interviewees told us they were involved in joint ventures, restructurings and M&A deals as well as going on jaunts to Companies House to create companies. Winckworth created a dedicated tax team in early 2014, hiring two partners from other firms. *"It's just one of the signs that corporate is going from strength to strength,"* trainees believed. *"I think you'll be hearing a lot more about it in the next few years."*

On the contentious side, trainees can do a seat in either commercial or property litigation. One interviewee said of their time in the former: *"There's a fastidious approach to detail, which can mean a lot of pressure to get things right."* Work includes drafting witness statements and the particulars of debt claims as well as attending court.

Separation of church and state

We trailed the more unusual practices above, so let's tell you a bit more about them: Winckworth employs three 'Roll A' Parliamentary Agents, who are registered to draft and promote private bills in Parliament. Lawyers in the six-strong parliamentary team also work on other primary legislation and statutory instruments, and even trainees get stuck into *"drafting bills and explanatory notes."* Lots of the work involves planning major infrastructure projects like HS2 and Crossrail, so *"you never get to see things all the way through – some of the matters run for five to ten years so in six months you only get a snapshot."*

The *Chambers*-ranked education team is home to 12 solicitors. One of the department's main activities is Academy conversions. *"They tend to last three to four months, so the team tries to get every trainee who sits in the department to oversee one end to end."* Other work includes advising schools on immigration, IT and employment issues. Clients include the Catholic Education Service and several Church of England Diocesan Boards of Education, which brings us to the firm's most esoteric practice area: ecclesiastical law. This department's clients include eight C of E dioceses, which the firm advises on canon law and all manner of commercial, employment and property issues. So a trainee might find themselves dealing with *"the systemic registration of unregistered church land,"* involving *"interesting obscure research tasks like having to burrow through 19th century church documents."*

Besides the fascinating unusual work on offer, one of the major perks of training at Winckworth is the humane approach to hours. *"Nobody judges you for working reasonable hours,"* said one trainee, before adding: *"That's not to say we don't work hard when we are in the office."* There are occasional late nights but staying beyond 8pm is considered a rarity – the latest any of our interviewees had ever been in the office was 11.30pm.

"We're a very friendly firm and I think that's shaped by the client base," a trainee told us when we asked about the atmosphere in the office. *"We work with a lot of honest and decent people like the church and the social housing sector,"* another added. *"These aren't City slickers with dollar signs in their eyes, making money hand over fist – they're trying to do what's best."* But don't let the client list of established institutions make you think this is a particularly traditional place. *"We're a modern, progressive firm and we take equal opportunities seriously,"* commented one trainee. And the figures support this: 42% of partners are female, as are 64% of associates.

And finally...

Winckworth encourages its trainees to get involved in CSR and pro bono activities, for example by helping out at the Southwark Citizens Advice Bureau rent arrears clinic.

Withers LLP

The facts

Location: London
Number of UK partners/solicitors: 54/90
Partners who trained at firm: c.33%
Total number of trainees: 25
Seats: 4x6 months
Alternative seats: overseas seats
Extras: pro bono – RCJ family division, Peckham CAB, LawWorks; language classes

On chambersstudent.co.uk...

How to get into Withers
Interview with training partner
  Suzanne Todd
Landmark divorce cases
Literary heroines

Who gets the private plane? Who inherits the luxury yacht? What's that art collection really worth? These are questions you'll actually be faced with at Withers.

Everywhere you go, always take the Withers with you

As a private client heavyweight – this practice, like family and employment, secures a top *Chambers UK* ranking – *"Withers' global strategy is to be wherever wealthy individuals want us to be."* This isn't just Withers. This is WithersWorldwide. International expansion became the order of the day following a merger with American firm Bergman Horowitz & Reynolds in 2002, and now the firm has 11 overseas offices – its most recent outpost, in San Francisco, opened in 2014. And these days the super-rich are to be found in Hong Kong and Singapore as well as London, Geneva, Milan and New York. So Withers is there too. *"All our major office openings have been client-driven,"* observed one source. The opening over in Cali was no different: the Golden State has the largest population of ultra-high net worth individuals in the US, with many based in San Fran or nearby Silicon Valley.

While trainees were attracted to Withers for its private client work and international scope, the training contract on offer is much broader than this, taking in areas like corporate/commercial, litigation and employment. About a month before each seat rotation trainees can put forward three preferences for their next move. Partner mentors are on hand to *"offer guidance if you need it and fight your corner as much as possible,"* but HR *"do their best to allocate you the seats you want."* Nobody we'd spoken to had ever been posted somewhere outside their top three picks. While no seats are compulsory, most people will pass through either the wealth planning or family departments. The employment team is also a popular destination – it only takes one trainee at a time.

Are you FITT or FAB?

The wealth planning department does much of the work we at the *Student Guide* would class as 'private client'. The department used to be divided into three sub-groups which offered a seat each: funds, investments, tax and trusts (FITTs); family and business planning (FAB); and international. While wealth planning now technically operates as one big team, trainees told us they still unofficially 'belong' to one of the three sub-groups.

The FITTs arm *"acts for big trusts, institutions, and high-net-worth individuals who have assets structured in offshore jurisdictions"* and *"advises on tax issues internationally."* One trainee told us: *"I had to do a lot of document management, but I was also taken along to client meetings and took attendance notes, and towards the end of my seat I even helped prepare tax reports."* Another told us: *"My supervisor was great and gave me a lot of responsibility. For example, I wrote tax opinions for clients who were buying property in the UK."* This type of work often leads to crossovers with corporate – trainees told us they'd helped out on things like restructuring companies for tax purposes or converting them into trusts.

The FAB team offers trainees the opportunity to do *"the first drafts of deeds and wills."* Interviewees said that they also *"deal with lasting powers of attorney"* and conduct research into tax structures. *"The partners offer a lot of*

Seat options: litigation; family; real estate; wealth planning; commercial

Chambers UK rankings

Administrative & Public Law	Employment
Agriculture & Rural Affairs	Family/Matrimonial
Charities	Private Client
Court of Protection	Professional Negligence
Defamation/Reputation Management	Tax

support and are a fantastic resource," reflected a first-year. *"They really want to get you involved. I got to sit with one client while they signed a will. It was a well-known, wealthy individual too – I was actually a bit star struck!"* And no, we can't tell you who this rich star was – all the department's clients are confidential.

A seat in the international team gives trainees the chance to advise foreigners on UK residency claims and offshore tax issues. This is where the firm's international network of offices really comes into its own. *"There are some great opportunities to work with lawyers in the US,"* said one source. And don't think you'll miss out on high-profile work by taking on international matters – *Chambers Global* awards Withers a top-tier ranking for its global-wide international private client work. The wealth planning department also has quite a few French and Italian clients, so language skills are in high demand. At the time of our calls the 26-strong trainee group contained five French speakers and four Italian speakers.

Contentious private client work is done by the contentious trusts and succession group (CTSG). The team delves into probate litigation as well as working on *"huge international trust cases worth millions and millions!"* Of one such dispute, a source told us: *"It involved a huge number of jurisdictions because the client had property and art collections based all over the world."* There's also a charities team here, which handles disputes arising from money left to non-profits in wills. *"I was able to handle some of those cases on my own under supervision,"* a second-year told us. *"I got to project manage them and drive them forward."* The team also advises elderly and vulnerable clients in the Court of Protection, a practice that is top-ranked nationally by *Chambers UK*.

Withers possesses one of the largest family law teams in London. It has vast experience in complex international cases involving money, tax and/or children, with a client base largely consisting of City professionals. *"For the first three months you'll spend all your time honing your attention to detail, learning best practice, and picking up on how the team works,"* explained a trainee. A lot of the matters that come through the door are *"big-money cases,"* so for trainees there's plenty of bundling on the menu. *"Once you've proved yourself through working hard, you can get your teeth into more substantive work,"*

said one trainee. This includes having a go at drafting pre-nups, pleadings and witness statements. There are also quite a few opportunities to go to court and attend mediations.

I'm too sexy for my...

The employment team is a popular destination (but hard to secure a seat in) – from the testimony we received it's easy to see why. *"We represent both employees and employers, so one day you might be acting for an employee and get to see all the tactics used on that side, while the next day you might be acting for a company, and see things from a completely different perspective."* The department is home to just 17 qualified lawyers and only one trainee so *"you get to work very closely with partners. You're taken to meetings and get to see how they deal with clients. They are brilliant legal professionals, but also have fantastic soft skills – it's incredible to watch."*

The commercial litigation and arbitration department assists clients with a range of employment, fraud, corporate crime, and professional negligence disputes, and is active internationally too in countries like Italy, Greece and Cyprus. *"Every client has a different story,"* reflected a trainee. *"One day you might be looking at a breach of contract for a pharmaceutical company, and the next at an individual suing their accountant."* One source who'd clearly been seduced by the excitement of it all told us: *"It's one of the sexier departments. We do the beefy money claims in the high millions."* Not that this pushed trainees from the front line: *"I got to draft instructions to counsel and prepare witness statements,"* an interviewee told us, adding: *"One trainee was even flown out to meet a client abroad – on their own. They said it was scary, but a lot of fun!"*

Withers' corporate group is known for working with luxury brands and creative individuals, recently securing investment deals for young British designers Nicholas Kirkwood and JW Anderson from LVMH (a tie-up between Louis Vuitton, champagne producer Moët & Chandon and cognac manufacturer Hennessy). Trainees reported doing due diligence but also had client contact via email. An interviewee reported that the department is *"very fast moving and throws up longer hours than other seats."*

Hours commitments are, on the whole, very reasonable. *"They're not like the hours at a big corporate firm,"* said one source. 9am to 6.30pm is par for the course, although interviewees did stress that *"trainees are expected to work hard,"* so when needs must, they sometimes stay until as late as midnight. *"It can be quite demanding,"* we heard. *"Clients want things done in their time frames and we know they have to be done properly and quickly."* Not that this means trainees are hung out to dry. *"I've never come across anyone senior who has shied away from answering questions,"* said one. *"You can easily approach people without being ridiculed or shouted at."* The time trainees put in is always appreciated, too. *"When we worked a few late nights on a case we were taken out for a drink afterwards to say thank you."*

Bow ties and Baltis

In the past we've reported that Withers' trainee cohort is always quite Oxbridge heavy. At the time of our calls the trainee group of 26 contained eight Oxford and three Cambridge graduates. Not a huge number, but not insignificantly few either. Just seven of the 26 had studied law at undergraduate – language, art and history degrees are commonplace here. And we'll mention language skills again: Withers likes to recruit at least some trainees who speak French and Italian every year, and at the time of our calls the trainee group also contained Spanish, German, Mandarin, Greek and Hebrew speakers. You might be wondering how we found out all this great insider information. Well... Withers very helpfully has extensive profiles of all its trainees on its website, so if you're wondering what type of person this firm recruits, then go check them out.

As you might expect from a private client firm founded nearly 120 years ago, Withers is home to some *"big personalities"* and *"eccentric characters who wear bow ties."* So perhaps it's understandable that some of our interviewees joined *"fearing everybody would be conservative, stuffy and old fashioned."* Once on the ground, they found Withers' *"progressive"* approach came as a breath of fresh air. The firm is female-heavy: Margaret Robertson has been managing director since 2007, and the current training partner is also a woman, Suzanne Todd. This is no coincidence: 33% of current partners are female as are 64% of associates.

Overall trainees gave the firm's working atmosphere a thumbs up. *"The people here don't have a huge competitive streak,"* interviewees agreed. *"Nobody is dobbing each other in or doing any back-stabbing. There's a real camaraderie between us."* Trainee intakes – usually 13 or 14 souls strong – are pretty close and *"regularly do dinners and drinks at each other's houses."* The firm also provides a budget for an annual trainee Christmas party. *"In 2013 we went for a curry on Brick Lane, which was a slightly dodgy choice if you ask me, but it was great fun."* Trainees can also let their hair down with a pint after work in All Bar One, Corney & Barrow, or Jamies Wine Bar. Additional stresses were alleviated by a *"much quicker"* qualification process in 2014 (there had been complaints in the past) and in the end ten of 13 qualifiers were retained.

And finally...
A top private client firm, Withers acts for an impressive 33% of the Sunday Times Rich List.

Wragge Lawrence Graham & Co

The facts

Location: Birmingham, London

Number of UK partners/solicitors: 157/388

Total number of trainees: 63

Seats: 4x6 months

Alternative seats: secondments, overseas seats

Extras: pro bono – LawWorks, Birmingham Legal Advice Clinic, Human Dignity Trust, Birmingham Employment Rights Advice Line, The Pensions Advisory Service

On chambersstudent.co.uk...

How to get into Wragge Lawrence Graham & Co

More on seats

Interview with training partner Baljit Chohan

Fresh from their May 1st merger, London's Lawrence Graham and Birmingham's Wragge & Co are now getting together.

Meet in the middle

Wragges had been casting around for a London merger since 2009, and Lawrence Graham was in need of a bigger buddy firm to pull it out of the financial quagmire it'd been in since 2008. LG's debt burden and falling revenue (down by a quarter between 2006 and 2012) clearly weren't a turn off for Wragge & Co, and the happy pair tied the knot on 1 May 2014.

While Wragges was twice LG's size and had double the number of trainees, the Birmingham firm also had a dozen trainees in London, so the two offices are now evenly balanced: WLG is recruiting 15 trainees in London and 15 in Brum for 2017. Candidates apply to work in a specific office and complete their training in a single location. Wragge & Co's retention rate has always been about average, while LG recently had a few below-average years. In 2014, 30 of 39 WLG qualifiers were kept on.

Trainees must do one real estate, one transactional and one contentious seat. Luckily in London *"the merger means that there are loads more seat options. It's a bit like starting again at another firm!"* From September 2014 all seat options are open to all trainees (though for a brief period legacy Wragges trainees will get first dibs on legacy Wragges seats, and ditto LG trainees). Before each rotation a seat list is circulated, and trainees are asked to list their top three preferred destinations, with motivation. Each trainee then has a meeting with HR to discuss their preferences.

At both legacy firms real estate was the largest practice group, complemented by significant corporate and litigation departments. *"But it's surprising how little overlap there's been in our market presence,"* says training partner Baljit Chohan. Wragge & Co's real estate work was development-led, whereas Lawrence Graham's was for institutional investors and financial institutions. *"On the corporate side,"* Chohan adds, *"LG's strength was in funds, equity capital markets and AIM work, while Wragges did more mainstream M&A."* Businesses from the pharma, hospitality, automotive and manufacturing industries now sit alongside banks, private equity houses and investment funds on the merged firm's client books. At the level of smaller departments there are differences too: LG had a well-regarded private client department, while Wragges sported a highly respectable pensions team. Go to our website for more.

Price match

Chambers UK 2014 awarded Wragge & Co's real estate department a top-tier UK-wide ranking for firms out-

> **Seat options:** corporate finance; projects; non-contentious construction; commercial; private capital; commercial litigation; construction; finance litigation; insurance litigation; IT disputes; IP; employment and pensions; competition; real estate; development; retail and property; asset management; real estate; litigation; property finance

Chambers UK rankings

Banking & Finance	Life Sciences
Banking Litigation	Litigation
Capital Markets	Local Government
Competition/European Law	Outsourcing
	Pensions
Construction	Pensions Litigation
Corporate/M&A	Planning
Employment	Private Client
Energy & Natural Resources	Projects
Environment	Public Procurement
Fraud	Real Estate
Health & Safety	Real Estate Finance
Healthcare	Real Estate Litigation
Information Technology	Restructuring/Insolvency
Insurance	Retail
Intellectual Property	Social Housing
Investment Funds	Tax
	Telecommunications

side London, while LG was ranked in three London real estate categories. At WLG the department is split into seven subgroups: commercial development and investment (CDI); property litigation; retail, energy, leisure and management (RELM); specialist transactions; housing development and regeneration; and planning. Trainees sit in one of these groups but *"there is quite a lot of cross-departmental work."* In Birmingham the firm is best known for *"big regeneration and building projects – things like shopping centres – which you'll see reported in the news."* It also runs property portfolios for their owners or managers. *"When I first started I was given a bunch of my own files to look after,"* a trainee reported. *"They included new leases, licences to renew and licences to alter. I did all the drafting and negotiating, and kept the client up to date."* While some of the work is Brum-based – for example, advising Birmingham City University on its £125m relocation to make way for High Speed 2 – quite a bit is national in scope.

LG's real estate team was always most noted for its retail, hospitality and leisure work, as well as its expertise in the field of real estate finance. Clients include The Crown Estate, Sainsbury's and British Land, and the team recently advised a joint venture between Legal & General and Schroders on the £500m plan for the regeneration of Bracknell town centre, which includes leases for Primark, H&M, Carluccios and Las Iguanas. The real estate finance team acts for property funds like Longbow – *"managing the property portfolio of big shopping centres"*– and advises banks like HSBC on *"the rejigging of property portfolios"* and *"risky debt deals."*

WLG's corporate team sits comfortably in the London mid-market, doing work for AIM-listed businesses as well as large corporates. For example, it recently advised long-standing client Arthur J. Gallagher & Co, an insurance broker listed on the New York Stock Exchange, on its £233m acquisition of Giles Insurance Brokers from Charterhouse Capital. *"The experience is quite different from real estate,"* observed one trainee. *"You work with the team on larger matters rather than having your own files. That means you have less independence and are often responsible for the administrative tasks, although that's not all you do!"* Tasks might include share purchase agreements, as well as compiling ancillary documents like board minutes and letters of resignation.

Birmingham's corporate work is also mid-market – *"deal value tends to be between £20m and £100m."* The firm recently advised on the acquisition a £90m security company based in Dunedin and on the purchase of Amber Taverns which runs 95 pubs in the North West. *"The advantage of working on smaller transactions is that you get to do more than a trainee at a firm which does mega-deals,"* said one source.

Eastern promise

In London, LG's litigation team was always especially recognised for its corporate investigations, fraud and asset tracing work. Lawyers recently acted for Grant Thornton as liquidator of Stanford Bank in litigation brought by the Serious Fraud Office over the massive Ponzi scheme revealed when the bank collapsed in 2009. And back in March 2013 Lawrence Graham was commissioned by the now-ousted Ukrainian president Viktor Yanukovych to look into the misappropriation of assets by former prime minister Yulia Tymoshenko. A London trainee reported on their experience in litigation: *"Sometimes you do have to do the less crucial tasks – bundling, costs – because some of the matters are huge."* Another source added: *"There are also smaller matters, which allow you to get more involved. I've been to meetings with counsel, and worked on claim forms and witness statements."*

Over in Brum cases tend to be less finance-heavy and less international. For example, the firm acted for Sandwell Borough Council in a £50m outsourcing contract dispute with BT, and represented Scottish F1 driver Paul di Resta in a dispute with Lewis Hamilton's dad over the axing of a management agreement. Besides contractual disputes, the department works on *"everything from corporate crime to personal injury, social housing, construction and finance."* One satisfied party told us: *"I worked with just a partner on a big multimillion-pound construction case. I drafted witness statements and attended hearings. I also worked on smaller cases that I ran myself: debt recovery files worth up to £50,000. That enabled me to gain experience of negotiation and day-to-day client contact, and see a matter from beginning to end."*

Head to our website for more on the other seats as well as the two overseas options: Dubai and Guangzhou. We heard rumours that a stint in Singapore could soon be in the offing too. Besides these three locations WLG also has offices in Brussels, Monaco, Moscow, Munich and Paris. International expansion is one of the new firm's chief ambitions. And according to trainees: *"There are rumours swirling around about further international offices opening up."* Hong Kong and Frankfurt?

Tear down this wall

Back to Blighty and the big question: why did this merger happen, and how good a fit is it? Well, both Wragge & Co and Lawrence Graham had reputations for being friendly, forward-looking places intent on modernising and establishing a fresh, contemporary brand. But Wragges had perhaps been a bit more successful at doing this than LG: a few wobbly years during the recession were followed by steady revenue growth and international expansion. Meanwhile, Lawrence Graham struggled. It was bedevilled by a failed rebrand (the firm was officially known as 'LG' from 2007 to 2013), several years of revenue shrinkage, rising debt and cumbersome property overheads. *"It was no secret that we needed a merger,"* a legacy LG trainee told us. *"When the merger was announced, people felt better about everything; previous concerns were lifted."* Commentary from ex-Wragges trainees was notably more upbeat: *"Wragge & Co really wanted to grow in London, and the best and quickest way to do that was through a merger. There was quite a buzz in the office the day the merger was announced."*

Post-merger integration was already well underway by the time of our calls in July 2014. All litigators are now in Waterhouse Square, while real estate and corporate have headed over to More London. As a result, said one ex-LG trainee, *"I already have a relationship with the head of commercial litigation, who is an ex-Wragges person."* And sources from both legacy firms told us of working with trainees from the other. A point to note: while Wragges' London office was, like Birmingham, open plan, LG's More London digs had individual offices. *"I do find it strange moving from one to the other,"* an interviewee admitted, but it seems office layout is up in the air: *"They've been knocking down a few walls,"* a source at More London told us. We wonder what the legacy LG partners will think of that.

Integration is not just a London affair. Although *"the merger is not likely to affect Birmingham in terms of office culture,"* we were told *"the firm has made an effort to get LG lawyers up to Birmingham and Wragges people down to London to meet the teams there."* There was also a post-merger all-trainee social in London in early May, and there have been team integration socials too.

Looking back at our research from the last five years, Wragges has always had a bubbly, sociable and chatty trainee cohort. The Lawrence Graham group were also a nice, polite bunch but perhaps a little more reserved and serious than their Wragges counterparts. So is this difference causing a culture clash? Well, no, say trainees. *"Culturally I don't think there will be any problems,"* one observed. *"All the trainees are really positive about the merger – we're on the same wavelength and have the same approach to work. Everyone is really friendly and has been making an effort to introduce themselves. The two cultures are blending."*

Supervision and on-the-job training stood out as big positives for our interviewees. In Birmingham, training is given especially huge priority. *"My current supervisor is very good,"* a source there said. *"He actively keeps track of what I'm doing and sends out emails to the team to find particular types of work for me to do."* End-of-seat and mid-seat reviews are supplemented by a start-of-seat *"objective-setting"* meeting. Each trainee also has a partner mentor (or 'training principal') who sits in on every review and is "the person you can go to if you have any problems or concerns." Supervision and appraisals were historically a bit more informal and *"hands-off"* at Lawrence Graham, but we heard from trainees that the Wragges system is to be rolled-out across the whole firm in future.

Supervision and appraisal structure is one area where Wragge & Co is firmly in the driving seat of post-merger changes. (The application system is another – go to our website to find out more.) In addition, all but one of WLG's practice groups is now led by a legacy Wragges lawyer, and only two ex-LG partners have spots on the new management board. And note that WLG's training partner, Baljit Chohan, is ex-Wragge & Co too. Also, the salary of ex-LG trainees has now been raised to the same *"more competitive"* level enjoyed by Wragges trainees. We think you can guess who's calling the shots on this one.

And finally...

Wragge & Co wanted to expand in London and internationally, and Lawrence Graham needed support to pull it out of the financial doldrums. That's why this merger happened.

Refine your search

Applications and Selection

Firm Name	Degree Class	Number of contracts	Number of applications
Addleshaw Goddard	2:1	30	Not known
Allen & Overy	2:1	c. 85	Not known
Arnold & Porter	2:1	2	700
Ashfords	2:1	10	400
Ashurst	2:1	40	2,500
Baker & McKenzie	2:1	30	Not known
Bates Wells & Braithwaite	2:1	4	750+
Berwin Leighton Paisner	2:1	40-45	Not known
Bingham McCutchen	High 2:1	Up to 3	Not known
Bircham Dyson Bell	2:1 preferred	5	700
Bird & Bird	2:1	16-18	2,000
Bond Dickinson	Not known	Not known	Not known
Boodle Hatfield	2:1	5	Not known
BP Collins	2:1	3-4	Not known
BPE Solicitors	2:1	4	100
Brabners	2:1 or postgraduate degree	6	Not known
Bristows	2:1 preferred	Up to 10	1,800
Browne Jacobson	Not known	10	500
Burges Salmon	2:1	25	1,500
Capsticks	2:1	8	508
Charles Russell	2:1	15	Not known
Cleary Gottlieb Steen & Hamilton	2:1	10-14	Not known
Clyde & Co	2:1	45-50	2,000
CMS Cameron McKenna	2:1	80	1,000
Collyer Bristow	2:1	Not known	Not known
Covington & Burling	2:1	6	Not known
Cripps LLP	2:1	8	200
Curtis	2:1	2	300
Davis Polk & Wardwell	2:1	4	Not known
Dechert	2:1	10-12	1,000+
Dentons	2:1	20	1,000
DLA Piper	2:1	80	3,800
DWF	2:1	48	c.3,000
Edwards Wildman Palmer	2:1	6	c.550
Eversheds	2:1	Not known	Not known
Farrer & Co	2:1	10	1,000
Fladgate	2:1	4	Not known
Foot Anstey	2:1	4-6	300
Freeths	2:1	10	750
Freshfields Bruckhaus Deringer	2:1	Up to 90	c.2,000
Gateley	2:1	Not known	Not known
Gide Loyrette Nouel	2:1	6-8	100

Applications and Selection

Firm Name	Degree Class	Number of contracts	Number of applications
Gordons	2:1	4	400
Government Legal Service	2:2	25-30	3,000+
Harbottle & Lewis	2:1	5	500
Herbert Smith Freehills	2:1	c.70	Not known
Hewitsons	2:1	10	850
Higgs & Sons	2:1 preferred	4-6	350+
Hill Dickinson	2:1	Up to 14	Not known
Hogan Lovells	2:1	Up to 60	1,500
Holman Fenwick Willan	2:1	15	Not known
Ince & Co	2:1	10	861
Irwin Mitchell	None	50	2,000-2,500
Jones Day	2:1	20	1,800
K&L Gates	2:1	Up to 15	1,000
Kennedys	2:1	c.18	900
King & Wood Mallesons	2:1	30	2,000
Kingsley Napley	2:1	5	250
Kirkland & Ellis	2:1	Not known	Not known
Latham & Watkins	2:1	20	Not known
Leigh Day & Co	2:1 preferred	Not known	Not known
Lester Aldridge	2:1	6	Not known
Lewis Silkin	2:1	Up to 6	600
Linklaters	2:1	110	4,500
Macfarlanes	2:1	27	1,000
Maclay Murray & Spens	2:1	20-25	450
Mayer Brown	2:1	c.15-20	2,000+
McDermott Will & Emery	2:1	Not known	Not known
Memery Crystal	2:1	4	300
Michelmores	2:1	8	200
Mills & Reeve	2:1	17	980
Mishcon de Reya	2:1	8-12	1,000+
Morgan Lewis & Bockius	High 2:1	5	Not known
Muckle	2:1 preferred	4	230-240
Nabarro	2:1	25	950
Norton Rose Fulbright	2:1	Up to 55	2,000
Olswang	2:1	12	2,000
O'Melveny & Myers	2:1	Up to 4	Not known
Orrick	2:1	4	Not known
Osborne Clarke	2:1	20	1,200
Paul Hastings	2:1	3-4	Not known
Peters & Peters	2:1	2	c.200
Pinsent Masons	High 2:1	75	1,500+
PwC Legal	2:1	Not known	Not known

Applications and Selection

Firm Name	Degree Class	Number of contracts	Number of applications
Reed Smith	2:1	24	1,000
RPC	2:1	22	Not known
SGH Martineau	2:1	10	600
Shearman & Sterling	2:1	c.15	Not known
Sheridans	2:1	1-2	Not known
Shoosmiths	2:1	20	1,600+
Sidley Austin	2:1	10	600
Simmons & Simmons	2:1	c.40	2,500
Skadden	2:1	10-12	1,000
Slaughter and May	High 2:1	c.75-80	c.2,000
Speechly Bircham	2:1	9	600
Squire Patton Boggs	2:1	20	1,500
Stephenson Harwood	2:1	16	c.1,500
Stevens & Bolton	2:1	4	350
Sullivan & Cromwell	2:1	4-6	750
Taylor Wessing	2:1	c.22	Not known
Thomas Cooper	2:1	4	Not known
TLT	2:1	Up to 15	c.700
Travers Smith	2:1	25	1,000
Trethowans	2:1	3-4	100+
Trowers & Hamlins	2:1	20	c.1,600
Veale Wasbrough Vizards	2:1 preferred	8-10	Not known
Vinson & Elkins	2:1	3-4	492
Ward Hadaway	2:1	10	600+
Watson, Farley & Williams	2:1	15	700
Wedlake Bell	2:1	6	Not known
Weil, Gotshal & Manges	2:1	Up to 14	Not known
White & Case	2:1	30	1,500
Wilsons	Not known	4	Not known
Winckworth Sherwood	2:1	6	350
Withers	2:1	10	900
Wragge Lawrence Graham & Co	None	30	1,000+

Refine Your Search

Salaries and Benefits

Firm Name	1st year salary	2nd year salary	Qualification salary	Sponsorship/ Awards	Other benefits
Addleshaw Goddard	£37,000 (London) £25,000 (Leeds/ Manchester)	Not known	Not known	GDL & LPC: fees + £7,000 (London) £4,500 (elsewhere)	Corporate gym m'ship, STL, subsd restaurant, pension, pte healthcare
Arnold & Porter	Not known	Not known	Not known	GDL & LPC: fees + £8,000	Bonus, childcare vouchers, PHI, pte dental ins, life ass, STL
Ashfords	Not known (Bristol, London uplift)	Not known	Not known (Bristol, London uplift)	LPC: £9,000 grant towards LPC	Pension, holiday purchase scheme, childcare vouchers, CTW, EAP, life ass, employee rates and discounts, free legal services
Ashurst	£40,000	£45,000	£63,000	GDL & LPC: fees + £8,000 (London), £7,000 (elsewhere), £500 for first-class degree, language bursaries	Pension, life ass, STL, subsd gym m'ship, PMI, income protection, in-house medical facilities, restaurant, CTW
Baker & McKenzie	£39,500 + £3,000 bonus	£44,000	£65,000	GDL: fees + £6,000 LPC: fees + £8,000	Health ins, life ass, pte medical ins, group pension, subsd gym m'ship, STL, subsd staff restaurant
Bates Wells & Braithwaite	£32,000	£34,000	£46,575	GDL: discretionary support LPC: £7,000 + interest paid on student loans	Pension, STL, PHI, death-in-service benefit, subsd gym, CTW, subsd restaurant, holiday purchase scheme, one month's unpaid leave on qualification
Berwin Leighton Paisner	£39,000	£44,000	£63,000	GDL & LPC: fees + £7,200	Not known
Bingham McCutchen	£40,000	£45,000	£100,000	GDL & LPC: fees + £8,000	PHI, travel ins, disability ins, STL, life ass, critical illness scheme, discretionary bonus, subsd gym m'ship
Bircham Dyson Bell	£32,000	£33,500	£52,000	GDL & LPC: fees	Bonus scheme, group health care, life ass, pension, STL
Bird & Bird	£36,000	£38,000	£59,000	Not known	Not known
Bond Dickinson	Not known	Not known	Not known	Not known	Not known
Boodle Hatfield	£33,500	£35,500	£54,000	GDL & LPC: fees+ maintenance	PHI, life ass, STL, pension, enhanced maternity pay, conveyancing grant, pte healthcare, EAP, childcare vouchers, CTW, give as you earn scheme
BP Collins	£25,370	£26,370	Not known	Not known	Not known
BPE Solicitors	£20,000	£20,000	Not known	Not known	Pension, income protection, death-in-service benefit, sabbatical scheme
Brabners	No less than £22,000	No less than £22,000	Not known	Assistance with LPC funding	Not known

Salaries and Benefits

Firm Name	1st year salary	2nd year salary	Qualification salary	Sponsorship/ Awards	Other benefits
Bristows	£36,000	£39,000	£58,000	GDL & LPC: fees + £8,000	Flexible: life ass, pension, PMI, dental and , critical illness ins, holiday purchase scheme, eye care, health assessment, EAP, CTW, childcare voucher, STL
Browne Jacobson	£25,500	£26,500	Not known	GDL & LPC: fees + £5,000	Life ass, income protection, pension, pte healthcare, dental ins, travel ins, critical illness cover, childcare vouchers, corporate discounts
Burges Salmon	£33,000	£34,000	£42,500	GDL & LPC: fees + £7,000	Bonus, pension, pte healthcare, life ass, mobile phone, Christmas gift, corporate gym m'ship, sports and social club
Capsticks	£30,000 (London)	£31,000 (London)	£47,000	GDL & LPC: financial support	Bonus, pension, income protection, PMI, life ass, CTW, corporate gym m'ship, childcare vouchers, STL
Charles Russell	Not known	Not known	Not known	GDL & LPC: fees + £6,000 (London)	Bupa, PHI, life ass, STL, subsd canteen, pension
Cleary Gottlieb Steen & Hamilton	£42,000	£47,000	£96,000	GDL & LPC: fees + £8,000	Pension, gym m'ship, PHI, life ins, disability ins, EAP, subsd restaurant
Clyde & Co	£36,000	£38,000	£59,000	GDL & LPC: fees + maintenance	Pension, life ass, dental ins, PMI, subsd gym, STL, optional interest free loan, subsd restaurant
CMS Cameron McKenna	£38,000 (London) £32,000 (Bristol)	£43,000 (London) £34,000 (Bristol)	£63,000 (London) £45,000 (Bristol)	GDL & LPC: fees + £7,500	Subsd gym m'ship, life ass, pension, pte healthcare, STL, confidential careline, subsd restaurant, optional holiday purchase
Collyer Bristow	£28,500	£31,500	Not known	Not known	Not known
Covington & Burling	£40,000	£44,000	£80,000	GDL & LPC: fees + £8,000	PMI, life ass, PHI, pension, STL, EAP
Cripps Harries Hall	Not known	Not known	Not known	(Discretionary) LPC fees: 50% interest free loan, 50% bursary	Not known
Curtis	£38,000	£42,000	Not known	Not known	Pte healthcare, STL, pension, income protection
Davis Polk & Wardwell	£50,000	£55,000	£100,000	GDL & LPC: fees + maintenance	PMI, life ins, pension, STL, subsd gym m'ship, EAP.
Dechert	£41,000	£46,000	£68,000	LPC: fees + £10,000	Not known
Dentons	£39,000 (London) £25,500 (Milton Keynes)	£44,000 (London) £27,500 (Milton Keynes)	£61,000	GDL & LPC: fees + £6,000 (London) £5,000 (elsewhere)	Flexible: Pte health ins, income protection, life ass, pension and others
DLA Piper	£40,000 (London) £26,500 (Regions)	£44,000 (London) £28,500 (Regions)	£62,000 (London) £38,500 (Regions)	GDL & LPC: fees + maintenance	Not known

Salaries and Benefits

Firm Name	1st year salary	2nd year salary	Qualification salary	Sponsorship/ Awards	Other benefits
DWF	£35,000 (London) up to £26,000 (Regions)	Not known	Not known	LPC: funding available	Flexible: insurance, life ass, pension and others
Edwards Wildman Palmer	£38,000	£42,000	£61,000	GDL & LPC: fees & £7,000 (London) £6,500 (elsewhere)	Bupa, STL, subsd gym m'ship, pension, life ass, subsd cafe, CTW, EAP, eye tests
Farrer & Co	£35,000	£38,000	£58,500	GDL & LPC: fees + £6,000	Flexible: STL, group income protection, life ass, company doctor, subsd gym m'ship, subsd yoga/pilates, pension, PMI
Fladgate	£32,000	Not known	£55,000	Not known	Pension, PHI, life ass, STL, PMI, sports club loan
Foot Anstey	Not known	Not known	£35,000	LPC: grants towards fees + maintenance	Holiday purchase scheme, pension, life ass, CTW, childcare vouchers
Freeth Cartwright	£21,500	Not known	£35,000	GDL & LPC: interest-free loan	Pte healthcare, pension
Freshfields Bruckhaus Deringer	£40,500	£45,500	£67,500	GDL & LPC: fees + maintenance	Flexible scheme
Gateley	£20,000-£22,000 (Midlands)	£22,000-£24,000 (Midlands)	£33,000 (Midlands)	LPC: maintenance grant of £5,000	Pte healthcare, life ass, pension, STL, library
Gide Loyrette Nouel	£38,000	£42,000	£65,000	GDL & LPC: fees + maintenance, partial refund in certain circumstance	Not known
Gordons	£20,000	£22,000	Not known	LPC: £5,000	Pension, life ass, interest-free travel loan, childcare vouchers, sports and social club, free fruit
Government Legal Service	£23,900-£24,600	£25,300-£26,500	£32,000-£40,000	LPC: fees BPTC: fees + £7,000	Pension, flexible working
Harbottle & Lewis	£30,000	£31,000	£50,000	LPC: fees + interest-free loan	Lunch, STL, pension, life ass, childcare vouchers, CTW, EAP
Herbert Smith Freehills	£39,500	£44,000	£65,000	GDL & LPC: fees + maintenance	Not known
Higgs & Sons	£21,500	£24,000	£32,000	No	PMI, pension, life ass, BTSS m'ship
Hill Dickinson	£32,000 (London) £24,000 (elsewhere)	£34,000 (London) £26,000 (elsewhere)	Not known	LPC: fees + maintenance	Pension, travel ins, holiday purchase scheme, PHI, life ass, STL, Bupa
Hogan Lovells	£39,500	£45,000	£65,000	GDL & LPC: fees+ maintenance	PMI, life ass, STL, gym, dentist, GP & physio, subsd restaurant, local retail discounts
Holman Fenwick Willan	£36,000	£38,000	£58,000	Study assistance + grants	Pension, subsd gym, STL, life ass, medical ins, CTW, dental ins, free GP service
Ince & Co	£36,000	£39,000	£58,000	GDL: fees + £6,500 (London and Guildford), £6,000 (elsewhere) LPC: fees £7,000 (London and Guildford) £6,500 (elsewhere)	STL, corporate health cover, PHI, pension, fitness subsidy

Salaries and Benefits

Firm Name	1st year salary	2nd year salary	Qualification salary	Sponsorship/ Awards	Other benefits
Irwin Mitchell	£36,000 (London) £25,000 (elsewhere)	£38,000 (London) £27,000 (elsewhere)	Not known	GDL & LPC: fees + £4,500	Pension, healthcare, death in service, critical illness cover
Jones Day	£42,000 rising to £47,000 after 10 months	£47,000 rising to £51,000 after 22 months	£75,000	GDL & LPC: fees + £8,000	Pte healthcare, STL, subsd sports club m'ship, life cover, salary sacrifice scheme, pension
K&L Gates	£37,500	£41,000	£62,000	GDL: fees + £5,000 LPC: fees + £7,000	Subsd sports club m'ship, STL, PHI, life ass, GP, pension
Kennedys	£34,000 (London)	£37,000 (London)	Not known	Not known	PHI, pension, PMI, life ins, STL, gym m'ship, CTW, childcare assistance, EAP, corporate GP, conveyancing fees contribution, eye care vouchers
King & Wood Mallesons SJB	£39,250	£43,500	£63,000	Not known	Pte healthcare, subsd gym m'ship, life ass, pension, STL, lunch
Kingsley Napley	£30,000	£32,000	£52,000	Not known	PHI, income protection ins, life ass, pension, corporate cash plan
Kirkland & Ellis	£41,000	£44,000	£97,560	GDL & LPC: fees + £8,000	PMI, travel ins, life ins, EAP, corp gym m'ship, bonus, STL
Latham & Watkins	£42,000	£45,000	£96,970	GDL & LPC: fees + £8,000 + £500 for LPC distinction	Healthcare +dental, pension, life ass
Lester Aldridge	Not known	Not known	Not known	Not known	Not known
Lewis Silkin	£32,500	£34,500	Up to £52,000	GDL & LPC: fees + £5,000	Bonus, life ass, income protection, health ins, STL, pension, subsd gym m'ship
Linklaters	£40,000	Not known	£65,000	GDL & LPC: fees + maintenance	Bonus, pension, PMI, life ass, income protection, subsd gym m'ship, STL and others
Macfarlanes	£39,000	£44,000	£64,000	GDL & LPC: fees + maintenance	Life ass, pension, pte healthcare, bonus, STL, subsd restaurant, subsd gym m'ship, childcare vouchers and eye care vouchers
Maclay Murray & Spens	£32,000 (London)	Not known	Not known	LPC: assistance	Pension, death-in-service benefit, income protection insurance, CTW, STL and others
Mayer Brown	£37,500	£42,300	£62,500	GDL & LPC: fees + £7,000	STL, subsd sports club, m'ship, pte healthcare
McDermott Will & Emery	£39,000	£43,000	Not known	GDL & LPC: fees + maintenance	Pte medical and dental ins, life ass, PHI, pension, STL, subsd gym m'ship, EAP.
Memery Crystal	£30,000	£32,000	Not known	GDL& LPC: fees	Not known
Michelmores	£20,000 (Exeter)	£21,000 (Exeter)	£33,000 (Exeter)	LPC: contribution	PMI, pension, subsd restaurant, subsd gym with personal trainer

Salaries and Benefits

Firm Name	1st year salary	2nd year salary	Qualification salary	Sponsorship/ Awards	Other benefits
Mills & Reeve	£25,000	£26,500	Not known	GDL & LPC: fees + maintenance	Flexbile: life ass, pension, bonus, sports and social club, subsd restaurant, STL
Mishcon de Reya	£33,000	Not known	Not known	GDL & LPC: fees + £5,000	Life ass, dental ins, critical illness cover, gym m'ship, STL, pension, yoga, childcare vouchers, in-house doctor, bonus and other
Morgan Lewis	£40,000	£43,000	£75,000	GDL & LPC: fees + £7,500	Life ins, health and travel ins, dental ins, long-term disability ins, STL
Muckle	£22,000	Not known	£34,000	LPC: fees subject to eligibility	Pension, PHI, life ass, corporate discounts, salary sacrifice scheme, car parking discounts
Nabarro	£37,000 (London), £25,000 (Sheffield)	£40,000 (London), £28,000 (Sheffield)	£59,000 (London), £38,000 (Sheffield)	GDL & LPC: fees + (or 50% respectively) £6,000 (London GDL) £5,000 (Regions GDL) £7,000 (London LPC) £6,000 (Regions LPC)	PMI, pension, STL, subsd gym m'ship, subsd restaurant, life ass, healthcare.
Norton Rose Fulbright	£39,500	£44,500	Not known	Not known	Not known
Olswang	£37,000	£41,500	£60,000	GDL & LPC: fees + £7,000 (London) £6,500 (elsewhere)	Life ass, PMI, dental, subsd gym m'ship, subsd restaurant, STL, medicals, CTW, childcare vouchers, pensions, PHI
O'Melveny & Myers	£41,000	£44,000	Not known	GDL & LPC: fees + £8,000	Pension, life ins, long-term disability ins, PHI, travel ins, STL, corporate gym m'ship
Orrick	£38,000	£42,500	Not known	GDL & LPC: fees + £7,000	Pension, income protection, life ass, PMI, dental, subsd gym m'ship, STL, childcare vouchers
Osborne Clarke	£33,000-£37,500	£35,000-£40,000	£40,000-£60,000	GDL & LPC: fees + maintenance	Pension, PHI, PMI, life ass, STL
Paul Hastings	£40,000	£45,000	£88,000	GDL & LPC: fees + maintenance	Pte healthcare, life ass, pension, STL, subsd gym
Peters & Peters	£37,000	£39,000	£52,000	Not known	Pension, Bupa, STL, subsd gym m'ship, CTW, life ass, childcare vouchers
Pinsent Masons	Not known	Not known	Not known	Not known	Not known
PwC Legal	£37,000	Not known	Not known	GDL & LPC: scholarship for fees + maintenance	Not known
Reed Smith	£37,000	Not known	£60,000	GDL: fees + £6,000 LPC: fees + £7,000	Flexible: PHI, subsd cafeteria, life ins, lifestyle discounts +concierge, pension, STL
RPC	£37,000 (London) £32,000 (Bristol)	£40,000 (London) £35,000 (Bristol)	Not known	GDL & LPC: bursaries for fees + up to £7,000	Not known
SGH Martineau	c. £23,000	c. £25,000	£36,000	LPC: fees + maintenance	PHI, life ins, PMI, pension, STL, CTW

Salaries and Benefits

Firm Name	1st year salary	2nd year salary	Qualification salary	Sponsorship/ Awards	Other benefits
Shearman & Sterling	£39,000	£44,000	£83,000	GDL & LPC: fees + £7,000	PHI, life ins, dental, gym, pension, disability ins, travel ins
Sheridans	Not known	Not known	Not known	Not known	Not known
Shoosmiths	£24,000	£25,000	£38,000	GDL & LPC: financial assistance + maintenance	Pension, life ass, corporate discounts
Sidley Austin	£41,000	£43,000	Not known	GDL & LPC: fees + £7,000	PHI, life ass, subsd gym m'ship, STL, income protection scheme, pension, subsd restaurant
Simmons & Simmons	£37,500	£41,750	£63,000	GDL: fees + £6,500 LPC: fees + £7,500	Not known
Skadden	£42,000	£45,000	Not known	GDL & LPC: fees + £8,000	Life ins, PHI, PMI, travel ins, subsd gym, subsd restaurant, EAP, technology allowance
Slaughter and May	£39,500	£45,000	£65,000	GDL & LPC: fees + maintenance	PMI, STL, pension, interest-free loan, subsd gym m'ship, accident cover, CTW, childcare vouchers, and others
Speechly Bircham	£34,000	£36,000	£57,000	GDL & LPC: fees + maintenance	PMI, life ass, pension, STL, subsd restaurant, corporate discount for gym membership
Squire Patton Boggs	£35,000 (London) £23,500 (Regions)	£37,000 (London) £26,000 (Regions)	£58,000 (London) £37,000 (Regions)	GDL: fees + £6,000 (London) £4,500 (Regions), LPC: fees + £7,000 (London) £5,000 (Regions)	Flexible: pension, life ass, subsd gym m'ship, STL
Stephenson Harwood	£37,000	£40,000	£60,000	GDL & LPC: fees + up to £6,000	Subsd gym m'ship, PHI, pension, life ass, private GP, critical illness cover, dental ins, retail vouchers, subsd cafe, STL + others
Stevens & Bolton	£30,000	Not known	Not known	GDL & LPC: fees + £4,000	Pension, pte healthcare, life ass, interest-free loan for travel or car parking
Sullivan & Cromwell	£50,000	£55,000	£97,500	GDL & LPC: fees + £9,000	Pte healthcare, dental ins, life ins, travel ins, pension, subsd gym m'ship, concierge
Taylor Wessing	£37,000	£41,000	£60,000	GDL & LPC: fees + maintenance	Not known
Thomas Cooper	£33,000	£36,500	Not known	LPC: fees	PMI, PHI, life ass, pension, dental ins loan, STL, gym m'ship loan
TLT	Not known	Not known	Not known	GDL & LPC: fee sponsorship	Flexible scheme
Travers Smith	£40,000	£44,000	£65,000	GDL & LPC: fees + £7,000 (London) £6,500 (elsewhere)	PHI, life ass, pte health ins, pension, CTW, subsd bistro, childcare vouchers, STL, corporate gym m'ship loan

Refine Your Search

Salaries and Benefits

Firm Name	1st year salary	2nd year salary	Qualification salary	Sponsorship/ Awards	Other benefits
Trethowans	Not known	Not known	Not known	No	Pension, death-in-service benefit, PHI, bonus, car parking, new recruit bonus, childcare vouchers, EAP
Trowers & Hamlins	£36,000	£39,000	£58,000	GDL & LPC: fees + maintenance	Not known
Veale Wasbrough Vizards	£23,000	£25,000	£35,000	LPC: potential sponsorship comprising fees + interest-free loan	Not known
Vinson & Elkins	£40,000	£42,000	£80,000	GDL: fees LPC: fees + up to £7,200	Pte medical + dental, STL, life ass
Ward Hadaway	£22,000	£24,000	£34,000	GDL & LPC: fees + maintenance	Flexible: death in service insurance, pension, travel scheme
Watson, Farley & Williams	£39,000	£44,000	£65,000	GDL & LPC: fees + £6,500/£5,500 depending on location	Income protection, life ass, EAP, pension, STL, subsd gym and healthcare m'ship
Wedlake Bell	£33,000	£35,000	Not known	LPC: funding available	Pension, travel loans, gym m'ship, PMI, life ass, PHI, CTW, EAP
Weil, Gotshal & Manges	£41,000	£45,000 by fourth seat	£95,500	GDL & LPC: fees + £8,000	Pte health cover, PHI, life ass, pension
White & Case	£43,000	£46,000	£75,000	GDL & LPC: fees + maintenance + awards for commendation + distinction on LPC	Flexible: PMI, dental ins, life ass, pension, critical illness insurance, travel ins, STL and others
Wilsons	Not known	Not known	Not known	Not known	Pension, life ass, PMI, optional benefits
Winckworth Sherwood	£32,000	Not known	Not known	GDL & LPC: financial support in certain circumstances	Not known
Withers	£34,000	£36,000	£56,000	GDL & LPC: fees + £5,000	Not known
Wragge Lawrence Graham & Co	£36,250 (London) £26,250 (Birmingham)	£39,250 (London) £29,250 (Birmingham)	Not known	GDL & LPC: fees + maintenance +prizes for first class degree and distinction GDL/LP	Pension, life ass, PHI, PMI and others

Refine Your Search

Picking a firm for its overseas opportunities

The idea of the international law firm is far from new; UK firms have ventured overseas since the 19th century. What has changed is the number of firms with offices overseas and the increasing desire to plant flags around the globe.

Big firms are canny operators. They understand that thriving in a competitive international legal market requires a network of overseas offices (or relationships with overseas firms) in regions with strong economic growth. China and the Far East are of real interest at present, as are Central and Eastern Europe, the Middle East, Africa and resource-rich parts of Central Asia. Despite its economic draws, India has so far avoided invasions due to its strict Bar Association rules. The downturn in the world economy has, largely, not dampened this thirst for expansion, with firms becoming ever more determined to invest in developing countries where growth has been affected less. The global recession did, however, see some of the magic circle firms retreating in regions such as CEE.

There are so many firms with overseas networks that keeping track of the fluctuation of office openings and closings is almost a full-time occupation. Wherever possible, we've mentioned the main changes from the past year in our True Picture reports. Predicting which firms will open new overseas offices and who will merge with whom is always a gamble, but palpable trends crop up here and there. Anglo-American mergers are particularly in vogue – Squire Patton Boggs, Norton Rose Fulbright and Dentons are all the product of transatlantic tie-ups in recent years. Several firms – Ashurst, Norton Rose, Clifford Chance, DLA Piper and most recently Herbert Smith Freehills – have made similar gestures towards the Australian market, while SJ Berwin's tie up with King & Wood Mallesons makes the first global firm headquartered in Asia.

There is no question that practising abroad does make your CV shine. Of course, competition for seats can get tough, and not all firms can guarantee opportunities abroad ahead of time, but the True Picture reports should give you a better idea of where your luck lies. An important thing to bear in mind is language capability – some firms earmark their fluent Russian speakers for Moscow, regardless of whether they'd prefer to head to New York. Language skills in general are undeniably attractive to recruiters, particularly those who actively recruit with certain needs in mind. International private client firm

Withers, for example, likes to enlist a few fluent Italian speakers in each intake to fill its coveted corporate seat in Milan.

Although time abroad gives you experience of working in another jurisdiction, chances are you won't actually practise foreign law. Still, an overseas seat is without a doubt a very rewarding and challenging experience. For UK firms at least, your overseas outpost will be smaller than your home office, so you're likely to receive a greater amount of responsibility. Securing the most popular overseas seats often involves waging a campaign of self-promotion back at home. Sometimes you'll also need to gain experience in a certain department in the UK office before you go.

Overseas trainees need not worry about feeling isolated in their host country as the local lawyers and staff invariably give a warm welcome to newcomers. In cities with a large influx of UK trainees there's usually a ready-made social scene, so it's likely the first thing to pop up in your inbox will be an invitation to meet other new arrivals. In Singapore, it's not unheard of for trainees to jet off for group weekends on Indonesian islands. Another big plus is free accommodation on the firm. Trainees are usually housed in centrally located private apartments. In fact, it may be some time before they can afford such plush digs and domestic perks back home. For more on life as a trainee in an overseas seat, check out our website.

The following table outlines where the overseas seat opportunities are this year. Back in the UK, a firm's international footprint will determine what trainees do day to day. At White & Case there's project finance work conducted in conjunction with Eastern European offices, while Dentons' energy and natural resources work across Africa and the Middle East rakes in heaps of work for London lawyers. Likewise, Trowers & Hamlins' predominance in Islamic finance keeps its City side busy, as do Curtis Mallet's and Wragge Lawrence Graham's respective relationships with Middle Eastern governments and major film studios in Los Angeles. See our True Picture reports for more details on each.

489

Overseas seats: Who goes where?

Location	Firms
Abu Dhabi	Berwin Leighton Paisner, Cleary Gottlieb Steen & Hamilton, Clifford Chance, Clyde & Co, Dentons, DLA Piper, Herbert Smith Freehills, Linklaters, Reed Smith, Shearman & Sterling, Simmons & Simmons, Trowers & Hamlins, White & Case
Almaty	White & Case
Amsterdam	Clifford Chance, Freshfields, Linklaters, Norton Rose Fulbright, Slaughter and May
Athens	Watson Farley & Williams
Auckland	Slaughter and May
Bahrain	Trowers & Hamlins
Bangkok	DLA Piper, Watson Farley & Williams
Barcelona	Slaughter and May
Beijing	Cleary Gottlieb Steen & Hamilton, Clifford Chance, CMS, White & Case
Berlin	Freshfields
Brussels	Baker & McKenzie, Berwin Leighton Paisner, Bird & Bird, Cleary Gottlieb Steen & Hamilton, Clifford Chance, Dechert, Freshfields, Herbert Smith Freehills, Hogan Lovells, Holman Fenwick Willan, King & Wood Mallesons, Linklaters, Morgan, Lewis & Bockius, Nabarro, Olswang, Shearman & Sterling, Sidley Austin, Skadden, Slaughter and May, Squire Patton Boggs, White & Case
Bucharest	CMS
Dar es Salaam	Clyde & Co
Doha	Clyde & Co, Eversheds, Herbert Smith Freehills
Dubai	Addleshaw Goddard, Ashurst, Clifford Chance, Clyde & Co, CMS, Dentons, DLA Piper, Freshfields, Gateley, Herbert Smith Freehills, Hogan Lovells, Holman Fenwick Willan, King & Wood Mallesons, Latham & Watkins, Linklaters, Morgan, Lewis & Bockius, Norton Rose Fulbright, Pinsent Masons, Simmons & Simmons, Stephenson Harwood, Trowers & Hamlins, Vinson & Elkins, Wragge Lawrence Graham & Co
Dublin	Dechert
Düsseldorf	McDermott Will & Emery
Falkland Is.	Pinsent Masons
Frankfurt	Clifford Chance, Freshfields, King & Wood Mallesons, Linklaters, White & Case
Geneva	Charles Russell, Holman Fenwick Willan
Guangzhou	Wragge Lawrence Graham & Co
Hamburg	Ince & Co, Watson Farley & Williams
Helsinki	Slaughter and May
Hong Kong	Addleshaw Goddard, Ashurst, Baker & McKenzie, Berwin Leighton Paisner, Cleary Gottlieb Steen & Hamilton, Clifford Chance, Clyde & Co, DLA Piper, Eversheds, Freshfields, Gide, Herbert Smith Freehills, Hogan Lovells, Holman Fenwick Willan, Kennedys, Kirkland & Ellis, Latham & Watkins, Linklaters, Mayer Brown, Simmons & Simmons, Skadden, Slaughter and May, Stephenson Harwood, Vinson & Elkins, White & Case, Withers
Houston	Vinson & Elkins
Istanbul	White & Case
Johannesburg	Baker & McKenzie, Norton Rose Fulbright, White & Case
Luxembourg	King & Wood Mallesons SJ Berwin
Madrid	Ashurst, Clifford Chance, DLA Piper, King & Wood Mallesons, Linklaters, Slaughter and May
Melbourne	Norton Rose Fulbright
Mexico City	CMS
Milan	Clifford Chance, Linklaters, Norton Rose Fulbright, Slaughter and May, Withers
Moscow	Baker & McKenzie, Berwin Leighton Paisner, Cleary Gottlieb Steen & Hamilton, Clifford Chance, CMS Cameron McKenna, DLA Piper, Freshfields, Gide, Herbert Smith Freehills, Latham & Watkins, Linklaters, Morgan, Lewis & Bockius, Skadden, White & Case
Munich	Clifford Chance, CMS, Slaughter and May
Muscat	Addleshaw Goddard, Dentons, Trowers & Hamlins

Overseas seats: Who goes where?

Location	Firms
New York	Ashurst, Cleary Gottlieb Steen & Hamilton, Curtis, Davis Polk, Freshfields, Hogan Lovells, Kirkland & Ellis, Latham & Watkins, Mayer Brown, Shearman & Sterling, Slaughter and May, Weil, Gotshal & Manges, White & Case
Oslo	Slaughter and May
Paris	Cleary Gottlieb Steen & Hamilton, Eversheds, Freshfields, Gide, Herbert Smith Freehills, Hogan Lovells, Holman Fenwick Willan, King & Wood Mallesons, Latham & Watkins, Linklaters, McDermott Will & Emery, Norton Rose Fulbright, Olswang, Simmons & Simmons, Slaughter and May, Squire Patton Boggs, Travers Smith, Watson Farley & Williams, Weil, Gotshal & Manges, White & Case
Perth	Holman Fenwick Willan, Norton Rose Fulbright
Piraeus	Holman Fenwick Willan, Ince & Co, Reed Smith, Thomas Cooper
Prague	CMS, White & Case
Rio de Janeiro	CMS
San Francisco	Clyde & Co
São Paulo	Clifford Chance
Seoul	Herbert Smith Freehills, Linklaters
Shanghai	Clyde & Co, Eversheds, Holman Fenwick Willan, Linklaters
Singapore	Ashurst, Baker & McKenzie, Berwin Leighton Paisner, Clifford Chance, DLA Piper, Eversheds, Freshfields, Herbert Smith Freehills, Hill Dickinson, Hogan Lovells, Holman Fenwick Willan, Latham & Watkins, Linklaters, Norton Rose Fulbright, Shearman & Sterling, Simmons & Simmons, Stephenson Harwood, Thomas Cooper, Watson Farley & Williams, White & Case
Stockholm	Slaughter and May
Sydney	Baker & McKenzie, DLA Piper, Herbert Smith Freehills, Norton Rose Fulbright, Slaughter and May
Tokyo	Ashurst, Clifford Chance, Freshfields, Herbert Smith Freehills, Linklaters, Norton Rose Fulbright, Simmons & Simmons, White & Case
Vienna	CMS Cameron McKenna
Washington DC	Cleary Gottlieb Steen & Hamilton, Freshfields

Refine Your Search

From our foreign correspondents: *Chambers Student*'s guide to overseas seats can be found on chambersstudent.co.uk

"I often find unsuccessful candidates are the ones who err towards rehearsed answers. Some people just spout off research they've done on the internet but can't actually apply it to the day-to-day operations of the firm or its clients. As a future trainee you have to have a certain degree of commercial awareness and know about the challenges the firm you're applying to faces."

City training partner

A-Z of Solicitors

Addleshaw Goddard

Milton Gate, 60 Chiswell St, London EC1Y 4AG
Tel: (020) 7606 8855 Fax: (020) 7606 4390
Email: grad@addleshawgoddard.com
Website: www.addleshawgoddard.com/graduates

Firm profile

Addleshaw Goddard is an international law firm committed to creating and delivering outstanding value. We are exceptional lawyers and market leaders in client investment and understanding. Fun to work with and for, we are known for our constant enquiry and innovation and combine insight with business knowledge to deliver the best results for our clients, whenever and wherever required. Wherever you are based, you'll also be part of the team from day one, getting first-hand experience of working with bluechip clients within a supportive yet challenging environment and benefit from a structured training programme designed with your future success in mind.

Main areas of work

The firm's client portfolio is testament to its strength and range of expertise and includes financial institutions, public sector bodies, successful businesses and private individuals. It is a leading advisor to FTSE100 companies and a market leader across its business divisions – commercial services, corporate, finance and projects, litigation and real estate – as well as in specialist fields such as private capital and across its chosen sectors: financial services, government, energy and infrastructure, retail and consumer and real estate.

Trainee profile

Graduates who are capable of achieving a 2:1 and can demonstrate commercial awareness, teamwork, motivation and drive. Applications from law and non-law graduates are welcomed, as are applications from students who may be considering a change of direction. We also have a Legal access scheme for applicants on GDL or LPC with less conventional academic backgrounds. Further details can be found on our website.

Training environment

During each six-month seat, there will be regular two-way performance reviews with the supervising partner or solicitor. Trainees may have the opportunity to spend a seat in one of the firm's other offices and there are a number of secondments to clients available. Seated with a qualified solicitor or partner and working as part of a team enables trainees to develop the professional skills necessary to deal with the demanding and challenging work the firm carries out for its clients. Practical training is complemented by high-quality training courses provided by both the in-house team and external training providers. A trainee buddy programme is in place with the trainee predecessor for the first seat. All trainees have a mentor for the duration of their training contract and beyond.

Placement schemes

We run placement schemes in our Leeds, London and Manchester offices. The schemes are integral to our training contract recruitment. The schemes last for one or two weeks and take place over Easter, June, July and August. Applications should be made online by 31 January 2015 and interviews start early February.

Sponsorship & benefits

GDL and LPC fees are paid, plus a maintenance grant of £7,000 (London) or £4,500 (elsewhere in the UK). Benefits include corporate gym membership, season ticket loan, subsidised restaurant, pension and private healthcare.

Partners 177
Trainees 65
Total Staff 1250

Contact
grad@addleshawgoddard.com

Closing date for 2017
Candidates must complete our online application at www.addleshawgoddard.com/graduates by 31 July 2015 to begin September 2017 or March 2018.

Application
Training contracts p.a. 30
Required degree grade 2:1
BBB at A Level (excluding General Studies)

Training
Starting salary
£37,000 (London)
£25,000 (Leeds/Manchester)

Overseas offices
Dubai, Hong Kong, Oman, Qatar and Singapore

Arnold & Porter (UK) LLP

Tower 42, 25 Old Broad Street, London, EC2N 1HQ
Tel: (020) 7786 6100 Fax: (020) 7786 6299
Email: graduates@aporter.com
Website: www.arnoldporter.com

Firm profile
Arnold & Porter is a US-based firm with a deserved reputation for its quality of service and expertise in handling the most complex legal and business problems requiring innovative and practical solutions. The firm's global reach, experience and deep knowledge allows it to work across geographic, cultural, technological and ideological borders, serving clients whose business needs require US, EU or cross-border regulatory, litigation and transactional services.

Main areas of work
The London office is home to the firm's European regulatory, life sciences, IP, competition, corporate, financial services, white collar crime, international arbitration, employment and telecoms practices. Chambers UK recently ranked its London office as a top ranked leading firm in EU Competition, Intellectual Property, Media and Entertainment, Corporate: M&A, Life Sciences, Product Liability, Telecommunications and Retail.

Trainee profile
The firm looks for talented law and non-law graduates from all backgrounds who share the firm's commitment to excellence, and want to be part of the continued growth of its London office. Candidates need to demonstrate a consistently high academic background; the firm looks for well-rounded individuals who can demonstrate their participation in a range of extra-curricular activities and achievements.

Training environment
Four six-month seats: pharmaceuticals, IP, corporate and securities, financial services, competition, international arbitration or white collar crime. The firm encourages individuals to work across specialisms and emphasises teamwork, so trainees may find that whilst they are working in one group, they undertake work in a variety of different areas throughout the firm. Trainees will be expected to work on several matters at once, and assume responsibility at an early stage. Trainees may also have an opportunity to work in the firm's Brussels office and where the occasion permits, to work on projects in one of the firm's US offices.

An important aspect of the firm's culture is its commitment to pro bono. Trainees and all lawyers at the firm are encouraged to take part and devote 15% of their time to it, which helps young lawyers develop client management skills from an early stage.

Vacation schemes
The firm takes around eight summer vacation students each recruiting year. Whether you are a law or non-law student, the firm will introduce you to life in a busy City law firm, spending two weeks working on a variety of projects and workshops with partners and associates throughout the London office. Apply via the firm's website by 8 March 2015.

Benefits
Healthy incentive bonus, Christmas bonus, child care vouchers, private health insurance, private dental insurance, life assurance, season ticket loan.

Sponsorship & awards
GDL/LPC: fees paid; £8,000 per course maintenance.

Partners 19
Assistant Solicitors 25
Total Trainees 2

Contact
Graduate Recruitment

Method of application
Apply via website

Selection procedure
Interview with partners and associates; written assessment

Closing date for 2017
3 August 2015

Application
Training contracts p.a. 2
Applications p.a 700
% interviewed 2%
Required degree grade 2:1

Training
Salary
1st year US firm market rate
2nd year US firm market rate
Holiday entitlement 25 days

Post-qualification
% of trainees offered job on qualification 100%

Overseas, regional offices
London, Washington DC, New York, Los Angeles, Denver, Houston, San Francisco, Silicon Valley, Brussels

ARNOLD & PORTER (UK)LLP

Ashfords LLP

Grenadier Road, Exeter EX1 3LH
Tel: (01392) 333634
Email: graduaterecruitment@ashfords.co.uk
Website: www.ashfords.co.uk

Firm profile

Ashfords is recognised nationally as a leading provider of legal and related professional services. We deliver commercially focused advice to our clients across a range of industries and sectors. Our aim is straightforward – to help our clients get the results that they want. Our commitment to excellence is reflected by the quality of our staff and partners, our client testimonials and industry awards. We are also delighted to have been voted a Guardian UK 300 employer by students and graduates in the UK for the third year running.

Main areas of work

Our three core divisions – commercial services, real estate and infrastructure and private client – cover a wide range of practice areas, including corporate, commercial property, dispute resolution, projects, local government, employment, intellectual property, information technology, trusts and estates, family, residential property and equity release. We have a wealth of experience in the specific sector areas of technology, waste, energy and resource management, local government, and bulk commodity services and, through our ADVOC network of independent law firms, we have experts in more than 60 countries across the world.

Trainee profile

We are looking for applicants that demonstrate our own values of teamwork, quality client service and innovation with a forward thinking commercial focus. We want our trainees to be engaged and motivated, ready to immerse themselves in real client matters, providing our clients with the benefit of a fresh and expert approach. You will need to be an excellent communicator with the ability to adapt to and embrace the challenges that a career in law can throw at you. Committed to a 'recruit to retain' policy we want our trainees to be our partners of the future.

Training environment

You will experience four areas of law during your training contract, spending six months getting to grips with each department. You have a choice of either a Bristol-based or a South West-based training contract. Our South West trainees will have the opportunity to work across our Exeter, Taunton and Plymouth offices. We also offer flexibility for trainees to complete a seat in another office if the opportunity arises, including London.

As an Ashfords trainee, you will experience first-hand the work of a commercial law firm. We offer the opportunity of hands-on experience, early responsibility and client involvement. To make sure that everything is on track you will meet with your supervisor during each seat to monitor your development. You will also have a mentor to provide personalised support and give you the opportunity to discuss all those burning questions. Our trainees also play an integral role in our CSR programme and business development and marketing events, which provide exposure to our diverse client base.

In addition to a comprehensive induction to the firm, the dedicated Learning and Development Team will support you through your mandatory PSC training, as well as providing a variety of client focused and soft skills courses, underpinning and complementing your on-the-job training.

Benefits

Pension scheme, holiday purchase, childcare voucher and cycle schemes, employee assistance programme, life assurance, employee rates and discounts and free legal services.

Sponsorship

A £9,000 grant is available towards your LPC.

Partners 74
Fee-Earners 176
Total Staff 505
Total Trainees 20

Contact
graduaterecruitment
@ashfords.co.uk

Method of application
Online application form

Selection procedure
Assessment days

Closing date
Summer scheme
28 February 2015
Training contract
31 July 2015

Application
Training contracts p.a. 10
Applications p.a. 400
% interviewed 15%
Required degree grade 2:1

Training
Salary Competitive
(Bristol and London uplift
will apply)
Holiday entitlement 22 days
(rising to 27 on qualification)

Post-qualification
Salary Competitive
(Bristol and London uplift
will apply)

Offices
Bristol, Exeter, London,
Plymouth, Taunton and
Tiverton.

A-Z of Solicitors

ashfords

Ashurst LLP

Broadwalk House, 5 Appold St, London EC2A 2HA
Tel: (020) 7638 1111 Fax: (020) 7638 1112
Email: gradrec@ashurst.com
Website: www.ashurst.com/trainees
Facebook: www.facebook.com/AshurstTrainees

Firm profile

Ashurst offers its clients and trainees a clear alternative to other elite law firms by cutting through complexity. With 28 offices spanning the world's leading financial and resource centres in Europe, Asia-Pacific, Middle East and the USA, we offer the scale to attract global mandates. We operate at the cutting edge of the financial, corporate, infrastructure, disputes and resources markets with advice that is commercially acute as well as technically accurate. For our clients this means getting to the heart of issues with speed and clarity. For trainees, our strong culture of collegiality means you will be encouraged to apply your intellect and make your presence felt right from the outset.

Trainee profile

As with other law firms at the top of the market there will be challenges, late nights and pressure to perform. However, we also prize our culture of teamwork, client service, innovation and fun. We are looking for exceptional people who can contribute fully in all these areas. You will need to be totally committed to delivering for our clients and at home expressing yourself on paper and out loud, with your team and within a client's board room. If you share our vision, have a track record of achievement and are determined to be the best, multi-faceted lawyer you can be, we would like to hear from you.

Training environment

In addition to the obvious legal skills taught by all leading law firms, we will help you to develop the broad based acumen that will one day make you a trusted advisor to governments and the world's leading businesses. Your role at Ashurst will require you to become not only a highly technical lawyer, but also a shrewd negotiator, an incisive reader of any balance sheet and a business strategist with deep understanding of specific industries. In setting out to learn these skills you will complete four seats of six months, each of which will be planned in collaboration with you. You will also be encouraged to join an overseas office or go on secondment to one of our most valued clients.

Benefits

Private medical cover, pension, life assurance, income protection, interest-free season ticket loan, cycle to work scheme, in-house medical facilities, subsidised gym membership and staff restaurant and 25 days holiday per year during training.

Vacation placements

The best way to learn what it's really like to work at Ashurst is to join one of our vacation schemes. Have a look at our website to find out which one would be best for you to join us on.

Sponsorship & awards

Full fees paid for the GDL and LPC, plus maintenance allowances of £8,000 per annum (for study in London), or £7,000 (outside of London). First class degree awards of £500 and language tuition bursaries.

Partners 420
Assistant Solicitors 1700
Total Trainees 85 (London)

Contact
Emma Young, Senior HR Manager, Graduate Recruitment and Development
For general enquiries contact us on gradrec@ashurst.com

Method of application
Online

Selection procedure
An assessment day - see our website for full details

Closing date for 2017
31 July 2015

Application
Training contracts p.a. 40
Applications p.a. 2,500
% interviewed p.a. 10%
Required degree grade 2:1 (or equivalent)

Training
Salary (2014)
1st year £40,000
2nd year £45,000
Holiday entitlement 25 days
% of trainees with a non-law degree 50%
Number of seats abroad available p.a. 14

Post-qualification
Salary (2014) £63,000
% of trainees offered job on qualification 96%

Overseas offices
28 offices in 16 countries: Australia, Belgium, China, France, Germany, Indonesia, Italy, Japan, Papua New Guinea, Saudi Arabia, Singapore, Spain, Sweden, UAE, UK and USA.

Baker & McKenzie LLP

100 New Bridge Street, London EC4V 6JA
Tel: (020) 7919 1000 Fax: (020) 7919 1999
Email: londongraduates@bakermckenzie.com
Website: www.bakermckenzie.com/londongraduates

Firm profile
Baker & McKenzie is a leading global law firm based in over 70 locations across 47 countries. With a presence in nearly all of the world's leading financial and commercial centres, our strategy is to provide the best combination of local legal and commercial knowledge, international expertise and resources. Our trainee solicitors are a vital part of that strategy, exposed to the international scope of the firm from the moment they start. There is also the possibility of an overseas secondment, recent secondees have spent time in San Francisco, Brussels, Moscow, Johannesburg and Hong Kong.

Main areas of work
London is home to the firm's largest office where Baker & McKenzie has been well established since opening in 1961. With more than 400 legal professionals, we have a substantial presence in the legal and business community.

We deliver high-quality local solutions across a broad range of practices and global advice in conjunction with our international offices. Our client base consists primarily of multinational corporates, based in the UK and elsewhere, and financial institutions. As may be expected of a firm with a very strong international client base, we have considerable expertise in acting on, and co-ordinating, cross-border transactions and disputes.

Our Corporate and Finance teams regularly advise on, and co-ordinate, complex, cross-border transactions for our clients. As a full service office, we cover all the practices expected of a major law firm in the UK, many of which are acclaimed and market-leading.

Trainee profile
The firm strives to enable trainees to be the best they can be. We are looking for trainees who are stimulated by intellectual challenge and respect and enjoy the diversity of cultural, social and academic backgrounds found in the firm. Effective communication skills, together with the ability to be creative and practical problem solvers, team players and to have a sense of humour, are qualities which will help them stand out from the crowd.

Training environment
The two-year training contract comprises of four six-month seats which include a corporate and a contentious seat, usually within our highly regarded dispute resolution department, together with the possibility of a secondment abroad or with a client. During each seat you will have formal and informal reviews to discuss your progress and regular meetings to explore subsequent seat preferences. Your training contract commences with a highly interactive and practical induction programme which focuses on key skills including practical problem solving, presenting and the application of information technology. The firm's training programmes include important components on management and other business skills, as well as seminars and workshops on key legal topics for each practice area. There is a Trainee Solicitor Liaison Committee which acts as a forum for any new ideas which may occur during the training contract.

Benefits
Permanent health insurance, life insurance, private medical insurance, group personal pension, subsidised gym membership, season ticket loan, subsidised staff restaurant.

Sponsorship & awards
CPE/GDL funding: fees paid plus £6,000 maintenance.

LPC funding: fees paid plus £8,000 maintenance.

Partners 84
Assistant Solicitors 202
Trainees 78

Contact
The Graduate Recruitment
Team 020 7919 1000

Method of application
Online via our website
www.bakermckenzie.com/
londongraduates

Selection procedure
Online application, online
tests, telephone interview and
assessment centre

Application
No. of training contracts p.a 30
Required degree grade 2:1 or
equivalent
AAB at A Level or equivalent.

Training
Salary for each year of training
1st year £39,500 + £3,000
'joining bonus'
2nd year £44,000

Post-qualification
Salary £65,000

Overseas offices
Over 70 offices across 47
countries

A-Z of Solicitors

BAKER & M^cKENZIE

Bates Wells Braithwaite

2-6 Cannon Street, London EC4M 6YH
Tel: (020) 7551 7777 Fax: (020) 7551 7800
Email: training@bwbllp.com
Website: www.bwbllp.com

Firm profile
Bates Wells Braithwaite is a commercial law firm servicing a wide range of commercial statutory, charity and social enterprises. The firm is expanding, progressive and is doing high quality work for clients and providing high quality training for those who work with the firm.

Whilst the firm is ranked first in three areas of law by the Legal 500 and ranked by them or Chambers in 15 other areas of law, the firm also believes in its staff enjoying a good work/life balance and living a life outside as well as inside the office.

Main areas of work
The firm is well known for its work for a wide range and variety of clients. This includes working with the charities and social enterprise sector, commercial organisations, regulators and individuals. The firm also has particular expertise in the arts and media, sports and immigration arenas together with strong departments dealing with employment, property and dispute resolution.

Trainee profile
The firm is looking for trainees with not only a sound academic background and the ability to communicate clearly and effectively, but most importantly it is looking for trainees who positively want to join a firm such as Bates Wells Braithwaite. We want the applicant with the character and ability to prosper anywhere, who is positively looking to be in a firm with our work mix and approach.

Training environment
In the first year there are two six month seats, whilst in the second year there are three four month seats which, between them, cover a wide range of the work with which the firm is involved. From time to time the firm arranges secondments to clients on an ad hoc basis.

The firm runs a programme of internal seminars specifically addressed to trainees and operates a mentoring system, all designed to ensure that the trainees enjoy their time with the firm and to maximise the opportunities that are available for them during their training contract and beyond.

Benefits
Firm pension scheme with match funding provided, interest-free loan for season ticket travel, Permanent Health Insurance (PHI), Death in Service Scheme, subsidised use of gym/corporate gym membership, wellbeing classes and squash court access, cycle to work scheme, subsidised restaurant, Buying Annual leave and one month's unpaid leave on qualification.

Vacation placements
Places for 2015: 12 people for a duration of two weeks each (£300 paid expenses). Closing date: March 2015. See website for details and to apply.

Sponsorship & awards
We will provide financial support to the value of £7,000 for LPC course fees which commence after the offer has been accepted. Similar support is given for the GDL on a discretionary basis. We also pay interest on student loans on either of these courses from the signing of the training contract to the contract end.

Partners 29
Assistant Solicitors 49
Trainees 8

Graduate recruitment contact
Jemma Oleary
(020) 7551 7777

Method of application
Online via website

Selection procedure
Interviews

Closing date for 2017
June 2015 - see website

Application
Training contracts per annum 4
Applications p.a. 750+
% interviewed p.a. 5%
Required degree 2:1

Training
Salary
1st year £32,000
2nd year £34,000
Holiday entitlement
5 weeks

Post-qualification
Salary £46,575
% of trainees offered job
on qualification (last 3 years)
92%

Bates Wells Braithwaite

Berwin Leighton Paisner

Adelaide House, London Bridge, London EC4R 9HA
Tel: (020) 3400 1000 Fax: (020) 3400 1111
Website: www.blplaw.com/trainee

Firm profile
BLP is an exciting, ambitious, and dynamic full service international law firm with over 820 fee-earners, including more than 200 partners. BLP currently has offices in eleven international locations, and has acted for or completed work in 130 countries in the last two years.

Main areas of work
Our client base includes more than 30 FTSE 100 companies and some of the world's top banks. We support each of the country's largest retail, water and construction companies. There are over 70 legal disciplines in which we are ranked. These include: commercial contracts; corporate finance; dispute resolution; energy and natural resources; EU and competition; finance; hotels, leisure and gaming; human resources; insurance; intellectual property; outsourcing; public sector; real estate; retail; regulatory and compliance; restructuring and insolvency; tax; and transport and infrastructure.

Trainee profile
In addition to talented individuals with brilliant minds and bright attitudes, we are looking for people who can take complex, often pressurised, commercial situations in their stride. The sort of people our clients want on their side and will ask for by name. People they can trust to help them succeed.

Training environment
Trainees spend six months in four seats and progress is reviewed every three months. Client secondments are a popular choice, and there is the opportunity to undertake an international seat in either our Brussels, Moscow, Singapore, Hong Kong or Abu Dhabi offices.

LLM+/ GDL+
The firm developed and runs a tailor-made LPC Course, called the LLM+. All trainees study at the University of Law, where tutors are joined by BLP lawyers and trainers who help to deliver some of the sessions, using BLP precedents and documents, and discuss how theory is applied to real cases and transactions. In 2011 we also introduced the GDL+; a programme of BLP led workshops which supplement the content that you study on the GDL course.

Sponsorship
CPE/GDL and LLM+ fees paid and £7,200 maintenance p.a

Partners 209
Assistant Solicitors 395
Associate Directors 32
Total Trainees 84

Contact
Alan Demirkaya, Graduate Recruitment & Trainee Manager

Method of application
Online application form

Selection procedure
Telephone interview, assessment centre, partner interview

Closing date for 2016/2017
31 July 2015

Application
Training contracts p.a. 40-45
Required degree grade 2:1
Required UCAs points 340

Training
Salary
1st year (2014)
£39,000
2nd year (2014)
£44,000
Holiday entitlement 25 days
% of trainees with a
non-law degree p.a. 50%
No. of seats available
abroad p.a. 5

Post-qualification
Salary (2014) £63,000
% of trainees offered job
on qualification (March 2014)
89%

Offices
Abu Dhabi, Beijing, Berlin, Brussels, Dubai, Frankfurt, Hong Kong, London, Moscow, Paris and Singapore

Bingham McCutchen (London) LLP

41 Lothbury, London EC2R 7HF
Tel: (020) 7661 5300 Fax: (020) 7661 5400
Email: graduaterecruitment@bingham.com
Website: www.bingham.com

Firm profile

Bingham London offers you the opportunity to work alongside outstanding individuals in a personal and collegial environment. Our team of over 50 finance, litigation and corporate lawyers is dedicated to providing a seamless and responsive service to the firm's international financial institution clients. Our London office capabilities have been carefully shaped to meet the complex needs of a demanding client base. Through practical experience and in-depth study of the legal and business issues facing these clients, the firm's London lawyers provide counsel in an intelligent and focused way. Widely recognised as one of the world's top-tier financial restructuring firms, Bingham has played a leading role representing creditors in numerous high-profile, precedent-setting workouts and restructurings throughout Europe including the senior noteholders on the restructurings of Royal Imtech N.V., Uralita, Technicolor S.A. (formerly Thomson S.A.) and the Quinn Group; the public noteholders of Dannemora Minerals AB, Northland Resources, Invitel, the OSX group, Wind Hellas, Preem, Petroplus, Sevan Marine, the Icelandic Banks (Kaupthing, Landsbanki and Glitnir), Anglo Irish Bank and Irish Nationwide Building Society; the mezzanine lenders to Gala Coral, Bulgaria Telecommunications/Vivacom, European Directories, Alliance Medical and Findus Foods; the senior lenders of Klöckner Pentaplast and the Terreal Group; the informal group of equity and note investors in connection with the planned financial restructuring of the Punch A and Punch B securitisation structures; the administrators of Comet Group Limited; and the bondholders on the majority of restructurings of high yield bonds in Norway including Petrojack and Remedial Offshore. Our Financial Restructuring Practice is ranked in Band 1 by Chambers UK, Legal 500 UK and IFLR 1000 and was named Insolvency and Restructuring Firm of the Year by Who's Who Legal for the third time in 10 years in 2014. We have 14 locations spanning the US, Europe and Asia.

Main areas of work

Bingham's London office capabilities include financial restructuring, finance, securities and financial institutions litigation, financial regulatory, UK funds, corporate, EU/UK competition and tax.

Trainee profile

We are looking for high-quality candidates who have an exceptional academic record combined with evidence of extracurricular achievement. Prospective trainees will show initiative, be solution-driven and seek to be part of a challenging, yet friendly, environment.

Training environment

We recruit up to three trainee solicitors each year. The training contract consists of four six-month seats, rotating between the following practice areas: financial restructuring, finance, corporate, financial regulatory, competition, tax and litigation. The intimate nature of our London office means that you will benefit from a bespoke training programme with a high level of partner involvement. You will assume responsibilities from day one.

Benefits

As well as a competitive salary, the firm offers private health insurance, travel insurance, long-term disability insurance, season ticket loan, life assurance, a critical illness scheme and subsidised gym membership. A discretionary bonus is also payable.

Sponsorship & awards

On acceptance of our offer for a training contract, we will provide LPC and PgDL fees and a maintenance grant of £8,000 per year.

Assistant solicitors 31
Total Trainees 4

Contact
Vicky Widdows, Senior Manager, Legal Recruiting/Learning and Development
(020) 7661 5300

Method of application
Online application via firm website at www.bingham.com or via CV Mail

Selection procedure
Currently face to face interviews

Closing date for 2017
31 July 2015

Application
Training contracts p.a. up to 3
Required degree grade
High 2:1 from a leading university and excellent A-levels

Training
Salary
1st year £40,000
2nd year £45,000
Holiday entitlement 25 days

Post-qualification
Salary (2014) £100,000

Overseas offices
Beijing, Boston, Frankfurt, Hartford, Hong Kong, Los Angeles, New York, Orange County, San Francisco, Santa Monica, Silicon Valley, Tokyo, Washington

BINGHAM

Bircham Dyson Bell LLP

50 Broadway, London SW1H 0BL
Tel: (020) 7227 7000

Firm profile

BDB is a multi-disciplinary UK law firm advising private companies, public sector bodies, not-for-profit organisations and individuals since 1834. The firm's approach and track record has enabled it to attract and retain some of the most talented people in the profession. This is achieved through the breadth and variety of work that the firm does.

The firm is a leading member of Lexwork International, a network of 45 mid-sized independent law firms with over 2,500 lawyers in major cities across North America and Europe.

Main areas of work

The firm is a top 100 London-based LLP with around 170 partners, solicitors and experts, all based in Westminster. It works with clients across a variety of major practice areas, with a focus on planning and major projects, public law, corporate and commercial and real estate. These skills compliment the traditional strengths the firm has in private wealth, family, employment, litigation, charity and the not-for-profit sectors – practice areas recently strengthened by the firm's merger with private client boutique, Ambrose Appelbe.

Trainee profile

Applications are welcome from both law and non-law students who can demonstrate a consistently high academic record. BDB is looking for candidates with high professional standards, who demonstrate commercial awareness, drive to deliver quality results, effective teamwork and communication skills, and enthusiasm for a career in law. As we hope our trainees won't just be here to train but to take our success forward, successful candidates are ambitious, forward-looking and have leadership potential.

Training environment

We've built a culture that encourages talent to flourish and an environment where people enjoy working. A training contract with Bircham Dyson Bell will bring you real responsibility right from the start, combined with the right level of support to ensure you never feel overwhelmed. The two-year training contract consists of four six-month seats during which you will work alongside partners and other senior lawyers, some of whom are leaders in their field. After a comprehensive induction programme our trainees receive extensive training to ensure their expertise and career skills are constantly developing. Trainees undergo specific technical training in each seat in addition to the mandatory Professional Skills Course (PSC). Great emphasis is also placed on interpersonal skills such as networking and client management so when you qualify you have the breadth of skills required to be an excellent solicitor.

Benefits

Bonus scheme, group health care, life assurance, pension scheme, season ticket loan.

Sponsorship

Bircham Dyson Bell provides funding for GDL and LPC fees.

Partners 47
Fee Earners 113
Total Trainees 14

Contact
Graduate Recruitment Team
(020) 7227 7000

Method of application
Please visit the firm's website,
www.bdb-law.co.uk

Selection procedure
Two interviews with members of the Graduate Recruitment Panel, comprising of a number of partners, associates and HR. In addition you will be required to complete an online test and assessment centre exercise.

Closing date for 2017
31 July 2015

Application
Training contracts p.a. 5
Applications p.a. 700
% interviewed p.a. 5%
Required degree grade
2:1 or above degree preferred

Training
Salary
1st year £32,000
2nd year £33,500
Holiday entitlement 25 days

Post-qualification
Salary £52,000
% of trainees offered job on qualification (2013) 86%

BIRCHAM DYSON BELL

Bird & Bird

15 Fetter Lane, London EC4A 1JP
Tel: (020) 7415 6003 Fax: (020) 7415 6111
Website: www.twobirds.com/londongraduates

Firm profile

Over the course of nearly 190 years, Bird & Bird has evolved into a respected global business, serving clients in 118 countries from 26 offices across Europe, the Middle East and Asia. Today, our clients include the owners of seven of the ten most valuable brands on the planet and more than half of those listed by Forbes as the world's 100 most innovative companies. They need legal advisors who can work in partnership with them, develop a deep understanding of their sector and add real value to their business. It's the reason they turn to Bird & Bird.

The firm is ambitious and it manages to combine a resilient business approach with a hugely supportive attitude to its employees. With offices in Abu Dhabi, Beijing, Bratislava, Brussels, Budapest, Copenhagen, Dubai, Düsseldorf, Frankfurt, The Hague, Hamburg, Helsinki, Hong Kong, London, Lyon, Madrid, Milan, Munich, Paris, Prague, Rome, Shanghai, Singapore, Skanderborg, Stockholm, Warsaw and close ties with firms in other key centres in Europe, Asia and the United States, the firm is well placed to offer its clients local expertise within a global context.

The firm is proud of its friendly, stimulating environment where individuals are able to develop first class legal, business and interpersonal skills. It has an open and collegiate culture reflected in its strong retention rate and assistant involvement. The firm is structured with a very strong international perspective to its culture – integrated teams working for cross-border clients as well as a range of international sport and social activities enables this.

At Bird & Bird, there is a genuine commitment to acting as a responsible employer and also as a proactive member of its local and wider international communities. The firm has a full programme of corporate social responsibility initiatives and policies in place, which fall under three broad areas: people, community and environment.

Main areas of work

We operate at the forefront of a range of sectors including: aviation and defence, automotive, communications, electronics, energy and utilities, financial services, food, healthcare, information technology, life sciences, media and sports.

Across these sectors, we cover the following practice areas: arbitration, banking and finance, commercial, corporate, corporate restructuring and insolvency, dispute resolution, EU and competition, intellectual property, international HR services, outsourcing, privacy and data protection, public sector, real estate, regulatory and administrative, tax, trade and customs and pro bono.

Trainee profile

We look to recruit trainees who have the potential and ambition to meet our clients' exacting standards.

Not only will you need to develop technical legal skills to deliver high-quality legal advice, but you must also have an inquisitive, down-to-earth and pragmatic approach. If you think you have what it takes, we can offer you a challenging career in a fast-paced international environment. It's your chance to help shape the future of the clients we work for and the industries they serve.

If you are interested in a training contract at Bird & Bird, the summer placement scheme is a fantastic way to get started. We take on 30 students for two three-week schemes throughout June and July. Apply online at londongraduates.twobirds.com/apply/ by 31 January 2015 for summer placement applications or by 31 July 2015 for training contract applications.

Partners Over 280*
Assistant Solicitors Over 680*
Total Trainees 36 in London
*denotes worldwide figures

Contact
Graduate Recruitment and
Trainee Development Team
london.graduates@twobirds.com

Method of application
Online application form via the
firm website

Selection procedure
Insight and selection days in
March 2015 for summer
placements and September
2015 for training contracts

Closing date for 2017
31 July 2015 for law and non-
law students

Application
Training contracts p.a. 16-18
Applications p.a. 2,000
% interviewed at first stage
p.a. 20%
Required degree grade 2:1

Training
Salary
1st year (2014) £36,000
2nd year (2014) £38,000
Holiday entitlement 25 days
% of trainees with a non-law
degree p.a. Varies

Post-qualification
Salary (2013) £59,000
% of trainees offered job on
qualification (2014) 94%

Overseas offices
Abu Dhabi, Beijing, Bratislava,
Brussels, Budapest, Copenhagen,
Dubai, Düsseldorf, Frankfurt,
The Hague, Hamburg, Helsinki,
Hong Kong, Lyon, Madrid, Milan,
Munich, Paris, Prague, Rome,
Shanghai, Singapore, Skander-
borg, Stockholm and Warsaw.

Bond Dickinson

St. Ann's Wharf, 112 Quayside, Newcastle upon Tyne NE1 3DX
Tel: (0844) 984 1500 Fax: (0844) 984 1501
Email: graduates@bonddickinson.com
Website: www.bonddickinson.com

Firm profile

It's been a year of change for Bond Dickinson since our merger last year. In that time we've continued to grow our business by strengthening client relationships, winning new business and investing in our people. It's been challenging but it's been exciting and we're looking forward to what the future now has in store for us. One thing is for certain, we're ambitious and committed to growing the business and that makes it an exciting time for anyone at the start of their legal career to be joining us.

The merger has given us a nationwide footprint and we now have more than 700 lawyers, 148 partners across 8 locations, namely Aberdeen, Bristol, Leeds, London, Plymouth, Southampton and Tees Valley.

Main areas of work

We are a full service law firm with a focus on 7 major sectors: energy, waste and natural resources; retail and fast moving consumer goods (FMCG); real estate; financial institutions; chemicals and manufacturing; transport and infrastructure; private wealth. We also have 3 other areas which are growing: technology; hospitality and leisure; education.

Trainee profile

The firm is looking for intellectually able, motivated and enthusiastic graduates from any discipline. Successful applicants will understand the need to provide practical, commercial advice to clients. You will share the firm's commitment to self-development and teamwork and its desire to provide clients with services which match their highest expectations.

Training environment

Our approach to trainee recruitment is one of long-term investment.

Trainees at Bond Dickinson will have an opportunity to spend six months in four Business Groups, gaining a real breadth of experience along the way. Your personal preferences are taken into consideration during the seat rotation process.

Our supervisors are trained and fully supported on an ongoing basis. You will have access to high quality work and senior client contacts. We regularly second trainees to our most high profile clients.

We keep our trainee intake relatively small which is great for you. You are generally one trainee in a team which provides you with some great opportunities. We're looking for trainees across six of our locations, namely, Bristol, Leeds, Newcastle, Plymouth, Southampton and Tees Valley, with opportunities to spend time in our Aberdeen or London offices.

Work placements

The firm's work placement weeks are part of the recruitment process and all applicants should apply online at www.bonddickinson.com.

The first stage is an online application form which assesses the core competencies we look for: analytical thinking, communication and influencing skills, an ability to build strong and lasting relationships, commercial awareness, an ability to adapt and innovate and drive and motivation. If you are successful in getting through this stage, you will be invited to complete an online SHL verbal reasoning assessment. The next step will be to attend an assessment day in the location of your choice.

The day consists of a number of exercises as well as time to meet with trainees, partners and other people from around the business. By the end of the day we hope that you can make an informed decision about whether we are right for you.

Partners 148
Total Staff 1,200
Total Trainees 45

Contact
Graduate Recruitment Team

Method of application
Apply online at
www.bonddickinson.com

Selection procedure
Online application, aptitude
and ability tests, assessment
day, presentation, interview

Closing date for 2017
31 July 2015 for 2017
31 January 2015 for Easter
and summer placements

Application
Training contracts are based
in Newcastle, Tees Valley,
Leeds, Bristol, Plymouth and
Southampton

Training
Salary
1st year Please see the firm's
website
2nd year Please see the firm's
website
Holiday entitlement 25 days
% of trainees with a non-law
degree p.a. 50-60%
No. of seats available abroad 0

Post-qualification
% of trainees offered job on
qualification (2013) 89%

Other offices
London, Aberdeen

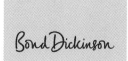

Boodle Hatfield LLP

240 Blackfriars Road, London SE1 8NW
Tel: (020) 7629 7411
Email: traineesolicitors@boodlehatfield.com
Website: www.boodlehatfield.com

Firm profile
Boodle Hatfield is a highly successful law firm which has been providing bespoke legal services for nearly 300 years. They still act for some of their very first clients and are proud to do so. The firm has grown into a substantial practice, serving the full spectrum of commercial and private clients, both domestically and internationally.

Main areas of work
The ethos of facilitating private capital activity and private businesses underpins the work of the whole firm. The interplay of skills between five major areas – private client and tax, property, family, corporate and litigation – makes Boodle Hatfield particularly well placed to serve these individuals and businesses.

Trainee profile
The qualities the firm looks for in its trainees are commitment, flexibility and the ability to work as part of a team. Applicants who have obtained, or who are predicted to obtain a 2:1 degree in any discipline and a minimum of AAB at A-level should apply.

Training environment
Trainees spend six months in up to four of the firm's main areas: property, corporate, family, private client and tax and litigation. Boodle Hatfield is well known for the high quality of its training. All trainees are involved in client work from the start and are encouraged to handle their own files personally as soon as they are able to do so, (with the appropriate supervision). The firm's trainees therefore have a greater degree of client contact than in many firms with the result that they should be able to take on more responsibility at an early stage. Trainees are given formal appraisals every three months which are designed as a two-way process and give trainees the chance to discuss their progress and to indicate where more can be done to help in their ongoing training and development.

Benefits
Private healthcare, life assurance, season ticket loan, pension scheme, enhanced maternity pay, conveyancing grant, permanent health insurance, employee assistance line, childcare vouchers, cycle to work scheme, give as you earn scheme.

Vacation placements
Two week placement in July, for which six students are accepted each year. Applicants should apply via the application form on the website at www.boodlehatfield.com. The form will be available from 1 November 2014.

Sponsorship & awards
LPC and GDL fees paid in full plus maintenance grant.

Partners 34
Other Fee-earners 50
Total Trainees 11

Contact
Nicky Goodwin
(020) 7079 8240

Method of application
Online application

Selection procedure
Interviews with the Training Principal, a Partner and the HR Director plus an ability test in verbal reasoning

Closing date for 2017
31 July 2015

Application
Training contracts p.a. 5
Required degree grade 2:1

Training
Salary
1st year £33,500
2nd year £35,500
Holiday entitlement 25 days

Post-qualification
Salary £54,000

Regional offices
Oxford

B P Collins LLP

Collins House, 32-38 Station Road, Gerrards Cross SL9 8EL
Tel: (01753) 889995 Fax: (01753) 889851
Email: jacqui.symons@bpcollins.co.uk
Website: www.bpcollins.co.uk

Firm profile

B P Collins LLP was established in 1966 and has expanded significantly to become one of Buckinghamshire's largest and best-known practices with an enviable reputation within the Thames Valley Region. Based to the west of London, our easily accessible offices in Gerrards Cross are close to the M25/M40 interchange and city rail links as well as Heathrow airport. This location enables us to deliver city quality legal services at highly competitive rates.

The firm's emphasis is on offering the full range of commercial and private client legal services to all our clients from business start-ups to multi-nationals, successful entrepreneurs to retired professionals.

Most of our partners and associates have worked in London but have now opted to work in more congenial surroundings and enjoy a higher quality lifestyle. Gerrards Cross is a very pleasant town surrounded by beautiful countryside but within 30 minutes commuting distance of central London. It is an affluent area and we are conveniently located to serve the extremely active business community which includes West London, Heathrow, Uxbridge, Slough and High Wycombe.

Types of Work
- Corporate and commercial
- Commercial and residential property
- Employment law
- Family law
- Litigation and dispute resolution
- Private client

Training programme

The firm aims to have six to eight trainee solicitors at different stages of their training contracts at all times. Trainees complete five months in four different practice groups of their choice. The final four months is spent in the practice group in which the trainee intends to specialise. The firm has a partner with overall responsibility for all trainees and each practice group has its own supervisor who is responsible for day to day supervision. Trainees are given early responsibility which includes plenty of client contact and professional work. There are regular meetings between the supervisors and trainees to monitor progress as well as a review meeting with the training partner both midway through and at the end of each practice group seat. Trainees are encouraged to participate in social and marketing events. The firm has a very high trainee retention rate.

Trainee profile

Bright, hard working, lateral thinkers who are good communicators with plenty of initiative will thrive in the B P Collins environment. You should be adaptable and self starting in approach and possess a degree of robustness to cope with the changing demands which you will face during the contract.

Partners 15
Assistant Solicitors 30
Total Trainees 7

Contact
HR Manager Mrs Jacqui Symons

Method of application
Handwritten covering letter & CV

Selection procedure
Screening interview & assessment day
Applications for the firm's 2016 intake will be accepted from 1st March to 31 May 2015

Application
Required degree grade 2:1, Grades A & B at A level

Training
Salary
1st year £25,370
2nd year £26,370

BPE Solicitors

St James' House, St James' Square, Cheltenham GL50 3PR
Tel: (01242) 224433 Fax: (01242) 574285
Email: bpe@bpe.co.uk
Website: www.bpe.co.uk

Firm profile

BPE thrives on being different to many other law firms.

It is prepared to pioneer new approaches to provide a better service for its clients, and invests time and resources in new teams where it sees potential for growth. The firm's partners do not hide behind closed doors but instead work alongside their assistants and trainees so you have an opportunity to learn from their experience every step of the way. Our only office is in Cheltenham but we have access points in Cirencester, Oxford, Bristol and London.

Main areas of work

BPE offers a full range of services including: corporate, commercial property, commercial, employment, commercial litigation, construction and engineering, private client, science and technology, and family. Clients range from blue-chip multi-nationals, property developers and entrepreneurs to charities and local authorities.

Trainee profile

BPE looks for high-calibre, commercially astute individuals with character. The firm's 'work hard, play hard' ethos makes it an ideal workplace for dedicated and driven lawyers-to-be who are keen to socialise with colleagues outside of the office. Applications from law and non-law graduates are welcome provided you have a 2:1 degree.

Training environment

BPE adopt a flexible approach to your training. If you suspect commercial property may be your eventual specialisation or you have a passion for corporate work the firm will try to accommodate you.

Trainees at the firm are required to spend a six month seat in each of the following disciplines and are encouraged to spend their last six-month seat in the team of their choice: corporate; commercial property; commercial litigation; commercial. Although your training will be handson, the firm offers a comprehensive trainee induction programme to help you understand the firm's style of working, its culture, policies and procedures.

Benefits

A contributory pension scheme, 25 days holiday, income protection to cover long-term illness, death in service benefits and a sabbatical scheme.

Sponsorship & awards

BPE supports trainees in attending the Professional Skills Course (PSC).

Equity Partners 6
Partners 15
Associates 7
Total Trainees 4

Contact
Amanda Coleman
(01242) 248231

Method of application
Application form, available on website

Selection procedure
Shortlisted applicants are invited to attend an open day in August/September each year. A final shortlist of applicants is invited to attend an assessment day which includes formal interview, case studies and a numerical and verbal reasoning test.

Closing date for 2017
31st July 2015

Application
Training contracts p.a. 4
Applications p.a. 100
% interviewed p.a. 25%
Required degree grade 2:1

Training
Salary
£20,000
Holiday entitlement 25 days

Post-qualification
Salary Market rate
% of trainees offered job
on qualification 80%

Brabners LLP

Horton House, Exchange Flags, Liverpool L2 3YL
Tel: (0151) 600 3000 Fax: (0151) 227 3185
55 King Street, Manchester M2 4LQ Tel: (0161) 236 5800 Fax: (0161) 228 6862
7-8 Chapel Street, Preston PR1 8AN Tel: (01772) 823921 Fax: (01772) 201918
Email: trainees@brabners.com
Website: www.brabners.com

Firm profile
One of the top North West commercial firms, Brabners LLP, in Liverpool, Manchester and Preston, has the experience, talent and prestige of a firm that has a 200-plus-year history. Brabners LLP is a dynamic, client-led specialist in the provision of excellent legal services to clients ranging from large plcs to private individuals.

Main areas of work
The LLP carries out a wide range of specialist legal services and Brabner's client base includes plcs, public sector bodies, banks and other commercial, corporate and professional businesses. The LLP's client focused departments include banking, corporate, commercial (including sports law), employment, litigation (including media and sports law), property (including housing association and construction) and private client.

Trainee profile
Graduates and those undertaking CPE or LPC, who can demonstrate intelligence, intuition, humour, approachability and commitment.

Training environment
The LLP is one of the few law firms that holds Investor in People status and has a comprehensive training and development programme. It has been listed 6 times in the Sunday Times Best 100 Employers to work for. Trainees are given a high degree of responsibility and are an integral part of the culture of the firm. Each trainee will have partner-level supervision. Personal development appraisals are conducted at three and six-monthly intervals to ensure that trainee progress is valuable and informed. The training programme is overseen by the firm's Director of Training, Dr Tony Harvey, and each centre has a designated Trainee Partner. It is not all hard work and the firm has an excellent social programme.

Sponsorship & awards
Assistance with LPC funding is available.

Partners 77
Associates 51
Assistant Solicitors 46
Fee Earners 50
Total Trainees 12

Contact
Liverpool office
Dr Tony Harvey
Director of Training, Risk and Compliance

Method of application
Online

Selection procedure
Interview & assessment day

Closing date for 2017
Apply by 30 June 2015 for training contracts commencing in September 2017

Application
Training contracts p.a. 6
Required degree grade
2:1 or post-graduate degree

Training
Salary
Not less than £22,000
Holiday entitlement 25 days

Offices
Liverpool, Manchester, Preston

Brabners

Bristows LLP

100 Victoria Embankment, London EC4Y 0DH
Tel: (020) 7400 8000 Fax: (020) 7400 8050
Email: trainee.recruitment@bristows.com
Website: www.training.bristows.com
Twitter: twitter.com/BristowsGrad

Firm profile

Bristows is a medium-sized firm that handles the kind of work that might normally be associated with only the very largest firms. Established over 175 years ago, the firm has built up a client list that includes leading businesses from a variety of sectors, whether global corporations, fast-growing start-ups, high profile charities or financial institutions. Working with so many ambitious organisations, the firm is often advising on issues that shape entire industries and on which a company's future might depend. For example, advising on whether the business is entitled to launch a new product or assisting a client to buy a rival business.

Main areas of work

Bristows has one of the foremost intellectual property practices in the world. The firm's lawyers are also recognised as leading authorities in a wide variety of other legal disciplines and as a firm offer a true breadth of expertise. These are our core practice areas: intellectual property; information technology and data protection; corporate; commercial disputes; real estate; regulatory; EU and competition; media and marketing; employment and tax.

Trainee profile

The size of the firm makes this an ideal environment for trainees. As part of a small intake, the trainees work alongside the partners dealing directly with clients right from the start. There's plenty of responsibility but this is matched by an extremely supportive and friendly culture so you're never far from encouragement and advice when you need it. The firm recognises that its reputation as a leading city law firm is entirely down to the individuals who work here, so it places great stock in attracting talented people and doing all it can to make sure they enjoy life at Bristows.

Training environment

Each year the firm asks up to 10 graduates to join the Bristows team. The firm is extremely selective because it is seeking graduates who will become Bristows' future partners. As part of such a select and high calibre intake, the firm will give you real responsibility earlier that you might perhaps expect. During the two year traineeship, you'll spend time in each of the firm's main departments, developing your skills and knowledge. You will also work closely with the partners and senior associates. Part of this training may also involve a UK secondment to the in-house legal department of one of the firm's leading multinational clients. With the international spread of the firm's clients, the probability of overseas travel is high, especially following qualification.

Benefits

We offer a flexible benefits package including: life assurance; pension scheme; private medical insurance; permanent health insurance; dental and critical illness insurance; holiday "buy and sell"; eye care; health assessment; employee assistance programme; cycle to work scheme; childcare voucher scheme; and season ticket loan.

Work experience

For opportunities to spend time with the firm during Winter, Spring and Summer, please see the firm's website for full details.

Sponsorship & awards

GDL and LPC fees paid in full, plus an annual maintenance grant of £8,000 for each as required.

Partners 39
Assistant Solicitors 84
Total Trainees 19

Contact
Graduate Resourcing Manager

Method of application
Online

Selection procedure
A telephone interview with HR, 2 individual interviews and a written exercise

Closing date for 2017
31 January 2015 for February interviews,
31 July 2015 for August interviews

Application
Training contracts p.a.
Up to 10
Applications p.a. 1,800
% interviewed p.a. 5%
Required degree grade
2:1 (preferred)

Training
Salary
1st year (2014) £36,000
2nd year (2014) £39,000
Holiday entitlement
23 days
% of trainees with a non-law degree p.a. 75%

Post-qualification
Salary (2014) £58,000
% of trainees offered job on qualification (2014) 88%

BRISTOWS

Browne Jacobson LLP

Nottingham, Birmingham, London, Manchester, Exeter
Tel: (0808) 178 9064
Email: traineeapplications@brownejacobson.com
Website: www.brownejacobsoncareers.com

Firm profile

Browne Jacobson is a full service national law firm with an impressive international, national and regional private and public sector client portfolio and the firm is committed to delivering exceptional client service.

Browne Jacobson is large enough to attract talent from across the country, but small enough to foster a supportive and flexible working environment. The firm's people are the key to its success and it has a track record of attracting and retaining the best.

Browne Jacobson focuses on long-term relationships which are friendly, flexible and straightforward. The firm's forward thinking environment and friendly and open culture mean that its people really enjoy working there. This allows good working relationships to develop and provides consistency for clients. It's a simple tactic yet one that works, which is why a large proportion of the firm's client base has been with the firm for a number of years.

Main areas of work

Browne Jacobson offers a comprehensive range of quality legal services, with expertise in four key sectors – commercial, public, health and insurance.

Trainee profile

Browne Jacobson is looking for talented law and non-law graduates who can bring with them enthusiasm, tenacity, commitment and client focus combined with a flexible and friendly attitude. For more information about life as a trainee visit their blog at www.traineetalk.co.uk or follow them on twitter at www.twitter.com/brownejtrainees.

Training environment

Trainees start with a comprehensive induction programme, a fast track professional skills course and then go on to undertake an extensive internal trainee development programme. They spend four periods of six months in some of the principle areas of the firm, gaining an overview of the practice. Trainees get great training, a friendly and supportive working environment and real career opportunities. They are also given quality work and exposure to clients from early on, but are supported in achieving results and recognised for their contribution.

Sponsorship & awards

LPC/GDL tuition fees paid, plus £5,000 maintenance grant. These will not be paid retrospectively.

Placement schemes

Browne Jacobson runs a placement scheme in the summer. The application deadline for a 2015 work placement is 17 March 2015. Apply online at www.brownejacobsoncareers.com

Benefits

Browne Jacobson offers a flexible benefits package with life assurance, income protection and pension as standard, plus private medical care, dental care, travel insurance, critical illness cover, childcare vouchers, Ride2Work and discounted shopping.

Partners 98
Associates 74
Assistant Solicitors 108
Total Trainees 16
Total Staff 738

Contact
Sophie Potter, HR Manager

Method of application
Apply online at
www.brownejacobsoncareers.com

Selection procedure
Telephone interview, assessment centre and partner interview

Closing date
31 July 2015 for 2017 training contracts

Application
Training contracts p.a. 10
Applications p.a. 500
% interviewed p.a. 4%

Training
Salary
1st year (2014) £25,500
2nd year (2014) £26,500
Holiday entitlement 25 days
% of trainees with a
non-law degree p.a. 60%

Post-qualification
Salary Market Rate
Holiday entitlement 25 days
% of trainees offered a job on qualification (2013) 100%

brownejacobson
law, less ordinary

Burges Salmon

1 Glass Wharf, Bristol BS2 0ZX
Tel: (0117) 939 2229 Fax: (0117) 902 4400
Email: frances.lambton@burges-salmon.com
Website: www.burges-salmon.com

Firm profile
Burges Salmon is consistently ranked among the UK's most successful commercial law firms. We pride ourselves on delivering an excellent standard of legal and business advice to our clients, which has led to many of our practice areas and sectors winning awards and recognition as best in class. Our national and international client base ranges from private individuals to government departments and FTSE 100 companies including The Crown Estate, Nationwide, Lloyds Banking Group, The Nuclear Decommissioning Authority and FirstGroup.

Main areas of work
We provide a full commercial service through five main departments: corporate and financial institutions (CFI); commercial; real estate; private client and wealth structuring; and disputes, environment and planning. Our sector specialisms include energy, infrastructure, financial services, real estate, food, farming and land and transport.

Trainee profile
Our people are ambitious and forward thinking with a determination to deliver top quality work for our clients. We therefore recruit hardworking and motivated individuals who are able to drive the business forward and contribute to our formidable reputation as a leading UK law firm.

We accept applications from penultimate and final year law students, final year non-law students, graduates and those who are looking for a change in career. Successful candidates will have achieved or expect to achieve a 2.1 at degree level in any discipline and have achievements which demonstrate the exceptional personal skills necessary to become a lawyer at Burges Salmon.

Training environment
Our training contract incorporates six seats which we believe ensures our trainees gain maximum exposure to our varied practice areas.

Trainees are given early responsibility balanced with an open door policy for advice and guidance from experienced supervisors. This enables our trainees to develop themselves as trusted business advisers quickly, contributing to the firm and deepening their professional expertise in a supportive and encouraging environment.

Vacation schemes
We run two assessment days in February and offer 36 places over 4 two-week vacation schemes during the summer. Individuals visit two departments of their choice supervised by a partner or senior solicitor. Current trainees run skills training sessions, sports and social events. Vacation schemes are open to to penultimate and final year law students, final year non-law students, graduates and those considering a change in career.

Remuneration: £250 per week.

Sponsorship & awards
The firm pays GDL and LPC fees. Maintenance grants of £7,000 are paid to LPC students and £14,000 to students studying for both the GDL and LPC (£7,000 p.a.).

Benefits
Annually reviewed competitive salary, 24 days paid annual leave, bonus scheme, pension scheme, private health care membership, life assurance, mobile phone, Christmas gift, corporate gym membership, sports and social club.

Partners 81
Assistant Solicitors 350
Trainees 46

Contact
Frances Lambton, Recruitment
Advisor (Trainee Solicitors)

Method of application
Application form available via
our website

Selection procedure
Assessment centres held in
August include a psychometric
test, a group exercise and a
written exercise. Successful
candidates will be invited back
for an interview conducted by
a partner and member of the
HR team.

Closing date for 2017
31 July 2015

Application
Training contracts p.a. 25
Applications p.a. 1,500 approx.
% interviewed p.a. 10%
Required degree grade 2:1 in
any discipline

Training
Salary
1st year (2013) £33,000
2nd year (2013) £34,000
Holiday entitlement 24 days

Post-qualification
Salary (2013) £42,500
% of trainees offered job
on qualification (2013) 91%

Capsticks

1 St George's Road, Wimbledon SW19 4DR
Tel: (020) 8780 2211 Fax: (020) 8780 4811
Email: career@capsticks.com
Website: www.capsticks.com

Firm profile

Capsticks is one of the leading providers of legal services within health and social care, professional discipline and social housing. The firm has over 230 fee earners across its 4 offices in London, Birmingham, Leeds and Southampton.

Main areas of work

The firm acts for over 200 clients, including all forms of NHS provider and commissioner organisations, the Department of Health, the NHSLA, regulatory bodies, charities, independent healthcare providers, housing associations, medical malpractice insurers and defence organisations.

Trainee profile

The firm is committed to recruiting the best people to maintain its market leading position. The firm plans to recruit eight (five in London, one in Birmingham, Leeds and Southampton) trainee solicitors in 2017 and welcomes applications from candidates who are either on course for or have achieved at least a 2:1 (or equivalent) in their undergraduate degree. The firm expects candidates to be committed to a career in healthcare law and to be able to demonstrate they are highly driven, but well rounded, team players, with good problem solving and communication skills.

Training environment

The firm's broad range of practice areas and health and social care clients enables it to give its trainees an opportunity to experience a wide variety of legal work. Trainees are therefore able to acquire an in-depth knowledge of both health and social care law and industry, in addition to developing the skills that any good lawyer needs.

The training contract is designed to give trainees maximum exposure to the work of the firm and trainees undertake seats in all of the firm's practice areas, including clinical law, corporate/commercial, dispute resolution, employment and real estate.

Benefits

Bonus scheme, 25 days holiday, pension contribution, income protection, private medical insurance, life assurance benefit, cycle to work scheme, corporate gym 'membership', childcare voucher scheme and season ticket loan.

Vacation placements

The firm's vacation scheme in each office runs from the end of June through to the middle of August and placements last for two weeks each. In order to be eligible for the 2015 vacation scheme you should be looking to secure a training contract with the firm in September 2017. The firm welcomes applications for a place on its 2015 vacation scheme between 10 November 2014 and 13 February 2015. Further details are available from the website.

The firm encourages all prospective trainee solicitors to participate in the vacation scheme as this is their primary means for selecting future trainee solicitors.

Sponsorship & awards

The firm offers its future trainees financial support for both the Graduate Diploma in Law and the Legal Practice Course.

Partners 51
Assistant Solicitors 163
Total Trainees 14
Other Fee-earners 44

Contact
HR department,
career@capsticks.com

Method of application
Online application form found under graduate recruitment page on website

Selection procedure
Interview with Partner and Head of HR

Closing date for 2017
11 August 2015

Application
Training contracts p.a. 8
Applications p.a. 508
% interviewed p.a. 9.4%
Required degree grade 2:1 or above

Training
Salary
1st year £30,000 p.a. (London)
2nd year £31,000 p.a.(London)

Holiday entitlement
25 days p.a.
% of trainees with a non-law degree p.a. 50%

Post-qualification
Salary (2014)
£47,000 p.a.
% of trainees offered job on qualification (2014) 100%

Charles Russell LLP

5 Fleet Place, London EC4M 7RD
Tel: (020) 7203 5000 Fax: (020) 7203 5307
Website: www.charlesrussell.co.uk

Partners 93	
Other fee earners 286	
Total trainees 37	
Total staff 653	

Contact
trainee.recruitment@charles-russell.co.uk

Method of application
Online application via www.charlesrussell.co.uk

Selection procedure
Assessment days includes an interview and other exercises designed to assess identified performance criteria.

Firm profile

Charles Russell is a leading law firm with a rich heritage and a clear vision of our future. We are headquartered in London and have UK regional and international offices providing efficient solutions through specialist teams.

We are highly regarded in our chosen areas of expertise, advising clients on the contentious and non-contentious business and personal legal issues they face.

The practice is well known as a friendly place to work and is committed to fostering a strong team spirit and encouraging personal development, which combined with good quality work and good quality people, makes it a winning combination.

Charles Russell people are actively involved in CSR; helping to promote and organise pro bono, volunteering and fundraising initiatives.

Main areas of work

There are experts in a number of legal service areas, including: corporate and commercial; employment and pensions; litigation and dispute resolution; family; private client; property.

These services are focussed on the following sector areas: charities and not-for-profit; energy and natural resources; family; healthcare; private wealth; property; retail and leisure; sport; technology, media and telecommunications; financial services.

Trainee profile

Trainees are expected to get involved with all aspects of the role; so aside from the drafting and research tasks, trainees can also expect to get more involved directly with clients, run their own files with close support, develop their commercial awareness and participate in business development.

The firm wants to recruit trainees of the highest standard. Trainees will usually have a consistent and strong academic background and will have demonstrated other key attributes outside of academia, such as teamwork, leadership, communication skills and initiative. The firm is looking for a diverse make up of trainees and welcomes individuals who will bring something different to the role.

Training environment

A small number of trainees are recruited and this allows trainees to undergo the best possible training.

Trainees can expect to be challenged and encouraged to go beyond their comfort zone, all with the full guidance, support and encouragement of the team. Formal training is in place from day one and the first two weeks are spent completing induction and Professional Skills Course modules. This training provides trainees with the key skills required for their first day in the service area.

Regular feedback is important and mid and end seat appraisals take place to discuss performance and to give guidance on how to develop further.

Benefits

BUPA; PHI; life assurance; pension; season ticket loan; 25 days' holiday; subsidised canteen (London).

Sponsorship & awards

GDL/LPC funding plus £6,000 maintenance grant (London) whilst you are at law school.

Charles Russell is to merge with Speechly Bircham on 1st November 2014 to become Charles Russell Speechlys. The merger will create one of the world's leading private wealth and business law firms with 170 partners and a total of 500 lawyers and combined revenues of £135m, placing it within the UK top 30 law firms.

Cleary Gottlieb Steen & Hamilton LLP

City Place House, 55 Basinghall Street, London EC2V 5EH
Tel: (020) 7847 6860 Fax: (020) 7600 1698
Email: longraduaterecruit@cgsh.com
Website: www.cgsh.com/careers/london

Firm profile

Founded in 1946 by lawyers committed to legal excellence, internationalism and diversity, Cleary Gottlieb Steen & Hamilton LLP is a leading international law firm with 16 closely integrated offices located in major financial and political centres around the world. For more than 60 years, the firm has been pre-eminent in shaping the internationalisation of the legal profession. Cleary's "one firm" approach enables them to deliver all their resources to all their clients, wherever in the world they may be.

Main areas of work

Core areas of practice in London are mergers and acquisitions, financing, capital markets, international litigation and arbitration, and competition. In addition, there are successful self-standing practices in tax, financial regulation and intellectual property and information technology. Lawyers who focus on different practices work closely together according to the requirements of a particular transaction.

Trainee profile

Cleary looks for candidates who are enthusiastic about the practice of law in a challenging and dynamic international setting. While academic excellence is a pre-requisite, Cleary places particular emphasis on recruiting candidates with whom they and their clients will enjoy working. A sense of humour is as important as the ability to think critically and creatively about cutting-edge legal issues.

Training environment

Cleary does not believe in a "one size fits all" training solution. By recruiting 10-14 trainees each year, Cleary are able to offer bespoke training that is tailored to their trainees' interests, experience and aptitudes. Nor do they believe that the transition from trainee solicitor to associate occurs overnight on qualification. So, they encourage their trainee solicitors to accept increased responsibility as soon as they are ready to do so. Given appropriate levels of supervision and support, their trainees operate as lawyers from the day that they join Cleary.

Benefits

5% employer pension contribution, 25 day's holiday, fully funded gym membership, private health insurance (personal and family), life insurance of twice annual salary, long-term disability insurance, employee assistance programme and subsidised staff restaurant.

Vacation schemes

The firm's London office offers 35 vacation places each year (five in winter, ten in spring and ten in each of two summer schemes). The firm actively encourages all candidates that are considering applying for a trainee solicitor position to undertake a vacation placement with the firm. Applications for winter vacation placements should be received by 15 November. The deadline for spring and summer vacation scheme applications is 28 January.

Sponsorship & awards

Cleary funds the LPC for all future trainee solicitors. For non-law graduates, the firm also funds the GDL. A maintenance grant of £8,000 is paid for each year of professional study.

Trainees 24

Partners 197
(20 in London)

Total Staff 2500
(200 in London)

Contact
Graduate Recruitment

Method of application
Cover letter and CV

Selection procedure
Future trainees are primarily selected from among those having completed a vacation scheme with the firm

Closing date for 2017
July 31 2015

Application
Training contracts p.a. 10-14
Required degree grade
High 2:1

Training
Salary
1st year £42,000
2nd year £47,000

Post-qualification
Salary £96,000

Overseas offices
New York, Washington DC, Paris, Brussels, Moscow, Frankfurt, Cologne, Rome, Milan, Hong Kong, Beijing, Buenos Aires, Sao Paulo, Abu Dhabi and Seoul

A-Z of Solicitors

Clyde & Co

The St Botolph Building, 138 Houndsditch, London EC3A 7AR
Tel: (020) 7876 5555 Fax: (020) 7876 5111
Email: theanswers@clydeco.com
Website: www.careers.clydeco.com/trainees

Firm profile

Clyde & Co is an international law firm with a pioneering heritage and a resolute focus on its core sectors of aviation, energy, healthcare, infrastructure, industrials, insurance, professional practices, shipping and trade. With over 1,440 lawyers operating from 37 offices and associated offices across six continents, the firm advises corporations, financial institutions, private individuals and governments on a wide range of contentious and transactional matters.

Main areas of work

Core sectors: aviation, energy, healthcare, industrials, infrastructure, insurance, professional practices, shipping, trade and commodities.

Core practice areas: commercial, competition, corporate, dispute resolution, employment, finance, global governance, insolvency and reorganisation, international arbitration, projects and construction, real estate.

Trainee profile

An excellent academic record (including a 2:1 degree) is expected but equally important are your commercial and transferable skills. We look for trainees who take an interest in our clients' business, can apply their knowledge and intellect to practical legal problems, have the confidence to build relationships with clients and colleagues and are committed to a career in commercial law.

Training environment

You will gain early responsibility and be supported through close personal supervision and day-to-day coaching complemented by a wide range of training courses. You will undertake four six-month seats, which will cover both transactional and contentious work. You may also choose to be seconded to one of our overseas offices or have the opportunity for a client secondment.

Benefits

An optional £1,000 interest free loan on joining, pension, life assurance, dental insurance, private medical insurance, subsidised gym membership, interest-free season ticket loan, 25 days holiday per year, we also have a subsidised restaurant.

Vacation placements

The firm runs two-week summer and Easter schemes. Applications are made online at www.apply4law.com/clydeco. The closing date for applications is 31 January 2015. The vacation students have the opportunity to get involved in a range of training sessions along with a tour of Lloyd's of London and the Royal Courts of Justice. In addition to working in their chosen practice group, students have the opportunity to network with employees at a variety of social events.

Sponsorship & awards

GDL and LPC fees paid plus a maintenance grant.

Partners 297*
Assistant Solicitors 1,497*
Trainees 100*
*denotes worldwide figures

Contact
Caroline Walsh, Head of Legal Trainee Recruitment and Development

Method of application
Online

Selection procedure
Assessment day

Closing date for 2017
31 July 2015

Application
Training contracts p.a. 45-50
Applications p.a. 2000
% interviewed p.a. 10%
Required degree grade 2:1

Training
Salary
1st year £36,000
2nd year £38,000
Holiday entitlement 25 days

Post-qualification
Salary (2013) £59,000
% of trainees offered job on qualification (2013) 92%

Overseas offices
Abu Dhabi, Atlanta, Beijing, Cape Town, Caracas, Chongqing, Dar es Salaam, Doha, Dubai, Hong Kong, Jakarta*, Johannesburg, Madrid, Melbourne, Montreal, Mumbai*, Nantes, New Delhi*, New Jersey, New York, Paris, Perth, Piraeus, Riyadh*, São Paulo, San Francisco, Shanghai, Singapore, St Petersburg*, Sydney, Toronto, Tripoli
*associate offices
Alliances: Mongolia - Khan Lex Advocates, Zimbabwe - Scanlen and Holderness

CLYDE&CO

CMS Cameron McKenna

Mitre House, 160 Aldersgate Street, London EC1A 4DD
Tel: (020) 7367 3000 Fax: (020) 7367 2000
Email: gradrec@cms-cmck.com
Website: www.cms-cmck.com/chambers

Firm profile
What's in a name? A lot, when it's CMS. Firstly, CMS Cameron McKenna forms part of a leading network of firms known as CMS. We have 58 offices in 32 countries, with the most extensive footprint in Europe of any other firm. Secondly, we take a genuine, client-focused approach that attracts some of the world's biggest organisations. Last but not least, we know how to take talented people much, much further – geographically, intellectually and professionally.

Main areas of work
Our lawyers advise international clients across all types of commercial law, including corporate, banking and finance, energy, intellectual property and real estate.

Trainee profile
We welcome both non-law and law graduates who can contribute fresh thinking, an international outlook and formidable communication and analytical skills. The work we do is intellectually demanding and professionally stretching – something you'll find provides you with an excellent grounding for your career in law.

Training environment
We offer two-year training contracts in London, Bristol, Aberdeen, Edinburgh and Glasgow. During this time you'll undertake four seats across our broad range of practice areas, such as energy, intellectual property, corporate or EU competition. Alongside this, you're guaranteed to spend a seat outside of your 'home' office – an exciting prospect. You might be seconded to one of our top clients based in London or Europe, or spend time in one of our international offices including Rio de Janeiro, Edinburgh or Moscow.

Vacation placements
Places for 2015: 80 over spring and summer. Duration: 2 weeks. Remuneration: £250pw. Closing date for applications: 31 January 2015.

Benefits
Gym membership/subsidy, life assurance, pension scheme with firm contributions, private healthcare, season ticket loan, confidential care line, subsidised restaurant and 25 days' holiday with options to buy a further five days. You are also guaranteed to spend a seat outside your home office on a client, regional or international secondment.

Sponsorship & awards
The firm will cover fees for the GDL and LPC (or PEAT for Scotland) and provide you with a maintenance grant of up to £7,500. Please see our website for further details.

Partners 800 (global)
Assistant Solicitors 3,000
Total Trainees 160

Contact
Jess Heading (020) 7367 3000

Method of application
Online

Selection procedure
Stage one: online application and psychometric testing. Stage two: assessment day (commercial analysis, group exercises and partner interview)

Closing dates
Training contracts
London & Bristol
31 July 2015
Aberdeen, Edinburgh & Glasgow
11 October 2015
All vacation schemes
31 January 2015

Application
Training contracts p.a. 80
Applications p.a. 1,000
% interviewed p.a. 10-15%
Required degree grade 2:1

Training
Salary
1st year
London £38,000
Bristol £32,000
Scotland £22,500
2nd year
London £43,000
Bristol £34,000
Scotland £25,000

Post-qualification
Salary
London £63,000
Bristol £45,500
Scotland Competitive
% of trainees offered job on qualification 82%

Overseas/regional offices
London, Bristol, Aberdeen, Edinburgh, Glasgow, Prague, Rio de Janeiro, Bucharest, Moscow

A-Z of Solicitors

Collyer Bristow LLP

4 Bedford Row, London WC1R 4TF
Tel: (020) 7242 7363 Fax: (020) 7405 0555
Email: recruitment@collyerbristow.com
Website: www.collyerbristow.com

Firm profile

This long-established London firm provides a complete legal service to businesses and private individuals. Collyer Bristow is committed to providing a commercial and innovative approach to clients' legal issues, combined with a discrete and personal service, often not available from a large city practice. The firm's client base includes: multinationals, public and private companies, partnerships, entrepreneurs, public sector organisations and high net worth individuals, both in the UK and throughout the world.

The firm's Geneva office provides a base from which to serve clients in Switzerland, Europe and worldwide and, increasingly, to service its expanded private client offering.

The firm is well known for its ground-breaking in-house art gallery and is passionate in its support for the contemporary arts.

Main areas of work

Collyer Bristow has an impressive client base in such diverse sectors as real estate, media and sports, hotels and leisure, financial services and fashion, as well as a substantial private client practice. The firm's main areas of practice include corporate and commercial, real estate, dispute resolution, tax and estate planning, family, defamation and reputation management.

Trainee profile

The firm is looking for individuals who are able to demonstrate a strong academic performance, having gained a 2:1 or at least on track to achieve this. Successful candidates will be motivated individuals who possess strong commercial awareness, common sense and an ability to understand a client's needs.

Training environment

The firm's trainees spend six months in four of the firm's five key practice areas, working with a range of people from senior partners to more recently qualified solicitors. The firm has mentoring, training and appraisal programmes which nurture the development of technical expertise and client advisory skills. Trainees are encouraged at an early stage to take responsibility for their own files and to participate in managing the client's work with appropriate supervision.

Benefits

25 days holiday and usual benefits.

Partners 31
Trainees 8
Total Staff 135

Contact
recruitment@collyerbristow.com

Method of application
Application form

Selection procedure
Testing and interview

Training
Salary
1st year (2013) £28,500
2nd year (2013) £31,500
(Both reviewed annually)

Covington & Burling LLP

265 Strand, London WC2R 1BH
Tel: (020) 7067 2000 Fax: (020) 7067 2222
Email: graduate@cov.com
Website: www.cov.com

Firm profile

Covington & Burling's LLP London office, situated next to the Royal Courts of Justice, encompasses a broad range of expertise and practice areas. The office, established in 1988, combines deep industry knowledge with lawyers experienced in advising on a wide variety of pioneering legal issues. The firm has over 800 lawyers globally, in offices in Beijing, Brussels, London, New York, San Diego, San Francisco, Seoul, Shanghai, Silicon Valley and Washington.

Covington has been rated a Top Ranked Leading Law Firm in Chambers UK 2014 and appears in The Lawyer Top 30 International Law Firm, as well as Legal Business Global 100 surveys.

At Covington & Burling, you will have an opportunity to work on cutting-edge deals for international and UK corporates such as Microsoft, Merck and Samsung, Fortune 100 businesses and leading technology, life sciences and media companies.

Main areas of work

Corporate advisory (including capital markets, M&A, finance, private equity, venture capital and funds), commercial litigation, data privacy, employment, financial services, insurance coverage disputes, intellectual property, internal investigations and compliance, international arbitration, life sciences, tax, technology and media. In addition, all our lawyers, including trainees, are encouraged to undertake pro bono work.

Trainee profile

We are looking for consistently high academic results (on target for a 2:1 degree or above and with strong A level results), commercial awareness, strong interpersonal skills and ability to work well in a team.

Training environment

You will do four six-month seats, rotating between departments. All trainees will undertake a seat in corporate and a seat in dispute resolution. We can offer optional seats in the following areas: employment, intellectual property, life sciences regulatory, life sciences transactional, tax, technology and media. Client secondments may also be available.

We aim to distinguish our trainee programme by offering a genuine support network which includes assigning associate buddies and undertaking regular performance reviews. We have an excellent record of retaining trainees on qualification and we aim to recruit trainees who are interested in making a long term commitment to the firm.

Benefits

Private medical insurance, life assurance, permanent health insurance, pension, 25 days holiday, season ticket loan and access to an employee assistance programme. We also have an active social calendar which includes regular firm drinks and sports activities.

Vacation placements

Summer Placements for 2015: We offer up to 24 summer placements, split into three, week-long programmes. You will be paid £300 per week. Apply by 31 January 2015, online at www.cov.com.

Sponsorship

GDL and LPC course fees and a maintenance grant of up to £8,000 are paid.

Partners 260*	
Associate Lawyers & Others 627*	
Total Trainees London	
2010	14
2011	13
2012	13
2013	14
2014	14

*denotes worldwide figures

Contact
Graduate Recruitment Team
(020) 7067 2000
graduate@cov.com

Method of application
Online application form
See website www.cov.com

Selection procedure
1st & 2nd interview

Closing date for 2017
31 July 2015

Application
Training contracts p.a. 6
Required degree grade 2:1

Training
Salary
1st year £40,000
2nd year £44,000
Holiday entitlement 25 days

Post-qualification
Salary currently £80,000 p.a.

Overseas offices
Beijing, Brussels, New York, San Diego, San Francisco, Seoul, Shanghai, Silicon Valley, Washington

COVINGTON
COVINGTON & BURLING LLP

Cripps LLP

Wallside House, 12 Mount Ephraim Road, Tunbridge Wells TN1 1EG
Tel: (01892) 515 121 Fax: (01892) 544 878
Email: graduates@cripps.co.uk
Website: www.cripps.co.uk
Twitter: @crippslaw

Firm profile

Cripps is a key regional law firm serving clients nationally and internationally from offices in Kent and London. Recognised countrywide for both its commercial and private client work, the firm focuses on wealthier families, entrepreneurial businesses and the real estate sector.

Cripps has a particularly strong client service culture. With over 300 people, it is nonhierarchical, open and highly flexible. It works closely and sympathetically with clients, offering commercially astute solutions. Everything is designed around the needs of individual clients, with the firm adapting itself to each client and their particular objectives.

The unusual combination of personal, responsive service and the highest quality of advice is equally attractive to large businesses and institutions as it is to entrepreneurial organisations and wealthy individuals.

This makes Cripps an excellent choice for talented recruits. The firm is large enough to offer the right breadth of experience but not so big that individuals get lost in the machine. Our lawyers have a great deal of variety, working for a range of different client types, building close and highly effective personal relationships with them. Your six trainee seats could see you working with wealthy families, the owners of entrepreneurial businesses and private capital, and senior in-house lawyers at major corporates.

Internally, you'll meet and know all leaders and senior managers; you'll be part of a firm that knows where it's going, that's in control of its own destiny and that's nimble enough to flex and adapt to a rapidly changing legal market.

You'll work with lawyers of the highest quality (either home-grown or from City or other eminent firms). Business services professionals will work closely with you to ensure you're properly supported.

Main areas of work

Commercial 23%, dispute resolution 17%, private client 16%, property 44%.

Trainee profile

Cripps is looking for confident and lively people who want to work in a nonhierarchical, energetic and positive business. Dynamic and multi-disciplinary teams are looking for people who can use their intelligence and interpersonal skills to get clients where they need to be. Many clients are successful entrepreneurs and the firm needs lawyers who can work with them as part of their team.

Training environment

The firm offers a comprehensive induction course, a well structured training programme, frequent one to one reviews, regular in-house courses and seminars, good levels of support and real responsibility.

The training programme is broader than most other firms and typically includes six seats in both commercial and private client areas. Trainees usually share a room with a partner or an associate and gain varied and challenging first hand experience.

Sponsorship awards

Discretionary LPC funding: Fees – 50% interest free loan, 50% bursary.

Partners 47
Assistant Solicitors 82
Total Trainees 16

Contact
Emma Brooks
Head of HR

Method of application
Application form available on website

Selection procedure
First stage interview with a partner and an associate. Successful candidates are invited back to a second stage interview with the Managing Partner, Divisional Partners and the Head of HR.

Closing date for 2017
31 July 2015

Application
Training contracts p.a. 8
Applications p.a. up to 200
% interviewed p.a. 20%
Required degree grade 2:1

Training
Holiday entitlement 25 days
% of trainees with a non-law degree p.a. 19%

Post-qualification
% of trainees offered job on qualification (2013) 100%
% of assistants/associates (as at 2013) who joined as trainees 58%
% of partners (as at 1/5/2013) who joined as trainees 16%

A-Z of Solicitors

Curtis, Mallet-Prevost, Colt & Mosle LLP

99 Gresham Street, London EC2V 7NG
Tel: (020) 7710 9800 Fax: (020) 7710 9801
Website: www.curtis.com

Firm profile

Curtis is one of the longest established international firms in either London or New York. It was one of the first US firms to open in Mexico City in 1985, remains the only US-headquartered law firm licensed to practice in Oman and was the first international law firm to open an office in Turkmenistan. The firm operates out of 16 offices across Europe, the Middle East, Asia and the Americas.

Main areas of work

Curtis' core practices in London are: international arbitration, investment management and corporate/commercial law. The latter includes M&A; private placements; public offerings; venture capital and private equity; fund formation; joint ventures; infrastructure projects; and debt finance. The firm is well known for representing state-owned energy companies and governments around the world.

Trainee profile

Curtis provides an international and dynamic environment. Applicants will need energy, enthusiasm and an ability to get on well with people of all kinds, as well as excellent academics. A proactive approach is a plus, as are languages and a willingness to travel.

Training environment

Curtis' London office is small and friendly as well as diverse and internationally minded. As a key hub for the firm's European and African activities, many of our overseas partners and colleagues visit regularly. Instead of a traditional four seat method, we offer flexible but non-rotational training. This allows for a highly tailored approach that plays to individual interests and talents. Our second year trainees spend up to ten weeks participating in the summer associate programme in New York.

Benefits

The range of benefits includes private health care, travel season ticket loan, pension and income protection.

Partners 6
Counsel 1
Associates 9
Total Trainees 2

Contact
Tuula Davis, Office Manager
(020) 7710 9800

Method of application
Candidates should e-mail a CV and cover letter to
recruitmentlondon@curtis.com

Selection procedure
Three rounds of interviews with partners and the chance to meet current associates and trainees.

Closing date for 2015
Applicants for September 2015 should apply by end March 2015.

Application
Training contracts p.a. 2
Applications p.a. c. 300
% interviewed p.a. 8%
Required degree grade 2:1

Training
Salary
1st year £38,000
2nd year salary £42,000
Holiday entitlement 25 days

Post-qualification
100% of trainees offered job on qualification

Overseas and regional offices
We have offices in Almaty, Ashgabat, Astana, Beijing, Buenos Aires, Dubai, Frankfurt, Houston, Istanbul, London, Mexico City, Milan, Muscat, New York, Paris and Washington DC.

A-Z of Solicitors

CURTIS
Curtis, Mallet-Prevost, Colt & Mosle LLP

Davis Polk & Wardwell London LLP

99 Gresham Street London EC2V 7NG
Tel: (020) 7418 1300 Fax: (020) 7418 1400
Website: careers.davispolk.com

Firm profile
Davis Polk is a global law firm. For more than 160 years, its lawyers have advised industry-leading companies and major financial institutions on their most challenging legal and business matters. Davis Polk ranks among the world's preeminent law firms across the entire range of its practice. With more than 750 lawyers in New York, Menlo Park, Washington DC, London, Paris, Madrid, Hong Kong, Beijing, Tokyo and Sao Paulo, the firm operates from key business centres around the world to provide clients with seamlessly integrated legal services of the highest calibre.

Main areas of work
We advise European companies, private equity firms, financial institutions and governments on all areas of business and finance, and we are regularly involved in the largest and most important securities offerings and M&A transactions in Europe. Trainee profile We seek to hire applicants from a variety of backgrounds with outstanding academic and nonacademic achievements, personal skills and creativity, and with a demonstrated willingness to take initiative. We strive to find exceptional lawyers who share our commitment to excellence and who will be collaborative and supportive colleagues.

Trainee profile
We seek to hire applicants from a variety of backgrounds with outstanding academic and non-academic achievements, personal skills and creativity, and with a demonstrated willingness to take initiative. We strive to find exceptional lawyers who share our commitment to excellence and who will be collaborative and supportive colleagues.

Training environment
Davis Polk trainees will work closely with and learn from our senior lawyers in London and in our offices around the world as we advise leading British, European and global corporations across the spectrum of their most complex legal matters. Given the quality of instruction, the meaningful legal experience gained on major global transactions and the opportunity to be a part of a dynamic and rapidly expanding practice at one of the world's truly preeminent law firms, there is no better place than Davis Polk for an aspiring solicitor to begin a career. Davis Polk trainees will also have the opportunity to work for a period in our New York office.

Benefits
Private medical insurance, life insurance, pension scheme, season ticket loan, subsidised gym membership, Employee Assistance Programme.

Vacation schemes
Davis Polk offers two-week vacation schemes in the summer for students interested in training contracts. During each vacation scheme, students will have the opportunity to work on international transactions for a variety of the firm's clients and attend training programs designed to teach skills required to become an effective solicitor as well as information sessions focused on the work of our UK practice. Students will also have the opportunity to experience Davis Polk's culture through interactions with lawyer mentors and attendance at social events. We will be accepting applications for 2015 summer vacation schemes (please visit our website at www.careers.davispolk. com for information on how to apply) from 1st November 2014 through to 28th January 2015. We expect to offer approximately 20 places on our vacation schemes in 2015.

Sponsorship & awards
GDL and LPC fees and maintenance grants are paid.

Partners 10 (over 150 world-wide)
Other fee-earners Over 40 (over 700 worldwide)
Total trainees 5

Contact
martha.jeacle@davispolk.com

Method of application
Please visit our website at careers.davispolk.com for information on how to apply

Selection procedure
Cover letter and accompanying CV followed by an interview

Closing date for 2017
31 July 2015

Application
Training contracts p.a.
Approx. 4
Required degree grade 2:1 or higher

Training
Salary
1st year £50,000
2nd year £55,000

Post-qualification
Compensation £100,000

Overseas offices
New York, Menlo Park, Washington DC, São Paulo, Paris, Madrid, Tokyo, Beijing and Hong Kong

A-Z of Solicitors

Dechert LLP

160 Queen Victoria Street, London EC4V 4QQ
Tel: (020) 7184 7000 Fax: (020) 7184 7001
Email: application@dechert.com
Website: www.dechert.com www.careers.dechert.com

Firm profile
Dechert LLP is a dynamic international law firm, with 2,000 professionals across the USA, Europe, Middle East and Asia. London is the third largest office, after Philadelphia and New York.

Main areas of work
The London office has particular strengths in investment funds, corporate and securities (including private equity), litigation (including international dispute resolution, white collar and securities, EU trade and government affairs and arbitration) and finance and real estate; and smaller teams in employment, IP and tax.

Trainee profile
Dechert looks for enthusiasm, intelligence, an ability to find practical solutions and for powers of expression and persuasion. Undergraduates and graduates from any discipline are welcome to apply.

Training environment
The highly personalised six seat rotation system allows trainees to structure their training contract to their interests and aspirations and allows opportunity for secondments to overseas offices as well as to clients. Your seat plan and professional development are guided by the graduate recruitment manager, the graduate recruitment partners and your dedicated trainee partner. Your trainee partner is allocated to you when you start your training contract and acts as a sounding board and a source of support until you qualify.

Vacation placements
Dechert runs a two week vacation placement in the summer and Insight Days in the spring. During our placements visitors are supervised by a partner or senior associate and they undertake a variety of tasks such as research projects and attending client meetings. Training sessions are also hosted throughout the scheme, on a range of topics, such as presentation and client pitch skills. The closing date for applications is 31 January 2015. The Insight Days are designed to give participants an overview of the firm, its practice areas and its work. Participants also have the opportunity to meet trainees and associates and take part in a legal case study.

Sponsorship & awards
The firm pays law school fees plus a £10,000 maintenance grant.

Partners 41*
Assistant Solicitors 87*
Total Trainees 24*
*denotes London figure

Contact
application@dechert.com or
Graduate Recruitment Team
020 7184 7576

Method of application
Online

Selection procedure
An assessment morning or afternoon which includes interviews with partners, associates and recruiters and written tests

Closing date for 2017
31 July 2015

Application
Training contracts p.a. 12
Applications p.a. 500
% interviewed p.a. 5-10%
Required degree grade 2:1 (or capability of attaining a 2:1)

Training
Salary Current trainee salaries as of September 2014 £41,000 and £46,000. Trainee salaries are reviewed annually.
Holiday entitlement 25 days
% of trainees with a non-law degree p.a. Varies
No. of seats available abroad p.a. Varies

Post-qualification
Salary £69,000
% of trainees offered job on qualification 70% (2014)

Overseas offices
Almaty, Austin, Beijing, Boston, Brussels, Charlotte, Chicago, Dubai, Dublin, Frankfurt, Hartford, Hong Kong, LA, Luxembourg, Moscow, Munich, New York, Orange County, Paris, Philadelphia, Princeton, San Francisco, Silicon Valley, Tblisi, Washington

A-Z of Solicitors

Dentons

One Fleet Place, London EC4M 7WS
Tel: (020) 7242 1212 Fax: (020) 7320 6555
Email: graduaterecruitment@dentons.com
Website: www.dentons.com/uk-graduates

Firm profile

Dentons is a global firm driven to provide a competitive edge in an increasingly complex and interconnected world. It was formed in March 2013 by the combination of international law firm Salans LLP, Canadian law firm Fraser Milner Casgrain LLP (FMC) and international law firm SNR Denton. Dentons is built on the solid foundations of these three highly valued law firms.

Dentons' clients now benefit from approximately 2,600 lawyers and professionals in more than 75 locations spanning 50-plus countries across Africa, Asia Pacific, Canada, Central Asia, Europe, the Middle East, Russia and the CIS, the UK and the US who are committed to challenge the status quo and offer creative, dynamic business and legal solutions.

Main areas of work

Dentons offers an international legal practice focused on quality in the following industry sectors: energy, transport and infrastructure, financial institutions and funds, government, health and life sciences, insurance, manufacturing, real estate, retail and hotels, technology, media and telecommunications.

Trainee profile

There's no typical candidate for our training contract programme. The expertise within our firm is as diverse as the needs of our global clients – and we want to keep it that way. We look for people with a wide range of skills, aptitudes and personalities, with the potential to contribute to our growing success.

Being a team player is important as is having the drive and ambition to succeed in a highly demanding work environment.

We need to see a strong record of academic and extra-curricular achievement. We accept degrees in any discipline (minimum 2:1 or equivalent) and we look for a minimum of AAB at 'A' level.

Training environment

As a trainee you will undertake four six-month seats, including a contentious seat or attending an external litigation course. Your transactional experience will include banking (if in London) and corporate, construction or real estate (if in Milton Keynes). Middle East trainees will spend two seats in the UK and two in the Middle East.

Benefits

You'll earn a competitive salary. In London £39,000 in your first year, rising to £44,000 in your second year. In Milton Keynes you'll earn £25,500 in your first year, rising to £27,500 in your second. On top of that, during your training contract you'll enjoy numerous benefits – and you'll get to choose the ones that best fit your lifestyle, from 24 days' holiday, private health cover, income protection insurance, life assurance, pension and many others.

Vacation placements

We offer a one-week summer scheme in London for law students (July) and in Milton Keynes for both law and non-law students (July).

In London we also offer open days for final year non-law students and for first year law students.

These placements consist of business games, department visits and social events, giving potential trainees an insight into commercial law and our way of life at Dentons.

Sponsorship & awards

We'll pay your GDL/LPC law school fees during actual years of study, as well as study maintenance grants of £5,000 per year of study (£6,000 in London).

Partners 157
Fee-earners 404
Total Trainees 45

Contact
Alexandra Mundy

Method of application
Online application form

Selection procedure
Selection test; occupational personality questionnaire; first interview; second interview and case study

Closing date for 2017
Non-law – 31 March 2015
Law – 31 July 2015

Application
Training contracts p.a. 20
Applications p.a. 1,000
% interviewed p.a. 10%
Required degree grade 2:1

Training
Salary in London
1st year £39,000
2nd year £44,000
Salary in Milton Keynes
1st year £25,500
2nd year £27,500
Holiday entitlement 24 days
% of trainees with a
non-law degree p.a. 30%
No. of seats available
abroad p.a. Currently 2

Post-qualification
Salary (2014) £61,000
% of trainees offered job
on qualification (2014) 85%

Dentons Offices
London and Milton Keynes
in the UK and across Europe,
Middle East, CIS, America,
Canada, Africa, South East
Asia and Central Asia. For
more location details please
see our website.

DENTONS

DLA Piper UK LLP

3 Noble Street, London EC2V 7EE
Tel: (0870) 0111 111
Email: recruitment.graduate@dlapiper.com
Website: www.dlapipergraduates.co.uk

Firm profile

DLA Piper is a global law firm with 4,200 lawyers located in more than 30 countries. In the UK the firm provides full service legal advice from London and the other major business centres. DLA Piper was built to serve clients wherever in the world they do business – quickly, efficiently and with a genuine knowledge of both local and international considerations.

Main areas of work

DLA Piper is organised to provide clients with a range of essential business advice, not just on large scale mergers and acquisitions and banking deals but also on people and employment, commercial dealings, litigation, insurance, real estate, IT, intellectual property, plans for restructuring and tax.

Trainee profile

Within their trainee cohort DLA Piper requires a diverse group of talented individuals who have a consistently strong academic performance, formidable commercial acumen, who are articulate, ambitious and driven with sharp minds, enthusiasm and intellectual curiosity.

Training environment

Trainees complete four six-month seats and are given an opportunity to express the areas of law they would like to experience during their training contracts. They also have the opportunity to do a seat abroad, or a client secondment.

The firm's approach to learning and development, which encourages people to take on early responsibility, combined with an open door policy and their award winning training programmes, provide trainees with an excellent foundation on which to build their careers.

Sponsorship & awards

Where training contracts are secured prior to course completion, DLA Piper fully fund the LPC and GDL, as well as offering a maintenance grant.

Work placement scheme

There are 130 placements offered by DLA Piper. Participants are fully immersed into life at the firm for two weeks. They are given real work to develop their skills and demonstrate their ability. They also take part in work shadowing, court visits, bespoke presentations, group activities and social events.

Contact
Sally Carthy, Head of Graduate Recruitment

Method of application
Online

Selection procedure
Interviews, group exercise, assessment day

Closing date for 2017
31 July 2015

Application
Training contracts p.a. 80
Applications pa 3,800
% Interviewed p.a. 13%
Required degree grade 2.1

Training
Salary
1st year
£40,000 (London)
£26,500 (English Regions)
£23,000 (Scotland)
2nd year
£44,000 (London)
£28,500 (English Regions)
£25,000 (Scotland)
Holiday entitlement 25 days

Post-qualification
Salary
£62,000 (London)
£38,500 (English Regions)
£34,000 (Scotland)
% of trainees offered a job on qualification 80% (2014)

Overseas offices
Australia, Austria, Bahrain, Belgium, Brazil, China, Czech Republic, France, Georgia, Germany, Hong Kong, Hungary, Italy, Japan, Korea, Kuwait, Mexico, Netherlands, Norway, Oman, Poland, Qatar, Romania, Russia, Saudi Arabia, Singapore, Slovak Republic, Spain, Thailand, UAE, Ukraine, USA

A-Z of Solicitors

DLA PIPER

DWF LLP

1 Scott Place, 2 Hardman Street, Manchester M3 3AA
Tel: (0333) 320 2220 Fax: (0333) 320 4440
Email: trainees@dwf.co.uk
Website: www.dwf.co.uk

Firm profile

Described by market commentators as "blazing a trail", DWF is one of the UK's largest law firms and has an award-winning reputation for client service excellence and effective operational management.

Independently ranked 1st of all top 20 law firms for the quality of its legal advice and joint 1st of all national law firms for its service delivery and responsiveness, DWF has recently been named 'Best Managed National Firm' at the Managing Partners' Forum Awards for Management Excellence 2014, which recognise management excellence in professional services firms across Europe.

Main areas of work

Employing over 2,500 people across 12 locations in the UK and Ireland, the firm has core strengths in insurance, corporate and banking, real estate and litigation, and in-depth industry expertise in six chosen sectors including central and local government; energy and industrials; financial services; retail, food and hospitality; technology; and transport.

DWF is focused on delivering client service excellence to all of its clients, which include major household names and FTSE-listed companies such as Virgin Trains, adidas, Leeds City Council, Whitbread, De Vere Group, Greene King, Barclays and the Royal Bank of Scotland, and has invested significantly in its client care programme developing a number of strategic account leadership for its clients across the UK and internationally.

Trainee profile

We're looking for people who are committed to a career in law, who enjoy working as part of a busy team and respond positively to a challenge.

Our trainees share ambition and the ability to bring something new and valuable to our team. Commercial acumen, good organisational skills and a fresh way of thinking about client needs are all hallmarks of a DWF team member. We also like to see candidates who have spent some time pursuing interests outside of academia.

Training environment

Our unique training contract is divided into six four-month 'seats'. This allows trainees to get a real taste of the variety of work we offer and make informed decisions about their future career. Trainees have the opportunity to sit in specialist departments within all of our practice groups and return to a preferred department for their final seat; enabling up to eight months pre-qualification experience in their chosen field.

Halfway through each seat, a senior member of our dedicated HR team will meet with each trainee to discuss progress. Trainees are also able to discuss which practice area they would like to target for their next seat rotation. We always do our best to accommodate seat preferences. Having completed four seats our trainees have a detailed discussion with the training principal about their future aspirations.

Vacation placements

The summer vacation scheme is an excellent way to learn more about the firm and experience first-hand life as a DWF trainee. During the two weeks you will become fully immersed in two of our many practice groups, complete legal skills training and attend numerous social events.

Partners 358
Other fee-earners 1,199
Total Trainees c. 100

Contact
Matthew Akin
Emerging Talent Specialist

Method of application
Apply online via www.dwf.co.uk

Selection procedure
Application form, video interview, Partner interview, assessment centre and final selection day

Closing date for 2016/2017
Undergraduates 31 July 2015

Application
Training contracts p.a. 48
Applications p.a. c. 3,000
% interviewed p.a. 10%
Required degree grade 2:1

Training
Salary
1st year (2014)
up to £26,000 (Regional)
£35,000 (London)
Holiday entitlement
25 days p.a.

Post-qualification
% of trainees offered job on qualification
2013 76% 2014 84%

Benefits
Flexible benefits scheme including insurance, life assurance, contributory pension and others

Sponsorship & awards
LPC / Scottish Diploma

Offices
Birmingham, Bristol, Dublin, Edinburgh, Glasgow, Leeds, Liverpool, London, Manchester, Milton Keynes, Newcastle, Preston

Edwards Wildman Palmer UK LLP

Dashwood, 69 Old Broad Street London EC2M 1QS
Tel: 020 7583 4055
Fax: 020 7353 7377
Email: swarnes@edwardswildman.com
Web: www.trainee.edwardswildman.com

Firm profile
Edwards Wildman is a growing international firm working with Fortune 500, FTSE 250 clients and start-up companies alike in a full spectrum of industries. We serve clients across the globe and they know us as trusted legal and business advisers. Recent accolades include 2012 London Office of the Year by Legal Week and 2012 Most Innovative Law Firm by the Financial Times in recognition of the firm's litigation practice. In 2013 Edwards Wildman was named in a report listing 1000 companies to inspire Britain by the London Stock Exchange.

Main areas of work
Our lawyers are known internationally for their work in private equity, venture capital, corporate and finance, complex litigation, insurance and reinsurance and intellectual property. We also have other specialisms in our London office. We advise multi-national corporates, financial institutions and governments worldwide on a range of multi-jurisdictional and cross-border disputes, transactions and regulatory matters.

Trainee Profile
Our trainees need to be stimulated by solving business and legal challenges; therefore academic excellence, great analytical skills and a rigorous approach are essential. We seek engaging individuals with the dynamism, initiative and drive to make their mark. We value good commercial judgement, adaptability and those capable of thinking on their feet. Understanding teamwork, evidence of leadership and seeking responsibilities are vital. Interesting achievements and making the most of non-academic opportunities will help applicants stand-out.

Training environment
We believe you learn best by doing, making substantive contributions to the matters you work on. Trainees meet clients, develop responsibility for their own work and get involved in marketing and client development activities. Trainees spend six months in four of the firm's key practice areas. There are also secondment opportunities to clients. Our tailored training programme develops the technical skills and knowledge needed in those areas. A varied support network enables you to build on and maximise the knowledge and skills gained.

Benefits
Bupa, STL, subsidised gym membership, pension scheme, life assurance, subsidised café, cycle to work scheme, EAP, eye tests, social events and sports.

Vacation placements
Places for 2015: 8; Duration: 2 weeks; Remuneration: £300.

Open days
3 per year.

Sponsorship
CPE/GDL and LPC full funding, maintenance allowance of £7,000 (London) / £6,500 (outside London).

Partners 29
Assistant Solicitors 41
Total Trainees 12

Contact
Sarah Warnes
020 7556 4414

Method of application
Online applications only
www.trainee.edwardswildman.com

Selection procedure
Assessment day. Successful candidates are interviewed by partners/senior associates.

Closing dates
Training Contracts (2017) 31 July 2015
Summer placements (2015) 31 January 2015
Open days (2014/15) rolling until 1 June 2015

Application
Training contracts p.a 6
Applications p.a 550 approx
% interviewed p.a 5-8 %
Required degree grade 2:1

Training
Salary
1st year £38,000
2nd year £42,000
Holiday entitlement 25 days

Post-qualification
Salary £61,000
Trainees offered job on qualification 60% (2014)

Offices
UK: London. US: New York, Boston, Chicago, Hartford, Los Angeles, Orange County, Providence, Stamford, Washington DC, West Palm Beach, Morristown NJ, Ft Lauderdale. Asia: Hong Kong, Tokyo. Europe: Istanbul.

A-Z of Solicitors

Farrer & Co LLP

66 Lincoln's Inn Fields, London WC2A 3LH
Tel: (020) 3375 7000 Fax: (020) 3375 7001
Email: graduaterecruitment@farrer.co.uk
Website: www.farrer.co.uk

Firm profile

Farrer & Co is a mid-sized London law firm. The firm provides specialist advice to a large number of prominent private, institutional and commercial clients. Farrer & Co has built a successful law firm based on the goodwill of close client relationships, outstanding expertise in niche sectors and a careful attention to personal service and quality.

Main areas of work

The firm's breadth of expertise is reflected by the fact that it has an outstanding reputation in fields as diverse as matrimonial law, offshore tax planning, employment, heritage work, charity law, defamation and sports law.

Trainee profile

Trainees are expected to be highly motivated individuals with keen intellects and interesting and engaging personalities. Those applicants who appear to break the mould – as shown by their initiative for organisation, leadership, exploration, or enterprise – are far more likely to get an interview than the erudite, but otherwise unimpressive, student.

Training environment

The training programme involves each trainee in the widest range of cases, clients and issues possible in a single law firm, taking full advantage of the wide range of practice areas at Farrer & Co by offering six seats, rather than the more usual four. This provides a broad foundation of knowledge and experience and the opportunity to make an informed choice about the area of law in which to specialise. A high degree of involvement is encouraged under the direct supervision of solicitors and partners. Trainees attend an induction programme and regular internal lectures. The training partner reviews trainees' progress at the end of each seat and extensive feedback is given. The firm has a very friendly atmosphere and regular sporting and social events.

Benefits

Flexible benefits scheme, sporting teams/clubs, season ticket loan, 25 days' holiday, group income protection, group life assurance, company doctor, subsidised gym membership, subsidised yoga/pilates, pension scheme, private medical insurance after one year, wellwoman/wellman checks.

Vacation placements

Places for 2015: 30; Duration: 2 weeks at Easter, two schemes for 2 weeks in summer; Remuneration: £275 p.w.; Closing date: 31 January 2015.

Sponsorship & awards

CPE Funding: Fees paid plus £6,000 maintenance. LPC Funding: Fees paid plus £6,000 maintenance.

Partners 73
Assistant Solicitors 167
Total Trainees 20

Contact
Trainee Recruitment Consultant

Method of application
Online via the firm's website

Selection procedure
Interviews with Trainee Recruitment Partner and partners

Closing date for 2017
31 July 2015

Application
Training contracts p.a.10
Applications p.a. 1000
% interviewed p.a. 5%
Required degree grade 2:1

Training
Salary
1st year (Sept 2014) £35,000
2nd year (Sept 2014) £38,000
Holiday entitlement 25 days
% of trainees with non-law
degrees p.a. 40-60%

Post-qualification
Salary (2014) £58,500
% of trainees offered job
on qualification (2013) 100%
% of partners (as at 2014)
who joined as trainees over
60%

FARRER&Co

Fladgate LLP

16 Great Queen Street, London WC2B 5DG
Tel: (020) 3036 7000 Fax: (020) 3036 7600
Email: trainees@fladgate.com
Website: www.fladgate.com

Firm profile
Fladgate LLP is an innovative, progressive and thriving law firm which prides itself on its friendly and professional working environment. We are based in modern, attractive offices in London's Covent Garden.

Main areas of work
The firm provides a wide range of legal services to a portfolio of prestigious clients in the UK and overseas, including multinationals, major institutions and listed companies, clearing banks, lenders and entrepreneurs. Fladgate LLP's lawyers have experience in most major areas of practice and the firm combines an accessible and responsive style of service with first-class technical skills and in-depth expertise.

The firm has a strong international dimension based on multi-lingual and multi-qualified lawyers working in London and complemented by access to an extensive network of overseas lawyers. The firm operates specialist teams which serve continental Europe, India, Israel, South Africa, the US and the Middle East.

The firm's principal departments comprise corporate (which includes tax, private capital, restructuring, employment, IP and technology), litigation and real estate (which includes planning, construction and real estate litigation). These are supported by specialist cross-departmental teams that provide co-ordinated advice on a range of issues.

Trainee profile
Fladgate LLP seeks trainees with enthusiasm, confidence and excellent interpersonal skills. You must be able to work both independently and in a team, and will be expected to show common sense and initiative. Awareness of the commercial interests of clients is essential. You will have a minimum of a 2:1 degree, although not necessarily in law, together with three excellent A levels or equivalent.

Training environment
Typically, you will complete four six-month seats. Each seat will bring you into contact with new clients and colleagues, and you can expect to gain real hands-on experience of a variety of deals and projects, both large and small. In each seat you will work alongside senior lawyers who will supervise your development and ensure that you are involved in challenging and interesting work. In addition to on-the-job training, each department has a comprehensive training schedule of seminars and workshops covering a range of legal and skills training.

The firm has a modern culture and an open-door policy where trainees are given early responsibility and encouraged to achieve their full potential.

Benefits
Pension, permanent health insurance, life assurance, season ticket loan, sports club loan, private medical.

Partners 63
Assistant Solicitors 38
Total Trainees 8

Contact
Mrs Annabelle Lawrence,
Senior Human Resources
Manager

Method of application
Information and an application
form are available at the firm's
website www.fladgate.com

Selection procedure
Assessment day plus interview

Application
For more details please visit
www.fladgate.com
Training contracts p.a. 4
Required degree grade 2:1

Training
Starting salary £32,000
Holiday entitlement
25 days

Post-qualification
Salary £55,000

A-Z of Solicitors

Foot Anstey LLP

Salt Quay House, 4 North East Quay, Sutton Harbour, Plymouth, PL4 0BN
Tel: (01752) 675000 Fax: (01752) 675500
Website: www.footanstey.com

Firm profile

Leading regional law firm Foot Anstey is a major presence in the South West. A Top 100 law firm with five offices across the region, our lawyers offer a range of specialist legal services to our regional, national and international clients, both businesses and individuals.

The firm has significantly grown over recent years; the strategy created by Managing Partner John Westwell and the management team has completely realigned the business and accelerated our growth. Investment is constant; we've achieved consistent growth, strong financial performance and are on track to achieve our ambitious financial targets. We've grown organically through our bold, agile strategy that has attracted the attention of the industry; we've been named in numerous awards that include the British Legal Awards, MPF Awards for Management Excellence and most recently by LawCareers.Net for the strength of our training.

And while our business may have changed considerably over our 100 year history, we are proud of our South West roots and support our local communities and economies whenever we can.

Main areas of work

Foot Anstey advises a wide variety of clients on a wider range of services. Advising regional, national and international clients, the pace is fast and interesting.

The firm is arranged into six main groups; Clinical Negligence, Real Estate, Commercial, Corporate, Dispute Resolution and Employment. We also have a niche expertise in Islamic Finance.

Trainee profile

We welcome applications from all law and non-law graduates who have a strong academic background, exceptional communication skills and the vision to be part of our future.

We are an ambitious firm; we want people that will help take us there.

Training environment

Our training programme is designed to help you reach your full potential. Our trainees undertake four seats of six months with regular, open communication between the trainees and supervisors as standard. You'll get exposure to situations to develop your legal and commercial expertise, in an environment that is friendly and supportive.

The trainees at Foot Anstey also play a key role in the firm's CSR and charitable activities and are encouraged to be fully involved in the firm's social calendar.

Benefits

All trainees are entitled to the flexible, forward thinking 'Choices' benefits package which includes: 25 days holiday, options to buy/sell holiday, contributory pension scheme, life assurance, cycle scheme and childcare vouchers. In addition, we offer a popular Lifestyle Hour, the chance to take one hour off work each week to promote a healthy work/life balance.

Vacation placements

Our summer placement scheme offers a week of unpaid work experience, providing a valuable insight into our business and the different areas of legal expertise. Apply online by 30 April 2015 at www.footanstey.com.

Sponsorship

Grants available towards LPC and living expenses.

Partners 45
Assistant Solicitors 71
Trainees 12

Contact
Jenna.Wickham@footanstey.com

Method of application
Online at www.footanstey.com

Selection procedure
Online Training Contract Application Form and Assessment Day

Closing date for 2017
Applications for a 2017 training contract should be made by 1 June 2015. The deadline for the 2015 summer placement scheme is 30 April 2015.

Application
Training Contracts p.a. 4-6
Applications p.a. 300
% interviewed 10%
Required degree grade Usually 2:1 degree

Training
Starting salaries TBC

Post-qualification
Salary (2014) £35,000
% of trainees offered job on qualification (2014) 71%
% of assistant solicitors who joined as trainees 46%
% of partners who joined as trainees 8%

Offices
Bristol, Taunton, Exeter, Plymouth, Truro

Freeths

Cumberland Court, 80 Mount Street, Nottingham NG1 6HH
Tel: (0845) 634 2600 Fax: (0115) 859 9600
Email: carole.wigley@freeths.co.uk
Website: www.freeths.co.uk

Firm profile

Freeths is a national law firm offering services to a wide range of commercial and private clients. The firm has clients throughout the UK and many of those clients have strong international connections. The firm is the 66th largest in the UK, with a team of over 600 operating from offices in Birmingham, Derby, Leeds, Leicester, London, Manchester, Milton Keynes, Nottingham, Oxford, Sheffield and Stoke on Trent.

In recognition of organisations that demonstrate high levels of employee engagement, the firm has been awarded star status by Best Companies for 2013. The Legal 500's UK rankings also put the firm as a regional leader in no less than 28 categories and 61 partners are recognised by Chambers UK as leaders in their field. The firm has also won awards for training and recruitment and its IT infrastructure.

Main areas of work

Real estate and construction; commercial services; private client and personal litigation.

Trainee profile

Individuality. There's no such thing as a typical Freeths candidate! We are open-minded and interested in people who share this quality. We are looking for individuals who can demonstrate strong academic performance – and would expect candidates to be able to demonstrate the ability to achieve a 2.1 degree or higher at university, in any degree discipline, and have 320 UCAS points (ABB) at A Level (or equivalent). Beyond this we want to see evidence of teamwork, motivation and drive, communication skills, planning and organisation, critical thinking, commercial awareness and commitment – both to a career in law and to a career with Freeths.

Training environment

Your training contract will be based on six month rotations through a number of departmental or practice seats. You will sit with a partner or an associate and actively contribute to the day-to-day work of that department – working on transactions and cases, taking real responsibility and gaining plenty of client exposure. Your supervisor will give you regular feedback and conduct an appraisal with you at the end of the seat so you are fully aware of your progress.

Benefits

Trainees with the firm are entitled to 25 days annual holiday, private healthcare and a non-contributory pension.

Sponsorship & awards

An interest free loan is available to cover the cost of the GDL and LPC.

Partners 129
Assistant Solicitors 61
Total Trainees 20

Contact
Carole Wigley, HR Director
0845 274 6815

Method of application
Online application form

Selection procedure
Interview and selection day

Closing date for August 2017
12/07/2015

Application
No. of training contracts
p.a 10
Applications p.a. 750
% interviewed 10%
Required degree grade 2:1

Training
Salary for each year of training
Starting salary £21,500 (September 2012)
Holiday entitlement 25 days

Post-qualification
% trainees offered job on qualification 90%
Salary £35,000

Overseas / regional offices
Birmingham, Derby, Leeds, Leicester, London, Manchester, Milton Keynes, Nottingham, Oxford, Sheffield and Stoke on Trent.

FREETHS

Freshfields Bruckhaus Deringer LLP

65 Fleet Street, London EC4Y 1HS
Tel: (020) 7785 5554
Email: uktrainees@freshfields.com
Website: www.freshfields.com/uktrainees

Firm profile

As an international law firm, Freshfields Bruckhaus Deringer LLP advises some of the world's most well-known businesses. For graduates keen to pursue a career in commercial law, we offer challenging work that demands a strong intellect and a desire to help ambitious businesses achieve long-term success.

Our lawyers provide clients with a global service from our network of offices across Europe, the Americas and Asia. It is essential that our service is consistent and of the highest quality.

Main areas of work

Our lawyers work in teams, often of no more than three: a partner, an associate and a trainee. Whatever our clients want to achieve, the team's job is to work out how. Is it possible? What will be the most effective way of structuring the deal or tackling the problem? What are the risks? How should it be documented? The team has to provide real commercial solutions, not just what is right or wrong in law.

Organisationally, our lawyers work in one of seven practice areas: antitrust, competition and trade; corporate; dispute resolution; employment, pensions and benefits; finance; real estate; and tax.

Trainee profile

Background, university and the degree studied are immaterial. But every successful candidate has three qualities that are non-negotiable: intellectual talent, excellent English (written and verbal), and a generous spirit.

We pursue premium, cross-border work that is nearly always complicated. This means that the learning curve is steep, so the graduates who do best are those who like to be challenged.

Training environment

Graduates who accept a training contract with us have the opportunity to experience up to eight areas of law – twice the number offered by most law firms. The training is largely provided from our London office but many trainees will also spend time on secondment to a client or to one of our US, European or Asian offices.

Benefits

The firm offers a flexible and competitive benefits package.

Vacation placements

We normally take students on our vacation schemes who are in their penultimate year of an undergraduate degree. Again, you will need to submit an online application. The application window for our 2015 schemes is from 1 October 2014 to 6 January 2015. Since we offer places as we go along, the sooner you apply the better.

Sponsorship & awards

Before a training contract starts all graduates complete the Legal Practice Course; and non-law graduates also need to take the Graduate Diploma in Law before the LPC. The firm meets the cost and provides a maintenance grant for both.

Partners 427
Associates 1,611
Total Trainees 163*
(* London based)

Contact
uktrainees@freshfields.com

Method of application
Online application form

Selection procedure
Online verbal reasoning test, 2 interviews and written test

Closing date for 2017
Please see website

Application
Training contracts p.a. up to 90
Applications p.a. c. 2,000
% interviewed p.a. c.12%

Training
Salary
1st year £40,500
2nd year £45,500
Holiday entitlement 25 days
% of trainees with a non-law degree p.a. c. 40%
No. of seats available abroad p.a. c. 42

Post-qualification
Salary £67,500
% of trainees offered job on qualification 84% (as at Autumn 2014)

Overseas offices
Abu Dhabi, Amsterdam, Bahrain, Beijing, Berlin, Brussels, Cologne, Dubai, Düsseldorf, Frankfurt, Hamburg, Hanoi, Ho Chi Minh City, Hong Kong, Madrid, Milan, Moscow, Munich, New York, Paris, Rome, Shanghai, Singapore, Tokyo, Vienna, Washington DC

FRESHFIELDS

Gateley LLP

One Eleven, Edmund Street, Birmingham B3 2HJ
Tel: (0121) 234 0000 Fax: (0121) 234 0079
Website: www.gateleyuk.com
Twitter: @GateleyLLP
Blog: talkingtrainees.gateleyuk.com

Firm profile

A top 50 UK based practice with an excellent reputation for commercial work and a particular expertise in corporate, plc, commercial, employment, property, construction, insolvency, commercial dispute resolution, banking, tax and shipping.

The firm also offers individual clients a complete private client service including FSA-approved financial advice. The firm is expanding (768 employees) and offers a practical, commercial and fast-paced working environment. It has built an outstanding reputation across the UK for its practical approach, sound advice and professional commitment to clients. The firm is a full service, multi-disciplinary legal business with expertise in many areas.

Gateley has an enviable reputation as a friendly and sociable place to work and is committed to equality and diversity throughout its offices.

Trainee profile

To apply for a placement in England, applications are invited from second year law students and final year non-law students and graduates. Applicants should have (or be heading for) a minimum 2.1 degree, and should have at least three Bs (or equivalent) at A-level. Individuals should be hardworking team players capable of using initiative and demonstrating commercial awareness.

Training environment

Four six-month seats with ongoing supervision and appraisals every three months. PSC taken internally. In-house courses on skills such as time management, negotiation, IT, drafting, business skills, marketing, presenting and writing in plain English.

Benefits

One of our current trainees is offered as a 'buddy' – a point of contact within the firm, library access, private health care, life assurance (death in service), pension scheme and season ticket loan.

Vacation placements

Two-week placement over the summer. Deadline for next year's vacation placement scheme is 31 January 2015 and the closing date for 2017 training contracts is 31 July 2015. Apply online at www.gateleyuk.com. Paper/email applications not accepted.

Sponsorship & awards

LPC maintenance grant of £5,000.

Partners 150 (firmwide)
Vacancies 11 (England)
Total Trainees 30 (England)
Total Staff 768 (firmwide)

Contact
graduaterecruitmentengland@
gateley.co.uk

Closing date for 2017
Training contracts
31 July 2015
Vacation placements
31 January 2015

Training
Salary
1st year £20,000-22,000
(Midlands)
2nd year £22,000-24,000
(Midlands)

Post-qualification
Salary £33,000 (Midlands)

Offices
Birmingham, Dubai, Edinburgh, Glasgow, Leeds, Leicester, London, Nottingham and Manchester.

Gide Loyrette Nouel LLP (Gide)

125 Old Broad Street, London EC2N 1AR
Tel: (020) 7382 5500 Fax: (020) 7382 5501
Website: www.gide.com

Firm profile

Gide Loyrette Nouel is a premier international French law firm with 17 offices in 14 countries. The firm was recently named French Law Firm of the Year 2014 by Chambers and rivals the best English and US firms in the international business arena.

Main areas of work

Gide London is a niche finance and international dispute resolution practice in the City of London. Our lawyers play a vital role in the firm's global strategy, spear-heading the firm's common law finance practice worldwide. Our English, US and French lawyers work closely to provide integrated solutions to our clients within rapidly changing markets, advising on structured finance and derivatives, international banking, projects and infrastructure, capital markets and securitisation.

Gide London is also home to our flourishing International Dispute Resolution and Arbitration team and International Tax Group.

Trainee profile

We are recruiting 4-6 trainees for 2017 and are looking for candidates with an interest in international business and finance. They must be confident, capable of thinking and working independently and unafraid of a challenge. Our trainees are flexible, commercial and open to new experiences. Life at Gide is constantly changing and we need lawyers who are capable of adapting easily.

Training environment

Because finance is a very important part of what we do, our trainees are given an unparalleled start to their careers as finance lawyers and you will be exposed to a far wider variety of finance law than in a more generalist practice. We offer four seats of six months, at least one of which will be in Hong Kong, Moscow and/or Paris. You will also complete a seat in International Dispute Resolution, as well as being offered a seat with the International Tax Group. We believe in treating our trainees as professionals and we allocate a training budget to each person, which they can spend on any external training that may interest them. You will work directly with senior lawyers and partners in London and in our network of international offices, thereby giving you the opportunity to learn from practice area experts. Our trainees also benefit from one-to-one coaching from an accredited business coach.

Sponsorship & awards

We sponsor successful candidates through their GDL and/or LPC (fees and maintenance grant), but we only refund fees paid in the three months prior to offer.

Partners 9
Associates 18
Trainees 8

Contact
Paula McMullan/Stéphanie Leduc
tcapplications@gide.com

Method of application
Firm's own application form

Selection procedure
Assessment day, interview

Closing date for 2017
15 July 2015

Application
Training contracts p.a. 4-6
Applications p.a. 130
% interviewed 5-10%
2:1 degree or equivalent in any subject

Training
Salary
1st year £38,000
2nd year £42,000
Holiday entitlement
5 weeks

Post-qualification
Salary £65,000
Trainees offered job on qualification (2014) 4 out of 4

Other offices which take English trainees
Hong Kong, Paris, Moscow

Gordons LLP

Riverside West, Whitehall Road, Leeds, LS1 4AW
Tel: (0113) 227 0100 Fax: (0113) 227 0113
Forward House, 8 Duke Street, Bradford, BD1 3QX
Tel: (01274) 202202 Fax: (01274) 202100
Email: recruitment@gordonsllp.com
Website: www.gordonsllp.com

Firm profile
Gordons is a UK Top 100 law firm and one of the largest law firms based entirely in Yorkshire, with offices in Leeds and Bradford. We provide commercial and personal legal services to a wide range of businesses and individuals across the region and beyond, from the individual entrepreneur and small family business to the large PLC, and our private client service is equally as comprehensive. Our approach is that of a straight-talking, ambitious law firm that puts its clients' success before our own. We are a modern firm with traditional values operating in the real world, which means we believe in hard work and professionalism combined with a personal touch. We aim to be the law firm of choice in Yorkshire, providing a genuine alternative to the national firms.

Main areas of work
Commercial property; planning and environmental; construction; corporate; pensions; banking; insolvency; commercial litigation; intellectual property; employment; personal injury; private client; family law and residential property.

Trainee profile
We are looking for trainees who are eager to learn, have good interpersonal skills, can relate well to clients and who welcome responsibility at an early stage. Initiative, commercial awareness, IT skills and a friendly and professional manner are all essential qualities along with ambition to succeed. We see our trainees as our partners of tomorrow!

Training environment
Trainees spend a minimum of six months in at least three different departments. During the second year of the training contract they may state their preference for a particular department and we will try to accommodate the request where possible. Our trainees work closely with a partner or senior solicitor in each seat and get 'hands on' training with plenty of client contact. They are actively encouraged to get involved with marketing, networking, training, and other events hosted by the firm and/or clients, and the firm itself has regular social activities on offer, both formal and informal. The environment is supportive and friendly with an open door policy across the firm, and the trainees have regular meetings with their supervisors to ensure their progress. We aim to offer our trainees positions within the firm on qualification wherever possible.

Benefits
Group personal pension; life assurance; interest-free travel loan; childcare vouchers scheme; 24 days holiday per year plus statutory holidays; free fruit; sports and social club.

Sponsorship & awards
The firm contributes £5,000 towards LPC course fees.

Partners 35
Assistant Solicitors 65
Total Trainees 9

Contact
Karen Mills, HR Manager

Method of application
Online application via website
www.gordonsllp.com

Selection procedure
One stage interview process,
including practical exercise
and opportunity to meet current trainees

Closing date for 2017
31 July 2015

Application
Training contracts p.a. 4
Applications p.a. 400
% interviewed p.a. 8%
Required degree grade 2:1

Training
Salary
1st year £20,000
2nd year £22,000
(Reviewed annually)
Holiday entitlement 24 days
and statutory
% of trainees with a
non-law degree p.a. 50%

Post-qualification
NQ Salary reviewed annually

A-Z of Solicitors

Government Legal Service

Tel: 0845 300 0793
Email: glstrainees@tmpw.co.uk
Web: www.gov.uk/gls

Firm profile

The Government Legal Service (GLS) is the collective term for the 2000 lawyers working in the legal teams of over 30 of the largest government departments and agencies. These include departments such as the Department for Business, Innovation and Skills, Department of Energy and Climate Change, HM Revenue and Customs, the Home Office, the Ministry of Justice and the Treasury Solicitor's Department but there are many more.

Main areas of work

Military action overseas. Immigration policy. Welfare reform. Measures to protect the public from anti-social behaviour. Reforms to improve the quality of care vulnerable children receive. These are just some examples of the work our lawyers have been involved in recently. The diversity of our work reflects the wide range of activities within government. These range across issues of national and international significance and across public and private law, embracing advisory and legislative work, litigation and a wealth of specialist areas.

Trainee profile

To join the GLS as a trainee solicitor or pupil barrister, you'll need at least a 2:2 degree (which need not be in law). You must also provide evidence of strong analytical ability, excellent communication and interpersonal skills and motivation for working in public service.

Training environment

The GLS provides a unique and varied training environment for trainees and pupils. Trainee solicitors work in four different areas of practice ('seats') over a two year period. At least one of these seats will be in a litigation team and one in an advisory team. Pupil barristers divide their year's pupillage between their department and chambers. The GLS prides itself on involving trainees and pupils in the full range of casework conducted by their department. This frequently includes high profile matters and will be under the supervision of senior colleagues.

Benefits

These include professional development opportunities, pension scheme, civilised working hours, generous holiday entitlement and flexible working opportunities.

Vacation placements

10-15 placements are usually available each year. Please check www.gov.uk/gls for further information.

Sponsorship & awards

LPC and BPTC fees as well as other compulsory Professional Skills Course fees. The GLS also provides a grant of around £7,000 for the vocational year. The GLS is unable to provide funding for the GDL.

Total trainees around 50 currently working for the Government Legal Service

Contact
glstrainees@tmpw.co.uk or visit www.gov.uk/gls

Method of application
Online application form, situational judgement test, verbal reasoning test and critical reasoning test

Selection procedure
Half day assessment centre involving a written exercise and competency based interview

Closing date for 2017
31 July 2015

Application
Training contracts p.a. 25-30
Applications p.a. 3000+
4% p.a. interviewed
Required degree grade (need not be in law) 2:2

Training
Salary
1st year salary £23,900-£24,600
2nd year salary £25,300-£26,500
Holiday entitlement 25 days on entry

Post-qualification
Salary
£32,000-£40,000
% of trainees accepting job on qualification (2013) 100%

A-Z of Solicitors

Harbottle & Lewis LLP

Hanover House, 14 Hanover Square, London W1S 1HP
Tel: (020) 7667 5000 Fax: (020) 7667 5100
Email: kathy.beilby@harbottle.com
Website: www.harbottle.com

Firm profile

Harbottle & Lewis provides pro-active legal advice to dynamic and creative clients operating primarily in the following sectors: media and entertainment; technology; advertising, marketing and sponsorship; sport; charities; retail; property; travel and leisure.

Recent highlights include acting for Emirates on the terms of its 10 year sponsorship of the Transport for London cable car, "Emirates Air Line"; acting for Zattikka on its initial incorporation and the acquisition of other gaming companies; advising Comic Relief on matters relating to Comic Relief television programmes, fundraising and challenges overseas; undertaking all financing and production work on "Call the Midwife", advising Conor Maynard in relation to his recording and publishing agreements; and advising Tom Daley on the establishment of his image rights company and on endorsements deals.

In 2012 the firm won the FT's award for the Most Innovative Law Firm in Private Client work and became the British Legal Awards' Private Client / Family Team of the Year.

Main areas of work

Harbottle & Lewis advises businesses and other organisations on corporate, commercial, charity, data protection, employment, family, finance, intellectual property, litigation, property, reputation management and regulatory matters. It advises individuals on issues including asset freezing, family law, high-value residential property, mediation, personal injury, philanthropy, privacy, probate, tax and trusts.

Having been at the centre of many of the entertainment industries' largest and most high profile transactions and cases it has a strong reputation for providing specialist advice to clients in industries such as broadcasting, digital media, fashion, film, interactive entertainment, live events, media finance, music, publishing, television and theatre.

Trainee profile

Trainees will have demonstrated the high academic abilities, commercial awareness, and initiative necessary to become part of a team advising clients in dynamic and demanding industries.

Training environment

The two year training contract is divided into four six-month seats where trainees will be given experience in a variety of legal skills. Seats include, corporate, employment, family/tax/private client, litigation, property, a secondment to a long-standing client as well as a seat in the firm's core industries, including film, interactive entertainment, music, publishing, sport, television and theatre. The firm has a policy of accepting a small number of trainees to ensure they are given relevant and challenging work and are exposed to and have responsibility for a full range of legal tasks. The firm has its own seminar programme in both legal topics and industry know-how. An open door policy and a pragmatic entrepreneurial approach to legal practice provides a stimulating working environment.

Benefits

Lunch provided; season ticket loans; group personal pension scheme; life assurance; 23 days holiday; childcare vouchers; cycle to work scheme; employee assistance scheme.

Sponsorship & awards

LPC fees paid and interest-free loans towards maintenance.

Partners 34
Assistant Solicitors 38
Total Trainees 11

Contact
Kathy Beilby

Method of application
Application form to download from website

Selection procedure
Interview

Closing date for 2017
31 July 2015

Application
Training contracts p.a. 5
Applications p.a. 500
% interviewed p.a. 15%
Required degree grade 2:1

Training
Salary
1st year £30,000 (2013)
2nd year £31,000 (2013)
Holiday entitlement
in the first year 23 days
in the second year 26 days
% of trainees with
a non-law degree p.a. 40%

Post-qualification
Salary (2013) £50k

Harbottle & Lewis

Herbert Smith Freehills LLP

Exchange House, Primrose Street, London EC2A 2EG
Tel: (020) 7374 8000
Email: graduatesuk@hsf.com

Firm profile

As one of the world's leading law firms, Herbert Smith Freehills advises many of the biggest and most ambitious organisations across all major regions of the globe. The firm's clients trust it with their most important transactions, disputes and projects.

The firm is committed to excellence, providing tailored legal advice of the highest quality to major corporations, governments, financial institutions and all types of commercial organisations.

Main areas of work

Herbert Smith Freehills' disputes practice is acknowledged as the number one in the UK and Asia and includes the firm's leading international arbitration practice and award winning in-house advocacy unit, offering a complete litigation service and a realistic alternative to the bar. The firm is a market leader in corporate with a particular strength in the energy sector. Allied to this is a deep vein of quality that runs through its other practice areas, including finance, competition, regulation and trade, real estate and employment, pensions and incentives. The firm also has specialist areas such as intellectual property and tax.

Trainee profile

The firm seeks to recruit people with the desire to be exceptional at what they do. As well as a solid academic record, applicants should have a strong level of commercial awareness and understand the importance of building relationships with clients and colleagues. Herbert Smith Freehills chooses people who are assured, perceptive, ambitious and empathetic. Combine these qualities with a creative and questioning mind and Herbert Smith Freehills will offer you great challenges and rewards.

Training environment

The strength and breadth of the firm's practice areas guarantees excellent training and development opportunities for trainees. Trainees rotate through four six month seats and most trainees will go on international or client secondments.

Sponsorship & awards

The firm provides funding and a maintenance allowance for GDL and LPC courses.

Vacation placements

Herbert Smith Freehills run winter, spring and summer vacation schemes. The firm also runs two day workshops exclusively for first year students around Easter time, designed to give students an early insight into a career at an international law firm. Finalists and graduates can apply to winter, spring or summer schemes and penultimate year students should apply for summer. Applications open for a winter scheme from 1 to 31 October 2014 and applications for spring and summer open from 1 December 2014 to 16 January 2015.

Partners 453
Total Staff 4,725
Total Trainees 143

Contact
graduatesuk@hsf.com
020 7374 8000

Method of application
Online at www.herbertsmith-freehills.com/careers/london/graduates

Selection procedure
Online tests: Verbal reasoning, critical reasoning and situational judgement
Assessment Centre: Group exercise, case study presentation and a competency interview

Application
Required degree grade 2:1

Closing date for 2014/5 vacation schemes
Winter 31 October 2014
Spring/Summer 16 January 2015

Closing date for 2017 training contracts
Finalists and graduates should apply between 1 October 2014 and 16 January 2015

Training
Salary
1st year £39,500
2nd year £44,000
25 days holiday (rising to 27 on qualification)

Post-qualification
Salary £65,000
% of trainees offered job on qualification (March 2014) 90%

Overseas Offices
Asia, Australia, Europe, the Middle East and the US

Hewitsons LLP

42 Newmarket Road, Cambridge CB5 8EP
Tel: (01604) 233233 Fax: (01223) 316511
Email: mail@hewitsons.com (for all offices)
Website: www.hewitsons.com (for all offices)

Firm profile
Established in 1865, the firm handles mostly company and commercial work, but has a growing body of public sector clients. The firm has three offices: Cambridge, Northampton and Milton Keynes.

Main areas of work
Seven Business Units: Property, Corporate, Private Client, Contentious, Employment, Agriculture and Residential Property.

Trainee profile
The firm is interested in applications from candidates who have achieved a high degree of success in academic studies and who are bright, personable and able to take the initiative.

Training environment
The firm offers four six-month seats.

Benefits
The PSC is provided during the first year of the training contract. This is coupled with an extensive programme of Trainee Solicitor Seminars provided by specialist in-house lawyers.

Vacation placements
Places for 2015: A few placements are available, application is by way of letter and CV to Caroline Lewis.

Sponsorship & awards
Funding for the CPE and/or LPC is not provided.

Partners 40
Assistant Solicitors 33
Total Trainees 11

Contact
Caroline Lewis
Elgin House, Billing Road,
Northampton, NN1 5AU

Method of application
Firm's application form

Selection procedure
Interview

Closing date for 2017
31 August 2015

Application
Training contracts p.a. 10
Applications p.a. 850
% interviewed p.a. 10%
Required degree grade
2:1 min

Training
Salary
1st year £23,500
2nd year £23,500
Holiday entitlement 20 days
% of trainees with a non-law
degree p.a. 50%

Post-qualification
Salary £36,500
% of trainees offered job on
qualification (2013) 75%

Higgs & Sons

3 Waterfront Business Park, Brierley Hill DY5 1LX
Tel: (0845) 111 5050 Fax: (01384) 327291
Email: growyourfuture@higgsandsons.co.uk
Website: www.higgsandsons.co.uk

Firm profile

Higgs & Sons is one of the largest and most respected law firms in the West Midlands, operating out of offices in Brierley Hill and employing over 200 staff. The firm's headquarters are situated in a modern, purpose designed facility at the prestigious Waterfront Business Park. The firm is well recognised in the Legal 500 and Chambers Guide to the Legal Profession.

Higgs & Sons is different from the typical law firm. The firm successfully combines traditional values with an innovative approach to legal problems which has helped to attract an impressive client base whilst also staying true to the local community. Clients and staff alike are attracted to Higgs' ability to offer an all round service in a number of areas. The firm is proud to provide a supportive and friendly working environment within which colleagues can thrive. The opportunity for career progression is clear as more than half of the firm's partners trained with the firm.

Main areas of work

For the business client: corporate and commercial, insolvency, employment, commercial litigation, commercial property and regulatory.

For the private client: wills, probate, trusts and tax, employment, personal injury, clinical negligence, conveyancing, dispute resolution, matrimonial/family, motoring and private criminal.

Trainee profile

Applications are welcome from law and non law students who can demonstrate consistently high academic records, a broad range of interpersonal skills and extra curricular activities and interests. The firm would like to hear about what you have done to develop your wider skills and awareness. It is looking for people who want to get involved and participate fully in the business.

Training environment

A training contract at Higgs is different from those offered by other firms. There is the unique opportunity to undertake six four-month seats in a variety of departments, including a double seat in the department in to which you wish to qualify as you approach the end of your training contract. Throughout the training contract you will receive a mix of contentious and non-contentious work and an open door policy means that there is always someone on hand to answer questions and supervise your work. Regular appraisals take place at the end of each seat and a designated partner oversees you throughout the duration of your training contract, acting as a mentor. Participation in BTSS events and an active Higgs social environment ensures an effective work life balance.

Benefits

Private medical insurance, contributory pension, life assurance and BTSS membership.

Sponsorship

Professional Skills Course.

Partners 31
Fee earners 115
Total trainees 8
Contact
Gemma Dipple
Method of application
Online application form
Selection procedure
Assesment day including interview
Closing date for 2017
31 July 2015
Application
Training contracts p.a. 4/6
Applications p.a. 350 plus
% interviewed p.a. varies
Required degree grade preferably 2:1
Training
Salary reviewed annually
1st year £21,500
2nd year £24,000
Holiday entitlement
25 days p.a.
Post-qualification
Salary £32,000
% of trainees offered job on qualification 100%

Hill Dickinson

No. 1 St Paul's Square, Liverpool, L3 9SJ
Tel: (0151) 600 8000
Email: recruitment@hilldickinson.com
Website: www.hilldickinsontrainees.com

Firm profile
We're an award-winning, full service international law firm with big clients, great people and fantastic opportunities. With around 1300 people, including 180 partners, we have offices in Liverpool, London, Manchester and Sheffield in the UK, alongside international bases in Singapore, Piraeus, Monaco and Hong Kong.

Main areas of work
We're a full service commercial law firm, so we cover all areas of law and work across a number of sectors, including: insurance, retail, aviation, sports, media, health and marine.

Trainee profile
Academically, you'll need at least a 2:1 and ABB or equivalent. We want our trainees to show a commitment to learning throughout their careers. We want trainees with the insight and awareness to understand our clients' demands and what is expected of us as an international law firm, so we want to hear about your business background. You will need to have experiences that demonstrate your passion for a career in law and the motivation you've got to get there.

Training environment
Modest numbers: we recruit to retain, so for 2017, we're taking on up to 14 trainees which means we'll have the resources and time to give you as much support as you need.

Immediate responsibilities: because of our small intake, there's lots of interesting work to go around and you will be given challenges from the start.

Choices: you will work four seats and select preferences from a variety of different areas of law.

A mentor: your mentor (a Hill Dickinson solicitor) will be on hand from day one and throughout your training contract to offer advice, guidance and support.

Office sharing: you will share an office with a partner, who will help you develop your legal knowledge and be there to support you.

A brilliant start: before you officially start your training contract, you will spend a number of days in our offices learning about our business, as part of our LPC+ scheme.

A social scene: our trainees work really hard and as you'd expect, it's not all fun and games. But when they do let their hair down, they get together and do it properly! You're welcome to get involved in the firm's sports and CSR teams, too.

Benefits
As well as a host of fantastic training opportunities, we also provide some pretty good perks: pension, travel insurance, buying and selling holiday entitlement, permanent health insurance and life assurance, season ticket loans, BUPA cover, and we'll even give you your birthday off (paid).

Sponsorship & awards
We'll pay your LPC fees in full and provide a maintenance grant.

Vacation placements
We have up to 48 places available in our Northern offices and 20 in London. Apply online by 31 January 2015.

Open days
Come and meet us at our offices in Liverpool on 6 February 2015 and in London on 20 February 2015.

Partners 180
Assistant Solicitors 159
Associates 87
Total Trainees 34

Contact
Emma McAvinchey/Jen Hulse/
Hannah Williams in the Talent
and Development Team
recruitment@hilldickinson.com

Selection procedure
You will need to have completed an online application, a video interview and a psychometric test by the closing dates, so apply early and please ensure you give yourself plenty of time.

Closing dates for 2017
Open days 1 December 2015
Vacation schemes 31 Jan 2015
Training contracts 20 July 2015

Training
Salary
1st year £24,000
2nd year £26,000
1st year (London) £32,000
2nd year (London) £34,000

Post-qualification
% of trainees offered job
on qualification (2014) 79%

Offices
Liverpool, Manchester,
Sheffield, London, Singapore,
Piraeus, Monaco, Hong Kong

HILL DICKINSON

Hogan Lovells

Hogan Lovells, Atlantic House, Holborn Viaduct, London EC1A 2FG
Tel: (020) 7296 2000 Fax: (020) 7296 2001
Email: graduate.recruitment@hoganlovells.com
Website: www.hoganlovells.com/graduates

Firm profile
Hogan Lovells is a top global law firm, with over 2,500 lawyers working in over 40 offices in Asia, Europe, Latin America, Africa, the Middle East and the United States. Our unique balance of ambition and approachability attracts prestigious clients and creates a working culture where the ambition of our trainee solicitors is supported to ensure their success.

Main areas of work
Our global diversity and wide range of practice areas gives us a strong reputation for corporate finance, dispute resolution, government regulatory and intellectual property. Exposure to a variety of legal disciplines provides good training and development opportunities for those joining us.

Trainee profile
We are looking for graduates whose combination of academic excellence and desire for specialist knowledge will contribute to developing business and taking it forward. Although we are one of the largest global legal practices, we work in small, hard-working teams where everybody is committed to our collective success.

The personal qualities our people possess are as important as their qualifications. You need to be happy collaborating with a team yet capable of, and used to, independent action. You will need to demonstrate an ability and desire for lateral thinking, be capable of close attention to detail, and have the energy, resilience and ambition to succeed in a top global law firm.

Training environment
As a trainee solicitor at Hogan Lovells, you will be offered work that sharpens your mind. You will take on as much responsibility as you can handle relating to client work, as well as a comprehensive legal skills training programme, regular reviews and appraisals. After qualification, continuous training and development remain a priority – you will deepen your professional and business expertise throughout your career. Making the best of your expertise enhances the quality of advice we provide to clients, maintains our reputation and helps you build your career.

We require every prospective trainee solicitor to undertake the accelerated LPC at BPP University. The course will prepare you for practice in the City.

Our two-year training contract is split into four six-month periods of work experience known as 'seats'. As a trainee solicitor, you will move around four different practice areas during this time to gain as much experience as possible – one of your seats will be in either our corporate or finance group, and another in one of our litigation teams. You will also have the option of spending time in the second year of training on secondment to one of our international offices or to the in-house legal team of a major client.

Benefits
PPP medical insurance, life assurance, season ticket loan, in-house gym, access to dentist, doctor and physiotherapist, subsidised staff restaurant, discounts at local retailers.

Sponsorship
GDL and LPC course fees are paid and maintenance grants are provided for both the GDL and LPC.

Partners 800+
Assistant Solicitors 2,500+
Total Trainees 129

Method of application
Online application form

Selection procedure
Assessment day

Closing date for February & August 2017
Law applications 31 July 2015
Non-Law applications 31 March 2015

Application
Training contracts p.a. up to 60
Applications p.a. 1,500
% interviewed p.a. 25%
Required degree grade 2:1

Training
Salary
1st year £39,500
2nd year £45,000
Holiday entitlement 25 days
% of trainees with a non-law degree p.a. 50%
No. of seats available abroad p.a. 25

Post-qualification
Salary £65,000

International offices
Alicante, Amsterdam, Baltimore, Beijing, Brussels, Budapest, Caracas, Colorado, Denver, Dubai, Dusseldorf, Frankfurt, Hamburg, Hanoi, Ho Chi Minh City, Hong Kong, Houston, Jakarta, Jeddah, Johannesburg, London, Los Angeles, Luxembourg, Madrid, Miami, Milan, Moscow, Munich, New York, Northern Virginia, Paris, Philadelphia, Rio de Janeiro, Riyadh, Rome, San Francisco, Sao Paulo, Shanghai, Silicon Valley, Singapore, Tokyo, Ulaanbaatar, Warsaw, Washington DC, Zagreb

A-Z of Solicitors

Holman Fenwick Willan LLP

Friary Court, 65 Crutched Friars, London EC3N 2AE
Tel: (020) 7264 8000
Email: grad.recruitment@hfw.com
Website: www.hfw.com

Firm profile
We are an international law firm with over 475 lawyers worldwide and a market-leading reputation for advising businesses on the legal aspects of international commerce. We have developed our transactional, regulatory and dispute resolution services across a number of core sectors, including aviation, commodities, energy, offshore mining, insurance, and shipping and transport. We offer our trainees an environment where they will be working alongside some of the most respected and talented lawyers in their field, embracing opportunities that include international seats and client secondments. If you are driven, enjoy challenges and are motivated by the idea of completing a training contract in a global environment, then we would like to hear from you.

Main areas of work
Aviation, commodities, construction, energy, financial institutions, insurance and reinsurance, logistics, mining, ports and terminals, shipping, space, superyachts, travel, cruise and leisure.

Trainee profile
We look for trainees with sharp minds, common sense, enthusiasm, ingenuity and a good sense of humour. We look for team players and good communicators who work hard and are client focused. As our training contract is truly international, we look for individuals who have a global perspective and an interest in completing international work. We accept applications from all disciplines and backgrounds; from students and experienced graduates alike.

Training environment
Trainees are involved in a combination of trainee workshops, departmental know-how discussions, mentoring by experienced lawyers and on-the-job training. All our trainees are also encouraged to spend time on our numerous worldwide pro bono and CSR initiatives.

Each year we recruit only a small number of trainees – 15 per year split across a September and a March intake. This enables us to give every trainee our full attention, and means that your individual contribution makes a big difference. You will do interesting, stretching work, very often with an international element. During your training you will have four six-month seats, sitting with a partner or a senior associate. Most trainees have the opportunity to work in one of our overseas offices (recently trainees have completed seats in Brussels, Dubai, Geneva, Hong Kong, Paris, Perth, Piraeus, Singapore and Shanghai), or to be seconded to a client.

Benefits
Our salaries are competitive. Trainees receive an annual salary of £36,000, increasing to £38,000 after the first year of the training contract. On top of that, we offer additional benefits, which include: study assistance and grants; generous contributory pension; subsidised gym membership; season ticket loan; life assurance; non-contributory medical insurance; cycle to work scheme; dental insurance, free GP service.

Vacation placements
We run a 1 week spring vacation scheme and 2 x 2 week summer vacation schemes. We have up to 10 places on each scheme (30 in total). Vacation scheme participants gain practical experience and exposure, as well as attending a final round interview for a training contract as part of the scheme.

The closing date for 2015 vacation schemes will be 14 February 2015.

Partners 145
Associates 214
Total Trainees 30

Contact
Sarah Burson

Method of application
Online application form

Selection procedure
Online application form, assessment centre, vacation scheme (if applied for), final round interview with 2 partners

Closing date for September 2017 / March 2018
31 July 2015

Application
Training contracts p.a. 15
Required degree grade 2:1

Training
Salary (2014)
1st year £36,000
2nd year £38,000
Holiday entitlement 25 days
Number of seats available abroad 9 (2014)

Post-qualification
Salary £58,000 (2014)

Overseas offices
Paris, Brussels, Geneva, Piraeus, Dubai, Shanghai, Hong Kong, Singapore, Perth, Melbourne, Sydney, Sao Paulo

A-Z of Solicitors

Ince & Co LLP

International House, 1 St Katharine's Way, London E1W 1AY
Email: recruitment@incelaw.com

Firm profile
With over 140 years of experience, Ince & Co is one of the oldest law firms in the City. We've built our success by always taking an innovative approach, looking for new ways to apply legal strategies and create new law. Ince & Co is frequently at the forefront of developments in contract and tort law.

Main areas of work
With a world leading reputation initially built on shipping and insurance, over the decades we have successfully explored new territory and established our expertise across a number of specific industries. We have five core business groups: aviation, energy and offshore, insurance and reinsurance, international trade and shipping.

Trainee profile
Hardworking, competitive individuals with initiative who relish challenge and responsibility within a team environment. Academic achievements, positions of responsibility, sport and travel are all taken into account. Not only do we regard our trainees as future solicitors and potential partners, but our training programme is different too. Ince trainees get involved in real legal work from day one, and the cases they assist on stay with them throughout their training period and sometimes beyond.

Training environment
Our training contract is unique as we do not have a rigid seat structure which confines trainees to a specific department. Instead, trainees are encouraged to be proactive and take on tasks from any of our business groups.

Our open and friendly culture allows our trainees to make a real contribution and get involved in all aspects of our practice. Trainees will sit with four different partners for six months at a time throughout their training. Under close supervision, trainees are encouraged from an early stage to meet and visit clients, interview witnesses, liaise with counsel, deal with technical experts and handle opposing lawyers. As a result they quickly build up a portfolio of cases from a number of partners involved in a cross-section of the firm's practice.

Benefits
Season ticket loan; corporate health cover; private health insurance; contributory pension scheme; Well Man/Well Woman health checks; fitness subsidy.

Vacation placements
Places for 2015 10; Duration 2 weeks; Remuneration £250 p/w.; Closing Date 31 January 2015.

Sponsorship & awards
LPC fees; £7,000 grant for study in London and Guildford, £6,500 grant for study elsewhere.
GDL fees; £6,500 grant for study in London and Guildford, £6,000 grant for study elsewhere.

Partners 96*
Senior Associates 50*
Solicitors 121*
Total Trainees 25*
* denotes worldwide figures

Contact
Rebecca Withers, Recruitment and Resourcing Manager

Method of application
Online at http://graduates.incelaw.com

Selection procedure
Interview with HR and a Partner from the Recruitment Committee & 4 tests

Closing date for 2017
31 July 2015

Application
Training contracts p.a. 10
Applications p.a. 861
% interviewed p.a. 10%
Required degree grade 2:1

Training
Salary
1st year £36,000
2nd year £39,000
Holiday entitlement 25 days
% of trainees with a non-law degree p.a. 50%

Post-qualification
Salary £58,000
% of trainees offered job on qualification (2013) 67%
% of partners (as at 2013) who joined as trainees approx 70%

Overseas offices
Beijing, Dubai, Hamburg, Hong Kong, Le Havre, Monaco, Paris, Piraeus, Shanghai, Singapore.

INCE &CO | INTERNATIONAL LAW FIRM

Irwin Mitchell

Riverside East, 2 Millsands, Sheffield S3 8DT
Tel: (0870) 1500 100 Fax: (0870) 197 3549
Email: graduaterecruitment@irwinmitchell.com
Website: www.irwinmitchell.com/graduates

Firm profile

Irwin Mitchell is unique, both in its culture and its approach to law. Nationally acclaimed, it is one of a few law firms to provide a diverse range of legal services to businesses and private individuals. It has a strong customer service culture and a high level of client retention. It has an established office network and employs more than 2100 staff. In August 2012, it was one of the first firms to become an Alternative Business Structure (ABS), and the first to be granted multiple ABS licences by the SRA. The firm was awarded the best graduate trainee recruitment campaign and most effective diversity programme (gender) at The Lawyer Workplace & Diversity Awards (2012). Other accolades include being ranked in the Stonewall Workplace Equality Index for 2013, as well as being one of the leading companies to sign up to the Business Compact scheme to create fairer job opportunities for all.

Main areas of work

Personal Legal Services: The firm remains one of the leading personal injury and medical negligence litigation practices in the UK, covering all the key injury types from road traffic accidents, to product liability claims and serious head/spinal injury cases. A comprehensive range of private client services are also provided, including a national family team. In addition, it provides a national probate, contentious probate, public law and conveyancing service and is the UK's leading court of protection practice.

Business Legal Services: The firm offers a wide range of commercial services and in recent years has expanded its corporate, commercial litigation and real estate services. The aim is to develop a cutting edge commercial service that will challenge the traditional City and national firms. Areas of expertise include business investigations, commercial litigation and dispute resolution, construction, corporate, employment, environmental, finance, insolvency, international, pensions, planning, real estate, recoveries, restructuring and tax.

Trainee profile

The firm is looking for ambitious and well-motivated individuals who have a real commitment to the law and who can demonstrate a positive approach to work-life balance. Irwin Mitchell recruits law and non-law graduates and views social ability as important as academic achievement.

Training environment

The firm's training contracts are streamed so that as a trainee you would either undertake a training contract based within the Personal Legal Services or Business Legal Services divisions. Trainees will have three training seats and a qualification seat. This allows trainees to gain practical experience in diverse areas of law, whilst maximising retention opportunities.

Benefits

Pension, professional subscriptions, health plan, death in service and critical illness cover.

Sponsorship & awards

GDL and LPC funding, if you have not started or completed your studies when offered a training contract, plus a maintenance grant of £4,500.

Work placements

Each summer the firm runs a formal work placement programme which is a great way to get a real insight into what life is like as a trainee at Irwin Mitchell. An increasing number of training contracts go to people who have undertaken a work placement, so the firm encourages all those interested in joining to apply. Closing date for applications is the 31 January 2015.

Partners 201
Other fee-earners 1200+
Total Trainees 79

Contact
Nicola Stanley
Graduate Manager
graduaterecruitment@
irwinmitchell.com

Method of application
Please visit the firm's website
www.irwinmitchell.com/
graduates and complete the
online application

Selection procedure
Telephone interview and assessment centre

Closing date for 2017
31 July 2015

Application
Training contracts p.a. 50
Applications p.a. 2,000-2,500
% interviewed p.a. 20%
Required degree grade
The firm does not require a
specific degree grade

Training
Salary
Outside London
1st year £25,000
2nd year £27,000
London
1st year £36,000
2nd year £38,000
reviewed annually in July
Holiday entitlement
24.5 days

Post-qualification
% of trainees offered job on
qualification 80%+

Overseas / Regional offices
Birmingham, Bristol, Cambridge,
Leeds, Leicester (consulting
office), London, Manchester,
Newcastle, Sheffield and
Southampton.

A-Z of Solicitors

irwinmitchell (IM)
solicitors

Jones Day

21 Tudor Street, London EC4Y 0DJ
Tel: (020) 7039 5959 Fax: (020) 7039 5999
Email: recruit.london@jonesday.com
Website: www.jonesdaylondon.com
Facebook: Jones Day UK Graduate Recruitment

Firm profile
Jones Day is a truly global law firm – probably the most integrated in the world. Our 2,400 lawyers across 41 locations in major business and finance centres worldwide have vast transactional and contentious experience and are at the forefront of globalisation and the advancement of the rule of law. Our strengths in London reflect those of the firm: our 200 London lawyers (including around 65 partners and 35 trainees) have a sophisticated understanding of risk and draw on specialist insights and skills from across the globe to guide clients through their toughest challenges and most significant, corporate life events.

Main areas of work
In London's critical financial centre, our lawyers are perfectly placed to address the most demanding and complex global matters; including cross-border M&A; real estate and finance transactions (including banking, capital markets, investment funds, private equity and structured finance); global disputes; and regulatory matters involving the UK, US and other authorities. Additional specialist areas include business restructuring; competition/antitrust; corporate tax planning; employment and pensions; energy; intellectual property; and projects and infrastructure.

Trainee profile
We look to recruit people who want to work on global deals, be challenged on an international level, and can become partners of the future, not just trainees who will qualify with us. Successful candidates have either a law or non-law degree; strong intellectual ability; good communication skills; and demonstrate resourcefulness, drive and dedication.

Training environment
The firm operates a unique, non-rotational system of training (whereby trainees receive work simultaneously from all departments) to provide flexibility, responsibility, faster development of potential and the opportunity to compare and contrast different disciplines alongside one another. Work will vary from small cases which trainees may handle alone (under the supervision of a senior lawyer) to larger matters where they will assist a partner or an associate solicitor. The firm runs a structured seminar programme to support the practical teaching trainees receive from associates and partners they work with.

Placement schemes
70 places for two-week placement schemes. Allowance of £400 per week. Apply for a placement if you want to train at Jones Day. We expect to recruit all trainees from our placement candidates. They see how the firm's non-rotational training system works in practice by taking on real work from a variety of practice areas and meet a range of lawyers at various social events. All our placement schemes are open to final year law and non-law students, graduates and postgraduates, as well as career changers. Our summer placement schemes are also open to penultimate year students undertaking a qualifying law degree. We recruit on a rolling basis, so cannot guarantee availability. Final deadlines (unless places fill earlier) are 31 October 2014 (winter scheme); 19 December 2014 (spring scheme); 16 January 2015 (summer scheme).

Trainee benefits
Private healthcare, season ticket loan, subsidised sports club membership, group life cover, salary sacrifice schemes and personal pension.

Sponsorship & awards
GDL and LPC fees paid and £8,000 maintenance p.a. Fast track LPC for sponsored students from August to February each year, allowing for a 6 month gap before training starts.

Partners approx 65
Assistant Solicitors approx 100
Total Trainees approx 35

Contact
Diana Spoudeas
Manager - Trainee Recruitment
& Development

Method of application
Online via our website:
www.jonesdaylondon.com

Selection procedure
We recruit all trainees from our placement schemes:
1 interview with 2 partners for placement scheme; further interview with 2 partners for training contract whilst on placement scheme.
Applications open early on 1 September 2014.

Closing date for 2014/15 placement schemes and 2017 training contracts
16 January 2015 (unless places fill earlier). We close when full, so apply early.

Application
Placements p.a. 70
Training contracts p.a. 20
Applications p.a. 1,800
% interviewed p.a. 25%
Required degree grade 2:1
Required A-Levels/IB AAA/36

Training
Salary (2014)
Start £42,000
After 10 months £47,000
After 22 months £51,000
Holiday entitlement
5 weeks

Post-qualification
Salary (2014) £75,000
% of trainees offered job on qualification (2014) 100%

Overseas offices
Continental Europe, Asia, USA, Latin America, Middle East, Asia Pacific

 JONES DAY One Firm Worldwide™

K&L Gates LLP

One New Change, London, EC4M 9AF
Tel: (020) 7648 9000 Fax: (020) 7648 9001
Email: traineerecruitment@klgates.com
Website: www.klgates.com

Firm profile

K&L Gates LLP comprises more than 2,000 lawyers who practice in 48 offices located on five continents. K&L Gates represents leading global corporations, growth and middle-market companies, capital markets participants and entrepreneurs in every major industry group as well as public sector entities, educational institutions, philanthropic organisations and individuals. The firm's practice is a robust full market practice – cutting edge, complex and dynamic, at once regional, national and international in scope. Over each of the last 5 years our revenues exceeded $1 billion and, as stated in the July 2010 issue of the UK publication Legal Business, the firm 'has further cemented its position as the Global 100's fastest growing firm.'

Main areas of work

K&L Gates is active in the areas of corporate/M&A, capital markets, private equity, restructuring and insolvency, finance, derivatives, funds, antitrust, competition and trade regulation, real estate, planning and environment, intellectual property, media and sport, construction, insurance coverage, regulatory, tax, employment, pensions and incentives, litigation, international arbitration, white collar crime and other forms of dispute resolution.

Trainee profile

The firm welcomes applications from both law and non-law students. Law students should generally be in their penultimate year of study and non-law students should be in their final year of study. The firm also welcomes applications from relevant postgraduates or others who have satisfied the 'academic stage of training' as required by the Solicitors Regulation Authority (SRA). You should be highly motivated, intellectually curious, with an interest in commercial law and be looking for comprehensive training.

Training environment

The firm ensures each trainee is given exceptional opportunities to learn, experience and develop so that they can achieve their maximum potential. Trainees spend six month seats in four of the areas mentioned above. Each trainee sits with a supervisor and is allocated an individual mentor to ensure all round supervision and training. The firm has a thorough induction scheme, and has won awards for its career development programme. High importance is placed on the acquisition of business and professional skills, with considerable emphasis on client contact and early responsibility. The training programme consists of weekly legal education seminars, workshops and a full programme of skills electives. Pro bono and corporate social responsibility activities are also encouraged.

Benefits

25 days holiday per annum, subsidised sports club membership, season ticket loan, permanent health insurance, life assurance, GP service and pension.

Legal work placements

The firm's formal legal work placement scheme is open to penultimate year law students, final year non-law students, other relevant post graduates or others who have satisfied the 'academic stage of training' as required by the SRA.

Sponsorship

GDL funding: fees paid plus £5,000 maintenance grant. LPC funding: fees paid plus £7,000 maintenance grant.

Partners 55
Trainees 16
Total Staff 275

Contact
Hayley Atherton

Method of application
Online at www.klgates.com

Selection procedure
Online testing, full assessment centre and interview

Closing date for 2017
31 July 2015

Application
Training contracts p.a. TBD
Applications p.a. 1,000
% interviewed p.a. 10%
Required degree grade 2:1

Training
Salary
1st year £37,500
2nd year £41,000
% of trainees with a non-law degree p.a. Varies

Post-qualification
Salary £62,000
% of trainees offered job on qualification 80%

Overseas offices
Anchorage, Austin, Beijing, Berlin, Boston, Brisbane, Brussels, Charleston, Charlotte, Chicago, Dallas, Doha, Dubai, Fort Worth, Frankfurt, Harrisburg, Hong Kong, Houston, Los Angeles, Melbourne, Miami, Milan, Moscow, Newark, New York, Orange County, Palo Alto, Paris, Perth, Pittsburgh, Portland, Raleigh, Research Triangle Park, San Diego, San Francisco, Sao Paulo, Seattle, Seoul, Shanghai, Singapore, Spokane, Sydney, Taipei, Tokyo, Warsaw, Washington and Wilmington.

K&L GATES

Kennedys

25 Fenchurch Avenue, London, EC3M 5AD
Tel: (020) 7667 9667 Fax: (020) 7667 9777
Email: r.bubb@kennedys-law.com
Website: www.kennedys-law.com

Firm profile
Kennedys is a specialist national and international legal firm with unrivalled expertise in litigation and dispute resolution. The firm has over 1240 people globally, across nine UK and 10 international locations. Kennedys is a top 30 law firm. Kennedys is regarded as a leader, not just because it has some of the most respected legal minds in their field – but because they know the importance of being practical, commercial and approachable. Kennedys prides itself on offering its clients clear legal advice.

Main areas of work
Kennedys lawyers provide a range of specialist legal services for many industries including: insurance/reinsurance, healthcare, construction, rail, maritime and international trade, aviation and transport – with a particular focus on dispute resolution and litigation.

Trainee profile
The firm is looking for graduates who are articulate, self aware and resourceful. Kennedys' trainees experience early responsibility and client contact, therefore it essential to have a mature and confident approach. Trainees with the firm must have commercial awareness and a strong appreciation of the interests of the client. As Kennedys has a vibrant and supportive working environment it is also looking for sociable, energetic team players.

Training environment
The purpose of the training contract is to give the trainees a mix of experience and skills that will set them up in their legal career as a solicitor with Kennedys. The firm's ability to consistently offer the majority of its trainees positions on qualification is attributable to producing newly qualified lawyers who are competent, confident and commercially driven. A balance of responsibility, supervision and formal training achieves this. Kennedys ensures that their trainee solicitors are given sound training in the core disciplines. All partners and supervisors are readily accessible and always ready to offer support when needed.

Placement schemes
Kennedys runs summer vacation schemes during June and July. Applications should be made online for the 2015 schemes by 31 January 2015.

Benefits
Permanent health insurance, pension, private medial insurance, life insurance, 25 days holiday increasing to 27 days after five years, interest-free season ticket loan, gym membership, cycle to work scheme, child care assistance scheme, employee assistance scheme, corporate GP, contribution towards conveyancing fees and eye care vouchers.

Partners 173
Fee-Earners 565
Total Trainees 36
Total Staff 1240

Contact
Rowena Bubb
Graduate Recruitment Advisor
r.bubb@kennedys-law.com

Method of application
Online Application Form

Selection procedure
Assessment Day

Closing date for 2017
31 July 2015

Application
Training contracts approx 18
Applications 900 (London)
Required degree grade 2:1 and 300 UCAS points or equivalent at A-level

Training
Salary
1st Year £34,000 (London)
2nd Year £37,000 (London)

Post-qualification
% of trainees offered job on qualification 95%

Offices
Auckland, Belfast, Birmingham, Brussels, Cambridge, Chelmsford, Dubai, Dublin, Hong Kong, Lisbon, London, Madrid, Maidstone, Manchester, Miami, Sheffield, Singapore, Sydney, Taunton

Kennedys
Legal advice in black and white

King & Wood Mallesons

10 Queen Street Place, London EC4R 1BE
Tel: (020) 7111 2268 Fax: (020) 7111 2000
Email: graduate.recruitment@eu.kwm.com
Website: careers.kwm.com/en-uk

Firm profile

King & Wood Mallesons was formed by a game changing combination of the Asian powerhouse with SJ Berwin's first tier capabilities in Europe and the Middle East on 1 November 2013. King & Wood Mallesons is a new choice of law firm bringing a fresh perspective to commercial thinking and client experience. Strategically positioned in the world's growth markets, more than 2,700 lawyers in more than 30 international offices are cutting through the challenges facing business, providing commercial solutions and transforming the way legal services are delivered.

Main areas of work

King & Wood Mallesons advises clients on the full spectrum of commercial, financial and specialist legal services, with a principle focus on: antitrust and regulatory, banking and finance, corporate M&A and securities, DR/litigation, projects (energy and resources), funds / private equity, intellectual property, real estate and tax.

Trainee profile

The firm wants ambitious, commercially minded individuals who seek a high level of involvement from day one. Candidates must have a strong academic record, be on track for, or have achieved, a 2:1 or equivalent in their undergraduate degree, and have demonstrated strong team and leadership potential.

Training environment

The two-year training contract is divided into four six-month seats. Trainees will spend two seats (which may include a seat abroad or client secondment) within the following areas: finance, mergers and aquisitions, equity capital markets, private equity, venture capital and investment funds. Trainees are given early responsibility and are supported throughout the training contract.

How to apply

The firm welcomes applications from all disciplines and all universities. Applications must be made using the firm's online form available at careers.kwm.com/en-uk. The same form can be used to indicate your interest in an open day, a vacation scheme and/or a training contract.

Benefits

25 days holiday, private healthcare, gym membership/subsidy, life assurance, pension scheme, season ticket loan, free lunch.

Partners 550
Assistant Solicitors 2230
Total Trainees 72

Contact
Graduate Recruitment Team

Method of application
Online application form

Selection procedure
2 interviews / case study / critical reasoning test

Closing date for 2017
31 July 2015
2015 Easter and summer vacation schemes 31 January 2015

Application
Training contracts p.a. 30
Applications p.a. 2,000
10% interviewed p.a.
Required degree grade 2:1

Training
Salary
1st year £39,250
2nd year £43,500
Holiday entitlement 25 days
% of trainees with a non-law degree p.a. 50%

Post-qualification
Salary (2013) £63,000
% of trainees offered job on qualification (as at September 2014) 73%

Overseas offices
Over 30 offices across Asia, Australia, Europe and the Middle East.

A-Z of Solicitors

KING&WOOD
MALLESONS

Kingsley Napley LLP

Knights Quarter, 14 St John's Lane, London EC1M 4AJ
Tel: (020) 7814 1200 Fax: (020) 7490 2288 DX 22 Chancery Lane
Website: www.kingsleynapley.co.uk

Firm profile

Kingsley Napley is an internationally recognised law firm based in central London. Our wide range of expertise means that we can provide support for our clients in all areas of their business and private life. Many of our lawyers are leaders in their field and our practice areas are highly ranked by the legal directories.

We are known for combining creative solutions with pragmatism and a friendly, sensitive approach. The relationship between lawyer and client is key. We work hard to match clients with lawyers who have the right mix of skills, experience and approach in order to achieve the best possible outcome.

Main areas of work

Clinical negligence and personal injury, corporate and commercial, criminal litigation, dispute resolution, employment, family, immigration, private client, public law, real estate and regulatory and professional discipline.

Trainee profile

The firm looks for both legal and non-legal graduates who have a strong academic background (achieved a 2:1 degree). A trainee will need to demonstrate commercial awareness, motivation and enthusiasm. To be successful you will need excellent communication skills with the ability to be a creative, practical problem solver. We look for team players who bring something to the table and have a long-term interest in Kingsley Napley and the areas of legal practice it focuses on.

Training environment

The training contract will consist of four seats in both contentious and non-contentious practice areas, which aim to provide trainees with a wide range skills and practical experience. Individual preferences for seats will be taken into account, but will also be balanced with the firm's needs.

Trainees work closely with partners and solicitors at all levels in a supportive team structure, and have regular reviews to assist with development. The firm has a friendly and open environment which gives trainees the chance to meet clients, be responsible for their own work and join in marketing and client development activities.

Benefits

Private health insurance, income protection insurance, life assurance, pension, corporate cash plan and 25 days holiday per year during training. Trainees are also eligible to participate in the firm's flexible benefits scheme.

Partners 45
Assistant Solicitors 76
Total Trainees 10

Contact
Jemimah Cook, HR Director or
Vicki Tavener, HR Officer
Tel 020 7814 1200

Method of application
Online application form

Selection Procedure
Assessment centre. Candidates who are successful at this stage will then be invited to an interview.

Closing date for September 2016
31st May 2015

Application
Training contracts p.a. 5
Applications p.a. 250
% interviewed p.a 10%
Required degree grade 2:1

Training
Salary (2014)
First year £30,000
Second year £32,000
Holiday entitlement 25 days
% of trainees with a non-law degree 60%

Post qualification
Salary (2014) £52,000
% of trainees offered job on qualification 80%

A-Z of Solicitors

Kirkland & Ellis International LLP

30 St Mary Axe, London EC3A 8AF
Tel: (020) 7469 2000 Fax: (020) 7469 2001
Website: www.kirkland.com/ukgraduate

Partners 733	
Assistant solicitors 839	
Contact	
Kate Osborne	
Method of application	
Online application form	
Selection procedure	
Interview	
Closing date for 2017	
31 July 2015	
Training	
Salary	
1st year (2013) £41,000	
2nd year (2013) £44,000	
Holiday entitlement 25 days	
Post-qualification	
Salary	
1st year £97,560	
% of trainees offered job on	
qualification 100%	
Overseas/regional offices	
Beijing, Chicago, Hong Kong,	
Houston, Los Angeles, Munich,	
New York, Palo Alto, San	
Francisco, Shanghai,	
Washington DC	

Firm profile
Kirkland & Ellis International LLP is a 1,600-attorney law firm representing global clients in offices around the world.

For over 100 years, major national and international clients have called upon Kirkland & Ellis to provide superior legal advice and client services. The firm's London office has been the hub of European operations since 1994. Here, approximately 140 lawyers offer detailed expertise to a wide range of UK and international clients.

Main areas of work
The firm handles complex corporate, debt finance, restructuring, funds, capital markets, tax, intellectual property, regulatory, antitrust and competition, litigation and counselling matters. Kirkland & Ellis operates as a strategic network, committing the full resources of an international firm to any matter in any territory as appropriate.

Trainee profile
Your academic record will be excellent, probably culminating in an expected or achieved 2:1. You will have the initiative, the drive and the work ethic to thrive in the firm's meritocratic culture and arrive with an understanding of the work undertaken in the firm's London office.

Training environment
As one of a select number of trainees, you will be given early responsibility to work on complex multi jurisdictional matters.

The principal focus of your training will be on corporate law with a specialism in private equity. You will complete four, six month seats and obtain training in areas such as debt finance, funds, arbitration, IP, regulatory, antitrust and competition, restructuring and tax. In addition there will be opportunities to undertake an overseas secondment to enable you to experience the international resources and capabilities of Kirkland & Ellis.

Your on the job training will be actively supported by an extensive education programme, carefully tailored to meet your needs.

Benefits
Private medical insurance, travel insurance, life insurance, employee assistance plan, corporate gym membership, bonus scheme and season ticket loan.

Vacation placements
Places for 2015: 16-18. Duration: 2 weeks. Remuneration: £350 per week. Closing date for applications: 16 January 2015.

Sponsorship & awards
GDL and LPC course fees and a maintenance grant of £8,000 p.a.

KIRKLAND & ELLIS

Latham & Watkins

99 Bishopsgate, London EC2M 3XF
Tel: (020) 7710 1000 Fax: (020) 7374 4460
Email: lograduate.recruitment@lw.com
Website: www.lw.com

Partners 65+	
Associates 150	
Trainees 40	

Contact
Graduate Recruitment Team
lograduate.recruitment@
lw.com

Method of application
Online application form at
www.lw.com

Selection procedure
2 x 30 minute interviews with
a partner and an associate,
plus a case study

Closing date for 2017
31 July 2015

Application
Training contracts p.a. 20
Required degree grade 2:1

Training
Salary
1st year (2014) £42,000
2nd year (2014) £45,000

Post-qualification
Salary (2014) £96,970

Overseas/regional offices
Abu Dhabi, Barcelona, Beijing,
Boston, Brussels, Chicago,
Doha, Dubai, Frankfurt, Hamburg, Hong Kong, Houston,
London, Los Angeles, Madrid,
Milan, Moscow, Munich, New
Jersey, New York, Orange
County, Paris, Riyadh, Rome,
San Diego, San Francisco,
Shanghai, Silicon Valley,
Singapore, Tokyo,
Washington DC

Firm profile
Latham & Watkins has more than 2,000 fee earners in 31 offices across Europe, the US, the Middle East and Asia and the London office advises on some of the most significant and groundbreaking cross-border transactions in Europe. The firm believes that its non-hierarchical management style and 'one firm' culture makes Latham & Watkins unique.

Main areas of work
Latham & Watkins provides clients with a strong, full-service offering, including banking and finance, corporate, capital markets, litigation, real estate, employment and tax practices. Many of the firm's practice groups are award-winning industry leaders, as are many of the firm's partners.

The firm offers clients unrivalled legal resources and strategic commercial thinking to provide innovative solutions to even the most complex issues, and serves multinational companies, startups, investment banks, private equity funds, venture capital firms, sovereign wealth funds, governments and other organisations around the world.

Trainee profile
Candidates should be entrepreneurial and thrive on early responsibility. Those with a strong academic background, excellent communication skills and a consistent record of personal and/or professional achievement will be rewarded with first-class training in a stimulating environment.

The firm is dedicated to diversity and equal opportunity and values originality and creative thinking.

Training environment
Latham & Watkins can provide a very different training experience to that offered by other elite law firms. Each trainee receives bespoke supervision and outstanding support while being encouraged to recognise that they have their own part to play in the growth and success of the firm.

Each trainee has meaningful responsibility from the outset and significant legal experience on qualification. It is also common for trainees to be given the opportunity to spend one of their four six-month seats in one of the firm's overseas offices.

Benefits
Healthcare and dental scheme, pension scheme and life assurance.

Sponsorship & awards
All GDL and LPC costs are paid and trainees receive a maintenance grant of £8,000 per year whilst studying. A bonus of £500 is provided by the firm if a distinction is achieved in the LPC.

Vacation placements
The firm runs 2 vacation schemes during summer. Students are paid £350 per week.

Please visit our website www.lw.com for application deadlines and eligibility requirements as well as for further information regarding other recruitment opportunities and events.

LATHAM&WATKINS

A-Z of Solicitors

Lester Aldridge LLP

Russell House, Oxford Road, Bournemouth BH8 8EX
Tel: (01202) 786161 Fax: (01202) 786110
Email: humanresources@LA-law.com
Website: www.lesteraldridge.com

Firm profile

Lester Aldridge LLP is an energetic business providing both commercial and private client servic-es on a local, regional, national and international scale. The firm's reputation rests on the expertise of its people who are first-class in every respect, and on the firm's astute approach to its clients. Client satisfaction is always the firm's aim.

History is important in any business – it shows a commitment to its industry and its clients and the firm is proud of its own history. Lester Aldridge's positioning on the south coast offers a positive working environment and a great work life balance; while providing opportunities to work with first class lawyers, impressive clients and opportunity for City experience via LA's London office.

Excellent legal advice is standard. Each client can expect a commitment to excellent service from its staff, a partner led approach, leading legal expertise, comprehensive and cohesive advice, in-novative and technological support and value for money.

Main areas of work

LA's work is divided up into 5 groups – Dispute Resolution, Corporate and Commercial, Banking and Finance, Real Estate and Private Client. Within these groups the firm has a number of sec-tors which offer a cross section of work – these include marine, charities, fertility and same sex couples, development, care and medical practices. As a trainee, you will get involved in the broad range giving you choice and experience for your future career in law.

Trainee profile

Candidates should have a consistently strong academic record, be commercially aware and possess a broad range of interpersonal skills. Applicants should be highly motivated and have a desire to succeed working with teams to advise clients in dynamic and demanding industries.

Training environment

When you start at LA you'll be given responsibilities and real jobs to get your teeth into. Direct client involvement is encouraged and you will become an integral part of each team you join.

During the course of your two year contract you will complete four seats of six months duration. This gives you exposure to different areas of the firm and hopefully will help you decide what you would like to specialise in.

Giving constructive feedback is always encouraged at LA, so you can expect to hear the good things about your work from your team (and a few things you need to improve). LA also has an appraisal system where you work with your team leader to set objectives and create an action plan that will measure your progress. In addition each trainee is assigned a mentor to provide guidance and encouragement and regular review meetings are arranged with the Managing Partner where you'll be encouraged to voice your views and opinions.

Vacation placements

The firm offers 2 week work placements in the summer of each year. The application deadline is usually 31 March but please check the firm's website for further details on how to apply.

Sponsorship

LPC loan currently under review.

Vacancies 6
Trainees 13
Total Staff 290

Contact
HR Team

Method of application
Apply to human resources application form

Selection procedure
Interview by a panel of part-ners as part of assessment and development day

Closing date for 2017
30 June 2015

Application
Training contracts p.a. 6
Minimum required degree grade 2:1

Training
Starting salary Competitive market rate for a south coast firm plus additional London allowance where appropriate
Holiday entitlement 22 days

Offices
Bournemouth (2), Southamp-ton & London

Lewis Silkin

5 Chancery Lane, Clifford's Inn, London EC4A 1BL
Tel: (020) 7074 8000 Fax: (020) 7864 1200
Email: train@lewissilkin.com
Website: www.lewissilkin.com

Firm profile

Lewis Silkin is a commercial firm with 60 partners. Due to its expertise and the number of leaders in their respective fields, it has an impressive list of household name clients, ranging from large multinational corporations to brands to government agencies and entrepreneurs, across a wide range of sectors. What distinguishes them is a matter of personality. For lawyers, they are notably informal, unstuffy…well, human really. They are 'people people'; as committed and professional as any good law firm, but perhaps more adept at the inter-personal skills that make relationships work and go on working. They place a high priority on the excellent technical ability and commercial thinking of their lawyers and also on their relationships with clients. Clients find them refreshingly easy to deal with. The firm has a friendly, lively style with a commitment to continuous improvement.

Main areas of work

Lewis Silkin provides services through five departments: Corporate; Employment, Reward and Immigration; Litigation and Dispute Resolution; Real Estate and Development; and Media, Brands and Technology. The major work areas include: commercial litigation and dispute resolution; corporate services, which includes company commercial and corporate finance; intellectual property; media and entertainment; reputation management; employment; marketing services, embracing advertising and marketing law; real estate (including social housing); and technology and communications. They are recognised by commentators as a leading firm in employment and all aspects of brand management.

Trainee profile

They are looking for up to six trainees with keen minds and personalities, who will fit into a professional but informal team.

Training environment

The firm provides a comprehensive induction and training programme, with practical hands-on experience from day one. You will sit with either a partner or senior associate giving you access to day-to-day supervision and guidance. The training contract consists of four six-month seats, working in the firm's five departments and/or client secondments.

Benefits

These include individual and firm bonus schemes, life assurance, group income protection, health insurance, season ticket loan, group pension plan and subsidised gym membership.

Work placements

Please refer to the firm's website for further information.

Sponsorship & awards

Funding for GDL and LPC fees is provided plus a £5,000 maintenance grant for each.

lewissilkin

Partners 60
Assistant Solicitors 94
Total Trainees 12

Contact
Human Resources

Method of application
Online application form

Selection procedure
Assessment day, including an interview with 2 partners, a group exercise, analytical and aptitude test

Closing date for 2017 intake
Please refer to website

Application
Training contracts p.a. up to 6
Applications p.a. 600
Required degree grade 2:1

Training
Salary
1st year £32,500
2nd year £34,500
Holiday entitlement 25 days

Post-qualification
Salary (2014) up to £52,000

Linklaters LLP

One Silk Street, London EC2Y 8HQ
Tel: (020) 7456 2000 Fax: (020) 7456 2222
Email: graduate.recruitment@linklaters.com
Website: www.linklaters.com/ukgrads

Firm profile

Live your ambition at Linklaters. Whatever career goals you have, as one of the world's most prestigious law firms, we can help you to achieve them. We're committed to maximising potential in all of our people. So, we'll give you a training contract that plays to your strengths, plus a wealth of dedicated support – allowing you to develop a long and rewarding career in law.

Main areas of work

Many law firms are strong in particular areas. Linklaters is the only firm to have market-leading teams across the globe covering a full range of practice areas. This, combined with the breadth of our client base (including leading financial institutions, governments and high-profile companies), sets us apart from our competitors.

Trainee profile

Linklaters attracts and recruits people from a range of subject disciplines and backgrounds who are talented, motivated and expect a lot from themselves. What they all have in common is a desire to achieve their full potential through a career in law. In return, we offer a wealth of opportunity, entrepreneurial freedom and incredible rewards.

Training environment

Linklaters helps you achieve your ambition by providing an outstanding environment in which to succeed. For non-law graduates, it starts with the Graduate Diploma in Law (GDL), giving you all the legal knowledge required to start your professional training. All graduates then come together to complete the bespoke Legal Practice Course (LPC).

Your two-year training contract covers six-month seats in four practice areas, typically including an international or client secondment, so you will have the opportunity to develop a breadth and depth of knowledge and to enjoy the highest quality training in commercial law – allowing you to develop as a lawyer and consider qualification options for your career. We believe in continuous learning and so the unique Linklaters Law and Business School will deliver the tools, knowledge and confidence for you throughout your career.

Sponsorship & benefits

GDL and LPC fees are paid in full, plus a maintenance grant provided for each. Benefits include eligibility for a personal performance-related bonus, pension, private medical insurance, life assurance, income protection, in-house healthcare services, family friendly benefits, in-house gym, subsidised staff restaurant, interest-free season ticket loan, holiday travel insurance, time bank scheme, cycle2work and give as you earn.

Vacation placements

Linklaters offers vacation schemes for penultimate year undergraduates at UK and Irish universities (law and non-law), which take place over the summer, as well as vacation schemes for final year students and graduates (law and non-law), which take place in the spring. We also offer first year undergraduates structured work experience through a two-day insight programme called Pathfinder. All applications begin with an online application form.

Partners 460
Associates 2,200
Trainees 230+*
*(London)

Contact
Graduate Recruitment

Method of application
Online application form

Selection procedure
Critical thinking test, work simulation exercise and two interviews

Application
Training contracts p.a. 110
Applications p.a. 4,500
Required degree grade 2:1

Training
Salary
1st year £40,000
Holiday entitlement 25 days
% of trainees with a non-law degree p.a. 40%

Post-qualification
Salary £65,000 + discretionary performance-related bonus

Offices
Abu Dhabi, Amsterdam, Antwerp, Bangkok, Beijing, Berlin, Brussels, Dubai, Düsseldorf, Frankfurt, Hong Kong, Lisbon, London, Luxembourg, Madrid, Milan, Moscow, Munich, New York, Paris, Rome, São Paulo, Seoul, Shanghai, Singapore, Stockholm, Tokyo, Warsaw, Washington DC

Linklaters

Macfarlanes LLP

20 Cursitor Street, London, EC4A 1LT
Tel: (020) 7831 9222 Fax: (020) 7831 9607
Email: gradrec@macfarlanes.com
Website: www.macfarlanes.com

Firm profile

Macfarlanes is a leading City law firm with a straightforward, independently-minded approach. We bring smart, thoughtful solutions to the complex legal challenges faced by our clients around the world. We are recognised for the quality of our work, not just in dealing with a full range of corporate and commercial matters, but in advising clients on their private affairs. Clients trust Macfarlanes' judgement and the firm is in a unique position to advise on their most complex matters, whilst at the same time remaining smaller than its competitors.

As advisers to many of the world's leading businesses and business leaders, the firm manages international matters in an effective and seamless manner. It gives clients a single point of contact and co-ordinates advice across all relevant jurisdictions.

Main areas of work

The firm's main areas of practice are in banking and finance; commercial; competition; corporate and M&A; corporate and regulatory investigations; data privacy; employment; financial services regulation; hedge funds; investment management; IP and IT; litigation and dispute resolution; pensions; private client; private equity; projects; real estate; restructuring and insolvency; and tax.

Trainee profile

Macfarlanes believes the strongest firm is achieved by choosing a mix of people – reflecting different styles so as to meet the needs that it – and its varied range of clients – will have in the future. The firm looks for a rare combination of intellectual curiosity, character and drive. It is looking for ambitious trainees who will thrive on responsibility and challenge and who are ready to begin their careers on day one.

Training environment

Woven into every aspect of life at the firm is an enduring commitment to the development of trainees. Training begins with tailored electives on the LPC and a week-long induction course at the start of your training contract.

During the two-year training contract you'll be working on real cases, doing real work for real clients from day one. As a trainee you will complete four six-month seats in different areas of practice; typically it is one seat in corporate and M&A, two seats in either private client, litigation, commercial real estate or tax, and then a seat in one of the firm's specialised practice areas within corporate. The precise allocation of seats is flexible so that it can offer you as broad a legal training as possible. Support and guidance are, of course, vital and you will find your supervisor a valuable source of information and inspiration.

Benefits

Life assurance, pension scheme with company contributions, private healthcare, discretionary performance related bonus scheme, season ticket loan, subsidised restaurant, gym membership assistance, eyecare vouchers and childcare vouchers.

Vacation placements

Places for 2015: 55; Duration 2 weeks; Remuneration: £300 p.w.; Closing date: 31 January 2015.

Sponsorship & awards

CPE/GDL and LPC fees paid in full and a £7,000 maintenance allowance.

Partners 80
Assistant Solicitors 185
Total Trainees 56

Contact
Vicki Wood

Method of application
Online via website

Selection procedure
Assessment day

Closing date for 2017
31 July 2015

Application
Training contracts p.a. 27
Applications p.a. 1,000
% interviewed p.a. 15%
Required degree grade 2:1

Training
Salary
1st year £39,000
2nd year £44,000
Holiday entitlement 25 days,
rising to 26 on qualification

Post-qualification
Salary (2014) £64,000
% of trainees offered job
on qualification (2014) 80%
% of partners (as at 21/5/14)
who joined as trainees 59%

Maclay Murray & Spens LLP

1 George Square, Glasgow, G2 1AL
Website: www.mms.co.uk

Firm profile
Maclay Murray & Spens LLP is a full service, independent, commercial law firm offering legal solutions and advice to clients throughout the UK and beyond. With offices in Aberdeen, Glasgow, Edinburgh and London the firm's objective is to provide a consistently excellent quality of service across the firm's entire service range and from every UK office.

Main areas of work
Banking and finance, capital projects, commercial dispute resolution, construction and engineering, corporate, employment, pensions, EU, competition and regulatory, IP and technology, oil and gas, planning and environmental, private client, property, public sector and tax.

Trainee profile
Applicants should have a strong academic background (minimum 2:1 degree) as well as demonstrate a number of key skills including an inquiring mind and a keenness to learn, commitment, professionalism, determination to see a job through, first class communication skills, the ability to get on with colleagues and clients at all levels, an ability to operate under pressure in a team environment, as well as a sense of humour. The firm welcomes bright non-law graduates.

Training environment
Trainees will have three seats of eight months where you will be provided with a very broad range of practical experience, including legal writing, drafting, research work and an element of client contact. This is one of the firm's strengths as a business and a long standing attraction for candidates.

In addition to on-the-job training, the firm also offers trainees the opportunity of attending in-house seminars and workshops in order to develop their legal and general business skills. By working as a team member on more complex transactions, you are given the opportunity to gain experience over a broad range of work. You will also be encouraged to meet and work alongside clients from different backgrounds and diverse areas of industry and commerce. The firm has an open plan office environment which allows trainees the benefit of working closely alongside solicitors at all levels. This promotes greater communication and team working. Trainees are also able to participate in CSR activities which take place across our offices.

Benefits
At MMS trainees are paid competitive salaries as well as provided with an attractive benefits package. All of the firm's employees receive a combination of fixed and variable holidays totalling 34 days each year. The firm also offers a contributory pension scheme, death in service benefit worth four times your annual salary, support with conveyancing fees, enhanced maternity and paternity pay, income protection insurance, cycle to work scheme, Give As You Earn, season ticket loan for travel, childcare voucher scheme and discounted access to medical and dental plans.

Vacation scheme
MMS offers students the opportunity of a three week summer placement. To apply please visit our website for more details on our application process. The closing date is January 2015.

Sponsorship
Assistance with LPC is available.

Partners 60
Assistant Solicitors 130
Total Trainees 40

Contact
Karen Falconer, HR Assistant
karen.falconer@mms.co.uk

Method of application
Application forms only, accessed at www.mms.co.uk/careers/ traineeship

Selection procedure
Two stage interview process. During the second stage candidates will be asked to complete a role-play and research exercise.

Closing date for 2016 and 2017
London traineeship August 2015
Scottish traineeship October 2015

Application
Training contracts p.a. 20-25
Applications p.a. 450
Required degree grade 2:1

Training
Salary (2013)
(Scotland) 1st year £18,000
(London) 1st year £32,000
Holiday entitlement 34 days per year, including public holidays

Mayer Brown[1]

201 Bishopsgate, London EC2M 3AF
Email: graduaterecruitment@mayerbrown.com
Website: www.mayerbrowngraduates.com

Firm profile

Mayer Brown was one of the first law firms to develop a global platform in recognition of the fact that many of its clients increasingly needed an integrated, cross border legal advice. The firm is now one of the world's leading global law firms with offices in key business centres across Asia, Europe and the Americas. In Brazil, the firm has an association with Tauil & Chequer Avogados. Through the association, the extensive international expertise of its lawyers and its presence in the leading financial centres around the world, Mayer Brown provides high quality legal advice and client-focussed solutions to support many of the world's leading businesses, governments and individuals. This includes a significant proportion of the Fortune 100, FTSE 100 and DAX and Hang Seng Index and organisations in the banking, insurance, communications, industrials, energy, construction, professional services, pharmaceuticals, chemicals and mining sectors.

Main areas of work

Our lawyers have expertise across a wide range of areas including corporate, finance, litigation and dispute resolution, real estate, insurance and reinsurance, pensions and employment, competition and trade, tax, intellectual property and information technology.

Trainee profile

We are looking for candidates who not only have a consistently strong academic record, but also who have a wide range of interests and achievements outside their academic career. Additionally, the firm would like to see innovative candidates who can demonstrate a drive for results, good verbal and written communication skills and an ability to analyse, with good judgement and excellent interpersonal skills.

Training environment

One of the advantages of joining Mayer Brown are the choices available to you. As a trainee at the firm, you will be able to tailor your training contract across a broad range of seats, including our main practice areas in London (as listed above), and international secondments in either Hong Kong or New York. If you don't want to stray too far, you have the option to gain valuable in house experience by going on secondment to one of the firm's major clients. Whilst Mayer Brown is a global law firm, our London office remains a tightly knit team with an open and inclusive culture. You will be given significant opportunities to assist on matters which may be multi-disciplinary, cross-border, complex and high-profile in nature.

Benefits

Benefits include 25 days holiday per annum, an interest free season ticket loan, subsidised sports club membership and membership of private health scheme.

Work experience programmes

The firm runs three work experience programmes each year; two three-week schemes in the summer and one two-week programme in the spring. You will gain experience in two key practice areas and be involved in seminars and social events, including a trip to one of our European offices.

Sponsorship & awards

The firm will cover the cost of the GDL and LPC fees and provide a maintenance grant of £7,000.

[1] Mayer Brown International LLP operates in combination with its associated Illinois limited liability partnerships, a SELAS established in France, a Hong Kong partnership, and its associated entities in Asia, and is associated with Tauil & Chequer Advogados, a Brazilian law partnership.

Partners 100
Assistant Solicitors 130
Total Trainees 30

Contact
Caroline Sarson,
Graduate Recruitment Manager

Method of application
Online application form

Selection procedure
One stage assessment process including an interview, a written exercise, a group exercise and an online verbal reasoning test

Closing date for September 2016/March 2017
31 July 2015

Application
Training contracts p.a. approx 15-20
Applications p.a. 2,000+
% interviewed p.a. 8%
Required degree grade 2:1

Training
1st year £37,500
2nd year £42,300
Holiday entitlement 25 days
% of trainees with a non-law degree p.a. 50%

Post-qualification
NQ salary £62,500

Overseas offices
Bangkok, Beijing, Brussels, Charlotte, Chicago, Dusseldorf, Frankfurt, Guangzhou, Hanoi, Ho Chi Minh City, Hong Kong, Houston, London, Los Angeles, New York, Palo Alto, Paris, Shanghai, Singapore and Washington DC

MAYER·BROWN

McDermott Will & Emery UK LLP

Heron Tower, 110 Bishopsgate, London EC2N 4AY
Tel: (020) 7577 6900 Fax: (020) 7577 6950
Website: www.mwe.com
Email: graduate.recruitment@mwe.com

Partners 592 (worldwide)	
Associate Lawyers & Other Fee-earners 660 (worldwide)	
Total Trainees 5 (London)	

Contact
Graduate Recruitment

Method of application
Apply online at www.mwe.com

Selection procedure
Assessment day, written test and Partner interview

Closing date for 2017
17 July 2015

Training
Salary
1st year £39,000 (2014)
2nd year £43,000 (2014)

Firm profile

McDermott Will & Emery UK LLP is a leading international law firm with offices in Boston, Brussels, Chicago, Düsseldorf, Frankfurt, Houston, London, Los Angeles, Miami, Milan, Munich, New York, Orange County, Paris, Rome, Seoul, Silicon Valley and Washington DC, and a strategic alliance with MWE China Law Offices (Shanghai). The firm's client base includes some of the world's leading financial institutions, largest corporations, mid-cap businesses, and individuals. The firm represents more than 77% of the companies in the Fortune 100 in addition to clients in the FTSE 100. Rated as one of the leading firms in The American Lawyer's Top 100, by a number of indicators, including gross revenues and profits per Partner.

London Office: The London office was founded in 1998. The firm has around 45 lawyers at present in London, all of whom are English-qualified. The firm provides business oriented legal advice to multinational and national corporates, financial institutions, investment banks and private clients. Many of the firm's partners were head of practice at their former firms and are recognised as leaders in their respective fields by the most respected professional directories and market commentators.

Chambers UK 2013 – "McDermott is recommended for complex cross-border issues leveraging its US/UK strength to conduct high-end work."

Main areas of work

Energy and commodities advisory; corporate advisory; financial institutions advisory; employee benefits, compensation, labour and employment; US and international tax; private client; international dispute avoidance and resolution; and IP litigation. London is the hub for the firm's European expansions and the firm coordinates legal advice from here for all multinational clients across Europe and elsewhere.

Trainee profile

The firm is looking for the brightest, best and most entrepreneurial trainees. You will need to convince the firm that you have made a deliberate choice to apply to McDermott Will & Emery.

Training environment

The primary focus is to provide a practical foundation for your career with the firm. You will experience four seats over the two-year period and a deliberately small number of trainees means that the firm is able to provide a degree of flexibility in tailoring seats to the individual. Trainees get regular support and feedback.

Benefits

Private medical and dental insurance, life assurance, permanent health insurance, pension, season ticket loan, subsidised gym membership, employee assistance programme, 25 days holiday.

Sponsorship & awards

GDL and LPC funding and maintenance grant.

McDermott
Will & Emery

A-Z of Solicitors

Memery Crystal LLP

44 Southampton Buildings, London WC2A 1AP
Tel: (020) 7242 5905 Fax: (020) 7242 2058
Email: hseaward@memerycrystal.com Web: www.memerycrystal.com

Partners 20
Solicitors 35
Total Trainees 8

Contact
Helen Seaward

Method of application
Online application form

Selection procedure
First interview followed by
assessment centre

Closing date for training
contracts starting September
2017
31 July 2015

Application
Training contracts p.a. 4.
Applications p.a. 300
% interviewed 15%
Required degree grade 2:1

Training
Salary
1st yr (2013) £30,000
2nd yr (2013) £32,000

Post qualification
Competitive NQ salary
Holiday entitlement 25 days
p.a.
% of trainees with a non-law
degree 80%

Firm profile
Memery Crystal LLP has an enviable reputation as a commercial legal practice. We have a strong internal culture, based upon a set of core values, which underpins our individuality, our emphasis on long-term client relationships and our collegiate and entrepreneurial approach. We act for a broad range of clients, from individual entrepreneurs and owner-managed businesses, to City institutions, educational organisations and multi-national corporations.

We offer a partner-led service and pride ourselves on the strength of our client relationships. We set ourselves apart from our competitors through our pragmatism and pro-activity and we have a reputation for punching well above our weight. Unusually for a single-office firm, we have a strong international focus, which we see as vital to our vision of remaining independent in a globalising economy. We have considerable cross-border transactional experience and have built strong relationships with other independent law firms around the world.

Our key strength lies in the quality of our award winning people. We seek to recruit and retain leading individuals, who provide the highest level of service to our clients.

Main areas of work
Our main practice areas include equity capital markets, M&A, banking/debt finance, tax, employment, employee incentives, IP, commercial contracts, real estate and dispute resolution. Much of our work has an international dimension and we have a strong focus in key sectors including natural resources and technology. We are ranked amongst the leading firms acting for AIM-listed companies and we were named "Dispute Resolution Team of the Year" at the 2014 Legal Business Awards.

Trainee profile
We welcome applications from candidates who have achieved a high standard of education in any discipline and who demonstrate a willingness to take on responsibility. We are looking for enthusiastic and ambitious individuals, who are commercially aware and want to build a career at the firm.

Training environment
During your training contact you will rotate departments every 6 months with the aim to give second year trainees their choice in seats. You will sit with a partner or senior associate who will monitor your progress on a regular basis, with appraisals being carried out every three months. You will also have support from a mentor (normally a junior lawyer) for guidance throughout your training contact. We run a high number of internal legal, client focused and soft skill training courses throughout the year which all trainees are invited to.

We believe that trainees should be integrated into the firm from their first day; you are encouraged to get involved in various firm initiatives and committee groups. Ultimately, we believe that if you accept a training contract here then you are worth investing in. We are looking for individuals to become and remain Memery Crystal career lawyers.

Work placements
We offer two Open Evenings in July, which aim to provide an insight to the firm and the trainee recruitment process. Please see our website for more details and for information on how to apply.

Sponsorship
The firm funds the GDL and the LPC.

MemeryCrystal

Michelmores LLP

Woodwater House, Pynes Hill, Exeter EX2 5WR
Tel: (01392) 688 688 Fax: (01392) 360 563
Email: graduaterecruitment@michelmores.com Website: www.michelmores.com

Firm profile
As a top 100 law firm, Michelmores is a dynamic, full-service practice with a total complement of over 400 staff. From its Exeter, Bristol and London offices, the firm provides a first-class service to a wide range of local, national (including several central government departments) and international clients. Our teams include corporate and commercial, real estate and private client and cross practice sector focused teams including energy and renewables, manufacturing and international trade.

The firm has an established track record of attracting quality lawyers at every level, enabling its trainees to learn from solicitors who are leaders in their fields. The partnership has retained a collegiate style, which has helped to foster a happy law firm renowned for the enthusiasm of its lawyers, from the managing partner to the first-year trainees. We have won a number of awards and accolades, including Regional Law Firm of the Year 2013 at the Citywealth Magic Circle Awards and UK & Ireland Regional Legal Team of the Year at the STEP Private Client Awards 2013/14. Furthermore we have achieved our 'One Star' accreditation in the prestigious Best Companies Awards 2014 for the second year running.

Main areas of work
The firm has an excellent reputation for its work in company commercial law, dispute resolution and commercial property while the firm's Private Client Group (including the firm's Clinical Negligance and Family teams) continues to thrive. The firm also has specialist teams in areas such as projects/PFI, technology, media and communications, construction and business, insolvency and restructuring.

Trainee profile
The firm welcomes applications from both law and non-law graduates. The firm is looking for trainees with a strong academic background who are team players and who genuinely want to share in the firm's success and help it to continue to grow. We are looking to recruit future associates and partners of the firm. Retaining our trainees on qualification is very important to us and we have an excellent retention track record of 100% for the past 3 years. In 2014 we were delighted to have our trainees qualify into each of our offices.

Training environment
As a Michelmores trainee you will usually spend six months in each of the firm's main departments (business, real estate and private client). You will work closely with your supervisor in each department and will be pleasantly surprised at the level of client exposure, responsibility and client involvement. The firm's trainees are given both the opportunity to handle work themselves (while under supervision) and to work as part of a team. The quality of the firm's training is high. You will be expected to attend relevant training sessions on areas such as marketing, IT skills and time management, and will also be encouraged to attend conferences, seminars and marketing events. As well as the Exeter office we also have thriving Bristol and London offices where trainees have the opportunity to spend six months of their training contract. We run a structured trainee training development programme, which aims to equip our trainees with the key skills needed to be a successful solicitor, on a technical and personal level.

Sponsorship & benefits
Optional private medical insurance, pension scheme, payment towards of LPC fees, subsidised staff restaurant, subsidised gym with personal trainer (Exeter).

Vacation placements
The firm runs an annual vacation placement scheme in July in the firm's Exeter office for one week. Apply via our online application. Completed forms should arrive by 28 February 2015.

Partners 60
Total Staff (inc. Partners) 410
Trainees 13

Contact
graduaterecruitment
@michelmores.com

Method of application
Online application form

Selection procedure
Assessment days and vacation placement assessments

Closing date for 2017
1 July 2015
Vacation placement 28 February 2015

Application
Training contracts p.a. 8
Applications p.a. 200
% interviewed 15%
Required degree grade 2:1

Training
Salary (Exeter)
1st year (2013) £20,000
2nd year (2013) £21,000

Holiday entitlement
25 days p.a.
% of trainees with a non-law degree 10%
Number of seats available abroad 0 (although occasional foreign secondments available)

Post-qualification
Salary (Exeter 2014) £33,000
% offered job 100%

Mills & Reeve

100 Hills Road, Cambridge CB2 1PH
Tel: (01223) 222336 Fax: (01223) 355848
Email: graduate.recruitment@mills-reeve.com
Web: www.mills-reeve.com/graduates

Firm profile

Mills & Reeve is a major UK law firm operating from offices in Birmingham, Cambridge, Leeds, London, Manchester and Norwich.

Our business model is straightforward – the highest quality advice, outstanding client service and value for money. We advise more than 120 universities, colleges and education bodies and over 100 healthcare organisations, as well as leading international insurers. Our commercial clients include global and UK-based businesses, FTSE and AIM listed organisations, private companies and startups. We have the largest private tax team outside of London and one of the largest family teams in Europe.

For the 11th year running Mills & Reeve has been listed in The Sunday Times Top 100 Best Companies to Work For, which recognises that we put people at the centre of our business.

Main areas of work

Mills & Reeve's services are delivered through firm-wide core groups: corporate and commercial, disputes, employment, family, health, insurance, private wealth sectors, projects and construction and real estate. Further specialist sector teams focus on agriculture, charities, education, food and beverage, real estate investment, sport and technology.

Trainee profile

We welcome applications from penultimate year law students, final year non-law students and graduates. Candidates should already have or expect a 2.1 degree or equivalent from either a law or non-law background.

You'll have a good balance between academic ability, interpersonal skills, drafting skills, common sense, commercial awareness, confidence and a professional attitude.

We look for candidates who have the potential to develop into our solicitors of the future.

Training environment

Trainees complete six four-month seats and are recruited to the Birmingham, Cambridge, Manchester and Norwich offices. Trainees work alongside a partner or senior solicitor. Regular feedback is given to aid development. Performance is assessed by a formal review at the end of each seat.

Training is supported by a full induction, in-house training programme developed by our team of professional support lawyers and the professional skills course (PSC).

Benefits

Life assurance, a contributory pension scheme, 25 days holiday, bonus scheme, sports and social club, subsidised staff restaurants, season ticket loan. The firm runs a flexible benefits scheme.

Vacation schemes

Applications for two week placements during the summer must be received by 31 January 2015.

Sponsorship & awards

The firm pays the full costs of the CPE/GDL and LPC fees and a maintenance grant during the GDL and LPC.

Partners 116	
Assistant solicitors 490	
Total trainees 33	

Contact
Fiona Medlock
01223 222336

Method of application
Online

Selection procedure
Normally one day assessment centre

Closing date for 2017
31 July 2015 for training contracts
31 January 2015 for work placements

Application
Training contracts 17 per annum
Applications 980 per annum
% interviewed per annum 8%
Required grade 2:1

Training
Salary
1st year £25,000
2nd year £26,500
Holiday entitlement 25 days per annum
% of current trainees with a non-law degree 40%

Post qualification
% of trainees offered job on qualification 84%

Offices
Birmingham, Cambridge, Leeds, London, Manchester, Norwich

MILLS & REEVE

Mishcon de Reya

Summit House, 12 Red Lion Square, London WC1R 4QD
Tel: (020) 7440 7000
Email: trainee.recruitment@mishcon.com
Website: www.mishcongraduates.com

Firm profile

Founded in 1937, Mishcon de Reya is a law firm with offices in London and New York, offering a wide range of legal services to companies and individuals.

Our clients are dynamic and sophisticated and we reflect that in our belief in challenging the conventional or accepted ways of working. We like to solve problems quickly. To achieve this consistently, we employ a diverse collection of talented people, from varied backgrounds with differing perspectives, who are capable of addressing issues in a collaborative, non-hierarchical environment.

In every area of the law that we operate, Mishcon de Reya prides itself in providing a best in class service to its clients. Our expertise covers five areas: analysing risk, protection of assets, managing wealth, resolving disputes and building business.

Main areas of work

We are organised internally into six different departments: corporate, employment, dispute resolution, family, Mishcon private and real estate. The firm also has a growing number of specialist groups which include: art; betting and gaming; finance and banking; fraud; immigration; insolvency and IP.

Trainee profile

Our trainees are typically high-achieving and intelligent individuals with good interpersonal skills and outgoing personalities. Strength of character and ability to think laterally are also important.

Training environment

Trainees have the opportunity to gain experience, skills and knowledge from across the firm in four six-month seats involving contentious and non-contentious work. Because of the relatively few training contracts offered, trainees can be exposed to high-quality work with lots of responsibility early on. Trainees are supported with a wide ranging training and development programme in addition to the Professional Skills Course. Trainee performance is monitored closely and trainees can expect to receive regular feedback in addition to mid-seat and end-of-seat appraisals.

Sponsorship & benefits

The firm provides full LPC and GDL funding, and a maintenance grant of £5,000 payable in the GDL and LPC year. Benefits include 25 days holiday, health screening, life assurance, dental insurance, income replacement insurance, private medical insurance, travel insurance, critical illness cover, gym membership, season ticket loan, stakeholder pension scheme, yoga classes, childcare vouchers, cycle scheme, in-house doctor, bonus scheme and give-as-you-earn schemes.

Vacation placements

Places for Easter 2015: 10

Places for Summer 2015: 20

Duration: 2 weeks; closing date: 15 January 2015

Candidates will only be considered for a training contract once they have completed a vacation scheme.

Our Easter and summer vacation schemes have been designed to provide students with an opportunity to gain an insight into the role of a trainee, our culture and our people. We run a fun and informative workshop programme covering all practice areas of the firm, combined with individual and group work sessions.

Partners 94
Solicitors 177
Total Trainees 24

Contact
Charlotte Lynch,
Recruitment Advisor

Method of application
Online application form

Closing date for 2017
15 July 2015

Application
Training contracts p.a. 8-12
Applications p.a. 1,000+
% interviewed p.a. 5%
Required degree grade 2:1

Training
Salary
1st year £33,000
Holiday entitlement 25 days
Occasional secondments
available

Overseas / Regional Offices
London, New York

Mishcon de Reya

Morgan Lewis & Bockius

Condor House, 5-10 St. Paul's Churchyard, London EC4M 8AL
Tel: (020) 3201 5000 Fax: (020) 3201 5001
Email: Londontrainingprogramme@morganlewis.com
Website: www.morganlewis.co.uk

Firm profile
With 25 offices in the United States, Europe, Asia and the Middle East, Morgan Lewis provides comprehensive corporate, transactional, regulatory and litigation services to clients of all sizes and across all major industries. Founded in 1873, Morgan Lewis comprises more than 1,600 legal professionals – including lawyers, patent agents, benefits advisers, regulatory scientists and other specialists. The firm has expanded significantly in London in the past year through the addition of several new teams.

Main areas of work
Debt and equity capital markets; finance and restructuring; labour and employment including employment litigation and immigration advice; private investment fund formation and operation; UK and US tax planning and structuring; international commercial dispute, arbitration, insurance recovery and white collar matters: life sciences, financial services, energy and technology sector work.

Trainee profile
Morgan Lewis is seeking candidates with a consistently strong academic record, who would respond with confidence to opportunities to work on challenging assignments across a wide variety of areas. Candidates should be able to demonstrate strong interpersonal, communication and client service skills and analytical ability, as well as a proven ability to work effectively both independently and within a team.

Training environment
Following a full induction into the firm, our programme will provide trainees with consistently high-quality, challenging assignments, working directly with senior lawyers across a range of practices and industry groups on complex and frequently cross-border matters. Through this hands-on and varied experience, trainees can expect to gather a thorough understanding of the firm's business and of working with international, high-profile clients. Over two years you will complete four, six-month seats with the opportunity to gain experience in at least three distinct areas of law. International secondments to our Moscow and Dubai offices may also be available. In addition to formal appraisals, the office environment allows regular contact with, and feedback from, the training principal, supervisors and other lawyers.

Trainees will attend Professional Skills Courses throughout their contract and will have the opportunity to actively participate in all in-house associate training sessions, and to take part in pro bono work and business development activities. They will experience regular interaction amongst the trainee and associate groups and have the opportunity to become a member of the firm's social committee.

Vacation scheme
Morgan Lewis offer a limited number of placements during the summer each year. The aim of our placement scheme is to provide candidates the opportunity to gain an insight into life as a trainee at the firm. To apply for a place on our summer programme applicants should complete the firm's online application form which is available on our website www.morganlewis.com. The closing date for applications is 31 January 2015.

Benefits
Life insurance, health and travel insurance, dental insurance, long-term disability insurance and season ticket loan.

Sponsorship & awards
Sponsorship of LPC and GDL. A maintenance grant of £7,500 will be provided.

Partners 23
Assistant Solicitors 29
Total Trainees 10

Contact
Georgia Shearman
(020) 3201 5620

Method of application
Via our website

Closing date for 2017
31 July 2015

Selection procedure
Interviews

Application
No. of training contracts 5 p.a
Required degree grade
high 2:1

Training
Salary
1st year £40,000
2nd year £43,000

Holiday entitlement
25 days p.a

Post-qualification
Salary £75,000

Overseas offices
Almaty, Beijing, Boston, Brussels, Chicago, Dallas, Dubai, Frankfurt, Harrisburg, Houston, Irvine, London, Los Angeles, Miami, Moscow, New York, Palo Alto, Paris, Philadelphia, Pittsburgh, Princeton, San Francisco, Tokyo, Washington, Wilmington

Morgan Lewis

Muckle LLP

Time Central, 32 Gallowgate, Newcastle upon Tyne NE1 4BF
Tel: (0191) 211 7777 Fax: (0191) 211 7788
Email: kerry.irving@muckle-llp.com
Website: www.muckle-llp.com

Firm profile
Muckle LLP is a leading commercial law firm in the North East of England. The firm has an excellent client base of successful private and public companies, property investors and developers, financial institutions and public sector and educational organisations, which recognise that its innovative commercial skills are a major benefit in enhancing its service delivery to them.

Main areas of work
The firm provides the following services – corporate, banking and restructuring, commercial, construction and engineering, real estate, employment, dispute resolution and private client.

Trainee profile
The firm recruits four trainees a year. The firm is looking to recruit talented individuals who can demonstrate their enthusiasm and desire to become business advisers and a commitment to building their career in the North East. Trainees must have good academic qualifications, interpersonal skills, be team players and embrace our culture and values.

Training environment
The firm runs an excellent training programme that focuses on the trainees' legal, IT, management and business development skills. During your training contract you may experience training within the following areas: corporate finance, commercial, property, employment, dispute resolution, construction and banking. Training is a combination of on-the-job experience, partner and other lawyer mentoring as well as in-house and external courses. Trainees are encouraged to participate in all aspects of the firm which include engagement, community and 'green' teams.

Benefits
25 days holiday a year and flexible holiday option; pension after six months service; permanent health insurance; life assurance; corporate discounts; salary sacrifice schemes; car parking discounts.

Sponsorship & awards
LPC fees are paid subject to eligibility.

Partners 27
Fee earners 89
Total Trainees 7

Contact
Kerry Irving
0191 211 7866

Method of application
Apply online via our website
www.muckle-llp.com

Selection procedure
Interviews and an assessment day

Closing date for 2015 summer vacation scheme
Saturday 31st January 2015

Closing date for 2017 training contracts
Friday 31st July 2015

Application
Training contracts p.a. 4
Applications p.a. 230-240
% interviewed p.a. 25%
Required degree grade preferably 2:1

Training
Salary
Starting salary £22,000 (2012) with regular reviews throughout training contract
Holiday entitlement
25 days holiday a year and flexible holiday option

Post-qualification
Salary
Starting salary £34,000 (2013) with regular reviews
Aim to retain 100% of trainees on qualification

Office
Only Newcastle upon Tyne

A-Z of Solicitors

Nabarro LLP

125 London Wall, London EC2Y 5AS
Tel: (020) 7524 6000 Fax: (020) 7524 6524
Website: www.nabarro.com/graduates
Twitter: @nabarrograds

Firm profile
Nabarro is a full service commercial law firm. We have over 100 partners leading 300 lawyers focused on delivering practical, business-savvy legal advice; we offer our clients clarity. From the most successful companies in the world to fast growth startups, we work with a diverse range of clients across many sectors.

Main areas of work
Banking and finance, corporate, infrastructure, construction and energy, dispute resolution, employment, financial services, funds and indirect real estate, intellectual property, pensions, planning, real estate, restructuring and insolvency, tax.

Trainee profile
You will need to demonstrate strong academic achievement, commercial awareness, excellent interpersonal skills and teamwork, motivation and drive. Applications are welcomed from law and non-law students and we are committed to making the most of diverse skills, expertise and experience. Accordingly there is no typical Nabarro trainee and we aim to recruit from a wide range of universities.

Training environment
Our trainees undertake six four-month seats to ensure maximum exposure to the firm's core practice areas (corporate, real estate and litigation). In addition, trainees have the opportunity to gain further experience by spending time in specialist areas, in our Brussels office or on a client secondment. Trainees usually return to their qualification department for their final seat, ensuring a smooth transition from trainee to qualified solicitor. We are committed to retaining our trainees on qualification and achieve consistently high retention rates.

Benefits
Private medical insurance, 26 days holiday, occupational contributory pension scheme, interest-free season ticket loan, subsidised gym membership, subsidised restaurant facilities, life assurance, occupational healthcare.

Vacation placements
Places for 2015: 55

Duration: Three schemes of three weeks duration (two in London, one in Sheffield) between mid June and early August.

Our multi-award winning summer schemes are an excellent way to learn about the firm and experience first-hand life as a Nabarro trainee. The three weeks are spent in one department with support from a supervisor and buddy. There is a comprehensive programme including induction, IT and research training, breakfast briefings and social events, designed to ensure you meet a wide range of people across the firm. We recruit all our future trainees through our summer schemes.

Sponsorship and awards
GDL funding: full fees plus a maintenance grant (London £6000, regions £5000).

LPC funding: full fees plus a maintenance grant (London £7000, regions £6000).

We will refund 50% of your fees retrospectively if you have already completed the GDL/LPC.

Partners 104
Assistant Solicitors 270
Total trainees 50

Contact
Jane Drew

Method of application
Online

Selection procedure
Assessment day (full details on our microsite) and summer scheme

Closing date for 2017
15 January 2015

Application
Training contracts 25 pa
Applications 950 pa
Required degree grade 2.1

Training salary
London £37,000 (1st Year)
£40,000 (2nd year)
Sheffield £25,000 (1st year)
£28,000 (2nd year)

Post-qualification
Salary
London £59,000
Sheffield £38,000

Firm offices
London, Manchester, Sheffield, Brussels, Dubai and Singapore. In Europe the firm has an alliance with GSK Stockmann & Kollegen in Germany, Nunziante Magrone in Italy and Roca Junyent in Spain.

N A B A R R O

Norton Rose Fulbright LLP

3 More London Riverside, London, SE1 2AQ
Tel: (020) 7444 2113 Fax: (020) 7283 6500
Email: graduate.recruitment@nortonrosefulbright.com
Website: www.nortonrosefulbrightgraduates.com

Firm profile

Norton Rose Fulbright is a global legal practice. We provide the world's pre-eminent corporations and financial institutions with a full business law service. We have more than 3800 lawyers based in over 50 cities across Europe, the United States, Canada, Latin America, Asia, Australia, Africa, the Middle East and Central Asia.

Wherever we are, we operate in accordance with our global business principles of quality, unity and integrity. We aim to provide the highest possible standard of legal service in each of our offices and to maintain that level of quality at every point of contact.

Main areas of work

Recognised for our industry focus, we are strong across all the key industry sectors: financial institutions; energy; infrastructure, mining and commodities; transport; technology and innovation; and life sciences and healthcare.

Trainee profile

Based on a four-seat pattern, you will get the widest possible exposure to different practice areas and offices around the world, enabling you to make the best and most informed choice of qualification area. Choosing the practice area that suits your skills and engages your interest is crucial.

When we hire you, we are making an investment. We ensure we obtain the maximum return on this by providing the highest standards of training. Becoming an outstanding lawyer is about continuous development – we will make sure you are challenged and rewarded in equal measure.

Our mentoring scheme will help you make the most of the vast breadth of knowledge and experience across the organisation. Your partner mentor will offer you everything from career insights to resolving any concerns you may have about a particular transaction you are working on, your client or international secondments, or your general progress.

To be successful here you will understand and embrace our strategy and our focus on six key industry sectors. An impeccable academic record and intellectual rigour are prerequisites. We expect successful candidates to have at least AAB at A-Level (or equivalent) and be on track for a strong 2.1 (or equivalent). You will have an enquiring mind with a profound and genuine interest in the world of international business and the commercial environment of our clients. Your global mindset means that you will embrace the international opportunities on offer. Your interpersonal skills will be second to none and you will have the confidence to build long term, trusting relationships with clients and colleagues.

Placement programmes

We offer three vacation programmes (winter and summer) and a number of open days throughout the year. Our winter vacation programme is for finalists and graduates. Please apply from 1st to 31st October 2014 for assessment days in mid-November. Our two summer vacation programmes are for penultimate year undergraduates. Please apply from 1st November 2014 to 31st January 2015 for assessment days in January to mid-February. Open day applications will be open from 1st November 2014 to 31st January 2015 for all candidates except first year undergraduates. First year undergraduates should apply from 1st March to 30th April 2015.

Partners 1250*
Assistant Solicitors 3800*
Total Trainees 110
*denotes worldwide figures

Contact
Caroline Lindner

Method of application
Online

Selection procedure
Application form and assessment day including written exercise, group exercise and interview.

Closing date for 2017
31 July 2015

Application
Training contracts p.a. Up to 55
Applications p.a. 2,000+
% interviewed p.a. 5-10%
Required degree grade 2:1

Training
Salary
1st year £39,500
2nd year £44,500
Holiday entitlement 25 days
% of trainees with a non-law degree p.a. 50%
No. of seats available abroad p.a. 20

Overseas offices
Abu Dhabi, Almaty, Amsterdam, Athens, Austin, Bahrain, Bangkok, Beijing, Bogotá, Brisbane, Brussels, Calgary, Canberra, Cape Town, Caracas, Casablanca, Dallas, Dar es Salaam, Denver, Dubai, Durban, Frankfurt, Hamburg, Hong Kong, Houston, Jakarta*, Johannesburg, Los Angeles, Melbourne, Milan, Minneapolis, Montréal, Moscow, Munich, New York, Ottawa, Paris, Perth, Piraeus, Pittsburgh-Southpointe, Québec, Rio de Janeiro, Riyadh*, Rome, St Louis, San Antonio, Shanghai, Singapore, Sydney, Tokyo, Toronto, Warsaw, Washington DC
*associate offices

Olswang LLP

90 High Holborn, London WC1V 6XX
Tel: (020) 7067 3000 Fax: (020) 7067 3999
Email: traineesolicitor@olswang.com
Website: www.olswangtrainees.com

Firm profile

Olswang is a passionate and pioneering firm with a business-minded approach to the law. Our decisive, connected and highly-commercial people are committed to changing the face of business, impacting sectors ranging from real estate to retail and life sciences to leisure. Our progressive culture gives us a definitive edge and has won us an unparalleled reputation in industries such as technology, media and telecoms.

Headquartered in London, our firm comprises over 750 people spanning a network of offices in Belgium, France, Germany, Spain, Singapore and the UK. Our rapidly expanding presence across Europe, combined with our ambitious plans for growth in the territories our clients demand, makes us the firm of choice for true innovation, wherever it may be emerging across the globe.

Main areas of work

Olswang provides expertise across a wide range of practice areas including commercial contracts, competition and regulatory, corporate, employment, pensions and benefits, finance, intellectual property, litigation, real estate, sourcing, procurement and supply chain, restructuring and special situations and tax.

Trainee profile

Being a trainee at Olswang is both demanding and rewarding. The firm is interested in hearing from individuals who have achieved, or are on course for, a 2:1 degree or above and possess enthusiasm, energy, confidence and commitment. Olswang aims to be a liberating and exciting place to work with a unique culture that suits open-minded, collaborative and engaging people.

Training environment

Olswang wants to help trainees match their expectations and needs with those of the firm. Training consists of four six-month seats in corporate, real estate, litigation, finance, commercial or IP. You will be assigned a mentor, usually a partner, to assist and advise you throughout your training contract. In-house lectures supplement general training, three-monthly appraisals assess development and regular social events with the other trainees encourage stronger, lasting relationships.

Benefits

Immediately: 4 x life assurance, private medical insurance, dental cover, subsidised gym membership, subsidised staff restaurant, season ticket loan, medicals, cycle to work scheme, childcare vouchers, pension contributions matched up to 5%. After 12 months: PHI.

Vacation placements

Places for 2015: Spring and Summer; Remuneration: £275 p.w.; 10 students per scheme; Closing Date: 15 January 2015.

Sponsorship & awards

LPC and GDL fees paid in full. Maintenance grant of £7,000 (inside London), £6,500 (outside).

Partners 122
Fee-earners 355
Total Trainees 27

Contact
Katharine Banbury
Graduate Recruitment &
Development

Method of application
Online

Selection procedure
Commercial exercise, competency based interviews, psychometric tests and written exercises

Closing date for 2017
31 July 2015

Application
Training contracts p.a. 12
Applications p.a. 2,000
% interviewed p.a. 4%
Required degree grade 2:1

Training
Salary
1st year (2014) £37,000
2nd year (2014) £41,500
Holiday entitlement 25 days
% of trainees with a non-law degree p.a. 50%

Post-qualification
Salary (2014) £60,000

Overseas offices
Brussels, Berlin, Madrid, Paris, Munich, Singapore

OLSWANG

O'Melveny & Myers LLP

Warwick Court, 5 Paternoster Square, London EC4M 7DX
Tel: (020) 7088 0000 Fax: (020) 7088 0001
Email: graduate-recruitment@omm.com
Website: www.omm.com/careers/london

Firm profile
O'Melveny & Myers is a leading international law firm with approximately 800 lawyers practicing in 16 offices in the key US, Asian and European economic and political centres. The London office provides transactional and litigation legal services to a diverse groups of prominent private equity houses, financial institutions and corporate clients. The team in London comprises mainly English qualified lawyers, as well as some dual qualified (US and UK) lawyers. They advise on cross-border English law matters and work closely with the firm's international network to provide a seamless global service. The London office is known for its entrepreneurial leadership and commitment to excellence, both of which underpin its approach to recruitment. Each year a number of our partners and senior counsel are recognised in the Chambers UK guide as leaders in their practice areas.

Main areas of work
Globally, O'Melveny's capabilities span virtually every area of legal practice. The London office has both a transactions department - which advises on private equity, corporate finance, entertainment, sports and media, M&A and investment funds matters - as well as an international litigation department, with antitrust and competition services support provided through the Brussels office. London also has the key transactional support functions which are essential to a leading corporate practice, such as tax and regulatory.

Trainee profile
The London office recruits up to four high calibre graduates for training contracts each year. Successful candidates will have proven academic ability, sound commercial awareness, be keen team players and have the ability to carry real responsibility from the outset.

Training environment
Individual preferences can usually be taken into account when tailoring the London training programme, subject to completing the core competencies. Trainees complete seats with partners or senior lawyers usually in each of the corporate, finance, funds and litigation practices. O'Melveny trainees are also regularly seconded overseas to the Hong Kong, Singapore and Brussels offices. They are encouraged to be proactive and take responsibility at an early stage. Trainees work in a very supportive and inclusive environment, with regular formal and informal feedback. Great importance is placed on training for lawyers at all levels, and so trainees participate in both legal and non-legal skills training programmes.

Vacation schemes
Vacation placements are available each summer. All applications for 2015 placements must be submitted online via www.apply4law.com/omm by 31st January 2015.

Benefits
Benefits include: 25 days holiday, pension, life insurance, long term disability insurance, private health insurance, travel insurance, interest-free season ticket loan, corporate rate gym membership.

Sponsorship & awards
O'Melveny & Myers sponsors GDL/LPC fees incurred post-recruitment and awards a maintenance grant (currently £8,000 per annum) during the GDL/LPC course.

Partners 8
Counsel & Associates 19
Trainees 7

Contact
Natalie Beacroft
HR Officer

Method of application
Online application
www.apply4law.com/omm

Application
Training contracts p.a. up to 4
Required degree grade 2:1, any discipline

Closing date for 2017
30 June 2015

Training
Salary
1st year (2014) £41,000
2nd year (2014) £44,000
Post-qualification
Market rate

Overseas offices/ regional offices
Beijing, Brussels, Century City, Hong Kong, Jakarta (in association with Tumbuan & Partners) Los Angeles, Newport Beach, New York, San Francisco, Seoul, Shanghai, Silicon Valley, Singapore, Tokyo and Washington DC

A-Z of Solicitors

Orrick, Herrington & Sutcliffe

107 Cheapside, London, EC2V 6DN
Tel: (020) 7862 4600 Fax: (020) 7862 4800
Email: recruitlondon@orrick.com
Website: www.orrick.com/careers/london/graduate-recruitment

Firm profile

Orrick is a leading international law firm with more than 1,100 lawyers in 25 offices located throughout North America, Europe and Asia. Orrick has earned a global reputation advising both established and emerging companies, banks and international financial institutions. Much of Orrick's client work involves cross-border transactions which have increased substantially in recent years with the development of the firm's network of global offices.

Main areas of work

Antitrust and competition, banking and debt capital markets, commercial litigation, emerging companies, employment law, energy and infrastructure, capital markets, financial institutions and market regulation, intellectual property, international dispute resolution, mergers and acquisitions, professional negligence, real estate, structured finance and tax.

Trainee profile

If you set your standards high, have a strong work ethic and are a bright, talented graduate of any discipline looking for a firm offering a broad-based training contract, then Orrick could be for you. Applicants should have at least three A level passes at grades A and B and a 2:1 degree.

Training environment

Orrick is a firm for those looking for a high level of responsibility from day one. The firm values team players and rewards collaboration over competition. It aims to give individuals the opportunity to flourish in a lively and supportive work environment and encourage interaction among lawyers across international offices at every level of experience within the firm. It supports learning through a steadfast focus on training and a mentoring programme that will provide you with the right foundation for building your legal career and for working with clients. A genuine open door policy means trainees work closely with partners and of counsel as well as associates to gain practical experience in research, drafting, procedural and client-related skills. There are regular training sessions on legal and soft skills to enhance your development as a lawyer. The two-year training programme is made up of four six-month seats, with regular appraisals throughout. Trainees undertake the Professional Skills Course during their induction programme.

Benefits

Pension, group income protection scheme, life assurance, private medical insurance, dental care, subsidised gym membership, season ticket loan and childcare voucher scheme.

Sponsorship & awards

GDL and LPC: fees paid plus £7,000 maintenance.

Open days

We hold open days during the year which provide a good opportunity to see the London office of a US law firm in action. Applicants spend the day learning more about the firm and the work on offer in the London office as well as participating in a business game designed to give a flavour of the work of a City lawyer. Applications should be made online via our graduate recruitment website.

Partners 19 (London)
Associates 33 (incl Of Counsel) (London)
Total Trainees 8

Contact
Halina Kasprowiak

Method of application
Online at
www.orrick.com/careers/
london/graduate-recruitment

Selection procedure
2 interviews: 1st round with Recruitment Manager and a senior associate/of counsel; 2nd round with two partners

Closing date for 2017
31 July 2015

Application
Training contracts p.a. 4
Required degree grade 2:1

Training
Salary
1st year (2014) £38,000
2nd year (2014) £42,500
Holiday entitlement 25 days

Overseas offices
Beijing, Berlin, Brussels, Dusseldorf, Frankfurt, Hong Kong, Los Angeles, Milan, Moscow, Munich, New York, Orange County, Paris, Portland, Rome, Sacramento, San Francisco, Seattle, Shanghai, Silicon Valley, Taipei, Tokyo, Washington DC and Wheeling (GOC).

ORRICK

Osborne Clarke

2 Temple Back East, Temple Quay, Bristol BS1 6EG
Tel: (0117) 917 3484
Email: trainee.recruitment@osborneclarke.com
Website: www.osborneclarke.com

Firm profile

A few years ago a legal magazine described us as 'one of the UK's most distinctive legal practices'. So, what is it that makes us distinctive?

What makes us tick, of course, is legal expertise. Our high profile clients expect us to be brilliant, whether we are corporate, commercial or litigation lawyers, so we put a lot of effort into helping our lawyers be the best they can throughout their careers – not just at the start of it.

Over the past two years, we've grown rapidly, worldwide and now have 19 united offices throughout Europe and the US. For our clients, it means that we are on the ground with local legal expertise, when they need us; and it adds an exciting international dimension to much of our work.

The sectors we work in all thrive on technology, energy and innovation: digital business, energy, financial services, life sciences, real estate, recruitment or transport. Our sector teams include lawyers from all legal disciplines, so in our structure expertise, insight and enthusiasm go hand-in-hand.

The final piece in the jigsaw is our culture. When we asked our recent recruits what attracted them to OC, they used words like 'friendly', 'inclusive', 'open' and 'fun'. To our clients we are 'approachable', 'proactive', 'understanding' and 'formidable'. For us, our culture is all about building relationships, gaining and providing insights and getting valuable results for our clients and our people. We like to think that our culture underpins our exceptional track record.

Main areas of work

Main areas of expertise include; banking and finance, business regulation, commercial, corporate, employment and benefits, litigation, pensions, projects, real estate, restructuring and insolvency and tax.

Trainee profile

Osborne Clarke is looking for candidates who can: communicate effectively; think commercially and practically; solve problems creatively; build effective relationships; and demonstrate initiative. Foreign language skills are also an advantage.

Training environment

We group all of our trainee training and development into one coherent programme, which can be tailored to your individual needs. You'll receive on the job training, dedicated technical workshops, all the IT and compliance training you need and personal development workshops.

Throughout your training contract we want you to experience the broad range of work available at Osborne Clarke. As a trainee, you'll complete four seats: corporate or banking, real estate or tax, litigation, and one other. In each seat, a senior lawyer will supervise your day-to-day progress and give you regular feedback, so you know how you're doing. They're there to help you up your game. Every three months, you'll have a formal progress review to help you track your development.

Our trainees get lots of responsibility. And they find that it's what differentiates their training contracts from others.

Benefits

25 days' holiday (plus a Christmas shopping day), pension, permanent health insurance, private medical insurance, life assurance and season ticket loan. GDL/LPC sponsorship and maintenance grant.

Vacation schemes

Each of our vacation scheme placements runs for two weeks over the summer and offers a great opportunity for candidates to really get to know the firm. The placement follows a structured programme which allows candidates to spend time in two different departments and get involved in real client work. Beyond work there are plenty of social events organised by our trainees.

Partners 185
Lawyers 469
Trainees 37

Contact
Zoe Reid, Recruitment Officer

Method of application
Online application form

Selection procedure
Assessment centre comprises of group exercises, psychometric test, partner interview, written exercise

Closing date for 2017
31 July 2015

Application
Training contracts p.a. 20
Applications p.a. 1,200
% interviewed p.a. 10%
Required degree grade: 2:1, any discipline

Training
1st year £33,000 - £37,500
2nd year £35,000 - £40,000
Holiday entitlement 25 days
% of trainees with a non-law degree p.a. 46%

Post-qualification
Salary
£40,000 - £60,000

Overseas / Regional offices
Amsterdam, Barcelona, Brescia, Bristol, Brussels, Cologne, Hamburg, London, Madrid, Milan, Munich, New York, Padua, Paris, Rome, San Francisco, Silicon Valley, Thames Valley.

A-Z of Solicitors

Paul Hastings (Europe) LLP

10 Bishops Square, 8th Floor, London, E1 6EG
Tel: (020) 3023 5100 Fax: (020) 3023 5109
Email: yvettecroucher@paulhastings.com
Website: www.paulhastings.com

Firm profile

With lawyers serving clients from 20 worldwide offices, Paul Hastings provides a wide range of services across Europe, America and Asia. Through a collaborative approach, entrepreneurial spirit and firm commitment to client service, the legal professionals of Paul Hastings deliver innovative solutions to many of the world's top financial institutions and Fortune 500 companies.

Main areas of work

Paul Hastings' London office focuses on corporate and real estate finance transactions, M&A, restructuring, capital markets, litigation, payment systems and financial services, employment and tax. The London office has particular experience in multi-jurisdictional European transactions, working together with our offices in Frankfurt, Milan, Paris and Brussels.

Trainee profile

The firm seeks individuals with a wide variety of skills who combine intellectual ability with enthusiasm, creativity and a demonstrable ability to thrive in a challenging environment. The firm expects candidates to have a high level of achievement both at A level (or equivalent) and degree level. This would typically mean an upper second or first class degree. The firm recruits both law and non-law graduates.

Training environment

Paul Hastings will provide you with a first class training and development program, combining on-the-job training and professional courses. You will gain experience in four practice areas, including a client secondment. Your progress will be monitored on a formal and informal basis and you will have the opportunity to give feedback on the program itself and on those areas that are most important to you.

Benefits

Private healthcare, life assurance, pension scheme, season ticket loan and gym subsidy.

Sponsorship & awards

Paul Hastings offers a maintenance grant and also offers sponsorship for the GDL and/or LPC.

Partners 22
Assistant Solicitors 28
Total Trainees 7-8

Contact
yvettecroucher
@paulhastings.com

Method of application
Online application form available on website

Selection procedure
Interview and written assessment

Closing date for 2017
31 July 2015

Application
Training contracts p.a. 3-4
Required degree grade 2:1

Training
Salary
1st year £40,000
2nd year £45,000
Holiday entitlement
25 days

Post-qualification
Salary (2014) £88,000

Overseas/regional offices
Atlanta, Beijing, Brussels, Chicago, Frankfurt, Hong Kong, Houston, London, Los Angeles, Milan, New York, Orange County, Palo Alto, Paris, San Diego, San Francisco, Seoul, Shanghai, Tokyo, Washington DC

PAUL
HASTINGS

A-Z of Solicitors

Peters & Peters Solicitors LLP

15 Fetter Lane, London EC4A 1BW
Tel: (020) 7822 7777 Fax: (020) 7822 7788
Website: www.petersandpeters.com

Firm profile
This specialist practice is best known as a leading firm in fraud, financial crime, commercial litigation and regulatory work, for which it attracts an impressive client base. It was previously recognised as 'Niche Firm of The Year' at The Lawyer Awards and as a 'Stand-Out Firm' for dispute resolution at The FT Innovative Lawyers Awards. Peters & Peters was one of the first practices to develop a key multi-disciplinary approach and the firm has built up a high level of expertise across its practice areas. Much of its work is high-profile and international in scope and as well as advising corporate and individual clients, it provides advice to foreign regulators, worldwide organisations and governments. In doing so it has forged close working relationships with overseas law firms.

Main areas of work
Business crime, civil fraud, commercial litigation and regulatory work. Its key practice areas include anti-money laundering, anti-bribery and corruption, commercial and trust litigation, competition litigation, corporate investigations, criminal antitrust (cartels), economic sanctions, extradition and mutual legal assistance, financial regulation, fraud (civil and criminal), HMRC inquiries and investigations, insider dealing, international asset training and private prosecutions.

Trainee profile
We are a friendly firm with a supportive culture. We regard our trainees highly and make every effort to help them become fully integrated into the practice both in our work and socially. We have an excellent retention rate reflected by the fact that many of our partners trained with us. We are looking for trainees with strong academic qualifications. We recruit from a wide range of universities, taking both law and non-law graduates who have achieved a degree at 2:1 level or above. Given the nature of our international practice, we are particularly interested in meeting candidates with fluency in foreign languages. You must be committed to hard work and to a steep learning curve. Ideal candidates will have drive, enthusiasm and a sense of humour. Ours is very much a people business so you will also have to demonstrate strong presentation and communication skills. To hear from the head of human resources, Sue Bachorski about the trainee recruitment process, please watch the film at www.petersandpeters.com/careers

Training environment
You will sit with a partner or your principal supervisor who will be the main source of your work during that seat, although you will have a good deal of contact with the other fee earners in the department. Your training contract will consist of three seats: business crime; commercial litigation/civil fraud; a non-contentious area of law e.g. corporate, dependent upon which particular secondment you undertake.

Benefits
25 days holiday, pension scheme, BUPA private medical insurance, interest free season ticket loan, subsidised gym membership, interest free cycle purchase loan, life assurance and a childcare voucher scheme.

Partners (and equivalent) 12
Associates 17
Total Trainees 5

Contact
Julie Beckwith
020 7822 7721
jbeckwith@petersandpeters.com

Method of application
Application form from the careers section of the Peters & Peters' website and send it to Julie Beckwith (see contact details above). Peters & Peters is an equal opportunities employer. If you apply for this job, please also complete the equal opportunities monitoring form.

Selection procedure
First stage, two hour written testing session (admin test and topical essay). Second stage, interview with a partner and the HR and Training Manager, Sue Bachorski. Third stage, interview with two senior partners.

Closing date for 2016
Ongoing

Application
Training contracts p.a. 2
Applications p.a. c. 200
% interviewed p.a. 1st stage (testing) 30%, interviewed 5%
Required degree grade 2:1

Training
Salary (2014)
1st year £37,000
2nd year £39,000
Holiday entitlement 25 days
% of trainees with a non-law degree varies year on year

Post-qualification
Salary (2014) £52,000

PETERS & PETERS

Pinsent Masons LLP

30 Crown Place, London EC2A 4ES
Email: graduate@pinsentmasons.com
Website: www.pinsentmasons.com/graduate

Firm profile

Pinsent Masons is a full service international law firm and ranks amongst the top 75 global law firms. We provide legal services to a wide variety of clients, in particular across our four global sectors of Advanced Manufacturing & Technology Services, Energy & Natural Resources, Financial Services and Infrastructure. We work with clients including FTSE 100 and AIM listed companies, government departments and public sector institutions. Pinsent Masons is the only firm to operate across all three UK jurisdictions and more recently we have been developing our overseas network of offices in the Asia-Pacific region, Europe and the Middle East. This reflects our strategy to become a firm of truly international reach, offering world-class service and excellent value.

Main areas of work

At Pinsent Masons you can expect to get involved in interesting, highly commercial, client-facing work from the earliest stage in your career. Our aim is to develop you as a fully-rounded commercial lawyer and business adviser. To achieve that, we work with you to develop your technical legal expertise, alongside your knowledge of the sectors in which our clients operate.

The firm is organised into seven key practice areas: Construction Advisory & Disputes; Corporate; Financial Institutions & Human Capital (Banking & Restructuring, Employment, Financial Regulation and Pensions); Litigation & Compliance (including EU & Competition and Tax); Projects; Property; and Strategic Business Services (Commercial, Intellectual Property and Technology, Media & Telecommunications).

Trainee profile

Pinsent Masons needs exceptional individuals with drive, ability and confidence. It is not about the school or university you attended, but your unique qualities as an individual and what you can bring to our organisation, which will make you successful. Excellent analytical and problem-solving skills are essential, as well as the ability to develop strong working relationships with both clients and colleagues, because fundamentally, the law is about people. How you develop and demonstrate these attributes is up to you.

Training environment

A training contract at Pinsent Masons represents the first stage of a focussed development programme that will enable you to reach your full potential. Our training programme has been developed in-house, which ensures you receive a balanced and comprehensive introduction to the profession.

Trainees move departments every six months. This gives you the necessary time to develop the legal and commercial depth of understanding required to take on real client-facing responsibility. During the second year of training you may also have the opportunity to undertake a secondment to either a client organisation or one of our international offices.

Vacation placements

We believe that a vacation placement is the best way for you to understand whether a career in commercial law at Pinsent Masons is right for you. We typically recruit 70% of our trainee solicitors through our vacation placement programme and strongly recommend this application route to candidates.

We typically offer c.100 vacation placements across the UK. The dates of our placements and the deadline for applications can be found on our website.

Partners 350+
Lawyers 1500+
Trainees 150

Contact
The Graduate Team

Method of application
Online application form

Selection Process
Psychometric test and assessment centre

Closing date for 2017
Dates available on website
(varies by location)

Application
Training contracts p.a. 75
Applications p.a. 1500+
% interviewed p.a. c.15%
Required degree grade strong
2:1 (or equivalent)
Salaries Highly Competitive
(details available on website)

Regional Offices
London, Birmingham, Leeds, Manchester, Aberdeen, Edinburgh, Glasgow, Belfast and the Falkland Islands

Overseas Offices
Istanbul, Munich, Paris, Doha, Dubai, Beijing, Hong Kong, Shanghai and Singapore

PwC Legal

1 Embankment Place, London, WC2N 6RH
Tel: (0808) 100 1500
Website: www.pwc.com/uk/careers
Facebook: www.facebook.com/PwCCareersUK

Firm profile

PwC Legal is a member of the PwC international network of firms and an exciting place to launch your legal career. With more than 2,000 lawyers in over 80 countries, we have the most extensive legal services network in the world. What's more, although we're independent, our services are embedded within the powerful, multi-disciplinary capabilities and broad geographic footprint of a global professional services leader. Our links to PwC mean we can offer our clients rounded solutions incorporating multi-disciplinary advice. Yet we're not so large as to be impersonal. You'll feel respected and encouraged to be the best you can be – thanks to the quality of our legal training plus daily exposure to the highest standards of work and broad business skills.

Training environment

You'll be training in a stimulating, multifaceted environment and learning from exceptional people. You'll quickly gain practical, hands-on experience and lateral thinking skills as part of teams generating creative ways to tackle complex problems. The practice groups you could work in include Mergers and Acquisitions, Banking, Commercial Litigation, Commercial Fraud, Corporate Structuring, Employment, Immigration, Intellectual Property and Information Technology, Pensions, Real Estate and Tax Litigation. You may also complete a seat in Dubai.

Vacation schemes

Our three-week paid Summer Vacation Scheme is a great way to find out how we work and see for yourself the ways in which we're truly unique in the legal marketplace. And you'll get a highly-competitive wage while you're here. You'll have the opportunity to join client meetings and calls, conduct research, practise legal drafting, join our seminar and training programme and work directly alongside our lawyers. The scheme is our principal route towards securing a training contract with us.

The next available scheme is the Summer Vacation 2015. All successful applicants from the 2015 scheme will be offered a Training Contract to join in 2016 or more usually 2017. Apply by 29 January 2015.

Sponsorship & awards

Trainees can apply for a scholarship award to help with the costs of the Graduate Diploma and the Legal Practice Course. If successful, you'll receive the total cost of the tuition and examination fees plus a significant contribution towards living expenses. You can find out more on our website.

Take the opportunity of a lifetime.

Vacancies 16
Trainees 20
Partners 23
Total staff 215

Method of application
Visit www.pwc.com/uk/careers to submit your online application form.

Closing dates
For our summer vacation scheme apply by January 29 2015

Application
Penultimate-year law students and final-year non-law students with at least a 2.1 honours degree (or equivalent), a 320+ UCAS tariff (or equivalent) and a keen interest in business law

Training
Salary (London)
Summer vacation scheme £400 per week
Training contract £37,000

PricewaterhouseCoopers Legal LLP

Reed Smith

The Broadgate Tower, 20 Primrose Street, London EC2A 2RS
Tel: (020) 3116 3000 Fax: (020) 3116 3999
Email: graduate.recruitment@reedsmith.com
Website: www.reedsmith.com

Firm profile

Key to Reed Smith's success is its ability to build lasting relationships: with clients and with each other. United through a culture defined by commitment to professional development, team-work, diversity, pro bono and community support, the firm has grown to become one of the largest law firms in the world. Its 25 offices span three continents and London is currently the largest with over 600 people. While the offices benefit from an international framework, each one retains key elements of the local business culture.

Main areas of work

The firm is particularly well known for its work advising leading companies in the areas of financial services, life sciences, shipping, energy and natural resources, advertising, technology and media. It provides a wide range of commercial legal services for all these clients, including a full spectrum of corporate, commercial and financial services, dispute resolution, real estate and employment advice. Much of the work is multi-jurisdictional.

Trainee profile

The firm is looking for individuals with the drive and potential to become world-class business lawyers. They want 'players' rather than 'onlookers' with strong intellect, initiative, the ability to thrive in a challenging profession and the personal qualities to build strong relationships with colleagues and clients.

Training environment

Given the range of different work undertaken in the London office, trainees get the chance to have a varied training contract and develop a wide range of skills. The firm runs a 4 seat rotation system and trainees will be supervised by either a senior associate or partner. In addition to seats in the London office, trainees have the opportunity to spend six months on secondment, either abroad or with a client.

The firm has developed a new version of the Legal Practice Course (LPC) that fully integrates legal and business learning and leads to a unique Master's qualification, the MA (LPC with Business). This bespoke programme was the first of its kind and allows students to study commercial and legal aspects in parallel, and not separately, so that they complete the course before entering a training contract with the firm.

There are vacancies for training contracts commencing in August 2017 and February 2018.

Benefits

Permanent health insurance, subsidised cafeteria, life insurance, lifestyle discounts and concierge service, contributory pension scheme, season ticket loan and a flexible benefits package.

Vacation placements

Every summer, the firm offers the opportunity for up to 24 students to experience working life at Reed Smith as part of their vacation scheme. It is also an excellent opportunity for the firm to meet with prospective trainees in a relaxed environment and to provide them with a realistic representation of what trainee life may be like. The schemes are two weeks in duration and students will have the opportunity to work in two different practice areas. On arrival, students will have completed at least two years of undergraduate study.

Sponsorship & awards

GDL Funding: Fees paid plus £6,000 maintenance. LPC Funding: Fees paid plus £7,000 maintenance.

Partners 111*
Fee-earners 293* (excluding partners, but including trainees)
Total Trainees 50
* denotes UK figures

Contact
Lucy Crittenden

Method of application
Online application form

Selection procedure
Assessment centre

Closing date for 2017/2018
31 July 2015

Application
Training contracts p.a. approximately 24
Applications p.a. 1000
% interviewed p.a. 7%
Required degree grade 2:1

Training
Salary
1st year (2014) £37,000
Holiday entitlement 25 days
% of trainees with a non-law degree p.a. 40%
No. of seats available abroad p.a. 2

Post-qualification
Salary (2014)
£60,000 plus bonus
% of assistants who joined as trainees 43%
% of partners who joined as trainees 45%

Overseas offices
New York, London, Hong Kong, Chicago, Washington DC, Beijing, Paris, Los Angeles, San Francisco, Philadelphia, Pittsburg, Munich, Abu Dhabi, Princeton, N Virginia, Dubai, Century City, Piraeus, Richmond, Silicon Valley, Shanghai, Houston, Singapore, Kazakhstan, Wilmington

RPC

Tower Bridge House, St Katharine's Way, London E1W 1AA
Tel: (020) 3060 6000
Website: www.rpc.co.uk/manifesto

Firm profile

Leading lawyers. Great clients. And an unrivalled commercial approach to business. At RPC we offer a depth of knowledge and creativity that few firms can rival and combine this with high quality training programmes that are consistently lauded in the leading directories.

Headquartered in a state of the art site in the City of London, we also have stunning offices in Bristol, Hong Kong and Singapore. Our open plan, collaborative working environment – where knowledge is easily shared and access to partners an everyday reality – is designed to bring out the best in our people and to ensure that the service we offer our clients is second to none. And it is.

We provide top quality legal services to global businesses across a wide range of industry sectors and practices, including insurance, commercial litigation, construction, engineering and projects, corporate/M&A, IP and technology, media, real estate, employment and pensions, outsourcing, regulatory, tax and competition.

In June 2014 we were named Law Firm of the Year at The Lawyer Awards having been nominated four times before over the previous 18 months. We also won Competition Team of the Year at the Legal Business Awards 2014. Last year we picked up gongs as Best Tax Team in a Law Firm and Best Trainee Recruitment Campaign. And, in 2012, we won Insurance Team of the Year at The Legal Business Awards and Corporate Team of the Year (midcap) at The Lawyer Awards, as well as Service Provider of the Year at the British Insurance Awards; we were also voted by the Financial Times as one of the most innovative firms in Europe.

Main areas of work

Banking and finance, commercial litigation, corporate, corporate insurance, competition, construction, corporate finance, dispute resolution, employment, energy/transport/infrastructure, insolvency, insurance and reinsurance, intellectual property, IT, media, personal injury, pensions and benefits, real estate, regulatory, tax, technology and outsourcing.

Trainee profile

Although proven academic ability is important (we require a 2:1 degree or above, not necessarily in Law) we value energy, enthusiasm, business sense, commitment and the ability to relate well to others just as highly.

Benefits

We feel it is important to offer our employees a creative and competitive benefits package with choice and flexibility. Our full range of benefits can be viewed via our website.

Funding

Bursaries are available for the GDL, if applicable, and the LPC. Bursaries comprise course and examination fees and maintenance grants of up to £7,000. We request that all our trainees complete their LPC and GDL at BPP law school.

Partners 76
Associates 214
Total trainees 39

Contact
Trainee Recruitment Team
020 3060 6000
RPC, Tower Bridge House,
St Katharine's Way,
London, E1W 1AA
www.rpc.co.uk/manifesto

Method of application
Online

Selection procedure
First interview face to face,
presentations, aptitude tests,
case studies

Closing date for 2017
Training contract
31 July 2015
Vacation scheme
31 January 2015

Application
Training contracts p.a.
London 20
Bristol 2
Required degree grade London
& Bristol 2:1

Training
Salary
London 1st year £37,000
Bristol 1st year £32,000
London 2nd year £40,000
Bristol 2nd year £35,000

Post-qualification
Salary Merit-based
% of trainees offered job
on qualification (2013) 81%

Overseas/Regional offices
Hong Kong and Singapore

SGH Martineau

No 1 Colmore Square, Birmingham B4 6AA
One America Square, Crosswall, London EC3N 2SG
Tel: 0800 763 1000 Fax: 0800 763 1001
Email: training.contracts@sghmartineau.com
Website: www.sghmartineau.com

Firm profile
We are a top 100, commercially orientated law firm that offers the full spectrum of legal services.

Main areas of work
We offer a range of legal services to clients from a diverse range of sectors, with a focus on banking and financial services, education, energy, industry and manufacturing, investment funds, leisure and retail, private wealth and restructuring and insolvency.

Trainee profile
We work in partnership with our trainees and provide mentoring, supervision, support and exposure to the key areas of the firm's practice. Trainees are encouraged to deliver legal solutions to clients while benefiting from quality work.

Trainees benefit from a structured career training programme tailored to their personal development needs. It covers not only legal technical matters but also a business and commercial approach which has never been more central to successful professional careers.

Trainees rotate every four months which results in gaining a broad experience and also the possibility of repeating a seat.

Benefits
Permanent health insurance, life insurance, private medical insurance, pension, season ticket loan, cycle to work.

Sponsorship
LPC fees are paid and a maintenance grant available.

Vacation placements
Our 2 day mini vacation schemes give an excellent opportunity to meet a range of people from the firm and see what life is like as a trainee. They involve presentations, interactive workshops and legal activities from various teams, networking opportunities and much more.

Partners 50
Fee earners 120
Total Trainees 18

Contact
Jennifer Nicholson

Method of application
Online application form
www.sghmartineau.com/
trainingcontracts

Selection procedure
Mini vacation scheme and
assessment centre

Closing date for 2017 training
contracts
31 July 2015

Closing date for 2015 mini
vacation schemes
31 January 2015

Application
Training contracts p.a. 10
Applications p.a. 600
& interviewed p.a. 10%
Required degree grade 2:1

Training
Salary
1st year (2014)
c. £23,000 (regional)
2nd year (2014)
c. £25,000 (regional)
Holiday entitlement 25 days
% of trainees with a non-law
degree 25%

Post-qualification
Salary (2013) £36,000
(regional)
% of trainees offered job on
qualification (2013) 64%

Overseas offices
Belgium

sgh | martineau llp

Sheridans

Seventy Six Wardour Street, London W1F 0UR
Tel: (020) 7079 0100 Fax: (020) 7079 0200
Email: enquiries@sheridans.co.uk
Website: www.sheridans.co.uk

Firm profile

Sheridans is a leading leisure, media and entertainment law firm with an established reputation across the creative industries. The firm represents a number of leading organisations, brands and talent across sectors including computer games, entertainment, fashion, film, interactive media, music, sport, television and theatre. Sheridans complements this expertise with a thriving commercial practice offering corporate, dispute resolution, real estate and employment services.

Main areas of work

Media & Entertainment: The music department advises recording artists and recording and management companies, on contract negotiation, popular and classical music publishing, merchandising and sponsorship. The film and television departments advise broadcasters, television and feature film production companies, distribution and sales agents, financiers and talent. Other specialist areas include theatre, sport, advertising and branding, fashion and design, trade marks and domain names, technology, computer games and interactive and digital media.

Dispute Resolution: The firm provides advice and representation in relation to disputes arising in the media and entertainment industries. The disputes typically range from privacy and defamation claims against the national press to rights disputes.

Corporate/Commercial: The firm advises on commercial contracts, mergers, acquisitions and disposals, management buy-outs and buy-ins, corporate finance, joint ventures, corporate reorganisations, company formations and insolvency.

Real Estate: Services include the sale and purchase of commercial property, involving investment, leasehold and planning matters, secured lending, building and development schemes and property financing, as well as domestic conveyancing for high net worth individuals.

Employment: The employment practice handles contentious and non-contentious matters, representing both employers and senior executives on a wide range of matters from recruitment to severence and change management to TUPE.

Trainee profile

Excellent academic background (2:1 and above, good A levels), commercial awareness, great interpersonal skills and an ability to think strategically. Trainees should have an enthusiasm for, and a demonstrable commitment to, the firm's areas of practice.

Training

The training contract is divided into four six-month seats, although trainees are expected to be flexible and assist any department as required. Trainees are given a challenging range of work and exposure to a significant level of responsibility.

Partners 35
Consultants 1
Assistant solicitors 22
Total trainees 3

Contact
Claire Lewis (Training Principal)

Method of application
CV and covering letter, by email to trainees@sheridans.co.uk between 01 June 2015 to 31 July 2015

Selection procedure
2 stage interview process

Closing date for 2017
31 July 2015

Application
Training contracts p.a. 1/2
Required degree grade 2:1

Training
Salary
1st year competitive with similar firms
2nd year competitive with similar firms
Holiday entitlement
20 days

Post-qualification
Salary Competitive with similar firms
% of trainees offered job on qualification (in last two years) 100%

Shoosmiths

The Lakes, Northampton NN4 7SH
Tel: (0370) 086 3075 Fax: (0370) 086 3001
Email: join.us@shoosmiths.co.uk
Website: www.shoosmiths.co.uk
Twitter: www.twitter.com/shoosmithsgrads

Firm profile

You'll find us a modern, forward-looking national commercial firm. Achieving this is a dedicated team of lawyers along with a strong support team, in 10 offices throughout the UK, from Southampton to Edinburgh.

Our client list speaks volumes for the quality of our lawyers and the experience they provide. From Hewlett-Packard to Krispy Kreme and property developers to some of the UK's largest banks, we work with a growing number of the FTSE 250 and some of the world's most exciting and ambitious growth businesses.

Main areas of work

Shoosmiths is a full service law firm offering you experience in a variety of areas, including commercial, corporate, employment, real estate, intellectual property, banking, planning and dispute resolution. Through our Access Legal consumer brand, we also offer private client, personal injury, medical negligence and conveyancing.

Trainee Profile

You'll be open-minded, forward-thinking, creative and innovative, and be trained in a non-hierarchal, open plan environment.

As a trainee, you will value a social life outside the office. Work-wise, you will care about the quality of service you give to clients, and will want to make a direct contribution to the firm's success.

Shoosmiths Trainees take an active part in the CR (Corporate Responsibility) around the firm, and drive initiatives of their own including "New Friday" a networking event for young professionals.

Training environment

There's nothing like diving straight in and having a go and, while we would not ask you to do something you are not comfortable in tackling, we expect you to relish the opportunity to get experience of real cases and deals from the start. In our opinion, it's the best way to learn.

Over two years, you will complete four, six-month placements, one of which could be an external secondment to a client's in-house legal team, providing an invaluable insight from the client's perspective.

Your experience will be built around a practical workload, complemented by technical and business skills training. We allocate no more than one trainee to each team, which means trainees enjoy high levels of involvement with the team, and are given good quality work and contact with clients.

Benefits

Regular involvement in sporting and social events, flexible holiday, pension, life assurance, corporate discounts. Please see our website for full details of our benefits package.

Vacation placements

Placements provide invaluable experience, allowing you to choose the right firm for you, and can even fast track you to a place on the assessment day for a training contract.

During your time with us, you'll be buddied with a trainee and spend time working with clients, partners and qualified lawyers, making a valuable contribution to the business.

Sponsorship & awards

We are happy to offer you financial assistance in relation to your GDL and/or LPC whilst you are studying. We will also provide a living allowance whilst you are studying.

Partners 130
Total Staff 1,300
Total Trainees 42

Contact
Samantha Hope

Method of application
Online application form

Selection procedure
Application & assessment day

Closing date for 2016
31st July 2014

Application
No. of Training Contracts 20
Applications pa 1600+
% Interviewed 10%
Required degree grade 2:1

Training
Salary
£24,000 / £25,000
Holiday entitlement p.a
23 days + flex

Post-qualification
Salary £38,000
% of trainees offered job on qualification (2012) 100%

Offices
Birmingham, Edinburgh, Manchester, Milton Keynes, Nottingham, Northampton, Reading, Solent (please see our website for locations we are currently recruiting to)

A-Z of Solicitors

Sidley Austin LLP

Woolgate Exchange, 25 Basinghall Street, London EC2V 5HA
Tel: (020) 7360 3600
Email: ukrecruitment@sidley.com
Website: www.sidley.com

Firm profile

Sidley Austin LLP is one of the world's largest full-service law firms. With approximately 1,800 lawyers practising on four continents (North America, Europe, Australasia and Asia), the firm provides a broad range of integrated services to meet the needs of its clients across a multitude of industries.

Main areas of work

Corporate, competition, corporate reorganisation and bankruptcy, debt restructuring, debt finance and structured finance, equity capital markets, employment, financial services regulatory, hedge funds, insurance, IP/IT, litigation, real estate and real estate finance, tax.

Trainee profile

Sidley Austin LLP looks for focused, intelligent and enthusiastic individuals with personality and humour who have a real interest in practising law in the commercial world. Trainees should have a consistently strong academic record and a 2:1 degree (not necessarily in law).

Training environment

The firm is not a typical City firm and it is not a 'legal factory' so there is no risk of being just a number. Everyone is encouraged to be proactive and to create their own niche when they are ready to do so. Trainees spend time in the firm's main groups. In each group trainees will sit with a partner or senior associate to ensure individual training based on 'hands on' experience. You will be encouraged to take responsibility where appropriate. Regular meetings with your supervisor ensure both the quality and quantity of your experience. In addition, there is a structured timetable of training on a cross-section of subjects.

Benefits

Private health insurance, life assurance, contribution to gym membership, interest-free season ticket loan, income protection scheme, pension and subsidised restaurant.

Sponsorship & awards

Tuition fees for the GDL/CPE and the LPC. Maintenance grant of £7,000 p.a.

Sidley Austin LLP, a Delaware limited liability partnership which operates at the firm's offices other than Chicago, London, Hong Kong, Singapore and Sydney, is affiliated with other partnerships, including Sidley Austin LLP, an Illinois limited liability partnership (Chicago); Sidley Austin LLP, a separate Delaware limited liability partnership (London); Sidley Austin LLP, a separate Delaware limited liability partnership (Singapore); Sidley Austin, a New York general partnership (Hong Kong); Sidley Austin, a Delaware general partnership of registered foreign lawyers restricted to practising foreign law (Sydney); and Sidley Austin Nishikawa Foreign Law Joint Enterprise (Tokyo). The affiliated partnerships are referred to herein collectively as Sidley Austin, Sidley, or the firm.

Partners 39
Assistant Solicitors 73
Total Trainees 22

Contact
Lucy Slater
Graduate Recruitment Officer

Method of application
Apply online at
www.sidley.com

Selection procedure
Interview and verbal reasoning test

Closing date for 2017
31 July 2015

Application
Training contracts p.a. 10
Applications p.a. 600
% interviewed p.a. 15
Required degree grade 2:1

Training
Salary
1st year (2014) £41,000
2nd year (2014) £43,000
Holiday entitlement 25 days
% of trainees with a
non-law degree p.a. 50%

Overseas offices
Beijing, Boston, Brussels, Chicago, Dallas, Geneva, Hong Kong, Houston, Los Angeles, New York, Palo Alto, San Francisco, Shanghai, Singapore, Sydney, Tokyo, Washington DC

Simmons & Simmons

CityPoint, One Ropemaker Street, London EC2Y 9SS
Tel: (020) 7628 2020 Fax: (020) 7628 2070
Email: recruitment@simmons-simmons.com
Website: www.simmons-simmons.com/graduates

Firm profile

Simmons & Simmons is a leading international law firm with fully integrated teams working throughout offices in Europe, the Middle East and Asia. The firm's strategy is designed to ensure it provides its clients with high quality advice and to deliver value through new ways of working.

Main areas of work

From our offices in major business and financial centres throughout Europe, the Middle East and Asia, we view the world through the lens of our key sectors: asset management & investment funds, energy & infrastructure, financial institutions, life sciences, and technology, media & telecommunications. These five sector teams are drawn from the core practice areas of: corporate, dispute resolution, competition & regulatory, employment, pensions & employee benefits, financial markets, intellectual property, projects, real estate, information, communications & technology, and tax.

Trainee profile

Simmons & Simmons is interested in finding out about your academic successes but will also explore your ability to form excellent interpersonal relations and work within a team environment, as well as your levels of motivation, drive and ambition. Show us evidence of a rich 'life experience' as well as examples of your intellectual capabilities and we will provide you with everything you need to become a successful member of our firm.

Training environment

The training programme is constantly evolving to build the skills you will need to be successful in the fast moving world of international business. Our groundbreaking MBA programme is designed to provide our trainees and junior lawyers with a unique opportunity to gain valuable business and commercial skills early in their career. During the training contract we will also ensure trainees have a broad legal experience, and a balanced, integrated approach to gaining the knowledge, expertise and abilities you will need to qualify in the practice area of your choice.

Vacation placements

The firm's internship schemes are one of the primary means of selecting candidates for a career at Simmons & Simmons. Your placement will enable you to gain a first-hand experience of a busy and dynamic international law firm, with exposure to the deals and transactions the firm works on.

Winter vacation scheme: one week scheme aimed specifically at final year law and non-law students, graduates of non-law subjects and career changers. Applications open 01 October 2014.

Spring insight scheme: two day workshop, designed to equip you with a range of key skills and commercial knowledge you will need, to help you make your first steps towards your career in law. Applications open 01 January 2015.

Summer vacation scheme: three week scheme open to penultimate year law students, final year non-law students and graduates. Applications open 01 November 2014.

A series of open days are also available to all students and graduates and are run throughout the year.

Sponsorship

The firm will cover your full tuition fees for law school and offer a maintenance grant of £6,500 for the GDL and £7,500 for the LPC.

Partners 230+
Fee earners 800+
Total Trainees 80+

Contact
Jenny Daniel, Graduate
Recruitment Advisor

Method of application
Online application form, at
www.simmons-simmons.com/
graduates

Selection procedure
Online application, remote
online critical reasoning test,
assessment day

Application dates for Training
Contracts in 2017/18
Non law finalists and all
graduates
01 Nov 2014 - 31 March 2015
Law undergraduates
01 June - 31 July 2015

Application
Training contracts p.a. circa 40
Applications p.a. 2,500
Required degree grade 2:1

Training
Salary
£37,500 1st and 2nd seat
£41,750 3rd and 4th seat
Holiday entitlement 25 days
% of trainees with a
non-law degree p.a. 50%
No. of seats available
abroad p.a. varies

Post-qualification
Salary (2014) £63,000

Overseas offices
Abu Dhabi, Amsterdam,
Beijing, Bristol, Brussels, Doha,
Dubai, Düsseldorf, Frankfurt,
Funchal*, Hong Kong, Jeddah*, Lisbon*, Madrid, Milan,
Munich, Paris, Rome, Shanghai,
Singapore, Tokyo
*Associated office

Simmons & Simmons

Skadden, Arps, Slate, Meagher & Flom (UK) LLP

40 Bank Street, Canary Wharf, London E14 5DS
Tel: (020) 7519 7000 Fax: (020) 7519 7070
Email: graduate.hiring@skadden.com
Website: www.skadden.com/uktraineesolicitor

Firm profile
Skadden is one of the leading law firms in the world with approximately 2,000 lawyers in 24 offices across the globe. Clients include corporate, industrial, financial institutions and government entities. The London office is the gateway to the firm's European practice and has some 250 lawyers dedicated to top-end, cross-border corporate transactions and international arbitration and litigation. The firm has handled matters in nearly every country in the greater European region and in Africa and the Middle East. The firm is consistently ranked as a leader in all disciplines and amongst a whole host of accolades, the firm has been voted 'Global Corporate Law Firm of the Year' (Chambers and Partners), 'Best US Law Firm in London' (Legal Business) 'Best Trainer' and 'Best Recruiter' in the US law firm in London category (Law Careers.Net Training and Recruitment Awards).

Main areas of work
Lawyers across the European network focus primarily on corporate transactions, including domestic and cross-border mergers and acquisitions, private equity, capital markets, leveraged finance and banking, tax, corporate restructuring and energy and projects. The firm also advises in international arbitration, litigation and regulatory matters.

Trainee profile
The firm seeks to recruit a small number of high-calibre graduates from any discipline to join their highly successful London office as trainee solicitors. The firm is looking for candidates who combine intellectual ability with enthusiasm, creativity and a demonstrable ability to rise to a challenge and to work with others towards a common goal.

Training environment
The firm can offer you the chance to develop your career in a uniquely rewarding and professional environment. You will join a close-knit but diverse team in which you will be given ample opportunity to work on complex matters, almost all with an international aspect, whilst benefiting from highly personalised training and supervision in an informal and friendly environment. The first year of your training contract will be divided into two six month seats where you will gain experience in corporate transactions and international litigation and arbitration. In the second year of your training contract, you will have the opportunity to discuss your preferences for your remaining two seats. The firm also offers the opportunity for second year trainees to be seconded to our Hong Kong office for a six month seat.

Benefits
Life insurance, private health insurance, private medical insurance, travel insurance, joining fee paid at Canary Wharf gym, subsidised restaurant, employee assistance programme and technology allowance.

Work placements
Skadden offers the opportunity for penultimate year law and non-law students to experience the culture and working environment of the firm through two week work placements. Placements are paid and take place during Easter and over the course of the summer. The deadline for applications is 12 January 2015 for placements in 2015.

Sponsorship & awards
The firm pays for GDL and LPC course fees and provides a £8,000 grant for each year of these courses.

Partners 31*
Assistant Solicitors 115
Trainees 15*
*London office

Contact
Aidan Connor
Graduate Recruitment
Specialist

Method of application
Online application

Selection procedure
A selection event comprising of an interview and a short exercise
Closing date for 2017
31 July 2015

Application
Training contracts p.a. 10-12
Applications p.a. 1000
% interviewed p.a. 8%
Required degree grade 2:1

Training
Salary
1st year £42,000
2nd year £45,000
Holiday entitlement 25 days
% of trainees with a non-law degree p.a. 50%

Overseas offices
Beijing, Boston, Brussels, Chicago, Frankfurt, Hong Kong, Houston, Los Angeles, Moscow, Munich, New York, Palo Alto, Paris, San Francisco, São Paulo, Seoul, Shanghai, Singapore, Sydney, Tokyo, Toronto, Washington DC, Wilmington

A-Z of Solicitors

Skadden, Arps, Slate, Meagher & Flom (UK) LLP

Slaughter and May

One Bunhill Row, London EC1Y 8YY
Tel: (020) 7600 1200
Email: trainee.recruit@slaughterandmay.com (enquiries only)
Website: www.slaughterandmay.com

Firm profile
One of the most prestigious law firms in the world, Slaughter and May enjoys a reputation for quality and expertise. The corporate, commercial and financing practice is particularly strong and lawyers are known for their business acumen and technical excellence. As well as its London, Brussels, Beijing and Hong Kong offices, the firm nurtures long-standing relationships with the leading independent law firms in other jurisdictions in order to provide the best advice and service across the world.

Main areas of work
Corporate, commercial and financing; tax; competition; financial regulation; dispute resolution; technology, media and telecommunications; intellectual property; real estate; pensions and employment.

Trainee profile
The work is demanding and the firm looks for intellectual agility and the ability to work with people from different countries and walks of life. Common sense, the ability to communicate clearly and the willingness to accept responsibility are all essential. The firm expects to provide training in everything except the fundamental principles of law, so does not expect applicants to know much of commercial life.

Training environment
Each trainee completes four or five seats of three or six months duration. Two or three seats will be spent in one of the firm's corporate, commercial and financing groups. The remaining time can be divided between some of the specialist groups and can also include an overseas secondment to one of the firm's offices or to one of its best friend firms. In each seat a partner is responsible for monitoring your progress and reviewing your work. There is an extensive training programme which includes the PSC. There are also discussion groups covering general and specialised legal topics.

Benefits
Private medical insurance, season ticket loan, pension scheme, interest free loan, subsidised membership of health club, 24 hour accident cover, Cycle to Work scheme, childcare vouchers, subsidised restaurant and coffee bar, concierge service and health screenings.

Vacation placements
Work experience schemes are available at Easter and during the summer period for penultimate year students. We also offer a first year open day for law students at Easter and workshops for finalists and graduates during the winter. Please visit the website for full details.

Sponsorship & awards
GDL and LPC fees and maintenance grants are paid.

Partners 112
Associates Over 400
Total Trainees 169

Contact
The Trainee Recruitment Team

Method of application
Online (via website)

Selection procedure
Interview

Application
Training contracts p.a. approx 75-80
Applications p.a. 2,000 approx
Required degree grade Strong 2:1

Training
Salary (May 2014)
1st year £39,500
2nd year £45,000
Holiday entitlement
25 days p.a.
% of trainees with a non-law degree Approx 50%
No of seats available abroad p.a. Approx 20

Post-qualification
Salary (May 2014) £65,000
% of trainees offered job on qualification (March 2014) 90%

Overseas offices
Brussels, Beijing and Hong Kong, plus 'Best Friend' firms in all the major jurisdictions.

SLAUGHTER AND MAY

A-Z of Solicitors

Speechly Bircham LLP

6 New Street Square, London EC4A 3LX
Tel: (020) 7427 6400 Fax: (020) 7427 4456
Website: www.speechlys.com

Firm profile
Speechly Bircham is an ambitious, full-service City firm with a fascinating mix of clients. We do not see ourselves purely as legal advisers to our clients. Instead, we aim to offer a more rounded, tailored service, where our insight and expertise helps clients achieve their wider aims. We combine expertise, professionalism and hands-on involvement to help our clients both in the UK and internationally with a complete offering across four sectors – financial services, private wealth, technology and real estate and construction.

The firm's international capabilities span five key European centres, with offices in London, Luxembourg, Paris, Geneva and Zurich, making it one of the few UK law firms to offer intergrated corporate, tax, regulatory, funds and private client work to companies, banks, fund managers, wealthy individuals and private offices in Europe.

Main areas of work
Banking and finance, construction, engineering and projects, corporate, dispute resolution, employment and immigration, family, financial services and tax, IP, technology and data, pensions, real estate, real estate litigation, residential property and tax, trust and succession.

Trainee profile
We require candidates to achieve a minimum of a 2:1 in their degree and look for smart, ambitious and intellectually curious individuals. People come to us from all backgrounds and degree disciplines, with a range of views that combine to give us our distinctive perspective on the law.

Training environment
Speechly Bircham divides the training contract into four six-month seats. We only take on 9 trainees per year and emphasis is given to early responsibility and supervised client contact to provide you with a practical learning environment. Trainees are supported by a partner or solicitor and are given in-house legal training complemented by regular performance reviews to promote development. Most of our trainees are selected from our summer schemes however we also accept direct training contract applications and interviews for these take place during August each year.

Vacation scheme
Our scheme offers a detailed introduction to the legal world. Each week is spent in a different practice area where you will carry out fee-earning work that could include attending client meetings and going to court. Support is always close at hand, with a current trainee as mentor and a solicitor as sponsor for each placement. Our summer scheme also has a programme of sports and social events which help both parties see if we are right for each other personally as well as professionally.

Benefits
Benefits include private medical insurance, life assurance, pension scheme, 25 days holiday, interest-free season ticket loan, subsidised restaurant, 4 weeks unpaid leave on qualification, corporate discount for gym membership.

Sponsorship
GDL and LPC fees paid together with a maintenance grant

Speechly Bircham is to merge with Charles Russell on 1st November 2014 to become Charles Russell Speechlys. The merger will create one of the world's leading private wealth and business law firms with 170 partners and a total of 500 lawyers and combined revenues of £135m, placing it within the UK top 30 law firms.

Partners 80
Assistant Solicitors 120
Total Trainees 22

Contact
Hayley Halvatzis
HR Officer

Method of application
Online application via
www.dolawthinkbusiness.co.uk

Selection procedure
Interview and psychometric testing

Closing date for 2017
31 July 2015

Application
Training contracts p.a. 9
Applications p.a. 600
% interviewed p.a. 10%
Required degree grade 2:1

Training
Salary
1st year £34,000
2nd year £36,000
Holiday entitlement 25 days

Post-qualification
Salary (2014) £57,000

SpeechlyBircham

Squire Patton Boggs

Rutland House, 148 Edmund Street, Birmingham B3 2JR
7 Devonshire Square, Cutlers Gardens, London EC2M 4YH
2 Park Lane, Leeds LS3 1ES
Trinity Court, 16 John Dalton Street, Manchester M60 8HS
Tel: (0800) 163 498   Email: traineerecruitment@squirepb.com
Website: www.squirepattonboggs.com

Firm profile

We combine sound legal advice with a deep knowledge of our clients' businesses to resolve their legal challenges. We care about the quality of our services, the success of our clients and the relationships that are forged through those successes.

With over 1,500 lawyers in 44 offices located in 21 countries around the world, our global legal practice is in the markets where our clients do business. We also have strong working relationships with independent firms in Europe and the Middle East, as well as the Squire Patton Boggs Legal Counsel Worldwide Network, which includes independent firms across Latin America.

The client base of our global legal practice spans every type of business, both private and public, worldwide. We advise a diverse mix of clients, from Fortune 100 and FTSE 100 corporations to emerging companies and from individuals to local and national governments.

Main areas of work

Banking and financial services, corporate/corporate finance, environment, safety and health, intellectual property, commercial and IT, international dispute resolution, labour and employment, litigation/disputes, pensions, real estate, regulatory, restructuring and insolvency and tax.

Trainee profile

Squire Patton Boggs seeks applications from law and non-law graduates, and we also welcome applications from individuals seeking a career change. A strong academic background will be key and you will have, or would expect, a 2:1 degree. It is an advantage for applicants to have language skills, but this is not essential. You should also be motivated and ambitious and have a wish to succeed in a client-focused business. Evidence of work experience in the legal sector, excellent communication skills and significant achievement in non-academic pursuits is advisable.

Training environment

20 trainee solicitors recruited each year. Trainees undertake six four-month seats during their training contract. Trainees have input in choice of seats and are encouraged to undertake a broad selection of seats to benefit their knowledge on qualification. Trainees benefit from two-tier supervision and challenging work. The firm provides a comprehensive induction programme including on-going departmental training, seminars and workshops throughout the training contract. Trainees undertake formal appraisal meetings with their supervisors during each seat. Trainees also benefit from exposure to clients, cross-border work and opportunity for seats on secondment. Trainees are involved in all aspects of professional life.

Benefits

Pension, life assurance, subsidised gym membership, interest free season ticket loan and a flexible benefits package.

Vacation placements

Places for 2015: 40 summer scheme; Duration: 2 weeks; Remuneration: £240 p.w. (London) £225 p.w. (Birmingham, Leeds, Manchester); Closing date: 31 January 2015.

Sponsorship & awards

PgDL and LPC fees paid and maintenance grant provided. Maintenance grant presently:

GDL: London, £6,000; Regional, £4,500

LPC: London, £7,000; Regional, £5,000

Assistant Solicitors 1,500
Total Trainees 40

Contact
Graduate Recruitment Team

Method of application
Online application form

Selection procedure
Assessment and interview

Closing date for 2017
31 July 2015

Application
Training contracts p.a. 20
Applications p.a. 1,500
% interviewed p.a. 10%
Required degree grade 2:1

Training
Salary
1st year (2014)
£23,500 regional
£35,000 London
2nd year (2014)
£26,000 regional
£37,000 London
Holiday entitlement 25 days
% of trainees with a non-law degree p.a. 30%
No. of seats available abroad p.a. 6

Post-qualification
Salary (2014)
London £58,000
Other £37,000
% of trainees accepting job on qualification (2014) 80%

Overseas offices
Squire Patton Boggs Legal Counsel World Wide has offices in the USA, South America, Asia, Europe and the Middle East. For a complete list of our offices, please visit our website.

Stephenson Harwood LLP

1 Finsbury Circus, London EC2M 7SH
Tel: (020) 7809 2812 Fax: (020) 7003 8346
Email: graduate.recruitment@shlegal.com
Website: www.shlegal.com/graduate

Firm profile
Stephenson Harwood is a thriving, international law firm with over 120 partners and more than 700 staff worldwide. We act for a wide range of listed and private companies, institutions and successful entrepreneurs. We also offer a full range of services in a wide variety of sectors.

Join a firm that's ambitious, growing and delivering ground breaking deals. You'll work in tight, focused teams alongside associates and partners, and will be right at the heart of the action.

Main areas of work
Commercial litigation; corporate; employment and pensions; finance; marine and international trade; and real estate.

Trainee profile
Firstly we look for a quick intellect. As well as at least a 2:1 in any subject area plus 320 UCAS points or equivalent, you'll need strong analytical skills, sound judgement, imagination and meticulous attention to detail.

Also vital are the communication skills to be persuasive and build rapport, plenty of drive and determination, plus a keen interest in business. Mandarin Chinese language skills are useful.

Training environment
We take just 16 trainees on each year. So you can look forward to a huge amount of individual attention, coaching and mentoring. Your structured programme involves four six-month seats in our contentious and non-contentious practice groups. You can expect on-the-job training complemented by in-house seminars; to share an office with a partner or senior associate; and to benefit from a continuous review of your career development. You could also have the chance to spend one of your six-month seats in Hong Kong, Singapore or Dubai and to take advantage of client secondment opportunities. We'll give you your own caseload and as much responsibility as you can shoulder.

Benefits
These include subsidised health club membership, private health insurance and screening, pension, life assurance, private GP services, critical illness cover, dental insurance, retail vouchers, subsidised cafe, season ticket loan, 25 days' paid holiday a year and language tuition where appropriate.

Vacation placements
Places for 2014/2015: 40

Duration: 1 week winter; 2 weeks spring and summer

Remuneration: £260 p.w.

Closing date: 2 November 2014 for winter; 31 January 2015 for spring and summer.

Open days
14 January 2015, 11 February 2015, 18 March 2015, 22 April 2015

Closing date: 31 January 2014

Sponsorship & awards
Fees paid for GDL and LPC at BPP Law School London and maintenance awards of up to £6,000 (if still studying).

Partners 120+
Associates 200+
Total Trainees 32

Contact
Sarah Jackson (graduate.
recruitment@shlegal.com)

Method of application
Online application form via
www.shlegal.com/graduate

Selection procedure
Application screening, online verbal and numerical testing, face to face interview and assessment centre

Closing date for TC commencing March/Sept 2017
31 July 2015

Application
Applications p.a. circa 1,500
Training contracts p.a. 16
Required degree grade 2:1

Training
Salary
1st year £37,000
2nd year £40,000
Holiday entitlement 25 days
% of trainees with a non-law degree p.a. 50%
Overseas secondment opportunities

Post-qualification
Salary £60,000
86% of trainees offered job

Overseas offices
Paris, Piraeus, Hong Kong, Singapore, Shanghai, Guangzhou, Dubai, Beijing

Associated offices
Athens, Bucharest, Jakarta, Yangon

STEPHENSON HARWOOD

Stevens & Bolton LLP

Wey House, Farnham Road, Guildford GUI 4YD
Tel: (01483) 302264 Fax: (01483) 302254
Email: julie.bounden@stevens-bolton.com
Website: www.stevens-bolton.com

Firm profile

Stevens & Bolton LLP is recognised as a leading national law firm, offering a full range of commercial legal services. We are recommended in 24 specialist practice areas by leading independent legal directories and have received widespread awards recognition. Over the years we have been named and shortlisted Best Recruiter and Best Trainer in the LawCareers.Net Training & Recruitment Awards.

Based in Guildford, our single office approach ensures excellent communication and efficient co-ordination of our resources. We provide legal services both nationally and internationally, with unswerving focus on quality. From the outset, our trainees get first class experience of the business world. We advise a number of the top 100 and other UK FTSE companies, as well as many other substantial international groups, owner managed businesses and SMEs. As such, the work we carry out is both interesting and challenging and equal to work handled by City firms.

Main areas of work

Corporate and commercial; finance; real estate; dispute resolution; IP; employment, pensions and immigration; tax, trusts and charities; and family.

Trainee profile

We welcome applications from candidates with either a law or non-law background, with at least 320 UCAS points and one grade A at A level, who have achieved (or expect to achieve) a 2:1 degree or higher. Essential qualities include: very good communication skills, drive and ambition, intelligence, attention to detail, business interest and genuine enthusiasm for wanting to be a lawyer.

Training environment

Our trainees have genuine responsibility and experience of dealing with clients – and are made to feel part of the team from day one. Trainee seats will be available in most of the key business areas we specialise in, namely M&A and other corporate work, finance, commercial contracts, tax, real estate, IP, commercial disputes and employment. We do our best to maximise your ability to experience as many of those areas as possible as part of our six, four month seat rotation.

We are dedicated to encouraging continuous professional development, delivered in a variety of ways to give our trainees the best chance to become rounded, assured and respected professionals. Training in technical and business skills and early exposure to stimulating work with a variety of clients is instrumental in providing a solid foundation. In addition, the value to be gained from a unique combination of factors – supervision when you need it, support from colleagues and the opportunity to embrace early responsibility as soon as you are ready – creates a compelling proposition at the outset of your career.

Benefits

25 days holiday, pension, private healthcare, life assurance and an interest free loan for rail travel or car parking.

Sponsorship & awards

We pay the fees for the CPE/GDL and LPC and a £4,000 maintenance grant for each course of study. Any future trainees who are yet to take their LPC or the GDL are required to attend the College of Law Guildford.

Vacation placements

We run two programmes each summer of one week duration. Applications are accepted between 1 December 2014 and 31 January 2015.

Partners 35
Associates 73
Total Trainees 8

Contact
Julie Bounden
(01483) 302264

Method of application
Online application form available from website

Selection procedure
Two interviews and other processes

Closing date for 2017
31st July 2015

Application
Training contracts p.a. 4
Applications p.a. 350
% interviewed 20%
Required degree grade 2:1

Training
Salary
£30,000
Holiday entitlement 25 days

Overseas/regional offices
Guildford only

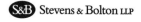 Stevens & Bolton LLP

A-Z of Solicitors

Sullivan & Cromwell LLP

1 New Fetter Lane, London EC4A 1AN
Tel: (020) 7959 8900 Fax: (020) 7959 8950
Email: traineesolicitors@sullcrom.com
Website: www.sullcrom.com/uk-trainee-solicitor-recruitment

Firm profile

Sullivan & Cromwell provides the highest quality legal advice and representation to clients around the world. The results we achieve have set us apart for more than 130 years and serve as a model for the modern practice of law. At S&C there is no such thing as second best. Meritocracy, responsibility and opportunity foster the success of each new employee. S&C has approximately 800 lawyers across an international network of twelve offices on four continents. We maintain a unified firm culture worldwide and provide our clients with highly integrated advice on a global basis.

The London office, established in 1972, is S&C's largest office excepting its New York City headquarters. There are approximately 80 English, US and dual-qualified lawyers working in the office across of number of practice areas.

Main areas of work

S&C London is perhaps unique in the scale, complexity and significance of the work carried out in an office of its size. Our practice areas include: M&A and private equity, capital markets, finance (credit, leveraged and acquisition), restructuring, project finance, competition law, criminal defence and investigations, and tax.

Trainee profile

We seek trainees who have an excellent prior academic record along with strong academic credentials, including a projected or achieved First or Upper Second Class honours degree, or the equivalent. You should possess genuine intellectual curiosity, integrity, strong interpersonal skills, commercial awareness and an ambition to succeed at one of the world's leading law firms. We expect most of our applicants to be penultimate year law students and final year non-law students. Graduates and post-graduates are also eligible.

Training environment

We will offer our trainees the opportunity to do superior work, meet exceptional people and grow in a supportive culture. We aim to distinguish our trainee programme by offering genuine mentoring from partners and other senior lawyers who will take a keen interest in your career development. Training contracts with S&C will be divided into four six-month seats, covering at least three practice areas. You will be supervised in each seat by a partner who is a leader in his or her field, along with other senior lawyers. They will provide the guidance you need to help you make the transition from academic study to legal practice.

Benefits

Include private health insurance, dental insurance, life insurance, travel insurance, a group personal pension scheme, subsidised gym membership, concierge service and 24 vacation days each year.

Vacation placements

Places for 2015: a two-week summer placement scheme primarily aimed at penultimate year law students and final year non-law students. Remuneration £500 p.w. Apply by CV (including a full classification and percentage breakdown of all academic results) and a covering letter to traineesolicitors@sullcrom.com. We will be accepting applications for our 2015 summer vacation scheme from 3 November 2014 through 30 January 2015.

Sponsorship & awards

GDL and LPC full funding and a maintenance grant of £9000.

Partners 19
Assistant Solicitors 65
Total Trainees 4

Contact
Kirsten Davies, Trainee Solicitor Recruitment Manager

Method of application
CV and covering letter

Selection procedure
Interview with Graduate Recruitment and two Partners, meeting with 1-2 associates

Closing date for 2017
31 July 2015

Application
Training contracts p.a. 4-6
Applications p.a. 750
Required degree grade 2:1

Training
Salary (2014)
First year £50,000
Second year £55,000
Holiday entitlement 24 days

Post-qualification
Salary (2014) £97,500

Overseas/regional offices
Beijing, Frankfurt, Hong Kong, London, Los Angeles, Melbourne, New York, Palo Alto, Paris, Sydney, Tokyo, Washington DC

SULLIVAN & CROMWELL LLP

Taylor Wessing LLP

5 New Street Square, London EC4A 3TW
Tel: (020) 7300 7000 Fax: (020) 7300 7100
Email: graduate@taylorwessing.com
Website: graduate.taylorwessing.com

Firm profile

Taylor Wessing is a leading international law firm where you can move your career forward, faster. We are looking for the trusted advisors of tomorrow who can think creatively, be proactive and stay close to our clients and identify and deliver innovative solutions that help their businesses grow. Our clients include large and medium size, private and public companies, financial institutions, professional service firms, public sector bodies and wealthy individuals. Our focus is on the sectors that we believe are the industries of tomorrow: energy; life sciences; private wealth; technology; media and communications.

We are experts in providing a seamless, high-quality service to global clients across many jurisdictions. Combining a pan-European network with a strong presence in the Middle East, India, China and North America, we are the leading firm for inward investment from North America and experts in IP protection and enforcement rights across the globe. That's why we advise half of the world's top 100 brands.

Main areas of work

We offer industry-focused advice and in-depth sector experience by grouping together lawyers from different legal disciplines including: banking and finance; capital markets; copyright and media law; corporate; commercial agreements; construction and engineering; employment and pensions; EU competition, IT and telecoms; litigation and dispute resolution; patents; planning and environment; private client; projects; real estate; restructuring and corporate recovery; tax; trade marks and designs.

Trainee profile

We look for people with a minimum of ABB grades at A-level and a 2:1 degree in any discipline. You'll need to be a team player with the communication skills to build vibrant relationships with our clients. You'll have the energy, ambition and creativity to take early responsibility and have a real impact on our business and our clients' business. You'll also be committed to a career in law, with a genuine drive to learn and explore new boundaries.

Training environment

Our award winning training programme (lawcareers.net best trainer – large city firm 2014) combines the in-house Professional Skills Course with six-month seats in four different practice groups, including one contentious seat and one in our corporate or finance areas.

Working closely with partners and associates on high-quality work from the outset, you'll get regular support and feedback every step of the way to align your career to the growth and needs of the firm and our clients. There are also secondment opportunities to our clients.

Vacation schemes

Our vacation schemes are designed for you to experience life as a trainee solicitor in a uniquely innovative City law firm. You'll spend two weeks in two different practice groups gaining firsthand experience under the supervision of associates and partners.

Places: 40. Duration: 2 weeks. Remuneration: £250 per week. Closing date: 30 January 2015.

Sponsorship

GDL and LPC fees at BPP London sponsored. A maintenance grant is provided.

Partners 400
Trainees 47
Vacancies Circa 22

Application
All candidates are required to complete our online application form, which can be found on our website
www.taylorwessing.com/graduate

Training
Salary
1st year £37,000
2nd year £41,000

Post qualification
Salary £60,000

Offices
Berlin, Bratislava, Brussels, Budapest, Cambridge, Dubai, Dusseldorf, Frankfurt, Hamburg, Jakarta, Kiev, London, London Tech City, Munich, Paris, Prague, Seoul, Singapore, Vienna and Warsaw

Representative Offices
Beijing, Brno, Klagenfurt and Shanghai

TaylorWessing

Thomas Cooper LLP

Ibex House, 42-47 Minories, London EC3N 1HA
Tel: (020) 7481 8851 Fax: (020) 7480 6097
Email: recruitment@thomascooperlaw.com
Website: www.thomascooperlaw.com

Firm profile

Thomas Cooper is an international law firm which was founded in 1825.

Thomas Cooper has experience of dealing with the law in key jurisdictions around the world, with offices in London, Athens, Madrid, Paris, Sao Paulo and Singapore. The firm takes a pragmatic approach, providing clear advice that helps clients navigate through the complexity of international commerce.

The firm is recommended by and recognised by the major legal directories for its expertise.

The firm's clients operate globally and range from shipowners to charterers and traders, from banks and other financial institutions to underwriters and P&I clubs, from blue chip companies to small businesses and private individuals.

The firm gives insightful and pragmatic advice to clients and allows them to manage their exposure to risk more effectively.

Main areas of work

The firm's core practice areas are maritime, trade, finance, company and commercial, international arbitration, insurance, oil and gas.

Trainee profile

As a trainee with the firm you will be exposed to clients and fee earning work from your first seat. Thomas Cooper works for a wide variety of clients and as such, you can expect to find yourself dealing with finance, personal injury, wet or dry shipping claims.

Thomas Cooper values its trainees because they are vital for the future of the business. If you are bright, confident and a self starter who has a keen interest in maritime then the firm would encourage you to apply to its trainee programme.

Thomas Cooper recruits a maximum of 4 trainees per year.

Training environment

Thomas Cooper has a four-seat trainee programme over two years: two seats in shipping, one in defence and personal injury; and one in finance and international trade. There is also opportunity to do a seat in one of the firm's international offices, this is dependent upon language skills and team workload.

Benefits

Private medical insurance; permanent health insurance; life assurance; 25 days holiday; pension scheme; loan for dental insurance; season ticket loan; loan for gym membership. LPC course fees are paid by the firm.

Partners 24
Assistant solicitors 31
Total trainees 7/8

Contact
Karan Tapley - Human Resources Manager
Tel (020) 7481 8851

Method of application
Online application form

Selection procedure
Interviews and assessments

Closing date for 2017
31 July 2015

Application
Required degree grade 2:1

Training
Salary
Starting salary for trainees is
Year 1 £33,000
Year 2 £36,500 (based on 2014 salaries)
25 days holiday

Overseas/regional offices
Athens, Madrid, Paris, Sao Paulo and Singapore

TLT LLP

One Redcliff St, Bristol BS1 6TP
Tel: (0117) 917 8905 Fax: (0117) 917 7649
Email: graduate@TLTsolicitors.com
Website: www.TLTcareers.com/trainee

Firm profile
Here, the firm is open. Open to connected working, open plan and open minded. We have reshaped the traditional law firm model into a fresh, bright, inclusive and creative place to work.

And the approach seems to be working. Since 2002 TLT has more than tripled in size; we've opened new offices in Belfast and Manchester, bringing in interesting clients including Boohoo.com and E.ON. We're also expanding in Scotland, building on our strong financial services profile with clients in the leisure and energy and renewables sectors.

Voted as a top five UK law firm for client service in Legal Week's Client Satisfaction Report 2013, we are driven around the needs of clients. Our enviable roster of large corporates, public institutions and high growth businesses includes Punch Taverns, Merlin Entertainments, Dyson, WHSmith, Barclays Bank and EDF Energy. With revenues hitting £57.9m in 2013/14, we are going places – quickly. If you want to make your mark and work progressively, then this is where your career really begins.

Main areas of work
TLT's legal services span the financial services, leisure, retail and consumer goods, technology and media, renewables, housing and public sectors. Our core legal specialisms include real estate, banking and finance, commercial, corporate, employment, dispute resolution and litigation, but we believe there's more to legal work than being a lawyer – you need to embrace management, technology and business skills too.

Trainee profile
Genuinely ambitious, talented and technically impressive, you don't just tick all the boxes – you open them up, reshape them and connect them all together. You'll stand out, stand up for what's right, and stand shoulder to shoulder with your colleagues – embracing team working and sharing a passion for exceptional client service. And while academic achievement is important, your personal qualities also count for a lot here.

Training environment
Whether you join us for your training contract or a one week vacation scheme placement, you'll work on live cases for real clients, get input from a partner and develop a broad range of legal and business skills. Our training contracts are designed to have more in them so you get more out, something recognised by The Lex 100 who awarded us Recommended Firm status in 2012/13. With TLT, you'll gain invaluable technical knowledge and professional skills, all backed up by a one-to-one mentor, expert guidance and unlimited support throughout.

Benefits
We offer a full and flexible benefits plan designed to meet your lifestyle needs. As part of the firm's commitment to giving something back, you'll also get involved in community support work, pro bono legal advice, fundraising and environmental initiatives.

Vacation placements
Spend a week with TLT and you'll pick up unparalleled experience and a real taste of life at a leading law firm - especially when you consider the amount of partner contact you'll enjoy, and we've built assessments into the week, which means you won't have to make a separate training contract application or attend an assessment day.

Sponsorship & awards
We will sponsor the completion of GDL and LPC if you've not already undertaken them.

Partners 83
Solicitors c. 200
Total Trainees 32 (from September 2014)

Contact
Gemma Cowley, HR Recruitment Officer - Trainees
Tel 0117 917 8905

Method of application
Online application form at www.TLTcareers.com/trainee

Selection procedure
Application form, telephone screening, verbal reasoning testing, assessment centre

Closing date
31 July each year

Application
Training contracts up to 15 p.a.
Applications circa 700 p.a.
% interviewed 12% p.a.
Required degree grade
2:1 or above in any discipline at degree level and a minimum of 300/24 UCAS points at A level

Training
Salary See website for details
Holiday entitlement 25 days

Post-qualification
Salary
See website for details
% trainees offered job on qualification 80-100%

Offices
Bristol, London, Manchester, Glasgow, Edinburgh, Belfast, Piraeus (Greece)

A-Z of Solicitors

Travers Smith LLP

10 Snow Hill, London EC1A 2AL
Tel: (020) 7295 3000 Fax: (020) 7295 3500
Email: graduate.recruitment@traverssmith.com
Website: www.traverssmith.com

Firm profile
Travers Smith is an award-winning independent law firm with a reputation for excellence in all of its chosen fields. Less than a quarter of the size of the largest firms, Travers Smith handles high profile and top quality work, much of which has an international dimension.

Main areas of work
Corporate law (including takeovers and mergers, private equity, IPOs, equity capital markets and funds), environment and operational regulatory, commercial, intellectual property and technology law, dispute resolution, banking, restructuring, financial services and markets, competition, tax, employment, pensions and real estate.

Trainee profile
The firm looks for people who combine academic excellence with common sense; who are determined and articulate, who can think on their feet, and who take their work but not themselves seriously. Applications are welcome from law and non-law undergraduates and graduates.

Training environment
The firm has a comprehensive training programme which ensures that trainees experience a broad range of work. All trainee solicitors sit in rooms with partners and associates, which leads to a refreshing lack of hierarchy. It also means that trainees receive an individual and extensive training from experienced lawyers, enjoying client contact, and the responsibility that goes with it, from day one.

During the two year training contract, trainees spend six months in the corporate department and one of either the dispute resolution or the employment departments. The other two six-month seats are spent in two of the other specialist departments. Trainees may also have the opportunity to spend six months in the firm's Paris office.

Benefits
Private health and permanent health insurance, life assurance, health screening programme, pension scheme, 25 days holiday, Ride2Work scheme, subsidised bistro, childcare vouchers, season ticket and corporate health club membership loan.

Vacation placements
Summer 2015: Three schemes with 15 places on each; duration is two weeks; remuneration of £275 per week; deadline is 31 January 2015. The firm also offers a two-week Christmas scheme for 15 students.

Sponsorship & awards
GDL and LPC paid in full, plus maintenance of £7,000 per annum to those in London and £6,500 per annum to those outside of London.

Partners 66
Associates 240
Total Trainees 46

Contact
Germaine VanGeyzel

Method of application
Online

Selection procedure
Interviews (2 stage process)

Closing date for 2017
31 July 2015

Application
Training contracts p.a. 25
Applications p.a. 1,000
% interviewed p.a. 30%
Required degree grade 2:1

Training
Salary
1st year (2014) £40,000
2nd year (2014) £44,000
Holiday entitlement 25 days

Post-qualification
Salary (2014) £65,000
% of trainees offered job
on qualification (2014) 94%

TRAVERS SMITH

A-Z of Solicitors

Trethowans LLP

London Road, Salisbury, Wiltshire, SP1 3HP
The Director General's House, 15 Rockstone Place, Southampton SO15 2EP
Tel: 0845 302 4695 Fax: 01722 333 011
Email: recruitment@trethowans.com
Web: www.trethowans.com

Firm profile

Trethowans is a premier law firm based in the South with a team of over 140 including 26 partners and 46 lawyers. The firm has a diverse and expanding client base. Our continued success is due to the quality of our people and the growing strength and reputation of our brand. With offices in Salisbury and Southampton our partners and staff enjoy the benefit of living close to the south coast whilst having the quality of work and clients often associated with a city firm. Many of our clients are household name clients. Service excellence is a priority – clients value the firm's ability to deliver top-quality, expert advice, on time, in a very personable manner and at a competitive price.

Main areas of work

On the commercial side, we represent international and national household brand names, owner-managed businesses, entrepreneurs and major regional employers across the UK. When acting for individuals, we represent landowners, entrepreneurs, local families, property developers and trustees amongst others.

Legal advice to businesses include: corporate, commercial, commercial property, commercial litigation, insurance litigation, employment and licensing. Legal advice to individuals includes: personal injury, private client (wills, trusts and tax; wealth structuring and inheritance planning; court of protection and mental capacity), agriculture and rural property, family and residential property.

Many of our teams and individuals are rated in both the Chambers Guide to the Legal Profession and Legal 500, the two independent guides to the legal profession in the UK.

Trainee profile

Trainees should possess sound academic abilities and be able to demonstrate commercial acumen. Flexibility, ambition and enthusiasm are valued. Candidates should be good communicators and adopt a problem solving approach to client work.

Training environment

Trainee solicitors usually undertake four separate specialist seats, each lasting six months. The firm offers a flexible approach in deciding trainees' seats to suit individual needs, while providing a broad training programme in accordance with the Solicitors Regulation Authority guidelines. Trainees work closely with the supervising lawyer/partner to whom they are responsible. They are considered an important part of each team and become closely involved in the team's work to obtain first-hand legal experience. Each trainee's performance is reviewed regularly by their supervisor and Training Partner and regular feedback is provided. This enables the trainee scheme to be continually evaluated and also ensures that the highest possible standards are maintained. Prospects for trainees are excellent. Most trainees are offered a position as solicitors at the end of their training contract. Trainees are an integral part of the firm from day one. They are responsible for the firm's staff newsletter, participate in business development, and actively communicate via twitter about their work and progress as a trainee (www.twitter.com/trethtrainees).

Benefits

Incremental holiday entitlement up to 28 days, contributory pension scheme, death in service benefit, Simply Health Cash Plan Scheme, PHI scheme, performance-related bonus scheme, car parking, new staff recruitment bonus, childcare voucher scheme and employee assistance programme.

Sponsorship & awards

None.

Partners 26
Solicitors 46
Total Trainees 7

Contact
Kate Ellis
02380 820503

Method of application
Applications by online application form and covering letter

Selection procedure
Two stage process; interview and assessment day

Closing date for 2016
31 July 2015

Application
Training contracts p.a. 3-4
Applications p.a. 100+
% interviewed p.a. 25-30%
Required degree grade 2:1

Training
Salary Competitive market rate with regular reviews
Holiday entitlement 23 days

Post-qualification
Salary Competitive market rate with regular reviews
% of trainees offered position on qualification 100% (Nov 2009), 67% (Nov 2010), 75% (Nov 2011), 67% (Nov 2012), 50% (Nov 2013)
Holiday entitlement 25 days

Regional offices
Salisbury, Southampton

Trowers & Hamlins LLP

3 Bunhill Row, London, EC1Y 8YZ
Tel: (020) 7423 8312 Fax: (020) 7423 8001
Email: avithlani@trowers.com
Website: www.trowers.com/careers/students

Firm profile

We are a City, national and international full-service firm with a unique mixture of practice areas. We are the number one firm in the UK for Housing and Public Sector work, and we are consistently ranked as one of the leading firms in the Middle East. We pride ourselves on providing down-to-earth and commercially savvy advice to our clients and, no matter where our clients are, they have access to a connected network of lawyers across disciplines, jurisdictions and sectors.

Main areas of work

Banking and finance, corporate, dispute resolution and litigation, employment and pensions, international (based in London, the Middle East and the Far East), projects and construction, public sector, real estate (including commercial property and housing), tax and private wealth.

Trainee profile

We usually recruit around 20 trainees every year, split between September and March intakes. The majority of our trainees will be recruited for our London office, with a small number of trainees taken on in our Birmingham, Exeter and Manchester offices respectively. However, we expect our trainees to be ready to undertake seats in any of our UK or overseas offices.

Excellent academic results are essential. However, we also look for other attributes in our potential trainees, including enthusiasm and a drive to succeed, teamworking skills, good humour, an analytical and logical mind, excellent communication skills, good commercial awareness, and a genuine passion for the law and the firm.

Training environment

The training contract itself is divided into four six-month seats and you can expect to experience a broad range of departments over the course of the two-year period. You will be allocated a supervisor and will be appraised every three months (mid-seat appraisal and end-of-seat appraisal). This gives you a great opportunity to receive detailed feedback on your performance and allows us to see that you are developing at an appropriate pace.

We believe in learning by experience. Throughout your training contract, you will be given responsibility and you will be challenged. However, you will benefit from a strong network of support around you in addition to that which is provided departmentally. Our Graduate Recruitment & Development Manager is always on hand, along with the Training Principal and the Trainee Solicitors' Committee. The Committee meets regularly to discuss training, selection and trainee events, and includes four trainee solicitor representatives (one from each intake).

Vacation placements

The firm runs two fortnight-long summer vacation schemes that are open to candidates looking to secure a training contract commencing in 2017. We only consider applications submitted to us through our online application system, which can be accessed via our dedicated graduate recruitment webpages on the firm's website.

Sponsorship & awards

If you join us and have yet to complete the Graduate Diploma in Law (GDL) and/or the Legal Practice Course (LPC), we will cover your course fees in full. We will also provide you with a maintenance grant. All future trainees intending to study the GDL and/or the LPC in London are required to attend Kaplan Law School. For those wishing to study the course(s) outside of London, we are flexible with your choice of institution.

Partners 132
Assistant Solicitors 160
Total Trainees 39

Contact
Anup Vithlani, Graduate Recruitment & Development Manager

Method of application
Online application form

Selection procedure
Assessment centre, interviews, psychometric tests & practical test

Closing date for 2017
1 August 2015

Application
Applications p.a. circa 1,600
% interviewed p.a. 4%
Required grades
minimum of 320 UCAS points (ABB) and 2.1 degree or above

Training
London Salary
1st year £36,000
2nd year £39,000
Holiday entitlement 25 days
% of trainees with a
non-law degree p.a. 50% / 50%
No of seats available abroad p.a. 14

Post-qualification
Salary £58,000
% of trainees offered job on qualification (March 2014) 100%

Offices
London, Birmingham, Exeter, Manchester, Abu Dhabi, Bahrain, Dubai, Malaysia and Oman

A-Z of Solicitors

Veale Wasbrough Vizards

Orchard Court, Orchard Lane, Bristol BS1 5WS
Tel: (0117) 925 2020 Fax: (0117) 925 2025
Barnards Inn, 86 Fetter Lane, London EC4A 1AD
Tel: (020) 7405 1234 Fax: (020) 7405 4171
Email: careers@vwv.co.uk
Website: www.vwv.co.uk Twitter: @VWVCareers

Firm profile

Veale Wasbrough Vizards (VWV) is a full service commercial law firm and leading sector specialist acting for clients nationally from offices in London, Bristol and Birmingham. The firm also offers a dedicated service to individuals.

VWV places a strong emphasis on the development of the skill and expertise of all staff, quality of service and regulatory compliance. They are accredited to Investors in People (IIP) Bronze level and Lexcel, the Law Society's management standard.

It is the combination of specialist expertise, genuine teamwork and client commitment that sets VWV apart from competitors.

People and culture are important to VWV. They are proud to have the reputation of being a friendly firm to work for and with. Many new joiners comment on the open culture and approachability of all staff, no matter what their role or position.

The fact that 94% of clients say that they would recommend VWV to others is a strong indicator that it is the culture, and not just experience, that gives clients the confidence to continue to instruct.

Main areas of work

VWV has a deep expertise in all areas of business law. The sector focus is underpinned by core legal services including real estate, corporate, commercial (including IP and technology), employment, dispute resolution and tax.

The firm also manages two distinctly branded divisions, Augustines Injury Law and Convey Direct, handling residential conveyancing.

Sectors include academies and maintained schools, aerospace and defence, agriculture and estates, charities, central government, energy and utilities, family-owned businesses, further education, healthcare, higher education, independent schools, local government and emergency services, property investment and development, private wealth and technology.

Trainee profile

The firm recruits 8-10 trainees annually for training contracts based in its Bristol or London offices. It is looking for graduates who will become dynamic lawyers, who will make the most of the training opportunities and positively contribute to the future of the firm. Applicants should have proven academic ability, be good team players, with strong communication skills and commercial awareness.

Training environment

The firm offers its trainees early responsibility. It provides four seats of six months each in a variety of teams, currently including charities, commercial, commercial litigation, commercial property, construction, corporate, employment, private client and property litigation. Many of the firm's partners and senior lawyers trained with the firm and are now widely respected experts in their chosen field.

Sponsorship & awards

Successful candidates may be eligible for sponsorship for the Legal Practice Course, consisting of a grant for LPC fees and an interest-free loan.

Vacation scheme

The firm's popular summer vacation scheme offers a week's unpaid work experience, providing an insight into the day to day workings of a large firm of commercial lawyers as students spend time across a range of different legal teams.

Partners 51
Assistant Solicitors 90
Total Trainees 17

Contact
Ellen Marsh, HR Advisor

Method of application
Online application at
www.vwv.co.uk/careers

Selection procedure
Interview

Closing date for September 2017
30 June 2015

Application
Training contracts p.a. 8-10
% interviewed (2013) 10%
Required degree grade Preferably 2:1

Training
1st year min £23,000
2nd year min £25,000
Holiday entitlement 25 days plus bank holidays

Post-qualification
Salary min £35,000
% of trainees offered job on qualification (2013) 72%

Veale Wasbrough Vizards

Vinson & Elkins

CityPoint, 33rd Floor, One Ropemaker Street, London EC2Y 9UE
Tel: (020) 7065 6000 Fax: (020) 7065 6001

Firm profile

Vinson & Elkins RLLP is one of the largest international law firms and has been repeatedly ranked as the world's leading energy law firm. Founded in Houston in 1917 (and with an office in London for over 40 years), Vinson & Elkins currently has over 700 lawyers with offices in Abu Dhabi, Austin, Beijing, Dallas, Dubai, Hong Kong, Houston, London, Moscow, New York, Palo Alto, Riyadh, San Francisco, Tokyo and Washington, DC.

Main areas of work

Cross-border M&A, private equity, corporate finance and securities advice (including London Main Market and AIM listings and international equity and debt capital markets), banking and finance, international energy transactions, construction, project development and finance transactions, litigation and arbitration and tax.

Trainee profile

The firm is looking for ambitious individuals with strong academic results, sound commercial awareness and rounded personalities. The ability to think laterally and creatively is essential, as is a need for common-sense and a willingness to take the initiative.

Training environment

The firm currently offers three to four training contracts commencing each September. These are not run on a rigid seat system, but instead a trainee will gain wide experience in many different areas, working with a wide variety of associates and partners from across the firm. V&E is proud of the fact it has twice won LawCareers.Net awards for the quality of its training with a further six nominations.

Whilst the trainees are based in London, the firm is currently regularly seconding its trainees to other offices (particularly its offices in Abu Dhabi, Dubai, Hong Kong and Houston).

Benefits

Private medical and dental, pension, season ticket loan, life assurance.

Vacation placements

We view vacation placements as a key part of our recruitment process. For summer 2015 apply by 31 January 2015, by way of online application form.

Sponsorship & awards

The firm pays all GDL and LPC course fees and a discretionary stipend (of up to £7,200) to assist with the LPC year.

Partners 15
Assistant Solicitors 17
Total Trainees 8

Contact
Natalie Perkin
(020) 7065 6048

Method of application
Online application form

Selection procedure
Interview

Closing date for 2017
31 July 2015

Application
Training contracts p.a. 3-4
Applications p.a. 492
% interviewed p.a. 10%
Required degree grade 2:1

Training
Salary
1st year £40,000
2nd year £42,000
Holiday entitlement 25 days
% of trainees with a
non-law degree p.a. 62.5%
No. of seats available
abroad p.a. 4

Post-qualification
Salary £80,000
% of trainees offered job
on qualification 87.5%

Overseas / Regional offices
Abu Dhabi, Austin, Beijing,
Dallas, Dubai, Hong Kong,
Houston, London, Moscow,
New York, Palo Alto, Riyadh,
San Francisco, Tokyo and
Washington DC.

A-Z of Solicitors

597

Ward Hadaway

Sandgate House, 102 Quayside, Newcastle upon Tyne NE1 3DX
Tel: (0191) 204 4000 Fax: (0191) 204 4098
Email: recruitment@wardhadaway.com
Website: www.wardhadaway.com

Firm profile
Ward Hadaway is one of the most progressive law firms in the North of England and is firmly established as one of the region's legal heavyweights. Operating from offices in Newcastle, Leeds and Manchester, the firm attracts some of the most ambitious businesses in the region and has a substantial client base of regional, national and international clients from the private and public sectors.

As a business founded and located in the North, the firm has grown rapidly, investing heavily in developing its existing people and recruiting further outstanding individuals from inside and outside of the region. The firm is listed in the top 75 UK law firms.

Main areas of work
The firm is divided into five main departments; litigation, property, corporate, commercial and private client, with a number of cross departmental teams. The firm is commercially based, satisfying the needs of the business community in both business and private life. Clients vary from international plcs to local, private clients. The firm is on a number of panels including; the Arts Council, NHS (four panels), English Heritage, Department of Education and the General Teaching Council.

Trainee profile
The usual academic and professional qualifications are sought. Sound commercial and business awareness are essential as is the need to demonstrate strong communication skills, enthusiasm and flexibility. Candidates will be able to demonstrate excellent interpersonal and analytical skills.

Training environment
The training contract is structured around four seats, each of six months duration. At regular intervals, and each time you are due to change seat, you will have the opportunity to discuss the experience you would like to gain during your training contract. The firm will give high priority to your preferences. You will work closely with a Partner or associate who will supervise and encourage you as you become involved in more complex work. Your practical experience will also be complemented by an extensive programme of seminars and lectures. All trainees are allocated a 'buddy', usually a second year trainee or newly qualified solicitor, who can provide as much practical advice and guidance as possible during your training. The firm has an active social committee and offers a full range of sporting and social events.

Benefits
25 days holiday (27 after five years service), death in service insurance, contributory pension, flexible benefits package, travel scheme.

Vacation placements
Vacation placements run spring/summer between June and July and are of 1 week's duration. Applications should be received by 28 February 2015.

Sponsorship & awards
CPE/GDL and LPC fees paid and maintenance grants in accordance with the terms of the firm's offer.

Partners 80
Total Trainees 18

Contact
Graduate recruitment team

Method of application
Firm's application form

Selection procedure
Assessment Centre and interview

Closing date for 2017
31 July 2015

Application
Training contracts p.a. 10
Applications p.a. 600+
% interviewed p.a. 10%
Required degree grade 2:1

Training
Salary 2014
1st year £22,000
2nd year £24,000
Holiday entitlement 25 days
% of trainees with a
non-law degree p.a. Varies

Post-qualification
Salary (2014)
£34,000

Watson, Farley & Williams LLP

15 Appold Street, London EC2A 2HB
Tel: (020) 7814 8000 Fax: (020) 7814 8017
Email: graduates@wfw.com
Website: www.wfw.com/trainee

Firm Profile

WFW was founded in 1982 in the City of London. It has since grown rapidly to over 130 partners and a total staff of over 800. The firm has offices in London, New York, Paris, Frankfurt, Hamburg, Munich, Rome, Milan, Madrid, Athens, Singapore, Bangkok and Hong Kong.

Main areas of work

WFW is a distinctive law firm with a leading market position in international finance and investment, maritime and energy.

In our chosen sectors we compete successfully with some of the best law firms in the world. Building on our origins in ship finance, demand for our maritime work remains as strong as ever. At the same time we have seized opportunities to excel in related areas where our finance expertise has most relevance, such as energy, natural resources, transport, real estate and technology.

Trainee profile

Although there is no typical WFW trainee, there are certain attributes that we look for. You will need a 2:1 or above and at least ABB – from A-level results, or their equivalent. We also particularly value applicants with initiative, drive and commercial awareness.

Training environment

At WFW we deal with training and ongoing development in an individual way. During each seat we discuss with you plans for the next one to ensure you gain valuable insight from the six seat programme, including one seat in either Paris, Singapore, Athens, Bangkok or Hamburg.

Your training contract will be hands-on, with as much experience of clients and real, high-profile work as possible. You'll also benefit from plenty of exposure to senior lawyers, many acknowledged leaders in their field.

The firm has a reputation for challenging work. Yours will be no exception as we believe that only total immersion can provide you with the experience you require.

Benefits

Various benefits are available to trainees after a qualifying period of service e.g. 25 days holiday, bank holidays, income protection scheme, life assurance, employee assistance scheme, pension scheme, interest-free season ticket loan, £250 contribution towards a sports club and healthcare membership.

Vacation placements

Our vacation scheme is the best way to really familiarise yourself with WFW. The two-week placements are at our London office, throughout the year. To appreciate first-hand the kind of work trainees undertake day to day, you will work with solicitors in one of our practice groups for the whole period. To complement this focus on one area, you will also participate in a variety of training and social events designed to give you a general overview of the firm. Deadline to apply: 31 January 2015.

Sponsorship & awards

GDL and LPC fees are paid depending on point of offer plus a maintenance grant of £6,500/£5,500 dependant on location.

Partners 130+
Total fee-earners 400+
Total Trainees 28

Contact
Graduate Recruitment Manager

Method of application
Online application

Selection procedure
Assessment centre and interview

Closing date for 2017
31 July 2015

Application
Training contracts p.a. 15
Applications p.a. 700
% interviewed p.a. 30%
Required degree grade
Minimum 2:1 ABB or equivalent

Training
Salary
1st year (2014) £39,000
2nd year (2014) £44,000
Holiday entitlement 25 days
% of trainees with a non-law degree p.a. 50%
No of seats available abroad p.a. 15

Post-qualification
Salary (2014)
£65,000
% of trainees offered job on qualification 92%
% of assistants who joined as trainees 54%
% of partners who joined as trainees 10%

Overseas offices
New York, Paris, Frankfurt, Hamburg, Munich, Rome, Milan, Madrid, Athens, Singapore, Bangkok, Hong Kong

WATSON FARLEY
&
WILLIAMS

Wedlake Bell

52 Bedford Row, London, WC1R 4LR
Tel: (020) 7395 3000 Fax: (020) 7395 3100
Email: recruitment@wedlakebell.com
Website: www.wedlakebell.com

Firm profile
Wedlake Bell LLP is a medium-sized law firm providing legal advice to businesses and high net worth individuals from around the world. The firm's services are based on a high degree of partner involvement, extensive business and commercial experience and strong technical expertise. The firm has approximately 130 lawyers in central London and affiliations with law firms throughout Europe and in the United States.

Main areas of work
For the firm's business clients: banking and asset finance; corporate; corporate tax; business recoveries; commercial; intellectual property; information technology; media; commercial property; construction; residential property.

For private individuals: family, tax, trusts and wealth protection; offshore services; residential property.

Trainee profile
In addition to academic excellence, Wedlake Bell LLP looks for commercial aptitude, flexibility, enthusiasm, a personable nature, confidence, mental agility and computer literacy in its candidates. Languages are not crucial.

Training environment
Trainees have four seats of six months across the following areas: business recoveries, commercial property, construction, corporate, employment, family, IP and commercial, private client, pensions, property litigation and residential property. As a trainee, the firm encourages you to have direct contact and involvement with clients from an early stage. Trainees will work within highly specialised teams and have a high degree of responsibility. Trainees will be closely supervised by a partner or senior solicitor and become involved in high quality and varied work. The firm is committed to the training and career development of its lawyers and many of its trainees continue their careers with the firm, often through to partnership. Wedlake Bell LLP has an informal, creative and co-operative culture with a balanced approach to life.

Sponsorship & benefits
LPC funding available subject to the terms and conditions of any offer. During the training contract: pension, travel loans, gym membership, private medical insurance, life assurance, permanent health insurance, cycle to work scheme, employee assistance scheme.

Vacation placements
Places for 2015: 8; Duration: 3 weeks in July; Closing date: End of February, 2015.

Partners 55
Assistant Solicitors 78
Total Trainees 12

Contact
The Graduate Recruitment Department

Method of application
Application form

Selection procedure
Two interviews & open day

Closing date for 2017
End of July 2015

Application
Training contracts p.a. 6
Required degree grade 2:1

Training
Salary
1st year £33,000
2nd year £35,000
Holiday entitlement 25 days

Weil, Gotshal & Manges

110 Fetter Lane, London EC4A 1AY
Tel: (020) 7903 1000 Fax: (020) 7903 0990
Email: graduate.recruitment@weil.com
Website: www.weil.com

Partners 28	
Solicitors 89	
Total Trainees 23	

Contact
Lisa Wells

Method of application
Online application form

Closing date for 2017
31 July 2015

Application
Training contracts p.a. up to 14
Required degree grade 2:1

Training
Salary
1st year (2014) £41,000 rising to £45,000 in 4th seat
Holiday entitlement 23 days rising by 1 day for each year of service up to 28 days

Overseas offices
Beijing, Boston, Budapest, Dallas, Dubai, Frankfurt, Hong Kong, Houston, London, Miami, Munich, New York, Paris, Prague, Princeton, Providence, Shanghai, Silicon Valley, Warsaw and Washington DC

Firm profile
Weil is one of the world's truly elite international firms. The firm has over 1,200 lawyers in 20 cities throughout the US, Europe, Asia and the Middle East.

The London office was established in 1996 and has grown to become the second largest of the firm's worldwide offices, with over 95% of lawyers in London being English-qualified and around 80% of our work home grown.

Weil's strategy is focused on long-term investment in recruiting and retaining exceptional talent at all levels. Our people celebrate diversity and inclusion, and our award-winning pro-bono programme is deeply ingrained in the firm's culture.

Main areas of work
Private equity/M&A, private funds; banking & finance; restructuring; dispute resolution; full-service transactional support including competition; employment; environment; IP/IT; pensions; real estate and tax.

Trainee profile
We are looking for business minded high achievers with confidence and self-belief. Individuals that will always push themselves to keep developing and improving and who can work effectively in a team.

Training environment
We offer a comprehensive and sophisticated training programme with direct input from leading partners alongside a tailor made approach to mentoring, career progression and development for each lawyer. Working in close knit partner-led teams provides much greater responsibility and early exposure to our global network of clients and contacts.

Benefits
Starting salary £41,000 increasing to £45,000 in final seat of the Training Contract. Our NQ salary is currently £95,500.

Private health cover, permanent health insurance, life assurance, pension (the firm will contribute to the Group Personal Pension Plan at the rate of 5% of your basic salary) and birthday holiday.

23 days' leave, with holiday entitlement increasing by one day after each year of service, up to a maximum of 28 days.

Sponsorship
GDL and LPC funding plus maintenance allowances of £8,000 per annum.

White & Case LLP

5 Old Broad Street, London EC2N 1DW
Tel: (020) 7532 1000 Fax: (020) 7532 1001
Email: trainee@whitecase.com
Website: www.whitecasetrainee.com

Firm profile

White & Case LLP is a global law firm with more than 2,200 lawyers worldwide. The firm has a network of 40 offices, providing the full range of legal services of the highest quality in virtually every major commercial centre and emerging market. They work with international businesses, financial institutions and governments worldwide on corporate and financial transactions and dispute resolution proceedings. Their clients range from some of the world's longest established and most respected names to many start-up visionaries. The firm's lawyers work on a variety of sophisticated, high-value transactions, many of which feature in the legal press worldwide as the firm's clients achieve firsts in privatisation, cross-border business deals, or major development projects.

Main areas of work

Banking and capital markets; construction and engineering; corporate (including M&A and private equity); dispute resolution (including arbitration and mediation); employment and benefits; energy, infrastructure, project and asset finance; IP, PPP/PFI; real estate; tax; and telecommunications.

Trainee profile

Trainees should be ambitious, creative and work well in teams. They should have an understanding of international commercial issues and have a desire to be involved in high profile, cross-border legal matters.

Training environment

Trainees undertake four seats, each of six months in duration. The firm guarantees that one of these seats can be spent overseas. Regardless of where they work, trainees get a high level of partner and senior associate contact from day one, ensuring they receive high quality, stimulating and rewarding work. Trainees are encouraged to take early responsibility and there is a strong emphasis on practical hands-on training, together with plenty of support and feedback. The firm recruits and develops trainee solicitors with the aim of retaining them on qualification.

Benefits

The firm operates a flexible benefits scheme, through which you can select the benefits you wish to receive. Currently, the benefits include private medical insurance, dental insurance, life assurance, pension, critical illness insurance, travel insurance, retail vouchers, gym membership, season ticket loan and green bikes.

Vacation placements

Places for 2015: 15 places available on one two-week spring placement and 60 places available across our summer placements. Remuneration: £350 per week; Closing Date: 31 January 2014.

Sponsorship & awards

GDL and LPC fees and maintenance paid p.a. Awards for commendation and distinction for LPC.

Partners 79
Assistant Solicitors 223
Total Trainees 63

Contact
Christina Churchman

Method of application
Online application via firm website

Selection procedure
Interview

Closing date for August 2017/ February 2018
31 July 2015

Application
Training contracts p.a. 30
Applications p.a. 1,500
Required degree grade 2:1

Training
Salary
1st year £43,000
2nd year £46,000
Holiday entitlement 25 days
All trainees are guaranteed to spend a seat overseas

Post-qualification
Salary £75,000

Overseas offices
Abu Dhabi, Almaty, Ankara, Beijing, Berlin, Bratislava, Brussels, Bucharest, Budapest, Doha, Düsseldorf, Frankfurt, Geneva, Hamburg, Helsinki, Hong Kong, Istanbul, Johannesburg, London, Los Angeles, Madrid, Mexico City, Miami, Milan, Monterrey, Moscow, Munich, New York, Paris, Prague, Riyadh, São Paulo, Silicon Valley, Singapore, Shanghai, Stockholm, Tokyo, Warsaw, Washington DC

WHITE & CASE

Wilsons Solicitors LLP

Alexandra House, St Johns Street, Salisbury, Wiltshire SP1 2SB
Tel: (01722) 412 412 Fax: (01722) 427 610
Email: jo.ratcliffe@wilsonslaw.com
Website: www.wilsonslaw.com

Firm profile
Ranked as one of the top private client and charity law firms in the country, our 280-year heritage, combined with lawyers who are recognised leaders in their fields, enables Wilsons to provide a unique combination of skills and experience to our clients. Our lawyers are dedicated to ensuring a detailed understanding of their clients' interests and a seamless working relationship across the different specialities of the practice.

Main areas of work
Private Client: We act for clients with business interests, landed and inherited wealth, foreign domiciliaries, UK and offshore trustees and non-resident individuals with links to the UK. Services including tax planning, estate and succession planning, asset structuring, UK and offshore trust formation and advice, wills and trusts and estate administration and probates and intestacies valued at up to £50m.

The family team's expertise ranges from pre-nuptial agreements and civil partnerships to divorce and children's arrangements.

Charity: Wilsons has one of the most highly ranked teams in the UK. We advise on the complete range of legal needs and have a particular specialism in contentious and noncontentious legacy work. The constitutional and governance team has considerable expertise in advising military charities and the charitable care sector.

Agriculture: Wilsons' rural team has developed a practice centred on the needs of rural business and landowners. These include complex sales and purchases, development options for landowners, grants and diversification advice and property litigation, including landlord and tenant, partnership matters, boundary, title and rights of way disputes.

Commercial: The commercial team specialises in employment, commercial property and corporate work. Corporate work focuses on commercial tax and asset planning, transactions and refinancing. The team deals with an unusual breadth of work requiring high-quality, bespoke commercial advice.

Property: Our clients have substantial commercial, agricultural and residential property interests and the firm advises on purchasing, letting and sales, and has a reputation for gaining excellent results in the options over and sales of development land.

Litigation and dispute resolution: Wilsons has one of the largest teams outside London. We advise clients on a wide range of contentious matters to provide an efficient and effective means of dispute resolution. In addition to its expertise in agricultural and probate disputes, the firm has specialists who can advise on all aspects of commercial dispute claims.

Trainee profile
We aim to employ the highest quality people; our reputation relies upon this. We place considerable emphasis on teamwork and look for applicants who are clear team players.

Training environment
The firm has attracted several senior City lawyers and an enviable client base and being based in Salisbury ensures an exceptional quality of work within beautiful surroundings.

Benefits
Pension, life assurance, choice of optional benefits and private medical insurance.

Work experience placements
One week available in July at our head office in Salisbury.

Partners 33
Trainees 8
Total Staff 150

Contact
Mrs J Ratcliffe
jo.ratcliffe@wilsonslaw.com

Method of application
Application via website

Selection procedure
Interview and assessment day

Closing dates for training scheme
30 June 2017 for training contract to commence in September 2017

Application
Training contracts p.a. 4

Salary
Above market rate
Holiday entitlement 22 days

Offices
Salisbury, London

Winckworth Sherwood

Minerva House, 5 Montague Close, London SE1 9BB
Tel: (020) 7593 5000   Fax: (020) 7593 5099
Email: trainees@wslaw.co.uk
Website: www.wslaw.co.uk

Firm profile
The firm has a long established pedigree. It is a full service firm and is particularly recognised for its specialist practices.

Main areas of practice
Corporate & Commercial: We advise on transactional, structuring, commercial, tax, financing, real estate, licensing and dispute resolution matters.

Employment & Partnership: We provide contentious and non contentious advice covering financial, insurance, retail, hotel, media, publishing, real estate and educational establishments. We also advise senior executives and on partnership disputes, as well as specialist non contentious partnership advice.

Infrastructure Projects: We specialise in private legislation promoting projects of major strategic importance. We also advise central and local government bodies, developers and operators on infrastructure planning, development, construction, procurement, structuring and finance.

Not for profit: We advise a large number of educational and affordable housing operators, charitable and religious organisations and cultural and leisure services providers, delivering a full range of legal expertise.

Private Wealth & Tax: We advise high net worth individuals, families, senior executives, private trustees and executors on a full range of private legal matters, including complex residential property solutions, tax and succession issues, pre-marital advice, divorce and family.

Real Estate & Planning: We work for many of the leading national residential and commercial developers, national house builders, investors and fund managers. This includes commercial real estate and regeneration, planning, development, corporate finance, funds, tax, construction, asset management and property litigation capability.

Trainee profile
We require a strong academic record both at school and university and we also look for other attributes such as drive and determination, enthusiasm and resilience, team-working and excellent communication skills and an analytical and logical approach.

Training environment
Trainees will be placed in four departments in six month placements. We encourage early responsibility and substantial client interaction. You will usually sit with a partner or associate and may be given the opportunity to manage your own files, subject to suitable supervision.

We have a well developed in-house CPD programme which draws upon the expertise of partners, associates and guest professionals. As well as legal training, we also provide business skills training such as presentation skills, project management, networking and client development.

Sponsorship & awards
Under certain conditions the firm provides financial assistance for course fees to trainees attending the Legal Practice Course (LPC) or in exceptional circumstances studying for a Graduate Diploma in Law (GDL).

Partners 49
Assistant Solicitors 77
Total Trainees 12

Contact
Heather Cornish
020 7593 5077

Method of application
Online application form
(https://www.apply4law.com/winckworths/)

Selection procedure
Summer Vacation Scheme,
Trainee Assessment Day and
Panel Interviews

Closing date for September 2017
30 June 2015

Application
No. of training contracts p.a. 6
Applications p.a. 350
% interviewed 15%
Required degree grade 2.1

Training
Starting salary £32K
Holiday entitlement 24 days
plus Bank Holidays and one
extra day at Christmas

Post-qualification
% trainees offered job on
qualification 80% (2013)

Overseas/regional offices
London

Withers LLP

16 Old Bailey, London EC4M 7EG
Tel: (020) 7597 6000 Fax: (020) 7329 2534
Email: jaya.louvre@withersworldwide.com
Website: www.withersworldwide.com

Firm profile

Withers LLP is a leading international law firm dedicated to the business, personal and philanthropic interests of successful people, their families, their businesses and their advisers.

The firm's mission is to offer a truly integrated legal service to people with sophisticated global wealth, management and business needs. Withers' reputation in commercial law along with its status as the largest Private Client Team in Europe and leading Family Team sets it apart from other City firms. The firm has been recognised for its great working environment having been listed in both The Sunday Times 100 Best Companies to work for and in receiving Legal Week's Best Legal Employer Award for the past two years. The firm also won the Financial Mail's 2013 Breaking the Mould Award for its work promoting and supporting women.

Main areas of work

The wealth of today's private client has increased considerably and many are institutions in their own right. Withers has been able to respond to these changing legal needs and offers integrated solutions to the international legal and tax needs of its clients. The firm has unparalleled expertise in commercial and tax law, trusts, estate planning, litigation, charities, employment, family law and other legal issues facing high net worth individuals. Work is often international due to the complexity of our client base which includes some of the wealthiest global citizens. Currently we act for around a quarter of the UK Sunday Times 'Rich List' and a significant number from the US 'Forbes' and Asian 'Huran' rich lists. Trainees who speak a relevant language may have the opportunity to complete a seat in one of our offices abroad.

Trainee profile

Each year the firm looks for a diverse mix of trainees who are excited by the prospect of working with leaders in their field. Trainees must have an excellent academic background and great attention to detail. Team players with leadership potential are of interest to the firm, as is an international outlook and foreign language skills.

Training environment

Trainees spend six months in four different departments. Working in a team with a partner and an assistant solicitor provides autonomy, responsibility and fast development. Buddy and mentor systems as well as on the job training ensure trainees are fully supported from the outset.

Application

Apply online by 31 July 2015 to begin training in September 2017. Interviews take place between June and September.

Vacation scheme

The firm runs two-week long placements at Easter and over the summer in London. Apply online by 31 January 2015 for places in 2015. Interviews take place between January and March.

Sponsorship

Fees plus £5,000 maintenance for both the GDL and/or LPC are paid.

Partners 108
Total Staff 761
Trainees 26

Contact
Jaya Louvre,
Recruitment Manager

Method of application
Application form (available online)

Selection procedure
2 interviews incl. written exercise and presentation

Closing dates for 2016/2017
2017 training scheme
31 July 2015
2015 vacation placements
31 January 2015

Application
Training contracts p.a. 10
Applications p.a. 900
% interviewed p.a. 20%
Required grades 2:1, AAB at A-Level

Training
Salary
1st year (2012) £34,000
2nd year (2012) £36,000
Holiday entitlement 23 days
% of trainees with a non-law degree p.a. 50%

Post-qualification
Salary £56,000

Offices
London, Milan, Geneva, Zurich, New York, New Haven (Connecticut), Greenwich (USA), Hong Kong, Singapore, BVI

A-Z of Solicitors

Wragge Lawrence Graham & Co

55 Colmore Row, Birmingham B3 2AS
3 Waterhouse Square, 142 Holborn, London EC1N 2SW
4 More, London Riverside, London SE1 2AU
Tel: (0870) 903 1000 / (0870) 904 1099
Email: mail@wragge-law.com

Firm profile
Wragge Lawrence Graham & Co is a UK-headquartered international law firm providing a full service to clients worldwide. Businesses around the world choose us to help them thrive, prosper and become their best. And the key to our success? Our people, of course. Bright, talented individuals who work together to deliver a first-class legal service to first-class legal clients.

Main areas of work
We are a full-service law firm, and our key practice areas are: commercial and projects; corporate, finance and private capital; dispute resolution; human resources; and real estate.

We are sector-focused. We bring together dedicated teams of insightful experts in a wide range of industries, including aerospace, technology, energy, food and drink, healthcare and life sciences, public sector and retail, commercial, energy and natural resources, intellectual property, IT, outsourcing, PFI, projects and regulatory issues.

Trainee profile
First and foremost, it's talent that matters. Talent and potential. As well as having an enviable work ethic, you'll share our passion for working together to deliver brilliant legal services.

We're the sum of our parts here, a powerful collective of individuals. Diversity is our strength: age, ethnic origin, gender, sexual orientation, religion, disability are irrelevant – when it comes to recruitment, ability is everything.

Training environment
We think that if you're intelligent, talented, willing to learn and work hard, you deserve the chance to prove yourself. This means challenging you with early responsibility and exposure to some of our top clients.

You may find yourself working on high-profile cases in your first few weeks, talking to clients and giving advice. If you can show that you're willing to take on more work and greater responsibility, then we'll trust you with exactly that. And we'll always give you the support you need.

Benefits
We offer all trainees the following: £1,000 interest-free loan, a prize for first class degree, a prize for GDL and LPC distinction, pension scheme (firm makes a contribution after six months), life assurance, permanent health insurance, access to discounted private medical insurance rates, 25 days holiday, optional unpaid leave, social club, access to corporate rates and discounts.

Sponsorship & awards
We cover your Legal Practice Course (LPC) and Graduate Diploma in Law (GDL) fees, as well as providing a maintenance grant for each course.

Partners 180
Assistance Solicitors 770
Total Trainees 60

Contact:
Hayley Basford (graduate recruitment team)

Method of application
Online application via the graduate website:
www.wragge-law.com/graduate

Selection procedure
Application form, verbal reasoning test, situational judgement test, telephone interview and assessment day.

Closing dates
2015 Vacation scheme applications from October
Training contract 2016 and 2017 applications close July 2015

Applications
No of training contracts p.a. 30
Applications p.a. 1,000+
% interviewed variable
Required degree grade N/A

Training
Salary for each year of training
1st year
Birmingham £26,250
London £36,250
2nd year
Birmingham £29,250
London £39,250
Holiday entitlement 25 days

Overseas/regional offices
London, Birmingham, Brussels, Dubai, Guangzhou, Monaco, Moscow, Munich, Paris and Singapore.

The Bar

Barcode

Don't let alien terms used at the Bar confuse or intimidate you.

Bar Council – the General Council of the Bar, to give it its full title, is the Bar's representative body. It can be found clashing regularly with the Ministry of Justice.

Bar Standards Board – or BSB, is the Bar's regulatory body.

Barrister – a member of the Bar of England and Wales.

Bench – the judiciary.

Bencher – a senior member of an Inn of Court. Usually silks and judges, known as Masters of the Bench.

Brief – the documents setting out case instructions.

BPTC – the Bar Professional Training Course. Successful completion entitles you to call yourself a barrister in non-legal circumstances (ie dinner parties), but does not give you rights of audience.

BPTC Online – the application system through which applications to Bar school must be made.

Cab-rank rule – Self-employed barristers cannot refuse instructions if they have the time and experience to undertake the case. You cannot refuse to represent someone because you find their opinions or actions objectionable.

Call – the ceremony whereby you become a barrister.

Chambers – a group of barristers in independent practice who have joined together to share the costs of practising. Chambers is also the name used for a judge's private office.

Chambers & Partners – that's us, remember? So called because the founder of the company is Michael Chambers, not because we write about the Bar.

Circuit – The courts of England and Wales are divided into six circuits: North Eastern, Northern, Midland, South Eastern, Western and Wales & Chester circuits.

Clerk – administrator/manager in chambers who organises work for barristers and payment of fees, etc.

Counsel – a barrister.

CPS – Crown Prosecution Service. Government body responsible for the prosecution of criminal offences in England and Wales.

Devilling – (paid) work done by a junior member of chambers for a more senior member.

Employed Bar – Some barristers do not engage in private practice at chambers, but are employed full-time by a company or public body.

First and second six – Pupillages are divided into two six-month periods. Most chambers now only offer 12-month pupillages; however, it is still possible to undertake the two sixes at different sets.

FRU – the Free Representation Unit. Provides real-life advocacy experience to budding barristers in Employment Tribunals and social security cases.

Independent Bar – the collective name for barristers who practise on a self-employed basis.

Inns of Court – ancient institutions that alone have the power to 'make' barristers. There was a time when there was a proliferation of them but now there are only four: Gray's Inn, Inner Temple, Lincoln's Inn and Middle Temple.

Junior – a barrister not yet appointed silk. Note: older juniors are known as senior juniors.

Junior brief – a case on which a junior is led by a senior. Such cases are too much work for one barrister alone and may involve a lot of research or run for a long time. Ordinarily, junior counsel will not conduct advocacy.

Keeping term – eating the dinners in hall required to be eligible for call to the Bar.

Marshalling – work experience in which you shadow a judge, normally lasting between one and five days.

Mess – the hierarchical groups of four in which students sit during dining sessions. 'Mixed messes' means that barristers and masters sit with students.

Mini-pupillage – work experience at a set of chambers, normally lasting between one and five days.

Moot – a legal debate in which students act as claimants or respondents in an appeal court (ie the Court of Appeal or Supreme Court). Typically, there will be two students on each team, acting as either senior or junior.

Pupillage – the year of training undertaken after Bar school and before tenancy.

Pupillage Gateway – the online application system for pupillage.

Pupil supervisor – a senior barrister with whom a pupil sits and who teaches the pupil. Some sets and barristers still refer to this position by its old title: pupil master (or mistress).

QC – one of Her Majesty's Counsel, formerly appointed by the Lord Chancellor. The system fell into abeyance in 2004 and has now been revived with a new, more open appointments system. In the reign of a male monarch, the term is KC (King's Counsel).

Set – as in a 'set of chambers'.

Silk – a QC, so named because of their silk robes.

Supervisor – the new name for a pupilmaster.

Tenant/tenancy – permission from chambers to join their set and work with them. A 'squatter' is someone who is permitted to use chambers' premises, but is not actually a member of the set. A 'door tenant' is someone who is affiliated with the set, but does not conduct business from chambers' premises.

Third six – when pupils are not successful in gaining tenancy, they can apply for a third six at another set in the hopes of success there.

A Career at the Bar

Being a barrister is, to quote one sage QC, *"quite simply, the best job in the world."* True, the Bar is an eminently competitive world in which the hours can be punishing and the work arduous, but the mix of high-octane excitement, advocacy opportunity and prestige is unique.

Essential Bar stats: a harsh reality

It's no secret the Bar is an incredibly competitive field. *"Becoming a barrister is a strenuous and difficult process which is not to be underestimated,"* a current pupil told us. The statistics alone are enough to put someone off: according to the 2014 Bar Barometer the number of students who successfully completed the BPTC in 2011/12 totalled 1,260, though only 438 pupillages were actually offered that same year. Add to that pool the BPTC grads from previous years still hunting for jobs and you can see just how diminutive that latter figure starts to look.

While the initial odds of landing a pupillage will probably discourage the casual applicant, the average would-be barrister is made of sterner stuff and usually has a deep-seated commitment to this branch of the profession.

In an effort to address this obvious problem of over-subscription, the Bar Standards Board raised its admission standards by introducing an official aptitude test for BPTC applicants in 2013. It's now compulsory for everyone who wants to do the BPTC and is designed to test logic, deduction and interpretation skills.

Will you make it?

If you're still soldiering on at this point, it's safe to say we've established your vocational drive. But do you have what it takes to distinguish yourself from the multitude of other applicants? This is a tough one. Meet enough pupils and barristers and you'll see what makes someone successful can vary hugely. That you're gobby/argumentative/confident doesn't necessarily mean you'll make it, nor is success guaranteed by superstar academic results and an ability to complete the *Times* crossword in three minutes.

Ask a chambers recruiter to define the qualities they look for, and they'll speak in fairly general terms (read: academic credentials, people skills, analytical skills, commitment, passion, an ability to express ideas), relying on the vague platitude that 'you know a good one when you see one.'

What is clear is that those who thrive at the Bar offer the right traits for their chosen area of practice. Crime is all about guts, personality and advocacy ability. Genius isn't necessary, but being to-the-point, down-to-earth and capable of assimilating and recalling facts easily is. Commercial practice, on the other hand, is a more sophisticated game. Intelligence, an analytical mind, commercial acumen and an easy manner with business clients are all musts, with specialisms like tax and insolvency attracting true brainboxes. Of course, advocacy is still important in commercial practice, though many would argue the ability to craft a masterpiece opinion or succinctly explain a complex legal argument is even more so.

Check out our **Chambers Reports** and **Practice areas at the Bar** features to learn more about the skills required in various specialist areas.

Another matter to consider upfront is how marketable your university is to recruiters. A common preconception is that only Oxbridge graduates have a shot at the Bar, but this is patently untrue. The most recently published Bar Council report shows that graduates of these two elite establishments only made up 35% of all pupils in 2010/11. That said, Oxford and Cambridge are undeniably happy hunting grounds for chambers, so the lower your university is in the rankings, the more you'll need to make up for it by way of stellar grades and worthwhile extracurriculars.

Is the cost of training prohibitive?

The GDL conversion course is expensive, and the BPTC is painfully steep, so it makes financial sense to be fairly confident about your prospects of succeeding at the Bar before setting out for law school. And then there's the pupillage year to consider: many criminal or general common law sets only pay their pupils the bare minimum award of £1,000 per month (as prescribed by the Bar Council). Of course, there are plenty of commercial sets that offer pupillage awards in line with trainee salaries at big City firms and even advance funds for the BPTC year – you've just got to apply in time.

Any way you slice it, getting through law school and pupillage is a pricey business and those without cash at their disposal or a locked-in funding deal will likely require loans from a bank or their parents. Read our **How to fund law school** feature on page 96 for more on the options at hand. Check out our info on the four Inns of Court too – of all the potential sponsors out there, they have the deepest pockets, offering nearly £5m each year to students.

Huge debts aren't as worrying for those guaranteed a fat income, but we should point out that the common perception that all barristers are rolling in it is pretty out of touch. Public funding for civil, family and criminal cases is rapidly dwindling as legal aid cuts start to bite, so those determined to serve their community will quite likely face a tough road in terms of remuneration, particularly at the lower levels.

On the other hand, privately paying clients still need legal advice, and commercial sets continue to thrive. There's no question that tenancy at one of the best commercial sets pays very well indeed: some Commercial Bar stars earn well over £1m a year, while the income of pupils who make it to tenancy at good-quality sets can quickly outstrip that of their solicitor peers. Do be aware that within each area of practice at the Bar are a few Premier League sets and many others in lower divisions. Unsurprisingly, a set's stature contributes greatly to its tenants' incomes, and the difference in earnings between the top and the bottom is not insubstantial.

Get Bar ready

If you're still at university there's plenty you can do to prepare yourself for a shot at the Bar. Landing a First is key, particularly if there's anything a little dicey about your CV – mature students and those with poor A levels, take note. Applicants with 2:1s are two a penny, and a 2:2 will almost certainly scupper your chances, bar those who can demonstrate some truly remarkable alternative qualities. On that note, chambers are generally more interested in your undergraduate performance than what you can muster up on the BPTC, but frankly you should try to get the best grades at every stage.

When it comes to postgraduate degrees, it's really up to you. Many of the Bar's most successful candidates have a master's degree from a good UK university or institution abroad, but simply holding an MA will not in and of itself help you score a pupillage.

The best way to demonstrate commitment to the Bar is to undertake mini-pupillages – ie, work experience at a barristers' chambers. Whether assessed or not, minis of-

How much do barristers earn? With barristers being essentially self-employed courtside commodities that fluctuate in desirability, tracking their earnings is no easy job. Visit www.chambersstudent.co.uk where we give it our best shot.

fer the opportunity to observe barristers in chambers and probably also in court, although the degree of involvement varies hugely from one set to another. A good mini will see you sit in on a pre-trial conference (with the client's permission) and included in discussions about the law.

Many applicants find three or so days an economical and sufficient amount of time to get a sense of a set's working style and culture. Assessed minis have the added element of paperwork or appraisal through oral discussion. A typical scenario will see mini-pupils instructed to analyse a set of papers and produce a piece of written work, which is usually discussed with a supervisor. Some sets use assessed minis as a formal part of the recruitment process, but most recognise that would-be pupils can't go everywhere and take applications from those who haven't yet spent time with chambers. Indeed, during this year's interviews we spoke to many pupils who didn't complete a mini at their own set.

A mini-pupillage is an important point of contact with a set and an opportunity to create a good impression for an application later on. It's also good CV and interview fodder, so make the most of the experience: take notes, don't be afraid to ask questions (at appropriate moments of course) and be sure to reflect on what was good and bad about your experiences. Recruiters often tell us that applicants who simply list or describe their legal work experience fall short in comparison to those who articulate just what they've learned from shadowing practitioners.

Not all sets offer mini-pupillages, and some will only take students in the final year of academic legal study (be it degree or GDL), so make sure to check their websites carefully for how and when to apply.

You should aim to secure as many minis as you think it'll take to decide which areas of practice are of real interest. One recruiter passed on some sage advice: "*Minis assist the candidates much more than they assist a set. It puts them in a position to have proper conversation in an interview about the issues, legal and practical, of being a barrister in their chosen area. While it's never a question of how many mini-pupillages a candidate has done, I'm always surprised if they've done none at all.*"

Unfair as it may seem, personal contacts can still go a long way in obtaining a mini – apply to an Inn of Court to be assigned a sponsor, or if you've started dining at your Inn, start schmoozing.

Stand out from the crowd

Ever increasing competition for careers at the Bar means that top grades and a short stint of work experience alone are no longer sufficient for scoring a pupillage. Consider the backgrounds of some of the pupils we've spoken with over the past few years: one worked as a human rights intern investigating genocide in Mexico and Guatemala, another ran a charity in South Africa and a third interned at the European Commission in Brussels before reporting on war crimes trials in Tanzania. With impressive rivals like these at every turn, it's up to you to make sure your credentials are up to scratch.

Of course, working abroad is by no means a requirement; there are plenty of things you can do from your home town to amp up your CV. Take pro bono experience, for example – the Bar Standards Board requires BPTC students to undertake a certain amount of pro bono work during their year of study. To ensure you land something that both interests you and adds weight to a pupillage application form, it's a good idea to investigate the options as soon as possible.

Getting involved with debating and mooting opportunities, entering mock trial events at law school and keeping an eye out for essay competitions are also good ways to beef up an application. *"I sacrificed my social life to get the best experience possible,"* a pupil at a top set told us, *"and in the end it paid off."* Don't forget that scholarships offered by the Inns are not just a way of funding your education either; such prizes go a long way in marking you out from other well-qualified candidates. It goes without saying that networking is also an important way to make sure you get noticed.

Through the Gateway

Most candidates coming straight from uni begin making pupillage applications during their final undergraduate year, although some of the top commercial sets encourage students to apply in their penultimate year in an attempt to snap up the best candidates early. In general, however, the majority of pupillage offers tend to be made to students following the completion of the BPTC.

Since March 2013 students have been able to make applications through the Pupillage Gateway, an online tool that lets users tailor their applications for each of the sets they apply to. The Gateway is a replacement for the Pupillage Portal, a system that existed from 2009 to 2012 and itself replaced an earlier online system called OLPAS.

Participation in the Gateway is voluntary for chambers, though if they run their own separate application schemes they still have to advertise vacancies on the Pupillage Gateway website and in the Pupillages Handbook, which is published in March each year to coincide with the National Pupillage Fair in London. You can find out which sets use the Gateway and how to apply to the ones that don't by reading our **Chambers Reports**.

Users can target a maximum of 12 sets through the Gateway each annual cycle. The site is open for vacancy browsing from March each year, and students have a window that lasts the whole of April to submit their applications. Participating chambers conduct interviews in June and July before making offers in August.

The Gateway application format requires users to be succinct. In most cases a maximum of 200 words or so is all you'll get to answer questions like 'Why do you wish to become a barrister?' and 'What areas of practice are you interested in and why?' Bear in mind that long answers are not necessarily better. *"Whoever reads your application will have to read a lot of them, so do them a favour and get to the point rather than trying to fill the boxes all the way,"* one pupil advised. Indeed, try to strike the right balance between detailed and snappy answers, and definitely leave out that one time you went to band camp.

A good number of sets recruit pupils outside the Gateway machinery because they don't like its format or feel applicants' interests will be better served by other means. The application method at each of these non-Gateway sets will be different. Some choose to mirror the Gateway timetable in their own application procedures, but others run on their own schedule, which can put candidates in a tough spot: what do you do, for example, if a non-Gateway set makes you an attractive offer before your 12 Gateway applications play out? At that point, the decision is yours.

Fortunately, most sets that eschew the Gateway lay out the specifics of their application processes on their websites, so read up accordingly before ruling yourself out for any opportunities.

Interviews: getting them right

So you've got an interview – congratulate yourself because that's already an achievement. Do yourself a favour and make sure you look the part by dressing neatly and discreetly: tidy up your hair, floss your teeth, straighten your tie, do up your jacket. Most chambers will be grading you on standard criteria, and that includes everything from intellect and personality to whether your suit is rumpled or not.

Most sets operate two rounds of interviews/assessments. The ins and outs of procedure at each chambers vary quite a bit, but thankfully most tell you what to expect on their website. The first round is often a standard sit-down interview, though these depart from tradition in their brevity – ten to 15 minutes is typical. The interview may focus on a topical legal question or a discussion of the current issues in your prospective practice area, and will most likely involve a short investigation into you and your application form.

An increasing number of sets ask specific pre-set questions to each candidate to probe for certain competencies, analytical ability and advocacy skills. You might also be asked to complete a written test or group exercise where you have to argue a point against or alongside others.

Remember: you'll face a panel that wants you to stand out, so do your best to impress by keeping up to date with industry ongoings. *The Times*' Law supplement, *Guardian Law* and *Current Awareness* – an excellent daily blog you can have emailed from the Inner Temple library – should all be on your radar. You should also think about your CV and how you can account for questionable circumstances like disappointing grades or a rather flimsy work experience section.

If you make it to a second interview round, you'll probably find yourself in front of a large panel comprised of a cross-section of people from chambers. By and large the panel will aim to assess the depth of your legal knowledge, advocacy potential and strength of character through some kind of legal problem given in advance.

This is your moment to show what a brilliant advocate you are. The interview panel will try to catch you out or play devil's advocate against whatever point of view you choose to argue, but don't let them push you around. If you can support your position then stick to it – resolve is just as necessary for a career at the Bar as receptivity, and recruiters want to know that you can fight your corner. As one observed, "*it's amazing how many people can't stand up for themselves, which is essentially what we want to see.*"

Criminal and mixed sets commonly give interviewees an advocacy exercise, such as a bail application or a plea in mitigation. (A word of advice: the basic structures to such matters fit on a post-it, so note them down and keep them with you at all times.) Additionally, the majority of sets pose a legal problem – for example, you might be asked to interpret a piece of statute or compare several judgments and give your view on a case study – with the amount of preparation time ranging from ten minutes to a week. Make sure you take along an appropriate practitioner's text to your interview unless you know that one will be made available to you.

Chambers generally aren't looking for faultless knowledge of substantive law so much as an insight into how your mind works. As one seasoned interviewer explained, "*we're more interested in seeing how a candidate ap-*proaches *a problem than whether or not they get the right* answer." Finally, a second interview is the time when a professional ethics question may raise its head. You can prepare by reading up on the Bar's Code of Conduct, available on the Bar Standards Board's website.

Try, try and try again?

All's not lost if you still don't have pupillage by the time you've finished the BPTC. While it may seem like a grim prospect, an enforced year out offers a good amount of time to bulk up your CV and make yourself more marketable. "*It's worth trying again next year if you plan to use your time wisely,*" said one pupil we spoke with who faced rejection a few times around. "*You've just got to be persistent and make sure you're helping yourself become a better candidate.*"

If you're interested in a specialist area of practice (like tax) you could consider a master's degree; however, do be aware that simply completing a year of postgraduate study will not in itself help you secure a pupillage. Seeking out some sort of useful practical work experience is a better way of boosting your chances.

The most obvious option is a stint as a paralegal or outdoor clerk at a solicitors' firm. Paralegal positions can be hard to come by, but the experience gives the chance to see cases and solicitors – your future clients – in action. Likewise, a bout of clerking will expose you to the inside of a courtroom and give insight into the procedures and politics of trials.

Working with an organisation that undertakes activities related to your area(s) of legal interest is a great way to make use of a year out. We've interviewed plenty of lawyers who secured pupillage following a period with a company, charity or non-profit organisation. And – though this may sound confusing – quite a few commercial sets like recruiting pupils who have previously completed a training contract at a City firm and qualified as a solicitor. While this isn't a route we recommend taking, it is a reflection of the advanced levels of background experience and knowledge that top sets now expect from their recruits.

Pupillage

If you manage the long, bumpy road that is gaining pupillage and come out the other end successful, many congratulations! Now the hard work really starts. The pupillage year is broadly split into a first, non-practising six months and a second six, when pupils may be permitted some court action. Most sets further divide the year to include a number of seats, often with a different supervisor for each.

During their first six, pupils are generally tethered to their supervisor(s), shadowing them at court and conferences and in chambers and getting to grips with tasks like research or drafting pleadings, advice and skeletons, usually for matters their supervisor is working on.

The nature of the second six depends on the specific area of practice. At a busy criminal set it can mean court every day. Likewise, many civil or commercial sets specialising in areas like employment, PI, construction or insurance send their pupils out up to three times a week. Big commercial or Chancery sets, on the other hand, often prefer to keep pupils in chambers throughout the year, either for the purposes of assessment or because the nature of the work means pupils are simply too inexperienced to do oral advocacy.

Check out our **Chambers Reports** to find out more about the day-to-day work of a pupil.

Tenancy

Tenancy is the prize at the end of the year-long interview that is pupillage. An offer of tenancy is effectively an invitation from a set to take a space in their chambers as a self-employed practitioner, sharing the services of the clerking and administrative teams.

How many tenants a set takes on post-pupillage generally depends as much on the amount of space and work that's available in chambers as it does on the quality of the candidates at hand. If you're curious about a set's growth, view the list of members on its website and check how many new tenants have joined in recent years, then compare that against the number of pupillages offered in the same period.

Tenancies are usually awarded after a vote of all members of chambers, following recommendations from a tenancy committee, clerks and possibly pupils' instructing solicitors. Decisions are commonly made in the July of the pupillage year, allowing unsuccessful pupils time to cast around for other tenancy offers or a 'third six' elsewhere.

There's evidence to suggest that civil and commercial sets have higher pupil-to-tenant conversion rates than criminal sets. Indeed, it is not uncommon for a twelve-month criminal pupillage to be followed by a third or subsequent six somewhere other than at a pupil's first set. That said, plenty of commercial pupils also find themselves in need of a third-sixer. The general rule is that if a third six is not successful, it is perhaps time to look outside the Bar.

And finally...

One thing is sure about a career at the Bar: applicants need to be resolute. Success won't come your way unless you're confident in your ambition and ability.

Mini-pupillages

"Honestly, I don't think any Pupillage Gateway application should go out without at least one mini-pupillage on it."

One of the most common queries we come across at law fairs is how a student can improve their chances of becoming a barrister. The most obvious answer is: 'Do some mini-pupillages'. Minis – that is, periods of work shadowing and/or assessment within barristers' chambers – demonstrate an interest in and commitment to the Bar and are a crucial part of the application process. Any pupillage application will look distinctly lacking if it doesn't have at least one or two minis on it.

Over the years we've quizzed numerous current and future pupils, some of whom completed as many as six or seven minis before attaining pupillage. Read on for their thoughts on the process.

What form do mini-pupillages take?

While large solicitors' firms take an almost universally structured approach to vacation schemes, work experience programmes at barristers' chambers can be more ad hoc affairs. Some sets (especially the most profitable, prestigious and forward-thinking) co-ordinate opportunities in a very methodical way; at others you might encounter a pretty disorganised exercise...

Length: As a rule mini-pupillages last two, three or five days and will be either assessed (ie there will be tests and feedback) or non-assessed. Our sources say: *"You don't need to do a five-day mini unless it's assessed. Three days is more than enough, especially during term-time. It's okay to ask for a three-day mini, even if it specifically says five days on the set's website. Barristers are pretty switched on to the fact that students have a lot of other stuff on their plate."*

A good mini-pupillage will expose you to the fundamentals of the job by offering the chance to shadow a barrister in court, attend conferences with clients and look at paperwork. *"These tasks allow chambers to see how your brain works. Students shouldn't expect to be in court the whole time as that's not actually what the barristers do all day."* Indeed, while a peek into the courtroom is undoubtedly beneficial for aspiring barristers, it's possible that chambers won't even have anything going on in court while you're there – all the more reason to complete as many minis as you can.

A bad mini-pupillage might see you abandoned in a room with a barrister who doesn't really want you there. *"I got stuck with a costs lawyer. Costs isn't an easily accessible area of law, even for other barristers. He gave me a load of bundles and told me to give them a read. I came back two hours later and asked: 'Where do I start?'"* We suggest making the most of it by trying to get a feeling for the atmosphere overall and chatting to other tenants about life at chambers if you get the chance.

An assessed mini will probably be relatively structured, with a couple of the days dedicated entirely to the assessment process itself. As such, expect to spend more time on your own than in a non-assessed mini. As one insider pointed out, *"there can be a certain prestige to assessed minis – a lot of the top chambers do them."* Indeed, while you may be asked to attend an interview for a place on any type of mini-pupillage, the odds go way up if it's an assessed one you're after. Be prepared to talk convincingly about why you've chosen the barrister route and perhaps even make a short presentation on a subject selected by the set.

Assessment problems often cover unfamiliar areas of law to give people at different stages of the learning process a fair shot. *"My written answer was supposed be in the form of an opinion,"* said one source, *"but it was clear chambers understood that those who hadn't done the BPTC yet would likely produce something more in line with a GDL-style answer. This is why the focus was on content rather than style – they wanted to know if, aided by the right research tools, I could go through the appropriate thought processes and come up with a sensible answer."*

Those who've been through the process suggest trying out some **unassessed minis** before an assessed one and advise waiting until you're at least started on the GDL to sign up. *"They can be very academic and textbooky, which is a challenge if you haven't encountered that type of material yet."*

Said the above source of their assessment: *"It kind of felt like an academic exercise, but at the same time I knew they wanted an 'advice' of sorts, so my efforts had to be fairly practical. I was given a factual scenario that filled about one side of A4, plus a few questions to answer about it. The other mini-pupil and I went to the nearest Inn library to research and answer the questions using Halsbury's Laws, Westlaw, LexisNexis, etc. I had a day to do this before handing my written answers to a barrister. The following afternoon I had about 30 minutes' worth of feedback with the barrister, who pointed out where I had done well and where I had gone wrong. Among other things, the exercise was marked on the quality of the legal analysis, the structure and the language."*

While it's your written work that's officially marked, don't think you're not also being judged on the quality of your queries, how quickly you pick things up and your overall manner. Make sure you're on form at all times, and don't forget it's reasonable to request feedback on your performance.

The social scene: A few chambers take as many as five mini-pupils at a time, though more often than not pupils find themselves alongside just one other. Sets with more formalised programmes may put on a drinks party, but at most it's unlikely you'll be invited to any social events.

This is not to say you can't use your visit for some subtle yet effective networking. How much mini-pupils achieve in this respect depends on how people in chambers take to them and whether or not their interaction is of the right type. It's all about striking a good balance with members of chambers and making sure you're remembered for the right things – enthusiasm, reliability, engagement with the cases you encounter – and not for being a nuisance or a drain on people's time. Pick your moments for questions and conversation carefully.

When should you start applying?

It's never too early to get a move on mini-pupillage applications. We've heard from sources who did them at all points in their studies – during their final undergraduate year, on the GDL course, in the middle of the BPTC. A lot of it comes down to when you decide to become a barrister – once you're sure that's your goal, why wait? There is no rule that says first and second-year undergrads can't do minis.

Of course the less advanced you are in your studies, the less you'll probably be able to understand, but that certainly doesn't mean a mini-pupillage will be a waste of time; on the contrary, each day you spend at chambers contributes to your understanding of how to act around barristers and the industry at large. And of course, many find the experience inspirational if nothing else. *"My time at various sets reaffirmed my belief that this was what I wanted to do with my life."*

Minis are usually available during term-time, and many sets run more than usual in the run up to the summer.

Check your intended set's website for details on the weeks they have available.

How do you get a mini?

Some of our sources used connections within the profession to pick up a couple of minis – don't hesitate to use these contacts if you have them – but most went through the usual application process.

The first step is checking if, where and when opportunities are available. Most sets offer details regarding mini-pupillages on their website, even if it's just a quick line saying 'we do them'. In the event that it's unclear whether a set offers minis, *"don't be afraid to ring up the clerks, find out who deals with the minis (it's usually a junior barrister) and ask to speak to them."* If it turns out they're unavailable you can at least obtain the correct individual's e-mail address for applications.

Most sources suggest applying for as many minis as you can *"as it's a numbers game."* Still, don't compromise the quality of your applications in your bid to up the quantity. Most sets' procedures involve a fairly standard CV-based form, or a covering letter and CV, so it shouldn't require too much brain-straining. Make sure your application explains why you're interested in visiting a particular set and shows you're serious about a career as a barrister. Given the amount of advocacy involved in the job, demonstrating some kind of mooting or public speaking experience should put you in good stead and indeed is a must for some sets.

The number of mini-pupillages you're offered should give you a rough indication of how credible a candidate you are. Likewise, looking at the reputation of the sets that have extended offers gives an idea of where you stand in the pecking order. If you're having no success with leading sets, take the hint and set your sights lower. If you don't hear back from anyone at all, take a long hard look at your CV and ask yourself what needs to be improved.

Don't expect any feedback after making mini-pupillage applications – many sets don't even bother to send out rejection letters. If you haven't heard back after a couple of months it's likely that you've been unsuccessful. Of course, it's possible a set simply didn't have the space to accommodate you at that point in time, or it may just be a bit disorganised, so don't get too disheartened. One of our contacts applied for a mini in March 2008, didn't hear back immediately, and was then surprised when the set contacted her over a year later asking her to come in for the summer 2009 vacation period – *"far too late for a Pupillage Gateway application that year!"* Another told of getting rejected for a mini at the set where he eventually gained pupillage.

How many should you do?

According to one barrister we spoke with, *"mini-pupillages show your commitment to the Bar, but doing ten ceases to impress. Three is a decent number."* Having said that, we've heard from more than one successful source who'd completed half a dozen. *"I personally found all of mine helpful,"* said one such insider, *"but I do get asked why I did so many. I think there's an idea that doing a lot can project uncertainty as to which area of law you're interested in."* In our opinion going past three is unlikely to hurt your chances, especially if you've got clear reasons for doing so. Few admissions committees will find fault with a clear-cut desire to sample different areas of practice.

Of course there is such a thing as overkill. If you've completed a long string of minis, it might make sense to list only the more impressive experiences on your application forms. Likewise, it's tactical to delineate a clear narrative when reporting your work experience. For example, if you're aiming for a criminal pupillage but have done a mix of crime and civil minis, you might consider leaving some of the latter experiences off of your CV. In the end, *"it's a case of striking the right balance between showing your commitment to a practice area and showing that you know what else is out there."*

Top tips for making a good impression

- *"At the end of every day of a mini-pupillage, mark down each thing you've done, no matter how small – every little legal point you've looked at, every chat about it you had with a barrister. You will forget it when it comes to subsequent interviews unless you make a note."*

- *"Things may go way over your head while you're in court, but make sure you stay focused. The barrister who takes you along may ask you how you think the hearing went."*

- *"Try to be relaxed while you're in chambers, and don't expect too much on a personal or social level. Barristers all differ. Some will be very intense. Some will have read your CV and talk to you about your interests. Some won't give a shit and will vaguely resent having to baby-sit you – and you'll know it. Don't take it personally."*

- *"Later minis are often of more use when it comes to the work. On my earlier ones I learned that I loved the surroundings of chambers and going to court but found it difficult to engage with the work as I didn't actually understand most of the legal principles at hand. Further into the year, however, it became much easier to make a good impression."*

- *"Be persistent with your applications and accept that you will get rejected from some places. If you really want a spot at a particular set, ask yourself whether it's worth trying again and go for it. I didn't get in the first time around, but after applying again I managed to land a mini-pupillage and now I'm a pupil."*

- *"Remember how important each mini-pupillage is, particularly those that are a requisite part of a set's pupillage application process. It's your chance to impress, so take it seriously."*

And finally...

It's important to keep in mind that although a mini is certainly step in the right direction, it alone won't take you all the way to pupillage. That said, *"a mini-pupillage is a real morale boost – it's a reminder that at least somebody thinks you're worth taking a look at."*

The Inns of Court

London's Inns of Court are oases of calm amid the hustle and bustle of the City's legal heartland. The four Inns – Lincoln's Inn, Inner Temple, Middle Temple and Gray's Inn – have more than a little of the Oxbridge college about them.

In addition to teaching, guidance and scholarships, the Inns provide a social network for members. A stroll through them offers a front row view of the history that's shaped the Inns as we know them today. Inside each you'll find a drove of baronial oil paintings, the austere expressions of past grandees, judges, heads of state and prime ministers gazing out from the wood panelling; meanwhile, their idyllic gardens preserve a bygone era of drinks and croquet on the lawn.

The Inns are the only institutions with the power to 'call' a person to the Bar. Students must join one of the four Inns before starting their BPTC and, seeing as membership is for life, it's a decision worth mulling over. Although all four offer similar services and facilities, each maintains its own flavour and atmosphere, thanks in large part to their differing sizes. We suggest visiting the Inns in person to see which one most appeals before settling on one.

You can also check out our Inns of Court Comparison Table (see opposite) for further details. There is an old rhyme that attempts to delineate each Inn's identity – 'Inner for the rich, Middle for the poor, Lincoln's for the scholar, Gray's for the bore' – but pay it no heed: it's been widely discredited and has no basis in fact.

It's a good idea to consider a head start on your membership seeing as the inns offer around £4.5m in scholarships between them. This money is reserved for GDL and BPTC students as well as pupils. The deadlines for scholarship applications usually occur in the calendar year before the course begins. Detailed information about these dates can be found on the Inns' websites or in their hardcopy brochures.

Landing a scholarship is a competitive business. Applicants face panels of current members (which occasionally include judges) who examine their academic records and set challenges to determine on-the-spot presentation and advocacy skills. Achievements such as 'overcoming hardship' are sometimes also considered, as are extracurricular activities like sporting or musical ability. The top scholarships are the prestigious 'named' scholarships, worth around £15,000 each. A huge number of smaller awards are also available.

Another plus of joining early is that there are additional funds to help facilitate mini-pupillages, internships and other forms of relevant work experience. Students living away from London can get access to financial assistance to cover transport costs to visit the Inns, and money is also available to cover the cost of 'qualifying sessions', 12 of which must be attended before being 'called to the Bar' (though the final one can be the call ceremony itself).

Some of the qualifying sessions are educational, while others are designed to help students socialise, network and absorb the customs of the Bar. Sessions range from time-honoured dinners in the halls to debates, music evenings, seminars, advocacy weekends and even weekend brunches. During one illuminating visit we saw pinball machines being set up by people who would later return for the evening's entertainment dressed as Elvis.

Once a member of an Inn, students can be mentored by practitioners in their chosen field and take part in marshalling schemes that see them shadow a judge for a week. There are also educational workshops to polish advocacy skills and seminars discussing specific areas of law or courtroom techniques. Beyond that are a range of societies for interests like drama, music and mooting/debating. All Inns offer mooting at internal, inter-Inn or national level, and we fully recommend you get involved in some capacity as mooting experience is often a big draw for chambers recruiters.

Joining an Inn is the first step of the undeniably long slog that is becoming a barrister. While excitement at the prospect is understandable, make sure you don't forget the following mantra: Securing a Pupillage is Extremely Hard. A BPTC provider is unlikely to turn you away if you've got the cash to spend, but you won't make your Lord Chief Justice fantasy come true by simply completing the course. Even with a much sought-after scholarship under your belt, the barrister route is neither cheap nor simple. That said, the Inns certainly provide resources that can improve your chances of gaining pupillage. Use them wisely.

	Lincoln's Inn	Inner Temple	Middle Temple	Gray's Inn
Contact	Tel: 020 7405 1393 www.lincolnsinn.org.uk	Tel: 020 7787 8250 www.innertemple.org.uk	Tel: 020 7427 4800 www.middletemple.org.uk	Tel: 020 7458 7800 www.graysinn.info
Architecture	The Old Hall was build in 1490 and the larger Great Hall in 1845, the same year as the library. The Stone Buildings are Regency. The largest Inn, it covers 11 acres.	12th-century Temple Church stands opposite the modern Hall, which was built after the original was destroyed in WWII and stands on the site of an ancient hall of the Knights of the Temple.	Grand style includes smoking rooms decked out in oak, Van Dyck paintings and a large private collection of silver. The splendid Elizabethan Hall has ornate carvings and is tucked down an intricate maze of alleys and narrow streets.	Its ancient Hall and Chapel are still intact, despite suffering serious war damage. The rest is largely a 1950s red-brick creation. One of the smaller Inns.
Gardens	Always open and especially popular at lunchtimes.	Well kept and stretch down to the Thames. Croquet, chess and giant Connect Four can be played.	Small and award-winning, with a handy bar.	Famous 'Walks' good for nearby City Law School students. Restaurant during the summer.
Style	Friendly, international and large.	Sociable, progressive and switched on.	Musical, arty and very sociable. Christmas revels are notorious.	Traditional and cosy with a personal touch.
Gastronomy	Meals in Hall are subsidised for students.	Lunch served every day. 15% discount for students.	Good-quality lunch served daily.	Lunch served in Hall every day, with subsidised rates for students.
Accommodation	14 flats available for students and 3 are let to pupils. All on-site.	Not for students.	Not for students.	Not for students.
Bar	The stylish Members' Common Room has a restaurant and a terrace bar.	The Pegasus Bar has a terraced open-air area. Good for people-watching but not a place to go incognito.	St. Clement's Bar closed recently and is looking for new digs.	The Bridge Bar is above the gateway between South and Gray's Inn Squares.
Old Members	John Donne, Lord Hailsham LC, Lord Denning MR, Muhammad Ali Jinnah, H. Rider Haggard, Wilkie Collins, some 16 British Prime Ministers.	Dr Ivy Williams (first woman called to the Bar), Bram Stoker, Judge Jeffreys of 'Bloody Assizes', M K Gandhi, Lord Falconer of Thoroton.	Sir Walter Raleigh, William Blackstone, Charles Dickens, William Makepeace Thackeray.	Sir Francis Bacon, Thomas Cromwell, Dame Rose Heilbron (the first female QC, first female Old Bailey judge and first female treasurer at an Inn).
Points of Interest	Together with the Royal Navy, Lincoln's Inn takes the Loyal Toast seated, which commemorates a meal with King Charles II during which the entire company got too drunk to stand. Inn offers subsidised trips to The Hague, Luxembourg & Strasbourg.	Temple Church includes part of the Knights Templar's round church, which was modelled on the Church of the Holy Sepulchre in Jerusalem and used as a film set in *The Da Vinci Code*.	Shakespeare's *Twelfth Night* enjoyed its first performance here. Hall has a table from the Golden Hind. Every new barrister signs their name in a book on this table.	The first performance of Shakespeare's *Comedy of Errors* took place here. Law has been taught on the site of Gray's Inn since the reign of Edward III. The ornate carved screen in the Hall is made from an Armada ship.
Scholarship Interview Process	Panel interview with no set question beforehand. Expect chat about preferred areas of practice and items of legal interest in the news. Scholarship awarded solely on merit, then weighted according to financial means.	Panel interview with set question. GDL scholars entitled to automatic funding for BPTC, but can apply for higher award. Merit and academic excellence prioritised, but all awards (save for the top ones) are means tested.	Every applicant interviewed in a 15 minute panel interview that tests a range of skills. Awards based on merit and then weighted according to financial means.	Shortlisted applicants interviewed by a three-person panel prioritising an ability to think on one's feet over legal knowledge. Extra-curricular achievements taken into consideration – eg music, sport or overcoming adversity.
Scholarship Money	Over £1.5m available each year through 122 scholarships and numerous awards and bursaries. GDL: up to 32 scholarships of between £2k and £7k. BPTC: up to 90 scholarships of between £6k and £18.5k, plus up to 20 bursaries of up to £3k each.	A total of £1.58m available. GDL: two major scholarships, plus various awards totalling £183k. BPTC: seven major scholarships worth between £20k and £22k, plus further awards totalling £1.16m.	A total of around £1m available. A fund of £900k for BPTC scholarships and awards. A fund of £90k for GDL scholarships and awards. Overseas scholarships totalling at least up to £15k	A total of over £800k available. GDL: Around 16 awards available of between £1k and £10k. BPTC: around 42 scholarships and awards of between £10k and £19k. Various overseas scholarships and miscellaneous awards – eg £10k Hebe Plunkett award for disabled.

The civil courts of England and Wales

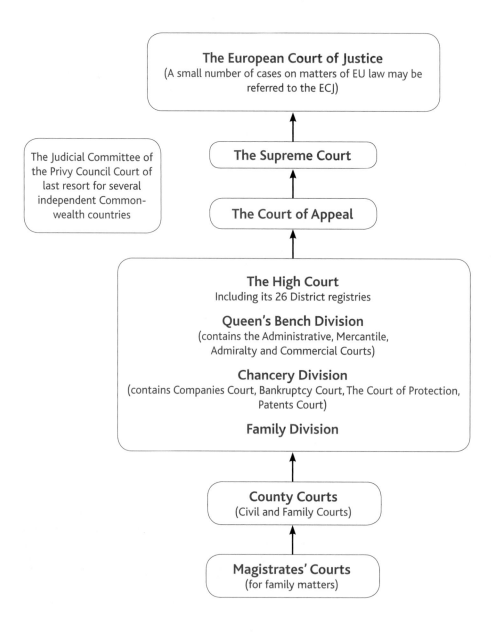

The European Court of Justice
(A small number of cases on matters of EU law may be referred to the ECJ)

The Judicial Committee of the Privy Council Court of last resort for several independent Common-wealth countries

The Supreme Court

The Court of Appeal

The High Court
Including its 26 District registries

Queen's Bench Division
(contains the Administrative, Mercantile, Admiralty and Commercial Courts)

Chancery Division
(contains Companies Court, Bankruptcy Court, The Court of Protection, Patents Court)

Family Division

County Courts
(Civil and Family Courts)

Magistrates' Courts
(for family matters)

Other Specialist Courts

Employment Tribunals	VAT and Duties Tribunals
Lands Tribunals	General and Special Commissioners (Tax)
Leasehold Valuation Tribunals	Asylum & Immigration Tribunals

Europe
ECJ: Any UK court can refer a point of law for determination if it relates to EU law.
The decision will be referred back to the court where the case originated.
European Court of Human Rights: Hears complaints regarding breaches of human rights.

Practice areas at the Bar

The Chancery Bar

In a nutshell

The Chancery Bar is tricky to define. The High Court has three divisions: Family, Queen's Bench (QBD) and Chancery, with cases allocated to and heard by the most appropriate division based on their subject matter. But what makes a case suitable for the Chancery Division? Historically it has been the venue for cases with an emphasis on legal principles, foremost among them the concept of equity (fairness). Cases are generally categorised as either 'traditional' Chancery (trusts, probate, real property, charities and mortgages) or 'commercial' Chancery (company law, shareholder cases, partnership, banking, pensions, financial services, insolvency, professional negligence, tax, media and IP). Most Chancery sets undertake both types of work, albeit with varying emphases. In practice, there is an overlap between Chancery practice and the work of the Commercial Bar (historically dealt with in the QBD). Barristers at commercial sets can frequently be found on Chancery cases and vice versa, though some areas, such as tax and IP, require specialisation.

The realities of the job

- This is an area of law for those who love to grapple with its most complex aspects. It's all about the application of long-standing legal principles to modern-day situations.
- Barristers must be very practical in the legal solutions they offer to clients. Complex and puzzling cases take significant unravelling and the legal arguments/principles must be explained coherently to the solicitor and the lay client. Suave and sophisticated presentation when before a judge is also vital.
- Advocacy is important, but the majority of time is spent in chambers perusing papers, considering arguments, drafting pleadings, skeletons and advices, or conducting settlement negotiations.
- Some instructions fly into chambers, need immediate attention and then disappear just as quickly. Others can rumble on for years.
- Variety is a key attraction. Traditional work can involve human interest: wills and inheritance can cause all sorts of ructions among families. Commercial Chancery practitioners deal with blood-on-the-boardroom-table disputes or bust-ups between co-writers of million-selling songs.
- Schedules aren't set by last-minute briefs for next-day court appearances, so barristers need self-discipline and good time management skills.
- The early years of practice feature low-value cases like straightforward possession proceedings in the County Court, winding-up applications in the Companies Court and appearances before the bankruptcy registrars. More prominent sets will involve baby barristers as second or third junior on larger, more complex cases.

Current issues

- The Chancery Bar attracts high-value, complex domestic cases and offshore and cross-border instructions. They might involve Russian and Eastern European business affairs or massive offshore trusts in the Cayman Islands, the British Virgin Islands, Bermuda and the Channel Islands.
- The scope of the Chancery Division means that practitioners get involved in some enormous commercial and public law matters.
- Following the introduction of the LASPO Act in 2012, new civil procedure rules for litigation have made the process more costs-conscious with stricter timetables.
- Litigation is very costly so settling before a case reaches court has become more popular. This means there's more mediation work around.

Some tips

- Most pupils at leading Chancery sets have a first-class degree. You should enjoy the analytical process involved in constructing arguments and evaluating the answers to problems. If you're not a natural essay writer, you're unlikely to be a natural-born Chancery practitioner.
- Don't wander into this area by accident. Are you actually interested in equity, trusts, company law, insolvency, IP or tax?
- Though not an accurate portrayal of modern practice, Dickens' novel *Bleak House* is the ultimate Chancery saga.

Read our Chambers Reports on...

Falcon Chambers	Serle Court
Maitland Chambers	South Square
XXIV Old Buildings	Wilberforce Chambers

The Commercial Bar

In a nutshell

The Commercial Bar handles a variety of business disputes. Commercial cases are classically defined as those heard by the Commercial Court – a subsection of the Queen's Bench Division of the High Court. But cases can also be heard in County Courts, by the Chancery Divisions or by the Technology and Construction Court (TCC). The Commercial Bar deals with disputes in all manner of industries from construction, shipping and insurance to banking, entertainment and manufacturing. Almost all disputes are contract and/or tort claims, and the Commercial Bar remains rooted in common law. That said, domestic and European legislation is increasingly important and commercial barristers' incomes now reflect the popularity of the English courts with overseas litigants. Cross-border issues including competition law, international public and trade law and conflicts of law are all growing in prominence. Alternative methods of dispute resolution – usually arbitration or mediation – are also popular because of the increased likelihood of preserving commercial relationships that would otherwise be destroyed by the litigation process.

The realities of the job

- Barristers steer solicitors and lay clients through the litigation process and advise on strategy, such as how clients can position themselves through witness statements, pleadings and pre-trial 'interlocutory' skirmishes.
- Advocacy is key, but as much of it is paper-based, written skills are just as important as oral skills.
- Commercial cases can be very fact-heavy and the evidence for a winning argument can be buried in a room full of papers. Barristers have to work closely with instructing solicitors to manage documentation.
- Not all commercial pupils will take on their own caseload in the second six. At first, new juniors commonly handle small cases including common law matters like personal injury, employment cases, possession proceedings and winding-up or bankruptcy applications.
- New juniors gain exposure to larger cases by assisting senior colleagues. As a 'second junior' they assist the 'first junior' and QC leading the case. They use this as an opportunity to pick up tips on cross-examining witnesses and how best to present arguments.
- In time, a junior's caseload increases in value and complexity. Most commercial barristers specialise by building up expertise on cases within a particular industry sector, eg shipping, insurance or entertainment.
- Developing a practice means working long hours, often under pressure. Your service standards must be impeccable and your style user-friendly, no matter how late or disorganised the solicitor's instruction. In a good set you can make an exceedingly good living.

Current issues

- The Commercial Bar is booming with cases involving ever larger sums of money, ever greater levels of complexity and ever larger teams of lawyers. One recent mega-case saw a Norwegian-owned investment firm bring an $8bn breach of contract claim against Deutsche Bank over purported trading losses in October 2008.
- As the above case shows, the fallout from the credit crunch continues to be felt in the courts. Financial, insurance and professional negligence disputes are all the rage in 2014 and this trend is set to continue. The number of cases brought to the High Court spiked in 2009, and has remained steady at pre-crunch levels since.
- With more claims being settled through mediation, only the big, multi-issue cases tend to reach court, as there are so many other opportunities for dealing with smaller, less complex cases.
- Third-party funding of litigation and costs risk-sharing arrangements are becoming more prevalent.

Some tips

- Competition for pupillage at the Commercial Bar is fierce. A first-class degree is commonplace and you'll need impressive references.
- Don't underestimate the value of non-legal work experience; commercial exposure of any kind is going to help you understand the client's perspective and motivations.
- Bear a set's specialities in mind when deciding where to accept pupillage – shipping is very different to banking, for example.
- Go to our website to read more about **Shipping** and **Construction** at the Bar.

Read our Chambers Reports on...

Atkin Chambers	Maitland Chambers
Blackstone Chambers	Monckton Chambers
Brick Court Chambers	4 New Square
Crown Office Chambers	XXIV Old Buildings
Essex Court Chambers	Pump Court Tax Chambers
One Essex Court	Quadrant Chambers
Thirty Nine Essex Street	Serle Court
Falcon Chambers	South Square
Henderson Chambers	3 Verulam Buildings
Keating Chambers	Wilberforce Chambers
7 King's Bench Walk	

The Common Law Bar

In a nutshell

English common law derives from the precedents set by judicial decisions rather than the contents of statutes. Most common law cases turn on principles of tort and contract and are dealt with in the Queen's Bench Division (QBD) of the High Court and the County Courts. At the edges, common law practice blurs into both Chancery and commercial practice, yet the work undertaken in common law sets is broader still, and one of the most appealing things about a career at one of these sets is the variety of instructions available.

Employment and personal injury are the bread and butter at the junior end, and such matters are interspersed with licensing, clinical negligence, landlord and tenant issues, the winding-up of companies and bankruptcy applications, as well as small commercial and contractual disputes. Some sets will even extend their remit to inquests and criminal cases.

The realities of the job

- Barristers tend to engage with a full range of cases throughout their careers, but there is an opportunity to begin to specialise at between five and ten years' call. Although you can express an interest in receiving certain work from the clerks, most sets expect their juniors to be common law generalists.
- Juniors can expect to be in court three days a week and second-six pupils often have their own cases. Small beginnings such as 'noting briefs' (where you attend court simply in order to report back on the proceedings) and masters' and district judges' appointments lead to lower-value 'fast-track' personal injury trials then longer, higher-value 'multi-track' trials and employment tribunals.
- Dealing with the volume and variety of cases requires a good grasp of the law and the procedural rules of the court, as well as an easy facility for assimilating the facts of each case.
- Interpersonal skills are important. A client who has never been to court before will be very nervous and needs to be put at ease.
- At the junior end, work comes in at short notice, so having to digest a file of documents quickly is commonplace.

Current issues

- The trend for mediation and arbitration of disputes, and the trend for solicitors to undertake more advocacy themselves, has reduced the amount of court work somewhat. Barristers remain involved with alternative dispute resolution, however, and while solicitor advocates frequently take on directions hearings, they are still rarely seen at trial.
- Britons have become increasingly litigious over the past few decades. Personal injury and clinical negligence claims (often against the NHS) are now an established part of the legal landscape, as individuals have become aware of the expanded protections afforded by health and safety regulation and professional codes of conduct.
- Since legal aid was cut from common law areas like PI in the 1990s, conditional fee agreements (aka 'no-win no-fee') and third-party funding of cases have helped sustain barristers' work volume.
- The Jackson reforms of civil litigation costs came into effect on 1 April 2013. The biggest change is that conditional fees and certain insurance premiums are no longer recoverable from the losing party. This lays a greater financial burden on claimants and is expected to result in less litigation and affect barristers' fees, especially in areas like PI.
- Other proposed changes – an increase in the small claims limit, changes to whiplash-related cases and restrictions on workplace-injury claims – could affect work at both the junior and senior end.

Some tips

- Though there are a lot of common law sets, pupillages and tenancies don't grow on trees. You'll have to impress to get a foot in the door and then make your mark to secure your next set of instructions. Personality and oral advocacy skills often matvter a lot.
- If you want to specialise, thoroughly research the sets you apply to – many want their juniors to retain a broad practice many years into tenancy, while others do allow some space to carve out a niche.

Read our Chambers Reports on...

Atkin Chambers	Littleton Chambers
Blackstone Chambers	Maitland Chambers
Brick Court Chambers	Matrix Chambers
Cloisters	4 New Square
Crown Office Chambers	XXIV Old Buildings
Essex Court Chambers	Old Square Chambers
One Essex Court	Serle Court
Thirty Nine Essex Street	South Square
Henderson Chambers	2 Temple Gardens
11KBW	3 Verulam Buildings
7 King's Bench Walk	Wilberforce Chambers

The Bar

The Criminal Bar

In a nutshell

Barristers are instructed by solicitors to provide advocacy or advice for individuals being prosecuted in cases brought before the UK's criminal courts. Lesser offences like driving charges, possession of drugs or benefit fraud are listed in the Magistrates' Courts, where solicitor advocates are increasingly active. More serious charges such as fraud, supplying drugs or murder go to the Crown Courts, which are essentially still the domain of barristers. Complex cases may reach the Court of Appeal or Supreme Court. A criminal set's caseload incorporates everything from theft, fraud, drugs and driving offences to assaults of varying degree of severity and murder.

The realities of the job

- Criminal barristers need a sense of theatre and dramatic timing, but good oratory skills are only half the story. Tactical sense, a level head and great time management skills are important.
- The barrister must be able to inspire confidence in clients from any kind of background.
- Some clients can be tricky, unpleasant or scary. Some will have pretty unfortunate lives, others will be addicted to alcohol or drugs, or have poor housing and little education.
- Barristers often handle several cases a day, frequently at different courts. Some of them will be poorly prepared by instructing solicitors. It is common to take on additional cases at short notice and to have to cope with missing defendants and witnesses. Stamina and adaptability are consequently a must.
- Sustained success rests on effective case preparation and an awareness of evolving law and sentencing policies.
- Pupils cut their teeth on motoring offences, committals and directions hearings in the Magistrates' Courts. By the end of pupillage they should expect to be instructed in their own right and make it into the Crown Court.
- Juniors quickly see the full gamut of cases. Trials start small – offences such as common assault – and move on to ABH, robbery and possession of drugs with intent to supply.
- It may be sexy work, but baby barrister pay on publicly funded cases can be abysmal. Increasingly, barristers earn as little as £10,000 annually for their first few years in practice.

Current issues

- Legal aid cuts and reforms are hitting the number of available criminal instructions and remuneration. This problem is fast becoming a crisis, especially at the junior end. Justice Secretary Chris Grayling has said he wants to cut an additional £220m a year from the criminal legal aid budget. A fair chunk of that will come out of barristers' fees. Cuts in criminal legal aid fees of 17.5% on average for solicitors and 6% for barristers were confirmed by Justice Secretary Chris Grayling in February 2014.
- Since 2013 there have been mass walkouts by barristers and solicitors in protest at the cuts, which will lead to 500,000 fewer instances of legal help to individuals and 45,000 fewer instances of legal representation. In June 2014, barristers and solicitors protested outside the Old Bailey and MoJ with a giant effigy of Chris Grayling.
- Partially as a consequence of legal aid cutbacks, many top-end criminal sets (and barristers themselves) are branching out into fraud, bribery, regulatory, VAT tribunal and professional discipline work.
- The traditionally close relationship between barristers and solicitors could be threatened by the rise of public access work, which allows barristers to bypass solicitors to gain clients, on fixed fees agreed in advance.
- Barristers are facing increasing competition for work from solicitor advocates, who can appear in court.
- Traditionally, freshly-minted tenants starting their practice at the Criminal Bar would be given a junior brief – a large case in which they'd be led by a senior member of chambers. This sort of work would provide a financial float for the junior. Nowadays it's hard to get the funding for two barristers on one case, so this traditional way into the Criminal Bar has declined. When a junior brief is available, often a solicitor with higher rights of audience will be the junior.
- Private paying criminal practice is as healthy as ever.

Some tips

- Mini-pupillage experience and plenty of mooting and debating is required before you can look like a serious applicant.
- The Criminal Bar tends to provide more pupillages than other areas, but these don't necessarily translate into tenancies. Third and fourth sixes are not uncommon.
- There are many ways of getting that all-important exposure to the criminal justice system. See our website for tips on useful voluntary opportunities.

Read our Chambers Reports on...

2 Bedford Row	Matrix Chambers
9-12 Bell Yard	

The Employment Bar

In a nutshell

The Employment Bar deals with any and every sort of claim arising from the relations or breakdown of relations between employees and employers. Disputes relating to individuals and small groups of employees are generally resolved at or before reaching an Employment Tribunal. Such 'statutory' claims may relate to redundancy; unfair dismissal; discrimination on the grounds of gender, sexual orientation, race, religion or age; workplace harassment; breach of contract; and whistle-blowing. Sometimes a tribunal will consist of an Employment Judge sitting with two 'wing members' (one from a trades union and one from a business background). In other tribunal cases – including unfair dismissals – the Employment Judge sits alone. Appeals are heard by the Employment Appeal Tribunal (EAT).

Accessibility is a key aim of the Employment Tribunal system, legal representation is not required, and many more cases proceed to a full hearing than in other areas of civil law. Such is the emphasis on user-friendliness that employment claims can even be issued online. Claimants often represent themselves, meaning a barrister acting for a respondent company faces a lay opponent. In complex, high-value cases both parties usually seek specialist legal representation from solicitors and barristers.

Employees and employers may also bring claims in civil court. High-value claims, applications for injunctions to prevent the breach of restrictive covenants, and disputes over team moves or use of trade secrets are usually dealt with in the County Courts or the High Court. These disputes make up a significant proportion of the work undertaken by senior members at sets at the top of the market.

The realities of the job

- For pupils and juniors, most advocacy takes place in Employment Tribunals or the EAT, where the atmosphere and proceedings are less formal. Hearings are conducted with everyone sitting down and barristers do not wear wigs. The emphasis is on oral advocacy, with witness statements generally read aloud.
- A corporate respondent might pay for a QC, while the applicant's pocket may only stretch to a junior. Solicitor advocates feature prominently in tribunals.
- Tribunals follow the basic pattern of examination in chief, cross-examination and closing submissions; however barristers have to modify their style, especially when appearing against someone who is unrepresented.

- Employment specialists need great people skills. Clients frequently become emotional or stressed, and the trend for respondent companies to name an individual (say a manager) as co-respondent means there may be several individuals in the room with complex personal, emotional and professional issues at stake.
- Few juniors act only for applicants or only for respondents. Most also undertake civil or commercial cases, some criminal matters.

Current issues

- The number of claims brought to employment tribunals rose greatly during the recession, up 50% in 2009/10 on the previous year. However, the government's introduction of tribunal fees in 2013 (up to £1,200 a pop) is arguably responsible for a sharp decline in the number of claims now taken to tribunal, with the Citizens Advice Bureau reporting that claims were down 73% in 2013/14 on the year before.
- The changes to legal aid introduced in April 2013 have removed public funding from all employment cases except discrimination claims. This has also adversely affected the volume of tribunal claims, and may mean that settlement becomes a popular option over the coming years.
- In a bid to boost economic recovery by encouraging employers to hire, the government has introduced a number of measures recently. One, dubbed 'shares for rights', was introduced in September 2013. It allows workers to sign away rights surrounding issues such as unfair dismissal, redundancy and flexible working in return for shares of up to £50,000 in the company they work for (provided both employee and employer agree to the scheme), though the option has not yet proved popular.

Some tips

- Get involved with the Free Representation Unit. No pupillage application will look complete without some involvement of this kind.
- Practically any kind of job will give you first-hand experience of being an employee – an experience that is not to be underestimated.
- High-profile cases are regularly reported in the press, so there's no excuse for not keeping abreast of the area.

Read our Chambers Reports on...

Blackstone Chambers	11KBW
Cloisters	Littleton Chambers
Essex Court Chambers	Matrix Chambers
5 Essex Court	Old Square Chambers
Thirty Nine Essex Street	

The Bar

The Family Bar

In a nutshell

Family law barristers deal with an array of cases arising from marital, civil union or cohabitation breakdown and related issues concerning children. Simple cases are heard in the County Courts, while complex or high-value cases are listed in the Family Division of the High Court. Around half of divorcing couples have at least one child aged under 16, and together divorces affect nearly 160,000 children a year. Consequently, a huge amount of court time is allotted to divorce, separation, adoption, child residence and contact orders, financial provision and domestic violence.

The realities of the job

- Emotional resilience is required, as is a capacity for empathy, as the work involves asking clients for intimate details of their private life, and breaking devastating news to the emotionally fragile. Private law children's cases can sometimes involve serious allegations between parents and require the input of child psychologists. The public law counterpart (care proceedings between local authorities and parents) invariably includes detailed and potentially distressing medical evidence.
- The job calls for communication, tact and maturity. Cases have a significant impact on the lives they involve, so finding the most appropriate course of action for each client is important. The best advocates are those who can differentiate between a case and client requiring a bullish approach and those crying out for settlement and concessions to be made.
- Where possible, mediation is used to resolve disputes in a more efficient and less unsettling fashion.
- Teamwork is crucial. As the barrister is the link between the client, the judge, solicitors and social workers, it is important to win the trust and confidence of all parties.
- The legislation affecting this area is comprehensive, and there's a large body of case law. Keeping abreast of developments is necessary because the job is more about negotiating general principles than adhering strictly to precedents.
- Finance-oriented barristers need an understanding of pensions and shares and a good grounding in the basics of trusts and property.
- The early years of practice involve a lot of private law children work (disputes between parents), small financial cases and injunctions in situations of domestic violence.

Current issues

- Compulsory mediation for divorcing couples was introduced in 2011, but has so far failed to bring down the number of cases going through the courts.
- Legal aid cuts are hitting the Family Bar hard, with funding removed from a majority of cases. An estimated 200,000 people a year are affected. Perversely, the result has been a massive increase in cases with more and more individuals representing themselves without consulting a lawyer.
- Big divorces involving wealthy couples are often big news and are often accompanied by strategic use of the media.
- A 2012 Law Commission report urged reform of the rules governing the division of assets on divorce, even going so far as to suggest a statutory formula could be introduced to determine how wealth is divided.
- The Marriage (Same Sex Couples) Act 2013 and further efforts to equalise marriage rights could affect divorce laws and civil partnerships.
- Since *Radmacher v Granatino*, prenuptial agreements are now part of the English legal landscape. Barristers are often involved in drafting the agreements too.

Some tips

- The Family Bar is quite small and competition for pupillage is intense. Think about how you can evidence your interest in family law. See our **Pro Bono and Volunteering** section.
- Younger pupils might find it daunting to advise on mortgages, marriages and children when they've never experienced any of these things personally. Those embarking on a second career, or who have delayed a year or two and acquired other life experiences, have a distinct advantage.
- Check a set's work orientation before applying for pupillage; some will specialise in a specific area like the financial aspects of divorce.

Read our Chambers Reports on...

1 Hare Court
Queen Elizabeth Building

Public Law at the Bar

In a nutshell

Centred on the Administrative Court, public law relates to the principles governing the exercise of power by public bodies. Those that most often appear as respondents in the High Court include government departments, local authorities, the prison service and NHS trusts. Often, headline cases are challenges to central government policies such as terror suspect control orders, the extradition of failed asylum seekers and the giving of evidence anonymously. Other big-ticket work comes from public inquires: the Chilcot, Leveson and Francis inquiries are all illustrative examples. However, for all the infamous cases reported in the media, there are hundreds of public bodies taking daily decisions that affect just about everyone in the country. It is decisions like these – on immigration, welfare, planning applications or a child's school allocation – that provide most work for private practitioners. The most important process in public practice is judicial review: the Administrative Court may order that any decision made unlawfully be overturned or reconsidered. Decisions are often reviewed on the basis of the Human Rights Act 1998. Many barristers also have practices in areas that dovetail with their public law practice. Criminal barristers will, for example, frequently handle issues relating to prisoners or breaches of procedure by police, whereas commercial barristers may handle judicial review of decisions made by the Department for Business, Innovation and Skills.

The realities of the job

- The Administrative Court is extremely busy, so an efficient style of advocacy is vital.
- Barristers need to cut straight to the chase and succinctly deliver pertinent information, case law or statutory regulations. Barristers need a genuine interest in the legislative process, and the fundamental laws by which we live.
- A real interest in academic law is a prerequisite. Complex arguments are more common than precise answers.
- While legal intellect is vital, public law's real world issues demand a practical outlook and an ability to stand back from the issue in question.
- Junior barristers often hone their nascent advocacy skills at the permissions stage of judicial review in short 30-minute hearings.

Current issues

- In response to terrorist attacks, a number of new laws have been introduced over the past decade or so, giving the government and police powers to sidestep traditional procedures. These measures, such as rights to stop and search, and the right to hold travelling passengers without 'reasonable suspicion' (introduced under the Terrorism Act 2000), have been criticised as inhumane and open to abuse. Cases involving challenges to these acts are becoming increasingly common, prompting some to suggest that civil liberties are slowly being reset on a case-by-case basis.
- At the same time, fresh controversy was raised when The Justice and Security Act 2013 expanded the use of closed material procedures (aka secret courts) in the civil courts. Evidence in these cases will only be seen by a judge and security-cleared special advocates, and the move has been widely criticised by public law practitioners.
- Prisoner voting rights are currently at the fore of politics, with the EU suggesting that the UK government's blanket ban on voting behind bars is an illegal breach of human rights. In August 2014, the European Court of Human Rights threw out claims that ten Scottish inmates were owed compensation from the UK government for their inability to vote.
- Administrative law cases are also on the up as public interest groups become increasingly alive to their powers to challenge administrative decisions, especially with proposed building developments.

Read our Chambers Reports on...

Blackstone Chambers	Henderson Chambers
Brick Court Chambers	Keating Chambers
Essex Court Chambers	11KBW
5 Essex Court	Matrix Chambers
Thirty Nine Essex Street	Monckton Chambers
Government Legal Service	

Chambers Reports: Introduction

Making an informed choice about where to apply for pupillage isn't easy. Once you establish your desired area of practice, you have to select a balanced collection of up to 12 Pupillage Gateway sets and figure out how many sets to apply to outside the scheme. But how do you know just where you'll fit in and who's interested in your particular working style?

These days the majority of chambers' websites display a lot of information – not just details about their size, nature of work and location, but also specifics on what to expect from their pupillage schemes. But internet surfing can only take you so far; there's no real substitute for the insights you'll gain into the inner workings of a set through a mini-pupillage. Of course, it's impossible to do minis at every set, so lucky for you we've done some digging.

For the last decade we've called in on various chambers regularly, taking time to speak with pupils, juniors, pupil supervisors, QCs, clerks and chief execs about life at their set. This is no small task, so we divvy up our approach, visiting each of our chosen sets every other year and refreshing the existing Chambers Report in the intervening year. This year's roll call of 34 sets includes 19 new features and 15 refreshed from our 2014 edition. We've tried to visit as many different types of sets as possible to paint a picture of the variety of practices available, from the grandeur of the Chancery Bar to the more modest publicly funded sets. Our selection strives to include something to suit most tastes, from commercial and common law to criminal, IP and tax. The wild card in our pack is the Government Legal Service, which admittedly isn't a chambers proper but still offers what we regard as a cracking pupillage.

All of the sets covered this year are located in London, where the majority of chambers and pupillages are based, but don't forget there are some excellent sets in the regions, mostly in larger cities like Leeds, Liverpool, Manchester, Birmingham and Bristol. We should also add that the on-the-record nature of our research at the Bar means we can't – and don't pretend to – give the same warts-and-all, anonymously sourced True Picture treatment to the following sets as we do to solicitors' firms. You'll have to find out about any warts yourself...

Whichever chambers you target, rest assured they're not expecting ready-formed barristers to turn up at their door. If you've done well academically and can prove your commitment to the relevant areas of practice through your extracurricular pursuits, most chambers will gladly make allowances for a lack of knowledge or experience on specific legal issues. Much has been said and written about how awful pupillage interviews can be, and from what we can tell that holds true in so far as interviews are a trying and disheartening process that can span anywhere from one to five years. However, the profession is increasingly business-oriented, with management taking greater notice of what constitutes good HR practice and acting more thoughtfully towards Bar hopefuls these days. You might also come across the occasional claims that pupillage itself amounts to little more than a year of pain and humiliation. We'd be remiss not to counter such claims. Sets don't try to push pupils to the edge of sanity – at least not on purpose; rather, their aim is to mentor and challenge pupils so as to gauge their compatibility with the set and overall potential at the Bar. Of course, that doesn't mean pupillage is a walk in the park by any means, though we can say with some conviction that any misery accompanying the year is likely driven by the demanding work at hand rather than any malevolence on behalf of chambers themselves.

The aim of our research for our Chambers Reports is not merely to get the low-down on pupillage at each set, but also to get a feel for each chambers' culture and to pick up tips for applicants. To this end we selflessly drank gallons of coffee, munched our way through kilos of biscuits and traipsed around numerous guided tours, checking out some crazy artwork and truly dishevelled libraries along the way. Now it's over to you to make your choices.

Set	Location	Head of Chambers	QCs/Juniors
Atkin Chambers	London	Andrew White QC	17/26
2 Bedford Row	London	William Clegg QC	18/51
9-12 Bell Yard	London	Mukul Chawla QC	11/54
Blackstone Chambers	London	Carss-Frisk QC/Peto QC	43/54
Brick Court Chambers	London	Hirst QC/Davies QC	36/48
Cloisters	London	Robin Allen QC	10/51
Crown Office Chambers	London	Richard Lynagh QC	13/78
Essex Court Chambers	London	Jacobs QC/Dunning QC	44/42
One Essex Court	London	Lord Grabiner QC	32/56
5 Essex Court	London	Fiona Barton QC	6/40
Thirty Nine Essex Street	London, Manchester, Singapore	Tromans QC/Block QC	40/86
Falcon Chambers	London	Derek Wood CBE QC	9/28
Fountain Court	London	Stephen Moriarty QC	29/39
Government Legal Service	London	N/A	411
1 Hare Court	London	Nicholas Cusworth QC	11/30
Henderson Chambers	London	Charles Gibson QC	10/39
11KBW	London	Cavanagh QC/Goudie QC	17/42
Keating Chambers	London	Paul Darling QC	27/30
7 King's Bench Walk	London	Gavin Kealey QC	24/31
Littleton Chambers	London	Bowers QC/Clarke QC	13/41
Maitland Chambers	London	Christopher Pymont QC	25/42
Matrix Chambers	London	Thomas Linden QC	23/38
Monckton Chambers	London	Paul Lasok QC	14/42
4 New Square	London	Ben Hubble QC	21/54
XXIV Old Buildings	London, Geneva	Mann QC/Steinfeld QC	11/32
Old Square Chambers	London, Bristol	Cooksley QC/McNeill QC	13/59
Pump Court Tax Chambers	London	Andrew Thornhill QC	11/23
Quadrant Chambers	London	Luke Parsons QC	19/41
Queen Elizabeth Building	London	Lewis Marks QC	4/28
Serle Court	London	Alan Boyle QC	20/36
South Square	London	William Trower QC	23/20
2 Temple Gardens	London	Benjamin Browne QC	12/47
3 Verulam Buildings	London	Ali Malek QC	23/47
Wilberforce Chambers	London	John Martin QC	22/32

The Bar

Atkin Chambers

The facts

Location: Gray's Inn, London
Number of QCs/juniors: 17/26 (10 women)
Apply though Pupillage Gateway
Pupils per year: 2
Seats: 2x3 and 1x6 months
Pupillage award: £60,000 (can advance £10,000 for BPTC)

In the past year, this set's caseload has spanned the world, from a power station on Teesside to cases relating to over a dozen overseas jurisdictions.

One of London's top two construction sets, Atkin is currently enjoying a wealth of interesting work, notably in the IT and in ternational arbitration fields.

Build me up buttercup

Although best known for its construction work, there's a lot more to Atkin than just bricks and mortar. Its practice extends into fields like renewable energy, engineering and IT. *"We've actually just completed one of the largest IT disputes ever,"* senior clerk Justin Wilson tells us. *"It was an 85-day arbitration worked on by eight of our barristers."* Much of the work centres around contracts and tort, and an interest in these areas is a must if you want to do a pupillage here. *"You don't have to come to your interview raving about construction law,"* one interviewee said. *"In fact, when we arrived most people here had never done any construction work – but you do need to be interested in contracts and tort."* Another source added: *"If you are interested in dealing with important questions of principle that arise in the law – for example, the approach to remedies in contract law or economic loss in tort law – then look at construction as a possible field to practice in. The tangible project-based nature of our work always makes getting your head around everything easier."*

Pupils at Atkin are exposed to a range of work, although there's no set programme. *"They'll probably encounter a lot of energy cases,"* pupillage committee member Fiona Parkin QC says, *"but what we're trying to ensure is that they develop the skillset to feel comfortable in any of our specialisms, be it pure construction or the computer/tech work that we're seeing more of."* Pupils themselves commented on the increasing amount of international work, as well as telling us that *"clients range from massive businesses to the privileged few who are still building swimming pools in their Mayfair homes."*

Justin Wilson confirms the set *"isn't looking to diversify from its construction core, but is always looking to adapt its skills to relevant sectors. The Bar is changing and there is a recognition that the status quo can't continue. We are still a referral profession and this set understands the importance of collaboration and building relationships."* Although the set retains certain traditional elements, such as afternoon tea and its classic Gray's Inn location, one member pointed out: *"We are modernising and always looking to approach the law with a strong commercial sense."* Another barrister added: *"We enjoy good relations with the biggest solicitors' firms in London, but we remain one of the smallest commercial sets at the Bar. We haven't undergone the same massive expansion which has made some sets more like law firms."* Perhaps it's this which gives Atkin its friendly atmosphere. *"Everyone is genuinely welcoming and deals with you on equal terms."* There's a *"super"* Christmas party, which in 2012 saw junior members belting out hits in a karaoke bar until the wee hours of the morn.

To err is human, to forgive divine

Pupillage is divided into three stages. In the first three months, until Christmas, pupils sit with their first supervisor. *"That's the period when mistakes are allowed,"* a pupil explained. *"They're happy for you to ask plenty of questions, and your supervisor understands that you will err. The general message is: just don't make the same mistake twice."* The second 'seat' lasts from January through to March. Pupils work on larger pleadings and advices, and research complex facts. *"Your lever arch files definitely get bigger as you go along..."* laughed one pupil.

Chambers UK rankings

Construction	Information Technology
Energy & Natural Resources	International Arbitration
	Professional Negligence

Throughout, *"you're always doing live work, rather than something your supervisor has dusted off for you to take a look at. This means you can learn more and get better feedback."* Pupils are also expected to complete set pieces of work for the pupillage committee throughout the period up to March. It's important to note that pupils do not spend any time on their feet. *"That's the nature of the Commercial Bar. If your main passion is oral advocacy then don't approach this set."* Pupils did assure us that they often attend court to observe members in action, and felt immersed in the process.

In April, pupils begin the assessment process for tenancy. *"We have a very structured programme,"* pupillage committee member Fiona Parkin says. A panel is made up, and all pupils have to submit five pieces of work to be assessed. *"You have three weeks to finish all five pieces,"* a pupil informed us. *"The exercises are really difficult and there is a lot of time pressure, but they do test your organisational skills and how you cope under pressure."* Each member of the panel then prepares a report on the work done which is submitted to the pupillage committee. Alongside the written pieces comes an advocacy exercise. *"You get two practice runs, then it's the real deal,"* a baby junior recalled. *"It's quite scary as it's actually assessed by a High Court judge."* In 2014 that was Mr Justice Edwards-Stuart, head of the Technology and Construction Court. Last but not least, pupils are given a week to complete a test paper – normally a piece of advice. *"Everything, including reports from the first two supervisors, is put together, marked and discussed. Then the tenancy decision is made."* Although it sounds tough junior members and pupils applauded the assessment process. *"The formalised system is very clear and distinct,"* one said. *"You know going in that if you meet the standard required, you will be kept on. It's as simple as that."* Another said: *"It never comes down to a choice between pupils. We always have the work and capacity to take on new tenants, they just have to meet our standards."* In 2014 one of the set's three pupils took up tenancy.

Hours, you'll be happy to hear, *"are better then expected,"* pupils and juniors agreed. Typical days range from 8.30am to 6pm during pupillage, with no weekend work. Naturally this increases dramatically during the assessment process. *"In that period you work round the clock, but that gives you a good sense of what junior practice is like."*

The third degree

Applications are made through the Pupillage Gateway, and the subsequent interview process consists of a single round split into three stages. In the first part, candidates have the opportunity to ask questions about pupillage and the set. The second part consists of a legal question designed to be accessible to both law and non-law graduates. Interviewees are given 20 minutes prior to the entire interview to prepare. Fiona Parkin tells us: *"The question allows us to see how candidates structure their response to an issue, but also how they respond to persistent questioning from several barristers. Can they think on their feet, or do they dry up?"* The final part is a discussion of a topical or ethical issue like organ donation or prenuptial agreements. 2014's question required candidates to present an argument for or against Scottish independence. *"Again, this tests a candidate's ability to structure an argument, and is normally the most important part of the interview for those who haven't done a law degree,"* says Fiona Parkin. *"The interview as a whole isn't designed to find out how many cases you know or whether you've read the most recent Lawtel decisions. Instead we're looking for an ability to approach problems logically and apply that logic to areas not encountered before."*

Applicants are required to have at least a 2:1, although one member admits that *"realistically, with the quality of applications we get, most pupils now have a First. However, if you have a 2:1 and are able to speak passionately and knowledgeably about matters at hand during your interview, that will put you in a strong position to compete with candidates with Firsts."* We spoke to some juniors with 2:1s, albeit ones with Masters degrees, additional Firsts and 'Outstandings' in their BPTC in the bag too.

And finally...

Atkin's tough pupillage assessments mean it is not for the fainthearted, but its stellar reputation makes it a great prospect for those with the right skills and interests.

2 Bedford Row

The facts

Location: Bedford Row, London

Number of QCs/juniors: 18/51 (15 women)

Applications: 400-600

Apply through Pupillage Gateway

Pupils per year: Up to 4

Seats: 2x6 months

Pupillage award: £12,000 + £10,000 guaranteed earnings

"On the first day of your second six you're in court on your own, and you go down to the cells to speak to a crack addict – they don't care which university you went to. They want you to be normal, to appreciate their position, to know the facts and the law."

Being ace at advocacy is essential to gaining pupillage at this esteemed crime set.

Prime time crime

Scampering through the doors of 2 Bedford Row, it's hard not to feel just a little bit starstruck (or Barstruck, perhaps). This set is, after all, one of the very top dogs at the Criminal Bar, as evidenced by its premier *Chambers UK* rankings for crime, criminal fraud and financial crime. The names on the door represent a pack of formidable silks under the leadership of William Clegg QC, *"probably the most famous barrister at the Bar."* Indeed, chambers takes some massive, headline-grabbing cases. Of late, Clegg has defended Mark Hanna, the former head of security at News International, against charges of conspiring to pervert the course of justice with Rebekah Brooks in the wake of the phone hacking scandal. He's also acted for drink and drug-addicted aristocrat Lord Edward Somerset, who stood trial for assaulting his wife over a period of 22 years.

While the set is *"prominent on the defence side,"* senior clerk John Grimmer highlights that *"we're very well covered"* when it comes to prosecution too, with barristers such as Brian Altman QC taking up positions like senior Treasury counsel at the Old Bailey and prosecuting high-profile cases such as the Birmingham terror plot. Although crime and fraud work are *"the bread and butter of the set and always will be,"* Grimmer notes that *"we have a number of practitioners who are very well known for professional discipline work, particularly in healthcare. Richard Matthews QC is the market leader for health and safety cases and Jim Sturman is the leading QC for sports law and frequently works for Premiership clubs."*

The big decision: concision is key

After admiring the reception area's bountiful fruit bowls and chocolate stash, we ascended in a tiny retro lift to an expansive room adorned with pastel renditions of courtroom scenes. Here we got the lowdown on recruitment from head of pupillage Stephen Vullo QC. So, what does the set look for? *"Advocacy – that's it."* Vullo elaborates: *"When we interview people we work on the assumption that they're well qualified or they wouldn't have got through the paper rounds. They will have done work experience, shown a dedication to the Bar, potentially even chambers itself, and saved koalas and pandas on their gap years. When they walk into the room it's about whether they can deliver."* The message is clear: if you're more at home behind a desk than on your feet then this isn't the place for you. Vullo continues: *"We take a mixed bag of people. We've had mature students in their 40s or 50s. This year we have four young women. We get people from privileged backgrounds and non-privileged backgrounds. It doesn't make any difference to us. It's about advocacy."* A baby junior confirmed this: *"There's certainly no mould. The reality is that on the first day of your second six you're in court on your own, and you go down to the cells to speak to a crack addict – they don't care which university you went to. They want you to be normal, to appreciate their position, to know the facts and the law."*

The set receives in the region of 700 to 800 applications through the Pupillage Gateway. Approximately 80 are invited to the first-round interview, which involves a short, non-legal advocacy exercise followed by a few questions based on the application form. For the former, *"a question is posed such as 'we should legalise drugs – give the two best reasons why.'*

Chambers UK rankings

Crime	Professional Discipline
Fraud	Sports Law
Health & Safety	

They have 15 minutes to prepare and 90 seconds to deliver. By and large it's usually enough to see how somebody deals with that." The challenge doesn't end there – a new set of instructions can be issued just before the preparation time elapses. *"We want to see whether somebody can adapt, follow instructions under pressure and be concise. About 30% of people go over the time limit."* Around 20 to 30 make it through to the longer second-round interviews. Again there's an advocacy exercise, though this time it's *"legally based and more technical. They'll be on their feet for about three minutes."* Both pupils we spoke to recalled preparing a plea in mitigation for this part of the interview, followed by discussion of legal and ethical points. Vullo adds: *"If we're interested in them then we'll ask difficult questions and grind down into more detail."*

Hoofing it

The first six, *"is the non-practising part of pupillage,"* so what you do is very dependent on your supervisor – the work you see is what they do."* It's a very *"close relationship,"* notes Vullo, although the supervisor will also *"ensure the pupil does work for a good cross-section of chambers so the tenancy committee have enough to work on"* when it comes to decision time. For the second half of the year, pupils switch to another supervisor. *You'll be out at court every day, so although that supervisor still gives you work to do and you can go to them for advice, it's more distant than with the first supervisor who you follow round all the time."* Pupils start to take on their own cases at the Magistrates' Court, a lot of which comes through legal aid. *"I've done a whole spectrum of things – trials, first appearances, sentences. There are lots of assault cases, plus harassment, petty theft and driving offences."*

Interviewees talked of handling *"smaller stuff in the Crown Court, like breaches of sentence, as well as covering the cases of more senior members if they're away."* Of course, pupils won't take on rape and murder cases in their own right, but they can get involved with these matters via their supervisor or other members. *"We'll go*

through papers, write case summaries, help with defence statements. An email might come through to all the pupils asking for help with a skeleton argument, an advice or a point of research." Pupils tend to see more defence work, although they do work on the prosecution side too. For the latter, *"you have to be booked with the CPS for a day, whereas with the defence work a solicitor will phone up and ask for someone to cover a trial the next day."* A baby junior told us: *"You're dealing with things at the last minute. It's about mastering the brief in a short period of time and getting the client to be confident in you."* Preparing for cases at such short notice means evening work is essential. *"Often the clerks will call you and send the papers through at about 5.30pm. I'll work here until about 8.30pm, leave and finish prepping at home. This week I've worked until about 11.30 or 12am."* Interviewees warned: *"I don't think anyone should have any illusions about the hours. It's a huge amount of work."* At least some of a pupil's weekend is dedicated to work, but on a Friday night they can be found at chambers' regular watering hole, The Old Nick. *"It's bizarre sometimes to see that these incredible advocates known for being brilliant are grounded, normal human beings."*

Don't wig out

Throughout the year pupils receive *"fast lane"* advocacy training from Stephen Vullo. *"He doesn't mince his words,"* laughed sources. *"He's not mean though. He's a perfectionist, like a craftsman."* The training culminates in a mock trial at Blackfriars Crown Court in which Bill Clegg acts as the judge with the tenancy committee as jury. Future pupils are invited to play the role of witnesses. *"It's pretty terrifying and purposefully difficult,"* admitted a baby junior. *"They put lots of points of law in there to see if you pick up on them."* However Vullo notes that *"it isn't the be-all and end-all – some people mess up slightly and still get taken on."*

The tenancy committee takes into account the pupillage committee's recommendation and the opinions of other members. From this year, pupils will complete a third six at chambers under a third supervisor and then apply for tenancy. *"They'll have experience on their feet for twelve months and everyone will know them well enough,"* explains Vullo. *"So there isn't a downside to this system."* A pupil concurred: *"An extra six months of experience will be a huge asset."*

And finally...

Afternoon tea doesn't happen here. *"Everyone's out at court!"* exclaimed interviewees. *"But there is a supply of tea, coffee and biscuits at all times."*

The Bar

9-12 Bell Yard

The facts

Location: Bell Yard, London
Number of QCs/juniors: 11/54
Applications: 400
Apply through Pupillage Gateway
Pupils per year: 2
Seats: 3x4 months
Pupillage award: £16,000 (+£10,000 guaranteed earnings)

"The first day of my second six was absolutely terrifying: I was in Hammersmith Magistrates' Court on a first appearance – I must have phoned a junior member of chambers at least three times with panicked questions."

Something wicked this way comes – and one of 9-12 Bell Yard's members may well be on hand to send down or defend the perpetrator.

London's burning

Arson, rape, murder, drug trafficking, possession of firearms, stabbings, insider trading, arms dealing, VAT fraud. Think of something unpleasant and members of this set have probably worked on it. And pupils get to see it all: from the cut and thrust of *"real knockabout"* cases in the Magistrates' Court on pickpocketing, ASBOs and neighbours kicking down doors to more *"paper-heavy"* corruption, money laundering and tax evasion trials.

9-12 Bell Yard is recognised by *Chambers UK* as one of the top dozen or so crime sets in London. It picks up similar recognition for its criminal fraud work. All members are crime specialists and about a quarter primarily work on fraud, with a further quarter dabbling in that area on occasion. 60% of the work is prosecution and 9-12 has close links to the CPS, HMRC, Royal Mail and regulatory bodies. There's also some extradition, professional discipline and asset recovery work, as well as involvement in public inquiries and investigations. (Junior members often go on secondment to external bodies like the SFO and the FCA to help with investigations.)

One recent 9-12 case saw a barrister prosecute a suspect who had to be extradited to stand trial for murder and arson, while another saw the conviction of a senior officer from the Met for misconduct in the wake of Operation Elveden. On the fraud side, head of chambers Mukul Chawla QC recently defended disgraced silk Rohan Pershad QC (formerly of 39 Essex Street) in his £600,000 VAT fraud trial. Another silk successfully defended a client against insider trading allegations brought by the (then) Financial Services Authority in *R v Sanders & Others*.

We should say a word about legal aid cuts at this point. They are affecting the Criminal Bar and at the time of writing around 70% of 9-12's work was publicly funded. *"The cuts have caused a reduction in turnover,"* admits first junior clerk Steve Parr. *"In response we have reduced overheads and cut costs for our members. We're also constantly looking at new areas of potential work."* Criminal regulatory, finance, tax and asset forfeiture are all areas 9-12 is looking to do more with in future (although we should note that the set is already active in all these fields). Recruitment has also been affected: the set now takes two pupils a year rather than the four it used to. There is usually room for a third-sixer though.

Lord of War

Pupils sit with three supervisors for four months each, usually spending time with the same three individuals. The first few months are mostly devoted to work for the supervisor, slowly branching out into assignments for other members too. That said, one baby junior recounted spending the first few weeks of pupillage *"shadowing the head of chambers in Southwark Crown Court – he was prosecuting an arms dealer."* The case was that of Gary Hyde, who helped sell 70,000 machine guns, 10,000 pistols and 32 million rounds of ammunition to China and Nigeria.

Written work in the first six typically includes taking notes of proceedings, helping with opening statements, and drafting skeleton arguments. One pupil told us they had worked for six or seven members by the time Christmas rolled around, and a baby junior recalled: *"When it came to the tenancy decision, it was particularly noted*

Chambers UK rankings

Crime	Fraud

that I had done work for a large number of members – around 20."

First-sixers also attend smaller Crown Court and Magistrates' Court trials and first appearances with newly minted tenants to get an idea of what their first time on their feet will be like. To further prep pupils, 9-12 runs an intensive advocacy training programme based on the Hampel Method. Sessions are fortnightly in the first six (and only slightly less frequent in the second), and revolve around cases based on real-life examples. Witness handling, cross-examination and first appearances all come up. *"The programme is taken very seriously. It's very useful in building up to the second six,"* a pupil told us. *"And in the second six it's a useful way to stop yourself picking up bad habits in the Magistrates' Courts!"*

Carry On Nurse

Pupils can expect to be on their feet from day one of the second six, with the number of appearances building up to one a day by the end of pupillage. Second-sixers usually start out with 'first appearances' in the Magistrates' Court – *"the defendant is just appearing in court to enter a plea. If they plead guilty they might be sentenced there and then. If they plead not guilty a date for trial is set."* The same source continued: *"Being the defence barrister at a first appearance is like being an A&E nurse. You might have no idea until you turn up what the facts of the case are. All you might hear is 'it's a burglary and they don't have bail'."*

Pupils' first trials start coming in quick and fast. *"My first one related to a chap who'd been caught pickpocketing in the West End,"* a pupil recalled. *"He was actually already in prison for another offence at the time the trial took place."* Trials soon become more paper-heavy, involving benefit fraud, for example. Pupils sometimes also prosecute CPS lists – spending a day in court prosecuting all the CPS's cases in a certain courtroom that day. Royal Mail prosecutions are also popular: they give pupils the chance to prosecute in a case based on a clear set of facts.

The tenancy decision is made at the end of August, start of September. The decision is based on a veritable smorgasbord of factors: the views of all members of chambers; feedback from members you've done work for; a report on the advocacy training sessions; a report from the clerks' room; three pieces of written work completed throughout the year; and your entry for that year's Kalisher Essay Competition. No wonder one pupil told us they felt they were being assessed on *"everything, right down to how you make a cup of tea for someone."* At the time we went to press the 2014 tenancy decision had yet to be made, but in 2013 one out of two pupils gained tenancy.

Peer pressure?

Despite having a Lib Dem peer (Lord Carlile of Berriew) as its former head, 9-12 is not a set with a particular political colour or thrust to it. *"We're a pretty eclectic bunch of people,"* reflected a baby junior. *"I don't really think we have a 'type'. But then you never can tell that from the inside!"* Perhaps because there's quite a lot of prosecution work, the same source said that a *"belief in being fair"* is what all members share. It's also clear that members value all their cases equally, whether it's a rough and tumble street violence affair or a complex Olympic ticketing fraud.

Interviewees said that while 9-12 isn't the most sociable of sets there are occasional pub, lunch and dinner outings, with members of similar seniority often clubbing together for these. But this isn't a set that makes a thing of hierarchy. Everyone's on first-name terms, and one baby junior told us this anecdote: *"When I was a pupil, Lord Carlile used to have an office on the same floor as the most junior barristers, and you'd occasionally hear his disembodied voice coming from his room to answer a tricky legal problem we'd been debating. He also came and spoke to me once just because he wanted a second opinion on a legal point."*

The application process is a pretty typical one: a panel interview followed by an oral advocacy exercise (usually a mock bail application or plea in mitigation). Go to our website to find out more.

And finally...

9-12 Bell Yard offers an excellent pupillage with court appearances galore, an arresting array of criminal cases, and an intensive in-house advocacy programme.

The Bar

Blackstone Chambers

The facts

Location: Middle Temple, London
Number of QCs/juniors: 43/54 (23 women)
Applications: 400+
Apply through Pupillage Gateway
Pupils per year: 4
Seats: 4x3 months
Pupillage Award: £60,000 (can advance £17,000 for BPTC)

Blackstone works on some fascinating commercial and public law cases, and attracts a diverse array of pupils.

This leading set marries a standard of excellence with a laid-back environment. It's none too shabby on the social front, either...

Smooth operator

Blackstone runs a slick operation. From its swish reception and glorious roof terrace to its swanky meeting rooms and frankly delightful biscuit selection, this set scores big points in the aesthetics department. Its practice is nothing to whine about, either: home to public law superstars like Dinah Rose QC, chambers boasts a sky-high reputation in the field and is up there with the best in many others. Along with its administrative and public law and its civil liberties and human rights practices, Blackstone scores top-tier *Chambers UK* rankings for its employment, financial services, fraud, sport, telecoms and media and entertainment work. A number of other areas – among them competition, environment and immigration – follow closely behind in the charts.

According to deputy chambers director Mat Swallow, commercial, public and employment law *"are at the heart of Blackstone, but so much of chambers' expertise falls under the broader regulatory banner, across the full spectrum of our practice areas including, for example, competition, financial services, energy and sport. We act for many of the regulators and our junior tenants regularly go on secondment to Ofgem, Ofcom and the FCA, among others."* While general commercial instructions technically account for the biggest spread of work – clocking in somewhere around 45% – it's Blackstone's public law undertakings that dominate the headlines. The BBC appointed Rose to spearhead its sexual harassment investigation following the Jimmy Savile scandal, while James Eadie QC acted for the government during the Leveson Inquiry and represented the Secretary of State for Health in the Francis Inquiry, the infamous probe into the disconcertingly high mortality rates at Stafford Hospital. Given Blackstone's commercial origins, it comes as little surprise that many of its public law cases bear a commercial tinge. *"A good example is the litigation surrounding tobacco advertising and calls for plain packaging legislation,"* Swallow says. *"In that kind of matter – which raises a blend of EU, competition, public law and human rights issues – we're likely to work with City firms or directly with the tobacco companies themselves."*

Of course, pure commercial work definitely makes its mark at Blackstone. Sports-related cases – for example, Pakistani cricketer Danish Kaneria's much publicised appeal against his lifetime ban for corruption – have gained the set a good deal of attention in recent years, as have crossover matters like Client Earth's Supreme Court appeal to reduce nitrogen dioxide levels, which combines elements of environmental, public, commercial and EU law. At the time of our visit, lawyers were grappling with the kick-off of the Madoff trial, *"one of the highest-profile pieces of commercial litigation to come to trial this year,"* according to Swallow. Pushpinder Saini QC is leading the way on multiple bankruptcy and insolvency disputes that have arisen out of the notorious Ponzi scheme. *"We're really driving our commercial work and are striving for more recognition on both the international and arbitration front,"* Swallow says, mentioning Blackstone's participation in one of India's biggest domestic arbitrations to date, a claim regarding cyclone damage to an oil refinery.

Learning from the best

Pupils rotate through four supervisors throughout their year, working exclusively for each. *"There's always someone who primarily practices commercial, and the*

Chambers UK rankings

Administrative & Public Law	Financial Services
Civil Liberties & Human Rights	Fraud
	Immigration
Commercial Dispute Resolution	Media & Entertainment
	Professional Discipline
Competition/European Law	Public International Law
	Public Procurement
Employment	Sports Law
Environment	Telecommunications

same goes for public and employment law – they want to ensure everybody sees our three main areas." Members of the current cohort praised this set-up for *"allowing you to see how four different people operate"* and *"offering the chance to impress a good number of people by the end of pupillage."* Under this system, our sources had encountered everything from telecoms and media cases to sports, fraud, regulatory and competition matters. *"I wouldn't recommend coming here if you're set on a particular type of law because the point is to expose you to a breadth of practice areas,"* advised one. That said, there was a warning to prospective applicants, particularly those keen on public law, that *"the bulk of your work as a pupil will quite likely fall under the general commercial and employment umbrellas. I've found pupillage to be less public law-oriented than Blackstone's reputation suggests."*

Pupils undertake six written assessments and a handful of advocacy exercises throughout their year. The former entails *"picking up a live piece of work, such as a legal note or opinion, at 8am on Monday and returning them by 6pm on Tuesday. These are marked and then a while later you sit down with somebody and get quizzed about what you wrote."* Only four of the seven or so advocacy assignments are assessed, with each filmed. *"It's the worst watching them back! You notice how rumpled your tie was or how much hair you had in your face. But the upside is that you end up righting a lot of wrongs. Also, knowing everyone is doing the same exercise keeps the assessment process fair and measured."* Additional feedback comes in the form of a sit-down between pupils and supervisors at the end of each seat.

Tenancy decisions are made in early July, and everyone in chambers gets a vote. *"At the meeting, the pupil supervisors are very influential of course, but everyone con-* *tributes to the decision,"* Jane Mulcahy QC, head of pupillage, assures us. *"We chat about our experiences with each pupil and where their strengths lie, and if they're good enough we'll take them all."* Our sources credited this attitude with eliminating a sense of competition among the intake. *"Knowing they have enough accommodation for everyone makes it possible to be friends and support each other."* In 2014 two of five stayed on as tenants.

Welcome to the family

It was clear right off the bat during our visit that Blackstone doesn't have a particularly formal environment. For starters, we encountered more than one tenant dressed *"like a student"* (their words), and one source actually guffawed when we asked about afternoon tea. *"I think because we've got so many fantastic people, nobody's pretending to try to be better or more professional by obsessing over sharp suits and outdated traditions,"* thought a junior. Indeed, a *"relaxed and co-operative"* vibe prevails, and several likened the set to *"a family"* in that *"people genuinely seem to like each other and many are deeply involved with one another's personal lives – they go on holiday together and socialise regularly outside of work."* As Mulcahy added: *"All of my daughters' godparents work in this building!"* A big factor is this genial atmosphere is an egalitarian attitude *"wielded from the top down – there's a big focus on fairness and equality, and everyone's opinion is valued. People naturally respect the work of their senior colleagues, but no one is asked to bow down to anyone else."* As such, even the relationship between barristers and clerks is *"relatively flat – we go out together for drinks all the time; they're not hidden away like you see at some sets."*

Pupils told of a *"civilised"* work/life balance in which they're *"rarely"* beholden to hours beyond the core 8.30am to 6.30pm. *"Supervisors do their best to make sure no one's overworked or too stressed out."* For junior members, this leaves plenty of time for socialising, which often takes place at the nearby Edgar Wallace or in the form of occasional dinners out. Chambers' roof terrace gets a good workout come summer, when there are Friday drinks outside, and various marketing events – such as football games and ping pong competitions with City firms – keep tenants busy during the rest of the year. There's a family-friendly Christmas do plus a cracking summer shindig, which we can confirm is just peachy, having attended ourselves.

And finally...
We've no space to talk about the application process, but our website provides plenty of detail on how to get into Blackstone.

Brick Court Chambers

The facts

Location: Essex Street, London
Number of QCs/juniors: 36/48
Number of applications: 400
Apply through Pupillage Gateway
Pupils per year: Up to 5
Seats: 3x4 months
Pupillage award: £60,000 (can advance £25,000 for BPTC)

This top commercial set accepts applications through both the Pupillage Gateway and its own website.

One of London's top commercial sets, Brick Court has a sterling reputation and snazzy offices, and is home to some A-list barristers.

Solid as a Brick

Brick Court's Essex Street home oozes effortless class. The slick, off-gold décor could easily be mistaken for that of a boutique hotel, but this set is in quite a different line of business. Brick is a leading light of the Commercial Bar, producing an exceptionally high standard of work in three core areas: EU/competition, public law and commercial. *"We're predominantly a commercial set with a strong competition and public law team,"* opined joint senior clerk Julian Hawes.

A glance at Brick's former members and door tenants gives you a sense of its pedigree. Sir Sydney Kentridge played a leading role in some of the most politically significant cases in apartheid-era South Africa, including Nelson Mandela's treason trial. Lord Phillips of Worth Matravers was the first president of the Supreme Court, while Jonathan Sumption – known for his work on the Hutton Inquiry and for successfully defending Roman Abramovich against claims made by fellow Russian oligarch Boris Berezovsky – was joint head of chambers until his appointment to the Supreme Court in 2011.

The current crop of barristers continues to be instructed on headline-grabbing cases. Recently members were involved in the *BSkyB v Ofcom* pay-TV dispute, Tottenham Hotspur's bid to use the Olympic Stadium, and the Pollard Review into the BBC and Newsnight amid the Jimmy Savile scandal. *"Brick Court's reputation for high quality work really appealed to me,"* remarked one pupil of their decision to apply. *Chambers UK* agrees on this point: Brick wins an impressive 14 rankings including top-tier recognition for competition, EU law, commercial disputes and civil fraud. Other ranked areas include banking, insurance and human rights.

Brick Court itself identifies 44 of its members as experts in commercial law, and 21 as active on public law (there isn't a huge amount of overlap between the two groups). A further 27 are competition professionals, with some overlap with the commercial group. Members frequently receive instructions from the City's biggest commercial beasts – Freshfields, Allen & Overy, Slaughter and May, Herbert Smith, Clyde & Co, Skadden – but also work with regional firms like Walker Morris and boutiques such as Harbottle & Lewis. Commercial work is wide-ranging, covering issues like the liability of state-owned corporations for a state's debts, and disputes relating to a mining project in Sierra Leone, and a row between Ukrainian oligarchs Viktor Pinchuk and Gennadiy Bogolyubov. Lay clients include Russian banks, Cayman Islands funds and Israeli entrepreneur Michael Cherney.

Master builders

Pupils sit with three (or four) supervisors – one from each of the set's three core areas. However, one source pointed out that *"a lot of the supervisors do crossover work,"* meaning that rookies *"gain the confidence to take instructions in a variety of different areas."* Pupils can expect their earliest tasks to involve *"doing research or making notes,"* before moving on to meatier writing and advisory work. *"I wrote skeleton arguments and opinions, and often prepared the first draft of pleadings, defences and claims,"* one source told us. These tasks continue into the second six; live oral advocacy is not part of pupillage here. *"There is plenty of opportunity to get on your feet after gaining tenancy though,"* a baby junior

Chambers UK rankings

Administrative & Public Law	Competition/European Law
Aviation	Energy & Natural Resources
Banking & Finance	Environment
Civil Liberties & Human Rights	Fraud
Commercial Dispute Resolution	Insurance
	International Arbitration
	Professional Negligence
	Telecommunications

said. The set also runs in-house oral advocacy exercises, which see pupils put to the test several times a year before a panel of QCs. The first few are unassessed and solely for training – latter exercises are assessed and pupils' performance weighs into the tenancy decision. Pupils also undertake six written assessments.

Is it daunting to face so many formal examinations? *"It is to some extent,"* confided one baby junior, *"but it's quite liberating too – the unassessed exercises give you the opportunity to fail, which can be a good learning experience."* Showing progress is paramount. *"You are given feedback throughout the year, and in return your performance is expected to show an upward trajectory,"* commented one baby junior. *"When you get to the end of the process, you know that if you don't gain tenancy, it's because you haven't met the standard."* The tenancy committee compiles a *"whacking great file"* on every single pupil. In it go the assessment exercises, reports on the oral advocacy exercises, reports on *every* piece of work pupils have done for their supervisors. Even notes on the pupils' original application, interview and mini-pupillage performance are taken into consideration.

2013 was a bumper year for pupils making it as tenants, as all five gained membership. In 2014 a further three out of five pupils stayed on, making for quite a growth spurt. Brick now has over 80 members, but our sources suggested there's no ceiling on size as long as quality is assured. This maxim extends to lateral hiring too: in 2013 Scottish advocate James Wolffe QC joined chambers and he was followed in early 2014 by Jeremy Gauntlett, a South African silk who helped draft that country's post-apartheid constitution. Julian Hawes estimated that 30% to 40% of the set's silks started out with other chambers.

Brick by Brick

Despite its bulky size, our sources said Brick Court has a cosy environment. This isn't a place where hard-nosed silks cordon themselves off from the world. *"People often stop by my office for a chat and gossip when the kettle boils,"* says Mike Bools QC. *"We're not down the pub together every evening, but the other night I did go for a drink with an ex-pupil who I supervised and some other juniors."* A pupil added: *"The junior end of chambers enjoys going for lunch together and sometimes for drinks on a Friday, but lots of people here have families so they'll head home once work is done."*

Securing a pupillage with this top-notch set is a challenging process. Brick is part of the Pupillage Gateway, but applications can also be made online during the rest of the year. Candidates who are invited to an initial interview find themselves faced with a problem question like 'Should lawyers be allowed to sit on juries?' *"It's a test of your ability to reason and express yourself clearly,"* a baby junior recalled. Those who impress at this first interview are invited to undertake an assessed mini-pupillage, during which they will also complete a marked written assessment. Pupillage committee chair Mike Bools explains why the set uses an assessed mini as part of its application process: *"We don't believe it's possible to recruit someone for a job which requires such particular interpersonal skills just on the basis of a 20-minute interview."*

Post-mini, around 20 applicants make it through to a final interview. They are sent a case a week in advance and asked to prepare an argument to make before a panel of five members. A baby junior said this interview is designed to allow candidates to show *"they can articulate themselves."* Overall, we'd venture to say that Brick Court is looking for a tad more than this: the set's ten most junior members are heavily laden with Oxbridge Firsts and Double Firsts. They also stand out for their international backgrounds: three did their undergraduate degrees in Australia or New Zealand, while five (!) studied at Harvard, and one in Paris. Among the group are also a Rhodes Scholar, a Fulbright Scholar and a former adviser to the Prime Minister of Iraq.

And finally...

Brick Court is often described as one of the Bar's 'magic circle' sets. Why? Its size, the complexity of its work, its commercial focus, and its humongous fee incomes: it raked in a whopping £63m in 2013/14, more than any other set.

The Bar

Cloisters

The facts

Location: Middle Temple, London
Number of QCs/juniors: 10/51 (24 women)
Applications: 350-450
Apply through Pupillage Gateway
Pupils per year: 2
Seats: 3x4 months
Pupillage award: £40,000 (can advance £6,000 for BPTC)

> *"Everyone here believes strongly in equality and social justice and we are generally pro-union as well."*

Splitting its work between employment, clinical negligence and personal injury, Cloisters is a leader in all these areas.

Big guys, little guys, good guys, bad guys

"Helping the little guy," is how one member summed up the ethos and outlook of this set. Its clin neg and PI practice is entirely claimant-side, and while employment is split between claimant and respondent work *"there is a slant towards discrimination and human rights focused cases."* In all, 60% of the set's practice is devoted to employment, 20% to PI and 20% to clin neg.

Cloisters works on some big, interesting cases defending the underprivileged. Back in 2010 two members represented the Nepalese Gurkhas in their Court of Appeal pensions battle with the MoD. Another member recently won £40,000 in compensation for a Co-op cashier after she was verbally harassed by her manager, while another defended former Travers Smith trainee Katie Tantum in her case claiming she was not offered an NQ job because she was pregnant.

Meanwhile, head of chambers Robin Allen QC (who was *Chambers UK*'s 2012 employment silk of the year) worked on *O'Brien v Ministry of Justice* establishing the right of part-time judges to receive a public pension. There are respondent cases too, which see barristers *"acting for the big guy."* One member recently represented Peter Stringfellow in the Employment Appeal Tribunal case over whether stripper Nadine Quashie was self-employed or not.

Being respondent counsel *"doesn't always mean acting for the bad guy"* and Cloisters is a set with a clear moral compass. *"Everyone here believes strongly in equality and social justice and we are generally pro-union as*

well," one member told us. The set has a *"lefty"* feel but it's *"not rammed down your throat"* and members are *"not uniformly of the same party-political persuasion."*

The bare bones

All pupillage applications are marked out of 20 by two members of chambers. Ten of those points are for academic achievement, while the other ten are for advocacy (worth three), communication skills (two), initiative and independence (two), commitment to the law (two) and suitability to Cloisters' areas of work (one). This gives each applicant a score out of 40 – in recent years a tally of 34 has been needed to get through to the first interview round. That first interview – to which around 80 are invited – consists of a non-legal problem question designed to assess presentation skills, analytical ability, common sense and time management. In 2012 the hypothetical question was about what action a head girl should take after discovering her school's model Santa Claus had had all of its clothes removed by a prankster.

Fifteen to 20 individuals make it through to a second interview – *"a fiendishly difficult legal problem"* based around a PI, clin neg or employment case. Applicants have one or two weeks to prepare and tons of legal research is required. *"The interview moves very quickly and you have to give every answer your best shot,"* a pupil recalled. At the end of the interview, applications are asked to argue for or against a political or moral question. In 2012, the question was 'Are lawful tax avoidance schemes morally wrong?'

Should aspiring pupils share the set's moral ethos? Pupillage committee head Lisa Sullivan told us that there are

Chambers UK rankings

Clinical Negligence	Personal Injury
Employment	

no specific marks for this in the recruitment process, but: *"Activities undertaken by people who share our ethos are likely to be one way of evidencing the competencies we do look for."* Sullivan also encourages applicants to ask themselves whether they *"really want pupillage or tenancy in a set where they don't share, at least to some extent, the ethos of that chambers."*

A summer in the heat

Pupils spend four three-month periods with four different supervisions, two practising in PI/clin neg and two in employment. During their first six, pupils shadow their supervisors, frequently attending court and taking on tasks like legal research for closing submission and first drafts of advices. *"There is also the opportunity to work for other members, although you are not required to do work for anyone in particular,"* a pupil said. *"They ease you in quite nicely,"* a baby junior recalled. *"I had little experience of employment law and I was given the time I needed to understand everything."* Also *"if you are here beyond 6.30 or 7pm people will usually pop in to ask what you are still doing at your desk. They'll tell you to save your energy for the second six!"*

And energy is what's required for the second half of pupillage. As well as continuing to shadow their supervisors pupils take on their own caseload, which eventually ramps up to court appearances several times a week. *"My first assignment was a two-day unfair dismissal case,"* a baby junior recalled, *"and by the end of my second six I was running a five-day discrimination trial."* Employment work gets pupils on their feet a lot and they'll also be running case management discussions and telephone hearings. A lot is expected of pupils here and we weren't surprised to hear one of our interviewees *"had gained some FRU advocacy experience before joining chambers."* Oral talents are highly valued for employment barristers, while drafting is the main skill for PI and clin neg specialists.

During the summer, from May onwards, pupils undergo four rigorous assessments. These constitute 90% of the basis of the tenancy decision (10% based on supervisor feedback looking at writing, research, court and client skills, as well as work for other members of chambers). The first assessment is a drafting exercise (worth 20%), usually particulars of claim or an ET1 form. Finally, a weight of 30% is given to an interview based around a legal problem question. Each exercise is assessed by different members of chambers, and a score of over 70% is required to be considered for tenancy, while a pupil getting 80% or above is unlikely to be turned away. It may seem harsh to judge someone based primarily on four exercises rather than their day-to-day work, but the pupil we spoke to saw the system's merits: *"It is fair and transparent and avoids the tendency for a set to pick members based on a personality match."* Pupils receive a lot of support in preparing for the exercises as well as time off to research and draft the written assessments. In 2014, both pupils took up tenancy with the set.

Doing good

We mustn't forget to mention that pro bono is a big thing at Cloisters. Its tenants are expected to do at least five days of unpaid work a year, *"but people do it because they want to and because it is interesting work,"* a baby junior said. Members can get involved with projects through FRU, the Bar Human Rights Committee, the Bar Pro Bono Unit and charities like Reprieve.

Sniffing the air at Cloisters, we found there was more than a whiff of egalitarianism about the place. *"It's not stuffy,"* a baby barrister said. *"All my friends are always disappointed that I can't dish the dirt on any Silk-style intrigues!"* That same baby barrister shared an office with a QC and a mid-ranking junior. We also noted that all members are listed on the website in alphabetical order rather than by seniority, and Cloisters is home to a higher proportion of female barristers than any other set in this year's *Student Guide*.

Furthermore, *"when you are new, people make an effort to talk to you at chambers drinks,"* the current pupil told us. Speaking of drinks, apparently *"some of the set's previous big drinkers have now had kids,"* so inebriation is not an obligatory part of life at Cloisters and *"there is no culture of presenteeism for pupils at social events."* But sometimes *"drinks are held for no particular reason"* and there's a *"fun Christmas party."*

And finally...

Shared interests among its members help make this set a strong one. *"Come to Cloisters – it's great,"* a junior said when we concluded our interview with them, giving the set a literal thumbs up.

The Bar

Crown Office Chambers

The facts

Location: Inner Temple, London
Number of QCs/juniors: 13/78 (24 women)
Applications: 150-200
Outside Pupillage Gateway
Pupils per year: 2-3
Seats: 2x3 and 1x6 months
Pupillage award: £50,000 + £10,000 guaranteed earnings
(can advance £15,000 for BPTC)

COC puts its pupils through an intense regime of assessments before they are considered for tenancy.

Pupils at the Bar's biggest common law set need to be the cat's pyjamas when it comes to advocacy – court appearances are customary in the second six.

It's health and safety gone mad

Overlooking the floral splendour of Inner Temple Gardens, Crown Office Chambers is *"going from strength to strength,"* according to senior managing clerk Andy Flanagan. COC was formed in 2000 by the merger of Two Crown Office Row and One Paper Buildings, *"both of which had quite a broad practice."* The result is the Bar's biggest common law set, a mighty prospect with 90 members.

The main areas of work are personal injury, health and safety, insurance, professional negligence, construction, product liability and clinical negligence. *"In 2011 we restructured our clerking team into groups that look after different practice areas,"* Andy Flanagan told us. *"This means we can align ourselves with our clients and it allows clerks to talk the talk as well as walk the walk."* Around 75% of instructions are on the defendant side. *"Another recent development has been that there is more commercial construction work coming into chambers,"* says Andy Flanagan.

The set is top ranked by *Chambers UK* for personal injury, health & safety and property damage work. Members are frequently involved in cases like *R v Lion Steel Equipment*, defending a director charged with gross negligence manslaughter after a factory worker fell to his death. And one senior junior recently represented Siemens after an employee at Harwich International Port was killed by a falling wind turbine blade during an attempt to move it from quayside to vessel. On the insurance side, members were involved in *AXN v Worboys*, which asked whether insurers were liable for damages because the crimes of 'black cab rapist' John Worboys were committed in his insured taxi. *"The lion's share of work comes from insurers' subrogation claims but that doesn't mean you're not representing a range of people or working on a variety of issues,"* explained a pupil. *"You could have to deal with a road traffic accident one day and property damage from a tree root the next. You can get insurance for just about everything – and if it's insurable you can argue about it in court!"*

Smooth talking

COC recruits two to three pupils every year. It operates outside the Pupillage Gateway and has its own online application form. *"The questions are pretty standard,"* recalled a current pupil. *"They ask about public speaking and work experience. You have to convey yourself in a succinct and clear way."* Stellar advocacy ability is crucial. *"We focus very much on advocacy during pupillage,"* says Patrick Blakesley, chair of the pupillage committee. *"Our pupils go to court a good deal in the second six, so they really do have to be fairly polished and mature performers from an early stage."* Another interviewee adds: *"The way we judge that from someone's CV is by looking for FRU or pro bono work, mooting, debating, or anything that's either client-facing or involves presenting something to a tribunal or judge of some description."*

The initial applications are filtered down to a first interview list of around forty. *"During my first interview, I was asked to explain a parliamentary system to a five-year-old,"* one pupil told us. *"It caught me off guard at first, but it's actually a good interview question because*

Chambers UK rankings

Clinical Negligence	Personal Injury
Construction	Product Liability
Health & Safety	Professional Negligence
Insurance	Property Damage
International Arbitration	

it allows you to demonstrate the skills needed to be a barrister, even if you haven't done a law degree." Approximately 12 to 14 candidates make it through to a second round of interviews, overseen by a panel of five barristers. Interviewees are given half an hour to prepare their views on a problem question such as an insurance issue.

On your toes

Pupils spend time with three supervisors. The first two seats last three months and the remaining six months are overseen by a final supervisor. *"You don't spend an even span of time with each supervisor because by the second six you're meant to be more independent and starting to become a self-employed practitioner,"* explained a pupil. There's an initial grace period of two months in which pupils aren't assessed. *"They appreciate that it's a baptism of fire and that you'll make mistakes. That's how you learn."*

Fledgling pupils often take on work that their supervisor has just completed. *"You have the opportunity to give it a try and then you'll get feedback straight afterwards – supervisors compare your work with theirs and tell you how to improve next time. It's very natural and not high-pressured. You don't get marks – they'll just sit with you and go through it."* Supervisors often have a roommate who'll also give work to a pupil, becoming *"like a quasi-supervisor."* The set makes sure that pupils see a broad spread of work. *"My first supervisor's practice was PI-orientated but his roommate was a construction specialist so I got a range of work from both,"* reported one interviewee.

From the start of the second six, pupils are on their feet in small claims trials and the like. *"Going to court so often absolutely distinguishes pupillage here,"* said one pupil. *"You have the opportunity to be in court all the time and so hopefully you'll be a confident advocate by the time you start tenancy. I've been up against people*

who are two or three years' call and they have been very complimentary of the pupils here, purely because we get so much experience in the second six." Natural talent for advocacy doesn't stop the first trial from being *"petrifying – I prepared the case within an inch of its life and then my appearance lasted all of two minutes. I thought, 'I've prepared for four days! What's wrong with you?! Let me show you my submissions!' Often as a pupil you'll be a lot younger than your lay client and the witnesses. You have to convince them that you're competent. It's nerve-racking because you want to do the job well."* In the second six especially, pupils are also encouraged to do written work for as many members as possible.

Shaken or stirred?

Starting two months in, pupils complete oral and written assessments which will inform the tenancy decision. First up are the advocacy assessments, in which pupils *"do things like applications before a panel. Afterwards they give you feedback on everything: whether you gesticulate too much, on the law – the whole nine yards."* Over time, these tests *"get more serious and harder. I had one before a High Court judge."* However, pupils remain sanguine about the process: *"It's a bit daunting but excellent practice for court."* As well as this, there are two to three written assessments which are blind marked. Pupils undertake these alongside their 'normal' duties. When it comes to the tenancy crunch, the pupillage committee *"only involves people in the decision-making process if they've had direct experience of pupils."* In 2014 both pupils were kept on.

Stepping into COC, we were impressed by the welcoming ambience, tasteful lithographs, soft coral carpet and suede tissue boxes (although we were disappointed not to spot Hunter the Inner Temple Garden cat on patrol outside). What do members and pupils have to say about the atmosphere? *"It's not particularly old-fashioned and definitely not stuffy,"* reported one. Instead of afternoon tea there are Friday drinks, which is *"basically a chambers cocktail night."* Pupils attested to the idea of COC's supportive atmosphere. *"The Bar can be off-putting for someone who is from a non-traditional background and is an ethnic minority like me,"* one pupil told us. *"I'd done mini-pupillages at more traditional sets where I perceived that it would be challenging to undertake pupillage. But here it's very friendly and open, and that's very important to me."*

And finally...

As well as good academics and talent as an advocate, this set is *"looking for people with extremely good interpersonal skills who will inspire confidence in their clients."*

The Bar

Essex Court Chambers

The facts

Location: Lincoln's Inn Fields, London
Number of QCs/juniors: 44/42 (13 women)
Applications: c.150
Apply through Pupillage Gateway
Pupils per year: Up to 4
Seats: 1x4 months + 3-week rotations
Pupillage award: £60,000 (can advance £20,000 for BPTC)

"Clients and solicitors don't want some brain in a room beavering away; they want someone who's going to roll up their sleeves and be part of a team."

The crème de la crème of the Commercial Bar congregates at Essex Court Chambers, where the work is wide-ranging and the members friendly.

Twenty years ago....

It was 1994. The Channel Tunnel opened, Tony Blair took the Labour Party reins, weekends took on new life thanks to the introduction of Sunday trading, and MI6 began its secret business in a new building on the banks of the Thames – all against a soundtrack of Brian Cox, now Britain's favourite physicist (BFPh), tinkling the keys for D:Ream. 1994 was also the year some major drama occurred at the London Bar. In an unprecedented move, commercial set Four Essex Court burst out of Temple, relocated to larger premises in Lincoln's Inn Fields and became known simply as Essex Court Chambers. Led by the mighty Gordon Pollock QC – who stepped down in 2013 after 21 years as head of chambers – the set grew to become the barristerial behemoth it is today. A bristling bunch of *Chambers UK* rankings, including top spots for commercial dispute resolution, civil fraud, international arbitration and public international law, attest to the elite status the set occupies in today's legal landscape.

Essex Court has a comprehensive spread of practices. *"Our first area of strength is general commercial work, which is a massive umbrella covering banking and finance, shipping, trade and commodities, and energy disputes,"* explains team leader Ben Perry. *"We also have bolt-ons to that like public international law and employment."* This breadth of work proved a big draw for the set's current pupils. *"I looked at Essex Court and just thought 'Wow! Look at all they do!' They cover pretty much any commercial sector work you could want."* Perry goes on to emphasise the *"huge amount of international work members take on – instructions come from every continent. Our members travel and appear in the Middle East, East Asia and Africa."* As you'd expect from a set of this stature, it's *"the blue-chip solicitors everyone's heard of"* – magic circlers plus big hitters like Ashurst and BLP – who instruct much of the time, though as Perry mentions, *"we also have relationships with provincial firms, which means juniors can cut their teeth on County Court stuff. It's important to us that they have access to advocacy."*

A major work highlight for Essex Court in recent years has been its members' involvement in a long-running €4.5bn dispute arising from the 2002 sinking of the 'Prestige' oil tanker off the coast of Galicia – the resultant oil spill caused the largest environmental disaster in Spanish and Portuguese history. Other high-profile cases of late include billionaire property mogul Robert Tchenguiz's huge damages claim against the Serious Fraud Office (SFO) after he and his brother were arrested in dawn raids back in 2011; a mega-dispute between three Ukrainian billionaires relating to the value of an iron ore company; and Russian financial group Otkritie's case against a former trader who defrauded the bank and distributed the money via a web of offshore accounts. The stolen dosh was spent on vintage Ferraris, luxury properties, jewellery and private jets – pretty high-octane stuff.

Nearly ripe advocates

The set takes up to four pupils each year. Academic excellence is high on the list of priorities when it comes to recruiting, as are *"tenacity, self-motivation and an ability to work as part of a team,"* says chair of the pupillage committee Claire Blanchard QC. The full list of objective criteria is available on Essex Court's website. Candidates apply through the Pupillage Gateway, and around 30 are invited for an interview – note there's only one. Interviewees are give a problem to look at for 45 min-

Chambers UK rankings

Banking & Finance	Fraud
Commercial Dispute Resolution	Insurance
Employment	International Arbitration
Energy & Natural Resources	Public International Law
	Shipping
	Tax

utes before being questioned by a panel of five who ask about the problem and try to gather additional evidence that the applicant satisfies the criteria above. *"The questions aren't scary – they don't try to upset you,"* current pupils said of the process. *"Rather it's about seeing how well you can reason and present. They want to see basic aptitude, not a fully formed advocate."* After this single interview, the set picks its newest batch of pupils.

"From the top to bottom of chambers you'll find people from a wide variety of backgrounds," Blanchard tells us. *"We absolutely do not seek out a specific type."* That said, as of July 2014, nine out of 11 of the most recently called members had a sparkling Oxbridge degree. For their part, a baby junior had this to say: *"A lot of people here have Oxbridge firsts, but there's definitely a determination to look outside of that."* In any case, *"personality is playing an increasingly bigger part in practice development,"* says Ben Perry. *"Clients and solicitors don't want some brain in a room beavering away; they want someone who's going to roll up their sleeves and be part of a team."* Additionally, he adds, *"commercial business sense is important – knowing when to give ground."*

Get ready to rota

Pupils spend their first four months with one supervisor. *"I helped out with whatever he was doing,"* recalled a junior. *"A week after I arrived there was a two-day shipping arbitration involving bills of lading – all quite mysterious to me at that stage. I interviewed some Nigerian witnesses over video link, which was quite fun, then went on to help out with some shipbuilding arbitrations and a massive insurance one. I wrote up some submissions and legal research, as well as an advice and a bit of pleading. I remember staying up till 11pm drafting submissions some nights. It was all very exciting!"*

After these initial months, which also include a training session on advocacy and conference skills, pupils should be *"at a baby junior standard"* in preparation for the next stage of their year – ominously entitled 'the rota'. *"Pupils spend three weeks at a time with members of different seniorities, including all the supervisors,"* explains Blanchard. This goes on for four to six months, and along the way pupils produce various pieces of work to be assessed, like advices and opinions. Afterwards *"all the people who've sat on the rota meet and make a recommendation as to whether a pupil should be offered tenancy."* Quite a big deal then.

"There was a bit of a myth about the rota as this horrendous experience," chuckled a baby junior who'd come out the other side, *"but funnily enough it isn't! It's gruelling in the way that practice can be gruelling, but it's doable, and you learn so much."* Alongside their assessed work, pupils attend conferences and court hearings. *"I came across so many different areas of law – shipping, insurance, commercial fraud, VAT, banking,"* said one. *"Knowing you're being assessed on it all can be quite stressful. You work hard. But you shouldn't be killing yourself. I found myself staying regularly until 8pm or 9pm."* For the remaining months of their pupillage, pupils either return to sit with their original supervisor, take up a spot alongside another member or scamper off on secondment. Note that pupils at Essex Court don't take on their own instructions until they're newly minted tenants. *"They want us to be as fully trained as possible and make all our mistakes now while we're still training."*

The social side of chambers life is relatively reserved. *"There's not that everybody going out for a drink after a day in court thing, but there are some very good friendships here."* There are weekly drinks gatherings and chambers lunches – we hear the latter is *"booming"* – though it can be hard to find time to attend both. *"There's a push to do things as a chambers, but ultimately we're a bunch of individuals rather than a corporate institution,"* summed up a junior. Apparently a choir is in the pipeline – watch this space. Sources went on to tell us that culturally speaking, *"we're not the poshest or the most institutional."* As one said, *"I thought I might have to act a certain way when I arrived, but I'm allowed to be my slightly kooky self. The fact that juniors can walk around like I do,"* they laughed, gesturing to a slightly rumpled shirt and trouser combo, *"is great."*

And finally...
In 2014 Essex Court made up three of five pupils to tenants.

The Bar

One Essex Court

The facts

Location: Middle Temple, London
Number of QCs/juniors: 32/56 (17 women)
Applications: c.200
Apply through Pupillage Gateway
Pupils per year: 5
Seats: 2x3 + 1x6 months
Pupillage award: £60,000 (can advance £20,000 for BPTC)

This top commercial set now offers a specialist IP pupillage too.

Top-of-the-tree commercial set One Essex Court is praised for its *"very good pupil supervision."* Only the best get a chance to sample its qualities.

In black and white

One Essex Court has spent the past half-century building up an extraordinarily strong reputation for high-end commercial work. One of the Bar's magic circle sets, it has grown membership by 25% in the past five years alone. The set's advocates remain a very popular choice for banks, businesses and investors of all kinds when resolving disputes.

Browse OEC's website and it's soon clear what its main areas of practice are. Low-angle shots of Canary Wharf, a share index and a wind farm loom large. Banking and finance, arbitration, civil fraud and energy are all key breadwinners, while the set also has a stash of specialists dealing with tax, competition, IP and insolvency disputes. Barristers often work with top City firms and *"direct instruction by in-house teams is increasingly prevalent,"* according to senior clerk Darren Burrows. *"In addition, the emergence of boutique litigation firms and international arbitration practices has provided a variety of new opportunities."*

Burrows also told us that 2013 was a record year for the set in revenue terms: *"We saw sustained periods of full engagement for all our members."* Or, as one member put it, *"everyone's been really busy making pots of money!"* The set's reputation and breadth of practice no doubt help a lot here. *"When your core practice is commercial disputes, you benefit from the broad umbrella of areas you can cover,"* says Burrows. OEC is also capitalising on London's increasing importance as an international disputes hub. To boost its international credentials, the set opened a representative office in Singapore in 2012. *"We do a huge amount of international work,"* one member observed.

One international dispute saw the set combine its expertise in energy and tax law: members acted for a subsidiary of Chiswick-based Tullow Oil on a $313m claim against Heritage Oil over unpaid tax liabilities in Uganda. The set has also been active on a large number of energy-related arbitrations. For example, three members acted for a Kuwaiti oil company in arbitration with Dow Chemical over whether Dow was entitled to claim damages after a failed merger between the two.

OEC's members act on a ton of disputes between banks and investors every year. A more unusual example saw Laurence Rabinowitz QC represent the Sisters of Charity of Jesus and Mary and other investors in a commercial case against Morgan Stanley over the loss of a $20m investment in a defunct German bank. Some clients are less saintly: one member is acting for newspaper proprietor Richard Desmond, who is suing Credit Suisse over a complex insurance swap investment contract. Members also frequently advise regulators like the FCA and Ofgem, sometimes going on secondments there too. And head of chambers Lord Grabiner was recently tapped by News Corporation to lead a £53m internal investigation in the wake of the phone-hacking scandal.

Purple prose

After an initial review of applications, approximately 50 applicants are invited in for a first interview. They are given a set of facts on a case, an analytical question and a copy of Chitty on Contracts, and get 90 minutes prep time. *"You are then asked to present your answer to the*

Chambers UK rankings

Banking & Finance	Energy & Natural Resources
Commercial Dispute Resolution	Fraud
Competition/European Law	Intellectual Property
	International Arbitration

interview panel, who challenge and cross-examine you," a pupil told us. The panel also asks some CV-based questions. The top 12 candidates go on to face a second-round interview.

By our count, around half of the present juniors under five years' call were Oxbridge undergraduates. To give you a further idea of their backgrounds, around one in three has a BCL, while a similar number studied overseas or worked (briefly) in academia. *"But we're not looking for a brain on a stick,"* a pupil supervisor said. *"We want persuasive advocates who can perform well in court and give focused commercial advice."* Another member added: *"If an applicant has a business background and it's relevant to the type of work we do, that could be advantageous. But if someone's background is not relevant to the job that doesn't count against them."*

Pupils sample all areas of practice during their year with the set. They spend time with three supervisors: two in the first six and one in the second. Each supervisor usually has a broad commercial practice, so pupils see a variety of cases during each seat. At present, pupils also have the option of completing a distinct IP seat. From 2014/15 onwards, OEC is offering a specialist IP pupillage alongside its four regular commercial slots. Applicants are given a different interview question and, although science or industry experience is not required, *"an interest and aptitude for IP"* is a must. It sounds like an interesting gig to us: the set's IP lawyers recently acted for M&S in its dispute with Interflora about Google search terms, and represented Cadbury in a case about the trade marking of its distinctive purple packaging.

Grabiner chance

From their first day, pupils work solely on active cases. *"They expect a lot of you from the start,"* a pupil said, *"but supervisors spend a lot of time getting you up to speed on their cases and they give good feedback."* Typical tasks in the first six include research, attending court and drafting skeleton arguments. From the off, pupils work for other members too. *"I met Lord Grabiner in my first week and was given the opportunity to shadow him in court,"* one pupil beamed. *"It was impressive to see him in action – being able to work with people like that is one of the reasons I came to this set."* Are working hours as long as the set's busy commercial vibe suggests? *"It varies,"* a pupil said. *"You're always going to be working from 9am to 6pm and that lengthens into the evening later in pupillage. And every hour you spend here is going to be quite intense and require a lot of brainpower."*

After six months, pupils are given an official review on their progress. There's no definite indication of whether tenancy is on the cards, but underperforming pupils are given a heads-up. In their second six, pupils get to spend time on their feet, appearing in small claims cases. *"We make a concerted effort to provide a steady stream of advocacy opportunities suitable for pupils and very junior members,"* says senior clerk Darren Burrows. Such cases may come from smaller provincial firms and are often RTAs or debt claims. *"My first case was an application to have a claim form extended,"* a pupil told us. *"It was in the High Court and in front of a judge, which I hadn't expected!"*

There are no advocacy or other exercises during pupillage. The tenancy decision is made by all members of chambers based on the three pupil supervisors' reports and score cards marking each piece of work done by a pupil for another member of chambers. In 2014 the set made tenants out of three of its five pupils.

As OEC is a fairly sizeable set, *"it's not the sort of place where members all rent a chalet and go on a skiing holiday together."* That said, on Fridays members often club together for lunch in halls and there are drinks in chambers at the end of the day. *"I usually go along as it's a good way to meet people,"* a pupil said, and there will often be *"cameo appearances"* from the top silks. A pupil told us that chambers *"isn't formal"* and *"you don't really notice the hierarchy,"* adding that *"at lunch in halls we'll have social conversations more than we have legal ones."* Members aren't required to buy into any prescriptive culture or traditions. *"I want to feel like I'm a member of a barristers chambers not a rugby club!"* said one.

And finally...

"Launching new junior tenants into practice is relatively straightforward when you have a strong position in the market, a high-quality product and a reputation for providing a first-class service," says OEC's senior clerk Darren Burrows.

5 Essex Court

The facts

Location: Middle Temple, London
Number of QCs/juniors: 6/40 (16 women)
Applications: 300
Apply through Pupillage Gateway
Pupils per year: 2
Seats: 3x4 months
Pupillage award: £25,000 + £15,000 guaranteed earnings

Offering a pupillage with plenty of live advocacy, 5 Essex Court has been instructed by the police in relation to Hillsborough, phone hacking, and the shooting of Mark Duggan.

While it will be no cakewalk securing a pupillage at this leading police law set, 5 Essex Court's impeccable retention rates and jovial atmosphere mean it's more than worth the effort.

Woop-woop! That's the sound of da police

According to senior clerk Mark Waller, the most important year in 5 Essex Court's recent history was 2004, when it switched from being a general common law set to being a purely civil set focused on police law. In the decade since, 5EC has kept its sights set on this area, winning a top-tier ranking from *Chambers UK* for ten years running. The set is instructed by virtually every police force in the country, with members appearing in an abundance of significant cases, inquests and inquires concerning law enforcement. Barristers have got their teeth into some high-profile matters, including the inquests into the Hillsborough disaster, the 7/7 bombings and the shooting of Jean Charles de Menezes. While work of this kind accounts for roughly two-thirds of the set's output, members are also active on employment, public law, personal injury and licensing matters.

Though it has an impeccable reputation, Mark Waller believes chambers would be foolhardy to rest on its laurels. There is currently a desire to develop the employment practice, with four new members welcomed into the mix from other sets in May 2014: Clare Harrington, Daniel Hobbs and Sarah Keogh hopped over from 13KBW, while Claire Palmer joined from Thomas More Chambers. Despite these new additions, 5EC has a very definite ceiling when it comes to numbers: no more than 45. *"Once you go beyond that,"* says Waller, *"you have to split the clerks' rooms. And once you split clerking, you split chambers."* This means any lateral recruitment is a careful and considered process – there is no inclination to stray from the *"small and boutique"* environment the set has cultivated. *"It's about bringing in barristers who are our kind of barrister,"* says Waller.

This ethos applies not only to those who have made their way in the profession, but also to those who've yet to make a mark. The set is very thorough in its search for new pupils, striving to find those it expects will flourish. *"That doesn't automatically mean they are the brightest person,"* says Waller. *"They might be someone outside the top 2% who has the right understanding of what our clients want."* Chair of the pupillage committee Jeremy Johnson QC agrees: *"You get people who sit there in interview and it's clear they have the best brain on the planet, but put them in court and they'd be bloody hopeless!"*

The interview process is therefore designed to get a glimpse into candidates' ability as advocates – *"challenging them in a way that will happen in court,"* according to Johnson. Those whose application forms pass muster – usually 30 or so – are invited to a first interview. Here they are given a problem question – often legal – *"to get them talking and for the panel to see how they analyse the problem."* Johnson adds: *"We're not looking for massive legal knowledge. We're looking for people who are good at communicating and structuring their thoughts."*

Only around ten applicants make it through to the second round. The scenario here is similar to the first interview but the set-up includes more in-depth legal questions. Candidates are expected to do some mock formal advocacy at this stage, with one member of the panel taking

Chambers UK rankings

Police Law	Professional Discipline

on the role of judge. Johnson explains: *"It's about seeing if a candidate can think on their feet, respond appropriately and be engaging in a persuasive manner."* He says no applicant would ever be shouted at, but *"they're not treated any differently than they would be by a benign but interventionist judge."* Clearly the system is working well: 5 Essex Court claims to have offered tenancy to every single one of its pupils for the past 14 years, and it kept on its single pupil in 2014.

Mistakes are the portals of discovery

Up to two pupils are taken on each year and they spend four months with three different supervisors. Each is usually focused on a different area of law – eg police, employment, public law – while juniors are also encouraged to work for other members of chambers throughout the year. *"It gives you a great insight into the spread of matters that come in,"* a pupil told us.

While the first six can be *"very demanding if your supervisor has a busy practice,"* expect the pressure to ramp up even more during the second. *"You have to juggle continuing to work for your supervisor with taking on cases yourself and building up a practice as best you can,"* remarked a baby junior. *"It's a big step up, mainly in terms of time management."* These demands are offset by the opportunity to get on your feet once or twice a week. *"It's just lower level court work to get you into the swing of things,"* a pupil reports. *"But it did get me really interested in the work I was doing."* Licensing work for TfL, civil orders for the police and a number of one-day applications were just some of things rookies delved into. Pupils also have the chance to do in-house work for police forces or personal injury firms.

There are no formal assessments during pupillage, but each piece of work pupils do plays at least some role in the tenancy decision. *"Everything is taken into account,"*

says Jeremy Johnson. *"But we all make mistakes – now if it was some gross ethical mistake, that would be difficult to get over. But if you were just out of your depth on a case or made the wrong judgement call, then we are much more interested in how you reacted to the problem. If you dealt with things maturely and responsibly, then sometimes mistakes can actually count in your favour."* Pupil supervisors submit a report of their underling to Johnson, who will also collect feedback from other members, the clerks and (on occasion) instructing solicitors. Pupils put forward an application for tenancy with two pieces of written work attached, so those members they haven't worked for can give their view too.

Dressed for the occasion

When we asked about day-to-day life at 5EC, we began to worry as interviewees started rolling out fluffy clichés about chambers being *"friendly"* and *"unstuffy."* Yet there were a few things we noticed during our visit which made us willing to believe these pretty words. First, our host for the day, junior junior Jonathan Dixey, took to the role with charm and gusto, taking the time to personally introduce us to every member present on the day of our visit. Considering he was merely standing in for the wonderfully enthusiastic yet court-ridden Georgina Wolfe (who was *"gutted"* she couldn't meet us), this spoke volumes about the set's camaraderie and amiable environment.

Something else that caught our attention was that at 5EC you don't need to be a big-name star of the Bar to be treated with the utmost respect. *"One of the cleaners, Vera, is just as much a part of chambers as anyone else,"* a pupil told us cheerfully. *"She's been here for about 30 years now and pretty much everyone is going to join the celebrations for her 70th birthday. It's going to be a wonderful party and she has a very nice dress to wear!"* Unstuffy? Sounds like it to us. But we'll let Jeremy Johnson have the last word: *"Well, I think we're a pretty relaxed set. At least, that's my justification for not wearing a suit and tie,"* he says, looking down at his jeans and what could charitably be described as an 'old' T-shirt he was wearing. *"Sorry – it's not a court day."*

And finally...

Pupils noted that 5 Essex Court has *"a good reputation in terms of gender and diversity."* Fiona Barton QC is head of chambers and *"you notice the presence of women across the generations; there's no sudden drop-off at age 30."*

The Bar

Thirty Nine Essex Street

The facts

Location:

Number of QCs/juniors: 40/86 (36 women)

Number of applications: 360

Apply through Pupillage Gateway

Pupils per year: Up to 4

Seats: 3x4 months

Pupillage award: £52,500 (can advance £12,500 for BPTC)

With a whopping 126 members, Thirty Nine Essex Street is London's biggest barristers' chambers.

The variety on offer at this all-rounder is ideal for those who want to maintain broad interests at the start of their career.

What's in a name?

"Thirty Nine Essex Street runs a slick, 21st-century outfit," a recent pupil told us. Indeed, nothing seems to stand in the way of progress for this business-driven chambers. An influx of 25 barristers from 4-5 Gray's Inn in 2012 made it the largest London-headquartered set. The opening of a Singapore office in 2013 saw it tap into the Asian market, and its opening of another in Kuala Lumpur in 2014 will make it the first UK chambers to have a branch in Malaysia. At home, rapid growth has posed certain issues: *"We've outgrown our current space,"* CEO David Barnes tells us. *"We're moving out of our three buildings around Essex Street to modern offices in Chancery Lane next year and are looking forward to having somewhere more fit for purpose."*

Propping up these new premises will be the set's four core practice areas: civil liability; public law; environmental and planning; and commercial, regulatory and construction. According to Barnes, the barristers from 4-5 Gray's Inn have really beefed up the set's financial services expertise of late, and the planning team has also grown: following a lull in UK development during the recession, its barristers are now busy on cases surrounding developments such as HS2.

Pupils spend a seat in each of the core areas, and while that might sound an awful lot like a solicitor's training contract, a current pupil was quick to stress that *"although the structure is similar, the role you play is very much that of the traditional pupil."* Being assigned two supervisors per seat (three in CRC) means *"you can ask for work from either and really follow where your interests lie. You get to know other members as well."*

From falls to floods

Pupillage follows a natural curve as *"expectations change and your work improves in quality."* Pupils are generally eased in *"with relatively simple document sifting, research and writing of legal notes."* In the second six, pupils are given cases to manage themselves – usually between ten and 20 overall. Recent pupils have taken road traffic accident matters, contractual disputes and negligence cases to the county and small claims courts, and one even donned robes to present an appeal and costs argument in the High Court.

The civil liability seat revolves mostly around clinical negligence matters. A current pupil was asked to draft a skeleton argument for a case concerning a 22-year-old tree surgeon rendered paraplegic after a fall in National Trust grounds. *"They're very generous here and from early on expose you to everything they can."* Interviewees found public law fascinating, having drafted legal submissions for the Special Immigration Appeals Commission and helped on terrorism cases. One had drafted a summary grounds for resisting the admission of two US anti-Islamic speakers into the country (it was believed they planned to attend an EDL march protesting the death of soldier Lee Rigby), and had conducted research on the legality of the badger cull.

The environmental and planning seat has seen one recent pupil travel around the country visiting wind farms, and given another the chance to do some pro bono work. The latter involved assisting conservation charity Save Britain's Heritage in a campaign to stop parts of Smithfield Market being demolished for conversion to office blocks – a development proposal which Eric Pickles subse-

Chambers UK rankings

Administrative & Public Law	Environment
Civil Liberties & Human Rights	Immigration
	International Arbitration
Clinical Negligence	Local Government
Construction	Personal Injury
Costs Litigation	Planning
Court of Protection	Product Liability
Energy & Natural Resources	Professional Discipline
	Professional Negligence
	Tax

quently rejected. In the CRC seat pupils can experience a spread of work, though one noted that *"it's easier to get involved in construction disputes since other cases are just so huge."* That same pupil had done research for a case concerning a flood in a block of flats that was heard in the Court of Appeal. *"It brought up an interesting legal point about how contractual indemnity works, since two parties had independently contributed to the damage – a real life manifestation of the old conundrum, 'if two guys shoot a man at exactly the same time, which one is to blame for his death?'"*

The 39 steps to success

The set is *"ultimately looking to recruit advocates,"* says David Barnes. For Barnes, this involves having a personality. *"We want people who are strong academically but also personable, who have wider interests. Whether arts, films or sport, we just like to see that candidates can speak passionately about something other than law."*

Gateway applications are blind sifted, and 50 or 60 are invited in for a first-round interview. Roughly 15-20 make it beyond the first panel to a second and final interview. *"You're pushed and challenged,"* pupils told us, though they also conceded that it's *"an interviewee-friendly set-up where you get chance to show the best of yourself."* The set also offers a mini-pupillage programme, which, though no necessity, Barnes does encourage candidates to apply for since the set looks for those *"who have spent time getting a feel for the Bar and the different areas of work on offer."*

Every piece of work pupils submit is assessed and fed back on, culminating in mid and end-of-seat reviews. Grades are awarded on the basis of an interplay between *"intellectual ability, expressional skills, interpersonal skills, an interest in the work of chambers, and any interests outside the law."* One pupil had been surprised to hear their weekend dog-walking stint and work with an orangutan charity in Borneo had sneaked their way into their performance review. *"They want to make sure you're not completely bookish and do have a life outside of work."*

Two formal written assessments also feed into the tenancy decision. These are *"almost always an opinion on a live issue that's come into chambers"* and are marked by silks. They're considered pretty tough but are *"used as a checking mechanism more than anything – if you're on the edge it can tip the decision in your favour,"* a recent pupil told us. Performance in a formal advocacy assessment in June is also taken into consideration. For this, pupils complete two training exercises *"to make sure we feel prepared,"* and then use their acquired skills to present something such as an interim injunction.

Lockout

39 enforces a strict Monday to Friday, 9am-6pm policy. *"We're not given a key to chambers and have no access to our e-mails outside those hours,"* a pupil confirmed. Every other week, a member sponsors a lunch in chambers which everyone is invited to, and drinks are held on Thursdays of the alternate week. *"These are all really enjoyable and friendly,"* a pupil told us, *"and there are e-mails shooting round all the time with invites to lunch or the Edgar Wallace after work."*

Though this set is a slicker operation than most chambers, the culture has remained down to earth. Everyone's on first-name terms, and the fact that pupils aren't competing for limited tenancies means they can become *"incredibly close."* *"They don't offer pupillages unless there's room for pupils to stay on,"* sources told us.

And finally...

All three pupils were kept on this year, contributing to the set's outstanding retention record. Over the past six years, Thirty Nine Essex Street has taken on 17 of the 19 pupils it trained.

The Bar

Falcon Chambers

The facts

Location: : Fleet Street, London
Number of QCs/juniors: 9/28 (9 women)
Number of applications: 100
Outside Pupillage Gateway
Pupils per year: Up to 2
Seats: 4x3 months
Pupillage award: £60,000 (can advance £20,000 for BPTC)

"Chambers makes a big effort not to pit pupils against each other. If you're good enough, there's space for you to stay."

This specialist set sits proudly at the top of the tree for property law.

Paragon Falcon

It's easy to miss Falcon Chambers during a casual trot through Fleet Street, nestled as it is down a narrow passageway between a Starbucks and a sushi shop. Despite its discreet roosting place, this set holds a distinctly lofty position within the legal market. Over the years it's maintained a reputation as the top-flight chambers for property law, netting premier spots in the *Chambers UK* rankings for real estate litigation and agriculture and rural affairs.

All of Falcon's 37 members are experts in landlord and tenant work, and cover commercial, agricultural and residential matters. Members also handle associated areas like restrictive covenants, property-related insolvency law, and professional negligence of solicitors and surveyors. Within this scope, certain senior members have particular métiers – Barry Denyer-Green, for example, literally wrote the book on the niche subject of the law of commonhold and of town and village greens.

Although chambers doesn't stray out of the property sphere, our sources emphasised the sheer breadth of its practice. *"Our clients range from the little old lady in a boundary dispute with a farmer to some of the largest commercial landlords in the business."* Instructions too come from a variety of sources, including *"in-house lawyers at pension funds, property investors and surveyors, magic circle and top City solicitors, big regional firms, and even one-man bands out in the regions."*

Of late, Falcon's silks have undertaken a case concerning the ownership of a huge, multimillion-pound steel plant in Kent, acted for Heathrow Airport in disputes with a pension fund and airline over parking rights, and helped a Swiss private bank possess a stately pile from a debt-plagued English aristocrat. *"Within my first few weeks here, I went on site visits to a megamillion-pound home in the West End and a grotty little shed somewhere with a tree growing through it. We get a lot of high-value work that can be heard about in the press, but even the low-value work about bits of land can be just as interesting in terms of the law involved,"* noted a junior. Another proclaimed: *"The value of a claim does not reflect its difficulty here. One of my most complex cases was worth £5,000. Some of the most boring cases are worth millions. That's the nature of property."*

No eggheads in this basket

Falcon recruits up to two pupils a year. It operates outside the Pupillage Gateway and has its own application form. These are anonymised during the initial sift. *"We take away the back sheet with the information about equality and diversity so that only the merits of the applicant are assessed,"* explains pupillage committee secretary Kester Lees. Inevitably, *"we look for academic excellence as a general rule,"* with recruiters appraising candidates' individual marks rather than overall grades to identify those with a record of consistent achievement. *"We have a high degree of people who are non-lawyers academically – it's not so much the subject that's important as how people have done in it."*

Of course, it's no use being royally clever but socially inept. *"Our area is very academically rigorous, but we don't just want a bunch of eggheads who can't communicate,"* stresses Lees. *"Communication is this business through and through. In property it's important to be someone who can get on with all sorts of people and*

Chambers UK rankings

Agriculture & Rural Affairs	Real Estate Litigation

empathise with clients." A pupil confirmed: *"I'm quite a sociable person, and I didn't want to do a commercial pupillage in which I'd only deal with banking clients. I wanted to meet real people, and that's the great thing about working here – you could act for a massive supermarket or equally deal with a bunch of neighbours in a block of flats who don't get along."*

Beyond exam results, the set searches for *"all the obvious traits one would expect to see from a decent applicant, like debating or mooting experience – it's rare that a successful applicant wouldn't have at least one or both of those on their CV,"* says Lees. Recruiters also keep an eye out for mini-pupillages. Although it's not necessary for applicants to have completed a mini at Falcon itself, a stint *"here or at one of our competitor sets shows someone is making an informed choice,"* Lees tells us. *"We're pre-eminent in our field and keen to add to that by recruiting people genuinely interested in our work. It's important to see applicants are at the very least interested in chancery work."*

Out of approximately 100 applicants, around 15 are selected for a first-round interview. This lasts roughly 20 minutes and is *"CV and reasoning-based."* Six or seven return for a lengthier and *"more probing"* second interview with a panel of six members. Beforehand, candidates are given time to look at a problem that's *"usually of a legal nature but designed so that those studying the GDL aren't at a disadvantage."* A pupil recalled: *"I was asked to present an argument either for or against something. When I went in, they grilled me on my view and then asked me to argue the opposing view."* After the second round is done and dusted, Falcon's fledglings are chosen.

Happy raptors

Pupils start their year with a week-long course on landlord and tenant law, then spend three months each with four supervisors. *"During my first seat I did everything my supervisor did,"* said a pupil. *"If she got a set of pa-*

pers and was in court the next day, then I'd work on a copy of them too. We compared advocacy so I could see why certain things do and don't work. It was the same with opinions – we'd both write it, and she'd give me feedback. We even had mock teleconferences so I could practise giving advice to a solicitor!"* Given the vertiginous learning curve, this initial stint is *"given less weight than others with respect to the tenancy decision."* According to our sources, a pupil's second and third seats generally involve opinion writing, drafting orders, researching points and watching their supervisor in court, plus the the chance to shadow junior members. Along the way are several advocacy training sessions.

During their second six, pupils are on their feet tackling possession hearings – *"the bread and butter of the junior end."* These could be *"against tenants for rent arrears, mortgage borrowers for non-payment or squatters who've taken over industrial estates or houses."* Pupils still remain partially under their supervisor's wing, though. *"We're keen that pupils continue to do work for their supervisor so they can be trained and assessed prior to the tenancy decision,"* Lees says. The moment of truth occurs in July when, having received reports from supervisors, the pupillage committee makes a recommendation that's then taken to a full chambers meeting.

The Chancery Bar is sometimes perceived as a bit on the stuffy side, but our interviewees at Falcon were keen to quash this perception. *"I was quite worried about that. When I set my mind to chancery I thought 'hmm that might not work, because I'm not that type of person!'"* chuckled a pupil. *"But actually it's extremely friendly – honestly! It's sort of like a family environment."* There's a daily afternoon tea – *"all talk of work is banned"* – and we hear members and pupils get together for lunch most days in the library. And on Fridays there's a tasty catered lunch for everyone. *"We're a very collegial set and proud of that,"* states Lees. *"Actually, I can't think of anyone who's left chambers to go elsewhere – other than in a coffin! Or to become a judge or retire."* One pupil offered this as further evidence of the set's lack of pomp: *"What struck me was that quite a lot of people go round chambers with no shoes on. I think that puts paid to any idea that it's stuck up or old school!"* Fortunately, for everyone's sake, *"socks are kept on. I haven't seen any toes – yet."*

The Bar

And finally...
In 2014 Falcon added two more to the flock, awarding tenancy to both of its pupils.

Fountain Court Chambers

The facts

Location: Middle Temple, London
Number of QCs/juniors: 29/39 (11 women)
Applications: c.175
Apply through Pupillage Gateway
Pupils per year: Up to 4
Seats: 3x4 months
Pupillage award: £60,000

"There is a degree of humility among people here. It's not brash and grandiose – everyone is very grounded and conscientious."

This leading light of the Commercial Bar offers a pupillage described in three words: *"challenging, stimulating, rewarding."*

He is a genius, a philosopher, an abstract thinker. He has a brain of the first order.

On a beautifully sunny day in May we journeyed to Fountain Court Chambers, reluctantly bypassing the barbecues burning in Temple Gardens on the way. As resplendent as the day itself was senior clerk Alex Taylor, bedecked in a black and gold pinstripe suit. *"We've always been at the cutting edge of the Commercial Bar,"* says Taylor, who's headed up the clerking team since 2008 (but clearly been at the cutting edge of fashion for a while longer). Fountain boasts a *"rich heritage,"* and previous members include former High Court Judge Sir Melford Stevenson and former Law Lord Leslie Scarman. The set has been home to the late Tom Bingham (who became Lord Chief Justice) while Lord Falconer of Thoroton and Lord Goldsmith both practised here before moving into politics. *"They're all big claims to fame,"* concludes Taylor, *"and a good demonstration of what this chambers is about."*

Fountain Court's members are frequently instructed on matters regarding aviation, banking and finance, commercial litigation, fraud, financial services, insurance/reinsurance, professional negligence and employment. In the first four areas it particularly flourishes (each is *Chambers UK Bar* top-ranked), but Taylor estimates that 50% of the set's output is banking and finance-related. Take this year's Alpstream case, where head of chambers Stephen Moriarty QC and Rosalind Phelps represented PK AirFinance in defence of a conspiracy action brought by Russian oligarch Alexander Lebedev's aircraft leasing business. *"It might be considered an aviation case,"* states Taylor, *"but some would say it was finance as it involved leases; you've also got some insurance slung in there as well. Quite a number of our cases are multifaceted in that sense."*

Fount of all knowledge

Up to three pupils are welcomed into Fountain Court each year. A new supervisor is assigned every three months, although pupils reconvene with their initial master for the concluding period. The first quarter of the year is non-assessed, and rookies work almost exclusively for their pupilmaster. *"We see it as a bedding-down period where they have a chance to make their mistakes and actually learn,"* says member of the pupillage committee James McClelland. Rebecca Loveridge, called in 2011, told us that pupils team up with another two supervisors for the middle six months. *"They are generally more responsible for organising your work at this point as you're trying to work with as many different members as possible."* McClelland concurs: *"Pupilmasters almost take on the job of a clerk. They have to solicit work that will be suitable from other members."*

There are no formal assessments, but each piece of work a newbie undertakes during this period is reviewed by the member they've collaborated with. McClelland informs us: *"The reviews are collected by the pupillage committee, who will ultimately reach a tenancy decision in reference to those and in discussion with the pupilmasters."* The committee will make a recommendation to chambers as a whole and that recommendation is *"almost always adopted."*

Chambers UK rankings

Aviation	Insurance
Banking & Finance	International Arbitration
Commercial Dispute Resolution	Product Liability
Financial Services	Professional Discipline
Fraud	Professional Negligence

This is indicative of how Fountain Court operates: *"We have committees responsible for the different functions within chambers, and they are predominantly run with a degree of autonomy,"* says McClelland. For example, the pupillage committee is not governed by the head of chambers. This ensures fairness is maintained when pupils are appraised.

The set goes to *"great pains"* to make sure pupils are given tasks that accurately inform members of their aptitude in each. *"We get them doing live pieces of work, not some artificial exercise,"* says McClelland. *"I've been doing skeleton arguments and other live pieces of work since my first months,"* a pupil said. *"It's not like you get half way through and only then are unleashed on pleadings."*

Advocacy, however, is not something to anticipate until you've been granted tenancy. *"Once you're taken on you have to learn a lot of things yourself, so it's nice to make the most of the opportunity of sitting in someone's room and seeing the day-to-day business of being a barrister. Observing is so useful and you never get that chance again."* That said, a pupil told us: *"Although I haven't presented in court I have attended frequently. It's a great way to learn – you see how your work plays out and what becomes important when the case gets to court."*

Fountain of youth

This is a set that pushes its residents to build amiable relationships with one another, and this starts right from the bottom rungs. By avoiding formal testing *"pupils can never be compared directly"* – a *"deliberate strategy,"*

according to Loveridge. *"It allows you to develop relationships with the other pupils in a non-competitive environment, as no one can say 'I've done better than you'. You're really encouraged to be friendly with them, go to lunch on a Friday and generally support one another."* McClelland recognises these traits as an important factor in why he signed on: *"It seems superficial, but I have been totally vindicated,"* he says. *"I'm now ten years' call and one thing I really value about chambers is that it has a supportive and friendly atmosphere. For example, I am now a godfather to one of my own pupilmaster's children."* He concludes: *"I don't mean this in a breast-beating way, but there is a degree of humility among people here. It's not brash and grandiose – everyone is very grounded and conscientious."*

Thus while FC was described as *"members-led,"* the role of the clerks was never understated. *"There is a very important, symbiotic relationship between the two,"* relays McClelland. Rebecca Loveridge adds: *"The clerks are excellent, well respected and everyone recognises the work they put in on our behalf."* Alex Taylor also sees no evidence of a fault line: *"It's not clerks and members – it's Fountain Court and we all represent that."*

Chambers has taken on 11 new tenants in the last three years and only one lateral hire for the set in eight years. Organic growth is clearly prioritised – two out of three pupils were retained in 2014 – but candidates must stack up to the requisite standard: *"The brand of Fountain Court should be strong enough to convince people there are no weak links,"* remarks Taylor. From the 2015 application round, a three-day mini-pupillage will form part of the application process. *"We want to have a more focused opportunity to consider the merits of candidates rather than purely by way of interviews."* Traditionally applicants have had to negotiate two interviews: the first a discussion of their application, followed by an analytical question that forces them to think on their feet; during the second, candidates are given a legal problem to consider before discussing it with the pupillage committee. Now a shorter first-round interview – akin to the one employed now – is used to earmark candidates for the mini itself.

And finally...

This set may have a long and decorated history, but it's not rigidly traditional. Afternoon tea is not a staple of life here, but *"cake does get put out in the kitchen every day at about 4pm."*

The Bar

Government Legal Service (GLS)

The facts

Location: London

Number of barristers: 411

Applications (solicitor and barrister route): 3,000+

Outside Pupillage Gateway

Pupils per year: 5-10

Seats: 2x6 or 3x4 months

Pupillage award: £32,000-£40,000. Plus BPTC fees and a £7,000 maintenance grant

On chambersstudent.co.uk...
The GLS's application process
More on government departments

If you're looking for advisory work of national importance, job security, favourable hours and a wide-reaching practice, the GLS is the place for you.

The rule of law

For many, the idea of a career at the independent Bar conjures up images of fame, fortune and fulfilment. The reality though can be very different – long periods without regular work, horrendous hours when a case finally comes through and no formal holiday allowance. No wonder the Government Legal Service gets 3,000 applicants each year for its solicitor and barrister training programmes – it offers stability, security, hours that won't kill you and a fascinating array of work. Junior barristers at the GLS work on everything from prisoners' rights to Welsh devolution to EU directives. *"Having the chance to advise central government on policies that shape the whole country is incredible,"* insiders agreed.

"I came here because I'm into law and politics; this is where the two meet and it's the only place you can really do both," said one source when asked about their reasons for choosing the GLS. *"The competitiveness of the independent Bar was a bit of a turn-off for me and I love the security that comes with working for the government."* So who gets in here? *"They want to see that you have certain skills, and that you're persuasive both orally and verbally,"* one interviewee observed, speaking of the competency-based application process (head over to our website for the full lowdown). We also heard that many successful applicants have previous experience: *"I noticed at the assessment day that there were very few young people there – it's not like everyone has come straight from uni."*

At the time of our research there were eight pupil barristers at the GLS: four at the Treasury Solicitor's Department (TSol), two at Business, Innovation & Skills (BIS), one at HMRC and one at the Home Office. TSol advises a plethora of government departments, including the Ministry of Defence (MoD), the Department for Transport (DfT), the Ministry of Justice (MoJ) and the Cabinet Office, while juniors at HMRC or BIS are (usually) tied to that department. After the year of pupillage ends, GLS juniors spend two years as 'legal officers', before shooting up the payscale again to become Grade 7 lawyers.

Decent exposure

During the course of their first year at the GLS, pupils are despatched for six months to one of the big London sets to work on public law matters. At the time of our calls there were GLS pupils at Monckton, Landmark, Thirty Nine Essex Street, Blackstone and 11KBW. *"It was a fantastic experience,"* one junior said of their time in chambers. *"I picked up some great experience and worked closely with a couple of QCs. Ultimately though, I came back to the GLS sure that I'd made the right decision to train here."* Something to bear in mind: if standing up in court defending the honour of your client is your goal, pupillage at the GLS probably isn't for you. *"Anyone coming here looking for tons of oral advocacy will inevitably be disappointed – it's pretty rare. You're much more likely to be doing advisory work,"* insiders agreed.

A junior who'd spent time in TSol's public law litigation team told us: *"I was running smaller cases myself; for example, judicial reviews brought by prisoners against the MoJ. I was involved in some seriously high-profile matters too, including litigation brought against the MoD in the wake of the wars in Iraq and Afghanistan. I was given plenty of responsibility but there was always someone to turn to when I needed supervision."*

The Bar

The Attorney General's Office – described as *"a small legal service unto itself"* – provides direct advice to government ministers and oversees a lot of the work done by the Crown Prosecution Service. Interviewees who'd spent time there reported working on Crown Court sentences that were considered unduly lenient, and working closely with both the Attorney General and his deputy, the Solicitor General, the two most senior lawyers in government. *"It's not unusual for you to meet with them once a week and give them briefings,"* said one interviewee. *"I found it incredibly nerve-racking to begin with, particularly when they were asking me to discuss the finer points of my work. That said, it's also very exciting!"*

Pupils at BIS often get stuck into its prosecution work. The criminal offences the department deals with include fraudulent trading, undischarged bankruptcy and failure to keep proper accounting records. Said one source: *"There's immediate responsibility – you're not just an understudy. The day I arrived there were five cases on my desk! We decide whether or not to prosecute and if we do you'll be involved in writing out the charges. There are also chances to do advocacy in the Crown Court from time to time – that's great. You come up against a lot of perjury and undisclosed assets, as well as dodgy business dealings and falsified documents – it's very interesting work."*

Tax to the max

Over at HMRC, the enforcement and insolvency litigation seat involves *"seriously complex and high-value cases – none of it is run of the mill. We're chasing unpaid tax bills and getting companies shut down on a daily basis."* Juniors spoke of drafting statements, instructing counsel and even running their own hearings. *"You're left to run cases yourself; I loved the level of trust,"* one source said. For those in the personal tax seat there's advisory and litigious work on offer. *"You're helping on work that affects an awful lot of people,"* we heard. Like what? *"I was drafting bits of secondary legislation on income tax, National Insurance and statutory sick pay."*

When we asked our sources about their time in chambers, we were told: *"They treat you as if you're one of their own pupils. The experience itself is certainly worthwhile – you learn a lot about drafting, preparing documents and going to court. I also found that a lot of the actual law that I learnt there was relevant to the work I was given when I got back to TSol."* A second source added: *"I was drafting advices and witness statements, doing research tasks and attending meetings on some seriously big cases. It's useful to spend time with a set because you get an idea of how the independent Bar works; you see the pressure external counsel is under and you make good contacts!"*

Besides the varied exposure it offers to the world of law, favourable office hours are another perk that comes with being a junior lawyer with the GLS. Sources we spoke to said that a standard day is 9.30am to 6pm. *"It's not like at the independent Bar – there's never any pressure to stay,"* one source said, while another added: *"I've had to work late from time to time but I've never had to stay as late as midnight or anything."*

All this leaves a good amount of time for socialising. *"We're a tight-knit bunch and we go out quite a lot with others across the GLS, as well as the staff in our department."* We heard about a weekend away in Snowdonia and trips to museums and galleries, as well as the usual pub and restaurant outings. Still, don't expect lavish corporate Christmas parties at the Dorchester or any of the trimmings that come with a job in the private sector. Government expenses are on a tight leash at the moment, so office budgets for social events and other activities are close to non-existent.

The broad opportunities for career development were also seen as an excellent benefit. *"There's a wealth of opportunity – you can move between departments at any time once you're qualified and that doesn't mean staying in London – people have gone to work in Strasbourg, Brussels and New York,"* said one source.

And finally...

"There's a real sense that this is a job for life. The GLS wants you to make your career here and they're not trying to burn you out. There's constant care."

The Bar

1 Hare Court

The facts

Location: Temple, London
Number of QCs/juniors: 11/30 (19 women)
Applications: 84
Outside Pupillage Gateway
Pupils per year: 2
Seats: 3x4 months
Pupillage award: £35,000

A specialist among specialists, 1 Hare Court's work is all about the D-word: divorce.

You can't choose your family, but you can choose this outstanding family law set with a *"family-esque"* atmosphere.

Kramer vs Kramer

Senior clerk Steve McCrone sat down with us and cast his mind back 20 years. *"When I first started in chambers,"* he mused, *"1 Hare Court used to do all kinds of family work. While we still do some children and legal aid cases at the bottom end, about 90% of our work is now ancillary relief."* This strand of family law – also known as 'matrimonial finance' – focuses on the divvying up of assets in divorce settlements. And *Chambers UK* awards 1 Hare Court a top-tier ranking for this type of work.

"There are a lot of eminent silks here," observed one junior, *"and family cases you read about in the press or the law reports often have 1 Hare Court members involved."* For example, in 2013 Richard Todd QC and Stephen Trowell represented Mrs Prest in the landmark *Petrodel v Prest* Supreme Court case. In their wisdom, the seven sitting justices ruled it is possible to 'pierce the corporate veil' – ie, that a divorcing spouse can stake a claim on their hubby's or wifey's assets, even if they are held in the name of a company. Todd was also active on the 2010 *Radmacher v Granatino* case, which pitted him against then fellow 1HCer and now High Court judge Nicholas Mostyn and upheld the legitimacy of prenups. More recently Nichola Gray was instructed on *Lawrence v Gallagher*, the first ever civil partnership division of assets case to reach the Court of Appeal.

Over the last few years the set has seen a significant increase in its international work. Steve McCrone told us members have recently been active on cases involving assets in the Cayman Islands, Gibraltar, Hong Kong, Singapore and the British Virgin Islands.

Think of the children!

Pupils spend four months each with three supervisors. *"It's a good amount of time,"* said one interviewee. *"You can see their practice, and they can see your skills, but after four months you feel like you're ready to move on to the next supervisor to show them what you've learnt."* Rookies are also encouraged to seek out work from other members. A baby junior recalled: *"If my supervisor was quiet, I would go and knock on doors or ask the clerks to see if anyone was going to court that day."*

Because of chambers' specialism in financial remedies, pupils' work consists mainly of preparing asset schedules, chronologies and research notes. In addition, we heard *"even early on you might be able to have a stab at the first draft of a skeleton argument."* In the second six the workload ramps up as pupils take on their own cases. *"That obviously changes the dynamic, as your own work is prioritised over helping your supervisor,"* one source said. During this period they can expect to be in court *"one or two times a week."* While big-money cases keep more senior members busy, pupils and baby juniors cut their teeth on children work – child abduction cases, for example – or domestic violence and cohabitation claims. *"It's all very interesting stuff and a great way to get court experience."* Two non-assessed advocacy exercises before the pupillage committee are thrown in to help pupils prepare.

When it comes to the tenancy decision, pupils make an application to the tenancy committee, complete with examples of their work and references from supervisors, other members, instructing solicitors or judges they've marshalled for. The decision is *"based more on the over-*

Chambers UK rankings

Family/Matrimonial

all impression of your work rather than assessment of every single thing you do." A final assessed advocacy exercise and interview before the tenancy committee round off the process. Pupillage committee member Rachel Spicer tells us: *"The final interview and exercise are fairly crucial. The decision is made on that day, and inevitably we look at how someone performs under pressure sitting in front of us."*

1 Hare Court used to take on three pupils, but from 2013 upped its pupillage award and lowered its intake to two per year. The initial plan was to offer tenancy to one of these two and then welcome outside applicants, but both of the set's pupils were in fact retained in 2014. Rachel Spicer told us this reflects a general change in outlook. *"The plan for the future is that the first two advocacy exercises will play a more formal role in the assessment process,"* she says. *"The reason for the change is that in the first instance we will now be looking to recruit tenants from our own pupils rather than looking externally."*

We are family

Chambers is not part of the Pupillage Gateway; applicants must send in a handwritten covering letter and CV to impress. *"We like the idea of having a covering letter specifically addressed to us,"* says Spicer. *"It gives us an opportunity to see a candidate's presentational style and allows them to sell themselves to us."* One pupil admitted: *"I have awful handwriting, so I kept my letter short and sharp, and presented my own case: 'This is why I want to work here, here are strongest points, please find my CV attached'."*

About 20 to 25 lucky applicants will make it through to a first-round interview. *"It's a short, getting-to-know-you affair and – we hope – a friendly interview, principally*

based on a candidate's CV and their interest in family law," says Spicer. A pupil confirmed: *"They asked me general questions and primarily wanted to know about me and my skills."*

The number of people invited to the last interview flits between eight and 12. Candidates are posed a problem question on a general area of family law, and presented with some relevant cases and materials to consider, prior to a 20-minute panel interview. *"We formulate the question and its materials so that it can be digested by someone who has limited knowledge of family law,"* says Spicer. *"We consider it to be a failure if someone in an interview freezes up, and we try to ask someone questions which they are able to answer."* After the interview, a drinks reception is held for all second-round candidates to meet other members of chambers.

"We've found that increasing our pupillage award and reducing the number of pupils has triggered a slight rise in the quality of applications," says Rachel Spicer. Given this, how does 1 Hare Court differentiate between such able candidates? *"We do look for academic success,"* Spicer says, *"but also for an expressed interest in chambers and the work we do. We want to see that people have explored extracurricular opportunities which allowed them to get to know family law."*

While some members are still addressed as 'Sir' of 'Ma'am' by the clerks, Steve McCrone say this is just because *"we have grown up doing it that way – this isn't a stuffy set."* Rachel Spicer adds: *"If you join us, then for better or for worse you are likely to spend a lot of time here, so it's worth building close relationships."* We were told there's a good social scene, and while *"pupils aren't going out drinking with the silks regularly, everyone has a good sense of humour, and nobody gets that stressed."* Chambers cricket is one social outlet, although one pupil admitted: *"I was terrible in the most recent match. I didn't get in to bat, I didn't manage to bowl, and I fell over picking up a ball. It wasn't the best display of my physical prowess."*

And finally...

This set specialises in divorces and matrimonial finance, so swotting up on these areas in particular – and some of the tax and money issues involved – will do you no harm if you want to apply here.

The Bar

Henderson Chambers

The facts

Location: Temple, London
Number of QCs/juniors: 10/39 (12 women)
Number of applications: 170+
Apply through Pupillage Gateway
Pupils per year: Up to 2
Seats: 4x3 months
Pupillage award: £50,000

A really friendly set, great advocacy opportunities, and interesting cases. What's not to love?

Henderson Chambers has successfully meshed a modern outlook with a traditional approach. Its tenants are charming and enthusiastic, and the work is top-quality.

Breaking Bad

"When people try to pigeonhole us," says Henderson's charismatic chief clerk John White, *"they soon realise that there isn't a pigeonhole wide enough. A lot of our major practices have overlaps, and we have members with their feet in many camps."* Now, while we're not trying to pigeonhole anyone, it's fair to say that this set's especially proficient in health and safety, product liability and consumer credit law. Its additional areas of expertise – personal injury, employment, property, commercial, and local government – interlink nicely with these core areas.

Henderson's health and safety expertise has seen it enlisted on many of the biggest cases in this arena in recent years. These include those arising from the Hatfield and Ladbroke Grove train crashes, and the claims made after the 2005 Buncefield oil depot explosion. In the past two decades members have also been instructed on some highly significant product liability claims, including group actions concerning Opren, Seroxat and benzodiazepines. More recently members have worked for surgeon defendants in proceedings arising out of the PIP breast implant scandal. *"Any product that gets taken to court – pharmaceuticals, knees, boobs, hips, you name it – Henderson will be involved in that case,"* one cheeky source told us.

Henderson regularly defends and prosecutes cases brought by the Health and Safety Executive (HSE) – there's somewhat more defendant than claimant work. For example, head of chambers Charlie Gibson recently advised on an HSE prosecution against UK Power Networks after an employee was electrocuted when working on an overhead power line. Another silk acted for a former subsidiary of BP in a group action brought by 100 Colombian farmers who say their farms were damaged by a defective oil pipeline. The same member also defended a go-kart manufacturer after it was sued by a woman who was left tetraplegic by a go-karting accident – she claimed the design of the go-kart was defective. On the consumer side one junior represented the defendant in a six-figure claim related to the sale of defective materials for making concrete bricks. Some of the work is finance-related, eg PPI claims, sales misrepresentations, and tiffs between banks and financiers over credit agreements.

Tussles and Brussels

Pupils spend three months with four different supervisors. These supervisors tend to practise in several areas at once, so pupils get exposure to a variety of fields including health and safety, product liability, employment and property. In the first six, pupils can expect to prepare pleadings, skeleton arguments, cross-examinations and advices for their supervisors. *"You're always doing live work that is necessary for a case,"* said one pupil. *"We're not given pieces of work which have been done before just to test us."* Pupils can anticipate a much more burdensome schedule once the second six rolls around. *"There's a huge shift from the first six,"* one informed us. *"I began to take on lots of my own cases, and I was on my feet three or four times a week!"* A junior tenant added: *"It's great to have the exposure and freedom, but it is difficult to juggle your own practice with the work you do for*

The Bar

Chambers UK rankings

Consumer Law	Product Liability
Health & Safety	Public Procurement
Information Technology	Real Estate Litigation

other members. *Fortunately the supervisors are on hand to assist you in managing your time.*" For pupils and baby juniors the *"bread-and-butter work"* consists of possession hearings and landlord/tenant cases. There might also be bigger interim applications to handle and one source had even had advocacy experience in the High Court.

For the first three months of pupillage *"you're not expected to be perfect, but after that you're conscious of the fact that each piece of work will make a certain impression on your supervisor."* After the first rotation pupils begin to take on work from other members, too, and *"each time you do they fill out a written feedback form with constructive criticism and comments. These then make up part of your tenancy application."*

This is one part of a *"very structured feedback process"* that should leave rookies in no doubt as to how they've performed throughout the year. In addition *"supervisors provide written reviews to pupils at the end of each seat, which is really useful in gauging how you're getting on."* Three or four mock advocacy exercises also act as a barometer of progress, as well as allowing pupils to hone their skills. The last of these actually takes place before a master at the Royal Courts of Justice. Another guaranteed part of the pupillage year is a month-long secondment to the competition department of US law firm McDermott Will & Emery's Brussels office.

By year end tenancy candidates will have *"a big binder"* comprising all their reports and assessments. This forms the basis of the tenancy decision made by the recruitment committee, although the opinions of the clerks, other members and instructing solicitors are taken into account too.

You better not kill the groove, DJ

Applications are scored out of 100 based on academics, other achievements, commitment to the Bar and an interest in Henderson. About 30 of the highest scorers make it through to a first-round interview. This lasts 15 minutes and takes place before a panel of three barristers. *"You're*

given a topic and asked to prepare for a discussion on it,"* a pupil informed us. *"Mine was about the reforms to legal aid which were going on at the time."* Another source said: *"You don't have to worry about preparing pleadings or making submissions in advance – it's an oral exercise. Legal knowledge is also not that important. What matters is your ability to analyse a situation and defend your point of view."* Those who make it to a second interview are met by the full recruitment panel. Candidates can expect a similar format to the first round, but with the set question *"digging a bit deeper into a tough legal dilemma."*

More than perhaps any other set Henderson has been working hard in the past few years to put out a clear message to students about what it is and what it does. As far as we know this is the only set with a dedicated 'graduate recruitment' website (launched in 2013) – www.hendersonpupillage.co.uk – and it's one of only two with a pupillage Twitter account, @HendersonPupils, which we definitely recommend you follow, as it cascades excellent advice about pupillage applications and interviews.

John White says this is a clear example of how Henderson *"is trying to be ahead of the curve in the legal world,"* and also pointed to the 2012 renovation of chambers' digs at 2 Harcourt Buildings in the Temple. *"We've modernised the building and upgraded the conference suites, which now have full video-conferencing facilities,"* he informs us. Chambers administrator Helen Ghalem says the rebuild hasn't sought to eviscerate Henderson's roots: *"We didn't want to produce a white clinical workplace. We wanted to marry the modern with the traditional and maintain chambers' warmth."*

There's certainly no chill to be found here. *"There's a collegiate atmosphere and a camaraderie that means you can walk into anyone's room and ask for assistance,"* a pupil told us. Henderson's members have a wide range of extracurricular interests and backgrounds, yet they all seem to mesh seamlessly together. Music is one thing which distinguishes members *and* brings them together. Junior Paul Skinner was a 2004 BBC Young Musician of the Year finalist (in the woodwind section, if you were wondering), while Charlie Gibson is very proud of the electric drum kit in his office and Prashant Popat QC actually has a set of decks in his – although we presume he didn't make silk for his DJing skills. *"It's pretty cool,"* said one interviewee, *"but he'll kill me for telling you about it!"*

The Bar

And finally...
Henderson Chambers took on both of its pupils in 2014, as it had done in 2013.

11KBW

The facts

Location: Inner Temple, London
Number of QCs/juniors: 17/42 (17 women)
Applications: 110
Pupils per year: 2-4
Seats: 2x3 and 1x6 months
Pupillage award: £55,000 (can advance £15,000 for BPTC)

"As a pupil, your work is a really interesting balance of long-running, intellectually tough matters and fairly straightforward assignments."

Public law is a strong suit at 11KBW, which handles education, local government and employment work.

Public frenemy

With just 32 years under its belt, 11KBW is still young in the grand scheme of things. But what this set lacks in age it more than makes up for in eminent alumni – former tenants include political power couple Tony and Cherie Blair and Alexander 'Derry' Irvine QC, founding member turned Lord Chancellor. The basic cornerstones of this set are public law, employment, commercial/business and information law work, each of which encompasses a number of sub-sectors – *"for example, community care, education, local government and mental health work all fall under the first bracket,"* joint senior clerk Lucy Barbet tells us. She estimates some 40% of instructions involve public law matters, while information law work accounts for 20% and employment and commercial issues together comprise the remaining 40%.

This spread of undertakings lends itself to *"an incredibly broad"* client base, from universities, investment banks and professional services firms to local authorities, central government bodies and trade unions. On the education front, 11KBW barristers represented both claimants and respondent examination boards in the headline-grabbing GCSE marking challenge of 2012 and acted for a Birmingham girls' school in a landmark appeal against the Secretary of State for Education's decision to remove it from the Register of Independent Schools. The set's education and local government practices are both top-ranked in *Chambers UK* and between them represent the likes of the Department of Education, the University of Oxford, Surrey County Council and the London Borough of Brent.

11KBW is also recognised as a top employment set, regularly handling discrimination, unfair dismissal, equal pay and trade law cases, often in the Employment Appeals Tribunal. Recent court appearances include acting on behalf of News International during an indemnity claim related to the infamous *News of the World* phone-hacking scandal and winning a female client's sex discrimination case against German financial giant Commerzbank. The set's also known for its human rights expertise, working across the immigration, mental health and social care sectors, and is upping its reputation on the informational law side, contending with a growing number of hot-button issues like late-term abortions and MPs' expenses.

The ailing economy has prompted 11KBW to expand its private sector capabilities in recent years. *"We've had to reconsider the level at which we pitch ourselves,"* Barbet says. *"The aim is to continue increasing turnover on the private side and add to our international offerings as well."* Much of the set's commercial work of late has involved the financial services sector, with members enjoying a growing involvement in high-profile City cases like the conspiracy wars between brokers Tullett Prebon and BGC Brokers and ContiCap's long-running claim under the Swiss Unfair Competition Act.

Checks and balances

Pupillage is split into two three-month seats followed by a six-month one. *"Over the year, pupils tend to spend three months with somebody who works at the commercial/employment end, then another three months with someone who predominately practises public law. After that, who they sit with depends on which areas of work they have yet to observe,"* chair of the pupillage committee Daniel Stilitz QC

The Bar

Chambers UK rankings

Administrative & Public Law	Data Protection
Civil Liberties & Human Rights	Education
	Employment
Competition/European Law	Local Government
	Public Procurement

tells us. *"It's all about providing a balanced legal education and making sure they see as wide a range of chambers' work as possible."* According to pupils, the first seat is *"a settling-in period – you're not expected to do a whole lot other than observe the work your supervisor is doing and absorb how that works."* Indeed, *"it's only after a few months that you assume a case management function and start working for other people in chambers."*

"As a pupil, your work is a really interesting balance of long-running, intellectually tough matters and fairly straightforward assignments," said one source. *"I've worked on a big judicial review exploring the extraterritorial application of the Human Rights Act with respect to drone strikes in Pakistan; equally, I've been asked to draft grounds for an individual's small employment claim."* While the public law arena often supplies the more *"prestigious"* cases, the employment side of things is hardly humdrum: *"The junior end involves a lot of claims made against big organisations, which tend to be pretty exciting because you've got to have a good case to take it to court."* One source estimated *"around a fifth"* of the year is spent in the courtroom.

Devil's advocate

Virtually all pupils are recruited via assessed mini-pupillages, which are obtained through written applications and offer *"an accurate insight into how chambers operates day-to-day."* Stints normally last a week and *"function essentially as a first interview. There's a lot of focus on your written work and ability to argue and express yourself orally."* According to Stilitz, plans are in place to make the interview stage – *"wherein we gather the ten or 12 who've impressed us during their mini-pupillage"*– more assessment-based. *"This year we'll judge candidates on a legal problem they're given in advance plus a short advocacy exercise. These exercises give us a much*

better idea of what a candidate will be like in practice than anything on his or her CV."

Between our interviewees, one had two undergrad degrees and a Master's in law, while another spent time as a philosopher and human rights volunteer abroad before opting for the Bar. Easy enough, right? Beyond pure academic success, advocacy experience is *"a definite plus"* in applicants, Stilitz says. *"Advocacy skills are as important as analytical ones at the Bar. Experience that shows your interest in and aptitude for being a strong advocate – whether it's through pro bono work or mooting or work experience – is invaluable."* Competition for spots is undeniably tough, but insiders assured us *"once you're in, you're only up against yourself. We're told we'll all be kept on if we're good enough."* After keeping on both pupils in 2013, the set retained one of two in 2014.

A *"sincere interest"* in pro bono work prevails at 11KBW. Recent activity includes representing anti-poverty charity Z2K in a challenge to the 2012 housing benefit freeze and spearheading a disability discrimination claim made by a law student suffering from multiple sclerosis. *"There's loads of scope to get involved, and just about everybody in chambers does. We get a lot of claimant public law cases going around as well as some tangential commercial matters."*

Despite chambers' *"rigorous academic approach,"* the day-to-day atmosphere is *"relaxed,"* sources agreed. *"Everyone has a friendly attitude and is supportive, even the silks with rock star practices. Nobody's ever told me off for taking up their time with a really basic question!"* Likewise, the relationship between tenants and clerks is *"pretty informal – you won't hear anyone addressed as 'mister' or 'ma'am' around here."* Pupils are *"fully incorporated"* into chambers' social scene, which includes holiday parties, regular networking events and a weekly tea one source characterised as *"kind of ironic – we all flock to it to grab some food and catch up; it's not like we're sitting silently around a table waiting for the senior clerk to speak."* Another weekly tradition is Friday night drinks at The Witness Box, though we heard this might change following the famous dive's decision to go down the trendy wine bar route. *"I'm just not sure how much longer our loyalty will last now they're charging us more,"* an interviewee grumbled.

And finally...

Our interviewees urged applicants to *"bear in mind how crucial it is to display clear, logical and concise writing skills in your application form and mini-pupillage assessments. We're a place that believes written advocacy is as important as oral advocacy, so you will be judged harshly."*

The Bar

Keating Chambers

The facts

Location: Essex Street, London
Number of QCs/juniors: 27/30 (15 women)
Applications: c. 150
Apply through Pupillage Gateway
Pupils per year: Up to 3
Seats: 4x3 months
Pupillage award: £60,000 (can advance £18,000 for BPTC)

"Don't think our construction tag means the work is limiting; I'd say about 65% of what I do is general commercial law."

Keating is synonymous with construction, but don't mistake this set's specialist angle for a narrow scope.

Bringing down the house

Keating wrote the book on construction law – literally. In fact its influential construction tome *Keating on Construction Contracts* is now in its ninth edition, just one of many nods to the set's authority in all things bricks and mortar. (That *Chambers UK* deems Keating one of London's top two construction sets also speaks volumes to this point.) For all its concentrated expertise, however, Keating's purview is surprisingly extensive, taking in sectors as varied as engineering, shipbuilding, energy, professional negligence and IT. *"Funnily enough, from the outside world it looks like we do just one thing: construction law,"* says pupillage committee head Alexander Nissen QC. *"But in fact that broad categorisation lends itself to so many strands of commercial disputes – barristers here might be dealing with a power station one day, then a road project the next, and then a warehouse the next."*

Over the years members have applied their expertise to cases involving some of London's most iconic landmarks, including the Millennium Bridge, the Shard, the London Eye and Wembley Stadium. Topping chambers' docket at the time of our visit in summer 2014 was its representation of Accolade Wines in a £170m property damage and business interruption claim against the builders of its bottling plant – one of the Technology and Construction Court's biggest cases of the year. Other noteworthy matters of late include a £700m account dispute over the construction of the East London line, and a multimillion-pound repair claim following a flood at Greenwich Millennium Village.

Keating originally built up its name working for contractors, but these days the client roster includes all sorts of industry professionals, from employers and architects to insurers and suppliers. In fact, such is the set's reputation that members are regularly called on to act on either side of the same dispute. *"The lion's share of work we do is domestic,"* says clerk Robert Cowup, nodding to Keating's strong links with UK-based contractors like Kier, Skanska and Balfour Beatty, *"but we also have a strong presence internationally, particularly in the Middle and Far East, thanks in part to our work with clients like Samsung."* The set's shipbuilding faction, one of its biggest growth areas, lends itself to a decent spread of cross-border claims, as does its energy wing, where disputes over offshore wind farms and oil rigs dot the cache. Meanwhile, the procurement practice has expanded beyond the construction sphere to include health and professional services too.

Hit the roof

Pupils here undertake four three-month seats, each with a different supervisor. *"The first quarter is about getting a grip on the nature of the disputes we do, while the second and third let you put that into action by working for members beyond your supervisor. Now I even have some of my own cases."*

Interviewees made it clear *"the construction industry doesn't confine you to a small area of law."* As a pupil pointed out: *"Building disputes affect so many different types of people – there are industry professionals dealing with contract issues, but you also get lay clients like homeowners who've had a wall fall down in their garden and don't understand why they have to indemnify their neighbour. It's an interesting challenge to explain*

Chambers UK rankings

Construction	International Arbitration
Energy & Natural Resources	Professional Negligence
	Public Procurement

the technical side of things in layman's terms." Demand heightens when matters involve cross-border elements. *"There's a lot of admin required to sort out when, for example, a construction project is governed by English law but carried out abroad, or perhaps the vehicle is overseas but the insurer is based here."*

Once pupils' rights of audience kick in during their second six, it's off to court. *"I've done four court appearances now: two possession orders, a strikeout and a resistance to an application to amend particulars.* Back at chambers, there's plenty of research and drafting to get on with. *"I recently wrote an advice for a dispute concerning the Party Wall Act,"* said one pupil, while the other recounted their role in a dispute involving an oil well off the coast of Equatorial Guinea: *"I got quite embroiled in the matter – researching the oil sector, meeting the other solicitors and taking the client out to dinner."*

Every piece of work a pupil completes is assessed, and halfway through their tenancy there's a formal feedback session with representatives from the pupillage committee. The results of this factor into the tenancy decision, as do the three oral advocacy exercises, each of which sees pupils go head-to-head against each other during a mock three-hour hearing. *"We're given our materials, have that week to prepare skeletons and then it's submissions for an hour each, plus replies. They're very stressful but a good way to get your head around an argument and learn how to make a good submission."*

In July the tenancy committee prepares a report on each pupil which includes a recommendation as to whether they should be offered tenancy. The decision is ultimately reviewed by the whole of chambers, but *"it's generally presumed the committee's recommendation will prevail,"* according to Nissen. In 2014 one of the set's two pupils took up tenancy.

Right at home
A stroll through Keating's buzzing office on Essex Street speaks to claims that it's a *"welcoming"* and *"decided-*

ly non-stuffy" place. *"There's a lot of moxie and good energy here. We're traditional in that we observe a conventional hierarchy, but on the whole chambers is very forward-thinking; there aren't huge divisions between members and clerks, and we don't go for afternoon tea or any of that."*

Indeed, the custom is spurned in favour of a weekly lunch – pupils aren't invited, but that's just as well since *"we're always out to lunch with each other anyway!"* It helps that there are plenty of other events for them to intend, including networking dos, cricket matches and holiday parties. *"Our last summer party was held at the Royal Artillery Gardens and featured a fairground,"* said a pupil, recalling the *"fantastic moment when I hammered it out on the dodgems with three silks and a couple of clients – I turned around and realised a really senior QC had just crashed into me!"*

Holding the fort
Keating's application process has changed in recent years. Now the top 50 applicants are given a written exercise, and the set invites around 25 for a first interview in which they're questioned on their background and application, then asked to debate another another applicant – all in the span of 15 minutes. From there a dozen are asked to a second, half-hour interview. This involves a discussion on their written exercise, plus some general questions and a five-minute presentation of a non-legal subject. Recent topics include women's rugby, the advantages of learning Mandarin and the social impact of the Australian impressionist movement. *"It's got to be something you're comfortable talking about and shows a bit of your personality."*

According to Nissen, *"first and foremost, we're looking for high intellectual ability and a motivation to practise commercial law."* Demonstrating an ability to work hard, withstand long hours and get on well with all sorts of people also stands applicants in good stead. Something that's *"categorically not required"* is a specialist background or previous knowledge of construction law, a point our sources were keen to stress. *"We understand construction is quite a niche, technical area and that most people have limited exposure to it,"* says Nissen, while a junior added: *"Chambers really focuses on people who show an aptitude for contract and tort law. If you impress in that sphere, you're not at a disadvantage at all."*

The Bar

And finally...
"It's important to possess a lively intelligence here – you've got to be able to move outside your books and show you're someone clients would get on with and perhaps even go for a beer with."

7 King's Bench Walk

The facts

Location: Inner Temple, London
Number of QCs/juniors: 24/31 (12 women)
Applications: 175-200
Apply through Pupillage Gateway
Pupils per year: 2-3
Seats: Usually 4 in the first 9 months
Pupillage award: £60,000 (can advance up to £15,000 for BPTC)

"We are a little bit more informal and slightly less corporate than other commercial sets."

7KBW has a sterling reputation for all things insurance and shipping, but there's more to discover at this top commercial set.

Knights of the round table

7KBW's premises have been home to a number of illustrious figures over the years. Former occupant William Tidd's 18th-century common-law tome *Practice of the Court of King's Bench* is mentioned in *David Copperfield*. Future Lord Chancellor Lord Halsbury practised here too before penning *Halsbury's Laws of England*, which is still in print today. More recently, many ex-tenants have joined the Bench including Supreme Court Justice Lord Mance and Lord Justices of Appeal Sir Andrew Longmore and Sir Stephen Tomlinson.

The set is top-ranked by *Chambers UK* for insurance litigation, which *"constitutes at least 50% of the practice."* But insurance isn't just one thing: it can be marine insurance for shipping firms or professional negligence insurance for accountants: *"There are many different bents to it!"* We mentioned marine insurance there as shipping is an area which *"90-something per cent"* of members spend at least some of their time on. Maritime law is paper-heavy and suffused with its own language and customs, so we were pleased to hear pupils refer to it lightly as *"contract law with boats"* and say that *"it's about things your granny would understand, like a ship hitting a rock."* True. In one recent case members were called in to represent the operator of a berth at a harbour in Ecuador after the 'CCNI Antártico' struck the quayside there. Other cases have involved vessels suddenly splitting in two, catching fire, or grounding in ecologically sensitive areas.

Other areas of expertise include professional negligence, banking and finance, trade and commodities, fraud, construction, media and communications, EU and competi-

tion law, and oil and gas. The last one of these is really on the up: five members worked on one of the largest commercial cases of the year, *Excalibur Ventures v Texas Keystone*, which centred on oil exploration concessions in Kurdistan. Arbitration is another area in which the set is well regarded and it adds an international dimension to the work, with members frequently sailing off to places like Singapore, the Bahamas and Hong Kong.

Exercise books

Pupils have four supervisors. They usually sit with the first until Christmas. This period *"focuses on learning, and you work mostly for your supervisor."* Subsequent seats usually last two or three months. Supervisors are usually senior juniors, though junior silks occasionally fulfil the role too.

Each supervisor's practice usually includes insurance, shipping and other work. A pupil we spoke to had come across reinsurance, professional negligence and energy cases, as well as what he termed *"general commercial matters – those cases which don't fit neatly into any one category but help keep everything more varied."* Pupils worked on the aforementioned Excalibur case too, which offered *"the fantastic opportunity to watch a senior silk do some cross-examination – there's no better way to learn than that."*

Opinions, skeleton arguments, pieces of advice, pleadings and defences are standard drafting fare for pupils. The work is overwhelmingly on live cases, although *"sometimes your supervisor will give you the brief for one of his past cases and have you draft the relevant documents, so you can learn about a particular point."* Su-

Chambers UK rankings

Commercial Dispute Resolution	International Arbitration
Insurance	Professional Negligence
	Shipping

pervisors' cases *"can last anywhere from two days to two weeks, which means that you get to see a lot of what goes on."* Lengthy cases can be real head-scratchers and hinge on verbose precedents and statute. Shipping, insurance and commercial law are known as fairly academic fields. *"People here spend a lot of time doing serious, challenging work and are often buried under difficult papers for days on end."* Our interviewees didn't feel they were forced to do book-heavy drudgework though: *"I haven't been sent off to the library for six months to go and read 50 million books to figure out the meaning of one word!"*

Pupils don't spend any time on their feet during the second six, but do complete two formal advocacy exercises. The first is an application for summary judgment while the second is more meaty – an appeal to the Supreme Court. *"They're fun and scary at the same time,"* a pupil told us, but luckily *"there's plenty of time to prepare."* Pupils draft a skeleton argument beforehand, which they submit to the panel of silks and juniors conducting the exercise.

During pupillage you're also asked to complete eight to ten written pieces of work for several named pupil assessors. These can be *"quite difficult,"* but then the aim is to allow members other than the four supervisors to test the mettle of the pupils. The tenancy decision is made based on feedback from supervisors, pupil assessors and those who oversaw the advocacy exercises. In 2014 two out of three pupils gained tenancy with the set.

Brain trust

Despite the tough intellectual demands of being a pupil and tenant at this set, recruiters told us that you needn't be put off from applying if you don't have an encyclopaedic knowledge of shipping or insurance: *"The learning curve is going to be very steep whatever your background, so we're looking for people with an ability to pick things up quickly."* We were told that *"a substantial number of people come here after doing the GDL"* – a quick snoop on the firm's website revealed that a third of the members under five years' call didn't do law at undergrad. But we would be lying if we didn't admit that we were very impressed by the academic calibre of 7KBW's baby barristers. At the time of our research, the five youngest members of chambers had, between them, a Double First in Japanese and jurisprudence, a PhD in mathematics, a ten-year career at the Bar in Australia, an LLM from Harvard and a year's lecturing experience at Oxford, as well as at least 25 prizes and scholarships.

If you think you live up to these high standards and want to win a pupillage here, then you'll have to pick 7KBW as one of your 12 Pupillage Gateway sets. Around 25 individuals make it through the initial application sift. The interview process consists of an advocacy exercise (which candidates are given a couple of weeks to prepare) and *"a more traditional interview with all the normal CV-related questions."* A current pupil told us that *"the interview panel wants to see how you respond to difficult, off-the-cuff questions and whether you can think on your feet and demonstrate the lively intellect required to work here."*

7KBW's tenants don't specialise in just one area, which means that *"all members will end up working with one another at some point, so you get to know everyone."* Perhaps as a consequence this is *"not a fusty, unfriendly place – quite the opposite."* Members also admitted that *"because of the work we do there is an academic atmosphere, but that doesn't mean people are weird and don't talk to each other!"* Another source added: *"We are less into the idea of developing a brand than some other sets, and our organisation is more in line with the traditional idea of how a barristers' chambers should work, but we're certainly not traditional in the sense of being stuffy."*

There's chambers tea every day, and *"at least six to ten members usually come along to have a chat."* One of our interviewees was keen to dispel the myth that teas are crusty and old-fashioned: *"Some people seem to be allergic to the idea of chambers tea, but I think it should be rehabilitated at the Bar: it's just like having a drink with your mates really, except that you go back to work afterwards."* There are also frequent lunches in halls, drinks in the clerks' room on Friday evenings, and a Christmas party which usually brings everybody together each year.

The Bar

And finally...
You need both a strong dose of academic intellect and a head for business law to work at this busy commercial set.

Littleton Chambers

The facts

Location: Inner Temple, London
Number of QCs/juniors: 13/41 (11 women)
Applications: c.200
Apply through Pupillage Gateway
Pupils per year: 2
Seats: 4x3 months
Pupillage award: £55,000 (can advance £15,000 for BPTC)

This top employment set is branching out into commercial work

Despite considerable growth over the past decade, Littleton has kept hold of that 'little town' feel: pupils still consider it a *"sociable and close-knit"* set.

Three's a crowd

Littleton has long been prized for its employment prowess – the practice wins a top ranking in *Chambers UK* and accounts for just over half of the work carried out by members. Other practices are catching up though. *"We're becoming increasingly dominated by commercial litigation,"* says commercial director Nigel McEwen. *"We're instructed by small solicitors' firms and huge international outfits."* That's good news for future pupils who might want to maintain a broad practice early in their careers. *"Most of our junior tenants start out doing a mix of employment and commercial litigation before deciding whether they'd like to practice exclusively in one area. Some continue to practice in both,"* administration director Felicity Schneider tells us.

In Littleton's case, you'd be wrong to equate employment work just with unfair dismissals and tribunal cases. Members frequently appear in the High Court on bonus claims, team move cases and breach of contract matters. Barristers also work on industrial action claims like the Communication Workers Union's case against Royal Mail in the run-up to its privatisation, and represented the 'fatal bug surgeon' (who unwittingly transmitted a fatal infection to five of his patients) in High Court proceedings against Nottingham University Hospital. Other claims range from the slightly bizarre to ideal tabloid fodder. One member recently acted for a City banker dismissed following accusations that he'd been moonlighting as boxer David Haye's PA (where on earth did he find the time?), while another saw a Tory MP cleared of accusations that he'd invited his lesbian housekeeper to drop the duster and join him in a threesome.

On the commercial disputes side, Littleton's barristers are regularly instructed on commercial fraud cases, share disputes, and breaches of fiduciary duty cases. The set is looking to make strides in Russia and other CIS countries, and *"a good proportion of the work already comes from that part of the world,"* McEwen points out. One of the set's QCs recently hit the headlines when he successfully represented a Jordanian businesswoman claiming $10m commission for the sale of an airliner to Colonel Gaddafi. Her commission had been decided by an oral contract rather than any written agreement so the cross-examination was at the heart of the case. Sports disputes are also popular at this set – a number of members have recently appeared at the Premier League Managers' Arbitration Panel on manager cases, and another represented a player before the FA Disciplinary Panel on charges of steroid use.

Saving face

Pupils sit with four supervisors over the course of pupillage, and while these are essentially four distinct seats, *"there's no set structure – most supervisors do a mix of employment and commercial disputes, and some work in other areas like sports law too."* The fact that pupils are also encouraged to work for other members means that they *"get to see a broad range of cases"* over the year.

Pupils work for both claimants and respondents, writing opinions, conducting legal research, and drafting pleadings and arguments. Our interviewees had attended Employment Tribunals, taken applications for summary judgment to the County Courts, brought contract claims to the small claims court and gone for costs in the Companies Court. On top of smaller matters like these,

Chambers UK rankings

Employment

second-sixers continue to help out on high-profile cases. One source had been involved in a High Court restrictive covenants case which saw an employee awarded £250,000 in damages, and accompanied a QC to the Supreme Court on a case concerning the rights of maxillofacial surgeons under their contract of employment. *"They even mentioned some of my research at the hearing, which felt great!"*

Pupils can also build up experience by working on pro bono claims – one had worked for the Bar Pro Bono Unit, helping a client who was *"very daunted by the whole system"* to have his disability discrimination claim heard at an Employment Tribunal. *"You have to be sensitive to your client's feelings in that kind of situation, and I expect it's a factor they consider when choosing pupils in the first place,"* our source confided. *"Everyone here is very down to earth and able to relate to others – you need particularly good interpersonal skills to be an employment barrister."*

In order to prepare pupils for taking on their own work in the second six, members train them in cross-examination and oral advocacy. Felicity Schneider assured us that pupillage training exercises such as these aren't assessed, as *"it's essential that pupils are provided with an opportunity to improve and refine their skills without being penalised."* That said, there are plenty of formal assessments too – usually about four advocacy and two written exercises over the year. The first isn't carried out until December, so pupils have a three-month *"informal grace period"* during which they can spend time shadowing members in court and getting to grips with their written work. When assessments do hit, they're *"not designed to trick you"* but can be *"very difficult,"* as ultimately they *"exist to test and challenge you."* The results of the assessments, along with supervisors' reports and feedback on work done for other members, all feed into the tenancy decision. Regular feedback means the ultimate decision shouldn't come as a huge surprise, but pupils did suggest you should also make an effort to socialise with

people in chambers if you really want to get your foot through the door.

Thirst for knowledge (and wine)

Members look out for an ability to interact throughout the recruitment process. *"We expect a truly excellent academic background, but we also prize social skills and the ability to get on well with others,"* Nigel McEwen confirms. *"Applicants should act naturally during their interviews and let their personality come through."* Two panel interviews sandwich a compulsory mini-pupillage, meaning candidates would struggle to pretend to be someone they're not. About 25 are invited to an initial interview, 15 to 17 go to the three-day mini-pupillage, and ten to 12 attend the final interview. Rather than being competency-based, all three rounds aim to test how applicants can approach a legal or ethical question, and candidates are given time to prepare before facing the panel. The mini-pupillage *"gives you a good amount of time to show what you're capable of,"* and culminates in an opportunity to chat to members over a glass of wine.

If personality is so important, then what exactly is Littleton looking for? Oddly enough, it seems a whole spectrum of people are welcome, from the *"quiet and introverted"* to the *"outspoken and boisterous."* Perhaps this is down to the fact that Littleton has tried to move away from the standard mould of traditional chambers. It was one of the first to appoint a CEO, before moving on to the current system of being headed by a commercial and administrative director. And the set's offices in the Inner Temple are modern and pretty swish. *"As soon as you become a tenant there's no real hierarchy and you can happily mix with the silks,"* a baby junior told us. *"And everyone's invited to all our social events."* Drinks tend to be held a couple of times a term, and members often head to the Pegasus Bar to quench their thirst after work.

As a pupil, you should be able to maintain a social and private life outside of the office as long as you remain focused during the day. Pupils are encouraged to come in at about 8.30am and leave by 6pm, and our interviewees hadn't worked many evenings or weekends. On taking up tenancy, the hours become *"a lot more intense,"* but a baby junior reported that their old supervisors had continued to support them.

And finally...
One of two pupils was offered tenancy in 2014, following on from two out of three the previous year.

Maitland Chambers

The facts

Location: Lincoln's Inn, London
Number of QCs/juniors: 25/42 (13 women)
Applications: 170+
Outside Pupillage Gateway
Pupils per year: Up to 3
Seats: 1x3 months and 4x2 months
Pupillage award: £60,000 (can advance £20,000 for BPTC)

"Maitland does all things commercial chancery – you're not signing up to go down a narrow path."

This leading commercial chancery set continues to thrive and is seeking out multi-jurisdictional opportunities.

Venn diagrams and international plans

Breaking down Maitland's practice areas is a potentially difficult task – *"you need a Venn diagram not a pie chart!"* joked one interviewee. *"Roughly 50 to 60% of what we do is commercial chancery while the rest is property, charity, private client, trusts, company law and insolvency."* Other areas of expertise include charities, fraud, offshore finance, partnership disputes and professional negligence. Most members *"span two to four of these areas"* but there are single-area specialists too. *Chambers UK* ranks the set in 11 distinct areas and has recognised Maitland as a top-tier commercial chancery set for 11 years running.

Members of this set have been involved in many of 2014's top commercial cases, with QCs appearing for both sides in the Supreme Court hearing of *FHR v Mankarious* (on proprietary remedies for bribes and commissions) and a team of barristers working on a 15-week Commercial Court trial in which three banks are suing a German water company for $600m. Other leading cases include that brought against video retailer GAME by its landlords over unpaid rents, litigation in the BVI over Russia's largest social network site, and the fall-out from the Madoff scandal.

Maitland has an internal business development committee, which – as part of an ongoing drive to draw in more international work – is scrutinising global geographical regions with a cautious eye. *"We are looking quite thoroughly at East Asia,"* says senior clerk John Wiggs, who queries whether the market there *"will take off in the same way as many people think it will."* Maitland definitely is interested in strengthening its hand in more established jurisdictions like the British Virgin Islands and the Cayman Islands. And while the recession has seen areas like property and private client dip slightly *"the beauty of Maitland is that as one area goes down another goes up."* Work from the financial sector has definitely picked up. Members have recently been working on disputes relating to the collapse of Lehman and the Madoff fraud. Wiggs anticipates that more lender claims, derivatives actions and hedge fund disputes will be coming Maitland's way.

Headaches and BVI breaks

Maitland recruits outside of the Pupillage Gateway, and maintains an early deadline: applications for pupillage in 2016/17 have to be in by January 2015. Pupils described the short application form as *"an advocacy exercise in itself"* and recommend giving *"punchy"* responses – *"avoid any rambling statements."* The set whittles down 150 paper applications to 30 for the first round of interviews. These are 20-minute affairs and *"an opportunity for the set to get to know the candidate and test some basic non-legal skills."* There's also a logical reasoning problem to contend with, and those on the panel will *"try to catch interviewees off guard by putting forward a contrary position, just to see if they can hold the line or judge appropriately when to back off from it."* Between ten and 12 candidates make it through to a second interview, which consists of a *"fuller legal problem."* The panel are *"not interested in testing legal knowledge,"* so *"don't get het up because you didn't revise this bit of law or that before the interview."* Interviewers are interested

Chambers UK rankings

Agriculture & Rural Affairs	Fraud
Chancery	Offshore
Charities	Partnership
Commercial Dispute Resolution	Professional Negligence
	Real Estate Litigation
Company	Restructuring/Insolvency

in candidates' ability to assimilate information quickly and *"distil a problem down to the actual issues."*

Four supervisors – usually between seven and 15 years' call – are chosen each year, and all pupils spend time with each one of them. *"We pick the supervisors so that they are representative of the spread of work in chambers: one might do commercial work, another property, and yet another traditional chancery."*

Pupils work alongside their supervisor *"doing everything they do."* They'll be given the papers on a case as it's ongoing and asked to draft an opinion or other documents while their supervisor is doing the same. A comparison between the two is then made and feedback provided. *"My supervisors give me their version so I can build up a dossier of good-quality work to look back at later on,"* a pupil told us. If a supervisor is *"stuck on a very big case"* pupils are given older work to do. One told us: *"Supervisors build up a bag of work which they think might be useful for a pupil to undertake. I enjoy being able to observe the litigation process on live cases and work on my own projects at the same time."* Another source added: *"Some of the work we do is unbelievably hard – I frequently leave chambers with a headache and I have to think about problems which are far more difficult than anything I ever encountered during my studies."*

The range of work experienced is *"quite something"* and pupils have to make *"rapid mental adjustments."* One told us: *"One week you might be drafting a skeleton argument for a possession hearing and the next you could be writing an opinion for a huge commercial fraud case."* The breadth of work experienced by pupils continues into the first year of tenancy. A baby junior told us they had recently been working on a bankruptcy case, a land possession hearing and a contractual contract dispute as well as *"winging off to the BVI."* Awesome! Well, *"it was a disclosure exercise so it was slightly less glamorous than it sounds...."*

Terror stakes and biscuit breaks

Pupils do not get to spend time on their feet, as the complexity of the set's work means *"it's not fair on pupils to give them their own cases during the second six."* That doesn't mean there's no advocacy though: an in-house programme consisting of six oral exercises fills the gap instead. *"Each one is based on a real set of papers and pupils will hand in a skeleton argument before conducting a hearing in front of members."* Pupils described the exercises as *"hard work"* and *"one of those terrifying experiences that you enjoy nonetheless."* Luckily, supervisors set aside preparation time and to ensure fairness the same members evaluate each exercise for all pupils. Interviewees also appreciated the *"quality and detail"* of the feedback provided afterwards.

Throughout their year with Maitland, pupils' progress is monitored by both their supervisors and the advocacy assessors. After each seat supervisors fill out an assessment form and twice during pupillage there's a sit-down chat to discuss the comments. Nine months in, supervisors and advocacy assessors get together to decide whether to recommend a pupil for tenancy. *"People who have seen your work have the most input into the ultimate tenancy decision."* In 2014, two out of the three pupils were kept on as tenants.

Despite its slick interior furnishings, Maitland is a *"relaxed set"* according to our interviewees. *"It's not the type of place where the most senior person gets the best choice of biscuits,"* but there's *"a respect and deference to senior people where it's due."* Pupils said that *"everyone is keen to make you feel as much a part of things as possible,"* while members called the set *"very democratic."* How so? *"There have been a number of occasions when decisions have effectively been dictated by the needs of the junior end rather than the senior one."*

Maitland's 'pubco' organises regular pub-based socials. *"Every Thursday someone will ping around an e-mail inviting people out for a drink. It's usually the juniors who attend, and it's good to have the opportunity to catch up with people who you usually only see fleetingly."* There's chambers tea every day, which is *"a little more formal: some people use it as a place to discuss legal problems, but it's a social gathering too and people enjoy gossiping about judges and funny things that have happened in court."*

And finally...

Some of the work may be so complicated it's headache-inducing, but pupils certainly enjoy the challenge and the breadth of work available at this set.

The Bar

Matrix Chambers

The facts:

Location: Gray's Inn, London
Number of QCs/juniors: 23/38 (24 women)
Applications: 200
Outside Pupillage Gateway
Pupils per year: Up to 2
Seats: 4x3 months
Pupillage award: £50,000 (can advance £10,000 for BPTC)

If Mark Darcy were a real person he would work at Matrix Chambers.

A thoroughly modern set with a golden reputation for human rights work, Matrix spans a vast range of disciplines.

Cutting through the crust

Those who think the Bar is as stuffy as a taxidermied grouse should consider Matrix Chambers. There's a strong whiff of modernity about this place, heralded not simply by its slick name and rejection of afternoon tea, but the progressive ethos that lies at its heart. Matrix, though situated in the traditional legal enclave of Gray's Inn, was designed to be different from the outset. The set was founded just 14 years ago, at the dawn of the new millennium, by 22 barristers from seven different chambers. *"They knew the Human Rights Act was coming in and wanted to be able to apply the legislation across practice areas beyond human rights – European, public, criminal, and now media and information law,"* CEO Lindsay Scott explains. *"They were determined to be unstuffy, client-focused and run in a modern, professional way."*

Hence, staid lawyerly tradition was swept aside to create a contemporary brand where clerks and pupils are plainly called 'practice managers' and 'trainees'. Matrix's focus on high-quality work has earned it a stellar batch of *Chambers UK* rankings and is now synonymous with its brand. Scan a sample of headline-grabbing civil liberties or public law matters and you're pretty much guaranteed to find a Matrix member on the case. Barristers have recently acted for David Miranda, partner of journalist Glenn Greenwald, who was detained at Heathrow under anti-terrorist laws following the Edward Snowden affair. They've also been representing several major news publications during the Litvinenko inquest and advising victims of torture under Muammar Gaddafi's regime on proceedings against UK government officials.

Of course, while its human rights and public law dabbles tend to generate the most press, Matrix is steadfastly multidisciplinary, handling financial crime, employment, competition and regulatory, and commercial and public international law cases, plus sports and tax matters. Accordingly, its client base is very broad: magic circle members like Clifford Chance and Linklaters, regional and domestic firms, public law outfits like Leigh Day and Bindmans, governments, NGOs and international corporations all instruct the firm regularly. On the public international law front, member Professor James Crawford recently secured a successful judgment for the Australian government against Japan after the International Court of Justice ordered a halt to the latter's routine slaughter of minke whales in the Antarctic. And over on the commercial end, barristers have been busy acting for the owners of Coventry City Football Club in a dispute regarding Coventry City Council's allegedly unlawful £14.4m loan to stadium operators. Members have also been acting for property tycoon Robert Tchenguiz throughout the Serious Fraud Office's investigation into the collapse of Icelandic bank Kaupthing.

Heavily grilled – no sweat

With a couple hundred applications each year for just two trainee spots, the competition to nab one is pretty intense. Luckily the application process is outlined clearly in the traineeship brochure, which applicants can download from the set's website. There's even a system of points candidates can use to assess their suitability for interview.

Chambers UK rankings

Administrative & Public Law	Environment
	Fraud
Civil Liberties & Human Rights	Immigration
Crime	POCA Work & Asset Forfeiture
Defamation/Privacy	Police Law
Education	Public International Law
Employment	

According to our sources, the first interviewee is *"over in a flash"* and consists of three members asking a question each *"about policy, current events or something going on in the law at the time."* Those who make it over this hurdle will find the next stage is a bit trickier. *"You're given a statute-based legal problem to prepare beforehand, then you go in and basically get grilled for what seems like hours and hours by a panel of five to eight people. They don't expect you to know all the right answers or analyse everything completely correctly, though – it's partly testing, how you react, and whether you can keep it together and give coherent, reasoned answers, even if they're the wrong ones."*

Of course, poise isn't all. Superb academic credentials are paramount, but this set isn't snobbish about whether you got your education among the dreaming spires. If you look among the junior tenants, yes, there are plenty with Oxbridge Firsts, but also individuals who went to Sheffield, Durham and LSE. Additionally, *"chambers look for people who subscribe to Matrix's core values, like independence and commitment to legal aid. Work experience is important too."* Indeed, you won't find a trainee here who's completely wet behind the ears. Between them, our interviewees had worked for the Law Commission, interned for a judge at the ICTY in The Hague, mooted copiously, worked at a boutique public international law firm, interned at the UN in New York, and worked for the UN Relief and Works Agency in Jerusalem.

Feet, feedback and fish

Trainees split their year evenly between four supervisors. *"The set takes into account areas you're interested in and people you might want to sit with, which is great."* As one baby junior recalled: *"I did judicial review, public law-type stuff for my first seat, then actions against the police*

with some public international law, then media, and finally public law and inquests." Others areas sources had been exposed to include prison and sentencing law, immigration and anti-terrorism legislation. Public law work is particularly wide-ranging and can cover anything from anti-busking legislation through to the Terrorist Prevention Investigative Measures (TPIM) Act.

During the first half of the year, *"you closely mirror your supervisor's work. You accompany them to court, and they might ask you to produce a note or piece of research, or draft some judicial review grounds, which they tinker with until it's finished product. There's a lot of drafting, actually – from grounds to submissions to skeleton arguments."* As they move through their traineeship *"there's more of an opportunity to look at a file from the beginning. Your supervisor teaches you how to carry out legal analysis and appraise cases."*

Matrix trainees aren't hastily shoved onto their feet, though. *"We only tend to appear on our own in court towards the end of the second six,"* said an interviewee. *"I've been called by myself a couple of times, but only on small things like listing hearings."* Is it still terrifying? *"Absolutely! The capacity to mess up is enormous on every level!"* Fortunately there are practice area and advocacy training sessions delivered over the course of the year – *"they'll highlight things like practising bail applications"* – and during their third seat trainees complete a written and oral advocacy assessment to boost their skills. Feedback on this is given swiftly, *"and there's also feedback at the end of every seat, where your supervisor will say, 'You need to work on this' or, 'At the moment I'd recommend you'. They don't want anybody to reach the end of the year with no idea how they'll fare during the membership decision."* On this matter, the traineeship committee makes a recommendation that's taken to a general meeting. All three trainees were awarded membership in 2014.

Inside Matrix's unfussy rooms, we found a vibrant bunch of chatty folk and even a couple of engaging mascot fish (with e-mailing capabilities, we're told). *"The atmosphere here is fantastic. Everyone is chilled out and dressed in sneakers half the time. I genuinely love working here, and I'm not being paid to say that!"* gushed a junior. *"You're treated as someone who deserves to be here, which is really nice when you're in the difficult position of trying to prove yourself."*

And finally...
In keeping with its modern outlook, this sociable set has a lunch every week instead of tea, and hosts frequent drinks events.

Monckton Chambers

The facts

Location: Gray's Inn, London

Number of QCs/Juniors: 14/42 (14 women)

Applications: 200+

Apply through Pupillage Gateway

Pupils per year: 2

Seats: 4x3 months

Pupillage award: £60,000 (can advance £20,000 for the BPTC)

Head over to chambersstudent. co.uk to read an extended version of this feature.

Monckton barristers *"work hard on brain-aching problems"* related to EU, competition and public law.

Monckey business

Monckton Chambers has been enjoying a boom period. According to a recent article in *The Lawyer*, its revenue swelled by 59% between 2007 and 2012 (to £21m), and it's the fastest growing set in the UK top 30.

"There's a sense that there's plenty of work in this area," says a member. Monckton's forte is EU and competition law, and with more and more cases going to the European courts, it's hard to argue with that. The other *"core areas"* in which chambers excels are public law and regulatory, procurement, telecoms and VAT – all recognised with top-tier *Chambers UK* rankings.

Furthermore, *"we're looking to develop areas that complement our core practices,"* says clerk John Keegan, *"so, for example, we're putting efforts into the financial services area, where there's a clear synergy with our regulatory experience."* Monckton was recently involved in the Icesave dispute, which resulted from the 2008 collapse of Landsbanki. The governments of the UK and the Netherlands sought to compensate those who had invested in the bank and went after Iceland for the money. Chambers will use its work on high-profile cases such as this as a *"springboard"* to win more work in that area. Among many other headline matters that members have worked on is *R (Shoesmith) v Ofsted & Others*, which arose out of the death of Baby P.

In competition for competition

A master's in competition law isn't required to get in here, though an interest in the field helps. If you don't know much about the areas and are wondering what the appeal might be, here's how a junior summed it up: *"The reason I love it is that it's a wonderful eclectic mix of work on big commercial cases which have public law points. You find yourself advising on public law while at the same time being stretched to think in a commercial way."* It is *"cerebral"* work, and there's no point pretending that anything other than the highest academic qualifications are necessary. Examine members' profiles on the set's website, and you'll see what we mean.

If you can demonstrate *"ambition"* and *"dynamism"* through your extracurriculars, your application may be one of the 40 or so that gets through to the first interview stage. This is *"as relaxed as an interview can be"* – a *"getting-to-know-you session"* with two or three juniors, covering mainly CV-related topics *"so they feel like they are on home ground, and we can see what they can do when they're comfortable."* After this stage, promising candidates who haven't yet done a mini-pupillage with Monckton are invited to do one. This isn't assessed, but it's a chance for both chambers and applicant to get a closer look at each other.

The second-round interview is the tough one. About 20 applicants get through to this and have half an hour to look at a problem which they'll then be quizzed on by silks and juniors acting the part of difficult clients. *"Our head of chambers always starts by saying, 'We're going to be horrible, but we are trying to see what you're capable of'. It's an insight into what people are like and how they do under pressure."* One member of the pupillage committee gave the example of a recent successful candidate: *"What swung the decision in their favour was that despite having got something very silly wrong, they held their own. Barristers are always under pressure and*

Chambers UK rankings

Administrative & Public Law	Environment
Competition/European Law	Public Procurement
	Tax
Data Protection	Telecommunications

do make mistakes, and you have to be professional about it. This person handled his mistake beautifully, and you could imagine putting him in front of a judge or a client and him handling that situation."

Just say no

Pupillage takes the form of four three-month seats, and there's an effort to ensure pupils see the whole spread of chambers' work. *"In my first seat I was sitting with a competition lawyer, my second supervisor did a mix of EU and commercial law, and my third did a mix of competition and human rights,"* recalled one source. The tenancy decision comes at the end of the third seat, so the final one is *"almost a handover seat"* to ease pupils into full practice.

Sources recalled starting by taking on discrete pieces of work mainly for their supervisor – *"typically they'll say, 'I've got to write an opinion on this by next week; why don't you try the first draft?'"* Gradually, other members of chambers will start to send over work: *"You'll tend to get asked to do the first draft of a skeleton or a research note so that they can see how you present things."* To ensure pupils are *"never put in a situation where you are killing yourself for too many people,"* all other barristers have to come through the supervisor to give pupils work, *"and if the supervisor says no, it means no."* Nor are pupils expected to regularly work longer than standard office hours.

Pupils receive oral feedback on every piece of work they do for barristers who aren't their supervisor, and written feedback, which pupils don't see, is sent to the tenancy committee. *"You also get quite a detailed report at the end of each seat."* Everything is assessed, and pupils' performance in totality is taken into account at the final

reckoning. One source joked that *"everyone is entitled to one complete screw-up!"* What pupils should have amassed, however, is *"something that looks representative of a good body of work."* Monckton has a really good record when it comes to keeping people on, and has offered tenancy to 17 out of 19 pupils since 2002, with both pupils kept on in 2014.

"I enjoy written advocacy as much as oral – I didn't have dreams of wearing the wig and doing the Rumpole act," said one baby. Just as well considering the nature of chambers' work means that *"there are fewer opportunities for second-sixers to get into court"* than in some sets. Monckton takes on a lot of very large cases which don't require rookies to get on their feet, *"but the good side to that,"* points out Tim Ward QC, *"is that pupils get to see some very heavy litigation, so they might end up as a de facto junior on a very big case worth tens of millions of pounds."* Clerks make an effort to get new tenants their own smaller cases, doing things like freedom of information and immigration tribunals which allow more opportunities for advocacy.

Smells like team spirit. Also anchovies

One junior described Monckton as *"horizontal"* in terms of hierarchy, while another cited its defining feature as *"team spirit"* – perhaps due to the fact that members are so often *"sitting on the floor together at midnight eating pizza from a box"* when working on those very big cases. There aren't many silks who could pass as the lead singer of an indie band, but Daniel Beard is probably one of them. Barristers like him and Tim Ward, senior figures who can still remember the days when their own wigs were pristine, are clearly appreciated by juniors.

Not that the older generation are unapproachable: one source recalled the only time they'd ever been reprimanded, on entering the office of a senior QC: *"I couldn't bring myself to enter without knocking, so I kept on doing it, and that's the only thing I've ever been told off for – not just walking straight in to someone's room!"* All in all, we left Monckton with the impression that it's a fairly level-headed place, with a sensible attitude to life at the Bar and members who keep calm even at stressful times.

And finally...
Monckton is a set in good shape with a lot to offer super-bright applicants. Fun facts: Sir Walter Monckton penned King Edward VIII's abdication speech, and during World War I George Allen, the founder of Allen & Overy, saved his life.

4 New Square

The facts

Location: Lincoln's Inn, London
Number of QCs/juniors: 21/54 (15 women)
Applications: 120
Outside Pupillage Gateway
Pupils per year: 2
Seats: 2x3 + 1x6 months
Pupillage award: £60,000 (can advance £15,000 for BPTC)

With a fine stable of professional negligence and insurance specialists, 4NS is one of the Bar's most commercially minded sets

Nearly a third of 4 New Square's 75 barristers are QCs, but don't let that intimidate you – pupils told us they couldn't imagine a friendlier set.

Horses for courses

4 New Square has been on an interesting journey in the past few decades. *"We started out as a general common law set,"* senior clerk Lizzy Stewart explains, *"but we became increasingly specialist and by the mid-1990s were considered the place to go for professional negligence."* Today around 50% of work falls under this header and the practice wins a top-tier ranking in *Chambers UK* (which also ranks all but three of the set's silks in this area). Members are also particularly active on construction, costs, insurance and product liability cases, while others practise in areas including sports, human rights and financial services.

4NS barristers have recently worked on professional negligence claims related to alleged misconduct by solicitors, accountants, bankers, auditors, financial advisers, insurance brokers, property managers and surveyors. Instructions are a mix of claimant and defence work. We note that members have worked on a lot of claims against solicitors recently: for example, Justin Fenwick QC acted for London Underground in a claim against Freshfields and Herbert Smith over alleged wording errors in a failed PFI contract. Meanwhile, Mark Cannon QC defended Liverpool conveyancers Goldsmith Williams as one of many firms being sued by former council tenants over negligent advice about their 'right to buy'.

The set has also worked on insurance claims relating to everything from defective breast implants to delayed infrastructure projects. Two members recently acted on opposite sides of a case that saw a wild boar farmer disputing the insurance coverage he got when he lost his herd as a result of a raid by the Animal Liberation Front.

In another animal-related case Graeme McPherson QC ensured justice was served on a trainer accused of using doping by the British Horseracing Authority.

Dead or alive

The first six is spent with two supervisors for three months each, and the second six with a single individual. Pupils' first six months consist mainly of *"dead work"* – cases which their supervisor has recently worked on. Our interviewees appreciated that this takes some of the stress out of the start of pupillage. The second six, by contrast, is devoted *"pretty much entirely to live work"* – conducting research for supervisors and taking a stab at drafting pleadings for them.

There's also advocacy galore. Lizzy Stewart tells us that *"while ten years ago pupils used to mainly work on professional negligence matters, that's no longer the case – we grab whatever advocacy we can for them."* For example, pupils take small claims such as mortgage repossessions to the county courts. Our interviewees confirmed that doing this work had got them on their feet plenty of times, but also pointed out that they had been involved in *"the full spread of chambers' work,"* for example by attending hearings with their supervisor.

Interviewees stressed the emphasis placed on training, development and assessment during pupillage. Every piece of work pupils submit is placed under scrutiny and formally graded; a pupil assured us that *"you soon get used to this"* and *"fall into a pattern of always trying your best."* On top of this, pupils are assessed by means of three formal pieces of 'panel work' and three moots.

The Bar

Chambers UK rankings

Construction	Professional Discipline
Costs Litigation	Professional Negligence
Insurance	Sports Law
Product Liability	

For the former, pupils are handed papers and instructions and given 24 hours to prepare a piece of drafting. Sometimes the task will have an advocacy or conference element to it, such as delivering a skeleton argument as if in the Court of Appeal or conducting a telephone conference with a solicitor. These assessments are by their very nature *"pretty stressful,"* but our sources considered the work *"manageable in the time you're given,"* and told us they certainly weren't expected to stay up all night working to complete it. The moots, too, were considered *"a friendly if exacting experience"* designed to test pupils without making them feel uncomfortable.

Pupils noted that mid-seat and end-of-seat reviews mean *"you always know where you stand and whether you're doing anything wrong."* Head of the recruitment committee Neil Hext adds: *"Pupils get to comment on their supervisors' reviews, so they can have an input in the process if they believe something unfair has been said."* The way the tenancy decision gets made is considered *"very transparent."* A pupil told us: *"There's a set standard you have to reach when it comes to the quality of your written work, advocacy skills and more nebulous things such as 'delivery'."* The final decision is made by all members of chambers, following a recommendation from the recruitment committee based on all reviews and assessed work. In 2014 both of the set's pupils were taken on as members.

Food for thought

4 New Square recruits outside the Pupillage Gateway, so potential candidates must submit a form via the set's website. If their application catches the recruitment committee's eye then they're invited to a relatively short initial interview. About 15 to 20 then progress from this stage to a full day of interviews, divided into two main parts. One of these, a panel interview, sees candidates choose from a list of ethical, legal and current affairs-based questions and spend 45 minutes preparing their responses, before facing an interview panel. *"Giving you that length of time to prepare is a good reflection of the nature of the job,"* a recent pupil reflected. The other part of the interview day consists of an advocacy exercise; again candidates get 45 minutes of prep time before making a short application to a member of chambers who's acting as a judge. In any downtime there's the chance to sit and chat informally to junior members, and at the end of the day applicants head to a nearby pub with members of the interview panel. Both pupils and recruiters assured us this isn't a sly way to suss out candidates, but rather *"just a nice way to end the day."* That said, you should be on best behaviour and keep in mind just which 'bar' it is you're here for.

So what does 4 New Square look for in pupils? *"We want people who can construct persuasive arguments and react sensibly to points they haven't necessarily thought about before,"* says Neil Hext. Lizzy Stewart adds, with marketing hat firmly on her head: *"We need people who want to drive the business forward – people who are commercially minded and hungry for success."* Perhaps literally: at the end of the panel interview candidates are given five minutes to give a presentation on a topic of their choice. Barristers were particularly impressed by a recent interviewee's entertaining discourse on spaghetti carbonara. Indeed, many of 4NS's members seem to be of a culinary persuasion, with some knowing how to structure a summer pudding as well as they do an oral argument – see senior junior Hugh Evans' recently published *Proper Puddings* if you need convincing.

Cookery books aside, 4NS has turned away from the traditions of the Bar in a number of ways. You may have noted above that Lizzy Stewart referred to chambers as a 'business' – this set has long been one of the Bar's most commercially minded getups. It's also not a stuffy or old-fashioned place. The offices smack slightly of a magnolia show home, everyone is on first-name terms, and there's no event that everybody isn't invited to. Fortnightly breakfasts are *"pretty relaxed"* and *"a good way to get to know people."* Christmas and summer parties are other good networking opportunities, and juniors can often be found at the Seven Stars on a Friday night. One pupil mused: *"Everyone is hard-working but the atmosphere is open and friendly, and juniors are always keen to integrate pupils and new tenants into the set."*

And finally...

4 New Square's supervisors are very strict about hours, but not in the way you might expect. *"Pupils are not normally expected to work outside of 8am to 6pm Mondays to Fridays."*

The Bar

XXIV Old Buildings

The facts

Location: Lincoln's Inn, London
Number of QCs/juniors: 11/32 (9 women)
Outside Pupillage Gateway
Pupils per year: 2
Seats: 4x3 months
Pupillage award: £68,000 (can advance £15,000 for BPTC)

Small but perfectly formed, XXIV is a multidisciplinary and multi-jurisdictional star.

Offshore work abounds at this dynamic commercial chancery set, where barristers juggle domestic will disputes with massive high-value arbitrations.

This ain't no Jarndyce and Jarndyce

On our journey to XXIV Old Buildings, we schlepped through ancient archways, got a bit lost and dodged a few Bentleys before finally arriving at a tranquil corner of Lincoln's Inn. The whole place looks more like an Oxbridge college than a London business district and we half expected to hear the merry thwack of a croquet ball in the distance. But despite the traditional Englishness of its surroundings, XXIV Old Buildings is a set with a thoroughly international, 21st-century disposition. It has an office in Geneva and barristers take on work from places like the British Virgin Islands, the Cayman Islands, Bermuda, Jersey, the Bahamas, Gibraltar, Hong Kong, Samoa and Malaysia. Just to prove its international prowess, XXIV nets a gleaming top-spot ranking for offshore work in *Chambers UK*, along with a premier score for traditional chancery and additional rankings for aviation, commercial chancery, company, fraud, partnership, professional negligence and restructuring/insolvency work.

"What we do can be summarised as follows: business disputes, and trusts and property disputes," explained pupillage committee member Edward Cumming. *"We are often engaged on a broad range of disputes involving the trust and private wealth industry, banking and financial services, hedge funds, accountants and insolvency practitioners, aviation, real estate investors and developers as well as all different sorts of individuals, like the little old lady diddled out of her inheritance. It's important that we also act for charities – you don't want to be working for big business CEOs all the time. It's no less meritorious to act for charities over bequests and wills than it is to be involved in blood-on-the-boardroom-table disputes."*

Since the set's formation over 30 years ago, it's blossomed beyond its chancery roots to become increasingly active in the Commercial Court. A source in the clerks; room told us: *"We've developed into a commercial chancery set and we do a lot of work in the Commercial Court as well as the Chancery Division. We see the bigger commercial sets like One Essex Court as our rivals."* And what's XXIV's strategy for the future? *"We aim to grow with the right people and into the right markets. We see ourselves as exporters of English law: we're looking at China, Africa and offshore common law jurisdictions."*

Currently around 55% of work is international. Barristers have, for example, represented the Turkish financial services regulator in a bid to recover the proceeds of a massive Turkish bank fraud and acted for a Chinese drinks entrepreneur accused of civil fraud and facing claims of €800m. Recently, a member advised administrator Grant Thornton over collapsed hedge funds in the BVI controlled by Germany's notorious 'mini-Madoff' Helmut Kiener, who has been accused of the theft of up to $350m.

Joining the jet set

"Good academics are only part of what we're looking for," says pupil supervisor Bajul Shah. *"It's not just about being clever – we want good advocates, people who can present orally and on paper."* As well as this, *"good people skills"* are essential. *"The Bar is people-related. You have to interact and get on with solicitors, lay clients, judges and clerks."*

Chambers UK rankings

Aviation	Offshore
Chancery	Partnership
Company	Professional Negligence
Fraud	Restructuring/Insolvency

In 2012 XXIV revamped its application process, introducing an online aptitude test to assess candidates' logic and reasoning abilities. After this first hurdle, applicants are invited to an initial interview. Then there's a final round: an assessment day for a short-listed group to test oral and written advocacy, and interaction skills. The advocacy exercise is a mock application to court, while interaction is examined through a mock negotiation. Last year the latter test involved *"four candidates sat around a table, each representing a different charity. The four then had to decide how a pot of money was to be divided."* A junior tenant noted: *"It was interesting to see how the candidates balanced wanting to do well and impress us with how they negotiated. A lot of the stuff we do here is adversarial, but sometimes you have to be able to take a step back too."* After all this, chambers offers pupillage to two lucky individuals.

"We also made some other important changes to the application process," adds Bajul Shah. *"We filtered out anything that could skew results because of background or university. We're testing ability irrespective of these factors. And we increased the pupillage award, because we want to be certain that we are attracting the very best people."*

Pupils complete four seats of three months each. The first three of these are overseen by the same three supervisors. After nine months, the tenancy decision is made and pupils (whether successful or not) are placed with a more junior supervisor. *"As a pupil, you're quite ferociously guarded because they recognise that you've got a long way to go,"* explained one interviewee. A pupil's diary and workload is actively managed by their supervisor. *"A lot of time is spent learning. There's a supportive approach – you can ask daft questions. They want to teach you first and assess second,"* a baby junior said. *"You don't just sit there and cower. You feel valued. From the second seat onwards you're expected to make a real contribution."*

Pupils highlighted that *"the pupillage committee makes sure you see all types of work which chambers does."* This broad spread might include *"everything from domestic disputes over wills to fraud disputes in Dubai and aviation cases about stolen aircraft – Boeing 747s are tricky to make off with!"* If something particularly interesting arises, supervisors will encourage pupils to come to court with them or they'll keep paperwork and points of research aside to set as an exercise later on. *"By the end, you look back and think 'There's nothing I haven't done!'"*

Ariadne's thread

Fledgling barristers aren't prematurely shoved out the door and off to court. *"They're quite protective – when you do get to court, you'll have had a lot of training beforehand."* In any case, *"in chancery there's very little court work. A lot of what chambers does is very high value or very complicated, usually both. The emphasis is on getting to grips with the complexities of the law."* Pupils find themselves *"grappling with tricky legal principles, reading cases, going to the library – and thinking."* In more commercial cases, pupils must deploy their *"powers of analysis and imagination to play with ideas."* One declared: *"This is a pupillage for someone who wants an intellectual challenge."*

Along the way, pupils have review meetings to go over their work with supervisors, each of whom writes an official report on each pupil. The pupillage committee then makes a tenancy recommendation to the whole of chambers and all members get to vote on who's kept on. Fortunately, pupils felt that there is margin to *"make errors all the way through pupillage"* without blighting your chances. *"I made some ghastly mistakes,"* laughed one tenant. *"But mistakes are an opportunity to learn rather than a reason not to grant you tenancy."* In 2014 one of the set's two pupils was kept on as a tenant.

The size of chambers – around 40 members – seems to affect the atmosphere. *"It's close-knit and you get to know people quite well."* The lack of a formal afternoon tea doesn't mean things are always quiet. *"There's more of a continuous thread of friendliness,"* enthused one junior tenant. *"Once you get us started we're pretty difficult to shut up. There's always a pot of tea brewing somewhere and people have time for each other."* This sense of openness extends into the clerks' room and members and clerks are all on first name terms. *"The clerks are keen to get to know the pupils and my supervisor basically pushed me into the clerks' room to encourage that."* In fact such is the level of jauntiness at XXIV that apparently *"even people at the most junior level can take the mick out of the head of chambers – well, one of them, there's two – to his face."*

And finally...

Members of XXIV Old Buildings become part of the set's *"collective pursuit of brilliance"* while still remaining *"lovely, funny human beings."*

The Bar

Old Square Chambers

The facts

Location: Bedford Row, London

Number of QCs/juniors: 13/59 (26 women)

Number of applications: 300

Apply through Pupillage Gateway

Pupils per year: 2

Seats: 4

Pupillage award: £30K plus £10K guaranteed income in second six (can advance £8,000 for BPTC)

"There's a focus on supporting you as a person so you can be the best barrister you can be."

Employment work may be on the wane, but this unpretentious set still gets a healthy slice of the PI.

Picture perfect

Unless you're a stately home tour guide, you're unlikely to get to work in the midst of 250-year-old murals, but this set's premises (misleadingly located on Bedford Row) are decorated with vast paintings eulogising George I in shining armour, on a white horse. But despite these historical royalist credentials, for a long time the set's reputation was strongest for rather less pro-establishment work with trade unions. But as the set's senior clerk William Meade tells us, *"the practice areas we specialise in have come under fire. The implications of the Jackson reforms on personal injury work haven't really kicked in yet, but unfortunately there has been a slight decline in Employment Tribunal work."*

Historically, employment cases have been among the highest-profile work done at the set, and the past few years have been no exception. *Chambers UK*-recognised QC John Hendy is an employment law star who represents trade unions including UNITE, which has recently been involved in cabin crew disputes with British Airways. He also represented dancer Ms Quashie in a high-profile case against sleazy 'restaurant' chain Stringfellows, successfully setting the precedent that she was in fact an employee of the club, rather than self-employed, because of her compulsory shift patterns, fees and attendance at unpaid meetings. Other matters handled at the set have included a disability discrimination case against the BBC, a holiday pay matter for British Gas involving millions of employees, and a sex discrimination case against The FA.

These days, employment work has dropped off from accounting for about half down to a quarter of the work the set does. Chambers earns respectable rankings in *Chambers UK* for its environment, health and safety, personal injury and product liability work, which make up the rest of the legal pie. Still, the set's employment experience has come in handy in the linked area of professional discipline, where work is on the up – including defending medical professionals against being struck off by the General Medical Council, and representing NHS trusts. Personal injury cases also continue to be a steady source of income from the set. Barristers represent insurance companies and local authorities as well as taking claimant work on fascinating issues including the case of a City trader who attributed her nervous breakdown to the stress of her £1m a year job and negligence of her employer. Industrial disease is a particular speciality of several members of chambers, who work with clients suffering from rare employment-related ailments including *"vibration white finger, carpal tunnel syndrome,"* and a steady stream of asbestos-related cases.

Hoop-la

There aren't too many hoops to jump through in Old Square's newly streamlined application process. From a daunting 300 to 500 application forms submitted each year, 16 prospective pupils are invited in for interview. This session consists of an interview in front of a panel made up of three barristers from the set, and a representative from the clerks' room, who doesn't score candidates but will, as senior clerk tells us, *"see how they are with people."* There are likely to be some ice-breaking

The Bar

Chambers UK rankings

Employment	Personal Injury
Environment	

questions based on their CVs, but the lion's share of the 30-minute interview is given over to a statutory interpretation problem, which they have half an hour beforehand to prepare. Head of the pupillage committee Betsan Criddle informs us that *"it's not a legal knowledge test, so we don't expect people to come in knowing the 15 leading cases which will enable them to answer that question. We want to see that they can think through a problem, defend a position, and abandon it if it's untenable. It's also about seeing whether they have the personality to deal with a grumpy judge on a sunny Friday afternoon."* There'll also be questions to test candidates on their ethical judgement.

Our junior sources at the firm also added that *"they're looking for advocates who can deal with client contact with people from all walks of life. You need people skills and the ability to deal with responsibility from an early stage."* This is especially important due to the set's emphasis on getting pupils on their feet from early on in their second six.

Pupils do four stints of three months with different pupilmasters. One junior reported that *"I saw most of the drafting work my supervisor handled, including injunctions covering the Boxing Day strikes by Tube drivers, discrimination cases and unfair dismissal. I was drafting pleadings, writing advices, and did a disclosure exercise for my second supervisor involving a difficult medical personal injury claim, which involved quite a lot of research."*

Courtroom blitz

Our sources reported that *"there's quite a big shift in the second six months – you still help senior members but you take on a lot of your work."* Pupils are likely to start out on the relatively straightforward infant approval cases *"in County Courts all over England. My first one involved a child injured following a small car crash – it was quite good practice in client care."* There's also work on low-value employment tribunals – *"people take their claims very personally, so it's really good experience having to explain the issues involved to them, and is very rewarding when you succeed."* One pupil reported *"arguing against a barrister of ten or 12 years' call, who'd brought his own pupil along just to watch."* Pupils find

that their hours soar alongside their responsibility levels. One alliterative source explained that *"there's a lot of travel in your second six. You'll be up at 6.30 to get the train to trial in Truro."* They have an allocated clerk who assigns them cases and will make sure they're not appearing in court more than four times a week. Pupils found that *"the ethos is that if you're here, you have the resourcefulness to learn on your feet."*

One source felt that *"there's a focus on supporting you as a person so you can be the best barrister you can be, which is reflected in the assessment. It's a very thorough and fair process, where you get a lot of feedback along the way."* Pupils are assessed on set tasks at the end of each three-month stint with a supervisor. As well as involving advocacy exercises, these *"reflect the practical things you'd have to do as a barrister, such as writing advices or skeleton arguments, or doing a client conference."* Both pupils are set the same tasks, which they then present in front of the assessment committee. Success is based on *"making sure you're showing potential and responding to learning points. You're never going to be the finished product when you arrive, so it's about showing you're taking on board what you've been told."* The tenancy committee then makes decisions on retention based both on the assessments and on feedback and scores from pupilmasters. *"It very much felt that we weren't in competition,"* reflected a source. *"Pupils here are quite supportive, and I also got a lot of help from people a few years senior, which I've been conscious to pass down."* In 2014, two out of two pupils were kept on.

Bedford Rowdy

"Although we're traditionally seen as quite left-leaning, we have all sorts of different opinions on things." One source joked that *"we're very much on first-name terms here – apart from a few leading silks who we just call God. Everybody's doors are genuinely open, and I end up chatting to people as I pass."* The set gangs together for informal drinks, and also reported that, especially since the fall in tribunal work, *"we make a big effort to go out and do marketing events as a set."* There's also a *"relatively successful"* football team, but by and large the set preserves its efforts in the field of organised fun for their annual summer party. At the time of our visit, the set had just closed off part of the street for a bash in aid of Great Ormond Street Hospital. *"There was a street party with a live band, a barbecue and a coconut shy – although sadly it rained, so a lot of people had to come inside."*

The Bar

And finally...

"We have a beautiful building with so much history. You feel quite proud that this is the place you work. Although at the same time there's no air con apart from in the clerk's room so it is a balance."

Pump Court Tax Chambers

The facts

Location: Bedford Row, London
Number of QCs/juniors: 11/23 (8 women)
Applications: 80
Outside Pupillage Gateway
Pupils per year: 1-3
Seats: 3-4
Pupillage award: £50,000 (can advance £12,000 for BPTC)

PCTC is, quite simply, the top tax chambers in London.

This top-flight set turns tax into an art form. Be warned: tax can be challenging, mind-mangling stuff, but the results are ingenious.

Tax for good

"There isn't any area of human activity that tax doesn't impact on," pupillage committee secretary Giles Goodfellow QC explains. *"And that means that as tax barristers we have to poke our noses into lots of different areas – and that makes our work very interesting."* Well, that is most certainly true at Pump Court Tax Chambers, a set with an unrivalled place at the top of the *Chambers UK* tax rankings. Members of this chambers work on some really interesting legal head-scratchers. For example, PCTC recently won a victory for the estate of the late Sir George Howard, arguing that a Joshua Reynolds painting among his assets counted as 'machinery or plant' for tax purposes thanks to its function of attracting visitors to Castle Howard, and hence is ineligible for capital gains tax. The set also recently tackled the age-old debate, when is a zoo not a zoo? When it's one of the Wildfowl & Wetland Trust's centres, HMRC tried to argue – but PCTC won zoo status and accompanying tax breaks for seven of the charity's nine attractions. A spate of recent celebrity prosecutions have shown that even stars can't escape the tax man's reach. Although Anne Robinson and Gary Barlow might not have much else in common, they're both implicated in a £1.2bn dispute with HMRC over their use of an elaborate tax dodging scheme.

PCTC acts both for HMRC ('the Revenue') and for tax-payers including private clients, corporations and public bodies. The set has a decades-strong status as home to the country's top tax lawyers, scooping up top rankings in *Chambers UK* across its three areas of business. These comprise direct tax (income tax, capital gains tax), indirect tax (VAT and customs duties), and private tax (trusts, inheritance and estates). One junior source told

us that *"people think that tax barristers sit around with calculators all day but actually we do huge amounts of litigation."* Senior clerk Nigel Jones informs us that *"there's public pressure to crack down on tax avoidance, and HMRC is bearing the brunt of that. Because there are so many well-known people involved, a lot of these schemes and tax cases are relatively interesting to the public."* But there's more to the work of a tax barrister than just litigation. Top experts – like those at PCTC – can also be brought in to advise on corporate transactions and other matters. *"As the economy starts growing again more transactional work in the market will mean more advisory work for us,"* says Giles Goodfellow.

Pupils here sink their teeth into *"complicated black-letter law. Tax is an area with very complicated legislation, which means you have to take a pretty methodical approach to your work. You need mastery of detail, to feel comfortable jumping around between different sets of facts and rules."* We also heard that *"it's important to be able to express yourself clearly because you're dealing with quite complicated thoughts – if you can't do that you'll get in a real tangle."* But if the path to becoming a tax wizard looks daunting, be reassured that *"there's nothing magical about the skills involved, and all sorts of people are capable of doing it."* Senior clerk Nigel Jones tells us that *"there's no one thing that makes a good pupil. We have some people who you might consider quite bookish, and some who are much more outgoing. All kinds of different types of people fit in at this chambers."*

Chambers UK rankings

Tax

It only tax a minute, girl (three months, actually)

Pupils spend their first three months with one supervisor. One source told us that *"I was told that it was kind of a bedding-in period, the point of which was to learn and appreciate that one didn't know anything about tax."* After Christmas, the pace intensifies as *"there's an increasing focus on assessment, and expectations are a bit higher."* Pupils then spend six weeks each with two further supervisors. After that, they spend time with eight to ten other senior members of chambers for periods of one or two weeks. The advantage of this system is that *"a lot of senior people get to see your work firsthand so when it comes to the tenancy decision you're not just relying on the impression you've made when you've passed people in the corridor."* Last year's only pupil got granted tenancy.

Pupils emphasised that *"when you're a junior tenant preparing for a case you might have piles and piles of documents to work through, but quite rightly that's not the kind of work they give you as a pupil. They prefer you to sit down and get on with learning, it's not like being in a criminal set where you'll be up on your feet right away."* Pupils do not undertake their own live advocacy; our sources reported *"conducting research, drafting court documents, and taking notes at conferences"* for their supervisors. Getting to grips with tax law *"requires a lot of concentration and is mentally quite draining, so it doesn't really lend itself to long hours."* Pupils tend to head home in the early evening, but can expect to work the odd weekend at busy times.

Relight my fire

Applicants to PCTC submit a CV and covering letter to the set at the start of February. First-round interviews involve a 30-minute session talking through a problem question. *"We give applicants a self-contained set of extracts from a piece of legislation and some facts relating to a problem, and then ask three or four questions about them,"* explains Giles Goodfellow. *"The exercise is designed such that it's not a massive advantage to have studied tax law."* The second round involves producing a piece of written work that can be up to 2,000 words long over a period of eight hours.

It goes without saying that a set with such a stellar reputation is looking for tip-top grades. Of PCTC's 12 most junior tenants (called since 2000), five went to Oxford while seven are Cambridge grads. Five have Firsts and five have *double* Firsts, though interestingly we note that only four did a law degree. Giles Goodfellow went to some length to tell us the set definitely recruits from a broader base than these figures would suggest: *"If someone has a First, we will consider interviewing them whatever university they went to. And pupils are most certainly judged on their performance, not their academic merits."*

PCTC is relatively small, which makes for a *"friendly, unhierarchical"* environment, say our interviewees. *"The set is still run as if it were a band of eight or so people, even though we now have 34 members. We're still very co-operative: as we all have the same specialism there's a lot of pooling of knowledge and helping each other out."* The seeds of this collaboration may well be sown at the daily 11am coffee morning. *"It's a combination between a nice chance to mingle with other members, and a brain trust,"* believed one junior. *"Barristers come in with a question to put to people, and chances are someone will have done a case that covers the point in question."* Pupils tend to stay quiet, but explained that *"it's not for any sinister reason, and actually it takes the pressure off – if there's a full-on technical discussion, chances are you won't know the answer anyway. And if there's more general social chit-chat going on, anyone feels free to pitch in."*

A pupil told us they were drawn to this set primarily for the opportunity to work with *"people who are absolutely at the top of their game. That can be very intimidating at first, but no one here is arrogant. There are quite a few characters and some very quick-witted people here who are exciting to watch in action, whether that's in court or just at chambers coffee."*

And finally...

Pupillage committee secretary Giles Goodfellow advises: *"Doing a mini-pupillage here is definitely worthwhile, because tax law is like Marmite: you either love it or you hate it."* Have a taste and you might well find it's your thing.

Quadrant Chambers

The facts

Location: Fleet Street, London
Number of QCs/juniors: 19/41 (11 women)
Applications: 200
Outside Pupillage Gateway
Pupils per year: 3
Seats: 2x3 months and 1x6 months
Pupillage award: £65,000 (part of which can be drawn down during the BPTC)

"I quite like the idea there's an enormous ship out there, and you're dealing with something very tangible and physical."

Housed in an ex-brothel and one of London's first coffee houses, this leading commercial set has got its premises a lot more ship-shape.

Quadratic equations

Quadrant Chambers did some simple maths when coming up with their legal USP. Shipping is their historic specialism, which squared nicely with the addition of aviation plus travel, the sum of which makes them the go-to chambers for disputes about getting things from A to B. The set is top-ranked in *Chambers UK* in shipping and commodities and in aviation, and also has strengths in travel, general commercial dispute resolution and international arbitration. As one source revealed, *"shipping throws up a lot of quite expensive litigation. Often clients are hard-nosed and have an appetite for a fight. Plus there's a large amount of fraud, which makes for some exciting cross-examinations."* There are also top-secret arbitrations worth hundreds of millions, involving wrecks or damages to ships at seas.

For one source, a more idiosyncratic side of shipping's appeal was that *"I quite like the idea there's an enormous ship out there, and you're dealing with something very tangible and physical. When I'm working on a matter I can point to 20,000 tons of soya beans or a ship that's run aground somewhere, whereas in banking it's all abstract numbers stored in computers."*

Quadrant Chambers' colourful senior clerk Gary Ventura told us that the set's work is 60% shipping, involving a mixture of wet and dry work. The vessel 'Cape Bird' had $7m of oil stolen from it by pirates off the Nigerian coast – barristers from the set are representing its owners in a case brought by the viscous cargo's owners. They also argued for environmental action group Sea Shepherd after they cut nets to free bluefin tuna that they claimed had been caught illegally.

The other 40% comprises a mix of commodities, aviation and insurance. These can include anything from aeroplane and helicopter crashes and mid-air collisions down to *"alleged drink spillages"* on commercial flights. Two growing areas are offshore work, which involves the construction and supply of oil rigs, and international arbitrations.

All at sea

Quadrant's application process is a bit more complicated than some. The set receives about 150 applications a year, which are blind-marked by three members of chambers, and the best 60-ish applicants are then asked to do a written opinion, often on a shipping issue, which again is blind-marked by different barristers. Candidates are whittled down to a final 16, who have half an hour to prepare an ethical question which they go over in front of a panel of four.

Pupillage secretary Natalie Wallis told us that *"they look for people who are quite confident and maybe good on their feet. If they see someone who's quite bolshy, confident and intelligent, that'll be a tickpoint."* Languages are also a plus, especially German or Mandarin, we were told. Wallis explained that *"we're branching out even further internationally, so having an interest in foreign places and dealing with international clients would be very helpful."* A junior member of the set elaborated that *"it's good to have a sense of what's going on in the wider world rather than having a narrowly English view of things."*

The Bar

Chambers UK rankings

Aviation	International Arbitration
Commercial Dispute Resolution	Shipping
	Travel

The junior continued: *"We look for academic excellence, obviously, but it's also about having the ability to deal with the consequences of your arguments. It's important to have the commercial awareness to find the best and most practical way forward through these knotty legal problems."*

Successful candidates spend three months each with three supervisors, then either switch supervisors for their final three months or stay on. They reported that *"there's not much you can do in your first three months that would throw your chances of getting taken on, but it does become more intense as time goes on."* In the second six, juniors found that *"there's no real step change so much as an expectation we'd do better, and produce a quality of work nearer to that of a qualified barrister."* There are reviews with supervisors after three and six months, where *"each of our supervisors writes a report at the end of the three-month period, which we saw and could comment on."* Natalie Wallis says: *"Attention to detail is something pupilmasters are looking for, as well as seeing pupils using their intelligence, thinking on their feet, and not overthinking too much."*

These appraisals are the most important contributing factor in the final tenancy decision. However, the set also considers pupils' performances in four advocacy exercises. A junior told us that *"the supervisors observe us, and we get a QC in to act as the judge. It's quite intense."* In 2014 three out of four pupils were granted tenancy.

Men in the wigging

"I was largely given live work to do," one source reported. *"My job was to have the first stab at it, drafting-wise, and then compare and contrast my version with what my supervisor did. The live work feels important as it keeps the momentum up, but it's also helpful to work on something that's already been sent out, as you get a different perspective. I enjoyed the chance to do both."* Pupils don't get on their feet in court, in general, although they may take on the small matters after a positive tenancy decision has been made. Still, they have plenty of opportunity to witness courtroom dramas – one pupil told us that *"my supervisors would always take me along to court appearances and conferences."* There's an emphasis on allowing pupils to observe the set's barristers in action, meaning that pupils must wear a court-ready suit every day.

Pupils are closely supervised in an approach that emphasises getting to grips with the law involved. Accordingly, they reported that *"there's no effort to test our stamina as pupils. I was always told that 'there's no need it to finish this today if you run out of time,' and I took that to heart and worked 9am to 6pm."* Although they don't generally take on their own matters, another source explained that *"we were shown that you had to not just stick your head round the door but to physically go in and pick one of the clerks and talk to them every morning, because you'll be working so closely with them later."*

Our sources agreed that *"occasionally the clerks will call the more senior members Mr or Mrs,"* but in general they referred to an informal atmosphere. Quadrant Chambers doesn't gather for traditional afternoon teas like many sets do, although they reported that *"fairly regularly we'll have some sort of meeting to update people on the running of chambers."* Pupils are able to attend, but reported that *"although there's no sense you should be seen and not heard, I didn't want to run the risk of saying something that would make me appear stupid."*

One source told us that *"Gary is our ringleader. He'll take us out for drinks to celebrate things every now and then,"* as well as getting clerks and junior members together for informal evening get-togethers like a glass of wine in the library. Junior members of the set also head out for *"drinks after work every few weeks,"* at Daly's Wine Bar or The Old Bank of England pub *"depending on our mood."* But there's plenty of socialising going on within Quadrant's own (rather more than) four walls too. Quadrant Chambers is inordinately proud of its unusual premises, which are made up of buildings including a former brothel and one of the first cafés in London to actually serve coffee. The set's library – complete with newly discovered Georgian stucco ceiling – is typically a venue for social events, including Christmas carols by chambers-sponsored choir The Sixteen.

And finally...

Although pupil life at Quadrant tends to be more desk-based than outward bound, one source told us that *"the interesting scenarios help to bring the facts to life. When you're thinking about pirates or ships getting sunk in very deep water it's just more interesting."*

The Bar

Queen Elizabeth Building

The facts

Location: Middle Temple, London

Number of QCs/juniors: 4/28 (14 women)

Apply through Pupillage Gateway

Pupils per year: Up to 3

Seats: 3x4 months

Pupillage award: £25,000 (plus second-six earnings)

This top-quality family law set can also boast a caring and supportive *"family atmosphere."*

"We take pupillage very seriously and spend a lot of time improving it, structuring it, teaching, assessing and feeding back. It's not a process of following the pupil supervisor around, being ignored, and grabbing a cup of tea every now and again."

Family history

Queen Elizabeth Building has been a big name on the family law circuit for over 100 years and *Chambers UK* consistently top-ranks the set for its work in this field. What's been the secret behind such prolonged success? *"Excellence,"* Tim Amos QC responded with absolute conviction. *"People don't care if lawyers are this, that or the other; it's all about the service that's delivered. Not only in terms of the academic argument, but also the client feeling as though they were looked after. We provide excellence in the law and in interpersonal relations."*

QEB is particularly known for dealing with the financial consequences of relationship breakdowns but has vast experience in all aspects of family law including jurisdictional disputes, foreign divorces, premarital agreements, civil partnerships, injunctions, forced marriage, Inheritance Act claims and child work. In addition, some members practise general common law, with personal injury and professional negligence work being the focus of their attention. Many members also continue into high judicial office and at present four Family Division judges are former QEB-ers while another, Lord Wilson of Culworth, sits in the Supreme Court. Legal Aid– despite the cuts – still accounts for a portion of the set's work, *"especially at the junior end,"* but chambers handles cases for an *"absolutely huge"* range of clients. One junior explained: *"Everybody has family problems and the most difficult of those go to court no matter who you are. We look after the whole spread – the rich and famous, all the way down to people who literally have nothing."*

Family ties

The set receives around 180 applications through the Pupillage Gateway each year, with up to three individuals then taken on as pupils. Tim Amos says: *"We've always been on the smaller side, even if it's bigger now than when I started* [in 1988]. *That enables us to keep a family atmosphere among the members of chambers."* However, pupils should feel no undue pressure to outdo their cohorts, as space can always be found for the right candidate. *"Because we don't deal in quotas, it's not a question of the pupils being in competition with each other. It's more subtle than that: it's a competition with themselves and a standard of excellence."* In 2014 the set took one of its two pupils on. QEB also swings the pendulum in favour of its pupils by not externally recruiting any new tenants.

Pupils are assigned three supervisors across the year, spending four months with the first, three-and-a-half months with the second, and a four-and-a-half-month stint with the third to allow pupils a longer period to show off their potential in the build up to the tenancy decision. *"The most important thing is that they get a breadth of experience with different supervisors so they can get the best out of the training system,"* says pupil supervisor Katie Cowton. Member of the pupillage committee Amy Kisser adds: *"Your day-to-day is spent with your supervisor and you do the work they're doing and receive feedback on it. It's not like you're not left in the pupils' room by yourself. You have to create a rapport, as you end up sharing your life with them for four months."*

Chambers UK rankings

Family/Matrimonial

Formal assessments kick in after the Christmas break and *"it's fair to say you're being informally assessed the rest of the time."* QEB follows the mantra of *"there's no such thing as a stupid question during your first three months. Nobody is perfect and it's very much a learning process. However, from Christmas onwards we expect pupils to know what they're doing."* A junior contact, usually a baby tenant, is also on hand *"to offer personal support or act as a go-to point for any issues you don't want to discuss with your supervisor."*

The second six provides ample opportunities to get into court. *"When you're first on your feet, you'll go once or twice a week to children hearings or simple money cases,"* says Amy Kisser. *"As a rule of thumb, you'll be in court three or four times a week by the end."* Making the transition from first to second six isn't always straightforward, though. A pupil commented: *"It's quite an adjustment to make as when you're with your supervisor you'll be doing quite high-end stuff, but when you go to court you'll come across a lot of run-of-the-mill legal aid cases. It can be difficult going from a family law injunction application in Southend to a multimillion-pound divorce the same afternoon – it's hard to make that jump in the mind."*

Family dinner

For the lucky few who secure themselves an interview, there's no need to fear an incessant grilling from people determined to catch you out. In fact you can expect a much more affable atmosphere. *"Our interview is designed to be fun,"* concludes Tim Amos. *"It's clearly challenging, but some people have likened it to a dinner party. That may sound flippant but it has this characteristic in common: it's a group of people talking as equals."* Katie Cowton concurs: *"We don't want to scare people or make them nervous because it doesn't work. We don't think we've done a good interview unless we've given the candidate the opportunity to show us what they've got."* What is QEB looking for in its potential recruits? *"Because of our specialism we're looking for a good analytical brain,"* continues Cowton. *"We need a rounded person who can relate to a wide range of different people because it's a people-facing area. We need people who*

are empathetic but able to be clear in their advice. We also look for a certain self-confidence and presence, because within six months they'll take on their own clients and have to be able to convince them they know what they're doing."

Tim Amos described the structure of the set as follows: *"When I arrived it was a benevolent dictatorship. It moved more into an oligarchy, and is now pretty close to mass democracy in the sense that we have a head of chambers* [Lewis Marks QC] *who is important, but he is assisted by a management committee drawn from all levels and sectors. That committee takes all the decisions."* However, there is one exception: when it comes to tenancy decisions the full set will converge for deliberations that Katie Cowton insists *"rarely take less than a few hours."*

Modern family

There's no denying a sense of the traditional remains at this family law stalwart. Afternoon tea runs like clockwork at 4pm every day and *"as a pupil it's a great way of hearing what cases are going on and to generally pick up what's happening in chambers."* Clerks will address members mister or missus, but this formality masks a much closer relationship between these two factions within the set. Amy Kisser told us: *"I was talking to my dad the other day and was adamant I'd told him something, but it turned out it was* [senior clerk] *Ivor* [Treherne] *that I'd spoken with. That was worrying. The clerks run your life for you and they really look after us. They treat you with the utmost respect regardless of whether you're the head of chambers or the bottom baby."*

QEB is more progressive than it may initially seem, though. *"Lots of people think we're really traditional – shooting, hunting, fishing types,"* says Kisser. *"That's not true at all. From the bottom end and now up, we're very modern. We may have traditional values in that we support and care for each other, but equally we have a wide array of members too. Nobody would ever feel like they don't fit the mould here, because there just isn't one."* Tim Amos also believes the set has progressed significantly since he joined: *"Definitely it's changed, and definitely for the better. At the time I arrived QEB was said to be rather stuck-up. There may have been some truth in that but I don't think people would say it about us now. We're all pretty outgoing and available to other people."*

The Bar

And finally...

"You feel safe and secure here," a pupil told us. *"You will have a nice year, and if you're successful you'll have a nice practice. If you're not, then you can guarantee you'll be taken on somewhere else."*

Serle Court

The facts

Location: Lincoln's Inn, London
Number of QCs/Juniors: 20/36 (9 women)
Applications: c.150
Outside Pupillage Gateway
Pupils per year: Up to 3
Seats: 4x3 months
Pupillage award: £60,000 (can advance £20,000 for BPTC)

> *"People might think that we just look at trust deeds all day, but that's not true. It's tough to convey the breadth of practice this set offers."*

Inclusive and innovative, this leading commercial chancery set continues to cultivate a diverse practice.

The times they are a-changin'

Serle Court has its roots in a 2000 merger between a chancery and a commercial set. An innovative move at the time, but as one member points out: *"It's interesting that other chancery sets have now moved into commercial work too, and vice-versa."* That may be the case, but Serle Court has gone on to become one of the largest in its field, and it brandishes 11 practice area rankings in *Chambers UK*. *"There's a lot of fraud, offshore, probate and contentious trusts work, some straightforward commercial work, quite a lot of partnership disputes and company cases,"* one member informed us. *"But our practice varies from one year to the next. If you had said ten years ago that today we would be working on lots of Russia-related litigation everybody would have laughed!"* Members were recently embroiled in one the largest group of fraud actions ever brought to the High Court, while other fraud cases have revolved around a Russian oil company, a gold mine in Kazakhstan and the privatisation of state property in Azerbaijan. Other commercial chancery work has plunged members into disputes over Liverpool Football Club and a Chinese accountancy firm.

Interviewees told us that one legacy of the 2000 merger is that this set *"continues to move forward and be open to people with new areas of expertise – cross-fertilisation of ideas can be really helpful."* A number of 'lateral hires' have joined Serle to do work which didn't exactly fall within its traditional remit. For example, Michael Edenborough QC joined the set in 2008 to do IP law, while Conor Quigley QC arrived in 2010 as an expert on all things EU law. *"These are both practice areas which we didn't have before these arrivals, but still these individuals came to us."* The trend continued in December 2013, when Suzanne Rab joined the set from King & Spalding after 15 years as a commercial solicitor.

Serle receives around 150 applications each year. Recruiters are on the lookout for advocacy ability, even at the paper stage. However, *"students often think it's all about oral advocacy,"* one member told us, *"but written advocacy is very important in this area of the law – we want people who can be persuasive and concise on paper."* In order to be in with a shot at starting a pupillage in October 2016, applications must be submitted by noon on 2 February 2015.

Between 30 and 45 candidates make it through to a first-round interview, which is *"fairly friendly but quite probing."* There's a *"part-legal"* problem question to mull over, but interviewees shouldn't expect to get bogged down by the finer points of the law at this stage. Around ten are invited back for a second interview – *"a role-play conference scenario which includes more legal reasoning."* One baby junior recounted that *"in retrospect the interview was hilarious – my interviewers had a bit of competition to see who could come up with the most fun problem."*

Liar liar

Each pupil has four supervisors throughout the year, and spends three months with each. *"We like to have a mixture of new supervisors and people who have done it before,"* said one source, and although *"very few people cover our entire spectrum of work,"* an effort is made to pick supervisors who work in several areas, rather than specialists.

Chambers UK rankings

Banking & Finance	Offshore
Chancery	Partnership
Commercial Dispute Resolution	Professional Negligence
Company	Real Estate Litigation
Fraud	Restructuring/Insolvency

The current set of pupils had experienced a wide variety of work, including offshore cases, company disputes and *"large commercial cases involving Russian oligarchs."* Supervisors *"get you involved in their current cases, which makes everything more exciting."* One pupil had experienced *"a three-week trial all the way through,"* and was surprised to see a strong human element in this large Russia-related fraud case: *"It had all the commercial complexity that you'd expect, but underlying it all was the question of whether these blokes had lied at some point. You can imagine that the characters involved were quite eccentric..."*

By the third seat, it's not uncommon to be doing work for other members too, *"partly so that your work gets seen by them, but also to give you a broader experience."* Work in given to pupils via their supervisors so *"you don't have that awkward situation of being asked to do work that you don't have time for."* Beyond drafting skeleton arguments, research notes, particulars of claim and defences, pupils spend a lot of time *"preparing for conferences, and trying to set down the ways in which we'll try to convince the client to do what's in their own best interest – that involves commercial as much as legal knowledge."*

Bridging the gap

Mock advocacy sessions take place once every two to three months: *"We do different types of exercises and put pupils in front of different members of chambers with different judging styles."* Exercises may involve *"straightforward applications"* or *"more intensive applications with skeleton arguments."* There's also a mock client conference. *"It's one of those things which you'd think would be quite easy, but in practice it's quite intimidat-*

ing." Pupils get plenty of time to prepare, and said that *"you get constructive feedback about what might happen in practice."*

Halfway through their time with the set, pupils are given feedback on their performance. If weaknesses are identified, then the conversation gives pupils a snap-shot of *"where you are now compared to where you should be. If someone is so far off that tenancy looks unlikely then we may advise them that the Bar isn't for them."* Any member who has seen a pupil's work *"gets some sort of input"* in the tenancy decision, but supervisors have the most influence. Pupils are told of the decision in either May or June each year. In 2014 both pupils were offered tenancy.

Pupils were struck by the fact that *"the atmosphere in chambers doesn't fit the stereotypical image of what a chancery set is like – we are far more laid back."* The most junior members occupy rooms *"right next to the head of chambers, and he'll pop in and say hello, meaning any potential gap in the hierarchy is bridged."* It's a *"very live and let live environment, and everybody is able to fashion the practice that they want. If you want to be working 20 hours a day then that's fine, and if you want a more varied practice that's fine too. There's a sense of collectivity, but that comes from recognising individual aspirations and not making value judgements about them."*

In this *"inclusive"* culture, future pupils are included from the outset: *"As soon as you accept the offer of pupillage, you are invited to celebratory drinks and chambers lunches to ensure you meet the members and current pupils."* This trend continues into pupillage, when pupils are invited to client events, including a client party which occurs every 18 months and was most recently held at the Museum of London. There's also a Christmas party each year and Friday drinks in the clerks' room. For caffeine lovers, there's daily morning coffee and afternoon tea, and pupils told us they *"feel comfortable making conversation – tea is quite far removed from the 'let a silk hold court' model and we're positively encouraged to speak!"* Informal drinks are also organised *"every now and again,"* and although the night *"often starts in the Members' Common Room in Lincoln's Inn,"* members have a free-spirited approach to how their evening will progress...

The Bar

And finally...
Offering a *"combination of incredible intellect and intense niceness,"* Serle Court remains a great choice for ambitious barristers.

South Square

The facts

Location: Gray's Inn, London
Number of QCs/juniors: 23/20 (7 women)
Number of applications: c.150
Outside Pupillage Gateway
Pupils per year: Up to 3
Seats: 6x6 weeks
Pupillage award: £60,000 (some can be advanced for BPTC)

This is a swish commercial set with more than a touch of the City about it.

South Square masters the meatiest of insolvency and restructuring cases, but manages to be hip and chilled with it.

A square deal

"I wanted to come to a set that is the best at what it does," a pupil recalled of their decision to apply to South Square. The set certainly fits this bill, and you can take *Chambers UK*'s word for it: *"Few sets monopolise a corner of the legal market as successfully as South Square. It dominates the insolvency and restructuring sector, and has members with unrivalled talent."* As you'd expect, the set earns top rankings on that end and has had a hand in some major insolvency cases in recent years, including the financial meltdowns of Lehman Brothers, Northern Rock, Glasgow Rangers and Coventry City.

Beyond the insolvency sphere South Square dabbles primarily in general business law – its banking and finance, commercial litigation, company and offshore practices are all particularly highly regarded. According to chambers director Ron Barclay-Smith, offshore work – much of which spans the Cayman Islands, the British Virgin Islands and Bermuda – now accounts for roughly 20% of chambers' overall business. He goes on to tell us that many of South Square's instructions come from the magic circle. *"Not all of them,"* he clarifies, *"but our big complex insolvency cases tend to come through those firms."* For example, Linklaters instructed the set a few years back when it was acting for PricewaterhouseCoopers during the auditor's dissolution of Lehman Brothers in the UK.

Preparing for battle

Chambers takes up to three pupils each year. They swap supervisor every six weeks, totting up a total of eight over the course of the year. This isn't hard and fast, though: *"It's flexible. During my first rotation I was involved in a long trial, so my rotation was extended to eight weeks,"* explained a pupil. *"If you're stuck into something interesting and want to stay, you can."* Our sources praised this system and mentioned they can work for members beyond their supervisor too, an option many take up after their first rotation. *"It's nice to get to know lots of people across chambers."*

Pupils generally assist with *"whatever our supervisor or other members we're working with are instructed on."* With some supervisors, *"writing opinions and research notes"* is the norm, while others spend much more time in court: *"In my first few weeks I helped out on the Bernie Ecclestone trial,"* one pupil reported. The Formula One boss was accused of paying a German banker €33m (£26m) to ensure that a company he favoured could buy a stake in F1. A German court ended the bribery trial in August after Ecclestone stumped up £60m. *"Funnily enough in my second six I've been to court a lot less."*

Given the nature of the work, pupils don't get on their feet until after they gain tenancy. *"The way they see it, the work is so complicated that you need the full year to learn about the law and the procedures. Our clients are mainly big banks and hedge funds, so the idea of a pupil standing up in court can seem a bit stupid,"* said one pupil. A junior member added: *"Pupillage is about showing exponential growth, so pre-decision they really look to push you. I spent my time as a pupil working for*

The Bar

Chambers UK rankings

Banking & Finance	Offshore
Chancery	Restructuring/Insolvency
Company	

QCs and completing my advocacy exercises. Now I'm in court every week battling away."

Pupils are continually assessed during the year, *"but not on anything specific. Essentially you'll do work for your supervisor – a skeleton argument, for example – and they'll look at how good it is and how you're progressing. Everything is reviewed, but it's not like certain pieces of work are marked and given more weight than others."* This approach was greatly appreciated among our sources. *"You don't want to feel like you're doing exams again,"* said a junior tenant. *"This is a more realistic gauge of our ability to practise."* Pupils are kept abreast of their progress throughout the year: informal reviews take place with their supervisor before each changeover, followed by a more formal appraisal at the six-month mark with members of the pupillage committee.

According to pupillage director Martin Pascoe, South Square takes the view that *"mistakes are part of the learning process. Pupils are here to be trained as much as they are to be assessed. There's a lot to learn, so we don't expect them to be already fully formed when they arrive in October."* As a pupil added, *"they know you're coming into an area of law you haven't done before, in a job you haven't done before. You can get away with the odd thing."* Indeed, pupils actually return to their first supervisor in May or June *"to ensure that if they did get off to a bad start they can redeem themselves,"* Pascoe tells us.

The tenancy decision is made by the executive committee – *"the body which takes all the final decisions within chambers"* – and is based on the recommendations of pupil supervisors and other members pupils have worked for. *"I liked how it was done,"* reflected a rookie tenant. *"It's not a vote of all chambers, which meant I was able to interact with the junior end a lot more."* A pupil took up the story: *"Shortly after I started the junior members took me out for drinks in the West End, and after our first*

six we all went out for a meal. They made it clear they have nothing to do with the tenancy decision, so I immediately felt I could relax around them."

Thinking outside the square

Our sources agreed: *"There's no typical member of South Square,"* telling us it's home to an eclectic bunch: *"I know one chap into his literature and art, another chap who studied Sanskrit and one who's really into cooking and surfing. And one of the pupils actually just returned from commanding a platoon in Afghanistan! You'd be surprised by how well everyone gets along."* As one junior informed us, *"an advantage of not being a mega-set is that we all know each other very well. If you have any problems or questions, be it legal or otherwise, you can knock on anyone's door. Just the other day I found myself asking a former supervisor about his opinions on certain types of wine."*

During our visit to chambers it became clear *"we don't subscribe to that corporate culture you get in a law firm."* Indeed, while the pupils were suited and booted (*"until you're a tenant you can't wear what you want"*), most other members we came across looked destined for a day at the beach rather than the courtroom. *"People think the Bar is really traditional and everyone wears gowns all the time, but members here often wear T-shirts and shorts in chambers."*

South Square is not part of the Pupillage Gateway, so applications are made through a form on the set's website. All submissions are reviewed, and anywhere from 40 to 60 candidates are invited for a first interview, where *"we give them a question to test their analytical ability in front of two members,"* says Martin Pascoe. Around 20 or so are invited back for a second interview, which is conducted by the whole pupillage committee. *"At this stage candidates receive a problem to read before being questioned on it. To make the process fairer, we ask everybody the same questions,"* Pascoe says. *"This doesn't require legal knowledge; we're more interested in someone who can think on their feet and deal with a problem as it faces them."* He goes on to tell us: *"We try to keep things fairly relaxed, but we're quite demanding of them – it is a difficult decision after all."*

And finally...

"We don't only take people straight from university and the BPTC," Martin Pascoe says. *"It isn't a drawback for us to have people who have pursued other careers beforehand."* In 2014 South Square retained both of its pupils.

2TG - 2 Temple Gardens

The facts

Location: Inner Temple, London

Number of QCs/juniors: 12/47 (21 women)

Applications: 200-250

Apply through Pupillage Gateway

Pupils per year: 1-4

Seats: 2x3 + 1x6 months

Pupillage award: £67,500 (can advance up to £25,500 for BPTC)

2TG is a sociable mixed commercial and common law set located in one of the finest spots in the Temple.

It might specialise in painful areas like personal injury and clinical negligence, but sources at this lively set find their pupillages anything but agonising.

Modern medicine

2 Temple Gardens sits pretty in an eccentric French chateau-style building overlooking the Thames, complete with sculpted cherubs, larger-than-life figures of Learning and Justice, and balconies perfect for a celebratory drink or two. One junior source admitted that *"you get lost a lot at first, because there are so many different staircases!"* But despite these trad surroundings, 2TG is a set that's moving with the times and working to keep its members fully engaged. The bulk of the work it handles is personal injury, an area which has been threatened by the recent Jackson reforms, which have cut costs and tightened up court schedules. Despite this the common law aficionados we spoke to remain perky. A baby junior told us: *"Although people feared that after the Jackson reforms anyone with a personal injury practice would be done for, if anything we're in court more often now – there certainly hasn't been a downturn or drop-off in my work."*

2TG is top-ranked in *Chambers UK* for property damage and travel, and also has Chambers-recognised strengths in insurance, clinical negligence and personal injury. These areas might not have the multimillion-pound sheen of corporate work, but they do throw up a lively variety of issues. There can still be big wads of cash at stake too. Head of chambers Benjamin Browne QC regularly advises on multimillion-pound claims, and recently acted for the defence in *Collier v Norton*, which ended in the injured party being awarded a record £15m settlement. Another silk, Martin Porter, has a specialism in cycling injuries, and recently secured a prison sentence for a truck driver who caused one of the first cyclist deaths on London's Cycle Super Highways. Other members have specialisms in areas including industrial, equestrian and psychiatric injuries.

The set's travel barristers appear for insurers in international cases involving individuals injured abroad while cross-country skiing, horse riding, motorcycling, yachting, bowling, or – more prosaically – leaning against a hotel sink which then collapsed. Property damage cases might relate to fires, floods, subsidence-causing tree roots, or spontaneously combusting bales of plastic waste. The set is also acting for Warburtons in a claim against the designers of a defective industrial oven that caused a disastrous factory fire, affecting the development of the now-shelved 'Chippidy-Doo-Da' pitta snacks. 2TG also has a developing specialism in sport, which has grown from its expertise in sporting injuries. Members have started taking on contractual disputes for West Ham United of late, and recently acted for Scottish F1 driver Paul Di Resta against his former manager Anthony Hamilton (father of Lewis), in a dispute involving a £4.6m energy drink deal. As these examples suggest, the set also does commercial work and has members who practise in fields like banking and finance, professional negligence and commercial fraud. For example, Charles Dougherty QC was instructed to act for the government of Brazil in a multimillion-dollar case over the reclaiming of bribes received by former São Paulo mayor Paulo Maluf.

Baby steps

Pupils spend their first three months with a supervisor picked by the pupillage committee. At a formal review at the end of that stint, they can express an interest in a particular practice area, and are allocated to a supervisor with that specialism. They finish up pupillage with a

Chambers UK rankings

Clinical Negligence	Professional Negligence
Insurance	Property Damage
Personal Injury	Travel

six-month stay with a third supervisor, and do work for other members throughout pupillage. Rookies are also matched up with a junior tenant for mentoring purposes.

This seat system means pupils see a real mix of work. One told us: *"In my first six I saw everything from car crashes to accidents on oil rigs off the coast of Ghana"* – thankfully not literally. Sources reported that as a pupil *"you look at a case to get an idea of what it's about, then write something like a defence. Your supervisor will write their own version and you will then sit down to discuss the differences between the two drafts. It's a great way of learning – after two or three times you find there are far fewer differences."*

Pupils get on their feet early in the second six. They're likely to start off on infant approval cases, where they present financial settlements reached for child injuries for court authorisation. A source told us: *"An infant approval is one of the most basic things you can do as an advocate, but it's a great experience as it means you learn to do things properly rather than just by watching."* The infant work is quickly complemented by small road traffic claims.

Pupils get a written report at the end of their time with each supervisor, then talk through that feedback with the supervisor and the head of pupillage. Pupillage committee member Anna Hughes explains that *"of course you are being monitored throughout pupillage, but pupils get feedback on all the work they do, and we don't allow them to keep making the same mistakes – any issues are ironed out."* The supervisor reports form the basis for the tenancy decision, although pupils' performances in several mock advocacy exercises may also be taken into account. In 2014, 2TG kept on all three of its pupils.

When it comes to gaining pupillage in the first place, says Anna Hughes, *"TG looks for strong academics and*

something that demonstrates an aptitude for the Bar, such as advocacy experience, public speaking or acting." Out of 200 to 250 initial applicants 45 are invited to an assessment day. Unfortunately, our sources kept schtum on what the day actually involves, revealing only that *"it's a chance for us to spend a day with applicants, and test skills needed at the Bar."* There's also lunch attended by at least ten members of chambers, from silks right down to the newest tenants.

Taking the cake

2TG meets weekly for afternoon tea, and *"one person is always appointed to bring cake."* Don't think this is some form of *Bake Off*-inspired hazing of juniors and pupils: the most senior silks are expected to pull on their pinnies and try their hand at creating one of Mary Berry's latest scrummy treats. Or at least, they get someone to do that for them: apparently Howard Palmer QC *"brought in some very good brownies once – I think his wife made them."* Nevertheless, this egalitarian approach to catering fits the social atmosphere at tea. *"There's no noticeable hierarchy,"* said a pupil. *"Everyone bounces ideas off each other, or just chats about their day."* It's also a chance to prepare for the rigours of getting on your feet – *"some of the silks are just fantastic to talk to. You hear a lot of amusing war stories from the most senior members about their first experiences in court. One of them literally had a book thrown at him by a judge."*

The need to attend trials all over the country means that junior members and pupils might not get as much time for socialising as they'd like. One told us that *"during the week we're all on the run, so lunches out are sometimes limited to a sandwich on the train back from Staines."* Chambers makes up for this by assembling for Friday drinks in one of its conference rooms, and we were also told that *"some members even go on holiday together, or go to Paris for concerts."* This is also a set where barristers have space to pursue their personal passions: Martin Porter maintains a blog at thecyclingsilk.blogspot.com and campaigns for better road safety rights for cyclists, while Jennifer Gray recently wrote a series of best-selling children's books while on maternity leave, using her legal expertise to pen *Atticus Claw Breaks the Law* about a green-eyed tabby cat burglar.

And finally...

"We're encouraged to be in court early on, rather than being kept locked away in chambers every day," said one pupil. This means impressing 2TG with your passion for spoken advocacy is a must at interview.

3 Verulam Buildings

The facts

Location: Gray's Inn, London

Number of QCs/juniors: 23/47 (14 women)

Applications: c.125

Apply through Pupillage Gateway

Pupils per year: Up to 3

Seats: 4x3 months

Pupillage award: £60,000 (can advance £20,000 for BPTC)

"We're relatively future-proof, we're very solid, and we're not going anywhere."
Richard Ansell, practice manager

3VB offers pupils top-end banking experience and a rare opportunity – for a commercial set – to gain advocacy experience.

Feathers in the cap

"We now have far greater recognition in the marketplace and the directories than we did five years ago," said one 3VB member. Top-ranked practices in *Chambers UK* include banking and finance, commercial dispute resolution and civil fraud, while the set's professional negligence, international arbitration and media and entertainment expertise is also ranked highly.

3VB's *"core work"* is in the banking and finance arena, and *"mis-selling work is high on the list, on both the claimant and the defendant side."* There's also a good flow of regulatory cases coming in, *"both on the government side – the regulators – and for the people who fall foul of the regulators."* According to practice manager Richard Ansell, *"regulation is something that's only on the increase."* Members have recently been doing work for the Parliamentary Commission on Banking Standards – *"it's a pat on the back for the banking work we do."* There's also a broad mix of commercial work on the table, covering areas like insurance, company, IT and telecoms, as well as a lot of arbitration.

One recent high-profile banking case saw the set act for Deutsche Bank during its dispute with Sebastian Holdings over unpaid margin calls equating to an estimated £150m. Sebastian Holdings responded with a counterclaim worth a staggering $7bn. Meanwhile, 3VB member Paul Lowenstein QC advised steel magnate Lakshmi Mittal on a multimillion-pound claim brought by 'rice king' Manmohan Varma over allegations that Mittal backtracked on a verbal agreement to pay Varma fees in relation to an oil deal.

Ansell says *"chambers is increasingly seeing international work,"* and the set has been casting an eye eastward, developing links with Singapore, the Middle East, India and Hong Kong. Links continue to be forged in the Caribbean and, closer to home, the Channel Islands and the Isle of Man. The set laterally hires *"when the right opportunity presents itself,"* but there's a strong commitment to *"looking to recruit from the stock of pupils that we have."*

All n my grill

3VB receives around 125 paper applications each year. *"We've discerned a trend,"* said one member, who relayed that *"applicants are getting older and more experienced – they tend to come with two degrees and very often have a bit of real world experience in law or something else."* One recent pupil spent seven years working for a bank before coming to chambers, while a baby junior started out as a solicitor at a magic circle firm. For its part, 3VB is *"keen to recruit both more mature and earlier stage applicants,"* we're told. 40 applicants make it through to the first round. It's *"partly structured"* in that each interviewee faces a panel of three who discuss the candidate's CV and also ask *"a set topical question. It's normally not a legal question, and it forms the basis for a discussion."*

The top 15 or so make it to the second round, which is a *"much more structured and lengthy affair."* Candidates are set a problem in advance and usually have around a week to prepare. *The panel of six takes on the role of the client – a slightly demanding client it has to be said! – and we grill the candidates."* What recruiters are judging is a candidate's *"persuasiveness, intellectual ability and flexibility."* The golden piece of advice: *"It's important*

The Bar

Chambers UK rankings

Banking & Finance	Insurance
Commercial Dispute Resolution	International Arbitration
	Media & Entertainment
Financial Services	Professional Negligence
Fraud	Restructuring/Insolvency
Information Technology	

to recognise structure – for example, setting out three headline points and delivering them one by one. Don't ramble."

Litigating all the way to the bank

Pupils sit with four supervisors for three months at a time. Efforts are made to sit pupils with *"a range of seniorities,"* including a *"fairly junior pupil supervisor"* so they can *"see the more junior style of work that they'll graduate onto."* The pupillage committee also *"does its best to match a pupil to a supervisor if there's a particular preference for a practice area."*

It's highly likely that pupils will see a range of banking work, touching on insolvency, professional negligence and fraud – *"all the types of cases that crop up regularly in the banking context."* Some of it comes down to *"pot luck, so one person might happen to see a judicial review based on a decision by the financial ombudsman, whereas another might see a big fraud case."* A pupil told us *"most of the work is to do with banking – there's lots of it, particularly at the moment, and it's quite exciting work."* The stakes in these cases are *"often quite high"* and involve *"fiddly bits of the law that you need to get right, so you need to be on your toes."* It's not all banking though; pupils get a taste of *"neighbouring areas"* like insurance. There are also *"some things you don't expect – my last supervisor gave me a case about water pollution, which was very interesting."*

The work itself involves *"shadowing your supervisor and pretending their work is your work, which is nice except that you can't hope to do it is nearly as well!"* This means pupils get to experience a *"whole range of things,"* such as producing statements of case, particulars of claim defences, skeleton arguments and notes for cross-examinations. *"If your supervisor doesn't have current work of the right type, then a call will go out to chambers to find something suitable."*

On your own two feet

By their second six, pupils start receiving their own work, which is *"unusual for a commercial set."* One pupil told of working on *"about half a dozen cases so far, and only one of them was paperwork; the rest were in front of a judge."* Usually there are three to four advocacy exercises throughout pupillage as well. These involve preparing a *"standard application, like a summary judgment, or an application to amend. They make it difficult because that is what the training is intended to be like. They're useful exercises, though."* That said, one member stated that although there's *"a certain amount of advocacy in the second six, it's not something that we push particularly hard – the pupillage year is important for learning, and the crucial part is spending time with your supervisor."* The pupillage committee makes a tenancy decision after *"receiving reports from all the people who have seen the pupil's work throughout the year."* In 2014 3VB kept on all three of its pupils as tenants.

"The sheer volume of work never seems to dry up, and chambers is very busy at the moment," said a baby junior. *"As a junior here, a large component of your work is retail banking – that's the steady diet of chambers and that's what gets you into court. If you're doing led work or devilling for more senior members, then it could be absolutely anything, though. I recently did some research in relation to an academic plagiarism case."*

"We're not a place where there are daggers drawn," said one member. *"We want to cultivate friendliness, humanity and diversity."* What 3VB definitely doesn't want is a *"chambers 'type'* – some of the people we recruit are formal and more old-fashioned, while others are progressive and so forth. We see it as a source of our strength that we have people of different political persuasions and backgrounds."*

One interviewee picked up on the collaborative nature of the set: *"We're all in it together, under the 3VB umbrella, doing the best we can to build up the reputation of the set – everyone has a part to play."* Some had come to 3VB expecting it to be *"one of the more conservative sets because you associate banking and finance work with that, but although people are very serious about their work, the culture is informal and we do socialise."* Pupils are welcomed to the set via a drinks party to which *"everyone is invited,"* and they also get to revel in the annual summer party. Junior tenants are *"good at going out for drinks on a Friday evening,"* and there are also *"once-a-term drinks between junior members and the clerking team."*

The Bar

And finally...

If a commercial set with a banking slant is on your radar, then 3VB should be on your list. Just remember to bring the *"zest and energy"* that recruiters expect to see.

Wilberforce Chambers

The facts

Location: Lincoln's Inn, London
Number of QCs/juniors: 22/32 (9 women)
Applications: c.150
Outside Pupillage Gateway
Pupils per year: 2
Seats: 6x2 months
Pupillage Award: £65,000 (can advance £20,000 for BTPC)

"Supreme intellectual ability – that's what we're about."
Martin Hutchings QC, chairman of the pupillage committee

Chancery law: for types who like a thorny legal problem. So where better to look than Wilberforce? Just be sure you bring your A-game.

Smart people

"Barristers here are frighteningly good at their jobs," reflected one pupil during our visit to Wilberforce Chambers. Sprawling across two sides of the handsome 17th-century New Square, this Lincoln's Inn set impresses in every respect. Its true forte is neatly summed up in a trio of top-tier *Chambers UK* rankings for chancery, offshore and pensions. The set amasses rafts of other rankings besides – commercial, fraud, professional negligence, real estate – but this is at its heart a *"traditional chancery set,"* albeit *"one of the first to overlap to cover chancery and commercial,"* senior clerk Declan Redmond told us in 2013. (Redmond has since left the set and been replaced as practice director by Nick Luckman.)

So what about the Wilberforce name – was this the famed 19th-century abolitionist's own set? It turns out his great-grandson, who was a dab hand at chancery, founded the set. The early-'90s name change came about partly because *"the old 3 New Square address was confusing,"* but it also heralded a new, more commercially savvy operation that set out to be the best at what it does. And it achieved it, if its latest accomplishments are any indication: it acted on *Rybolovleva v Rybolovlev*, the highest-value divorce ever ($12bn), and 11 of its barristers represented various parties in the £2bn Nortel pension deficit case.

"Supreme intellectual ability – that's what we're about," Martin Hutchings QC, chairman of the pupillage committee declares. Wilberforce people are pretty brainy – every interviewee stressed this. Scanning through its members online, *"you could be forgiven for thinking we're all Oxbridge males with firsts,"* admits Hutchings, but in fact *"the university you went to is irrelevant."* The set is concerned about the *"image issue with top chancery sets,"* asserting that it's *"not something we have deliberately engineered, and we're keen to de-engineer it."* Hutchings adds: *"We would love to have more women in chambers,"* and the set's bid to boost its diversity profile is *"something we need to do professionally, because our practice is becoming fantastically international."* This also means linguists should apply.

No bullshitters, please

That Wilberforce is *"looking for people of high intellectual calibre"* should not come as a shock, then, and there are more key qualities listed on the set's website. To get your application noticed (outside of the Pupillage Gateway) *"there's no substitute for clarity of expression,"* hinted one pupil. The 30-ish candidates invited to the long-list interview face a short test of their legal reasoning ability. *"We've just changed the system,"* Hutchings tells us. The old interview format of a non-legal problem *"played to the strengths of the debaters – the public school boys – who were more confident at bullshitting,"* explains Tiffany Scott, pupillage committee member. Women, being *"less prone to bullshit,"* now fare more equally with the men, now that they're tested on *"legal analysis and a logical application of your legal knowledge."*

About half make it to the shortlist interview. This 45-minute panel-facing session focuses on a legal problem *"designed to test legal reasoning skills, not legal knowledge."* Non-law undergrads can breathe a sigh of relief, as Hutchings emphasises: *"We make allowances for what*

The Bar

Chambers UK rankings

Chancery	Fraud
Charities	Offshore
Commercial Dispute Resolution	Pensions
	Professional Negligence
Company	Real Estate Litigation

we expect from non-law candidates," echoing one junior who had *"only looked at a law book in earnest a few months earlier."* One pupil explained: *"It tests whether you're able to cope with pressure, and able to come to a definitive view and then defend that view."* Hutchings expands on this: *"At this stage we're looking for an ability to reason, to sustain an argument, to switch a view, to appreciate the consequences of what they're arguing."* Scott stresses that the aim is *"to look beyond the terms of the contract and towards the commercial purpose of the agreement."* While the panel will rate your potential to *"engage with clients, your commercial nous"* and whether you're a *"forceful personality,"* one source did reassure us: *"I felt kind of bad because getting pupillage is meant to be a great self-flagellation process, but it was actually pretty simple."* The breezy riposte of the man who got the job? Perhaps, but in relative terms it appears true: *"They're just not looking to catch you out."*

Life in the shadows

Every year chambers takes on two pupils, who are each assigned to a supervisor to shadow for two months. They then rotate after every two-month period until the year is up. Scott elaborates: *"We tend to give them to the person they get the best experience from,"* with the plan being to expose them to *"all the main bases of our work here: property, commercial, pensions and trust/private client work."* Pupils tend to start with a very senior QC for the first seat, and diversify thereafter, shadowing those offering the most interesting cases in chambers. And there is no real distinction between the first and second six, incidentally. All juniors reported happily that *"none of them treated me like a subspecies,"* and that *"pupillage was a very, very positive experience!"*

A taster of a pupil's assignments might be: *"Big commercial breach of contracts, breach of confidence trials, or trusts and pensions disputes."* One pupil raved about *"seeing five trials during pupillage – I've been to the Supreme Court twice and the Court of Appeal twice."* Super-

visors will either give pupils 'dead' work (old cases) or 'live' work (current). Both scenarios presented *"a lot of paperwork,"* agreed sources, but also saw them *"contributing to skeleton arguments and pleadings."* 'Dead' work *"enables them to spend time giving you feedback,"* and pupils truly valued *"getting feedback from some of the best practitioners in their fields,"* although some would have appreciated more emphasis on this. All agreed, however, that the true buzz comes from the 'live' work, taking the barristers-to-be into their natural habitat: *"Outside of my comfort zone."*

Wilberforce bans slavery

"There's no expectation of hours," Scott confirms, and pupils appreciate this: *"The best thing was that no one screws you over, you didn't get unreasonable requests – everyone gave me enough time to do all the work."* Thankfully, this leaves pupils with enough time to devote to the new advocacy training coming in this year, culminating in a *"mock courtroom test."* Another big plus is that *"you're not in competition with your fellow pupil,"* one told us. While the set certainly doesn't go soft on pupils, there is *"an understanding that you're learning as well as being assessed, and you're allowed to make mistakes – but the key thing is learning from that,"* one pupil reflected. The tenancy decision is made in June – relatively early on – a bonus on the occasion that you'd have to find a third six. The decision is based principally on the views of the four supervisors who mentored the pupils until June, assessing them on broadly the same criteria that got them the job in the first place. In 2014 Wilberforce kept on both its pupils.

How does life change after tenancy? Aside from the obvious, *"you get your own room on the top floor, which I like a lot."* We detected a no-nonsense, businesslike vibe on our visit. Tenants, pupils and clerks work pragmatically together, everyone does their job but respects down time: *"You control your own time; I took a three-week holiday after a big case and they didn't bat an eyelid,"* said a junior. Be it supervisor lunches, fortnightly chambers lunches, cocktail parties with clients, karaoke, fireworks or pétanque, Wilberforce does enough to ensure no end of pastoral support and social hoopla. *"I was made to feel very welcome,"* one pupil told us – no more so than down the Seven Stars, where you'll find a Wilberforce crowd *"pretty much any night of the week."* *"There's no set type of person here,"* one source commented. *"It's as normal an existence as much as being a barrister can be."*

The Bar

And finally...

All our interviewees did something non-legal before joining Wilberforce. *"Some knowledge of the world does help,"* says pupillage committee chair Martin Hutchings.

A-Z of Barristers

Atkin Chambers

1 Atkin Building, Gray's Inn, London, WC1R 5AT
Tel: (020) 7404 0102 Fax: (020) 7405 7456
Email: clerks@atkinchambers.com
Website: www.atkinchambers.com

No of Silks 17
No of Juniors 25
No of Pupils 2

Contact
Andrew Burrows
pupillage@atkinchambers.com

Method of application
Pupillage Gateway

Pupillages (p.a.)
2 - 12 month pupillages

Income
£60,000

Tenancies
4 in the last three years

Chambers profile
Atkin Chambers is a leading commercial set specialising in construction, energy and technology disputes and related professional negligence claims. As well as leading in the domestic field, its barristers have a significant international practice spanning Europe, the Middle East, Asia, Africa and the Caribbean.

Type of work undertaken
Atkin Chambers is a leader in the fields of construction and engineering law. This specialism means that members of chambers are often instructed in related commercial disputes such as those pertaining to energy, information technology, shipbuilding (including repair and conversion) and general commercial law matters arising from such commercial projects. Members of chambers are recommended as leaders in their field in the areas of construction, energy and natural resources, information technology, international arbitration (construction/engineering) and professional negligence (technology and construction). Members of Atkin Chambers regularly appear at international arbitrations seated in the Gulf States, Hong Kong and Singapore.

Pupil profile
Chambers is committed to recruiting pupils and tenants (generally from its own pupils) that will participate in its continued success in international and domestic practice. Chambers looks for pupils who are well motivated and have an interest in practising in the areas of law in which chambers specialises.

Applicants for pupillage should have a first-class degree or a good upper second-class degree. Postgraduate qualifications are viewed favourably but are not essential. Applications from non-law graduates are welcomed. Pre-existing knowledge of construction law is not required, although candidates should have a strong grounding in contract and tort law.

Mini-pupillage
Although a mini-pupillage is not a pre-requisite to applying for a pupillage, prospective pupils are encouraged to apply for a mini-pupillage so as to gain some knowledge of the areas of law in which Atkin Chambers specialises. Six mini-pupillages are offered each year. Applicants are invited to apply by letter with CV during March 2015 (pupillage@atkinchambers.com).

Pupillage
Atkin Chambers takes recruitment to pupillage and tenancy extremely seriously. The pupillage year is structured to provide all of the Bar Council's minimum training requirements and the additional training chambers considers is necessary for successful entry into the high-quality commercial work of its practice. Atkin Chambers provides its own advocacy training and assessment in addition to that provided by the Inns of Court.

Full and up-to-date details of the structure and goals of Atkin Chambers' pupillage training programme may be reviewed on our website.

Funding
Chambers offers up to two 12-month pupillages, all of which are funded. The pupillage award is £60,000 for pupils starting in 2016-2017. A proportion of this award may be drawn down in advance to assist pupils during their BVC year.

In their first years of practice, new members may expect earning potential equivalent to peers at the largest commercial sets.

The Bar

AtkinChambers Barristers

2 Bedford Row (William Clegg QC)

2 Bedford Row, London WC1R 4BU
Tel: (020) 7440 8888 Fax: (020) 7242 1738
Email: clerks@2bedfordrow.co.uk
Website: www.2bedfordrow.co.uk

No of Silks **18**
No of Juniors **51**
No of Pupils **4**

Graduate recruitment contact
Stephen Vullo QC
(020) 7440 8888

Method of application
Pupillage Gateway

Pupillages (p.a.)
4 x 12 months
**Tenancies offered according
to ability**

Chambers profile

Widely regarded as one of the leading crime chambers in the country, 2 Bedford Row was awarded Crime Set of the Year 2013 by both Chambers and Partners and the Legal 500 legal directories. Chambers has been described by Chambers UK as *"the outstanding criminal set"*, *"probably the leading fraud set in the country"* that has *"quality tenants from top to bottom"*.

Type of work undertaken

Chambers has a broad-based criminal practice and its members have appeared in some of the most high-profile criminal cases of recent years (Sgt Danny Nightingale R v Barry George, R v Levi Bellfield, R v Mark Dixie, News International phone hacking case, Vincent Tabak, Dave Lee Travis and the Hillsborough Inquiry). In addition, members of chambers have particular experience in the fields of confiscation/restraint, health and safety, financial services law, sports law, professional regulation/discipline and inquests. Members are frequently instructed to appear before regulatory bodies such as the GMC, the FA, the VAT tribunal and the Police Disciplinary Tribunal.

Pupil profile

Chambers recruits candidates from all backgrounds who display the highest intellectual ability, excellent advocacy skills, sound judgement and a real commitment to criminal law and its related fields. Candidates will also be well-rounded individuals who are able to communicate effectively with a wide variety of people.

Pupillage

Chambers offers up to four 12-month pupillages each year but will require a 3rd six to be successfully completed before inviting applications for tenancy. Each pupil will have a different pupil supervisor in each of the 3 six month periods. This ensures that pupils are provided with a thorough grounding in all aspects of chambers' practice. Chambers also provides structured advocacy training throughout the pupillage year and will pay for pupils to attend the 'Advice to Counsel' and 'Forensic Accountancy' courses.

Mini-pupillages

Chambers welcomes applications for mini-pupillage. Please see the website for details.

Funding

Chambers provides a grant of £12,000 to each pupil, paid monthly throughout the year and, in addition, guaranteed earnings of £10,000 in second six. All earnings retained in 3rd six.

**2
BEDFORD ROW**

Blackstone Chambers (Monica Carss-Frisk QC and Anthony Peto QC)

Blackstone House, Temple, London EC4Y 9BW DX: 281 Chancery Lane
Tel: (020) 7583 1770 Fax: (020) 7822 7350
Email: pupillage@blackstonechambers.com
Website: www.blackstonechambers.com

Chambers profile
Blackstone Chambers occupies large and modern premises in the Temple.

Type of work undertaken
Chambers' formidable strengths lie in its principal areas of practice: commercial, employment and EU, public law, human rights and public international law. Commercial law includes financial/ business law, international trade, conflicts, sport, media and entertainment, intellectual property and professional negligence. All aspects of employment law, including discrimination, are covered by chambers' extensive employment law practice. Public law incorporates judicial review, acting both for and against central and local government agencies and other regulatory authorities, all areas affected by the impact of human rights and other aspects of administrative law. EU permeates practices across the board. Chambers recognises the increasingly important role which mediation has to play in dispute resolution. Seven members are CEDR accredited mediators.

Pupil profile
Chambers looks for articulate and intelligent applicants who are able to work well under pressure and demonstrate high intellectual ability. Successful candidates usually have at least a 2:1 honours degree, although not necessarily in law.

Pupillage
Chambers offers four 12-month pupillages to those wishing to practise full-time at the Bar, normally commencing in October each year. Pupillage is normally divided into four sections and every effort is made to ensure that pupils receive a broad training. The environment is a friendly one; pupils attend an induction week introducing them to chambers' working environment. Chambers prefers to recruit new tenants from pupils wherever possible. Chambers subscribes to Pupillage Gateway.

Mini-pupillages
Assessed mini-pupillages are an essential part of the pupillage procedure and no pupillage will be offered at Blackstone Chambers unless the applicant has undertaken an assessed mini-pupillage. Applications for mini-pupillages must be made by 1st April 2015; earlier applications are strongly advised and are preferred in the year before pupillage commences.

Funding
Awards of £60,000 per annum are available. The pupillage committee has a discretion to consider applications for up to £17,000 of the pupillage award to be advanced during the BTPC year. Since chambers insists on an assessed mini-pupillage as part of the overall application procedure, financial assistance is offered either in respect of out of pocket travelling or accommodation expenses incurred in attending the mini-pupillage, up to a maximum of £250 per pupil.

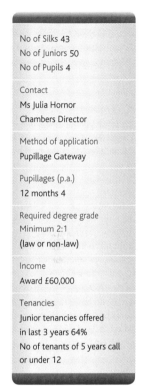

No of Silks 43
No of Juniors 50
No of Pupils 4

Contact
Ms Julia Hornor
Chambers Director

Method of application
Pupillage Gateway

Pupillages (p.a.)
12 months 4

Required degree grade
Minimum 2:1
(law or non-law)

Income
Award £60,000

Tenancies
Junior tenancies offered
in last 3 years 64%
No of tenants of 5 years call
or under 12

Blackstone
CHAMBERS

The Bar

Brick Court Chambers (Jonathan Hirst QC and Helen Davies QC)

7-8 Essex Street, London WC2R 3LD
Tel: (020) 7379 3550 Fax: (020) 7379 3558
Email: lyana.peniston@brickcourt.co.uk
Website: www.brickcourt.co.uk

No of Silks **36**
No of Juniors **45**
No of Pupils **5**

Contact
Mrs Lyana Peniston, Pupillage
Manager
Tel (020) 7520 9881

Method of application
Pupillage Gateway

Pupillages (p.a.)
12 months – 4-5

Tenancies
12 tenancies offered in the
last 3 years

Chambers profile

Brick Court Chambers has long been a leading commercial set of Chambers. We also have particular expertise in EU/competition law and in the fields of public law and human rights law. In all our practice areas, members of chambers are regularly involved in the leading cases of the day.

Pupillage

We take considerable care in providing a broad training to pupils. Some will wish to develop a commercial practice based primarily in the Commercial Court involving banking, reinsurance and international sale of goods, or a wider range of commercial work involving professional negligence, company law, private and public international law, takeovers and mergers, media and entertainment or sports law. Others will prefer to specialise in the EU or competition fields or in public law and human rights. Advocacy exercises under the supervision of senior members of chambers are an integral part of pupillage at Brick Court.

All twelve month pupillages carry an award of at least £60,000. Up to £25,000 of the award may be drawn down during the year prior to pupillage (subject to chambers' approval). Chambers also pays for all compulsory courses during pupillage, and for all pupils to accompany their pupil supervisor to a hearing before the European Courts if the opportunity arises.

Candidates are generally expected to have a first or good upper second degree and to demonstrate first class intellectual ability.

Mini-pupillages

Assessed mini-pupillages are an important part of our pupillage selection procedures. We do not expect to select pupils merely on interview, nor do we expect you to make your choice on such a limited basis. Please apply for a mini-pupillage, as early as possible and preferably prior to applying for pupillage, by way of the application form that can be found on the pupillage pages of our website.

The Bar

Cloisters

Cloisters, 1 Pump Court, Temple, London, EC4Y 7AA
Tel: (020) 7827 4000 Fax: (020) 7827 4100
Email: clerks@cloisters.com
Website: www.cloisters.com

No of Silks **9**
No of Juniors **42**
No of Pupils **2**

Contact
pupillage@cloisters.com

Method of application
Pupillage Gateway

Pupillages (p.a.)
2 for 12 months

Chambers profile
Cloisters is a leading set advising in employment, discrimination and equality, personal injury, clinical negligence, sports and commercial law with a reputation for delivering exceptional results. It provides responsive first-class client service combined with technical excellence and commercial perspective to resolve the most complex legal problems for individuals and organisations of all sizes.

Type of work undertaken
Employment, discrimination and equality: Cloisters is at the forefront of all aspects of employment law and has unrivalled expertise in discrimination and equality issues. Recent landmark cases include Bull and Bull v Hall and Preddy, the well-known case involving direct discrimination against a same sex couple by Christian hotel owners on the ground of the couple's sexual orientation; Stott v Thomas Cook, a case dealing with the rights of airline passengers with mobility problems to claim compensation for breach of the EC Disability Regulation and Howard v Metropolitan Police Service, a widely-reported case involving direct discrimination against a female police officer by a senior officer on the grounds of sex and race.

Personal injury and clinical negligence: Cloisters is consistently rated as a top-ranked clinical negligence and personal injury set in Chambers & Partners. We continue to be at the forefront of high value litigation involving catastrophic brain and spinal injury. Recent clinical negligence High Court trial successes include Pringle v Nestor Prime Care Services (amputation following negligent triage of septicaemia) and Coakley v Dr Rosie (GP failure to suspect bacterial meningitis); leading clinical negligence cases in the Court of Appeal include for example, Iqbal v Whipps Cross University Hospitals (lost years' earnings for children), Crofton v NHSLA (local authority payments and double recovery). Recent High Court PI trial successes include Farrugia v Burtenshaw (future care PPO), Collins v Serco (vicarious liability, attack on custody officer by detainee), Malvicini v Ealing PCT (disabling psychological injury, accident at work). Seminal Court of Appeal appearances include Connor v Surrey County Council (interplay of public and private law), Stanton v Collinson (seatbelts, contributory negligence), Noble v Owens (fraud/video surveillance). Members of chambers are also consistently instructed in the leading stress at work cases.

Pupil profile
Chambers welcomes applications from outstanding candidates from all backgrounds and academic disciplines including lawyers coming late to the Bar.

Pupillage
Chambers offers two 12 month pupillages for those wishing to practise full-time at the Bar, normally commencing in October each year. Each pupil is supervised and the supervisor changes every three months to show the pupil different areas of practice. Second six pupils will be allocated work by clerks subject to availability of work and pupil ability.

Mini-pupillages
Cloisters offers up to ten three day mini-pupillages each year. All applicants must have completed at least their first year at university in any subject. The mini-pupillage is not assessed and is not a requirement for applications for pupillage.

Funding
Cloisters offers two funded pupillages each year. Each pupil will receive an award (currently £40,000 per year). Pupils can also ask for an advance.

Crown Office Chambers

Head of Chambers: Richard Lynagh QC
2 Crown Office Row, Temple, London, EC4Y 7HJ
Tel: (020) 7797 8100 Fax: (020) 7797 8101
Email: mail@crownofficechambers.com
Website: www.crownofficechambers.com

No of Silks 13
No of Juniors 77
No of Pupils up to 3
Contact
Carlo Taczalski
Method of application
Chambers' application form, downloadable from chambers' website
Pupillages (p.a.)
Up to three per year, 12 months
£60,000, comprising £50,000 award plus £10,000 guaranteed earnings
Tenancies
No of tenancies offered in last 3 years 6

Chambers profile
Crown Office Chambers is one of the leading sets of chambers specialising in civil common law work. Chambers has an established reputation in the fields of construction, health and safety, insurance and reinsurance, personal injury, product liability, professional negligence and property damage. It is not a 'pure commercial' set, and pupils will see a range of work during pupillage.

Junior tenants also undertake a range of work with an emphasis on developing advocacy skills; in addition to working on their own paperwork and accepting junior briefs, junior tenants in their first years of practice are generally in court several times per week. Tenants have the opportunity to specialise as their practices develop, by which time chambers considers that their blend of early advocacy and advisory experience gives them the edge over their contemporaries at many 'pure commercial', and indeed 'pure' common law / personal injury sets. It also keeps work varied and allows members to make a more informed decisions to specialise in a given field or fields.

Pupil profile
Members pride themselves on their professionalism, an astute and business-orientated awareness of the practical needs of solicitors and lay clients, combined with an approachable and unstuffy attitude to their work. Chambers looks for the same in its pupils, all of whom are regarded as having strong tenancy potential. Pupils are expected to display the motivation, dedication and intelligence which are the hallmarks of a first-class barrister. Academically, they should have a first or upper second-class honours degree (not necessarily in law), a flair for oral and written advocacy, and a strong and committed work ethic.

Pupillage
Pupils rotate through three pupil supervisors during the course of the year. In their second six, pupils are briefed to attend County Court hearings on their own, probably at least two or three times per week. Generally these will be small personal injury cases. Pupils receive regular feedback on their work from pupil supervisors and other members of chambers. They also undertake a series of advocacy exercises in front of a panel of four members of chambers and receive extensive feedback after each exercise. There are also two to three assessed written exercises during the course of pupillage. Tenancy decisions are made in early July to enable any pupils who are not taken on to apply for third sixes.

Mini-pupillage
Limited number of mini-pupillages in selected weeks throughout the year. Online application form downloadable from chambers' website.

Essex Court Chambers

24 Lincoln's Inn Fields, London WC2A 3EG
Tel: (020) 7813 8000 Fax: (020) 7813 8080
Website: www.essexcourt.net

Chambers profile

We are a leading commercial set, with an international reputation for excellence.

Our members offer advisory and advocacy expertise on disputes relating to all aspects of business and commerce, both domestic and international. Our core areas of work include commercial litigation, civil fraud, international commercial arbitration, international trade, energy, shipping, PIL, insurance/reinsurance, banking and financial services. But our members enjoy the freedom to develop their own specialisms. Many have done so, in a wide range of areas. This means that pupils and junior tenants can see a broad range of work.

Pupil profile

Pupillage is primarily about training. We take that seriously. Our pupils can expect to be put through a rigorous but enjoyable training programme, including continuous feedback, regular appraisals and advocacy training. We also take career development seriously. Our members are supported by an enthusiastic, active clerking team from the earliest stage of their practice.

Our work is intellectually challenging. We seek to recruit the best and the brightest. A degree from Oxford or Cambridge is not a prerequisite of pupillage with us; not all of the top talent is concentrated in a small number of academic institutions. We encourage applications from all.

We are committed to equality of opportunity regardless of race, colour, ethnic or national origin, nationality, citizenship, sex, gender re-assignment, marital or civil partnership status, sexual orientation, age, disability, religion or belief, political persuasion, pregnancy or maternity. We will make reasonable adjustments for disabled applicants.

Pupillage

We typically offer up to four 12 month pupillages per year. Part of the first six months' award may be drawn down for the BPTC and/or relevant post-graduate study.

Undertaking a mini-pupillage is encouraged. Reasonable travel and other expenses are refunded.

Please see our website for full details of pupillage and mini-pupillage, including when and how to apply.

No of Silks 44
No of Juniors 43
No of Pupils at least 2

Contact
Petra Bailey
(020) 7147 7257

Method of application
Pupillage Gateway

Pupillages (p.a.)
Up to 4 12-month pupillages

Pupillage award
£60,000

Tenancies
Up to 4

The Bar

One Essex Court

Chambers of Lord Grabiner QC, One Essex Court, Temple, London EC4Y 9AR
Tel: (020) 7583 2000 Fax: (020) 7583 0118
Email: clerks@oeclaw.co.uk Website: www.oeclaw.co.uk

No of Silks **32**	
No of Juniors **56**	
No of Pupils **5+**	
Contact	
Joanne Huxley, Secretary to the Pupillage Committee	
Method of application	
Pupillage Gateway	
Pupillages (p.a.)	
5+ 12 months	
Required degree grade	
Ordinarily 1st Class (law or non-law)	
Income	
Award £60,000 + earnings during second-six	

Chambers profile
One Essex Court is a pre-eminent set of barristers' chambers, specialising in commercial litigation. Members provide specialist advice and advocacy services worldwide, which include all areas of dispute resolution, litigation and arbitration.

Type of work undertaken
Chambers' work embraces all aspects of domestic and international trade, commerce and finance. Members of chambers are recognised specialists in the many diverse fields characterised as commercial disputes, also regularly accepting nominations as arbitrators, mediators and experts. Chambers' work includes, but is not limited to: arbitration, banking and finance, civil fraud, commercial litigation, company and insolvency, competition and EU, energy (oil, gas and utilities), financial services, insurance, IP, professional negligence and revenue law.

Pupil profile
Chambers has for many years maintained a policy of active recruitment and expansion and only offers pupillage to those who are thought capable of becoming tenants. Provided a candidate is proven to have the requisite ability, no distinction is drawn between candidates who do and those who do not have a law degree. Pupils at One Essex Court do not compete against one another for a predetermined maximum intake.

Pupillage
At least four guaranteed 12-month pupillages are offered per year, each with substantial funding. In addition, chambers now offers a separate pupillage within their Intellectual Property group. From the beginning, pupils assist pupil supervisors with their papers, do legal research, draft opinions, pleadings and skeleton arguments. There are substantial opportunities for advocacy in the second six months of pupillage. Chambers subscribes to Pupillage Gateway.

Mini-pupillage
Mini-pupillages last for either one or two days. They are not assessed. A mini-pupillage is not a pre-requisite for pupillage although it is encouraged as it can provide a good opportunity both to see how chambers works and to meet members of chambers. Please visit chambers' website for the application process and deadlines.

Funding
Chambers offers each pupil £60,000, supplemented by earnings in the second six. It is understood that this is amongst the highest, if not the highest, remuneration package available to pupils. An advance of the Award is available, upon request, during a prospective pupil's Bar Professional Training Course ("BPTC") year.

5 Essex Court

5 Essex Court, Temple, London EC4Y 9AH
Tel: (020) 7410 2000   Fax: (020) 7129 8606
Email: clerks@5essexcourt.co.uk
Website: www.5essexcourt.co.uk

No of Silks **6**
No of Juniors **34**
No of Pupils **2**

Contact
Miss Georgina Wolfe
(020) 7410 2000

Method of application
Pupillage Gateway

Pupillages (p.a.)
Up to 2 12-month pupillages

Tenancies
% of pupils offered tenancy **100%**

Chambers profile
5 Essex Court is a leading civil set with particular specialisms in public law and human rights, police and employment law.

Chambers' work is exciting and often high profile with members of all levels involved in the majority of significant cases, public inquiries and inquests involving the police. Pupils and juniors in the last few years have been involved in such cases as the Leveson Inquiry, R (Roberts) v Commissioner of Police of the Metropolis (stop and search), R (Debbie Purdy) v DPP (assisted suicide) and the inquests arising from the Hillsborough disaster and the death of Mark Duggan. Junior tenants and pupils appear, alone or led, in a wide range of courts and tribunals, from the Magistrates' Court to the Supreme Court. Police law also emcompasses jury advocacy in civil trials for false imprisonment and malicious prosecution as well as inquests.

Types of work undertaken
5 Essex Court specialises in public law, police law, human rights, employment and personal injury. Chambers is widely acknowledged to be one of the leading sets for police law but also has leading practitioners in a variety of other areas such as employment, immigration and public inquiries.

Pupil profile
5 Essex Court looks to recruit up to two pupils of outstanding calibre each year. Applicants should be able to demonstrate good intellectual ability as well as a commitment to chambers' core practice areas. Successful candidates usually have a 2:1 degree or above, although not necessarily in law. No experience of police law is necessary.

Chambers operates an equal opportunities selection policy for pupils and tenants and particularly encourages applicants from minority groups and groups who are under represented at the Bar.

Pupillage
Chambers offers up to two pupillages each year to those wishing to practise full-time at the Bar. The pupillage year commences in September.

5 Essex Court prides itself on providing pupils with a supportive, friendly and constructive environment in which to learn and begin their practices. Chambers' commitment to pupils is reflected in the exceptional retention rate (100% in the last 7 years) and carefully structured pupillage year. Pupils have three supervisors and chambers aims to ensure that they experience the full range of chambers' work. Pupils also receive in-house advocacy training, funding for all required courses (such as Forensic Accounting) and a 'Pupils' Talks Programme' provided by members of chambers which is designed to introduce particular areas of chambers' practice and to provide more general guidance for a successful life at the Bar. Applications can be made through the Pupillage Gateway.

Mini-pupillages
A mini-pupillage at 5 Essex Court is an opportunity to experience life in chambers and to gain an insight into the work undertaken at 5 Essex Court by shadowing barristers over the course of a week.

Mini-pupillages are assessed but there is no requirement to complete a mini-pupillage in chambers in order to be considered for pupillage.

There are three mini-pupillage seasons and applications can be made online through the website.

Funding
5 Essex Court pupils receive a minimum of £40,000 during their pupillage year, comprising a £25,000 award and £15,000 guaranteed earnings.

The Bar

Thirty Nine Essex Street

39 Essex Street, London WC2R 3AT
Tel: (020) 7832 1111 Fax: (020) 7353 3978
82 Kings Street, Manchester, M2 4WQ
Tel: (0161) 870 0333 Fax: (020) 7353 3978
Email: clerks@39essex.com Website: www.39essex.com

No of Silks 40
No of Juniors 83
No of Pupils up to 3

Contact
Charles Cory-Wright QC &
Marion Smith
anna.markey@39essex.com
(020) 7832 1111

Method of application
Pupillage Gateway

Pupillages (p.a.)
Up to three

Other offices
Singapore

Chambers profile

Thirty Nine Essex Street is a long-established civil set. It currently has 123 members, including 40 QCs. Chambers has 17 members on the Attorney General's Panels for civil litigation. Chambers prides itself on its friendly and professional atmosphere. It was described by Chambers UK as 'home to some "extraordinarily bright people"'. Chambers is fully networked and its clerking and administrative services are of a high standard. Chambers works very hard but it also has extensive social, sporting and professional activities. Thirty Nine Essex Street is an equal opportunities employer.

Type of work undertaken

Commercial law: commercial regulation; construction and engineering; corporate restructuring; costs; employment; insurance and reinsurance; media, entertainment and sports; oil, gas and utilities; financial services; project finance; energy.

Civil liability: clinical negligence; health and safety; insurance; material loss claims; personal injury; product liability; professional negligence; sports injuries; toxic torts.

Planning, environmental and property: aviation; compulsory purchase; contaminated land; environmental civil liability; environmental regulation; international environmental law; licensing; marine environment; planning; nuisance; rating.

Administrative and public law: central and local government (including education, housing, immigration, prisons and VAT); European law; human rights; judicial review; mental health and community care; parliamentary and public affairs.

Regulatory and disciplinary: medical; legal; social care and education; financial services; broadcasting, communications and media; sport; transport; health and safety; building and housing; local government standards; licensing.

Pupillage

Chambers takes up to three 12-month pupils a year. During the pupillage year, each pupil will be rotated among four pupil supervisors, covering a broad range of chambers' work. The pupils will also do a number of assessed pieces of written work for other members of chambers. Pupils work only 9.00 am to 6.00 pm, Monday to Friday.

Chambers is a member of Pupillage Gateway. Applicants should consult the Pupillage Gateway timetable.

Mini-pupillage

Mini-pupillage is a very useful tool for the assessment by chambers of candidates and vice versa. It is not a prerequisite for potential pupils, but since it is likely to increase the chances of the able candidate in obtaining pupillage, we encourage those intending to seek pupillage to apply for mini-pupillage if they can. There are limited places available. Mini-pupillages are normally for three days. They commence in January and continue until June. Applications should be made between 1 September and 30 November, and (save in exceptional circumstances) while applicants are in their final year before undertaking the BPTC. Selection takes place between 1 December and early January (please check website for details). The deadline for acceptance of offers is mid-January.

Funding

Each 12-month pupillage comes with an award, currently £52,500. Of this, up to £12,500 may be drawn down during the year before pupillage commences. Awards and offers are all conditional upon passing the BPTC.

Falcon Chambers

Falcon Court, London EC4Y 1AA
Tel: (020) 7353 2484 Fax: (020) 7353 1261
Email: clerks@falcon-chambers.com
Website: www.falcon-chambers.com

No of Silks 9
No of Juniors 28
No of Pupils 2

Contact
Kester Lees
lees@falcon-chambers.com

Method of application
Application form available
from 1st December – see
Chambers website. Closing
date 31st December

Pupillages (p.a.)
Up to 2 12-month pupillages

Tenancies
3 offered in the last 3 years

Chambers profile

Falcon Chambers is recognised by the legal directories, solicitors and clients as the leading property chambers. Many of the major practitioner texts relating to property law are written by our members. We place a lot of importance on being a friendly, closely integrated group of colleagues. Many former members of chambers have become judges, including Lord Neuberger of Abbotsbury, President of The Supreme Court, Lord Justice Lewison and Mr Justice Morgan.

Type of work undertaken

Members of chambers are heavily involved in litigation in the real property, landlord and tenant and property-related fields, including cases involving insolvency, trusts, banking, revenue, professional negligence, environmental and treasury work. We are involved in both contentious and non-contentious work.

Pupil profile

Applications are welcome from all who have or expect to achieve a 2:1 or First in their degree, including students who have not yet completed a first degree, or non-law students who have not yet completed a GDL. The successful applicant will absorb complex information and identify essential points and practical solutions quickly; communicate clearly, concisely and persuasively, both orally and in writing; and remain calm, objective and confident while working under pressure.

Pupillage

Our current policy is to offer up to two pupillages each year, each of which is for 12 months. Pupils are allocated to a different pupil supervisor every three months in order to see a range of work and practices. We aim to give our pupils a good grounding in advocacy, in addition to the courses offered by the inns, by providing structured advocacy training throughout the year.

Few of our applicants will have studied our speciality in any depth, and therefore we provide an intensive course in landlord and tenant law at Falcon Chambers, usually held in the last week of September.

Applications should be made by chambers application form which is available from the website from the beginning of December 2014 for pupillages starting in October 2016. The closing date is the end of the year and interviews are held in January. More details are available on our website. Falcon Chambers does not receive applications through the Pupillage Gateway.

Mini-pupillages

Our mini-pupillages are not assessed and there is no requirement that you come to Chambers on a mini-pupillage before you apply for a pupillage. We do, however, encourage interested students to visit us for a few days to experience life at Falcon Chambers. We find that those who do so invariably apply to us for pupillage. The programme lasts for three days (usually Tuesday to Thursday), during which time we try to ensure that you will spend some time in court, sit in on a conference with clients and also sample some paperwork. We hold 4 mini-pupillage sessions each year, full details along with dates, when to apply and the application form are all available on our website.

Funding

Our pupillage award is up to £60,000 per pupil (for those starting in October 2016), of which up to £20,000 is available for draw-down during the BPTC year. In addition, in their second six months, pupils can expect to earn some additional income from their own work.

Successful pupils who become junior tenants are usually fully employed doing their own work shortly after being taken on.

Falcon Chambers

Fountain Court Chambers

Temple, London EC4Y 9DH
Tel: (020) 7583 3335 Fax: (020) 7353 0329
Email: chambers@fountaincourt.co.uk
Website: www.fountaincourt.co.uk

Chambers profile

Fountain Court Chambers is a magic circle set specialising in commercial work. In addition to general commercial and civil litigation, specific practice areas include banking and financial services, civil fraud, professional negligence, insurance and reinsurance and international arbitration.

Pupil profile

Each year, we expect to take up to three pupils who are selected based on academic and intellectual ability as well as oral and written communication skills. It is important for applicants to show an understanding of and interest in our work. Priority is given to applicants with high levels of academic achievement and successful applicants tend to have First class degrees. We welcome applications from law and non-law graduates.

Pupillage

Pupillage is divided into four periods of three months. The first three months and the last three months are spent with the same pupil supervisor, who retains overall responsibility for the pupil's training. The first two months are unassessed, following which pupils will be asked to complete specific pieces of work for different members, including silks, on ongoing cases. The work will be assessed and discussed. Pupillage does not involve competitive advocacy exercises or standard assessed pieces of work.

Mini-pupillages

With effect from the 2015 pupillage application round, mini-pupillages will be assessed and form part of the pupillage application process. We will generally expect a candidate to have completed or been offered a mini-pupillage before making their pupillage application.

Mini-pupillages typically last for three days, during which time you will sit with two or three members and learn about life at Fountain Court. You will be asked to complete a piece of written work which a member will review and discuss with you. We will pay £200 towards your expenses.

There are three mini-pupillage rounds each year (over the Christmas, Easter and Summer University holidays).

Funding

Each pupil receives £60,000 in the form of a first six month award of £40,000, with an additional £20,000 renewable for the second six months. A proportion can be drawn ahead of pupillage.

No of Silks 29
No of Juniors 37
No of pupils Currently 3

Contact
Lucy Scutt (Pupillage Coordinator)
lucy@fountaincourt.co.uk
(020) 7842 3702

Method of application
Pupillage Gateway

Pupillages (p.a.)
Up to four 12 month pupillages

Pupillage award
£60,000

Tenancies
Over the last 6 years, 16 out of 19 pupils have been offered tenancy

---

The Bar

1 Hare Court

1 Hare Court, Temple, London EC4Y 7BE
Tel: (020) 7797 7070 Fax: (020) 797 7435
Email: clerks@1hc.com
Website: www.1hc.com

No of Silks **12**	
No of Juniors **30**	
No of Pupils **2** (current)	
Contact	
Sarah Hardwicke	
Chambers Administrator	
Method of Application	
Curriculum Vitae with	
handwritten covering letter	
Pupillages (p.a.)	
2 12 month pupillages	
Tenancies offered	
7 in the last 5 years	

Chambers profile
Chambers is proud to be consistently identified as a market leader in family and matrimonial law, at the forefront of high-end financial remedy work.

Type of work undertaken
Chambers work involves the resolution of a broad range of disputes arising out of the breakdown of family relationships, including the dissolution of civil partnerships. Our reputation has been built upon our high net worth financial remedy work, increasingly with an international element. Members of chambers are also regularly instructed in property disputes arising from unmarried parties' cohabitation, Inheritance Act claims, Child Support Act appeals and private law children cases, including child abduction. We have a burgeoning reputation in the area of nuptial agreements.

Our work is undertaken predominantly in and around London, but can be as far a field as Hong Kong and the Cayman Islands. We represent clients at every level of Court and Tribunal, from the Family Proceedings and Magistrates Court to the Supreme Court and Privy Council.

In addition to advocacy and advice, 1 Hare Court provides a comprehensive dispute resolution service, including mediation, arbitration and collaborative law.

Pupil profile
Chambers looks to recruit pupils with ability, application and the potential to be first-rate advocates. Candidates should have excellent communication skills, sound judgement, a confident grasp of financial concepts and issues and good academic qualifications (at least a 2:1 honours degree).

Pupillage
Chambers offer two 12 months pupillages, commencing in October each year. Each pupil will have three different supervisors over the year and will be introduced to all aspects of chambers' work. We run in-house advocacy training and pupils will undertake a broad range of written work and research. We have a strong preference for recruiting tenants from our pupils.

Mini-pupillage
Mini-pupillages are available: for further details please consult our website at www.1hc.com/pupillages

Funding
Each pupil will receive an award of £35,000, of which £10,000 may be drawn down in the BTPC year.

1 HARE COURT

The Bar

Henderson Chambers

2 Harcourt Buildings, Temple, London EC4Y 9DB
Tel: (020) 7583 9020 Fax: (020) 7583 2686
Email: clerks@hendersonchambers.co.uk
Website: www.hendersonchambers.co.uk

Chambers profile

Henderson Chambers is a leading commercial/common law chambers with acknowledged expertise in all of its principal areas of practice. Members and pupils are frequently involved in high-profile commercial and common law litigation.

Type of work undertaken

Henderson Chambers has unrivalled expertise in product liability (which covers a wide range of commercial work including sale of goods and insurance disputes, multi-party pharmaceutical and medical device claims and regulatory and enforcement proceedings) and is consistently rated as the leading set in this area. Chambers is also widely recognised for the excellence of its health and safety work.

In addition, members are noted for their expertise and experience in areas including: banking and finance, consumer credit, employment law, regulatory and disciplinary proceedings, public law and judicial review, personal injury, property law, and technology and construction.

Pupil profile

Chambers looks for individuals who can demonstrate a first-class intellect whether via the traditional route of an outstanding higher education record or via proof of success in other professions, in business or in employment. It is a friendly and sociable set, and expects candidates to be able to show how they have both worked hard and played hard.

Pupillage

Pupillages are for 12 months, usually with four different pupil supervisors for three months each. Pupils have the opportunity to spend four weeks in Brussels at McDermott Will & Emery in order to experience European practice at first hand. Pupils will attend court regularly during their second six months.

Mini-pupillage

Chambers offers unassessed mini-pupillages. Our online application system operates to fixed appliation periods. Visit our pupillage website at www.hendersonpupillage.co.uk for details of how to apply.

Funding

Chambers offers two funded 12-month pupillages with minimum remuneration of £50,000 each. This consists of an award of £42,500 and guaranteed earnings of £7,500 during the second six months.

No of Silks 10
No of Juniors 37
No of Pupils 2

Contact
pupillages@hendersoncham-bers.co.uk
Method of application
Pupillage Gateway

Pupillages (p.a.)
2 12 month pupillages offered
Remuneration for pupil-lage £50,000 for 12 months
(£42,500 award, £7,500 guaranteed earnings)

Tenancies
6 in the last 3 years

HENDERSON CHAMBERS

The Bar

11KBW

11 King's Bench Walk, London EC4Y 7EQ
Tel: (020) 7632 8500 Fax: (020) 7583 9123
Email: clerksteam@11kbw.com
Web: www.11kbw.com

Chambers profile
We are a specialist civil law set providing high quality advice and advocacy to a wide range of private and public sector clients, both claimants and defendants.

Types of work undertaken
Pupils can expect to gain a range of experience across the following areas; public law and human rights; employment and discrimination law; commercial law; European community law; data protection; information law, public procurement, partnership, professional discipline and regulatory law and sports law.

Pupillage
The great majority of tenants are recruited from those who have done a 12 month pupillage here. We offer pupillages only to those who we believe have the potential to become tenants and our policy is to offer tenancy to all pupils who meet the required standard during their pupillage. We place a high premium on outstanding intellectual ability, but we are also looking for the strong advocacy skills, determination and practical common sense that will lead to a successful practice.

11KBW is a member of the Pupillage Gateway. Applications for pupillage commencing October 2016 should be made in the Pupillage Gateway summer round in 2015 (although we accept deferred applications). Interviews will be held in mid-July 2015 and offers of pupillage made in accordance with the Pupillage Gateway timetable. We require applicants for pupillage to do an assessed mini-pupillage in chambers. When we make pupillage selection decisions we take into account performance in assessed mini-pupillages, together with Pupillage Gateway application forms and performance at interview. Applicants must have a first or good upper second class degree (in any academic field).

Mini-pupillages
Chambers requires applicants for pupillage through Pupillage Gateway to do a one week assessed mini-pupillage in chambers. The deadline for applications for mini-pupillage is 1 March 2015 for those applying through Pupillage Gateway for pupillage commencing in October 2016. We will invite candidates for assessed mini-pupillages to a short interview in chambers in March 2015. If that causes particular difficulties, we will consider applications for alternative arrangements, such as interview by video conference. Assessed mini-pupillages will take place between April and June 2015. In exceptional circumstances, applicants for pupillage may ask to submit a written answer to a mini-pupillage problem instead of doing an assessed mini-pupillage in chambers. Any such application should also be made by 1 March 2015 for those applying for pupillage commencing in October 2016.

We also offer some unassessed mini pupillages for those who are at an earlier stage of their legal studies and who wish to consider practising as a barrister within our areas of expertise.

Awards
We offer a Pupillage Award of £55,000 (up to £15,000 of the pupillage award may be paid to prospective pupils as an advance in their BPTC year).

No of Silks 17
No of Juniors 38
No of Pupils 2 (current)

Contact
Ms Claire Halas – Operations Manager

Method of application
Pupillage Gateway

Pupillages (pa)
12 months – 2-3
Required degree first or upper second class (in any academic field)

Income
£55,000pa

Tenancies
No of tenancies offered in last 3 years: 5

The Bar

Keating Chambers

15 Essex Street, London, WC2R 3AA
Tel: (020) 7544 2600
Fax: (020) 7544 2700

No of Silks	27
No of Juniors	30
No of Pupils	up to 3

Contact
ebrowne@keatingchambers.com

Method of application
Pupillage Portal

Pupillages (p.a.)
Pupillages (p.a.) 3x12-month pupillages available

Tenancies
3 offered in last 3 years

Chambers profile

Keating Chambers is a leading commercial set specialising in construction, technology and related professional negligence disputes. These disputes often relate to high-profile projects in the UK and overseas and typically involve complex issues in the law of tort, contract and restitution. Chambers is based in modern premises just outside the Temple. In their first years of practice, tenants can expect earnings equivalent to those in other top sets of commercial chambers.

Type of work undertaken

Our members are involved in disputes of all shapes and sizes: from residential building works to multi-million pound projects for the construction of airports, dams, power stations and bridges. Members of chambers have been instructed on projects such as the Olympic venues, Wembley Stadium, the "Pinnacle", the "Shard", the "Gherkin", the Millennium Bridge, the London Eye and the Channel Tunnel. Work now also includes rapidly developing areas such as information technology, telecommunications, energy and EU law. Members of chambers act as advocates in litigation and arbitration throughout the UK.

We are often instructed to act in international hearings elsewhere in Europe and throughout Asia, Africa and the Caribbean. A number of our members specialise in international arbitration. New and alternative methods of dispute resolution are often used and several of our members are frequently appointed as mediators, arbitrators and adjudicators.

Chambers' area of practice is dynamic and challenging. The relevant principles of law are constantly developing and the technical complexity of disputes requires thorough analytical skills.

Members of Keating Chambers regularly publish books, articles and journals. Keating on Construction Contracts, the leading textbook in its field, is written and researched by current members of chambers, along with the Construction Law Reports. We also contribute to Halsbury's Laws of England and Chitty on Contracts.

Pupil profile

It must be emphasised that no specialist or technical knowledge of construction or engineering is required or assumed. However, a sound understanding of the principles of contract and tort law is essential. Save in exceptional cases, we expect applicants to have an upper second or first class degree, whether in law or not. Chambers assesses all applications using its own selection criteria.

Pupillage

Pupils are normally allocated four supervisors in the course of their 12 month pupillage. This ensures that each pupil sees a variety of work of differing levels of complexity within chambers.

Comprehensive training in the core skills required for practice in our field. To this end, pupils are encouraged to prepare drafts of pleadings, advices, letters and other documents that their supervisor or another member of chambers is instructed to prepare. Pupils are also asked to prepare skeleton arguments for hearings. They attend conferences with clients, both in and out of chambers and, of course, hearings in court, arbitration, adjudication and mediation.

Mini-pupillages

For details please see our website www.keatingchambers.com.

Funding

We offer up to three 12 month pupillages with an award for 2015 of £60,000. Of this, an advance of £18,000 is available in respect of BVC/BPTC fees (incurred or to be incurred).

The Bar

7 King's Bench Walk

7 King's Bench Walk, Temple, London, EC4Y 7DS
Tel: (020) 7910 8300 Fax: (020) 7910 8400
Website: www.7kbw.co.uk

Chambers profile
7 King's Bench Walk is a leading commercial set of chambers, with a reputation for excellence and intellectual rigour. The Legal 500 describes it as "One of the Bar's true elite".

Type of work undertaken
Chambers is at the forefront of commercial litigation, specialising in particular in the fields of insurance and reinsurance, shipping, international trade, professional negligence, commercial fraud, banking, energy, oil and gas and conflicts of laws. Most of its work has an international dimension. Members regularly appear in the High Court (particularly the Commercial Court), the Court of Appeal and the Supreme Court, as well as in arbitrations in London and overseas.

Pupil profile
Applicants must have at least a good 2:1, coupled with lively intelligence and strong advocacy skills (both oral and in writing). Chambers encourages applications from all outstanding candidates no matter what their background or academic discipline.

Pupillage
Chambers offers up to four (but typically two or three) 12 month pupillages each year (with a review after 6 months). Pupils will sit with four pupillage supervisors prior to the tenancy decision in July. Pupils will assist their pupil supervisors with their work and accompany them to hearings. Pupils will, particularly after completion of the first three months of pupillage, also do work for other members of chambers.

Mini-pupillage
Funded and non-funded mini-pupillages offered. Up to 12 funded mini-pupillages with an award of £250 together with a guaranteed pupillage interview upon subsequent application through Pupillage Gateway. Applications for funded mini-pupillages must be received by 30 November and will be scheduled in the period 1 February to 31 May. Applicants may be invited to a short interview.

Non-funded mini-pupillages are available in 2 periods during the year. Applications for the period from 1 June to 30 September (excluding August) must be received by 31 March; applications for mini-pupillages in the period 1 October to 31 January must be received by 31 July.

All applications are to be in the form of a covering letter and must be made to the mini-pupillage secretary by email to mini-pupillage@7kbw.co.uk

The CV should give a breakdown of all university examination results achieved to date.

Funding
A pupillage award of at least £60,000 will be available for the 2016/2017 and 2017/2018 years, of which up to £15,000 may be drawn down during the BPTC.

No of Silks 26
No of Juniors 31
No of Pupils at least 2 and up to 4

Contact
Emma Hilliard (pupillage secretary)
pupillage@7kbw.co.uk

Method of application
Pupillage Gateway

Pupillages (p.a.)
Up to 4 12-month pupillages offered
Required degree grade
Minimum 2:1 (law or non-law)
Remuneration for pupillage at least £60,000

Tenancies
Junior tenancies offered in last 3 years 4
No of tenants of 5 years call or under 8

7KBW
BARRISTERS

Littleton Chambers

3 King's Bench Walk North, Temple, London EC4Y 7HR
Tel: (020) 7797 8600 Fax: (020) 7797 8699
Email: fschneider@littletonchambers.co.uk
Website: www.littletonchambers.co.uk

No of Silks **13**	
No of Juniors **40**	
No of Pupils **currently 2**	
Contact	
Felicity Schneider, Administration Director	
Method of application	
Pupillage Gateway	
Pupillages (p.a.)	
12 month 2	
Required degree level 2:1 (law or non-law)	
Income	
£55,000 award. Earnings not included.	

Chambers profile

Littleton Chambers is acknowledged as being a top class set in each of its main practice areas. Its success is based upon both the desire to maintain high professional standards and a willingness to embrace change. It prides itself on the skills of its tenants, not only as advocates and advisers on the law, but also for their analytical and practical skills.

Type of work undertaken

Littleton Chambers specialises in commercial litigation, employment law, professional negligence, sports law, mediation and arbitration.

Pupil profile

Chambers takes a considerable amount of care in choosing its pupils and prefers to recruit its tenants from persons who have completed a full 12 months of pupillage with chambers. Chambers endeavours to take on pupils who not only have good academic skills, but who also show flair for advocacy and the ability to understand practical commercial issues.

Pupillage

Chambers generally offers pupillage to two people each year.

During your 12 month pupillage you will have the benefit of three pupil supervisors in succession. Your pupil supervisors will provide support and guidance to you throughout your pupillage, ensuring that you understand not only the nuts and bolts of a barrister's work, but also the ethical constraints which are such a distinctive feature of chambers' professional life.

After six months pupillage, you will be entitled to take on your own work. Typically, pupils in Littleton Chambers have been briefed once or twice a week. Your pupil supervisor will provide assistance in the preparation of these briefs to ensure that your client receives the best possible service from you.

Mini-pupillage

Assessed mini-pupillage forms part of the pupillage application process. Mini-pupillages are NOT offered outside of this process.

Funding

Each pupillage is funded (currently £55,000 per year) and, if necessary, it is possible to draw down some of this funding during the year of Bar Finals.

LITTLETON

Maitland Chambers

7 Stone Buildings, Lincoln's Inn, London WC2A 3SZ
Tel: (020) 7406 1200 Fax: (020) 7406 1300
Email: clerks@maitlandchambers.com
Website: www.maitlandchambers.com

Chambers profile
Chambers UK has rated Maitland in the top rank of commercial chancery sets every year since 2001.

Type of work undertaken
Maitland is instructed on a wide range of business and property related cases – from major international commercial litigation to disputes over the family home. Its core areas of practice include commercial litigation, banking, financial services and regulation, civil fraud, insolvency and restructuring, media law, pensions, professional negligence, real property, charity law, trusts and tax. Much of the set's work is done in London (as well as in other parts of England and Wales), although instructions often have an international aspect, involving acting for clients and appearing in court abroad. Chambers' work is predominantly concerned with dispute resolution; but it also does non-contentious work in the private client field.

Pupil profile
Academically, Maitland looks for a first or upper second class degree. Pupils must have a sense of commercial practicality, be stimulated by the challenge of written and oral advocacy and have an aptitude for and general enjoyment of complex legal argument.

Pupillage
Maitland offers up to three pupillages, all of which are funded. All pupils in chambers are regarded as potential tenants.

Pupils spend their first three months in chambers with one pupil supervisor in order that the pupil can find his or her feet and establish a point of contact. For the balance of the pupillage year each pupil will sit with different pupil supervisors, usually for two months at a time. The set believes that it is important for pupils to see all of the different kinds of work done in chambers.

Chambers believes that oral advocacy remains a core skill of the commercial chancery barrister. The set provides in-house advocacy exercises for pupils during their pupillage. These take the form of mock hearings, prepared in advance from adapted sets of papers, with senior members of chambers acting as the tribunal. They provide detailed feedback after each exercise. These exercises are part of the assessment process and help develop essential court skills.

Mini-pupillages
Applications are considered three times a year; please see chambers' website for current deadlines. Applications should be made with a covering letter and CV specifying degree classification obtained (or if you are still doing a law degree listing marks obtained in university examinations to date) and sent clearly marked 'Mini-pupillage' to the Pupillage Secretary.

Funding
Chambers offers up to three 12-month pupillages, all of which are funded (£60,000 for pupils starting in October 2016). Up to £20,000 of the award may be drawn down in advance during the BPTC year or to pay BPTC fees. There is also a cashflow assistance scheme available at the start of practice as a tenant.

No of Silks 25
No of Juniors 42
No of Pupils up to 3

Contact
Valerie Piper
(Pupillage Secretary)
pupillage
@maitlandchambers.com

Method of application
See Chambers' website from December 2014. Application deadline for pupillage in 2016-17 is 16 January 2015.

Pupillages (p.a.)
Up to 3 funded

Income
£60,000 p.a.

Tenancies
5 in last 3 years

maitland
CHAMBERS

Matrix Chambers

Griffin Building, Gray's Inn, London WC1R 5LN
Tel: (020) 7404 3447 Fax: (020) 7404 3448
Email: matrix@matrixlaw.co.uk
Website: www.matrixlaw.co.uk / www.matrixlawinternational.com
Twitter: @matrixchambers @matrixlawint

Chambers Profile

Matrix is an organisation committed to excellence in all areas of service delivery, to innovation in responding to change, and to working in new ways to meet the needs of clients.

Matrix uses paralegals and legal researchers to provide case and research support to members and clients. Matrix has associates worldwide and an office in Geneva. Matrix acts on the most complex and confidential cases providing advice, representation and advocacy at the highest level. Matrix prides itself on its extensive experience, unique knowledge and professional approach.

Matrix is founded on 'core values' including the independence of its practitioners, and a commitment to quality services, innovation, equality of opportunity and the provision of training opportunities.

Types of work undertaken

Although renowned for its high profile international and human rights work, Matrix also specialises in a unique crossover of practice areas including public, crime, EU/competition and commercial law. For the complete range of 25 international and domestic areas of law we cover, please visit the 'Areas of Practice' page on our website.

Pupil Profile

Matrix welcomes applications from exceptional candidates from all backgrounds. For further details please see our traineeship brochure on the 'Opportunities' page of our website.

Pupillage

Matrix offers up two traineeships, both starting 1 October for 12 months. Traineeships are organised into four periods of three months each. Trainees' preferences are taken into account in assigning them supervisors. In each three month period, trainees will be assigned to a different supervisor with the objective of providing experience or a full range of legal practice. In their second two seats, trainees are encouraged to take on their own cases in a supervised and well mentored way. Trainees will also be invited to attend internal and external continuing education seminars.

Mini-pupillages

Matrix do not offer mini-pupillages. Instead we run a Student Open Day in April for those considering applying for traineeship. For more details, please visit our website.

Funding

£50,000 (£10,000 to be drawn down during the BPTC).

No of Silks 28
No of Juniors 49
No of Pupils 3

Contact
Lindsay Scott
Tel: 0207 404 3447

Method of application
Our application form can be found on our website. We are not a member of the Pupillage Gateway.

Pupillages (p.a.)
Up to 2 per year – 12 months

Tenancies
5 out of 5 in the last 3 years

Monckton Chambers

1&2 Raymond Buildings, Gray's Inn, London WC1R 5NR
Tel: (020) 7405 7211 Fax: (020) 7405 2084
Email: pupillage@monckton.com
Website: www.monckton.com

No of Silks **13**	
No of Juniors **38**	
No of Pupils **3**	
Contact	
Claire Alderman	
020 7468 6345	
Method of application	
Pupillage Gateway	
Pupillages (p.a.)	
Two 12 month pupillages	

Chambers profile

Monckton Chambers is recognised by both Chambers UK and The Legal 500 as a leading set in our core areas of EU/competition, indirect tax and public and administrative law. We provide specialist advocacy services in courts and tribunals across many jurisdictions. Our members have a vast range of experience and an unrivalled knowledge of European and domestic law. We are renowned for our intellectual rigour and commercial focus.

Pupil profile

Monckton recruits pupils with the expectation of making an offer of tenancy, should they meet the required standard. Most candidates successful in their application for pupillage will have a First Class Honours degree (although it need not be in law) or a graduate degree in law.

Monckton is looking for candidates who have the ability, personal skills and willingness to learn, which will enable them to get the most out of our pupillage training programme and to go on to enjoy successful careers as tenants in our chambers. Successful candidates will therefore need to demonstrate: academic excellence, an ability and appetite for intellectually challenging legal work, excellent communication skills (both oral and written), an ability to reason and argue persuasively, and the spirit and personality needed to succeed at the self-employed Bar.

Pupillage

Monckton provides training of the highest quality delivered by, and through the opportunity of working with, barristers who are leaders in their fields and who fight cases and advise clients in the context of rapidly developing areas of law. Training is an interactive process in which we seek to accommodate the pupil's individual ambitions and interests, and help them to develop the legal knowledge, practical skills and sure judgement that will enable them to enjoy a lifetime of professional success.

Mini-pupillages

Please refer to www.monckton.com for further information on Monckton's mini pupillage scheme.

Funding

Monckton offer a pupillage award of £60,000.

4 New Square

4 New Square, Lincoln's Inn, London WC2A 3RJ
Tel: (020) 7822 2000 Fax: (020) 7822 2001
Website: www.4newsquare.com

No of Silks 21	
No of Juniors 56	
No of Pupils 2	
Contact	
Georgie Ruane	
Tel (020) 7822 2000	
Email	
pupillage@4newsquare.com	
Method of application	
Online www.4newsquare.com	
(from December each year)	

Chambers profile

4 New Square is a leading commercial and civil set of barristers comprising 77 members, of whom 21 are Queen's Counsel. 4 New Square enjoys a formidable reputation in its principal areas of work: commercial litigation and arbitration, insurance and reinsurance, professional liability, costs litigation and construction and engineering. Its members are also recognised as leading practitioners in the fields of chancery litigation, consumer law, financial services, pensions, product liability, professional discipline, public law and sports law. Members of 4 New Square appear in a wide range of tribunals (court and arbitral) and are regularly instructed to take landmark cases to the Court of Appeal and the Supreme Court. Recent examples of our work include, acting as counsel to the inquiry in the Hillsborough Inquests, the 'Trigger' Litigation (Supreme Court), the Atomic Veterans Litigation (Supreme Court), Jones v Kaney (Supreme Court) and Motto v Trafigura (Court of Appeal). Jackson & Powell on Professional Negligence (the main text in this area) is written and edited by current members of chambers. Chambers attracts a large amount of junior advocacy work which reflects the emphasis on developing pupils and junior tenants into experienced advocates to equip them for a successful career at the Bar.

Type of work undertaken

Professional liability, product liability, chancery, commercial dispute resolution, construction and engineering, costs, international arbitration, insurance and reinsurance, financial services and banking, offshore, human rights, administrative and public law and sports law.

Pupil profile

Chambers does not stream its pupils. Each has an equal prospect of securing a tenancy. Selection Criteria are: evidence of intellectual ability; potential as an advocate; personal qualities such as self reliance, integrity, reliability and the ability to work effectively with colleagues and clients; motivation.

Equal opportunities: Chambers observes a policy of equal opportunities in accordance with the Bar Code of Conduct.

Pupillage

The first six months: You will go to court and attend conferences with your pupil supervisor. You will also assist your pupil supervisor with their written work: carrying out written advisory and drafting work on their current papers and undertaking detailed research on the law.

The second six months: During your second six months, as well as continuing with work for your pupil supervisor, you will take on an increasing amount of your own court work. Chambers places a strong emphasis on advocacy and supports its pupils in gaining valuable practical experience. You can expect to be in court on your own about once a week up to the tenancy decision and potentially on a more regular basis thereafter. You will be expected to complete three assessed pieces of work for members of chambers who are not your pupil supervisors.

Advocacy: You will also take part in an assessed moot in front of a former member of Chambers who is now a Court of Appeal or High Court judge. Workshop training sessions are run to help you prepare for the moots.

Environment: Chambers aims to provide a friendly and sociable atmosphere. Pupils are included in chambers' social events throughout the year. Chambers is committed to investing in training its pupils. A "First Days on Your Feet" workshop is run by junior tenants for the pupils just before the second 6.

Mini-pupillages

Mini-pupillages generally last for two days and take place in specific weeks in May, July, November and December of each year. Chambers will pay travelling expenses of £50. Applications must be made on chambers' own mini-pupillage application form, which is available to download from our website.

NEW SQUARE

XXIV Old Buildings

XXIV Old Buildings, 24 Old Buildings, Lincoln's Inn, London, WC2A 3UP
Tel: (020) 7691 2424 Fax: (0870) 460 2178
Website: xxiv.co.uk

No of Silks 11	
No of Juniors 31	
No of Pupils 2	
Contact	
Steven Thompson	
Method of application	
Letter and CV. Please see www.xxiv.co.uk for guidance	
Pupillages (p.a.)	
2	
Tenancies	
Usually 1-2 per year	
Other offices	
Geneva	

Chambers profile
XXIV Old Buildings is a commercial Chancery chambers of 42 barristers based in Lincoln's Inn. Its members provide specialist legal advice and advocacy services in the UK and worldwide on a range of contentious, advisory and transactional matters to the financial, commercial and professional community and to private individuals. Our expertise covers all areas of dispute resolution, litigation and arbitration.

Type of work undertaken
The barristers at XXIV Old Buildings specialise in a variety of commercial Chancery areas with a particular emphasis on trusts and estates and commercial litigation. Areas in which members regularly take instructions include arbitration; aviation; charities; civil fraud, asset tracing and recovery; company; construction and projects; financial services; insolvency; international and offshore; partnership; pensions; professional negligence; real estate litigation and trusts, probate and estates.

XXIV Old Buildings is known for its pre-eminence in international and offshore work, both contentious and advisory. With offices in both London and Geneva, the barristers at XXIV Old Buildings regularly appear in courts and tribunals in offshore centres including the British Virgin Islands, the Cayman Islands, Bermuda, Jersey, the Isle of Man, the DIFC, the Bahamas, Gibraltar, Hong Kong and Malaysia.

Pupillage
The set likes to recruit its junior members from those who have undertaken pupillage with the set. Chambers are therefore careful that its pupils acquire all the skills necessary to make them successful commercial Chancery barristers. During a 12 month pupillage, a pupil will have, on average, four pupil supervisors with whom they will spend the majority of their time. Each year the set is looking for pupils with a first or 2:1 degree, though not necessarily in law, who have an enthusiasm for the type of work the set does, sound judgment and the application required to succeed in a very competitive and intellectually demanding environment. Application is by CV and covering letter.

Chambers will probably be recruiting for pupillage commencing in October 2016 early in 2015.

Mini-pupillages
Chambers accepts applications for mini-pupillages throughout the year. Application should be made by CV and covering letter. Please see our website www.xxiv.co.uk for details of how to apply.

Funding
Up to £68,000 per pupil.

The Bar

Pump Court Tax Chambers

16 Bedford Row, London WC1R 4EF
Tel: (0207) 414 8080 Fax: (0207) 414 8099
Email: clerks@pumptax.com
Website: www.pumptax.com

Chambers overview
Pump Court Tax Chambers is the largest specialist tax set.

Type of work undertaken
All areas of tax work (both contentious and non-contentious). Corporate tax clients range from major accountants and solicitors sending work such as M&A, reconstructions and demerger to (at the junior level) the corporation tax and VAT problems of small businesses. Private client work comes from a broad range of sources – city solicitors, regional firms, chartered tax advisers and IFAs, who act for private individuals, trustees and landed estates. Much of chambers' work concerns litigation and members of chambers regularly appear in the Tax Tribunals, the High Court, the Court of Appeal, the Supreme Court and the CJEU. Junior members' litigation tends to be led for the first couple of years, with an increasing amount of lower-value litigation on their own after that. Tax problems tend to bring in all other areas of the common law, and Chambers' VAT practice involves a great deal of EU law.

Pupil profile
Applicants who are intelligent, articulate and well-motivated. Successful candidates will have at least a 2:1 honours degree (although not necessarily in law). Prior experience of studying tax law is not required.

Pupillage
Chambers offers up to two 12-month pupillages (normally beginning in October and terminable early only for cause) to those wishing to practise full-time at the Bar.

Pupils will work with at least three pupil supervisors and will also sit with other members of chambers so as to receive a broad training in most aspects of Chambers' work.

Mini-pupillages
The programme runs throughout the year. Applications should be made via email to pupils@ pumptax.com with accompanying CV and marked for the attention of the Mini-Pupillage Secretary.

Funding
Award of up to £50,000. Up to £12,000 of the award may be advanced during the BPTC year.

No of Silks	11
No of Juniors	21
No of Pupils	1 to 2 in any given year

Contact
Thomas Chacko
pupils@pumptax.com

Method of application
CV and covering letter (non-Pupillage Gateway) by 2 February 2015

Pupillages (p.a.)
Up to 2 funded

Tenancies
3 new tenants in last 3 years

PUMP COURT
TAX CHAMBERS

Quadrant Chambers (Luke Parsons QC)

Quadrant House, 10 Fleet Street, London EC4Y 1AU
Tel: (020) 7583 4444 Fax: (020) 7583 4455
Email: pupillage@quadrantchambers.com
Website: www.quadrantchambers.com

No of Silks	19
No of Juniors	37

Contact
Pupillage Secretary

Method of application
Chambers' application form

Pupillages (p.a.)
1st 6 months 3
2nd 6 months 3
12 months
Required degree
1st or high 2:1

Income
1st 6 months
£32,500
2nd 6 months
£32,500
Earnings not included

Tenancies
Current tenants who served
pupillage in chambers 34
Junior tenancies offered
in last 3 years 5
No of tenants of 5 years
call or under 7

Chambers profile

Quadrant Chambers is a leading set of barristers specialising in commercial law. We act as advocates in courts, arbitrations and inquiries, and provide specialist legal advice to clients from around the world in a wide range of industry areas. Many of us are qualified to practice in other jurisdictions, including Australia, the BVI, California, Germany, Hong Kong, New York and South Africa. Distinguished former members of chambers have gone on to chair public enquiries and to sit as judges in the High Court (QBD, Commercial, Administrative and Admiralty Court), DIFC Courts, European General Court, Court of Appeal, House of Lords, Privy Council and UK Supreme Court.

Type of work undertaken

We undertake all types of commercial law. We are market leaders in shipping and aviation, and have an excellent reputation in banking and finance, energy, commercial Chancery, insurance and reinsurance, insolvency and restructuring, commodities and international trade, commercial litigation and arbitration, and sport and media. Our work has a strongly international flavour, and much of it involves international clients.

Pupil profile

We look for candidates with a very strong academic background. Successful applicants will generally have (or be predicted) a first class degree, and they must have / be predicted at least a high 2:1 to apply. They must have excellent analytical abilities, outstanding written and oral communication skills and the ability to perform under pressure. They must also be able to demonstrate that they have the commitment, energy and robustness to succeed at the Commercial Bar.

Successful candidates often read law for their first degree, and an increasing number also have postgraduate law degrees, but these are not pre-requisites, and we welcome applications from candidates who have studied any serious academic subject at university.

Pupillage

We offer up to three pupillages of 12 months' duration each year. We aim to develop in our pupils the skills, knowledge and judgment they will need to become successful commercial barristers. During their first six months, pupils sit with two pupil supervisors for three months each, and are exposed to a wide range of commercial work. Tenancy decisions are made at the end of June.

We hold an open day each December for those in the second year of university or above. This is an opportunity to meet the barristers and clerks, and learn about life at the Commercial Bar. Places are limited. See our website for details.

We do not use the Pupillage Gateway to manage our pupillage applications. There are three stages to our application process: (i) our own online application form, (ii) test set, and (iii) interview. See our website for details.

Mini-pupillages

Mini-pupillages are available in March / April, July and September of each year. Places are limited. See our website for details.

Funding

Pupils receive awards of £65,000, part of which may be advanced during the BPTC year. They also have the opportunity to do fee-earning work during their 2nd 6.

Queen Elizabeth Buildings (QEB) Chambers of Lewis Marks QC

Queen Elizabeth Building, Temple, London EC4Y 9BS
Tel: (020) 7797 7837 Fax: (020) 7353 5422
Email: clerks@qeb.co.uk
Website: www.qeb.co.uk

Chambers profile

QEB is a leading set of family law chambers, particularly well-known for dealing with the financial consequences of divorce, but with immense experience in all aspects of family law including: jurisdictional disputes, foreign divorces, pre-marital agreements, civil partnerships, injunctions both financial and domestic, private law child work, child abduction, Inheritance Act claims and disputes between former cohabitees. In addition some members practise in general common law, particularly personal injury and professional negligence work.

QEB has been established for well over 100 years and is consistently rated as one of the top-ranking sets for family law. Members of QEB have been involved in many of the most important cases of legal principle, including: White, Sorrell, Miller, Spencer, Marano, Robson, Schofield, Jones, Z v Z (No. 2) and Petrodel v Prest.

Many members of chambers have continued into high judicial office and Lord Wilson sits in the Supreme Court.

Pupil profile

The practice of family law is infinitely varied and clients come from all walks of life. International and conflict of laws issues arise increasingly often. An ability to deal not only with complex financial disputes, often involving commercial issues, but also with child-related or other emotionally fraught and sensitive situations, is essential. We are looking for applicants with a strong academic record (minimum 2:1 law or non-law degree save in exceptional circumstances), good legal and analytical skills, and an ability to communicate sensitively with a wide range of people at a critical time in their lives.

Pupillage

QEB offers up to three pupillages each year. A 12-month pupillage at QEB offers top-quality training and very good financial support in a busy, friendly environment. Pupils have three pupil supervisors, but are also encouraged to work with other tenants at all levels to gain a broad experience of our work. Pupils are automatically considered for tenancy, and our new tenants are only recruited from our pupils. QEB's reputation is such that where a pupil is not taken on, he/she is usually well placed elsewhere.

Chambers is a part of the Pupillage Gateway system. Applicants should apply in the summer 2015 season for a pupillage beginning in October 2016. Please consult the Pupillage Gateway website for details of the timetable.

Mini-pupillages

Applications for mini-pupillages are made by CV and covering letter to the Mini-Pupillage Secretary. Please consult our website at www.qeb.co.uk for full details.

Funding

Chambers offers a pupillage award of £25,000 pa minimum, plus earnings in the second six and from devilling. Pupils do not pay chambers' expenses or clerks' fees. Chambers also funds the compulsory Inn Advocacy and Practice Management Training Courses.

No of Silks 6
No of Juniors 27
No of Pupils up to 3

Contact
Miss Amy Kisser, Secretary to the Pupillage Committee

Method of Application
Pupilage Gateway

Pupillages
Up to three 12-month pupillages

Award
£25,000 minimum pupillage award + earnings in second six and from devilling

Tenancies
Four tenancies offered in the last three years

Annexes
None

The Bar

Serle Court

Serle Court, 6 New Square, Lincoln's Inn, London WC2A 3QS
Tel: (020) 7242 6105 Fax: (020) 7405 4004
Email: pupillage@serlecourt.co.uk
Website: www.serlecourt.co.uk

Chambers profile

Serle Court has "a phenomenally good reputation that is really well deserved", is a "'first port of call' for a wide range of commercial chancery cases" and they are "not simply very nice people, the are very, very good to work with" *(Chambers UK)*. Serle Court is one of the leading commercial chancery sets with 56 barristers including 20 silks. Widely recognised as a leading set, Chambers is recommended in 11 different areas of practice by the legal directories. Chambers has a stimulating and inclusive work environment and a forward looking approach.

Type of work undertaken

Litigation, arbitration, mediation and advisory services across the full range of chancery and commercial practice areas including: banking, civil fraud, commercial litigation, company, competition and state aid, financial services, insolvency, insurance and reinsurance, intellectual property, partnership and LLP, professional negligence, property, sports, entertainment and media and trusts and probate.

Pupil profile

Candidates are well-rounded people, from any background. Chambers looks for highly motivated individuals with outstanding intellectual ability, combined with a practical approach, sound judgement, an ability to develop good client relationships and the potential to become excellent advocates. Serle Court has a reputation for "consistent high quality" and for having "responsive and able team members" and seeks the same qualities in pupils. Chambers generally requires a degree classification of a good 2:1 as a minimum. Serle Court is committed to equality and diversity and encourages and welcomes applications from women, people of minority ethnic origin and people with disabilities, as well as candidates from other groups which are under represented in the legal sector.

Pupillage

Pupils sit with four pupil supervisors in order to experience a broad range of work. Up to three pupils are recruited each year and Chambers offers: an excellent preparation for successful practice; a genuinely friendly and supportive environment; the opportunity to learn from some of the leading barristers in their field; a good prospect of tenancy.

Mini-pupillages

About 30 available each year. The application form is available at www.serlecourt.co.uk.

Funding

Serle Court offers awards of £60,000 for 12 months, of which up to £20,000 can be drawn down during the BPTC year. It also provides an income guarantee worth up to £120,000 over the first two years of practice.

No of Silks 20
No of Juniors 36
No of Pupils 3

Contact
Kathryn Barry
Tel (020) 7242 6105

Method of application
Chambers application form, available from website or chambers. Not a member of Pupillage Gateway.

Pupillages
Up to three 12-month pupillages

Tenancies
Up to 3 per annum

serle court

South Square

3-4 South Square, Gray's Inn, London WC1R 5HP
Tel: (020) 7696 9900 Fax: (020) 7696 9911
Email: pupillage@southsquare.com
Website: www.southsquare.com

Chambers profile

Chambers is an established successful commercial set, involved in high-profile international and domestic commercial litigation. Members of chambers have been centrally involved in some of the most important commercial cases of the last decade including Lehman Brothers, Kaupthing, Landsbanki, Woolworths, Madoff Securities and Stanford International.

Type of work undertaken

South Square has a pre-eminent reputation in insolvency and restructuring law and specialist expertise in banking, commercial, company, financial services and fraud related disputes. Members regularly appeal in the courts and tribunals of various international jurisdictions in addition to those of England and Wales.

Pupil profile

Chambers seeks to recruit the highest calibre of candidates who must be prepared to commit themselves to establishing a successful practice and maintaining chambers' position at the forefront of the modern Commercial Bar. The minimum academic qualification is a 2:1 degree. A number of members have degrees in law, and some have BCL or other postgraduate qualifications. Others have non-law degrees and have gone on to take the Graduate Diploma in Law.

Pupillage

Pupils are welcomed into all areas of chambers' life and are provided with an organised programme designed to train and equip them for practice in a dynamic and challenging environment. Pupils sit with a number of pupil supervisors for periods of six to eight weeks and the set looks to recruit at least one tenant every year from its pupils.

Mini-pupillages

Chambers also offers funded and unfunded mini-pupillages – please see the set's website for further details.

Sponsorship & awards

Currently £60,000 per annum (reviewable annually). A proportion of the pupillage award may be paid for living expenses during the BPTC.

No of Silks 23
No of Juniors 18
No of Pupils 2

Contact
Pupillage Administrator
Tel (020) 7696 9900

Method of application
Mini-Pupillage - CV with covering letter
Pupillage - application form (available to download from the website)

Pupillages (p.a.)
Up to two 12-month pupillages offered each year

The Bar

2 Temple Gardens (Chambers of Benjamin Browne QC)

2 Temple Gardens, London EC4Y 9AY DX: 134 Chancery Lane
Tel: (020) 7822 1200 Fax: (020) 7822 1300
Email: clerks@2tg.co.uk
Website: www.2tg.co.uk

No of Silks 12	
No of Juniors 42	
No of Pupils 3	
Contact	
Katie Seingier	
Pupillage Administrator	
Method of application	
Pupillage Gateway (April)	
Pupillages (p.a.)	
Up to three 12-month pupillages	
Award 2015 £67,500	

Chambers profile
2tg is regarded as one of the leading commercial and civil law barristers' chambers. The firm specialises in professional negligence, insurance and personal injury and also has significant practices in banking, employment, technology, construction and clinical negligence, alongside strength in private international law.

Pupil profile
Academically, you will need at least a good 2:1 degree to be considered. Chambers look for applicants who work well in teams and have the ability to get on with solicitors, clients and other members of chambers.

Pupillage
Chambers offers one of the most generously funded, well-structured and enjoyable pupillages at the Bar. It takes pupillage very seriously and aims to recruit the best applicants, and to ensure that its pupils have an excellent foundation from which to start a successful career at the Bar. Pupils have three different pupil supervisors during pupillage, and will also do work for other members of chambers. The aim is for pupils to experience as much of chambers' work as possible during their pupillage year.

Mini-pupillages
Chambers welcomes 'mini-pupils'. Generally applicants will only be considered after their first year of a law degree or during CPE. Mini-pupillages are a good way to experience life at 2tg first hand. Most mini-pupillages are 2-3 days long. We aim to show you a wide range of barristers' work during your mini-pupillage. It offers an assessment at the completion of your mini-pupillage and encourages you to give feedback too. Chambers also offers help with reasonable expenses (up to £50).

Mini-pupillages are usually unfunded but a few funded mini-pupillages (maximum £250 per person) are also available.

Funding
Chambers offers up to three 12-month pupillages, all of which are funded. Its pupillage award for 2015 is £67,500. Please see our website www.2tg.co.uk for details of the award for 2015.

3 Verulam Buildings (Ali Malek QC)

3 Verulam Buildings, Gray's Inn, London WC1R 5NT DX: LDE 331
Tel: (020) 7831 8441 Fax: (020) 7831 8479
Email: chambers@3vb.com
Website: www.3vb.com

Chambers profile

Sitting comfortably and spaciously in a newly refurbished and expanded row of buildings in Gray's Inn, 3VB is one of the largest and most highly regarded commercial sets, its members being involved in many of the leading cases. Recent examples include the Beresovsky/Abramovitch dispute, Belmont Park Investments v BNY Corporate Trustees, The Rangers Football Club plc v Collyer Bristow LLP and Deutsche Bank v Sebastian Holdings.

Type of work undertaken

3VB's 23 silks and 44 juniors lead the field in banking and financial services, and are also among the top practitioners in the fields of professional negligence, civil fraud, insurance, arbitration and company and insolvency. Chambers also has significant expertise in IT and telecommunications, energy, construction, and media and entertainment.

Pupil profile

Commercial practice is intellectually demanding and 3VB seeks the brightest and the best. The typical successful applicant will have a first or upper second class degree (not necessarily in law) from a good university, with good mooting experience and proven experience of the commercial bar (generally through mini-pupillages with us or elsewhere). Many have a Master's degree or other legal or commercial experience.

Pupillage

Chambers seeks to recruit up to three 12-month pupils each year through the Pupillage Gateway. Chambers is committed to recruiting new tenants from its pupils whenever it can. Although tenancy is offered to all pupils who make the grade, on average two out of three pupils are successful in any one year.

Mini-pupillages

Two-day mini-pupillages are an essential part of chambers' selection procedure and it is strongly encouraged that prospective applicants for pupillage apply for a mini-pupillage (email minipupillage@3vb.com, attaching a detailed CV and covering letter).

Funding

For the year 2015/2016, the annual award will be at least £60,000, up to £20,000 of which may be drawn during the BPTC year.

No of Silks **23**
No of Juniors **44**
No of Pupils **3**

Contact
Please see the information on the pupillage pages at www.3vb.com

Method of application
Gateway (Pupillage); CV with detailed breakdown of examination results and covering letter explaining why 3VB (Mini-pupillage)

Pupillage
Pupillages p.a.12 months up to 3
Required degree grade High 2:1/First
Income In excess of £60,000 plus any earnings

Tenancies
Current tenants who served pupillage in Chambers approx 41
Junior tenancies offered in last 3 years 7
No of tenants of 5 years call or under 10

The Bar

Wilberforce Chambers

8 New Square, Lincoln's Inn, London WC2A 3QP
Tel: (020) 7306 0102 Fax: (020) 7306 0095
Email: pupillage@wilberforce.co.uk
Website: www.wilberforce.co.uk

No of Silks	**22**
No of Juniors	**30**

Method of application
Chambers application form available from website

Pupillages (p.a.)
2 x 12 months

Mini-pupillages
Total of 28 places
Award
£65,000

Minimum qualification
2:1 degree

Tenancies in last 3 years
5

Chambers profile

Wilberforce Chambers is a leading commercial chancery set of chambers and is involved in some of the most commercially important and cutting-edge litigation and advisory work undertaken by the Bar today. Members are recognised by the key legal directories as leaders in their fields. Instructions come from top UK and international law firms, providing a complex and rewarding range of work for international companies, financial institutions, well-known names, sports and media organisations, pension funds, commercial landlords and tenants, and private individuals. Clients demand high intellectual performance and client-care standards but in return the reward is a successful and fulfilling career at the Bar. Chambers has grown in size in recent years but retains a united and friendly 'family' atmosphere.

Type of work undertaken

All aspects of traditional and modern chancery work including property, pensions, private client, trust and taxation, professional negligence, general commercial litigation, banking, company, financial services, intellectual property and information technology, sports and media and charities.

Pupil profile

Chambers looks to offer two 12-month pupillages. You should possess high intellectual ability, excellent communication skills and a strong motivation to do commercial chancery work. You need to be mature and confident, have the ability to work with others and analyse legal problems clearly, demonstrating commercial and practical good sense. Chambers looks for people who have real potential to join as tenants at the end of their pupillage. Wilberforce takes great care in its selection process and puts effort into providing an excellent pupillage. There is a minimum requirement of a 2:1 degree in law or another subject, and Wilberforce has a track record of taking on GDL students.

Pupillage

Chambers operates a well-structured pupillage programme aimed at providing you with a broad experience of commercial chancery practice under several pupil supervisors with whom you will be able to develop your skills. Wilberforce aims to reach a decision about tenancy after approximately 9-10 months, but all pupils are entitled to stay for the remainder of their pupillage on a full pupillage award.

Mini-pupillages

Wilberforce encourages potential candidates for pupillage to undertake a mini-pupillage in order to learn how chambers operates, to meet its members and to see the type of work that they do - but a mini-pupillage is not a prerequisite for pupillage. Wilberforce runs four separate mini-pupillage weeks (two in December, one at Easter and one in July). Please visit the website for an application form and further information.

Funding

Wilberforce offers a generous and competitive pupillage award which is reviewed annually with the intention that it should be in line with the highest awards available. The award for 2015 is £65,000 for 12 months and is paid in monthly instalments. A proportion of the award (up to £20,000) can be drawn down during the BPTC year.

The Bar

Contacts

The Law Society
113 Chancery Lane,
London WC2A 1PL
Tel: 020 7242 1222
www.lawsociety.org.uk

Solicitors Regulation Authority
The Cube
199 Wharfside St
Birmingham B1 1RN
Tel: 0370 606 2555
E-mail: contactcentre@sra.org.uk
www.sra.org.uk

Junior Lawyers Division
The Law Society,
113 Chancery Lane,
London WC2 A 1PL
Helpline: 0207 320 5675
E-mail: juniorlawyers@lawsociety.org.uk
www.juniorlawyers.lawsociety.org.uk

The Bar Council
289-293 High Holborn,
London WC1V 7HZ
Tel: 020 7242 0082
www.barcouncil.org.uk

Bar Standards Board
289-293 High Holborn
London WC1V 7HZ
Tel: 020 7611 1444
www.barstandardsboard.org.uk

Gray's Inn, Education Department
8 South Square, Gray's Inn,
London WC1R 5ET
Tel: 020 7458 7900
E-mail: quinn.clarke@gray-sinn.org.uk
www.graysinn.info

Inner Temple, Education & Training Department
Treasury Building, Inner Temple,
London EC4Y 7HL
Tel: 020 7797 8208
E-mail: ffulton@innertemple.org.uk
www.innertemple.org.uk

Lincoln's Inn, Students' Department
Treasury Office, Lincoln's Inn,
London WC2A 3TL
Tel: 020 7405 1393
www.lincolnsinn.org.uk

Middle Temple, Students' Department
Treasury Office, Middle Temple Lane,
London EC4Y 9AT
Tel: 020 7427 4800
E-mail: members@middle-temple.co.uk
www.middletemple.org.uk

Chartered Institute of Legal Executives
Kempston Manor, Kempston,
Bedfordshire MK42 7AB
Tel: 01234 841000
E-mail: office@cilex.org.uk
www.ilex.org.uk

Institute of Paralegals
6 Graphite Square
Vauxhall Walk
London SE11 5EE
Tel: 020 7587 3917
E-mail: office@the iop.org
www.theiop.org

National Association of Licensed Paralegals
Canterbury Court,
Kennington Business Park,
1-3 Brixton Road,
London SW9 6DE
Tel: 0845 8627000
E-mail: info@nationalparalegals.co.uk
www.nationalparalegals.com

Crown Prosecution Service
Rose Court,
2 Southwark Bridge,
London SE1 9HS
Tel: 020 3357 0000
E-mail: strategic.resourcing@cps.gsi.gov.uk
www.cps.gov.uk

Citizens Advice Bureau
3rd Floor North
200 Aldersgate Street
London EC1A 4HD
Tel: 03000 231 231
Get Advice: 08444 111444
www.citizensadvice.org.uk

Law Centres Network
Floor 1, Tavis House
1-6 Tavistock Square
London WC1H 9NA
Tel: 020 3637 1330
www.lawcentres.org.uk
Email: via website

Free Representation Unit
Ground Floor
60 Gray's Inn Road,
London, WC1X 8LU
Tel: 020 7611 9555
www.thefru.org.uk

The Bar Lesbian & Gay Group
E-mail: contactus@blagg.org
www.blagg.org

Lesbian & Gay Lawyers Association
c/o Alternative Family Law,
3 Southwark Street,
London SE1 1RQ
Tel: 020 7407 4007
E-mail: andrea@lagla.org
www.lagla.org.uk

Interlaw Diversity Forum (LGBT)
Email: daniel.winterfeldt@cms-cmck.com
www.interlawdiversityforum.org

LawWorks
National Pro Bono Centre,
48 Chancery Lane,
London WCA2 1JF
Tel: 020 7092 3940
www.lawworks.org.uk

MLAW (The Association for Muslim Lawyers)
Meridien House, 42 Upper Berkeley Street,
London, W1H 5QJ
E-mail: info@muslimlawyer.co.uk
Tel: 020 37570066
www.muslimlawyer.co.uk

The Society of Asian Lawyers
nick@sethi.co.uk
www.societyofasianlawyers.co.uk

Society of Black Lawyers
www.blacklawyer.org

The Association of Women Barristers
E-mail: fj@33cllaw.com
www.womenbarristers.co.uk

Lawyers with Disabilities Division
The Law Society
113 Chancery Lane,
London WC1A 1PL
Tel: 020 7320 5793
E-mail: Judith.McDermott@lawsociety.org.uk

LPC/GDL Central Applications Board
Ground Floor
Suite 2
River House
Broadford Business Park
Shalford
Surrey GU4 8EP
Tel: 01483 301282
E-mail: applications@lawcabs.ac.uk
www.lawcabs.ac.uk

Pupillage Gateway
Tel: 0845 8350558
E-mail: pupillagegateway@barcouncil.org.uk

c/o The General Council of the Bar,
289-293 High Holborn,
London WC1V 7HZ
Tel: 020 7242 0082

Career Development Loans
Tel: 0800 100 900
www.gov.uk/career-development-loans/overview